MICROSOFT® OFFICE 97 PROFESSIONAL

Pamela R. Toliver
Yvonne Johnson

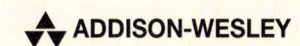

▲ ADDISON-WESLEY

An imprint of Addison Wesley Longman, Inc.

Reading, Massachusetts • Menlo Park, California • New York • Harlow, England
Don Mills, Ontario • Sydney • Mexico City • Madrid • Amsterdam

Senior Editor: Carol Crowell
Editorial Assistant: Kerry Connor
Production Supervision: Patty Mahtani/Diane Freed
Production Assistant: David Noyes
Copyeditor: Robin Drake/Barb Terry
Proofreader: Holly McLean-Aldis
Technical Editors: Martha Johnson, Robin Edwards, Deborah Minyard
Indexer: Mark Kmetzko
Composition: Compset, Inc.
Cover Illustration: © Frederic Joos/SIS
Cover Designer: Anthony Saizon
Cover Design Supervisor: Gina Hagen
Marketing Manager: Michelle Hudson
Manufacturing Manager: Hugh Crawford

Microsoft, Word, Excel, Access, and PowerPoint are registered trademarks of Microsoft Corporation.

Copyright © 1997 by Addison Wesley Longman, Inc.

All rights reserved. No part of this publication may be reproduced, stored in a retrieval system, or transmitted, in any form or by any means, electronic, mechanical, photocopying, recording, or otherwise, without the prior written permission of the publisher. Printed in the United States of America.

ISBN 0-201-30321-3
ISBN 0-201-32246-3
    (spiral)

Ordering from the SELECT System
For more information on ordering and pricing policies for the SELECT Lab Series and supplements, please contact your Addison Wesley Longman sales representative or call 1-800-552-2499.

Addison-Wesley Publishing Company
One Jacob Way
Reading, MA 01867
http://www.awl.com/he/is
is@awl.com

1 2 3 4 5 6 7 8 9 10-DOW-00999897

Preface to the Instructor

Welcome to the *Select: Office 97 Professional*. This new project-based visual text makes learning both the suite and applications easy and enjoyable. Students explore the essentials of software applications, learning the basic skills that are the foundation for business and academic success. Step-by-step exercises and full-color illustrations show the students what to do, how to do it, and the exact result.

Greater access to ideas and information is changing the way people work. With Office 97 applications, you have greater integration capabilities and easier access to Internet resources than ever before. The *Select Lab Series* helps you take advantage of these valuable resources, with special assignments devoted to the Internet and with additional connectivity resources that can be accessed through our Web site, **http://www.awl.com/he/is/.**

The *Select Lab Series* also offers individually bound texts for each *Office 97* application. Dozens of proven and class-tested lab manuals are available within the *Select Lab Series*, from the latest operating systems and browsers, to the most popular applications software for word processing, spreadsheets, databases, presentation graphics, desktop publishing, and integrated packages, to HTML and programming. We realize that you have specific needs for your lab course, so we offer the quick and affordable TechSuite program. For your lab course, you can choose what you want to combine; your choice of lab manuals will be sent to the bookstore, combined in a TechSuite, allowing students to purchase all books in one convenient package at a discount.

In addition, your school may qualify for full Office 97 upgrades or licenses. Your Addison Wesley Longman representative will be happy to work with you and your bookstore manager to provide the most current menu of *Select Lab Series* offerings, outline the ordering process, and provide pricing, ISBNs, and delivery information. Or call 1–800–447–2226 or visit our Web site at http://www.awl.com/he/is/.

Your Addison Wesley Longman representative will be happy to work with you and your bookstore manager to provide the most current menu of *Select Lab Series* offerings, outline the ordering process, and provide pricing, ISBNs, and delivery information. Or call 1-800-447-2226 or visit our Web site at http://www.awl.com/he/is/.

Organization

Select: Microsoft Office 97 Professional is divided into five parts: An Overview of Windows 95 and Office 97; Word 97; Excel 97; Access 97; and PowerPoint 97.

The "Overview of Windows 95, Outlook, and Internet Explorer 3.0" familiarizes students with Windows 95 and Office 97 before launching into the applications. Students learn the basics of starting Windows 95, using a mouse, using the essential features of Windows 95, organizing files, using Outlook for scheduling, recording tasks in the task list, sending e-mail, and using Internet Explorer.

Each Office 97 application is then covered in depth in five or six projects that teach beginning to intermediate skills. An overview introduces the basic concepts of the application and provides hands-on instructions to put students to work using the application immediately. Students learn problem-solving techniques while working through projects that provide practical, real-life scenarios that they can relate to.

Select: Microsoft Office 97 Professional provides several projects that help students learn how to use the integration capabilities in Office 97. The Integration projects introduce students to the exciting possibilities of document creation using the data-sharing capabilities available with OLE (Object Linking and Embedding).

Web assignments appear throughout the text at the end of each project, giving students practice using the Internet.

Approach

The *Select Lab Series* uses a document-centered approach to learning. Each project begins with a list of measurable objectives, a realistic scenario called the Challenge, a well-defined plan called the Solution, and an illustration of the final product. The Setup enables students to verify that the settings on the computer match those needed for the project. The project is arranged in carefully divided, highly visual objective-based tasks that foster confidence and self-reliance. Each project closes with a wrap-up of the project called the Conclusion, followed by summary questions, exercises, and assignments geared to reinforcing the information taught through the project.

Other Features

In addition to the document-centered, visual approach of each project, this book contains the following features:

- An overview of Windows 95 and Access 97 so that students feel comfortable and confident as they function in the working environment.
- Keycaps and toolbar button icons within each step so that the student can quickly perform the required action.
- A comprehensive and well-organized end-of-the-project Summary and Exercises section for reviewing, integrating, and applying new skills.
- An illustration or description of the results of each step so that students know they're on the right track all the time.

Preface to the Instructor **V**

PROJECT 2
Editing a Document

Creating a document is just the beginning of your work in word processing. After you create a document, you usually revise it several times. In this project, you will explore some of the most commonly used revision techniques.

Objectives

After completing this project, you will be able to:

- Open a document
- Move around in a document
- Select text to change the attributes
- Work with text
- Check spelling and grammar
- Create an envelope
- Change the view

The Challenge

After typing a letter for Mr. Williams to the Sports Marketing Professionals, Mr. Williams wants the letter retyped with the changes shown in Figure 2.1. Instead of sending additional information with the letter as previously planned, Mr. Williams has decided to send the information separately, so you will have to create an envelope for the letter.

WORD-41

The **Introduction** sets up the real-world scenario that serves as the environment for learning.

Clearly defined and measurable **objectives** give students the direction and focus they need to learn new material.

The **Challenge** introduces the goal of the project, the document, spreadsheet, database, or presentation to be created.

WORD-72

The Solution

You will format a document and set up the document to print across the long side of the paper in three columns. You will insert a graphic, modify and apply styles, create the bulleted and numbered lists, and format the brochure shown in Figure 3.1.

Figure 3.1

The Setup

So that your screen will match the illustrations and the tasks in this project will function as described, make sure that the Word 97 settings listed in Table 3.1 are selected on your computer.

The **Solution** describes the plan for completing the projects, the tasks leading to the final product.

An **illustration** shows the outcome of the project.

The **Setup** tells the students exactly which settings should be chosen to match those in the illustrations.

vi

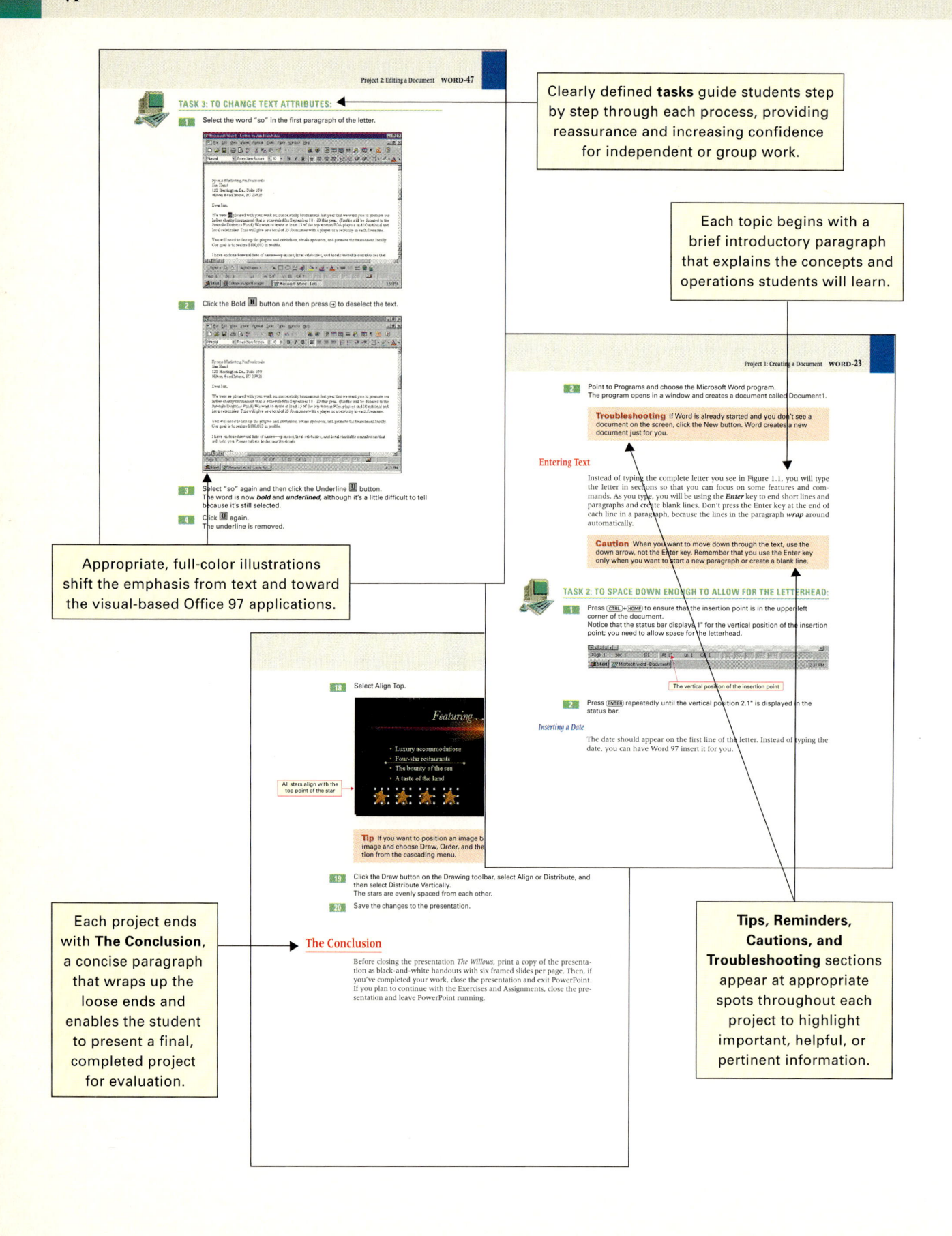

Clearly defined **tasks** guide students step by step through each process, providing reassurance and increasing confidence for independent or group work.

Each topic begins with a brief introductory paragraph that explains the concepts and operations students will learn.

Appropriate, full-color illustrations shift the emphasis from text and toward the visual-based Office 97 applications.

Each project ends with **The Conclusion**, a concise paragraph that wraps up the loose ends and enables the student to present a final, completed project for evaluation.

Tips, Reminders, Cautions, and Troubleshooting sections appear at appropriate spots throughout each project to highlight important, helpful, or pertinent information.

Preface to the Instructor **vii**

Summary and Exercises

Summary

- When you launch Word 97, it automatically creates a new document named Document 1.
- Word 97 can insert the current date in several formats.
- When typing text, you press ENTER to end a short line or paragraph or to create a blank line.
- Characters that can't be created by pressing a key on the keyboard can be inserted from the Symbols dialog box.
- Simple typing errors can be corrected using the Backspace key.
- The Undo command can undo multiple commands and tasks that you have performed.
- Misspelled words are marked with a wavy red line by Word 97 and replacement words can be selected from a pop-up menu.
- Documents can be saved with long filenames.
- Before you print a document, you can preview it to see if it looks acceptable.
- You can print a document using the Print button or the Print command on the File menu.
- When you close a file, if you haven't saved changes to the file, Word 97 asks if you want to save the changes.

Key Terms and Operations

Key Terms	Operations
AutoComplete	create new document
AutoCorrect	indent
Enter	insert special characters
new document	undo
SpellIt	save a document
Tab	preview a document
Wrap	print a document
	close a document

Study Questions

Multiple Choice

1. Which of the following should *not* be done when typing text in a document?
   a. Press BACKSPACE to erase the character to the left.
   b. Press ENTER at the end of every line.
   c. Press ENTER to create a blank line.
   d. Click the Undo button to undo the last operation.

2. After Word 97 launches,
   a. the screen is blank until you create a new document.
   b. a dialog box displays with the options to create a new document or edit an existing document.
   c. Document 1 is created automatically.
   d. the New File dialog box displays.

WORD-36

A bulleted **summary list** further reinforces the objectives and the material presented in the project.

Key Terms are boldface and italicized throughout each project and then listed for handy review in the summary section at the end of the project.

Twenty-four **study questions** (Multiple Choice, Short Answer, and For Discussion) bring the content of the project into focus again and allow for independent or group review of the material learned.

WORD-38

4. How do you insert a character that can't be entered from the keyboard?
5. How do you end a paragraph?
6. How do you magnify the document in the Print Preview mode?
7. What's the difference between using the Print command from the File menu and using the Print button?
8. What happens when you choose File, Close if you haven't saved the file?
9. Can you edit a document while viewing it in Print Preview mode?
10. Why don't you have to press Enter at the end of each line in a paragraph?

For Discussion

1. How does previewing a file before printing help the environment?
2. Why would you want to ignore a word that isn't in the dictionary rather than to add it to the dictionary?
3. Why is the Undo command so beneficial for novice users?
4. Under what circumstances would you click the New button to create a new document?

Review Exercises

1. Creating a New Letter

After meeting with Jim Hand to discuss promoting the golf tournament, Thomas Williams wants you to type a follow-up letter to confirm some of the topics they discussed.

Figure 1.3

---

8. Delete all the text below the horizontal line.
9. Type the title **Web Site Addresses and Sum**
10. Type **Address:** and press Enter. Type **Summ**
11. Copy the two lines typed in Step 3 and paste
12. Center the title and make it 12-point bold.
13. Fill in the addresses and summary with the in Web, making the Web addresses italic.
14. View the file in Page Layout view to see how bottom of the page. If the text isn't centered the text down by pressing Enter to insert blan line.
15. Save the file as *Golf Clubs.doc* and close the file

Assignments

1. Creating an Announcement

Create the announcement shown in Figure 2.6. shown and use fonts that appeal to you if you d shown in the figure. Be sure to center text as sho

Figure 2.6

Review Exercises present hands-on tasks for building on the skills acquired in the project.

Assignments invoke critical thinking and encourage integration of project skills.

- A durable, perforated, removable Function Reference Guide for each application. Functions are arranged alphabetically rather than by menu.
- Nearly all the topics in this book were designed to match the guidelines for the Microsoft Office 97 User Certification program, which certifies individuals as Proficient or Expert users. The performance-based tests, developed by an independent company and endorsed by Microsoft, test the skills that employers expect and require of employees. Since author Yvonne Johnson is on the certification test review panel, she has provided much guidance for the topical content of this book to help users prepare for certification. To view the complete list of guidelines, go to http://www.awl.com/is/select/.

Supplements

You get extra support for this text from supplemental materials, including the *Instructor's Manual* and the Instructor's Data Disk.

The *Instructor's Manual* includes a Test Bank and Transparency Masters for each project in the student text, as well as Expanded Student Objectives, Answers to Study Questions, and Additional Assessment Techniques. The Test Bank contains two separate tests with answers and consists of multiple-choice, true/false, and fill-in questions referenced to pages in the student text. Transparency Masters illustrate over one hundred key concepts and screen captures from the text.

The Instructor's Data Disk contains student data files, completed data files for Review Exercises and assignments, and the test files from the *Instructor's Manual* in ASCII format.

Thanks to . . .

When team members combine their knowledge and skills to produce a work designed to meet the needs of students and professors across the country, they take on an unenviable challenge.

To **Carol Crowell** and **Barb Terry,** thanks for the steady focus and refocus needed to get this project off the ground.

Thanks to **Martha Johnson, Robin Edwards,** and **Deborah Minyard,** who were more than just technical editors, but who also made sure things worked the way we said they would. Thanks to **Robin Drake**—without your great help and comments during development, nothing in this book would match; and to **Chuck Hutchinson,** for excellent editing. To those in production, especially to **Pat Mahtani,** your design efforts have paid off in a highly user friendly book!

To **Michelle Hudson,** thanks for your strong marketing insights for this book.

And, finally, thanks to everyone at Addison Wesley Longman who has followed this project from start to finish.

P. T. and Y. J.

Acknowledgments

Addison-Wesley Publishing Company would like to thank the following reviewers for their valuable contributions to the *SELECT Lab Series*.

James Agnew
Northern Virginia Community College

Joseph Aieta
Babson College

Dr. Muzaffar Ali
Bellarmine College

Tom Ashby
Oklahoma CC

Bob Barber
Lane CC

Robert Caruso
Santa Rosa Junior College

Robert Chi
California State Long Beach

Jill Davis
State University of New York at Stony Brook

Fredia Dillard
Samford University

Peter Drexel
Plymouth State College

David Egle
University of Texas, Pan American

Linda Ericksen
Lane Community College

Jonathan Frank
Suffolk University

Patrick Gilbert
University of Hawaii

Maureen Greenbaum
Union County College

Sally Ann Hanson
Mercer County CC

Sunil Hazari
East Carolina University

Gloria Henderson
Victor Valley College

Bruce Herniter
University of Hartford

Rick Homkes
Purdue University

Lisa Jackson
Henderson CC

Martha Johnson
(technical reviewer)
Delta State University

Cynthia Kachik
Santa Fe CC

Bennett Kramer
Massasoit CC

Charles Lake
Faulkner State Junior College

Ron Leake
Johnson County CC

Randy Marak
Hill College

Charles Mattox, Jr.
St. Mary's University

Jim McCullough
Porter and Chester Institute

Gail Miles
Lenoir-Rhyne College

Steve Moore
University of South Florida

Anthony Nowakowski
Buffalo State College

Gloria Oman
Portland State University

John Passafiume
Clemson University

Leonard Presby
William Paterson College

Louis Pryor
Garland County CC

Michael Reilly
University of Denver

Dick Ricketts
Lane CC

Dennis Santomauro
Kean College of New Jersey

Pamela Schmidt
Oakton CC

Gary Schubert
Alderson-Broaddus College

T. Michael Smith
Austin CC

Cynthia Thompson
Carl Sandburg College

Marion Tucker
Northern Oklahoma College

JoAnn Weathcrwax
Saddleback College

David Whitney
San Francisco State University

James Wood
Tri-County Technical College

Minnie Yen
University of Alaska Anchorage

Allen Zilbert
Long Island University

About the Authors

Pam Toliver has over fifteen years of experience teaching students and adults of all ages about the sometimes mysterious world of software. She bought her first computer for a high school classroom in 1979, and through necessity, began to develop teaching materials and exercises designed to strengthen student productivity and make learning fun. Since those early days, she has moved from teaching business education classes at the high school level to teaching software applications at the community college and university levels.

Pam has a bachelor's degree in business teacher education from Southern Illinois University, Carbondale and a master's degree in vocational education from Louisiana State University, Baton Rouge. She divides her personal time among her favorite activities: writing, learning new software, and teaching — but more often lately she finds herself "caught in the Web".

Yvonne Johnson has been involved in teaching and writing about PCs since they first came into use. For 12 years she owned and operated a successful computer training school, the first school of its kind in Kentucky. She authored all the training material for the school and has written 17 books published by Que, Osborne/McGraw-Hill and other publishers. Her training and writing background has made her exceptionally well-versed in database, word processing, graphic, spreadsheet, presentation, integrated, and publishing software.

She holds a BA degree from Centre College of Kentucky with a major in Education and English. She did her post graduate work at the University of South Florida.

Dedication

For Tancy Finkbiner, my teacher, roll-model, mentor, and friend—congratulations on your retirement. If all your students touch as many lives in as positive a way as you have, the world will be a much better place!

P.R.T.

Dedicated to my son Kirk, a student at the University of Illinois, and his friends Eric, Joe, Chip, and Weezie, who inspire me daily with all their hard work and dedication to the football team.

Y.J.

Contents

PART I Overview of Windows 95, Outlook, and Internet Explorer

Windows 95   WIN-1

Overview of Windows 95   WIN-2
Objectives   WIN-2
Launching Windows 95   WIN-3
Identifying the Desktop Elements   WIN-3
Using a Mouse   WIN-4
Using the Basic Features of
    Windows 95   WIN-5
  Using the Start Menu   WIN-5
  Using Windows   WIN-6
  Using Menu Bars and Toolbars   WIN-8
  Using Dialog Boxes   WIN-9
Organizing Your Computer   WIN-11
  Moving Files   WIN-14
  Deleting Files   WIN-16
  Restoring Files   WIN-16
Working with Multiple Programs   WIN-17
Getting Help   WIN-22
Exiting Windows 95   WIN-29

Outlook   OL-1

Overview of Outlook   OL-2

Objectives   OL-2
Identifying Outlook Features   OL-3
Launching Outlook   OL-3
Using the Outlook Bar   OL-4
Scheduling Appointments in
    the Calendar   OL-6
Recording Tasks in the Task List   OL-8
Tracking Computer Activities in
    the Journal   OL-10
Storing Contacts in the
    Contacts List   OL-12
Creating, Sending, and Receiving
    E-Mail   OL-15
Printing from Outlook   OL-18
Exiting Outlook   OL-20
Summary and Exercises   OL-21
Summary   OL-21
Key Terms and Operations   OL-21
  Key Terms   OL-21
  Operations   OL-21
Study Questions   OL-21
  Multiple Choice   OL-21
  Short Answer   OL-22
  For Discussion   OL-23
Review Exercises   OL-23
  1. Exploring Outlook   OL-23
  2. Scheduling Assignments   OL-23
Assignments   OL-23
  1. Adding Contacts to the Contacts List   OL-23
  2. Using Office Assistant   OL-24

Internet Explorer 3.0   IE-1

Overview of Internet Explorer 3.0   IE-2

Objectives   IE-2
Identifying the Structure and Purpose of the
    Internet   IE-3
  Connecting to the Internet   IE-3
    Identifying Services on the Internet   IE-3
  Launching Internet Explorer 3.0   IE-4
  Identifying the Internet Explorer 3.0 Screen
    Elements   IE-5
  Navigating the Internet   IE-6
    Following Links   IE-7
    Typing an Address   IE-7
    Selecting a Site from the Go Menu   IE-8
    Selecting a Site from the
      History Folder   IE-9
    Selecting a Favorite   IE-10
    Searching the Internet   IE-11
    Printing Information   IE-12
  Downloading a File Via FTP   IE-13
  Accessing Resources with a Gopher   IE-15
  Accessing Newsgroups   IE-18
    Launching Internet News   IE-19
  Creating, Sending, and
    Reading E-mail   IE-22
    Creating and Sending E-mail   IE-22
    Reading E-mail   IE-24
  Exiting Internet Explorer 3.0   IE-25
Summary and Exercises   IE-26
Summary   IE-26
Key Terms and Operations   IE-26
  Key Terms   IE-26
  Operations   IE-26
Study Questions   IE-26
  Multiple Choice   IE-26
  Short Answer   IE-28
  For Discussion   IE-28
Review Exercises   IE-28
  1. Finding Information with Gopher   IE-28

PART II Word 97

Overview   2

Objectives   2
   Identifying the Word 97 Features   2
   Launching Word 97   4
   Identifying Word 97 Screen Elements   4
      Working with Toolbars   6
      Hiding and Displaying the Ruler   8
   Getting Help   9
      Using the What's This? Help Feature   11
      Using the Office Assistant   11
      Getting Help from the World
        Wide Web   13
   Closing a Document and Exiting
      Word 97   14
Summary and Exercises   16
Summary   16
Key Terms and Operations   16
   Key Terms   16
   Operations   16
Study Questions   16
   Multiple Choice   16
   Short Answer   17
   For Discussion   18
Review Exercises   18
   1. Customizing the Screen   18
   2. Getting Help on the Web   19
Assignments   19
   1. Using Help to Explore and Use Buttons on the
      Drawing Toolbar   19
   2. Exploring the Microsoft Home Page   19

Project 1 Creating a Document   20

Objectives   20
The Challenge   20
The Solution   21
The Setup   21
   Creating a New Document   22
   Entering Text   23
      Inserting a Date   23
      Correcting Errors   25
      Inserting Special Characters   27
      Using AutoComplete   27
   Undoing Changes   28
   Correcting Errors Marked by SpellIt   29
   Saving a Document   30
   Previewing a Document   32
   Printing a Document   33
   Closing a File   34
The Conclusion   35
Summary and Exercises   36
Summary   36
Key Terms and Operations   36
   Key Terms   36
   Operations   36
Study Questions   36
   Multiple Choice   36
   Short Answer   37
   For Discussion   38
Review Exercises   38
   1. Creating a New Letter   39
   2. Getting Information from the Internet   39
Assignments   39
   1. Creating a Memo   39
   2. Creating a List of E-Mail Addresses   40

Project 2 Editing a Document   41

Objectives   41
The Challenge   41
The Solution   43
The Setup   43
   Opening a Document   43
   Moving Around in a Document   44
   Selecting Text to Change the Attributes   45
   Working with Text   50
   Checking Spelling and Grammar   57
   Creating an Envelope   59
   Changing the View   60
The Conclusion   62
Summary and Exercises   63
Summary   63
Key Terms and Operations   63
   Key Terms   63
   Operations   63
Study Questions   63
   Multiple Choice   63
   Short Answer   65
   For Discussion   65
Review Exercises   65
   1. Creating a List of Possible Sponsors   65
   2. Creating a List of Web Sites   67
Assignments   69
   1. Creating an Announcement   69
   2. Modifying the Announcement   70

Project 3 Using Advanced Formatting Features   71

Objectives   71
The Challenge   71
The Solution   72
The Setup   72
   Setting Up the Page   73
   Creating Columns   75
   Inserting and Manipulating a Graphic   76
   Formatting Paragraphs   80

Working with Tabs   83
  Applying and Modifying Styles   87
  Creating Bulleted and Numbered Lists   92
  Applying Borders and Shading   95
The Conclusion   98
Summary and Exercises   99
Summary   99
Key Terms and Operations   99
  Key Terms   99
  Operations   99
Study Questions   99
  Multiple Choice   99
  Short Answer   101
  For Discussion   101
Review Exercises   101
  1. Creating a List of Rules   101
  2. Creating a Camp Schedule   102
Assignments   103
  1. Creating an Award Certificate   103
  2. Creating a List of Summer Camps   104

Project 4 Creating a Table   105

Objectives   105
The Challenge   105
The Solution   105
The Setup   107
  Creating a Table   107
  Converting Existing Text to a Table   109
  Moving Around in a Table and
     Entering Data   110
  Inserting and Deleting Rows and Columns
     in a Table   111
  Formatting a Table Automatically   115
  Formatting a Table Manually   117
  Changing the Width of Columns   117
  Positioning Tables   119
  Drawing Tables   119
The Conclusion   124
Summary and Exercises   125
Summary   125
Key Terms and Operations   125
  Key Terms   125
  Operations   125
Study Questions   125
  Multiple Choice   125
  Short Answer   126
  For Discussion   127
Review Exercises   127
  1. Creating a Script for a Commercial   127
  2. Comparing the Competition   128
Assignments   129
  1. Creating a Form   129
  2. Creating a Golf FAQ   130

Project 5 Formatting a Long Document   131

Objectives   131
The Challenge   131
The Solution   132
The Setup   133
  Navigating Within a Long Document   133
  Inserting and Deleting Page Breaks   138
  Inserting Section Breaks   142
  Creating Headers and Footers   143
  Creating Footnotes   148
The Conclusion   151
Summary and Exercises   152
Summary   152
Key Terms and Operations   152
  Key Terms   152
  Operations   152
Study Questions   152
  Multiple Choice   152
  Short Answer   153
  For Discussion   154
Review Exercises   154
  1. Creating a Document with Two Sections   154
  2. Revising a Multi-Page Document   156
Assignments   158
  1. Creating a Document with Two Sections on the
     Same Page   158
  2. Downloading and Formatting an RFC   158

Project 6 Creating a Mail Merge   159

Objectives   159
The Challenge   159
The Solution   159
The Setup   160
  Creating the Data Source Document   160
  Creating the Main Document   164
  Merging the Documents   167
  Creating Another Main Document to Use
     with a Data Source Document   168
  Creating and Using Another Data Source
     Document with a Main Document   169
Summary and Exercises   172
Summary   172
Key Terms and Operations   172
  Key Terms   172
  Operations   172
Study Questions   172
  Multiple Choice   172
  Short Answer   173
  For Discussion   174
Review Exercises   174
  1. Creating a Data Source   174
  2. Creating a Main Document
     and Merging   175

Assignments 176
  1. *Creating a Form Letter to Send to Family and Friends* 176
  2. *Creating a Form Letter Requesting Catalogs* 176

PART III Excel 97

Overview 2

Objectives 2
  Identifying the Excel 97 Features 2
  Launching Excel 97 3
  Identifying Excel 97 Screen Elements 4
    Working with Toolbars 6
  Getting Help 8
    Using the Office Assistant 8
    Getting Help from the World Wide Web 10
  Closing a Workbook and Exiting Excel 97 11
Summary and Exercises 12
Summary 12
Key Terms and Operations 12
  Key Terms 12
  Operations 12
Study Questions 13
  Multiple Choice 13
  Short Answer 14
  For Discussion 14
Review Exercises 14
  1. *Starting Excel and Exploring the Workbook* 14
  2. *Getting Help on the Web* 15
Assignments 15
  1. *Getting Online Help* 15
  2. *Using the Web Toolbar* 15

Project 1 Creating a Workbook 17

Objectives 17
The Challenge 17
The Solution 18
The Setup 18
  Creating a New Workbook 19
  Moving Around in a Worksheet and a Workbook 19
  Naming Worksheets 23
  Entering Data 25
    Entering Text 25
    Entering Data on Multiple Worksheets 26
    Entering Numbers 31
  Entering Simple Formulas and Functions 32
  Saving a Workbook 37
  Previewing and Printing a Worksheet 39
  Closing a Workbook 41
The Conclusion 41
Summary and Exercises 42
Summary 42
Key Terms and Operations 42
  Key Terms 42
  Operations 42
Study Questions 42
  Multiple Choice 42
  Short Answer 43
  For Discussion 44
Review Exercises 44
  1. *Creating an Expense Account* 44
  2. *Calculating Savings* 45
Assignments 46
  1. *Creating a Timesheet* 46
  2. *Creating a Worksheet that Compares Menu Prices* 46

Project 2 Editing a Workbook 47

Objectives 47
The Challenge 47
The Solution 47
The Setup 48
  Opening a Workbook 49
  Finding Data 50
  Editing Data 52
  Working with Data 55
    Selecting Cells 55
    Copying Data 58
    Deleting Data 61
    Moving Data 63
  Adding Comments 65
  Checking Spelling 69
Conclusion 70
Summary and Exercises 71
Summary 71
Key Terms and Operations 71
  Key Terms 71
  Operations 71
Study Questions 71
  Multiple Choice 71
  Short Answer 72
  For Discussion 73
Review Exercises 73
  1. *Revising the Restaurant Sales Worksheet* 73
  2. *Revising a Time Sheet* 74
Assignments 74
  1. *Creating and Revising a Budget* 74
  2. *Tracking the American Stock Exchange* 74

Contents   xvii

Project 3 Enhancing the Appearance of a Workbook   75

Objectives   75
The Challenge   76
The Solution   76
The Setup   76
   Formatting Text   77
   Changing Cell Alignment   78
   Formatting Numbers   81
   Formatting Dates   84
   Formatting Numbers as Text   86
   Adding Borders and Fill   88
   Viewing and Changing a Page Break   91
   Using AutoFormat   92
The Conclusion   93
Summary and Exercises   94
Summary   94
Key Terms and Operations   94
   Key Terms   94
   Operations   94
Study Questions   94
   Multiple Choice   94
   Short Answer   95
   For Discussion   96
Review Exercises   96
   1. Enhancing the Restaurant Sales Worksheet   96
   2. Creating a Concert List   97
Assignments   97
   1. Reformatting the Income.xls *File*   97
   2. Using AutoFormat   98

Project 4 Editing the Structure of a Worksheet and a Workbook   99

Objectives   99
The Challenge   99
The Solution   100
The Setup   100
   Inserting, Deleting, and Arranging Worksheets   101
   Changing the Size of Columns and Rows   104
   Using AutoFit   106
   Adjusting Row Height   107
   Inserting Columns, Rows, and Cells   109
   Deleting Columns, Rows, and Cells   112
   Creating Headers and Footers   114
      Creating a Custom Header and Footer   117
The Conclusion   119
Summary and Exercises   120
Summary   120
Key Terms and Operations   120
   Key Terms   120
   Operations   120
Study Questions   120
   Multiple Choice   120
   Short Answer   121
   For Discussion   122
Review Exercises   122
   1. Editing the MarApr2 Workbook   122
   2. Creating a Sales Workbook for the Sandwich Shops and Snack Bars   123
Assignments   123
   1. Creating a Banquet Workbook   123
   2. Creating a Shopping List   124

Project 5 Creating a More Complex Workbook   125

Objectives   125
The Challenge   125
The Solution   126
The Setup   126
   Copying Data from Another Workbook   126
   Sorting Data   129
   Entering Formulas with Relative References   130
   Using Headings in Formulas   133
   Entering Formulas with Absolute References   133
      Pointing to Enter Absolute References   135
      Using Headings with Absolute References   136
   Creating and Modifying a Chart   136
      Moving and Sizing a Chart   139
      Changing Chart Data   140
      Formatting Chart Elements   143
      Changing the Chart Type   145
      Changing the Chart Options   146
      Creating a Pie Chart   147
The Conclusion   152
Summary and Exercises   153
Summary   153
Key Terms and Operations   153
   Key Terms   153
   Operations   153
Study Questions   153
   Multiple Choice   153
   Short Answer   155
   For Discussion   155

Review Exercises 155
   *1. Revising the Gift Inventory and
      Sales Workbook* 155
   2. Creating a New Items Workbook 156
Assignments 157
   1. Creating a Chart of Expenditures 157
   2. Completing a Vacation Package Workbook 157

Integrated Project 1: Integrating Word and Excel   IP1-1

Objectives   IP1-1
The Challenge   IP1-1
The Solution   IP1-2
The Setup   IP1-2
   Creating the Excel Worksheet   IP1-3
   Creating an Excel Chart   IP1-5
   Creating a Word Document   IP1-8
   Adding WordArt to a
      Word Document   IP1-12
   Copying Excel Data to a
      Word Document   IP1-15
   Linking an Excel Chart to a Word
      Document   IP1-19
The Conclusion   IP1-21
Summary and Exercises   IP1-22
Summary   IP1-22
Key Terms and Operations   IP1-22
   Key Terms   IP1-22
   Operations   IP1-22
Study Questions   IP1-22
   Multiple Choice   IP1-22
   Short Answer   IP1-23
   For Discussion   IP1-24
Review Exercise   IP1-24
   Linking Excel data to a Word document   IP1-24

PART IV   Access 97

Overview   2

Objectives   2
   Defining Database Terminology   2
      Defining Database Terms   3
   Designing a Database   6
   Launching Microsoft Access   7
   Creating and Saving a Database   8
   Identifying Microsoft Access
      Screen Elements   10
   Working with Menus, Dialog Boxes,
      and Toolbars   11
      Identifying Menu Features   11
      Working with Toolbars   12
      Working with Dialog Boxes   12
   Getting Help   14
      Using the Office Assistant   14
      Using What's This? Help   16
      Using Help Contents   17
      Using the Help Index   18
      Getting Help from the Microsoft
         Web Site   19
   Closing a Database and Exiting
      Microsoft Access   20
Summary and Exercises   21
Summary   21
Key Terms and Operations   21
   Key Terms   21
   Operations   21
Study Questions   21
   Multiple Choice   21
   Short Answer   22
   For Discussion   23
Review Exercises   23
   1. Designing a New Database   23
   2. Getting Help About Wizards   23
Assignments   23
   *1. Identifying Fields to Include in Database for
      The Willows*   23
   *2. Exploring the Microsoft Access Forum to Look for
      Jobs on the Web*   24

Project 1 Building a Database   25

Objectives   25
The Challenge   25
The Solution   26
The Setup   26
   Opening an Access Database   27
   Creating an Access Database Table   28
      Defining Table Fields   29
      Saving and Closing a Database Table   32
   Opening an Access Database Table   33
   Adding Records to an Access
      Database Table   34
   Checking the Spelling of Data in a
      Database Table   36
   Creating and Saving an AutoForm   37
   Navigating Datasheets and Forms   38
   Previewing and Printing
      Database Data   40
The Conclusion   42
Summary and Exercises   43
Summary   43
Key Terms and Operations   43
   Key Terms   43
   Operations   43
Study Questions   43
   Multiple Choice   43

Short Answer 44
For Discussion 45
Review Exercises 45
   1. Creating a Database and a Database Table 45
   2. Adding Records to a Database Table 47
Assignments 47
   1. Creating a New Table and Adding Records to the Table 47
   2. Finding Competitors on the Internet 49

Project 2 Maintaining a Database 50

Objectives 50
The Challenge 50
The Solution 51
The Setup 51
   Finding Records 52
   Updating Records 53
   Inserting Records 55
   Using the Replace Feature 57
   Deleting Records 59
   Sorting Records 60
   Filtering Records by Selection 62
   Filtering Records by Form 63
The Conclusion 66
Summary and Exercises 67
Summary 67
Key Terms and Operations 67
   Key Terms 67
   Operations 67
Study Questions 67
   Multiple Choice 67
   Short Answer 69
   For Discussion 69
Review Exercises 69
   1. Sorting Data, Finding and Replacing Data, and Updating a Database Table 69
   2. Filtering Data in a Database Table 72
Assignments 73
   1. Sorting, Filtering, Finding, and Updating Database Records 73
   2. Updating and Sorting a Database 73

Project 3 Altering the Table Design 74

Objectives 74
The Challenge 74
The Solution 75
The Setup 76
   Inserting Table Fields 76
   Rearranging Fields in a Table 78
   Deleting Table Fields 81
   Creating a Key Field 82
   Creating and Saving an AutoReport 83
   Copying a Table Structure 84

The Conclusion 85
Summary and Exercises 86
Summary 86
Key Terms and Operations 86
   Key Terms 86
   Operations 86
Study Questions 86
   Multiple Choice 86
   Short Answer 87
   For Discussion 88
Review Exercises 88
   1. Insert and Delete Fields, Assign a Key Field, and Update a Table 88
   2. Rearranging Fields in a Table and Creating an AutoReport 89
Assignments 90
   1. Insert Fields, Delete Fields, Set Key Field, and Set Field Properties 90
   2. Editing and Copying the Structure of a Database Table 90

Project 4 Creating Queries 92

Objectives 92
The Challenge 92
The Solution 93
The Setup 93
   Creating a New Query 94
   Adding Fields to the Query Grid 96
   Running a Query 97
   Saving and Closing a Query 98
   Opening and Running a Query 99
   Setting Query Sort Order and Criteria 100
   Editing a Query 104
The Conclusion 108
Summary and Exercises 109
Summary 109
Key Terms and Operations 109
   Key Terms 109
   Operations 109
Study Questions 109
   Multiple Choice 109
   Short Answer 110
   For Discussion 110
Review Exercises 111
   1. Creating and Saving a Simple Query 111
   2. Creating, Running, Saving, Editing, and Using Criteria in a Multi-Table Query 112
Assignments 113
   1. Creating a Query; Saving, Editing, Opening, and Running a Query 113
   2. Creating Queries from Data on the World Wide Web 114

Project 5 Creating and Modifying Forms   115

Objectives   115
The Challenge   116
The Solution   116
The Setup   116
   Creating a New Form and Displaying Form
      Design View   117
   Identifying Form Design
      View Features   118
   Selecting and Removing Fields from
      a Form   119
   Rearranging Fields on a Form   120
   Saving a Form   122
   Aligning Fields on a Form   122
   Changing Form Field Labels   123
   Adjusting Field Length on a Form   124
   Adding Titles to Forms   125
The Conclusion   128
Summary and Exercises   129
Key Terms and Operations   129
   Key Terms   129
   Operations   129
Study Questions   129
   Multiple Choice   129
   Short Answer   130
   For Discussion   131
Review Exercises   131
   1. Creating a New Form, Rearranging Fields, and
      Saving a Form   131
   2. Editing Field Labels, Adjusting Field Length,
      and Adding a Form Title   132
Assignments   132
   1. Creating a Form: Rearranging Fields,
      Removing Fields, Changing Field Labels,
      Adjusting Field Length, Adding a Title, and
      Saving   132
   2. Locating Forms on the Internet   133

Project 6 Customizing AutoReports   134

Objectives   134
The Challenge   134
The Solution   135
The Setup   135
   Opening a Report and Identifying Report
      Design Screen Features   135
   Selecting and Removing Fields from
      a Report   137
   Saving and Viewing Reports   139
   Modify a Report Design   140
   Printing Reports   148
The Conclusion   149
Summary and Exercises   150
Summary   150
Key Terms and Operations   150
   Key Terms   150
   Operations   150
Study Questions   150
   Multiple Choice   150
   Short Answer   152
   For Discussion   152
Review Exercises   152
   1. Creating a new AutoReport, rearranging fields,
      and saving a report   152
   2. Editing fields labels, adjusting field length, and
      adding a report title   153
Assignments   154
   1. Creating a new query to use for creating,
      designing, modifying, and saving
      a report   154
   2. Locating report layouts on the Internet   155

Integrated Project 2: Integrating Word, Excel, and Access   IP2-1

Objectives   IP2-1
The Challenge   IP2-1
The Solution   IP2-2
The Setup   IP2-2
Copying Excel Data to an
   Access Database   IP2-3
Updating the Access Table Design   IP2-7
Merging Access Data with a
   Word Document   IP2-9
The Conclusion   IP2-11
Summary and Exercises   IP2-12
Summary   IP2-12
Key Terms and Operations   IP2-12
   Key Terms   IP2-12
   Operations   IP2-12
Study Questions   IP2-12
   Multiple Choice   IP2-12
   Short Answer   IP2-13
   For Discussion   IP2-14
Exercise   IP2-14
   Creating a new Access database and tables from
      Excel data   IP2-14
Assignment   IP2-15
   Merging Access database table data with a Word
      document and publishing Access report data to a
      Word document   IP2-15

PART V PowerPoint 97

Overview   2

Objectives   2
   Defining PowerPoint Terminology   2

Designing a Presentation 4
Launching Microsoft PowerPoint 4
Identifying PowerPoint
  Screen Elements 5
Creating a Presentation 7
Displaying Presentations in
  Different Views 8
Working with Menus, Dialog Boxes,
  and Toolbars 11
    Identifying Menu Features 11
    Working with Toolbars 12
    Working with Dialog Boxes 13
Getting Help 16
  Using the Office Assistant 17
  Getting Help from the Microsoft
    Web Site 18
  Closing a Presentation and Exiting
    Microsoft PowerPoint 20
Summary and Exercises 21
Summary 21
Key Terms and Operations 21
  Key Terms 21
  Operations 21
Study Questions 21
  Multiple Choice 21
  Short Answer 23
  For Discussion 23
Review Exercises 23
  1. Designing a New Presentation 23
  2. Getting Help 24
Assignments 25
  1. Designing a Personal Presentation 25
  2. Searching the Internet for Images 25

Project 1 Building a Presentation 26

Objectives 26
The Challenge 26
The Solution 27
The Setup 28
  Creating a Blank Presentation and a
    Title Slide 28
  Saving and Closing a Presentation 32
  Opening a Presentation and
    Adding Slides 33
  Navigating a Presentation 37
  Applying a Template 37
  Switching Views 39
  Adding Text in Outline View 41
  Printing Slides, Handouts, and
    Presentation Outlines 43
The Conclusion 45
Summary and Exercises 46
Summary 46

Key Terms and Operations 46
  Key Terms 46
  Operations 46
Study Questions 46
  Multiple Choice 46
  Short Answer 47
  For Discussion 48
Review Exercises 48
  *1. Creating, Saving, and Adding Slides and
    Text to Presentations 48*
  *2. Switching Views, Navigating Presentation
    Slides, Applying a Template, and
    Printing Handouts 49*
Assignments 50
  *1. Creating, Formatting, and Saving a
    Multi-Slide Presentation 50*
  2. Finding Templates on the Internet 50

Project 2 Editing Slide Text 51

Objectives 51
The Challenge 51
The Solution 53
The Setup 53
  Selecting and Editing Placeholder Text 53
  Changing the Appearance of Text 57
  Finding and Replacing Text 60
  Checking the Style and Spelling of Text 63
  Formatting Text Placeholders 65
  Changing the Page Setup 68
  Creating a Presentation Using a Wizard 69
The Conclusion 73
Summary and Exercises 74
Summary 74
Key Terms and Operations 74
  Key Terms 74
  Operations 74
Study Questions 74
  Multiple Choice 74
  Short Answer 75
  For Discussion 76
Review Exercises 76
  1. Editing Text in an Existing Presentation 76
  *2. Formatting Placeholders, Changing the Page
    Setup, and Checking the Style of Slides in a
    Presentation 77*
Assignments 79
  *1. Editing and Formatting Slide Text and
    Placeholders 79*
  2. Creating a Presentation Using the Wizard 81

Project 3 Adding Art to a Presentation 82

Objectives 82
The Challenge 82

The Solution   83
The Setup   83
  Inserting Clip Art   84
  Moving and Sizing Clip Art   87
  Downloading and Inserting Clip Art from the PowerPoint Web Site   89
  Creating WordArt   94
  Formatting WordArt   96
  Creating Drawings   99
  Manipulating Art   104
The Conclusion   109
Summary and Exercises   110
Summary   110
Key Terms and Operations   110
  Key Terms   110
  Operations   110
Study Questions   110
  Multiple Choice   110
  Short Answer   111
  For Discussion   112
Review Exercises   112
  1. Adding, Moving, and Sizing Clip Art Images   112
  2. Adding WordArt and Drawings to Slides   113
Assignments   114
  1. Adding, Formatting, and Manipulating Clip Art, WordArt, and Drawings   114
  2. Searching the Internet for Pictures to Enhance Presentations   115

Project 4 Viewing and Editing a Presentation   116

Objectives   116
The Challenge   117
The Solution   117
The Setup   117
  Presenting a Slide Show   118
  Using the Slide Show Shortcut Menu   119
  Rearranging Slides in a Presentation   120
  Adding Slide Transitions   121
  Animating Text   123
  Expanding Slides   124
  Hiding Slides and Displaying Hidden Slides   127
The Conclusion   128
Summary and Exercises   129
Summary   129
Key Terms and Operations   129
  Key Terms   129
  Operations   129
Study Questions   129
  Multiple Choice   129
  Short Answer   131
  For Discussion   131
Review Exercises   131
  1. Rearranging, Hiding, and Expanding Slides and Showing a Presentation   131
  2. Editing, Enhancing, and Viewing a Presentation as a Slide Show   133
Assignments   134
  1. Editing and Enhancing a Presentation and Viewing a Slide Show   134
  2. Editing and Enhancing a Presentation and Posting It to the WWW   134

Project 5 Enhancing a Presentation   136

Objectives   136
The Challenge   136
The Solution   137
The Setup   137
  Animating Slides with Sound   137
  Setting Action Buttons   141
  Adding Slide Timings   144
  Setting a Presentation to Run Continuously   146
  Creating Notes Pages   147
  Packing a Presentation to Go   149
The Conclusion   151
Summary and Exercises   152
Summary   152
Key Terms and Operations   152
  Key Terms   152
  Operations   152
Study Questions   152
  Multiple Choice   152
  Short Answer   153
  For Discussion   154
Review Exercises   154
  1. Adding Sound Effects to Animated Text, Setting Action Buttons to Display Hidden Slides, Adding Text to a Slide   154
  2. Adding Action Buttons, Animating with Sound, Adding Slide Timings, Setting a Presentation to Run Continuously, Creating Notes Pages   155
Assignments   156
  1. Finalizing a Presentation to Run Continuously   156
  2. Packing Presentations to Go and Sending Them Via a Mail Message   157

Integrated Project 3: Integrating Word, Excel, Access, and Powerpoint   IP3-1

Objectives   IP3-1
The Challenge   IP3-1
The Solution   IP3-2
The Setup   IP3-3

Embedding a Word Table on a PowerPoint
    Slide   IP3-4
Linking Data from Excel to a PowerPoint
    Slide   IP3-8
Creating a Word Document from a
    PowerPoint Presentation Outline   IP3-12
Saving a PowerPoint Slide as a Graphic
    and Adding the Image to a
    Word Document   IP3-14
Creating a Hyperlink Between a Word
    Document and a PowerPoint
    Presentation   IP3-16
Saving a Presentation as an
    HTML File   IP3-18
The Conclusion   IP3-20
Summary and Exercises   IP3-21
Summary   *IP3-21*
Key Terms and Operations   *IP3-21*
   Key Terms   *IP3-21*
   Operations   *IP3-21*

Study Questions   *IP3-21*
   Multiple Choice   *IP3-21*
   Short Answer   *IP3-22*
   For Discussion   *IP3-23*
Exercises   *IP3-23*
   *Creating a PowerPoint presentation from a
      Word outline and saving a slide as
      a graphic*   *IP3-23*
Assignments   *IP3-25*
   *Embedding a new object in a PowerPoint
      presentation, linking an Excel worksheet to a
      PowerPoint slide, and creating a hyperlink to
      display the Excel worksheet*   *IP3-25*

Glossary   GL-1–6

Index   Index-1–11

Overview of Windows 95, Outlook, and Internet Explorer 3.0

Windows 95

Overview of Windows 95

Microsoft Windows 95 is an *operating system*, a special kind of computer program that performs three major functions. First, an operating system controls the actual *hardware* of the computer (the screen, the keyboard, the disk drives, and so on). Second, an operating system enables other software programs such as word processing or spreadsheet *applications* to run. Finally, an operating system determines how the user operates the computer and its programs or applications.

As an operating system, Windows 95 and all other programs written to run under it provide *graphics* (or pictures) called *icons* to carry out commands and run programs. For this reason, Windows 95 is referred to as a *Graphical User Interface* or GUI (pronounced *gooey*). You can use the keyboard or a device called a *mouse* to activate the icons.

This overview explains the basics of Windows 95 so that you can begin using your computer quickly and easily.

Objectives

After completing this project, you will be able to:

- ▶ **Launch Windows 95**
- ▶ **Identify the desktop elements**
- ▶ **Use a mouse**
- ▶ **Use the basic features of Windows 95**
- ▶ **Organize your computer**
- ▶ **Work with multiple programs**
- ▶ **Get help**
- ▶ **Exit Windows 95**

Launching Windows 95

Because Windows 95 is an operating system, it launches immediately when you turn on the computer. Depending on the way your computer is set up you may have to type your user name and password to log on — to get permission to begin using the program. After Windows 95 launches, the working environment, called the *desktop,* displays on the screen.

Identifying the Desktop Elements

Figure W.1 shows the Windows 95 desktop with several icons that represent the hardware and the software installed on the computer. *My Computer* enables you to organize your work. The *Recycle Bin* is a temporary storage area for files deleted from the hard disk. At the bottom of the desktop is the *Taskbar* for starting programs, accessing various areas of Windows 95, and switching among programs.

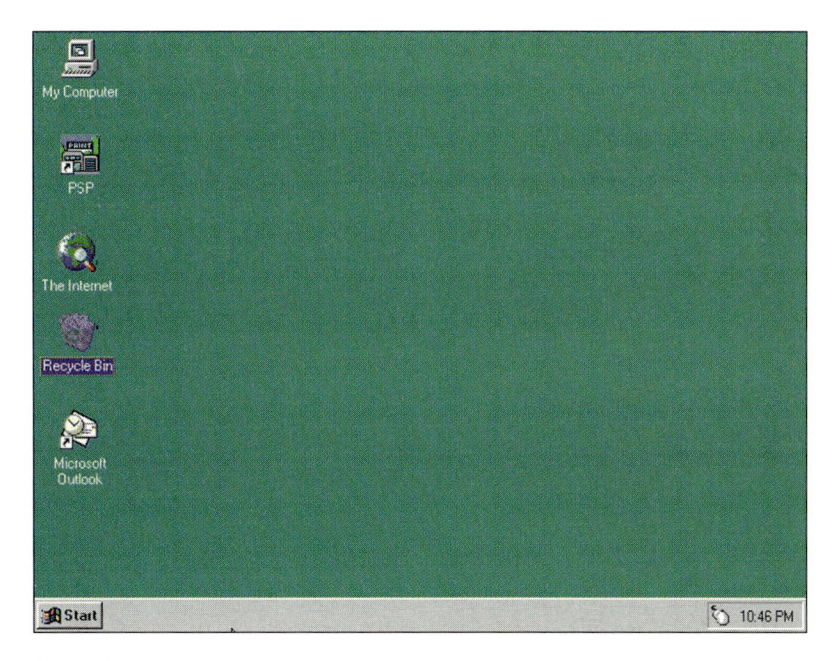

Figure W.1

> **Note** The desktop can be customized, so the desktop on the computer you're using will not look exactly like the one shown in the illustrations in this overview.

Using a Mouse

A pointing device is almost an indispensable tool for using Windows 95. Although you can use the keyboard to navigate and make selections, using a mouse is often more convenient and efficient.

When you move the mouse on your desk, a pointer moves on the screen. When the pointer is on the object you want to use, you can take one of the actions described in Table W.1 to give Windows 95 an instruction.

Table W.1   Mouse Actions

Action	Description
Point	Slide the mouse across a smooth surface (preferably a mouse pad) until the pointer on the screen is on the object.
Click	Press and release the left mouse button once.
Drag	Press and hold down the left mouse button while you move the mouse, and then release the mouse button to complete the action.
Right-click	Press and release the right mouse button once. Right-clicking usually displays a shortcut menu.
Double-click	Press and release the left mouse button twice in rapid succession.

TASK 1: TO PRACTICE USING THE MOUSE:

1. Point to the My Computer icon, press and hold down the left mouse button, and then drag the mouse across the desk.
   The icon moves.

2. Drag the My Computer icon back to its original location.

3. Right-click the icon.

Your shortcut menu may not match this menu

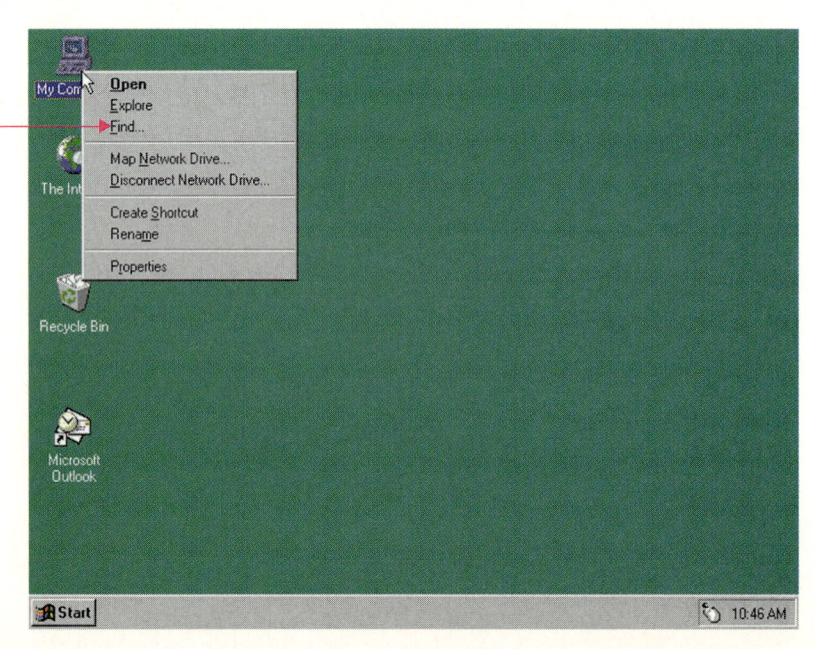

4 Click a blank space on the screen.
The shortcut menu closes.

5 Double-click the My Computer icon.

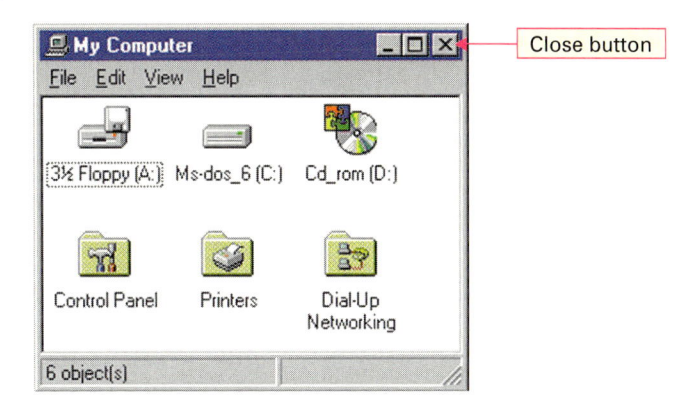

Close button

6 Click the Close [X] button to close the My Computer window.

Using the Basic Features of Windows 95

The basic features of Windows 95 are menus, windows, menu bars, dialog boxes, and toolbars. These features are used in all programs that are written to run under Windows 95.

Using the Start Menu

Menus contain the commands you use to perform tasks. In Windows 95, you can use the Start menu shown in Figure W.2 to start programs and to access other Windows options.

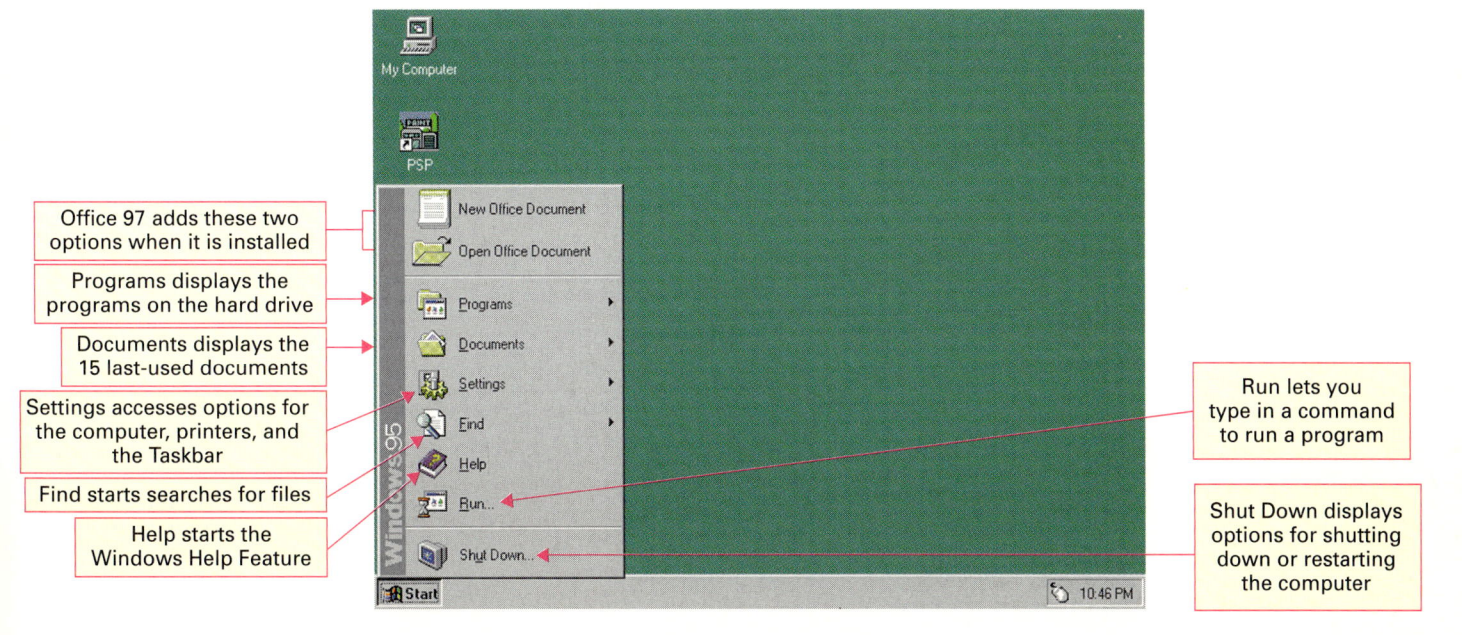

Office 97 adds these two options when it is installed

Programs displays the programs on the hard drive

Documents displays the 15 last-used documents

Settings accesses options for the computer, printers, and the Taskbar

Find starts searches for files

Help starts the Windows Help Feature

Run lets you type in a command to run a program

Shut Down displays options for shutting down or restarting the computer

Figure W.2

TASK 2: TO USE THE START MENU TO LAUNCH A PROGRAM:

1. Click the Start button.
   The triangles beside several of the menu options indicate that the options will display another menu.

2. Point to Programs and click the Windows Explorer icon.
   The Exploring window opens (see Figure W.3). You can use this feature of Windows 95 to manage files.

Using Windows

Clicking on the Windows Explorer icon opened a *window,* a Windows 95 feature that you saw earlier when you opened the My Computer window. Figure W.3 shows the common elements that most windows contain.

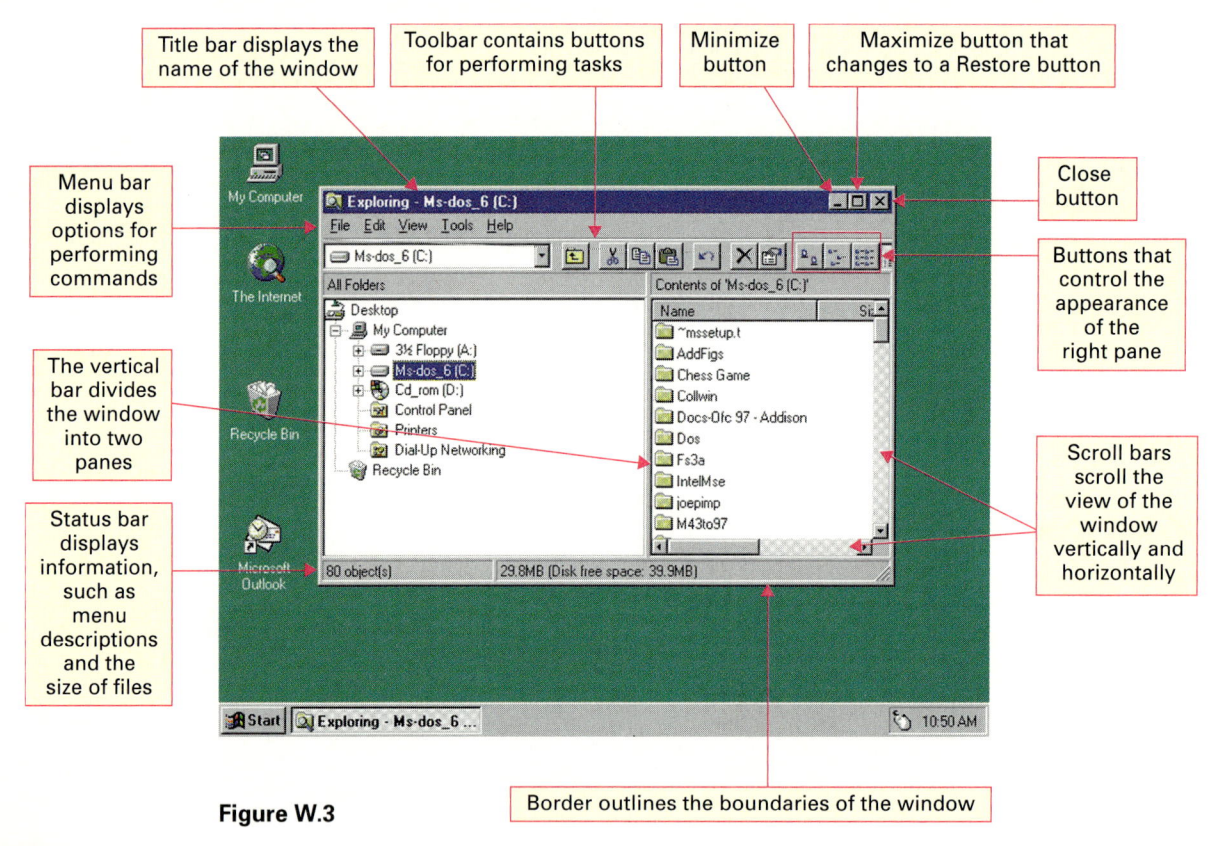

- Title bar displays the name of the window
- Toolbar contains buttons for performing tasks
- Minimize button
- Maximize button that changes to a Restore button
- Close button
- Menu bar displays options for performing commands
- Buttons that control the appearance of the right pane
- The vertical bar divides the window into two panes
- Scroll bars scroll the view of the window vertically and horizontally
- Status bar displays information, such as menu descriptions and the size of files
- Border outlines the boundaries of the window

Figure W.3

TASK 3: TO WORK WITH A WINDOW:

1. Click the Maximize button if it is displayed. If it is not displayed, click the Restore button, and then click the Maximize button.
   The Maximize button changes to a Restore button.

2. Click the Minimize button.

Overview **WIN-7**

Exploring window button

Warning When you minimize a window, the program in the window is still running and therefore using computer memory. To exit a program that is running in a window, you must click the Close button, not the Minimize button.

3 Click the Exploring button on the Taskbar and then click ⬜.

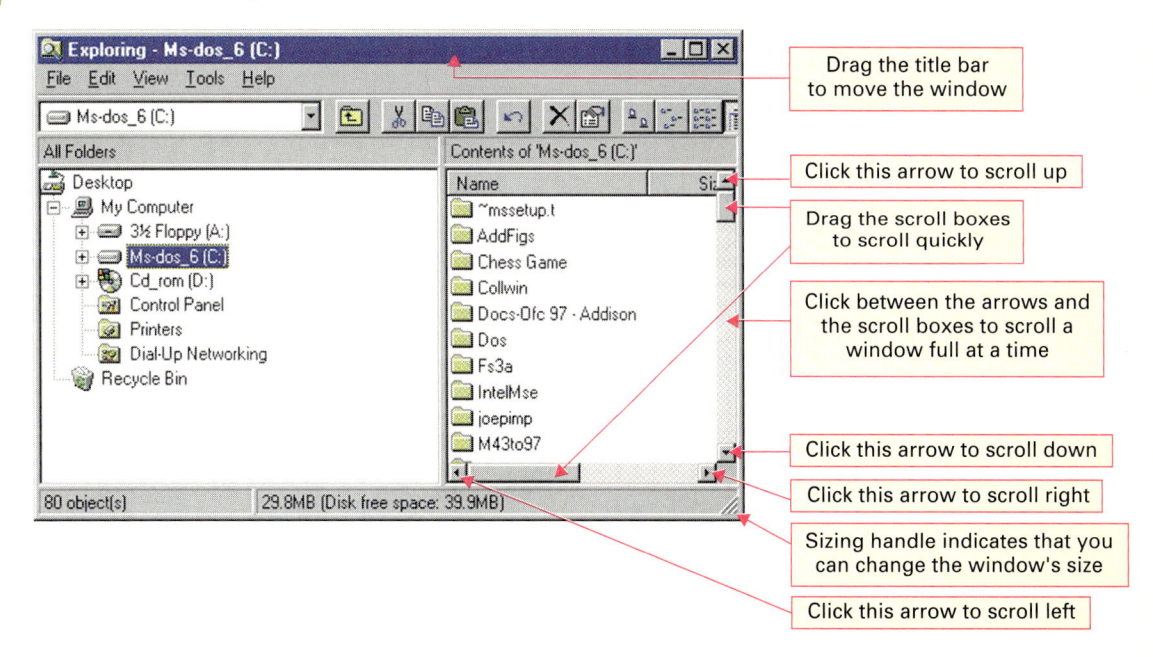

- Drag the title bar to move the window
- Click this arrow to scroll up
- Drag the scroll boxes to scroll quickly
- Click between the arrows and the scroll boxes to scroll a window full at a time
- Click this arrow to scroll down
- Click this arrow to scroll right
- Sizing handle indicates that you can change the window's size
- Click this arrow to scroll left

4 Point to the border of the Exploring window until the pointer changes to a double-headed black arrow, and then drag the border to make the window wider. (Be sure that all the buttons in the toolbar are visible.)

5 Practice scrolling.

6 When you are comfortable with your scrolling expertise, click ⬜.

Using Menu Bars and Toolbars

Menu bars and toolbars are generally located at the top of a window. You can select a menu option in a menu bar by clicking the option or by pressing ALT and then typing the underlined letter for the option. When you select an option, a drop-down menu appears. Figure W.4 shows a menu with many of the elements common to menus.

Note Because you can select menu commands in two ways, the steps with instructions to select a menu command will use the word choose instead of dictating the method of selection.

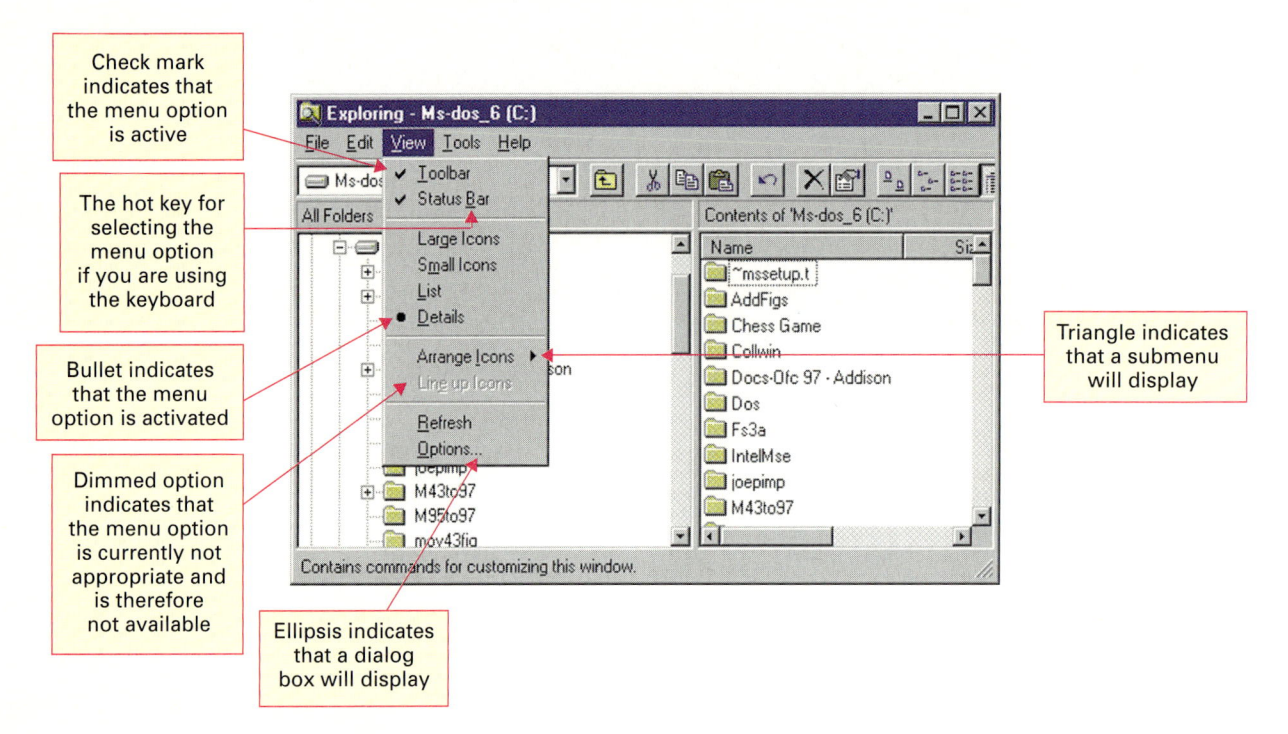

Check mark indicates that the menu option is active

The hot key for selecting the menu option if you are using the keyboard

Bullet indicates that the menu option is activated

Dimmed option indicates that the menu option is currently not appropriate and is therefore not available

Ellipsis indicates that a dialog box will display

Triangle indicates that a submenu will display

Figure W.4

Toolbars contain buttons that perform many of the same commands found on menus. To use a toolbar button, click the button; Windows 95 takes an immediate action, depending on the button's function.

Tip If you don't know what a button on the toolbar does, point to the button; a ToolTip, a brief description of the button, appears near the button.

TASK 4: TO USE MENUS AND TOOLBARS:

1. Choose View in the Exploring window.
   The View menu shown in Figure W.4 displays.

2. Choose Large Icons.

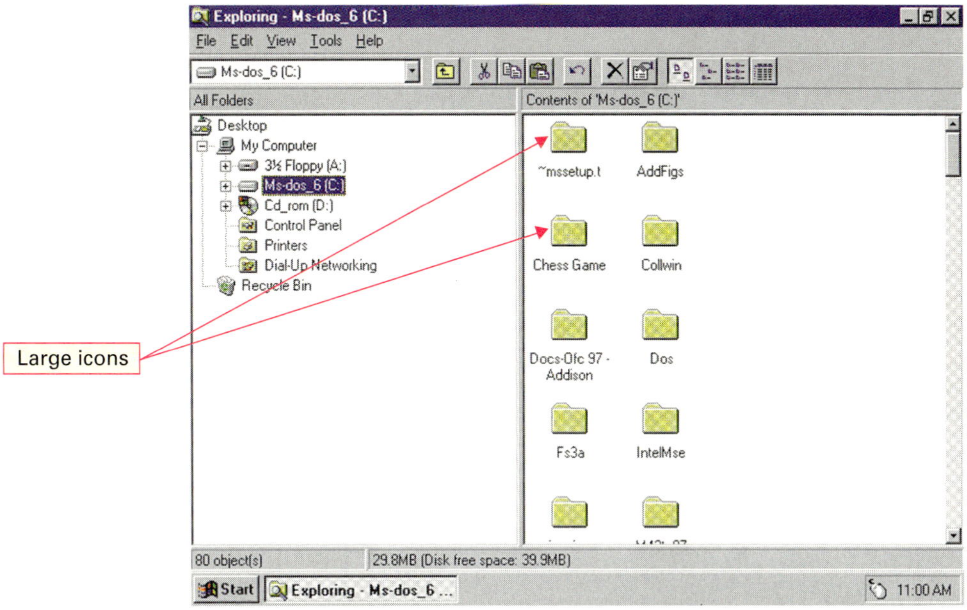
Large icons

3 Click the Details button on the toolbar.

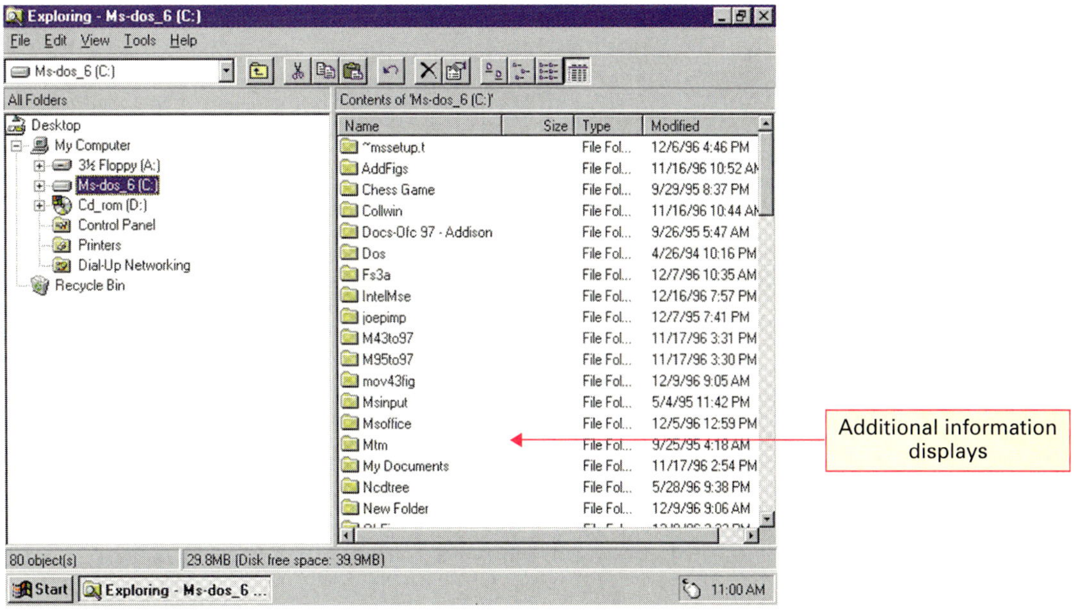
Additional information displays

Using Dialog Boxes

When many options are available for a single task, Windows 95 conveniently groups the options in one place, called a ***dialog box.*** Some functions have so many options that Windows 95 divides them further into groups and places them on separate pages in the dialog box. Figures W.5 and W.6 show dialog boxes with different types of options. Throughout the remainder of this project, you practice using dialog boxes.

win-10

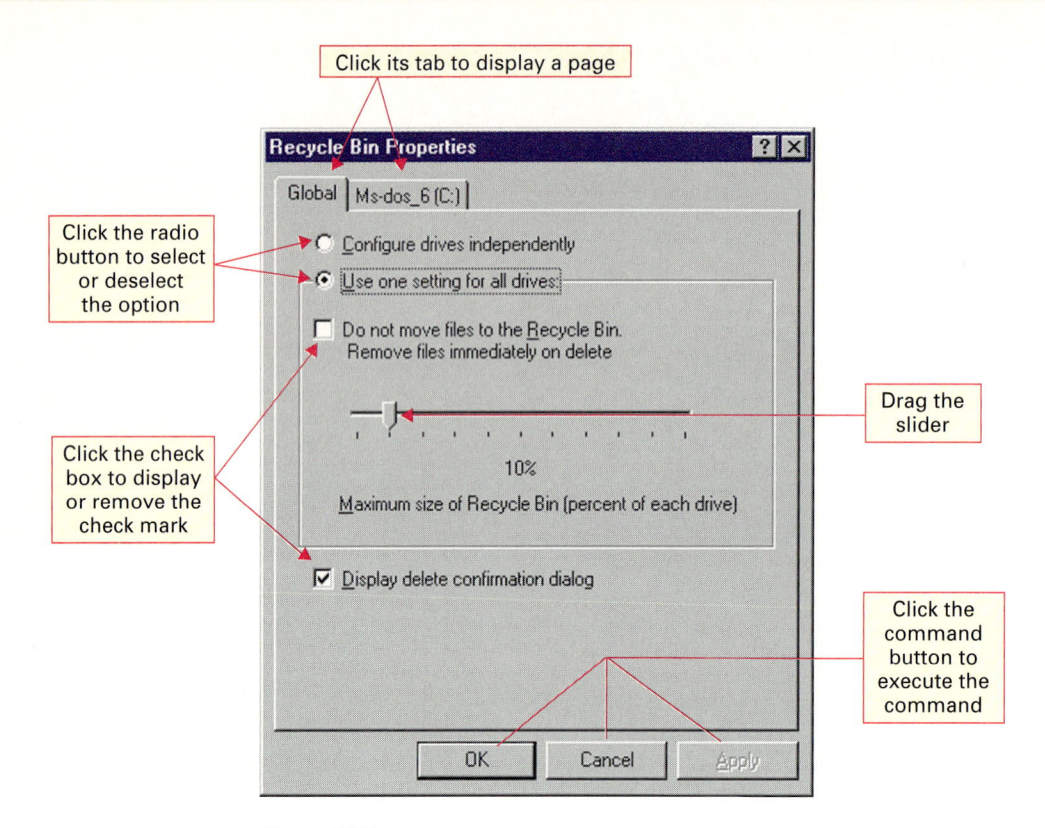

Figure W.5

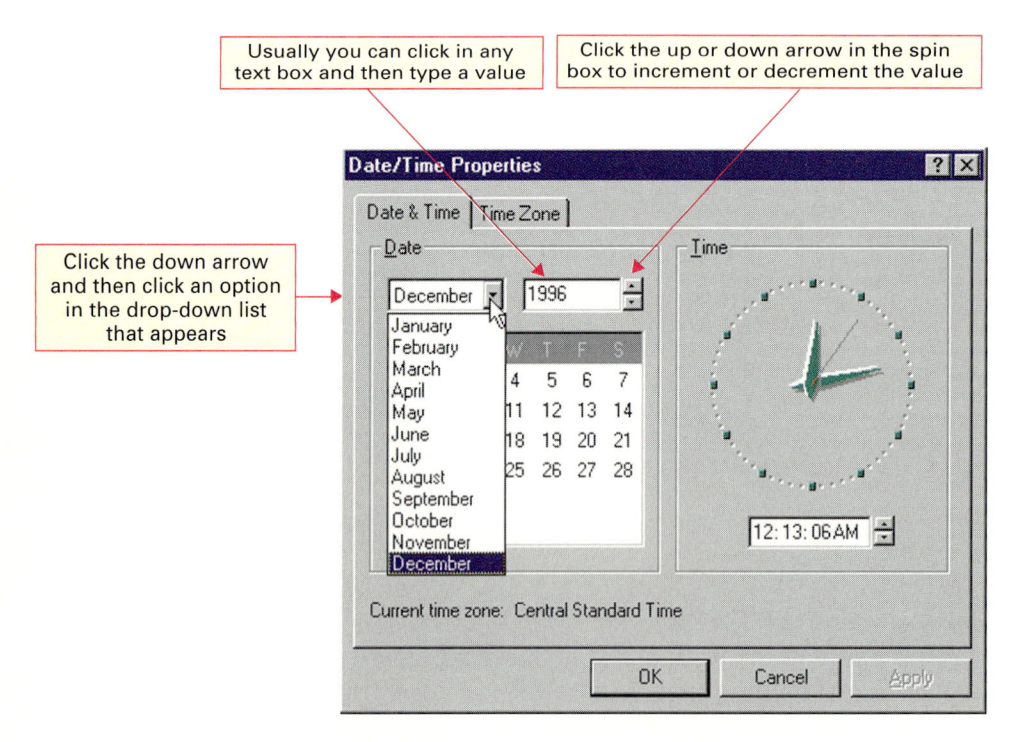

Callouts:
- Click its tab to display a page
- Click the radio button to select or deselect the option
- Click the check box to display or remove the check mark
- Drag the slider
- Click the command button to execute the command

Figure W.6

Callouts:
- Usually you can click in any text box and then type a value
- Click the up or down arrow in the spin box to increment or decrement the value
- Click the down arrow and then click an option in the drop-down list that appears

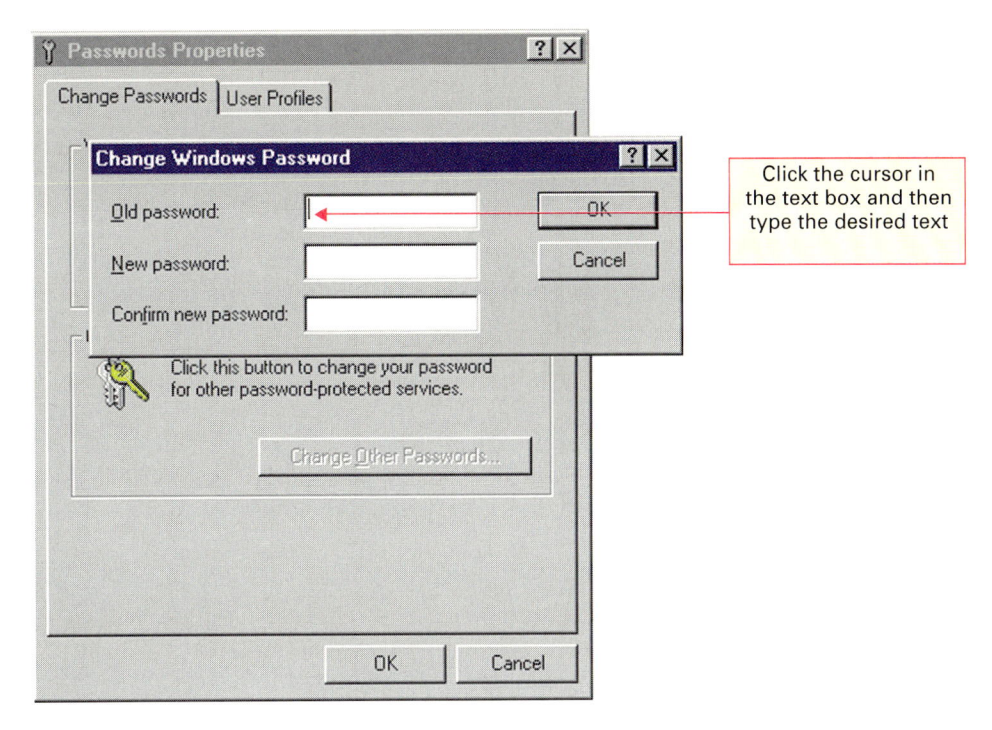

Figure W.7

Organizing Your Computer

A *disk drive* is designed to store the *files* you create (word processing documents, workbooks, databases, and so on). The computer you are using probably has at least two disk drives: a *hard disk drive* with a permanent disk and a *floppy disk drive* that uses a removable 5¼-inch or 3½-inch floppy disk (the floppy part of the disk is inside the protective covering). You also might have a *CD ROM drive.* If you are not sure what drives your computer has, you can find out by double-clicking the My Computer icon on the desktop. My Computer displays a window with icons for the elements installed on the computer.

Floppy drives are usually named with letters A or B. The hard drive is always C, and the CD ROM drive is D if there is only one hard drive.

> **Note** Before a computer can use a floppy disk, the disk must be formatted. Normally you format a disk only when it is new because formatting erases all files stored on a disk. If you need to format a new disk, place it in the floppy disk drive, right-click the floppy disk drive icon in Windows Explorer, click Format, click Full, and click Start. If you get a message that Windows cannot format the disk, go back to Windows Explorer, click on a different drive and then right-click the drive you want to format. After Windows 95 completes the formatting, click Close and then close the dialog box.

Creating Folders

The main directory (called the *root*) of any disk can hold only a limited number of files. Because you can have hundreds or thousands of files on a disk, you must create *folders* (also called *directories*) and store the files in the folders.

> **Tip** Do not store your data files in the same folders that contain program files. Create separate folders for data files.

TASK 5: TO CREATE A FOLDER ON DRIVE A:

1. Insert a formatted disk into drive A and click the drive A icon in the left pane, scrolling, if necessary.
   The icon is highlighted.

2. Choose File, New, Folder.

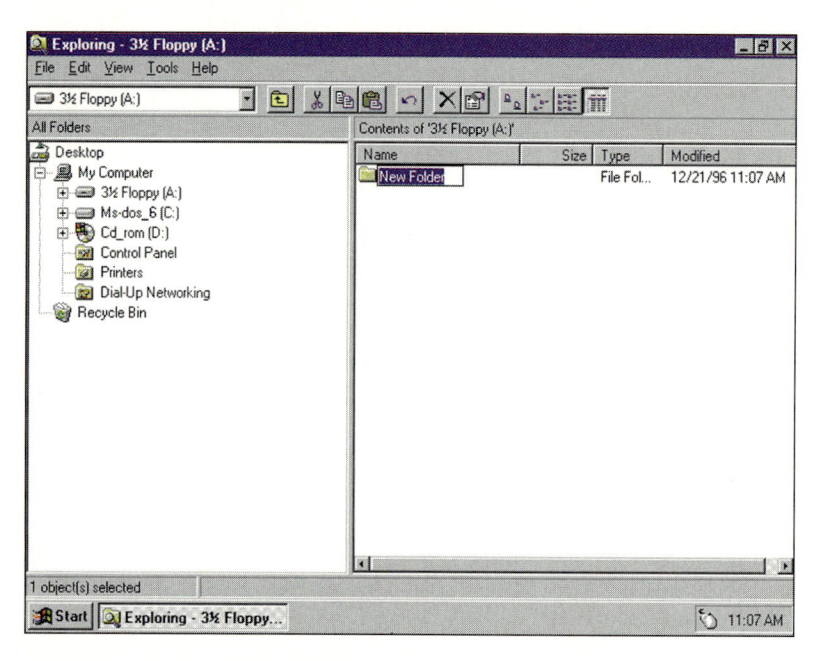

3. Type **Pictures** and press Enter.
   The word Pictures replaces the words *New Folder*.

Copying and Renaming Files

One of the primary purposes of Windows Explorer is to enable users to manage files. Using Windows Explorer, you can easily copy files and rename them.

TASK 6: TO COPY FILES:

1. Click the plus beside drive C and then scroll if necessary and click the Windows folder.

Overview **WIN-13**

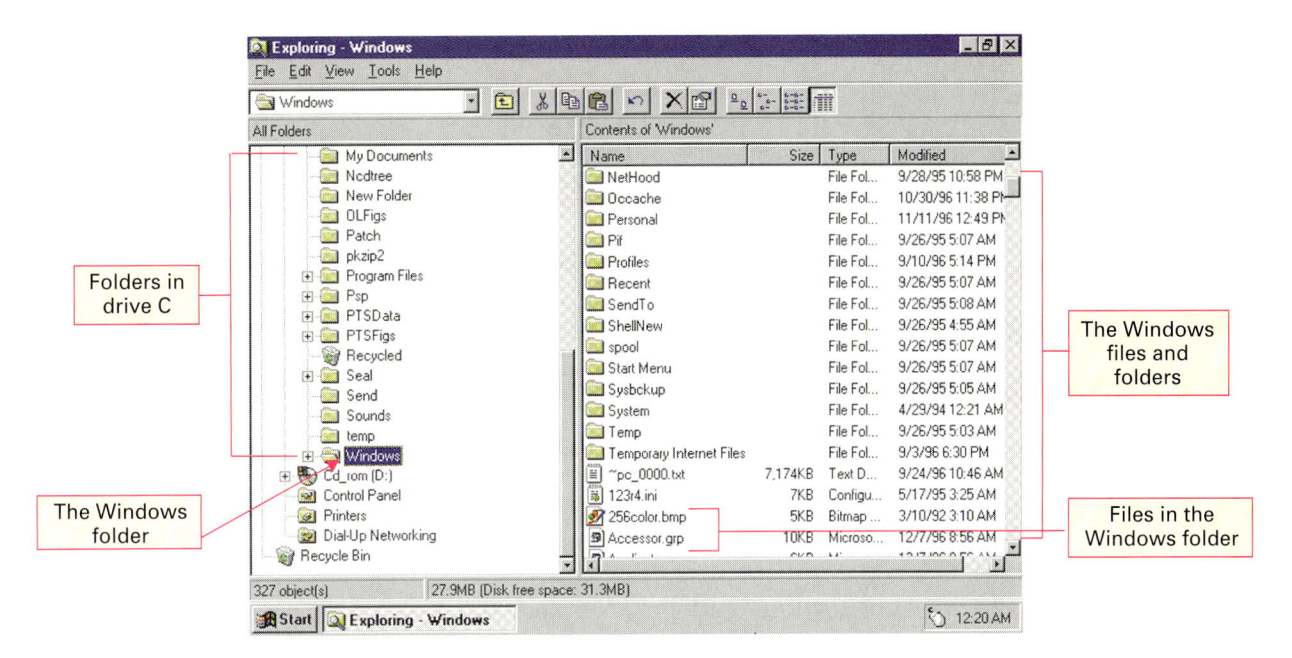

[Screenshot of Exploring - Windows file manager, with labels:
- Folders in drive C
- The Windows folder
- The Windows files and folders
- Files in the Windows folder]

2 Scroll the right pane until you see files with a bmp extension and then click any bmp file. You don't need to select the files shown in the figure.

> **Note** If you don't see file extensions on your screen, choose View, Options, and click the View tab if necessary. Deselect Hide Ms-DOS file extensions for file types that are registered and then click OK.

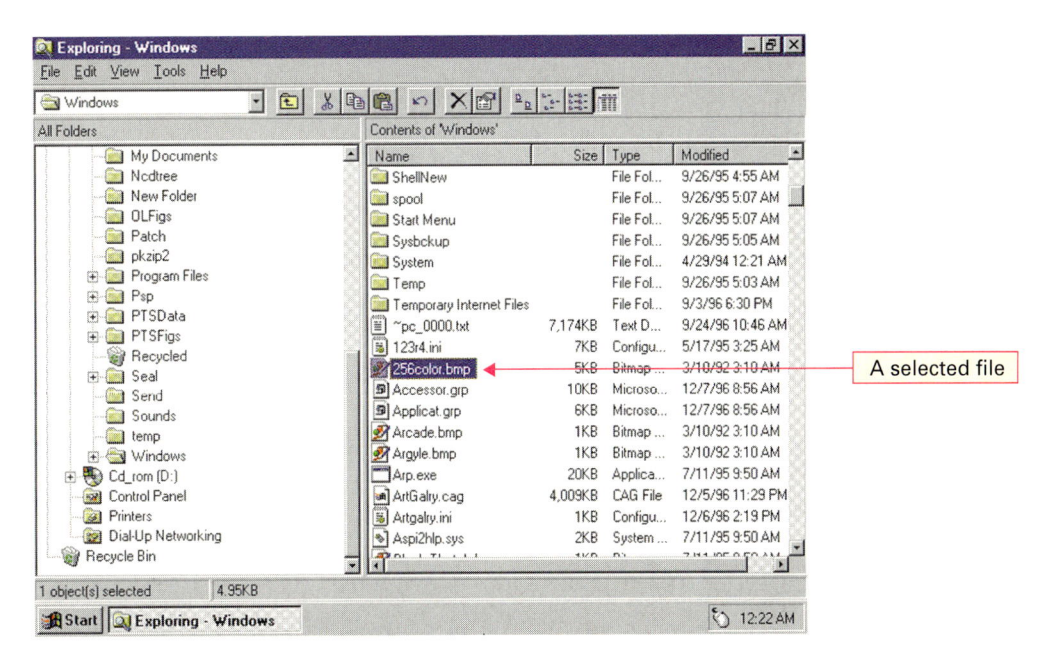

[Screenshot of Exploring - Windows file manager with 256color.bmp highlighted, labeled "A selected file"]

3 Press and hold down CTRL and then click another bmp file. Both files are selected.

4 Click the Copy button in the toolbar.
The files are copied and held in a memory storage area referred to as the *Clipboard*.

5 Scroll if necessary and click drive A in the left pane; then click the Paste button.

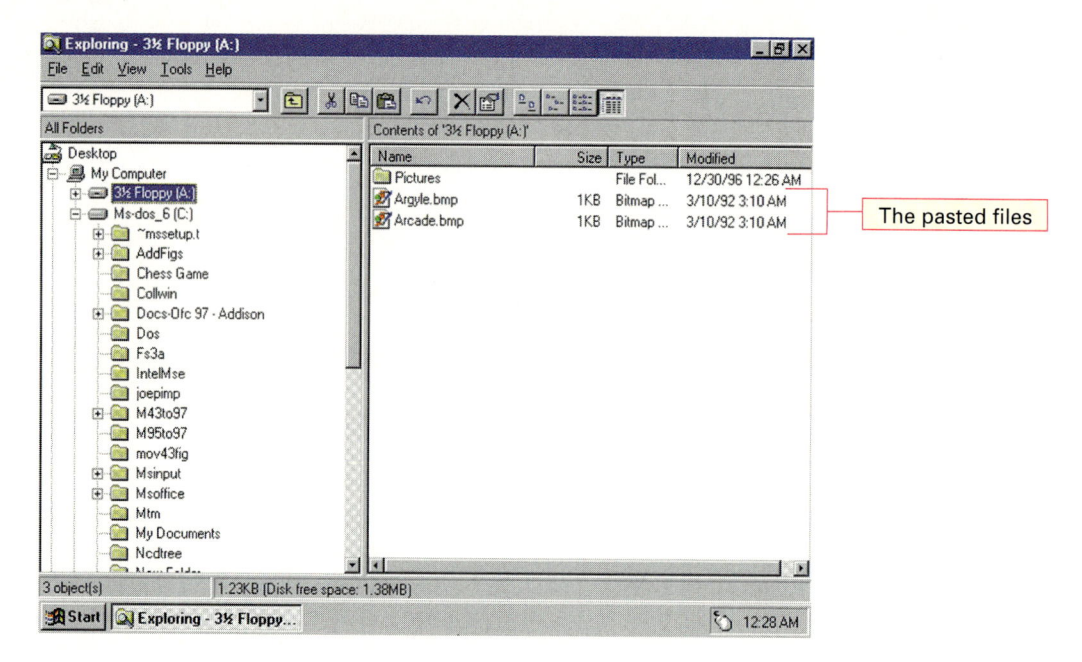

The pasted files (Argyle.bmp, Arcade.bmp shown in Contents of '3½ Floppy (A:)')

Note If you paste a file to the same location, Windows renames the file Copy of xxxxxxx.xxx (where xxxxxxx.xxx is the original file name).

Tip When copying files from the hard drive to a floppy drive, you also can right-click the files and choose Send to.

If you want to change the name of a file, you can rename it. When renaming files, you should use the same extension.

TASK 7: TO RENAME A FILE:

1 Click one of the files you just copied to drive A.
The file is selected.

2 Click the name of the file.
The name is selected.

3 Type **Figure 1.bmp** and press (ENTER).
The file is renamed.

Moving Files

Occasionally you may want to reorganize the files and folders on a disk by moving them. The steps to move files are very similar to the steps for copying.

TASK 8: TO MOVE A FILE:

1 Click the plus beside the drive A icon.

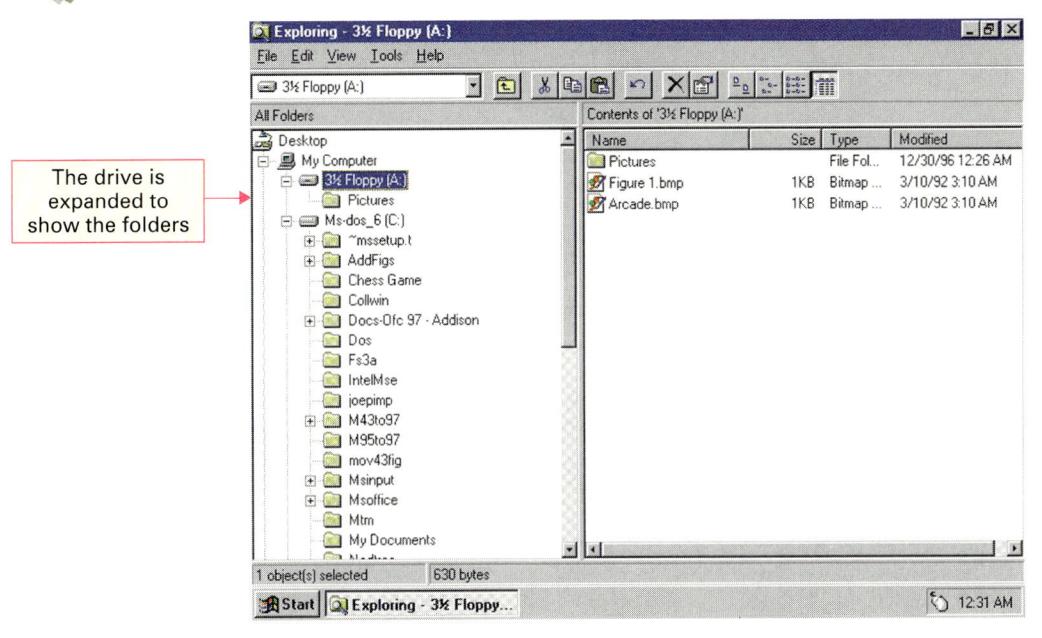

The drive is expanded to show the folders

2 Point to Figure 1.bmp in the right pane and press the right mouse button while you drag the files to the Pictures folder in the left pane. (Be careful to release the mouse button only when the Pictures folder is selected.)
A shortcut menu displays when you release the mouse button.

3 Click Move Here.
Windows 95 moves the file into the folder.

4 Click the Pictures folder in the left pane.

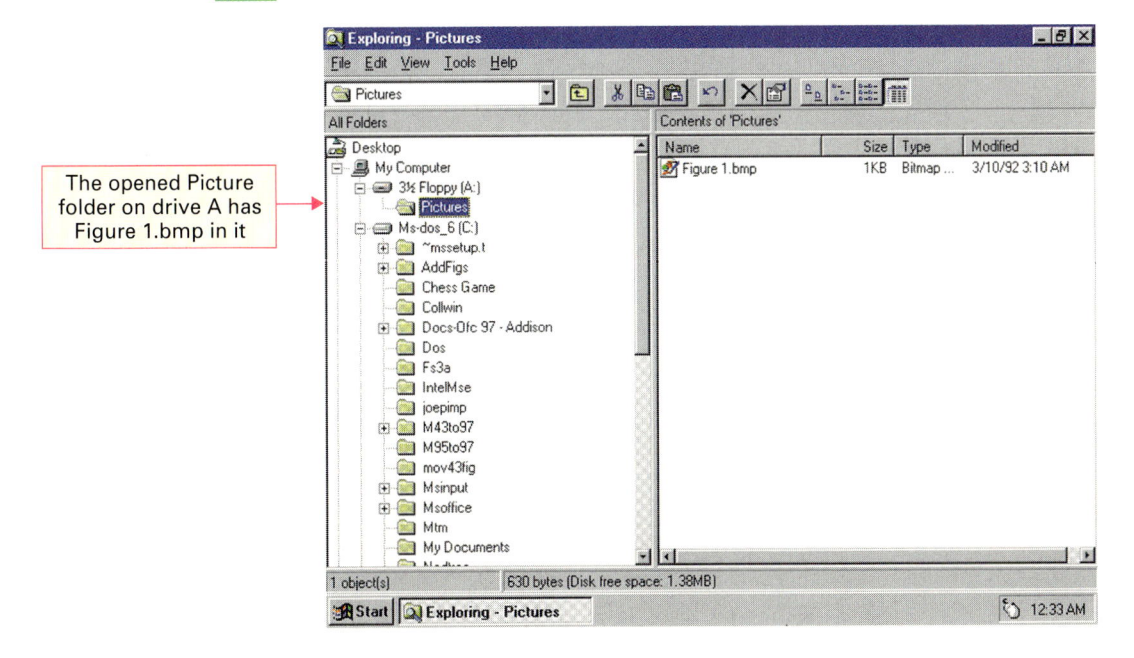

The opened Picture folder on drive A has Figure 1.bmp in it

Deleting Files

When you delete a file on the hard disk, the file just moves into the Recycle Bin where it stays until it is deleted or restored. When you delete a file from a floppy disk, the file is removed and doesn't go into the Recycle Bin on the hard drive.

> **Tip** If you are deleting files in order to reclaim hard disk space, you must empty the Recycle Bin after you delete the files.

TASK 9: TO DELETE FILES:

1. Ensure that the icon for drive A is selected in the left pane and then click the bmp file in the right pane and press DEL.

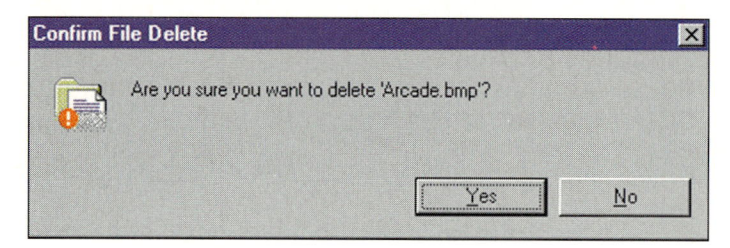

2. Click Yes to tell Windows 95 that you know what you're doing; you really do want to delete the file.
   The file is deleted.

3. Select the Setup.bmp file in the Windows folder in drive C, write the name down, and then delete it.
   The file is moved to the Recycle Bin.

> **Note** If you don't have a file named Setup.bmp, you can delete another file, but you should make a note of the filename so that you can restore the correct file in the next task.

Restoring Files

If you accidentally delete a file from the hard drive, you can restore it to its original location if the file is still in the Recycle Bin. (The Recycle Bin has a limited size. When the Recycle Bin fills up, older files are replaced by newer deleted files.)

TASK 10: TO RESTORE A FILE:

1. Click the Recycled folder in the left pane.

Overview **WIN-17**

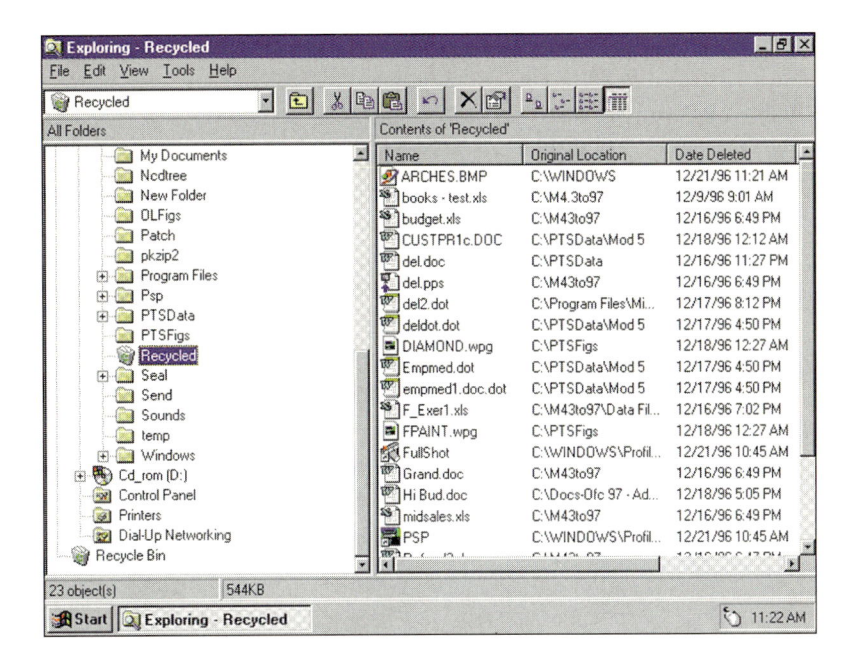

[Screenshot of Windows Explorer showing "Exploring - Recycled" window with folder tree on left and file contents on right, including files like ARCHES.BMP, books-test.xls, budget.xls, etc.]

2 Click the name of the bmp file you deleted in the previous task. You did write the name down, didn't you? Just in case you didn't, it's Setup.bmp.
The file is selected.

3 Click File and then click Restore.
Windows 95 restore the file to its original location.

4 Click ⊠.
The Windows Explorer closes.

Working with Multiple Programs

Windows 95's ***multitasking*** feature allows you to launch multiple programs and switch back and forth between them. Each open program is represented by a button on the Taskbar.

TASK 11: TO SWITCH BETWEEN WINDOWS:

1 Click Start and point to Programs.

WIN-18

2 Point to Accessories and click Paint. (Maximize the window if necessary.)

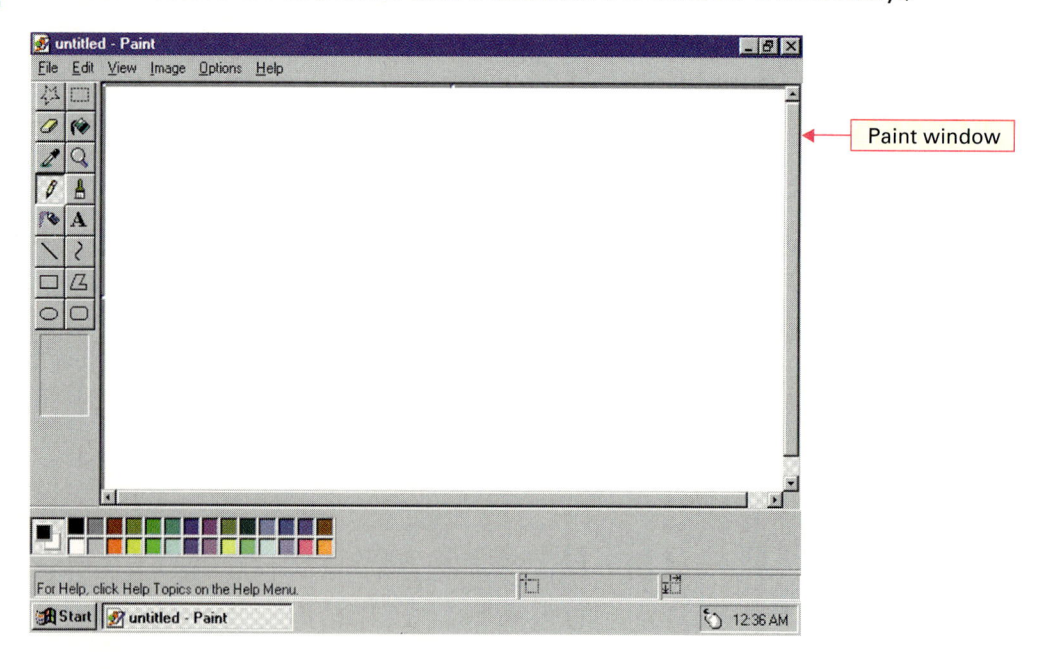

3 Click Start, point to Programs, point to Accessories, and click WordPad. (Maximize the window if necessary.)

Overview **WIN-19**

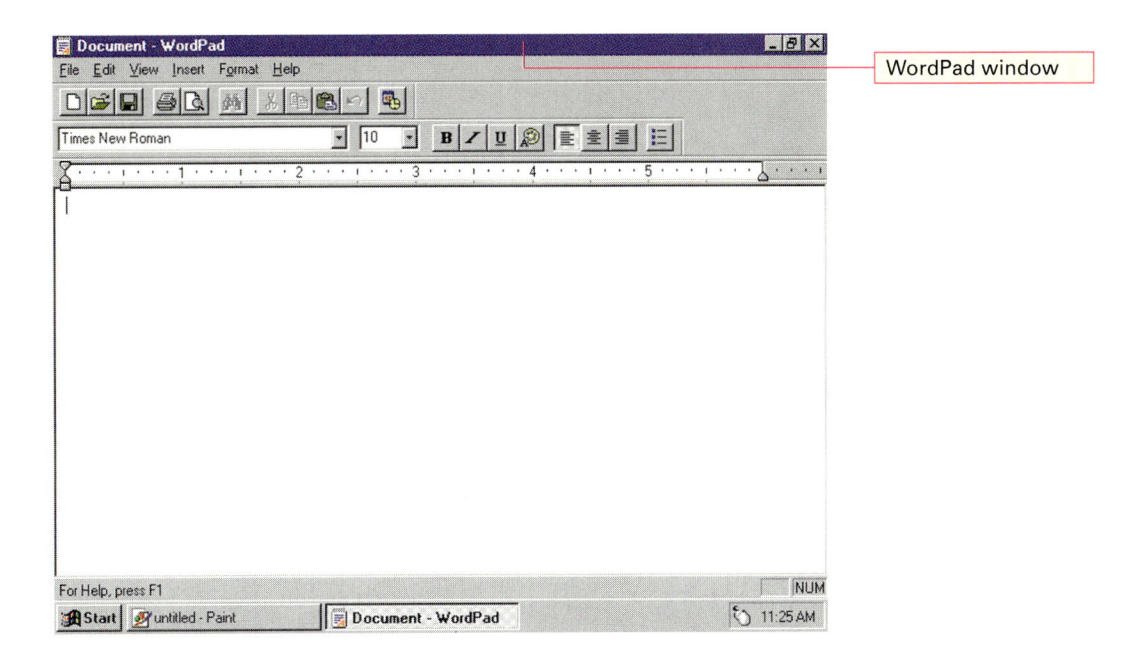

→ WordPad window

4 Type **What do you think of this graphic?** and press ENTER twice.

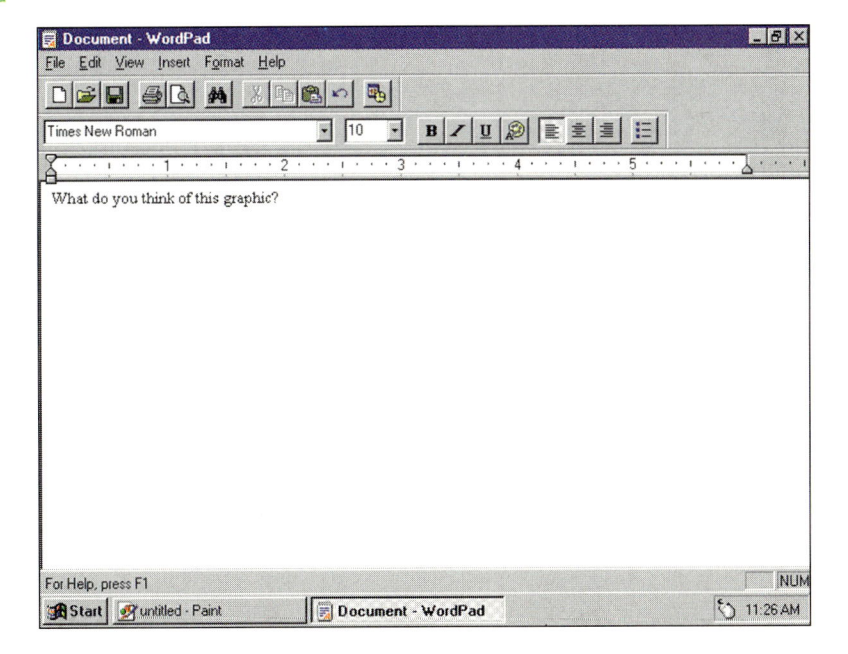

5 Click the Paint button in the Taskbar.
Windows switches to the Paint program.

6 Choose File, Open.

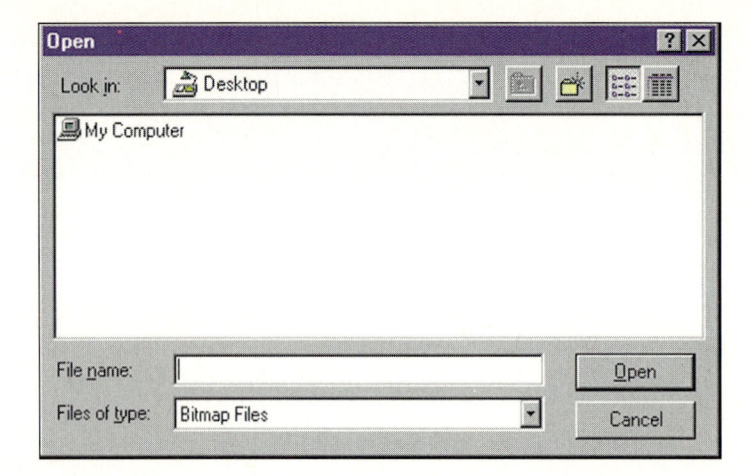

[Open dialog box screenshot showing Look in: Desktop, with My Computer listed, File name field, Files of type: Bitmap Files, Open and Cancel buttons]

7 Click the down arrow to access the Look in drop-down list box and click drive A icon.

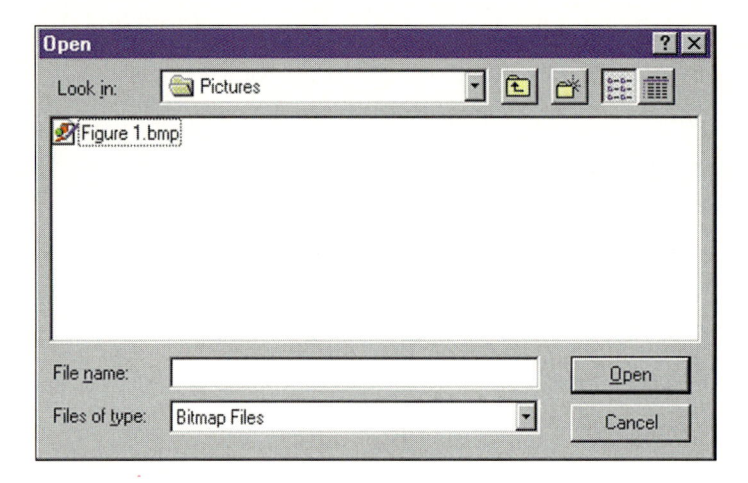

[Open dialog box screenshot showing Look in: Pictures, with Figure 1.bmp listed, File name field, Files of type: Bitmap Files, Open and Cancel buttons]

8 Double-click the Pictures folder.

9 Double-click the Figure 1.bmp file.
The Paint window opens with the graphic file in it.

10 Click Edit and then click Select All.

Overview **WIN-21**

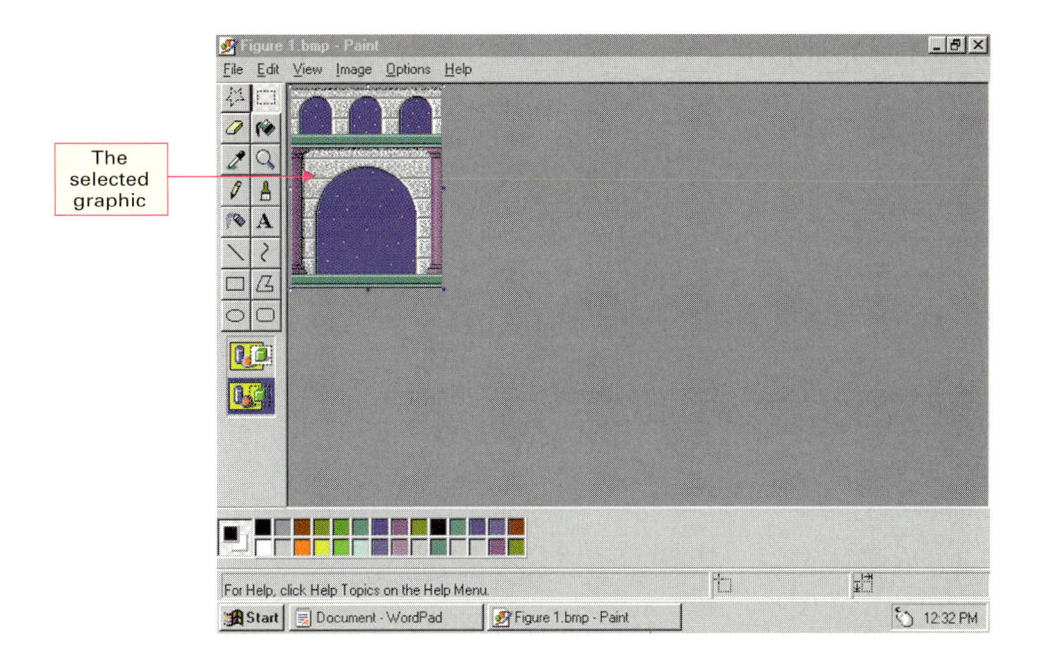

The selected graphic

Remember Your graphic may not match the illustration because you weren't told to copy a specific file.

11 Click Edit and then click Copy.
Windows 95 copies the image to the Clipboard memory area you used when you copied files.

12 Click the WordPad button in the Taskbar.
Windows switches to the WordPad program.

13 Click Edit and then click Paste.

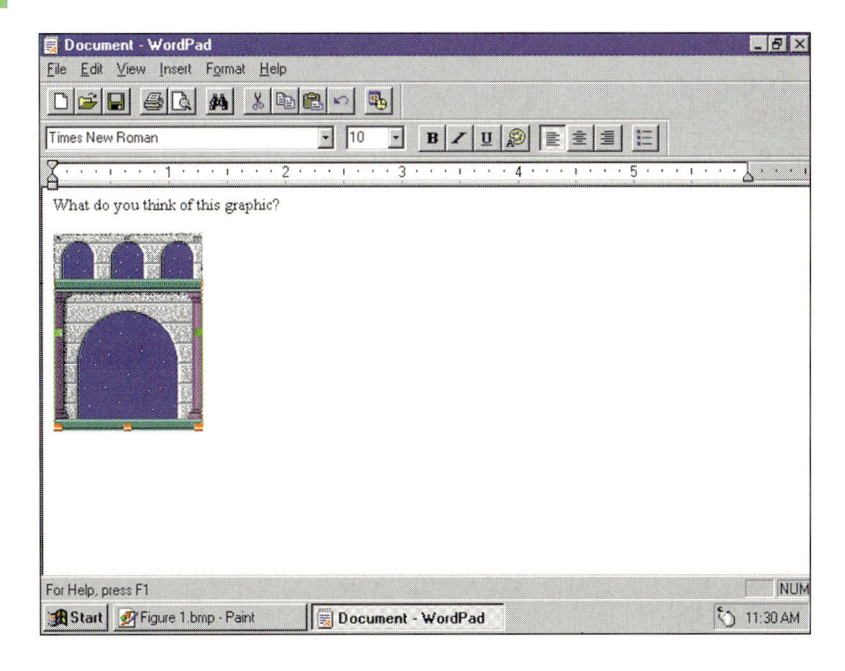

14 Click File, Save.

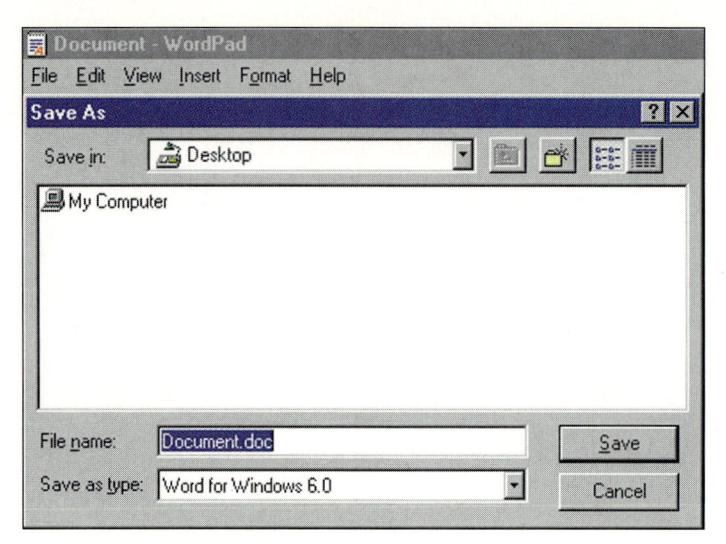

15 Type **a:\pictures\My File** in the File name text box and click Save. Windows 95 saves the file to the Pictures folder on drive A.

16 Click ✕ in the WordPad window.
The WordPad program closes.

17 Click ✕ in the Paint window.
The Paint window closes, and the Windows 95 desktop is visible again.

Getting Help

Windows 95 provides you with three methods of accessing help information: You can look up information in a table of contents; you can search for information in an index; or you can find a specific word or phrase in a database maintained by the Find feature.

Additionally, Windows 95 provides **context-sensitive help,** called **What's This?** for the topic you are working on. This type of help is generally found in dialog boxes.

After you learn to use Help in Windows 95, you can use help in any Windows program because all programs use the same help format.

TASK 12: TO USE HELP CONTENTS, INDEX, AND FIND:

1 Click the Start button on the Taskbar and click Help.

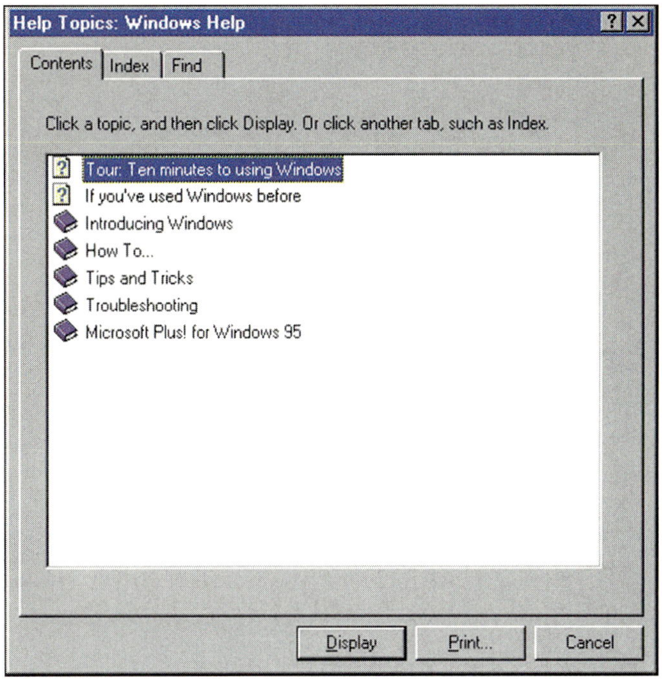
Help Topics: Windows Help
Contents
Index
Find
Click a topic, and then click Display. Or click another tab, such as Index.
Tour: Ten minutes to using Windows
If you've used Windows before
Introducing Windows
How To...
Tips and Tricks
Troubleshooting
Microsoft Plus! for Windows 95
Display
Print...
Cancel

2 Click the Contents tab if a different page is displayed. The Contents page displays.

3 Double-click Tips and Tricks.

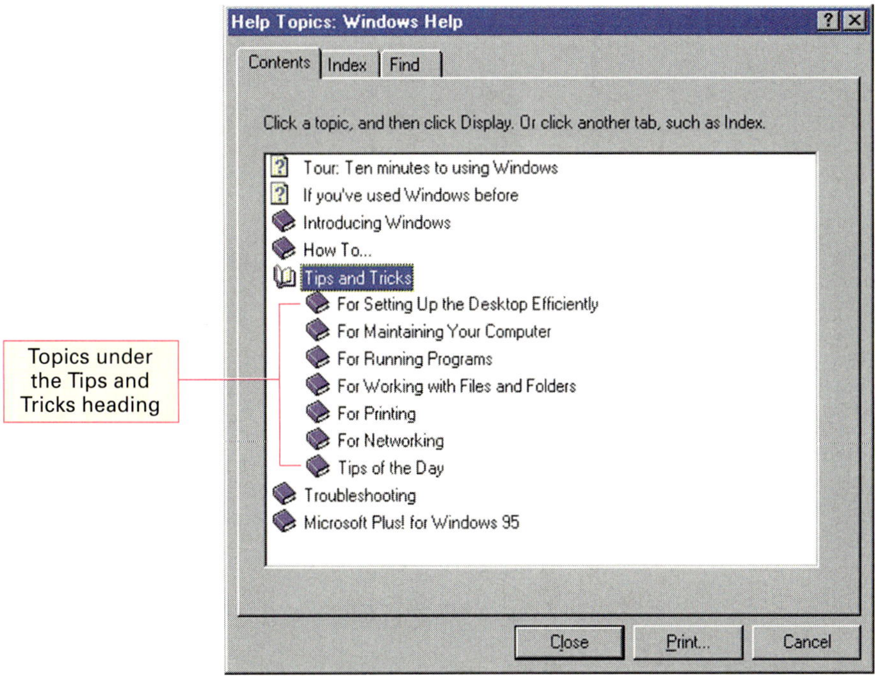
Help Topics: Windows Help
Contents
Index
Find
Click a topic, and then click Display. Or click another tab, such as Index.
Tour: Ten minutes to using Windows
If you've used Windows before
Introducing Windows
How To...
Tips and Tricks
For Setting Up the Desktop Efficiently
For Maintaining Your Computer
For Running Programs
For Working with Files and Folders
For Printing
For Networking
Tips of the Day
Troubleshooting
Microsoft Plus! for Windows 95
Close
Print...
Cancel
Topics under the Tips and Tricks heading

4 Double-click Tips of the Day.

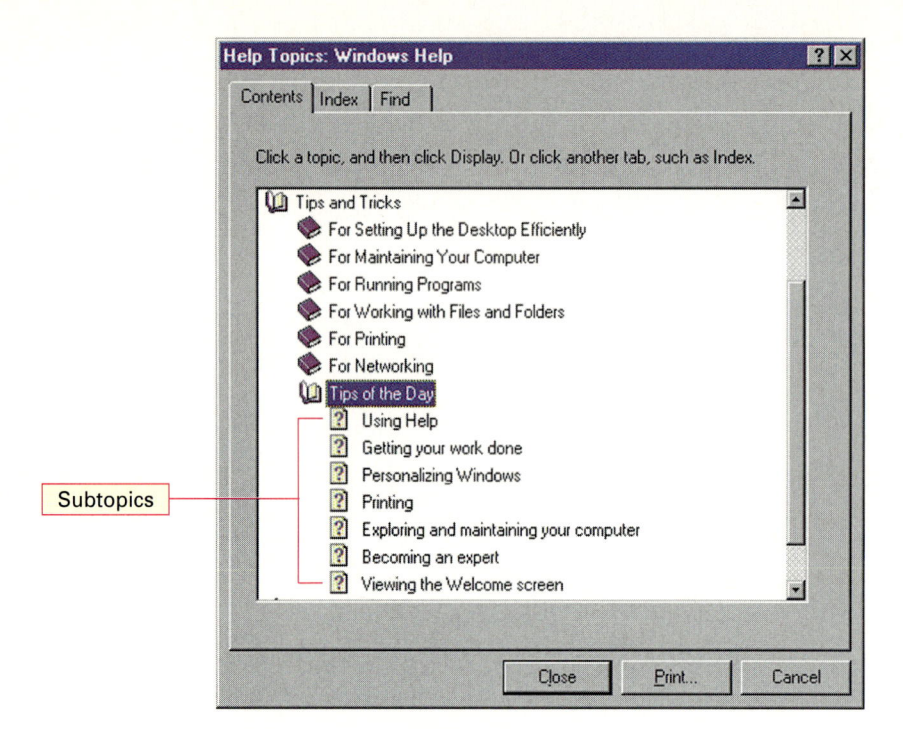

Subtopics

5 Double-click Using Help.

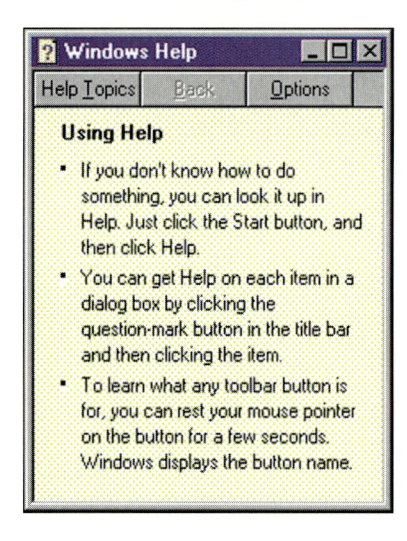

6 Read the information, click the Help Topics button, and then click the Index tab.

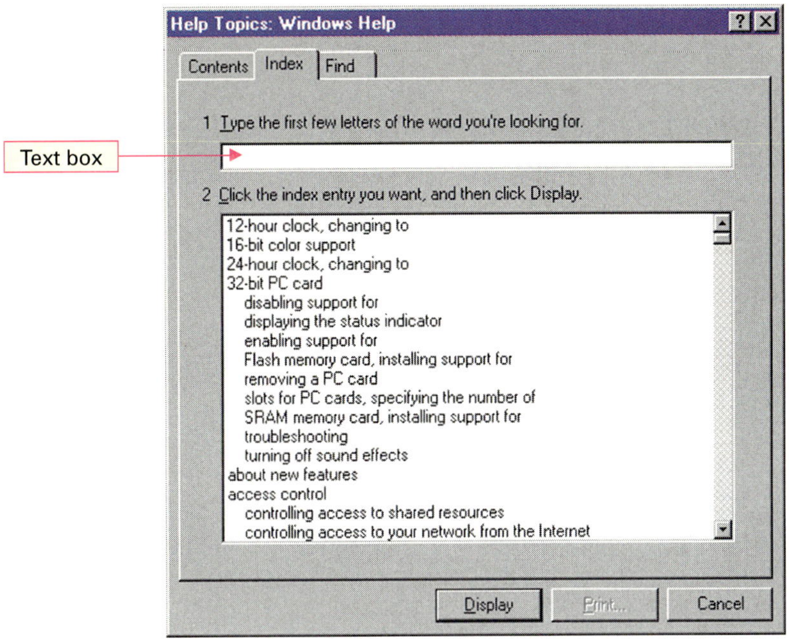
Help Topics: Windows Help
Contents
Index
Find
1 Type the first few letters of the word you're looking for.
2 Click the index entry you want, and then click Display.
12-hour clock, changing to
16-bit color support
24-hour clock, changing to
32-bit PC card
disabling support for
displaying the status indicator
enabling support for
Flash memory card, installing support for
removing a PC card
slots for PC cards, specifying the number of
SRAM memory card, installing support for
troubleshooting
turning off sound effects
about new features
access control
controlling access to shared resources
controlling access to your network from the Internet
Display
Print...
Cancel
Text box

7 Type **shortcut** in the textbox.

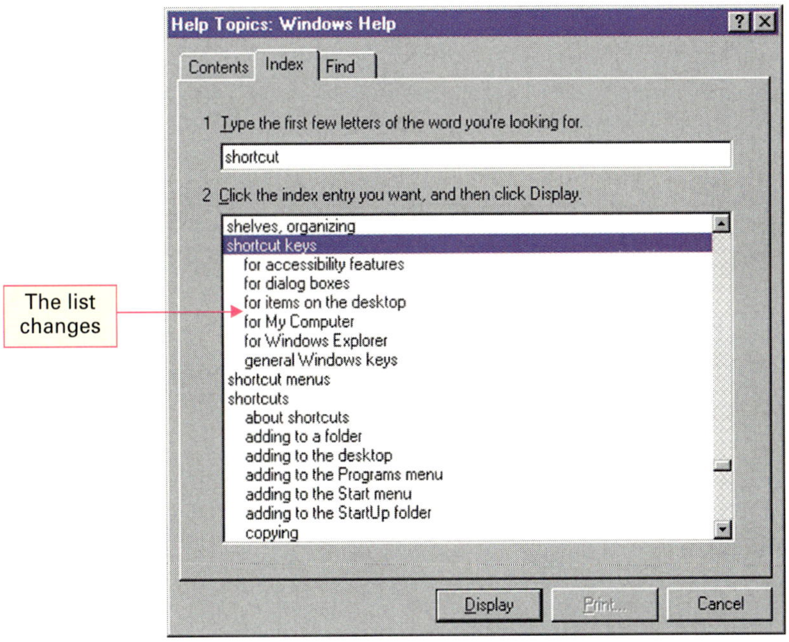
Help Topics: Windows Help
Contents
Index
Find
1 Type the first few letters of the word you're looking for.
shortcut
2 Click the index entry you want, and then click Display.
shelves, organizing
shortcut keys
for accessibility features
for dialog boxes
for items on the desktop
for My Computer
for Windows Explorer
general Windows keys
shortcut menus
shortcuts
about shortcuts
adding to a folder
adding to the desktop
adding to the Programs menu
adding to the Start menu
adding to the StartUp folder
copying
Display
Print...
Cancel
The list changes

8 Double-click "shortcut menus" in the list.

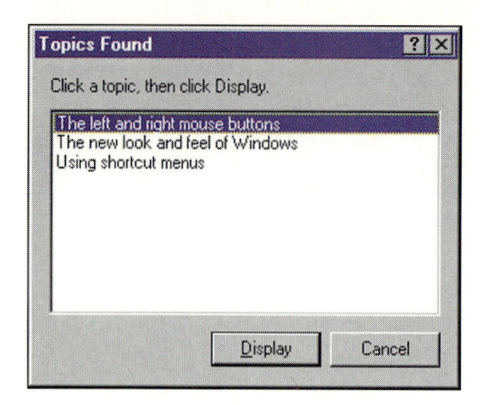

9 Double-click "Using shortcut menus."

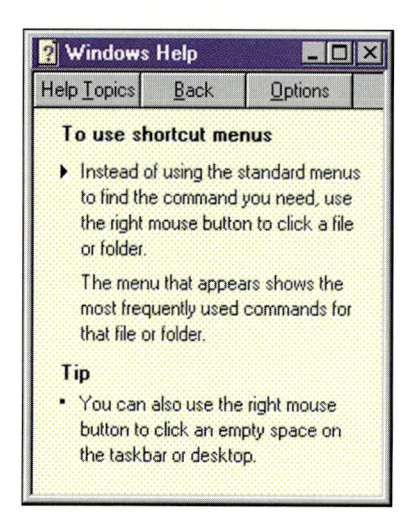

10 Read the information, click the Help Topics button, and then click the Find tab.

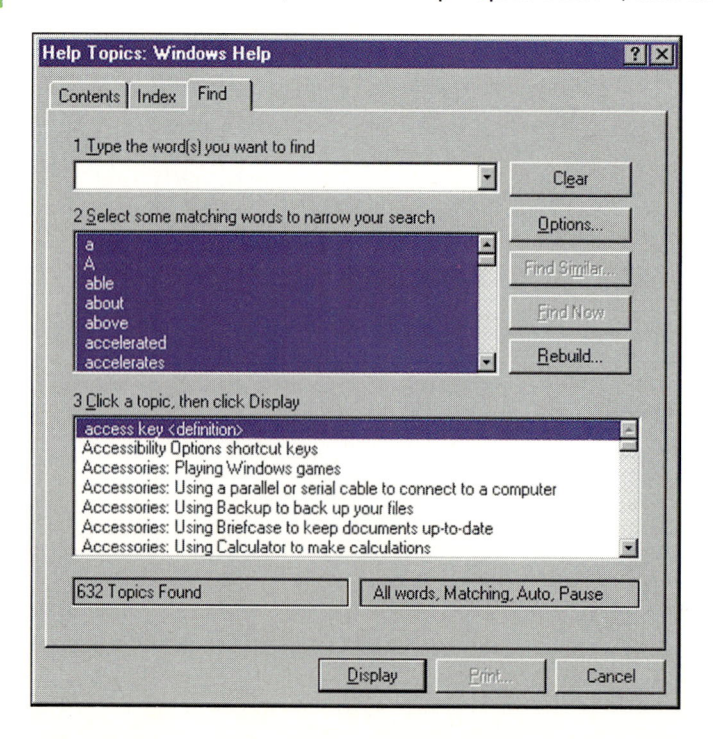

Overview **WIN-27**

11 Click the What's This [?] button in the Help Topics title bar.
A question mark is attached to the mouse pointer.

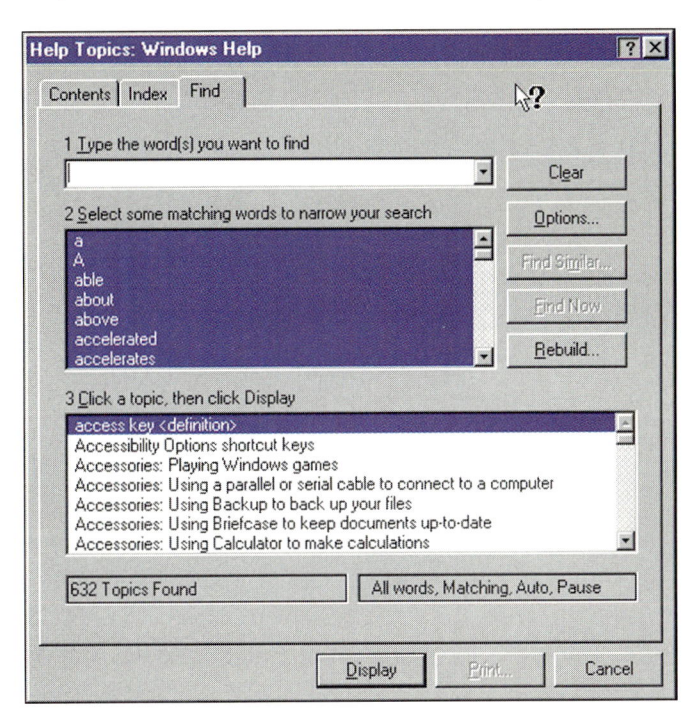

12 Click the Options button.

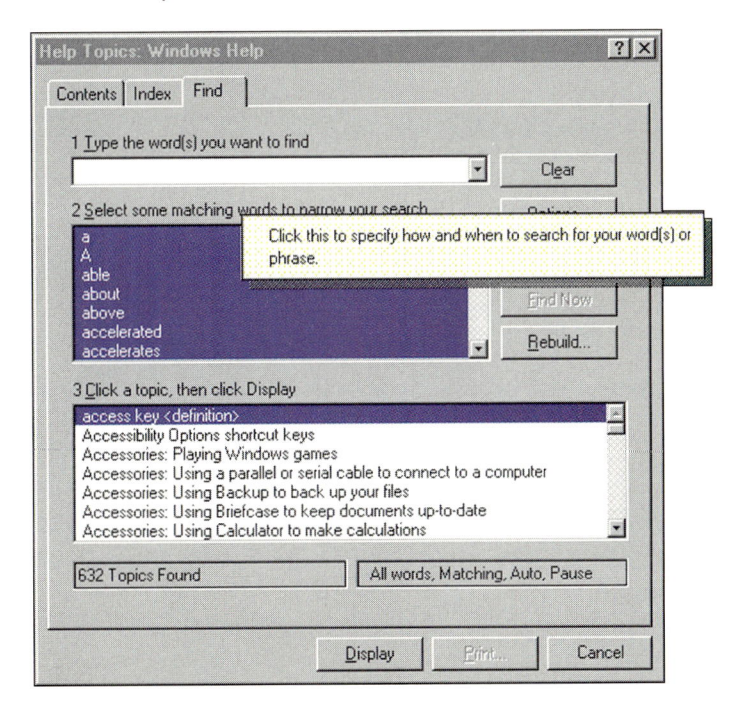

13 Read the pop-up message and then click it.
The message closes.

14 Type **printing help.** (If the list at the bottom of the screen doesn't change, click the Find Now button.

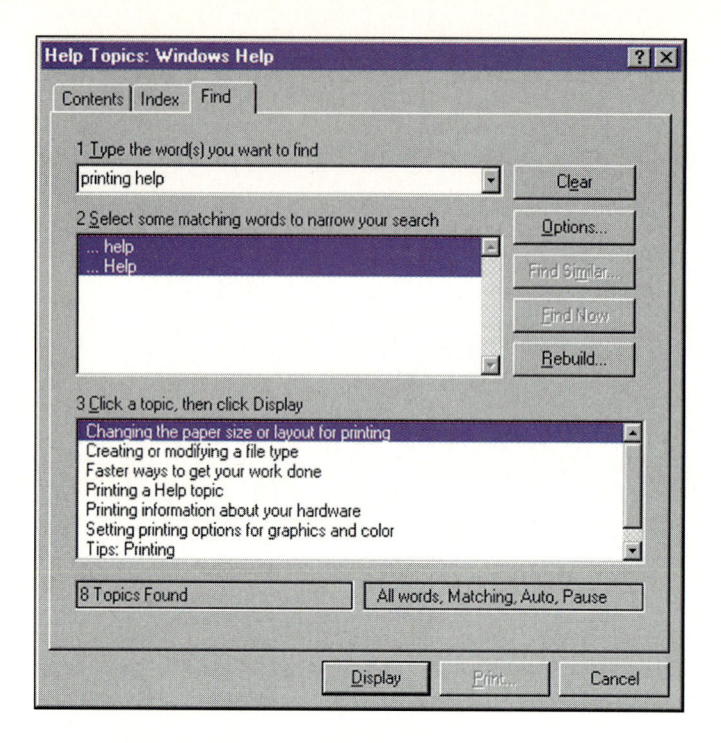

15 If necessary, scroll to "Printing a Help topic" in the list that displays and then double-click it.

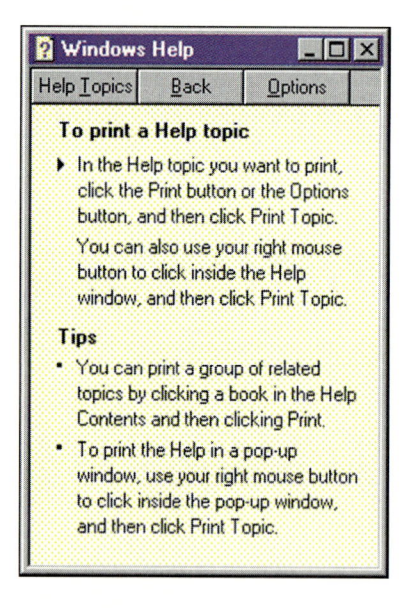

16 Click ⊠.
The Help dialog box closes.

> **Tip** You can print any help article by right-clicking anywhere in the article and choosing Print Topic.

Exiting Windows 95

When you are ready to turn off the computer, you must exit Windows 95 first. You should never turn off the computer without following the proper exit procedure because Windows 95 has to do some utility tasks before it shuts down. Unlike most of us, Windows 95 likes to put everything away when it's finished. When you shut down improperly, you can cause serious problems in Windows 95.

TASK 13: TO EXIT WINDOWS 95:

1. Click the Start button and then click Shut Down.

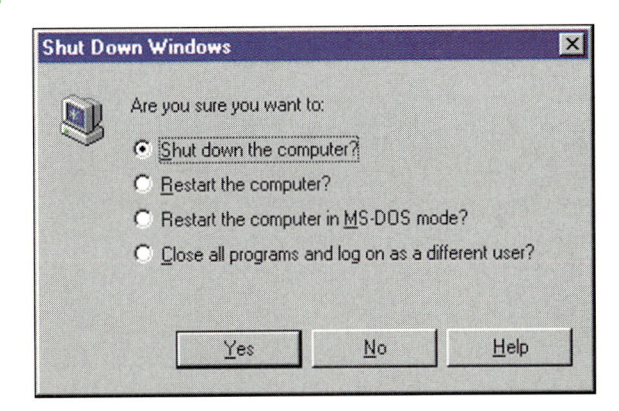

2. Click Shut down the computer? and then click Yes.

3. When the message "It's now safe to turn off your computer" appears, turn off the computer.

Outlook

Overview of Outlook

Microsoft Outlook, a personal desktop organizer similar to Daytimer and Franklin Planner, is installed as an integral part of Microsoft Office 97. The features in Outlook help you track appointments, send and receive messages, maintain a list of "to do" tasks, monitor computer activities, and update business and personal contacts in an instant.

Objectives

After completing this project, you will be able to:

- ▶ **Identify Outlook features**
- ▶ **Launch Outlook**
- ▶ **Use the Outlook Bar**
- ▶ **Schedule appointments in the Calendar**
- ▶ **Record tasks in the Task List**
- ▶ **Track computer activities in the Journal**
- ▶ **Store contacts in the Contacts List**
- ▶ **Create, send, and receive e-mail**
- ▶ **Print from Outlook**
- ▶ **Exit Outlook**

Identifying Outlook Features

Outlook comes with a number of features designed to keep you organized. You can keep Outlook open as you work in other applications and use it as a reference more easily. Table O.1 lists the features available in Outlook.

Table O.1: Outlook Features

Use this feature	to do this:
Calendar	Schedule appointments and meetings.
Task List	Record things to do, prioritize the list, and check tasks off as they are completed.
Inbox	Keep track of messages you receive.
Journal	Monitor computer activities as they happen and create a timeline of events for projects.
Contacts	Record business and personal contacts on a Rolodex-type file for easy access.
Notes	Store notes during phone conversations and meetings using the mini-word processor or that lets you type electronic Post-It notes.
Deleted Items	Retrieve "thrown out" items from the wastebasket as long as it hasn't been emptied.
Outlook Bar	Access other features by clicking the feature icon located on the Outlook screen.

Launching Outlook

The typical installation of Microsoft Office 97 creates a desktop shortcut to Outlook for easy access. Double-click the Microsoft Outlook shortcut icon to launch the program.

TASK 1: TO LAUNCH MICROSOFT OUTLOOK:

1. Turn on the computer and launch Windows 95.
2. Double-click the desktop Microsoft Outlook shortcut icon.

OL-4

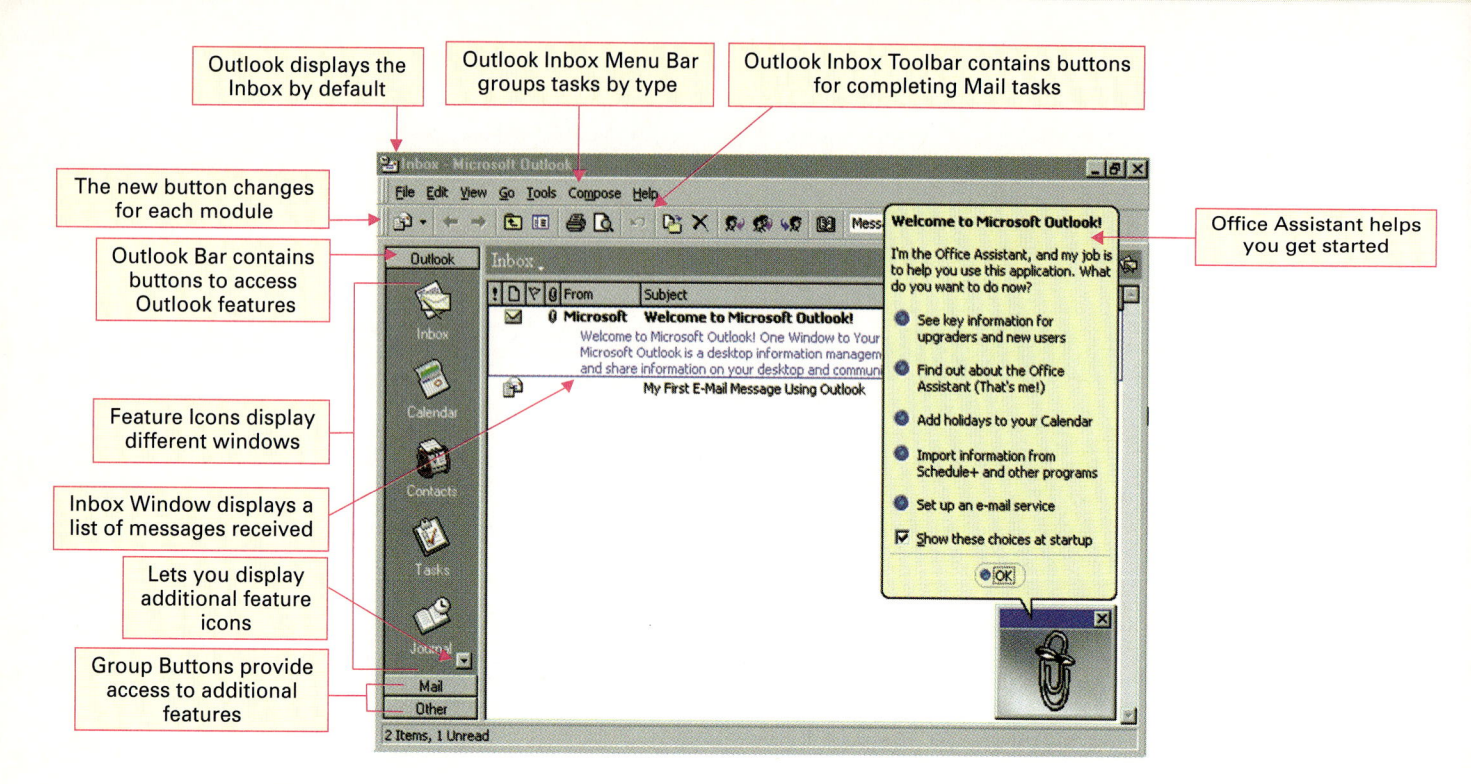

- Outlook displays the Inbox by default
- Outlook Inbox Menu Bar groups tasks by type
- Outlook Inbox Toolbar contains buttons for completing Mail tasks
- The new button changes for each module
- Outlook Bar contains buttons to access Outlook features
- Office Assistant helps you get started
- Feature Icons display different windows
- Inbox Window displays a list of messages received
- Lets you display additional feature icons
- Group Buttons provide access to additional features

3 Review the information the Office Assistant provides and then click OK.

Using the Outlook Bar

The Outlook Bar groups Outlook features into three different categories: Outlook, Mail, and Other. Category names appear on buttons on the Outlook Bar. When you click a category button, icons representing features within the category appear. When you click the icons on the Outlook Bar, the Outlook window changes, sometimes dividing into multiple window panes.

TASK 2: TO ACCESS OUTLOOK FEATURES:

1 Click the Outlook group button at the top of the Outlook Bar. The Outlook default icons appear.

Overview **OL-5**

2. Click the Mail group button at the bottom of the Outlook Bar.

   Displays feature buttons for the Mail group

3. Click the Other group button at the bottom of the Outlook Bar.

   Displays other feature buttons

4 Click the Outlook group button on the Outlook Bar.
The Outlook Bar displays the buttons for accessing the Outlook features.

5 Click the scroll down button at the bottom of the Outlook Bar to display additional features.

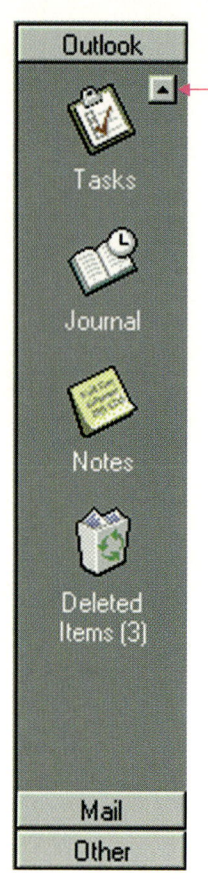

Scroll up button redisplays original feature buttons

Note Scroll buttons disappear when you reach the top or bottom of the Outlook Bar. If a scroll button isn't available, the first or last icon is on-screen.

6 Click the up scroll button at the top of the Outlook Bar.
The original feature icons redisplay.

Scheduling Appointments in the Calendar

Whether you use the Calendar to keep track of appointments or assignments, recording entries in the Calendar is easy. You can enter appointments directly in the Calendar window or use the Appointment dialog box to enter the appointment and set options.

TASK 3: TO SCHEDULE APPOINTMENTS IN THE CALENDAR:

1 Click the Calendar icon on the Outlook Bar.

Overview OL-7

Calendar toolbar

Current month

Type daily appointments beside the appropriate time in the daily calendar pane

Current date is highlighted in the monthly calendar pane

Tasks list pane for the selected date

Accesses additional time slots

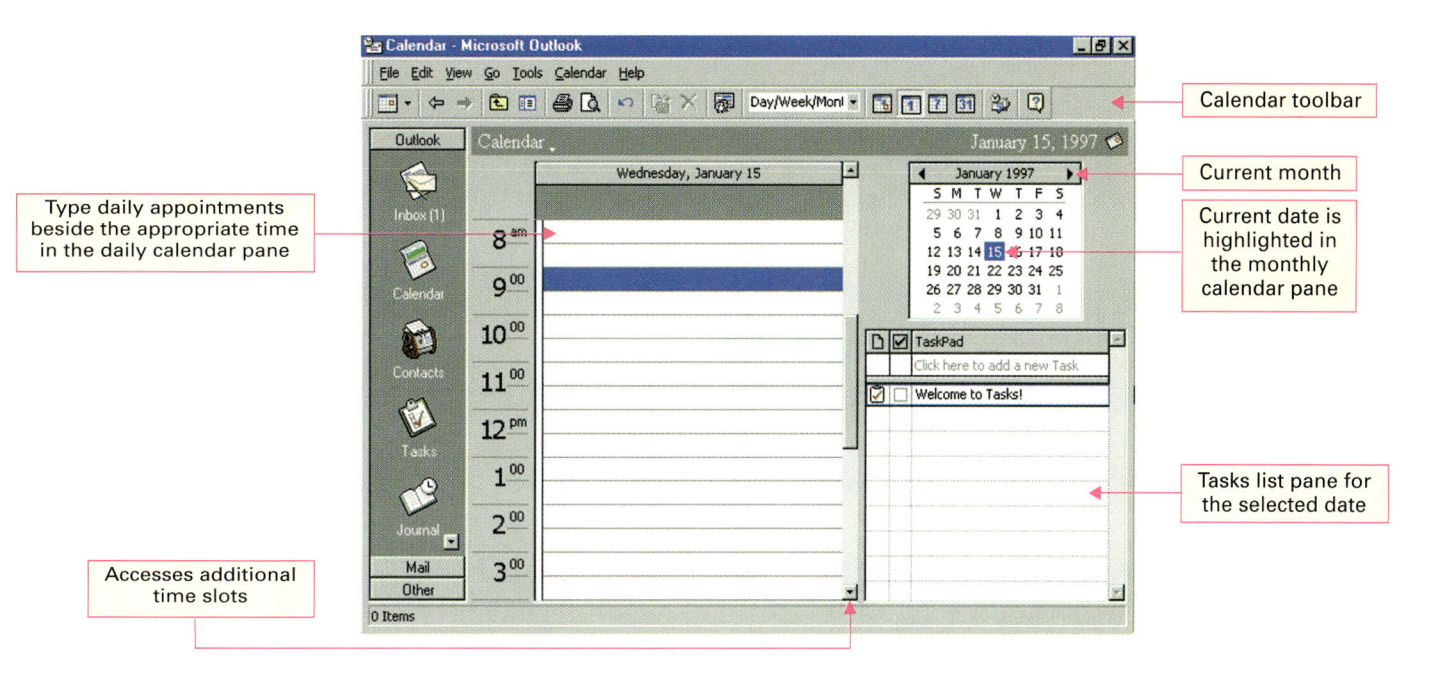

2 Double-click the 9:00 time slot on the Calendar appointment list.
The Appointment dialog box opens, offering more options than you have if you enter data directly into the Calendar window.

3 Enter the data indicated in the following Appointment dialog box, pressing TAB to advance from field to field.

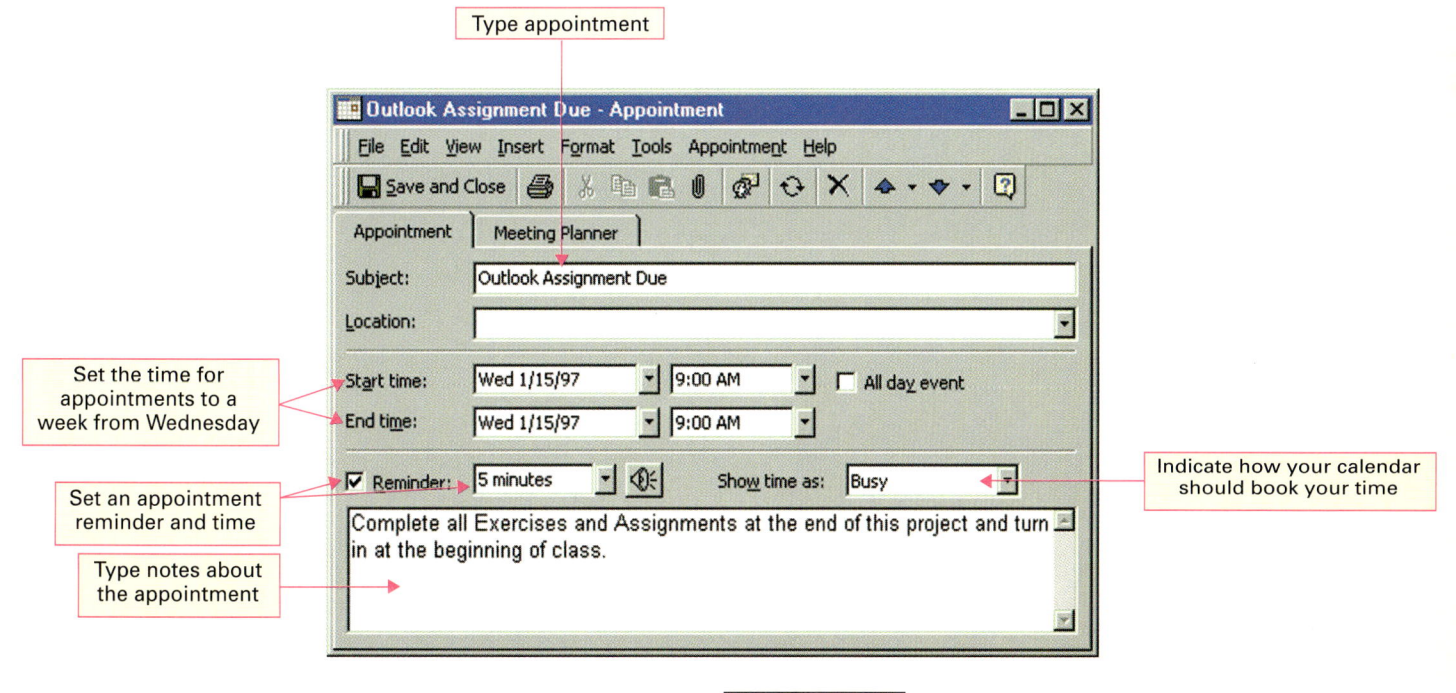

Type appointment

Set the time for appointments to a week from Wednesday

Set an appointment reminder and time

Type notes about the appointment

Indicate how your calendar should book your time

4 Click the toolbar Save and Close button.

Recording Tasks in the Task List

The Task List appears in a pane of the Calendar window for easy access. You can, however, display the Tasks in a full window. The procedures used to record entries in the Task List are the same regardless of which Task display you choose.

TASK 4: TO RECORD TASKS IN THE TASK LIST:

1. Click the Outlook Bar Tasks icon.

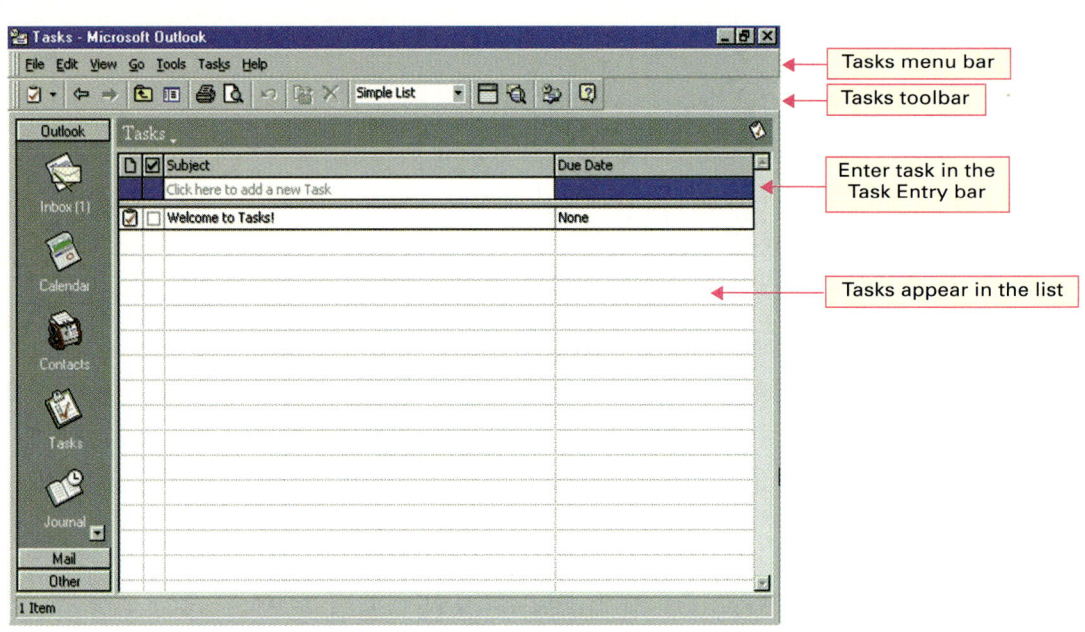

   (Screenshot of Tasks - Microsoft Outlook window with callouts: Tasks menu bar, Tasks toolbar, Enter task in the Task Entry bar, Tasks appear in the list)

2. Click the instruction *Click here to add a new task* in the task entry bar.

3. Type **Pick up forms from career center** and press (ENTER).
   The task appears in the task list.

4. Double-click the task entry bar.
   The Tasks dialog box opens.

Overview **OL-9**

5 Type the data shown in the following Tasks dialog box, pressing TAB to advance from field to field.

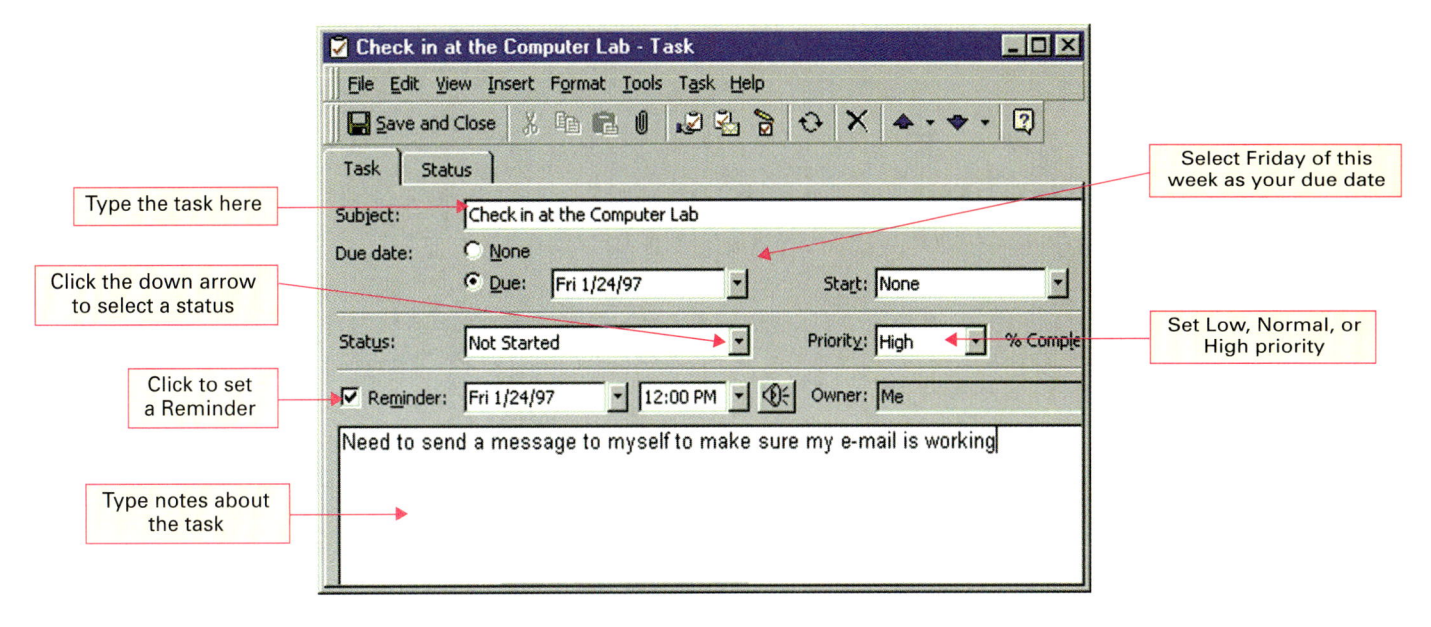

- Type the task here
- Click the down arrow to select a status
- Click to set a Reminder
- Type notes about the task
- Select Friday of this week as your due date
- Set Low, Normal, or High priority

Check in at the Computer Lab - Task

Subject: Check in at the Computer Lab
Due date: Due Fri 1/24/97   Start: None
Status: Not Started   Priority: High   % Complete
Reminder: Fri 1/24/97 12:00 PM   Owner: Me

Need to send a message to myself to make sure my e-mail is working

6 Click **Save and Close**.

Tip The text for overdue tasks is red. To quickly sort tasks by different columns, click the gray column heading button.

7 Double-click the line Welcome to Tasks! Information about the task displays in the notes area.

8 Click the Welcome to Tasks! window ⊠ to close the task window.

9 Click the check box for the *Pick up forms from career center* task.

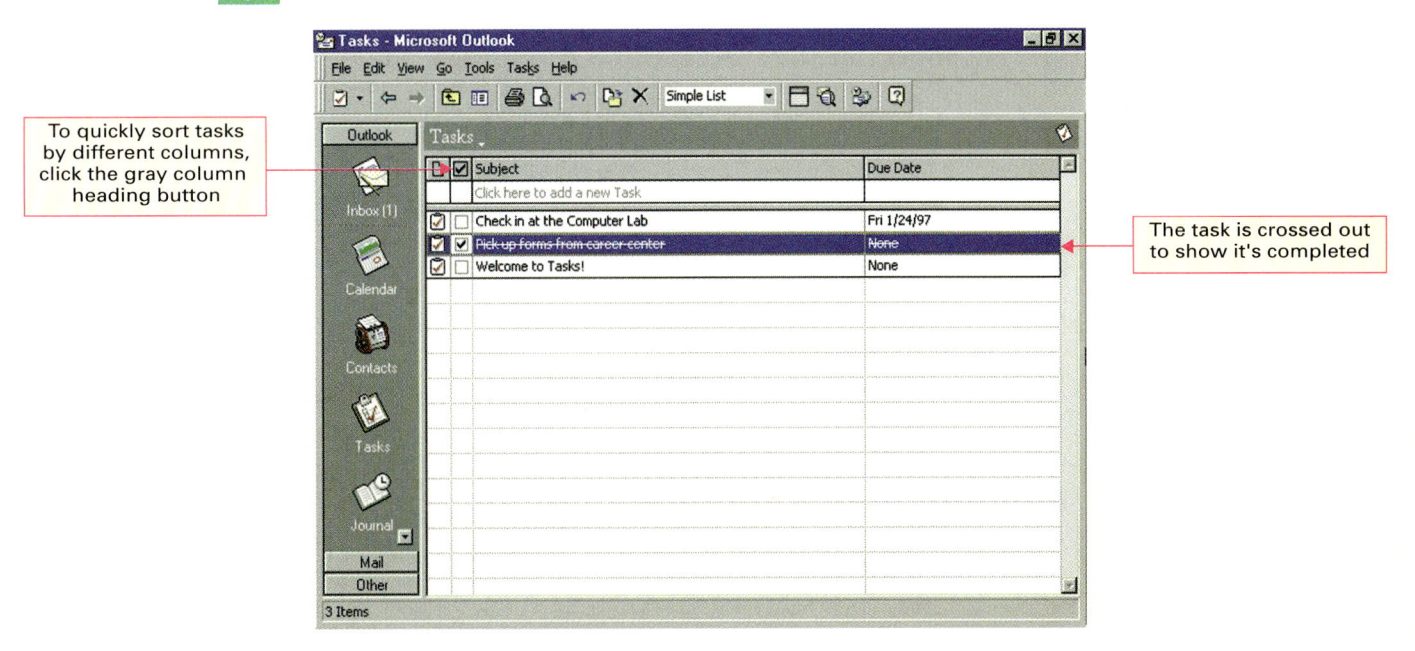

- To quickly sort tasks by different columns, click the gray column heading button
- The task is crossed out to show it's completed

Tasks - Microsoft Outlook

Subject	Due Date
Check in at the Computer Lab	Fri 1/24/97
~~Pick up forms from career center~~	~~None~~
Welcome to Tasks!	None

3 Items

10 Click ▦ to view the Task list in the Calendar window.

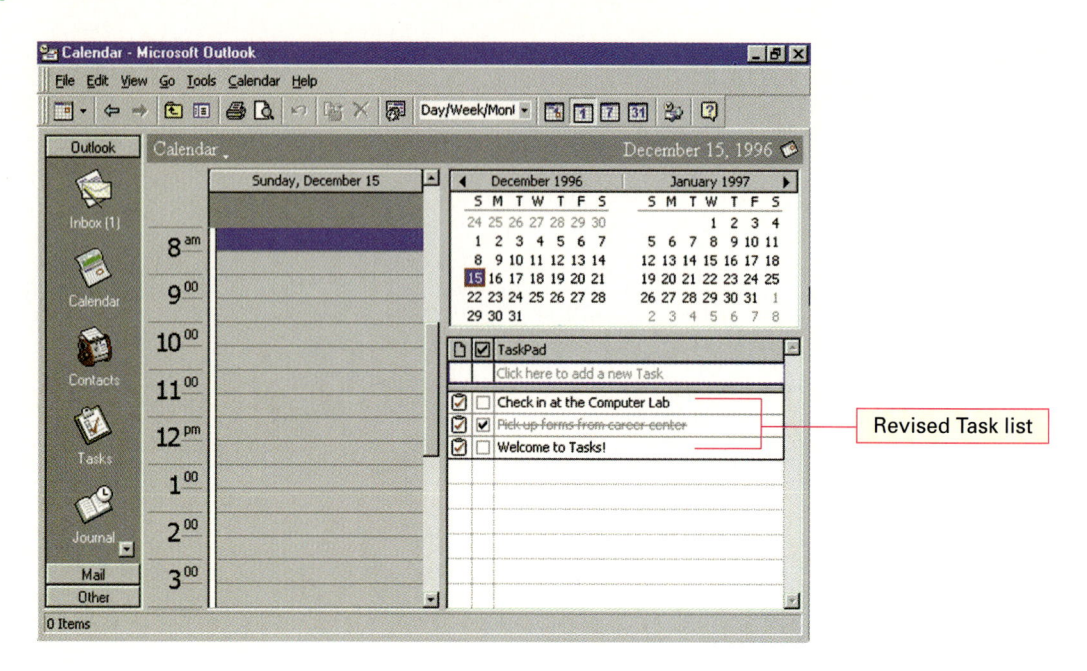

Revised Task list

Tracking Computer Activities in the Journal

The Journal feature in Outlook creates a timeline to record computer activities performed using Office 97 features and then groups journal entries by type to keep track of your activities. You also can use the Journal to manually record your thoughts, conversations, or notes.

TASK 5: TO DISPLAY JOURNAL ACTIVITIES AND RECORD ACTIVITIES MANUALLY:

1 Click the Outlook Bar Journal ▦ icon.

Overview **OL-11**

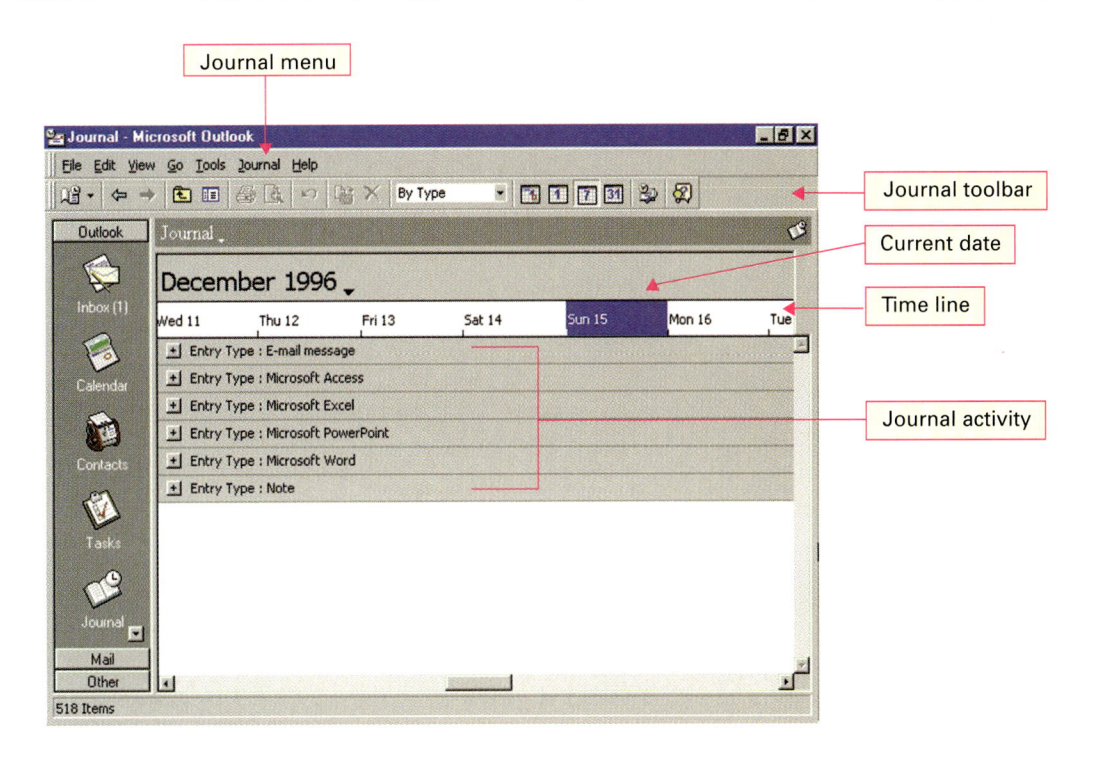

2 Click the plus ➕ button to display grouped activities for each journal entry.

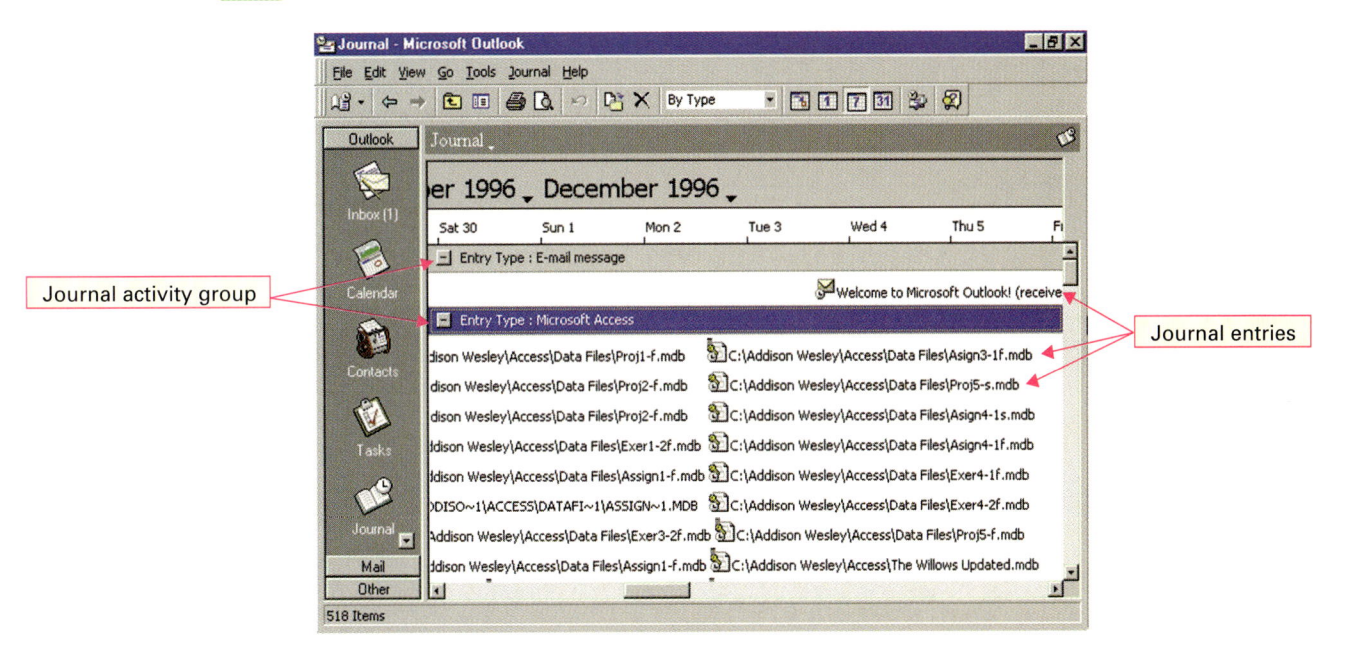

3 Choose Journal, New Journal Entry.
The Journal dialog box opens.

4 Type the data shown in the following Journal dialog box, pressing TAB to advance from field to field.

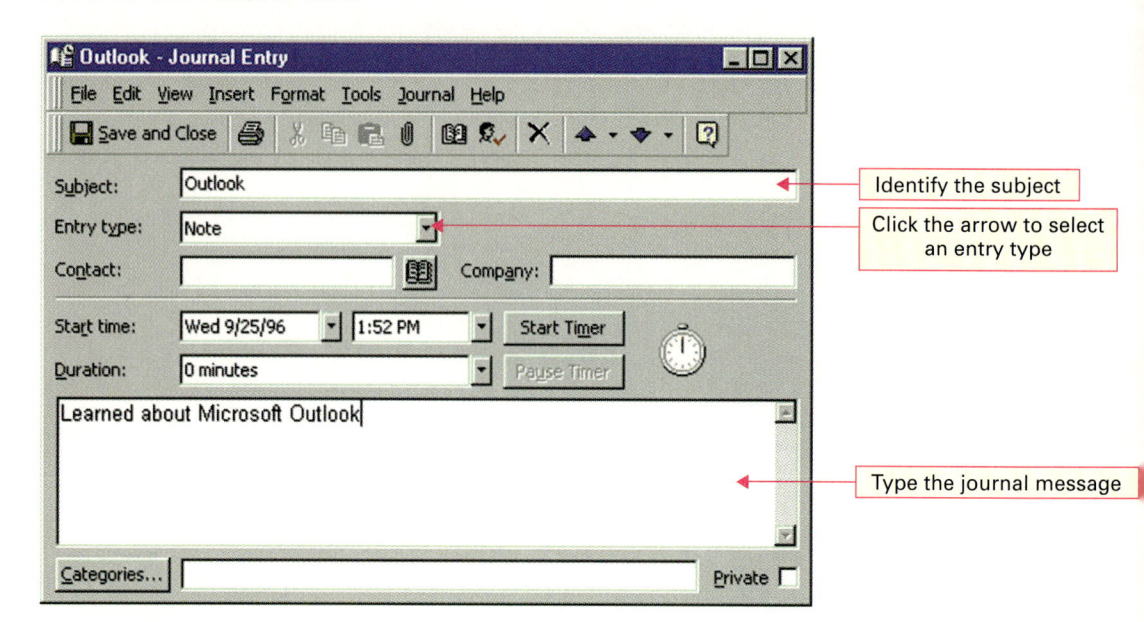

- Identify the subject
- Click the arrow to select an entry type
- Type the journal message

5 Click **Save and Close**.

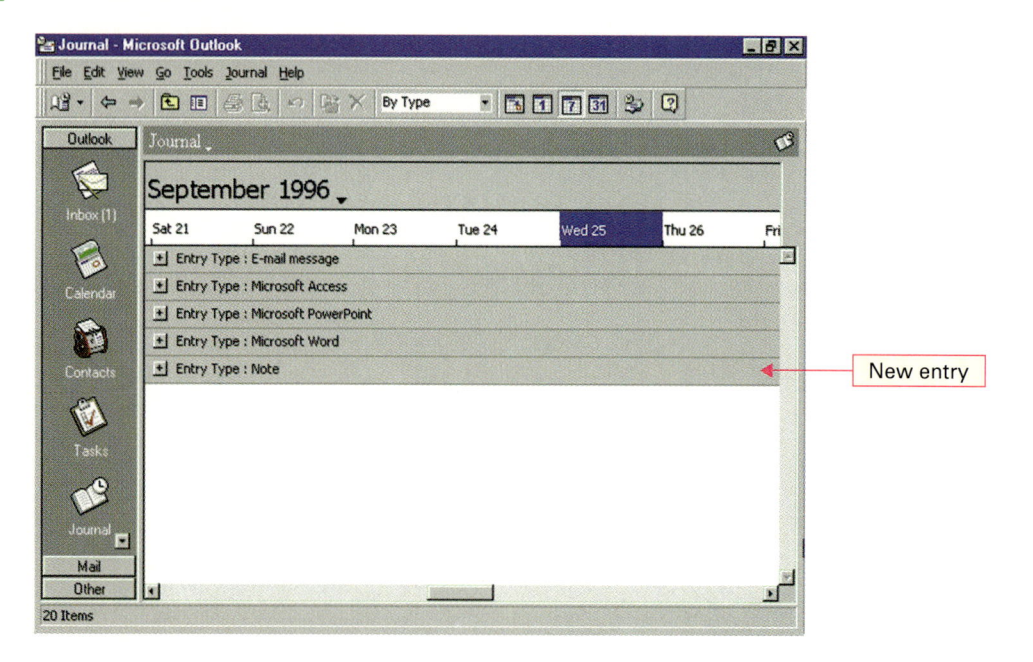

- New entry

Storing Contacts in the Contacts List

The Contacts List stores names, addresses, phone numbers, company names, and so forth about your personal and/or business contacts. You can use information you store in the Contacts List in letters and databases. In addition, you can send messages called *e-mail*, directly to those people in the Contact List who have e-mail addresses that your system can access.

Overview   OL-13

TASK 6: TO ADD CONTACTS TO THE CONTACT LIST:

1 Click the Outlook Bar Contacts icon.

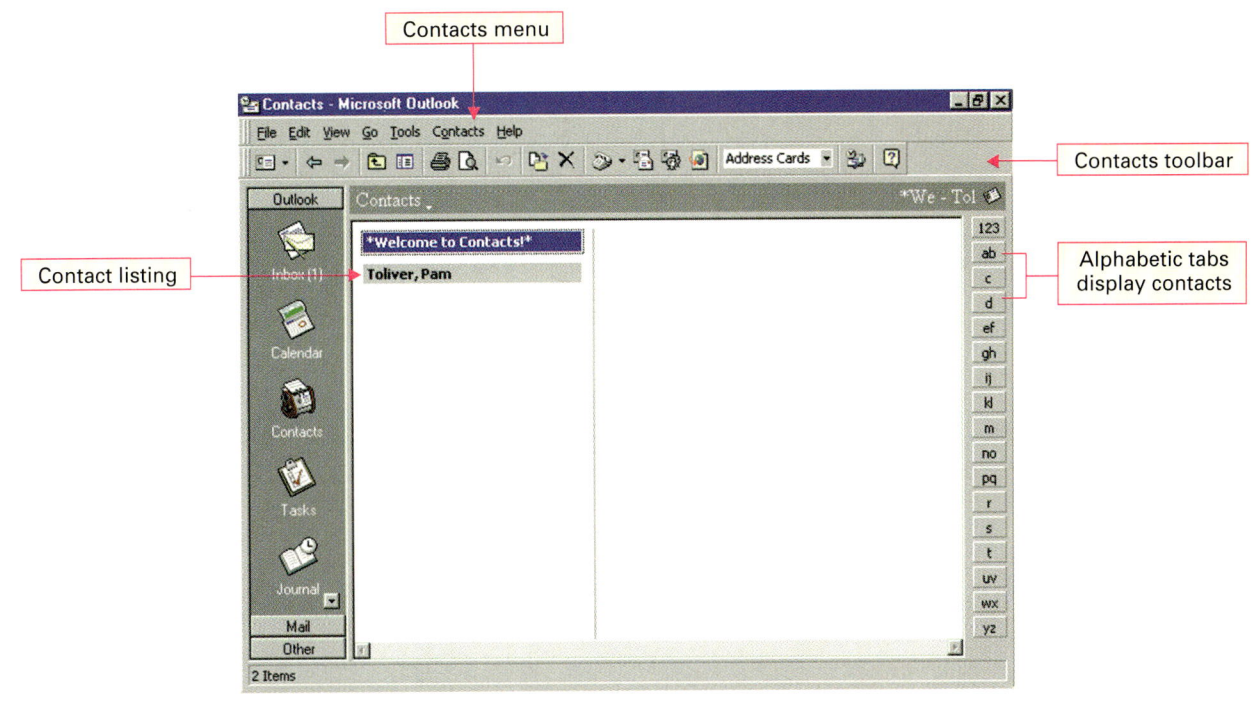

Contacts menu

Contacts toolbar

Contact listing

Alphabetic tabs display contacts

2 Double-click a blank area of the Contacts window. The Contacts dialog box opens.

3 Type the data shown in the following Contact dialog box, pressing TAB to advance from field to field.

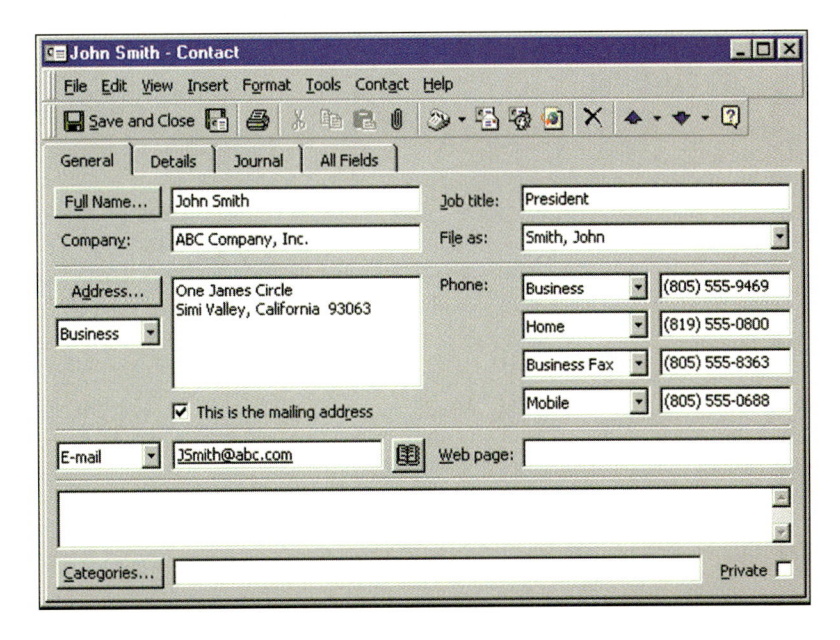

OL-14

4 Click **Save and Close** to save the contact.

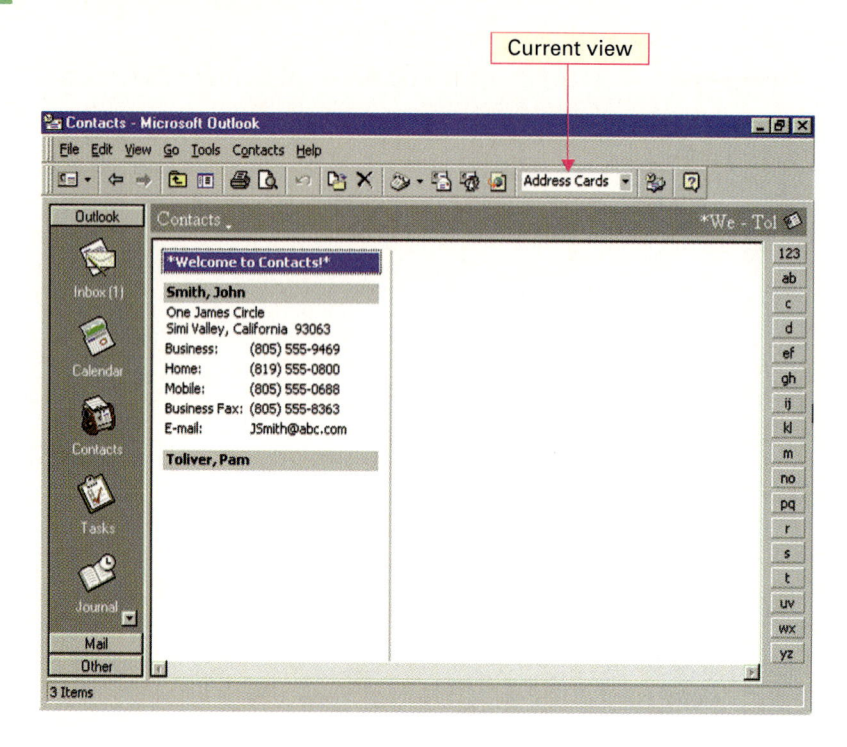

Current view

5 Click the drop-down list arrow beside the Current View area of the toolbar.

Address Cards
Detailed Address Cards
Phone List
By Category
By Company
By Location

6 Click *Detailed Address Cards*.

Overview **OL-15**

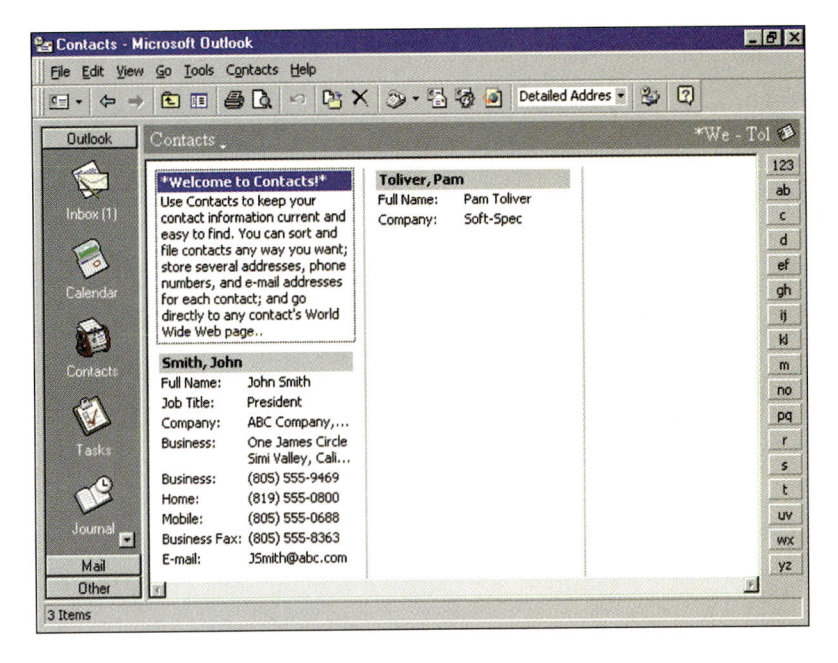

[Screenshot of Contacts - Microsoft Outlook window showing contact entries for Toliver, Pam and Smith, John]

7 Select *Address Cards* from the Current View list to return the previous display.

8 Add your name, address, and e-mail address as a contact in the Contacts List.

Creating, Sending, and Receiving E-Mail

Outlook comes equipped with an e-mail feature for communicating with people on a *local area network* (LAN) as well as with people on the *Internet,* the world-wide computer structure for sending information.

The Inbox stores messages you receive from others and automatically displays each time you launch Outlook to remind you to sign on or *log on* to the network and check for new messages. The Outbox stores messages you create until you log on to the network and send the messages.

TASK 7: TO USE THE OUTLOOK MAIL MESSAGE FEATURE:

1 Click the Inbox icon in the Outlook Bar.
The Inbox window opens.

> **Troubleshooting** By default, the Inbox automatically appears each time you launch Outlook. If your settings are different and display another Outlook feature, click the Outlook Bar Inbox icon to display the Inbox.

2 Click the New Mail Message icon on the Outlook toolbar.

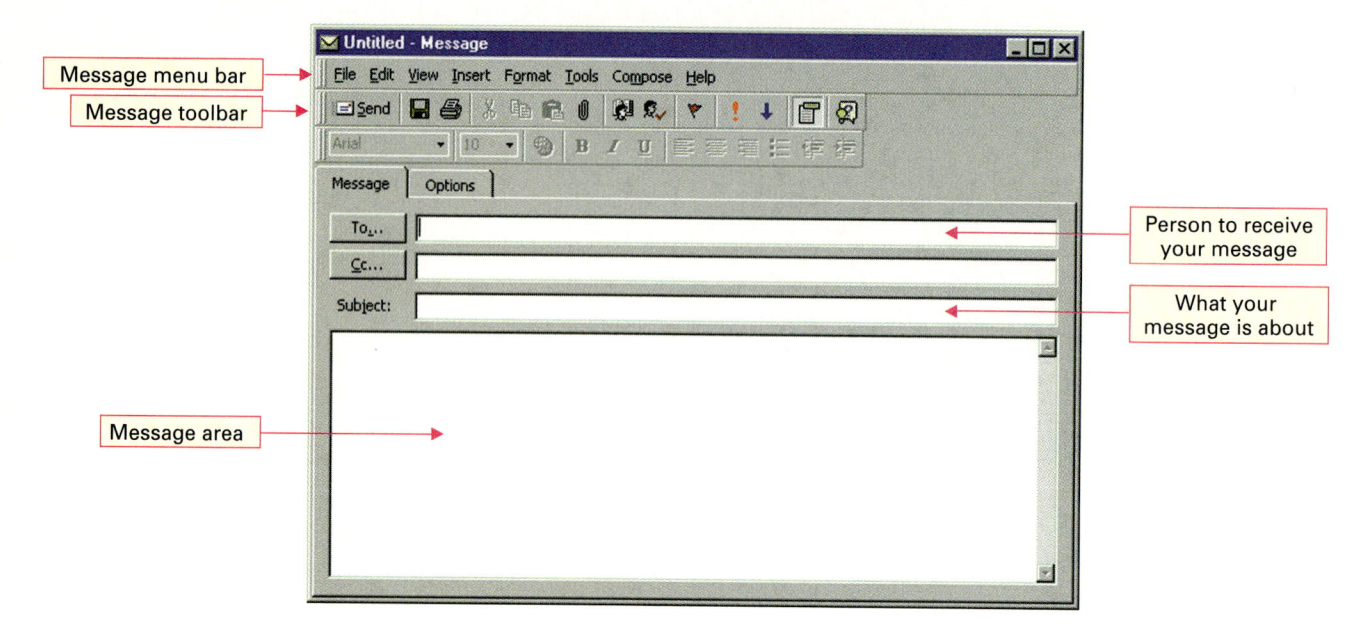

- Message menu bar
- Message toolbar
- Message area
- Person to receive your message
- What your message is about

Note If your system requires that you log on to the network to display a list of valid e-mail users, log on and type your password in the appropriate dialog box.

3 Click the To button to open the Select Names dialog box and either type or select your own e-mail address.

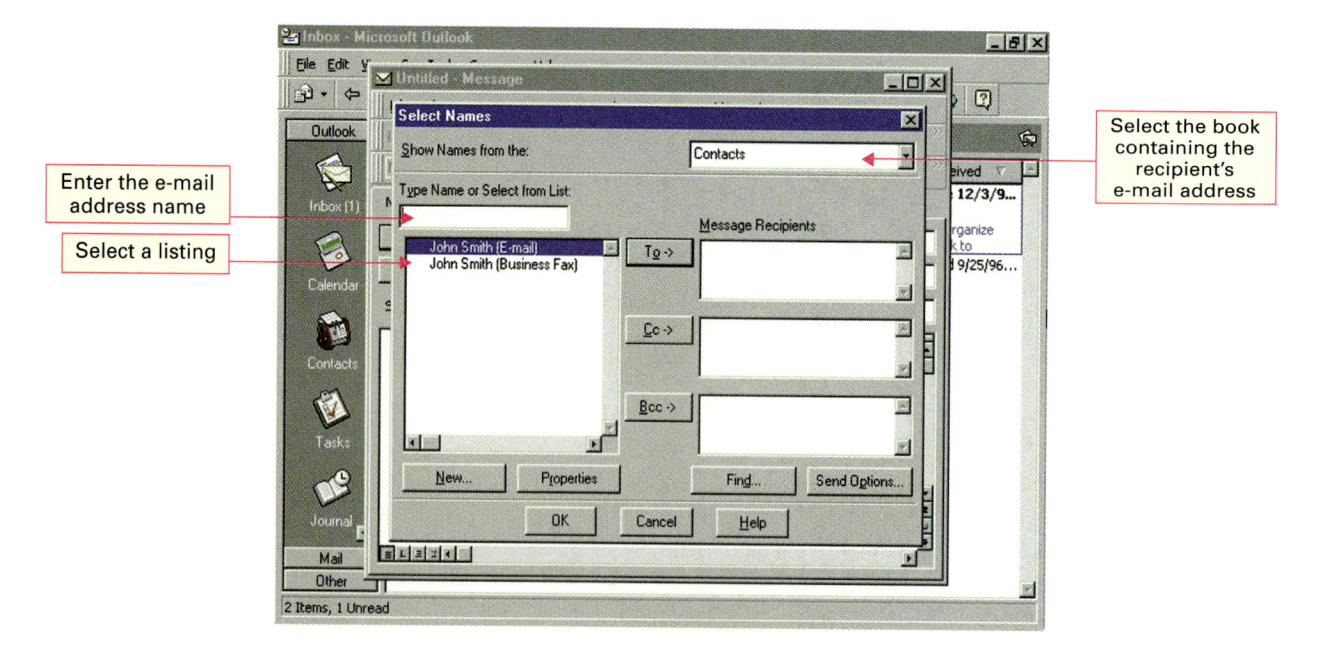

- Enter the e-mail address name
- Select a listing
- Select the book containing the recipient's e-mail address

4 Type the subject **My First E-Mail Message Using Outlook** and the following text as your e-mail message. Then click the Send button to mail it.

This is my first message typed using the Outlook Mail feature that came with Microsoft Office 97. If I receive this message, I will know that I am actively connected to the campus e-mail system and am able to send messages.

If you are logged on to the e-mail system when you click Send, your message is sent immediately. If you aren't currently logged on to the e-mail system, your message is stored in the Outbox. When you exit Outlook, it reminds you that the Outbox has messages. You can choose Yes to log on and send messages before exiting Outlook or choose No to exit Outlook and keep the messages in the Outbox for later delivery.

> **Note** The only reason to send a mail message to yourself is to test your e-mail delivery system, to have mail to read, or to determine approximately when messages you send are available to other recipients.

5 Choose Tools, Check for New Mail to log on to the e-mail system and access new mail sent to you since the last time you logged on.

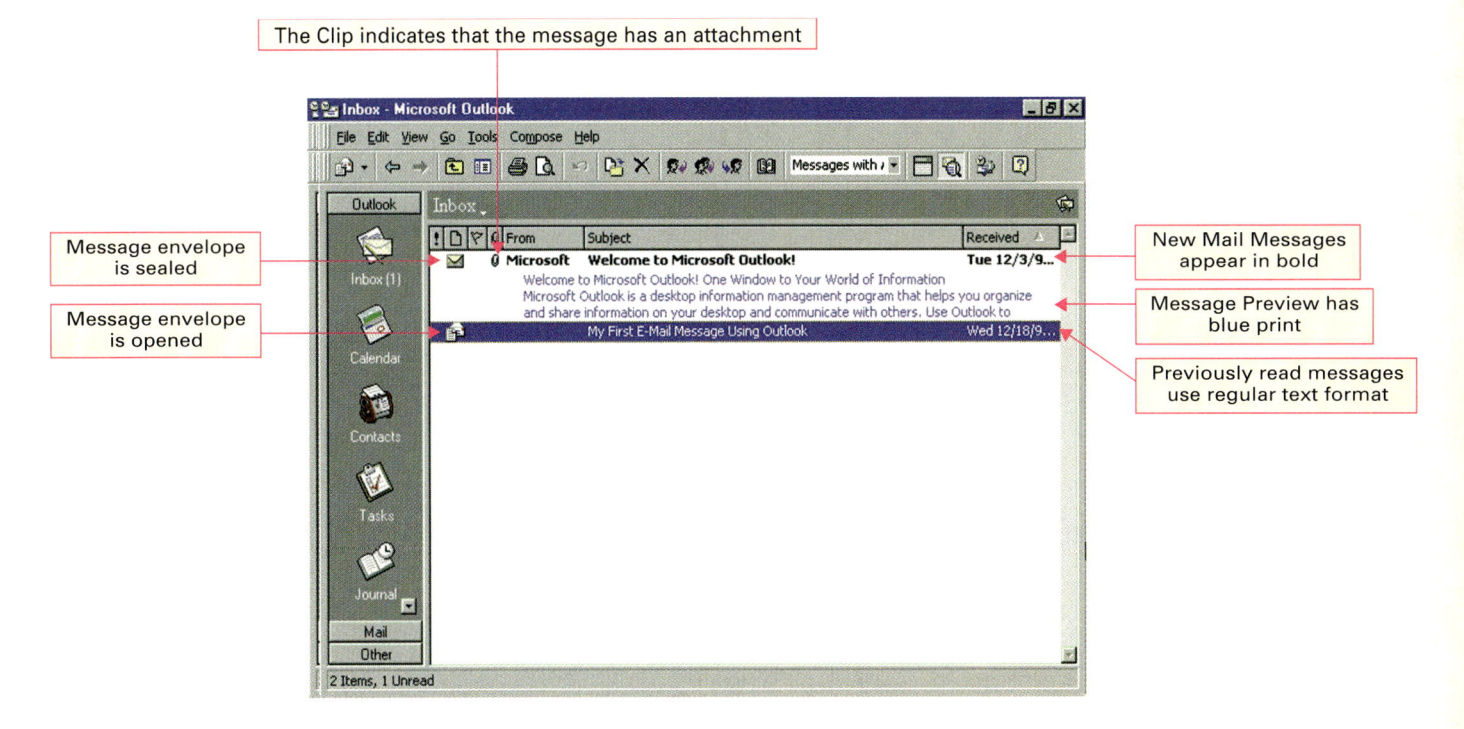

The Clip indicates that the message has an attachment

Message envelope is sealed

Message envelope is opened

New Mail Messages appear in bold

Message Preview has blue print

Previously read messages use regular text format

> **Note** An *attachment* can be a file, a picture, or some other type of object that you can transmit electronically.

OL-18

6 Double-click the message you received from yourself.
The full message appears in a window of its own. Use buttons on the toolbar to respond to the message, forward the message, or delete the message.

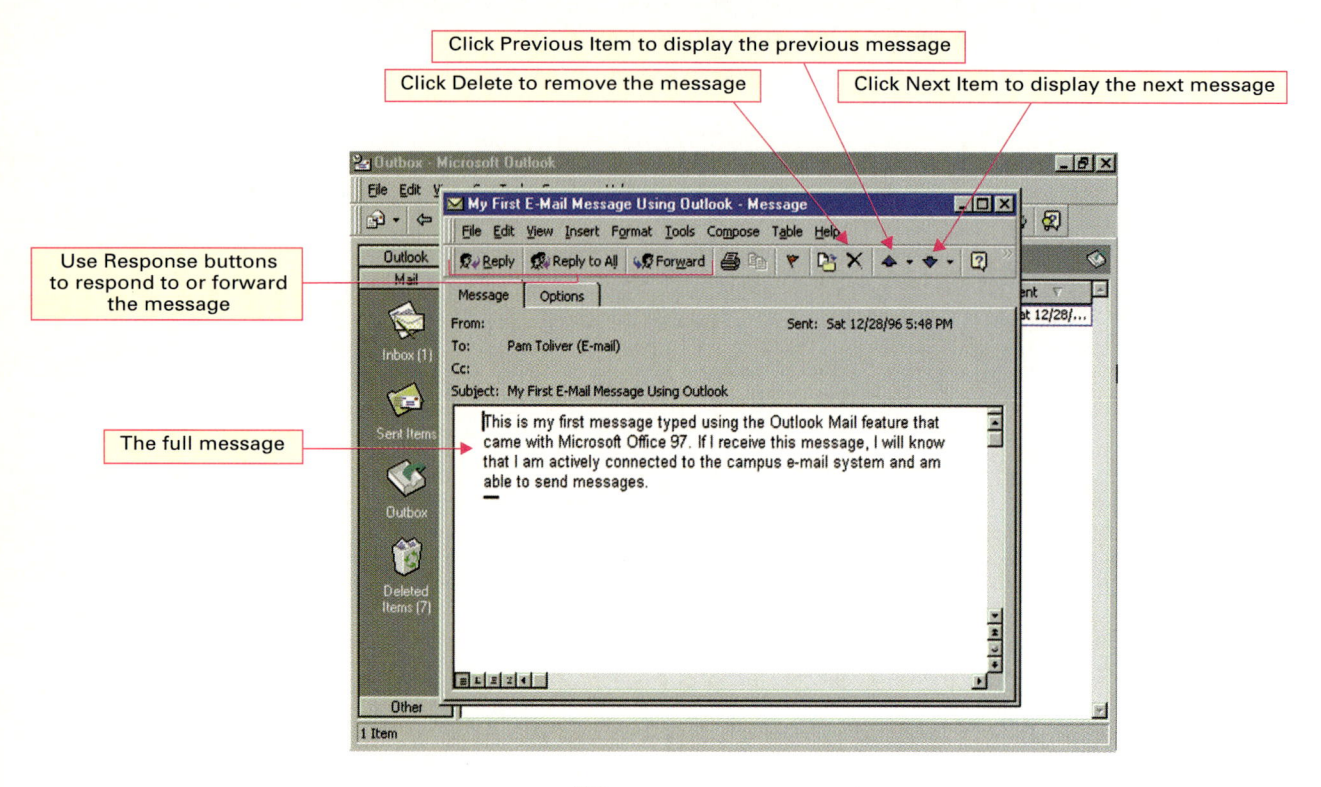

Click Previous Item to display the previous message

Click Delete to remove the message

Click Next Item to display the next message

Use Response buttons to respond to or forward the message

The full message

7 Click the message ⊠ to close the message window.

Printing from Outlook

You can print information contained in any of the Outlook modules using a variety of different formats. Regardless of which module in Outlook you are using, you can print information using the same basic procedures. Features and styles displayed in the Print dialog box vary according to the module you have active when you print.

TASK 8: TO PRINT FROM OUTLOOK:

1 Display your Outlook Calendar, display the current week, and choose File, Print.

Overview **OL-19**

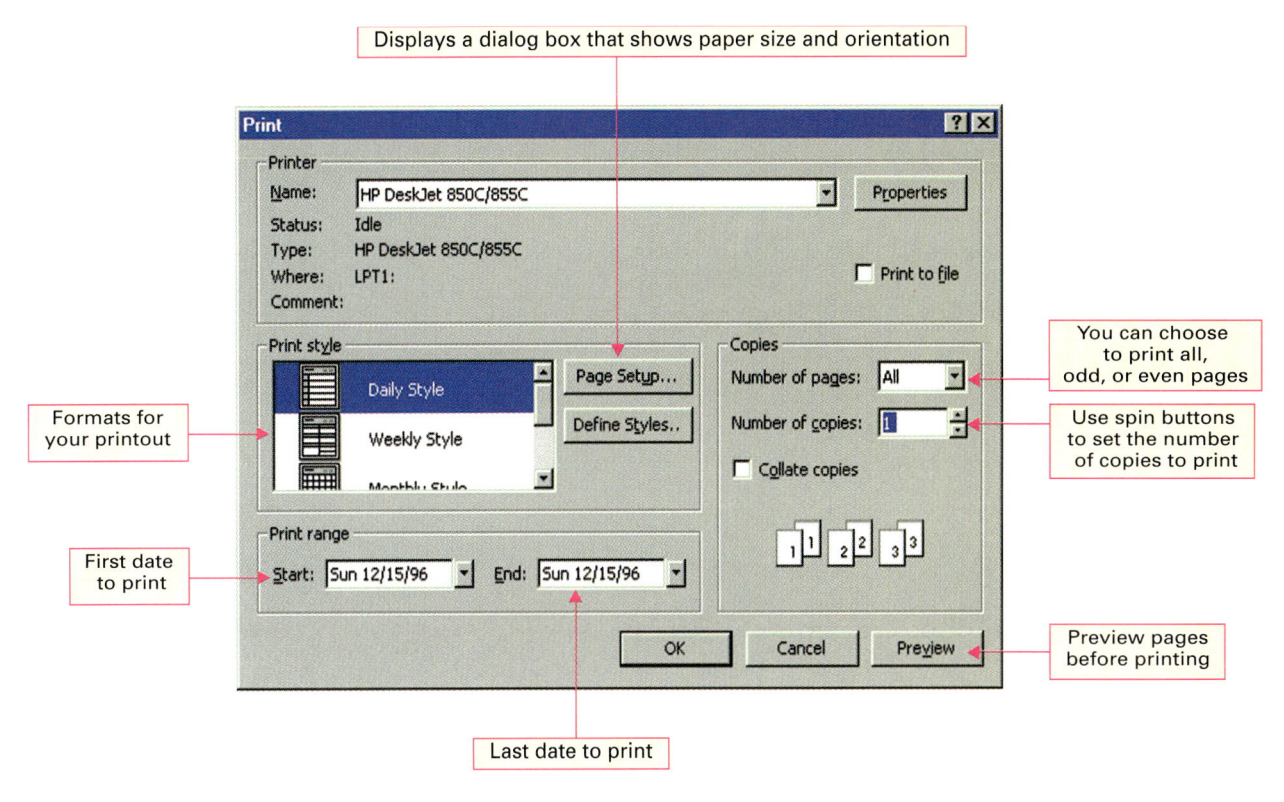

Displays a dialog box that shows paper size and orientation

- Formats for your printout
- You can choose to print all, odd, or even pages
- Use spin buttons to set the number of copies to print
- First date to print
- Preview pages before printing
- Last date to print

2 Select the Weekly Style from the Print style list, click the Page Setup button, and ensure that your settings match these:

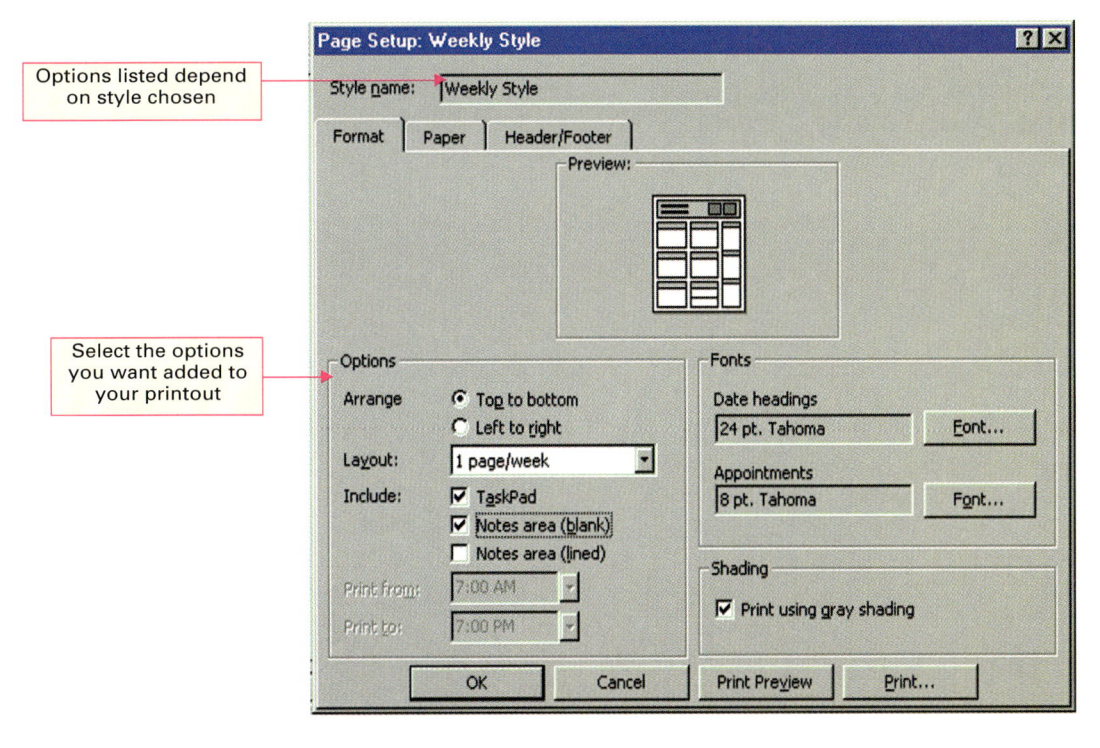

- Options listed depend on style chosen
- Select the options you want added to your printout

3 Click OK twice to print.

Exiting Outlook

Because Outlook is an application, you exit Outlook using the same techniques used to exit other applications designed for Windows 95.

TASK 9: TO EXIT OUTLOOK:

1. Click the Outlook application Close ☒ button.

   Note The Microsoft Outlook message box shown below appears only when you have messages in your Outbox that haven't yet been delivered. If the Outbox contains no messages, Outlook closes automatically.

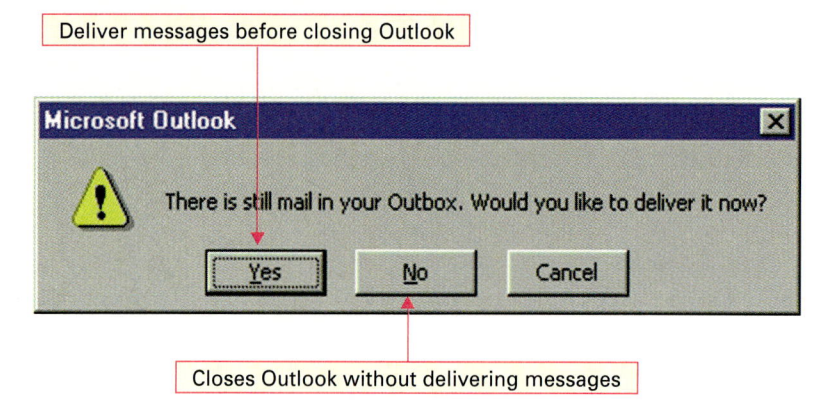

   Deliver messages before closing Outlook

   Microsoft Outlook dialog: "There is still mail in your Outbox. Would you like to deliver it now?" with Yes, No, Cancel buttons

   Closes Outlook without delivering messages

2. Click No if asked whether you want to deliver mail in the Outbox.

Summary and Exercises

Summary

- Microsoft Outlook is a personal desktop organizer designed after personal organizers such as Daytimer and Franklin Planner.
- Outlook combines a calendar, an address list, a task list, a journal, and an e-mail system into one efficient program.
- Microsoft Office 97 automatically creates a shortcut to access Outlook during a typical Office 97 installation; double click the shortcut icon on the desktop to launch Outlook.
- Because Outlook includes an e-mail program, you may be asked to provide log-on information when you launch Outlook.
- To use the e-mail feature of Outlook to communicate with others, you must have access to the Internet or be connected to a local area network.
- The Outlook Bar provides easy access to all features of Microsoft Outlook.
- The Print dialog box displays different options depending on the module of Outlook you have active when you print.

Key Terms and Operations

Key Terms
local area network (LAN)
e-mail
log on
Internet
Inbox
Outbox

Operations
Launch Microsoft Outlook
Access Microsoft Outlook Features
Record entries in the Outlook Calendar, Task List, Contacts List, and Journal
Send and receive e-mail
Print from Outlook modules

Study Questions

Multiple Choice

1. You launch Microsoft Outlook by
   a. clicking the Outlook shortcut icon on the desktop.
   b. double-clicking the Outlook shortcut icon on the desktop.
   c. choosing Start, Control, Microsoft Outlook.
   d. pressing (ENTER).

2. To change from one Outlook feature to another,
   a. click the feature icon on the Outlook Bar.
   b. press (CTRL)+(F6).
   c. double click the feature on the Outlook toolbar.
   d. press (ENTER).

3. The Outlook feature designed to keep track of meetings is the
   a. Schedule.
   b. Journal.
   c. Calendar.
   d. Task List.

OL-21

4. The Outlook feature designed to keep track of the things you need to do is the
   a. Calendar.
   b. Task List.
   c. Schedule.
   d. Journal.

5. The Outlook feature that tracks your computer activity is the
   a. Task List.
   b. Calendar.
   c. Journal.
   d. Schedule.

6. The Outlook feature that lists messages received is the
   a. e-mail.
   b. Inbox.
   c. Outbox.
   d. Trash Can.

7. The Outlook feature that stores messages you want to send is the
   a. e-mail.
   b. Inbox.
   c. Outbox.
   d. Trash Can.

8. The Outlook feature designed to store names and addresses of business associates is
   a. the Inbox.
   b. the Journal.
   c. the Calendar.
   d. Contacts.

9. To exit Outlook,
   a. click the application Close button.
   b. press ALT+F6.
   c. choose File, Close.
   d. press ENTER.

10. To schedule an appointment in the Calendar,
    a. Outlook must be running in the background.
    b. select the Calendar date and type the appointment.
    c. copy the appointment from the Journal.
    d. press ENTER

Short Answer

1. List the features in Microsoft Outlook.

2. What happens to messages you create and send when you aren't logged on to the e-mail system?

3. When viewing messages in the Inbox, how can you tell if a message has been read?

4. How are features arranged on the Outlook Bar?

5. In which Outlook Bar group does Outbox appear?

6. Which Outlook features can you use to record notes during a telephone conversation?

7. What computer activities does the Journal track?

8. How do you access a different month in the Calendar?

9. What is each section of the Calendar window called?

10. How do you access a blank form for adding contacts to the Contact List?

For Discussion

1. List and describe the features contained in Microsoft Outlook.

2. Describe the procedure for recording an entry in the Task List and how you would indicate that the task is complete.

3. Describe the Outlook feature you believe you would use most frequently and briefly tell how you would use the feature.

4. List your e-mail address and describe procedures for logging on to your local area network.

Review Exercises

1. Exploring Outlook
Launch Outlook and display Office Assistant. Ask the Office Assistant how to insert files to send with e-mail messages. After reviewing the information the Office Assistant displays, create an e-mail message to your instructor summarizing what you have discovered. Then print the message.

Ask the Office Assistant how to access the Outlook Web page. Then access the Outlook Web page and review some of the additional features available in Outlook. Look for some innovative ways others are using Outlook, if they are available. List the three most interesting features and try implementing them using Outlook on your computer. Type a summary of the features you discover in an e-mail message to your instructor, describe how the feature can benefit you in your work, and then print (but don't send) the message.

2. Scheduling Assignments
Launch Outlook and display the Outlook Calendar. Record the following items in your Outlook Calendar:
- All scheduled class assignments and tests for all classes
- Personal activities for the semester
- Important dates to remember
- Holidays
- Final Exam Week
- End of the Semester

Print a listing of each month's Calendar using the Monthly Style.

Create a list of tasks associated with the assignments and activities and record the tasks in the Tasks List.

Assignments

1. Adding Contacts to the Contacts List
Launch Outlook and display the Contacts screen. Create additional contact listings for the following:

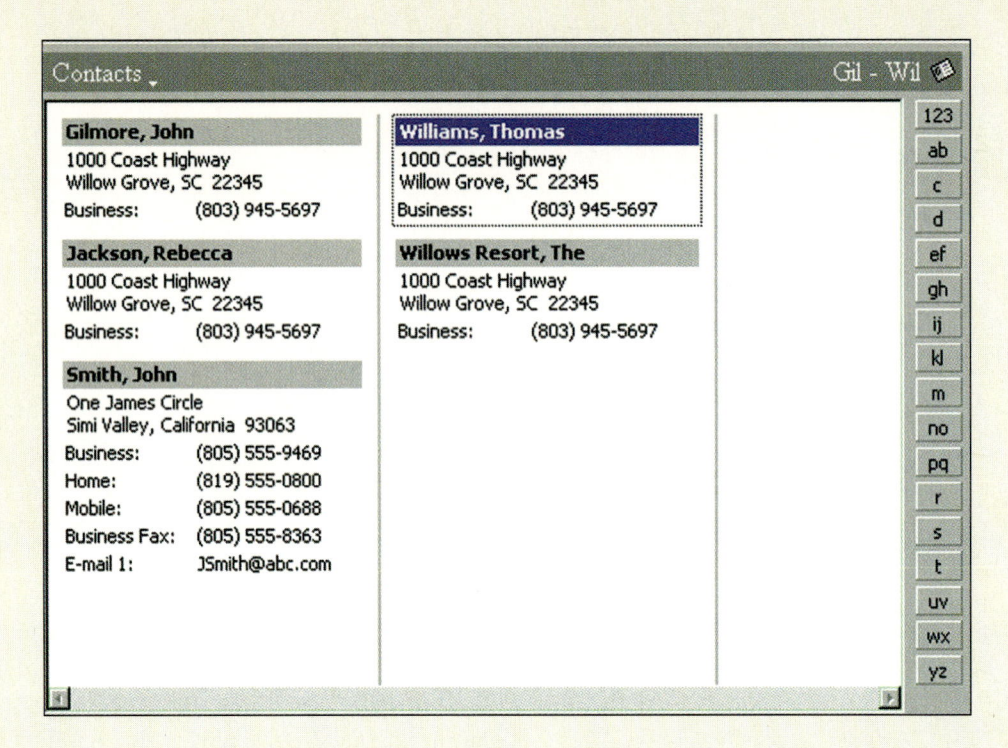

Your personal record will appear alphabetically among the contacts shown. The record for John Smith was added during the activities presented earlier in this overview. Print copies of the Contacts List in Small Booklet Style.

2. Using Office Assistant

Ask the Office Assistant how to set recurring appointments in the Calendar. Then use the information to set a recurring appointment for your Office 97 class. Print a copy of two months of classes using the monthly view format.

Print a list of tasks contained in the tasks list. Then mark completed tasks on your tasks list. Ask the Office Assistant how to prioritize tasks and then use the information to prioritize your tasks list. Prioritize incomplete tasks. Print a list of your revised tasks list.

Internet Explorer 3.0

Overview of Internet Explorer 3.0

Internet Explorer 3.0 is your "ride" on the information highway, taking you to places you want to go on the Internet and helping you obtain all sorts of information that you find there. This overview presents methods for using Internet Explorer 3.0 to access the basic resources on the Internet.

Objectives

After completing this project, you will be able to:

- ▶ **Identify the structure and purpose of the Internet**
- ▶ **Launch Internet Explorer 3.0**
- ▶ **Identify the Internet Explorer 3.0 screen elements**
- ▶ **Navigate the Internet**
- ▶ **Surf the Web**
- ▶ **Download a file via FTP**
- ▶ **Use a gopher to access resources**
- ▶ **Access newsgroups**
- ▶ **Create, send, and read e-mail on the Internet**
- ▶ **Exit Internet Explorer 3.0**

Identifying the Structure and Purpose of the Internet

The Internet is a network of networks consisting of millions of computers, located all over the world, all using a common set of signals called *Internet Protocol* (IP) to communicate. The Internet began with a network set up by the Department of Defense called ARPANET, Advanced Research Projects Agency Network. Soon the National Science Foundation joined the Internet, followed by many universities. The Internet quickly established a culture of free exchange of information and ideas.

The latest addition to the Internet, the Commercial Internet Exchange (CIX), seeks to profit from the Internet. Many traditional Internet users resent the addition of the CIX because its commercial orientation is in direct opposition to the original tenets of the Internet.

> **Note** A network generally consists of many satellite computers, called clients, that are attached to a main computer, called the server. The server provides the client computers with storage space, programs, a post office, and so on.

It is amazing that an entity as large as the Internet can operate without "someone in charge." No one organization or company "owns and operates" the Internet; however, InterNIC does issue unique server identifiers (IP addresses) to companies and organizations that want to join the Internet. Additionally, InterNIC keeps a database of all IP addresses on the Internet and makes this information available.

Connecting to the Internet

To connect to the Internet, you must be connected to a host computer. Many businesses, universities, colleges, and schools have host computers so that their employees, students, and staff have access to the Internet. If you don't have access to a host computer but your computer has a modem, you can connect to the Internet through an Internet Service Provider (ISP). ISPs usually charge a fee based on usage. If you find that you have no life and spend too much time on the Internet, you may want to find an ISP that offers an unlimited usage fee arrangement.

Identifying Services on the Internet

A variety of resources is available on the Internet. The most popular of these resources are described in Table I.1.

Table I.1 Resources Available on the Internet

Resources	Description
Electronic mail (e-mail)	Sends and receives electronic messages.
World Wide Web (WWW)	Provides information in a pictorial form, using hypertext links, a technology that allows you to jump from one Web page or Web site to another.
Newsgroups	Provides a bulletin board service for discussion groups.
Information retrieval — also called File Transfer Protocol (FTP)	Provides files for downloading and accepts files for uploading.
Internet Relay Chat (IRC)	Provides a connection for online discussions that are typed back and forth among users.
Gopher	Provides a menu system for locating resources on the Internet.
Telnet	Allows remote login to another computer or network.

To connect to any site on the Internet, you must have the address of the site. An address, also called a *Uniform Resource Locator* (URL), uses the following syntax:

> **protocol://domain_name/path/filename**

Table I.2 explains each part of the syntax.

Table I.2 Syntax of the URL

Syntax	Description
Protocol	Identifies the protocol used by the server. The World Wide Web uses HTTP protocol; File Transfer uses FTP; and gopher uses GOPHER.
Domain_name	Identifies the name assigned to the server (also called an IP address). The name is issued by InterNIC, an organization that regulates IP addresses. The name itself must follow a specific syntax. Typical domain names are microsoft.com, uiuc.edu, novell.com, netscape.com, and so on.
Path	Identifies the folders where the file is stored. The path may contain several folder names separated by slashes. This part of the syntax isn't used if the site is a home page (the first page of a site, often called the "front door") on the World Wide Web.
Filename	Identifies the name of the file. This part of the syntax also isn't used if the site is a home page.

Launching Internet Explorer 3.0

Internet Explorer 3.0 is a program designed for the Windows 95/Windows NT platform. Internet Explorer is classified as a *web browser* program because its interface is designed specifically for accessing the graphical features (the pictures, icons, buttons, and so on) of the World Wide Web; however, Internet Explorer also can be used for accessing FTP and gopher sites which use text-based formats.

TASK 1: TO LAUNCH INTERNET EXPLORER 3.0:

1 Double-click the Internet Explorer 3.0 icon [The Internet] on the desktop.
If the icon isn't on your desktop, choose Start, Programs, Internet Explorer. The following message may appear if you have other browsers installed. If it does appear, choose Yes or No as desired. You may also want to deselect "Always perform this check when starting Internet Explorer."

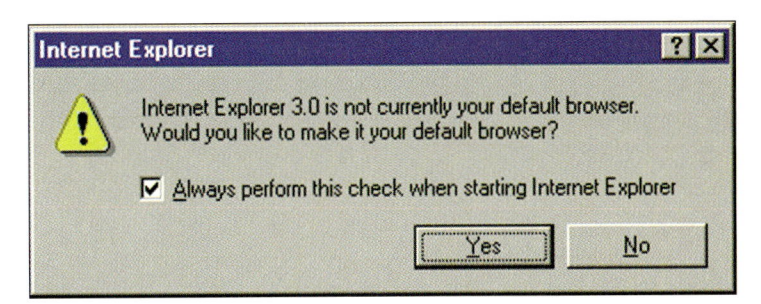

2 Respond to any prompts to log on to your service provider's network, if applicable.
The Microsoft start page displays. A **Start page,** also called a **home page,** is the starting point for browsing a Web site.

> **Tip** You also can launch Internet Explorer 3.0 from within each module of Office 97. Just click the Web toolbar button to display an abbreviated Internet Explorer 3.0 toolbar. When you type an Internet address and press (ENTER), Internet Explorer 3.0 launches and goes to the specified site.

Identifying the Internet Explorer 3.0 Screen Elements

Figure I.1 shows the basic elements of the Internet Explorer 3.0 start page. The page you see on your computer will not match the figure exactly because Microsoft changes the content of the page continually. The elements of the screen are described in Table I.3.

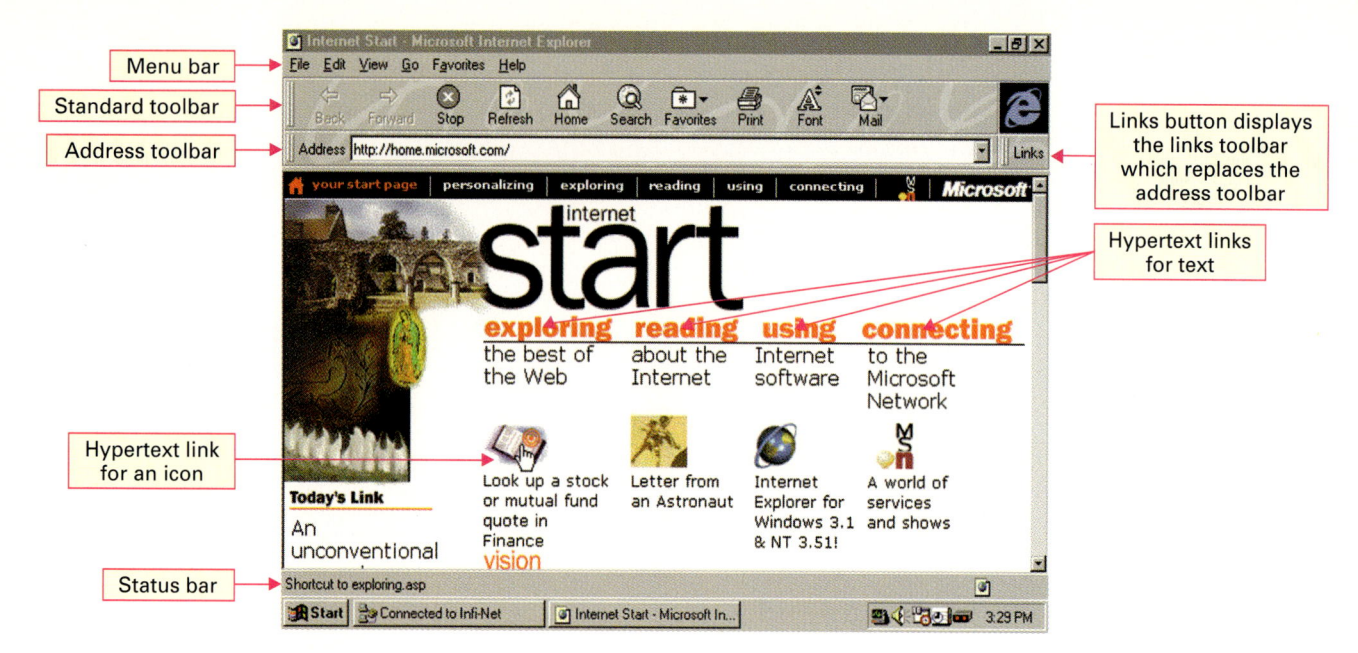

Figure I.1

Table I.3 Screen Elements

Screen Element	Description
Title bar	Displays the name of the application.
Menu bar	Contains the options File, Edit, View, Go, Favorites, and Help.
Address toolbar	Contains a text box in which you enter the address of the Internet site you want to visit. If this toolbar is displayed, the Links toolbar is not. To display the Links toolbar, click Links.
Links toolbar	Contains buttons that jump to specific Web sites. If this toolbar is displayed, the Address toolbar is not. To display the Address toolbar, click Address.
Status bar	Displays information about what is happening at the moment.

Tip As you navigate to other sites on the Internet, the text box in the Address toolbar displays the address of the current site.

Navigating the Internet

As soon as you launch Internet Explorer 3.0, you begin navigating the Internet automatically because Internet Explorer 3.0 takes you to its start page on the World Wide Web. To continue navigating on the Internet, you can use any of the following methods:

- Click on a hypertext link
- Type the address of the Internet site

- Select a site from the Go menu
- Select a site from the History folder
- Select a Favorite from the Favorites menu
- Click the Search button

> **Tip** To change to a different start page, go to the desired page and choose View, Options. Click the Navigation tab and choose the option *Use current to set the currently loaded page as the start page.* Then click OK. It is probably not advisable to change the start page in the lab.

Following Links

A Web page generally has text or graphic hypertext links that jump to a different Web page. The Web page may be located on the same Web server or a different server in another part of the world. Text links are generally bright blue and underlined. When you click on a text link, the color changes to purple to show that you have followed the link.

> **Tip** To find out whether text or a graphic is a hypertext link, point to the item with the mouse pointer. If the pointer changes to a hand with a pointing finger, the item is a hypertext link.

TASK 2: TO USE A HYPERTEXT LINK:

1. Point to text or a graphic that is a hypertext link and click.
   Internet Explorer 3.0 goes to another Web page.

2. Click another hypertext link.
   Internet Explorer 3.0 goes to the linked Web page.

Typing an Address

To get to any site on the Internet, you can enter the site address in the text box on the Address toolbar. However, because Internet sites may close or move to different addresses, the addresses used in the following tasks may not be valid when you try to use them. If you have difficulty visiting a particular address, ask for alternative addresses.

TASK 3: TO GO TO INTERNET SITES BY TYPING AN ADDRESS:

1. Click in the Address text box on the Address toolbar.
   The insertion point is positioned in the text box, and the address is highlighted.

IE-8

> The insertion point is positioned in the text box, and the address is highlighted.

2 Type **http://espnet.sportszone.com** and press ENTER.
The ESPN SportsZone page displays.

> **Tip** If you decide you don't want to go to a particular site, click the Stop button on the toolbar while the page is loading.

3 Type **ftp://ftp.microsoft.com** in the Address text box and press ENTER.
The Microsoft FTP site displays.

4 Type **gopher://gopher.tc.viewmn.edu** in the Address text box and press ENTER. The University of Minnesota Gopher site displays.

5 Click the Home button.
The start page displays.

> **Tip** Web pages with large graphic files (or other types of multimedia files) may take too long to display on the screen. You can turn off the downloading of multimedia by choosing View, Options, and clicking the General page, if necessary. Select or deselect the options in the Multimedia area and click OK. Check with your lab instructor before making changes to the View options.

Selecting a Site from the Go Menu

On the Go menu, Internet Explorer 3.0 lists the last five addresses you have visited in the current session. The addresses on the Go menu are deleted when you exit Internet Explorer 3.0.

TASK 4: TO RETURN TO A PAGE BY USING THE GO MENU:

1 Choose Go.

Overview **IE-9**

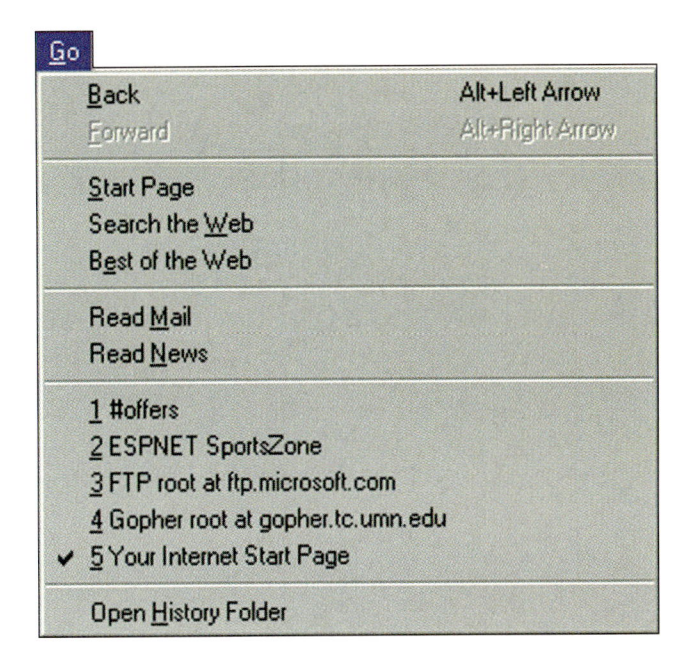

```
Go
    Back                          Alt+Left Arrow
    Forward                       Alt+Right Arrow

    Start Page
    Search the Web
    Best of the Web

    Read Mail
    Read News

    1 #offers
    2 ESPNET SportsZone
    3 FTP root at ftp.microsoft.com
    4 Gopher root at gopher.tc.umn.edu
  ✓ 5 Your Internet Start Page

    Open History Folder
```

2 Choose the site named FTP root at ftp.microsoft.com.
Internet Explorer 3.0 goes to the Microsoft FTP site.

Selecting a Site from the History Folder

The History folder stores links to all the addresses you have visited in the last 14 days. You can open the History folder to review the sites you have visited, or you can use a link in the folder to go to the site again. Sites that you visit aren't added to the History folder until you log off the Internet.

TASK 5: TO RETURN TO A PAGE BY USING THE HISTORY FOLDER:

1 Click ⊠ and then launch Internet Explorer 3.0 again.

2 Choose Go.
The Go menu displays.

3 Choose Open History Folder and scroll the list, if necessary, to display the address http://espnet.sportszone.com.

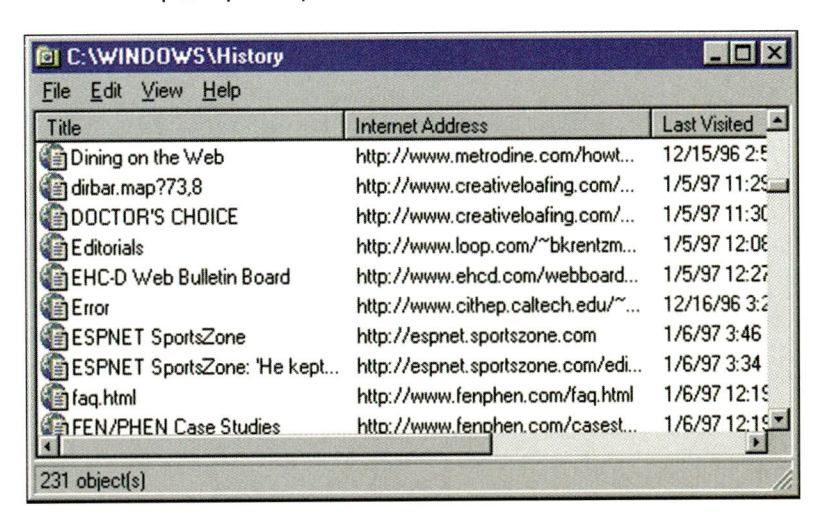

Title	Internet Address	Last Visited
Dining on the Web	http://www.metrodine.com/howt...	12/15/96 2:5
dirbar.map?73,8	http://www.creativeloafing.com/...	1/5/97 11:29
DOCTOR'S CHOICE	http://www.creativeloafing.com/...	1/5/97 11:30
Editorials	http://www.loop.com/~bkrentzm...	1/5/97 12:08
EHC-D Web Bulletin Board	http://www.ehcd.com/webboard...	1/5/97 12:27
Error	http://www.cithep.caltech.edu/~...	12/16/96 3:2
ESPNET SportsZone	http://espnet.sportszone.com	1/6/97 3:46
ESPNET SportsZone: 'He kept...	http://espnet.sportszone.com/edi...	1/6/97 3:34
faq.html	http://www.fenphen.com/faq.html	1/6/97 12:19
FEN/PHEN Case Studies	http://www.fenphen.com/casest...	1/6/97 12:19

C:\WINDOWS\History — File Edit View Help — 231 object(s)

IE-10

4 Double-click the address.
Internet Explorer 3.0 goes to the ESPNET SportsZone page.

5 Click ☒ in the History window.

Selecting a Favorite

Internet Explorer calls shortcuts to Internet sites Favorites and lists them on the Favorites menu. You can create shortcuts for your favorite sites if you can't remember the addresses or you don't want to type them.

TASK 6: TO ADD A FAVORITE:

1 Ensure that you are on the ESPNET SportsZone page and then choose Favorites.

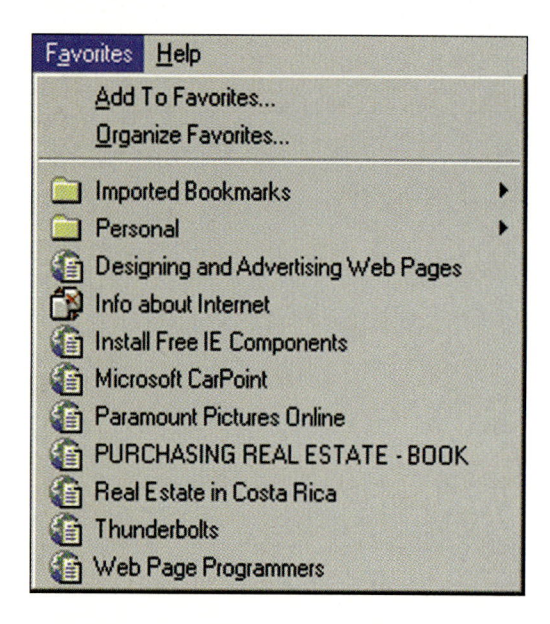

> **Note** If this site has already been added to the Favorites menu, choose another site to add.

2 Choose Add To Favorites.

3 Click OK.
The dialog box closes, and the ESPNET SportsZone page is added to the Favorites menu.

Overview **IE-11**

4 Click 🏠.
The start page displays.

5 Choose Favorites.
The Favorites menu shown in Step 1 displays.

6 Click ESPNET SportsZone.
Internet Explorer 3.0 goes to the ESPNET SportsZone site.

> **Tip** To go backward and forward through the pages you have opened in a session, click the Back button and the Forward button.

Searching the Internet

The Internet is so vast that finding information can be a challenge. To meet that challenge, several organizations and companies have created search engines, programs that search the Internet for text that users enter. Internet Explorer 3.0 gives you access to several popular search engines on one Web site.

TASK 7: TO SEARCH FOR INFORMATION USING A SEARCH ENGINE:

1 Click the Search 🔍 button.

The insertion point appears in the search text box

2 Type **beach resort** in the Search text box.

3 Choose InfoSeek.

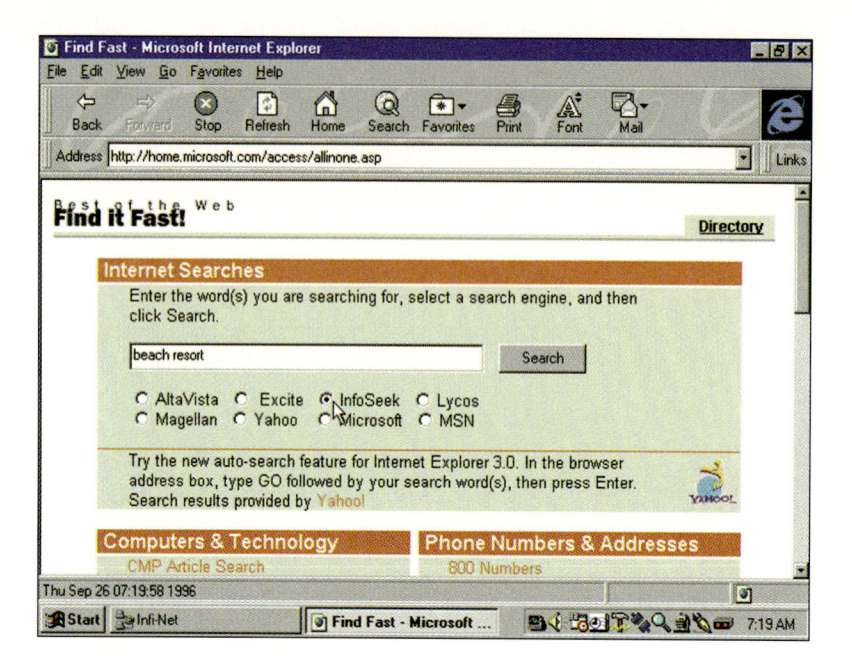

4 Click the Search button next to the Search text box.

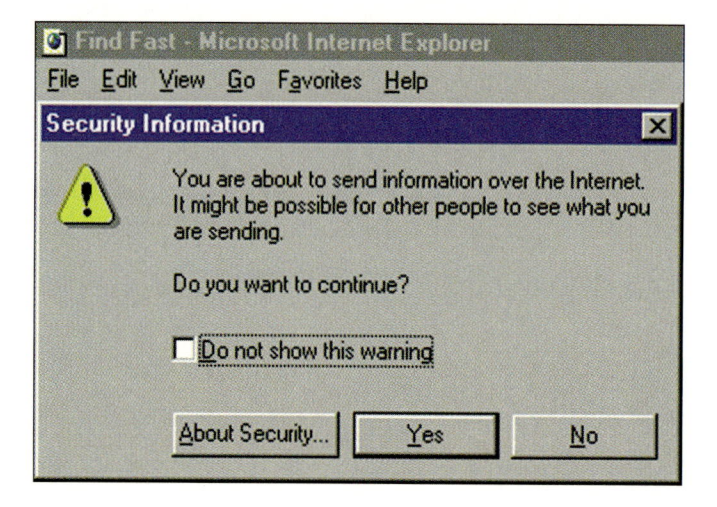

5 Choose Yes.

6 Scroll through the list of items found and click on any item that you want to read.

7 Click the Back ⬅ button.

8 Continue to scroll until you find another item you want to read and then click on it.

> **Tip** Use the Find command located on the Edit menu to search for specific text in the current document.

Printing Information

Often you may want to print the pages that you see displayed on the screen so that you can refer to them later.

TASK 8: TO PRINT A WEB PAGE:

1 Click 🏠.
The start page displays.

2 Ensure that you are connected to a printer and that the printer is online.

3 Click the Print 🖨 button.
The start page prints.

Downloading a File Via FTP

Many organizations maintain *anonymous* FTP sites that contain files for public downloading. The sites are called anonymous because anyone can log on with the user name "anonymous" and the e-mail address as the password. If you use Internet Explorer 3.0 to log on to an FTP site, you don't have to enter a password because this is done for you "behind the scenes." The steps for using Internet Explorer 3.0 to visit an FTP site are no different from the steps used when you visit a Web site; however, the appearance of an FTP site is *quite* different.

An FTP site provides a hierarchical list of directories and files, much like the list of directories and files you see in Windows Explorer. Each directory or filename in the list is a hypertext link. When you click a directory name, the directory displays its content. When you click a filename, the file opens (if Internet Explorer 3.0 recognizes the file type). If Internet Explorer 3.0 doesn't recognize the file type, a dialog box displays in which you can specify the program that will open the file or you can save the file to disk.

TASK 9: TO DOWNLOAD A FILE FROM AN FTP SITE:

1 Type **ftp://nis.nsf.net** in the Address text box and press ENTER.

IE-14

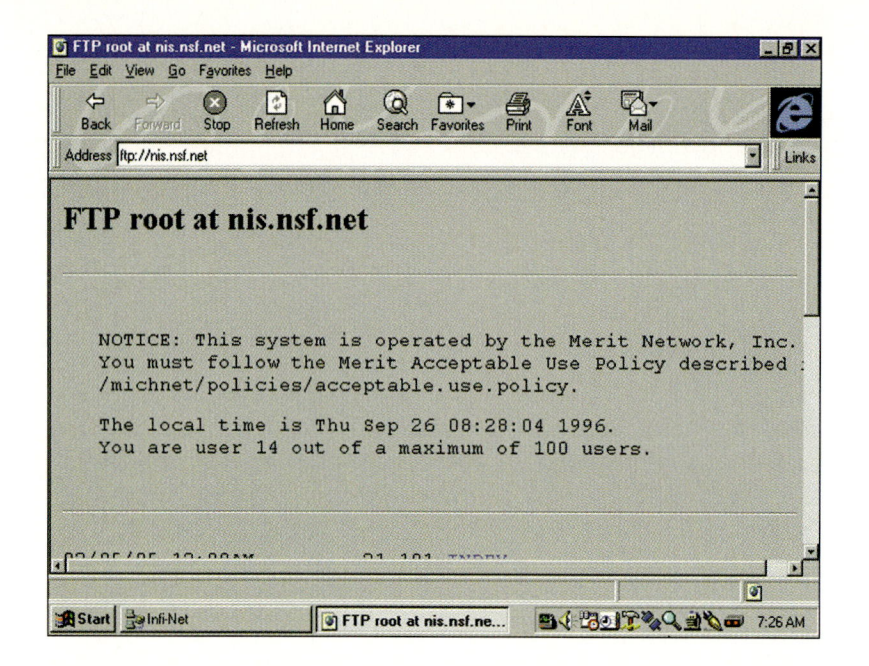

Note You may have to try to connect to this site at different times. It's often fairly busy.

2 Scroll down if necessary and click Documents.

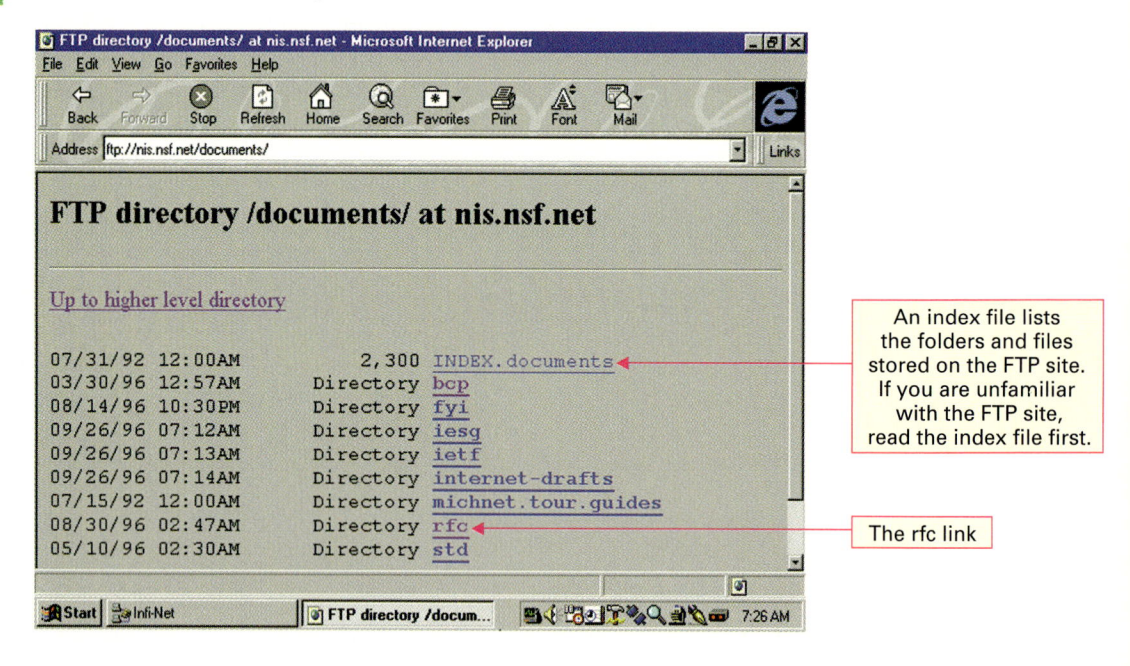

An index file lists the folders and files stored on the FTP site. If you are unfamiliar with the FTP site, read the index file first.

The rfc link

3 Click rfc.
Another FTP screen displays.

Overview **IE-15**

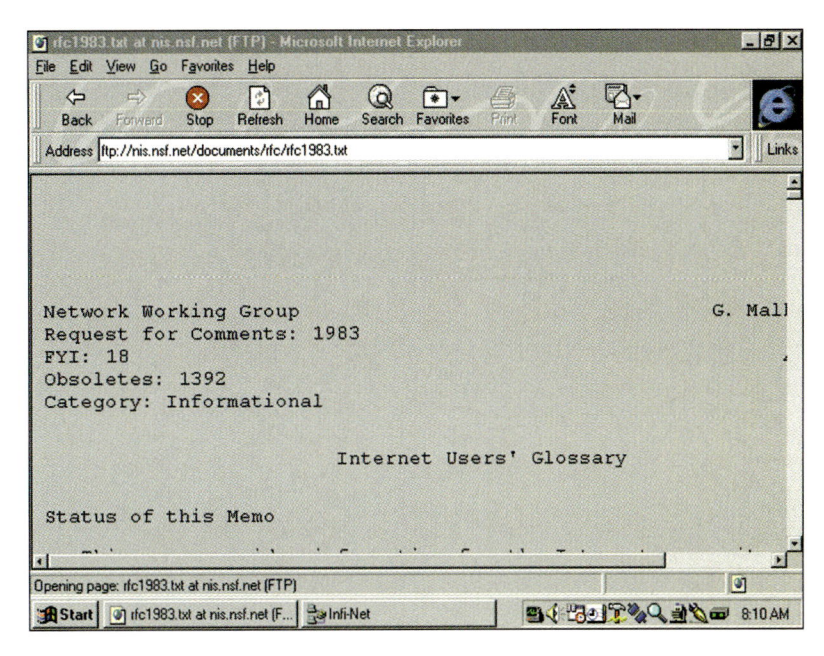

4 Scroll to rfc1983.txt and click it.

5 Choose File, Save As File.

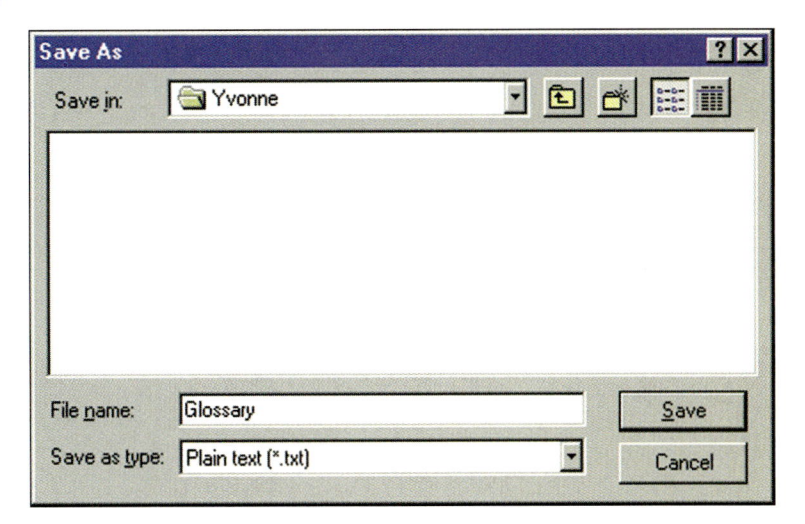

6 Select the desired Save in folder and type **Glossary** for the filename.

7 Click Save.
The file is downloaded to the specified folder.

> **Note** All FTP servers have a limit to the number of users that may log on at one time. When the limit is reached, new connections are denied and you just have to try the connection at a later time.

Accessing Resources with a Gopher

A gopher site provides a character-based, hierarchical lists that eventually lead to files you can download. Many gopher sites are linked to other gopher sites, so using a gopher is similar to using the Web because you may jump from one gopher site to another in your search for information. The difference is that you are moving down through a hierarchy until you reach specific information when you are using a gopher whereas you may be jumping around in random fashion when you are using the Web. Another difference between the Web and a gopher site is that the gopher site isn't graphical; it resembles an FTP site.

> **Note** The gopher site at the University of Minnesota is a good place to start a gopher search because the site is linked to most gopher sites on the Internet. The University of Minnesota, home of the Golden Gophers, originated the gopher protocol.

TASK 10: TO LOOK UP INFORMATION USING A GOPHER:

1. Type **gopher://gopher.tc.umn.edu** in the Address text box.
2. Press ENTER.

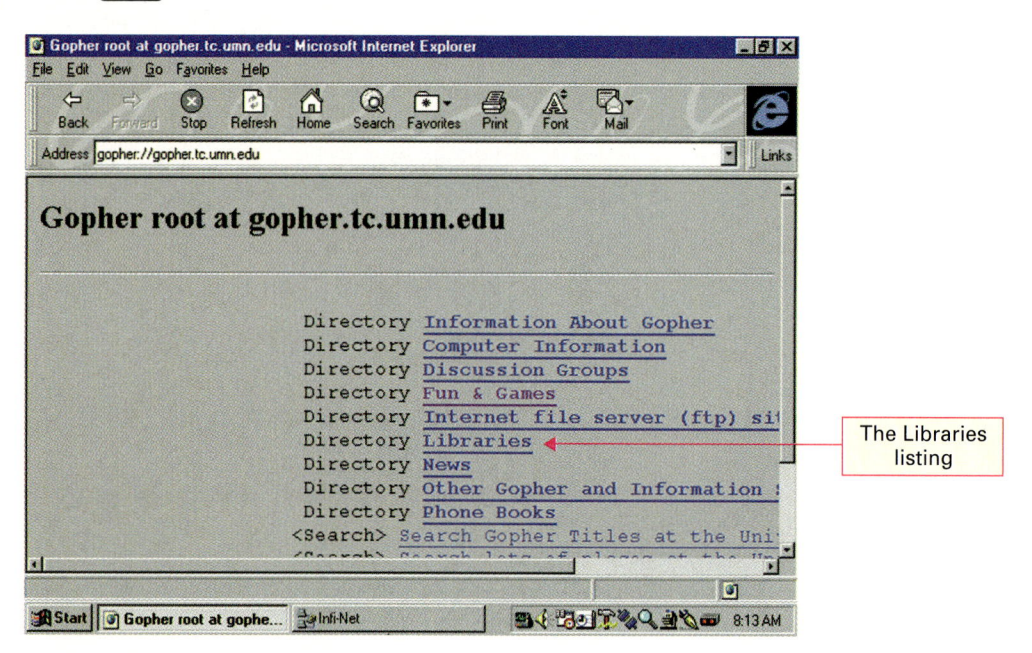

The Libraries listing

3. Click the Libraries listing.

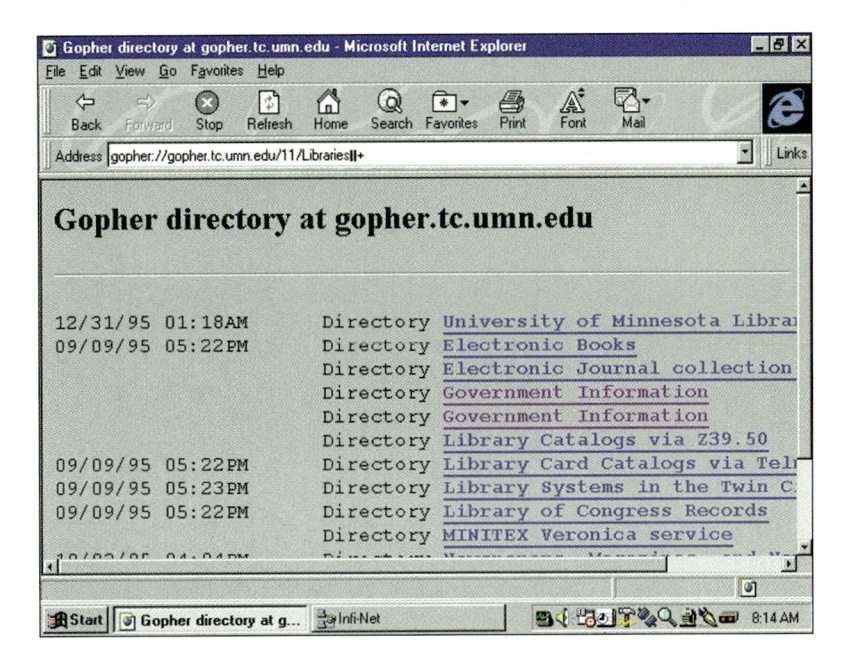

4 Click one of the Government Information listings.

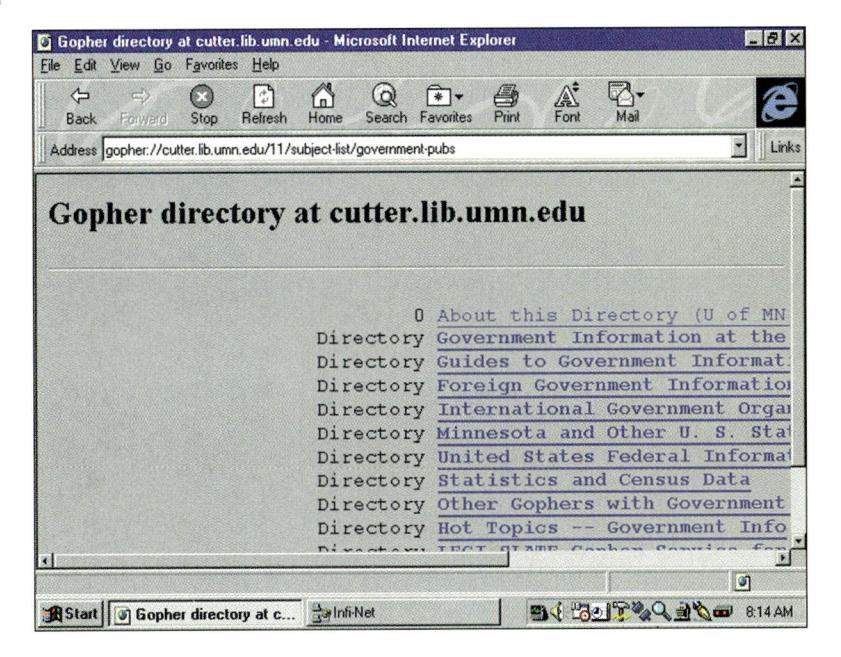

5 Click Statistics and Census Data.

6 Click 1990 Census: US Summaries (via UMich)

7 Click 1990 U.S. selected population and housing data (STF1C)

8 Scroll the page to find out what age group has the largest population.

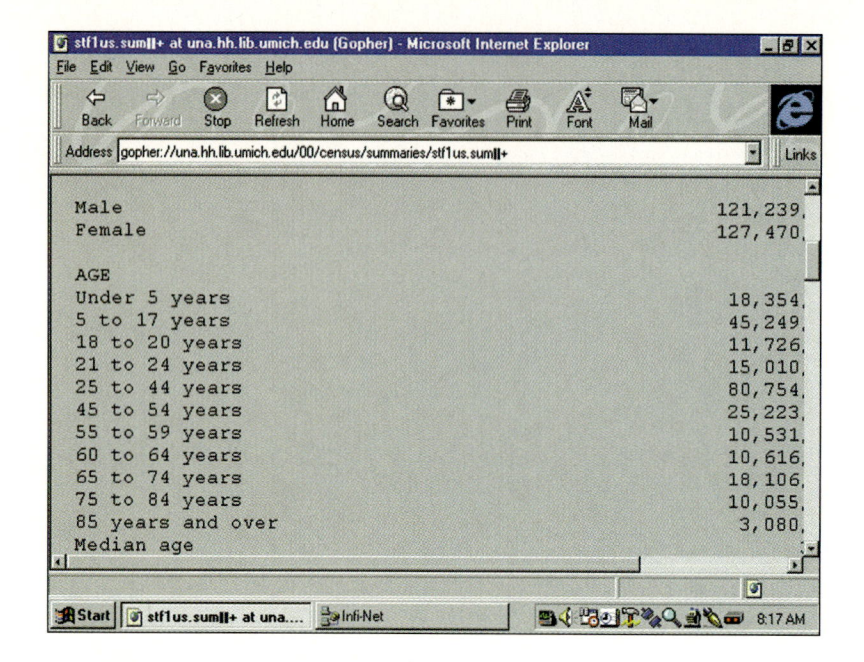

9 Click 🏠.
The start page appears.

Accessing Newsgroups

Newsgroups are collections of world-wide electronic discussion groups that allow network users to exchange ideas, opinions, and information. To participate in one of the more than 16,000 newsgroups available, you must have access to a news server and have a news reader program. Internet Explorer 3.0 has its own newsreader program, Internet News.

Usenet, the oldest organization of newsgroups, provides seven major news categories:

comp	computer-related topics
news	newsgroup information
rec	recreational topics
sci	scientific research topics
soc	social issues
talk	controversial debates
misc	everything else

Almost all news servers carry the seven major categories. Other categories which may or may not be carried by a news server include:

alt	alternative subjects
bionet	biological topics
bit	miscellaneous topics
biz	business related topics and advertisements
gnu	Free Software Foundation topics
k12	educational topics for kindergarten through 12th grade

Launching Internet News

Because so many newsgroups are available, you may want to select just the newsgroups that you are interested in so that you don't have to scroll through such a long list each time you want to participate in a group. Subscribing to a newsgroup simply lists the group on a separate page in Internet News so you can access it more easily.

TASK 11: TO LAUNCH INTERNET NEWS AND SUBSCRIBE TO SEVERAL NEWSGROUPS:

1 Choose Start, Programs, Internet News.

2 Respond to any prompts to logon to your service provider's network if applicable.
The newsgroup accessed when Internet News was last used displays, or a message displays telling you that there are new newsgroups. Click Yes to see them.

3 Click the Newsgroups button if a newsgroup displays or click the All tab if the Newsgroup dialog box displays.

This message may appear

4 Select the Don't ask me this again checkbox and then choose No if the message displays.

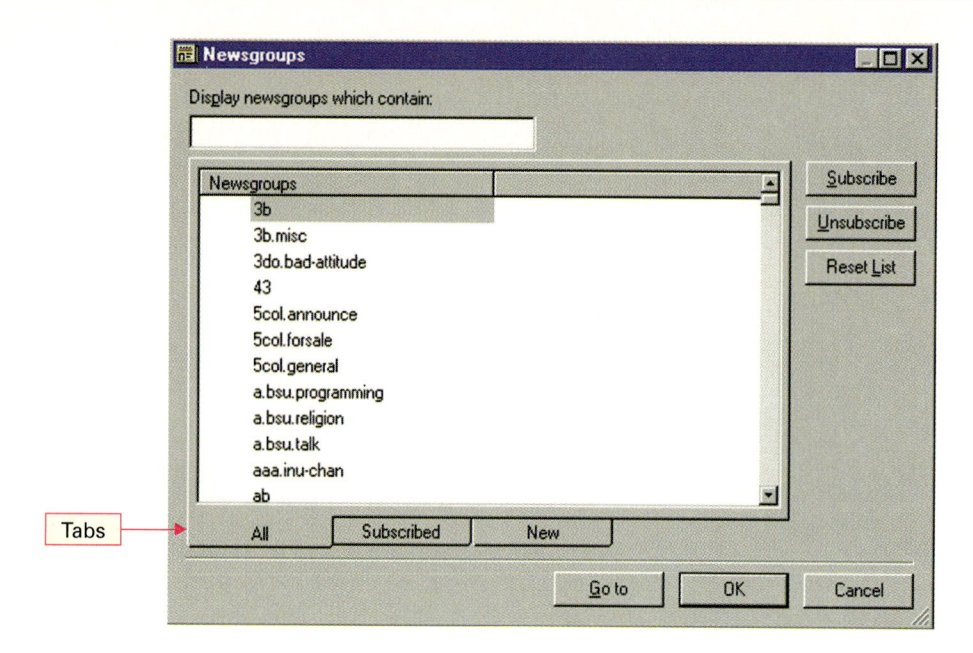

5 Scroll to and double-click the following newsgroups: rec.equestrian, rec.sport.golf, and rec.sport.tennis.
Double-clicking a newsgroup subscribes you to a newsgroup. Double-clicking again unsubscribes you. (You can "unsubscribe" by double-clicking also.)

Individual contributions to a newsgroup are called *articles* or *messages*. Submitting an article is called *posting*. Each posted message is part of a discussion *thread*. Posting a reply to a message adds a message to the thread. Posting a new message starts a new thread. Threads that have replies are marked with a plus sign (+).

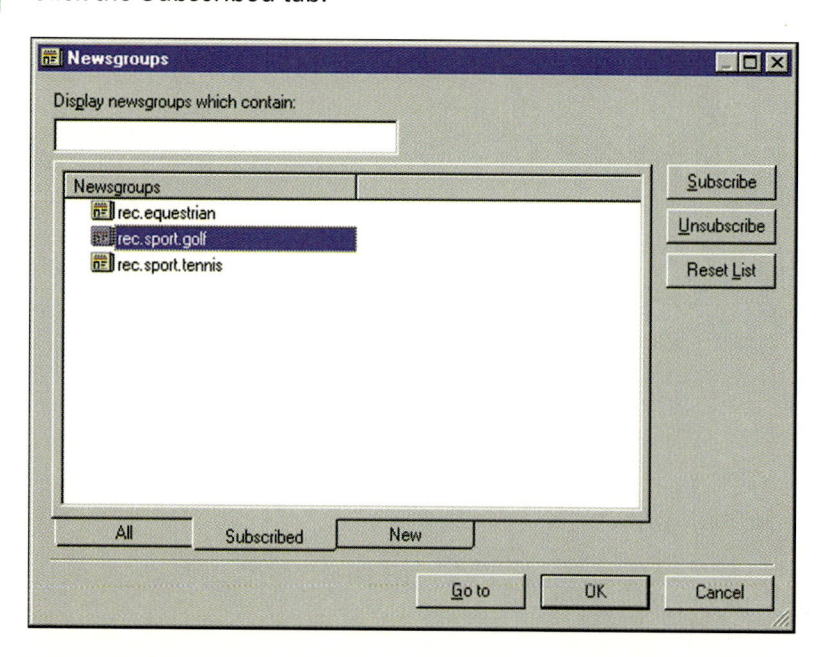

TASK 12: TO READ AN ARTICLE IN A NEWSGROUP:

1 Click the Subscribed tab.

2 Click rec.sport.golf.

3 Click Go to.

Indicates posting has replies. Clicking the plus displays the replies.

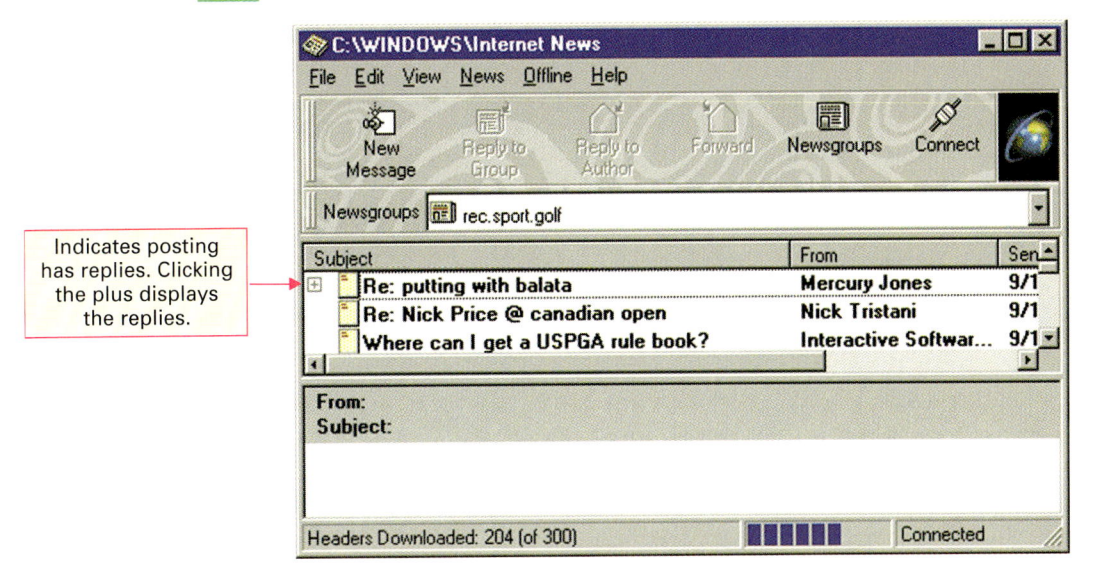

Note If a message appears about subscribing to a group, choose No.

4 Click 🔲.
The Internet News window maximizes.

5 Click any message in the upper pane.

The text of the message displays in the lower pane

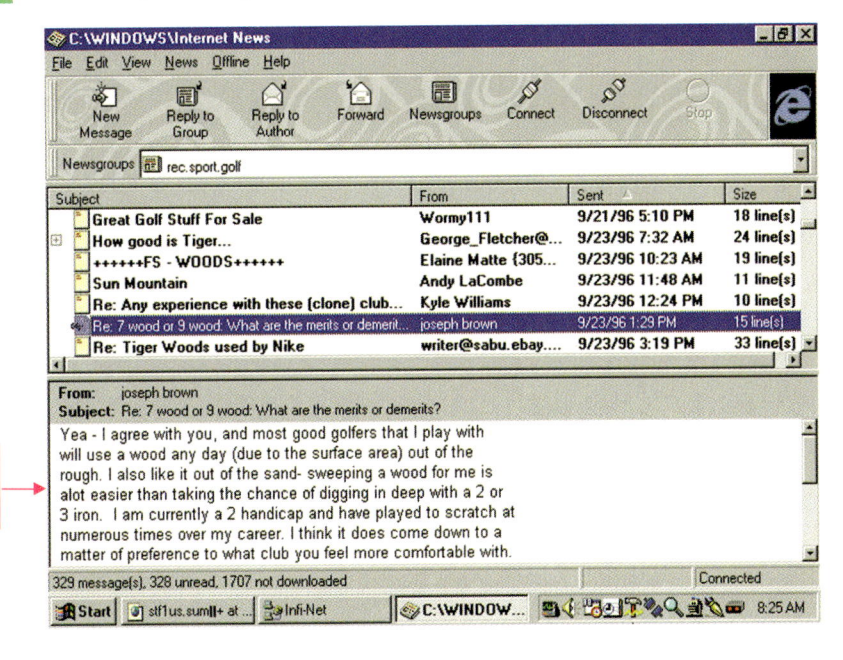

6 Read several more messages.

7 Click ✖.

8 Follow the on-screen steps if a message about disconnecting from the service provider displays.

Overview IE-21

> **Warning** You shouldn't post messages to newsgroups unless you know the informal rules that govern the newsgroup and are familiar with proper "netiquette," news etiquette. Look for the rules in a FAQ (frequently asked questions) posted on the newsgroup. If you don't see a FAQ posted, check the following address: ftp://ftp.rtfm.mit.edu/pub/usenet-by-group/news.answers. Also check the newsgroup news.announce.newusers for rules of net etiquette.

Creating, Sending, and Reading E-mail

Electronic mail (e-mail) is the most widely used resource on the Internet. Using e-mail, you can communicate with or send files to other people almost instantaneously without making expensive long distance calls or using overnight delivery services.

Creating and Sending E-mail

To send and receive e-mail messages on the Internet, you must have an e-mail program, be connected to a mail server, and have an e-mail address. The e-mail program that comes with Internet Explorer 3.0 is Internet Mail. The mail server may be provided by your organization's network or by a service provider. Your e-mail address is a combination of a user name, the at symbol (@), and the domain name of the server. For example, a student at the University of Illinois might have an e-mail address like this: SueBoggs2@ux10.uiuc.edu.

TASK 13: TO LAUNCH INTERNET MAIL AND CREATE AND SEND AN E-MAIL MESSAGE:

1. Choose Start, Programs, Internet Mail, and respond to any prompts to log on to your service provider's network.

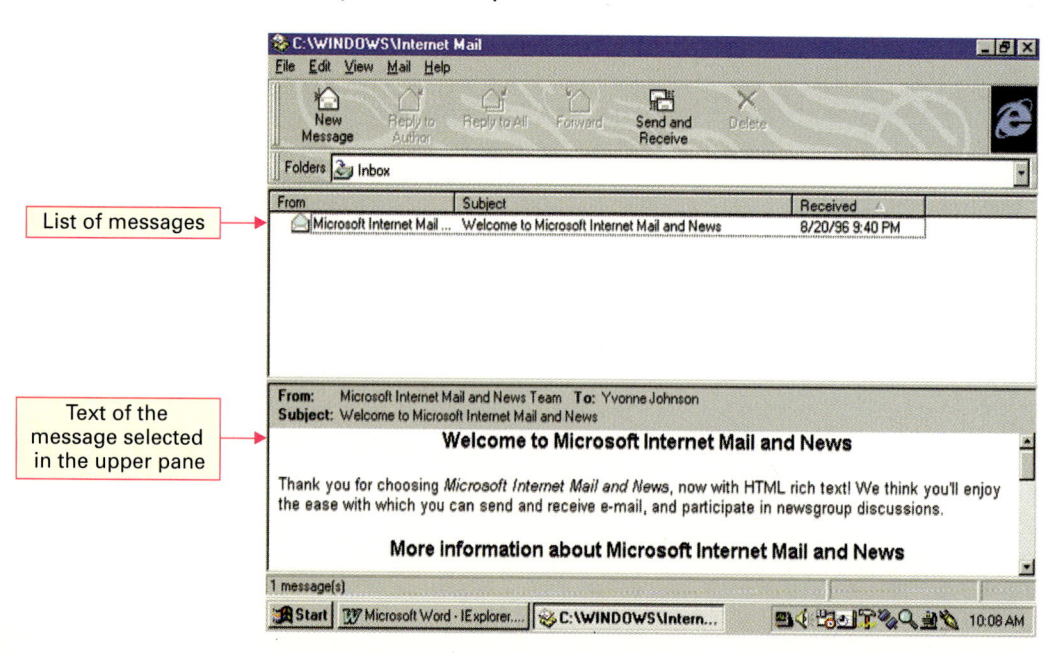

List of messages

Text of the message selected in the upper pane

Overview   IE-23

2 Click ▢.
The Internet Mail window is maximized.

3 Click the New Message button.

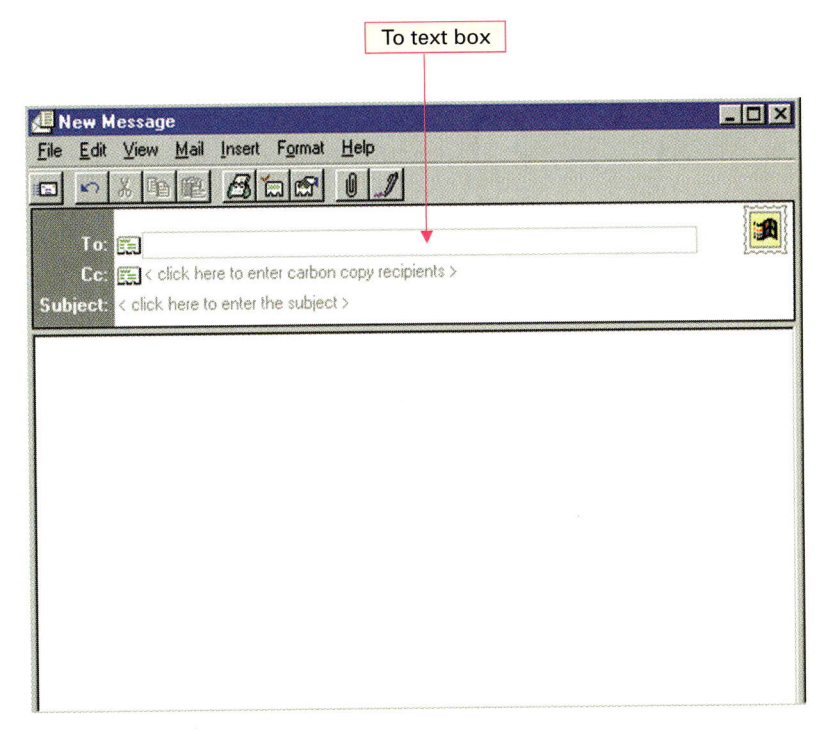

To text box

4 Type a friend or classmate's e-mail address in the To text box.

5 Click <click here to enter the subject> and type **Test**.

6 Click in the blank area under the Subject and type the message shown.

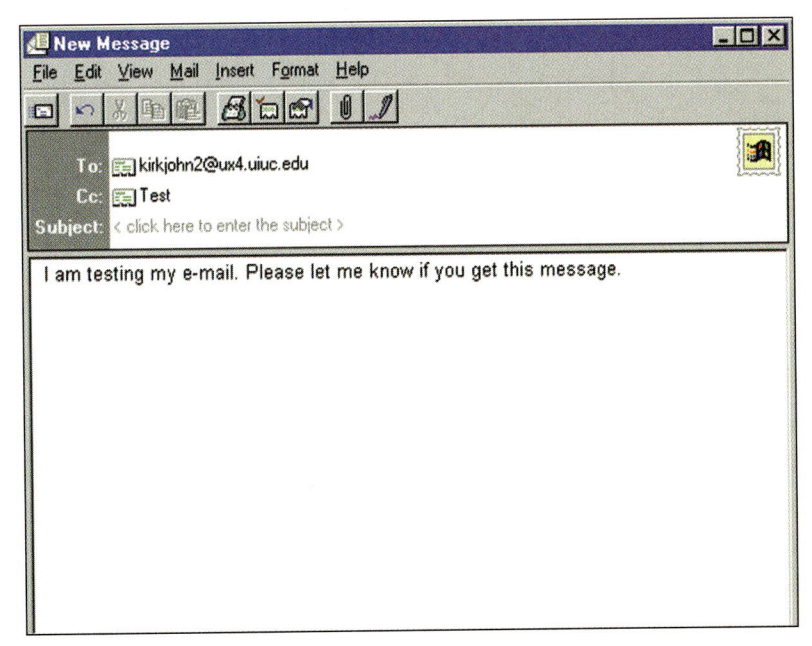

7 Click the Send [icon] button.
If you are logged on to the Network, the message is sent immediately; otherwise, the following message appears.

> **Send Mail**
>
> When you send an email message, it will be placed in your 'Outbox' folder ready to be sent the next time you choose the 'Send and Receive' command.
>
> ☐ Don't show me this message again.
>
> OK

8 Click OK.
The message is stored in the Outbox folder, and the New Message dialog box closes.

9 Click the arrow on the Folder drop-down list.

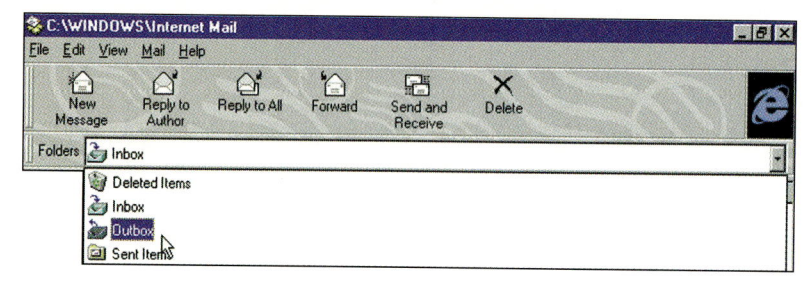

C:\WINDOWS\Internet Mail
File Edit View Mail Help
New Message | Reply to Author | Reply to All | Forward | Send and Receive | Delete
Folders: Inbox
- Deleted Items
- Inbox
- **Outbox**
- Sent Items

10 Click the Outbox folder.
The message displays.

11 Click the Send and Receive [icon] button.
A copy of the message is saved in the Sent Items folder and the message is sent.

Reading E-mail

E-mail that you receive is stored in your In-box.

Overview   IE-25

TASK 14: TO READ AN E-MAIL MESSAGE:

1 Launch Internet Mail.

2 Select Inbox from the Folder drop-down list if necessary.

3 Double-click any message in the upper pane.
A separate window opens with the text of the message.

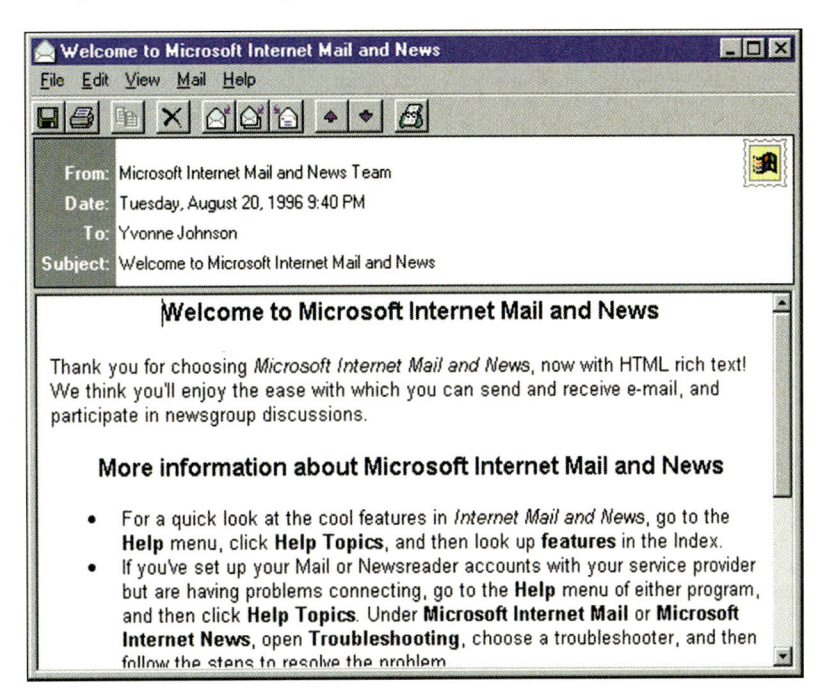

4 Click ⊠ after you read the message.
The message window closes.

5 Click ⊠.
Internet Mail closes.

6 Follow the steps given on-screen if a message about disconnecting from the service provider displays.

Exiting Internet Explorer 3.0

When you are finished using the Internet, exit Internet Explorer 3.0 and terminate your connection, if necessary.

TASK 15: TO EXIT INTERNET EXPLORER 3.0:

1 Choose File, Exit, or click ⊠.

2 Choose the appropriate option to disconnect, if you are prompted to disconnect from your Internet Service Provider's network.
Internet Explorer 3.0 closes.

Summary and Exercises

Summary

- The Internet is a network of networks all communicating with the IP protocol.
- Services on the Internet include e-mail, World Wide Web, newsgroups, FTP, gopher, relay chat, and telnet.
- Internet Explorer 3.0 provides many ways to navigate the Internet.
- FTP sites contain files for downloading.
- Gopher sites provide hierarchical menus to access resources.
- Newsgroups are discussion groups.
- E-mail is a fast, convenient, inexpensive way to communicate.

Key Terms and Operations

Key Terms
Address toolbar
client
domain name
e-mail
FAQ
Favorite
FTP
gopher
History folder
HTTP
Index
Internet Protocol (IP)
Internet Service Provider (ISP)
InterNIC
Links toolbar
Netiquette
newsgroups
posting
Relay Chat (IRC)
search engine
server
telnet
thread
URL
World Wide Web

Operations
Download a file
Exit Internet Explorer 3.0
Exit Internet Mail
Exit Internet News
Print a page
Read a newsgroup article
Read an e-mail message
Search the Internet
Send an e-mail message
Launch Internet Explorer 3.0
Launch Internet Mail
Launch Internet News
Subscribe to a newsgroup

Study Questions

Multiple Choice
1. URL is
   a. a protocol used on the World Wide Web.
   b. an acronym for Unspecified Resource Link.
   c. an acronym for Uniform Resource Locator.
   d. the organization that regulates the Internet.

IE-26

2. The gopher protocol was originated at
   a. University of Illinois.
   b. University of Minnesota.
   c. University of Wisconsin.
   d. the National Science Foundation.

3. A web browser is a
   a. user who browses the Web without actively participating.
   b. user who browses the Web and actively participates.
   c. program that accesses Web sites.
   d. search engine on a gopher site.

4. The oldest organization of newsgroups is
   a. Internet.
   b. Usenet.
   c. BITNET.
   d. Clarinet.

5. The syntax for an e-mail address is
   a. domain_name@user_name
   b. user_name@domain_name
   c. site@logon
   d. logonid@school

6. The Find command searches
   a. all Web sites for specified text.
   b. all FTP sites for specified text.
   c. only the current page for specified text.
   d. all gopher sites for specified text.

7. When you click a hypertext link,
   a. a pop-up box displays with a description of the hypertext link.
   b. the name of the linked file displays.
   c. another page or site on the Internet is accessed.
   d. you are automatically logged off the Internet.

8. The History folder stores
   a. a log of the dates and times you log on to the Internet.
   b. a list of Favorites.
   c. the Internet addresses accessed in the last 14 days.
   d. a list of user names that log on to the Internet.

9. When the pointer hovers over a hypertext link,
   a. the link changes color.
   b. the link blinks.
   c. the pointer changes to a hand with a pointing finger.
   d. the pointer changes color.

10. The last five addresses you have visited are listed on the
    a. Favorites menu.
    b. Go menu.
    c. Edit menu.
    d. View menu.

Short Answer
1. What was the name of the first network on the Internet?
2. What protocol does the World Wide Web use?
3. What does FTP stand for?
4. What are newsgroups?
5. What is a thread?
6. What is a home page?
7. What is a hypertext link?
8. What is an FAQ?
9. What is an Internet Service Provider?
10. From what Internet resource would you be most likely to download a file?

For Discussion
1. What is the difference between the way gopher accesses information and the way the World Wide Web accesses information?
2. Do you think that the traditional culture on the Internet is justified in feeling some resentment toward the Commercial Internet Exchange?
3. In what ways can you benefit from the Internet personally?
4. Why do you think that e-mail is the most popular service on the Internet?

Review Exercises

1. Finding Information with Gopher
The daily temperature is very important to the golf course manager, so you must check the temperature for the state of South Carolina.

1. Launch Internet Explorer 3.0 and go to gopher://gopher.utdallas.edu as shown.

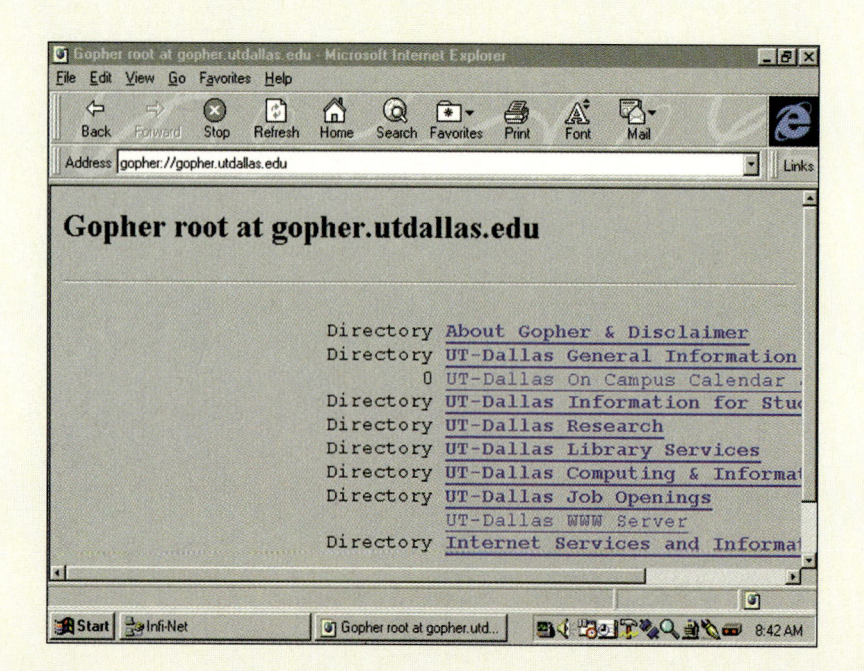

2. Click Internet Services and Information.

3. Click Internet Information by Subject.

4. Click Weather.

5. Click Weather forecasts and maps (the U of I Weather Machine).

6. Click States and Provinces.

7. Click South Carolina, US.

8. Click Surface Summary (with names).

9. Click the Print button.

2. Using the World Wide Web

1. Launch Internet Explorer 3.0 if necessary and go to the Microsoft start page.

2. Click the Links button in the Address toolbar.

3. Click Web Gallery.

4. Print the Web page.

5. Follow several links and print the Web pages that interest you most.

Assignments

1. Using Internet News
Using Internet News, explore the newsgroup categories more thoroughly and visit newsgroups that might be interesting or helpful to the manager of a resort hotel. Make a list of the newsgroups that you find.

2. Exploring FTP Sites
Explore several of the following FTP sites.

Novell: ftp://ftp.novell.com
Microsoft: ftp://ftp.microsoft.com
SCO: ftp://ftp.sco.com
Digital: ftp://ftp.digital.com
MIT FAQ Archive: ftp://rtfm.mit.edu
NSF Archives: ftp://nis.nsf.net
InterNIC Information Archives: ftp://ds.internic.net

Use the Index files on each site to get acquainted with the site. Then look for the following types of files to download: helpful information about the Internet, free software programs, and graphic files. Make a list of the files that you would like to download.

Notes

Notes

Notes

Word Processing
Using Microsoft Word 97

Overview

Before you can become productive with Word 97, you need to get acquainted with the program and learn how to perform some of the most basic functions of word processing. After you are comfortable with starting and exiting the program and getting help, you will be ready to tackle the tasks in the projects that follow.

Objectives

After completing this project, you will be able to:

- **Identify the Word 97 features**
- **Launch Word 97**
- **Identify Word 97 screen elements**
- **Get help**
- **Close a document**
- **Exit Word 97**

Identifying the Word 97 Features

The primary purpose of a word processing program is to create documents such as memos, letters, envelopes, reports, manuals, and so on. Word 97 is a powerful program that has all the features you need to create the most complex documents (see Figure 0.1), yet it's easy to use and easy to learn. Word 97 includes many features such as creating headers and footers, tables of contents and indexes, and tables and forms; checking spelling and grammar; using a thesaurus; inserting graphics and other objects; and creating form letters that are merged with address lists. Additionally, you can cut, copy, and move text; find text for editing without reading through the document, format a document automatically by making a selection from a gallery of formats,

Sports Marketing Professionals

Sports Marketing Professionals is a team of highly motivated sport enthusiasts and marketing experts that can make any sporting event a success. The team, headed by Jim Hand, has experience in all professional sports, including football, basketball, hockey, soccer, horse racing, auto racing, and golf. Sports Marketing Professionals can plan and execute all aspects of your events, solicit sponsors and advertisers, arrange transportation, publicize the event, recruit well known players and celebrities for charity events, and much more. When it comes to sports we are the experts!

You may recognize some of the events we handle each year: The Wild West Rodeo, Charlotte ProAm, The Phoenix Western Open, and The Avocado Bowl, to name a few. We can handle events anywhere in North America, and you can add your event to our long list of successes by contacting Jim Hand, Bill Radcliff, Mary Riley, or Frank Bentley. We will be proud to be your team behind the team.

If you are interested in holding a sporting event, fill out the information below and send it to us at the address below:

Company Name:			Phone:	
Address:				
City:		State:	Zip:	
Contact Name:			Phone:	
Event Location:				
Proposed Date:		Alternate Date:		
Please describe the type of event you want to have:				
If the event is for charity, please list the charity and explain your financial goals:				

123 Herrington Dr., Suite 550
Hilton Head Island, SC 22345

Figure 0.1

change the look of a paragraph by applying a predefined style, preview a document before you print it, and make a common typing error or misspell a common word without worrying because Word 97 corrects the mistake automatically.

Launching Word 97

When you start your computer, you may have to log on to a network or perform some other steps before Windows 95 starts. After the Windows 95 desktop displays on the screen, you're ready to launch Word 97.

TASK 1: TO LAUNCH WORD 97:

1. Click the Start **Start** button and point to Programs.

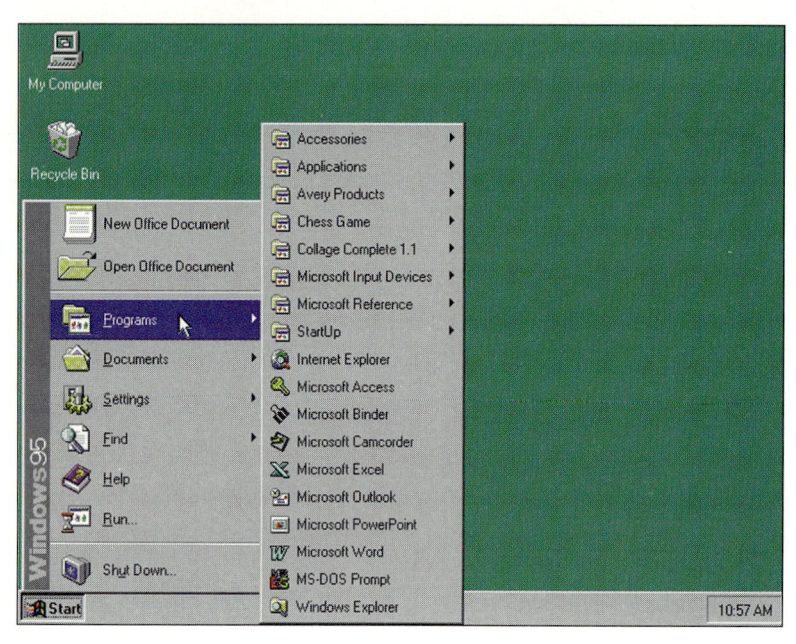

2. Point to the Microsoft Word program and click. The program opens in a window and creates a document called *Document1*.

Identifying Word 97 Screen Elements

The Word 97 screen has many of the common elements of a Windows 95 screen as well as some elements that are unique to the Word 97 program (see Figure 0.2). Because screen elements can be turned on and off, your screen may not look exactly like the screen in the figure.

> **Note** The screen displays two Close buttons. The button in the title bar closes Word 97; the button in the menu bar closes the current document.

Overview **WORD-5**

[Figure labels: Application title bar, Document buttons, Menu bar, Standard toolbar, Formatting toolbar, Ruler, Insertion point, Vertical ruler, Scroll bars, Status bar]

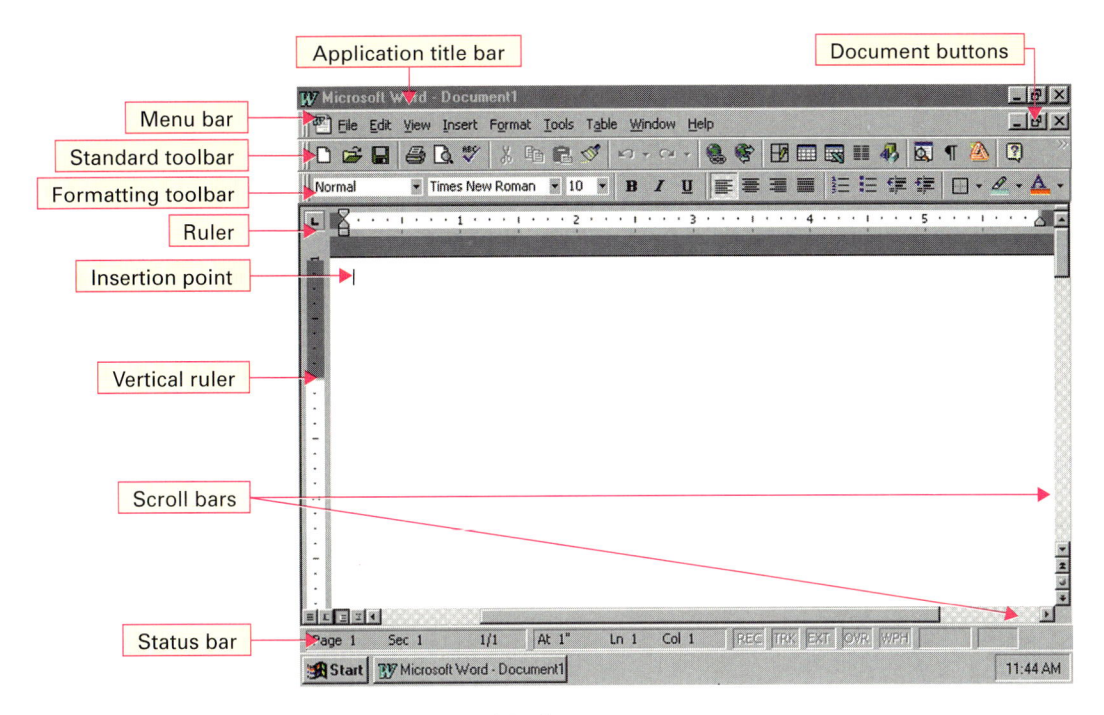

Figure 0.2 The Word 97 Screen

Elements of the screen include the following:

Element	Description
Application title bar	Displays the name of the application and the Minimize, Maximize/Restore, and Close buttons. If the document window is maximized, as in Figure 0.2, the name of the document also displays in the application title bar.
Document title bar	Displays the document title and the Minimize, Maximize/Restore, and Close buttons. If the window is maximized, no document title bar displays and the document buttons display in the menu bar.
Menu bar	Contains menu options. To use the menu, click an option to display a drop-down menu and then click an option on the drop-down menu to perform a command, view another menu, or view a dialog box.
Standard toolbar	Contains buttons for accomplishing commands. To use the toolbar, click a button to perform a command or view a dialog box.
Formatting toolbar	Contains buttons and controls for formatting. To use the toolbar, click a button to perform a command or view a dialog box.
Ruler	Displays the settings for the margins, tabs, and indents. The ruler also can be used to make these settings.
Insertion point	Marks the position with a blinking vertical line where a letter is inserted when you press a key.
Vertical and horizontal scroll bars	Scroll the screen vertically and horizontally.
Status bar	Displays information about the current document, including the page number and the position of the insertion point.

Working with Toolbars

Toolbars contain buttons that perform functions to accomplish a specific task or group of related tasks. Word 97 has several toolbars, but the Standard toolbar and the Formatting toolbar are the default toolbars, the ones that Word automatically displays. You can display or hide as many toolbars as you want.

You also can move toolbars to different locations on the screen. When a toolbar has been closed and then displayed again, Word places it where it was last located.

TASK 2: TO WORK WITH TOOLBARS:

1 Choose View, Toolbars.

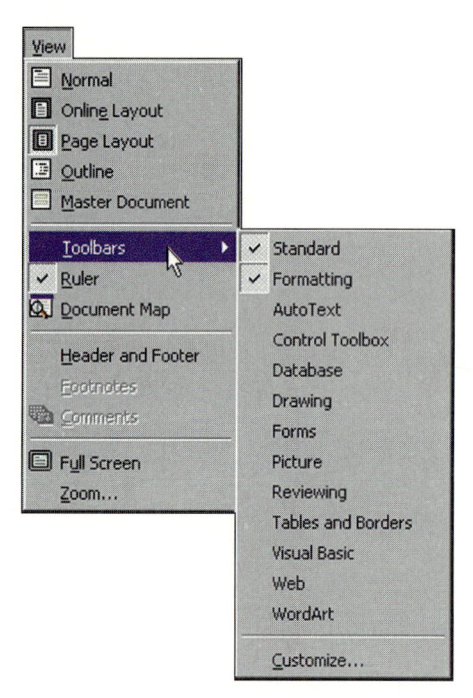

2 Click AutoText to display that toolbar.
The menu closes. Repeat for Control Toolbox, Database, and Drawing to display each toolbar (each time you choose a toolbar, the menu will close, requiring you to reopen it to select another toolbar).

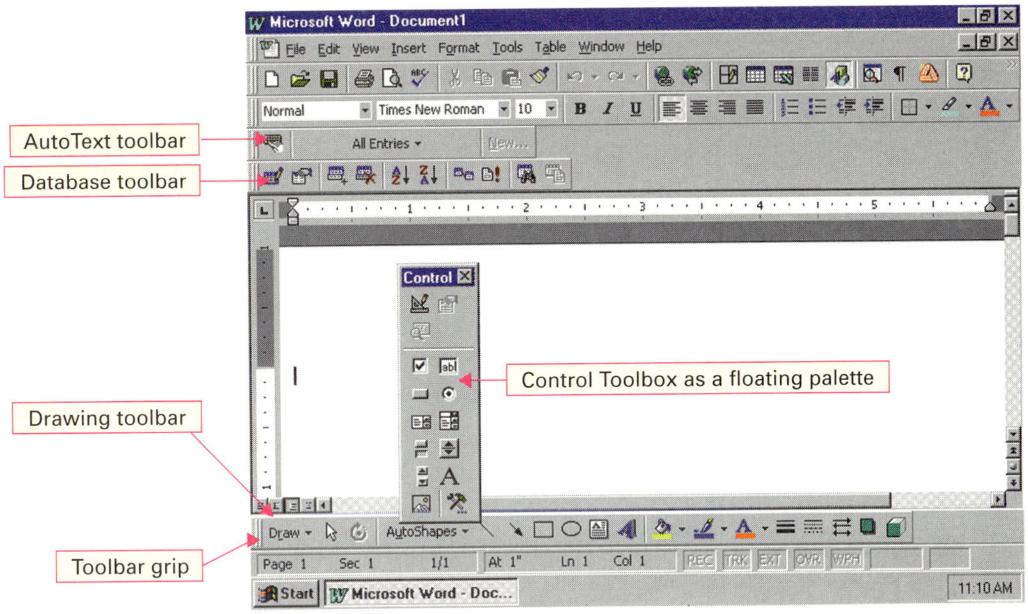
Microsoft Word - Document1
File Edit View Insert Format Tools Table Window Help
AutoText toolbar
Database toolbar
Control
Control Toolbox as a floating palette
Drawing toolbar
Toolbar grip
Draw
AutoShapes
Page 1 Sec 1 1/1 At 1" Ln 1 Col 1
Start
Microsoft Word - Doc...
11:10 AM

Your screen may not look exactly like this if Word 97 has been used by someone who previously moved the toolbars.

> **Tip** Some buttons on the Standard toolbar also display toolbars. The Web button displays the Web toolbar, for example, and the Drawing button displays the Drawing toolbar.

3 Point to the grip on any toolbar and drag the toolbar to the middle of the screen.

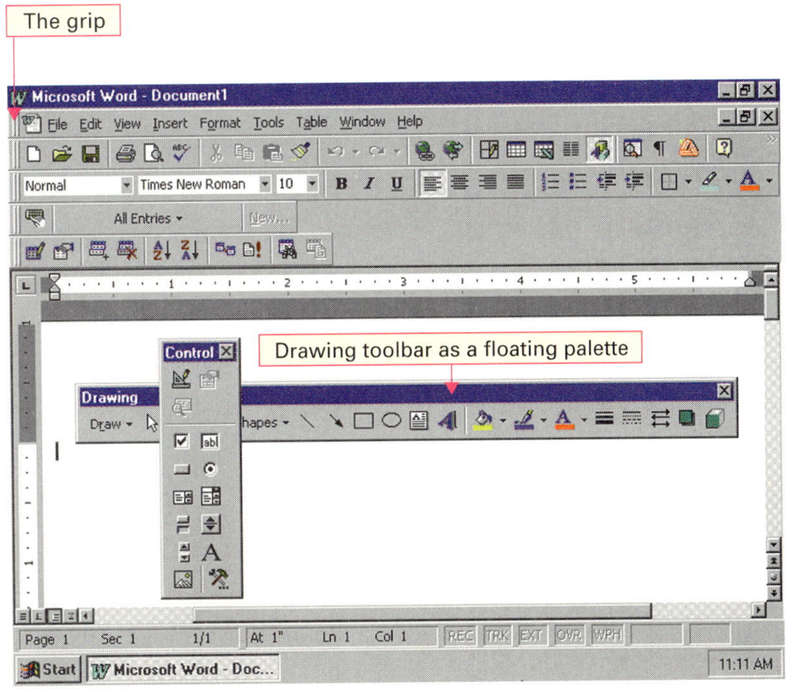
The grip
Microsoft Word - Document1
File Edit View Insert Format Tools Table Window Help
Control
Drawing
Drawing toolbar as a floating palette
Page 1 Sec 1 1/1 At 1" Ln 1 Col 1
Start
Microsoft Word - Doc...
11:11 AM

4 Click the Close ⊠ button of the palette you just moved.
The palette closes.

5 Point to the title bar of any floating palette and drag it to the top of the screen until it becomes a toolbar.
(If you don't have a floating palette, drag the toolbar until it becomes a palette and then drag it to the top of the screen until it becomes a toolbar.

6 Point to any toolbar and right-click.

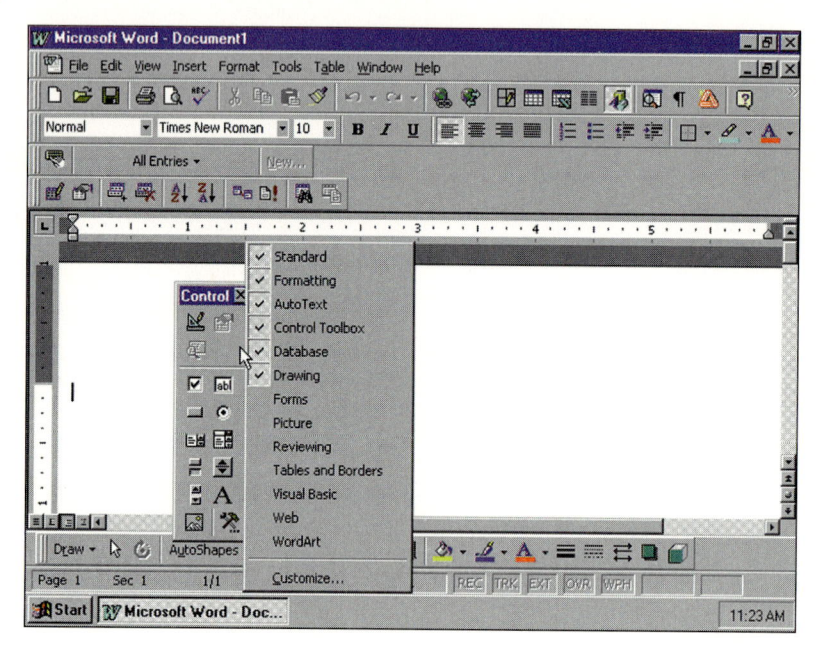

7 Click any toolbar that has a check mark beside it.
The toolbar closes.

8 Choose View, Toolbars and remove the check mark on each toolbar until only the Standard and Formatting toolbars are checked. (You may have to add check marks to the Standard and Formatting toolbars if you have closed them.)
Your screen should have the toolbars shown in Figure 0.2 displayed.

> **Note** If you want to hide a toolbar that you displayed by clicking a button on the Standard toolbar, just click the button again. The toolbar will disappear.

Hiding and Displaying the Ruler

The ruler provides an easy method of setting margins, tabs, and indents. If you don't need to use the ruler, you can hide it to provide more room on the screen. You use the same steps to hide or display the ruler.

Overview **WORD-9**

TASK 3: TO HIDE OR DISPLAY THE RULER:

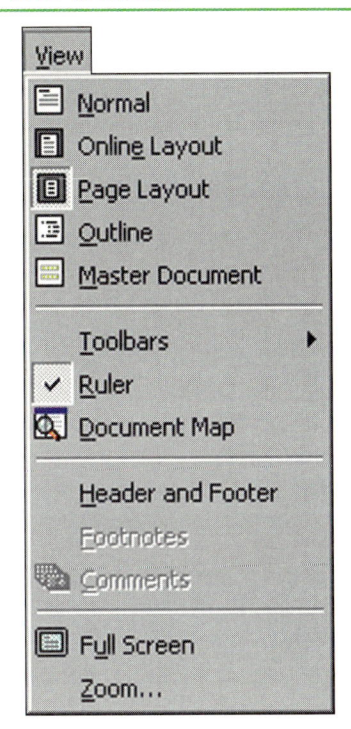

1 Choose View.

2 Choose Ruler.
The ruler displays if it wasn't displayed before.

3 Choose View, Ruler again, if necessary to redisplay the ruler.

Getting Help

Word 97 provides several ways to get help while you're learning and using the program. Previously, most software manufacturers went to great expense to produce printed user manuals that explained all the features of the program. Now the trend is to provide short Getting Started manuals and *online help* that explains all the features of the program. For online help, Word 97 offers several forms of help—the standard Windows 95 Help dialog box with three pages: Contents, Index, and Find; as well as What's This?, Office Assistant, and Help from the Microsoft Web site.

> **Note** The term *online help* refers to the help that is provided by the software and is accessible on the computer. Online help doesn't refer to "going online," which implies connecting with the Internet or some other network.

TASK 4: TO USE THE WORD HELP DIALOG BOX:

1 Choose Help, Contents and Index, and click the Index tab.

2 Type **splitting windows**.

WORD-10

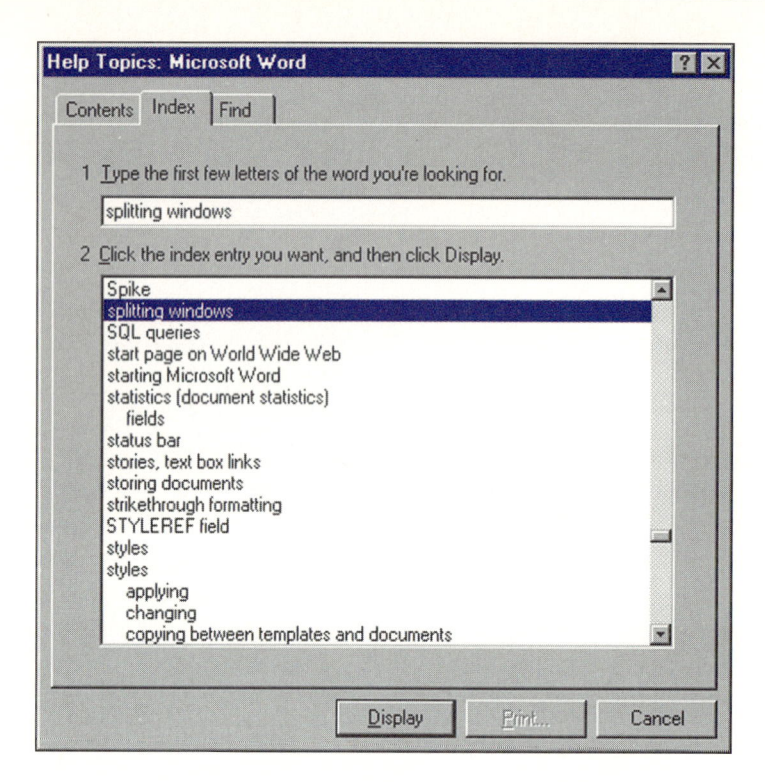

3 Double-click the topic "splitting windows" in the list.

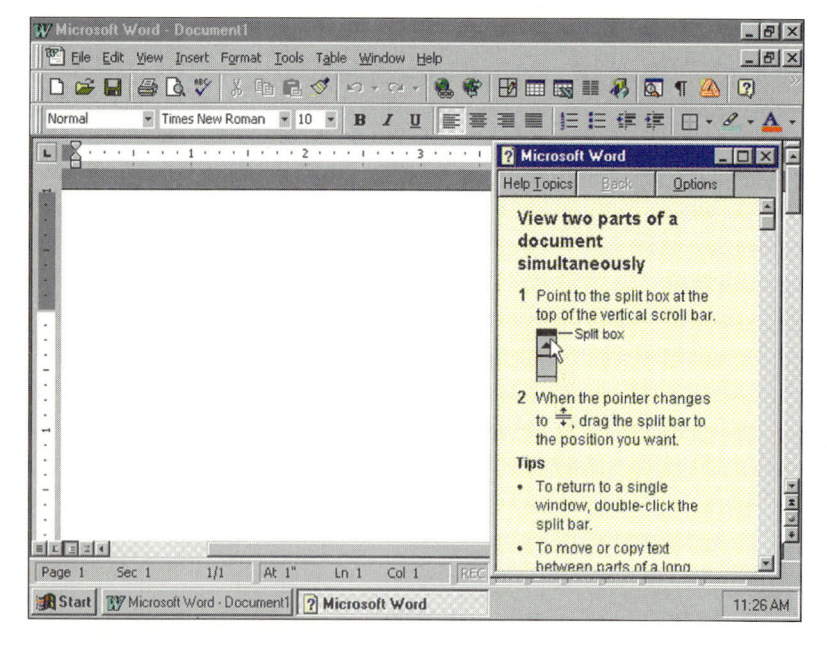

4 Read the Help information.

5 Click ⊠ when you finish reading the Help information. The dialog box closes.

Overview   WORD-11

Using the What's This? Help Feature

If you just want to know what something is, what something does, or what something means, you can use the ***What's This?*** Help feature. What's This? Help displays a short description in a pop-up box.

TASK 5: TO USE WHAT'S THIS? HELP:

1 Choose Tools, Language, Hyphenation.

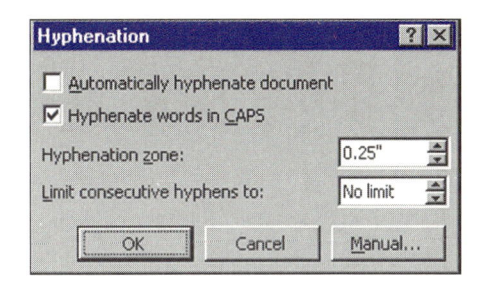

2 Click the What's This? button.
A question mark is attached to the mouse pointer.

3 Click Hyphenation zone.

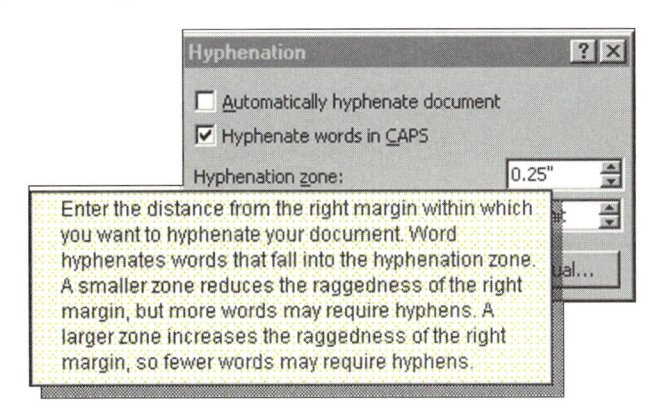

4 After reading the information, click the pop-up box. The pop-up box closes.

> **Tip** You can use What's This? help even if you aren't in a dialog box. Press Shift+F1 or choose Help, What's This? and then click the item you have a question about.

Using the Office Assistant

If you need some "hand-holding" help, use the new Help feature called ***Office Assistant***. Whenever possible, the Office Assistant offers help on the task you are performing, and is often referred to as ***context-sensitive help***. If the Office Assistant doesn't display the help you want, you can type a question to obtain the desired help.

TASK 6: TO USE THE OFFICE ASSISTANT:

1 Click the Office Assistant button.

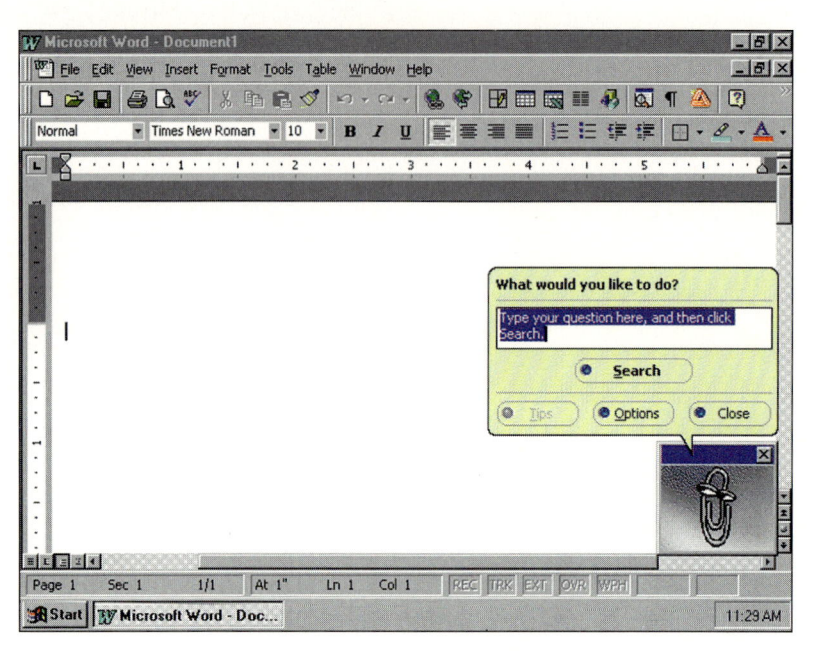

2 Type **How do you count the number of words in a document?** and click Search.

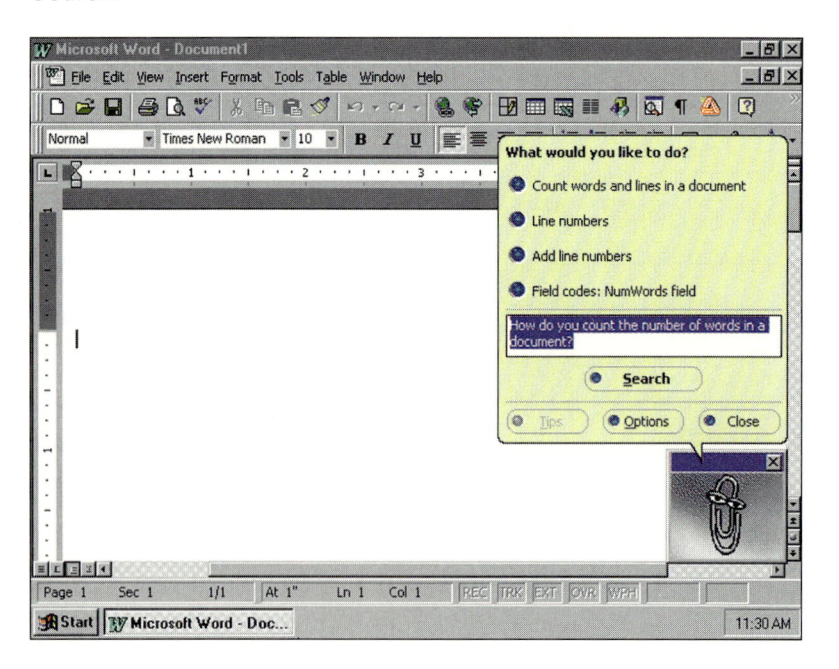

3 Click Count words and lines in a document.

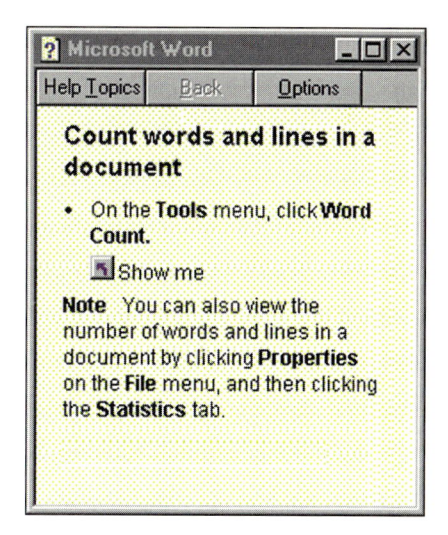

> **Count words and lines in a document**
> - On the **Tools** menu, click **Word Count.**
>   Show me
>
> **Note** You can also view the number of words and lines in a document by clicking **Properties** on the **File** menu, and then clicking the **Statistics** tab.

4 After reading the Help dialog box, click ☒.
The Help dialog box closes, but the Office Assistant window remains open.

5 Click the Office Assistant character in the Office Assistant window.
The Office Assistant asks what you want to do.

> **Note** The default Office Assistant is a paper clip named Clippit. Other assistants include Shakespeare, a robot, and a cat—to name a few.

6 Click Close.
The "bubble" closes.

7 Click ☒.
The Office Assistant winks at you, and the window closes.

Getting Help from the World Wide Web

Microsoft maintains several sites on the Web that have useful information, user support, product news, and free programs and files that you can download. If your system is connected to the Internet, you can access this type of help easily. The Microsoft sites are open to all users.

> **Note** When Microsoft is beta-testing a program, the company maintains "closed sites" open only to beta testers with a valid password.

TASK 7: TO READ ANSWERS TO FREQUENTLY ASKED QUESTIONS:

1 Choose Help, Microsoft on the Web.

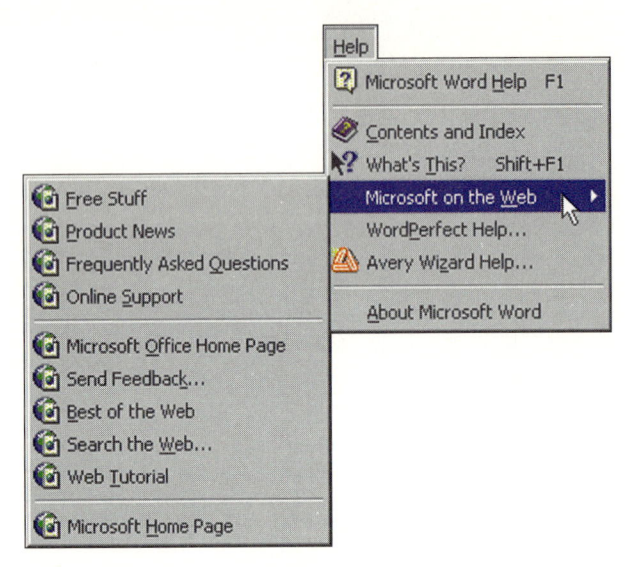

2 Choose Frequently Asked Questions.
The Internet browser program starts (usually Internet Explorer) and connects to the appropriate Web site.

3 When you finish browsing the Web, click ⊠ in the browser window.

Closing a Document and Exiting Word 97

Before you exit Word, you should always save any work that you want to keep and then close any open documents. When you exit Word 97, the program closes, and the Windows 95 desktop is visible again. If you have another program running in a maximized window, however, the program will be visible, not the desktop.

> **Tip** If you forget to save and close a changed file before you try to exit, Word 97 asks whether you want to save changes. You can choose Yes to save the changed file, No to exit without saving, or Cancel to cancel the exit request.

Overview **WORD-15**

TASK 8: TO CLOSE THE DOCUMENT AND EXIT WORD 97:

1 Click ⊠ in the document title bar.
Only the application window is open now.

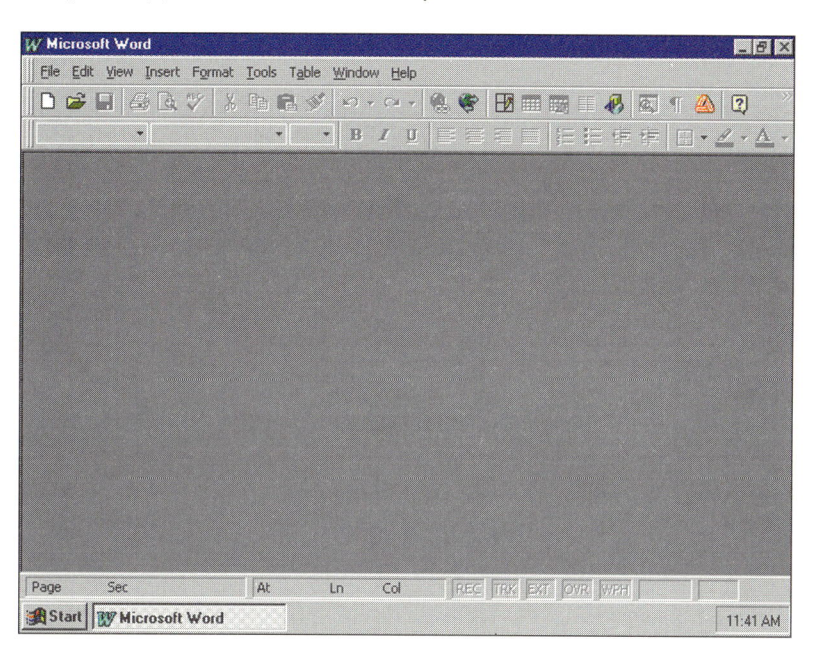

2 Click ⊠ in the application title bar.
The Word 97 program closes.

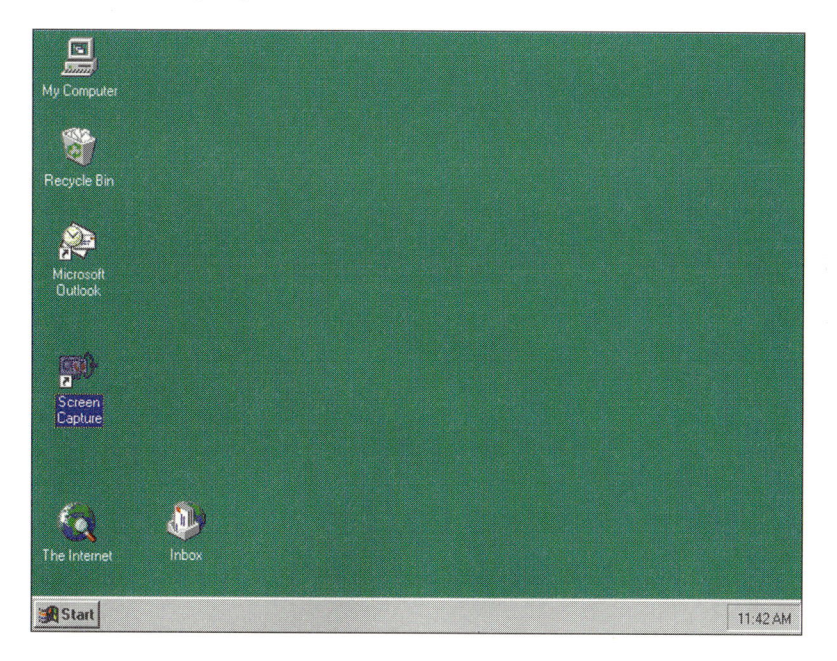

Summary and Exercises

Summary

- Word 97 is a full-featured word processing program that's easy to use.
- Many features of Word 97 streamline work by performing tasks automatically.
- You can hide or display many screen elements to suit your needs.
- If you don't understand a concept or you don't know how to do a task, you can get help from a variety of sources online or from the Web.
- Word 97 won't let you exit without reminding you to save a changed file if you haven't already done so.

Key Terms and Operations

Key Terms
application title bar
context-sensitive help
document title bar
floating palette
insertion point
menu bar
Office Assistant
online help
ruler
scroll bars
status bar
title bar
toolbar
toolbar grip
What's This?
word processing program

Operations
exit Word 97
get help from the Web
get online help
hide and display the ruler
hide and display toolbars
start Word 97
use Office Assistant

Study Questions

Multiple Choice

1. Which of the following methods starts Office Assistant?
    a. Choose Help, Office Assistant.
    b. Click the Office Assistant button.
    c. Press Shift+F1.
    d. Press F1.

2. To start Word 97,
    a. click Start and choose Run, Word 97.
    b. double-click the Outlook icon on the desktop.
    c. start Windows 95 and then press Alt+W.
    d. click Start and choose Programs, Microsoft Word.

3. Which two of the following aren't valid methods of moving a toolbar?
    a. Point to the toolbar and press the right mouse button while dragging the toolbar to a new location.
    b. Point to the toolbar grip and drag the toolbar to a new location.
    c. Point to the title bar of the toolbar and drag the toolbar to a new location.
    d. Choose View, Toolbar, Move.

WORD-16

Overview   WORD-17

4. To turn on the Web toolbar,
   a. point to the Standard toolbar, right-click, and click Web.
   b. point to any toolbar, right-click, and click Web.
   c. click the Web button on the Standard toolbar.
   d. All of the above.

5. The purpose of the ruler is
   a. to set the width of the page.
   b. to display the margins, tabs, and indents.
   c. to set the margins, tabs, and indents.
   d. Both B and C.

6. A shortcut menu
   a. appears when you right-click a toolbar.
   b. displays a list of shortcut keys.
   c. displays when you choose View, Shortcuts.
   d. displays shortcut icons.

7. To exit Word 97,
   a. choose File, Exit.
   b. click the Close button in the menu bar.
   c. click the Exit button in the Standard toolbar.
   d. Both A and B.

8. A question mark is attached to the mouse pointer when
   a. you press Shift+?.
   b. you press Shift+F1.
   c. you choose File, What's This?
   d. Both B and C.

9. To get help on the Web, you must
   a. be registered for support with Microsoft.
   b. have a connection to the Internet.
   c. know the password to logon to the Microsoft Web site.
   d. be a registered user of Office 97.

10. Which of the following is a false statement?
    a. The insertion point blinks.
    b. The insertion point marks the position where a letter will be inserted when you press a key.
    c. The insertion point is a vertical line.
    d. The insertion point can change shapes.

Short Answer

1. What are the two Word 97 default toolbars?
2. Can you exit Word 97 without saving your work?
3. What Help feature allows you to ask for help in your own words?
4. What's the grip on a toolbar?
5. What's the name of the document created automatically by Word 97 when you start the program?
6. What type of toolbar has a Close button?

7. What Help feature is equivalent to a printed user manual?

8. What's context-sensitive help?

9. How is it possible that Word 97 could be running on two different computers and the screens wouldn't look identical?

10. What happens if you click the Close button in the menu bar?

For Discussion

1. What features included in Word 97 do you think will be most useful for you?

2. What advantage is there to moving toolbars to different locations on the screen?

3. Discuss the pros and cons of using a printed user manual versus using online help.

4. Compare the value of the help information on the Web to the online help information that comes with Word 97.

Review Exercises

1. Customizing the Screen

Your work requires quite a bit of drawing, but you rarely make changes to margins, tabs, or indents. Customize your screen so that it accommodates your needs (see Figure 0.3).

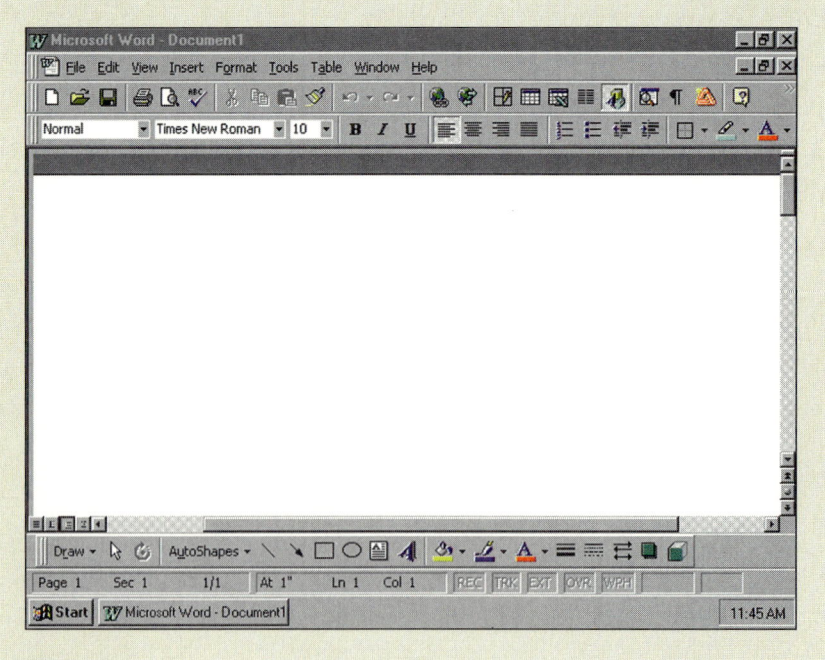

Figure 0.3

1. Start Word 97 if necessary.

2. Hide the Ruler if it's displayed.

3. Display the Drawing toolbar.

4. Drag the toolbar so it turns into a floating palette (if it isn't already floating) and move it to the location shown in Figure 0.3.

5. Exit Word 97 without saving the file.

2. Getting Help on the Web
Your company has a policy of upgrading software whenever a new release comes out. Find out whether Microsoft is developing any new software programs or upgrades at the current time.

1. Choose Help, Microsoft on the Web.
2. Choose Product News.
3. Follow appropriate hypertext links.
4. When you're finished, close Internet Explorer.

Assignments

1. Using Help to Explore and Use Buttons on the Drawing Toolbar
Display the Drawing toolbar, if necessary. Use What's This? help to display a description of the rectangle icon on the Drawing toolbar. Using the information What's This? provides, draw a rectangle as shown in Figure 0.4. Ask the Office Assistant how to add a fill color and then add a blue fill to the rectangle.

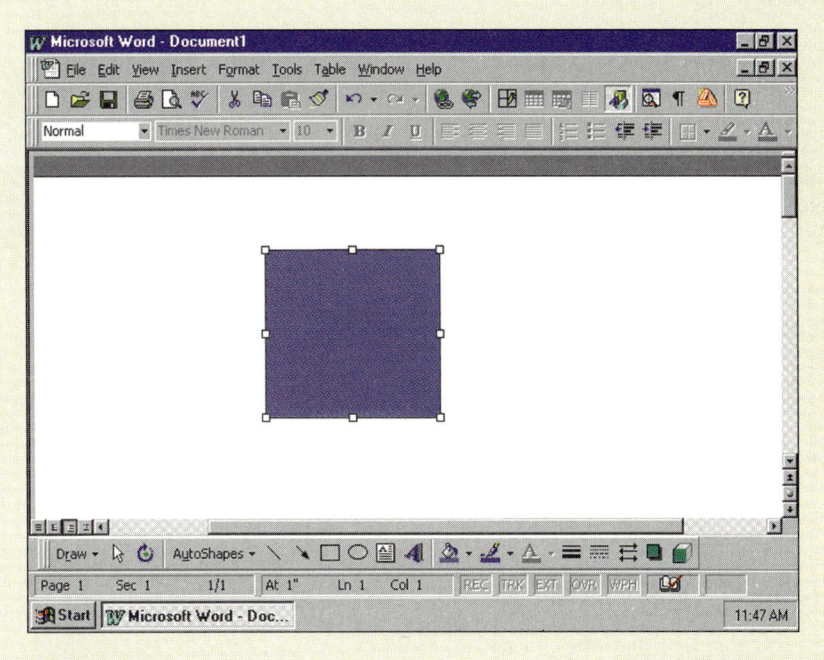

Figure 0.4

2. Exploring the Microsoft Home Page
The Microsoft home page has links to many interesting and helpful sites, and the home page changes frequently. Using Microsoft on the Web help, go to the Microsoft home page and see what's there. Print the page.

PROJECT 1

Creating a Document

Creating, saving, and printing are tasks that are basic to Word 97. Every user must have a good grasp of these skills in order to use Word 97 effectively.

Objectives

After completing this project, you will be able to:

- ➤ Create a new document
- ➤ Enter text
- ➤ Undo changes
- ➤ Correct errors marked by SpellIt
- ➤ Save a document
- ➤ Preview a document
- ➤ Print a document
- ➤ Close a file

The Challenge

In September, The Willows will host a golf tournament to benefit the Juvenile Diabetes Foundation. You must type a letter to a marketing firm asking Jim Hand to handle the tournament.

The Solution

Figure 1.1 shows the first draft of the document you will create and print on letterhead stationery. Because you will be enclosing the letter in a larger envelope with other enclosures, you don't need to create an envelope for this letter.

Space for letterhead →

<Insert date text here> ← Use the Word command to insert the current date here

Sports Marketing Professionals
Jim Hand
123 Herrington Dr., Suite 550
Hilton Head Island, SC 29928

Dear Jim,

We were so pleased with your work on our celebrity tournament last year that we want you to promote our ladies charity tournament scheduled for September 18 - 20 this year. (Profits will be donated to the Juvenile Diabetes Fund.) We want to invite at least 15 of the top women PGA players and 10 national and local celebrities. This will give us a total of 25 foursomes with a player or a celebrity in each foursome.

You will need to line up the players and celebrities, obtain sponsors, and promote the tournament locally. Our goal is to realize $100,000 in profits.

I have enclosed several lists of names (sponsors, local celebrities, and local charitable contributors) that will help you. Please call me to discuss the details.

Best regards,

Thomas Williams
Golf and Tennis Property Manager
The Willows

Cc: John Gilmore

Enclosures

YJ ← Initials of the typist

Figure 1.1

The Setup

So that your screen will match the illustrations and the tasks in this project will function as described, make sure that the Word 97 settings listed in Table 1.1 are selected on your computer.

Table 1.1　Word 97 Settings

Location	Make these settings:
View, Toolbars	Deselect all toolbars except the Standard and Formatting toolbars
View	Deselect the ruler
Standard toolbar	Deselect any buttons that are selected and set Zoom to 100%
Insert, AutoText, AutoText	Select the Show AutoComplete tip for AutoText and dates option
Tools, Options, Spelling & Grammar	Select the Check spelling as you type and the Check Grammar as you type options

Creating a New Document

When you launch Word 97, a blank *new document* named Document 1 automatically opens for you and you can begin to type.

TASK 1: TO CREATE A NEW DOCUMENT:

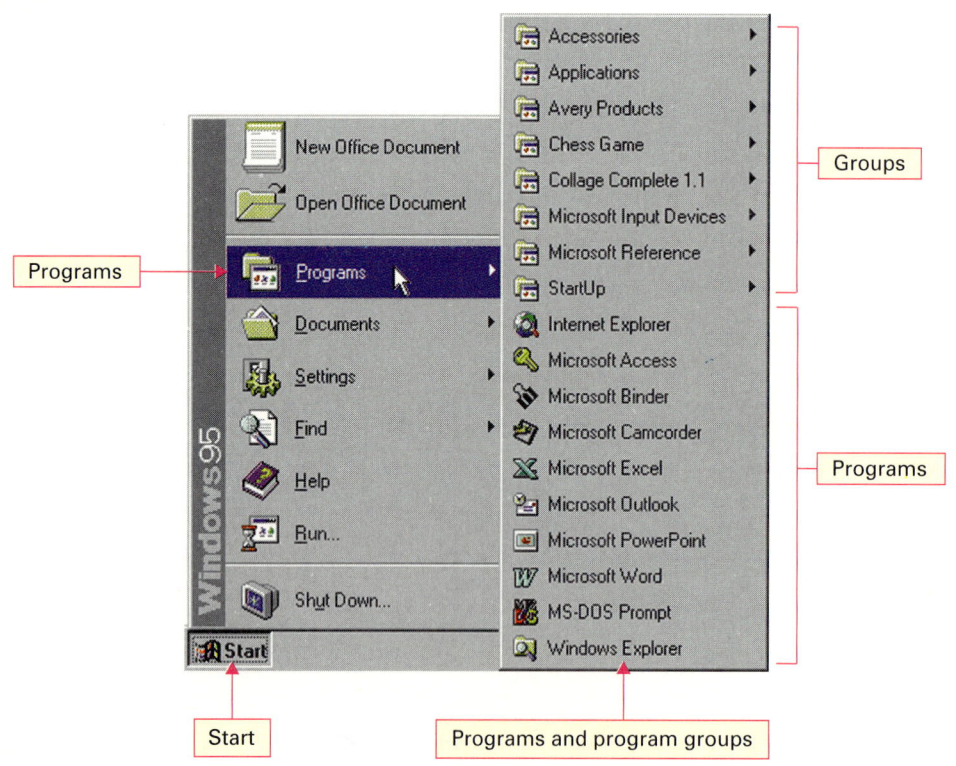

1. Click the Start button.

Project 1: Creating a Document   WORD-23

2 Point to Programs and choose the Microsoft Word program.
The program opens in a window and creates a document called Document1.

> **Troubleshooting** If Word is already started and you don't see a document on the screen, click the New button. Word creates a new document just for you.

Entering Text

Instead of typing the complete letter you see in Figure 1.1, you will type the letter in sections so that you can focus on some features and commands. As you type, you will be using the **Enter** key to end short lines and paragraphs and create blank lines. Don't press the Enter key at the end of each line in a paragraph, because the lines in the paragraph *wrap* around automatically.

> **Caution** When you want to move down through the text, use the down arrow, not the Enter key. Remember that you use the Enter key only when you want to start a new paragraph or create a blank line.

TASK 2: TO SPACE DOWN ENOUGH TO ALLOW FOR THE LETTERHEAD:

1 Press CTRL+HOME to ensure that the insertion point is in the upper-left corner of the document.
Notice that the status bar displays 1" for the vertical position of the insertion point; you need to allow space for the letterhead.

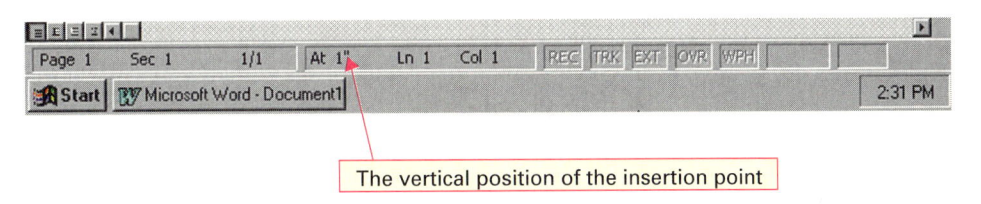

The vertical position of the insertion point (At 1")

2 Press ENTER repeatedly until the vertical position 2.1" is displayed in the status bar.

Inserting a Date

The date should appear on the first line of the letter. Instead of typing the date, you can have Word 97 insert it for you.

TASK 3: TO INSERT THE DATE:

1 Choose Insert from the menu bar.

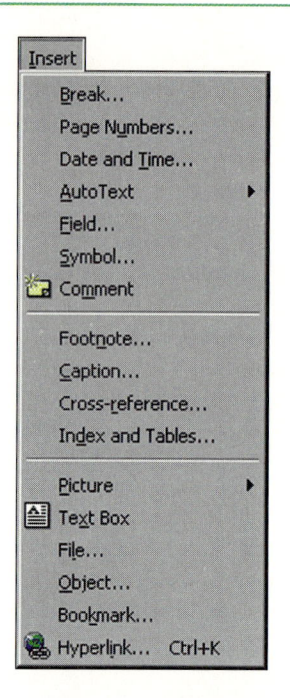

2 Choose Date and Time.

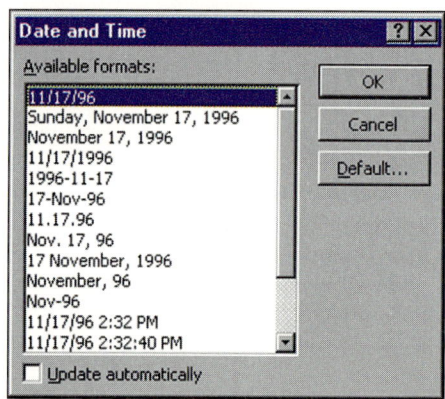

3 Select the third format.

Your computer will show the current date in this list

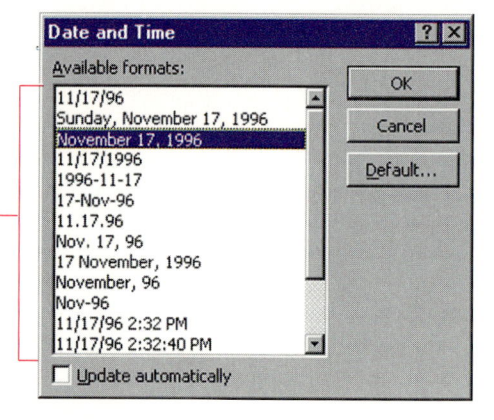

Project 1: Creating a Document   WORD-25

> **Tip** If you want to use the same date format in all your documents, click Default and choose Yes.

4 Click OK.
The current date (if the date in the computer is accurate) appears in the document.

Correcting Errors

As you type, you probably will make typos, but you may not see too many when you use this version of Word: the Word **AutoCorrect** feature automatically corrects many common typographical errors, such as *t-e-h* and *a-h-v-e*. When you see a word underlined with a wavy red line, you haven't gone crazy: Word is just pointing out a word that isn't in its dictionary. When you make a grammatical mistake, the Word Grammar feature underlines it with a wavy green line.

When you see a typo or a grammatical error, you can use the Backspace key to erase and then retype. Don't worry if you fail to catch and correct some mistakes while typing. You will have a chance in Project 2 to fix these little culprits when you are learning to make other revisions.

TASK 4: TO TYPE THE FIRST PART OF THE LETTER SHOWN IN FIGURE 1.1:

1 Press (ENTER) four times after the date.

2 Type **Sprots** (No, it's not a typo. Well, it is a typo, but it's deliberate so you can get some practice making corrections.)

3 Press (BACKSPACE) four times.
The last four letters you typed are erased.

4 Type **orts**.

5 Type **Marketing Professionals** and press (ENTER). Type each line of the remainder of the address, pressing (ENTER) after each line, as in:

Jim Hand
Sports Marketing Professionals
123 Harrington Dr., Suite 550
Hilton Head Island, SC 29928

6 Press (ENTER) again to create a blank line between the address and the greeting you are going to type.

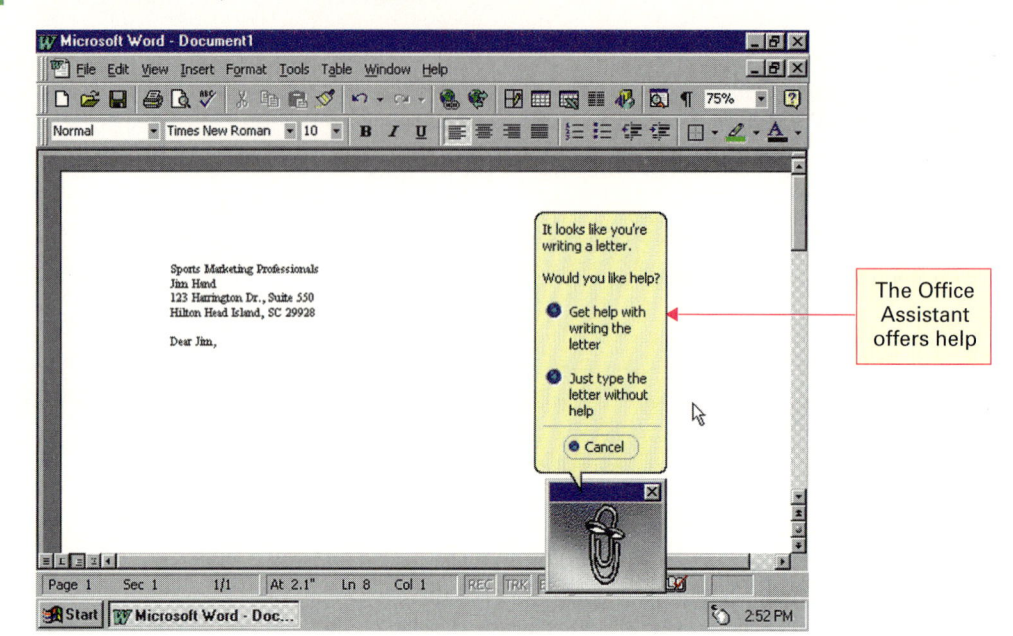

7 Type **Dear Jim,** and press ENTER twice.

The Office Assistant offers help

8 Click Cancel on the Office Assistant message.

9 Type the first paragraph until you reach the word "the," as in:

We were so pleased with your work on our celebrity tournament last year that we want you to promote our ladies charity tournament scheduled for September 18–20 this year. (Profits will be donated to

10 Type **teh** instead of "the" in this paragraph to see how AutoCorrect works.

11 Continue typing the first paragraph and press ENTER twice at the end of the paragraph, as in:

the Juvenile Diabetes Fund.) We want to invite at least 15 of the top women PGA players and 10 national and local celebrities. This will give us a total of 25 foursomes with a player or a celebrity in each foursome.

12 Type the second paragraph, and press ENTER twice at the end of the paragraph, as in:

You will need to line up the players and celebrities, obtain sponsors, and promote the tournament locally. Our goal is to realize $100,000 in profits.

Project 1: Creating a Document   **WORD-27**

Inserting Special Characters

The keyboard has a limited number of characters. Some of the characters you may want to include in text, such as © and ®, can't be typed from the keyboard, but you can insert them by using the Symbol dialog box.

TASK 5: TO INSERT A SYMBOL:

1 Type **I have enclosed several lists of names.** (Don't type the period.)

2 Choose Insert from the menu bar.
The Insert menu displays.

3 Choose Symbol and click the square that contains the em dash.

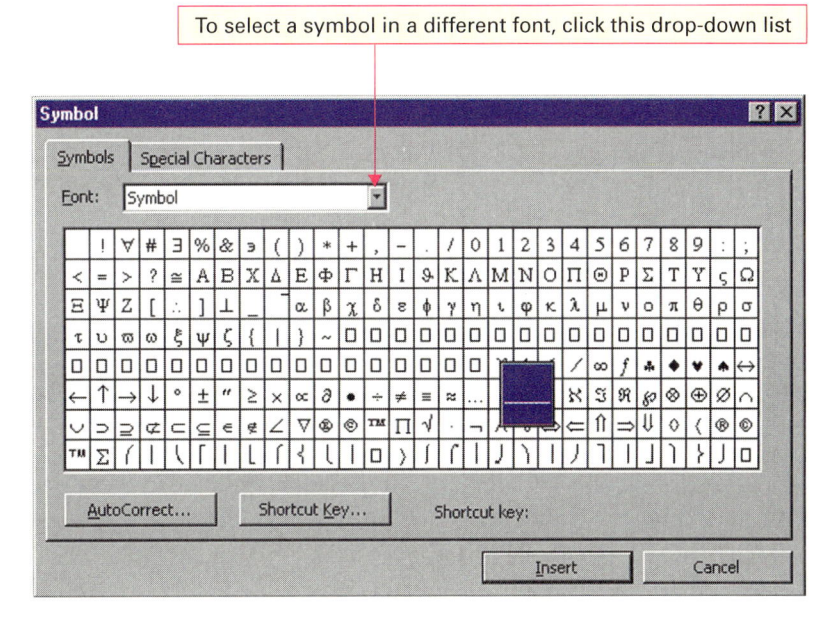

To select a symbol in a different font, click this drop-down list

4 Click Insert and then click Close.
The em dash is inserted into the document.

5 Type the rest of the paragraph and press ENTER twice, as in:

sponsors, local celebrities, and local charitable contributors that will help you. Please call me to discuss the details.

Using AutoComplete

The Word *AutoComplete* feature automatically completes many frequently typed words and phrases for you, such as *Best regards*. A pop-up box displays the word or phrase, and you can either accept it or keep on typing.

TASK 6: TO USE AUTOCOMPLETE:

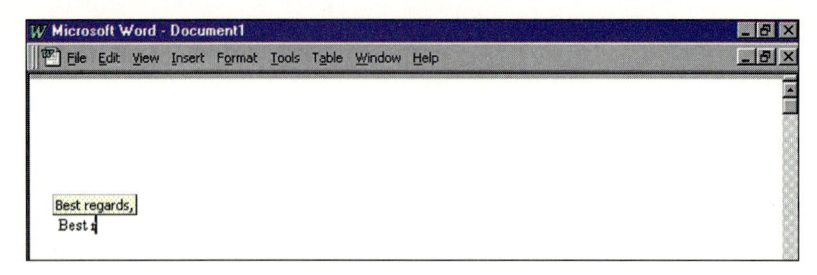

1 Type **Best r**.

2 Press ENTER.
Word automatically completes the phrase.

3 Press ENTER four times.

4 Type the rest of the text, as in:

Thomas Williams
Golf and Tennis Property Manager
The Willows

Undoing Changes

If you make a change to the text and decide that you shouldn't have, you can easily undo the change. Word 97 keeps a list of changes made in a document and allows you to undo all of them one by one.

> **Note** The Undo command is a lifesaver when some totally weird thing happens, and you don't know what you did to make it happen. Believe me; it will happen to you.

TASK 7: TO UNDO A CORRECTION:

1 Press ENTER twice and then type **Cc: John Gilmore**.

2 Press HOME and then press DELETE twice.
The insertion point moves to the beginning of the line and the first two characters are erased.

3 Point to the icon on the Undo button (not the down arrow) and click it twice.
The two previously erased characters are inserted again. Somehow, I have a feeling that Undo will become your new best friend. Just remember—I introduced you.

> **Tip** If you undo something accidentally or you change your mind, you can click the Redo button and everything will be back the way it was before you used Undo so over-zealously.

Project 1: Creating a Document   WORD-29

Correcting Errors Marked by SpellIt

SpellIt is the automatic spell-checking feature that puts all those wavy red lines in your documents. As you type, Word 97 checks the spelling of each word against the words in its dictionary. When you type a word that isn't in its dictionary—ZAP—a wavy red line. Instead of erasing the word with the Backspace key, you can correct the word by selecting the correct spelling from a shortcut menu.

TASK 8: TO CORRECT A SPELLING ERROR MARKED BY WORD 97:

1. Press ENTER twice, type **Encloseres**, and press the spacebar— another deliberate typo. (If you're like me, however, you make enough mistakes on your own! You really don't need to practice making them.)
   The word is underlined with a wavy red line to indicate that it's misspelled.

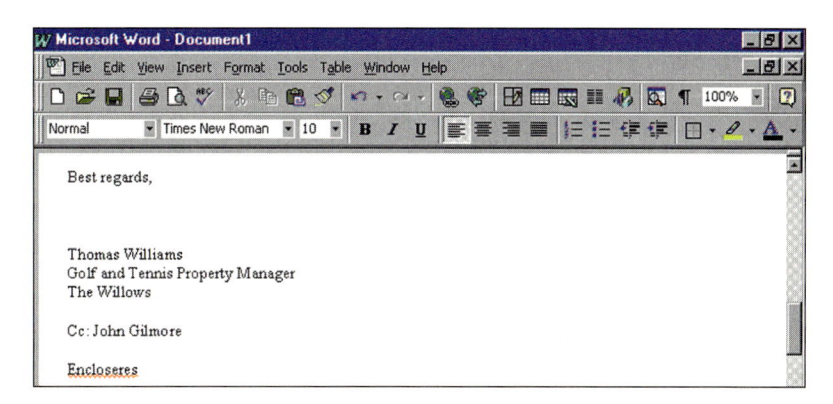

2. Point to the word and right-click.

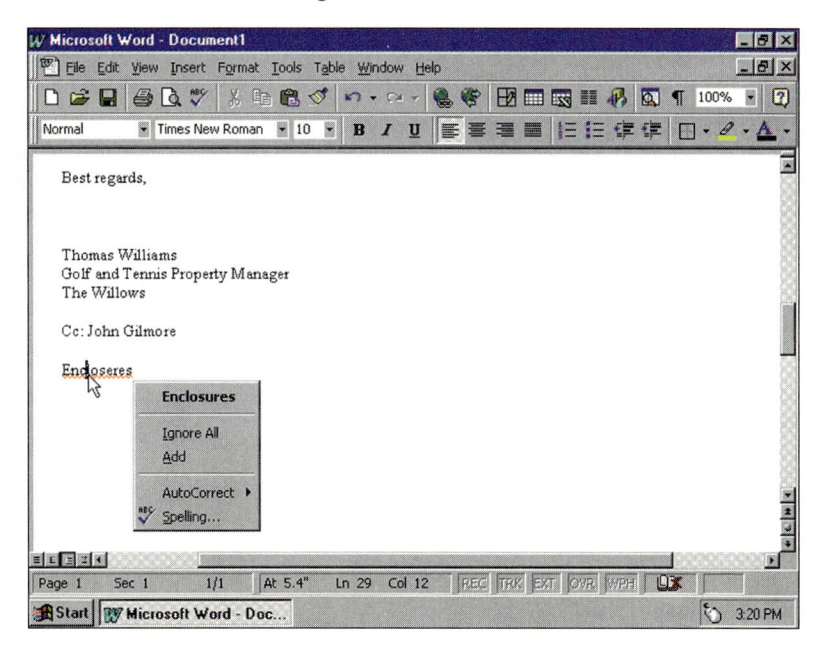

3 Click Enclosures.
Word corrects the spelling.

> **Tip** If a word is marked with a wavy red line but it isn't misspelled, you can add the word to the dictionary or ignore the word by right-clicking the word and choosing Add or Ignore. Don't add words to the dictionary when working in the lab, however, because the words that you add won't show up with wavy red lines for other students.

Saving a Document

If you want to keep a document for any period of time, you must save the document to disk. When saving the document, you specify a name for the document and a location where it will be stored.

> **Tip** Because Word 97 is written for Windows 95, the name can be a **long filename**. Long filenames (including the full path of the file) can have up to 255 characters. Although you can include as many spaces and periods in the filename as you want, you can't use ? or : or *. Older versions of Word (prior to Word 7.0) don't use long filenames, but a file with a long filename also has a conventional name that older versions of Word can read.

TASK 9: TO SAVE A NEW FILE:

1 Click the Save button.

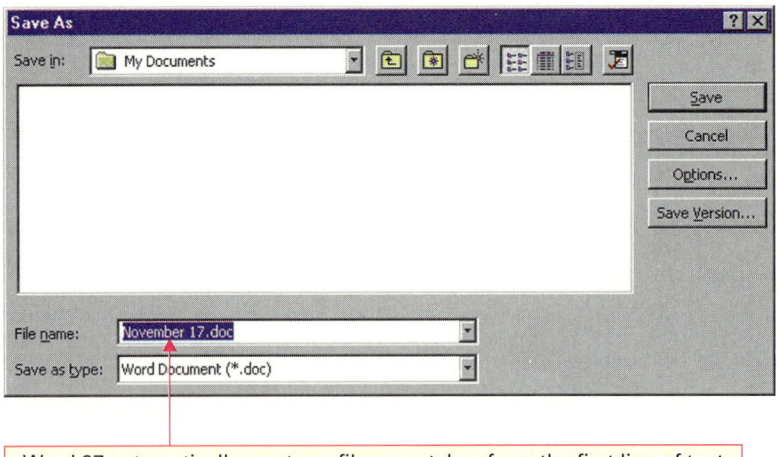

Word 97 automatically creates a filename taken from the first line of text

Project 1: Creating a Document   WORD-31

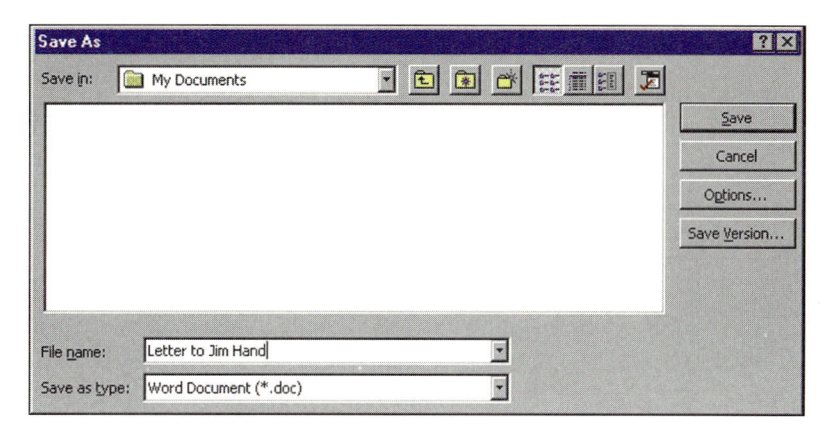

2 Type **Letter to Jim Hand** in the File Name text box.

Word 97 automatically adds the default extension .doc to the filename when the document is saved.

3 Click the down arrow in the Save In text box and choose drive A (or the drive and folder designated by your professor or lab assistant).

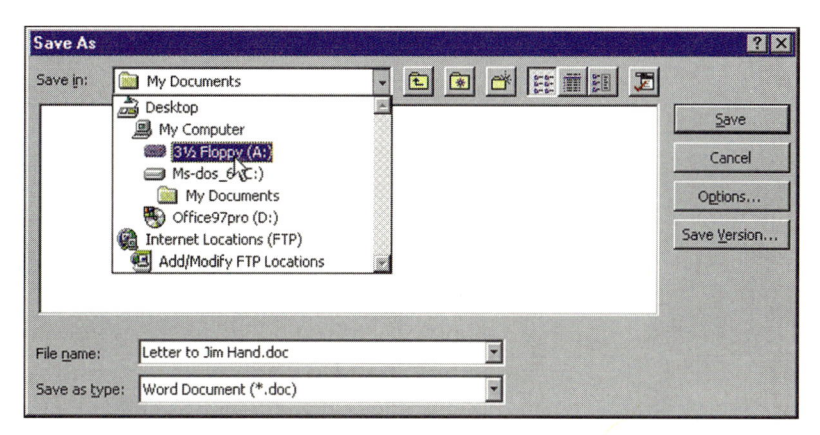

4 Click Save.
The dialog box closes, the file is saved on the disk, and the title bar displays the name of the file.

> **Tip** As you work on a document, you should save it periodically just in case your computer crashes or the electricity goes off.

TASK 10: TO SAVE AN EXISTING FILE:

1 Press (ENTER) twice and type your initials to indicate that you are the typist of the letter.

2 Click 🖫.
The Save As dialog box doesn't display. The file is simply saved with the same name in the same location.

> **Note** To save an existing document in a different location or with a different name, choose File, Save As.

Previewing a Document

Before printing a document, you should preview it to see if it looks the way you want it to look. The Print Preview mode shows the full page of a document (see Figure 1.2). While you're working in the Print Preview mode, you can magnify the page, edit text, and print the document as well.

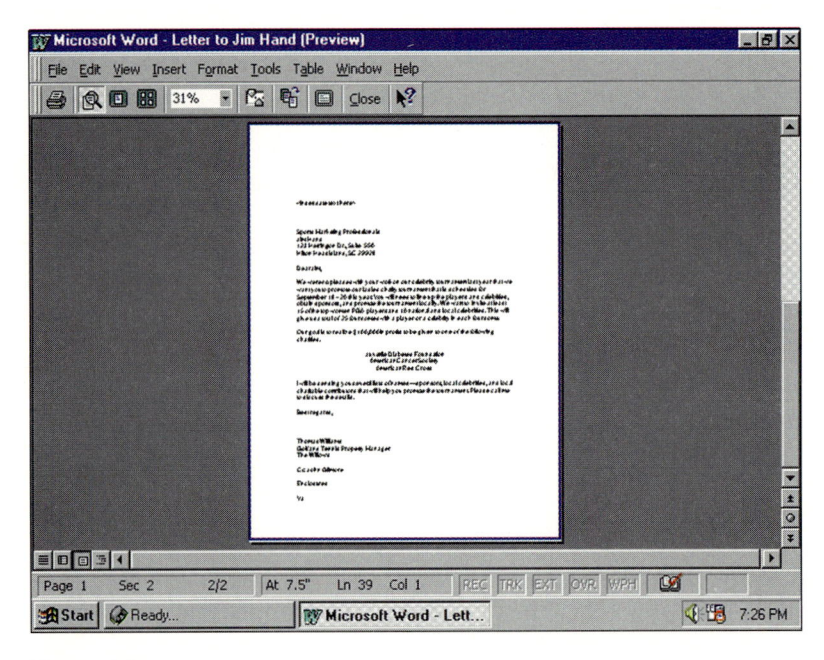

Figure 1.2

> **Tip** If you're previewing a multi-page document, you can show as many as six pages at a time.

TASK 11: TO VIEW A FILE IN PRINT PREVIEW MODE:

1 Click the Print Preview 🔍 button and notice the amount of blank space at the top of the page that is reserved for the letterhead.
The letter displays in the Print Preview mode, as shown in Figure 1.2.

2 Click the pointer, shaped like a magnifying glass, at the top of the letter where the address is typed.

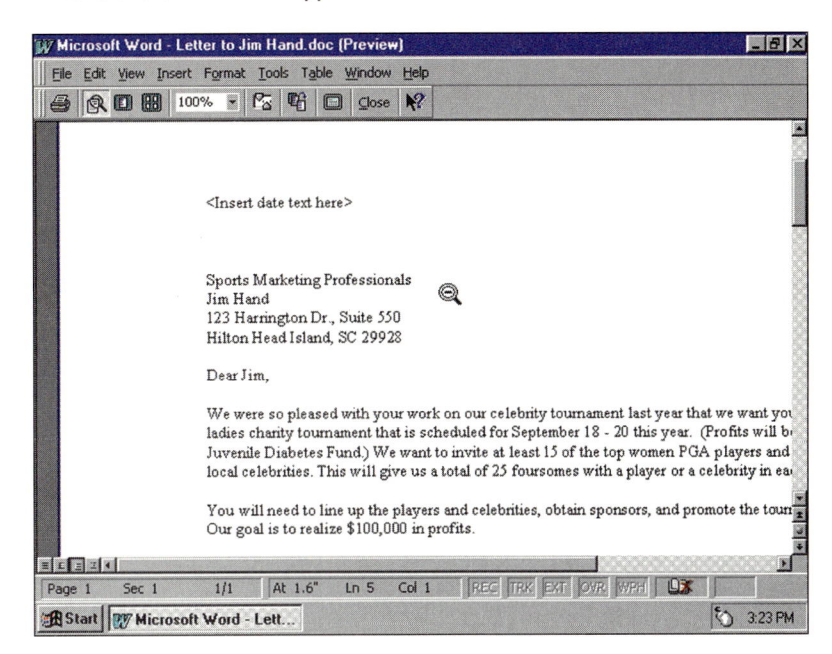

3 Click the Magnifier button.
The pointer changes to its normal shape.

4 Click before the "a" in "Harrington" in the street address.
The insertion point is positioned before the "a."

5 Press (DELETE) and type **e**.
Word corrects the spelling.

6 Click Close in the Print Preview toolbar.
The Print Preview mode closes, and the document screen displays.

7 Click .
The revised document is saved under the same name.

Printing a Document

You can print a document from the Print Preview window or from the document window. Clicking the Print button prints one copy of the complete document. If you want to print only part of the document or more than one copy, you should use the Print command from the File menu.

TASK 12: TO PRINT THE LETTER TO JIM HAND:

1 Ensure that the computer you are using is attached to a printer and that the printer is online.

2 Choose File from the menu bar.

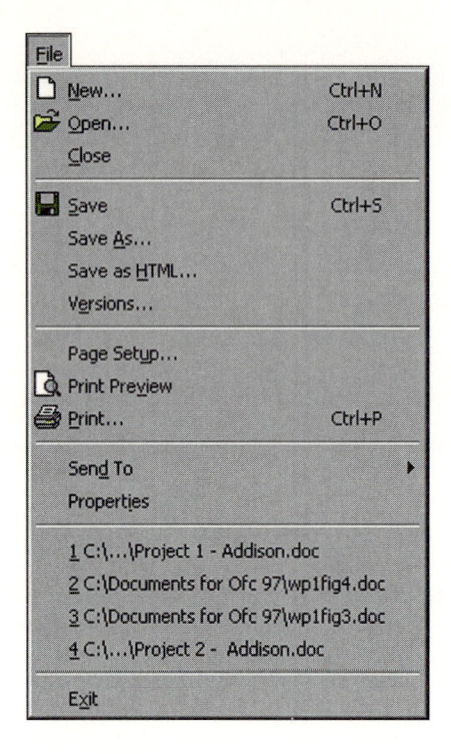

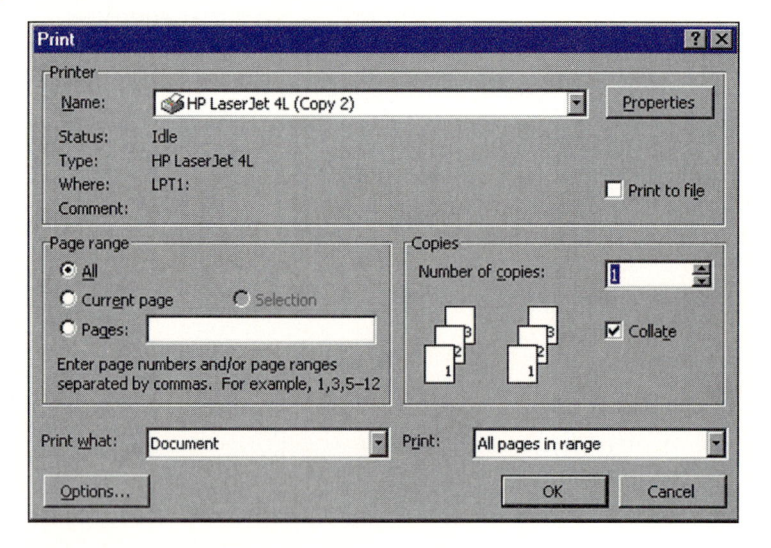

3 Choose Print.

4 Click OK.
The document prints.

Closing a File

When you are finished with a file, you can close it to "put it away." If you have made changes to the file that you want to keep, you should save the file before closing it. Don't worry, though. If you forget to save a file, Word 97 asks if you want to save changes.

TASK 13: TO CLOSE A FILE:

1. Choose File from the menu bar.
   The File menu displays.

2. Choose Close.

The Conclusion

You can exit Word 97 now by clicking the Close button, or you can work on the Review Exercises and Assignments.

Summary and Exercises

Summary

- When you launch Word 97, it automatically creates a new document named Document 1.
- Word 97 can insert the current date in several formats.
- When typing text, you press (ENTER) to end a short line or paragraph or to create a blank line.
- Characters that can't be created by pressing a key on the keyboard can be inserted from the Symbols dialog box.
- Simple typing errors can be corrected using the Backspace key.
- The Undo command can undo multiple commands and tasks that you have performed.
- Misspelled words are marked with a wavy red line by Word 97 and replacement words can be selected from a pop-up menu.
- Documents can be saved with long filenames.
- Before you print a document, you can preview it to see if it looks acceptable.
- You can print a document using the Print button or the Print command on the File menu.
- When you close a file, if you haven't saved changes to the file, Word 97 asks if you want to save the changes.

Key Terms and Operations

Key Terms	Operations
AutoComplete	create new document
AutoCorrect	indent
Enter	insert special characters
new document	undo
SpellIt	save a document
Tab	preview a document
Wrap	print a document
	close a document

Study Questions

Multiple Choice

1. Which of the following should *not* be done when typing text in a document?
    a. Press (BACKSPACE) to erase the character to the left.
    b. Press (ENTER) at the end of every line.
    c. Press (ENTER) to create a blank line.
    d. Click the Undo button to undo the last operation.

2. After Word 97 launches,
    a. the screen is blank until you create a new document.
    b. a dialog box displays with the options to create a new document or edit an existing document.
    c. Document 1 is created automatically.
    d. the New File dialog box displays.

WORD-36

3. The Undo command
   a. can undo the last operation.
   b. can undo deletions only.
   c. can undo the last five operations.
   d. can undo an unlimited number of operations.

4. A long filename
   a. is the name of a file that is more than ten pages long.
   b. can be as many characters as you want to use.
   c. can use a period only between the name and the extension.
   d. can't contain a question mark.

5. A word that has a wavy red line under it
   a. is misspelled.
   b. is marked for deletion.
   c. will print in bold.
   d. isn't in the Word 97 dictionary.

6. Which of the following names isn't a valid filename?
   a. *Letter to Mr. Hand . doc*
   b. *Letter to Mr. Hand.doc*
   c. *Letter:Mr. Hand.doc*
   d. *LttrHand.doc*

7. The Print Preview mode
   a. shows only one page at a time.
   b. can zoom to different magnifications.
   c. can display as many as ten pages.
   d. displays automatically before you print a document.

8. The Backspace key
   a. erases the character to the right.
   b. erases the character to the left.
   c. erases the character that the insertion point is on.
   d. moves the insertion point to the right but doesn't erase a character.

9. The status bar shows the
   a. left and right margins.
   b. vertical position of the insertion point.
   c. scroll bars.
   d. ruler.

10. If you click a word with a wavy red line,
    a. the line disappears.
    b. a menu displays.
    c. the Spell Checker starts.
    d. the insertion point is positioned in the word.

Short Answer

1. How do you save an existing file to a different location?
2. How many characters can a filename have, including the path?
3. How do you insert a date?

4. How do you insert a character that can't be entered from the keyboard?

5. How do you end a paragraph?

6. How do you magnify the document in the Print Preview mode?

7. What's the difference between using the Print command from the File menu and using the Print button?

8. What happens when you choose File, Close if you haven't saved the file?

9. Can you edit a document while viewing it in Print Preview mode?

10. Why don't you have to press Enter at the end of each line in a paragraph?

For Discussion

1. How does previewing a file before printing help the environment?

2. Why would you want to ignore a word that isn't in the dictionary rather than to add it to the dictionary?

3. Why is the Undo command so beneficial for novice users?

4. Under what circumstances would you click the New button to create a new document?

Review Exercises

1. Creating a New Letter

After meeting with Jim Hand to discuss promoting the golf tournament, Thomas Williams wants you to type a follow-up letter to confirm some of the topics they discussed.

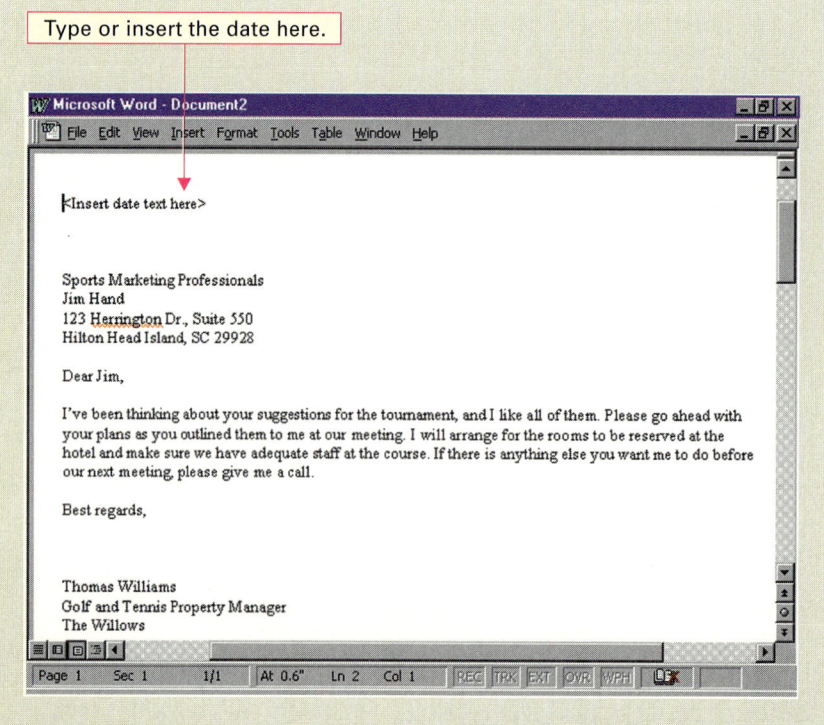

Figure 1.3

1. Create a new file and type the document shown in Figure 1.3. (Begin typing approximately 2 inches from the top of the page.)
2. Save the file as *Hand Follow-up.doc*.
3. Preview the file.
4. Add your initials to the end of the file while in Print Preview mode.
5. Save the file again and close it.

2. Getting Information from the Internet

Mr. Williams wants you to search the Internet for some ideas for the upcoming golf tournament. If you find anything useful, print it and give it to him with a short memo.

1. Search the Internet for topics related to golf.
2. Print several appropriate pages or files that you find.
3. Create a new file and type the memo shown in Figure 1.4.

Type your name and type or insert the date

Memo

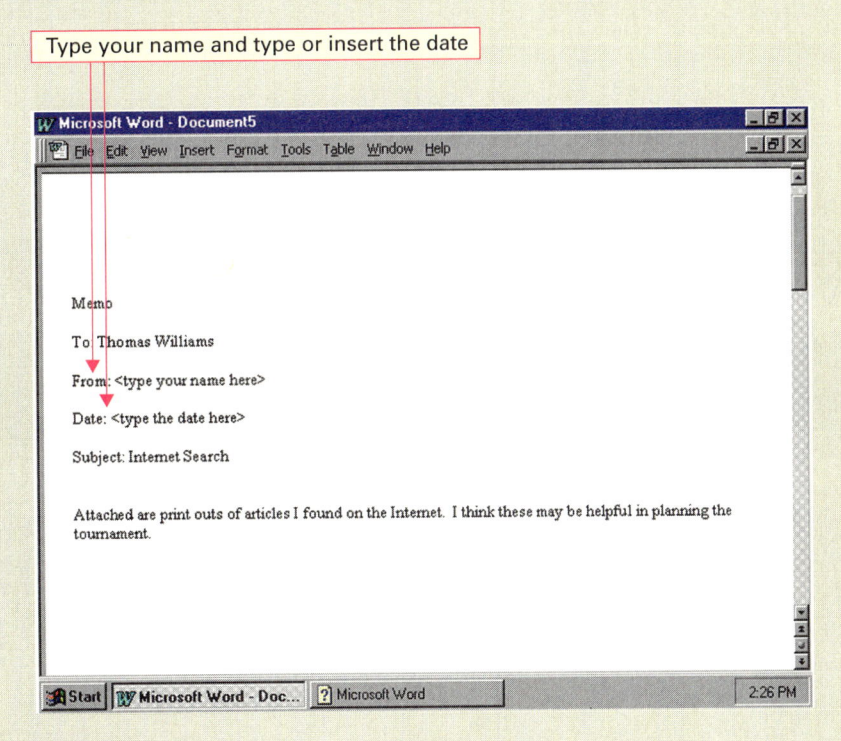

To: Thomas Williams

From: <type your name here>

Date: <type the date here>

Subject: Internet Search

Attached are print outs of articles I found on the Internet. I think these may be helpful in planning the tournament.

Figure 1.4

4. Save the file as *Internet Findings.doc* and close it.

Assignments

1. Creating a Memo

Type a memo to the Grande Hotel manager's administrative assistant, Lois Parks, asking her to reserve a block of 100 rooms for the golf tournament on September 18, 19, and 20.

2. Creating a List of E-Mail Addresses
Mr. Williams needs a list of the names of famous people whom he can contact about playing in the charity golf tournament. Use the Internet Explorer 3.0 search feature to find between five and ten e-mail addresses for several famous people, including TV and movie personalities, comedians, musicians and singers, politicians, and so on. Create a document listing the e-mail addresses you find and print the document.

PROJECT 2

Editing a Document

Creating a document is just the beginning of your work in word processing. After you create a document, you usually revise it several times. In this project, you will explore some of the most commonly used revision techniques.

Objectives

After completing this project, you will be able to:

- ▶ Open a document
- ▶ Move around in a document
- ▶ Select text to change the attributes
- ▶ Work with text
- ▶ Check spelling and grammar
- ▶ Create an envelope
- ▶ Change the view

The Challenge

After typing a letter for Mr. Williams to the Sports Marketing Professionals, Mr. Williams wants the letter retyped with the changes shown in Figure 2.1. Instead of sending additional information with the letter as previously planned, Mr. Williams has decided to send the information separately, so you will have to create an envelope for the letter.

WORD-41

Thomas Williams
The Willows Resort
1000 Coast Highway
Willow Grove, SC 22345

Sports Marketing Professionals
Jim Hand
123 Herrington Dr., Suite 550
Hilton Head Island, SC 29928

<Insert date text here>

Sports Marketing Professionals
Jim Hand
123 Herrington Dr., Suite 550
Hilton Head Island, SC 29928

Dear Jim,

We were **so** pleased with your work on our celebrity tournament last year that we want you to promote our ladies charity tournament that is scheduled for September 18 - 20 this year. You will need to line up the players and celebrities, obtain sponsors, and promote the tournament locally. We want to invite at least 15 of the top women PGA players and 10 national and local celebrities. This will give us a total of 25 foursomes with a player or a celebrity in each foursome.

Our goal is to realize $100,000 in profits to be given to one of the following charities.

Juvenile Diabetes Foundation
American Cancer Society
American Red Cross

I will be sending you several lists of names—sponsors, local celebrities, and local charitable contributors that will help you promote the tournament. Please call me to discuss the details.

Best regards,

Thomas Williams
Golf and Tennis Property Manager
The Willows

Cc: John Gilmore

Enclosures

YJ

Figure 2.1

The Solution

You will revise the original letter using several of Word's common revision techniques, and you will use the automatic feature in Word to create an envelope.

The Setup

So that your screen will match the illustrations and the tasks in this project will function as described, make sure that the Word 97 settings listed in Table 2.1 are selected on your computer.

Table 2.1 Word 97 Settings

Location	Make these settings:
View, Toolbars	Deselect all toolbars except the Standard and Formatting toolbars
View	Deselect the ruler
Standard toolbar	Deselect any buttons that are selected and set Zoom to 100%
Tools, Options, View	Select the Horizontal and Vertical scroll bars
Tools, Options, Edit	Select the Typing replaces selection option; deselect the Drag-and-drop text editing option; and select the option When selecting, automatically select entire word
Tools, Options, Spelling & Grammar	Select the Check spelling as you type, Check Grammar as you type, and Check grammar with spelling options

Opening a Document

When you want to view or revise a document that you have saved, you must open the document first.

> **Tip** If the document is one that you have opened recently, you may see it listed at the bottom of the File menu. To open the file, simply choose it from the menu.

TASK 1: TO OPEN A DOCUMENT:

1 Click the Open button.

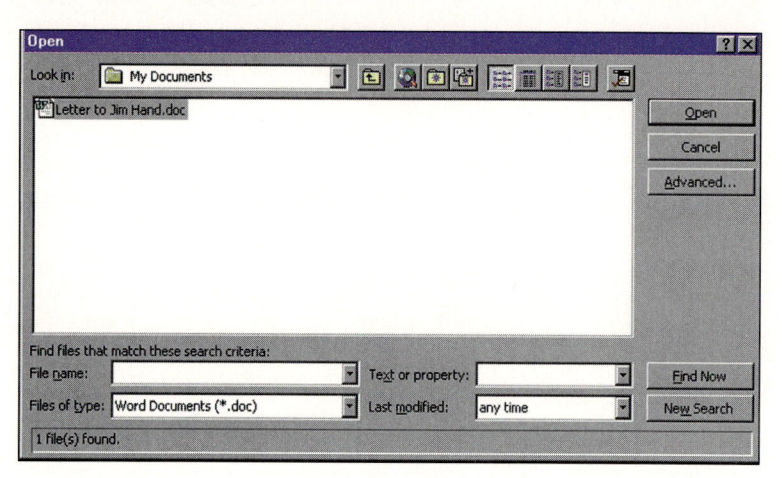

2 Double-click *Letter to Jim Hand.doc*
The file opens.

> **Troubleshooting** If the filename doesn't appear in the Open dialog box, click the down arrow in the Look in text box and click the drive where the file is stored. Type the filename in the File Name text box and click Advanced. Click Search subfolders and then click Find Now. If the file is on the drive, Word will find it. You can bet on it. Click Open when the results appear.

Moving Around in a Document

If the complete document isn't visible on the screen, you can use the scroll bars to scroll the text or just move the insertion point up or down one line at a time by pressing the up or down arrow.

When you are making revisions in a document, you need to move the insertion point to a specific location. The easiest way to move the insertion point is to scroll to the line of text using the scroll bar and then click the mouse pointer (shaped like an I-beam) in the desired location.

Instead of using the mouse to position the insertion point, you can use the keystrokes listed in Table 2.2.

Table 2.2 Navigation Keystrokes

To Move	Press
Down one line	↓
Up one line	↑
Left one character	←
Right one character	→
Left one word	CTRL+←
Right one word	CTRL+→
End of line	END
Beginning of line	HOME
Down one screen	PGDN
Up one screen	PGUP
End of the document	CTRL+END
Beginning of the document	CTRL+HOME

TASK 2: TO SCROLL THROUGH THE DOCUMENT:

1. Press ↓ to scroll through the document until you come to the bottom of the document.

2. Scroll back to the top of the document using the up arrow in the vertical scroll bar.
   You can't see the insertion point because it's still at the bottom of the document. Scrolling with the scroll bar doesn't move the insertion point.

3. Press PGDN.
   Now you can see the insertion point again.

Selecting Text to Change the Attributes

Several revision techniques, such as copying text or changing the text's size, require that you *select* the text first. Selected text is highlighted as shown in Figure 2.2. In most cases, the easiest way to select text is to drag the mouse pointer over the text, but Table 2.3 describes other ways of selecting text that are appropriate in many situations.

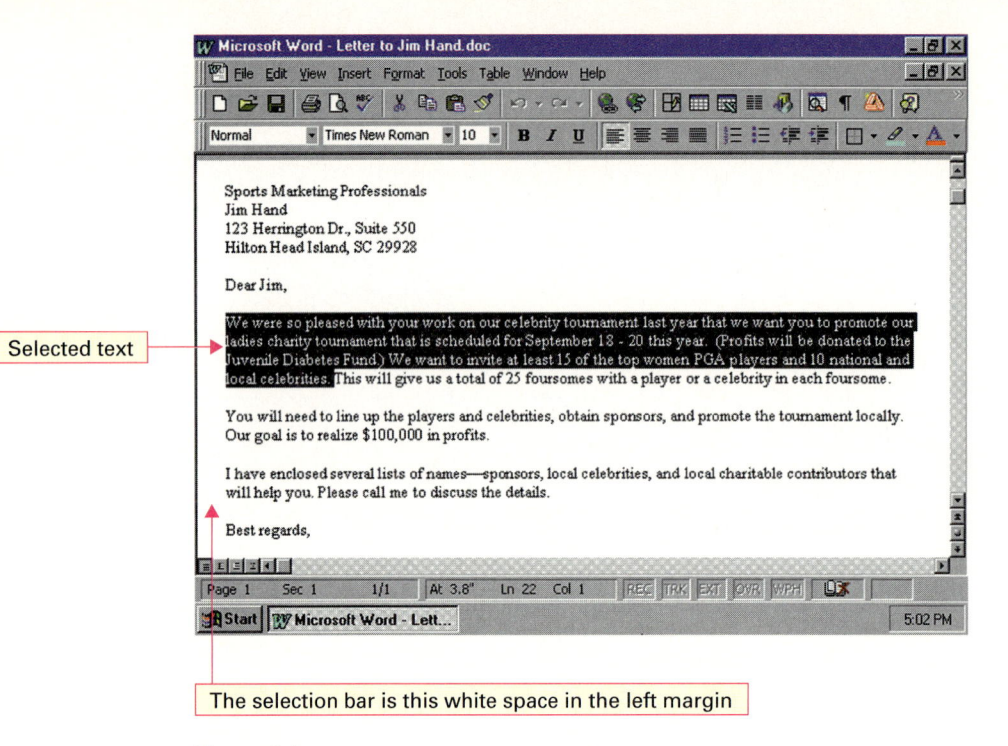

Selected text → [screenshot of Microsoft Word document showing a letter to Jim Hand with a highlighted paragraph]

The selection bar is this white space in the left margin

Figure 2.2

Table 2.3 Text Selection Methods

To Select	With the Mouse	With the Keyboard
A word	Double-click the word	Position the insertion point at the beginning of the word and press Shift+Ctrl+right arrow
A line	Click in the selection bar to the left of the line	Position the insertion point at the beginning of the line and press Shift+End
A sentence	Click anywhere in the sentence while pressing Ctrl	None
A paragraph	Triple-click anywhere in the paragraph	Position the insertion point at the beginning of the paragraph and press Shift+Ctrl+down arrow
An entire document	Click anywhere in the selection bar while pressing Ctrl	Press Ctrl+A or press Shift+Ctrl+End arrow at the top of the document or Choose Edit, Select All
A block of text	Drag the mouse pointer through the text	Position the insertion point at the beginning of the block, press and hold down Shift as you press any combination of arrow keys to move to the end of the block
A vertical block of text	Drag the mouse pointer through the text while pressing Alt	None

TASK 3: TO CHANGE TEXT ATTRIBUTES:

1 Select the word "so" in the first paragraph of the letter.

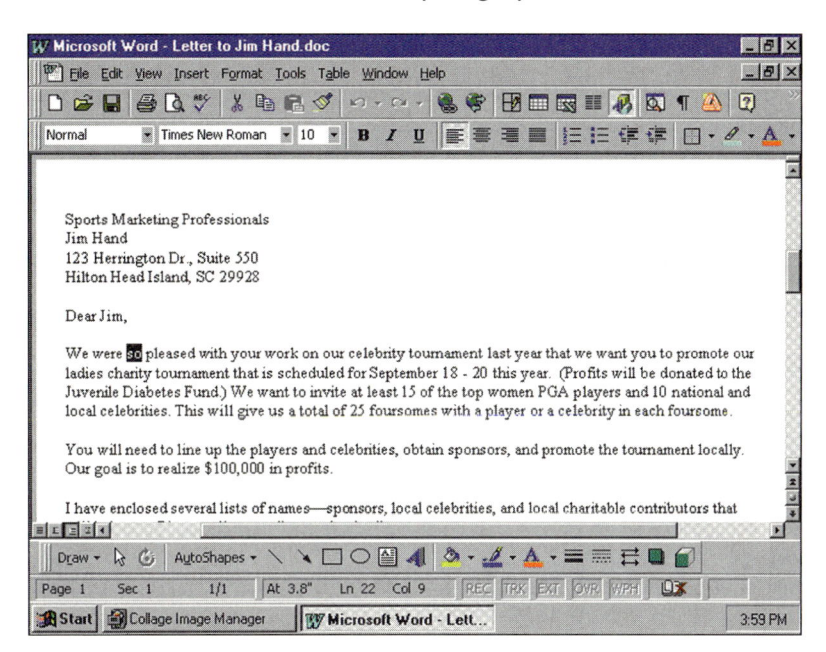

2 Click the Bold **B** button and then press → to deselect the text.

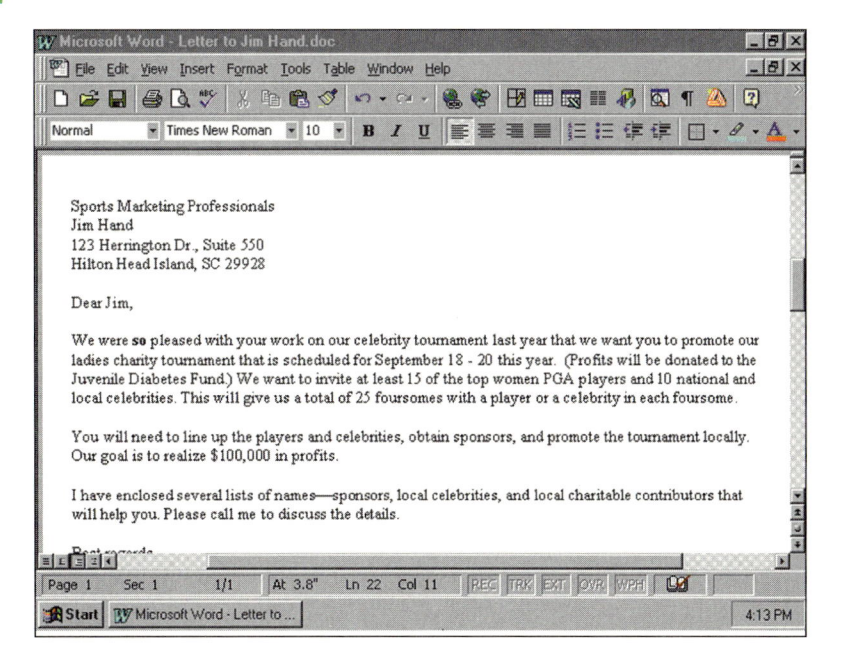

3 Select "so" again and then click the Underline **U** button.
The word is now **bold** and *underlined,* although it's a little difficult to tell because it's still selected.

4 Click **U** again.
The underline is removed.

5 Click the Italic **I** button and then press → to deselect the text.
The word is **bold** and *italic*.

6 Select "so" and press `CTRL`+I.
The word is just bold now.

7 Select the entire document.

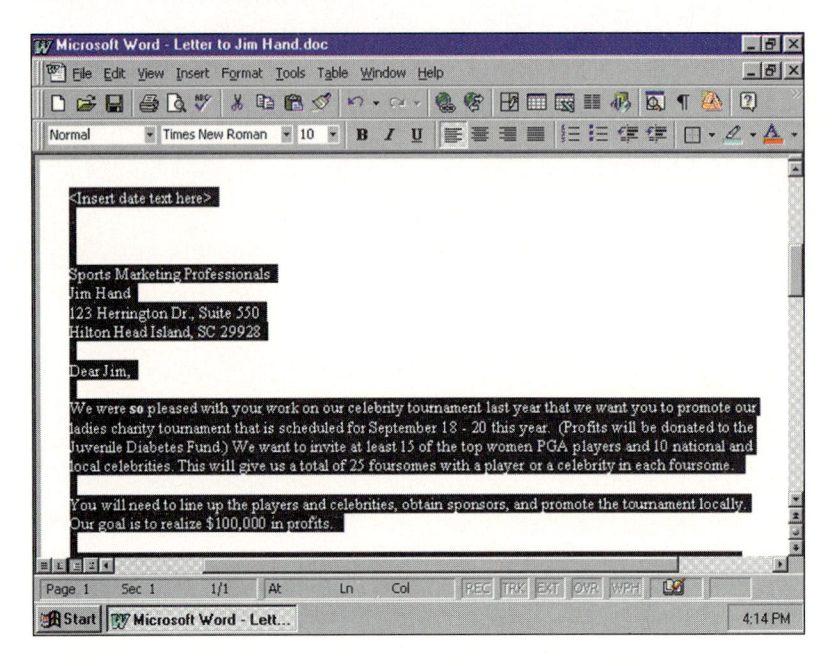

8 Click the down arrow in the Font Size drop-down list.

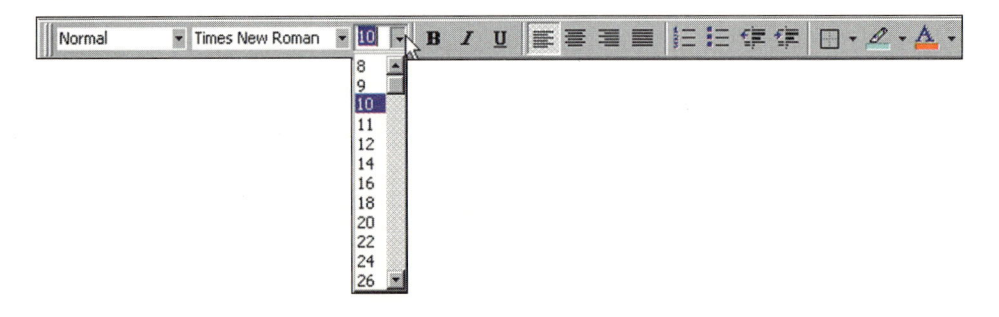

9 Choose 12.

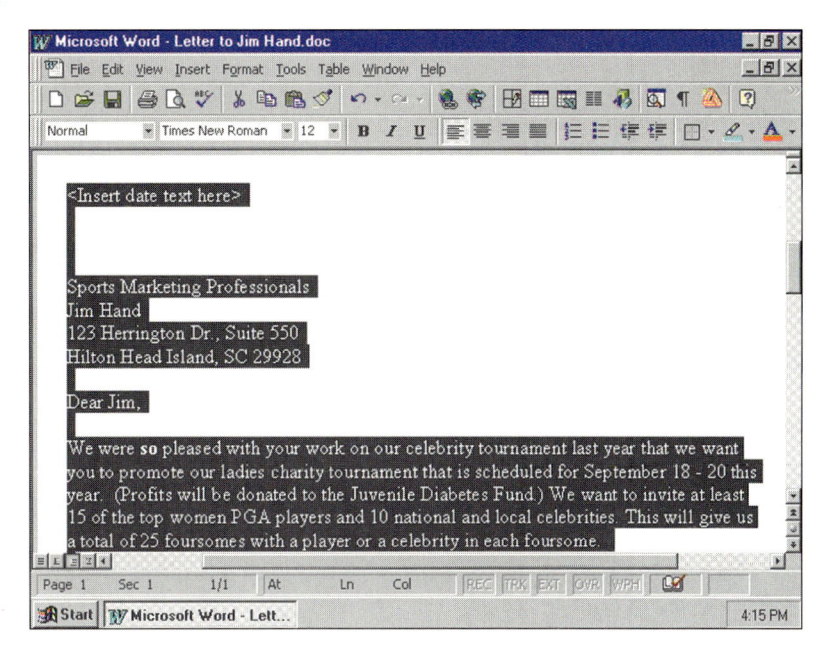

10 Click the down arrow in the Font drop-down list.

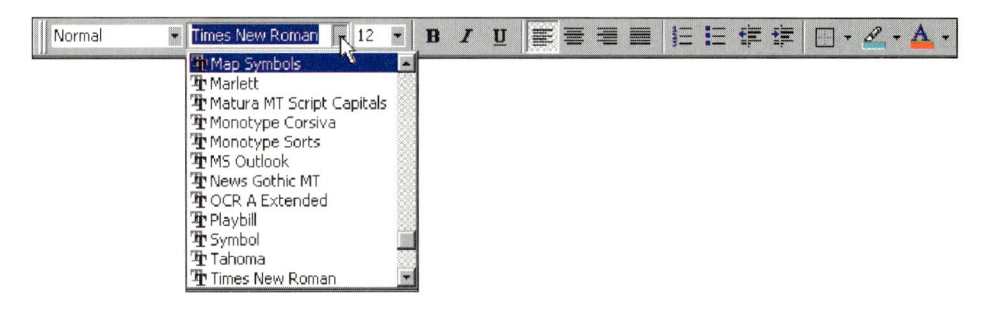

11 Scroll the list if necessary to display Arial.

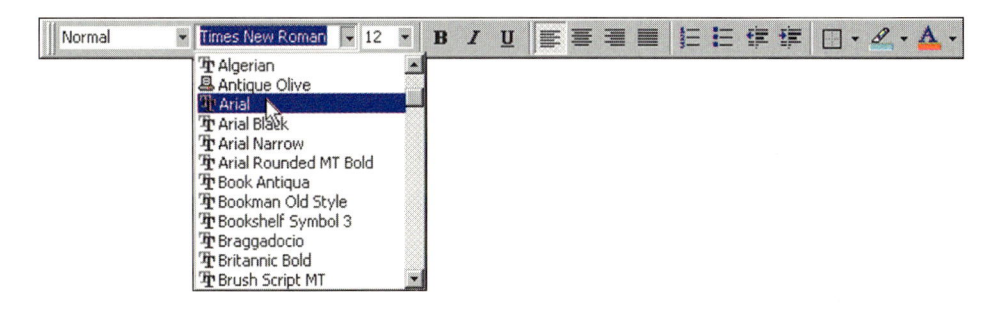

12 Click Arial.

All the text in the document changes to the Arial font.

> **Tip** To change the font, font size, and font attributes of selected text all at the same time, choose Format, Font to display the Font dialog box.

Working with Text

In addition to changing the appearance of text, often you have to delete, rearrange, realign, and copy text when you are making revisions. If you use a portion of text over and over again, you can make Word do your work for you by creating an AutoText entry for the text.

TASK 4: TO DELETE TEXT:

1 Select the text "(Profits will be donated to the Juvenile Diabetes Foundation.)"

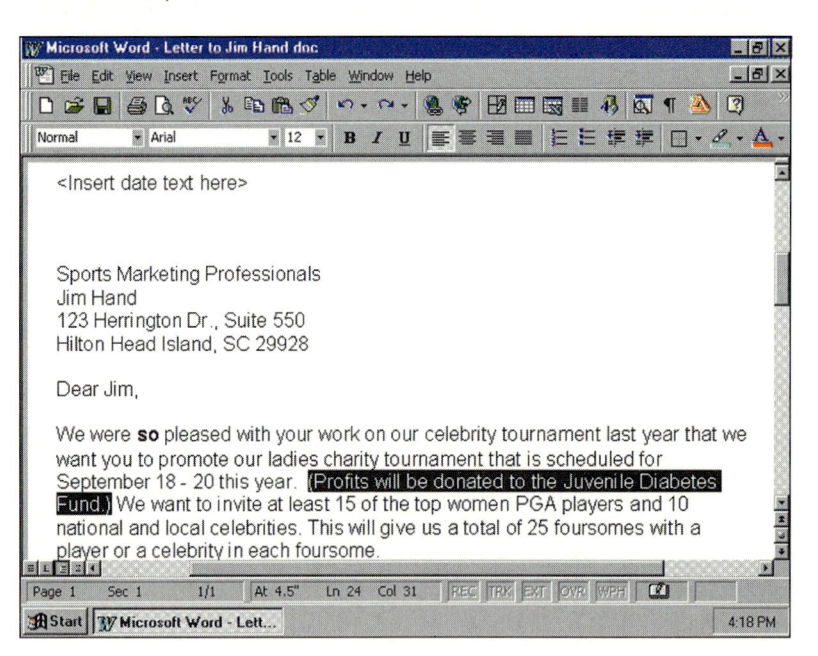

Project 2: Editing a Document   WORD-51

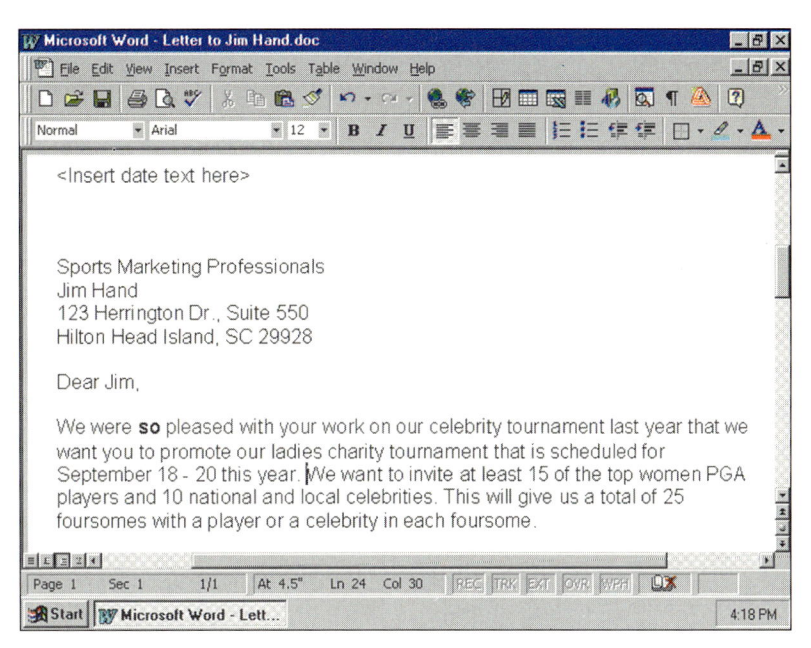

2 Press (DELETE).

TASK 5: TO MOVE TEXT:

1 Select the text "You will need to line up the players and celebrities, obtain sponsors, and promote the tournament locally."

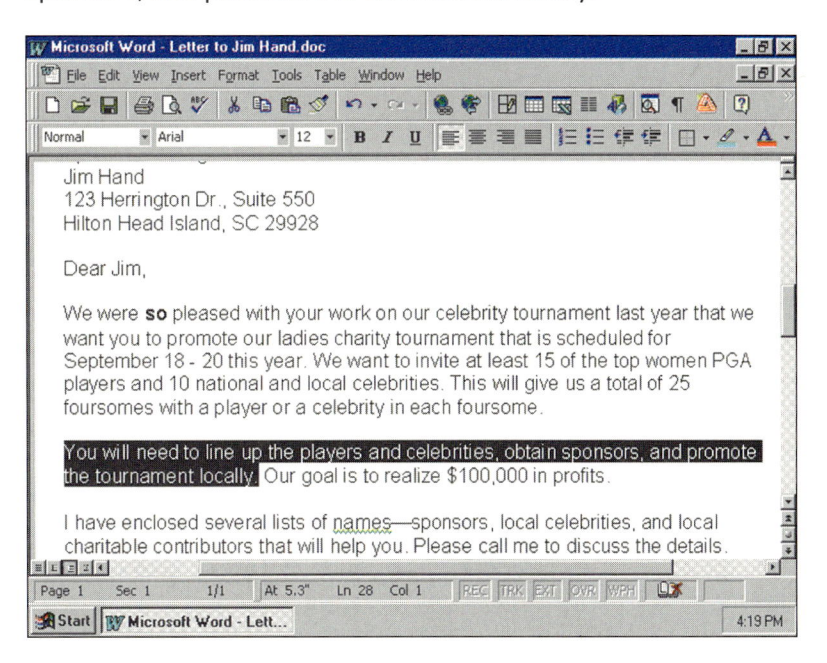

2 Click the Cut button.

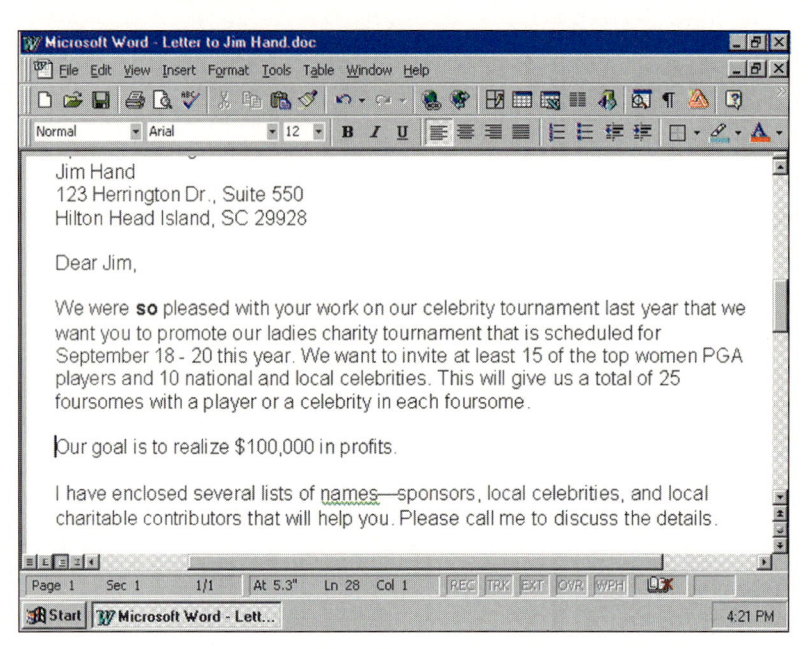

3 Click the insertion point after "September 18 - 20 this year."

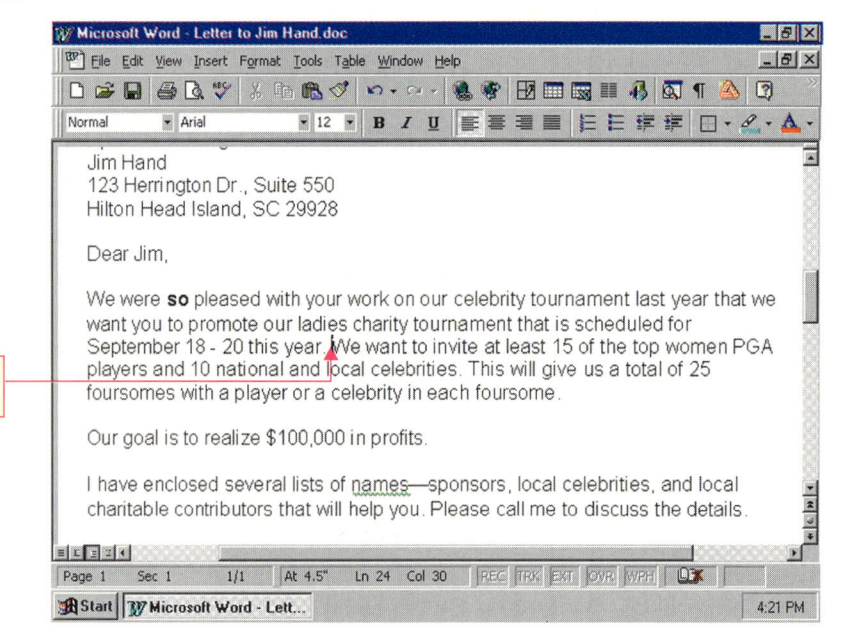

The insertion point should be here

4 Click the Paste button. Press SPACE if necessary.

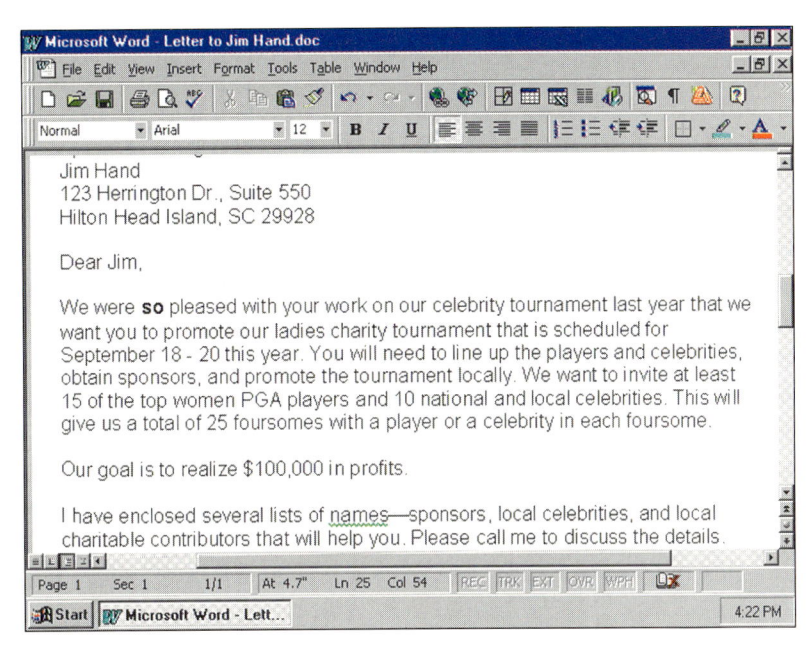

```
Microsoft Word - Letter to Jim Hand.doc
File  Edit  View  Insert  Format  Tools  Table  Window  Help

Normal    Arial        12    B  I  U

    Jim Hand
    123 Herrington Dr., Suite 550
    Hilton Head Island, SC 29928

    Dear Jim,

    We were **so** pleased with your work on our celebrity tournament last year that we
    want you to promote our ladies charity tournament that is scheduled for
    September 18 - 20 this year. You will need to line up the players and celebrities,
    obtain sponsors, and promote the tournament locally. We want to invite at least
    15 of the top women PGA players and 10 national and local celebrities. This will
    give us a total of 25 foursomes with a player or a celebrity in each foursome.

    Our goal is to realize $100,000 in profits.

    I have enclosed several lists of names—sponsors, local celebrities, and local
    charitable contributors that will help you. Please call me to discuss the details.

Page 1   Sec 1    1/1    At 4.7"   Ln 25  Col 54

Start   Microsoft Word - Lett...                              4:22 PM
```

> **Tip** Clicking the Cut button deletes text and stores it in a memory area called the Clipboard. When you delete text with the Delete key, the text isn't stored in the Clipboard, and you can't paste it in another location.

You can change the alignment of paragraphs in your document so that they are aligned at the left margin (*left-aligned*), at the right margin (*right-aligned*), *centered* between the margins, or *justified* (spread evenly between the margins). To align the text, you simply place the insertion point in the paragraph and click the Left, Right, Center, or Justify button on the Formatting toolbar. The paragraphs you type after setting the alignment keep the same alignment until you change it.

TASK 6: TO ALIGN TEXT:

1 Click the insertion point after "$100,000 in profits" just before the period and press SPACE.

2 Type **to be given to one of the following charities**, press →, and press ENTER twice.

3 Type **Juvenile Diabetes Foundation** and then click the Center button to center that line. Press ENTER to continue entering centered text in a list.

4 Type **American Cancer Society** and press ENTER.

5 Type **American Red Cross** and press ENTER again. The completed list is centered in the document.

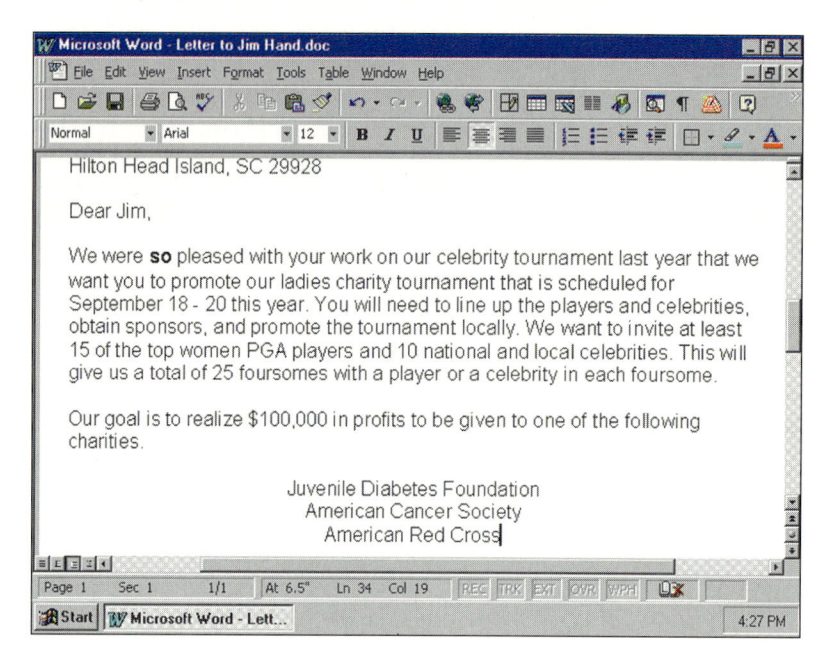

If you select text and then type something new, the selected text is replaced by the new text.

TASK 7: TO REPLACE TEXT:

1 Select the text "have enclosed."

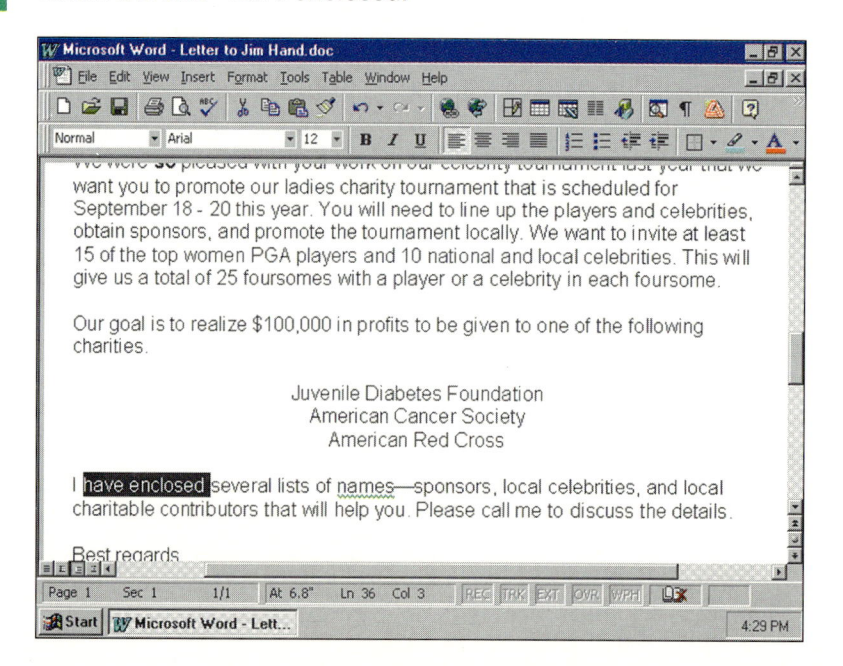

2 Type **will be sending you**.

If you want to have the same text repeated in the document, you can copy the text and paste it.

TASK 8: TO COPY TEXT:

1 In the first paragraph of the letter, select the text "promote the tournament."

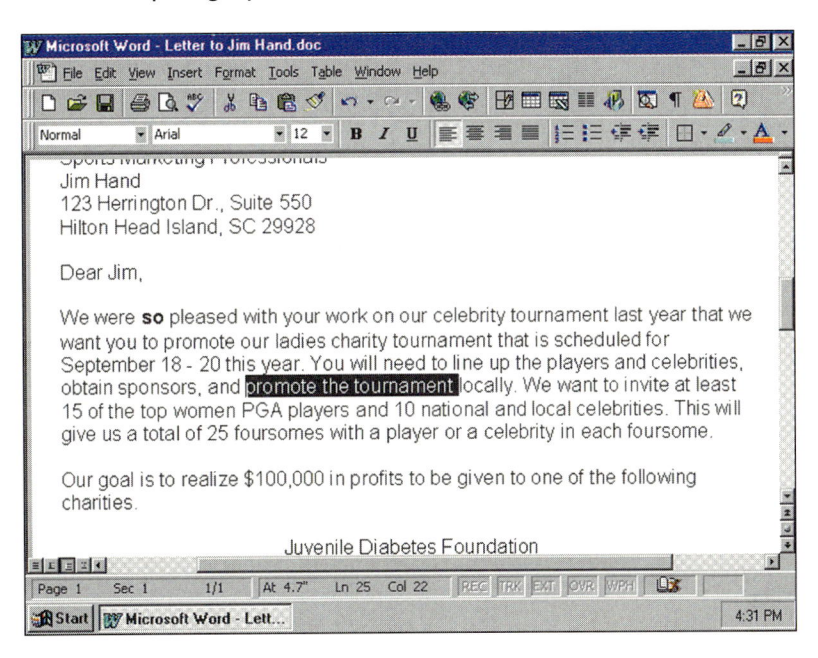

2 Click the Copy button.
The text is copied to the Clipboard.

3 Click the insertion point before the period in "that will help you."

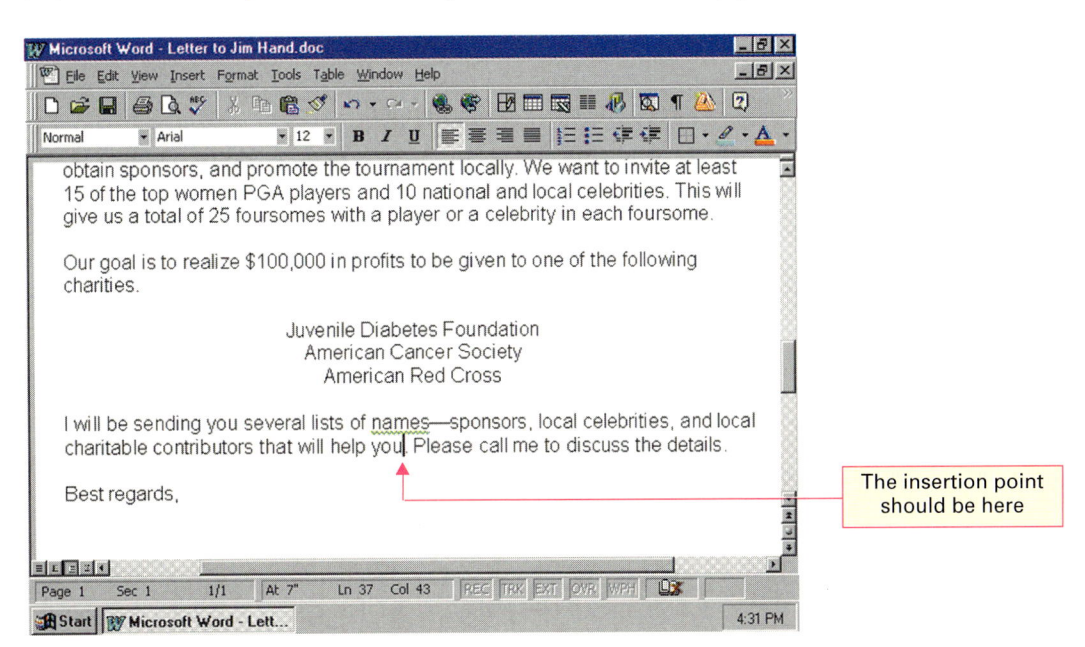

The insertion point should be here

4 Click 📋.

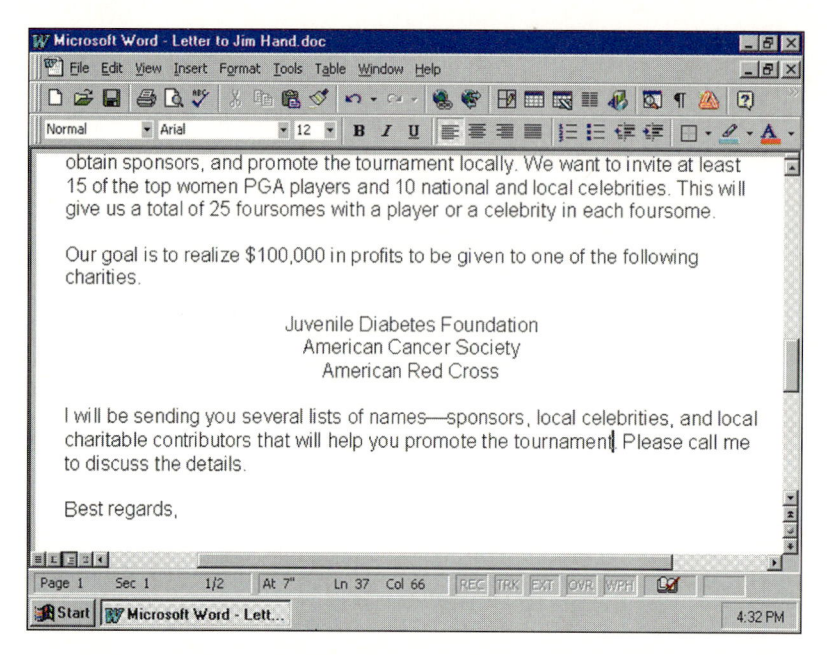

Tip The content of the Clipboard can be pasted over and over again. The content can even be pasted in other documents.

An *AutoText entry* is a portion of text that you can recall with a single keystroke. In the next task, you will create an AutoText entry for a letter closing.

TASK 9: TO CREATE AN AUTOTEXT ENTRY:

1 Select the signature block at the end of the letter.

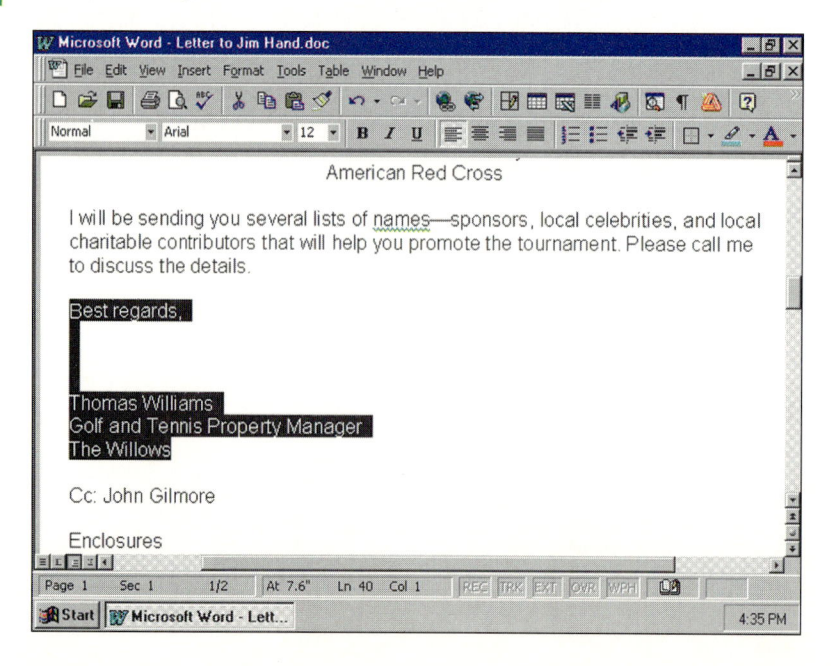

Project 2: Editing a Document **WORD-57**

2 Choose Insert, Autotext, New.

Create AutoText dialog box: "Word will create an AutoText entry from the current selection. Please name your AutoText entry: Best regards," [OK] [Cancel]

3 Type **twclose** and click OK.

4 Press (DELETE).
The signature block is deleted.

5 Type **twclose** and press (F3).
The signature block is inserted automatically.

> **Note** You can use this AutoText entry in any document. If you create enough AutoText entries, you may never have to type a complete sentence again.

Checking Spelling and Grammar

When you have made all the revisions in a document, you should give it one final check with the Spelling and Grammar checker. Because the automatic spelling and grammar features underline errors as you type, the final check will find only the errors you failed to correct as you went along.

TASK 10: TO CHECK SPELLING AND GRAMMAR:

1 Delete the "g" in the word "Marketing" in the address at the top of the letter.

2 Add another "s" in the middle of the word "Professionals."

3 Right-click on the word "Herrington" and choose Ignore so it doesn't show up in the spell check.

4 Press (CTRL)+(HOME) to move to the beginning of the document.

WORD-58

5 Click the Spelling & Grammar button.

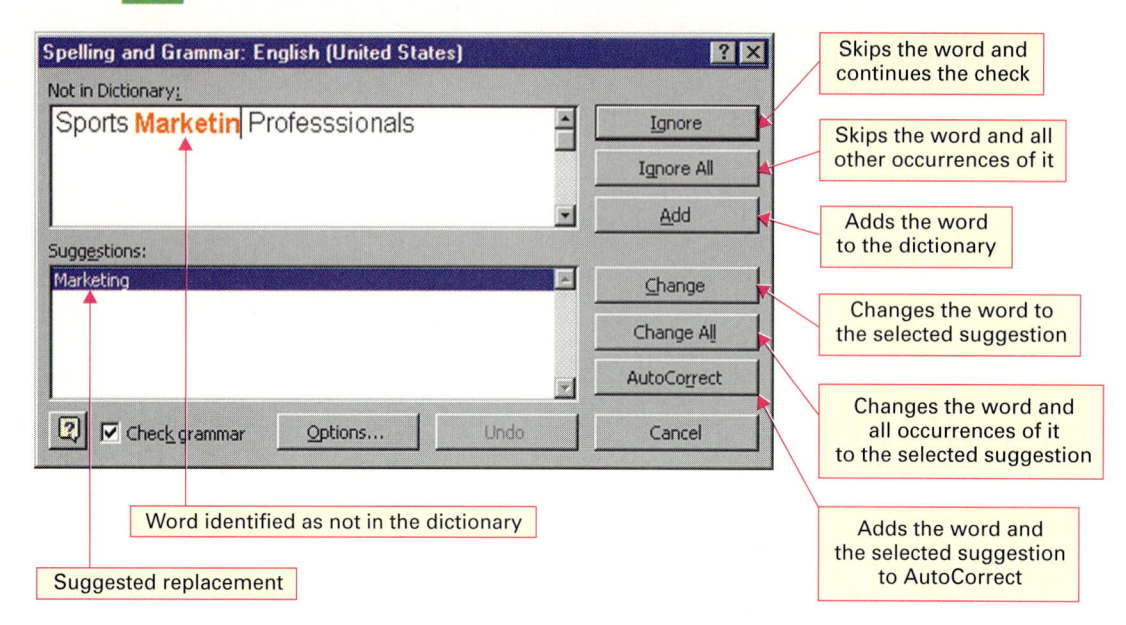

Skips the word and continues the check — Ignore

Skips the word and all other occurrences of it — Ignore All

Adds the word to the dictionary — Add

Changes the word to the selected suggestion — Change

Changes the word and all occurrences of it to the selected suggestion — Change All

Adds the word and the selected suggestion to AutoCorrect — AutoCorrect

Word identified as not in the dictionary

Suggested replacement

6 Click Change.

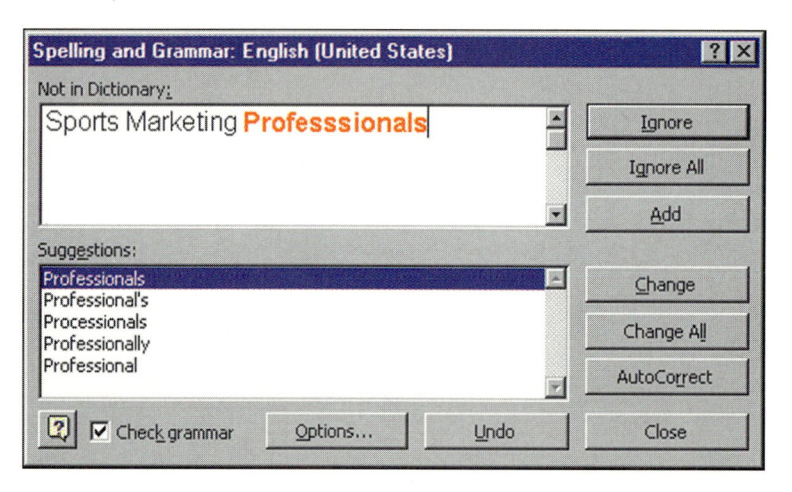

7 Click Change.

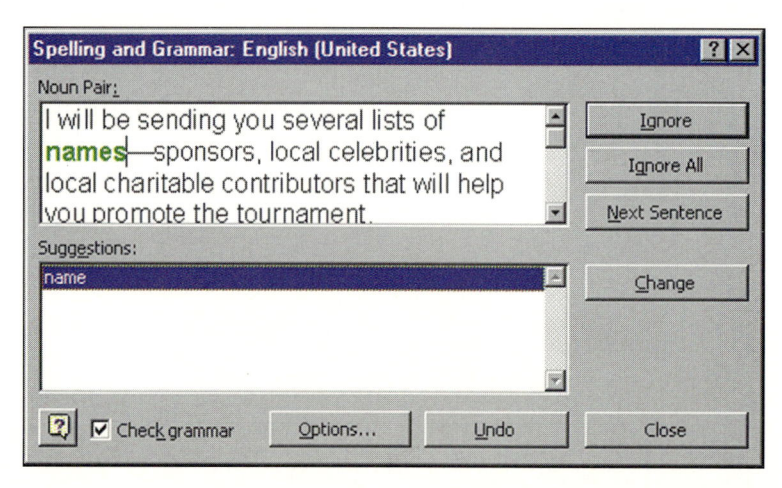

8 Click Ignore.

9 Click OK.
The dialog box closes.

Creating an Envelope

Word's Envelope tool makes it easy to create an envelope. In fact, you don't even have to type the address if you have an address at the top of the document.

TASK 11: TO CREATE AN ENVELOPE:

1 Choose Tools, Envelopes and Labels, and click the Envelopes tab if necessary.

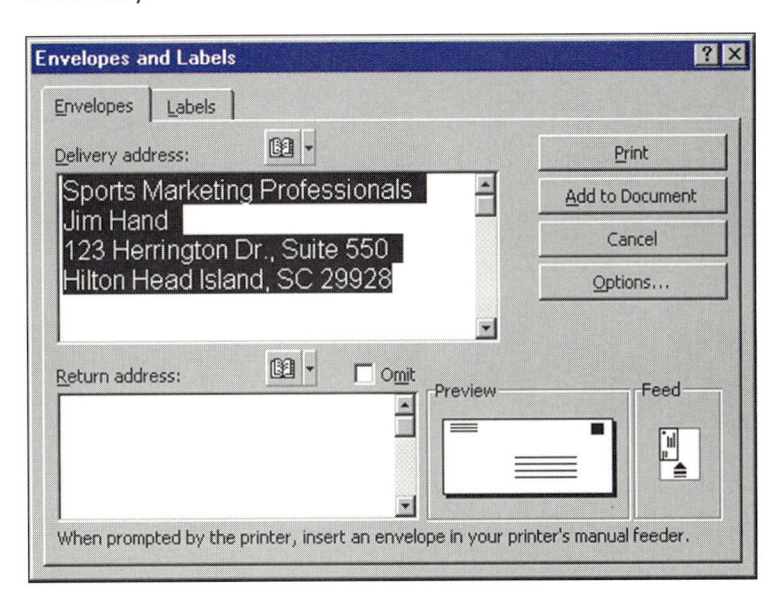

2 Click in the Return address area and type the address shown below.

Thomas Williams
The Willows Resort
1000 Coast Highway
Willow Grove, SC 22345

3 Click Add to Document and then click No when the message appears asking if you want to save the new address as the default address.

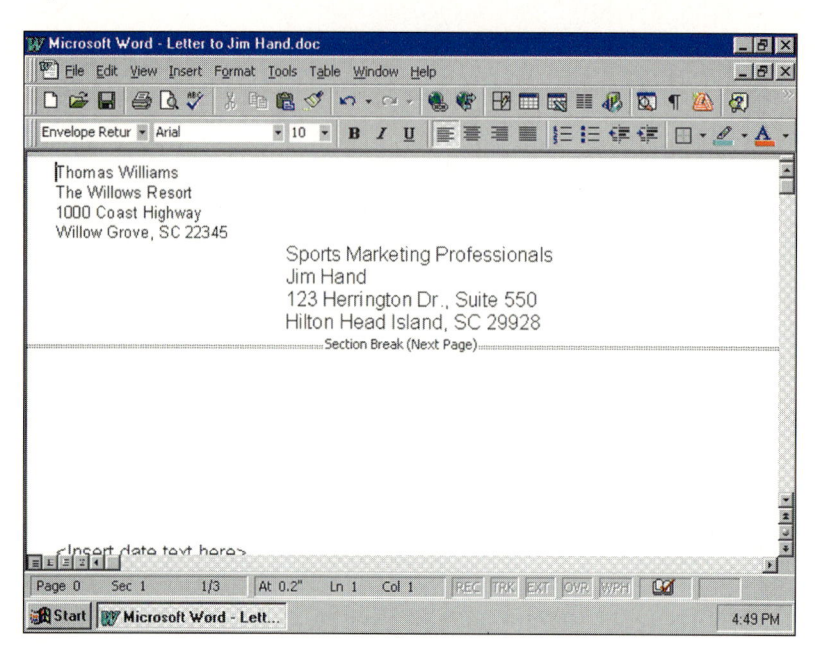

Word adds the envelope as the first page of the document, making the letter page two.

> **Tip** If you just want to print the envelope and not add it to the document, you can click Print instead of Add to Document.

Changing the View

Word provides several views for working with documents. Each view has features that are useful in different situations. The default view, Normal, doesn't show the white space for margins or the area on a page that hasn't been used; therefore, use the **Normal view** when you need to see the maximum amount of text. The *Page Layout view* shows margins and unused space as well as a visual *page break* between pages. Use the Page Layout view when you need an idea of what the page will look like when printed.

Project 2: Editing a Document   WORD-61

TASK 12: TO CHANGE THE VIEW TO PAGE LAYOUT VIEW:

1 Click the Page Layout View button in the horizontal scroll bar.

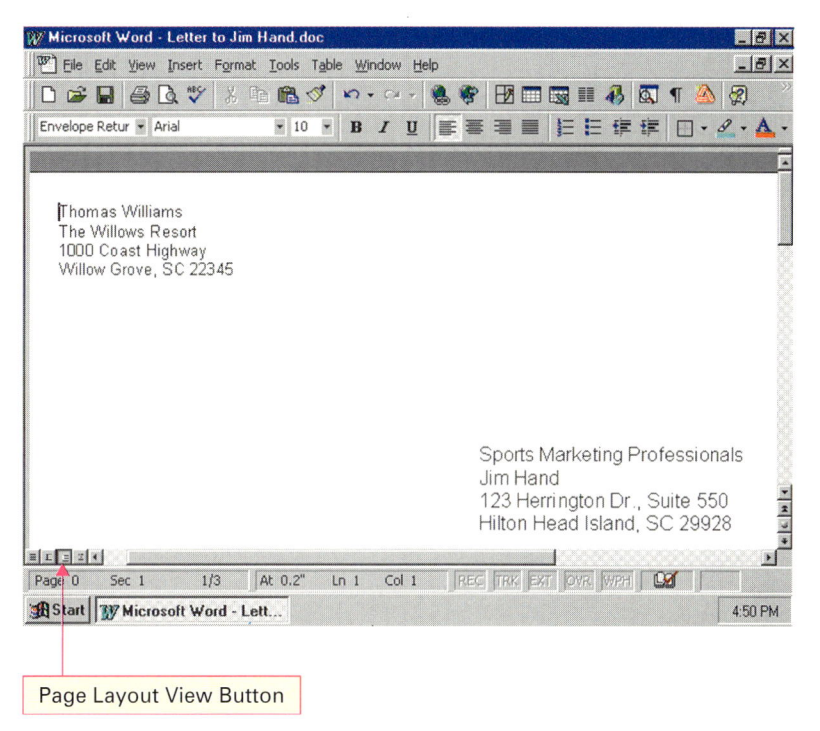

Page Layout View Button

2 Scroll down to see the page break.

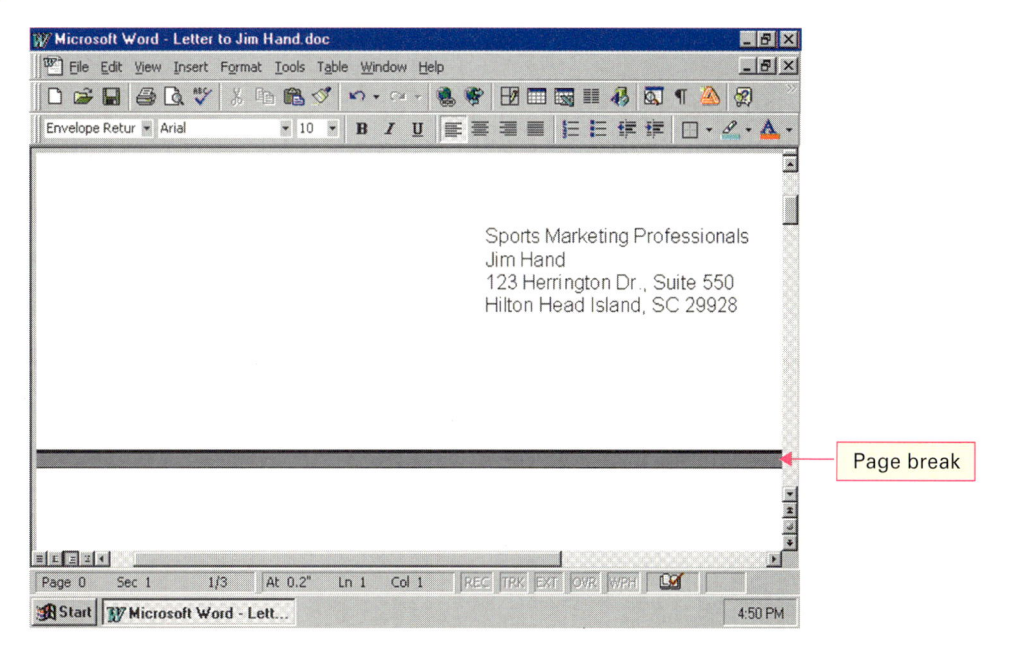

Page break

3 Scroll down to the bottom of the letter.
The letter won't fit on one page after you have revised it.

4 Scroll to the top of the letter and press DELETE.
One line at the top of the letter is deleted.

5 Press CTRL+END to go to the bottom of the document.
The letter fits on one page now.

> **Note** The view last used in a document is the view that displays when you open the document again.

The Conclusion

Edit the inside address and closing lines so they conform to standard business letter format as directed by your instructor. When you are finished with the document, click the Save button to save it; then choose File, Close to close the file.

Summary and Exercises

Summary

- You open a file to view it or revise it.
- To make revisions in a file, you must move the insertion point to the point of the revision.
- You can move the insertion point by clicking the mouse or by using different keystrokes.
- Scrolling with the scroll bar doesn't move the insertion point.
- Several revision techniques require selecting text.
- You can select text by highlighting it with the mouse or by using different keystrokes.
- You can change text attributes by clicking buttons or drop-down lists in the Formatting toolbar.
- You also can change text attributes by using the Font dialog box.
- The alignment buttons in the Formatting toolbar are Left, Center, Right, and Justify.
- The Clipboard stores text that has been cut or copied.
- The Paste button inserts text from the Clipboard.
- When using the Spelling and Grammar Checker, you can ignore or change words or add words to the dictionary or to the AutoCorrect list.
- Word creates and formats an envelope for you.
- The Normal view is the default view.
- The Page Layout view shows margins and unused space on a page.

Key Terms and Operations

Key Terms	Operations
bold	align text
center	change the view
Clipboard	copy text
italic	create an envelope
justify	delete text
left-align	move text
Normal view	open a document
page break	replace text
Page Layout view	scroll
right-align	select text
selection bar	spelling and grammar check
underline	

Study Questions

Multiple Choice

1. The selection bar is
   a. a toolbar.
   b. the blank area to the left of the text.
   c. the bar button in the status bar.
   d. the blank area to the right of the text.

2. Which of the following methods, if any, does *not* apply italic to text that's selected?
   a. Click the Italic button in the Formatting toolbar.
   b. Choose Format, Font, click Italic, and choose OK.
   c. Click the Italic button in the status bar.
   d. Press Ctrl+I.

3. Which of the following should *not* be used to scroll down through a document?
   a. Press the down arrow repeatedly.
   b. Press Enter repeatedly.
   c. Press PageDown repeatedly.
   d. Click the down scroll arrow repeatedly.

4. The Clipboard
   a. is an area in memory.
   b. holds excess text.
   c. is erased when you close a document.
   d. holds text that has been selected.

5. To store text in the Clipboard, you must first
   a. select the text.
   b. click the Copy or Cut button.
   c. click the Clipboard button.
   d. click the Paste button.

6. To move the insertion point to the end of a document,
   a. press Ctrl+PageDown.
   b. press Shift and click in the selection bar.
   c. double-click the box in the vertical scroll bar.
   d. press Ctrl+End.

7. To select a paragraph with the keyboard, position the insertion point at the beginning of the paragraph and press
   a. Shift+Ctrl+down arrow
   b. Shift+Alt+down arrow
   c. Shift+Ctrl+PageDown
   d. Shift+down arrow

8. Choosing Ignore All in the Spelling and Grammar dialog box
   a. ends the spell check.
   b. ignores all occurrences of the word.
   c. ignores all capitalization errors.
   d. ignores all suggestions.

9. The Copy button on the toolbar looks like
   a. a pair of scissors.
   b. two pieces of paper.
   c. a piece of paper with a magnifying glass.
   d. a clipboard with a piece of paper.

10. Which of the following methods, if any, does *not* select the entire document:
    a. Press Ctrl+A.
    b. Press and hold Ctrl and click in the selection bar.
    c. Position the insertion point at the top of the document and press Shift+Ctrl+Home.
    d. Choose Edit, Select All.

Short Answer
1. How do you remove bold, italic, or underline from text?
2. What do you choose in the Spelling and Grammar dialog box if you don't want to correct a word that has been identified as not being in the dictionary?
3. What two buttons do you use to move text?
4. What two buttons do you use to copy text?
5. How do you start the Spelling and Grammar checker?
6. How do you select a vertical block of text?
7. Describe two methods of selecting a word.
8. How can you open a document quickly if it has been opened recently?
9. Does scrolling with the vertical scroll bar move the insertion point?
10. How do you change the font of text?

For Discussion
1. Discuss the advantages of using the Normal view and the Page Layout view and when you would use both views.
2. In what circumstances would it be better to delete text with the Cut button than with the Delete key?
3. Describe the spelling and grammar checking tools available in Word.
4. How can you find a file and open it if you don't know where the file is located on the disk?

Review Exercises

1. Creating a List of Possible Sponsors
Mr. Williams has given you several Rolodex cards, some business cards, and some sticky notes with names, addresses, and phone numbers of potential sponsors in the area. He wants you to type a letter to Mr. Hand and include the alphabetical list (see Figure 2.3).

<Insert date text here>

Sports Marketing Professionals
Jim Hand
123 Herrington Dr., Suite 550
Hilton Head Island, SC 29928

Dear Jim,

I have been going through my files for possible sponsors in the area, and I have come up with the following list of companies and people that I think could be *major* sponsors:

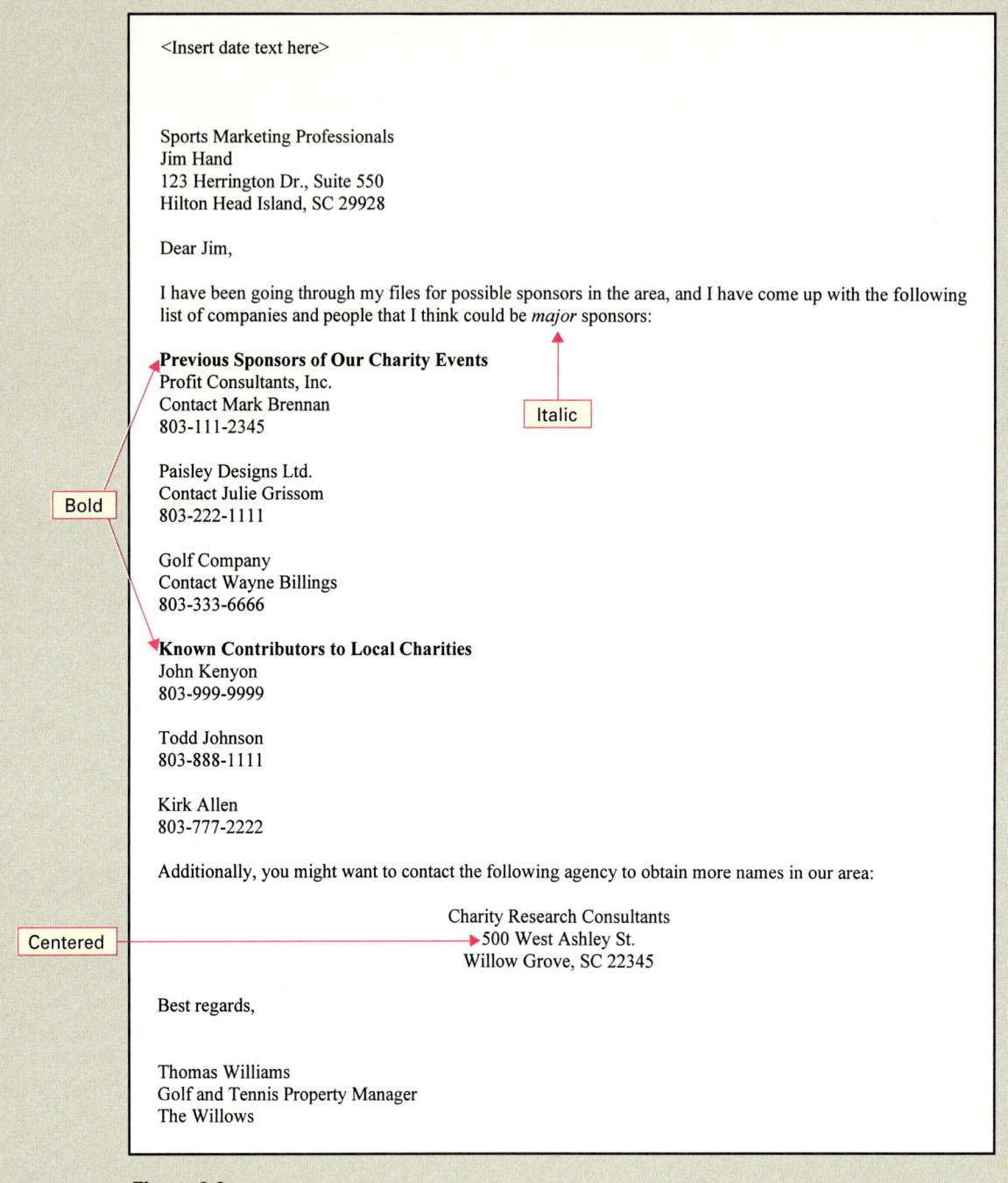

Previous Sponsors of Our Charity Events
Profit Consultants, Inc.
Contact Mark Brennan
803-111-2345

Paisley Designs Ltd.
Contact Julie Grissom
803-222-1111

Golf Company
Contact Wayne Billings
803-333-6666

Known Contributors to Local Charities
John Kenyon
803-999-9999

Todd Johnson
803-888-1111

Kirk Allen
803-777-2222

Additionally, you might want to contact the following agency to obtain more names in our area:

Charity Research Consultants
500 West Ashley St.
Willow Grove, SC 22345

Best regards,

Thomas Williams
Golf and Tennis Property Manager
The Willows

Figure 2.3

1. Create a new document and type the text shown in Figure 2.3, allowing approximately 2 inches at the top for letterhead. Notice the font attributes that have been used in the document.

2. Create an envelope and add it to the document. (Don't type a return address because the envelope has a preprinted return address.)

3. View the document in Page Layout view.

4. Make the changes shown in Figure 2.4.

5. Save the file as *Sponsors.doc* and close the file.

<Insert date text here>

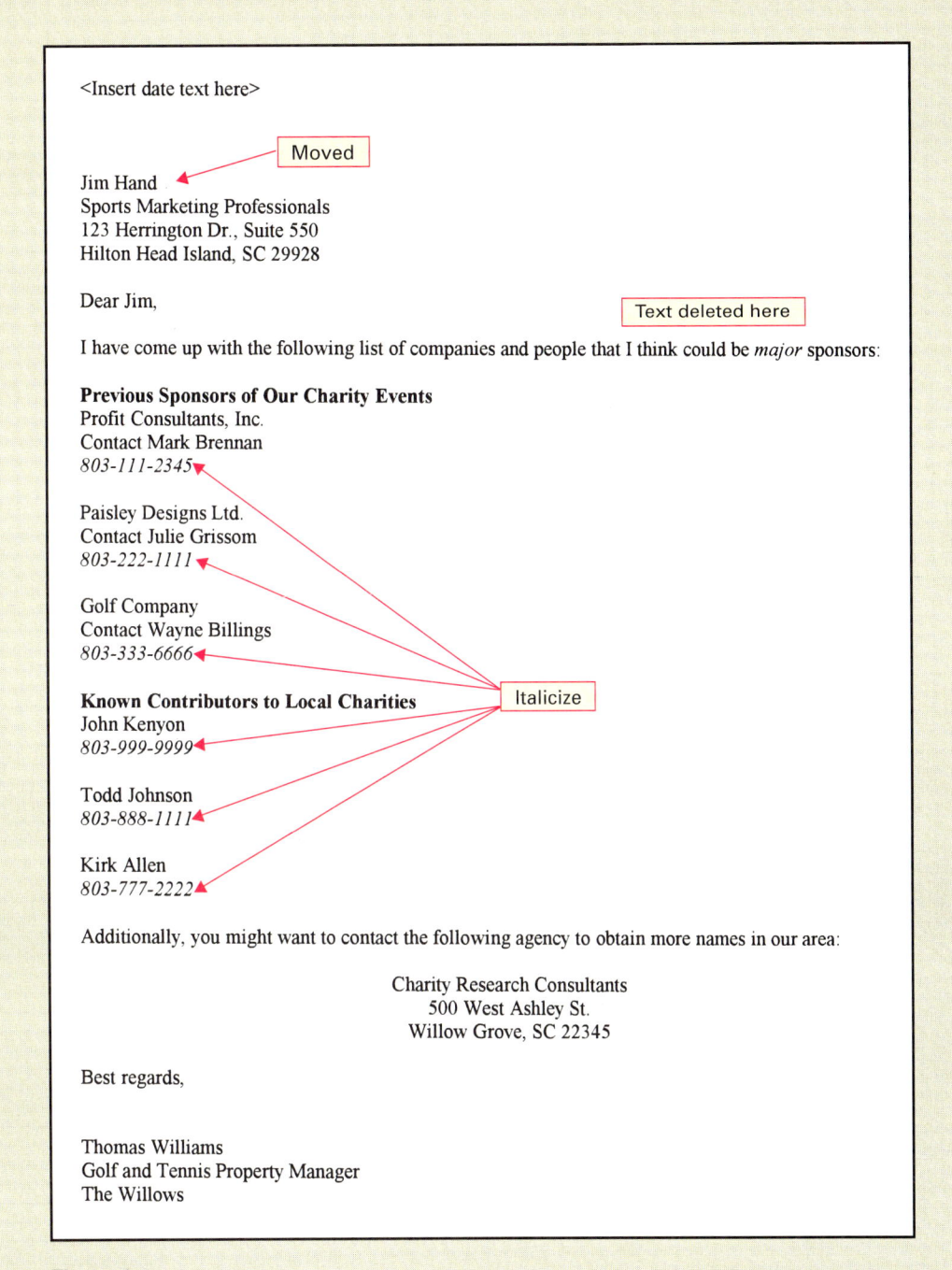

Jim Hand ← Moved
Sports Marketing Professionals
123 Herrington Dr., Suite 550
Hilton Head Island, SC 29928

Dear Jim,   Text deleted here

I have come up with the following list of companies and people that I think could be *major* sponsors:

Previous Sponsors of Our Charity Events
Profit Consultants, Inc.
Contact Mark Brennan
803-111-2345

Paisley Designs Ltd.
Contact Julie Grissom
803-222-1111

Golf Company
Contact Wayne Billings
803-333-6666

Known Contributors to Local Charities   ← Italicize
John Kenyon
803-999-9999

Todd Johnson
803-888-1111

Kirk Allen
803-777-2222

Additionally, you might want to contact the following agency to obtain more names in our area:

Charity Research Consultants
500 West Ashley St.
Willow Grove, SC 22345

Best regards,

Thomas Williams
Golf and Tennis Property Manager
The Willows

Figure 2.4

2. Creating a List of Web Sites

Mr. Williams wants you to spend some time on the Web exploring sites that have information about golf clubs and then give him the addresses of the five most informative sites. You will use a memo template to create a memo listing the sites and summarizing them (see Figure 2.5).

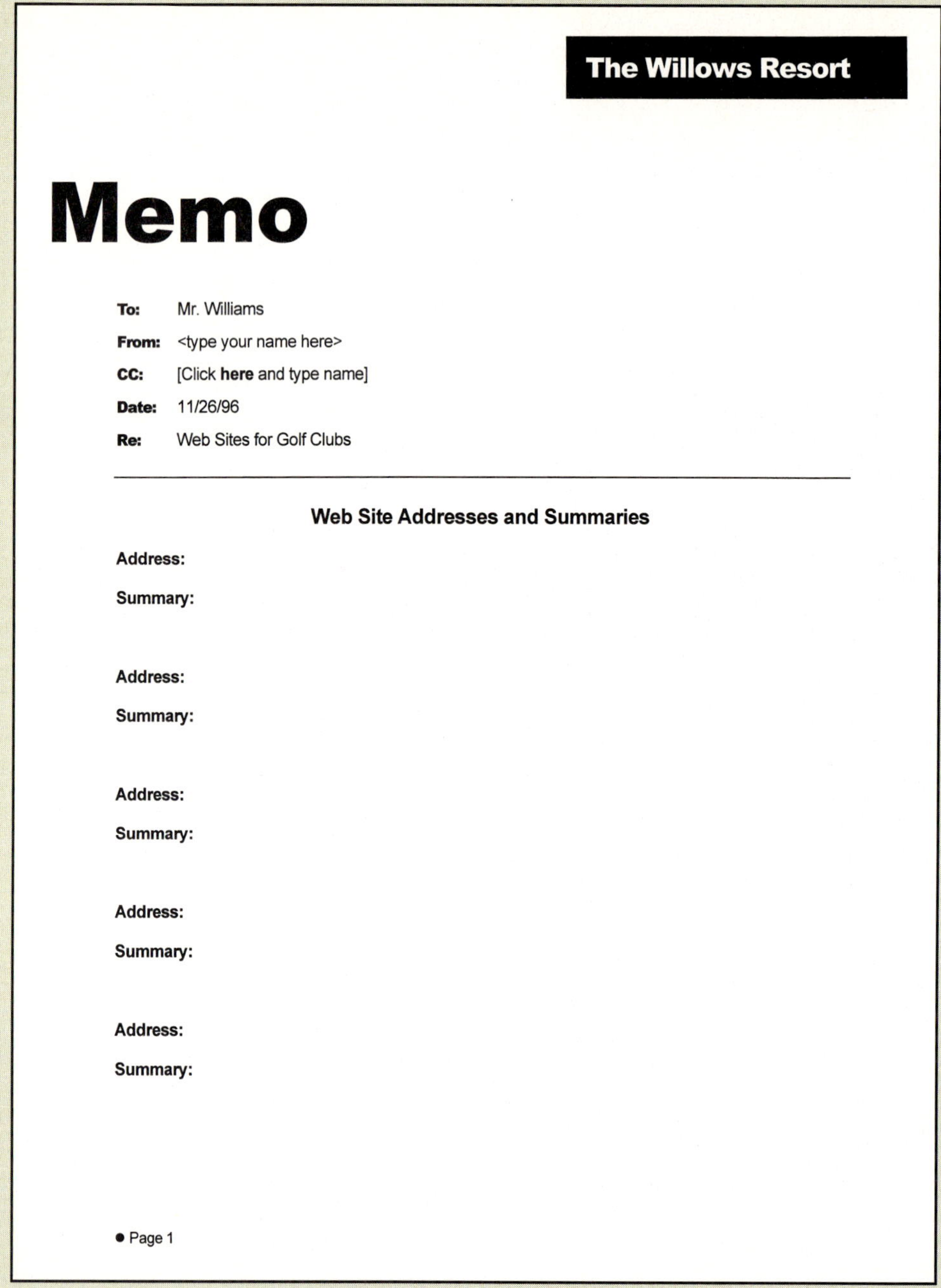

The Willows Resort

Memo

To: Mr. Williams
From: <type your name here>
CC: [Click here and type name]
Date: 11/26/96
Re: Web Sites for Golf Clubs

Web Site Addresses and Summaries

Address:

Summary:

Address:

Summary:

Address:

Summary:

Address:

Summary:

Address:

Summary:

• Page 1

Figure 2.5

1. Choose File, New.

2. Click the Memos tab.

3. Select *Professional Memo.dot* and click OK.

4. Select the text "Company Name Here" and type **The Willows Resort**.

5. Click beside "To:" and type **Mr. Williams**.

6. Click beside "From:" and type your name.

7. Click beside "Re:" and type **Web Sites for Golf Clubs**.

8. Delete all the text below the horizontal line.

9. Type the title **Web Site Addresses and Summaries**.

10. Type **Address:** and press Enter. Type **Summary:** and press Enter twice.

11. Copy the two lines typed in Step 3 and paste them four times.

12. Center the title and make it 12-point bold.

13. Fill in the addresses and summary with the information you obtain from the Web, making the Web addresses italic.

14. View the file in Page Layout view to see how much space is unused at the bottom of the page. If the text isn't centered under the horizontal line, move the text down by pressing Enter to insert blank lines after the horizontal line.

15. Save the file as *Golf Clubs.doc* and close the file.

Assignments

1. Creating an Announcement

Create the announcement shown in Figure 2.6. Use the bold and italic attributes shown and use fonts that appeal to you if you don't have fonts similar to those shown in the figure. Be sure to center text as shown in the figure.

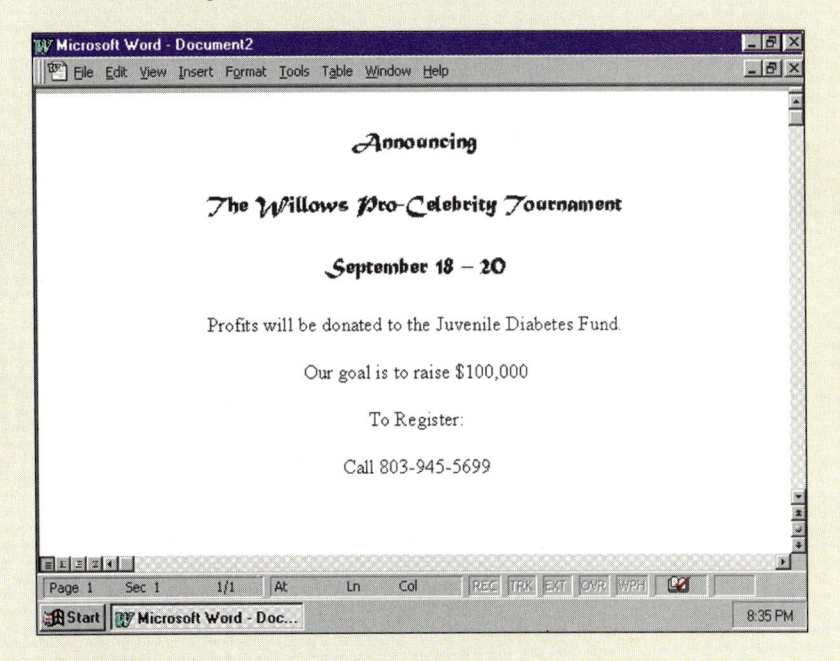

Figure 2.6

2. Modifying the Announcement

Make the changes shown in Figure 2.7. Search the Web to find an appropriate address to use in the last line of the announcement.

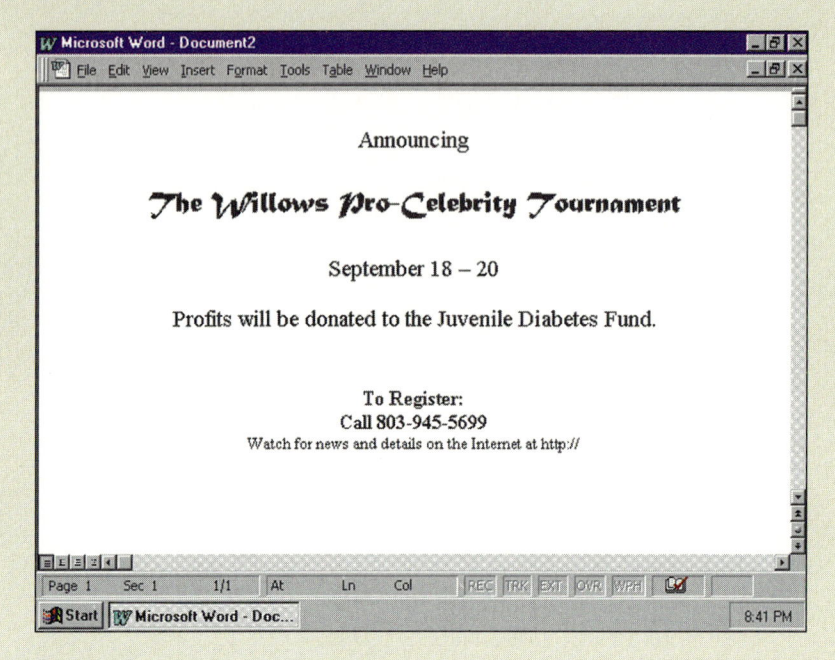

Figure 2.7

PROJECT 3

Using Advanced Formatting Features

In the first two projects, you worked with a simple document that used character formatting and alignment. In this project, you will use formatting techniques that produce a more sophisticated document that has multiple columns, a graphic, bulleted lists, indented paragraphs, styles, and more. You'll be out of breath when you finish this one!

Objectives

After completing this project, you will be able to:

- ➤ Set up the page
- ➤ Create columns
- ➤ Insert and manipulate a graphic
- ➤ Format paragraphs
- ➤ Work with tabs
- ➤ Apply and modify styles
- ➤ Create bulleted and numbered lists
- ➤ Apply borders and shading

The Challenge

The Willows needs a three-panel brochure for the summer camp program. The brochure gives the dates, ages, and costs; describes the facilities and excursions; lists items to bring; and provides directions for registering.

The Solution

You will format a document and set up the document to print across the long side of the paper in three columns. You will insert a graphic, modify and apply styles, create the bulleted and numbered lists, and format the brochure shown in Figure 3.1.

Camp Willows

Hit the bull's eye this summer at Camp Willows. You'll have plenty to say in that first school essay about what you did this summer - horseback riding, go-kart racing, hayrides, volleyball tournaments, fishing, jet-skiing, bicycling, golfing, camp fires, and more! The fun never stops at Camp Willows.

Space is limited, so make your reservations early. Each camp session is limited to 50 campers and 10 camp counselors - a maximum of five campers and one counselor per bungalow.

Camp Sessions

Date: June 9 - 13
Ages: 10 – 12
Cost: $500

Date: July 14 - 18
Ages: 13 – 15
Cost: $600

Date: August 4 - 8
Ages: 6 – 9
Cost: $400

Facilities

Campers stay in the Willow Beach Bungalows and all the facilities of The Willows are available for the campers' enjoyment.

Wild Hare Expo
Video games and electronic entertainment

Olympia Fitness Center
Free weights, exercise machines, saunas, whirlpools, indoor Olympic-size pool

Bye Bye Birdie and The Eagle's Nest
Two challenging miniature golf courses

Golf and Tennis
Three 18-hole PGA courses, two driving ranges, five putting greens, and ten tennis courses

Willow Pond Riding Stables
Guided horseback tours through open fields and wonderful wooded areas

Little Tree Playland
Playground equipment for younger children

Tree Top Water Park
Wave pool, water slides, swimming pools, diving pool

The Beach
White sand and the Board Walk, beach volleyball, jet skiing, water skiing

Excursions

Monday and Friday are camp excursion days. Campers are taken to outlying attractions that are located close to The Willows. Some excursions have an additional cost. Transportation is provided by hotel vans. Each camper may choose from the following excursions:

Cameron Caverns Tour
Cameron Caverns Tour is a 1 hour tour by an experienced guide through the complex maze of Cameron Caverns.

Haunted House Wax Museum
Nationally famous sculptor, Mark Hanson, fills the haunted house with life-like (and death-like) figures of your favorite ghosts and goblins.

Paul Bunyan's Action Park
Fun is guaranteed at Paul Bunyan's Action Park where you can race go-karts, play laser tag, ride bumper boats, ride the wild river, and test your batting skills in the cages.
   Additional Cost $30

Carolina Science Center
Explore technology at work today. Many hands on exhibits demonstrate the fundamentals of aviation, space flight, genetics, ecology, computers, and more.

Spring Mill Park
Visit the historic gristmill, the apothecary, the train station, and other restored buildings in Spring Mill Park, one of the first settlements in the state.

Hannibal Lake
Hannibal Lake offers some of the best crappie fishing in the state. Anglers will also find largemouth bass, bluegill, and a variety of catfish.
   Fishing license.. $11

What To Bring

Pack up your sense of adventure and these necessities:

- t-shirts and shorts
- tennis shoes
- a light jacket or sweatshirt
- socks and underwear
- bathing suit
- sunscreen and toiletries
- flashlight and batteries

How To Register

Follow these easy steps:

1. Fill out the enclosed registration.
2. Enclose a $100 non-refundable deposit.
3. Mail at least 60 days in advance.

Mail Your Registration Today!

Figure 3.1

The Setup

So that your screen will match the illustrations and the tasks in this project will function as described, make sure that the Word 97 settings listed in Table 3.1 are selected on your computer.

Table 3.1 Word 97 Settings.

Location	Make these settings:
View, Toolbars	Deselect all toolbars except the Standard and Formatting toolbars
View	Select the Ruler option and Page Layout view
Standard toolbar	Deselect any buttons that are selected and set Zoom to 100%
Tools, Options, View	Select the Vertical ruler option, the Horizontal scroll bar option, and the Vertical scroll bar option
Tools, Options, Edit	Select the Typing replaces selection option; deselect the Drag-and-drop text editing option; and select the option When selecting, automatically select entire word
Tools, Options, Spelling & Grammar	Select the Check spelling as you type and Check Grammar as you type options

Setting Up the Page

When you create a new document, Word chooses the setup options, including the margins, paper size, and orientation. The default margins are 1 for the top and bottom and 1.25" for the left and right. The paper size is 8½" by 11", and the *orientation* is portrait. Sometimes the defaults don't meet your needs, and you must change them.

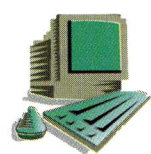

TASK 1: TO CHANGE MARGINS AND ORIENTATION:

1 Click the Open button.

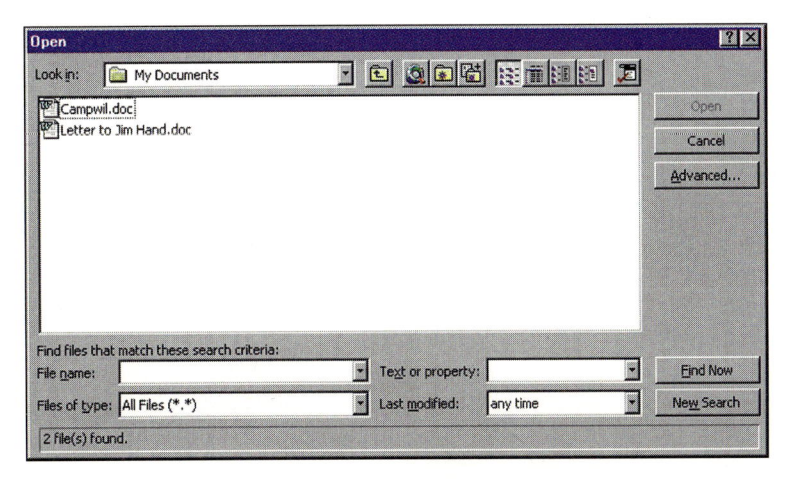

2 Change the Look in folder, if necessary, and then double-click *Campwil.doc*.

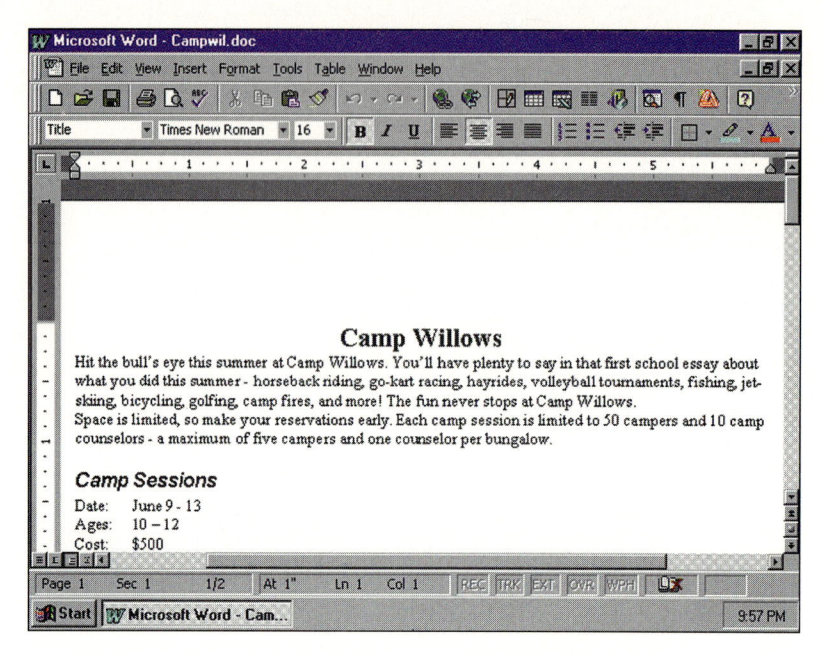

3 Choose File, Page Setup, and then click the Margins page tab, if necessary.

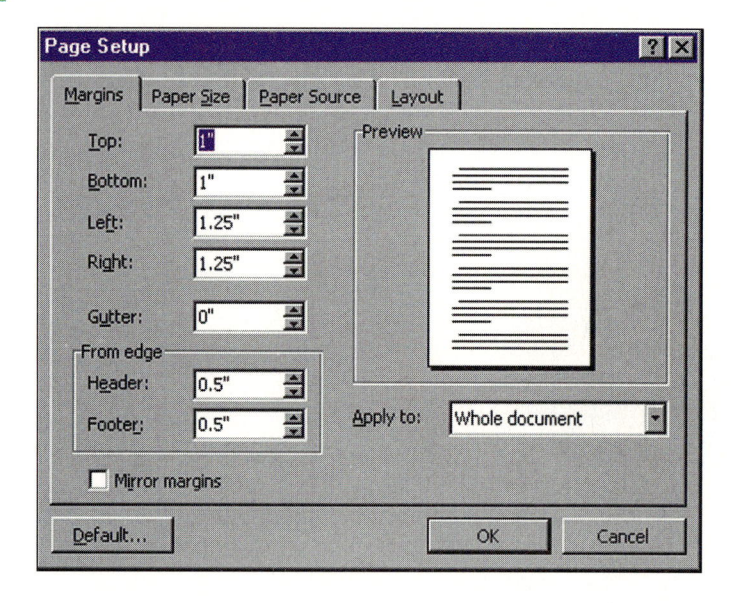

4 Change all margins to .5".

Project 3: Using Advanced Formatting Features **WORD-75**

5 Click the Paper Size page tab.

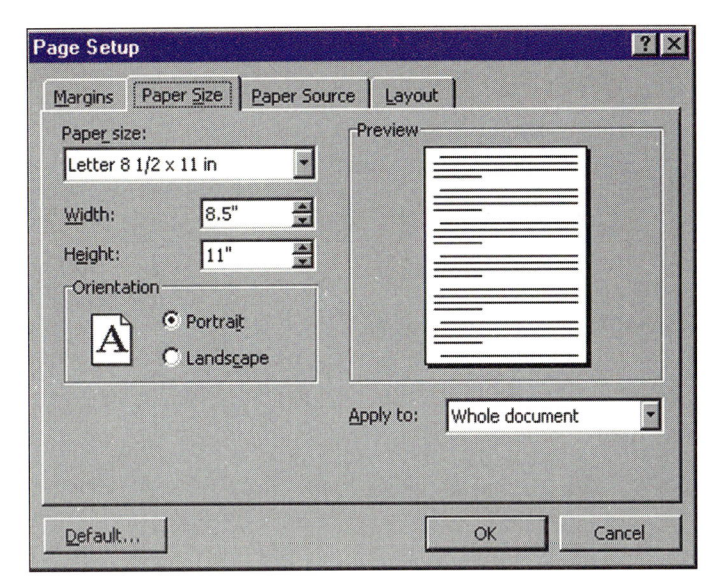

6 Select Landscape and click OK.
The dialog box closes.

Creating Columns

Word 97 can create multiple newspaper columns of equal or unequal widths. The text in newspaper columns flows from one column to the next when a column fills up.

TASK 2: TO CREATE THREE NEWSPAPER COLUMNS:

1 Choose Format.

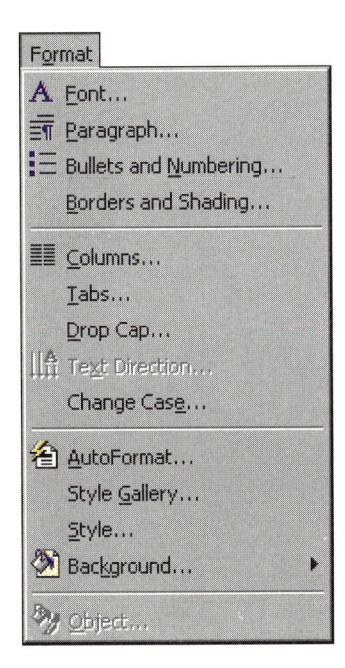

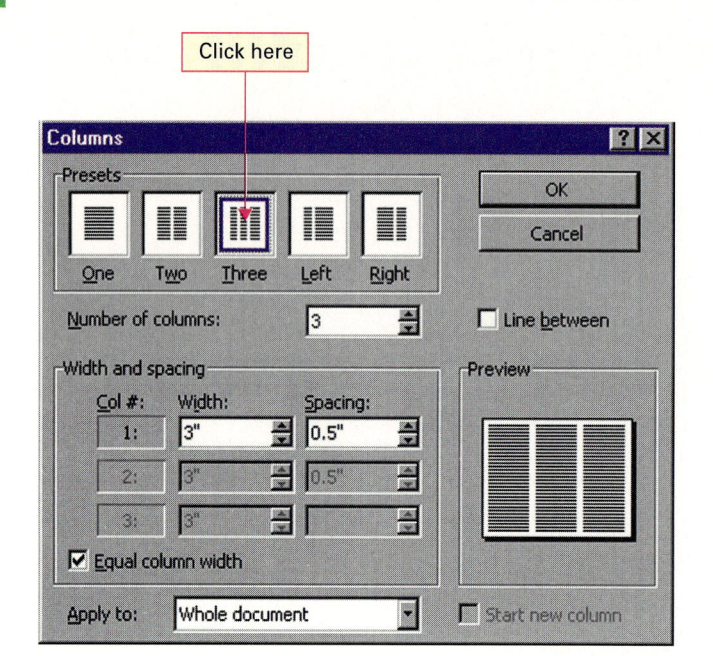

2 Choose Columns and click the Presets Three icon.

Click here

3 Click OK.
The dialog box closes.

4 Click the Print Preview button, view the new layout, and click the Close button.

> **Tip** To break a column before it fills up, choose Insert, Break, Column Break, OK.

Inserting and Manipulating a Graphic

Graphics add interest to a document, and Word 97 provides a Clip Gallery of graphics, called *clip art*, for you to use.

Project 3: Using Advanced Formatting Features   **WORD-77**

TASK 3: TO INSERT A GRAPHIC:

1 Choose Insert, Picture.

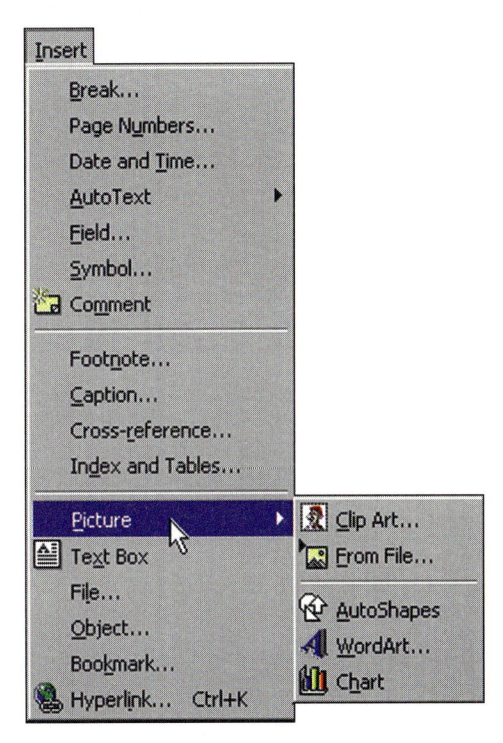

2 Choose Clip Art, choose OK if the "Additional Clips are Available on CD-ROM" message appears, and click the Clip Art page tab if necessary.

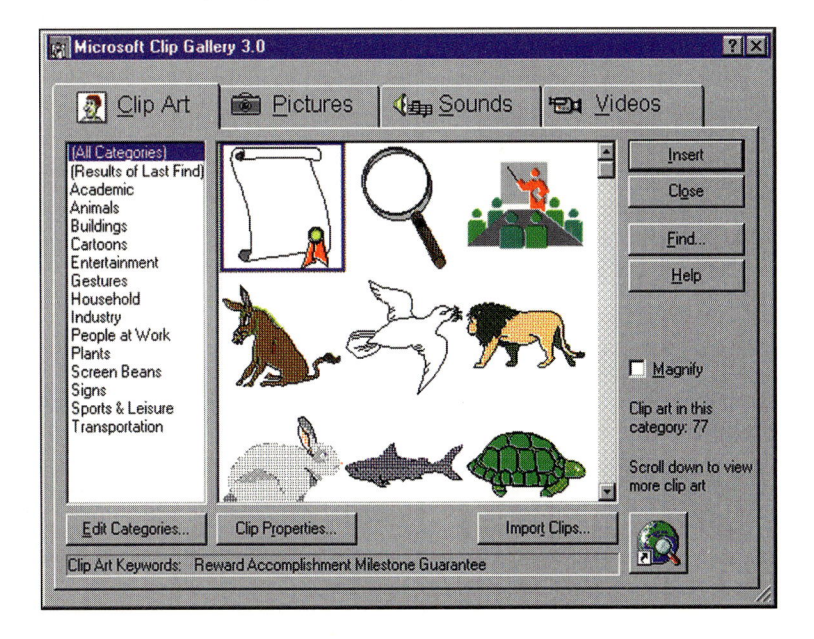

3 Click Sports & Leisure.

4 Click the graphic of the bull's eye if it isn't selected and click Insert.

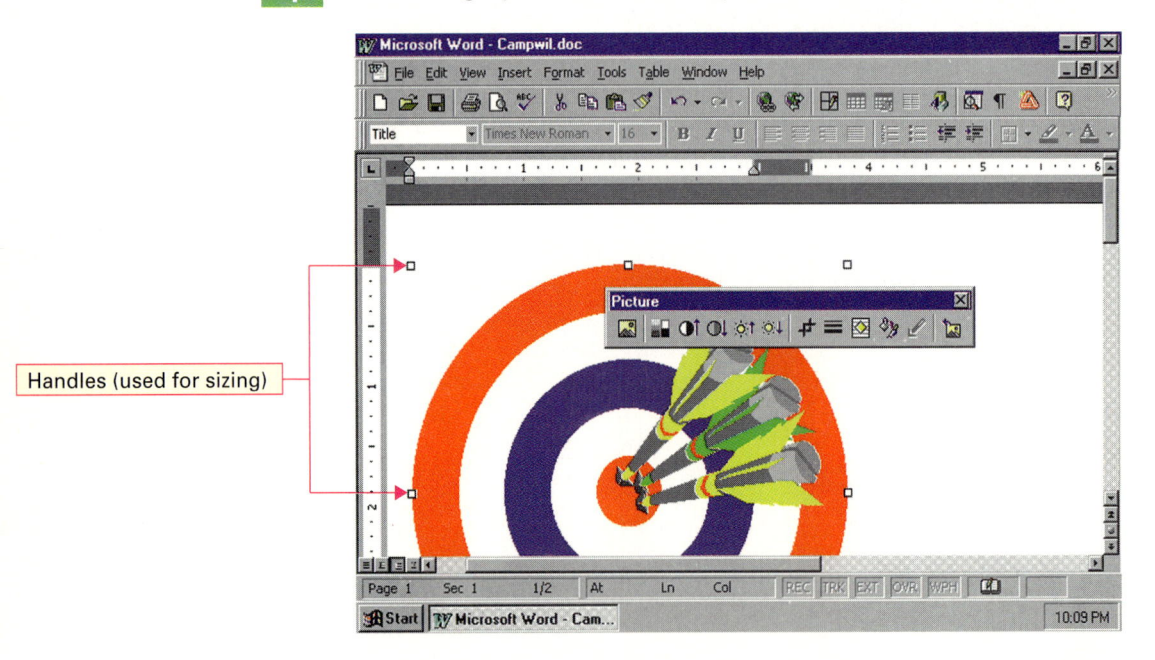

Handles (used for sizing)

The graphic inserted in the document is too large for the brochure. Also, you need to position it at the top of the first column. This looks to me like an excellent opportunity to practice manipulating graphics.

Project 3: Using Advanced Formatting Features WORD-79

TASK 4: TO SIZE AND MOVE A GRAPHIC:

1 Click the down arrow in the vertical scroll bar until you can see the bottom of the graphic.

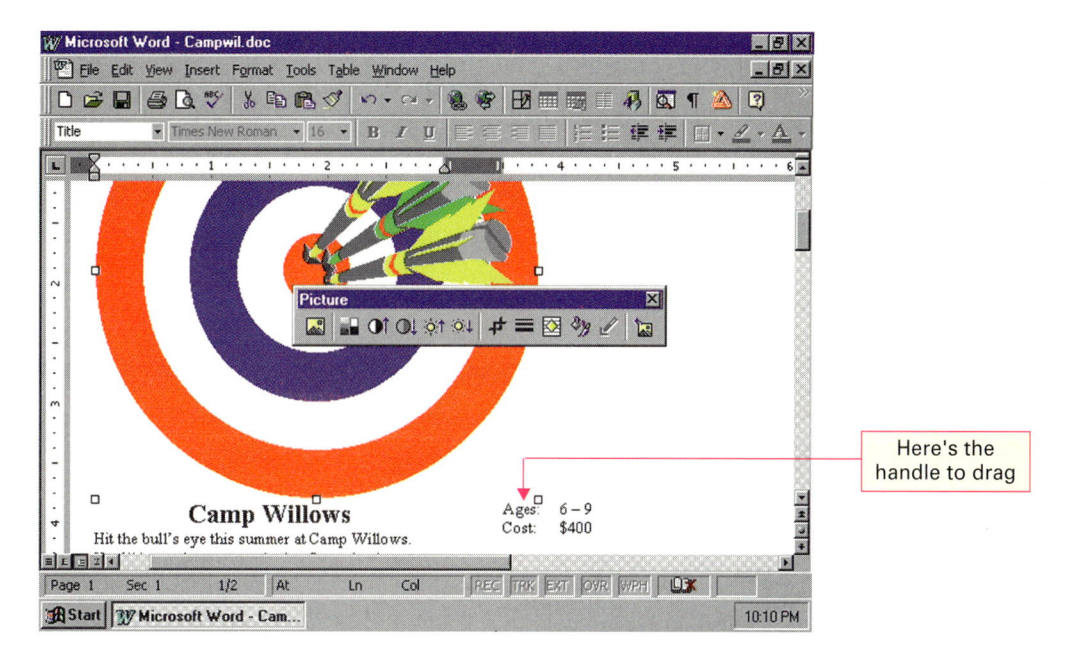

Here's the handle to drag

2 Drag the handle on the lower-right corner up and to the left until the graphic is about 1" wide.

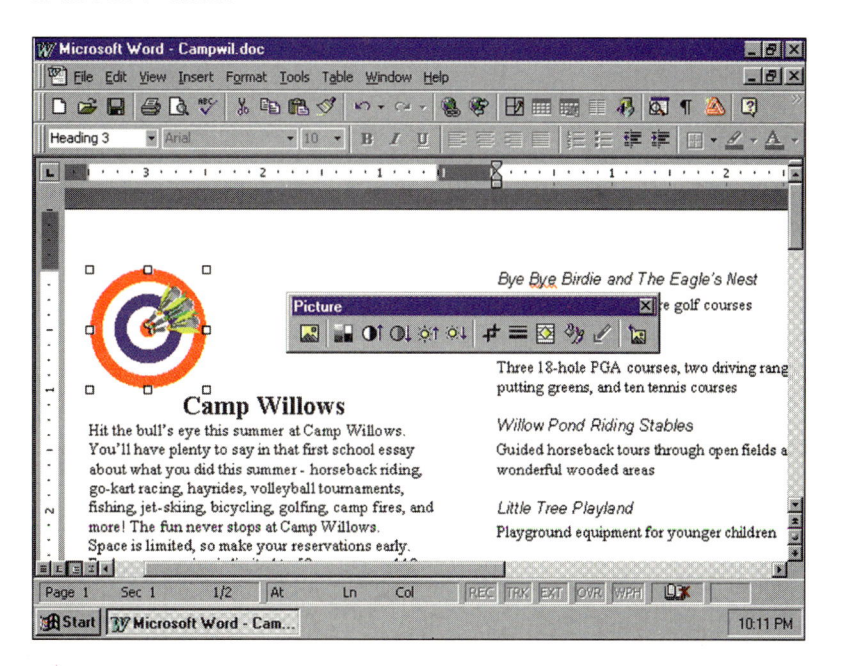

Tip Dragging a corner handle of a graphic keeps the graphic in proportion.

3 Click the up arrow in the vertical scroll bar to scroll to the top of the document, if necessary, and close the Picture palette.

4 Point to the middle of the graphic.
The mouse pointer changes to a four-headed arrow.

5 Drag the graphic to the center of the column.

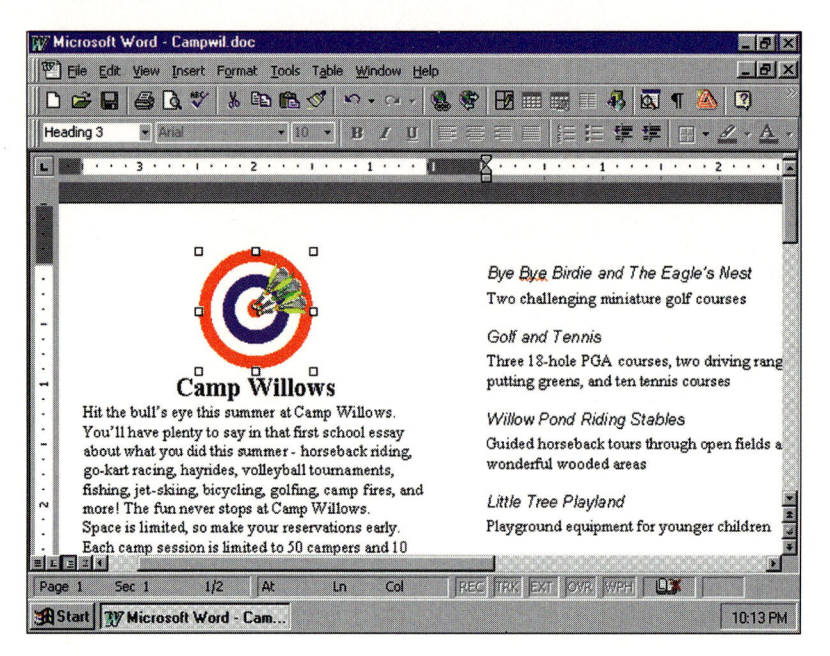

Formatting Paragraphs

In default paragraphs, all the lines line up with the left margin, are single-spaced, and have no spacing before or after them. By formatting a paragraph, you can indent the first line, indent all the lines of a paragraph on the left or right, change the line spacing, and add spacing before or after the paragraph.

Project 3: Using Advanced Formatting Features   WORD-81

TASK 5: TO INDENT THE FIRST LINE OF A PARAGRAPH AND ADD SPACING UNDER THE PARAGRAPH:

1 Click anywhere in the paragraph that begins "Hit the bull's eye...."

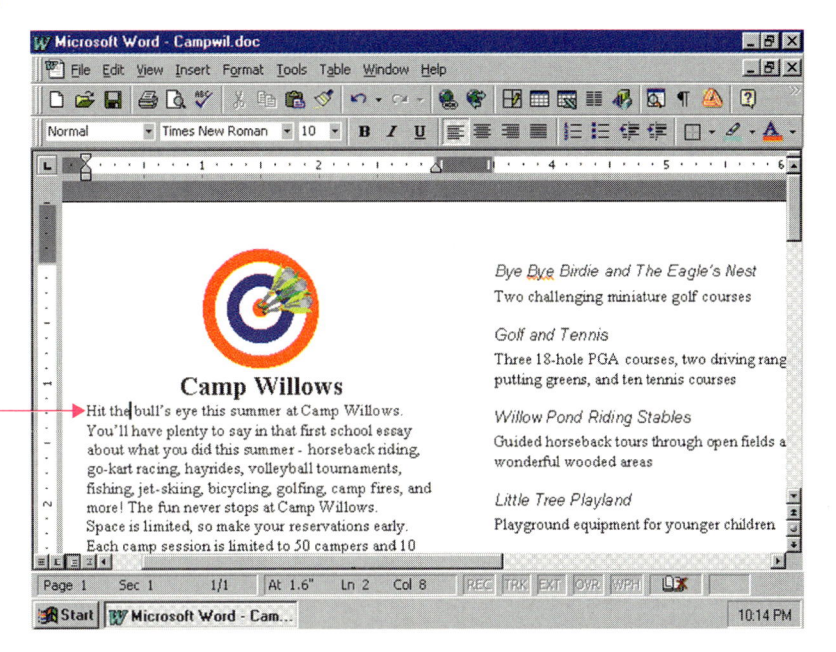

The clicked paragraph

2 Choose Format.

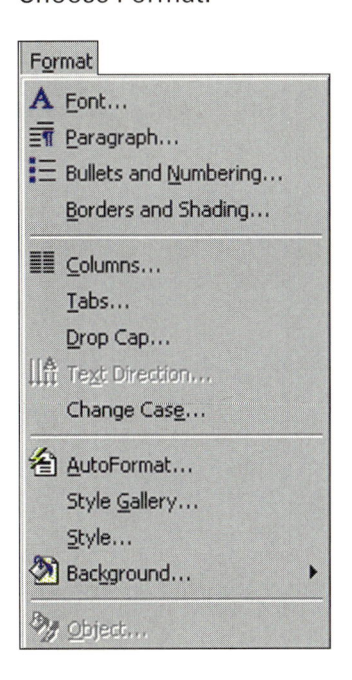

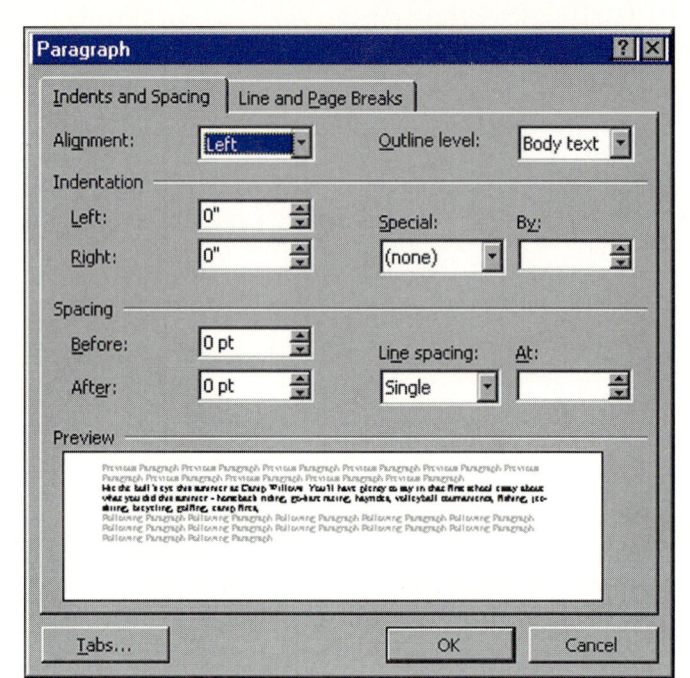

3. Choose Paragraph and click the Indents and Spacing tab if necessary.

4. Click the down arrow in the Special text box.
A drop-down list displays.

5. Click First Line.
The Special text box displays your choice.

6. Click the down arrow in the By spinner box until the measurement is 0.3".
Click the up arrow in the After spinner box until the measurement is 6 pt.

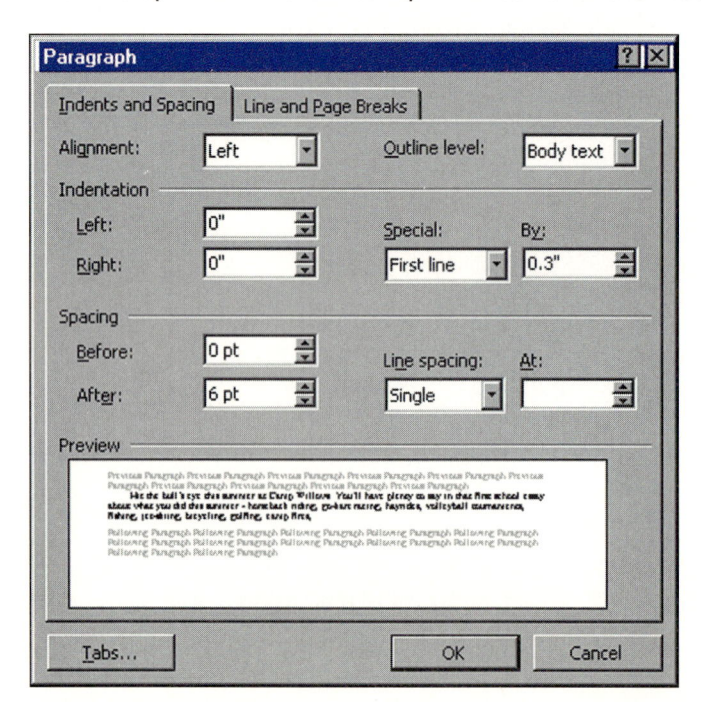

7 Click OK.
The dialog box closes.

8 Click anywhere in the paragraph that begins "Space is limited...."

9 Choose Format, Paragraph.
The Paragraph dialog box displays.

10 Click the down arrow in the Special text box and click First Line. Then click the down arrow in the By spinner box until the measurement is 0.3".

11 Click OK.
The two changed paragraphs should look like those in Figure 3.1.

Working with Tabs

When you want text within a paragraph to align differently, you can use *tabs*. They are shown as markers on the ruler. Table 3.2 describes the types of tabs available in Word 97.

Table 3.2   Types of Tabs

Type	Symbol	Description
Left	⌞	Aligns text on the left.
Center	⊥	Centers text on the tab stop.
Right	⌟	Aligns text on the right.
Decimal	⊥·	Aligns text on the decimal.
Bar	|	Inserts a vertical bar at the tab stop.
Leader		Displays characters, such as periods, before the tab. Any type of tab can have a leader.

TASK 6: TO SET A TAB:

1 Select all the text under the "Camp Sessions" heading.

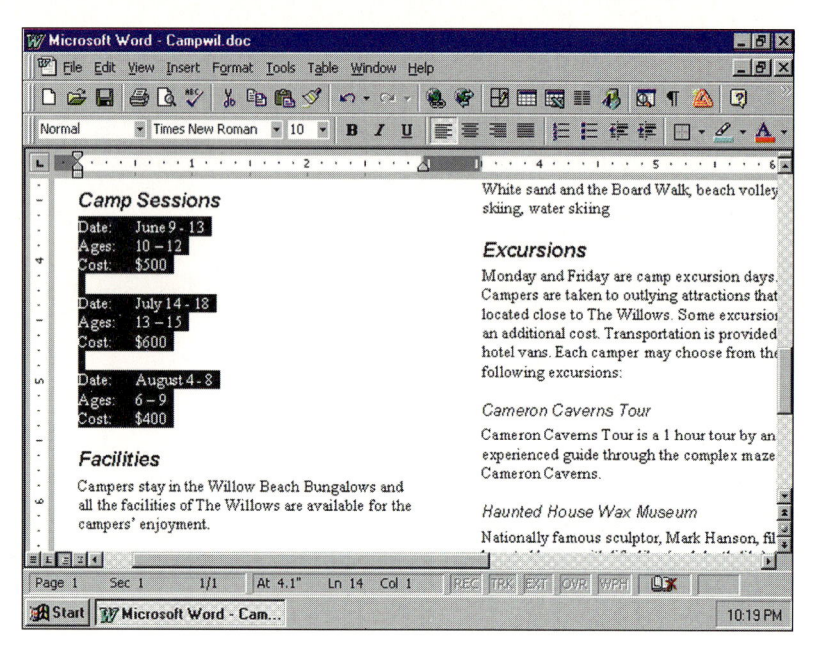

2 Click the dot in the ruler that is just to the left of the half-inch mark.

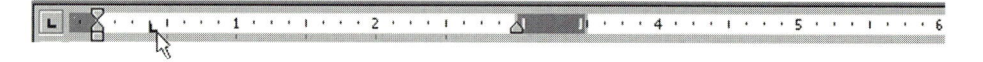

3 Scroll to the top of the third column by clicking the right arrow in the horizontal scroll bar and then clicking the up arrow in the vertical scroll bar.

4 Click after the period in "...in the cages." in the third column and then press ENTER.

5 Click the tab selector button until the right tab button displays.

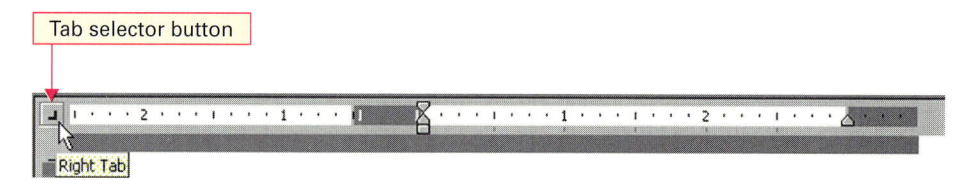

Tab selector button

6 Click the second dot to the right of the 2½" mark on the ruler.

Project 3: Using Advanced Formatting Features   WORD-85

7 Type **Additional cost**, press TAB, and type **$30**.

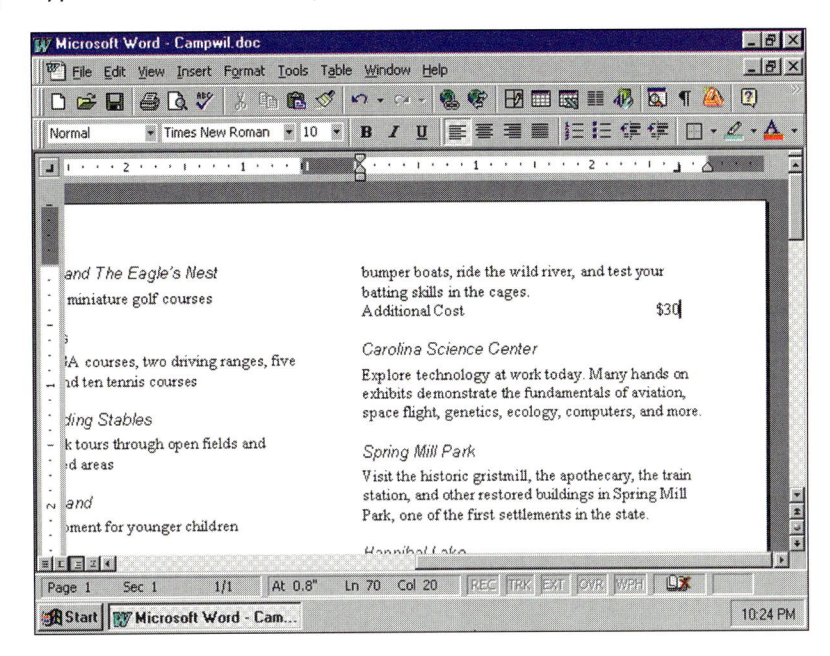

8 Choose Format, Tabs.

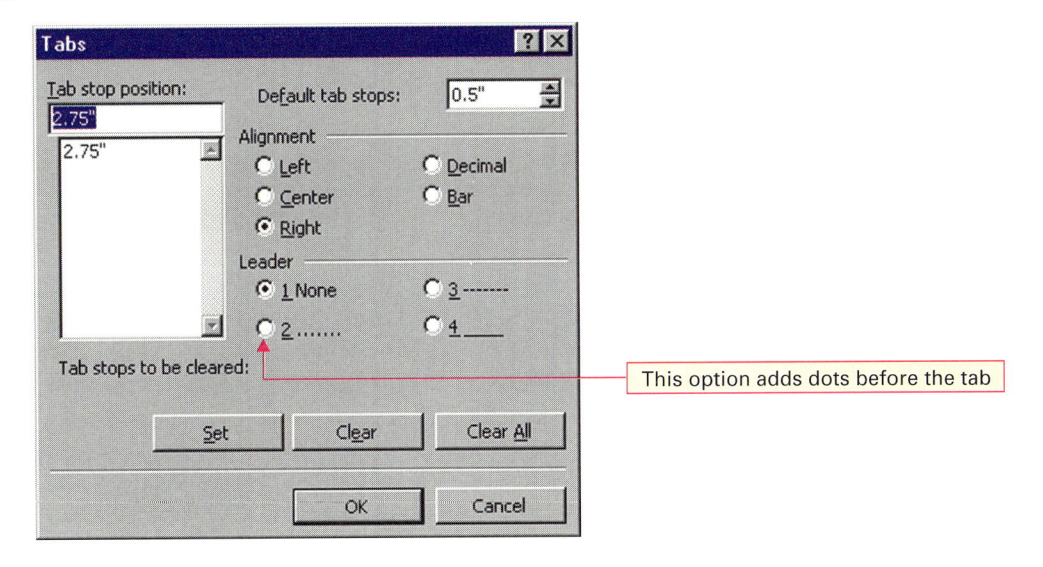

This option adds dots before the tab

9 Select 2 under Leader.

10 Click OK.

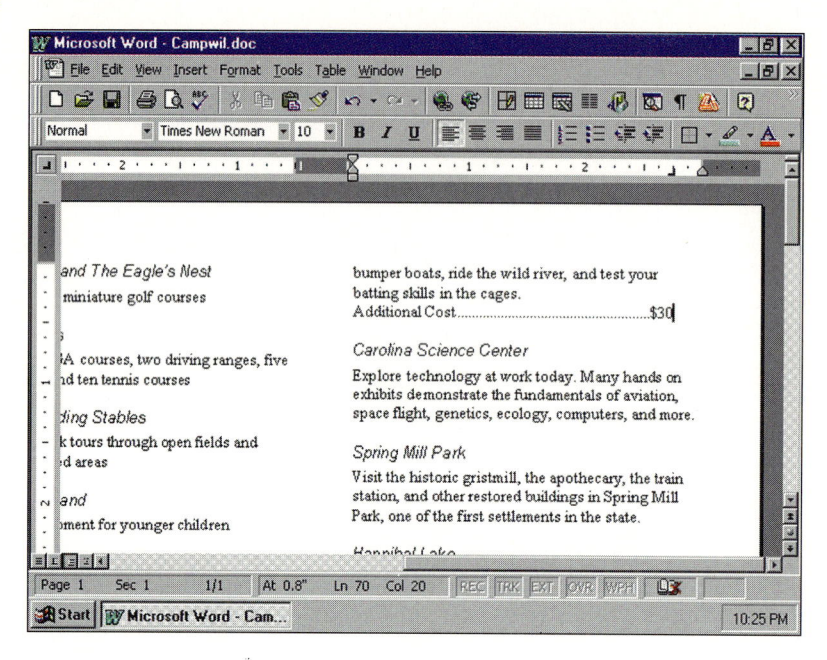

11 Click after the period in "...a variety of catfish." in the third column and press ENTER. A new, blank line is created.

12 Ensure that the tab selector button displays the right tab and click the second dot to the right of the 2½" mark on the ruler.

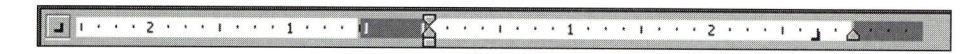

13 Type **Fishing license**, press TAB, and type **$11**.

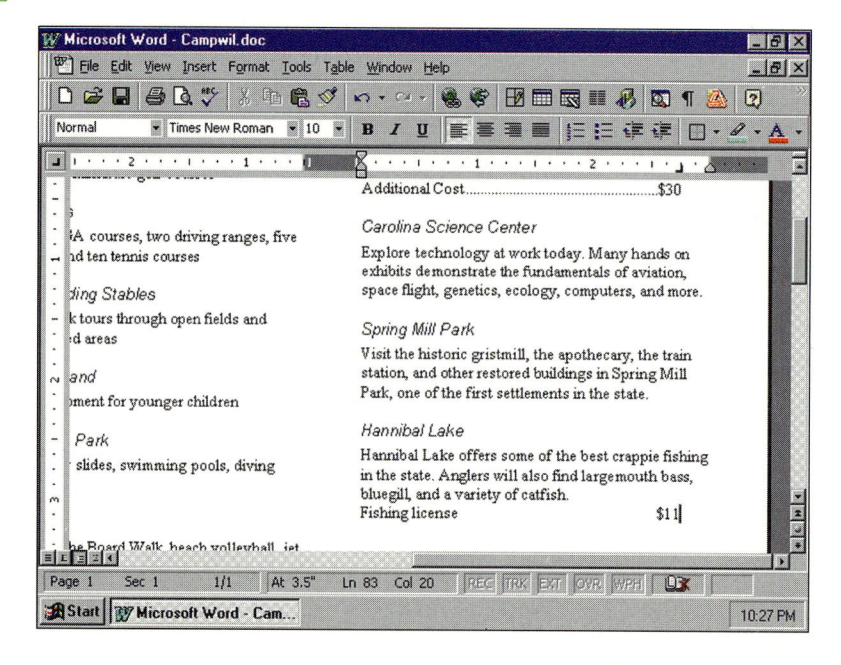

Project 3: Using Advanced Formatting Features   WORD-87

14 Choose Format, Tabs and select 2 under Leader again.

15 Click OK.

16 Press ENTER.
The insertion point moves to the next line.

Applying and Modifying Styles

A *style* is a collection of format settings that are grouped together and given a name. When you apply a style to a paragraph, the text of the paragraph takes on all the formatting stored in the style.

TASK 7: TO APPLY A STYLE:

1 Ensure the insertion point is on the line after "Fishing license..." and type **What To Bring**.

2 Press ENTER, type **Pack up your sense of adventure and these necessities:** and press ENTER.

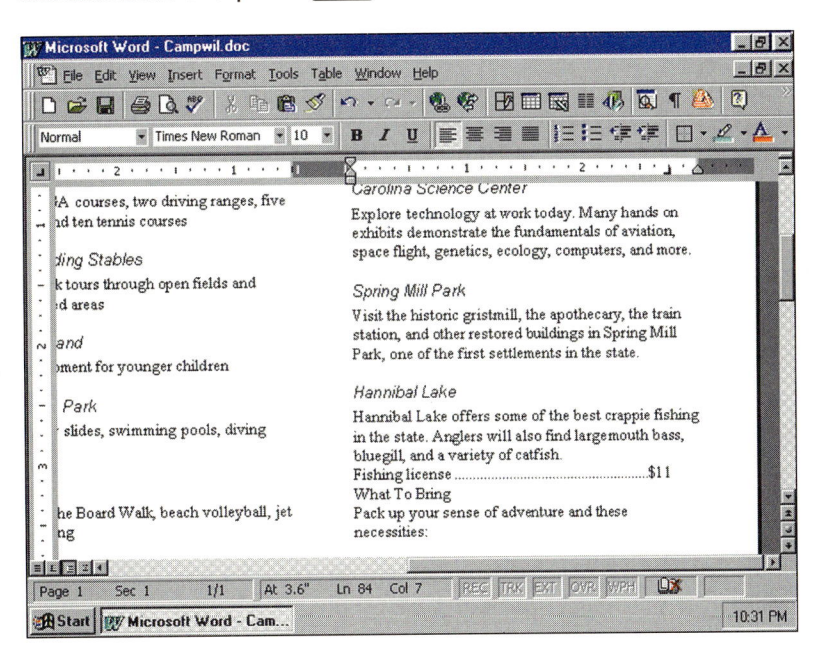

3 Type the list of items to bring, as in:

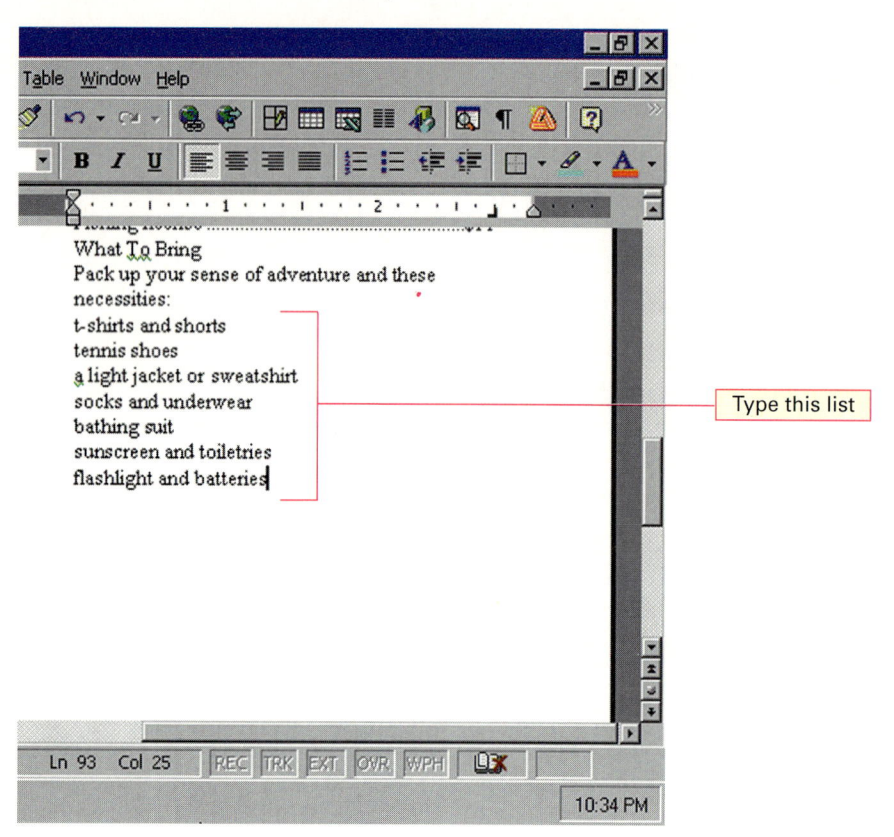

Type this list

4 Click anywhere in the text "What To Bring."

5 Click the down arrow in the Style list box in the Formatting toolbar.

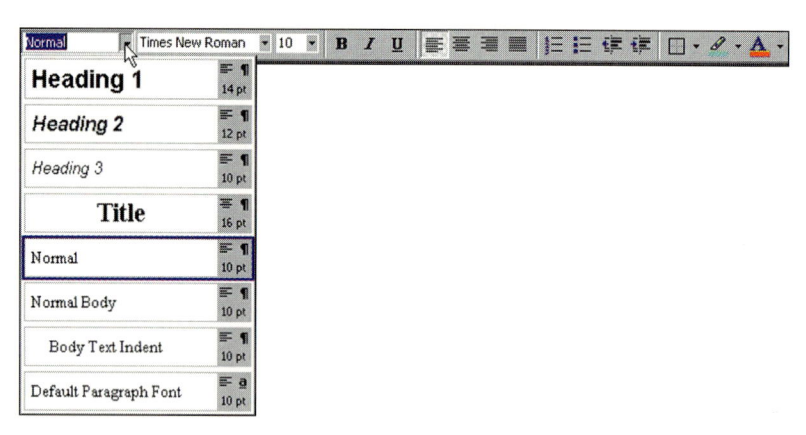

6 Click Heading 2.

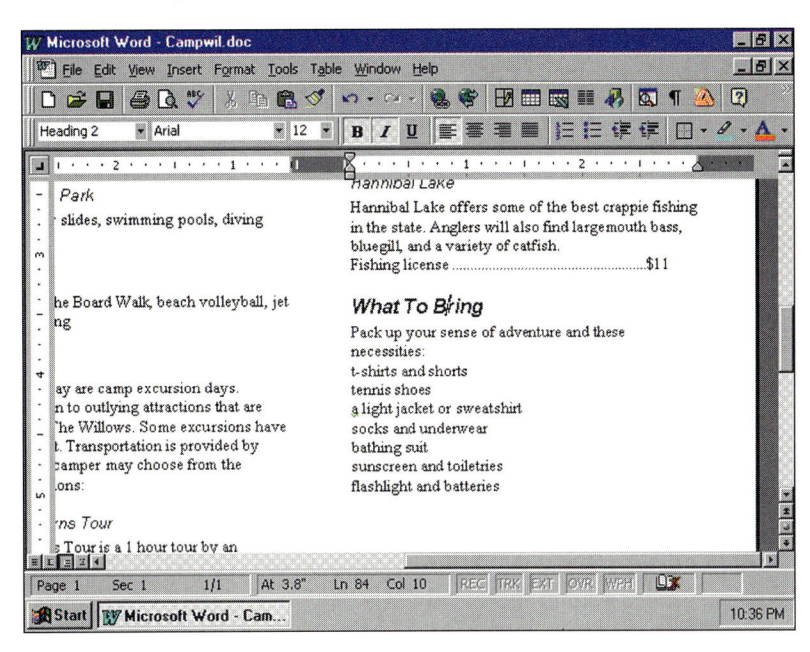

7 Click the insertion point anywhere in the paragraph that begins "Pack up your..."

8 Click the down arrow in the Style list box and click Normal Body.
You won't notice any change in the text when you complete this step; you'll just have to trust Word on this one.

In this document, the Normal Body style is used for paragraphs that follow Heading 2 styles. These paragraphs should have a first line indent and some space after them like the paragraphs you formatted at the top of the first column. Instead of formatting each paragraph individually, you can modify the Normal Body style, and the paragraphs that use the style will reflect the changes automatically—another example of how Word makes your life easier.

WORD-90

TASK 8: TO MODIFY A STYLE:

1 Choose Format, Style.

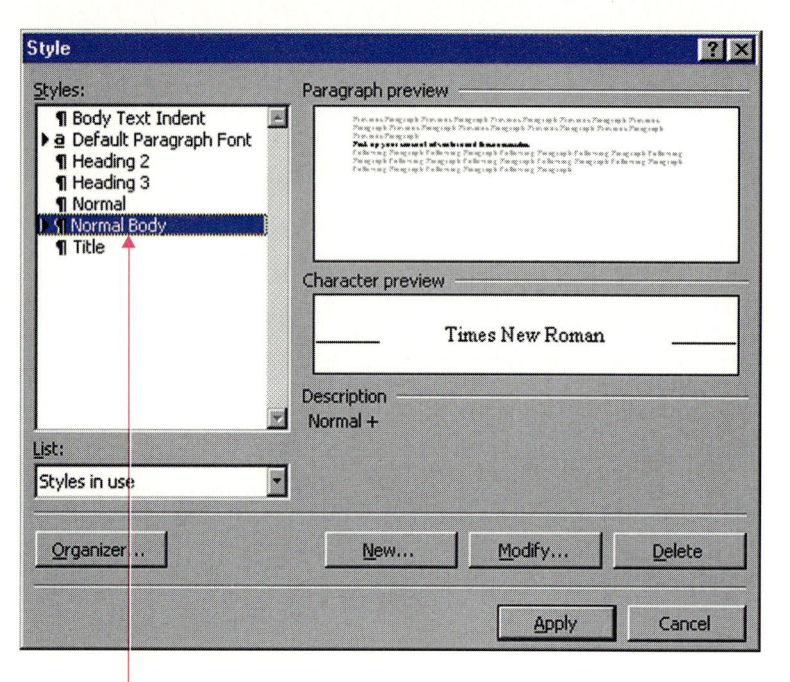

The style is selected because the insertion point is in a paragraph using that style

2 Click Modify.

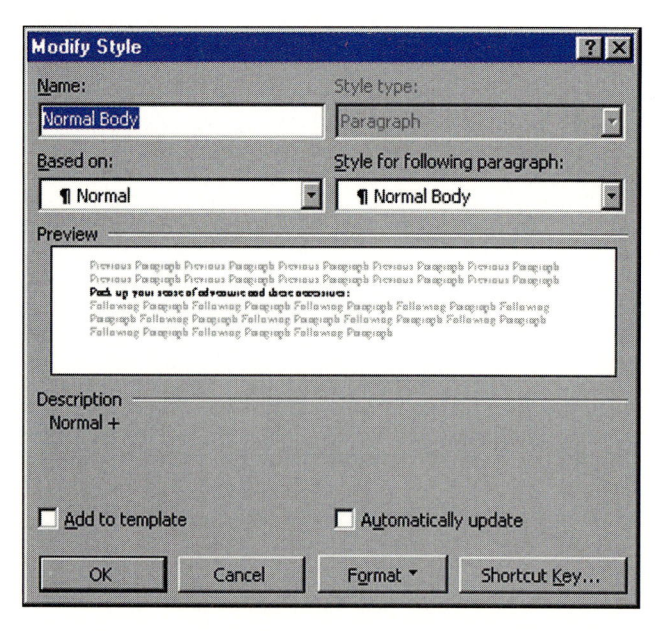

3 Click Format.

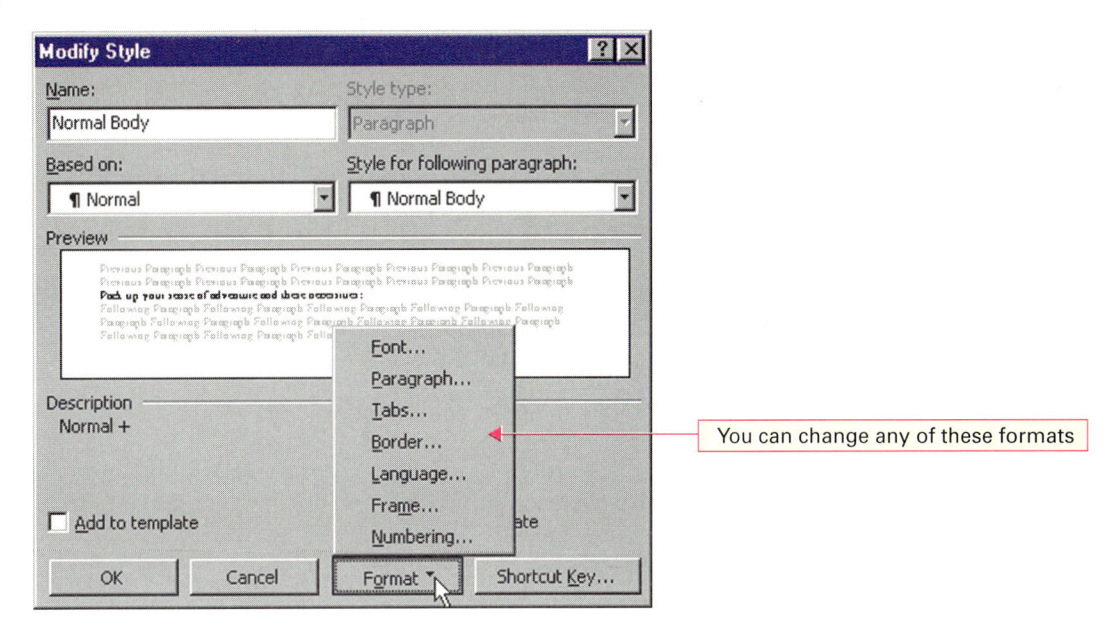

(Modify Style dialog box shown with Format menu open: Font..., Paragraph..., Tabs..., Border..., Language..., Frame..., Numbering...)

You can change any of these formats

4 Click Paragraph.
The Paragraph dialog box displays.

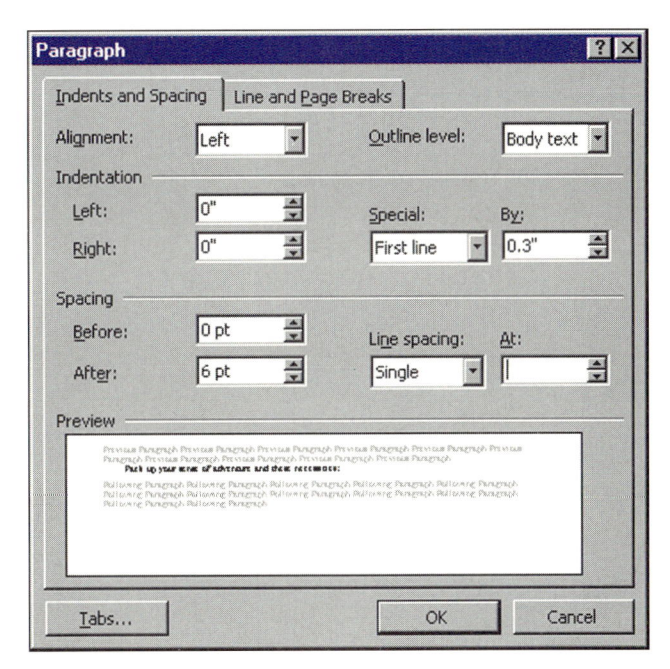

(Paragraph dialog box shown with Indents and Spacing tab active)

5 Under Specials, select First Line, specify 0.2" for the By option, and specify 6 pt for the After option.

6 Click OK.
The Modify Style dialog box redisplays.

7 Click OK.
The Style dialog box redisplays.

8 Click Close.

The modifications you made are applied to the paragraph that begins "Pack up your..." because you applied this style in the last task. The style is also applied to the next paragraph.

9 Click in the list that says "t-shirts and shorts" and apply the Normal style.

Creating Bulleted and Numbered Lists

To draw attention to a list, you can bullet the list or number it. A ***bullet*** is a symbol (usually a black circle) that precedes the text. Word 97 has two paragraph formats set up just for bulleting and numbering lists, and all you have to do is apply them.

> **Tip** Lists that have no particular order are usually bulleted rather than numbered.

TASK 9: TO CREATE A BULLETED LIST:

1 Select the text in the list under the "What To Bring" heading.

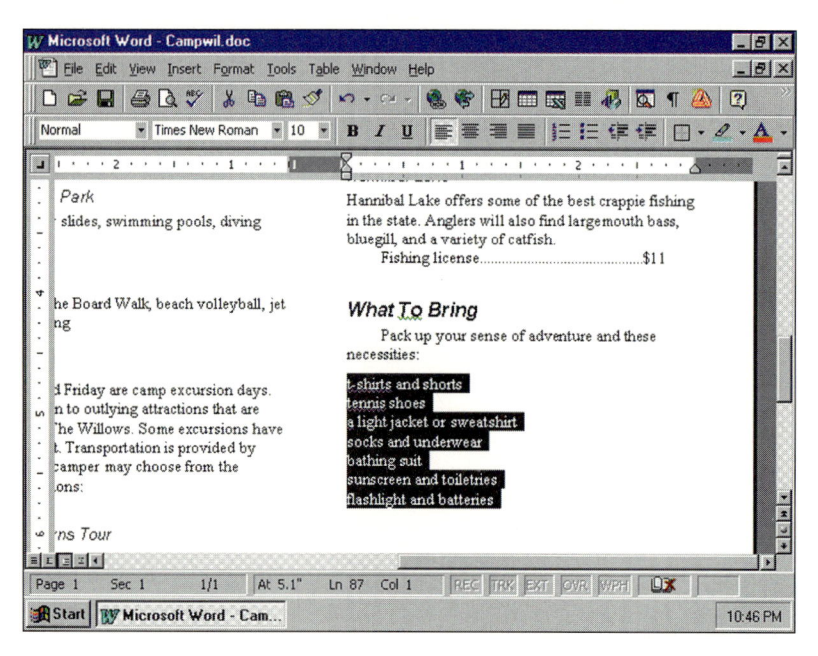

Project 3: Using Advanced Formatting Features   **WORD-93**

2 Click the Bullets button in the Formatting toolbar.

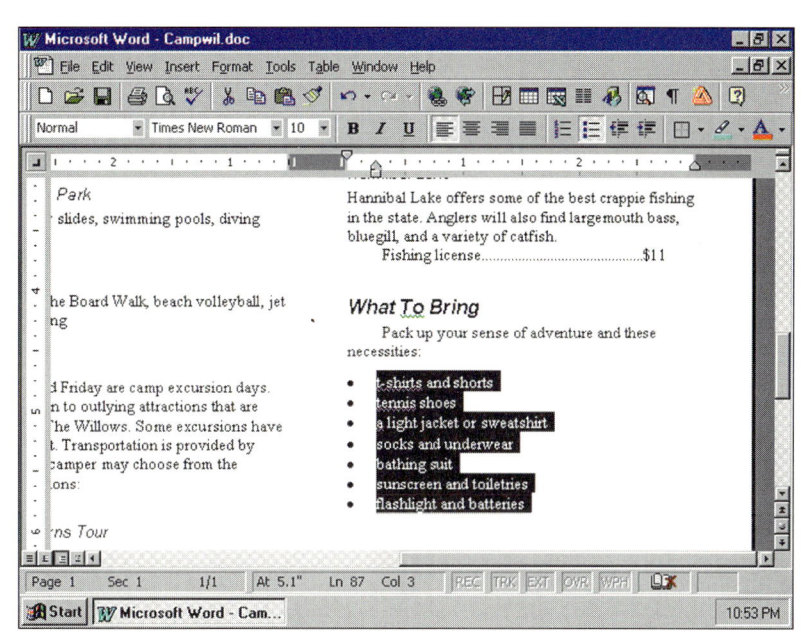

3 Click the Increase Indent button in the Formatting toolbar.

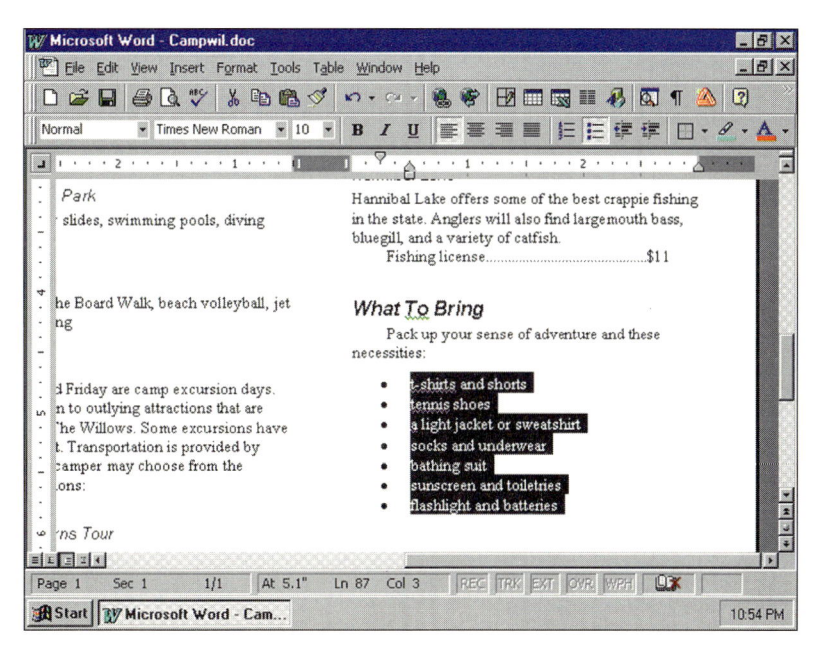

Tip If you don't like the bullet that Word automatically uses, choose Format, Bullets and Numbering to select a different bullet.

WORD-94

TASK 10: TO CREATE A NUMBERED LIST:

1 Click after "flashlight and batteries," press ENTER, and type **How To Register**.

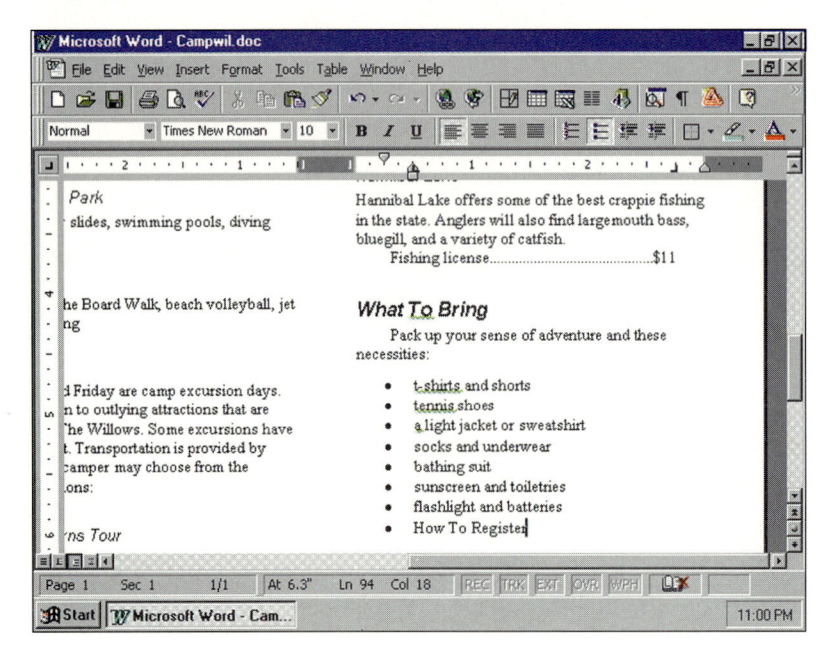

2 Select Heading 2 from the Styles drop-down list.

3 Press ENTER, type **Follow these easy steps:**, and press ENTER.

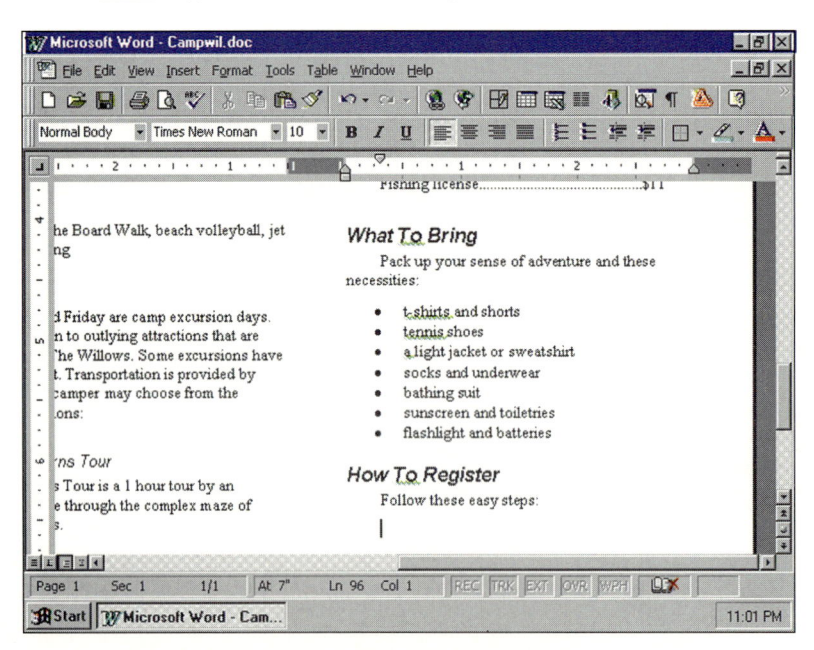

4 Choose Normal from the style drop-down list.

5 Click the Numbering button in the Formatting toolbar.
Word relieves you of the burden of numbering each item individually. Say thank you.

Project 3: Using Advanced Formatting Features   **WORD-95**

6 Type the following lines and press (ENTER) after each one:

Fill out the enclosed registration.
Enclose a $100 non-refundable deposit.
Mail at least 60 days in advance.

7 Click again.
The number is removed from the current line.

Applying Borders and Shading

Borders and shading draw attention to important text. *Borders* consist of a top, bottom, left, and right line, any of which can be displayed or hidden. *Shading* is available in various percentages of gray and in colors.

> **Caution** Be careful when you use shading. If the shading is too dark, people won't be able to read the text—especially if you're faxing the document.

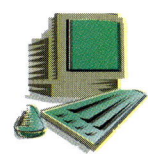

TASK 11: TO APPLY A BORDER AND SHADING:

1 Type **Mail Your Registration Today!** and press (ENTER).

2 Click the Show/Hide ¶ button in the Standard toolbar so that you can see the paragraph symbols.

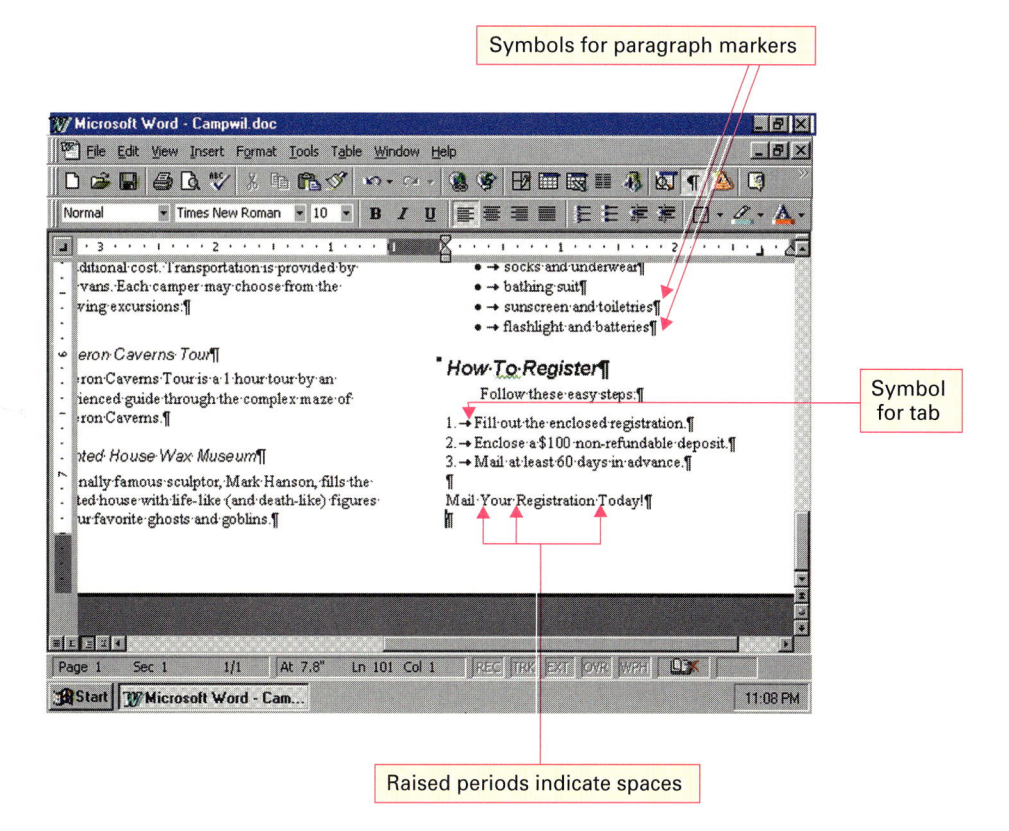

Symbols for paragraph markers

Symbol for tab

Raised periods indicate spaces

WORD-96

3 Select the paragraph symbol above the text, the text, and the paragraph symbol below the text.

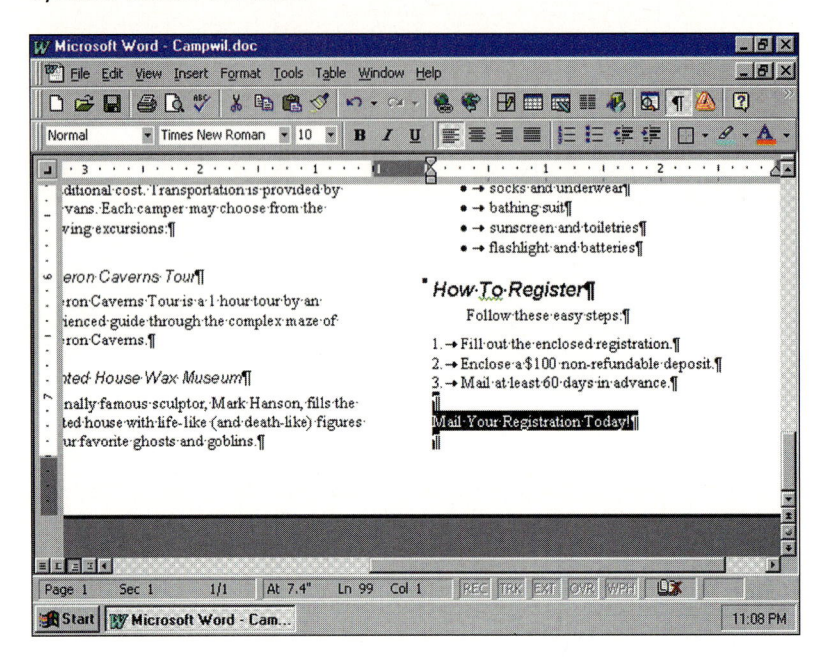

4 Choose Format, Borders and Shading, and click the Borders tab, if necessary.

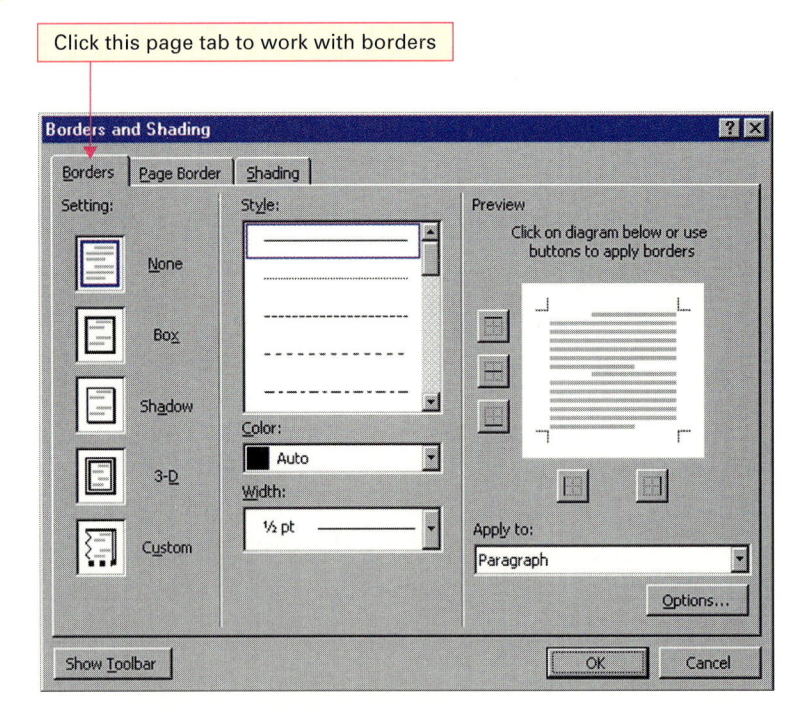

Click this page tab to work with borders

Project 3: Using Advanced Formatting Features   **WORD-97**

5 Click the icon beside the Box setting.

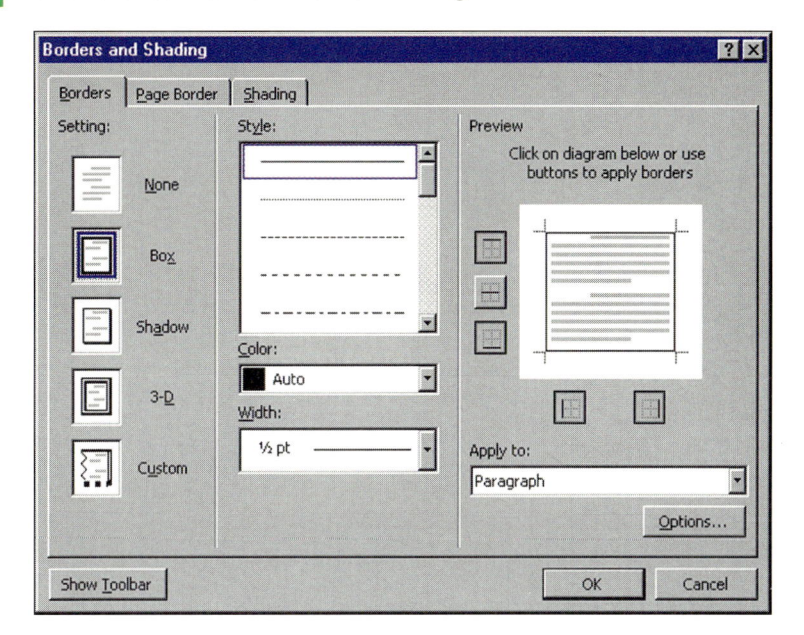

6 Click the Shading tab and click the fourth box in the first row.

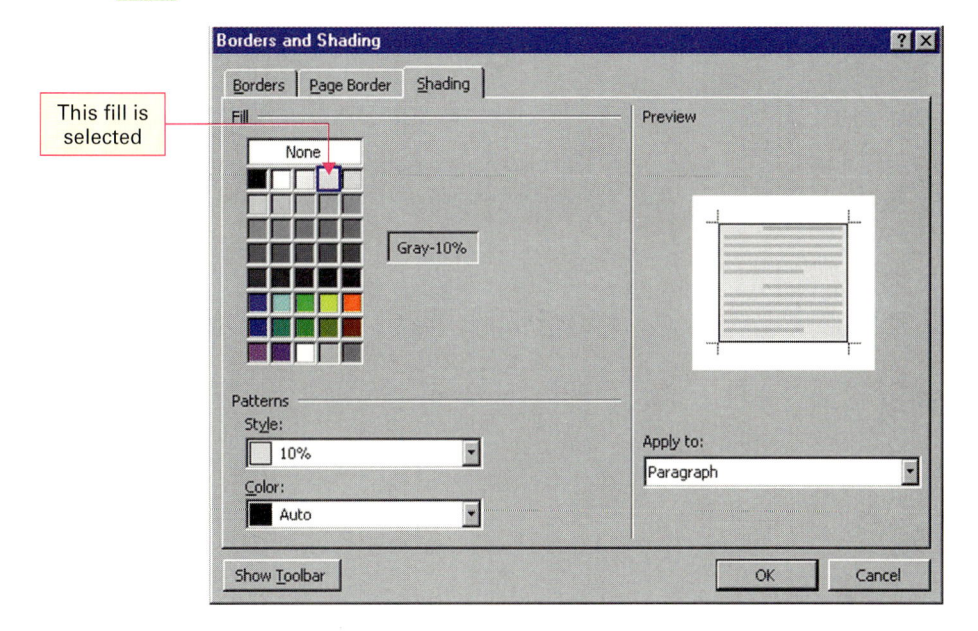

This fill is selected

7 Click OK.

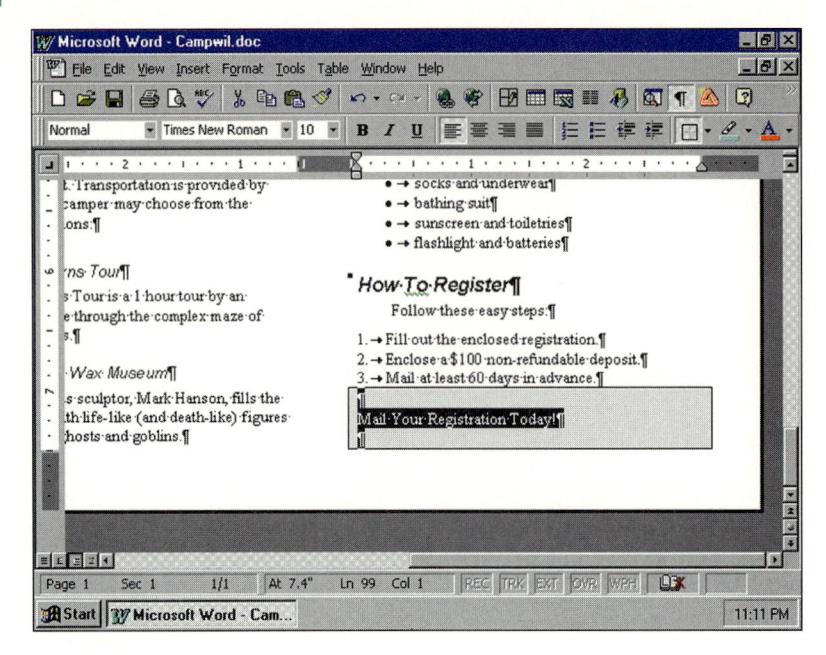

8 Click ¶.
Word hides the paragraph and space symbols.

9 Click the Center button.

> **Tip** To apply a border or shading to text within a paragraph, select the text before you choose Format, Borders and Shading.

The Conclusion

Check the file for spelling errors and then save the file as *Camp Willows.doc*. If you have access to a printer, preview the file and then print it and fold the paper in thirds to see how the brochure looks. If you don't have access to a printer, just preview the file. When you're finished, close the file.

Summary and Exercises

Summary

- Page setup options, including the margins, paper size, and orientation, are preset.
- The text in newspaper columns flows from column to column.
- The Clip Gallery has clip art for inserting in documents.
- Graphics can be sized and moved.
- Paragraph formats include alignment, line spacing, indention, and spacing before and after the paragraph.
- Tabs cause text to align in specific ways, depending on the type of tab.
- A leader can be added to any type of tab.
- A style is a collection of format settings.
- Word 97 has automatic formats for formatting bulleted lists and numbered lists.
- You can apply borders and shading to text.

Key Terms and Operations

Key Terms	Operations
border	apply a border
bulleted list	apply a style
center tab	apply shading
clip art	create a bulleted list
decimal tab	create a numbered list
graphic	create columns
indent	format a paragraph
leader	insert a graphic
left tab	modify a style
line spacing	move a graphic
margin	set a tab
newspaper column	set margins
numbered list	size a graphic
orientation	
page setup	
paper size	
right tab	
shading	
style	
tab	

Study Questions

Multiple Choice

1. You can add borders and shading to
   a. a paragraph only.
   b. a page only.
   c. a paragraph and a page only.
   d. any text, paragraphs, and a page.

2. The default page orientation is
   a. 8½" by 11".
   b. portrait.
   c. landscape.
   d. upright.

3. Normally paragraphs are aligned on the
   a. left.
   b. right.
   c. center.
   d. left and right.

4. A *leader* is
   a. a string of characters that displays before a tab.
   b. the first line of an indented paragraph.
   c. a type of bullet.
   d. a style.

5. To size a graphic,
   a. choose Format, AutoFormat.
   b. choose Insert, Picture, Clip Art, specify the size, and click Insert.
   c. right-click the graphic and choose Size.
   d. drag one of the handles.

6. To set a tab for a particular paragraph,
   a. position the insertion point at the beginning of the paragraph.
   b. position the insertion point at the end of the paragraph.
   c. position the insertion point anywhere in the paragraph.
   d. select the entire paragraph.

7. When you modify a style,
   a. the format changes aren't reflected in the paragraphs that already use the style.
   b. the format changes are reflected in the paragraphs that already use the style.
   c. you must give the style a new name.
   d. you must reapply the style to paragraphs that already use the style.

8. When you move a graphic, the mouse pointer has a
   a. two-headed arrow attached.
   b. three-headed arrow attached.
   c. four-headed arrow attached.
   d. five-headed arrow attached.

9. The default margins are
   a. 1" for the top, bottom, left, and right margins.
   b. 1.25" for the top and bottom margins and 1" for the left and right margins.
   c. 1" for the top and bottom margins and 1.25" for the left and right margins.
   d. 1.5" for the top margin and 1" for the bottom, left, and right margins.

10. When a style is applied to a paragraph,
    a. the name of the style appears in the selection bar.

b. the paragraph takes on the formatting of the style.
  c. the paragraph can't be edited.
  d. the formatting of the paragraph can't be changed.

Short Answer
1. Can you apply a border to a single word in a paragraph? If so, how?
2. What kind of borders can be applied to a paragraph?
3. List the options available for paragraph line spacing.
4. What other format options are available, in addition to paragraph formats, when you modify a style?
5. How do you apply a style?
6. Where is the tab selector button located?
7. How do you set a left tab at 3"?
8. How do you insert a graphic?
9. What kind of tab would you use to align the following numbers: 10.987, 1.1, and 123.45?
10. What does the Show/Hide ¶ button do?

For Discussion
1. When would you use numbers instead of bullets in a list?
2. Discuss the advantages of using styles.
3. When would it be better to format a paragraph rather than create a style to apply to the paragraph?
4. List and describe the types of tabs provided by Word 97.

Review Exercises

1. Creating a List of Rules
Now that you know how to format lists and work with styles, you can dress up the Rules document so that it looks like the one shown in Figure 3.2.

1. Open the file *Rules.doc*. Change the left and right margins to 1.5".
2. Insert the graphic from the Shapes category in the Clip Gallery.
3. Size and move the graphic so that it looks like the one in Figure 3.2.
4. Modify the Normal style and change the font to 12 and the spacing after the paragraph to 6 pt.
5. Go to the end of the document and create two equal columns. Select This point forward for the Apply to option.
6. Type the rules shown in the figure and apply numbering to the list.
7. Save the file as *Camp Willow Rules.doc* and close it.

Team Rules

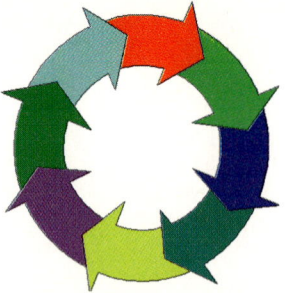

At Camp Willows, you are part of a team. Your mission is to be the best team player you can be and to help your team have the most fun it can have. To assist you in having a safe and fun-filled experience, we have some rules you must follow. These rules aren't like ordinary rules that are meant to restrain you. Just the opposite, these rules will knock down barriers and open doors.

1. Open doors slowly and watch out for buckets of water overhead.
2. Learn the names of at least two new people a day.
3. Don't lock your counselor in his or her room for more than two hours.
4. Eat whatever you want and as much as you want.
5. No jet skiing in the pool.
6. Write or call home at least once.
7. Don't pet the alligators on Tuesday unless they look like they're having a good day.
8. Don't put your team members' underwear in the freezer. Do it to members of opposing teams.
9. Stay with the group when we go on field trips to nearby attractions.
10. Don't play shuffleboard. Campers who break this rule will have to take Geritol and move to a retirement cottage.
11. All bonfires must be built on the beach and be approved by the fire marshall.
12. No skateboarding off the roof unless accompanied by an adult.

Figure 3.2

2. Creating a Camp Schedule

Now that you've created the brochure for Camp Willows, it's time to begin planning the Camp Willows schedule. Follow these easy steps to create the schedule shown in Figure 3.3.

1. Create a new document and type the title and the first paragraph as shown in Figure 3.3.

2. Set right tabs at 3.75" and 5.5". Set left tabs at 1" and 4.5". Type the schedule shown in the figure.

3. Explore the Internet for a historical site you can visit in South Carolina and describe it in the bordered box at the bottom of the document.

4. Save the file as *Schedule.doc* and close it.

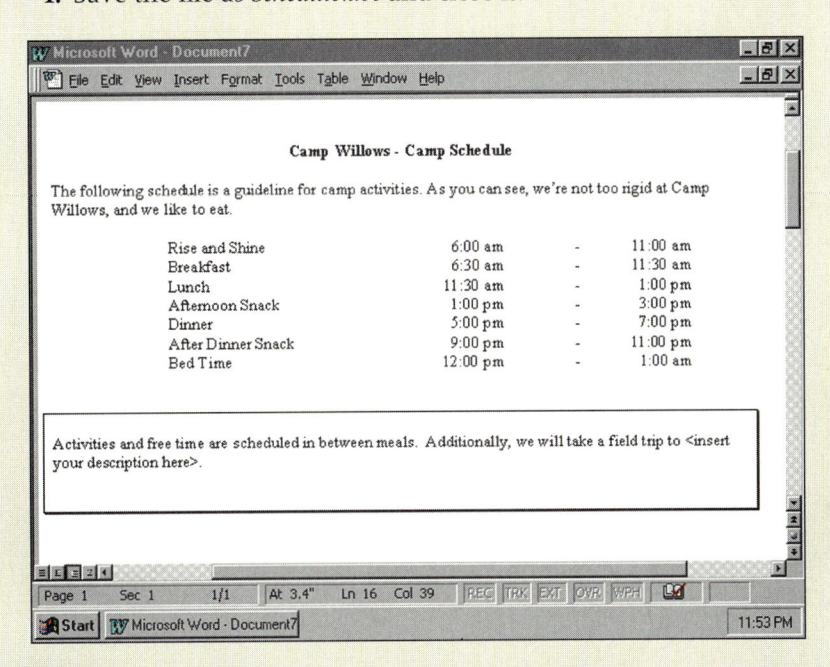

Figure 3.3

Assignments

1. Creating an Award Certificate
Create the award certificate shown in Figure 3.4. Choose Landscape for the orientation, use a page border, and insert the graphic from the Sports & Leisure category.

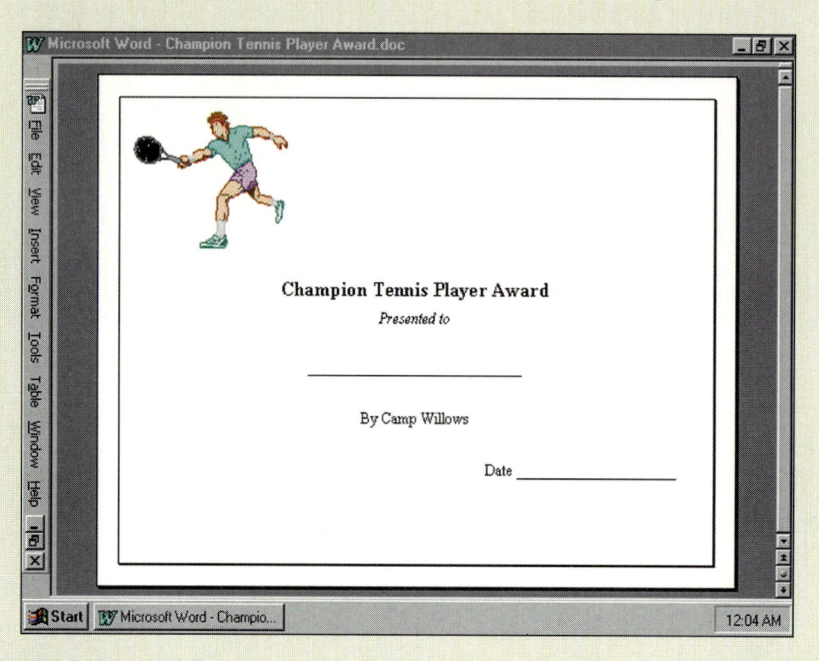

Figure 3.4

2. Creating a List of Summer Camps
Search the Web for information on summer camps. Create a new document listing at least five camps and give the following information for each: name of camp, location, cost, dates, Web address. List the information in columns separated by tabs. You may find it helpful to use landscape orientation.

PROJECT 4

Creating a Table

A table is a versatile tool for presenting data in an easy-to-read format. Often tables are used instead of tabs to present columnar information.

Objectives

After completing this project, you will be able to:

- ▶ Create a table
- ▶ Convert existing text to a table
- ▶ Move around in a table and enter data
- ▶ Insert and delete rows and columns in a table
- ▶ Format a table automatically
- ▶ Format a table manually
- ▶ Change the width of columns
- ▶ Position tables
- ▶ Draw a table

The Challenge

Mr. Williams wants you to complete the document that he drafted pertaining to entry fees and tee times for the upcoming golf tournament.

The Solution

You will open the document and add the tee times information in a table, and you will also convert some of the existing text into a table.

Then you will format the tables to make them easier to read, and finally you will draw a table to create a form. The complete document is shown in Figure 4.1.

The Willows Pro-Celebrity Golf Tournament
to aid the
Juvenile Diabetes Foundation
September 18 - 20

Entry Fees

Type	Sept. 18	Sept. 19	Sept. 20	All Three Days
Celebrity Foursome	$200	$400	$500	$900
Pro Foursome	$300	$500	$600	$1000

The Willows will donate the green fees. Carts will be charged at the regular price for 18 holes.

Tee Times

Group	Hole	Time
1	1	7:00 am
2	1	1:00 pm
1	3	7:00 am
2	3	1:00 pm
1	6	7:00 am
2	6	1:00 pm
1	9	7:10 am
2	9	1:10 pm
1	12	7:10 am
2	12	1:10 pm
1	15	7:10 am
2	15	1:10 pm
1	18	7:10 am
2	18	1:10 pm

✂ ---

Please detach the following form and mail with your nonrefundable deposit of $100 to:

The Willows Pro-Celebrity Tournament
The Willows Resort
1000 Coast Highway
Willow Grove, SC 22345

Name							
Address							
City			State		Zip		

Indicate your first, second and third choices for the type of foursome you want by placing the numbers 1, 2, and 3 in the appropriate boxes. We will make every effort to give you your first choice.

Celebrity Sept. 18	Pro Sept. 18	Celebrity Sept. 19	Pro Sept. 19	Celebrity Sept. 20	Pro Sept. 20	Celebrity 3-days	Pro 3-days

Figure 4.1

The Setup

So that your screen will match the illustrations and the tasks in this project will function as described, make sure that the Word 97 settings listed in Table 4.1 are selected on your computer.

Table 4.1 Word 97 Settings

Location	Make these settings:
View, Toolbars	Deselect all toolbars except the Standard and Formatting toolbars
View	Deselect the Ruler option and select Page Layout view
Standard toolbar	Deselect any buttons that are selected and set Zoom to 100%

Creating a Table

A *table* contains *columns* and *rows* (like a spreadsheet). The intersection of a column and a row is called a *cell*. Word 97 provides three methods of creating a table. You can insert a blank table, convert existing text to a table, or draw a table freehand. In this section, you will use the first two methods. Later in this project, after you have become more comfortable with using tables, you will draw one.

TASK 1: TO INSERT A TABLE:

1 Open the file *Fees.doc*.

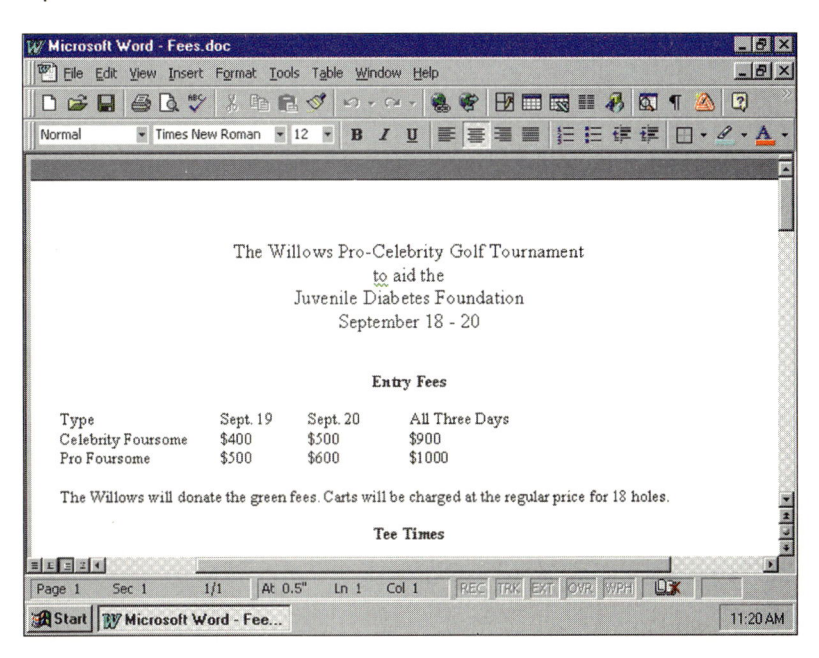

2 Click in the line that says "Tee Times" and press . twice. The insertion point moves two lines below the text.

3 Choose Table.

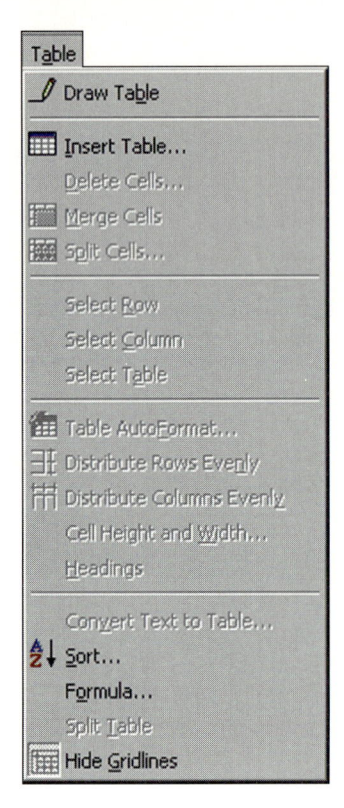

4 Choose Insert Table.

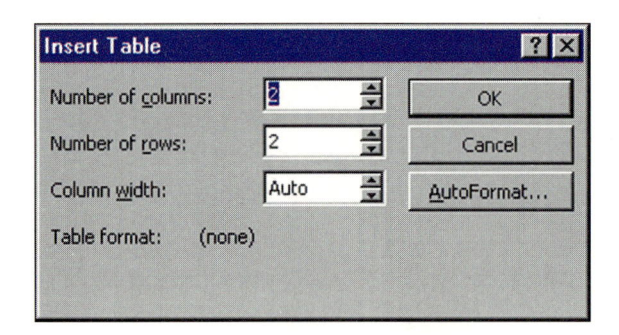

Project 4: Creating a Table   WORD-109

5 Type **4** for the number of columns; type **14** for the number of rows; and click OK.

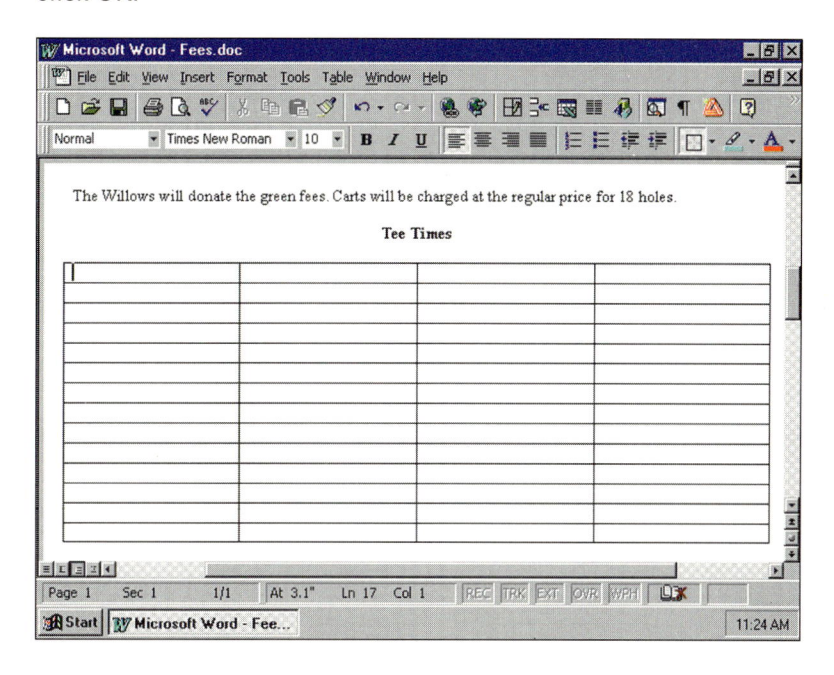

Converting Existing Text to a Table

If you have already typed the text that you want to include in a table, you can convert the text to a table without having to insert a blank table and copy the text or retype it. Generally the text that you convert is formatted in columns using tabs.

> **Tip** Be sure that only one tab exists between each item in the list; each tab creates a column in the table.

TASK 2: TO CREATE A TABLE FROM TEXT:

1 Click the Show/Hide ¶ button so that you can see the tabs and paragraph returns.

2 Select the three lines of text under the "Entry Fees" heading.

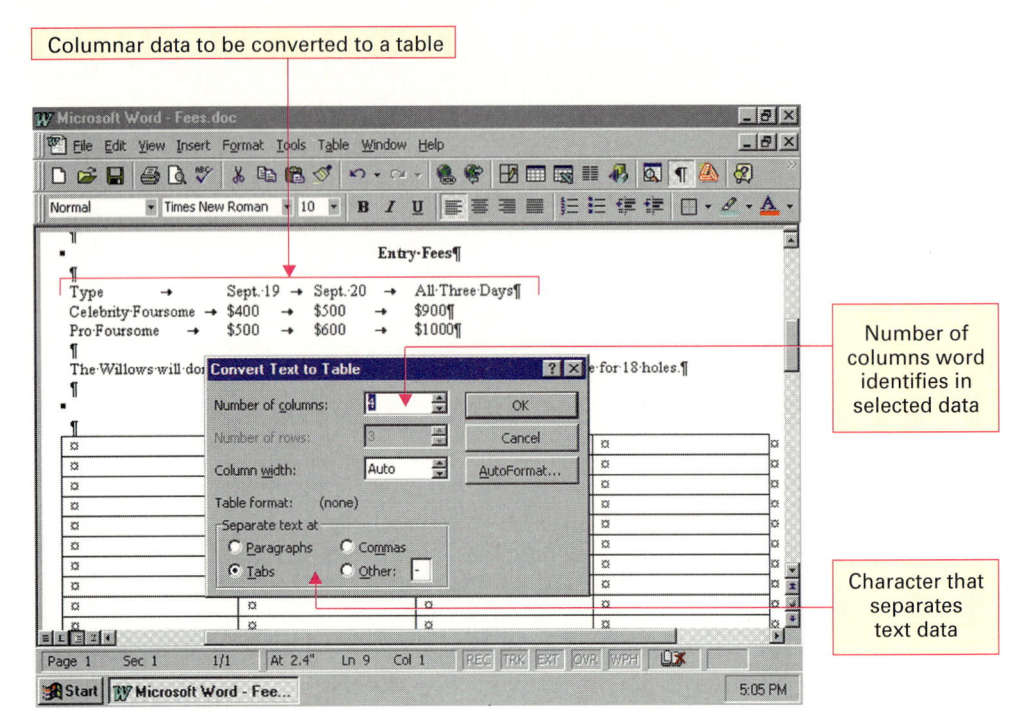

3 Choose Table, Convert Text to Table.

Columnar data to be converted to a table

Number of columns word identifies in selected data

Character that separates text data

4 Click OK.

Moving Around in a Table and Entering Data

The easiest way to go to a particular cell in a table is to click in the cell, but when you are entering data in blank cells it's more efficient to move around with the keyboard techniques described in Table 4.2.

As you type data in a cell, the text wraps to the next line automatically if the cell isn't wide enough to contain the text on one line. To create a new line in a cell, press the Enter key. To indent text in a cell, press and hold down the Ctrl key while you press the Tab key.

Table 4.2   Keyboard Navigation Techniques for a Blank Table

To go to	Press
The next cell	TAB or →
The previous cell	SHIFT + TAB or ←
The next row	↓
The previous row	↑

> **Note** When a table contains data, using the keyboard techniques described in Table 4.2 produces different results. For example, pressing TAB and SHIFT+TAB moves to the next and previous cells, but it also selects the text; pressing → moves to the next cell only when the insertion point is positioned after the last character in the current cell; and pressing ↓ moves to the next row only if the insertion point is positioned in the last line of the text in the current cell.

TASK 3: TO ENTER DATA IN A TABLE:

1 Click in the first cell of the blank table.
The insertion point blinks in the first cell.

2 Type **Group** and press TAB.
The text appears in the cell, and the insertion point moves to the next cell.

3 Type **Hole** and press TAB.
The text appears in the cell, and the insertion point moves to the next cell.

4 Type **Time** and press TAB.
The text appears in the cell, and the insertion point moves to the next cell.

5 Type **Cart Number** and press TAB.
The text appears in the cell, and the insertion point moves to the next cell.

6 Type the remaining text as in:

colspan="4"	Tee Times
Group	Hole	Time	Cart Number
1	1	7:00 am	1
2	1	1:00 pm	3
1	3	7:00 am	4
2	3	1:00 pm	5
1	6	7:00 am	7
2	6	1:00 pm	8
1	9	7:10 am	10
2	9	1:10 pm	12
1	12	7:10 am	13
2	12	1:10 pm	14
1	15	7:10 am	15
2	15	1:10 pm	16
1	18	7:10 am	20

Inserting and Deleting Rows and Columns in a Table

After you have created a table, you may need to add more rows or columns to insert additional data. You also may have to delete unwanted rows or columns. When you delete a row or column, all the data in the cells is deleted. To insert or delete rows or columns, you must select the appropriate rows or columns as described in Table 4.3. An inserted row is inserted above the selected row(s). An inserted column is inserted to the left of the selected column(s).

Table 4.3   Selection Techniques

To select	Technique
The contents of a single cell	Triple-click.
A row	Point to the row in the selection bar and click. (The selection bar is the white space to the left of the table.) If you want to insert only one row, you also can simply click in any cell in the row to select the row.
Several contiguous rows	Drag the pointer in the selection bar for all the desired rows.
A column	Point to the top border of the column until the pointer turns to a black arrow and then click.
Several contiguous columns	Point to the top border of the first column until the pointer turns to a black arrow and then click and drag across the other columns.
A block of cells	Drag the pointer through the cells.
The entire table	Press ALT+5. (NUM LOCK must be turned off.)

Tip Use the selection techniques in Table 4.3 when you want to select parts of a table for formatting.

TASK 4: TO INSERT AND DELETE ROWS AND COLUMNS:

1 Click in any cell in the second row of the table containing the tee times.
The insertion point blinks in the cell.

2 Choose Table, Insert Row.
A new row is inserted.

3 Click in the last cell in the last row of the table.
The insertion point blinks in the cell.

4 Press TAB.
A new row is added to the end of the table.

5 Type the following text in the new row at the bottom of the table:

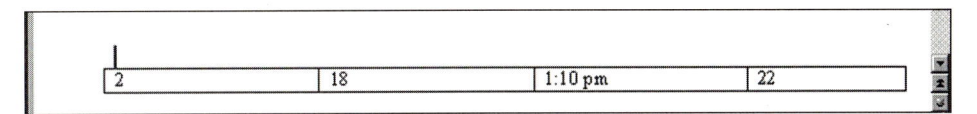

| 2 | 18 | 1:10 pm | 22 |

Tip If the insertion point is in the last cell in a table and you press the Tab key, Word adds a new row to the bottom of the table. To insert a new row below an existing row, click outside the table just to the right of the row's right border and then press the Enter key.

6 Select the second column in the Entry Fees table.

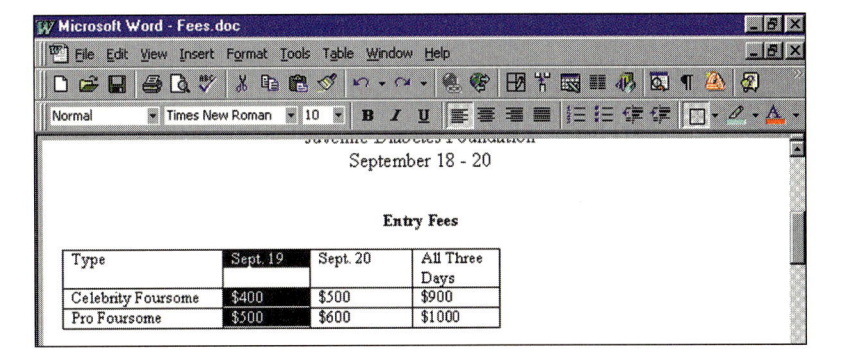

Microsoft Word - Fees.doc

September 18 - 20

Entry Fees

Type	Sept. 19	Sept. 20	All Three Days
Celebrity Foursome	$400	$500	$900
Pro Foursome	$500	$600	$1000

7 Choose Table, Insert Columns.
A new column is inserted to the left of the selected column.

WORD-114

8 Type the data in the column as in:

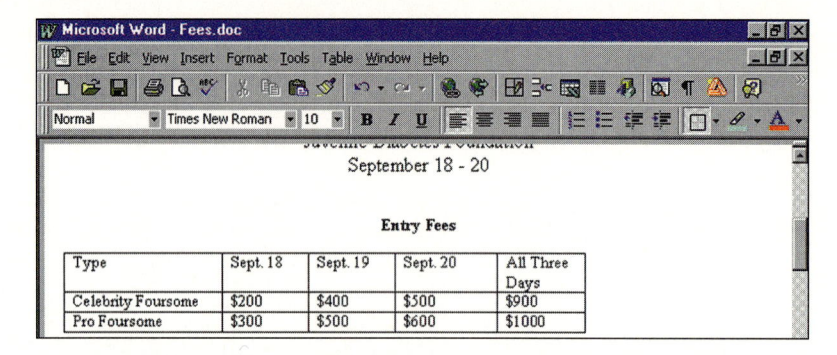

9 Click in the selection bar beside the second row in the Tee Times table.

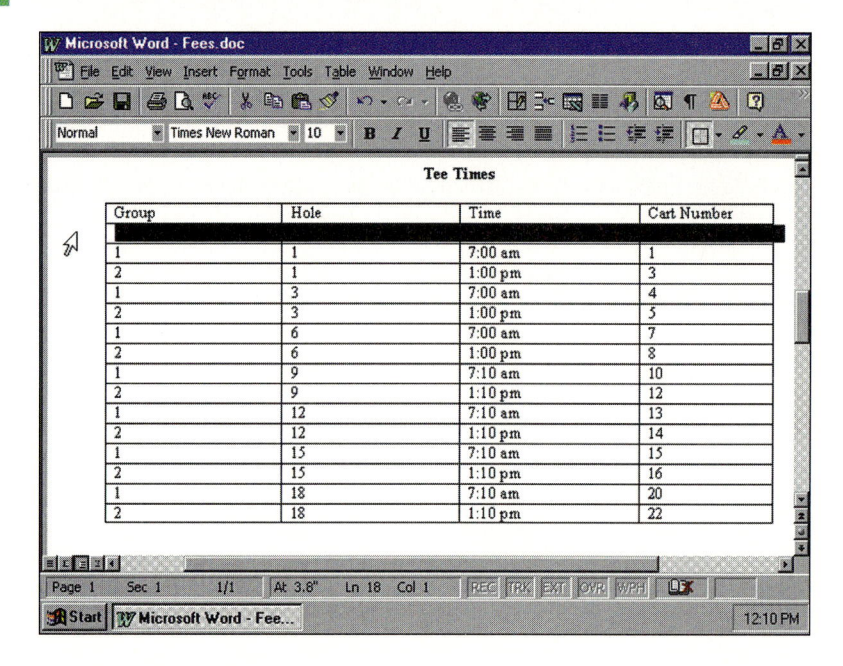

10 Choose Table, Delete Rows.
The row is deleted.

11 Select the fourth column in the Tee Times table.

12 Choose Table, Delete Columns.
The column is deleted.

Formatting a Table Automatically

Formatting a table is easy with Word 97's *AutoFormat* feature. AutoFormat provides many different formats for a table and allows you to preview the format before you select it.

TASK 5: TO FORMAT A TABLE WITH AUTOFORMAT:

1 Click in any cell in the second table.
The insertion point blinks in the cell.

2 Choose Table, Table AutoFormat.

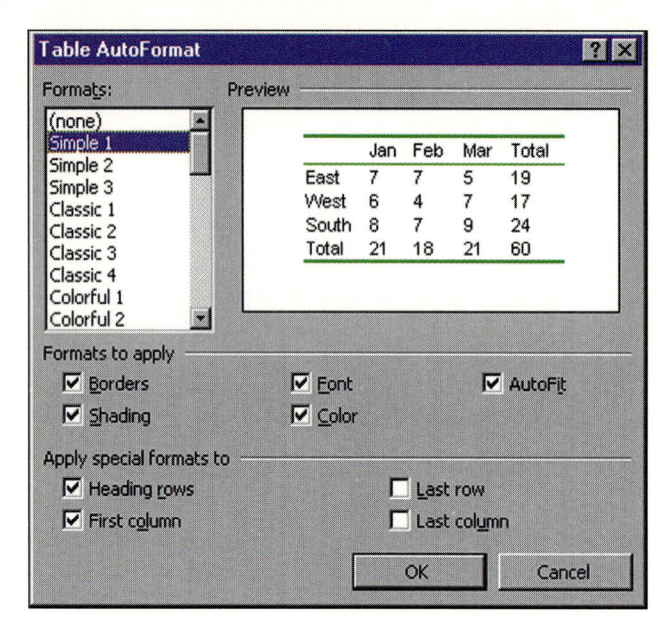

3 Scroll the Formats list, choose 3D effects 2, and deselect the First Column option.

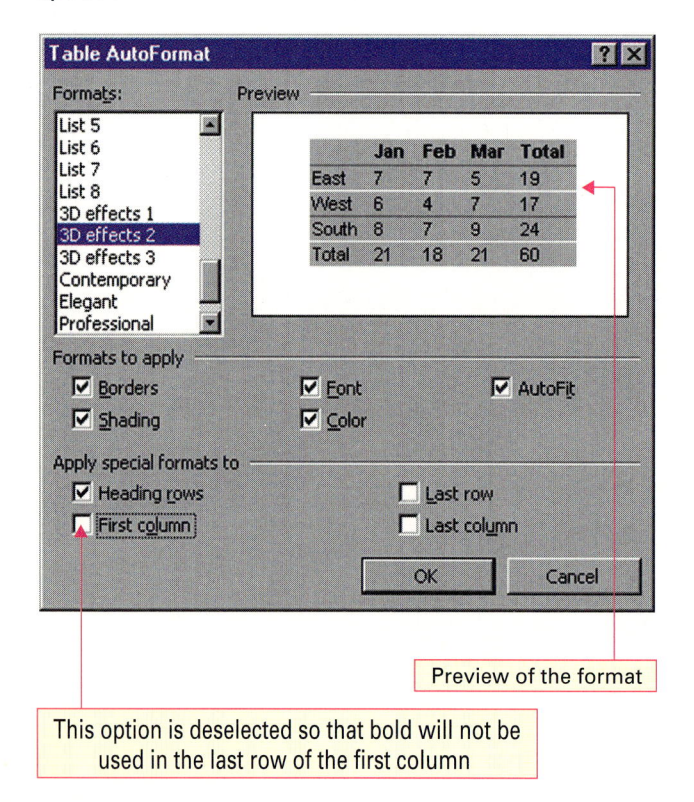

Preview of the format

This option is deselected so that bold will not be used in the last row of the first column

4 Click OK.

Project 4: Creating a Table   WORD-117

Formatting a Table Manually

In addition to using AutoFormat, you can manually apply other formatting techniques, such as bold and centered, to text in a table. The steps to apply any type of formatting to text in a table are the same as those for formatting paragraph text. Usually, you select the text in the table and then apply the formatting.

> **Note** Remember to select all the text in a cell, triple-click. To select a block of cells, drag the pointer through the cells.

TASK 6: TO CENTER TEXT IN A COLUMN:

1 Select the first and second columns in the Tee Times table.

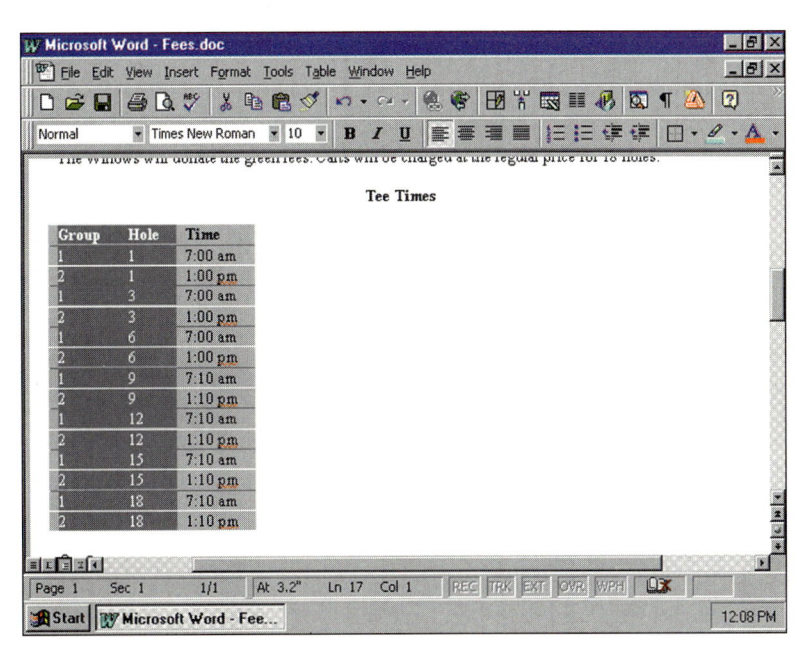

2 Click the Center button.
Text and numbers in each cell are centered.

> **Tip** You can also apply styles to the text in a table. Refer to Project 3 if you have forgotten how to apply styles, and don't feel guilty. You can't remember all this without a little review.

Changing the Width of Columns

If the text in a column wraps to another line, you can widen the column to keep the text on the same line. If the width of a column is too wide for the data it contains, you can narrow the column.

TASK 7: TO WIDEN A COLUMN:

1 Point to the cell border between "Hole" and "Time" in the first row of the Tee Times table until you see the double-headed arrow.

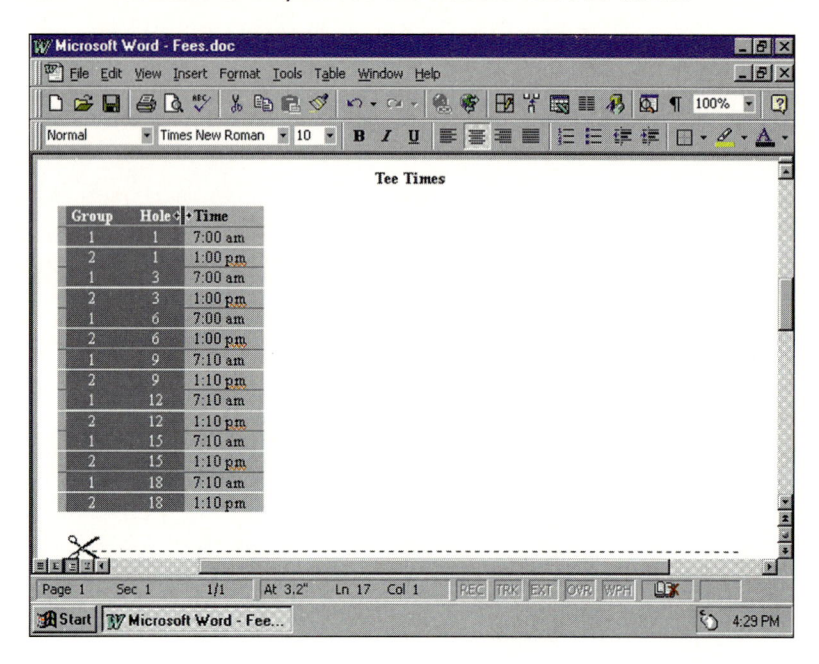

2 Drag to the right just a little bit to increase the width of the "Hole" column so it's about as wide as the first column.

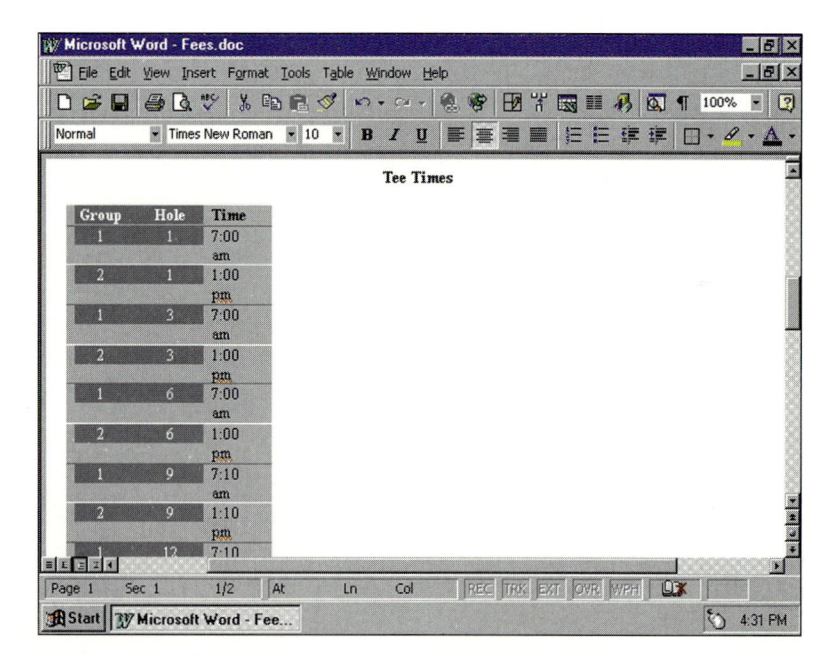

3 Point to the upper-right edge of the table until you see the double-headed arrow.

4 Drag to the right until the text in the last column doesn't wrap.

Project 4: Creating a Table   **WORD-119**

Positioning Tables

You can align tables on the left or right margins, center, or indent them a specific amount.

TASK 8: TO CENTER A TABLE:

1 Click in the first cell of the first row in the Tee Times table. The insertion point blinks in the cell.

2 Choose Table, Cell Height and Width.

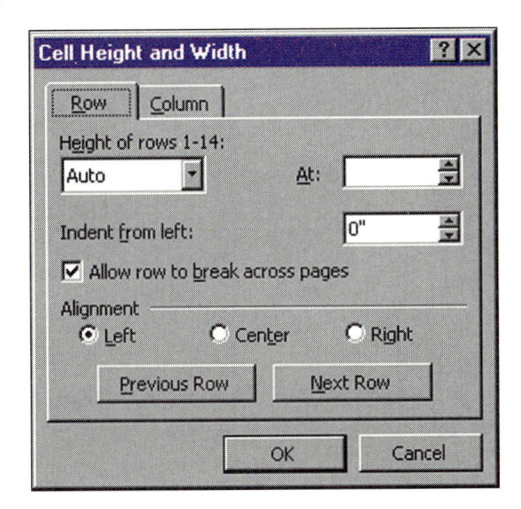

3 Choose Center for Alignment and click OK.

Drawing Tables

Sometimes you will want to create a table that has a very complex structure. Although you can create one by splitting and merging cells, why waste your time? Word 97 gives you a far easier method: You can draw the table so it looks perfect. Word even supplies an eraser you can use to remove unwanted lines and merge cells. When you draw a table, the Tables and Borders toolbar displays automatically.

TASK 9: TO DRAW A TABLE:

1 Scroll the page down so that you can see only the text "Willow Grove, SC 22345" at the top of the screen.

2 Choose Table, Draw Table.

If the Office Assistant displays, close it; you'll get all the help you need right now from this book.

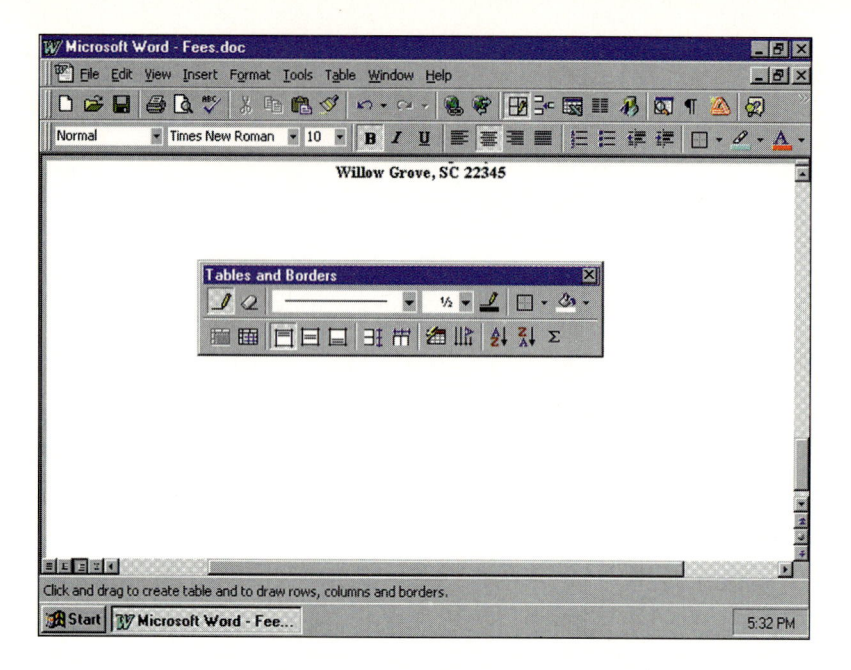

3 If the Tables and Borders toolbar appears as a palette, drag it to the bottom of the screen so that it becomes a bar.

4 Draw a rectangle below the text, starting at the left margin and extending to the right margin, that takes up most of the remainder of the screen.

5 Type **Name**, click the Draw Table button, and then draw a vertical line after the text and a horizontal line under the text.

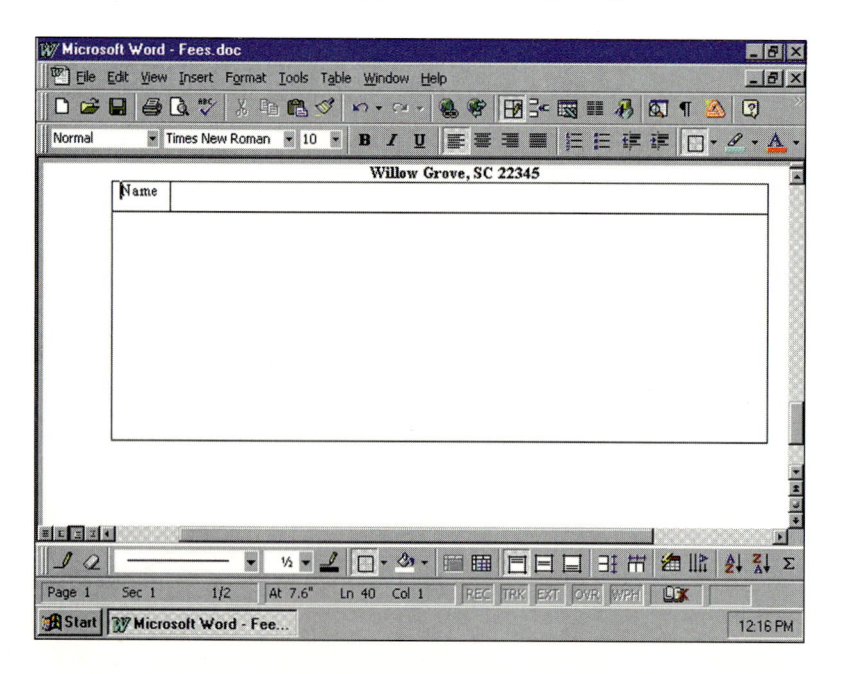

Tip If you draw a vertical line that's too close to the text and the text wraps, you can deselect the Draw Table button and then drag the column border to widen the column.

Project 4: Creating a Table   WORD-121

6 Click 🖉.
The pointer changes to the insertion point.

7 Click under "Name" and type **Address**.

8 Click 🖉 and draw a vertical line after "Address" and a horizontal line under "Address."

9 Continue using the same steps to type the following text and draw the following cells:

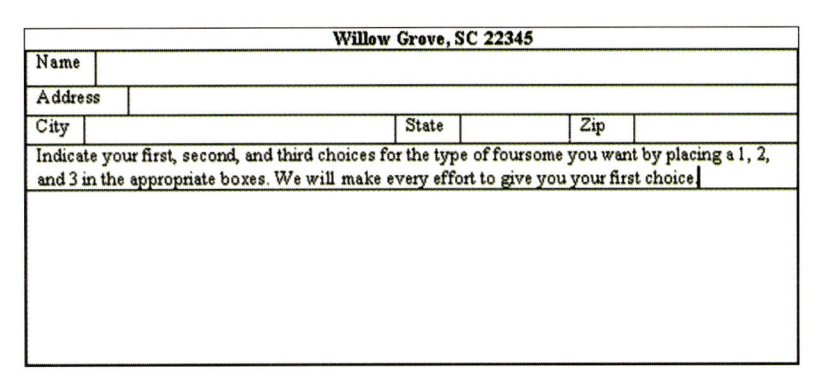

	Willow Grove, SC 22345				
Name					
Address					
City		State		Zip	
Indicate your first, second, and third choices for the type of foursome you want by placing a 1, 2, and 3 in the appropriate boxes. We will make every effort to give you your first choice.					

10 Draw seven vertical lines in the remaining space. Don't worry if the lines aren't equally spaced; Word will even them up for you later.

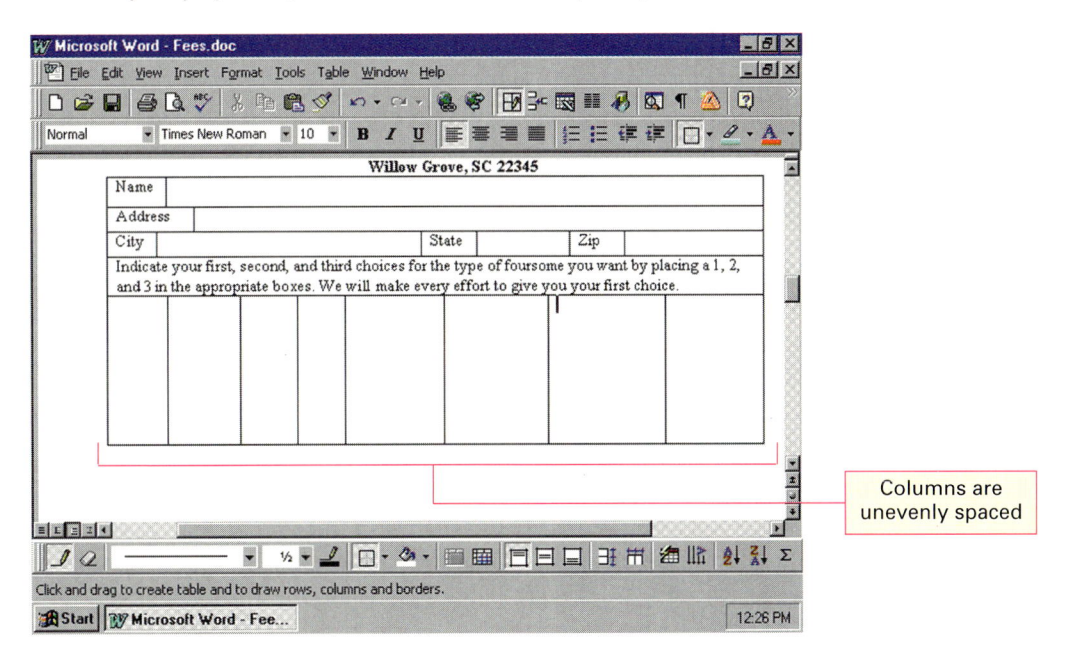

Columns are unevenly spaced

WORD-122

11 Select the last row by clicking in the selection bar.

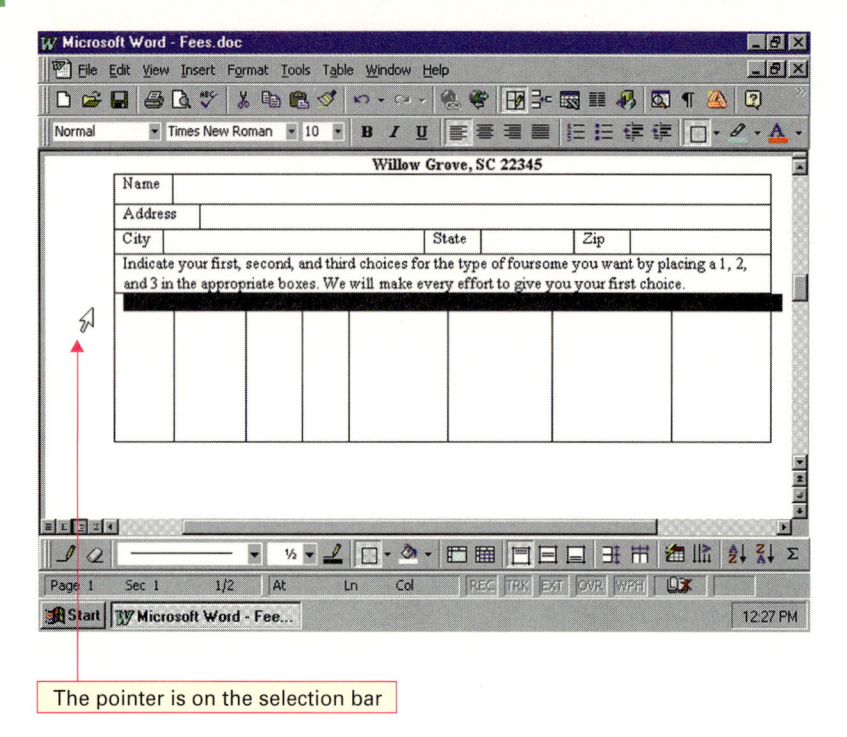

The pointer is on the selection bar

Note You can't select text, cells, columns, or rows when the Draw Table button is selected.

12 Click the Distribute Columns Evenly button.

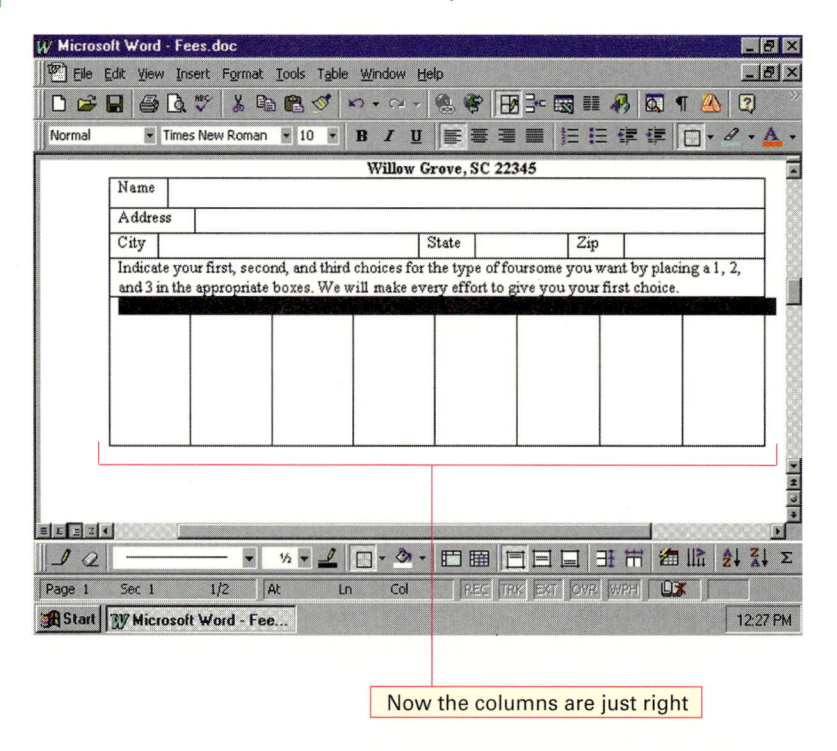

Now the columns are just right

13 Type the following text:

Name							
Address							
City				State		Zip	
Indicate your first, second, and third choices for the type of foursome you want by placing a 1, 2, and 3 in the appropriate boxes. We will make every effort to give you your first choice.							
Celebrity Sept. 18	Pro Sept. 18	Celebrity Sept. 19	Pro Sept. 19	Celebrity Sept. 20	Pro Sept. 20	Celebrity 3-days	Pro 3-days

14 Select the first four rows of the table.

15 Click the Distribute Rows Evenly button and then click the Center Vertically button.
The text is centered vertically in the rows.

16 Click the down arrow for Line Style and choose the line style shown here:

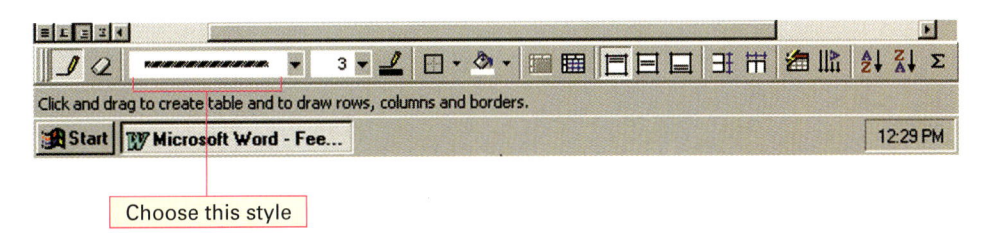

Choose this style

17 Click ![pencil icon] and trace over the top border line.
The line changes to the new style.

18 Trace over the other lines so that the form looks like the following:

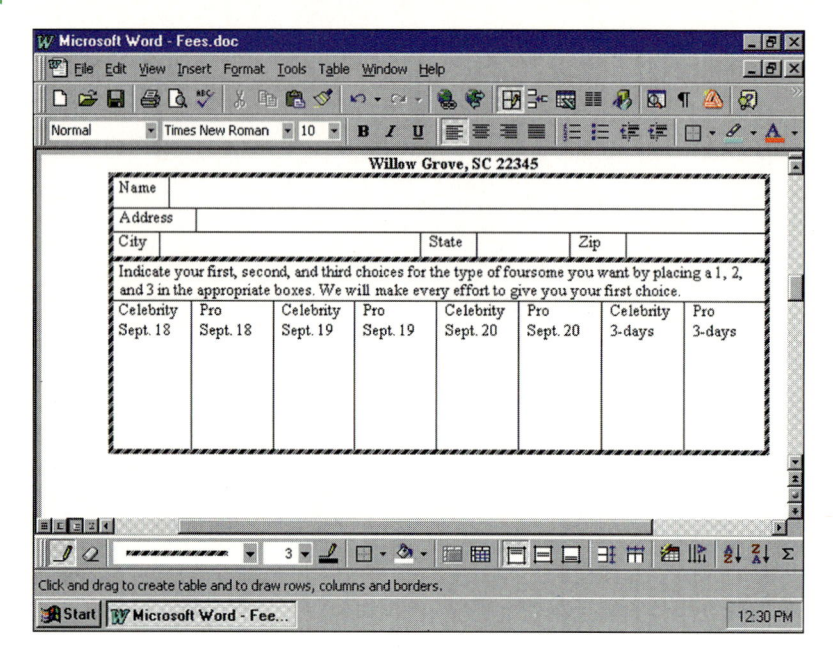

The Conclusion

Make adjustments to the table size if necessary. Widen the last column in the first table and then center the table. Save the file as *Fees-Times-Form.doc,* and then preview the file. If you have access to a printer, print the file and then close it.

Summary and Exercises

Summary

- You can insert a blank table, convert text to a table, or draw a table.
- To go to a cell in a table, you click in the cell.
- Text automatically wraps in a cell.
- You can insert and delete rows and columns.
- AutoFormat provides many formats for formatting a table automatically.
- You also can format a table manually.
- You can change the width of a column by dragging it.
- Tables can be aligned on the left or right margin, centered, or indented.
- The Tables and Borders toolbar contains the tools for drawing a table.

Key Terms and Operations

Key Terms	Operations
AutoFormat	align (position) a table
cell	AutoFormat a table
column	change the width of a column
row	convert text to a table
selection bar	create a table
table	delete a column
Tables and Borders toolbar	delete a row
	draw a table
	insert a column
	insert a row

Study Questions

Multiple Choice

1. To create a table, you
   a. must first type the text of the table.
   b. must create space for the table by inserting blank lines.
   c. choose Table, Insert Table.
   d. choose Table, Create Table.

2. To select a column,
   a. triple-click the first cell in the column.
   b. point to the top border of the column and click when the pointer is a black arrow.
   c. point to the top border of the column and click.
   d. point to the top border of the column and press (SHIFT) while you click.

3. To draw a horizontal or vertical line in a table, use
   a. the Draw Table button.
   b. the Draw Line button.
   c. the Line button.
   d. the Straight Line button.

WORD-125

4. You can't select a row
   a. if a column is selected.
   b. if a group of cells is selected.
   c. if the Draw Table button is selected.
   d. unless the table is selected.

5. To go to the previous cell, press
   a. ALT + TAB
   b. SHIFT + TAB
   c. CTRL + TAB
   d. TAB

6. If a table is blank, what keystroke moves down in a column from cell to cell?
   a. ↓
   b. ENTER
   c. TAB
   d. SHIFT + ↓

7. Which of the following statements are true, if any?
   a. An inserted row is inserted below the selected row(s).
   b. An inserted column is inserted to the left of the selected column(s).
   c. When you delete a row, all the data is added to the next row.
   d. When you delete a column, all the data is deleted as well.

8. Before using AutoFormat, you
   a. can click in any cell in the table.
   b. must select all the cells in the table.
   c. must manually align cells.
   d. must select the first row of the table.

9. To insert a row below the selected row,
   a. choose Table, Insert Rows.
   b. click in the last cell in the row and press ENTER.
   c. click in the last cell in the row and press TAB.
   d. click to the right of the right border of the last cell and press ENTER.

10. The Eraser button erases
    a. text in the document.
    b. text in a table only.
    c. lines in a table.
    d. any object in a table.

Short Answer

1. Describe two ways to add a row after the last row in the table.

2. What method of creating a table would you most likely use to create an employment application form?

3. How can you keep text from wrapping in a column?

4. How do you select multiple rows?

5. How do you indent text in a cell?

6. How do you center a table?

7. How do you change the style of a line in a table?

8. How do you widen a column?
9. How do you select multiple columns?
10. What's the name of the dialog box that has the options for positioning a table?

For Discussion
1. In what ways is the AutoFormat feature flexible?
2. Discuss the advantages of drawing a table.
3. Discuss the formatting that you can manually apply to the text in a table.
4. Describe the following AutoFormats: Simple 1, Classic 1, Columns 5, and List 1.

Review Exercises

1. Creating a Script for a Commercial

Mr. Williams has requested that you type up the script for a TV commercial about the golf tournament. Follow these steps to create the script.

1. Create a new document, using Figure 4.2 as your guide.
2. Type the text shown above the table, and press (ENTER) at the end of the text.
3. Create a table with 2 columns and 10 rows. Make the width of the first column narrower.
4. Type the following text:

Camera	Aerial view of golf course. Pan 9th hole. Zoom in on tee.
Action	Golfer 1 (back to the camera) seems to hit a terrific tee shot.
Golfer 2	Boy, you're having a good round. What's the secret?
Action	Other three golfers move closer to Golfer 1 to listen. (Golfer 1 still has back to camera)
Golfer 1	(Back is still to the camera) I think it's the environment. The course is great, the weather is beautiful, the resort is relaxing—everything a golfer could want.
Camera	Circles to reveal identity of Golfer 1.
Golfer 2	Yeah, and being a pro didn't hurt either, did it?
Action	Laughter from all golfers.
Camera	Fade out sound and zoom in on clubhouse.
Voice of announcer	Get together with friends at any one of the fine courses at The Willows Resort. You never know who might be in your foursome. Reservations accepted three days in advance. Call 803-945-5699 for available tee times.

5. Save the file as *Commercial.doc* and close it.

Script for 30 Second TV Spot

Characters: Golfer 1 (a well known professional), Golfers 2, 3, and 4 (unknowns), Announcer
Setting: 9th hole overlooking Green Jacket Clubhouse

Camera	Arial view of golf course. Pan 9th hole. Zoom in on tee.
Action	Golfer 1 (back to the camera) seems to hit a terrific tee shot.
Golfer 2	Boy, you're having a good round. What's the secret?
Action	Other three golfers move closer to Golfer 1 to listen. (Golfer 1 still has back to camera)
Golfer 1	(Back is still to the camera) I think it's the environment. The course is great, the weather is beautiful, the resort is relaxing – everything a golfer could want.
Camera	Circles to reveal identity of Golfer 1.
Golfer 2	Yeah, and being a pro didn't hurt either, did it?
Action	Laughter from all golfers.
Camera	Fade out sound and zoom in on clubhouse.
Voice of announcer	Get together with friends at any one of the fine courses at The Willows Resort. You never know who might be in your foursome. Reservations accepted three days in advance. Call 803-945-5699 for available tee times.

Figure 4.2

2. Comparing the Competition

To ensure that golf course standards at the Willows keeps up with the competition, the golf pro would like for you to check out fees at other resort courses. Follow these steps to create the *Competition* document:

1. Search the Web using the search string **"PGA golf course"** (include the quotation marks in the search).

2. Gather the information that appears in the table shown in Figure 4.3 for five golf courses.

3. Create a new document and change the page orientation to landscape.

4. Create a table with 8 columns and 6 rows.

5. Type the headings shown in the first row in Figure 4.3.

6. Delete the sample text in the second row and enter the information that you have found for the five golf courses.

7. Choose the Grid 5 AutoFormat.

8. Save the file as *Competition.doc* and close it.

Other Courses

Name	City	State	# of Courses	Lessons	Green Fees	Cart Fees	Annual Tournament
Sandy Beach Pines	Savannah	GA	3	Yes	$22	$18	None

Figure 4.3

Assignments

1. Creating a Form

Create the form shown in Figure 4.4. The table should be approximately 6½" by 9". The rows that appear to be the same height have been evenly distributed and the text is aligned vertically.

Employment Application Form				
For what position with our company are you applying?				
Last Name		First Name		Middle Initial
Street Address			Phone	
City		State	ZIP	
Education				
Institution Name			Dates	Diploma/Degree
Current Employer			Phone	
Employment History				
Company Name				Date/Position
Military Experience				
Have you ever been convicted of a felony?				
Will you submit to periodic drug testing?				
What skills do you have that qualify you for this position?				
References				
Name				Phone Number

Figure 4.4

2. Creating a Golf FAQ

The golf pro wants to have a FAQ sheet to give to novices who are taking golf lessons. Create a document with a two-column table. List the questions in the first column and the answers in the second column.

Search the Web for **"golf FAQ"** to answer the following questions. (Be sure to include the quotation marks in the search string.)
- What is *par*?
- What is a *foursome*?
- What is a *wood*?
- What is an *iron*?
- What does the number on the club mean?
- What is a *handicap*?
- What is a *hook*?
- What is a *slice*?

Apply an AutoFormat of your choice.

PROJECT 5

Formatting a Long Document

When working with long documents—documents that have several pages—you will have to use some features and techniques that aren't frequently used with one-page documents.

Objectives

After completing this project, you will be able to:

➤ Navigate in a long document
➤ Insert and delete page breaks
➤ Insert section breaks
➤ Create headers and footers
➤ Create footnotes

The Challenge

The golf pro has a file that's an excerpt from the PGA rule book written by the United States Golf Association (USGA). He wants you to add a title page as the first page and then number the second and subsequent pages starting with the number 1. He also wants a copyright notice on each page, and he wants to add some examples to the file as footnotes. No problem; you and Word 97 can handle anything.

The Solution

You will revise the file and add a page break to create the title page. Then you will create headers and footers for the file and insert the footnotes as shown in Figure 5.1.

The Rules of Play

The rules published within this document are a subset of the rules that belong to the United States Golf Association (USGA). This document is not intended to replace the complete set of rules as published by the USGA. The intent of this document is to promote the interests of golf and the rules of golf.

© USGA

Rule 14. Striking the Ball

Definition

A "stroke" is the forward movement of the club made with the intention of fairly striking at and moving the ball, but if a player checks his downswing voluntarily before the clubhead reaches the ball, he is deemed not to have made a stroke.

14-1. Ball to Be Fairly Struck At

The ball shall be fairly struck at with the head of the club and must not be pushed, scraped or spooned.[1]

14-2. Assistance

In making a stroke, a player shall not accept physical assistance or protection from the elements.[2]

14-4. Striking the Ball More than Once

If a player's club strikes the ball more than once in the course of a stroke, the player shall count the stroke and add a penalty stroke, making two strokes in all.

Rule 18. Ball at Rest Moved

Definitions

A ball is deemed to have "moved" if it leaves its position and comes to rest in any other place.

An "outside agency" is any agency not part of the match or, in stroke play, not part of the competitor's side, and includes a referee, a marker, an observer or a fore-caddie. Neither wind nor water is an outside agency.

"Equipment" is anything used, worn or carried by or for the player except any ball he has played at the hole being played and any small object, such as a coin or a tee, when used to mark the position of a ball or the extent of an area in which a ball is to be dropped. Equipment includes a golf cart, whether or not motorized. If such a cart is shared by two or more players, the cart and everything in it are deemed to be the equipment of the player whose ball is involved except that, when the cart is being moved by one of the players sharing it, the cart and everything in it are deemed to be that player's equipment.

Note: A ball played at the hole being played is equipment when it has been lifted and not put back into play.

[1] You cannot push a short putt all the way into the hole, for example.
[2] For example, a caddie cannot hold an umbrella over the golfer.

1

© USGA

A player has "addressed the ball" when he has taken his stance and has also grounded his club, except that in a hazard a player has addressed the ball when he has taken his stance.

Taking the "stance" consists in a player placing his feet in position for and preparatory to making a stroke.

18-1. By Outside Agency

If a ball at rest is moved by an outside agency, the player shall incur no penalty and the ball shall be replaced before the player plays another stroke.

18-2. By Player, Partner, Caddie or Equipment

a. General

When a player's ball is in play, if:

1. the player, his partner or either of their caddies lifts or moves it, touches it purposely (except with a club in the act of addressing it) or causes it to move except as permitted by a rule, or
2. equipment of the player or his partner causes the ball to move, the player shall incur a penalty stroke. The ball shall be replaced unless the movement of the ball occurs after the player has begun his swing and he does not discontinue his swing.

Under the Rules no penalty is incurred if a player accidentally causes his ball to move in the following circumstances:

- In measuring to determine which ball farther from hole -- Rule 10-4
- In searching for covered ball in hazard or for ball in casual water, ground under repair, etc. -- Rule 12-1
- In process of repairing hole plug or ball mark -- Rule 16-1c
- In process of removing loose impediment on putting green -- Rule 18-2c
- In process of lifting ball under a Rule -- Rule 20-1
- In process of placing or replacing ball under a Rule -- Rule 20-3a
- In complying with Rule 22 relating to lifting ball interfering with or assisting play
- In removal of movable obstruction-- Rule 24-1

b. Ball Moving After Address

If a player's ball in play moves after he has addressed it (other than as a result of a stroke), the player shall be deemed to have moved the ball and shall incur a penalty stroke. The player shall replace the ball unless the movement of the ball occurs after he has begun his swing and he does not discontinue his swing.

2

© USGA

c. Ball Moving After Loose Impediment Touched

Through the green, if the ball moves after any loose impediment lying within a club-length of it has been touched by the player, his partner or either of their caddies and before the player has addressed it, the player shall be deemed to have moved the ball and shall incur a penalty stroke. The player shall replace the ball unless the movement of the ball occurs after he has begun his swing and he does not discontinue his swing.

On the putting green, if the ball or ball-marker moves while removing a loose impediment, the ball or ball-marker shall be replaced. There is no penalty provided the movement of the ball or the ball-marker is directly attributable to the removal or the loose impediment. Otherwise, the player shall incur a penalty stroke under Rule 18-2a or 20-1.

18-3. By Opponent, Caddie or Equipment in Match Play

a. During Search

If, during search for a player's ball, it is moved by an opponent, his caddie or his equipment, no penalty is incurred and the player shall replace the ball.

b. Other Than During Search

If, other than during search for a ball, the ball is touched or moved by an opponent, his caddie or his equipment, except as otherwise provided in the Rules, the opponent shall incur a penalty stroke. The player shall replace the ball.

18-4. By Fellow-Competitor, Caddie or Equipment in Stroke Play

If a competitor's ball is moved by a fellow-competitor, his caddie or his equipment, no penalty is incurred. The competitor shall replace his ball.

18-5. By Another Ball

If a ball in play and at rest is moved by another ball in motion after a stroke, the moved ball shall be replaced.

Penalty for Breach of Rule:

Match play -- Loss of hole; Stroke play -- Two strokes.

*If a player who is required to replace a ball fails to do so, he shall incur the general penalty for breach of Rule 18 but no additional penalty under Rule 18 shall be applied.

Note 1: If a ball to be replaced under this Rule is not immediately recoverable, another ball may be substituted.

Note 2: If it is impossible to determine the spot on which a ball is to be placed, see Rule 20-3c.

3

Figure 5.1

Figure 5.1 *(continued)*

The Setup

So that your screen will match the illustrations and the tasks in this project will function as described, make sure that the Word 97 settings listed in Table 5.1 are selected on your computer.

Table 5.1 Word 97 Settings.

Location	Make these settings:
View, Toolbars	Deselect all toolbars except the Standard and Formatting toolbars
View	Deselect the Ruler option and select the Normal view
Standard toolbar	Deselect any buttons that are selected and set Zoom to 100%

Navigating Within a Long Document

Word 97 provides several ways to navigate within a document—Go To, Find, and Word's cool new Document Map feature. You can use buttons or scroll bars to go to each page, heading, graphic, or table. If you want to revise specific text in a long document, the easiest way to go to the text is to use the Find command. You also can use the Document Map to move to text under a specific heading.

TASK 1: TO GO TO A PAGE:

1 Open *Glfrules.doc*.
The first page of a multiple-page document displays.

2 Drag the box in the vertical scroll bar until you see Page 5 and then click the cursor in "b. Relief" in the document. (You may have to scroll up to find the text.)

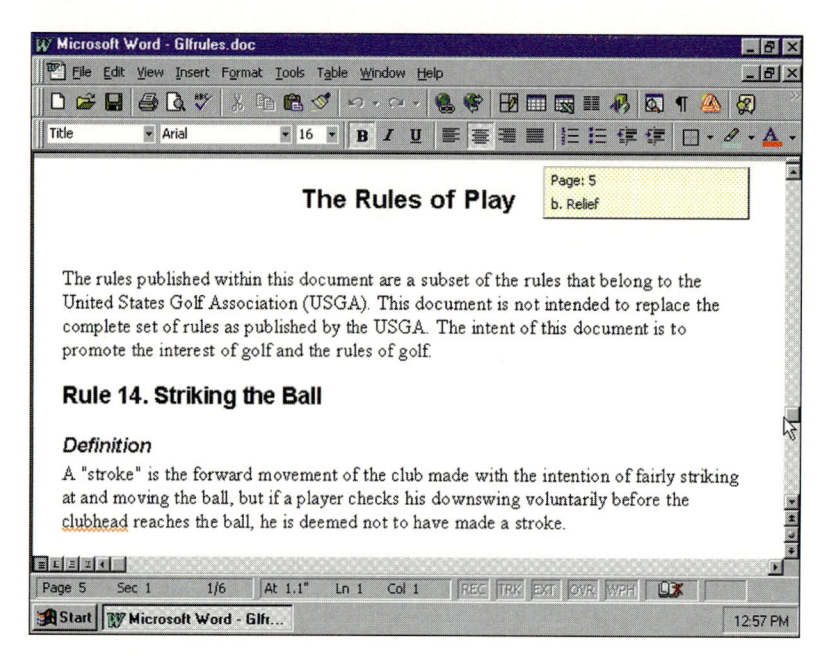

3 Choose View, Page Layout.
The view changes to Page Layout.

> **Tip** In Normal view, a page break that Word inserts automatically is a dotted line; in Page Layout view, the page break is a thick gray line with a thin black line at the top.

4 Click the Previous Page button twice.
Page 4 displays (as shown in the status bar).

5 Click the Next Page button.
Page 5 displays.

The new browsing feature allows you to navigate a document by jumping from one element to another. For example, you can jump from heading to heading or from table to table.

TASK 2: TO BROWSE BY HEADINGS:

1 Press CTRL+HOME.
The insertion point moves to the top of the first page.

2 Choose Edit, Go To.

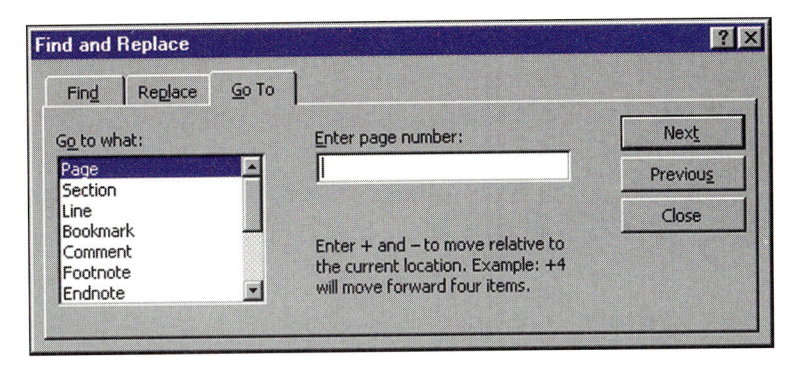

3 Choose Heading for Go to what, type **+1**, and click Close.
The dialog box closes, and the Previous Page and Next Page buttons turn blue, indicating that their functions have now changed to Previous Heading and Next Heading.

> **Tip** Pointing to the blue navigational buttons displays the current name of the button in a pop-up box.

4 Click the Next Heading button.
The insertion point moves to the first paragraph with a heading style. (Notice the name of the style in the Style box in the Formatting toolbar.)

5 Click repeatedly to browse through the entire document.
The insertion point moves to each paragraph with a heading style until it reaches the last paragraph with a heading style at the end of the document.

Finding a specific word or string of words is an efficient way to navigate in documents of more than one page, especially if you want to go to a specific portion of text to edit the text.

TASK 3: TO FIND TEXT IN A DOCUMENT:

1 Choose Edit, Find.

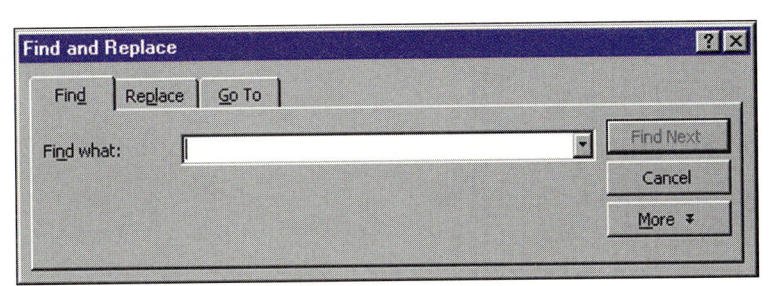

2 Type **club** and click Find Next.
The next occurrence of the word is highlighted and the dialog box remains open. If you get a message saying that Word has reached the end of the document, click Yes to continue searching from the beginning.

3 Click Find Next.
The word "clubhead" is highlighted.

4 Click More.

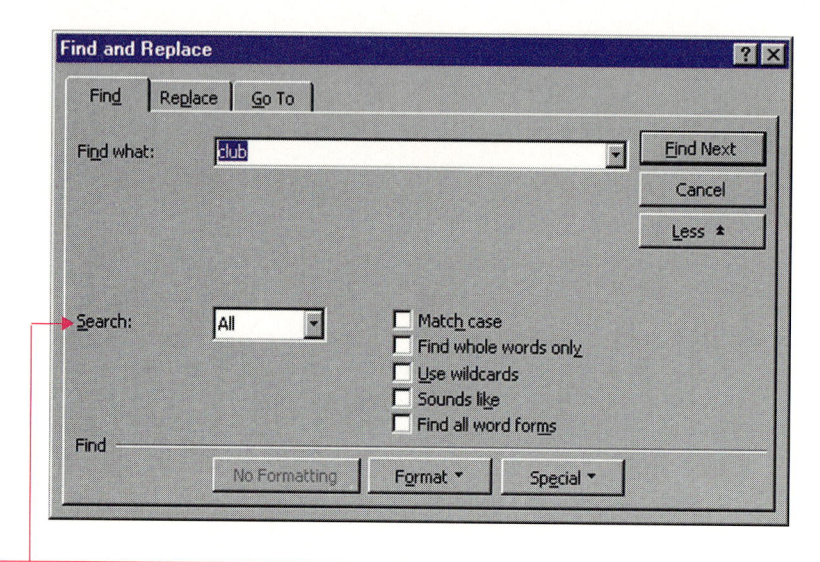

This option changes the direction of the search; the choices are All, Up, and Down

5 Choose the Find whole words only option and click Find Next.
The next occurrence is highlighted, but it's hidden by the dialog box.

6 Click [X].
The dialog box closes, the Previous Heading button changes to the Previous Find/Go To button, and the Next Heading button changes to the Next Find/Go To button.

7 Click [↓].
The next occurrence is highlighted.

> **Tip** To quickly change the navigation buttons back to Previous Page and Next Page, click the Select Browse Object button and click the Browse by Page button.

The **Document Map** is a new tool in Word 97 that lists all the document headings, similar to an outline, in a pane on the left. The headings are linked to the document so that you can click a heading and go directly to the text in the document.

TASK 4: TO NAVIGATE WITH THE DOCUMENT MAP:

1 Click the Document Map button.

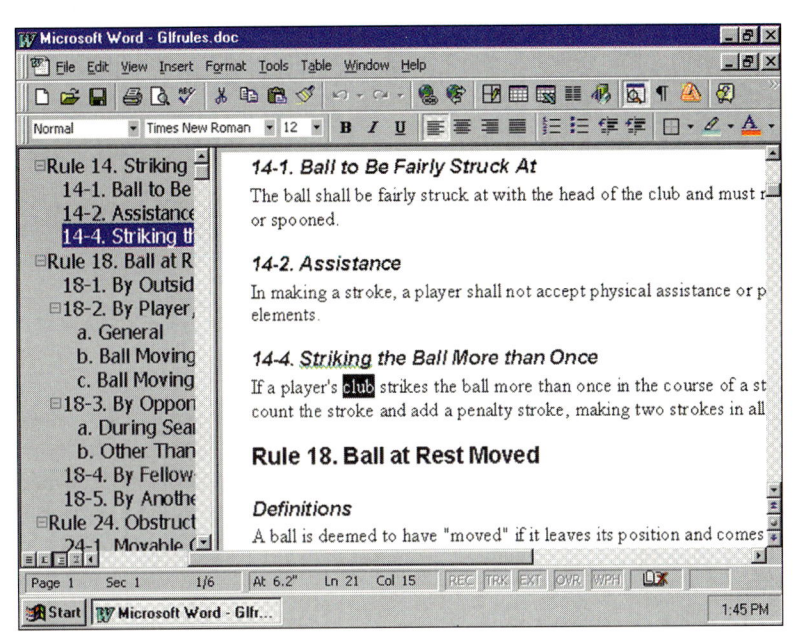

2 Click "Rule 14. Striking the Ball" in the left pane.

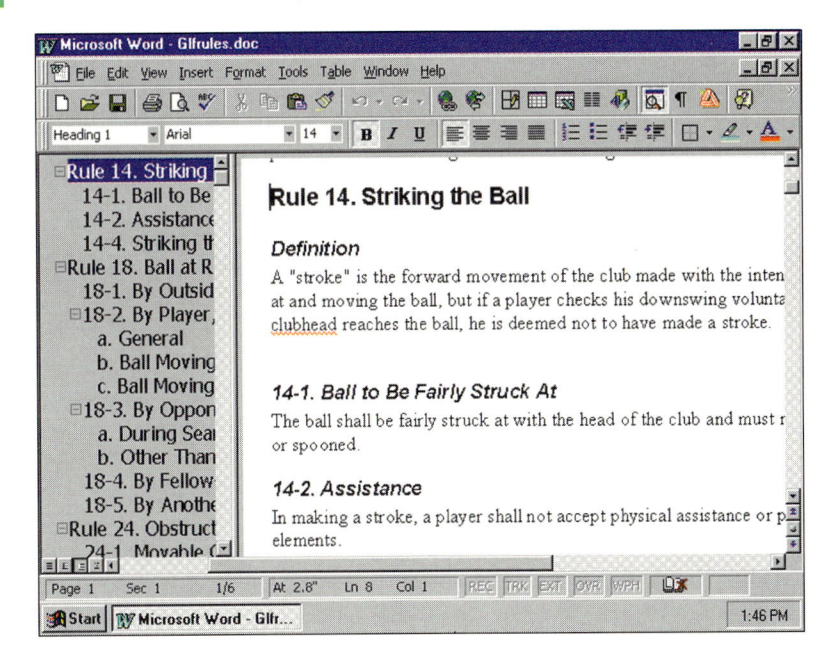

Project 5: Formatting a Long Document   WORD-137

3 Click "Rule 24. Obstructions" in the left pane.

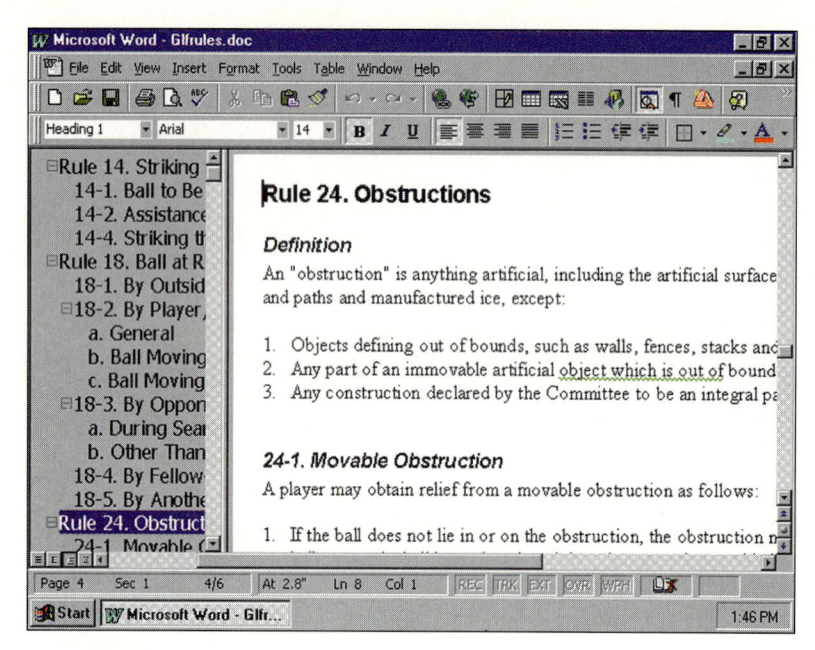

4 Click 🔍.
The view changes to Page Layout, the view originally selected.

> **Tip** To collapse a heading in the Document Map pane so that the subheadings are hidden, click the minus sign that appears to the left of the heading. To expand a heading to show the subheadings, click the plus sign that appears to the left of the heading.

Inserting and Deleting Page Breaks

When a page fills up with text, Word 97 automatically inserts a page break, referred to as a *soft page break*, and creates a new page. If you want a page to break before it's filled, you can insert a page break yourself. A user-defined page break is called a *hard page break*.

TASK 5: TO INSERT A PAGE BREAK FOR THE TITLE PAGE AND FOR EACH RULE

1 Press CTRL+HOME and click before "Rule 14. Striking the Ball."
The insertion point is positioned before the "R" in the text.

2 Press CTRL+ENTER.

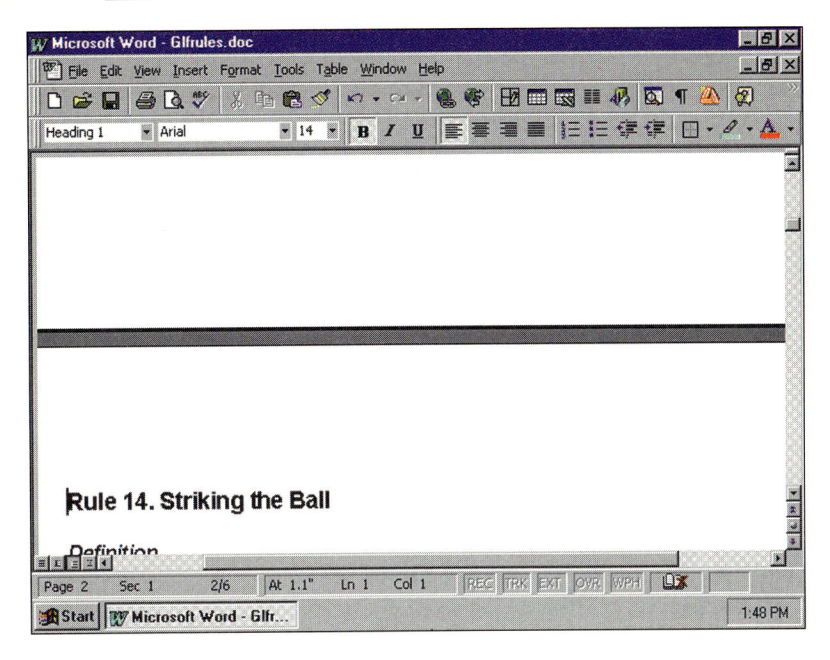

3 Choose View, Normal.
The view changes from Page Layout to Normal.

> **Tip** In Normal view, a hard page break has the words "Page Break" centered on the dotted line; a soft page break is simply a dotted line.

4 Choose Edit, Find.
The Find and Replace dialog box displays.

5 Type **Rule 18,** click Less, and then click Find Next.
"Rule 18" is highlighted.

6 Click Cancel.
The Find and Replace dialog box closes.

7 Press ←.
The insertion point moves to the beginning of the highlighted text, and the text is no longer highlighted.

8 Press CTRL+ENTER.
You just forced Word 97 to insert another page break. What power! What control!

9 Choose Edit, Find.
The Find and Replace dialog box displays.

10 Type **Rule 24,** click Find Next, and then click Find Next again to go to the next occurrence.
The text is highlighted.

11 Click Cancel.
The dialog box closes.

12 Press ←.
The insertion point moves to the beginning of the highlighted text, and the text is no longer highlighted.

13 Press CTRL+ENTER.
A page break is inserted.

TASK 6: TO DELETE A PAGE BREAK:

1 Press CTRL+HOME.
The insertion point moves to the top of the document.

> **Tip** If you want to delete a page break that you have inserted, it's advisable—though not mandatory—to switch to the Normal view. In the Normal view, you can actually see a symbol that you can delete.

2 Click the Select Browse Object button.

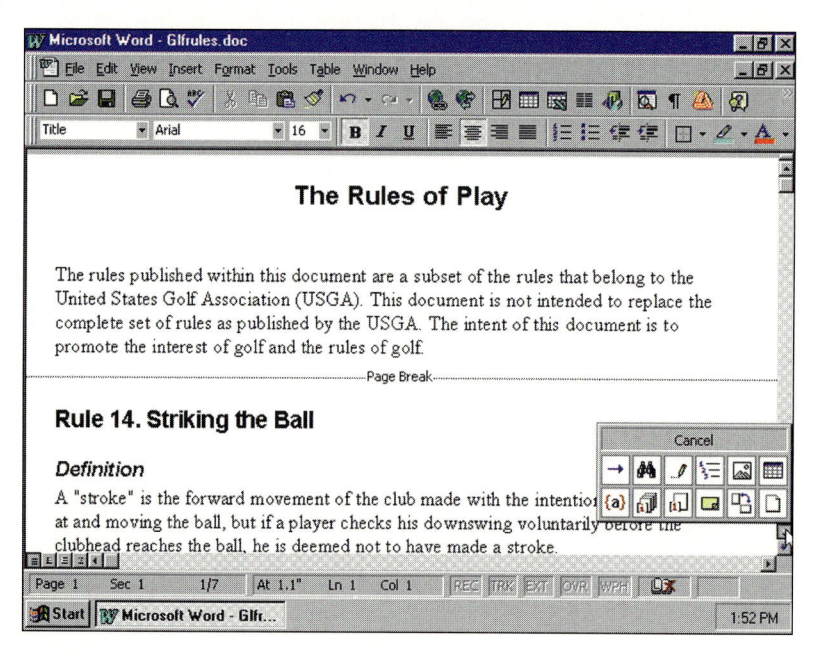

3 Click the Browse by Page button.
The Browse palette closes, and the navigational buttons change from blue to black.

4 Click ▼ twice.
The insertion point is blinking at the top of page 3.

5 Scroll up until you can see the page break.

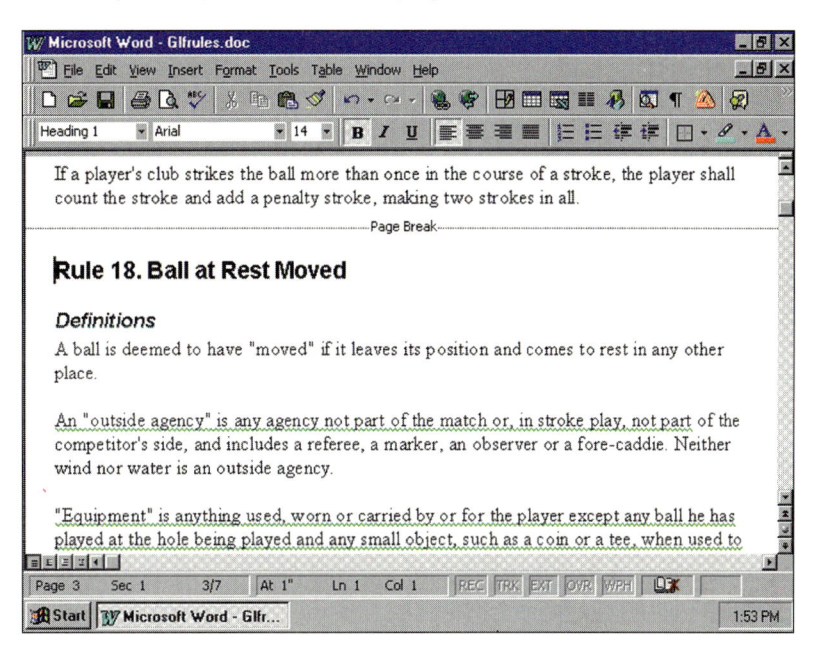

6 Click anywhere on the page break's dotted line.
The insertion point is positioned at the left margin on the dotted line.

7 Press (DELETE).
Zap! The page break is gone. Out of there. History.

8 Click ▼ three times to move to page 5, and scroll up so that you can see the page break.

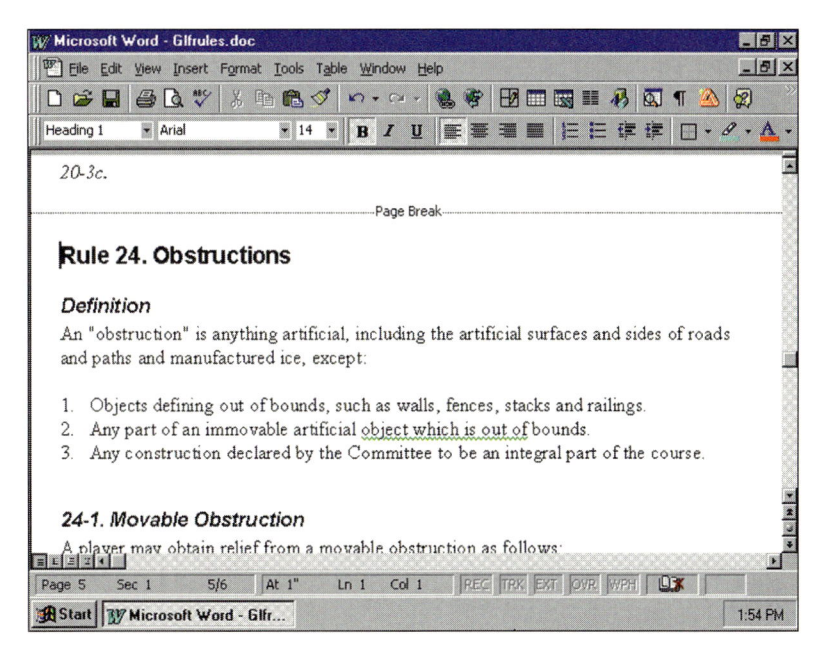

9 Click anywhere on the page break's dotted line.
The insertion point is positioned at the left margin on the dotted line.

10 Press (DELETE).
The page break is deleted.

> **Note** You can't delete a soft page break.

> **Tip** To delete a hard page break in the Page Layout view, click after the last character on the previous page and press Del or click before the first character on the page and press Backspace.

Inserting Section Breaks

A *section break* defines a new *section* in a document. You need to create a new section in a document if you want to use different formats, such as paper size and orientation, or if you want to create different headers and footers for each section.

> **Note** A *header* is text that prints at the top of every page in a section. A *footer* is text that prints at the bottom of every page in a section.

In the Rules of Play document, you will insert a section break between the title page and the first page so that you can create different headers and footers for these sections later. Because the type of section break you will insert carries a page break with it, you will have to delete the page break you inserted earlier, to avoid having a blank page. (Not all section breaks have page breaks.)

TASK 7: TO INSERT A SECTION BREAK:

1 Press (CTRL)+(HOME).
The insertion point moves to the top of the document.

2 Click before "Rule 14. Striking the Ball."
The insertion point is blinking before the "R" in the text.

3 Choose Insert, Break.

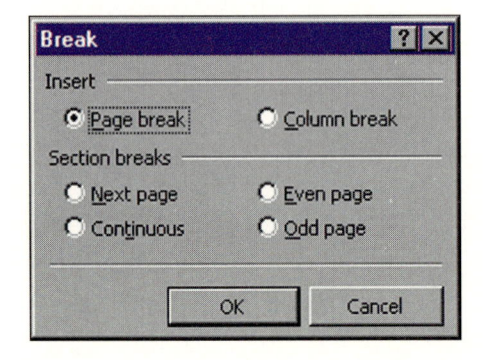

Project 5: Formatting a Long Document WORD-143

4 Select Next page and click OK.

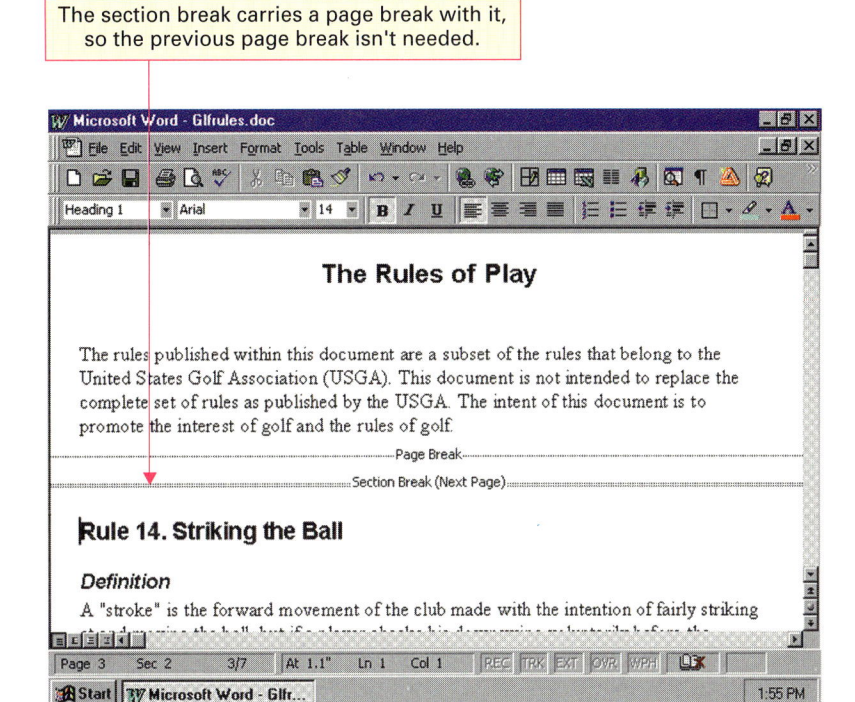

> The section break carries a page break with it, so the previous page break isn't needed.

5 Click the page break above the section break and press DELETE.
The page break is deleted.

> **Tip** To delete a section break, change to Normal view, click the section break, and press DELETE.

Creating Headers and Footers

When you create a header or a footer, a toolbar displays, and a header or footer space opens. Because text in a header or footer is normally printed in the center or flush with the left or right margins, the space has a center tab in the center and a right tab on the right margin.

TASK 8: TO CREATE A HEADER AND A FOOTER:

1 Click anywhere on page 2.
"Page 2 Sec 2" displays in the status bar.

2 Choose View, Header and Footer.

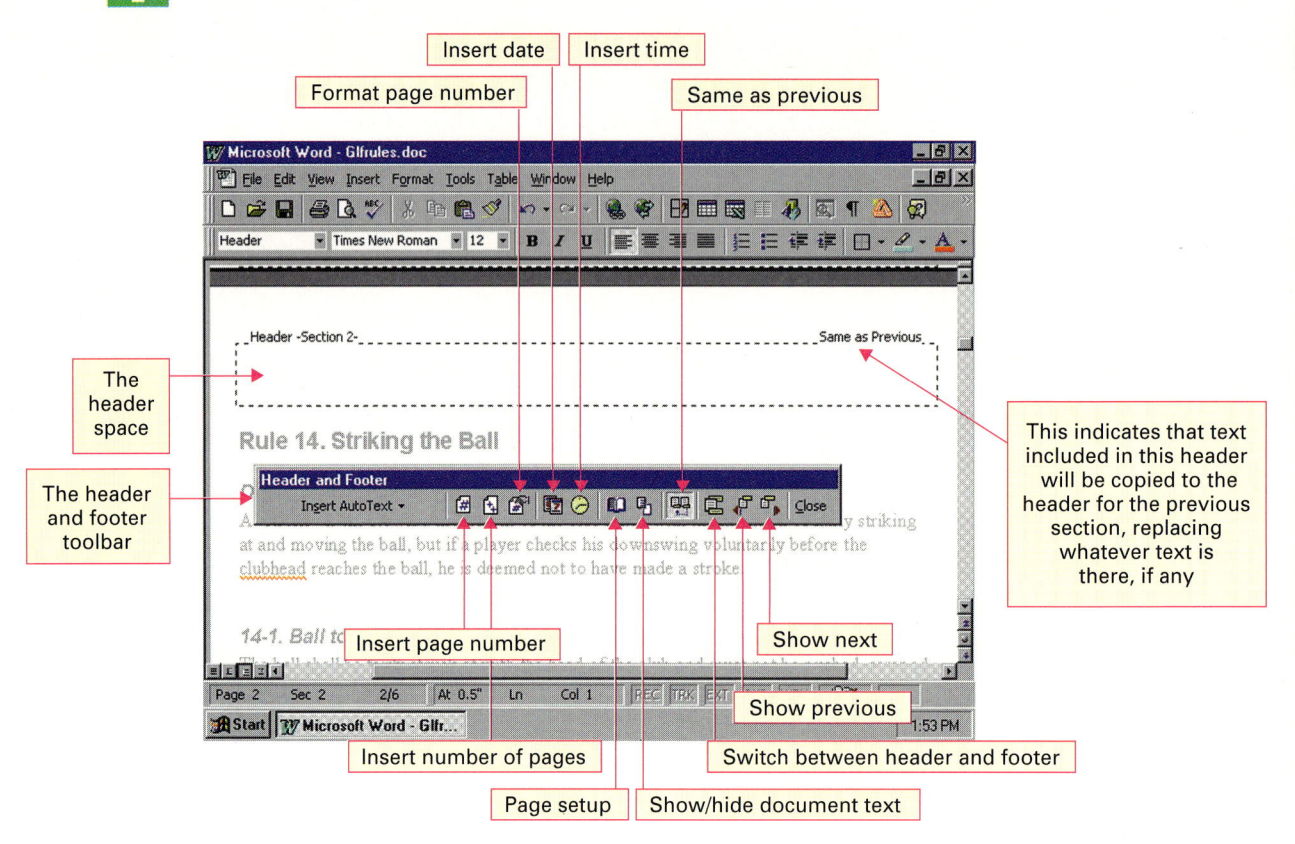

Callouts on the screenshot:
- Insert date
- Insert time
- Format page number
- Same as previous
- The header space
- The header and footer toolbar
- Insert page number
- Show next
- Insert number of pages
- Show previous
- Page setup
- Show/hide document text
- Switch between header and footer
- This indicates that text included in this header will be copied to the header for the previous section, replacing whatever text is there, if any

3 Click the Same as Previous button to deselect it so that this header doesn't influence the header in the previous section.
The words "Same as Previous" in the upper-right corner of the header are deleted.

4 Press TAB twice.
The insertion point moves to the right margin in the header space.

Project 5: Formatting a Long Document WORD-145

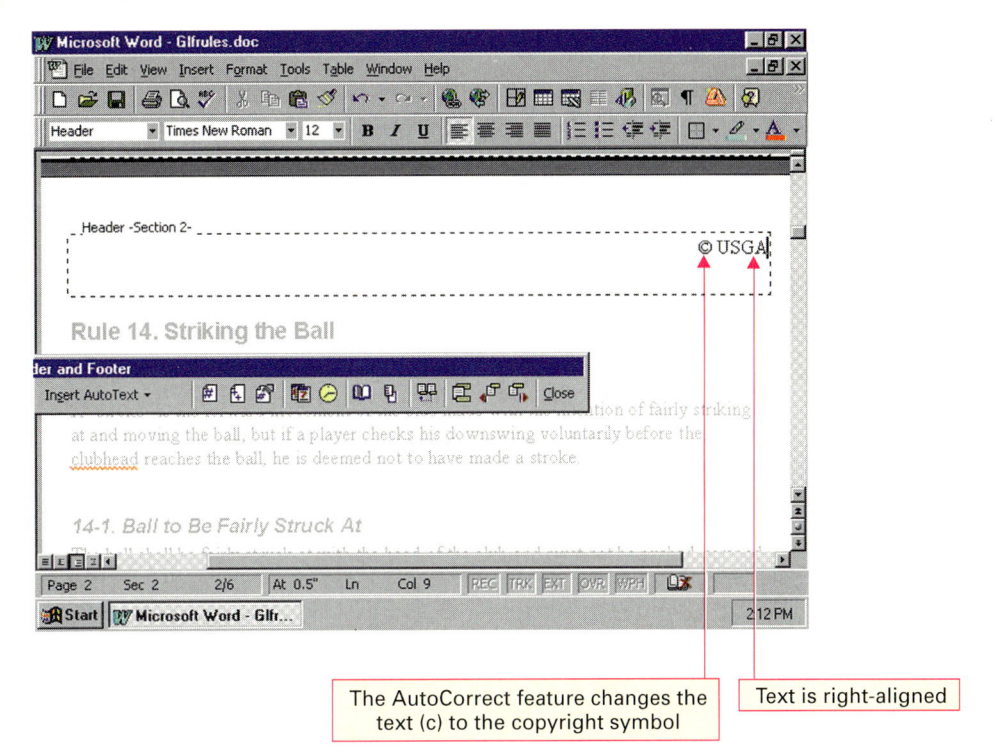

5 Type **(c) USGA**.

> The AutoCorrect feature changes the text (c) to the copyright symbol

> Text is right-aligned

6 Click the Show Previous button.

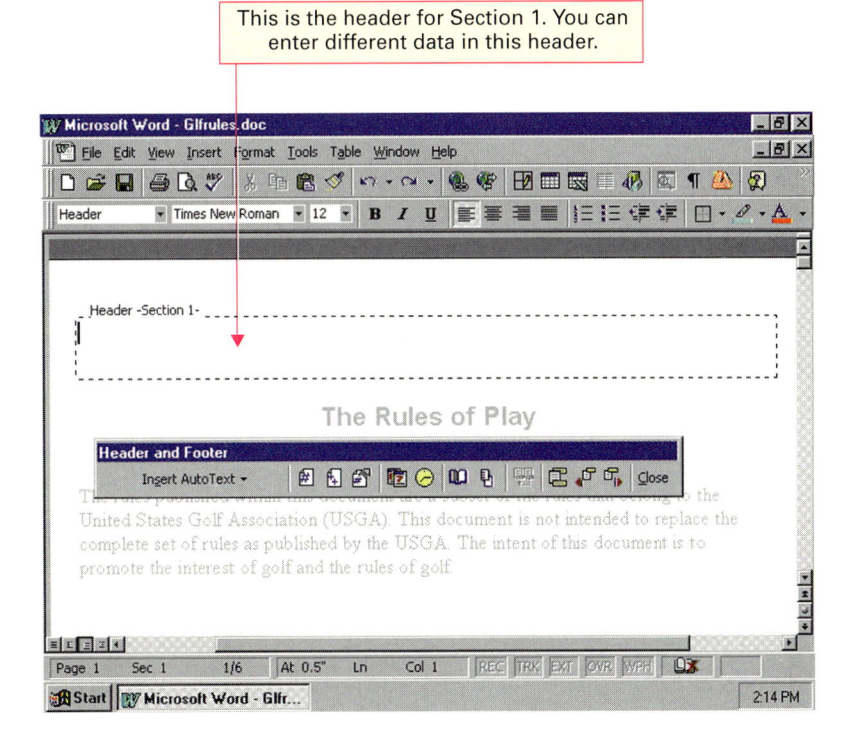

> This is the header for Section 1. You can enter different data in this header.

7 Click the Show Next button.
The header for Section 2 displays.

8 Click the Switch Between Header and Footer button.

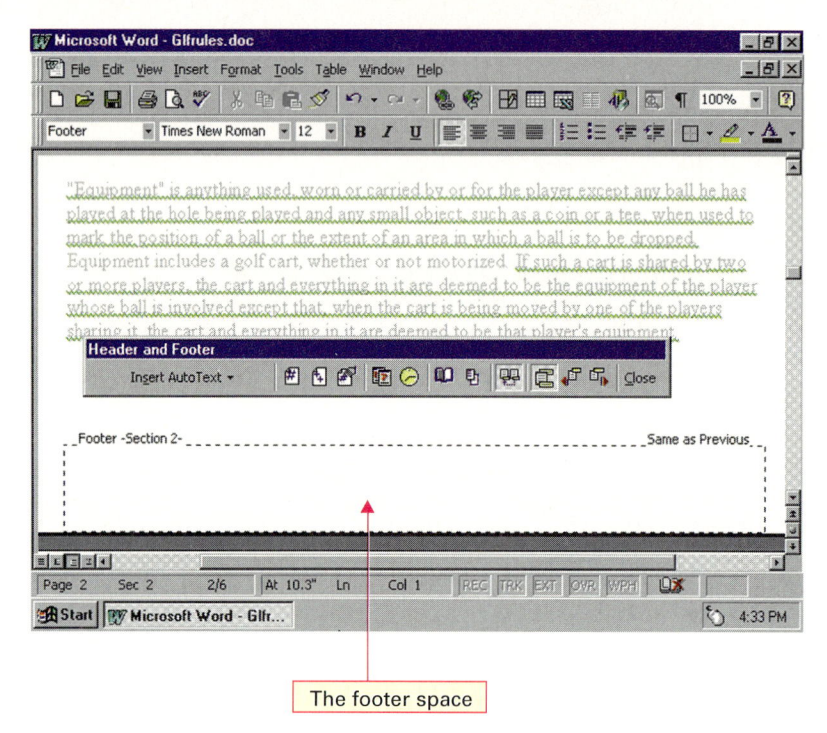

The footer space

9 Click .
The words "Same as Previous" in the upper-right corner of the footer are deleted.

10 Press TAB.
The insertion point moves to the middle of the footer space.

11 Click the Insert Page Number button.
The number "2" is inserted because Section 2 starts on page 2.

12 Click the Format Page Number button.

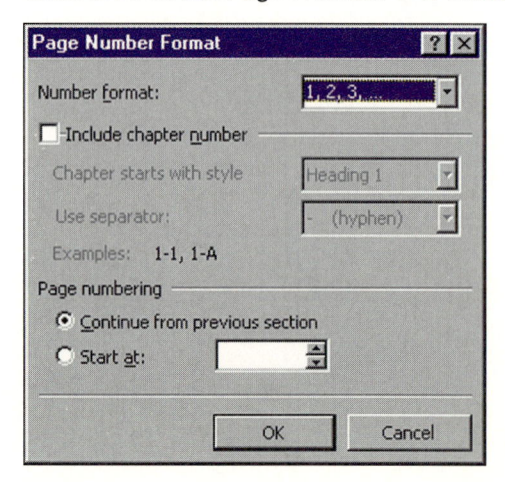

13 Select Start at.

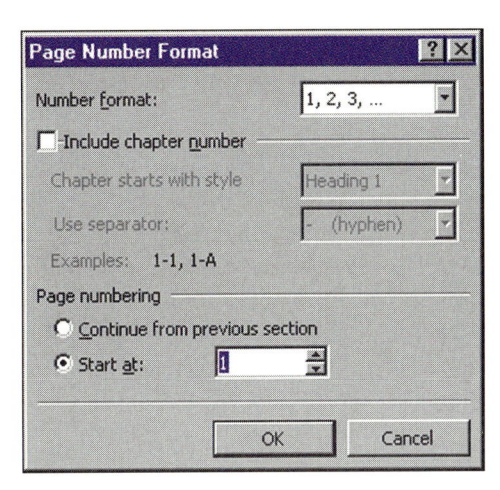

14 Click OK.

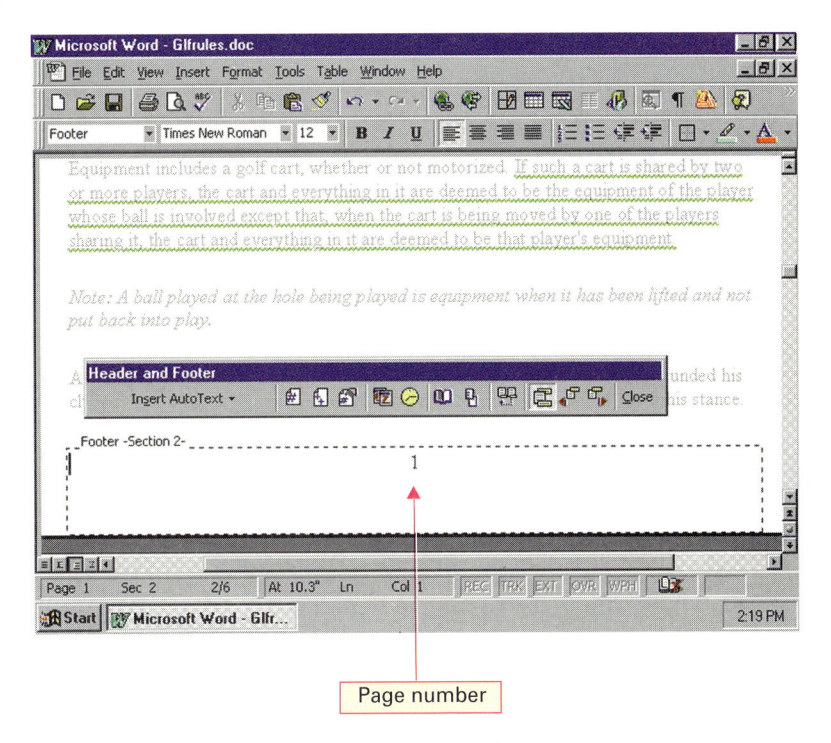

Page number

15 Click Close on the Header and Footer toolbar.
The footer space closes.

> **Tip** Headers and footers aren't visible in the Normal view.

16 Choose View, Page Layout, press (CTRL)+(HOME), and then scroll through the document to see the headers and footers.
No header or footer appears on the first page, but headers and footers appear on subsequent pages, and the page numbers are incremented.

17 Choose View, Normal.
The view changes to Normal and the headers and footers are no longer visible.

Creating Footnotes

A *footnote* is a comment or reference that appears at the bottom of the page. The reference in the text to which the footnote applies is generally numbered, and the footnote displays the same number. When you create a footnote, Word automatically numbers the footnote in the text and provides sufficient space at the bottom of the page for the footnote. You can create multiple footnotes on the same page. If you group the footnotes together at the end of the document, they're called *endnotes*.

You can insert footnotes in any order, and Word will number or renumber them consecutively throughout the document. Word is one accommodating word processing program.

TASK 9: TO INSERT A FOOTNOTE:

1 Choose Edit, Find.
The Find and Replace dialog box displays.

2 Type **protection from the elements.** and click Find Next.
The text is highlighted.

3 Click Cancel.
The Find and Replace dialog box closes.

4 Press → twice.
The insertion point moves to the end of the sentence and the highlight is removed.

5 Choose Insert, Footnote.

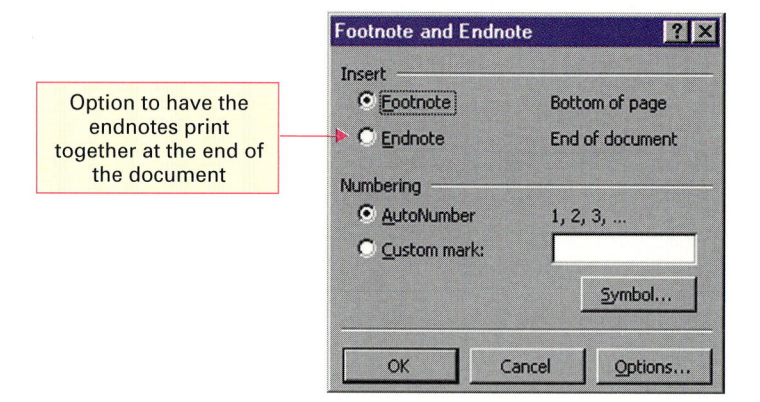

Option to have the endnotes print together at the end of the document

Project 5: Formatting a Long Document   WORD-149

6 Click OK.

The footnote space

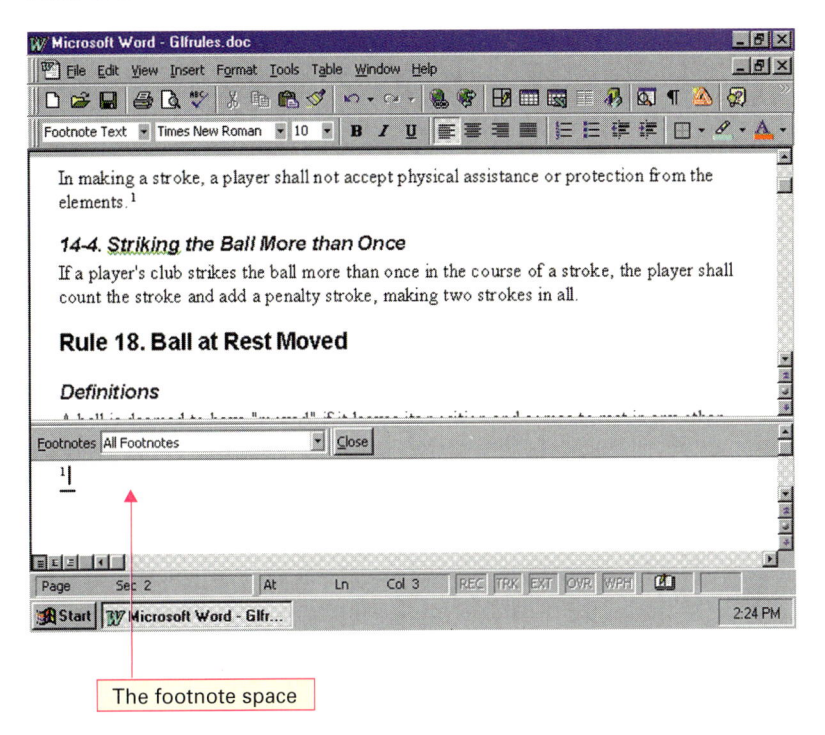

7 Type **For example, a caddie cannot hold an umbrella over the golfer.**

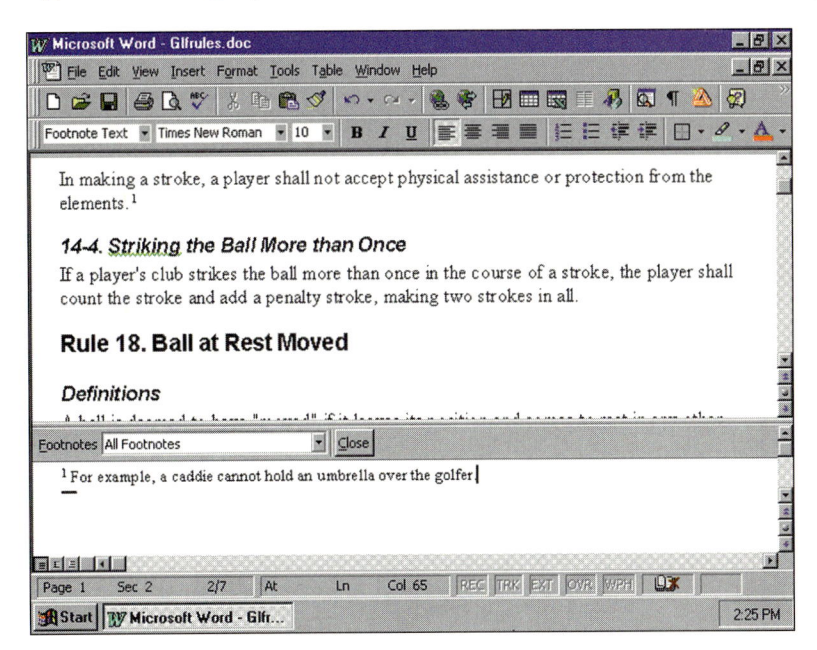

8 Click the up arrow in the vertical scroll bar until the previous heading is visible and click after "scraped or spooned."

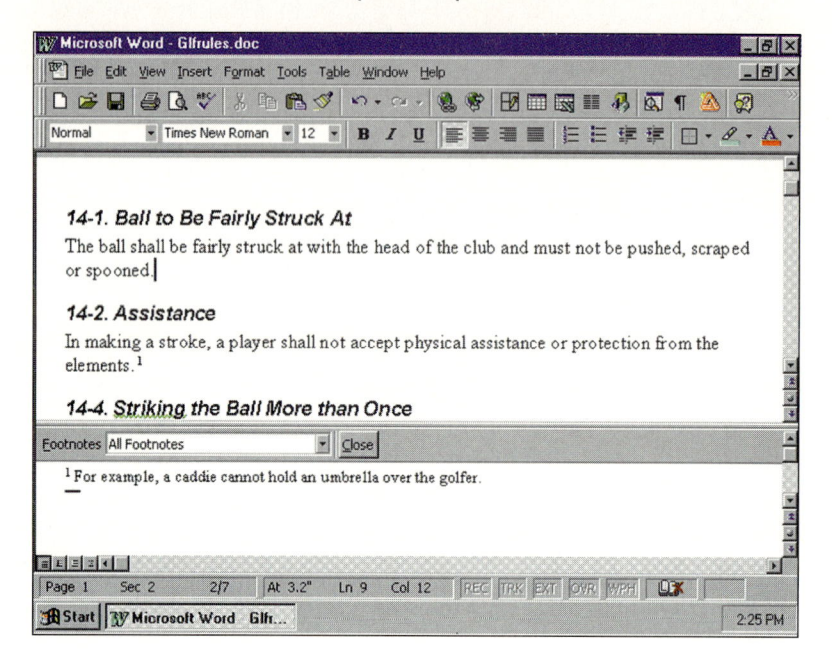

9 Choose Insert, Footnote, and click OK.
The reference number 1 is inserted and the previous reference changes to 2.

10 Type **You cannot push a short putt all the way into the hole, for example**.

11 Click Close.
The footnote space closes.

12 Change to Page Layout view if necessary and scroll to the end of the page to see the footnote.

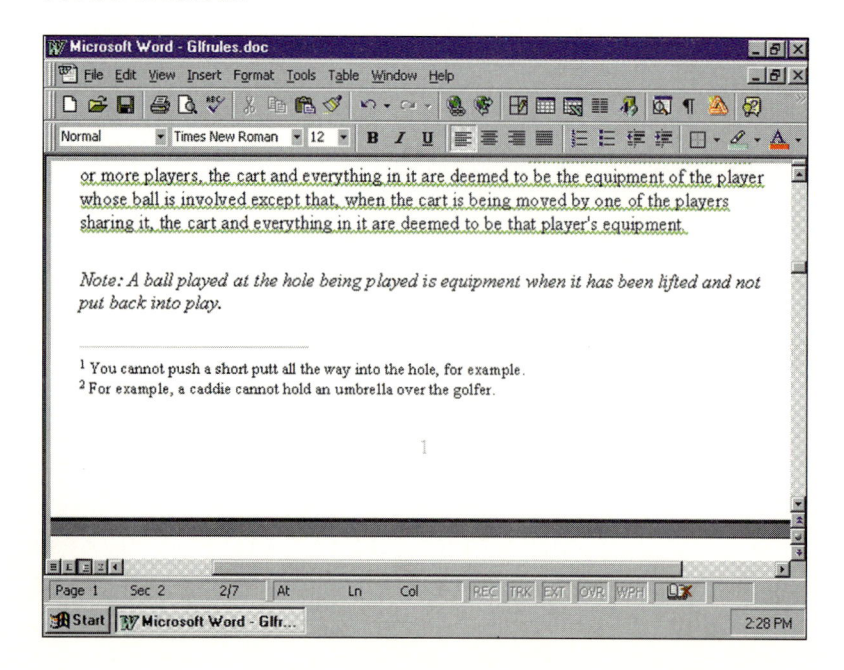

> **Tip** If you can't see a footnote, you're not blind. Just switch to Page Layout view. Footnotes aren't visible in Normal view.

The Conclusion

Save the file as *Rules of Golf.doc*. If you have access to a printer, practice printing portions of the document such as the current page or pages 2 and 3. When finished, close the file.

Summary and Exercises

Summary

- Word 97 provides several ways to navigate in a long document: Go To, Find, and Document Map.
- A page break creates a new page.
- A section break creates a new section.
- A header prints at the top of every page in a section.
- A footer prints at the bottom of every page in a section.
- Word 97 automatically numbers footnotes.

Key Terms and Operations

Key Terms
Document Map
endnote
footer
footnote
hard page break
header
page break
section break
Select Browse Object button
soft page break

Operations
delete a page break
delete a section break
find text
go to text
insert a page break
insert a section break

Study Questions

Multiple Choice

1. A footnote
   a. is automatically renumbered if you insert another footnote.
   b. is automatically renumbered if you insert another footnote before it.
   c. displays a subscripted number.
   d. doesn't display in Page Layout view.

2. A page break
   a. is inserted automatically by Word when a page fills up.
   b. is never inserted in the middle of a paragraph.
   c. can only be inserted by the user.
   d. allows you to use different orientation for different pages in the same document.

3. A footnote prints
   a. at the end of the document.
   b. at the bottom of the page on which the reference appears.
   c. only in the Page Layout view.
   d. only in the Normal view.

4. The Document Map
   a. is an outline.
   b. lists all the document headings in the right pane.

c. displays headings that are linked to the document.
d. displays all the headers, footers, footnotes, and other objects that aren't actually part of the body of the text.

5. A header prints
   a. at the top of every page.
   b. at the bottom of every page.
   c. at the top of every page in a section.
   d. at the top of every page in every section.

6. A section break
   a. always inserts a page break.
   b. allows you to use a different page orientation for different pages in the same document.
   c. is another name for a page break.
   d. must be applied to even or odd pages.

7. "Same as Previous" indicates that
   a. the section break will be like the one before it.
   b. the footnote will be like the one before it.
   c. the page break will be like the one before it.
   d. the header will be like the one before it.

8. A dotted line that spans the width of the screen indicates
   a. a soft page break.
   b. a section break.
   c. the footnote space.
   d. the header space.

9. The Select Browse Object button
   a. is located on the Standard toolbar.
   b. is located in the horizontal scroll bar.
   c. displays a palette.
   d. displays the Object toolbar.

10. If you want the first page of a document to have a portrait orientation and the next page to have a landscape orientation, you must
    a. insert a page break.
    b. create two different documents.
    c. insert a section break.
    d. insert a footer.

Short Answer

1. What happens if you click the Select Browse Object button?
2. List all the elements that you can go to using the Go To command.
3. What additional options are displayed in the Find dialog box if you click the More button?
4. What happens to the footnote numbers if you insert a footnote between two existing footnotes?
5. How can you change the navigational keys back to Previous Page and Next Page?

6. What elements can be automatically inserted in a header or footer?

7. How can you use two different page numbering formats in the same document?

8. How do you collapse the headings in the Document Map?

9. How do you display the Document Map?

10. What's the difference between footnotes and endnotes?

For Discussion

1. If you want to find several occurrences of a word, what's the best way to find the occurrences and read them in context?

2. Discuss the advantages of using a section break.

3. Why is it better to use a header or footer than to simply type the text that you want at the top or bottom of every page?

4. Discuss the benefits of using a word processing program to create a document that has many footnotes versus typing the document on a typewriter.

Review Exercises

1. Creating a Document with Two Sections

For the golf tournament, you need to type the memo and table pictured in Figure 5.2. Follow these steps to complete the task.

1. Create a new document using the *Professional Memo.dot* template.

2. Type the text for page 1 as shown in Figure 5.2.

3. Insert a Next Page section break at the end of the page.

4. Click page 2 and change the orientation to landscape.

5. Type the title and the footnote.

6. Create a table that's 13 columns by 7 rows.

7. Enter the data in the table as shown in Figure 5.2.

8. Save the file as *Golf Ball Sales.doc* and close it.

The Willows Resort

Memo

To: Thomas Williams
From: <type your name here>
Date: 11/29/96
Re: Golf Ball Sales for Last Year

I have looked up the sales records for last year for all sales of golf balls. The attached table includes sales in the pro shop **and all other** shops in The Willows Resort. If you want just the sales for the pro shop, let me know. I can easily obtain that information as well.

● Page 1

Golf Ball Sales for Last Year[1]

	Jan	Feb	Mar	Apr	May	Jun	Jul	Aug	Sep	Oct	Nov	Dec
MaxFli	500	900	700	760	800*	900	840	880	800	760*	900	900*
Titleist	520	610	720*	750	790	800*	910*	900	790	760	610*	800*
Dunlop	500	570	580	600*	510	400	500	600	510*	600	570	400*
Wilson	520	660	760	780	790	850	760	720*	790	820	660	850*
X-Out	540*	590*	600	580	590	600	780	800	590	580	590	600
Total	2580	3330	3360	3470	3480	3550	3790	3900	3480	3520	3330	3550

[1] Asterisk denotes that a sales promotion was run for that brand in that month.

● Page 2

Figure 5.2

2. Revising a Multi-Page Document

The Games.doc needs to be revised and references added for some of the information contained in the document. Follow these steps to edit the document.

1. Open the file named *Games.doc*.
2. Add this footnote to the title:

   See The Complete Book of Golf Games by Scott Johnston

3. View the Document Map so you can get an idea of what's contained in the file.
4. Click the Tournament Formats heading in the left pane.
5. Delete the page break after the "Tournament Formats" heading.
6. Insert a page break before the heading "Tournament Formats" heading.
7. Insert a Next Page section break between the first and second page.
8. On page 2, create a footer that contains a centered page number (starting with the number 2). Be sure there's no page number on page 1.
9. Insert a page break before the "Pink Ball" heading.
10. Search for "The Complete Book of Golf Games" on the Web and read the rules for the game called *Chicago*. Add the rules to the end of the document under the "Chicago" heading.
11. Save the file as *Games of Golf.doc* and close it.

Figure 5.3

Tournament Formats

Medal Play
Also known as Stroke Play
Comment: No gimmies
Handicap: Use handicaps from 80-100% - preferably on the lower side to prevent sandbagging.

Golfers play 18 holes and the winner is the player with the best gross scores and net scores.

Scramble
Comment: A shotgun start is generally used; seven or eight under is usually the score to beat
Handicap: Used to create teams but not used during play

Each foursome is a team competing against all other foursomes. Each player in the group drives off the tee, then all four golfers play their second shots from the best-driven ball. All then play their third shots from the best second ball, and so on. Each player in a foursome must have at least four of his or her drives used by the group during the game.

Flag Tournament
In a Flag Tournament, each player receives a certain number of strokes - usually the course par plus two-thirds of the player's full handicap. So, a 15-handicapper on a par-72 course gets 82 strokes.

There are then two options for play. The golfer can play all 82 shots and stops, planting a flag with her name on it on the spot where her 82nd shot landed, or she can stop when she has played 18 holes. The winner is the one who has planted the flag the farthest on the course or who has the most shots remaining after 18 holes. If the farthest two players both finish on the same green, the winner is the golfer closer to the hole.

Additional rule: You can't plant a flag past a hole that you haven't completed. For example, if you're five feet short of a green with one stroke left, you can't hit the ball onto the next fairway.

Pink Ball
Comment: A game for foursomes

Each foursome has a pink ball that rotates among players on each hole. Player 1 uses it on the first hole, player 2 on the second, and so on. Take the best net score on each hole and add it to the score of the player who used the pink ball.

Variation: Keep the overall net score for the pink ball separately, and give a prize to the team with the best pink ball score. If a team loses the pink ball, it's disqualified.

Trouble
Also known as Disaster
Comment: An excellent game for the intermediate player; encourages smart golf

Trouble is a point game in which the goal is to collect the least number of *trouble points* possible during a round.

Points are assigned as follows:

- out of bounds - 1
- water hazard - 1
- bunker - 1
- three-putt - 1
- leaving ball in bunker - 2
- hitting from one bunker to another - 2
- four-putt - 3
- whiffed ball - 4

A player can erase all the points accumulated on a given hole by making par. At the end of the round, simply net all the points against each other to see who wins.

Chicago
<type your description here>

Figure 5.3 *(continued)*

Assignments

1. Creating a Document with Two Sections on the Same Page

Create a new document and type the text that you see above the two columns in Figure 5.4. Insert a Continuous section break after the text. Create two columns and type the remaining text.

Games of Golf Seminar

The Willows Resort will be hosting a seminar in the Green Jacket Clubhouse every Tuesday for the month of March to discuss popular games of golf. The seminar will be taught by our own golf pro and the price is right – FREE.

Following is a brief description of some of the games the seminar will focus on.

Pick Up Sticks

Play is match play. Each time a player loses a hole, he may take one club in his opponent's bag out of play. (Best club to take away: the sand wedge, unless the player also carries a lob wedge.) Most players agree before the game to give the putter immunity because it's too much of a handicap not to have one.

No Alibis

Instead of using handicaps, players may replay shots during the round. The number of shots replayed is usually equal to three-fourths of a player's handicap. When replaying, the golfer must use the second shot, regardless of where it goes, and he can't replay the same shot twice.

Wolf

On each hole, the golfer with the drive that lands between the other two drives is the *wolf*. His opponents are the *hunters*. On par-three holes, the wolf is the second-closest to the pin after the first shot.

The wolf must match twice his net score on the hole against the combined net scores of the hunters. If there's a tie, players decide whether the points carry to the next hole. Any points carried over go to the next winning team.

Scotch Foursome

To play, a two-man team alternates shots from tee to green until the ball is in the hole. One player should drive all the odd holes and the other all the even. You must put some thought into who drives which holes.

Selected Score

Each golfer plays 36 holes. The final score is the combination of the two rounds, selecting the best net score from each of the 18 holes. Lowest score wins.

Medal Play

Golfers play 18 holes and the winner is the player with the best gross scores and net scores.

Scramble

Each foursome is a team competing against all other foursomes. Each player in the group drives off the tee, then all four golfers play their second shorts from the best-driven ball. All then play their third shots from the best second ball, and so on. Each player in a foursome must have at least four of their drives used by the group during the game.

Figure 5.4

2. Downloading and Formatting an RFC

Go to the Microsoft FTP site (ftp://ftp.microsoft.com) and download a file with an extension of .doc. Open the file in Word. View the headers and footers, if it has any. Add headers and footers of your own if the file doesn't have them. Add this footnote at the end of the document:

Downloaded from the Microsoft FTP site

PROJECT 6

Creating a Mail Merge

Mail merging is a process that inserts text from one file which contains a list of information into a second file such as a form letter. The process involves three steps: creating the file that contains the list of information, creating the form, and merging the two files.

Objectives

After completing this project, you will be able to:

- ➤ **Create the Data Source document**
- ➤ **Create the Main document**
- ➤ **Merge the documents**
- ➤ **Create another Main document to use with a Data Source document**
- ➤ **Create and use another Data Source document with a Main document**

The Challenge

The Olympia Fitness Center at The Willows Resort wants to offer a limited number of memberships to the general public in the surrounding area. Before advertising the memberships, the manager, Laura Carr, wants to send out personalized letters to a list of previous guests to give them an opportunity to join the club.

The Solution

You will create a **Data Source document** that contains the names and addresses of the guests to whom the letters will be sent. Then you will create the letter as a **Main document** and merge the letter with the list of names. Figure 6.1 shows a sample of a merged letter.

WORD-159

```
May 10, 1997

Mr. John A. Cartwright
ABC Printing
101 Main Street
Willow Grove, SC  22345

Dear Mr. Cartwright:

A limited number of memberships to the Olympia Fitness Center at The Willows Resort are available for
local patrons at a very reasonable price. Because you have been a guest at the fitness club in the past, we
would like to give you an opportunity to join the club before we advertise the memberships publicly. A
one-year membership is $1,500, and it includes full access to all the fitness club facilities as well as
discounts on the use of our golf and tennis facilities.

If you would like to take advantage of this special offer, please fill out and return the enclosed membership
form with a down payment of $500. You will be billed in two installments for the balance.

Sincerely,



Laura Carr
Manager, Olympia Fitness Center
```

Figure 6.1

The Setup

So that your screen will match the illustrations and the tasks in this project will function as described, make sure that the Word 97 settings listed in Table 6.1 are selected on your computer.

Table 6.1   Word 97 Settings

Location	Make these settings:
View, Toolbars	Deselect all toolbars except the Standard and Formatting toolbars
View	Deselect the Ruler option and select the Normal view
Standard toolbar	Deselect any buttons that are selected and set Zoom to 100%

Creating the Data Source Document

The Data Source document contains the *field names* of the *variables* as well as the variable information for each *record*. For example, the field named Address might contain the variable information "101 Main Street," "512 Southwinds Avenue," and so on.

Project 6: Creating a Mail Merge WORD-161

TASK 1: TO CREATE THE DATA SOURCE DOCUMENT:

1 In a blank document, choose Tools, Mail Merge.

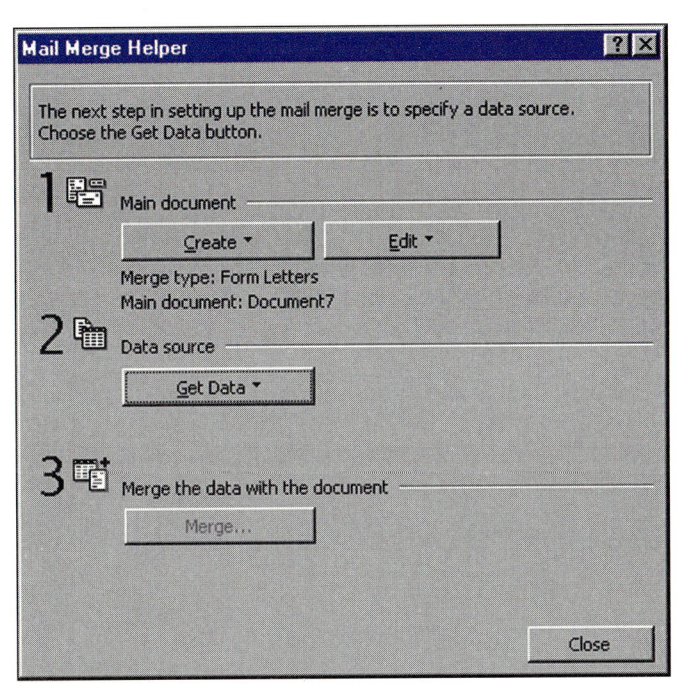

2 Select Create, Form Letters, Active Window.

3 Select Get Data.
A drop-down list displays.

4 Select Create Data Source.

> You can use this list of field names, or you can add additional fields that you need or remove fields that you don't need

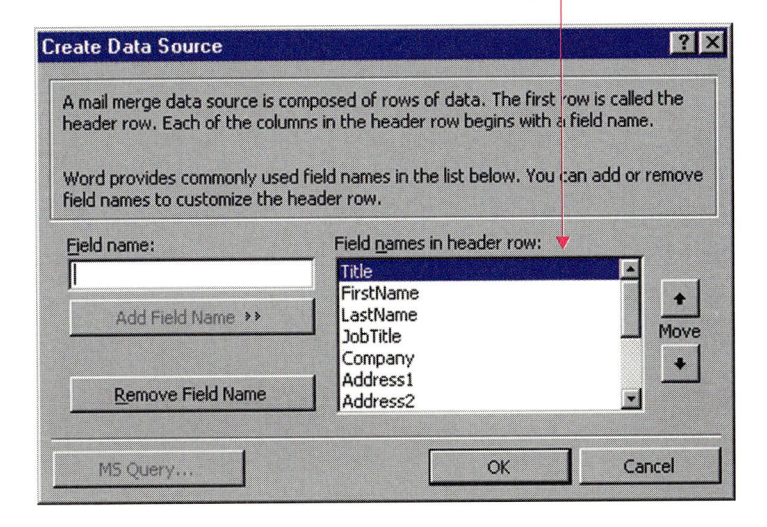

5 Select JobTitle in the Field names in header row list box.
The field is highlighted.

6 Click Remove Field Name.
The field is removed, appears in the Field name text box, and the next field is highlighted.

7 Following the same process, remove the Country, HomePhone, and WorkPhone fields.

8 Type **MiddleI**.
The name "WorkPhone" is replaced with the name "MiddleI" in the Field name text box.

9 Click Add Field Name.
The field name is added to the end of the Field names in header row list, and it's highlighted.

> **Note** A field name can't have a space in it.

10 Click the ▲ button (above the word "Move") seven times.
The field name moves up in the list until it's positioned after FirstName.

11 Click OK.
The Save As dialog box displays.

12 Type **Fitness List** for the filename, specify the Save in location that you're using for your work, and then click Save.

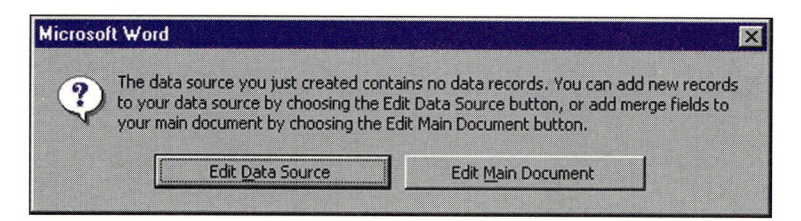

Microsoft Word dialog box: "The data source you just created contains no data records. You can add new records to your data source by choosing the Edit Data Source button, or add merge fields to your main document by choosing the Edit Main Document button." [Edit Data Source] [Edit Main Document]

13 Choose Edit Data Source.

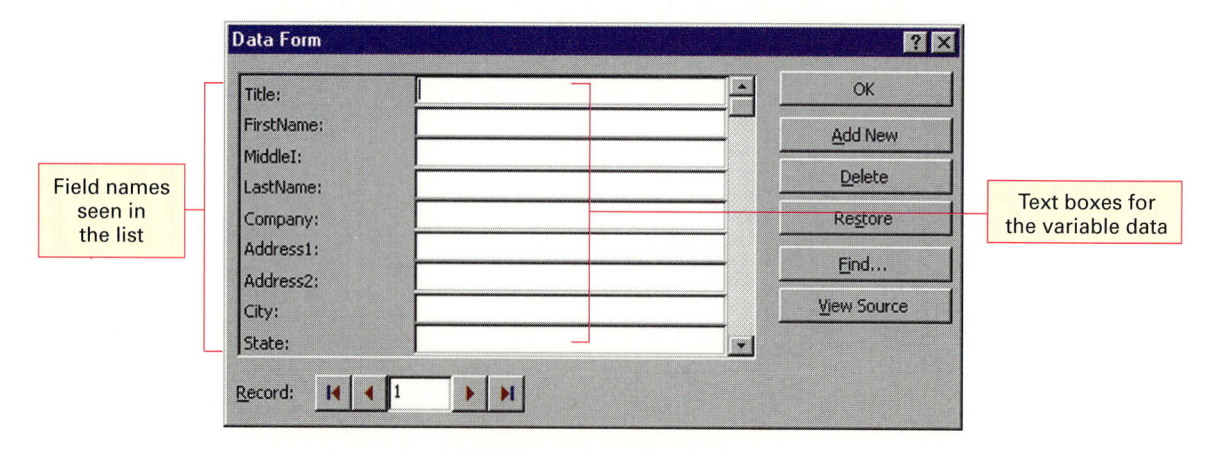

Data Form dialog box with fields: Title, FirstName, MiddleI, LastName, Company, Address1, Address2, City, State. Buttons: OK, Add New, Delete, Restore, Find..., View Source. Labels: "Field names seen in the list" and "Text boxes for the variable data".

14 Type **Mr.** and press (ENTER).
The text displays in the Title text box, and the insertion point moves to the next text box.

Project 6: Creating a Mail Merge WORD-163

15 Type **John** and press ENTER, type **A.** and press ENTER, and then type **Cartwright** and press ENTER.
The text displays in the appropriate name text boxes, and the insertion point moves to the Company text box.

16 Type **ABC Printing** and press ENTER.
The text displays in the Company text box, and the insertion point moves to the next text box.

17 Type **101 Main Street** and press ENTER twice.
The text displays in the Address1 text box, and the insertion point moves to the City text box.

> **Note** When Word 97 prints a letter that has a record with a blank field, Word skips the field without leaving a blank space or a blank line.

18 Type **Willow Grove** and press ENTER, type **SC** and press ENTER, and then type **22345** and press ENTER.
Record 1 is finished, and a new blank form displays for the next record.

19 Continue typing the following records:

Title	**Ms.**
FirstName	**Cynthia**
MiddleI	
LastName	**Baker**
Company	
Address1	**18 Winding Willows Road**
City	**Willow Grove**
State	**SC**
PostalCode	**22345**

Title	**Mrs.**
FirstName	**Jackie**
MiddleI	**B.**
LastName	**Taylor**
Company	
Address1	**Macon Estates**
Address2	**546 Seagrove Lane**
City	**Willow Grove**
State	**SC**
PostalCode	**22345**

Title	**Mr.**
FirstName	**Earl**
MiddleI	**W.**
LastName	**Thomas**
Company	**Highland Oil**
Address1	**2700 Highway 91**
Address2	
City	**Willow Grove**
State	**SC**
PostalCode	**22345**

20 Click OK.
The word processing document displays. In it, you will type the Main document for the mail merge in the next task. The Mail Merge toolbar displays automatically.

Mail Merge toolbar →

> **Note** At this point, the data you have typed in the Data Source document hasn't been saved. Only the field names have been saved.

Creating the Main Document

The Main document contains the text (usually a letter) to be merged with the names in the Data Source document. You insert the field names in the text of the Main document where you want the variable information to appear.

TASK 2: TO CREATE THE MAIN DOCUMENT:

1 Type or insert the current date and press (ENTER) four times.
The date appears at the top of the letter, and the insertion point is moved to the position where the inside address should appear.

2 Click Insert Merge Field.
A drop-down list of the fields in the Data Source document displays.

3 Click Title

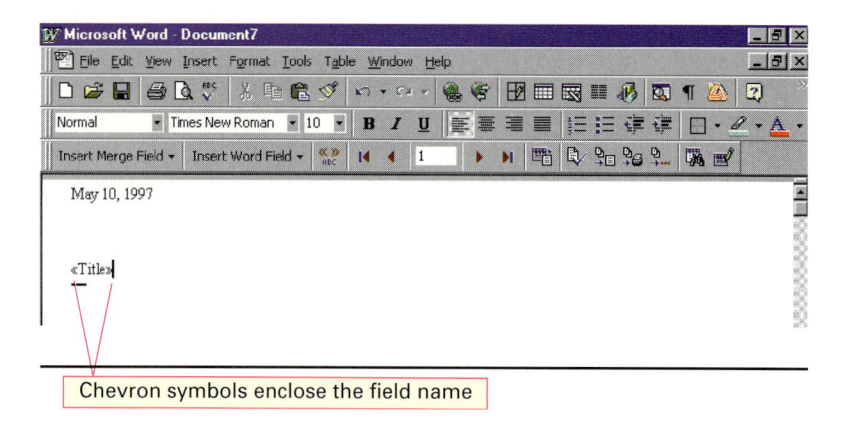

Chevron symbols enclose the field name

Project 6: Creating a Mail Merge   WORD-165

4 To complete the full name, press SPACE, click Insert Merge Field, and click FirstName. Press SPACE, click Insert Merge Field, and click MiddleI. Press SPACE, click Insert Merge Field, and click LastName. Then press ENTER.

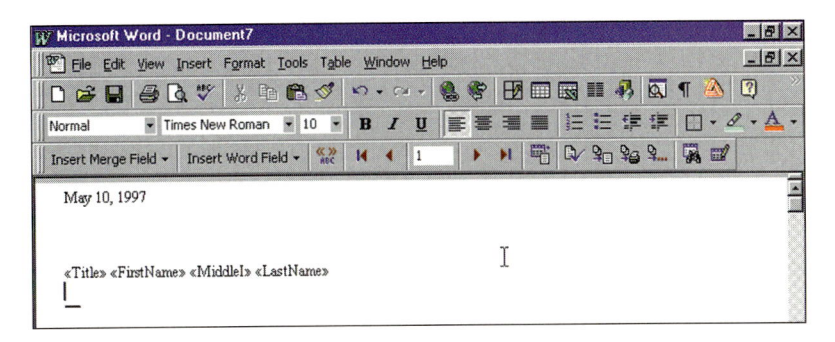

5 Click Insert Merge Field and click Company. Then press ENTER.

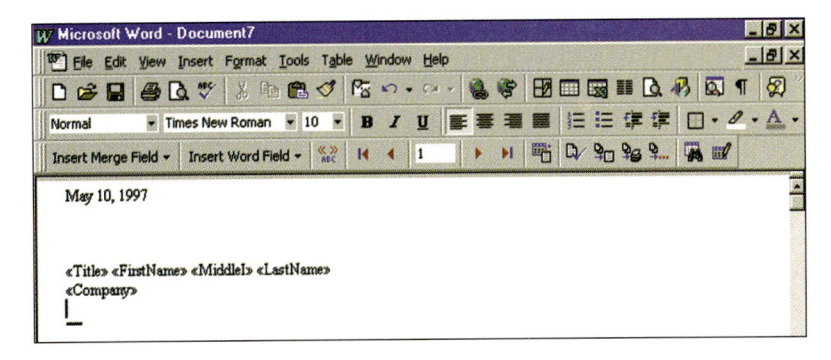

6 Click Insert Merge Field and click Address1. Then press ENTER.

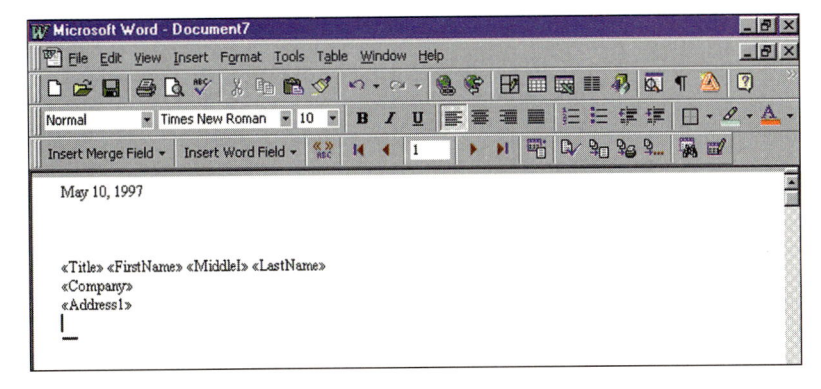

7 Click Insert Merge Field and click Address2. Then press ENTER.

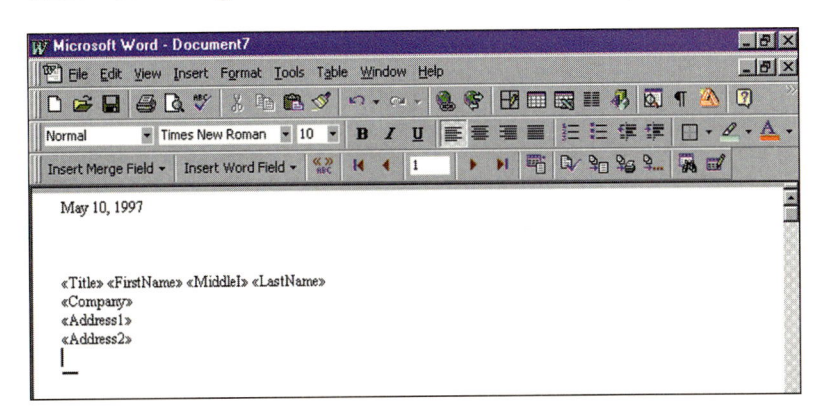

8 Click Insert Merge Field and click City. Type a comma, press SPACE, click Insert Merge Field, and click State. Press SPACE twice, click Insert Merge Field, and click PostalCode.

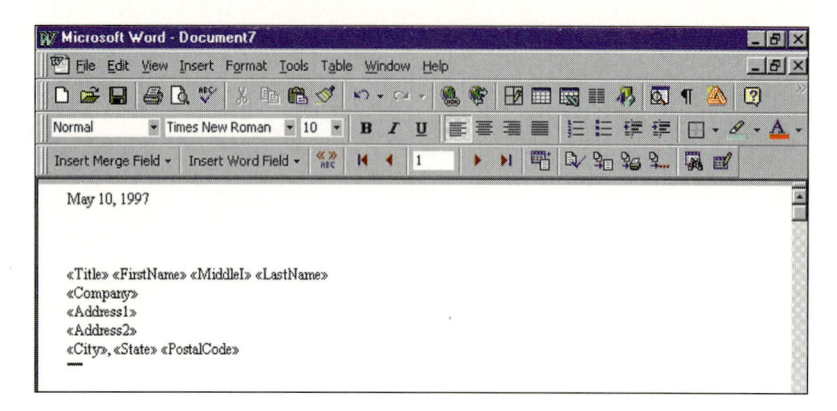

9 Press ENTER twice.
The insertion point moves into the position where the salutation should appear.

10 To create the salutation, type **Dear** and press SPACE. Click Insert Merge Field and click Title. Press SPACE, click Insert Merge Field, and click LastName. Type a colon and press ENTER twice.

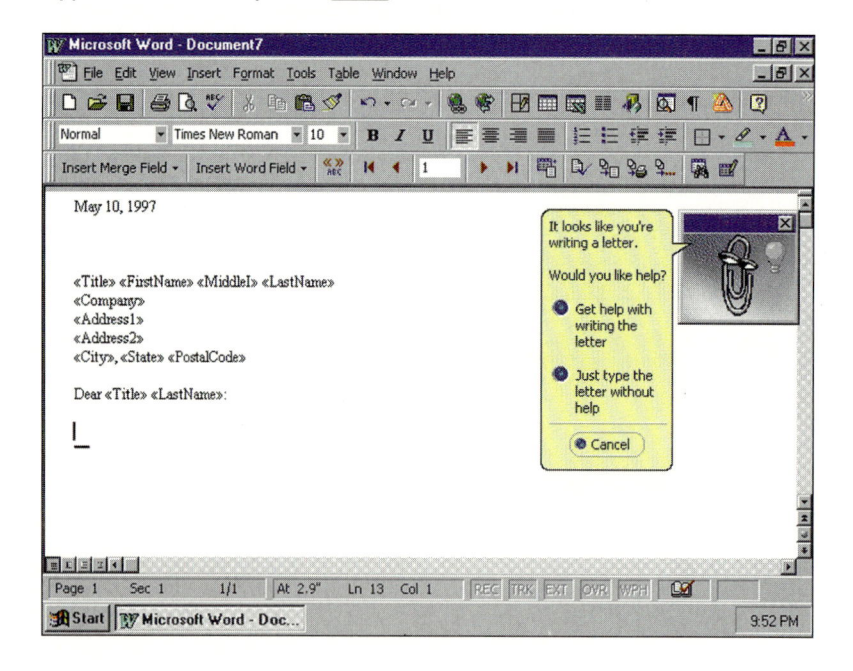

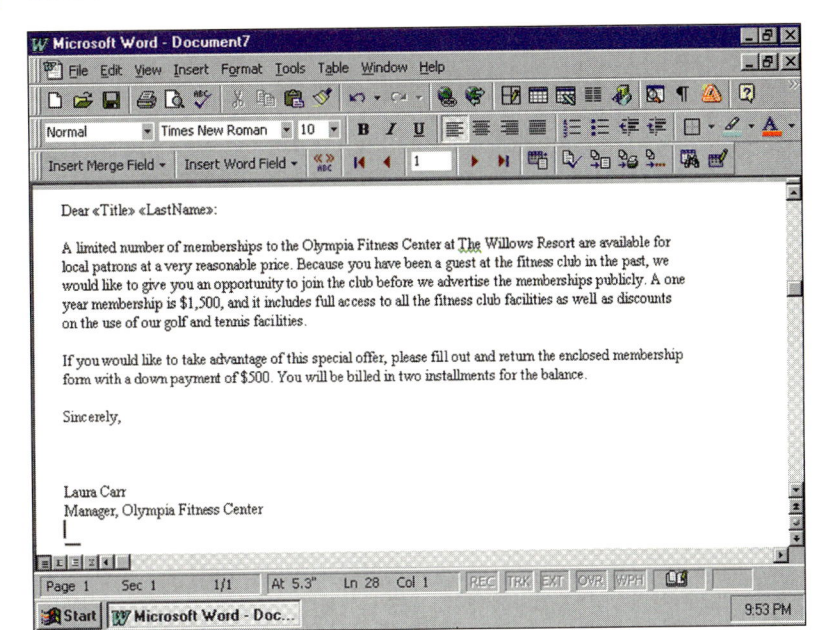

11 Click Cancel in the Office Assistant, and then type the text of the letter.

12 Save the file as *Membership Form Letter.doc* in the Save in location that you're using for your work. Leave the file open for the next exercise.

Merging the Documents

When you merge the Main document with the Data Source document, Word 97 matches the field names in the Main document with the field names in the Data Source document and inserts the appropriate data. Before you merge the Main document with the variable information in the Data Source document, you can see the variable information in the Main document by clicking the View Merged Data button.

TASK 3: TO MERGE THE DATA SOURCE DOCUMENT WITH THE MAIN DOCUMENT:

1 Click the Merge to New Document button.
A new document is created with a page for every record in the Data Source document.

> **Tip** If you don't want to create a new document, click the Merge to Printer button, and the merged documents will be printed instead.

2 Make desired revisions to the file.

3 Save the file if you want.

4 Print the file if you want.

5 Close the file when finished.

Project 6: Creating a Mail Merge WORD-167

6 Close the Main document.

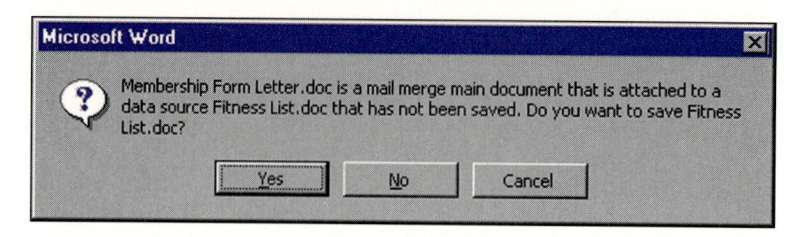

> **Microsoft Word**
> Membership Form Letter.doc is a mail merge main document that is attached to a data source Fitness List.doc that has not been saved. Do you want to save Fitness List.doc?
> [Yes] [No] [Cancel]

7 Click Yes.
The Data Source document is saved, and a message displays asking if you want to save changes made to the Main document.

8 Click Yes.
The Main document closes.

Creating Another Main Document to Use with a Data Source Document

You can create multiple Main documents to use with the same Data Source document. For example, you can create a series of several letters that you send to the same mailing list.

TASK 4: TO CREATE ANOTHER MAIN DOCUMENT TO USE WITH THE SAME DATA SOURCE DOCUMENT:

1 Click the New button.
A new file is created.

2 Choose Tools, Mail Merge, Create, Form Letters, Active Window.

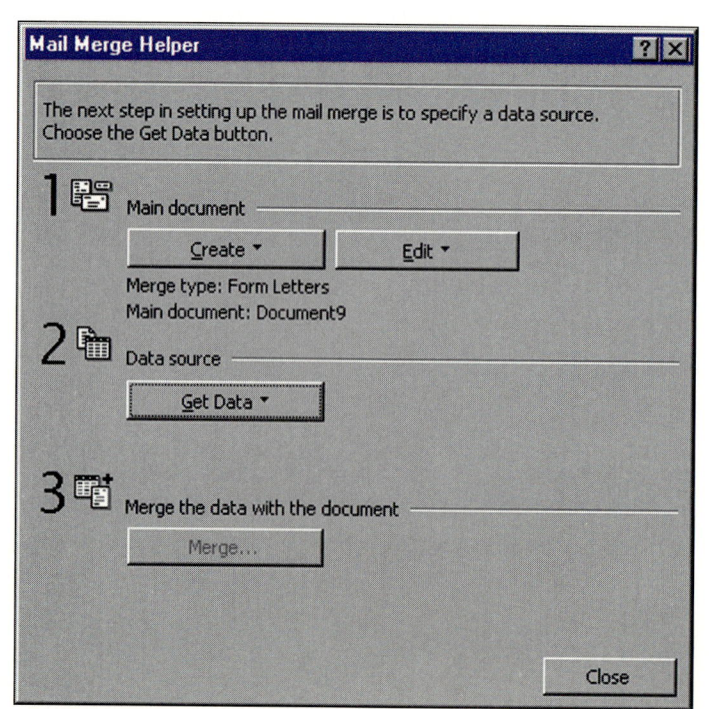

> **Mail Merge Helper**
> The next step in setting up the mail merge is to specify a data source. Choose the Get Data button.
>
> **1** Main document
> [Create ▼] [Edit ▼]
> Merge type: Form Letters
> Main document: Document9
>
> **2** Data source
> [Get Data ▼]
>
> **3** Merge the data with the document
> [Merge...]
>
> [Close]

Project 6: Creating a Mail Merge   WORD-169

3 Select Get Data, Open Data Source.
The Open Data Source dialog box displays.

4 Double-click the file named *Fitness List.doc*.

> **Microsoft Word**
> Word found no merge fields in your main document. Choose the Edit Main Document button to insert merge fields into your main document.
> [Edit Main Document]

5 Click Edit Main Document.
A blank Main document displays.

6 Type the following document:

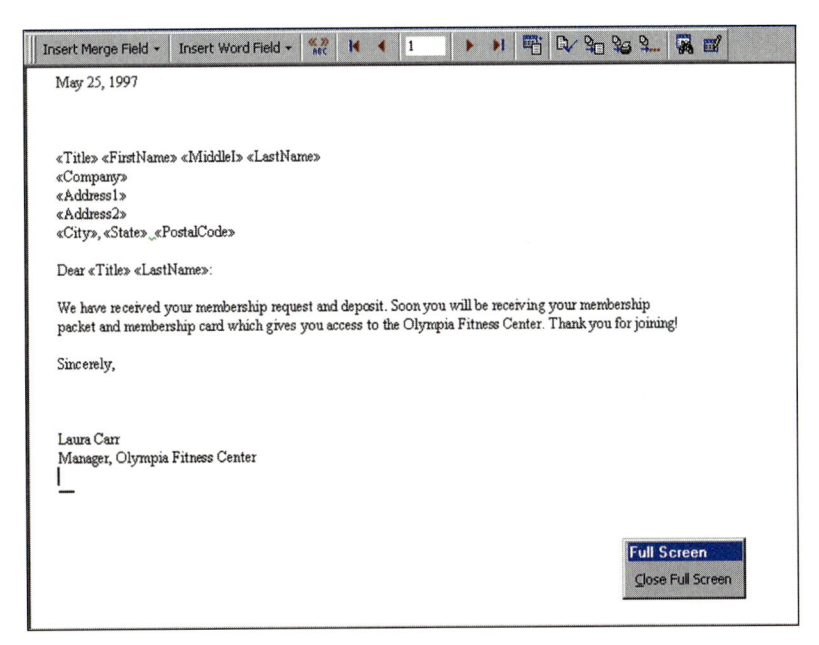

> May 25, 1997
>
> «Title» «FirstName» «MiddleI» «LastName»
> «Company»
> «Address1»
> «Address2»
> «City», «State» «PostalCode»
>
> Dear «Title» «LastName»:
>
> We have received your membership request and deposit. Soon you will be receiving your membership packet and membership card which gives you access to the Olympia Fitness Center. Thank you for joining!
>
> Sincerely,
>
> Laura Carr
> Manager, Olympia Fitness Center

7 Save the file as *Thank You.doc*.

8 Click [icon].
A new merged document displays.

9 Close the file without saving.

10 Close *Thank You.doc*.

11 Choose Yes to save the changes.

Creating and Using Another Data Source Document with a Main Document

Just as you can create multiple Main documents to merge with the same Data Source document, you also can create multiple Data Source documents to merge with the same Main document. The Data Source document may have fields that aren't used in the Main document, but all the fields used in the Main document must be contained in the Data Source document.

TASK 5: TO CREATE ANOTHER DATA SOURCE DOCUMENT FOR A MAIN DOCUMENT:

1 Open the file *Membership Form Letter.doc*.

2 Click the Mail Merge Helper button.

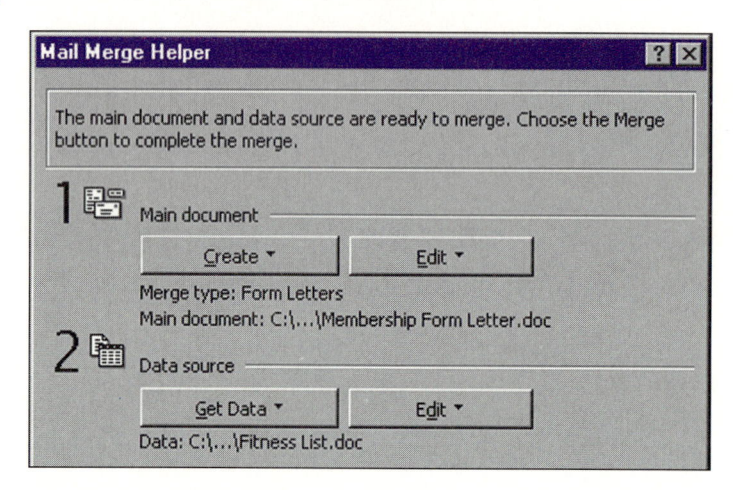

3 Select Get Data, Create Data Source.

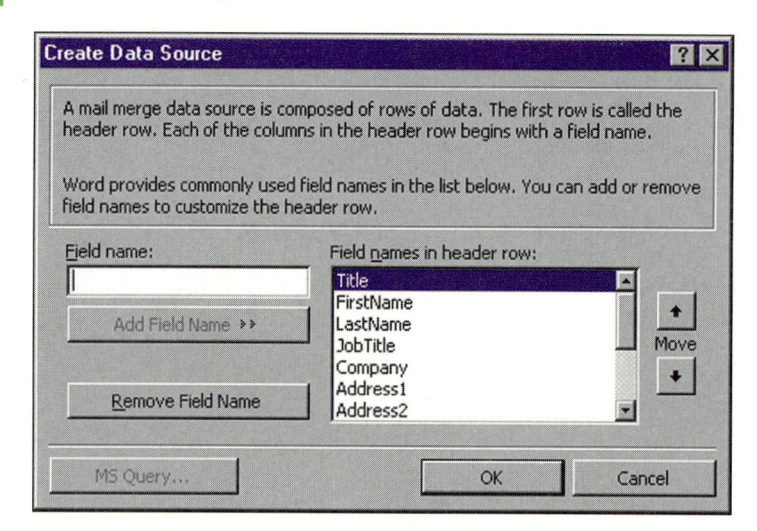

4 Remove the fields Job Title, Country, HomePhone, and WorkPhone. Add the field MiddleI and move it up under FirstName. Click OK.
The Save As dialog box displays.

5 Type **Fitness List 2** for the filename, specify the Save in location that you're using for your particular work, and click Save.
The Mail Merge Helper dialog box redisplays.

6 Click Edit (under Data source) and click Fitness List 2.
The Data Form displays.

7 Type the information for at least two records, and click OK when finished.
The Main document redisplays.

8 Save and close the Main document. A message displays asking if you want to save changes to the Data Source file.

9 Click Yes.

Project 6: Creating a Mail Merge WORD-171

TASK 6: TO SELECT A DATA SOURCE DOCUMENT:

1 Open the file *Membership Form Letter.doc*.

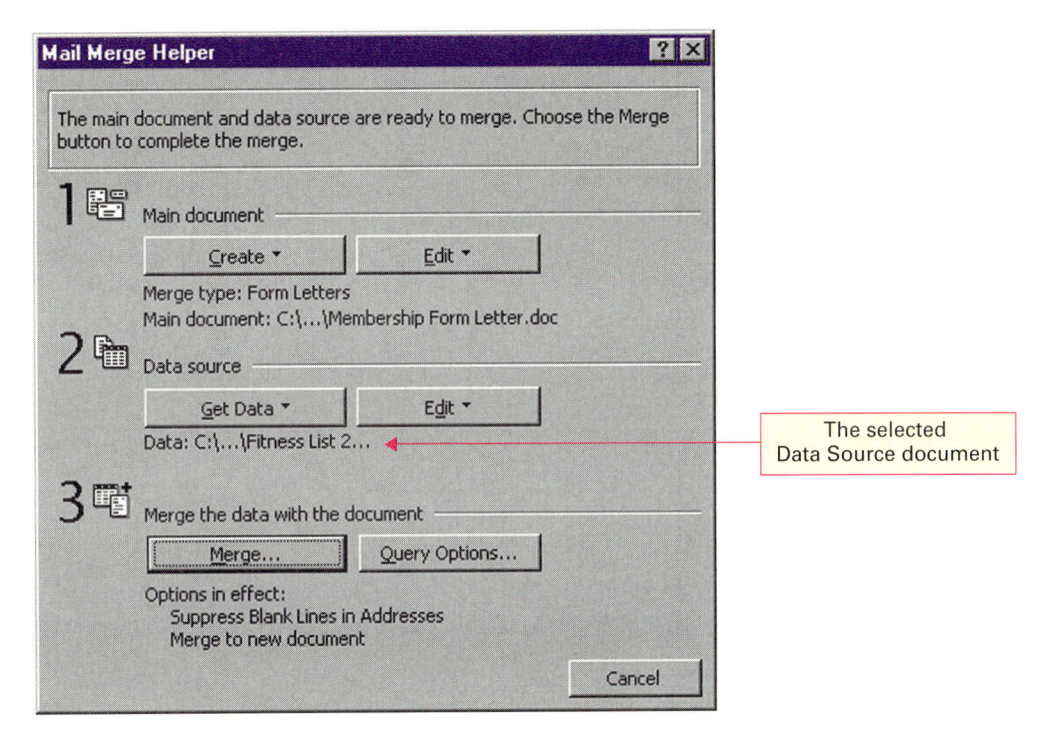

2 Click [icon].

The selected Data Source document (callout pointing to "Data: C:\...\Fitness List 2...")

3 Click Get Data and click Open Data Source.
The Open Data Source dialog box displays.

4 Double-click the file *Fitness List.doc*.
The selected Data Source document name changes from *Fitness List 2.doc* to *Fitness List.doc*.

5 Click Close.
The Main document redisplays.

6 Click [icon].
A new merged document displays.

The Conclusion

Make any desired revisions and then save the document. Print the document, if desired, and then close the file.

Close the Main document.

Summary and Exercises

Summary

- The Data Source document contains the field names of the variables as well as the variable information for each record.
- The Main document contains the text to be merged with the names in the Data Source document.
- During the merge process, Word 97 matches the field names in the Main document with the field names in the Data source document and inserts the appropriate data.
- You can create multiple Main documents to use with the same Data Source document.
- You can create multiple Data Source documents to merge with the same Main document.

Key Terms and Operations

Key Terms
Data Source document
field
Main document
mail merging
record

Operations
add records to the Data Source document
create a Main document
create a Date Source document
merge

Study Questions

Multiple Choice

1. The two documents used in a mail merge are
    a. the List document and the Form document.
    b. the Data Source document and the Form document.
    c. the List document and the Main document.
    d. the Data Source document and the Main document.

2. The file that contains the list of variable information is called the
    a. List document.
    b. Data Source document.
    c. Main document.
    d. Form document.

3. The file that contains the text (usually a letter) and the field names is called the
    a. List document.
    b. Data Source document.
    c. Main document.
    d. Form document.

4. To display the Mail Merge Helper dialog box,
    a. click the Mail Merger Helper button.
    b. choose Tools, Mail Merge.
    c. Both A and B.
    d. None of the above.

5. When you perform a merge,
    a. a new document is always created.
    b. the merged documents are always printed.
    c. you can choose to create a new document or send the document directly to the printer.
    d. the merged document replaces the form document.

6. Fields
    a. contain variable information.
    b. appear in the Data Form.
    c. can be inserted in the document that contains the form letter.
    d. All of the above.

7. When creating the list of fields,
    a. you must use the default list of fields.
    b. you can add your own fields to the default list and remove fields from the default list.
    c. you can remove fields from the default list, but you can't add fields.
    d. you must use only the fields in the default list, but you can move the fields to different locations.

8. To insert a field in a form letter,
    a. select the field from the Insert Merge Field drop-down list.
    b. choose Insert, Field.
    c. click the toolbar button that represents the field you want.
    d. None of the above.

9. Which two of the following statements are true?
    a. You can create several Data Source files to be used with a Main document.
    b. You can create only one List document to be used with a Form document.
    c. You can create several Main documents to be used with the same Data Source document.
    d. You can use the same Form document with several Main documents.

10. The merged document
    a. has one page for each record.
    b. displays all records on the same page.
    c. must be paginated to divide the records into pages.
    d. is saved automatically.

Short Answer

1. What happens when you click the Merge to New Document button?

2. What's the Data Form?

3. What's a field?

4. What's a record?

5. What happens when you click the Insert Merge Field button?

6. What's the Mail Merge Helper?

7. How can you see the variable information in the document that contains the form letter?

8. What symbols enclose an inserted field name?

9. If a record has a blank field, will the field print?

10. Can a field name be two words?

For Discussion

1. What process would you perform to create the same result as a mail merge if you didn't have the mail merge feature to use?

2. In what ways is the mail merge process flexible?

3. Open the file *Fitness List.doc* and discuss its structure.

4. Under what circumstances would you merge to a new document, and under what circumstances would you merge to the printer?

Review Exercises

1. Creating a Data Source

When equipment at the fitness center is replaced with new equipment, the used equipment is often sold to Fitness Club members who have expressed an interest. Create a Data Source which contains names of members who have asked to be notified when equipment is replaced.

1. Create a new file.

2. Create a Data Source document with the following fields: Title, FirstName, LastName, Address1, Address2, City, State, PostalCode, Salutation.

3. Save the Data Source as *Sale List.doc*.

4. Add these records to the Data Source document:

Title	Mr.	Ms.
FirstName	Alan	Barbara
LastName	Sheppard	Mavis
Address1	55 Frederick Lane	98 Jones Hollow Road
Address2		
City	Willow Grove	Willow Grove
State	SC	SC
PostalCode	22345	22345
Salutation	Dear Buzz,	Dear Ms. Mavis:
Title	Mrs.	Mr.
FirstName	Judy	William
LastName	Puckett	Turner
Address1	4351 Bay View Drive	Greenbriar Towers
Address2		101 Broad Way, Suite 100
City	Willow Grove	Willow Grove
State	SC	SC
PostalCode	22345	22345
Salutation	Dear Judy,	Dear Bill,

March 12, 1997

«Title» «FirstName» «LastName»
«Address1»
«Address2»
«City», «State» «PostalCode»

«Salutation»

From time to time the fitness center replaces equipment with newer or more advanced equipment. As a courtesy to our membership, we offer the equipment that we are replacing for sale. This month we are replacing all the Trimline 2200 treadmills.
Here are the specs on the treadmill:

Motor HP	
Continuous/Peak Speed	
Incline	
Belt Size	
Speed Control	
Deck	
Display	

The sale price is $500. If you are interested in purchasing one of the three machines we are replacing, please contact me.

Sincerely,

Laura Carr
Manager, Olympia Fitness Center

Figure 6.3

5. Save the blank document as *Sale Form Letter.doc* and close the file.

6. Save the Data Source document.

2. Creating a Main Document and Merging

Create the letter shown in Figure 6.3 to notify members about the equipment scheduled for replacement. Follow these steps to complete the document and merge the letter with names in the Data Source file.

1. Open *Sale Form Letter.doc*.

2. Type the letter shown in Figure 6.3, and insert the fields indicated.

3. Go to the Advanced Fitness home page (http://www.advancedfitness.com), and click the Fitness Equipment link. Click the Treadmills link, and find the information to fill in the second column in the table.

4. Merge the Main document with *Sale List.doc* and create a new document with the merged letters.

5. Save the new document as *Sale.doc* and close the file.

6. Close *Sale Form Letter.doc*.

Assignments

1. Creating a Form Letter to Send to Family and Friends
Merging data to documents can also improve your efficiency in corresponding with friends and family. Use your personal files to develop each of the following:

1. Create a Data Source document with the names and addresses of friends and family.

2. Create a Main document that contains general news about yourself and what you're doing.

3. Merge the Data Source document and the Main document to create a merged document.

2. Creating a Form Letter Requesting Catalogs
In your search for new items to sell in the shops at The Willows, you must keep up with the new items available from different vendors. Complete the following tasks to obtain information and catalogs from several vendors:

1. Go to the Web site http://www.cybermart.com/Home3/catalogs.html, and find the names and addresses of several companies. Create a Data Source file for the companies.

2. Create a form letter asking for information and/or catalogs from the companies, and merge the files to a new document.

3. Save the new file as *Catalogs.doc*.

Word 97 Function Guide

Function	Mouse Action or Button	Menu	Keyboard Shortcut
Bold	Select text and click **B**	Select text, choose Format, Font, and select Bold	Select text and press CTRL+**B**
Border, create	Select object and click	Select object and then choose Format, Borders and Shading, Borders tab	
Bulleted list, create	Select paragraph and click	Select paragraph and choose Format, Bullets and Numbering, Bulleted tab	
Columns, create	Click	Choose Format, Columns	
Document, close	Click	Choose File, Close	
Document, create new	Click	Choose File, New, and select template	Press CTRL+**N**
Document, open existing	Click	Choose File, Open	Press CTRL+**O**
Document, preview	Click	Choose File, Print Preview	
Document, print	Click	Choose File, Print	Press CTRL+**P**
Document, save	Click	Choose File, Save	Press CTRL+**S**
Document, select entire		Choose Edit, Select All	Press CTRL+**A**
Envelope, create		Choose Tools, Envelopes and Labels	
Go to		Choose Edit, Go To	Press CTRL+**G**
Grammar check	Click	Choose Tools, Spelling and Grammar	Press **F7**
Graphic, insert		Choose Insert, Picture	
Graphic, move	Select graphic and drag	Right-click graphic, choose Format Picture, Position tab	
Graphic, size	Select handle on graphic and drag	Right-click graphic, choose Format Picture, Size tab	
Header, Footer		Choose View, Header and Footer	
Help	Click	Choose Help, Microsoft Word Help	Press **F1**
Italicize	Select text and click *I*	Select text, choose Format, Font, and select Italic	Select text and press CTRL+**I**
Numbered list, create	Select paragraph and click	Select paragraph and choose Format, Bullets and Numbering, Numbered tab	
Paragraph align	Select paragraph and click , , , or	Select paragraph(s) and choose Format, Paragraph, Alignment	Press CTRL+**L** for left, CTRL+**R** for right, or CTRL+**E** for center

Word 97 Function Guide

Function	Mouse Action or Button	Menu	Keyboard Shortcut
Paragraph, format		Select paragraph(s) and choose Format, Paragraph	
Paragraph, indent	[icon]	Select paragraph(s) and choose Format, Paragraph	
Section break delete		Select section break and choose Edit, Clear	Select the section break and press (DELETE)
Section break, insert		Choose Insert, Break	
Shading apply		Select text, paragraph(s), or cells and choose Format, Borders, Shading tab	
Special characters, insert		Choose Insert, Symbol, Special Characters	
Spelling check	Click [icon]	Choose Tools, Spelling and Grammar	Press (F7)
Style apply	Select text, click Style drop-down arrow, and click style	Select text and choose Format, Style	
Tab change	Position insertion point in text and drag tab indicator to new location		
Tabs, set	Click tab indicator on ruler to select tab type and click ruler where you want the tab	Choose Format, Tabs	
Table, create		Choose Table, Insert Table	
Text copy	Select text and click [icon]	Select text and choose Edit, Copy	Press (CTRL)+**C**
Text, cut	Select text and click [icon]	Choose Edit, Cut	Press (CTRL)+**X**
Text, find		Choose Edit, Find	Press (CTRL)+**F**
Text, paste	Select text and click [icon]	Choose Edit, Paste	Press (CTRL)+**V**
Text, replace		Choose Edit, Replace	Press (CTRL)+**H**
Text, select	Position insertion point at beginning and drag through text		Press (SHIFT)+any cursor movement key, such as → or (END)
Toolbars, display/hide	Click [icon], [icon] or, [icon]	Choose View, Toolbars and select toolbar	
Underline	Select text and click [icon]	Select text, choose Format, Font, and select Underline	Select text and press (CTRL)+**U**
Undo	Click [icon]	Choose Edit, Undo	Press (CTRL)+**Z**
View, change	Click [icon], [icon], [icon], or [icon]	Choose View and select view	
Web	Click [icon]	Choose Help, Microsoft on the Web	
Zoom	Click [icon] in Preview	Choose View, Zoom	

Spreadsheets
Using Microsoft Excel 97

Overview

Excel is a tool you can use for organizing, calculating, and displaying numerical data. You might use Excel to record your checking account transactions, plan a budget, prepare a bid, control inventory, track sales, or create an expense report. Before you can become proficient with Excel 97, however, you need to get acquainted with the program and learn how to perform some of the most basic functions. Then you will be ready to start working on the projects in this part of the book.

Objectives

After completing this project, you will be able to:

- ▶ **Identify Excel 97 Features**
- ▶ **Launch Excel 97**
- ▶ **Identify Excel 97 Screen Elements**
- ▶ **Get help**
- ▶ **Close a workbook**
- ▶ **Exit Excel 97**

Identifying Excel 97 Features

Excel 97 is the electronic equivalent of one of those green (or buff color) columnar pads that bookkeepers and accountants use. Excel calls the area in which you work a *worksheet* — other programs call this a spreadsheet. An Excel worksheet has 256 *columns* and 65,536 *rows*, for a whopping total of 16,777,216 cells. Is that big or what?

Note A *cell* is the intersection of a column and a row.

An Excel worksheet is actually a page in a **workbook** file. By default, a new workbook file has three worksheets, but you can add additional worksheets if you need them — as many as your computer memory allows.

You can do more than store numbers with Excel 97; you can use it to perform calculations, recalculate formulas when numbers are changed, analyze data, and create charts and maps from the data that you enter. Many of the same text features available in a word processing program are also available in Excel. For example, you can check the spelling of words, use text styles, add headers and footers, and insert graphics and other objects. Figure 0.1 shows a worksheet with numbers, calculations, text formatted with styles, a graphic, and a chart.

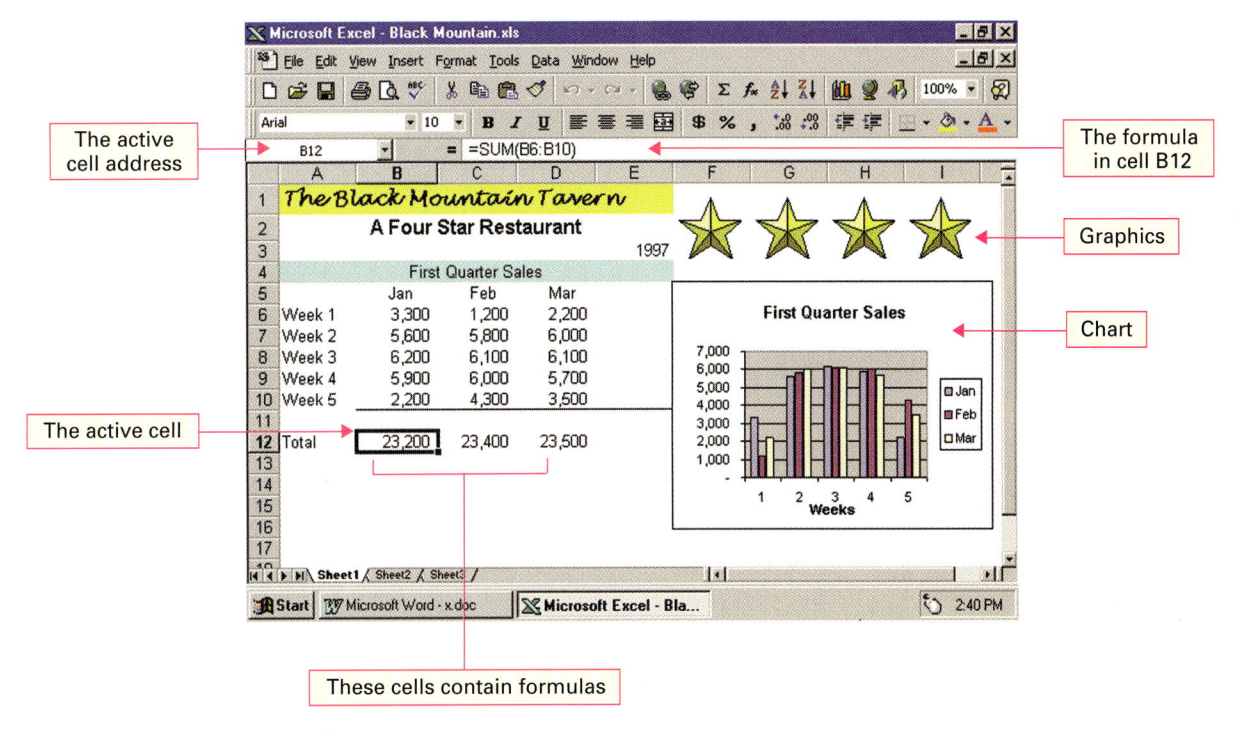

Figure O.1

Launching Excel 97

When you start your computer, you may have to log on to a network or perform some other steps before Windows 95 starts. After the Windows 95 desktop displays on the screen, you're ready to launch Excel 97.

TASK 1: TO LAUNCH EXCEL 97:

1. Click the Start **Start** button and point to Programs.

2 Point to Microsoft Excel and click.
The program opens in a window and creates a workbook called *Book1*.

Identifying Excel 97 Screen Elements

When you create a new workbook, the screen should look similar to the one shown in Figure 0.2. The Excel 97 screen has many of the common elements of a Windows 95 screen as well as some elements that are unique to the Excel 97 program.

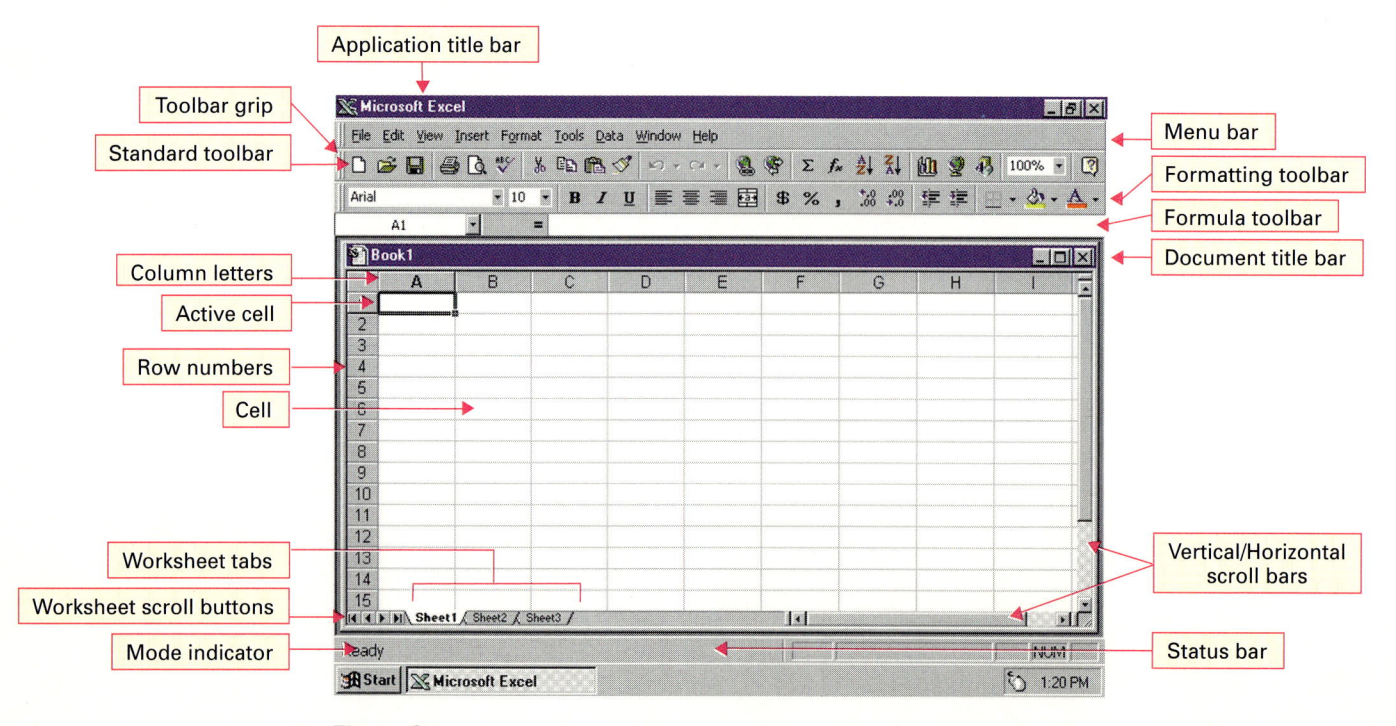

Figure O.2

> **Note** The screen displays two Close buttons. The button in the Application title bar closes Excel 97; the button in the document title bar closes the current workbook. If the document window is maximized, the Close button appears in the menu bar.

Table 0.1 lists the elements of the Excel 97 screen.

Table O.1   Elements of the Excel 97 Screen

Element	Description
Application title bar	Displays the name of the application and the Minimize, Maximize/Restore, and Close buttons. If the document window is maximized, the name of the workbook also displays in the application title bar.
Document title bar	Displays the name of the workbook file and the Minimize, Maximize/Restore, and Close buttons. If the window is maximized, there is no document title bar and the document buttons display in the menu bar.
Menu bar	Contains menu options. To use the menu, click an option to display a drop-down menu, and then click a command on the drop-down menu to perform the command, view another menu, or view a dialog box.
Standard toolbar	Contains buttons for accomplishing commands. To use the toolbar, click the button for the command you want to perform.
Formatting toolbar	Contains buttons and controls for formatting. To use the toolbar, click the button for the command you want to perform or click a drop-down list arrow to make a selection.
Formula bar	Displays the cell address and the contents of the active cell. Also used to enter and edit formulas.
Active cell	Marks the cell where data will be entered with a black border.
Scroll bars	Vertical and horizontal Scroll bars scroll the screen vertically and horizontally.
Worksheet tabs	Display the names of worksheets in the current workbook. Clicking a tab displays the worksheet.
Worksheet scroll buttons	Scroll the worksheet tabs (if you have too many worksheets to display all the tabs).
Status bar	Displays information about the current workbook. The Mode indicator displays on the far left side of the status bar.
Row numbers	Indicate the numbers associated with the rows.
Column letters	Indicate the letters associated with the columns.
Cell	The intersection of a column and a row, referred to with an address that combines the column letter(s) with the row number, such as A1, AA223, and so on.
Mode	Displays on the left side of the status bar and shows a word that describes the current working condition of the workbook. For example, the word *"Ready"* means that the worksheet is ready to receive data or execute a command. Other modes include *Edit, Enter, Point, Error,* and *Wait.*

> **Note** Although you can turn off the display of certain screen elements (toolbars, the Formula bar, and the Status bar), generally all the screen elements are displayed in Excel 97 because they are used so often.

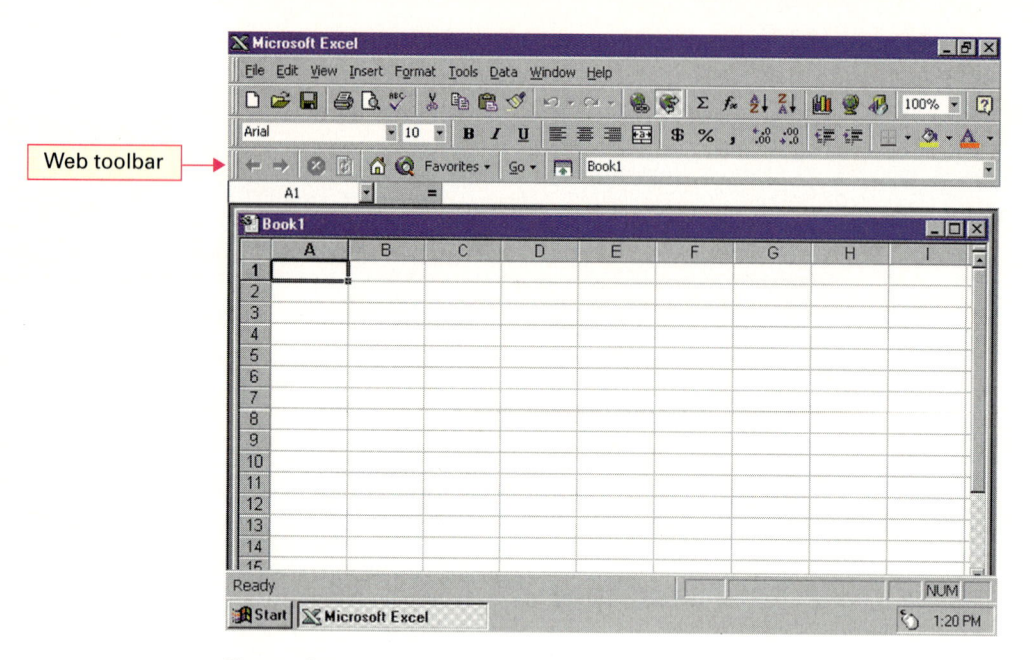

Figure O.3

Working with Toolbars

Toolbars contain buttons that perform functions. Usually the tools grouped together on a toolbar perform tasks that are all related. For example, the buttons on the Chart toolbar all perform tasks related to creating and modifying charts.

The Standard toolbar and the Formatting toolbar are the default toolbars, the ones that Excel 97 automatically displays. You can display or hide as many toolbars as desired. You also can move toolbars to different locations on the screen. When a toolbar is displayed, Excel places it where it was last located.

If you use the Internet frequently, you may want to display the **Web toolbar** by clicking the Web Toolbar button in the Standard toolbar. With the Web toolbar displayed, your screen should look like Figure O.3. To hide the Web toolbar, click the Web Toolbar button again.

Overview **EX-7**

TASK 2: TO WORK WITH TOOLBARS:

1 Choose View, Toolbars.

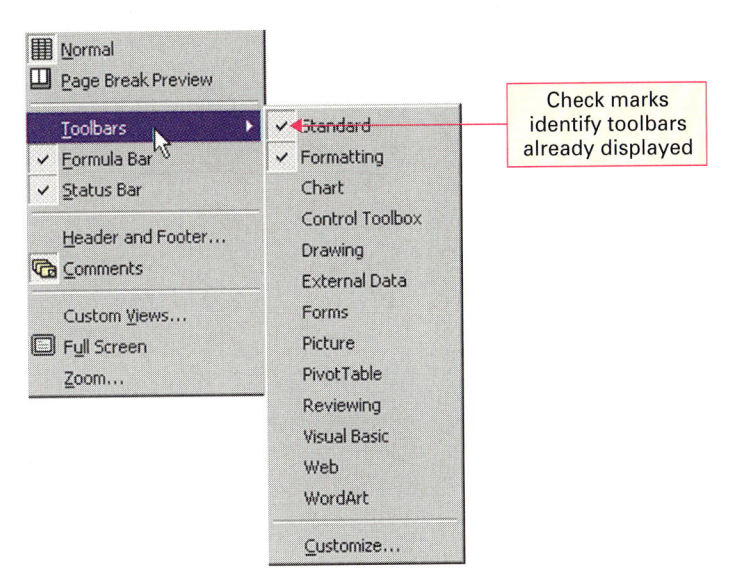

Check marks identify toolbars already displayed

2 Choose Chart.

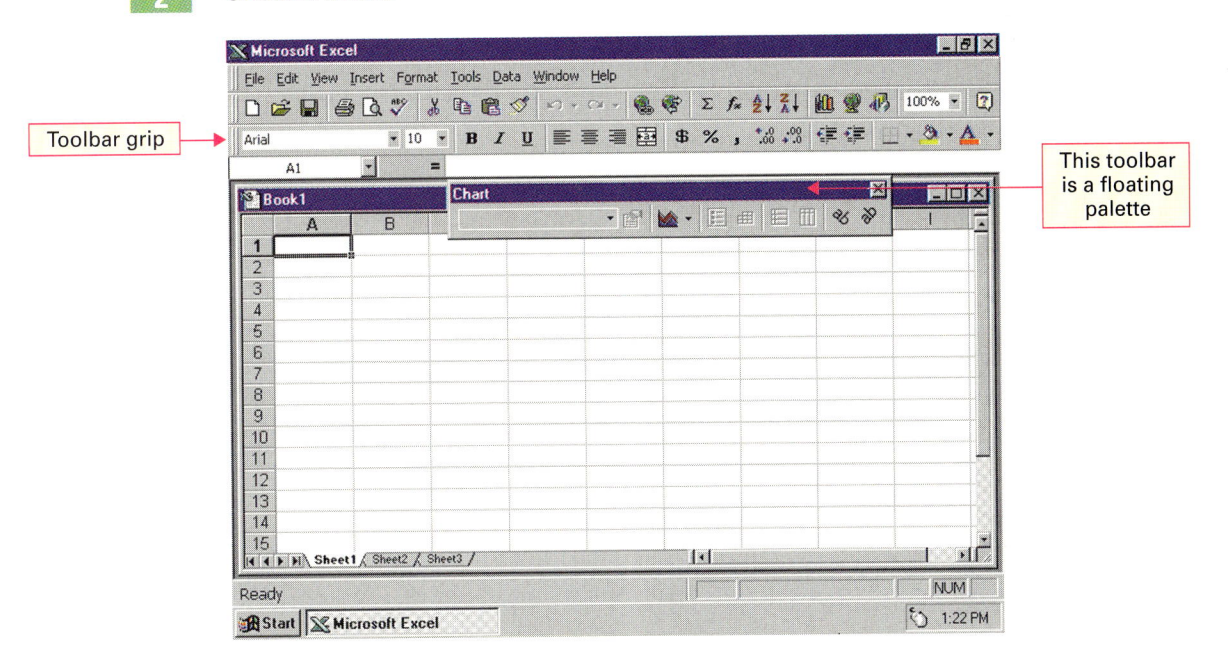

Toolbar grip

This toolbar is a floating palette

3 Point to the title bar of the Chart toolbar and drag the toolbar to a new location. If the toolbar doesn't appear as a palette, drag the toolbar by grabbing the grip. The toolbar moves.

4 Choose View, Toolbars, Chart.
The toolbar no longer displays.

Getting Help

Excel 97 provides several ways to get help. You can use the standard Windows 95 help dialog box that contains the Contents, Index, and Find pages and the What's This Help feature. Additionally, you can use the Office Assistant and Microsoft on the Web, both help features unique to Office 97.

Using the Office Assistant

The Office Assistant offers help on the task you are performing, often referred to as *context-sensitive help*. If the Office Assistant doesn't display the help you want, you can type a question to obtain the desired help.

TASK 3: TO USE THE OFFICE ASSISTANT:

1. Click the Office Assistant button if you don't see the Office Assistant.

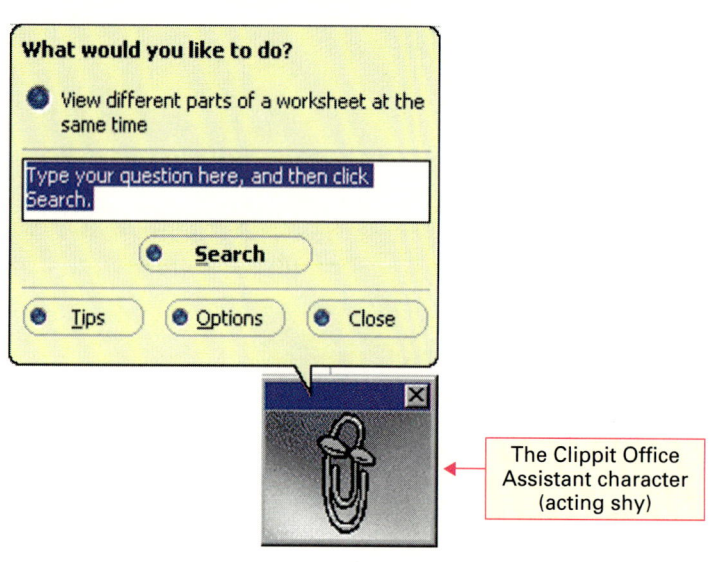

The Clippit Office Assistant character (acting shy)

Overview EX-9

2 Type **How do you enter a formula?**

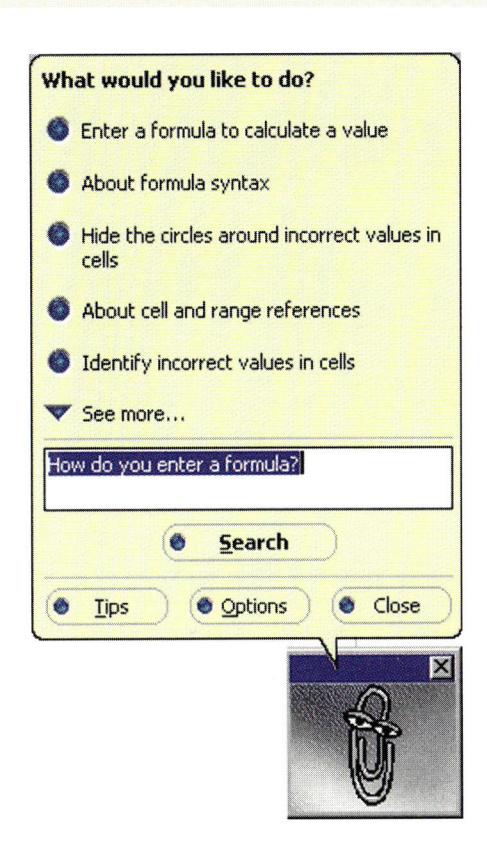

> **What would you like to do?**
> - Enter a formula to calculate a value
> - About formula syntax
> - Hide the circles around incorrect values in cells
> - About cell and range references
> - Identify incorrect values in cells
> - See more...
>
> How do you enter a formula?
>
> Search
>
> Tips   Options   Close

3 Click Search and then click About formula syntax.

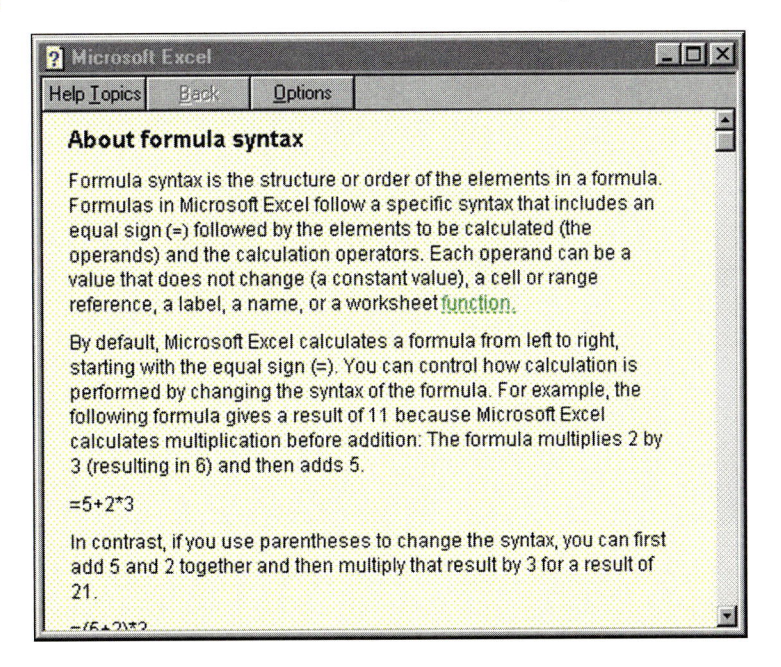

> **Microsoft Excel**
> Help Topics   Back   Options
>
> **About formula syntax**
>
> Formula syntax is the structure or order of the elements in a formula. Formulas in Microsoft Excel follow a specific syntax that includes an equal sign (=) followed by the elements to be calculated (the operands) and the calculation operators. Each operand can be a value that does not change (a constant value), a cell or range reference, a label, a name, or a worksheet function.
>
> By default, Microsoft Excel calculates a formula from left to right, starting with the equal sign (=). You can control how calculation is performed by changing the syntax of the formula. For example, the following formula gives a result of 11 because Microsoft Excel calculates multiplication before addition: The formula multiplies 2 by 3 (resulting in 6) and then adds 5.
>
> =5+2*3
>
> In contrast, if you use parentheses to change the syntax, you can first add 5 and 2 together and then multiply that result by 3 for a result of 21.

4 Read the Help dialog box and then click ⊠ on the Help title bar.
The Help dialog box closes, but the Office Assistant window remains open.

5 Click the Office Assistant character in the Office Assistant window.
The Office Assistant asks what you want to do.

> **Note** The default Office Assistant is a paper clip named Clippit. Other assistants include Shakespeare, a robot, and a cat — to name a few.

6 Click Close.
The "bubble" closes.

7 Click ⊠ on the Office Assistant title bar.
The Office Assistant window closes.

Getting Help from the World Wide Web

Microsoft maintains several sites on the Web that have useful information, user support, product news, and free programs and files that you can download. If your system is connected to the Internet, you can access this type of help easily. The Microsoft sites are open to all users.

> **Note** When Microsoft is beta testing a program, the company maintains "closed sites" open only to beta testers with a valid password.

TASK 4: TO READ ANSWERS TO FREQUENTLY ASKED QUESTIONS:

1 Choose Help, Microsoft on the Web.

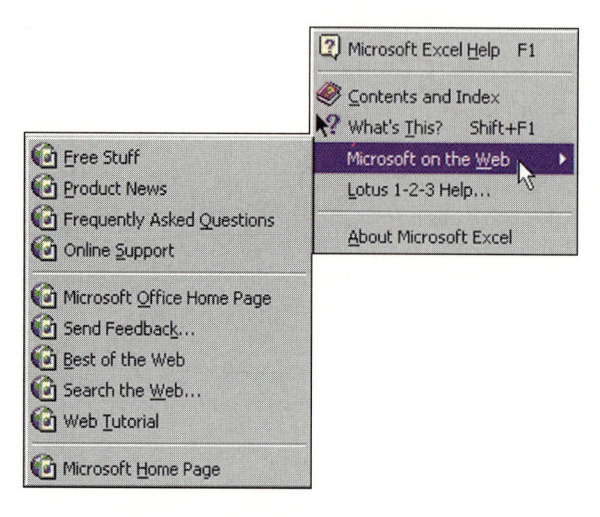

2 Choose Frequently Asked Questions.
The Internet browser program Internet Explorer starts and connects to the appropriate Web site.

3 When you finish browsing the Web, click ⊠ in the browser window. (I know you're tempted to start browsing around, but you can do that later.)

Overview   EX-11

Closing a Workbook and Exiting Excel 97

Before you exit Excel, you should always save any work that you want to keep and then close any open workbooks. When you exit Excel 97, the program closes, and the Windows 95 desktop is visible unless you have another program running in a maximized window, however, the program will be visible, not the desktop.

> **Tip** If you forget to save and close a changed file before you try to exit, Excel 97 asks whether you want to save changes. You can choose Yes to save the changed file, No to exit without saving, or Cancel to cancel the exit request.

TASK 5: TO CLOSE THE WORKBOOK AND EXIT EXCEL 97:

1 Click the Close ⊠ button in the document title bar.

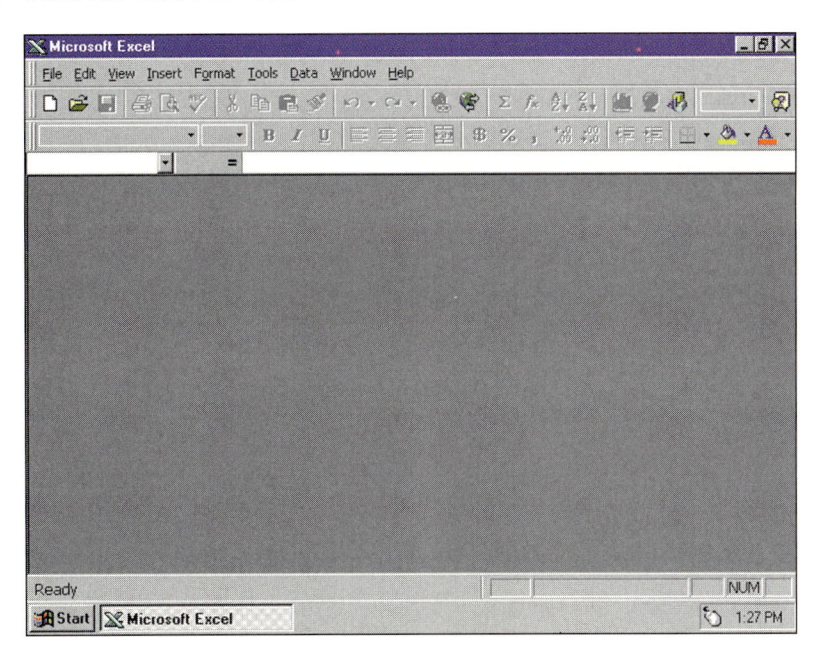

2 Click ⊠ in the application title bar.
   The Excel 97 program closes.

Summary and Exercises

Summary

- Excel 97 is a full-featured spreadsheet program that's easy to use.
- An Excel workbook includes three worksheets by default.
- Worksheets enable you to store numbers, perform calculations and recalculations, analyze data, and create charts and maps.
- Many features found in Word processing are also available in Excel 97.
- Excel 97 provides a variety of Help features.
- Excel 97 warns you if you try to exit the program without saving your work.

Key Terms and Operations

Key Terms
active cell
cell
column
column indicators
Edit mode
Enter mode
Error mode
Formatting toolbar
formula bar
menu bar
mode indicator
Office Assistant
Point mode
Ready mode
row
row indicators
scroll bars
Standard toolbar
status bar
title bar
toolbar
Wait mode
Web toolbar
What's This?
workbook
worksheet
worksheet scroll buttons
worksheet tab

Operations
exit Excel 97
get help from the Web
start Excel 97
use Office Assistant

Study Questions

Multiple Choice

1. Another name for a columnar worksheet is a
   a. workbook.
   b. spreadsheet.
   c. cell.
   d. booksheet.

2. The intersection of a column and a row is
   a. a worksheet tab.
   b. a cell.
   c. an active cell.
   d. an indicator.

3. The number of worksheets in a workbook is limited
   a. by default.
   b. to three.
   c. by memory.
   d. to 256.

4. The size of an Excel worksheet is
   a. 128 columns by 9,999 rows.
   b. 65,536 columns by 256 rows.
   c. over 256 million cells.
   d. 256 columns by 65,536 rows.

5. The name of a worksheet displays
   a. in the column letters.
   b. on the worksheet tab.
   c. in the row number.
   d. in the status bar.

6. Which of the following applications would most likely be created in Excel?
   a. a letter
   b. a budget
   c. a memo
   d. a meeting report

7. The standard Windows 95 help features used in Excel include all of the following except
   a. What's This?
   b. Contents.
   c. Index.
   d. Office Assistant.

8. Before exiting Excel 97, you should
   a. save and close all files.
   b. close all files, saving those that you want to keep.
   c. close all files without saving because Excel saves them automatically.
   d. close the Office Assistant.

9. Which of the following statements are false?
   a. The Office Assistant gives context-sensitive help and unsolicited help.
   b. The Office Assistant is an animated character.
   c. The Office Assistant can not be turned off.
   d. The Office Assistant displays help in a bubble.

10. Which of the following are false statements?
    a. The formula bar displays the cell address and the cell contents of the active cell.
    b. The formula bar is a floating palette.
    c. The formula bar is used for typing formulas.
    d. The formula bar can be hidden.

Short Answer
1. How do you start Excel?
2. What is a cell address? Give examples.
3. How are columns and rows identified?
4. How do you display the Web toolbar?
5. Why are screen elements not usually hidden in Excel?
6. Name some of the things that Excel can do.
7. Name some of the word processing features that are found in Excel.
8. Name and describe the different help features in Excel.
9. Name some of the mode indicators in Excel.
10. How many cells are in a worksheet?

For Discussion
1. Name some tasks that you could perform in Excel for your own personal use.
2. Discuss the advantages of using a program like Excel over keeping columnar records manually.
3. Name examples of situations that would benefit from having multiple worksheets in the same file.
4. Discuss the value of a chart in a worksheet.

Review Exercises

1. Starting Excel and Exploring the Workbook
In this exercise, you will start Excel 97 and move around in the workbook.

1. Start Excel 97.
2. Turn on the Web toolbar if it isn't displayed.
3. What text is displayed in the status bar?
4. What text is displayed in the formula bar?

5. Click the tab that says Sheet2.

6. Is there any change in the status bar and in the formula bar?

7. Turn the Web toolbar on if necessary and then turn it off.

2. Getting Help on the Web
In this exercise, you will explore the help feature on the World Wide Web.

1. Choose Help, Microsoft on the Web.

2. Choose Product News.

3. Print the initial Web page that displays.

4. Disconnect from the Internet and exit Internet Explorer.

Assignments

1. Getting Online Help
Start Excel 97 and use the Office Assistant to find a help topic about the Text Import Wizard. Choose Options and print the topic. When finished, close the Help dialog box.

2. Using the Web Toolbar
Start Excel 97 and display the Web toolbar in the new workbook if it isn't already displayed. Go to this address: http://www.dominis.com/Zines/ and explore the site. Give a brief description of what you find. When finished, close Internet Explorer, disconnect from the Internet, and exit Excel 97.

PROJECT 1

Creating a Workbook

In order to use Excel 97 effectively, you must know how to create, save, and print workbooks. In this project, you will enter text and numbers and calculate the numbers with formulas and functions to create a simple worksheet. (This might sound like a lot, but I promise you won't have to use all 16,777,216 cells!)

Objectives

After completing this project, you will be able to:

- ▶ Create a new workbook
- ▶ Move around in a worksheet and a workbook
- ▶ Name worksheets
- ▶ Enter data
- ▶ Enter simple formulas and functions
- ▶ Save a workbook
- ▶ Preview and print a worksheet
- ▶ Close a worksheet

The Challenge

Mr. Gilmore, manager of The Grande Hotel, wants a down-and-dirty worksheet to compare the January receipts to the February receipts for both restaurants in the hotel (the Atrium Café and the Willow Top Restaurant). Since the worksheet is just for him, you won't have to worry about formatting right now.

The Solution

You will create a workbook with a page for the Atrium Café and a page for the Willow Top Restaurant as shown in Figure 1.1. (For now, don't worry about aligning headings such as Jan and Feb. You'll learn this in a later project.)

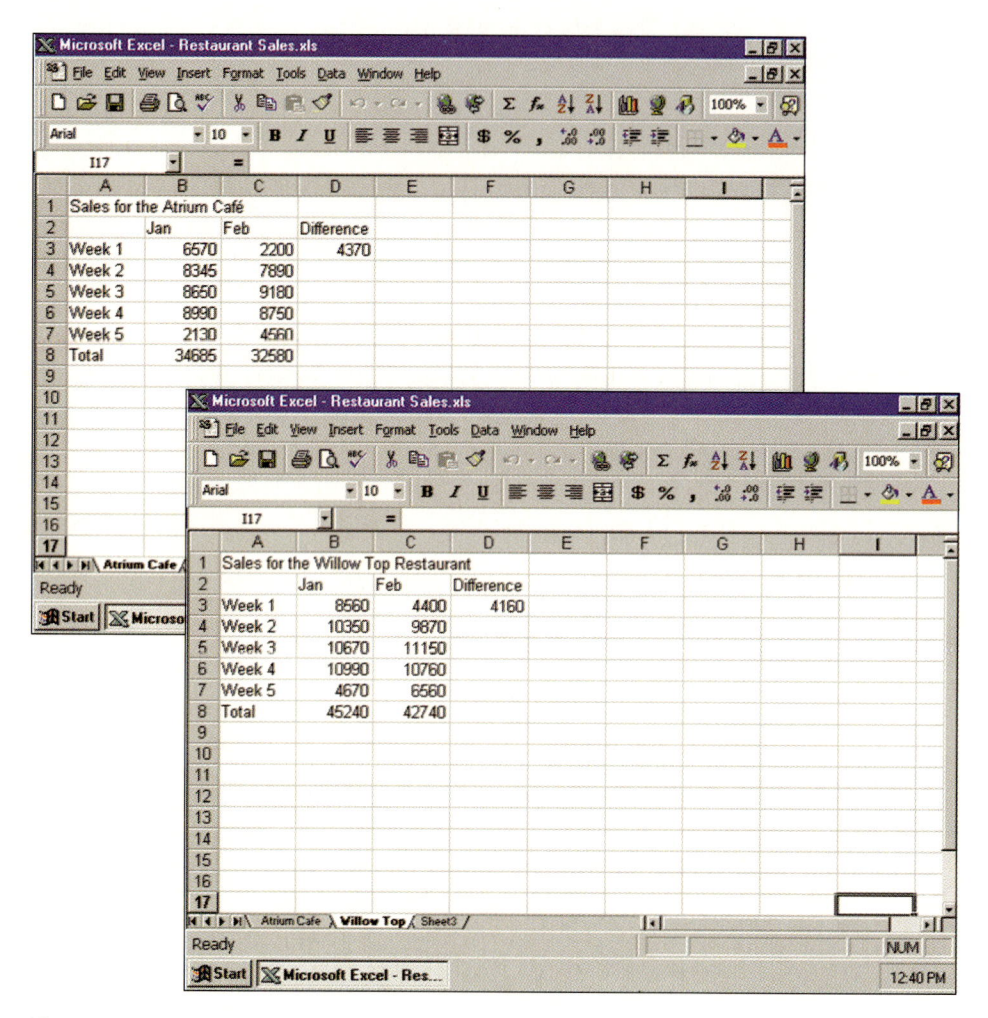

Figure 1.1

The Setup

So that your screen will match the illustrations in this chapter and to ensure that all the tasks in this project will function as described, you should set up Excel as described in Table 1.1. Because these are the default settings for the toolbars and view, you may not need to make any changes to your setup.

Project 1: Creating a Workbook   EX-19

Table 1.1   Excel Settings

Location	Make these settings:
View, Toolbars	Deselect all toolbars except the Standard and Formatting.
View	Use the Normal view and display the Formula Bar and the Status Bar.

Creating a New Workbook

When you launch Excel 97, a new blank workbook named Book1 automatically opens for you, and you can begin to enter data.

TASK 1: TO CREATE A NEW WORKBOOK:

1. Click the Start [Start] button and point to Programs.

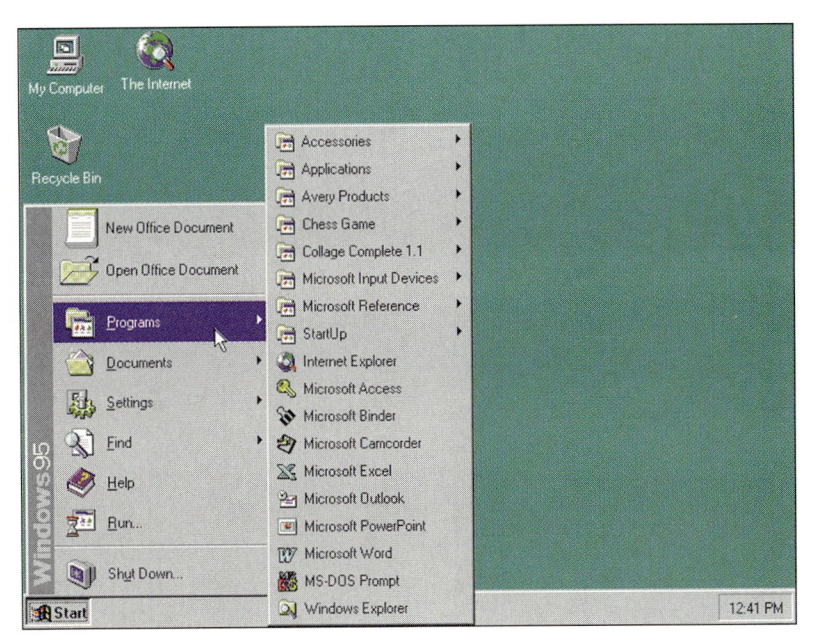

2. Choose Microsoft Excel.
   The program launches and creates a workbook called Book1.

   Note If Excel is already started and you don't see a workbook on the screen, click the New button, and Excel will create one for you.

Moving Around in a Worksheet and a Workbook

To enter data in a worksheet like the one shown in Figure 1.2, you must move to the desired cell. The ***active cell*** is outlined with a black border. You make a cell the active cell by clicking in the cell or by moving to the cell with keystrokes. Table 1.2 lists the navigational keystrokes used to move to the desired cell.

EX-20

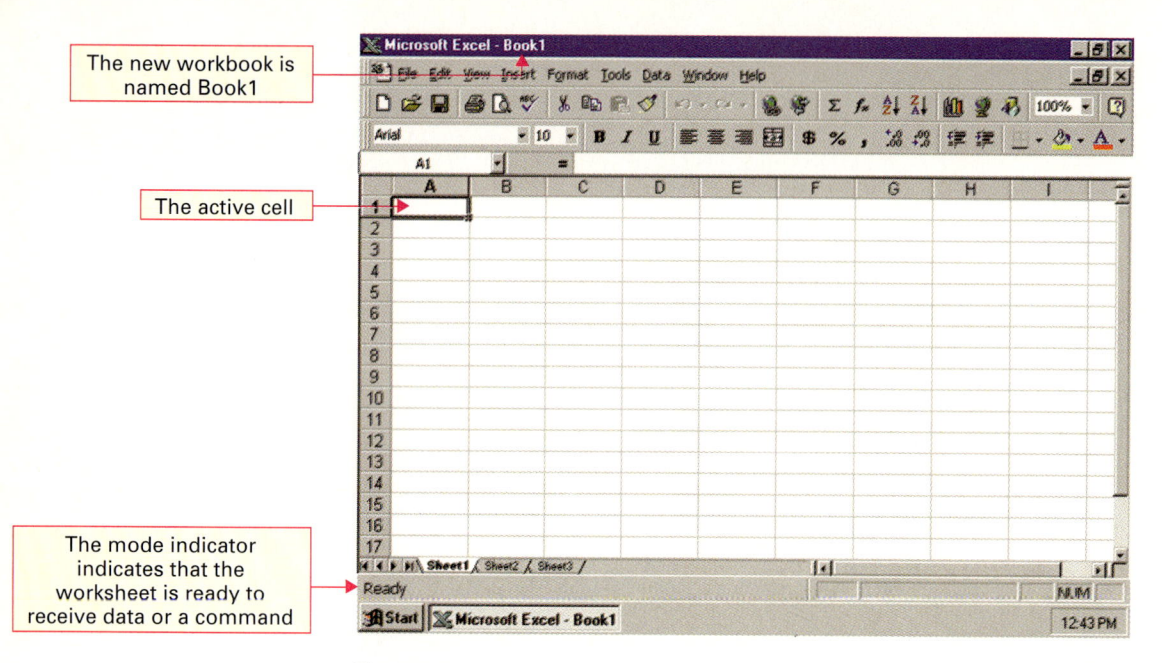

- The new workbook is named Book1
- The active cell
- The mode indicator indicates that the worksheet is ready to receive data or a command

Figure 1.2

> **Note** If you want to click in a cell you can't see on the screen, use the vertical or horizontal scroll bar to scroll the worksheet until you see the cell.

Table 1.2 Navigational Keystrokes

Target Location	Keystroke
Cell to the right of the active cell	→ or TAB
Cell to the left of the active cell	← or SHIFT+TAB
Cell below the active cell	↓ or ENTER
Cell above the active cell	↑ or SHIFT+ENTER
Upper-left corner of the worksheet	CTRL+HOME
Lower-right corner of the active area of the worksheet	CTRL+END
Down one screen	PGDN
Up one screen	PGUP
Right one screen	ALT+PGDN
Left one screen	ALT+PGUP

To display a different worksheet, click the worksheet tab. If you can't see the tab for the worksheet that you want to display, click the appropriate scroll button (the arrows just to the left of the worksheet tabs) to display the tab.

Project 1: Creating a Workbook   EX-21

TASK 2: TO MOVE AROUND IN A WORKSHEET AND A WORKBOOK:

1 Press PGDN.

Cell A18 becomes the active cell

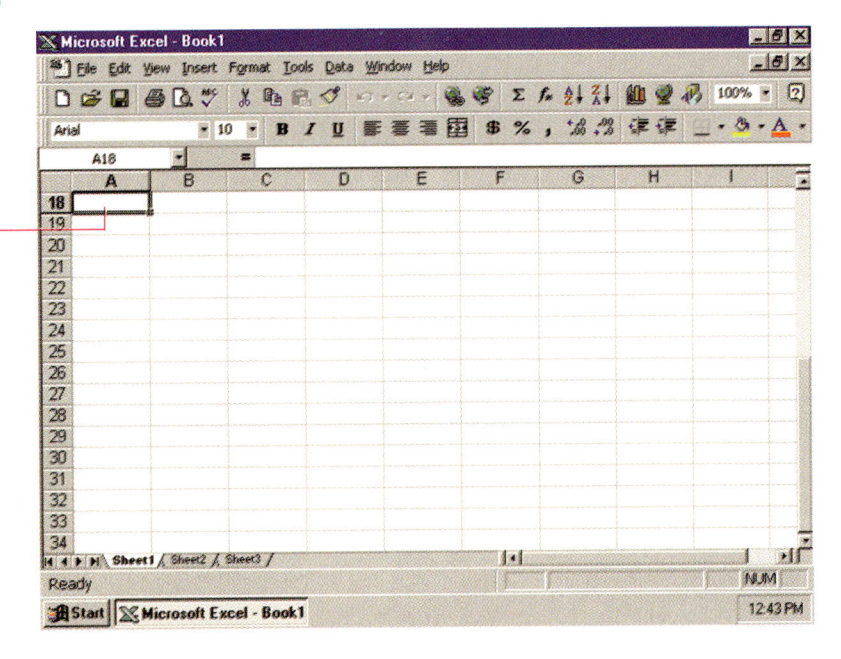

Note The monitor's size and resolution determine the number of columns and rows displayed on a screen. When you press PgDn, PgUp, Alt+PgDn, or Alt+PgUp, the active cell may be different from those shown in the illustrations.

2 Press → five times.

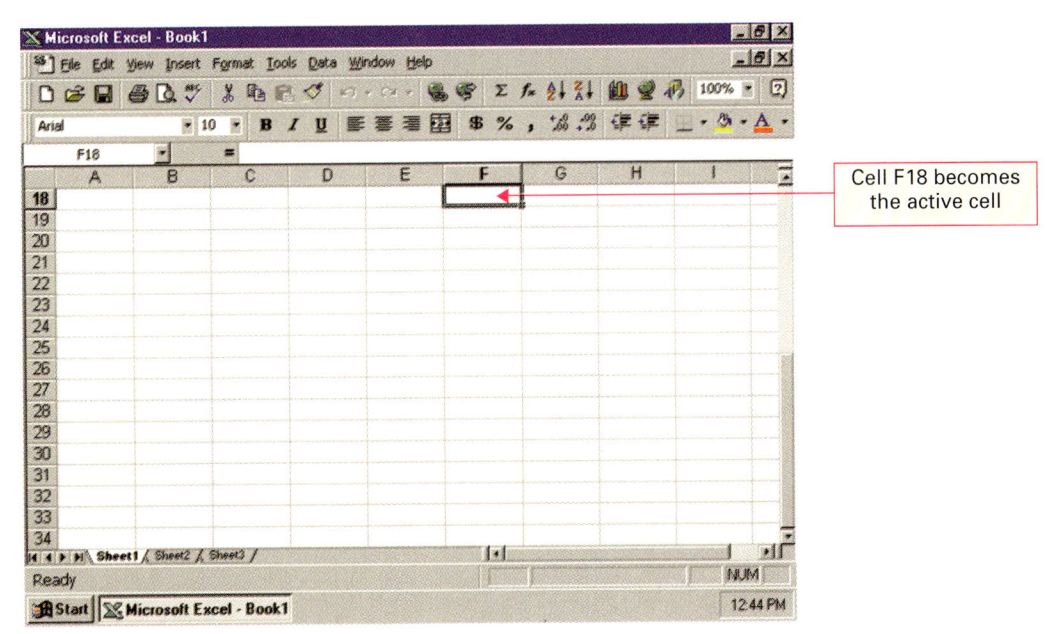

Cell F18 becomes the active cell

3 Type **88** and press ENTER.
The number displays in cell F18, and cell F19 becomes the active cell.

> **Note** Instead of pressing the Enter key to enter data in a cell, you can press any one of the arrow keys (Up, Down, Left, or Right) or any key that moves the cell pointer, such as the PgUp key or the PgDn key. When you enter data across a row, it's more efficient to use the Right arrow key than to use the Enter key.

4 Press CTRL+HOME.
Cell A1 becomes the active cell.

5 Drag the box in the vertical scroll bar until you see Row 4 in the ScrollTip box.

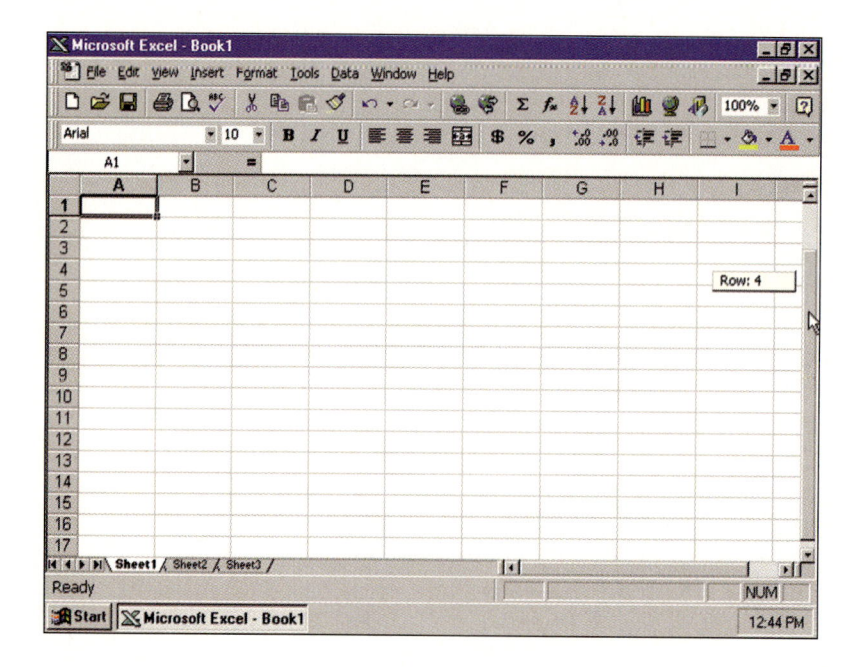

6 Click in cell D5.
Cell D5 becomes the active cell.

Project 1: Creating a Workbook   EX-23

7 Press CTRL+END.

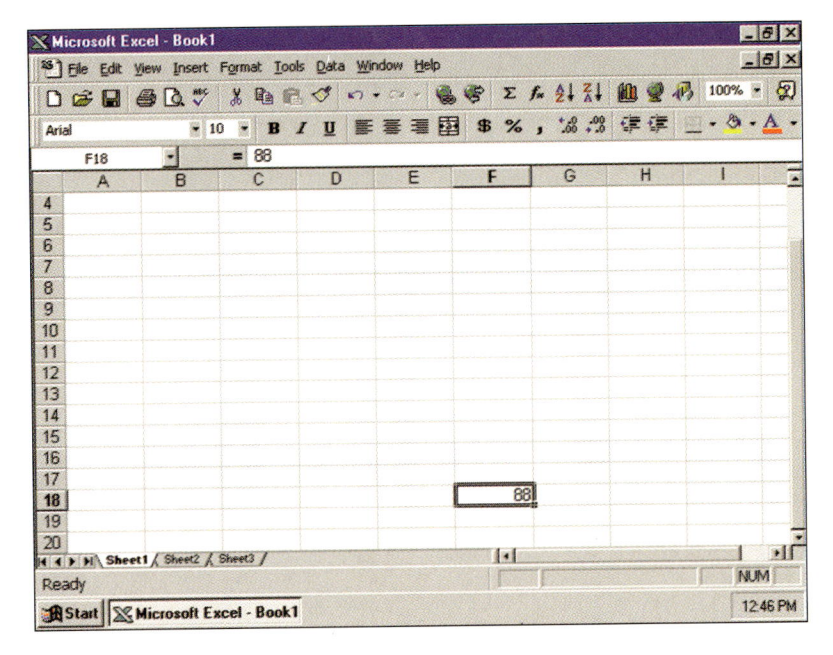

Note The lower right corner of the active worksheet is always the cell at the intersection of the last row and the last column used, and it doesn't necessarily contain data.

8 Press DEL.
The number is deleted.

9 Click the Sheet2 tab.
Sheet2 displays.

Naming Worksheets

The three worksheets created by default in a new workbook are named Sheet1, Sheet2, and Sheet3. Not very imaginative or meaningful names, are they? You can give the worksheets better names to help you identify the content of the worksheet.

TASK 3: TO NAME A WORKSHEET:

1 Point to the Sheet1 tab and right-click.

EX-24

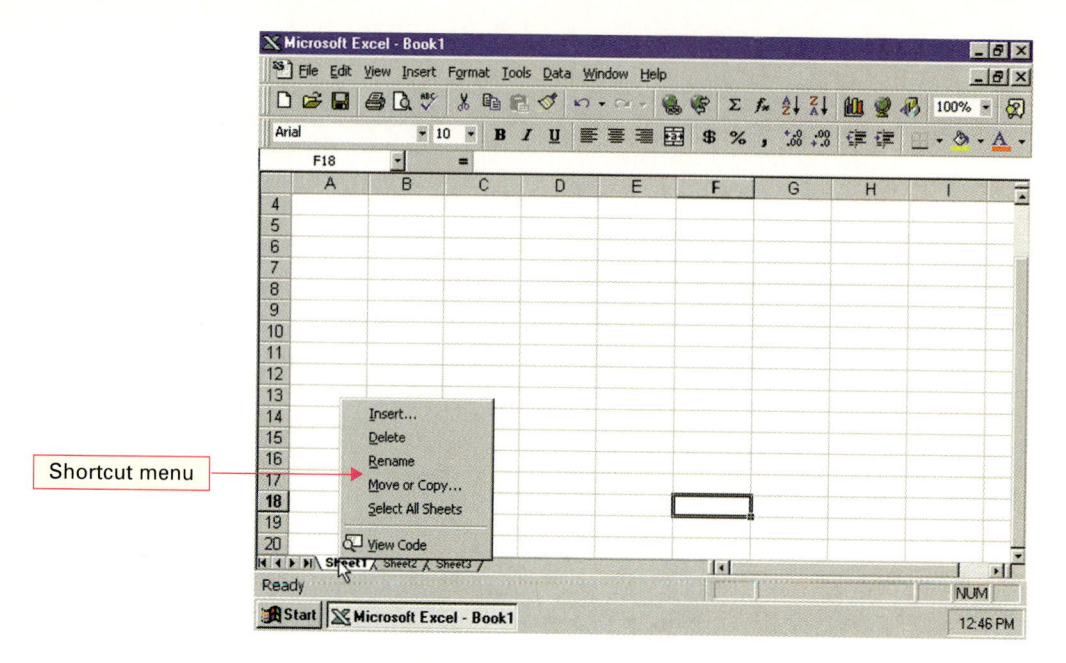

Shortcut menu (label pointing to screenshot)

2 Choose Rename.
The current name on the tab is highlighted.

3 Type **Atrium Cafe** and press ENTER.

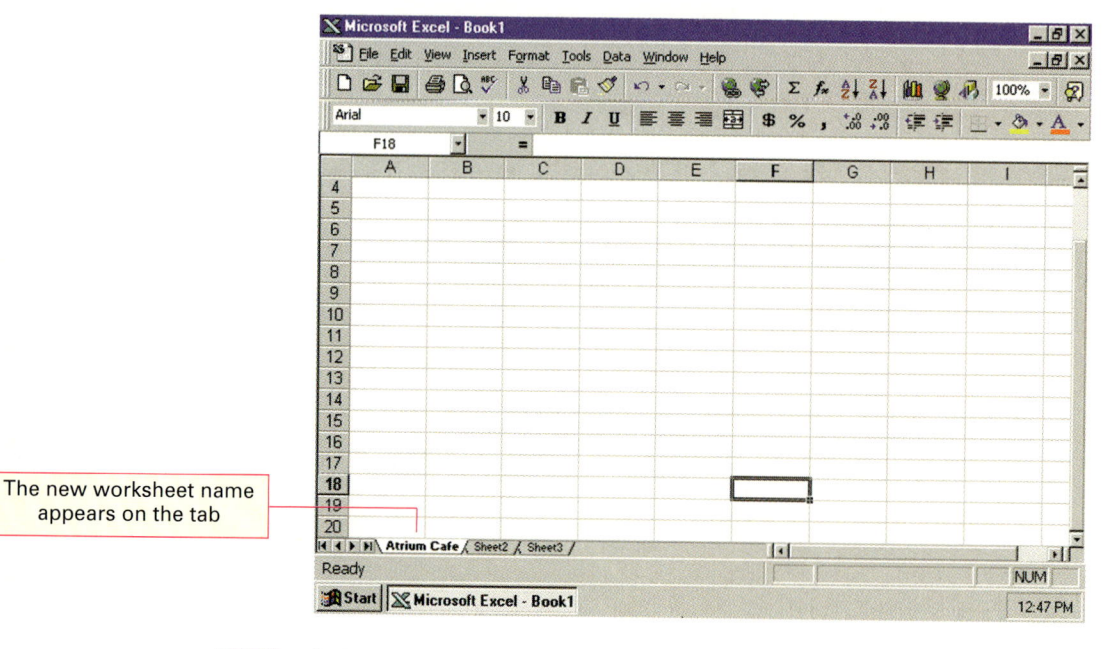

The new worksheet name appears on the tab (label pointing to screenshot)

4 Point to the Sheet2 tab and right-click.
The shortcut menu displays.

5 Choose Rename.
The current name on the tab is highlighted.

6 Type **Willow Top** and press ENTER.
The name displays on the tab.

Entering Data

Excel 97 recognizes several different types of data—text, dates, numbers, and formulas. Text can include any characters on the keyboard as well as special characters such as the symbols for the British pound or the Japanese Yen. Dates can be entered with numbers separated with a slash or a dash. Numbers can include only these characters:

1 2 3 4 5 6 7 8 9 0 + − ( ) , / $ % . E.

> **Tip** To enter a fraction instead of a date, precede the fraction with a zero. For example, to enter the fraction one-half, type 0 1/2 instead of 1/2 which Excel interprets as a date.

Entering Text

When you enter text in a cell, if the cell isn't wide enough to hold the text, the text will spill over into the next cell (if it's empty).

> **Tip** Any time you enter data that doesn't fit in a cell, you can widen the column and the data will display.

TASK 4: TO ENTER DATA IN THE WORKSHEET:

1 Click the Atrium Cafe tab.
The Atrium Cafe worksheet displays.

2 Click in cell A1.
Cell A1 becomes the active cell.

3 Type **Sales for the Atrium Cafe**.
Notice that the mode changes to **Enter** because you are entering data. Also notice that Excel adds an accent to the "e" in "cafe."

4 Press ENTER.

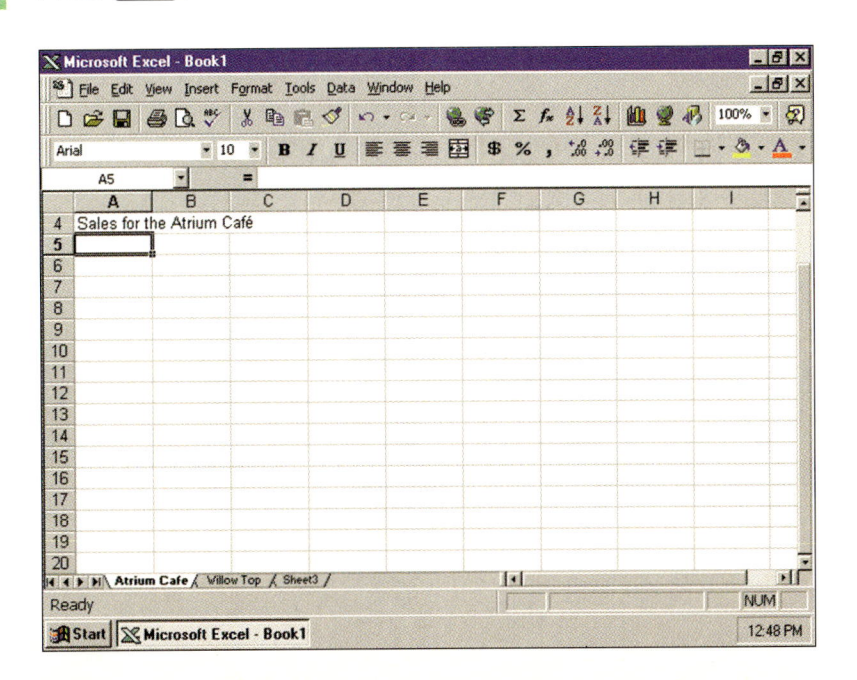

Tip If you make a mistake while typing, simply press the Backspace key and retype the text before you press Enter. If you change your mind about entering the data in the current cell, press ESC before Excel enters the data.

5 Click the Willow Top tab.
The Willow Top worksheet displays.

6 Click in cell A1 if necessary.
Cell A1 becomes the active cell.

7 Type **Sales for the Willow Top Restaurant** and press ENTER.

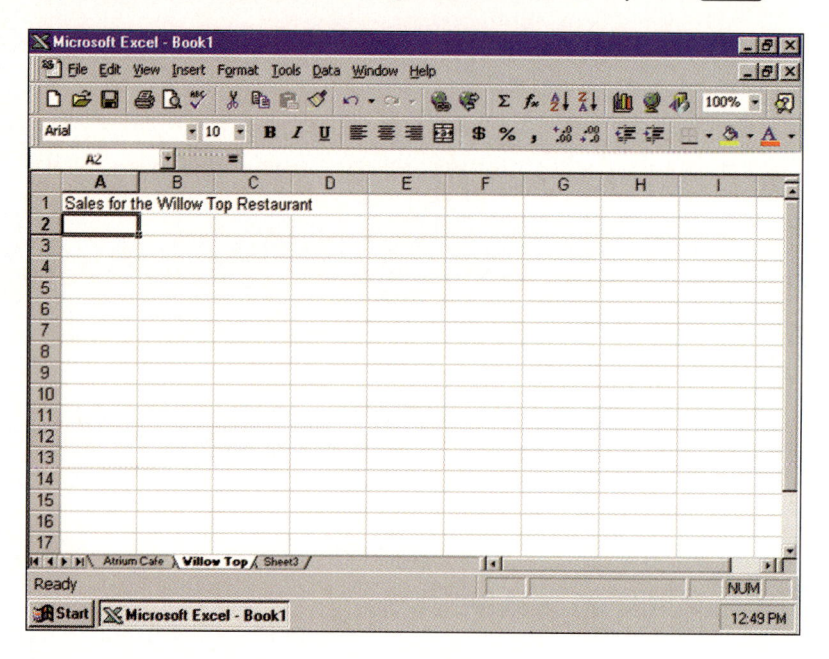

Entering Data on Multiple Worksheets

Sometimes the worksheets that you create have the same data entered several times. If the repetitive data that you are entering is text, the *Auto-Complete* feature of Excel 97 may complete the entry for you if the repetitive text appears in the same column. If the automatic completion isn't appropriate, just continue typing the text that you want.

If you are creating multiple worksheets in a workbook, you may want to use the same data for the column and row headings. To save time, you can enter the data that is the same on all worksheets at the same time.

TASK 5: TO ENTER THE SAME DATA ON MULTIPLE WORKSHEETS AT THE SAME TIME:

1 Press CTRL and click the Atrium Cafe tab.
Both the Atrium Cafe worksheet and the Willow Top worksheet are selected.

2 Click in cell B2 and type **Jan**.

Project 1: Creating a Workbook   EX-27

> **Note** The Group indicator displays in the title bar when multiple worksheets are selected.

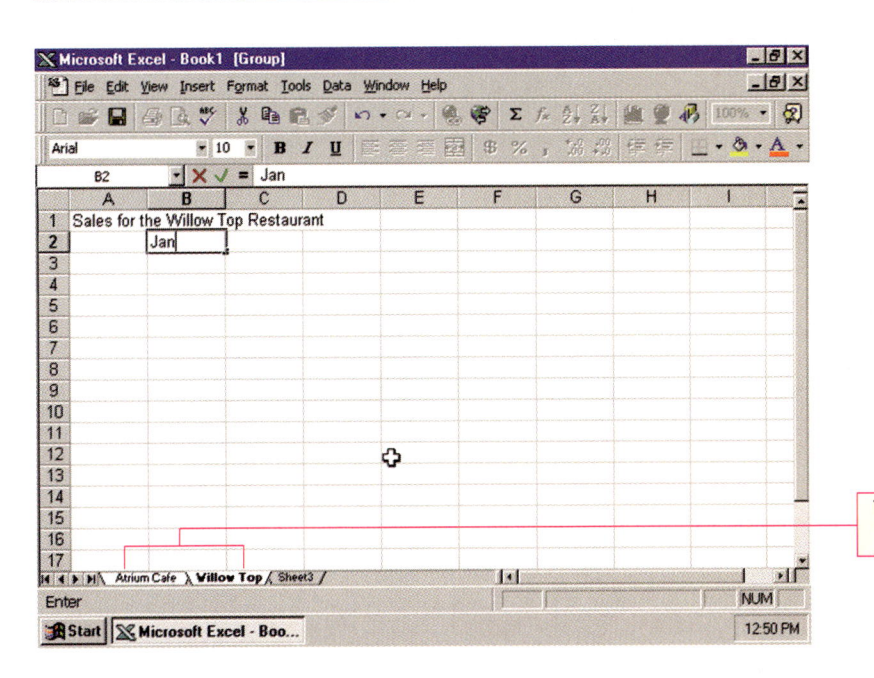

This indicates that more than one worksheet is selected

3 Press → and type **Feb**.

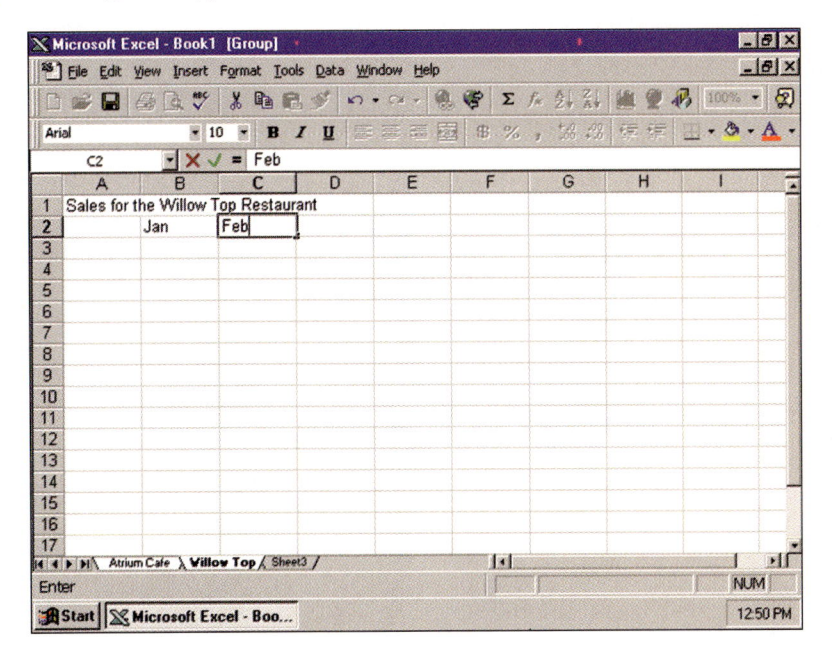

4 Press → and type **Difference**.

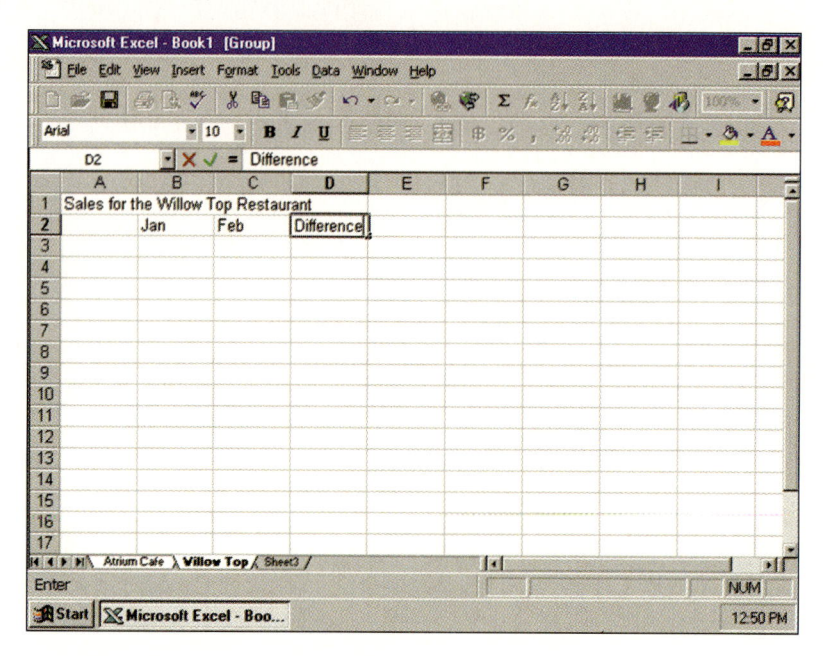

5 Click in cell A3 and type **Week 1**.

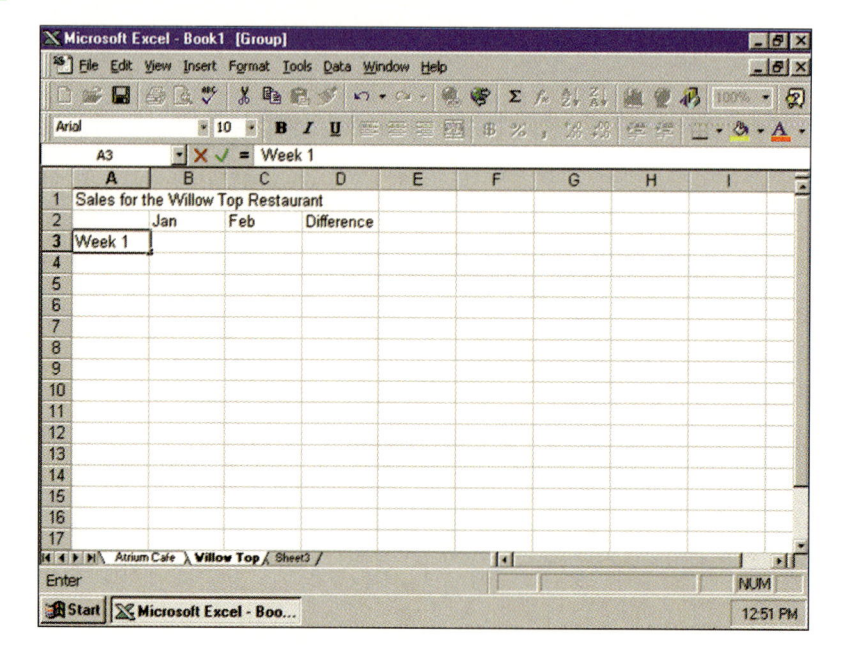

6 Press (ENTER) and type **Week**.
The AutoComplete feature completes the entry as Week 1.

Project 1: Creating a Workbook EX-29

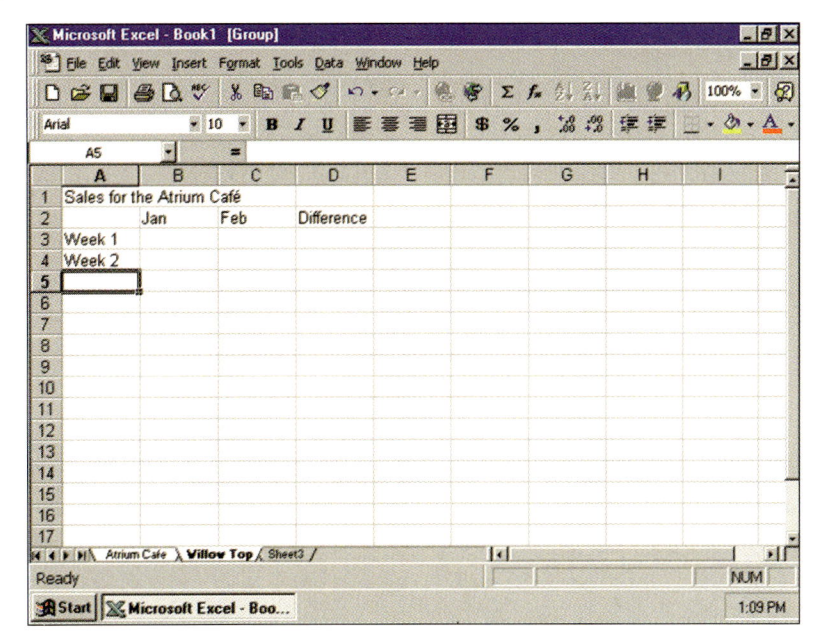

7 Continue typing so that the entry is "Week 2" and then press ENTER.

8 Click in cell A4.
Cell A4 becomes the active cell.

9 Point to the handle in the lower right corner of the cell.

> **Note** The pointer appears as a plus when you point to the handle.

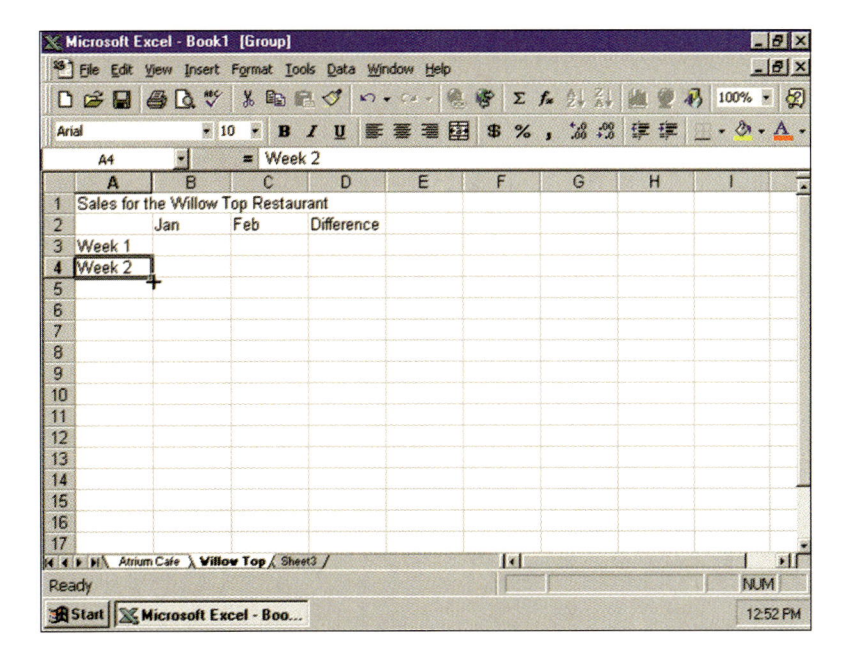

EX-30

10 Drag the handle to cell A7.

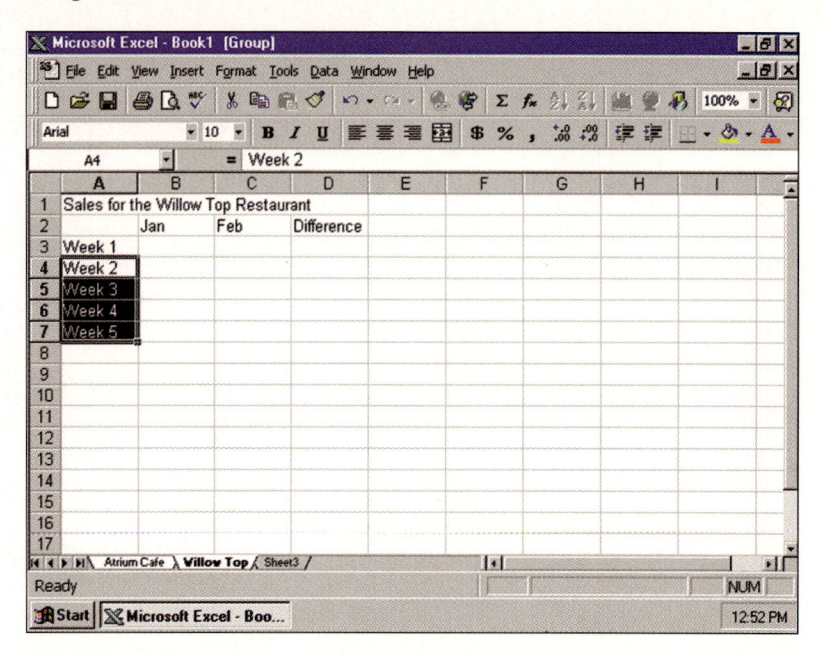

Tip You can use the dragging technique to enter almost any type of series (except the World Series, of course).

11 Click in cell A8, type **Total** and press ENTER.

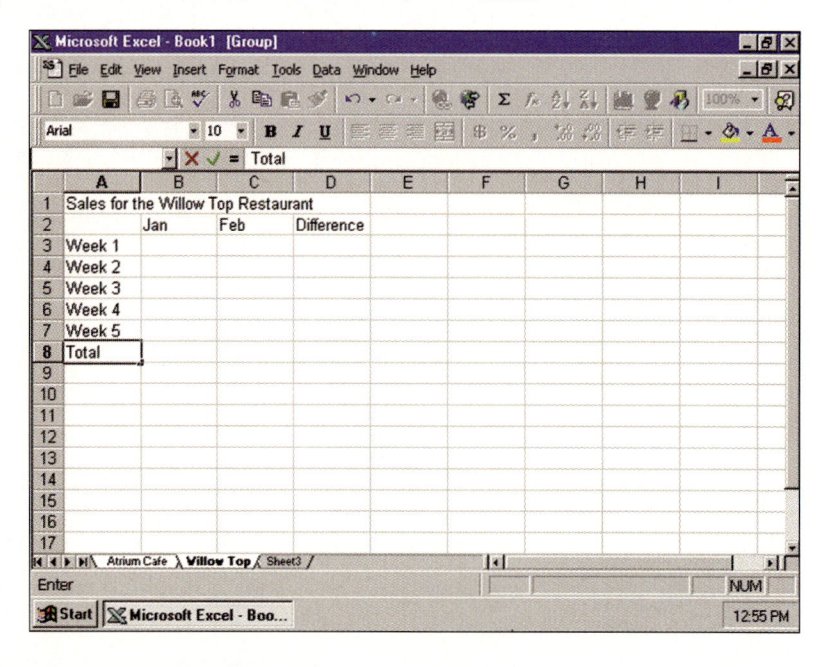

12 Click the Atrium Cafe tab.

Project 1: Creating a Workbook   EX-31

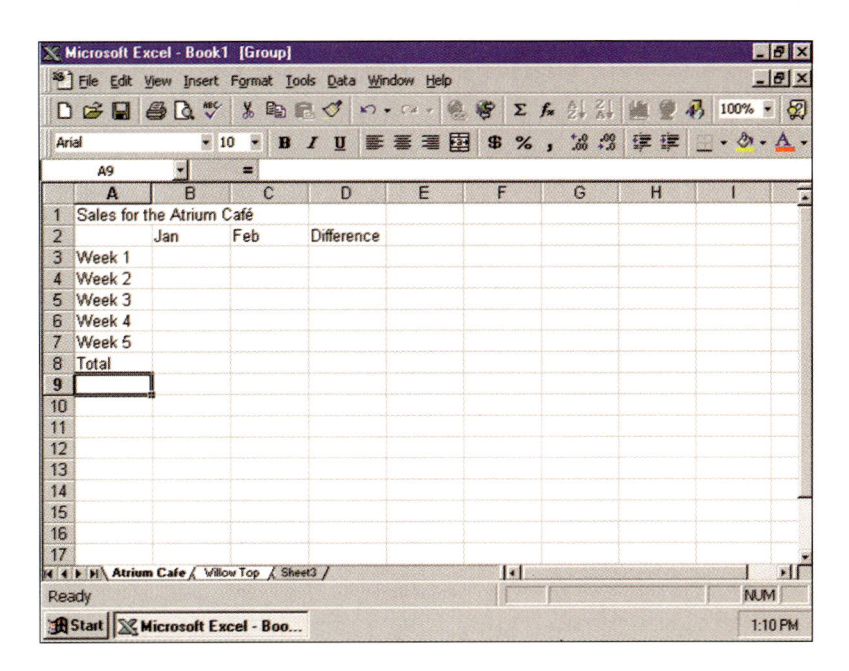

(screenshot of Microsoft Excel - Book1 [Group] showing the Atrium Cafe worksheet with "Sales for the Atrium Café" in A1, "Jan", "Feb", "Difference" in row 2, and "Week 1" through "Week 5" and "Total" in column A)

Now you will enter some numbers. The technique is the same.

Entering Numbers

If you enter a number that doesn't fit in a cell, Excel 97 either converts the number to *scientific notation* or displays pound signs (#) in the cell. If you enter a date that doesn't fit in a cell, Excel 97 displays pound signs.

> **Note** Scientific notation is a number format used for very large numbers and very small decimal numbers. For example, the scientific notation for 1,000,000,000 is 1E+09 which means 1 times 10 to the ninth power. Perhaps our government should consider using scientific notation to express the national debt; maybe it wouldn't look so bad.

TASK 6: TO ENTER NUMBERS IN THE WORKSHEETS:

1. Press CTRL and click the Willow Top tab.
   The Willow Top worksheet is deselected and the Group indicator no longer displays in the title bar.

2. Enter the following numbers in columns B and C on the Atrium Cafe worksheet:

COLUMN B	COLUMN C
6570	2200
8345	7890
8650	9180
8990	8750
2130	4560

EX-32

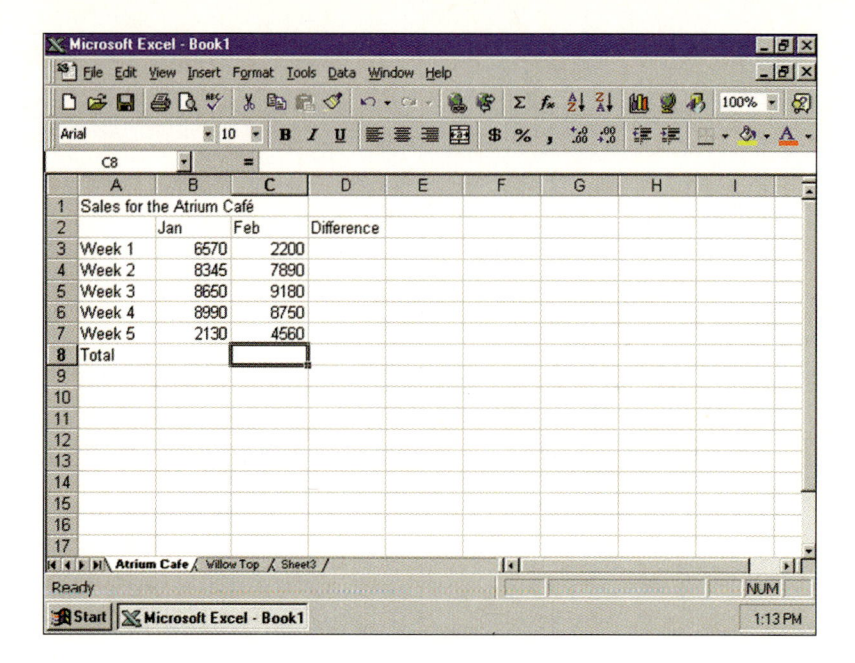

[Screenshot: Microsoft Excel - Book1, Atrium Cafe worksheet showing:
Sales for the Atrium Café
	Jan	Feb	Difference
Week 1	6570	2200	
Week 2	8345	7890	
Week 3	8650	9180	
Week 4	8990	8750	
Week 5	2130	4560	
Total			|]

3 Click the Willow Top tab.
The Willow Top worksheet displays.

4 Enter the following numbers in columns B and C on the Willow Top worksheet:

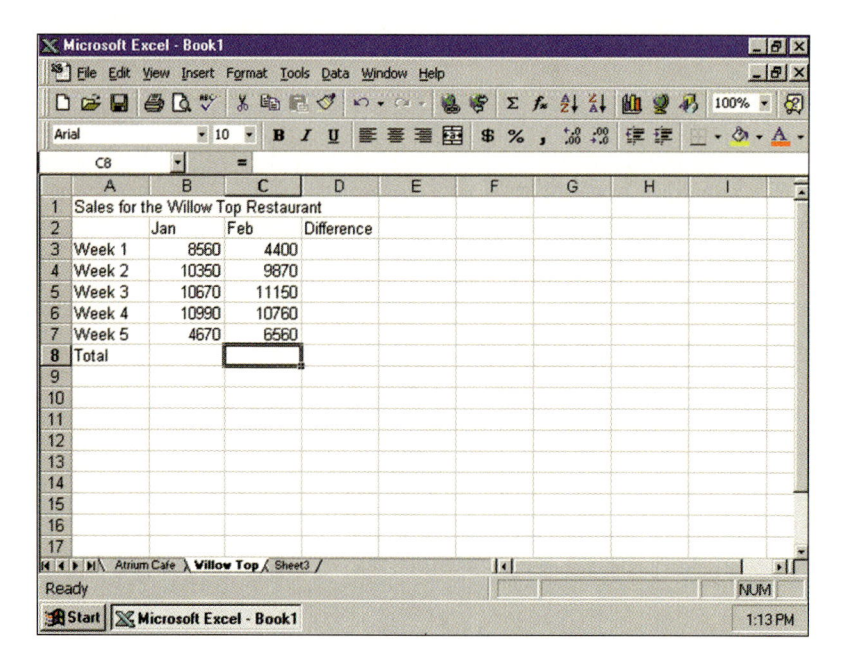

[Screenshot: Microsoft Excel - Book1, Willow Top worksheet showing:
Sales for the Willow Top Restaurant
	Jan	Feb	Difference
Week 1	8560	4400	
Week 2	10350	9870	
Week 3	10670	11150	
Week 4	10990	10760	
Week 5	4670	6560	
Total			|]

Entering Simple Formulas and Functions

Formulas and ***functions*** are mathematical statements that perform calculations. Formulas are made up and entered by the user to perform the specific calculation needed. Formulas and functions must start with the equal sign (=), and they can contain cell addresses, numbers, and ***arithmetic op-***

erators. Table 1.3 describes the arithmetic operators and gives examples. Table 1.4 lists some of the commonly used functions.

Functions are formulas that are included in Excel 97. They perform calculations that are commonly used such as calculating a sum or an average. Functions require specific information, called *arguments,* to perform the calculations.

> **Tip** Some formulas and functions refer to a block of cells, called a *range.* The address of a range includes the first and last cells in the range separated by a colon. For example, the address of the range from cell A1 through cell B10 is A1:B10.

Table 1.3 Arithmetic Operators

Operator	Meaning	Example	Result (if A1 = 20 and A2 = 2)
+	Addition	=A1+A2	22
−	Subtraction	=A1−A2	18
*	Multiplication	=A1*10	200
/	Division	=A1/A2	10
%	Percent	=A1%	.2
^	Exponentiation	=A1^A2	400

Table 1.4 Commonly Used Functions

Function	Meaning	Example	Result (if A1 = 1, A2 = 2 and A3 = 3)
=SUM(*argument*)	Calculates the sum of the cells in the argument	=SUM(A1:A3)	6
=AVERAGE(*argument*)	Calculates the average of the cells in the argument	=AVERAGE(A1:A3)	2
=MAX(*argument*)	Finds the largest value in the cells in the argument	=MAX(A1:A3)	3
=MIN(*argument*)	Finds the smallest value of the cells in the argument	=MIN(A1:A3)	1
=COUNT(*argument*)	Counts the number of cells in the argument that have a numeric value	=COUNT(A1:A3)	3

EX-34

TASK 7: TO ENTER FORMULAS AND FUNCTIONS:

1 Press CTRL and click the Atrium Cafe tab.
Both worksheets are selected, and the data you enter will display on both worksheets. Notice that the Group indicator displays in the title bar.

2 Click in cell D3 and click the equal sign in the formula bar. (If the Office Assistant opens, choose No, don't provide help now.)

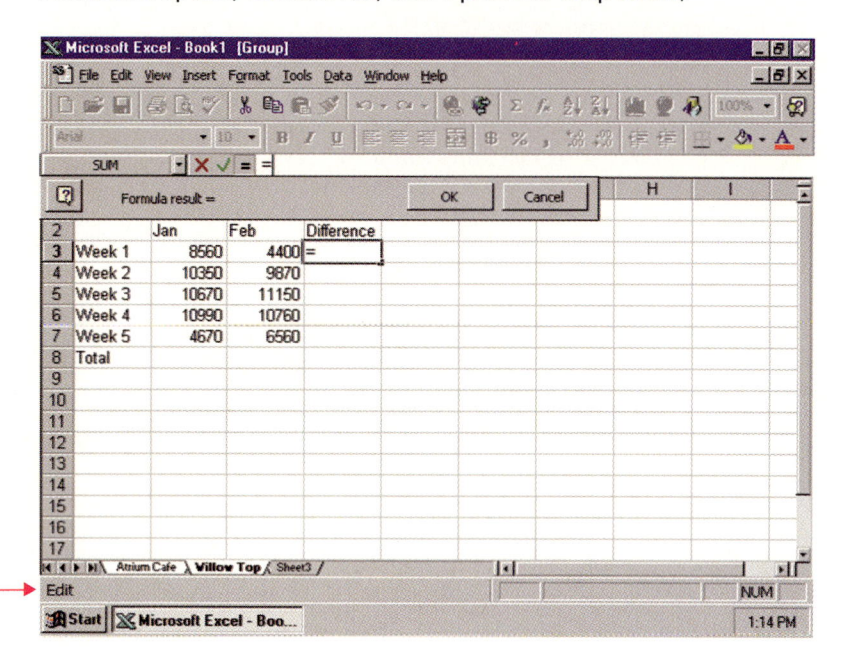

The mode changes to Edit because the data is being entered in the formula bar

3 Click in cell B3.
The mode changes to **Point** because you are pointing to cells to build the formula.

4 Type a minus sign (−).

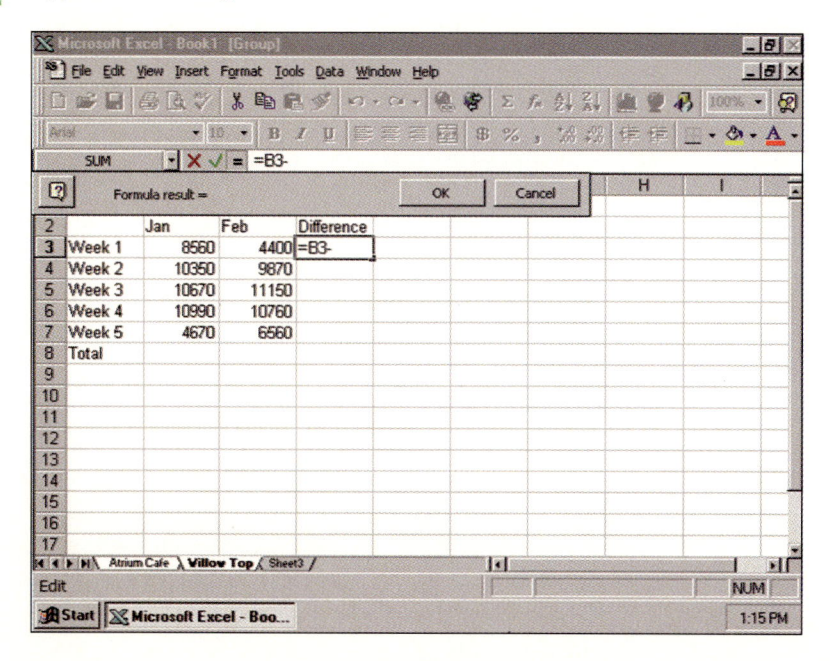

Project 1: Creating a Workbook EX-35

5 Click in cell C3 and the click the Enter ✓ button in the formula bar.

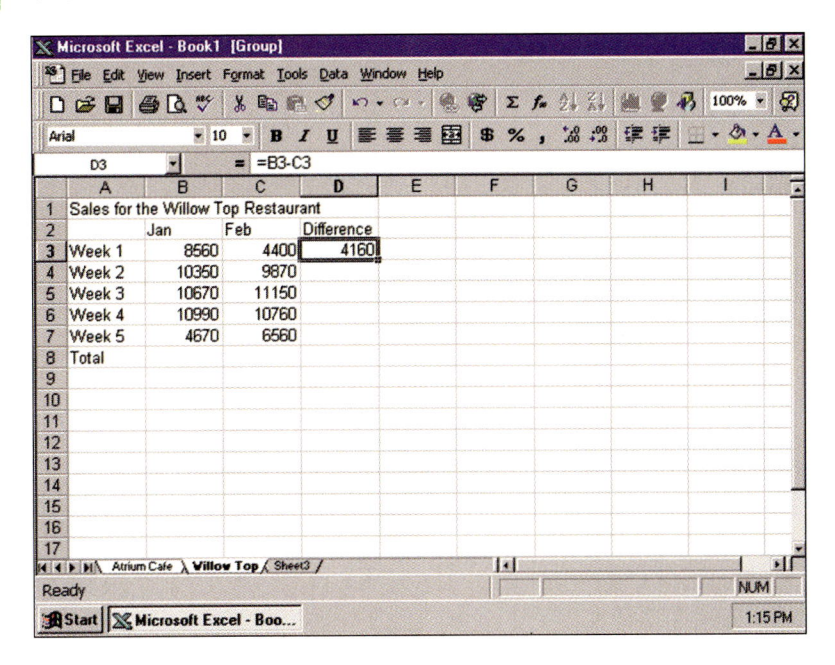

6 Click in cell B8 and type **=sum(**.

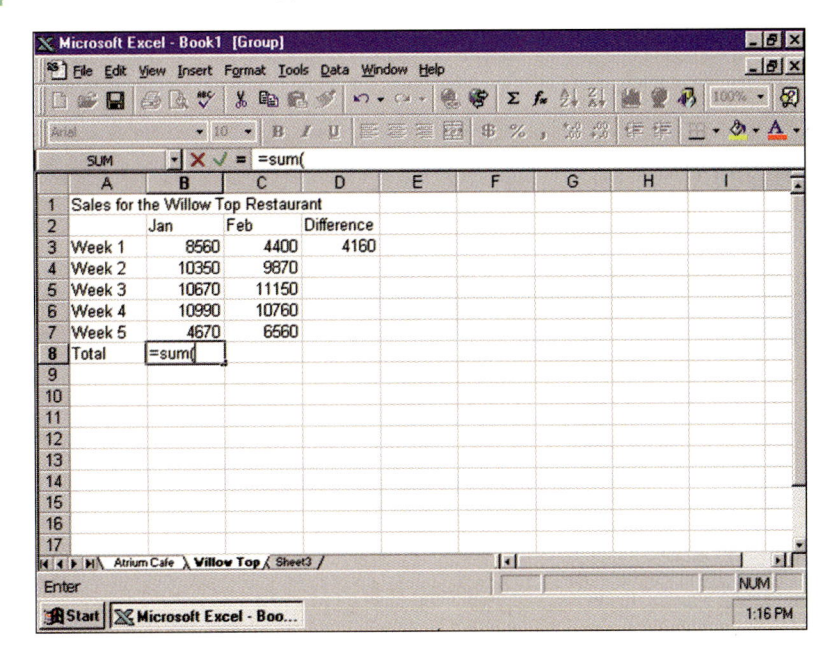

EX-36

7 Drag the cursor from cell B3 through cell B7.

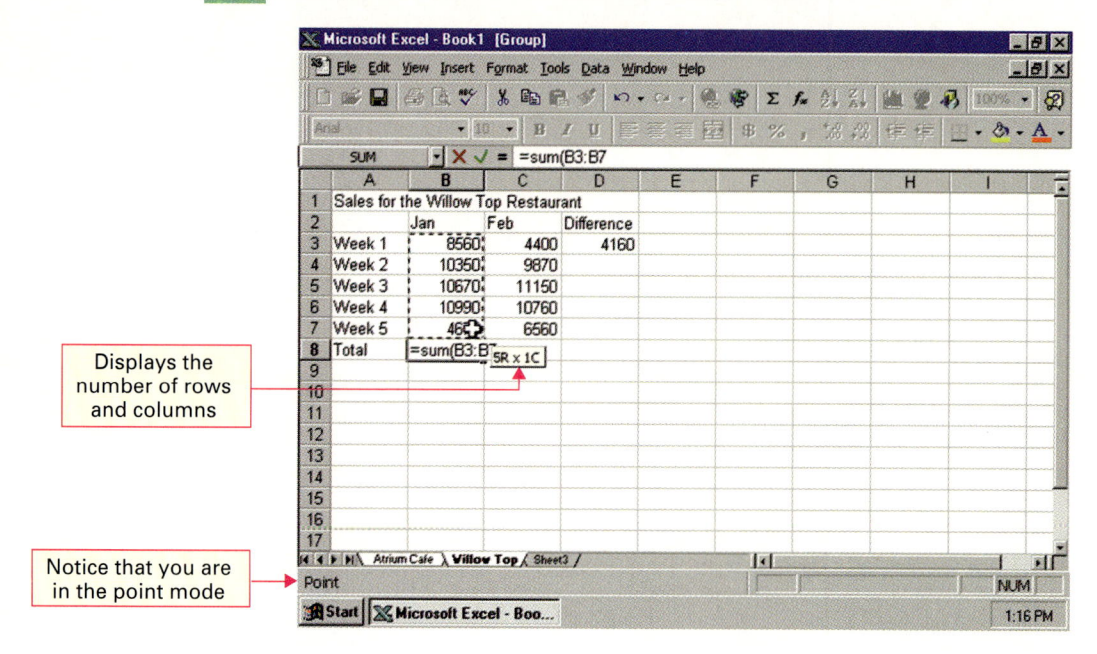

Displays the number of rows and columns

Notice that you are in the point mode

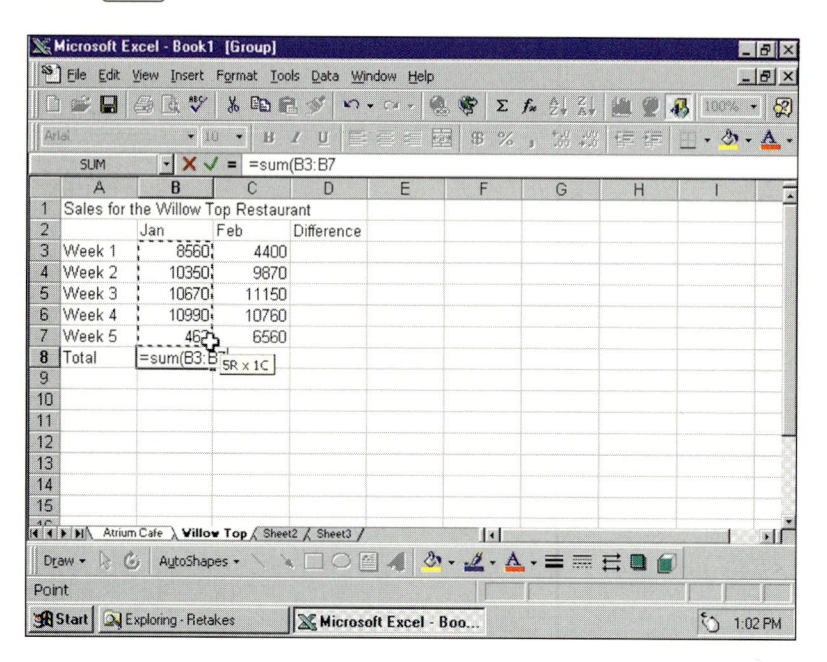

8 Press ENTER.

9 Click in cell C8 and click the AutoSum Σ button.

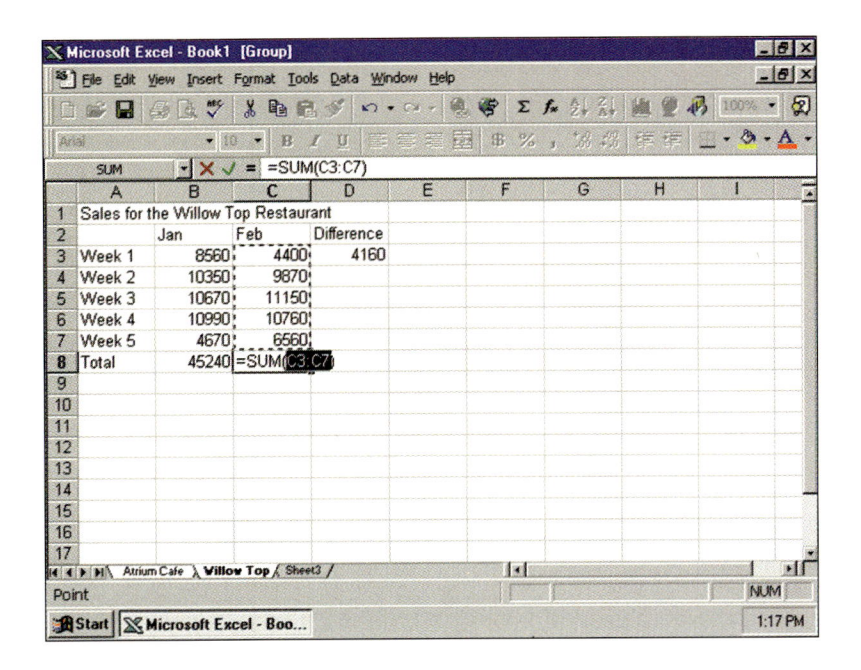

10 Press ENTER.
The numbers in column C are totaled.

> **Note** If you change a number in a cell, Excel 97 automatically recalculates all formulas or functions that might be affected.

> **Key Concept** When a formula has more than one operation, Excel 97 follows an order of precedence to determine the sequence in which each operation should be performed. The order is as follows: exponentiation first, then multiplication or division (from left to right), and finally addition or subtraction (from left to right). If the formula has parentheses, the operation(s) in the parentheses are performed first. You can use the phrase "Please excuse my dear Aunt Sally" to remember "p" for parentheses, "e" for exponent, "m" for multiplication, "d" for division, "a" for addition, and "s" for subtraction.

Saving a Workbook

If you want to keep the data that you have entered in a workbook, you must save the file. When saving the file, you specify a name for the document and a location where it will be stored.

> **Tip** Because Excel 97 is written for Windows 95, the name of a workbook can be a *long filename.* Long filenames (including the full path of the file) can use up to 255 characters. Although you can use as many spaces and periods in the filename as you want, you can't use ? or : or *. Older versions of Excel prior to Excel 7.0 do NOT use long filenames and will convert a long filename to eight characters (plus the extension).

EX-38

TASK 8: TO SAVE A WORKBOOK:

1 Click the Atrium Cafe tab if it isn't the displayed worksheet.
The Atrium Cafe worksheet displays.

2 Press CTRL and click the Willow Top tab.
The Willow Top worksheet is deselected.

> **Tip** When you are ready to save and close a workbook and you have more than one worksheet selected, you might want to deselect all but one worksheet by pressing CTRL and clicking the tabs you want to deselect. If you don't deselect worksheets, the next time you open the workbook, the worksheets will still be selected and any changes you make will be made on all worksheets.

3 Click the Save button.

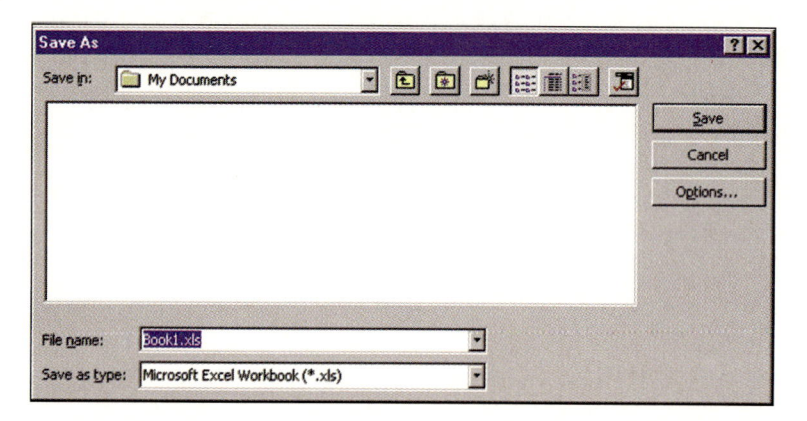

4 Type **Restaurant Sales** in the File Name text box.
Excel 97 adds the default extension xls to the filename when the file is saved.

5 Click the down arrow in the Save In text box and choose drive A: (or the drive and folder designated by your professor or lab assistant).

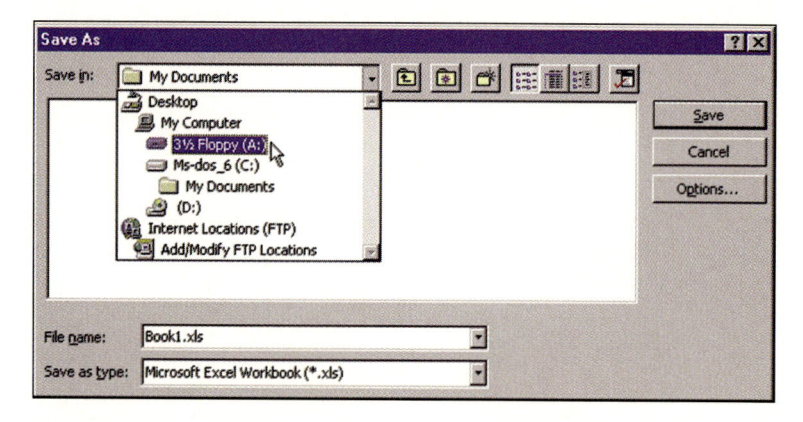

6 Click Save.
The dialog box closes, the file is saved on the disk, and the title bar displays the name of the file.

Project 1: Creating a Workbook   EX-39

> **Tip** After saving a file for the first time, you should save the document periodically as you continue to work on it in case your system goes down for some reason. After a file has a name, you can save the file again simply by clicking the Save button.

> **Note** To save a file in a different location or with a different name, choose File, Save As.

Previewing and Printing a Worksheet

Before you print a file, you should preview it to see if it looks like what you expect. (You don't want any surprises.) The ***Print Preview*** shows the full page of the current worksheet and allows you to zoom in on the worksheet so you can actually read the data, if necessary.

You can print a worksheet in the Print Preview mode or in Normal view. Clicking the Print button prints one copy of the complete workbook. If you want to print only part of the workbook or more than one copy, you should use the Print command from the File menu.

TASK 9: TO PREVIEW AND PRINT A WORKSHEET:

1 Click the Print Preview button.

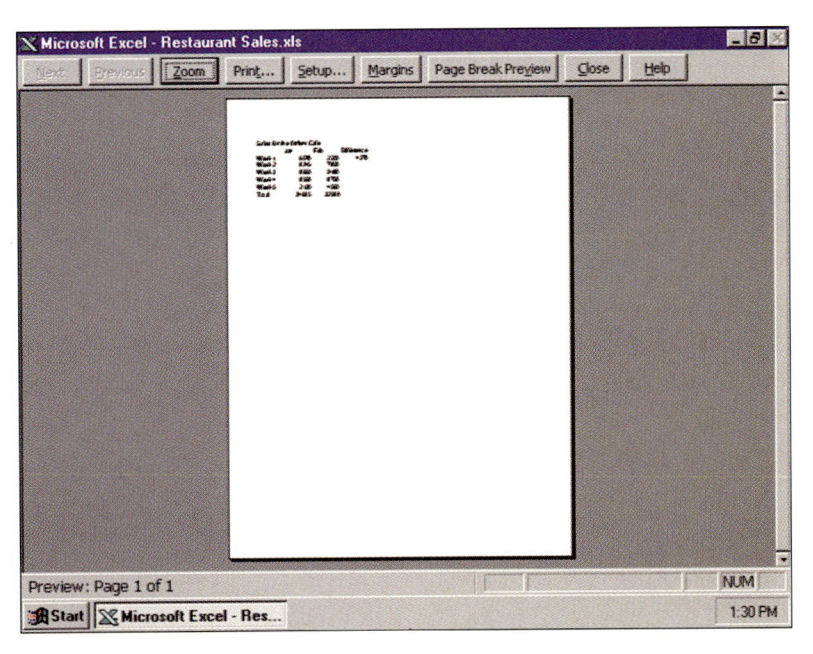

2 Click the pointer, shaped like a magnifying glass, at the top of the worksheet.

EX-40

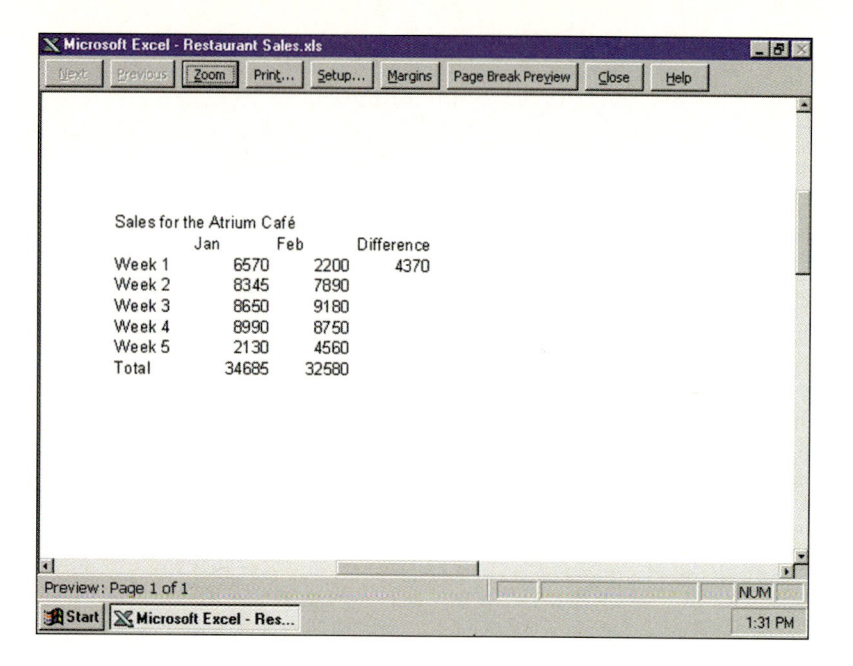

3 Click again.
The full page displays again.

4 Click Close in the Print Preview toolbar.
The Print Preview mode closes and the worksheet screen displays.

5 Ensure that the computer you are using is attached to a printer and that the printer is online.

6 Choose File from the menu bar.

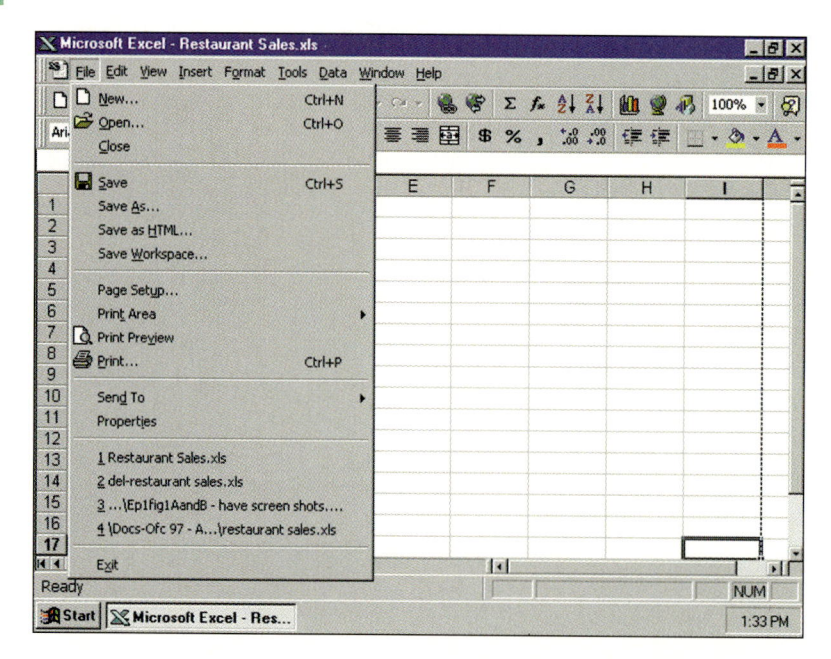

Project 1: Creating a Workbook EX-41

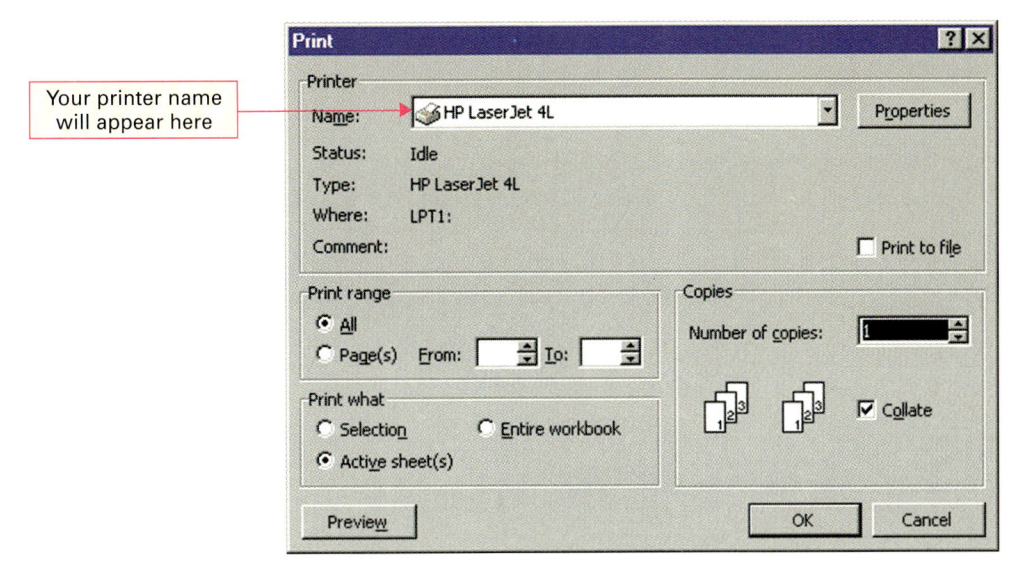

7 Choose Print.

Your printer name will appear here →

8 Click OK.
The workbook prints.

Closing a Workbook

When you are finished with a workbook, you can close it. If you have made changes that you want to keep, you should save the workbook before closing it. If you forget to save a workbook before closing, Excel 97 asks if you want to save changes.

TASK 11: TO CLOSE A FILE:

1 Click 💾.
The worksheet is saved.
The File menu displays.

2 Click ✖.
The file closes.

The Conclusion

You can exit Excel 97 now by clicking ✖, or you can work on the Review Exercises and Assignments.

Summary and Exercises

Summary

- When you launch Excel 97 a workbook named Book1 is created automatically.
- To enter data in a worksheet, the cell pointer must be positioned in the desired cell.
- By default, a new workbook has three worksheets.
- Excel 97 recognizes several different types of data: text, dates, numbers, and formulas.
- Formulas and functions are mathematical statements that perform calculations.
- Files can be saved with long filenames.
- Before you print a worksheet, you can preview it to see if it looks acceptable.
- When you close a file, if you haven't saved changes to the file, Excel 97 asks if you want to save the changes.

Key Terms and Operations

Key Terms
active cell
arithmetic operators
AutoComplete
Edit mode
Enter mode
formula
function
order of precedence
Point mode
Print Preview mode
range
scientific notation

Operations
close a workbook
create a workbook
enter data
enter formulas and functions
move in a workbook
name a workbook
preview a worksheet
print a worksheet
save a workbook

Study Questions

Multiple Choice

1. Using the order of precedence, solve the formula 5–2*(8+2). What is the answer?
    a. 26
    b. −15
    c. −9
    d. 30

2. To move to the cell below the active cell, press
    a. Enter.
    b. PageDown.
    c. Tab.
    d. Ctrl + the down arrow.

3. Which of the following is a range address?
   a. D1;D10
   b. D1,D10
   c. D1 D10
   d. D1:D10

4. Which of the following can not be included in numeric data?
   a. 1
   b. 2
   c. E
   d. $

5. Which of the following is an example of scientific notation?
   a. 1.5E+11
   b. 1^10
   c. 7.8!
   d. A2

6. If A1 is 10, A2 is 15, and A3 is 20, what is the result of =SUM(A1:A2)?
   a. 10
   b. 15
   c. 25
   d. 45

7. If A1 is 10, A2 is 15, and A3 is 20, what is the result of =AVERAGE(A1:A3)?
   a. 10
   b. 15
   c. 25
   d. 45

8. If A1 is 10, A2 is 15, A3 is 20, and A4 says "Total," what is the result of =COUNT(A1:A4)?
   a. 3
   b. 15
   c. 45
   d. 4

9. The Preview mode shows
   a. all pages of a workbook.
   b. the current page of the workbook.
   c. the formulas.
   d. the formulas and functions.

10. When you press Ctrl + End, what cell becomes the active cell?
    a. IV65536
    b. The last cell in the current column.
    c. The cell in the lower right corner.
    d. The cell in the lower right corner of the active area of the worksheet.

Short Answer

1. What happens when you change a number in a cell that is included in a formula?

2. What should you do before you close a workbook?

3. How do you rename a worksheet?
4. What is the order of precedence?
5. What displays in a cell if you enter 1/10?
6. How can you make 1/10 display as a fraction in a cell?
7. Write the formula to add the numbers in from cell A1 through cell A5.
8. Write the function to add the numbers in from cell A1 through cell A5.
9. How do you enter the same data on more than one worksheet?
10. What function finds the smallest value?

For Discussion
1. Describe a situation in which you would use several worksheets in the same workbook.
2. The cell displays #######. What caused the problem and how can you solve it?
3. Discuss the reasons you might rename worksheets in a workbook.
4. What is a range and how is it addressed?

Review Exercises

1. Creating an Expense Account
Your good friend Karl Klaus, the head chef at the 4-star restaurant in *The Grande Hotel*, has asked you to create an expense report for him because he can't type. In this exercise, you will create a worksheet that lists the expenses Karl had on a recent trip for the hotel.

You will learn to align headings in a later project

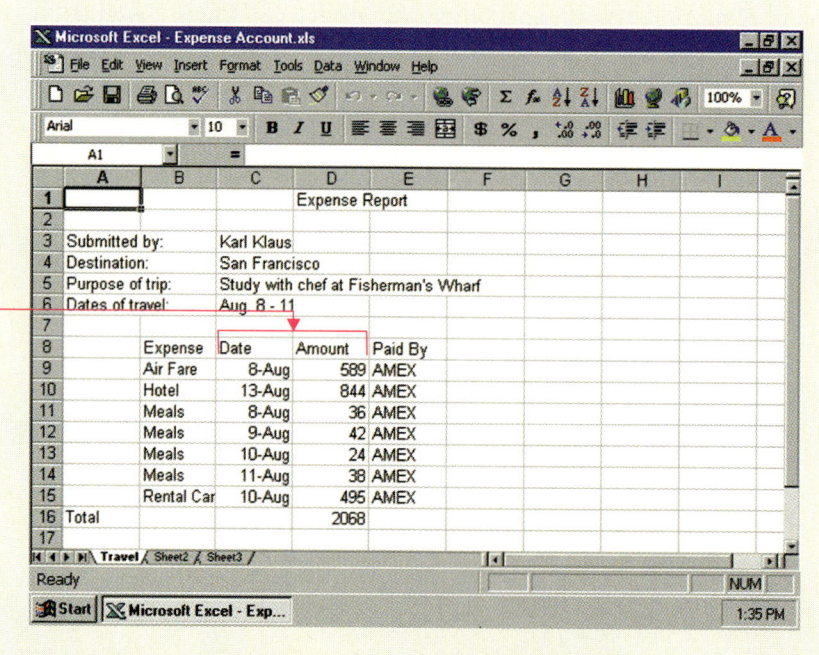

Figure 1.3

1. Create a new workbook.
2. Rename Sheet1 to Travel.

Project 1: Creating a Workbook   EX-45

3. Enter the data shown in Figure 1.3.

> **Note** The format for dates might be different on your computer.

4. Use the AutoSum button to calculate the total expenses.

5. Save the workbook as *Expense Account.xls*.

2. Calculating Savings

In this exercise, you will use a worksheet to calculate the amount of money you will have in twenty years, based on different variables such as the amount you can save each year and the rate of interest you earn.

[Screenshot of Microsoft Excel - Savings.xls showing:
- A1: Rate/Yr., B1: 0.05 (labeled "Interest rate")
- A2: No. of Years, B2: 20
- A3: Payment/Yr (labeled "Enter the amount of money you can save each year in this cell.")
- A4: Current Savings, B4: -1000
- A5: Future Value, B5: 2653.297705 (labeled "In 20 years, $1000 will grow to approximately $2653 at 5% interest.")]

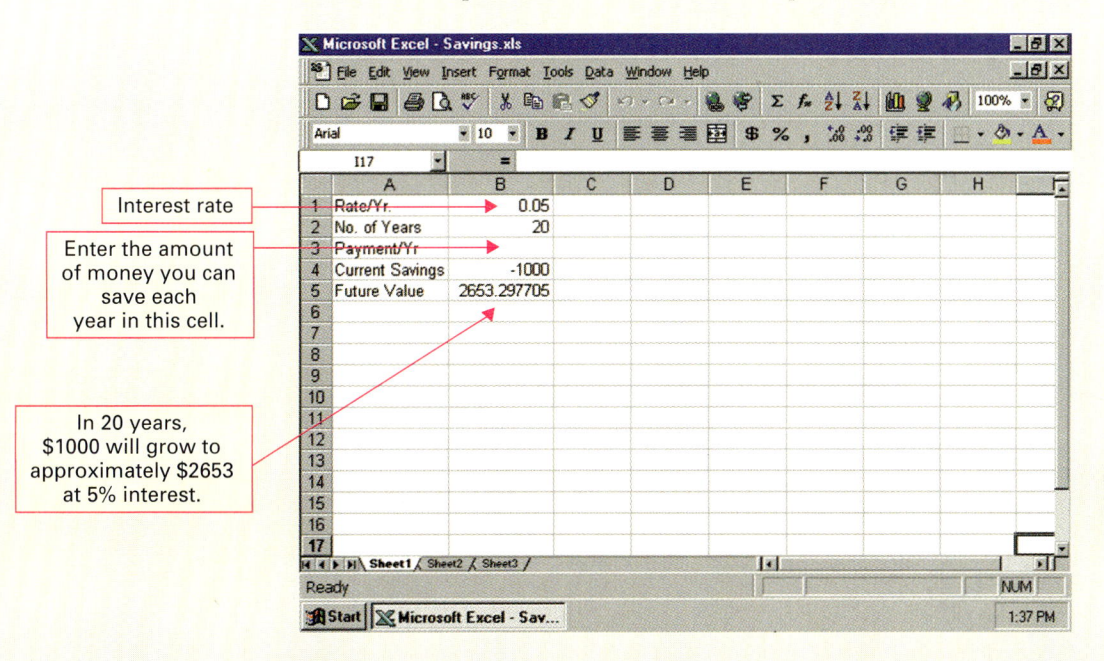

Figure 1.4

1. Go to this address on the Web:
   http://www.finaid.org/finaid/calculators/finaid_calc.html.

2. Select the Savings Plan Designer.

3. If you currently have $1000 in savings and you can get 5 percent interest, how much will you have to save each month to have $200,000 in 20 years?

4. Create a new worksheet and enter the data shown in Figure 1.4. Be sure to enter the data in the same cells shown in the figure.

> **Note** The values for current savings is a negative number due to the use of debits and credits in standard accounting procedures.

5. In cell B5, type this function: =FV(B1,B2,B3,B4,1).

6. In cell B3, enter the number that is 12 times the answer you got in step 3. Precede the number with a minus sign. The answer in cell B5 should be approximately 200,000.

7. Change the Payment/Yr amount to −2000 and change the Rate/Yr to .15.

8. Save the worksheet as *Savings.xls*.

Assignments

1. Creating a Timesheet
Create a workbook with a worksheet for each of your classes. List the dates and the number of hours that you spend for each class (including class time, lab time, and homework) in a week. Total the number of hours. Save the worksheets and workbook, using an appropriate filename.

2. Creating a Worksheet that Compares Menu Prices
Go to http://www.metrodine.com and follow links to find restaurant menus that list entrees and prices, or go to http://www.pvo.com/pvo/search.html and search for "menu." Create a worksheet that lists the entrees and prices for at least two restaurants. Use the MIN and MAX functions to show the lowest and highest priced entree for each restaurant. Save the worksheets and workbook, using an appropriate filename.

PROJECT 2

Editing a Workbook

Moving a title to a different location, deleting last week's totals, copying this month's totals to the summary worksheet, adding comments to a cell, checking the spelling — an Excel user's work is never done! In this project, you will edit a workbook and modify the data using some basic editing tasks.

Objectives

After completing this project, you will be able to:

- ➤ Open a workbook
- ➤ Find data
- ➤ Edit data
- ➤ Work with data
- ➤ Add comments
- ➤ Check spelling

The Challenge

Mr. Gilmore was impressed at how quickly you created his "down-and-dirty" worksheet, but he wants a few changes made to it. Specifically, he wants you to add some comments and create a new worksheet that includes the January sales figures from both restaurants.

The Solution

To make the changes Mr. Gilmore wants, you will open the Restaurant Sales workbook, revise some of the data, move and copy some of the cells, add comments, and check the spelling. The finished workbook will look like Figure 2.1.

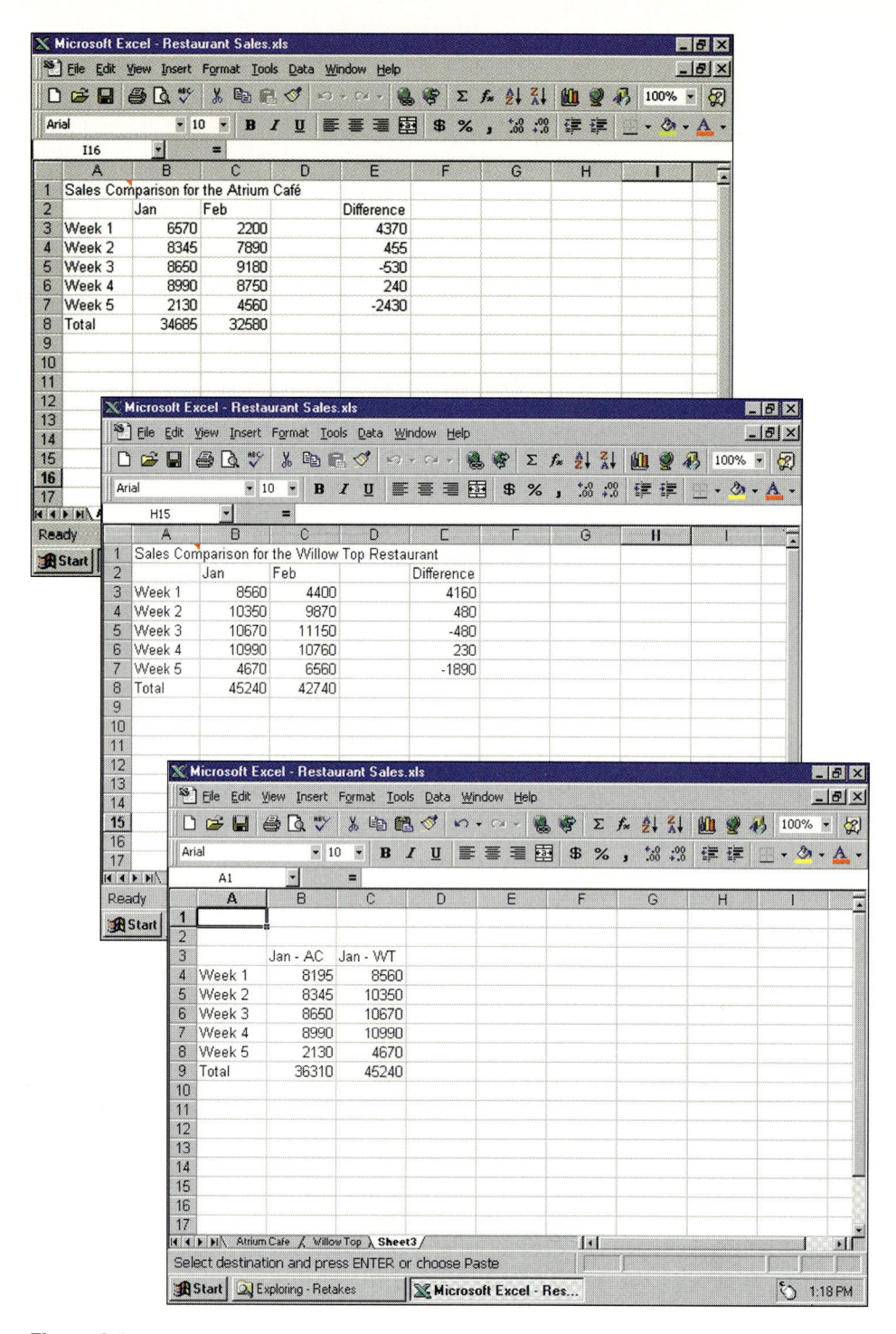

Figure 2.1

The Setup

So that your screen will match the illustrations in this chapter and to ensure that all the tasks in this project will function as described, you should set up Excel as described in Table 2.1. Because these are the default settings for the toolbars and view, you may not need to make any changes to your setup.

Table 2.1   Excel Settings

Location	Make these settings:
View, Toolbars	Deselect all toolbars except Standard and Formatting
View	Use Normal and display the Formula Bar and the Status Bar.

Opening a Workbook

When you want to view or revise a workbook that you have saved, you must open the workbook first. The worksheet and cell that were active when you last saved and closed the workbook are active when you open the workbook.

> **Tip** If the workbook is one that you have opened recently, you may see it listed at the bottom of the File menu. To open the file, simply select it from the menu.

TASK 1: TO OPEN A WORKBOOK:

1. Click the Open button.

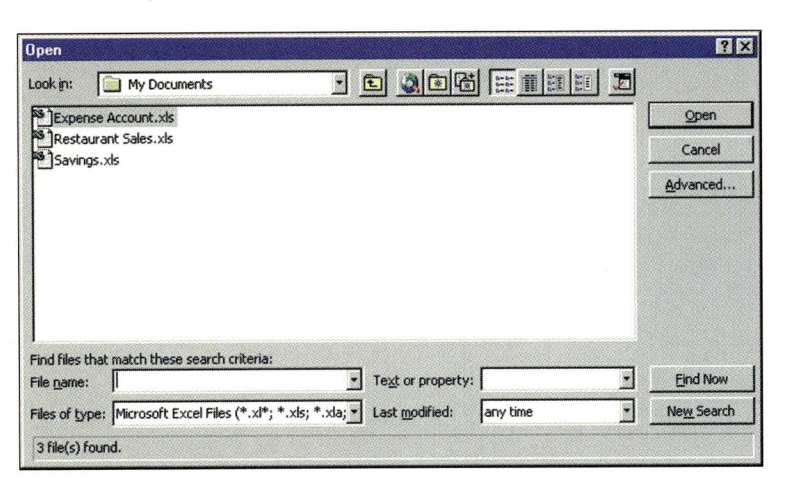

   Click on the arrow in the Look in text box to display the drop down list.

2. Select the correct path and folder.
   The folder name appears in the Look in text box.

3 Double-click *Restaurant Sales.xls*.

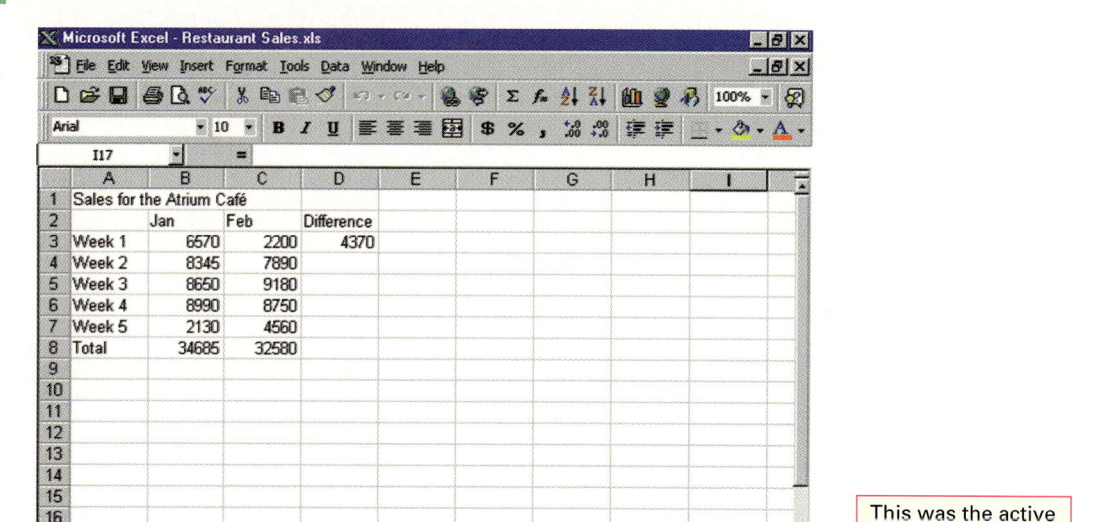

This was the active cell when the file was last saved

When you open a workbook, it opens to the location where you were when you last saved and closed it.

4 Click the Atrium Cafe tab if necessary.
The Atrium Cafe worksheet displays.

Finding Data

The Find command helps you find specific text or values in a worksheet. The command is very useful if the worksheet is large, but it also can be useful in small worksheets to find text and values that aren't shown on the screen. For example, you can use the Find command to find a word, number, or cell address that is in a formula.

Project 2: Editing a Workbook EX-51

TASK 2: TO FIND DATA:

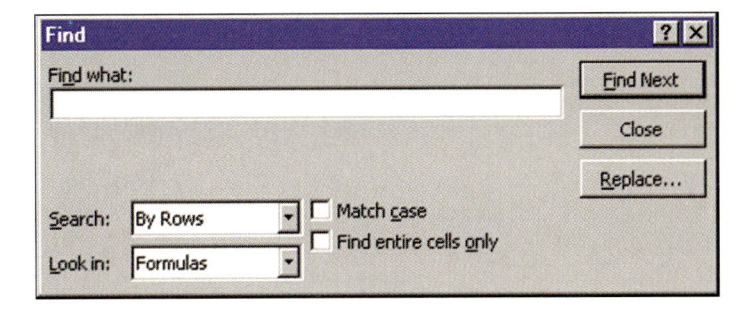

1 Choose Edit.

2 Choose Find.

3 Type **Sum** in the Find what text box and ensure that Formulas is selected in the Look in text box.

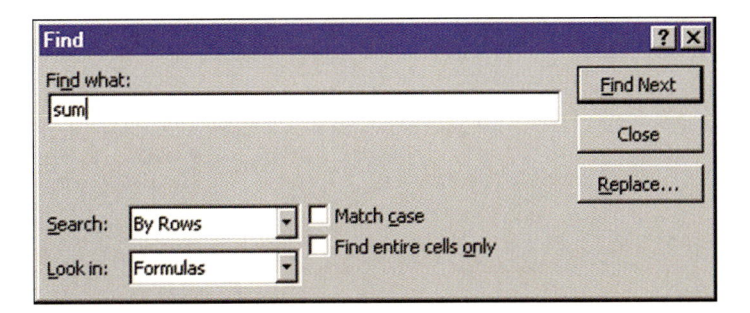

4 Click Find Next.
Cell B8 becomes the active cell.

5 Click Find Next.
Cell C8 becomes the active cell.

EX-52

6 Click Find Next.
Cell B8 becomes the active cell again even though the next worksheet has a SUM function.

> **Tip** The Find command searches only the current worksheet.

7 Click Close.
The Find dialog box closes.

Editing Data

If you want to change the data that is entered in a cell, just click in the cell and type the new data. If the data is lengthy, it is more efficient to edit the existing data unless the new data is completely different. If the cell that you edit is used in a formula or function, Excel 97 recalculates automatically to update the worksheet.

TASK 3: TO EDIT DATA IN A CELL:

1 Click in cell A1 in the Atrium Cafe worksheet.
Cell A1 becomes the active cell.

2 Click in the formula bar before the "f" in "for."

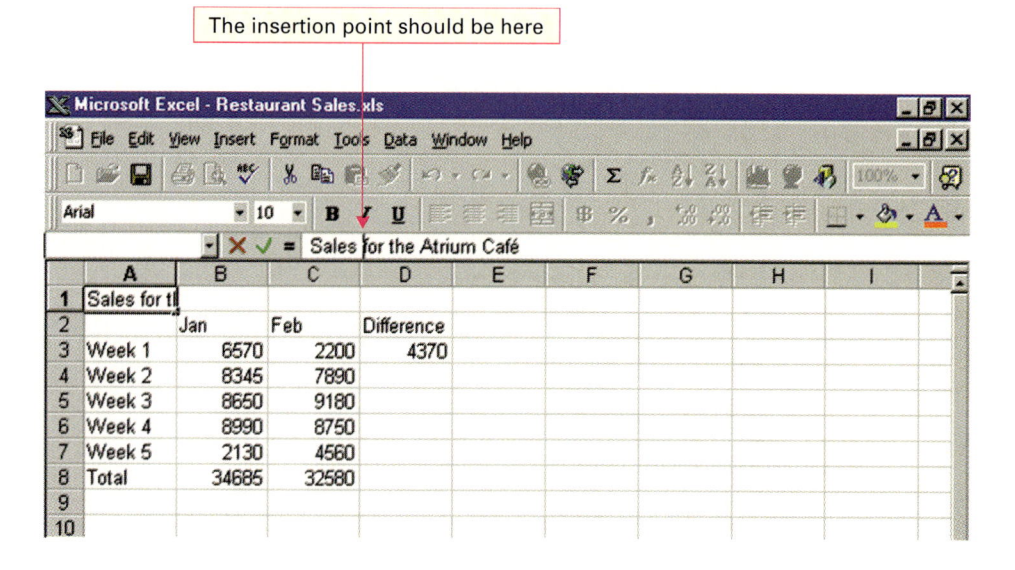

The insertion point should be here

Project 2: Editing a Workbook   EX-53

3 Type **Comparison** and then press (SPACE BAR).

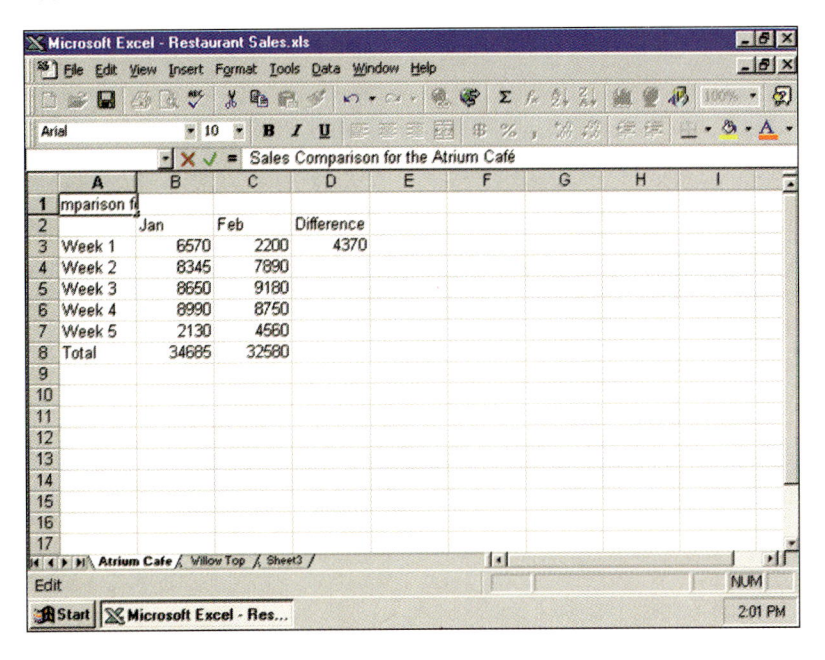

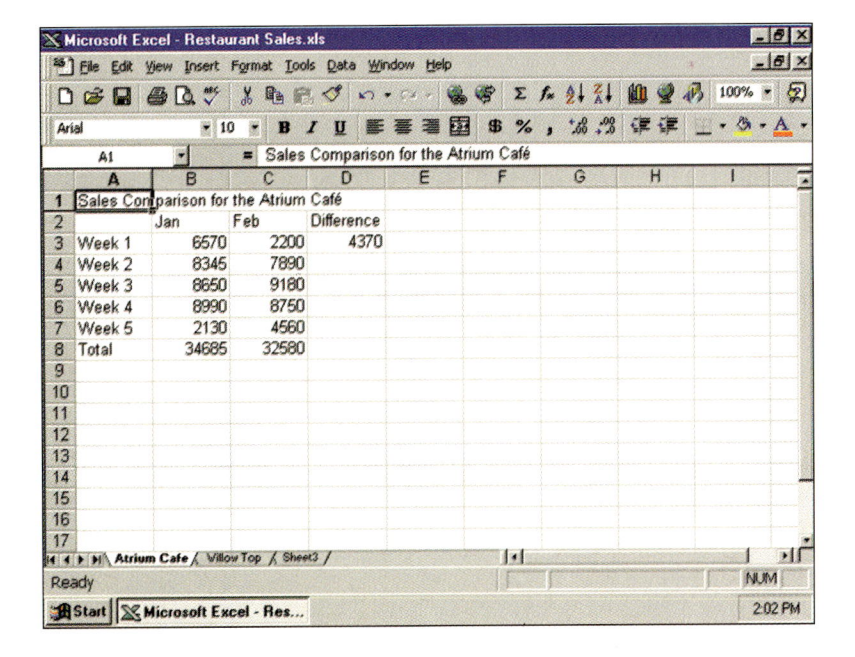

4 Press (ENTER).

5 Click the Willow Top tab.
The Willow Top worksheet displays.

6 Click in cell A1.
Cell A1 becomes the active cell.

EX-54

7 Click in the formula bar before the "f" in "for."

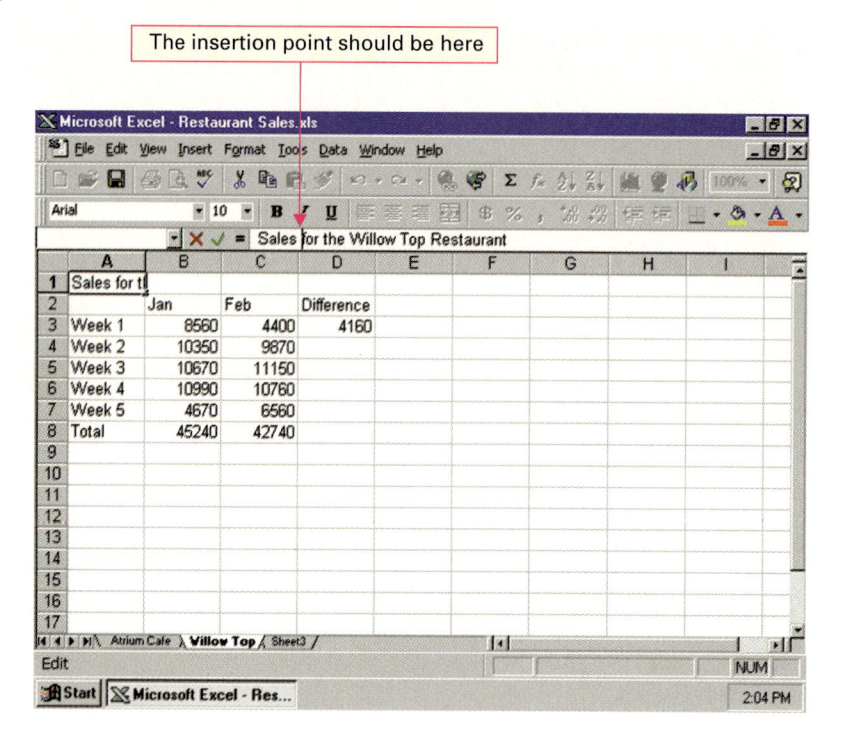

The insertion point should be here

8 Type **Comparison**, press SPACE BAR, and press ENTER.

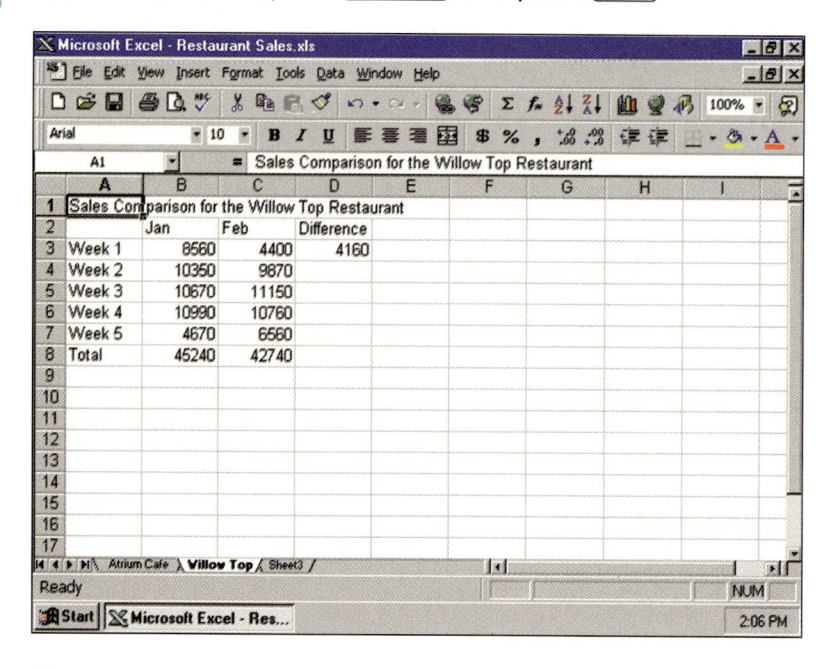

9 Click in cell B3.
Cell B3 becomes the active cell.

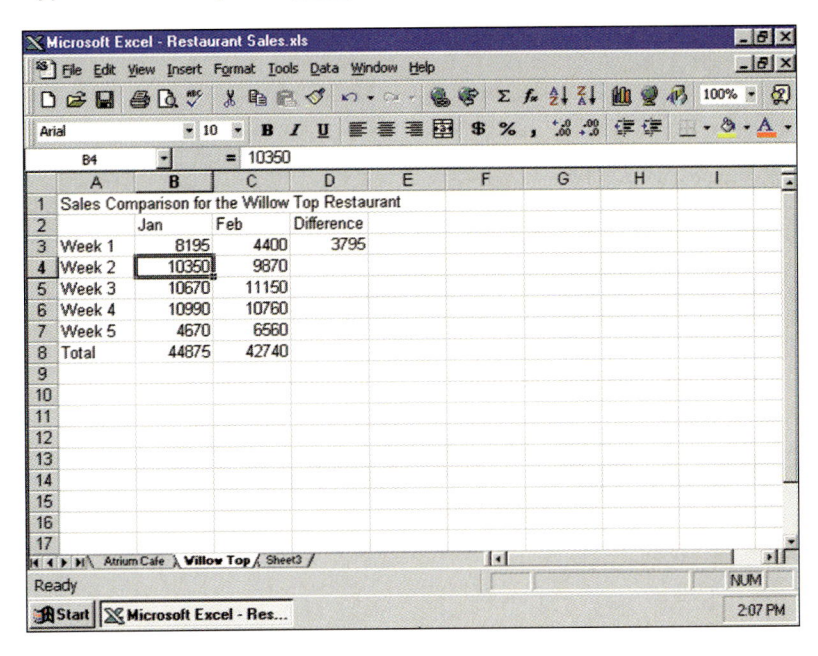

10 Type **8195** and press ENTER.

Working with Data

After you have entered data in a worksheet, you may find that you need to make some changes. You may have to copy, delete, or move the data. All of these types of revisions require selecting cells.

Selecting Cells

When you select cells, they are highlighted. In most cases, the easiest way to select cells is to drag the mouse pointer over the cells, but Table 2.2 describes other ways of selecting cells that are appropriate in many situations.

Table 2.2 Selection Methods

Selection	Method
Entire column	Click the column letter at the top of the column.
Entire row	Click the row number at the left of the row.
Entire worksheet	Click the blank button above the row numbers and to the left of the column letters.
Adjacent columns	Drag the pointer through the column letters.
Adjacent rows	Drag the pointer through the row numbers.
Non-adjacent ranges	Select the first range (the range can be an entire column or row) and then press CTRL while you select additional ranges.

EX-56

TASK 4: TO SELECT RANGES:

1 Click the column letter above column A.

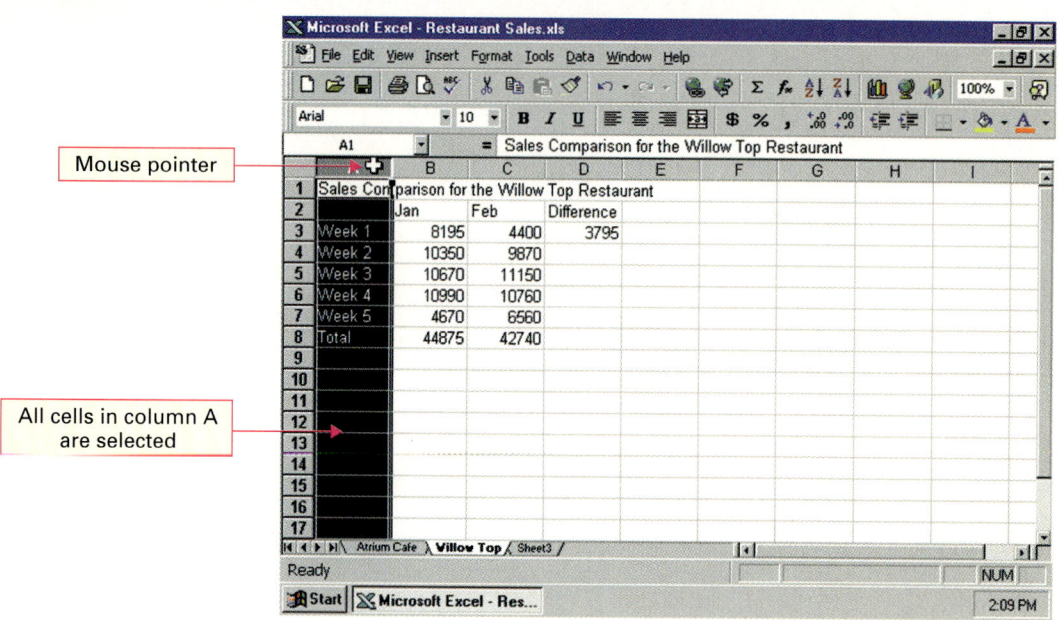

Mouse pointer

All cells in column A are selected

2 Drag the pointer through row numbers 3 and 4.

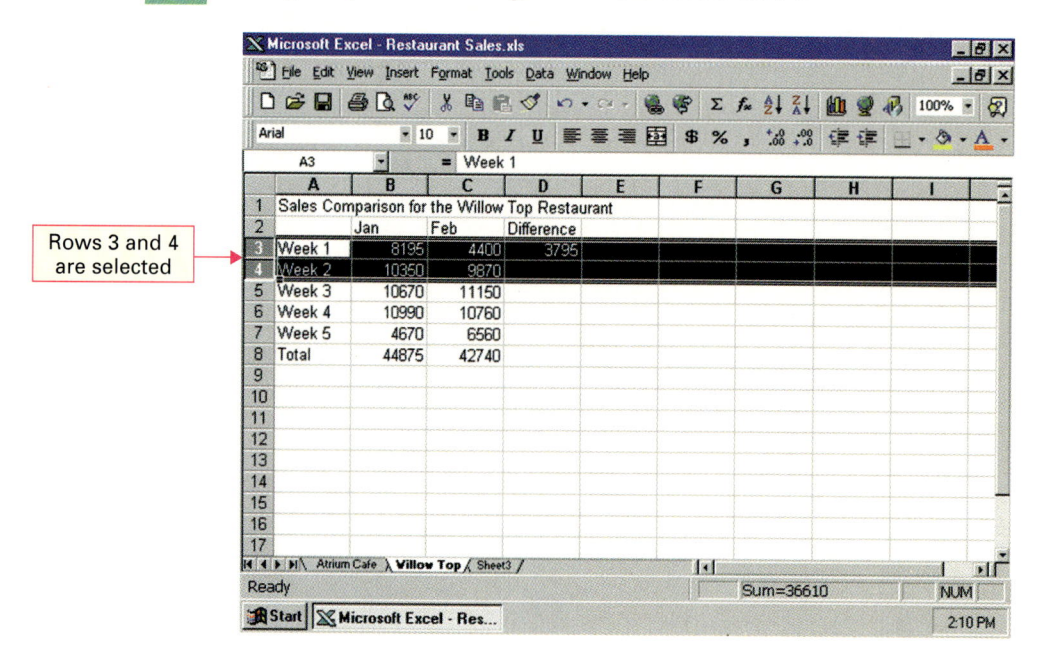

Rows 3 and 4 are selected

3 Select column C and then press CTRL while you select column F, row 8, and the range from cell H6 through cell I9.

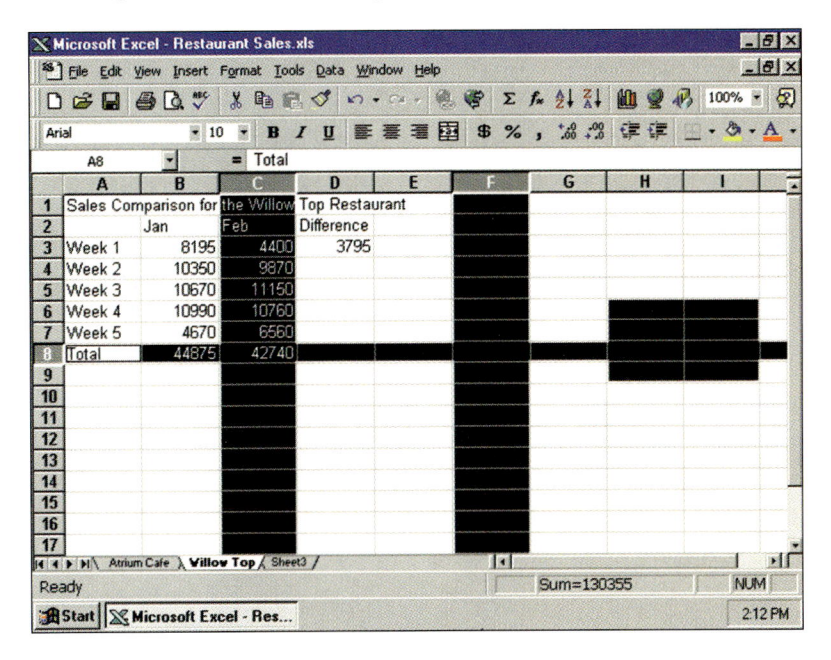

4 Select cell B3 through cell B7.

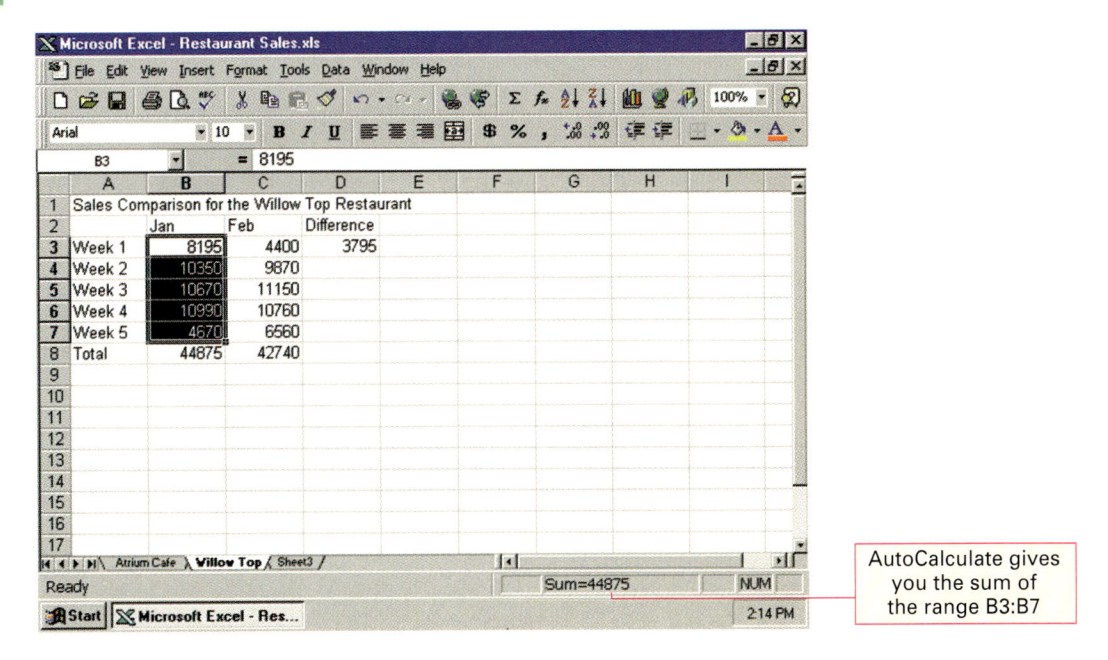

AutoCalculate gives you the sum of the range B3:B7

> **Tip** When you select a range with values, the *AutoCalculate* feature displays a calculation in the status bar. To change the type of calculation, right-click the calculation and choose a different one.

Copying Data

When you copy data, Excel 97 stores the data in a memory area called the *Clipboard*. Data in the Clipboard can be pasted in any cell, or range of cells in any worksheet or any workbook. If you copy or cut additional data, the new data replaces the existing data in the Clipboard. The Clipboard is erased when you exit Excel 97. Pasting data from the Clipboard does not remove data from the Clipboard; therefore, you can paste it repeatedly.

TASK 5: TO COPY DATA:

1. Press CTRL and click the Atrium Cafe tab.
   The Atrium Cafe worksheet and the Willow Top worksheet are both selected, and the Willow Top worksheet still displays.

2. Click in cell D3.
   Cell D3 becomes the active cell.

3. Click the Copy button.

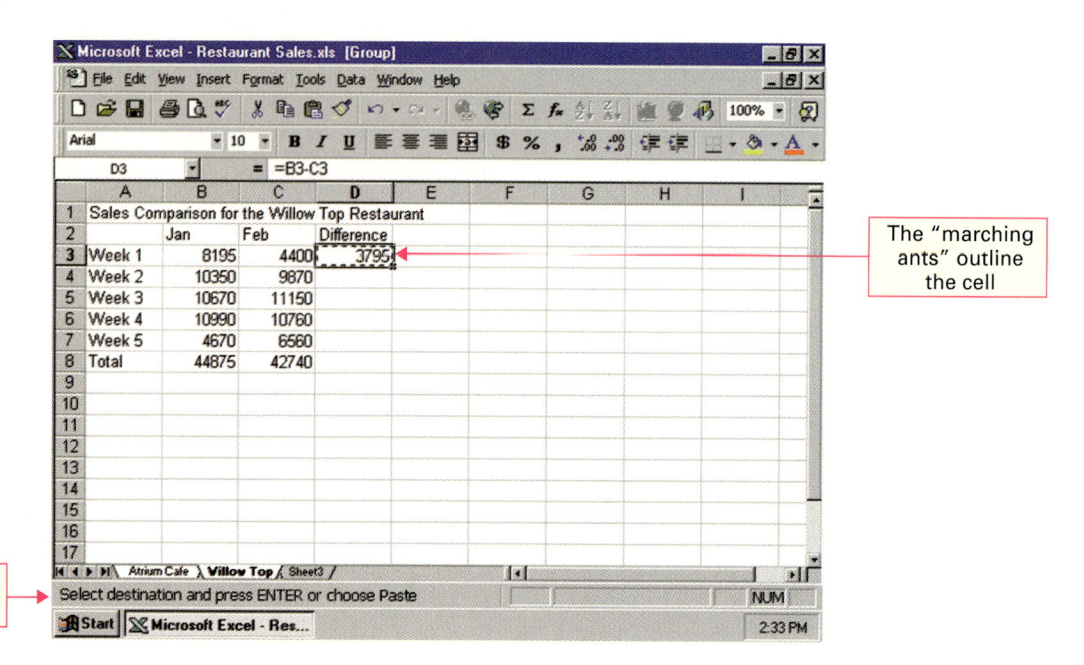

The "marching ants" outline the cell

The status bar tells you what to do next

Project 2: Editing a Workbook EX-59

4 Select the range from cell D4 through cell D7.

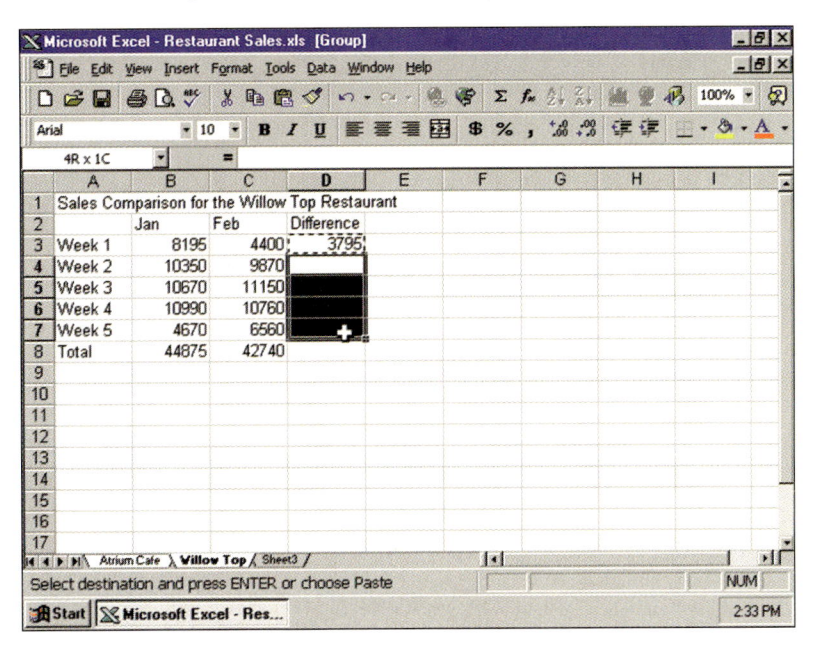

5 Click the Paste button.

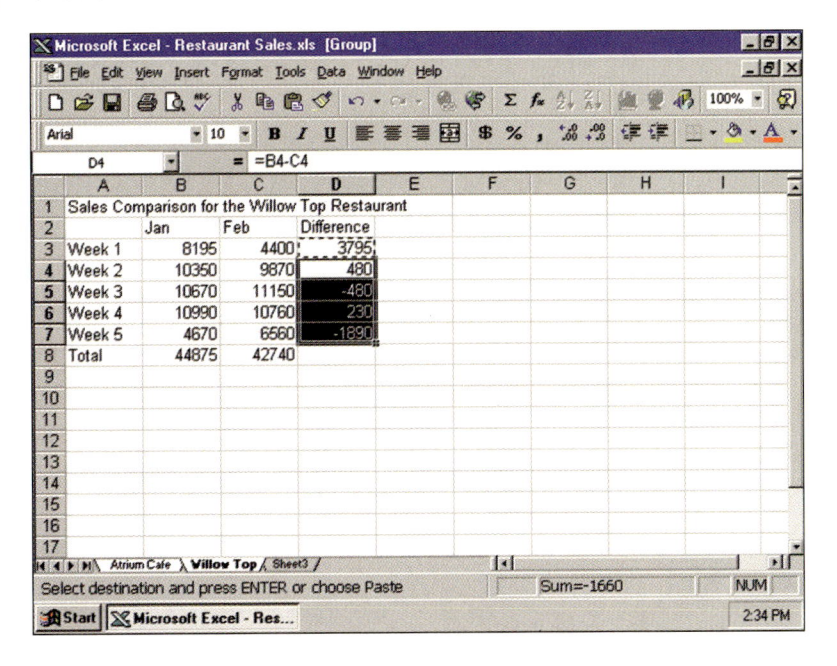

6 Click the Atrium Cafe tab.
The Copy command has been executed on this worksheet, too.

7 Press CTRL and click the Willow Top tab.
The Willow Top worksheet is deselected.

EX-60

8 Select the range from cell B2 through cell B8.

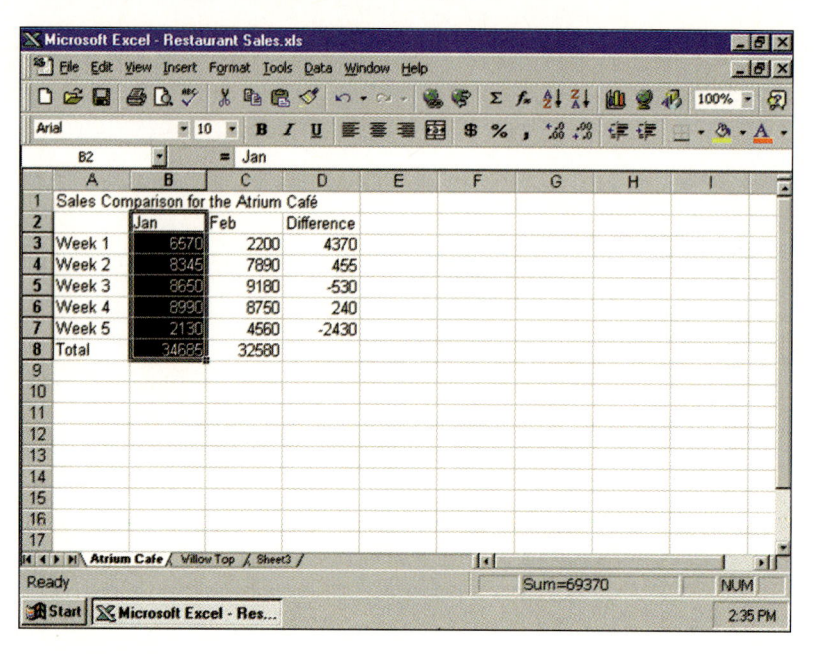

9 Click 📋.
The cells are copied to the Clipboard.

10 Click the Sheet3 tab.
The Sheet3 worksheet displays.

11 Click in cell A3.
Cell A3 becomes the active cell.

12 Click 📋.

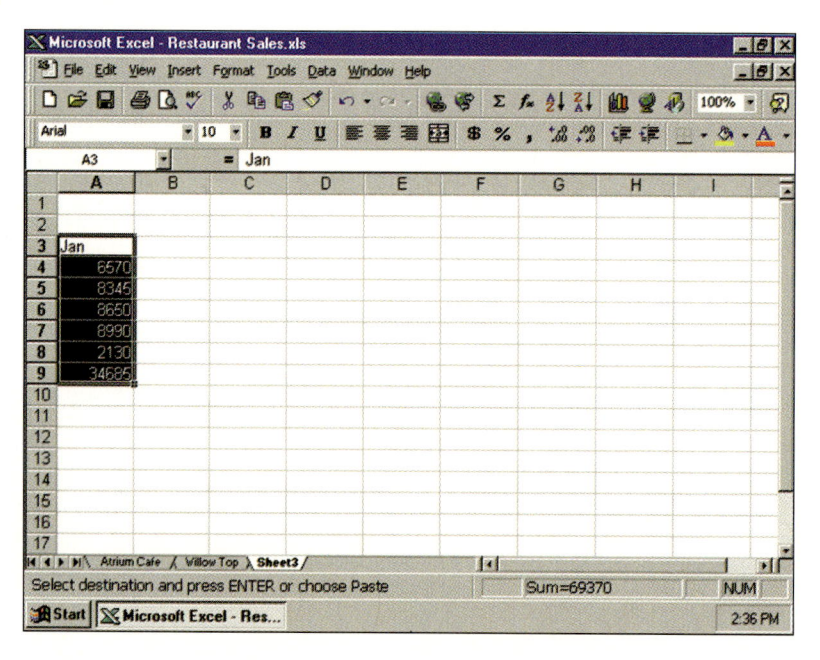

Project 2: Editing a Workbook EX-61

> **Caution** Pasting data into cells automatically replaces data already contained in the cells — without notice. Use the Undo feature to restore data, if necessary.

13 Copy and paste the same range from the Willow Top worksheet to cell B3 in Sheet3.

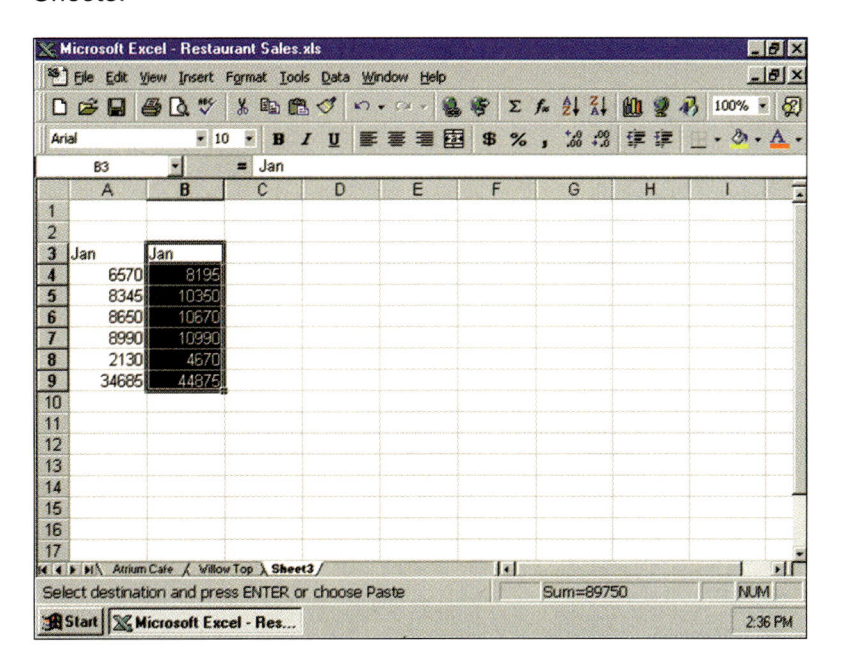

14 Rename Sheet3 to "January."
The name January appears on the tab.

Deleting Data

To erase the data in a cell or a range of cells, simply select the cells and press the Delete key. If you change your mind, click the Undo button.

> **Warning** Some users try to erase cells by passing the space bar. Although the cell looks blank, it really isn't; it contains the character for a space. You should never use this method to erase a cell; you could get arrested by the SSP (Special Spreadsheet Police).

> **Note** The Edit, Clear command accomplishes the same as pressing the Delete key.

EX-62

TASK 6: TO DELETE DATA:

1 Select cell A8 through cell B8 on the January worksheet.

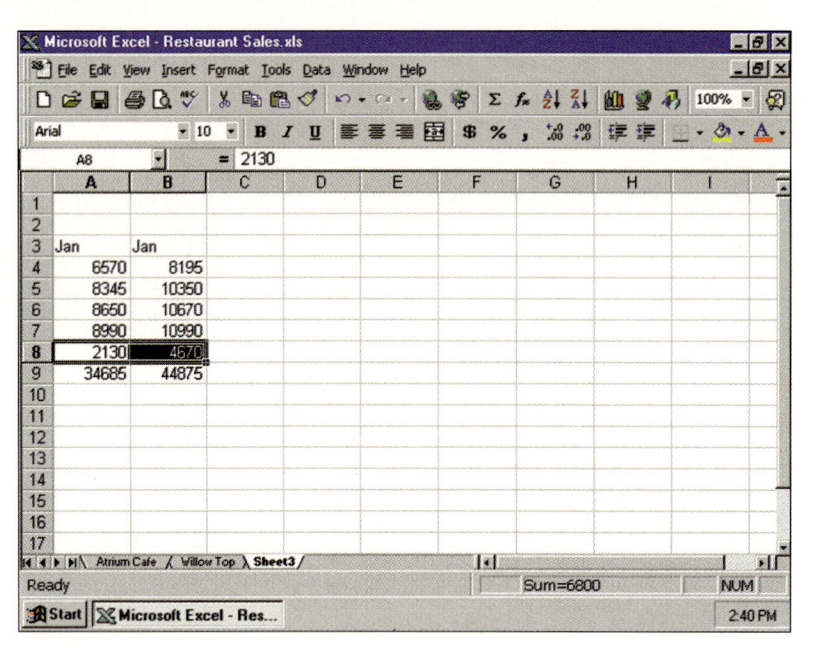

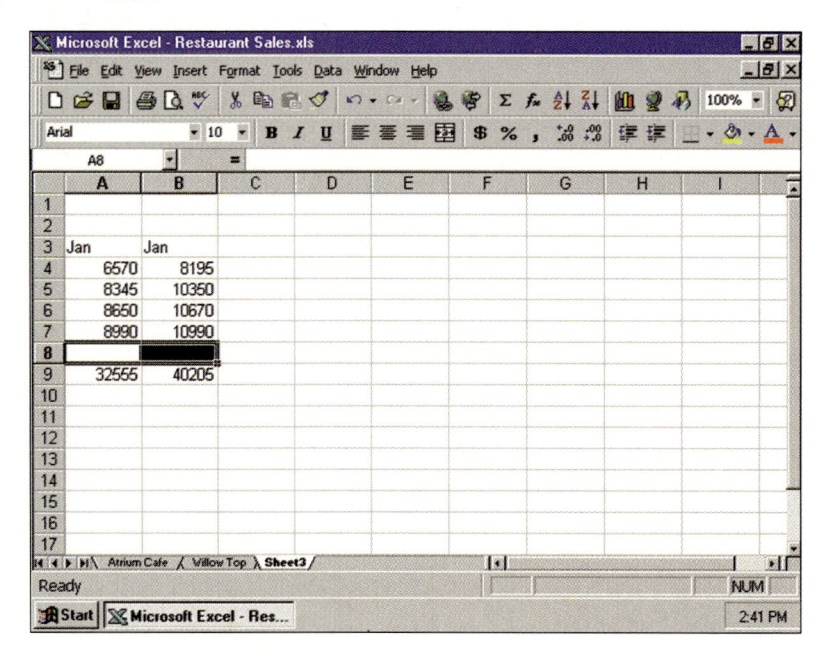

2 Press DEL.

3 Click the Undo button.
The data appears again.

Tip When you delete text with the Delete key, the text isn't stored in the Clipboard and therefore it can't be pasted in another location. You can press Shift+Delete or choose Edit, Delete if you want deleted text placed in the Clipboard.

Moving Data

You can move data to a different location in the same worksheet or to a location in a different worksheet.

TASK 7: TO MOVE DATA:

1. Click on the Atrium Cafe tab.
   The Atrium Cafe worksheet displays.

2. Select cell D2 through cell D7.

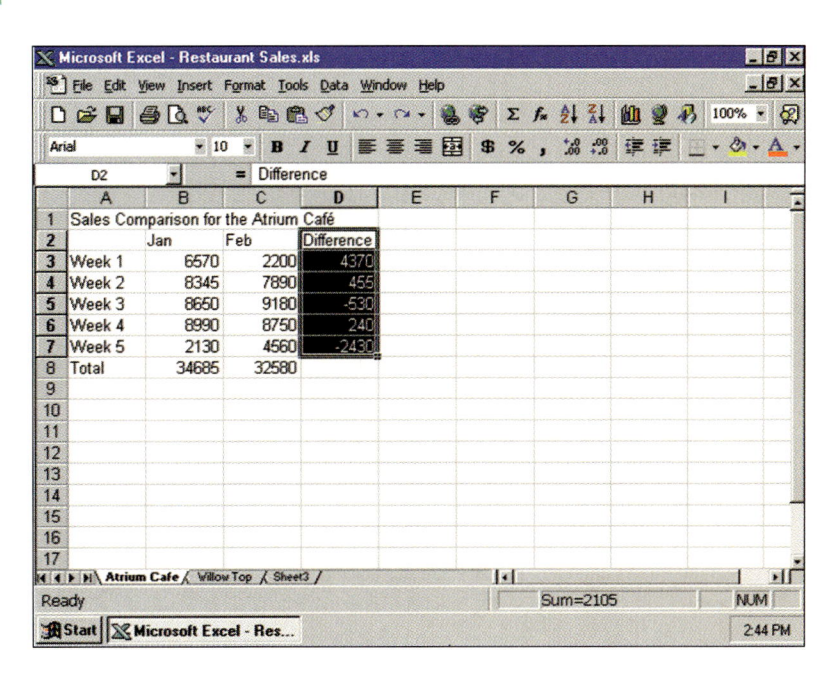

EX-64

3 Click the Cut button.

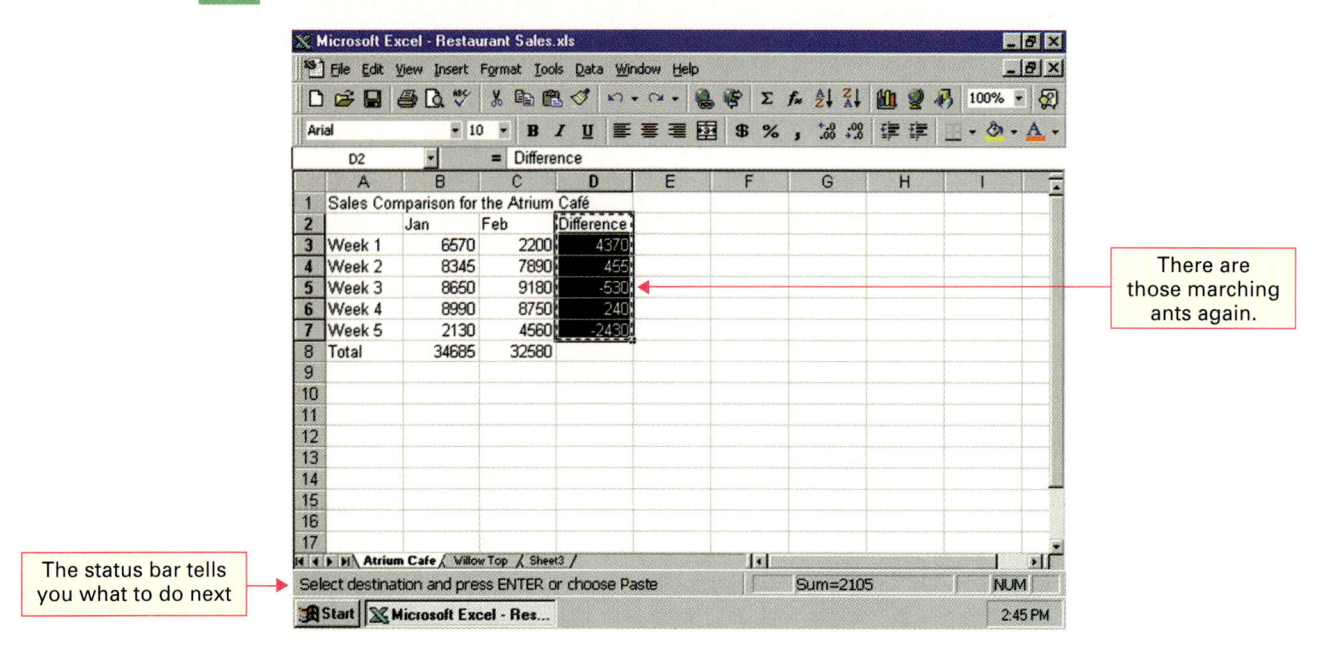

There are those marching ants again.

The status bar tells you what to do next

4 Click in cell E2.
Cell E2 becomes the active cell.

5 Click.

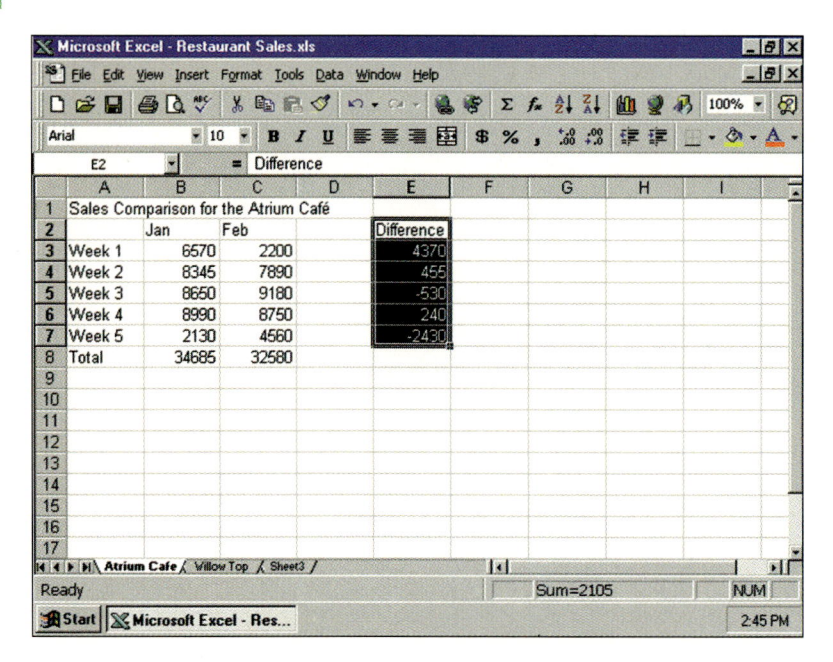

Warning Pasting anything that has been cut (or copied) to a new location that contains data overwrites the data.

Project 2: Editing a Workbook   EX-65

6   Display the Willow Top worksheet and move the range D2 through D7 to cell E2.

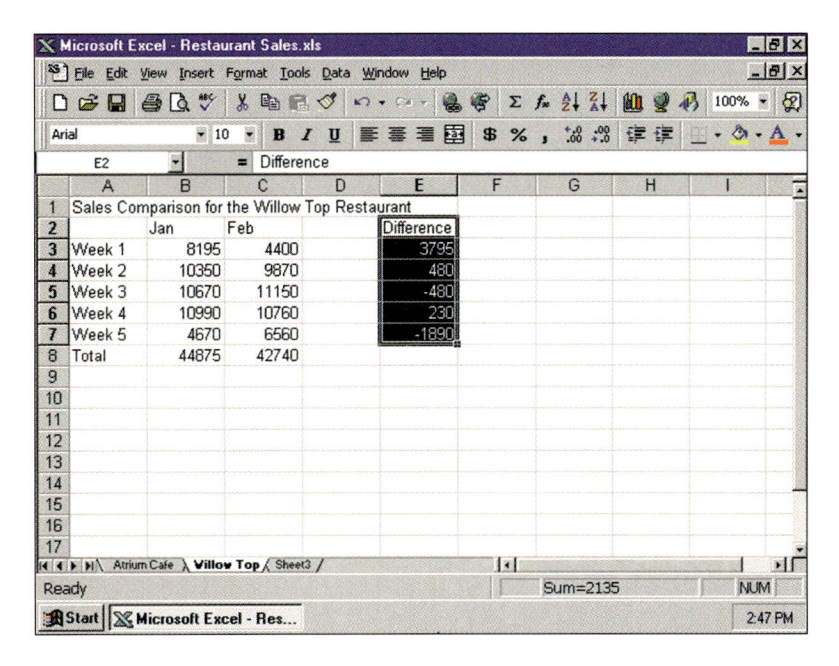

Adding Comments

You can attach **comments** to cells in a worksheet to provide additional information. The comment will contain the user name that is specified on the User Information page of the Options dialog box. The text in a comment displays on the screen and it can be made to print as well.

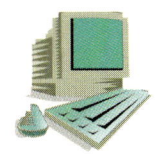

TASK 8: TO ADD COMMENTS:

1   Click in cell A1 on the Willow Top worksheet.
Cell A1 becomes the active cell.

2   Choose Insert.

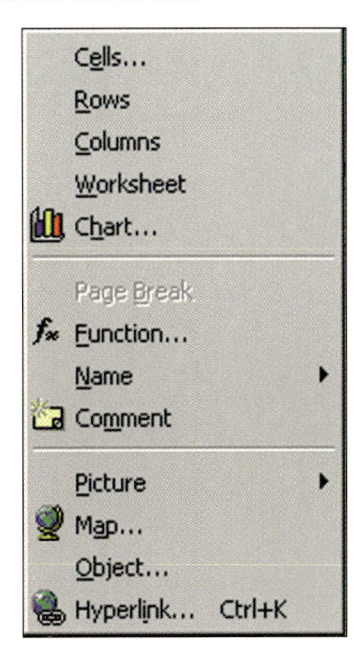

3 Choose Comment.

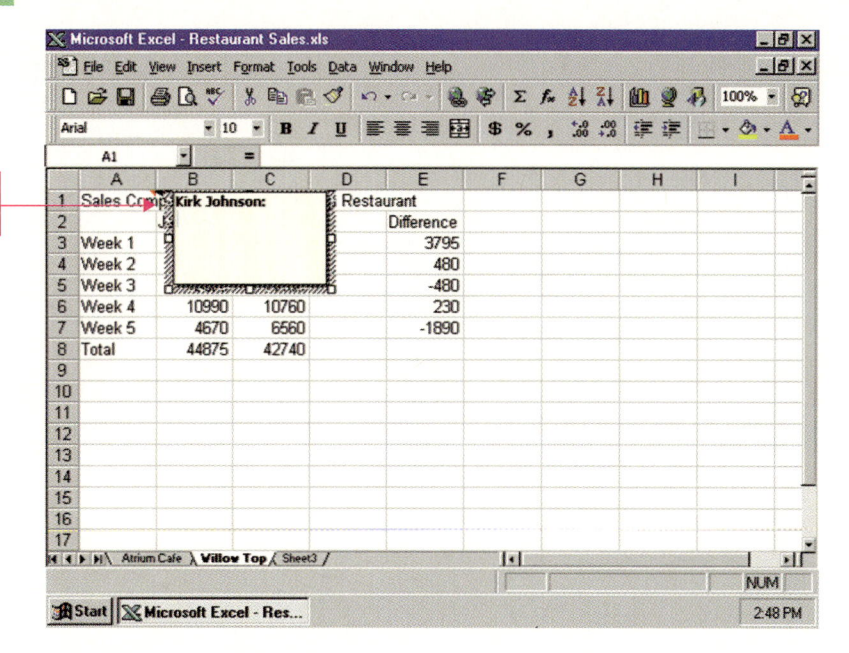

The user name precedes the comment

4 Type **Open for dinner only.**

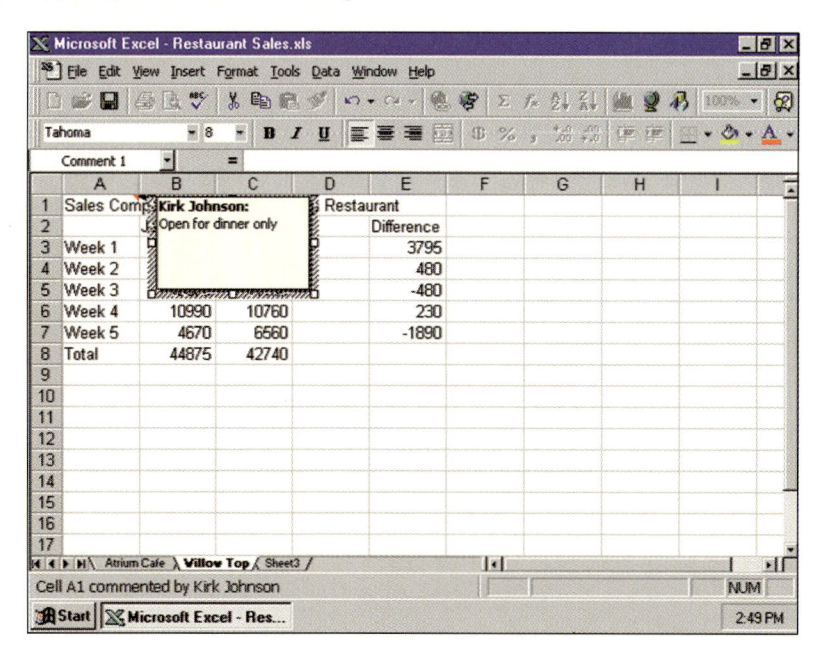

Project 2: Editing a Workbook   EX-67

5 Click anywhere outside the comment box.

The red mark denotes a comment

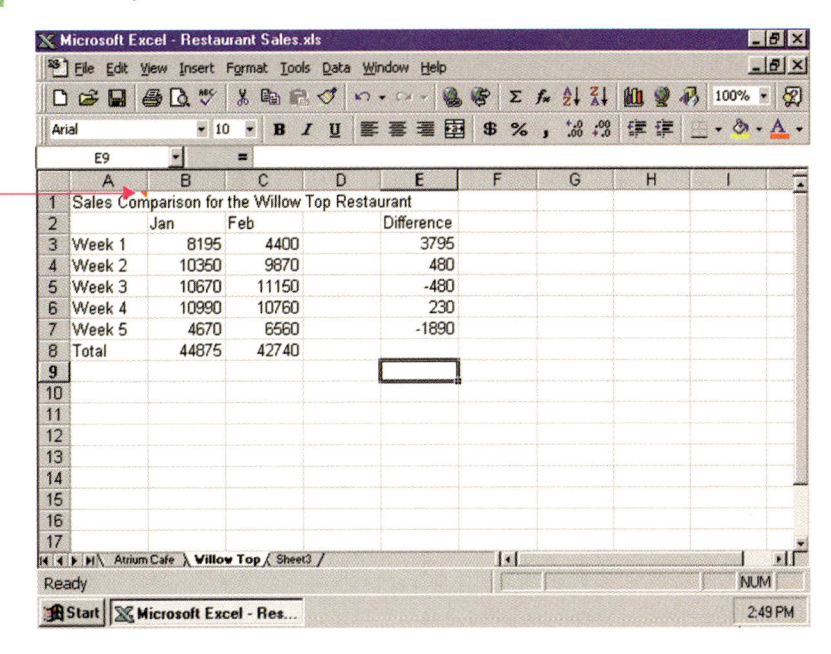

6 Click the Atrium Cafe tab.
The Atrium Cafe worksheet displays.

7 Click in cell A1.
Cell A1 becomes the active cell.

8 Choose Insert, Comment, and type **Open for breakfest, lunch, and dinner.**
Do not correct the spelling of "breakfast."

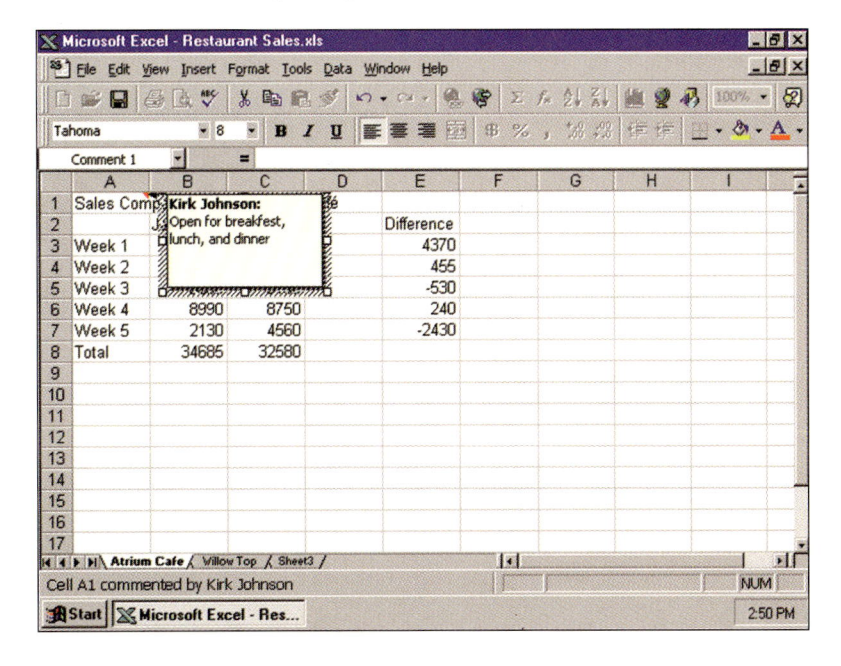

9 Click anywhere outside the comment box.
A red mark appears in cell A1.

EX-68

If you want to see the comments on a worksheet, you can point to the cell that has a red mark and the comment box will pop up, or you can turn on the Comment view and all the comments will be visible.

TASK 9: TO TURN ON THE COMMENT VIEW AND TURN IT OFF AGAIN:

1 Choose View.

2 Choose Comments.

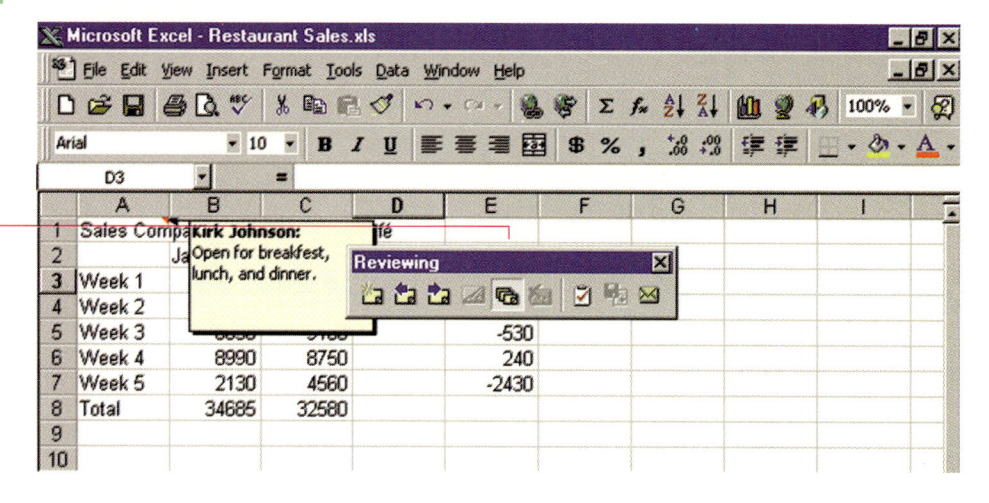

The Reviewing toolbar displays when you turn on the Comments view

3 Click the Willow Top tab.

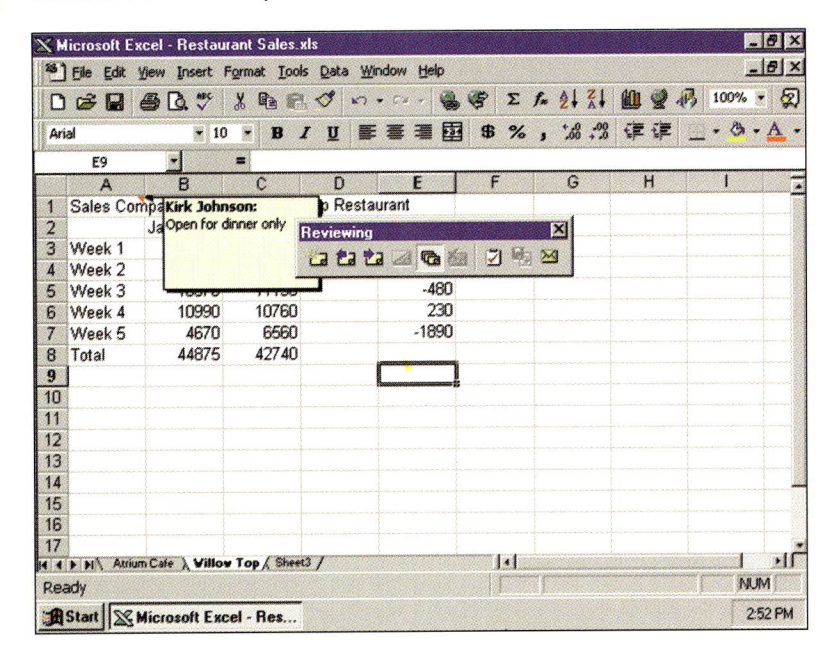

4 Click ⊠ on the Reviewing toolbar.
The toolbar closes.

5 Choose View, Comments.
The comments are hidden.

> **Tip** Use the Find command to find text or values in comments.

Checking Spelling

When you have made all the revisions in a worksheet, it is a good idea to check the spelling, especially since Excel 97 doesn't underline spelling errors as you make them (as Word 97 does).

> **Note** Even though Excel 97 doesn't check your spelling as you go, it does make automatic corrections for many typing errors.

TASK 10: TO CHECK THE SPELLING:

1 Click the Atrium Cafe tab.
The Atrium Cafe worksheet displays.

Project 2: Editing a Workbook EX-69

2 Click in cell A1.
Excel 97 will begin its check of the spelling with cell A1.

3 Click the Spelling button.

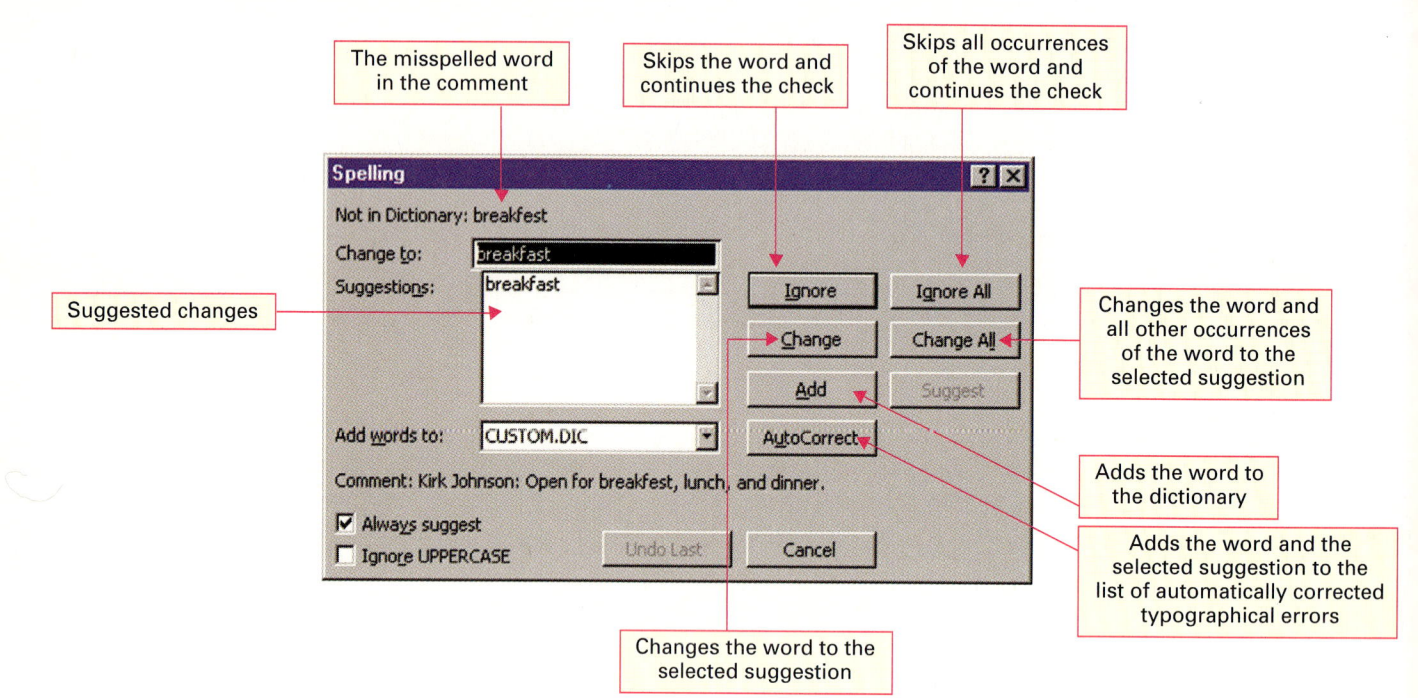

The misspelled word in the comment

Skips the word and continues the check

Skips all occurrences of the word and continues the check

Suggested changes

Changes the word and all other occurrences of the word to the selected suggestion

Adds the word to the dictionary

Adds the word and the selected suggestion to the list of automatically corrected typographical errors

Changes the word to the selected suggestion

Spelling
Not in Dictionary: breakfest
Change to: breakfast
Suggestions: breakfast
Add words to: CUSTOM.DIC
Comment: Kirk Johnson: Open for breakfest, lunch, and dinner.
☑ Always suggest
☐ Ignore UPPERCASE

Buttons: Ignore, Ignore All, Change, Change All, Add, Suggest, AutoCorrect, Undo Last, Cancel

4 Choose Change.
If there is another word not found in the dictionary, Excel 97 lists it, but if there are no more words, a message displays telling you that the spell check is complete.

5 Click OK.
The worksheet redisplays.

> **Note** If you have used multiple worksheets, you must spell check each sheet individually. Sorry!

Conclusion

If you have time, you may want to spell check the other worksheets. Then save the file and close it.

Summary and Exercises

Summary

- The Find command finds specific text or values in a worksheet.
- You can edit the data in a cell or simply reenter the data.
- Excel 97 automatically recalculates formulas if the numbers in the cells change.
- When you copy data it is stored in the Clipboard.
- Comments provide additional information in a workbook.
- You can check the spelling of worksheets in a workbook.

Key Terms and Operations

Key Terms
AutoCalculate
Clipboard
comment

Operations
add comments
copy data
delete data
edit data
find data
move data
open a workbook
paste data
select cells
spell check a worksheet

Study Questions

Multiple Choice

1. A workbook's name may appear at the bottom of the File menu,
   a. if it is in the current path.
   b. if the workbook has multiple worksheets.
   c. unless it is on a floppy disk.
   d. if it has been opened recently.

2. To edit a cell, first
   a. select the cell.
   b. click in the formula bar.
   c. activate the edit mode.
   d. press F4.

3. The easiest way to select the entire worksheet is to
   a. triple-click in any cell.
   b. click the button above the row numbers and to the left of the column letters.
   c. drag the pointer through all the cells in the worksheet.
   d. select all the rows in the worksheet.

4. The Find command can find
   a. only text.
   b. only numbers.
   c. only cell addresses.
   d. text in comments.

5. The Spell Checker will
   a. not check all worksheets at once.
   b. not check comments.
   c. only start in the first cell of a worksheet.
   d. not add words to the dictionary.

6. When you press Delete, the
   a. contents of the selected cells are erased.
   b. selected cells are removed from the worksheet.
   c. contents of the selected cells are stored in the Clipboard.
   d. same result is achieved as when you choose Edit, Delete.

7. The Find command
   a. searches only the current worksheet.
   b. searches all worksheets in the workbook.
   c. searches only formulas.
   d. is useful only in large worksheets.

8. Which of the following do not require pressing the CTRL key?
   a. non-adjacent columns
   b. non-adjacent rows
   c. adjacent columns
   d. a range of cells

9. To move data, use the
   a. Cut and Paste buttons.
   b. Copy and Paste buttons.
   c. Move and Paste buttons.
   d. Cut and Insert buttons.

10. A comment
    a. is attached to the worksheet.
    b. is attached to a cell.
    c. is only visible when you point to the cell.
    d. displays when you click a cell.

Short Answer

1. When you open a workbook, what is the location of the active cell?

2. How do you use the AutoCalculate feature?

3. What happens if you copy data to a range that already contains data?

4. What toolbar displays when you turn on the Comments view?

5. How would you select both Column C and the range A1 through A10?

6. How do you move data?

7. What happens to the data in the Clipboard when you copy new data?

8. What happens to the data in the Clipboard when you exit Excel 97?

9. How do you select several consecutive rows?

10. How do you insert a comment?

For Discussion

1. What do you do if you need to find all the formulas that reference cell B3?

2. Discuss the two methods of changing data in a cell and when you use each method.

3. Describe several scenarios in which comments are useful.

4. Describe several scenarios in which the AutoCalculate feature could be used.

Review Exercises

1. Revising the Restaurant Sales Worksheet

In this exercise, you will revise the Restaurant Sales worksheet, revising data and adding a comment.

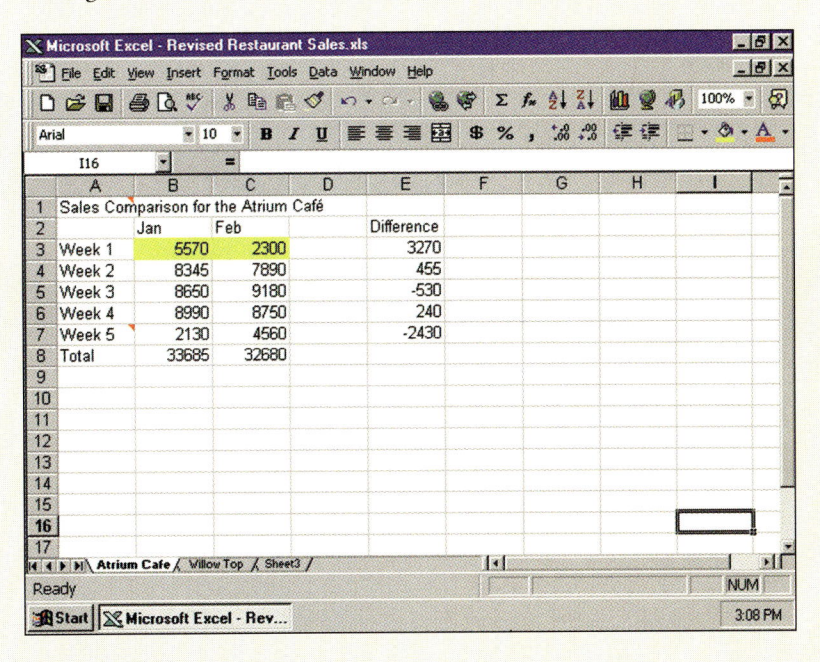

Figure 2.2

1. Open the workbook named *Restaurant Sales.xls*, unless it is already open.

2. Make the revisions (highlighted in yellow) shown in Figure 2.2.

3. Add a comment to cell A7 in the Atrium Cafe worksheet that says "This week had 4 days in January and 3 days in February."

4. Make sure the numbers on the January worksheet match the numbers on the Atrium Cafe and Willow Top worksheets.

5. Save the file as *Revised Restaurant Sales.xls* and close it.

2. Revising a Time Sheet
In this exercise, you will revise a time sheet workbook.

1. Ask your instructor how to obtain the file *Tmsheet.xls*. (If you have Internet access, you can download this file from the Addison Wesley Longman website at www.awl.com/is/select/).

2. Open the file and find the word "sum" in a formula in the Smith worksheet. Copy the formula to the next six cells on the right.

3. Delete the text in row 4.

4. Move the data in cell B1 to cell D1.

5. Copy A1:H9 to the Jones worksheet.

6. Save the file as *Times.xls* and close it.

Assignments

1. Creating and Revising a Budget
Create a worksheet that lists expenses for your personal budget. List expense items in column A starting in row 4. List the projected amounts for the next three months in columns B through D. Total each month at the bottom of the column. Save the worksheet as *My Budget.xls*. Revise the amounts so they are more conservative. Move the totals to row 3. Add comments for expenses that need further explanation. Save the revised worksheet as *Lower Budget.xls*.

2. Tracking the American Stock Exchange (Optional Exercise)
Go to the web site http://www.amex.com and click on the link Market Summary. Create a worksheet to contain the five columns of information shown in the summary. Save the worksheet as *Amex.xls*. Check the summary on several different days and add the information to the worksheet.

PROJECT 3

Enhancing the Appearance of a Workbook

Now that you can create and edit a worksheet, it's time for you to add a little pizzazz to the worksheet with various formatting techniques. In this project you will use borders and colors to give the worksheet a classy look.

Objectives

After completing this project, you will be able to:

- ➤ **Format text**
- ➤ **Change cell alignment**
- ➤ **Format numbers**
- ➤ **Format dates**
- ➤ **Format numbers as text**
- ➤ **Add borders and fill**
- ➤ **View and change a page break**
- ➤ **Use AutoFormat**

EX-76

The Challenge

Mr. Williams, the manager of the golf and tennis property at The Willows, has created a worksheet named *Income.xls* that estimates the income for the upcoming Pro-Celebrity Tournament. He has entered all the data and formulas, but he wants you to format the worksheet so it looks better and is easier to read.

The Solution

You will open the workbook, format the numbers and dates, add a border to the important information and emphasize the totals with shading. Additionally, you will format and align the data in some of the cells and use AutoFormat to format a group of cells automatically. The formatted worksheet will look like Figure 3.1 when you are finished. (The Full Screen view is used in Figure 3.1.)

Before you can begin you must download *Income.xls* from the Addison Wesley Longman web site. The file is stored at this address: www.awl.com/is/select/. If you are unable to download, obtain the file from your instructor.

Figure 3.1

The Setup

So that your screen will match the illustrations in this chapter and to ensure that all the tasks in this project will function as described, you should set up Excel as described in Table 3.1. Because these are the default settings for the toolbars and view, you may not need to make any changes to your setup.

Project 3: Enhancing the Appearance of a Workbook   EX-77

Table 3.1 Excel Settings

Location	Make these settings:
View, Toolbars	Deselect all toolbars except Standard and Formatting.
View	Use the Normal view and display the Formula Bar and Status Bar.

Formatting Text

You can format text in a number of ways. You can make it bold, italic, or underlined, or change the font, the font size, and the font color. The Formatting toolbar includes buttons for many of the text formatting options. Before you begin formatting the worksheet, you will save it as *Income2.xls* so you can use the original again later.

TASK 1: TO FORMAT TEXT:

1. Open *Income.xls* and choose File, Select the drive or folder, type *Income2.xls* in the filename text box and click Save.

2. Select cells D3, B4, and F4.

   Click the first cell to select it and then press Ctrl when you click the other cells

3. Click the Bold **B** button.
   The text in all three cells changes to bold.

4. Select cell D3. Click the drop-down arrow for Font Size and choose 12.
   The text in the cell changes from 10 point to 12 point.

EX-78

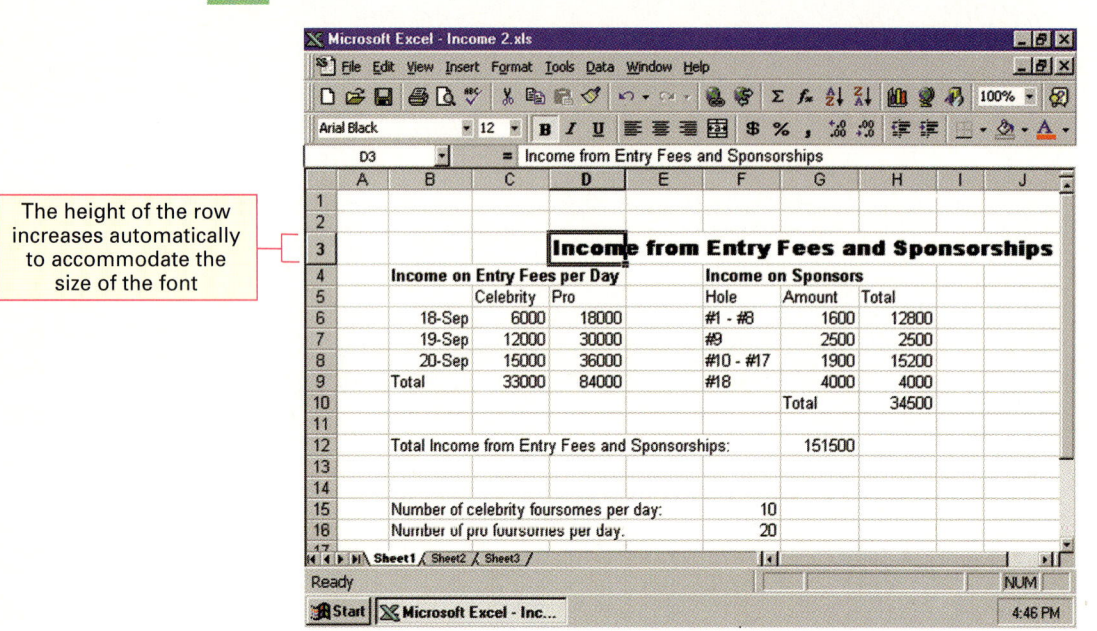

5 Click the drop-down arrow bar Font and choose Arial Black.

The height of the row increases automatically to accommodate the size of the font

Changing Cell Alignment

Data in a cell can be aligned on the left, in the center, or on the right. Each type of data that you enter uses a default alignment — text is left aligned and numbers and dates are right aligned.

You can change the alignment of data in a selected cell by clicking on one of the alignment buttons in the Formatting toolbar. Sometimes you may want to align data across several cells; for example, you might want to center a title in the first row so that the title spans the columns used in the worksheet. In this case, you can merge the cells into one wide cell, and then center the data in the wide cell.

TASK 2: TO CHANGE THE CELL ALIGNMENT:

1 Select A3:I3.
The cells are highlighted.

Project 3: Enhancing the Appearance of a Workbook   EX-79

2   Choose Format.

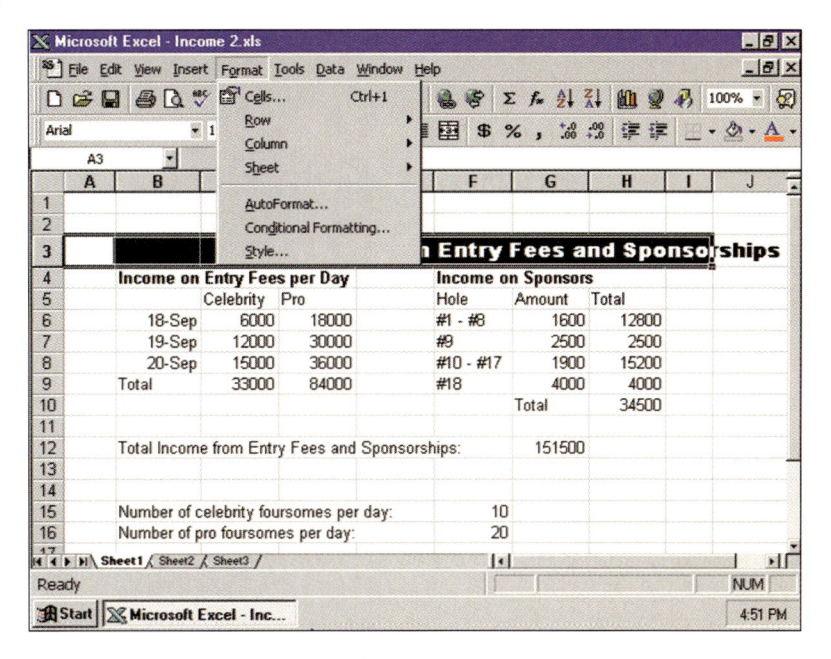

3   Choose Cells.

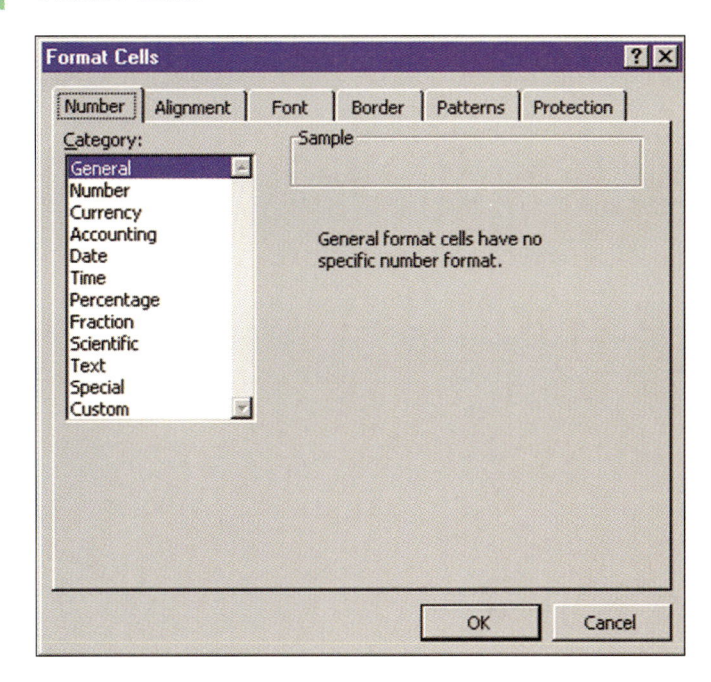

4 Click the Alignment tab.

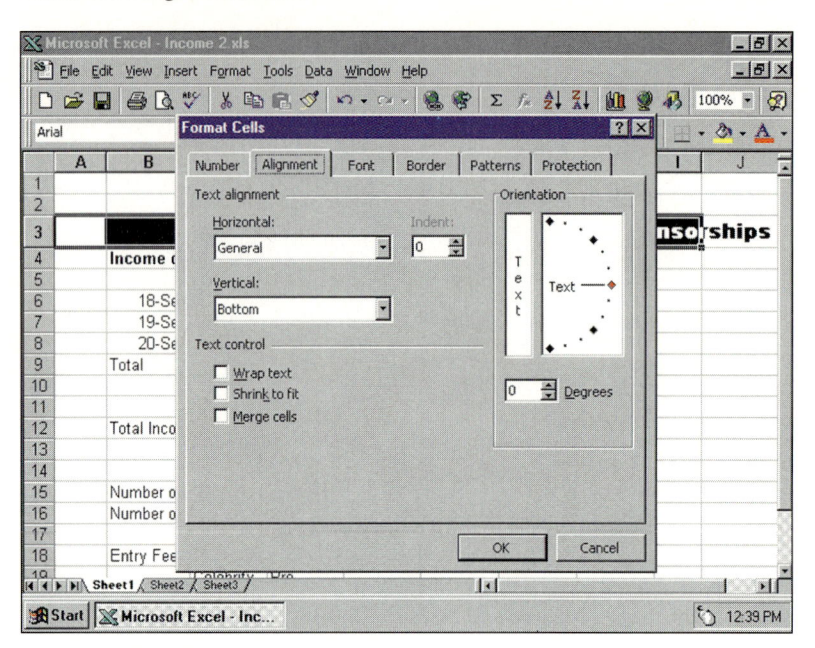

5 Choose Merge cells and click OK.
The cells become one cell.

6 Click the Center button.

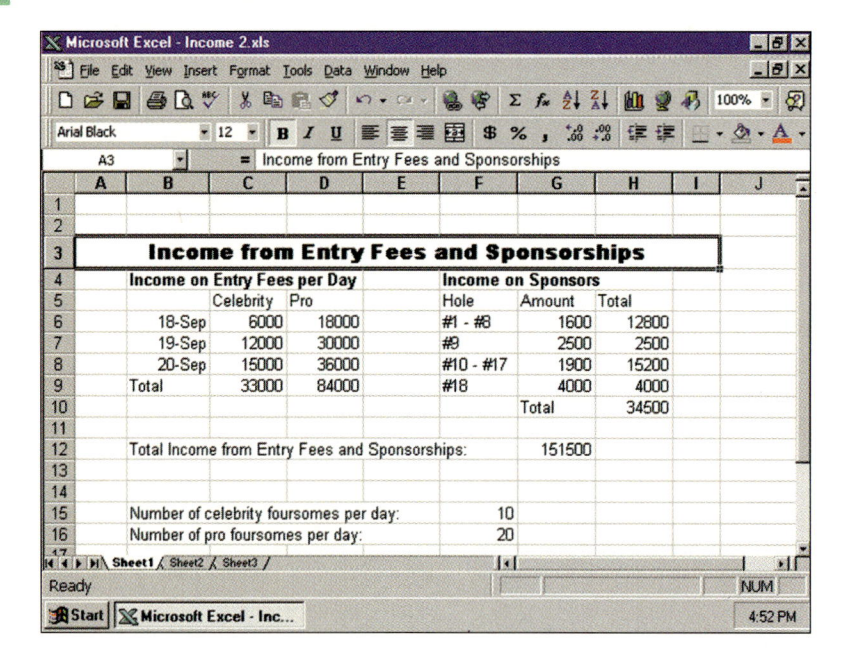

> **Tip** To merge and center at the same time, select the cells and click the Merge and Center button.

7 Merge and align the remaining cells:
Merge the cells B4:D4 into one cell and center the text in the cell. Merge the cells F4:H4 into one cell and center the text in the cell. Center the text in cell F5. Select cells C5, D5, G5, and H5 and click the Align Right button.

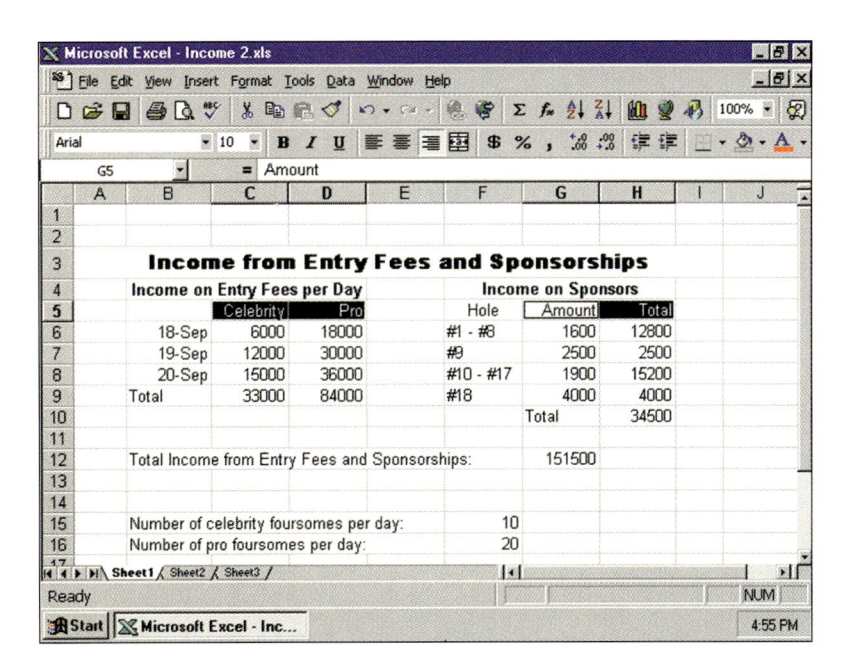

Formatting Numbers

The numbers you enter in a workbook can be "dressed up" with several different formats. As with text, you can make numbers bold, italic, change the font size, and font color. But there are other formatting options available for numbers. Table 3.2 describes the formats that are available in Excel and Figure 3.2 shows some examples.

Table 3.2 Number Formats

Format	Description
General	Numbers appear as entered except for fractions in the form of 1/2 which must be entered as **0 1/2**. Commas and decimal points can be entered with the numbers. If commas are not entered, they will not display automatically as in other formats. You can enter a minus or parentheses for negative numbers.
Number	Numbers have a fixed number of decimal places, comma separators can be displayed automatically, and negative numbers can be displayed with a minus, in red, with parentheses, or in red with parentheses.
Currency	Numbers have thousands separators and can have a fixed number of decimal places, a currency symbol, and negative numbers can be displayed with a minus, in red, with parentheses, or in red with parentheses.
Accounting	Numbers have thousands separators, a fixed number of decimal places, and can display a currency symbol. Currency symbols and decimal points line up in a column.
Date	Dates can display with numbers, such as 3/4/97 or 03/04/97, or with numbers and text, such as March 4, 1997 or March-97. Some date formats also display the time.
Time	Times can display as AM or PM or use the 24-hour clock, as in 13:15 for 1:15 PM.
Percentage	Numbers are multiplied by 100 and display a percent sign.
Fraction	Numbers display as one, two, or three digit fractions.
Scientific	Numbers display as a number times a power of 10 (represented by E).
Text	Numbers display exactly as entered but are treated as text; therefore, the number would not be used in a calculation.
Special	These formats are used for zip codes, phone numbers, and social security numbers.
Custom	Numbers display in a format created by the user.

	A	B	C	D	E
1	This column is formatted with the **General** Format which is the default.	This column is formatted with the **Number** format with two decimal places.	This column is formatted with the **Currency** format, two decimal places, a dollar sign, and negative numbers in red.	This column is formatted with the **Accounting** format and two decimal places.	This column is formatted with the **Scientific** format with two decimal places.
3	1.37512349	1.38	$1.38	$ 1.38	1.38E+00
4	1000000000	1000000000.00	$1,000,000,000.00	$ 1,000,000,000.00	1.00E+09
5	-98	-98.00	$98.00	$ (98.00)	-9.80E+01
6	12345.6	12345.60	$12,345.60	$ 12,345.60	1.23E+04
7	10	10.00	$10.00	$ 10.00	1.00E+01

Figure 3.2

Project 3: Enhancing the Appearance of a Workbook   EX-83

TASK 3: TO FORMAT NUMBERS:

1. Select cells C6:D9, G6:H9, H10, and G12.
   The cells are highlighted.

2. Choose Format, Cells, click the Number tab, and select Currency from the Category list.

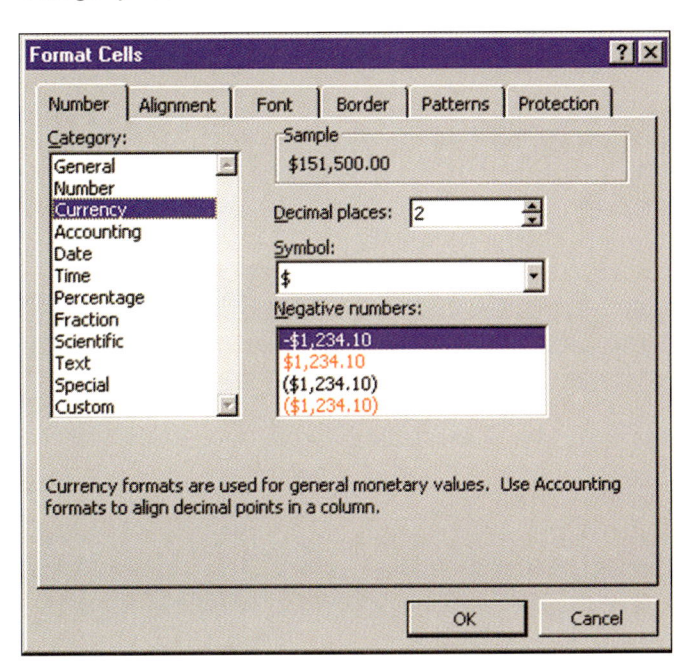

3. Select 0 for Decimal places and None for Symbol.

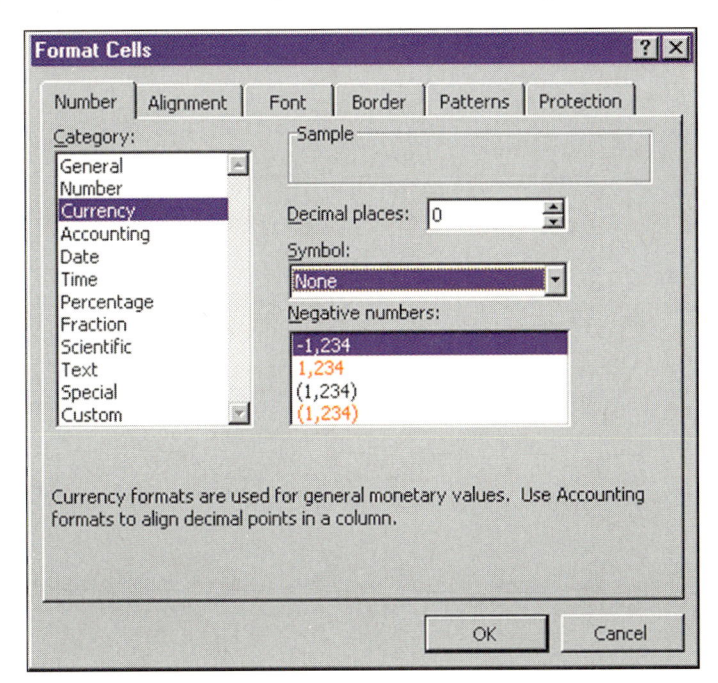

4. Click OK.
   The format is applied.

Formatting Dates

The date format is included in the number formats because Excel stores dates as numbers. You can format dates in several ways. For example, if you enter the date 3/4/97, you can format it to look like any of the following:

3/4	Mar-97
3/4/97	March-97
03/04/97	March 4, 1997
4-Mar	M
4-Mar-97	M-97
04-Mar-97	

Some numbers that you enter are really text. For example, in Figure 3.1, shown on page 77 and again below, the range of 1–8 refers to holes 1 through 8 on the golf course. If you do not format "1–8" as text, Excel will interpret the entry as a date. You will learn how to format dates in Tasks 4 and 5.

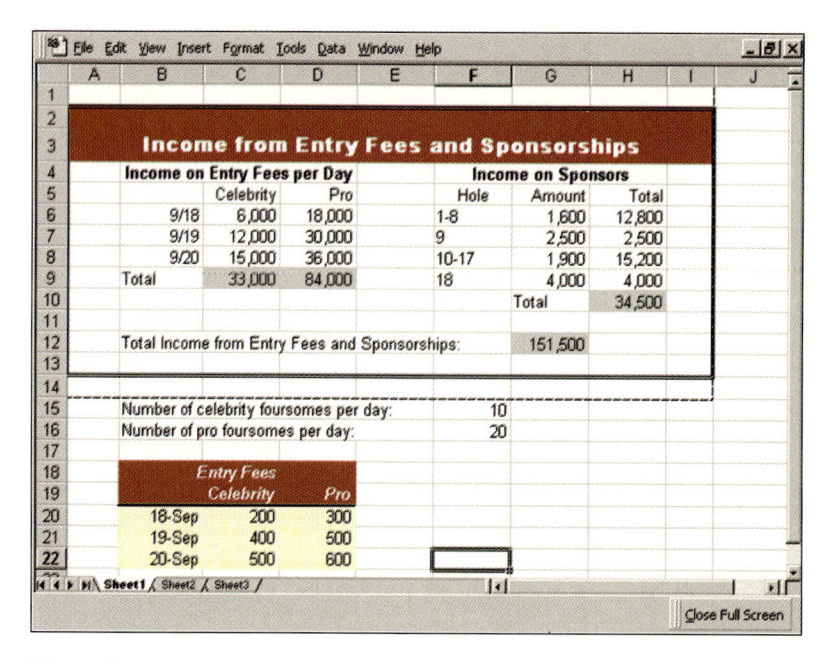

Figure 3.1

TASK 4: TO FORMAT DATES:

1 Select B6:B8.
The cells are highlighted.

2 Choose Format, Cells, and click on the Number tab (if necessary).
The default format is selected.

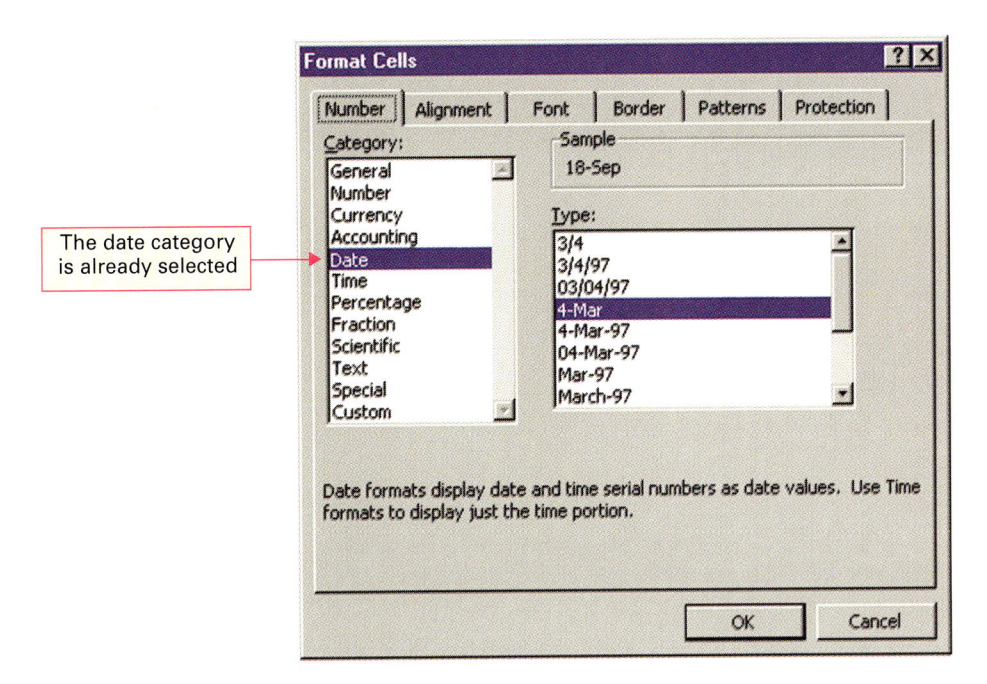

Project 3: Enhancing the Appearance of a Workbook   EX-85

The date category is already selected

3 Select the first option from the Type list (3/4) and click OK.

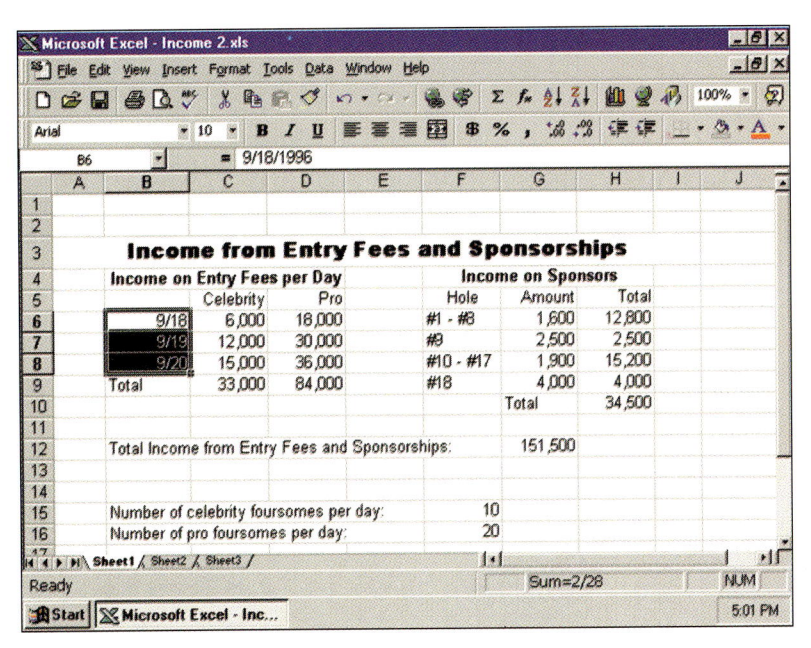

EX-86

Formatting Numbers as Text

When you enter numbers with dashes or slashes in a worksheet, as we did in golf course holes 1–8 and 10–17 shown below, Excel interprets the entry as a date. To avoid this, you must format the numbers as text.

TASK 5: TO FORMAT NUMBERS AS TEXT:

1 Reenter the data in cells F6:F9 exactly as shown:
F6: **1 - 8**
F7: **9**
F8: **10 - 17**
F9: **18**

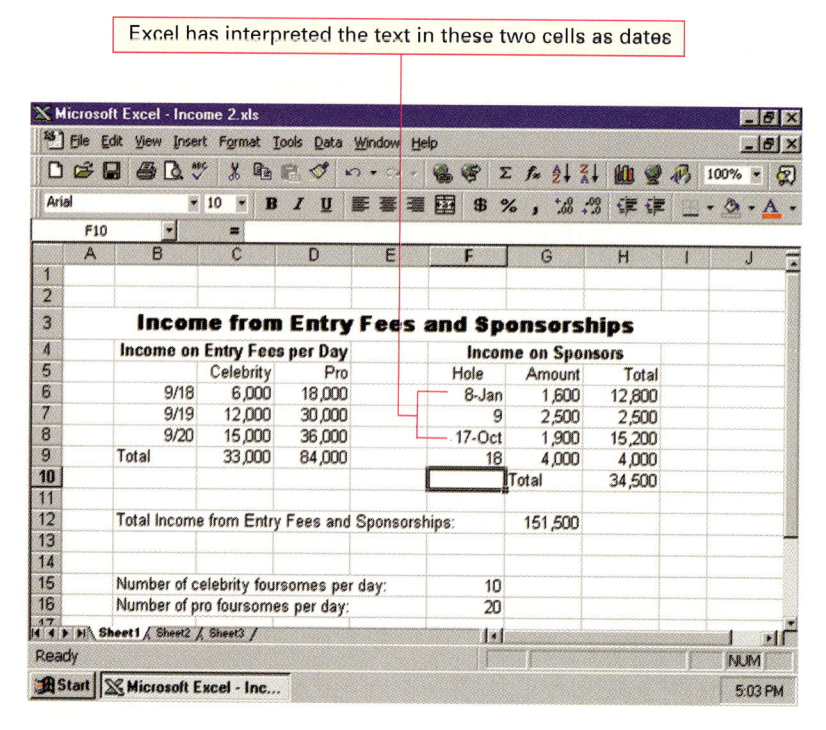

Excel has interpreted the text in these two cells as dates

2 Select cells F6:F9.
The cells are highlighted.

3 Choose Format, Cells, and click on the Number tab (if necessary). Select Text for the Category and click OK.

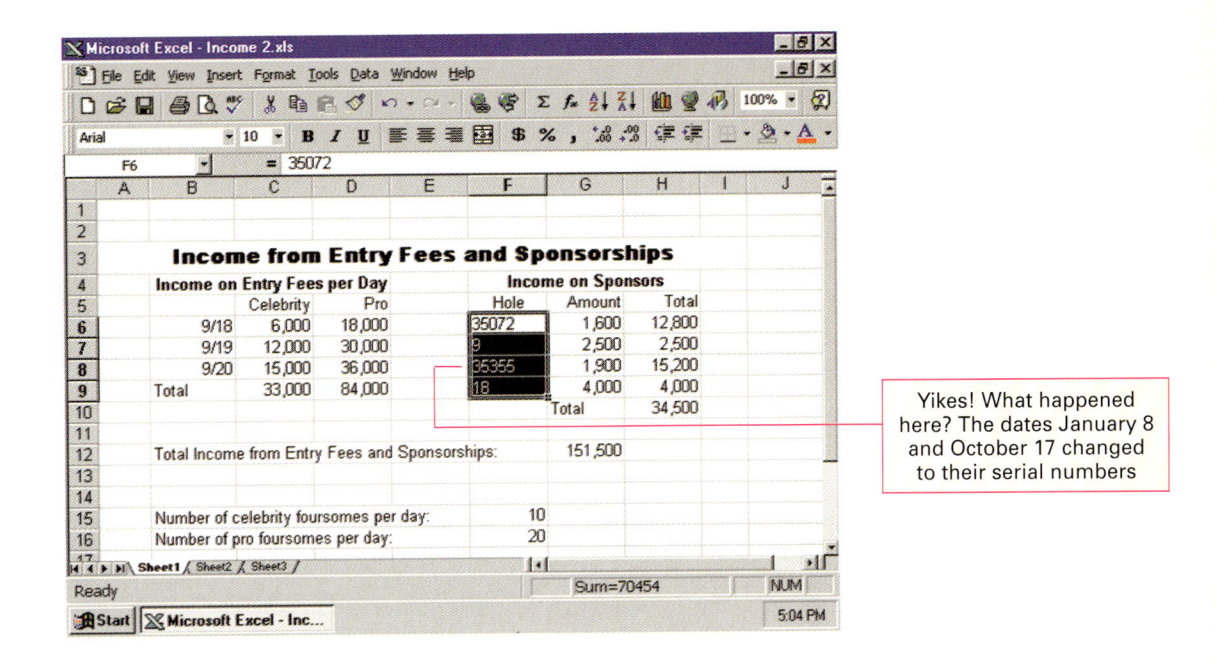

Project 3: Enhancing the Appearance of a Workbook   EX-87

Yikes! What happened here? The dates January 8 and October 17 changed to their serial numbers

Note A serial number is a sequential number given to every day of every year since the turn of the century. So the number 35072 means that January 8, 1997 is the 35,072nd day of the 20th century.

4 Type **1 - 8** in cell F6. Type **10 - 17** in cell F8.

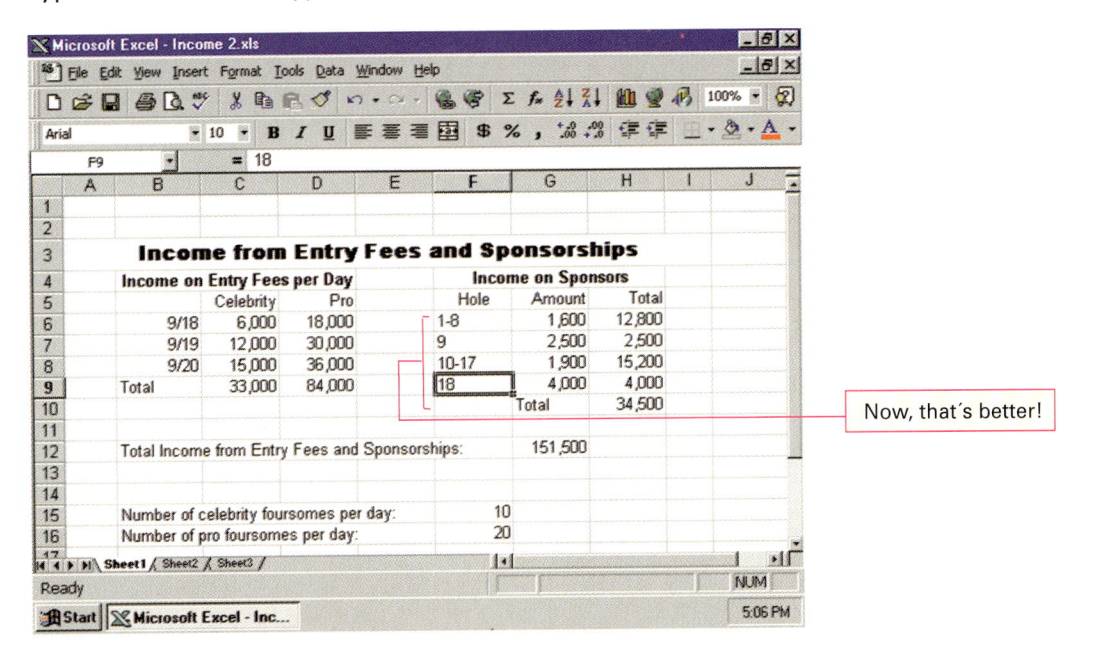

Now, that's better!

Adding Borders and Fill

A *border* is a line that displays on any side of a cell or group of cells. You can use borders in a variety of ways: to draw rectangles around cells, to create dividers between columns, to create a total line under a column of numbers, and so on.

Fill, also called *shading* or *patterns*, is a color or a shade of gray that you apply to the background of a cell. Use fill carefully if you do not have a color printer. Sometimes it doesn't look as good when it prints in black and white as it does on screen.

TASK 6: TO ADD A BORDER AND FILL:

1 Select cells A2:I13.
The cells are highlighted.

2 Choose Format, Cells, and click the Border tab.

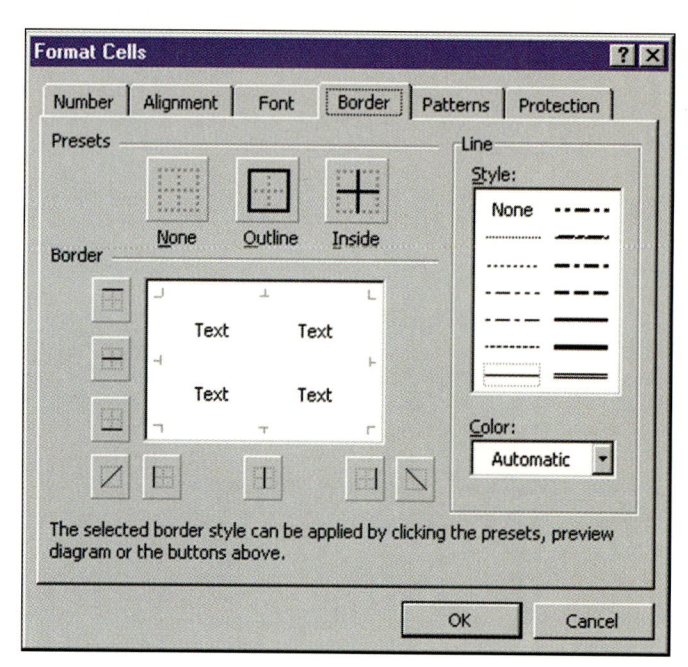

3 Select the double line in the Style box, click the Outline button, and click OK.

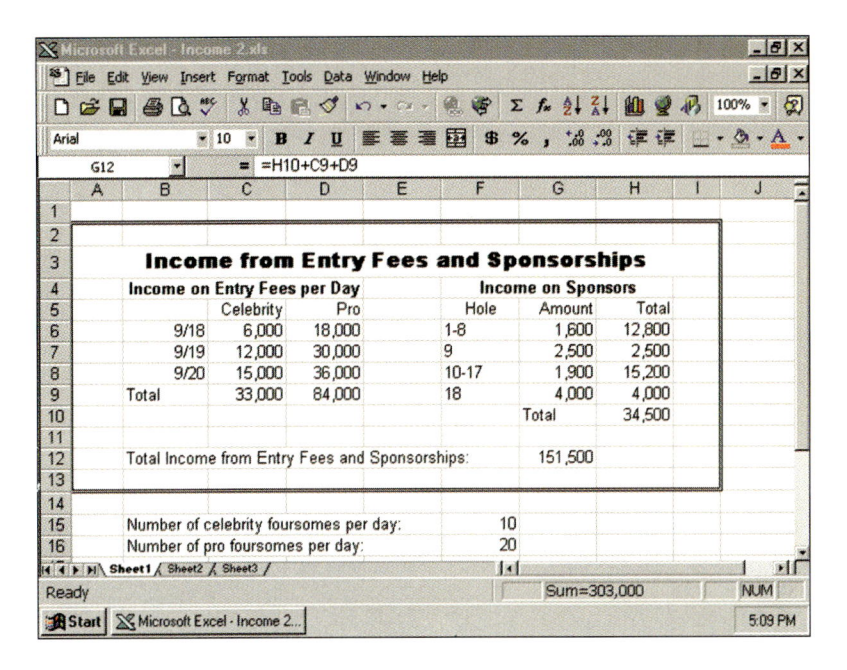

Project 3: Enhancing the Appearance of a Workbook   EX-89

4 Select cells C9:D9, H10, and G12.
The cells are highlighted.

5 Choose Format, Cells, and click the Patterns tab.

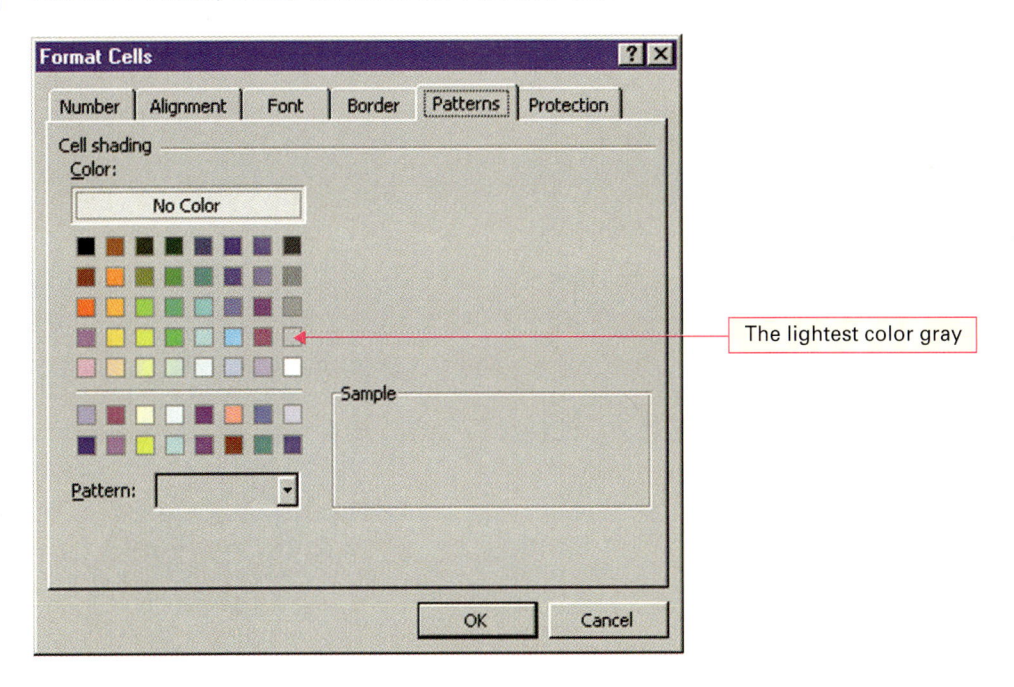

The lightest color gray

6 Select the lightest color gray and click OK.

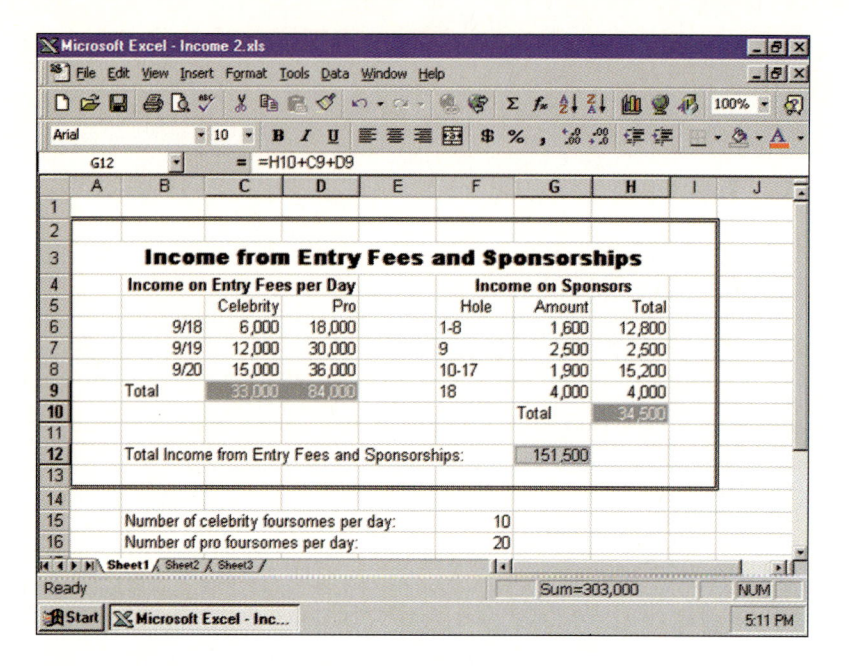

7 Select cells A2:I3 and format them with the first color on the second row of the color chart on the Patterns page.
The cells are shaded with the selected color.

> **Tip** You also can apply color by clicking the down arrow on the Fill Color button on the Formatting toolbar and selecting a color from a smaller palette.

8 Select cell A3.
The cell is highlighted.

9 To change the text color, click the down arrow in the Font Color button and click the white rectangle in the color palette.

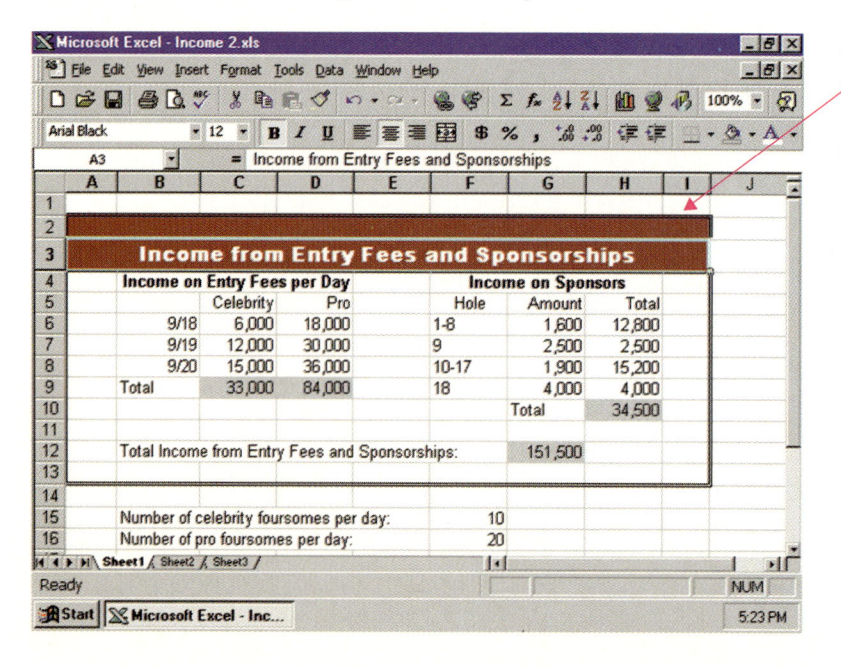

The border is in the same place, but it is hard to see because of the selected cells

Project 3: Enhancing the Appearance of a Workbook   EX-91

Viewing and Changing a Page Break

Unlike word processing documents, worksheets are not represented on the screen by pages. The complete worksheet, all 16,777,216 cells of it, is one big page on the screen. So that you can see where the pages will break when the worksheet prints, Excel provides a *Page Break view*. You can adjust the location of the *page breaks* in this view.

TASK 7: TO VIEW THE PAGE BREAK IN THE INCOME WORKSHEET AND CHANGE IT:

1 Click the Print Preview button.

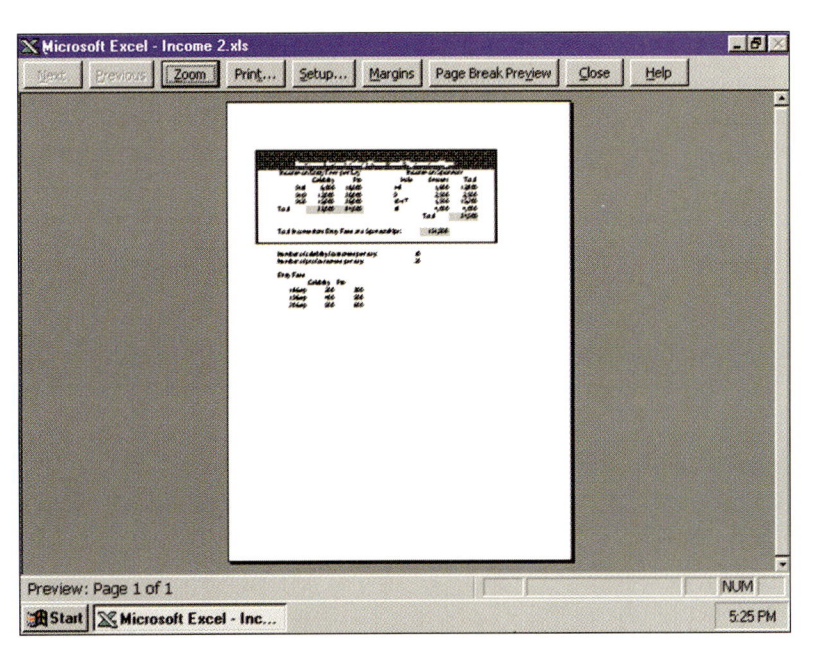

2 Click the Page Break Preview button. (Click OK if a message displays.)

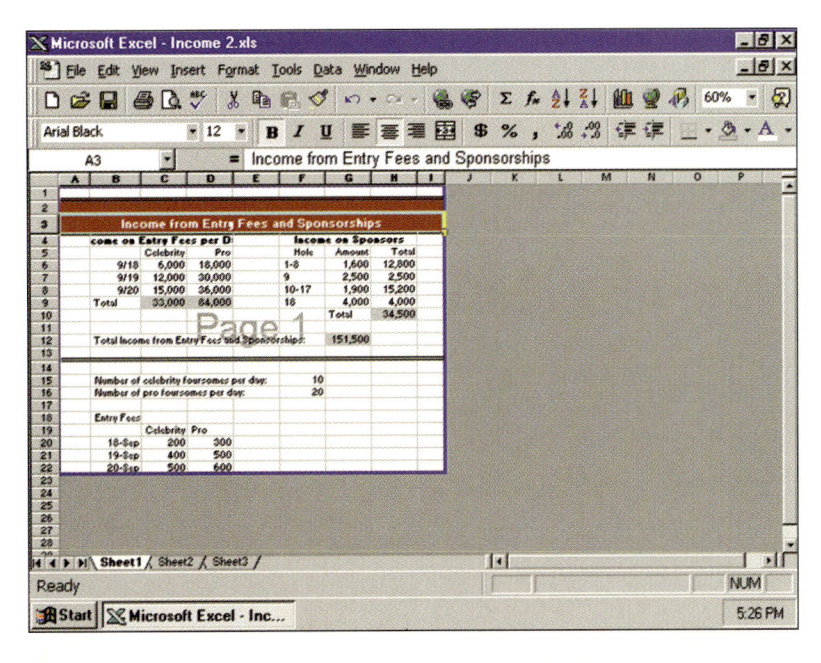

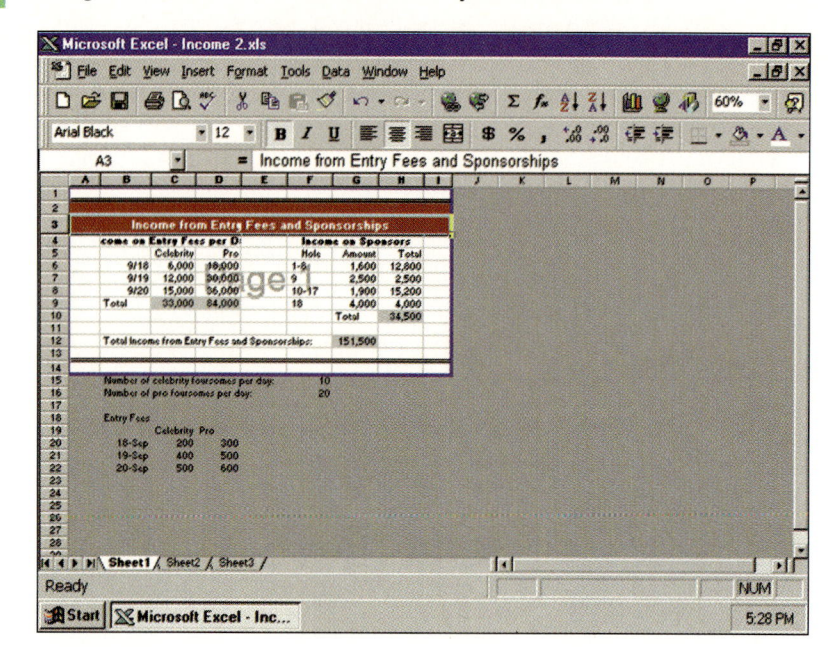

3 Drag the blue line at the bottom to just below row 14.

4 Click [icon].
Now, only the bordered text displays in the print preview for page 1.

5 Click the Normal View button.
The worksheet displays in Normal view. Notice that the page break location is indicated with a dotted line.

Using AutoFormat

Excel provides several formats that you can apply to a complete worksheet or to a single range. The **AutoFormat** feature enables you to apply many formatting features automatically, creating very professional looking worksheets without much effort on your part. (Excel works hard so you don't have to.)

> **Note** AutoFormats are designed for worksheets or ranges that have row headings in the first column and column headings in the first row.

TASK 8: TO APPLY AN AUTOFORMAT:

1 Select B18:D22.
The cells are highlighted.

Project 3: Enhancing the Appearance of a Workbook   EX-93

2   Choose Format, AutoFormat.

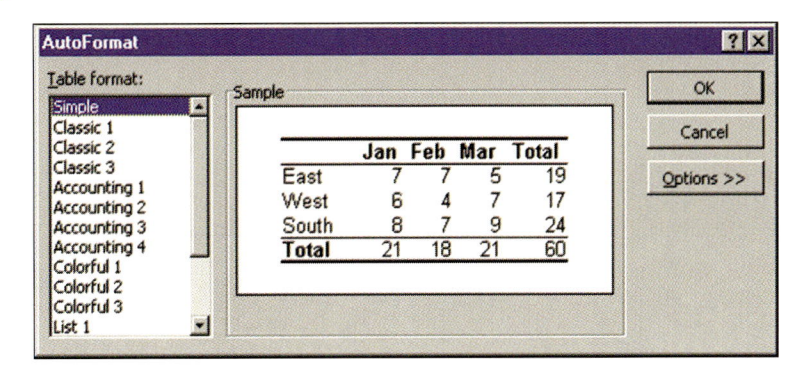

3   Select Colorful 2. Click Options, deselect Width/Height, and click OK. Click in a cell outside the selected range to see the true colors.

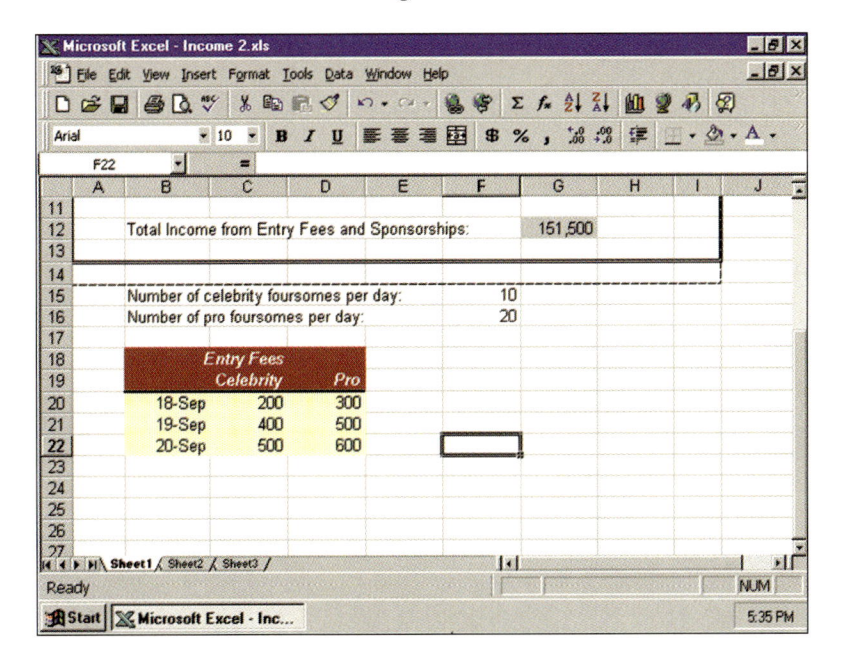

The Conclusion

If you have access to a printer, print page 1 of the worksheet. Save the workbook and close it.

Summary and Exercises

Summary

- You can format text with bold, italic, underline, different fonts and font sizes, and so on.
- Data in a cell can be left, right, or center aligned.
- Excel provides many formats for displaying numbers.
- You can apply a border to any side of a cell.
- You can apply a background color to a cell.
- The Page Break view shows where page breaks are located.
- An AutoFormat can be applied to a worksheet or a range.

Key Terms and Operations

Key Terms	Operations
border	add a border
fill	add fill
page break	align cells
Page Break view	AutoFormat
pattern	change a page break
shading	format dates
	format numbers
	format text
	view a page break

Study Questions

Multiple Choice

1. If you type text in cell A1 and you want to center the text across cells A1 through A5,
   - a. merge the cells and click the Center button.
   - b. select A1:A5 and click the Center button.
   - c. select A1:A5 and choose Format, Cells, Alignment, Center, and click OK.
   - d. merge the cells, and choose Format, Align, Center.

2. You can apply an AutoFormat
   - a. to a cell.
   - b. only to a complete worksheet.
   - c. to a single range.
   - d. to noncontiguous ranges.

3. To make text bold,
   - a. click in the cell, type the text, click the Bold button, and press Enter.
   - b. select the cell and click the Bold button.
   - c. select the cell and choose Format, Bold.
   - d. All of the above.

4. Borders can be applied to
   a. any side of a range.
   b. all sides of a range.
   c. the top and bottom sides of a range.
   d. All of the above.

5. To add shading to a cell, select the cell and
   a. click the drop-down arrow on the Shading button and choose the color.
   b. choose Format, Cells, Shading, select the color, and click OK.
   c. choose Format, Cells, Patterns, select the color, and click OK.
   d. choose Format, Shading, select the color, and click OK.

6. A page break is marked with
   a. a dotted line in the worksheet.
   b. a blue line in the Print Preview.
   c. a dotted line in the Page Break Preview.
   d. a blue line in the worksheet.

7. Which of the following format(s) (if any) would be used to achieve this format: $1,200.00?
   a. general format with a dollar sign symbol and two decimal places
   b. accounting format with a dollar sign symbol and two decimal places
   c. currency format with a dollar sign symbol and two decimal places
   d. number format with a dollar sign symbol and two decimal places

8. When you increase the point size of text,
   a. you must first increase the height of the row.
   b. the text may wrap in the cell if the cell is not wide enough to accommodate the new size.
   c. the row height increases automatically to accommodate the size of the text.
   d. the cell width increases automatically to accommodate the size of the text.

9. The option to rotate text in a cell is found
   a. on the Orientation page of the Format Cells dialog box.
   b. on the Format menu.
   c. on the Rotate button in the Formatting Toolbar.
   d. on the Alignment page of the Format Cells dialog box.

10. Excel stores a date as
    a. a number.
    b. a date.
    c. text.
    d. a mixture of text and numbers.

Short Answer

1. How are numbers aligned in a cell?

2. How can you enter 1–2–97 and make it appear as January 2, 1997?

3. How do you change the font of the text entered in a cell?

4. How do you change the color of the text entered in a cell?

5. Under what circumstances do you have to format a cell as text?

6. How do you merge cells?

7. How are dates aligned in a cell?

8. The entry 1.2E103 is an example of what number format?

9. What is a serial number?

10. What is the default alignment for text in a cell?

For Discussion

1. Describe the AutoFormat feature and discuss the advantages of using it.

2. How can you designate where the pages will break when the worksheet prints?

3. Compare the Page Break Preview with the Print Preview view.

4. Give examples of ways you could use borders.

Review Exercises

1. Enhancing the Restaurant Sales Worksheet

In this exercise, you will enhance the worksheet with border, shading, and number formats.

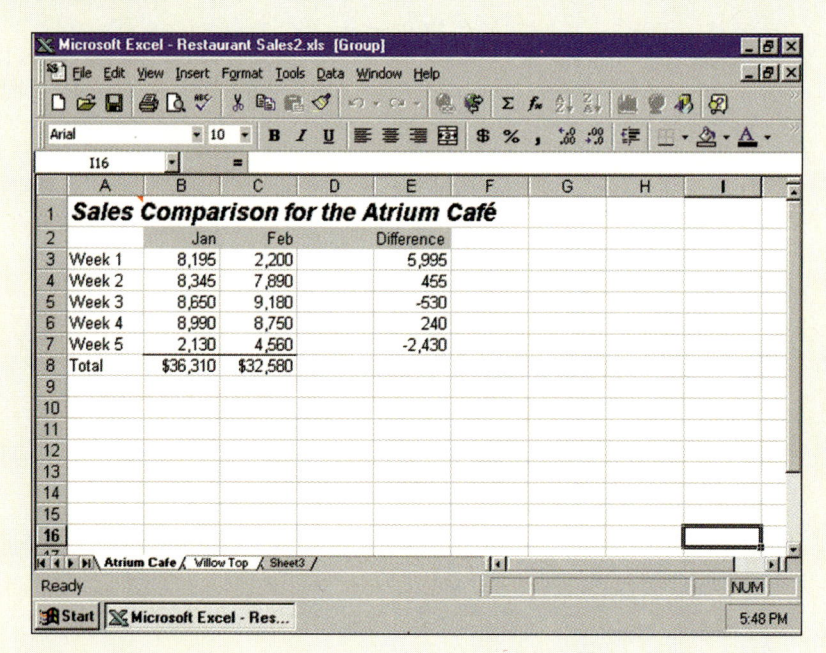

Figure 3.3

1. Open *Restaurant Sales.xls*, the file you saved at the end of Project 2.

2. Right align cells B2 and C2 on both worksheets.

3. Format all numbers on both worksheets (except for cells B8 and C8) with the Currency format, using no decimal places and no dollar sign. Format B8 and C8 on both worksheets with Currency, no decimal places, and a dollar sign.

4. Format cell A1 on both worksheets with bold, italic, 14 point.

5. Add a border to the bottom of cells B7 and C7 on both worksheets.

6. Add light gray fill to cells B2:E2 on both worksheets.

7. Save the file as *Restaurant Sales2.xls* and close it.

2. Creating a Concert List
In this exercise, you will create a workbook for a list of concerts and enhance the worksheet with formatting.

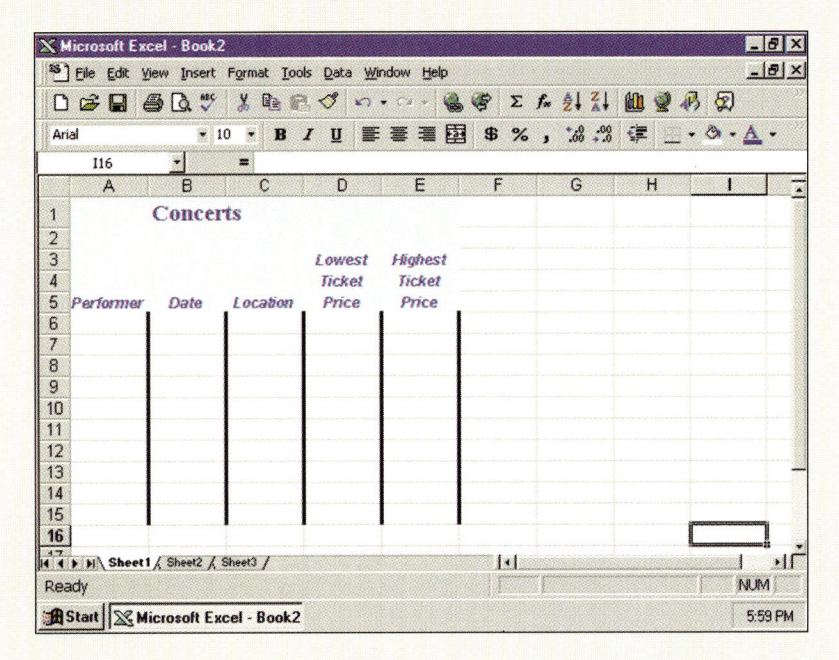

Figure 3.4

1. Go to http://www.ticketmaster.com and follow the link to the Box Office.

2. Search for at least 10 concerts by groups or performers that you like. Obtain information about when and where the concert will be and how much the tickets cost.

3. Create a worksheet with these column headings: Performer, Date, Location, Lowest Ticket Price, Highest Ticket Price.

4. Format the title with 14 point Times New Roman.

5. Format the column headings in bold, italic, 9 point and center them.

6. Use a thick border between each column.

7. Fill the range A1:E5 with light blue and change the color of the text in the range to dark blue.

8. Save the file as *Concerts.xls* and close it.

Assignments

1. Reformatting the *Income.xls* File
Open the Income.xls file. Move the data in cells B15:F22 to Sheet2. Format the data on Sheet1 using your own ideas for borders, shading, fonts, and so on. When finished, save the file as *Income 3.xls*.

2. Using AutoFormat

If you have Internet access, download *Revenues.xls* from www.awl.com/is/select/. If you are unable to download this file, ask your instructor how to obtain it. Experiment with different AutoFormats. Choose one of the formats you like and save the file as *Revenues2.xls*. Open *Revenues.xls* again and save it with another format that you like as *Revenues3.xls*. Open *Revenues.xls* and save it with another format that you like as *Revenues4.xls*.

PROJECT 4

Editing the Structure of a Worksheet and a Workbook

Think of yourself as an Excel architect. You design workbooks using the Excel "materials" — cells, columns, rows, and worksheets. When you want to edit the structure of a worksheet or a workbook, you have to request that materials be added to or removed from the file. Sometimes the design you want calls for different-sized materials or special materials — such as headers and footers. This project introduces you to the tools you'll need to modify the structure of a worksheet.

Objectives

After completing this project, you will be able to:

➤ Insert, delete, and arrange worksheets
➤ Change the size of columns and rows
➤ Insert columns, rows, and cells
➤ Delete columns, rows, and cells
➤ Create headers and footers

The Challenge

You have a workbook that contains March and April restaurant sales information that you have been preparing for the hotel manager, Mr. Gilmore.

You need to delete some information, add some information, make some adjustments in the columns and rows, and add a header and footer.

The Solution

You will begin your edits by deleting one of the worksheets, inserting a new worksheet, and rearranging worksheets. Then you will adjust the width of columns and the height of rows as needed. Next, you will insert and delete columns, rows, and cells, and, finally, you will add the headers and footers. Figure 4.1 shows the first worksheet in the workbook.

To obtain the files you need for this project, download them from the Addison Wesley Longman web site (http://www.awl.com/is/select/ or obtain them from your instructor.

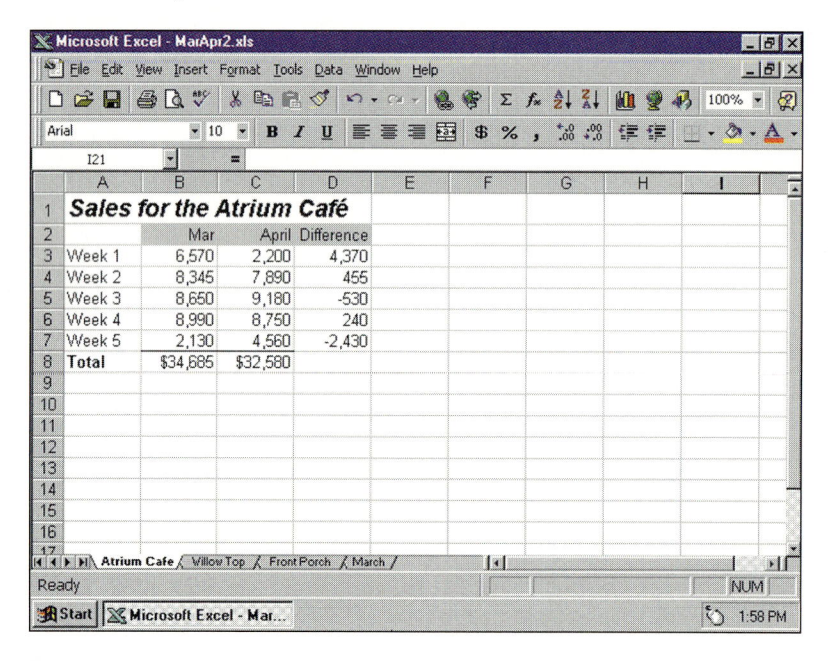

Figure 4.1

The Setup

So that your screen will match the illustrations and the tasks in this project will function as described, make sure that the Excel settings listed in Table 4.1 are selected on your computer. Because these are the default settings for the toolbars and view, you may not need to make any changes to your setup.

Table 4.1: Excel Settings

Location	Make these settings:
View, Toolbars	Deselect all toolbars except Standard and Formatting.
View	Use the Normal view and display the Formula Bar and Status Bar.

Inserting, Deleting, and Arranging Worksheets

As you remember (if you don't remember, just keep it to yourself and no one will be the wiser), a workbook starts out with three worksheets. You can add more worksheets or delete up to two of the three. You also can rearrange the order of worksheets.

TASK 1: TO INSERT AND DELETE PAGES:

1 Open *MarApr.xls*.

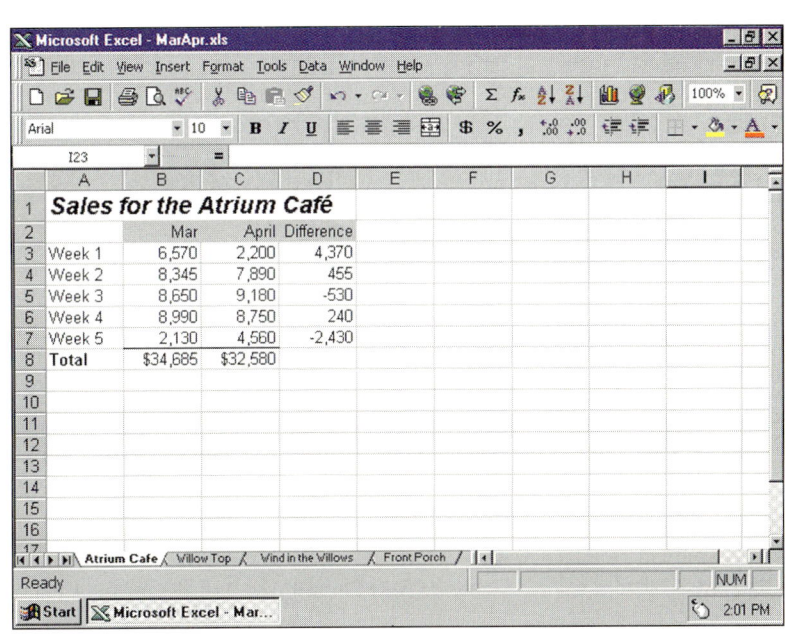

2 Click each worksheet tab to see each page of the workbook.

3 Right-click the tab for Wind in the Willows.

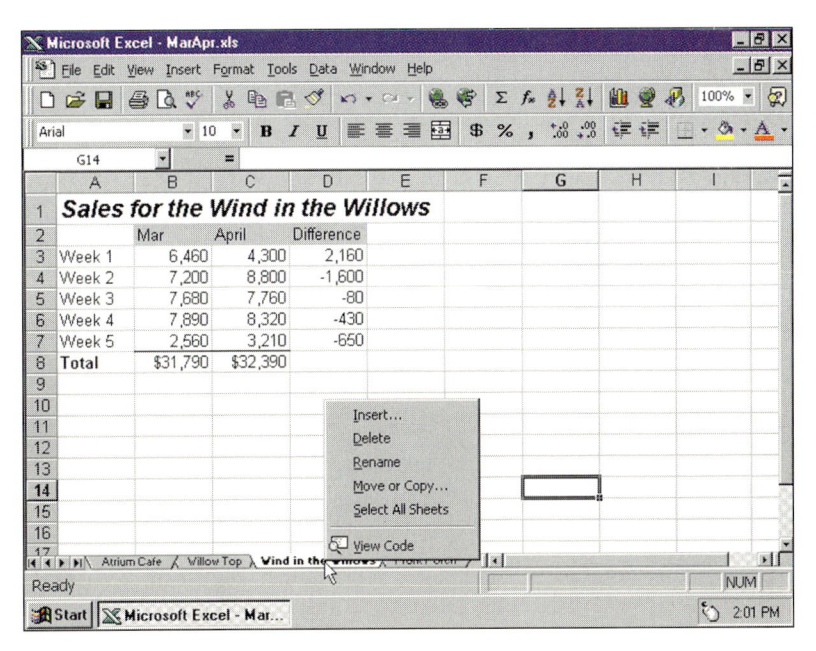

4 Choose Delete.

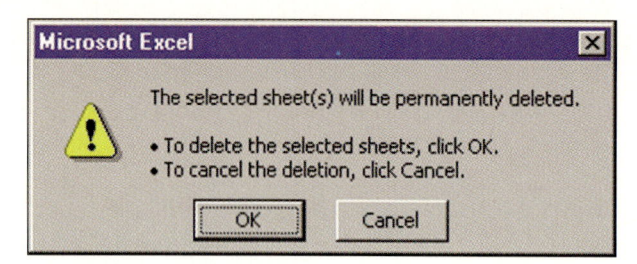

5 Click OK.
The worksheet is permanently deleted from the workbook, and no amount of clicking the Undo button will bring it back.

6 Right-click the Atrium Café tab and choose Insert.

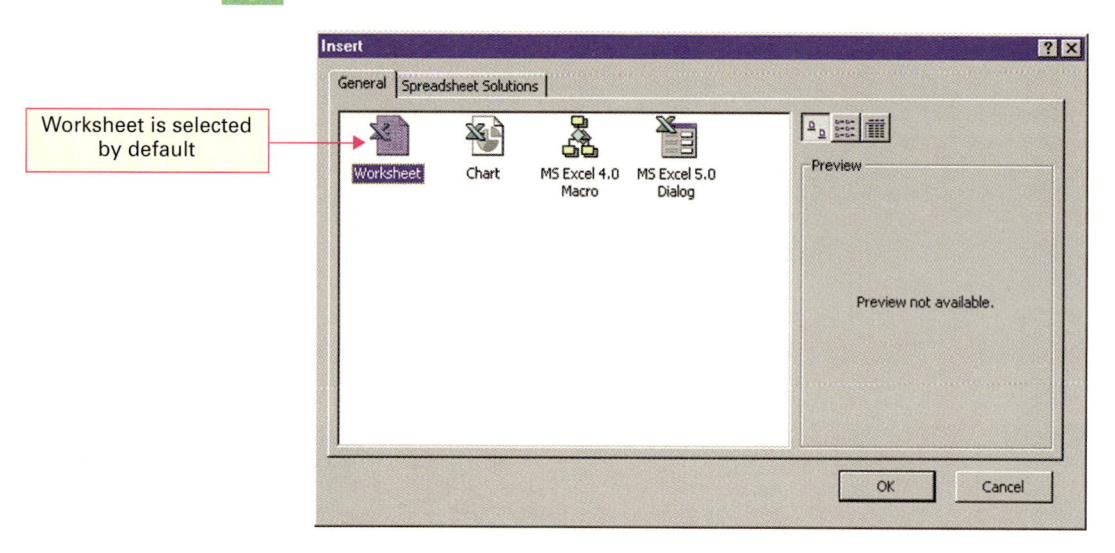

Worksheet is selected by default

7 Click OK.
A new blank worksheet is inserted before the selected worksheet.

8 Rename the new worksheet **March**.

Project 4: Editing the Structure of a Worksheet and a Workbook   EX-103

New worksheet

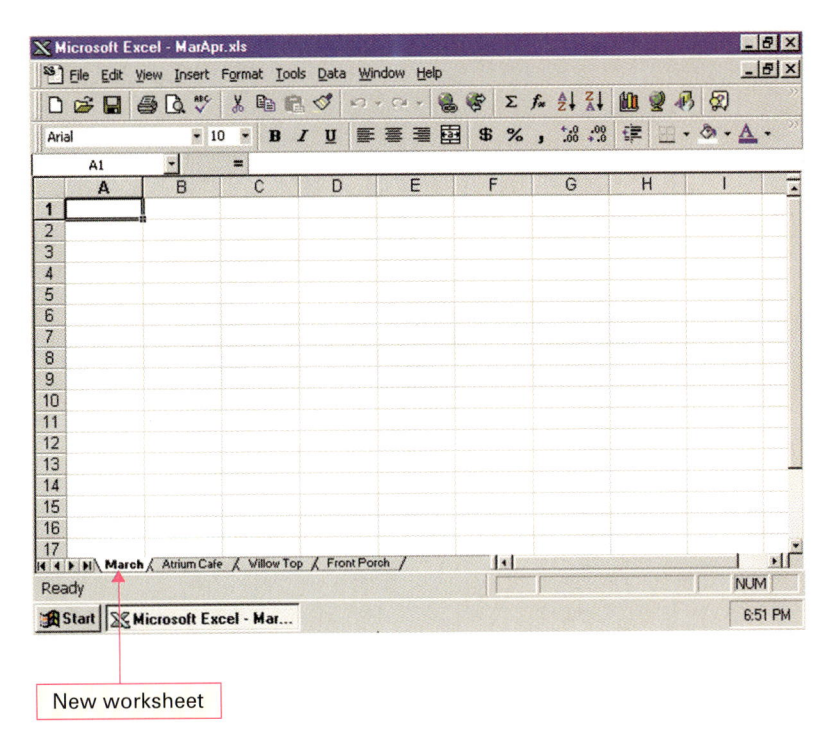

9 Drag the March tab to between the Atrium Café tab and the Willow Top tab, but don't release the mouse button yet.

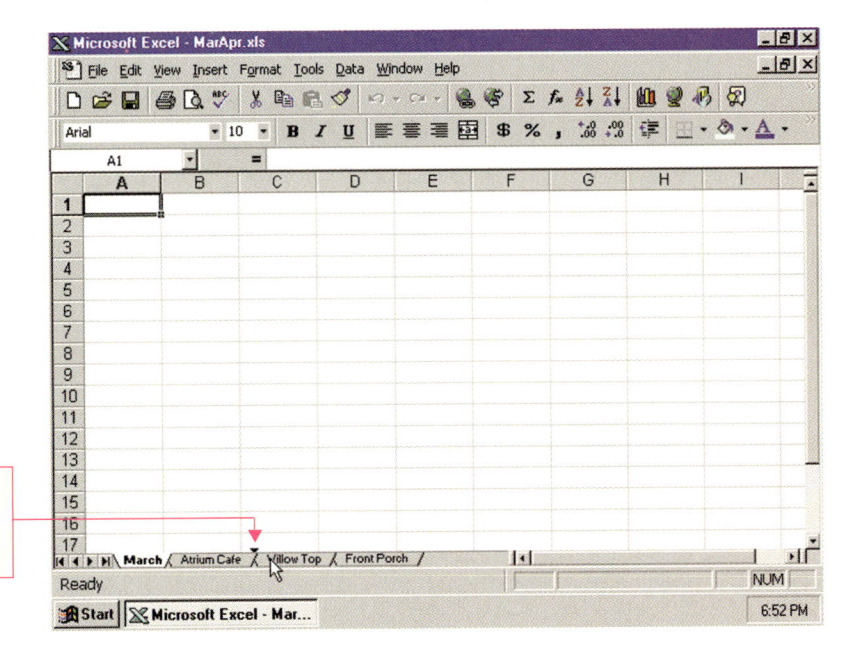

The black triangle marks the location where the new worksheet will be positioned

EX-104

10 Continue dragging to the end of the tabs and then release the mouse button.

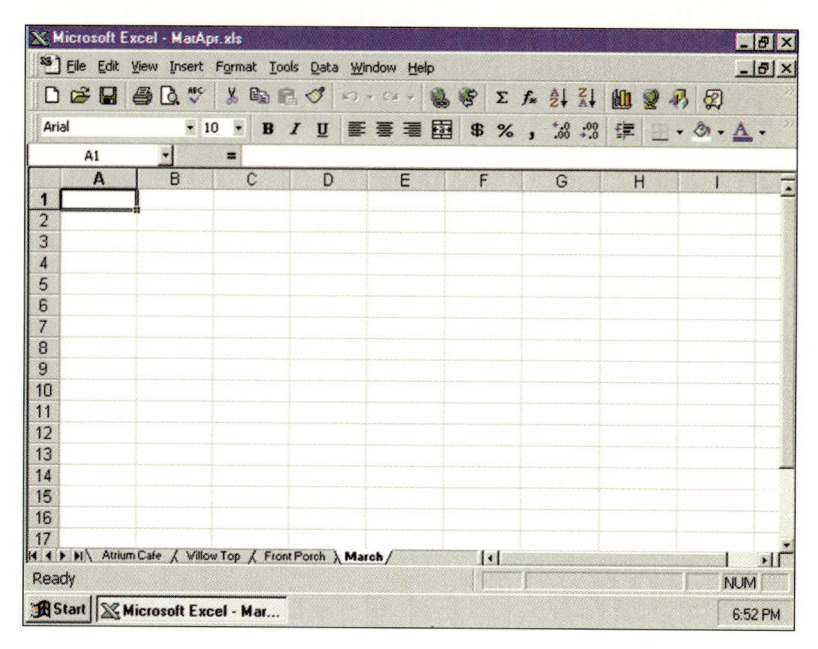

Changing the Size of Columns and Rows

When you create a new workbook, all the columns are the same width, and all the rows are the same height. When you add data to a worksheet, you often must change the row heights and column widths to accommodate the data. As you have already seen in a previous project, the height of a row increases or decreases automatically when you change the point size of the data; however, you may want to change the height of a row just to improve the spacing.

TASK 2: TO CHANGE THE WIDTH OF COLUMNS BY DRAGGING:

1 Type the following in the designated cells of the March worksheet:
A1: **March Sales**
A2: **Atrium Café**

> **Note** Excel will add the accent to the "e" in "café" automatically.

A3: **Willow Top Restaurant**
A4: **Front Porch Restaurant**

Project 4: Editing the Structure of a Worksheet and a Workbook EX-105

2 Point to the line that divides column letters A and B in the Column heading row.

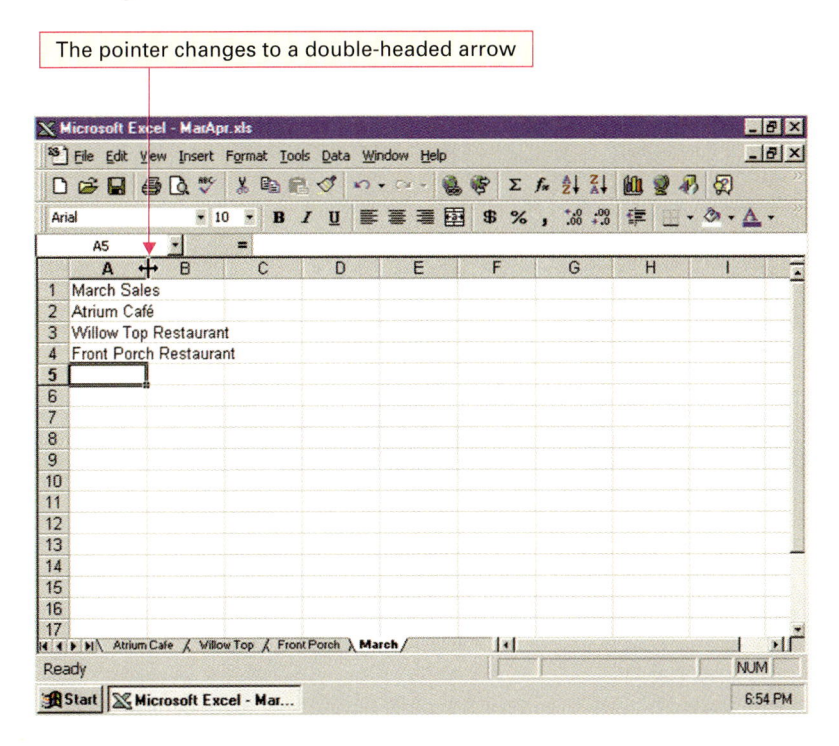

The pointer changes to a double-headed arrow

3 Drag the line to the right until the column is wide enough to hold the text.

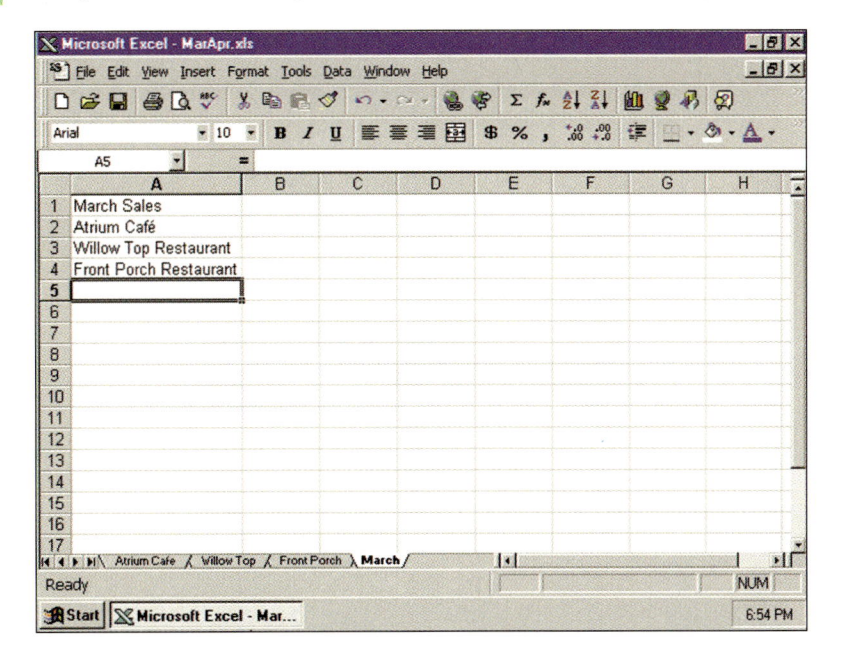

4 Drag the column until it is too wide as shown:

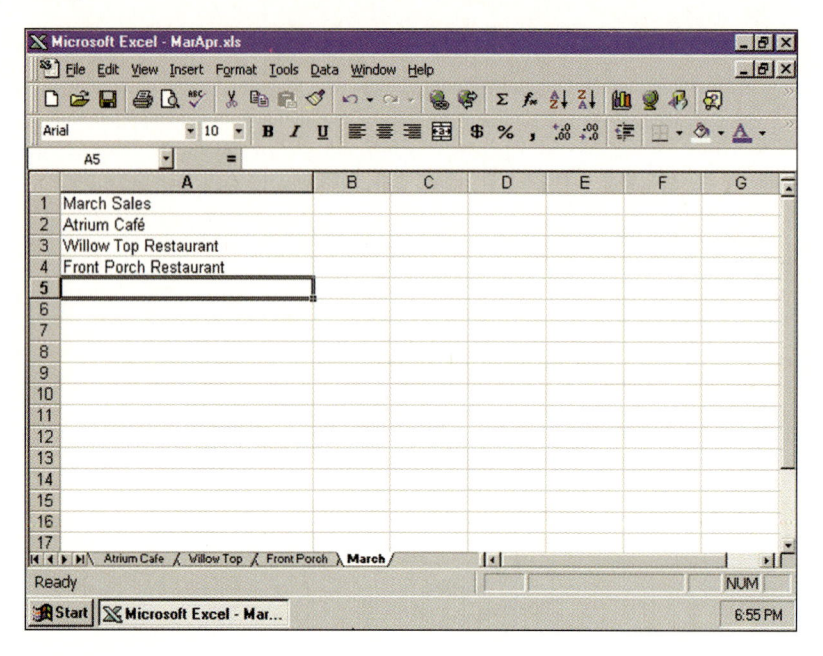

5 Type the following in the designated cells:
B2: **34685**
B3: **45240**
B4: **30835**

6 Drag the line between column letters B and C until column B is too wide as shown:

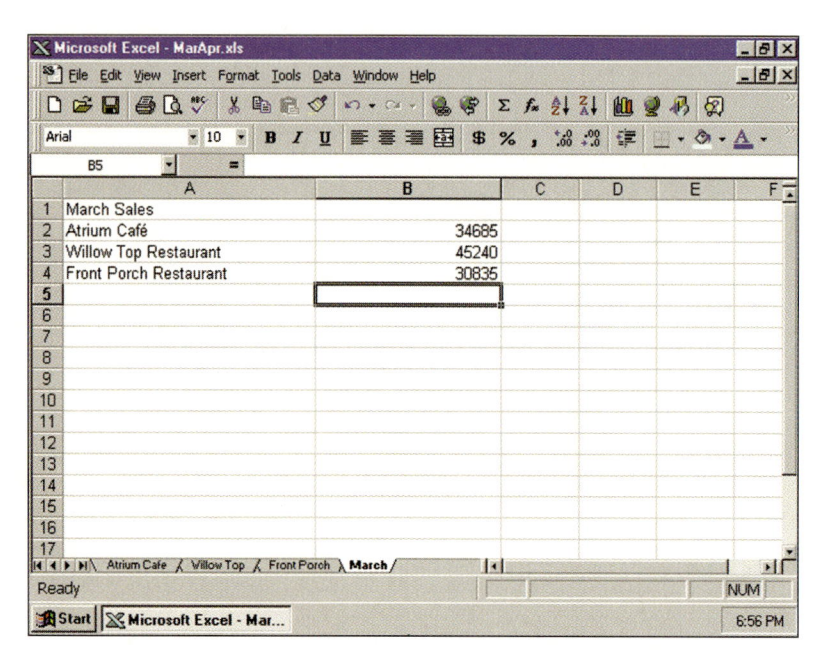

Using AutoFit

Another way to change the width of a column is to use AutoFit. *AutoFit* automatically adjusts columns to be just wide enough to accommodate the widest entry and can adjust the widths of several columns at once.

Project 4: Editing the Structure of a Worksheet and a Workbook EX-107

TASK 3: TO CHANGE THE WIDTH OF COLUMNS BY USING AUTOFIT:

1 Select columns A and B by dragging the mouse pointer through A and B at the top of the columns.
The columns are highlighted.

2 Choose Format, Column.

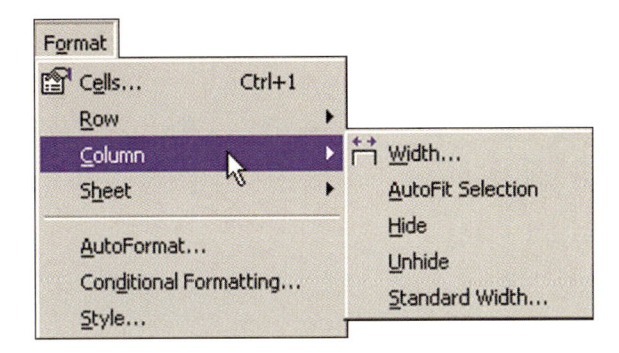

3 Choose AutoFit Selection.

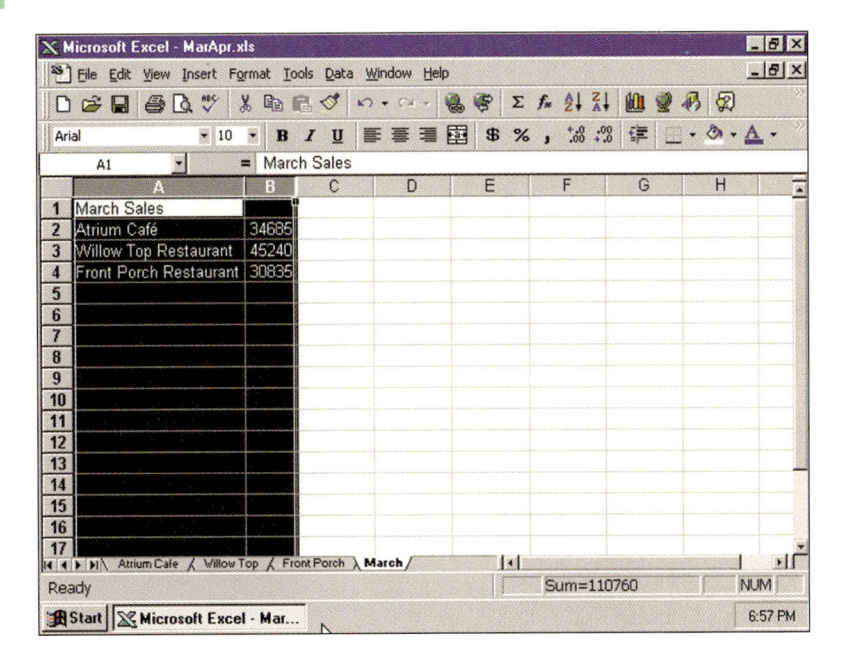

Tip You can select multiple columns and double-click a line between the column letters to AutoFit the selections.

Adjusting Row Height

If you want to control the spacing in a worksheet, you can make rows taller or shorter by dragging them to the desired height.

EX-108

TASK 4: TO CHANGE THE HEIGHT OF ROWS:

1 Point to the line that divides row numbers 1 and 2 in the row indicators column.

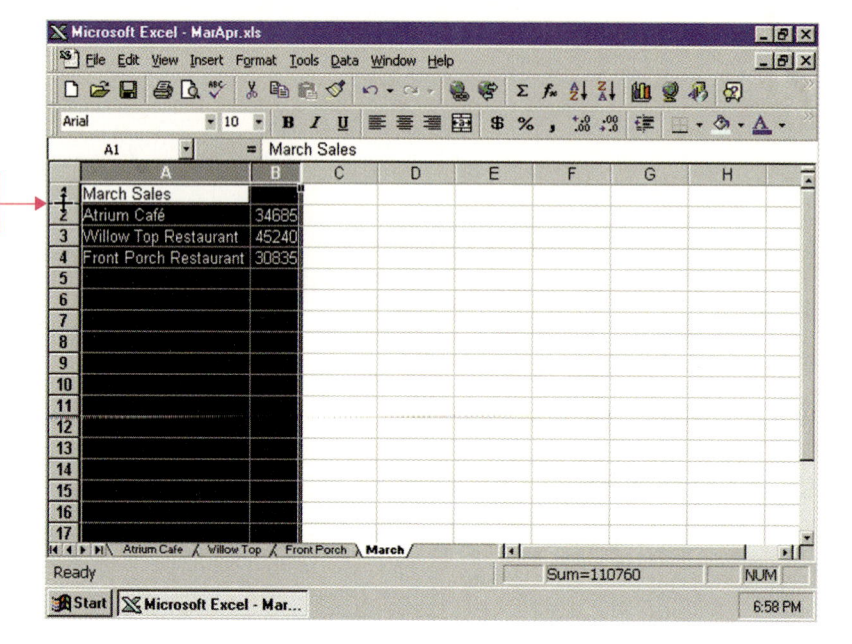

The pointer changes to a double-headed arrow

It doesn't matter if columns are selected when you change the row height because you don't have to select anything to change the height.

2 Drag down to make the row taller.

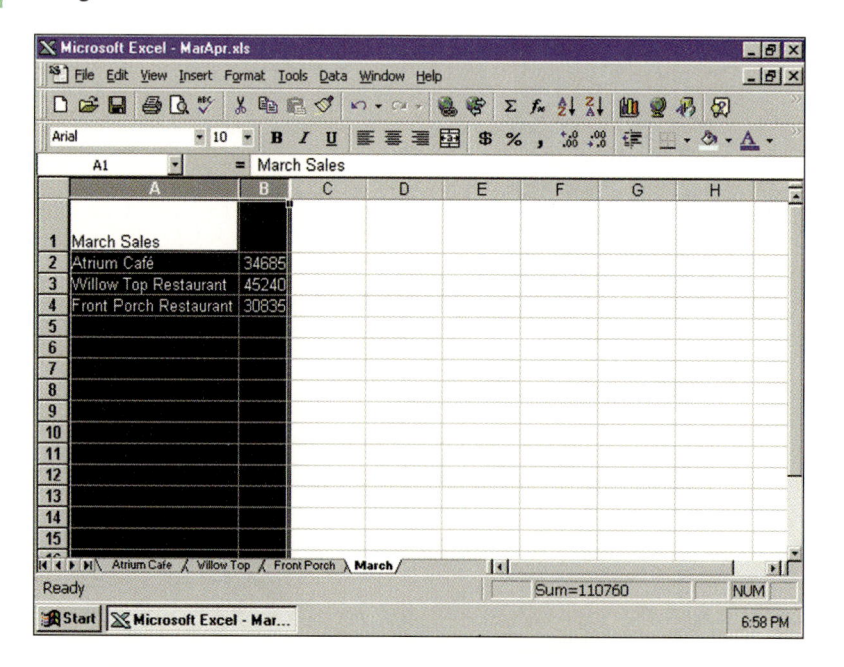

Tip You also can size rows with AutoFit. As you probably can guess, the command is under Format, Row or you can select the rows and double-click the line between the row numbers.

Project 4: Editing the Structure of a Worksheet and a Workbook   EX-109

Inserting Columns, Rows, and Cells

When you insert a column, all the other columns move to the right to give the new column room. When you insert rows, all the other rows move down, and when you insert cells, the other cells move to the right or move down. Excel is so polite!

TASK 5: TO INSERT A COLUMN, A ROW, AND A CELL:

1. Click anywhere in column A.
   The cell is selected.

2. Choose Insert.

3. Choose Columns.

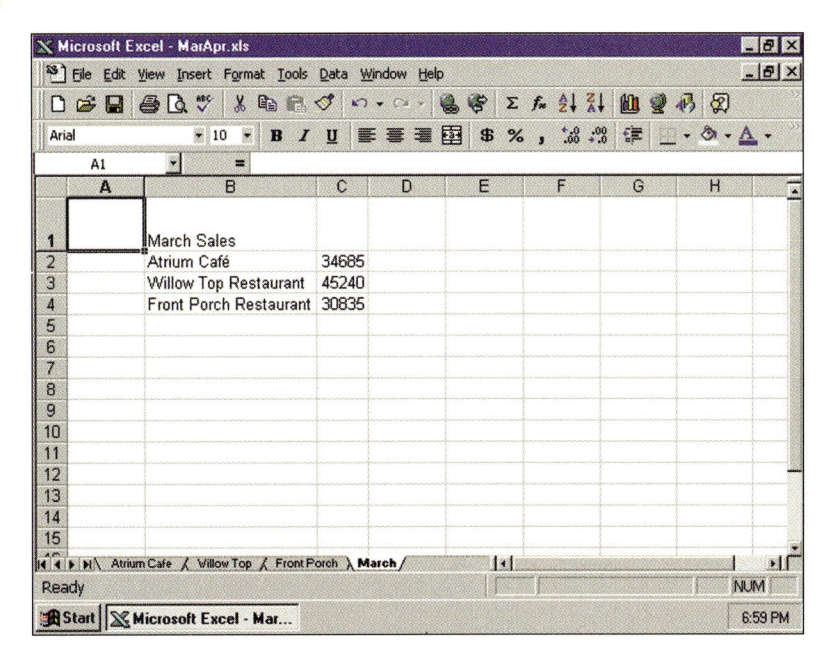

EX-110

> **Tip** To insert multiple columns, select the number of columns you want to insert in the location where you want to insert them, and then choose Insert, Columns.

4 Click anywhere in row 2.
The cell is selected.

5 Choose Insert, Rows. (The new rows take on the dimensions of the row above.)

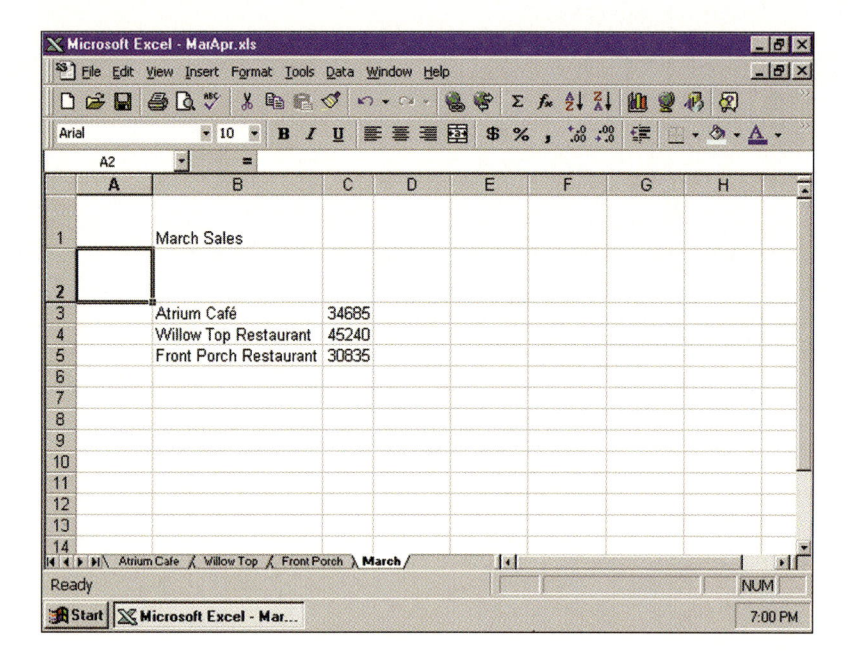

> **Tip** To insert multiple rows, select the number of rows you want to insert in the location where you want to insert them, and then choose Insert, Rows.

6 Type the following in the designated cells:
D1: **March Banquets**
D3: **D.A.R.**
D4: **L.W.V.**
D5: **B.S.A**
E3: **2560**
E4: **1500**
E5: **900**

7 Select cells D4 and E4.

8 Choose Insert, Cells.

The default is to shift the cells down →

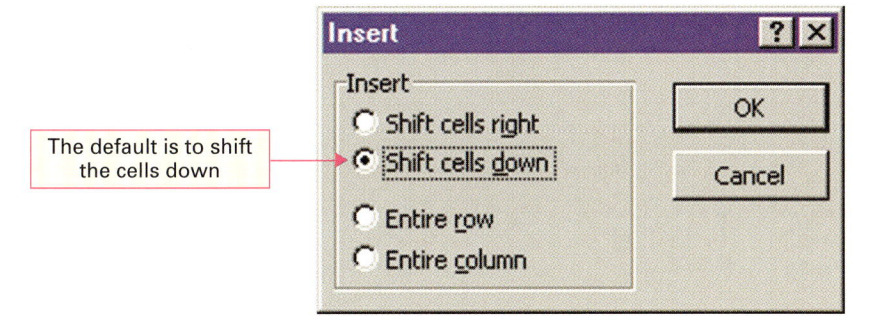

Insert dialog:
- ○ Shift cells right
- ● Shift cells down
- ○ Entire row
- ○ Entire column

[OK] [Cancel]

9 Click OK.

If you had inserted a row instead of a cell, cells B4 and C4 would be blank

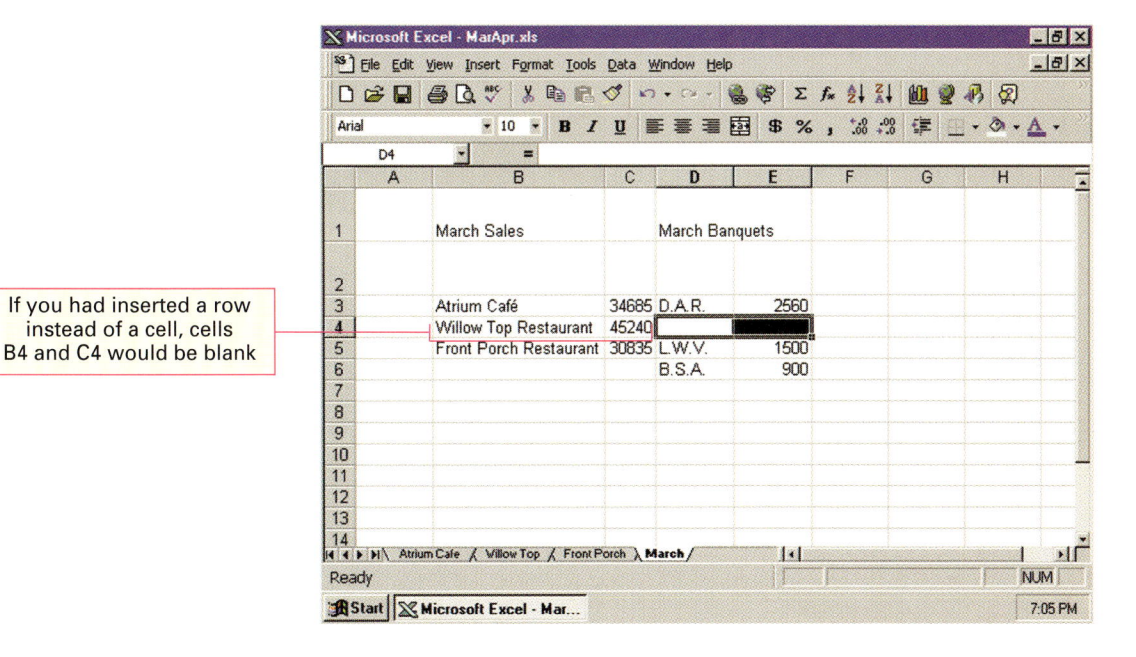

	A	B	C	D	E
1		March Sales		March Banquets	
2					
3		Atrium Café	34685	D.A.R.	2560
4		Willow Top Restaurant	45240		
5		Front Porch Restaurant	30835	L.W.V.	1500
6				B.S.A.	900

EX-112

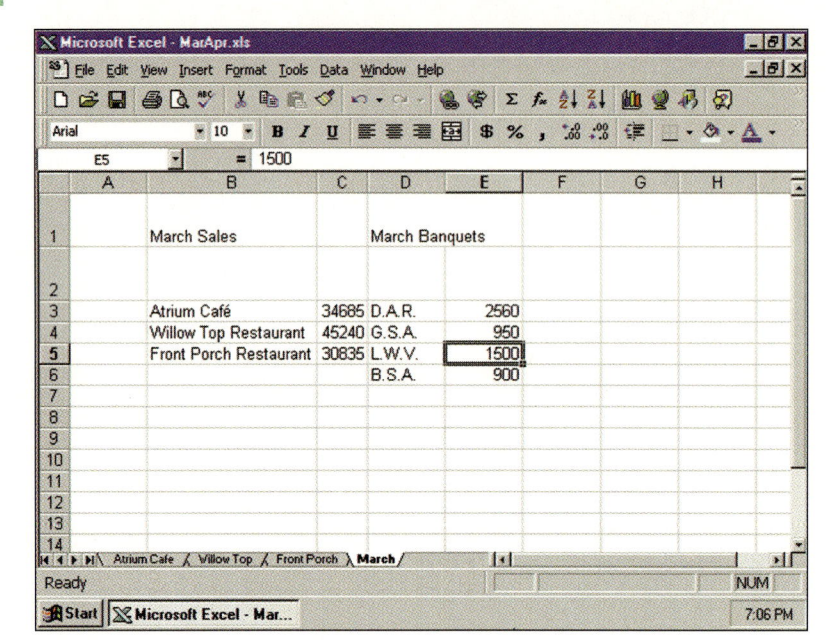

10 Type **G.S.A.** in cell D4, press →, type **950**, and press ENTER.

Deleting Columns, Rows, and Cells

When you delete columns, rows, or cells, you actually cut the space they occupy out of the worksheet. You don't just delete the data they contain.

Caution When you delete a column or row, the entire column or the entire row is deleted. Before deleting, be sure that the column or row doesn't contain data in a location that is off screen.

TASK 6: TO DELETE A COLUMN, A ROW, AND A CELL:

1 Select row 2 by clicking the row 2 button — at the left of the row. The row is highlighted.

2 Choose Edit, Delete.

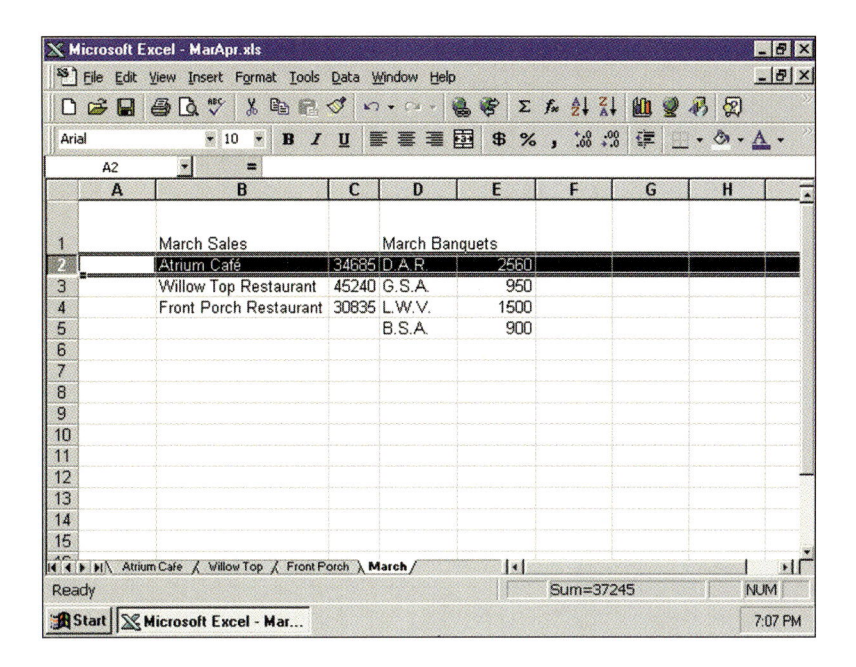

Project 4: Editing the Structure of a Worksheet and a Workbook EX-113

3 Select column A by clicking the column button A above the column. The column is highlighted.

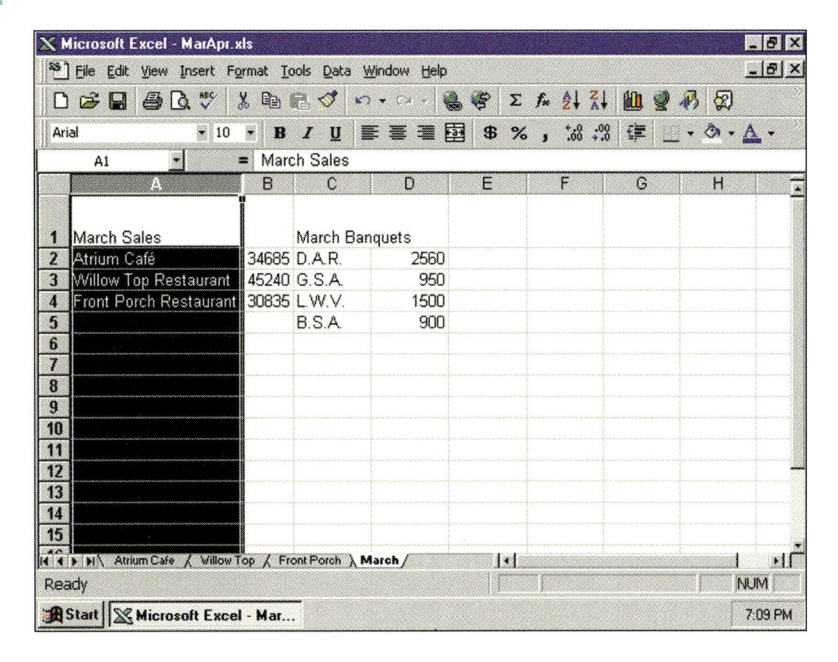

4 Choose Edit, Delete.

EX-114

5 Select cells C2 and D2 and choose Edit, Delete.

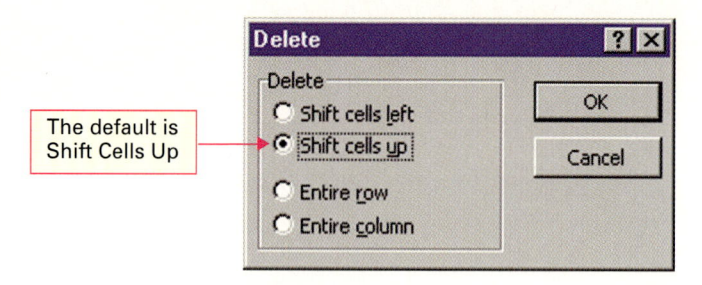

The default is Shift Cells Up → (Shift cells up option in Delete dialog box)

6 Click OK.

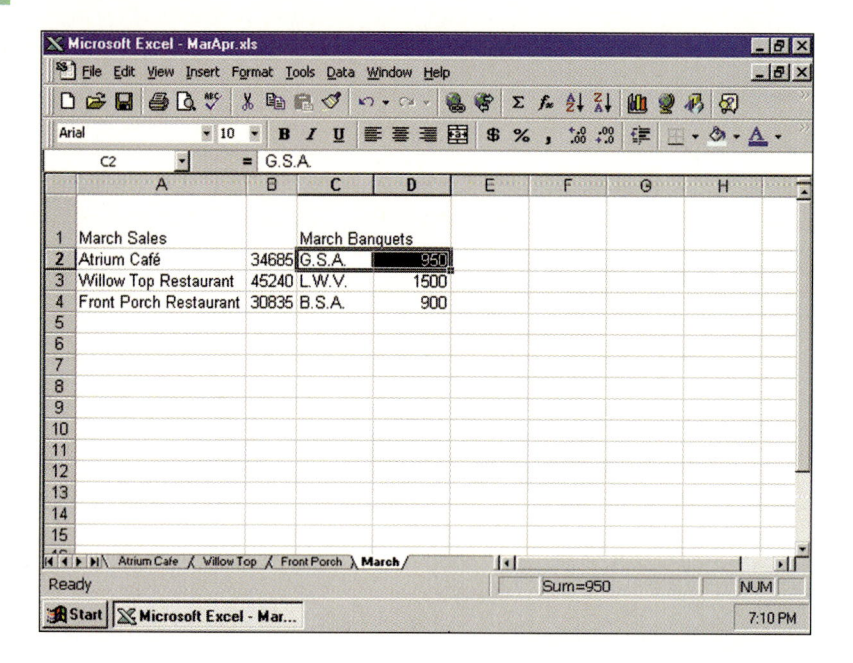

Creating Headers and Footers

A *header* prints at the top of every page of a worksheet, and a *footer* prints (you guessed it) at the bottom of every page. If the workbook has multiple worksheets, you can create headers and footers for each worksheet. A header or footer created for one worksheet doesn't print on any other worksheets in the same workbook.

Project 4: Editing the Structure of a Worksheet and a Workbook   EX-115

TASK 7: TO CREATE A SIMPLE HEADER AND A FOOTER:

1 Choose View.

2 Choose Header and Footer.

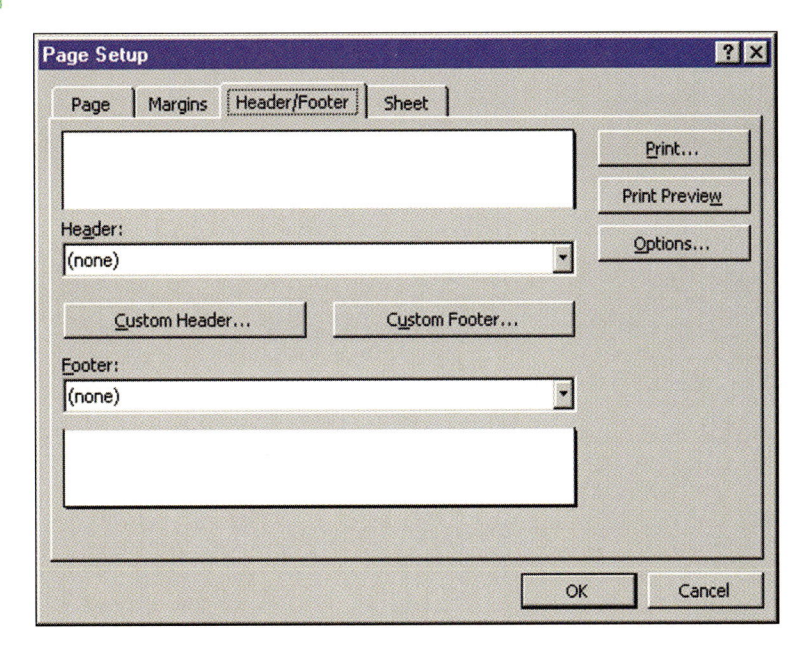

EX-116

3 Click the down arrow for the Header list and choose Page 1.

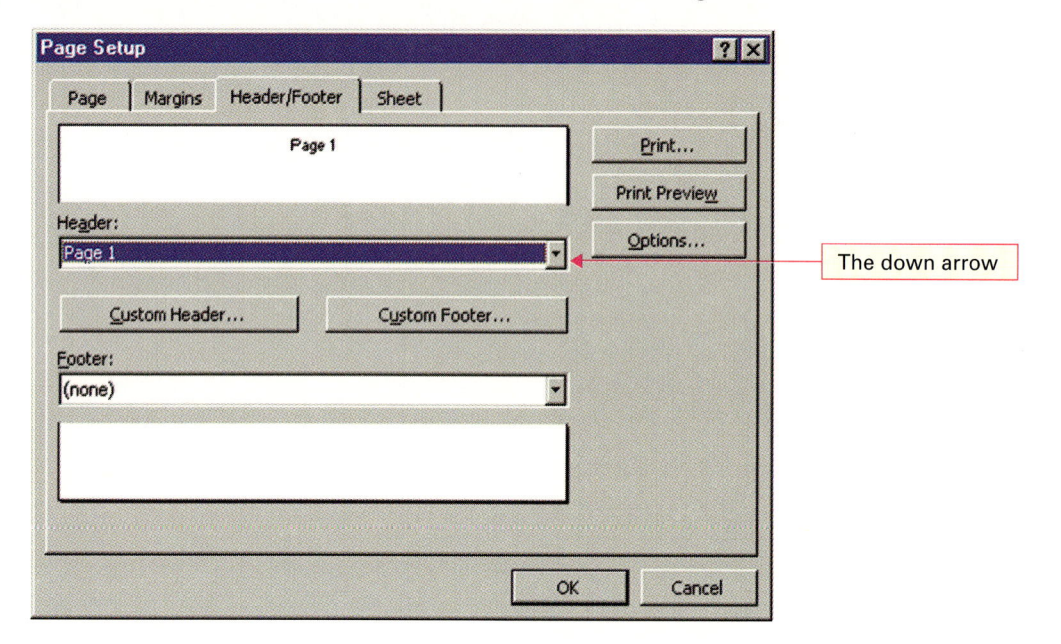

The down arrow

4 Click the down arrow for the Footer list and choose MarApr.xls.

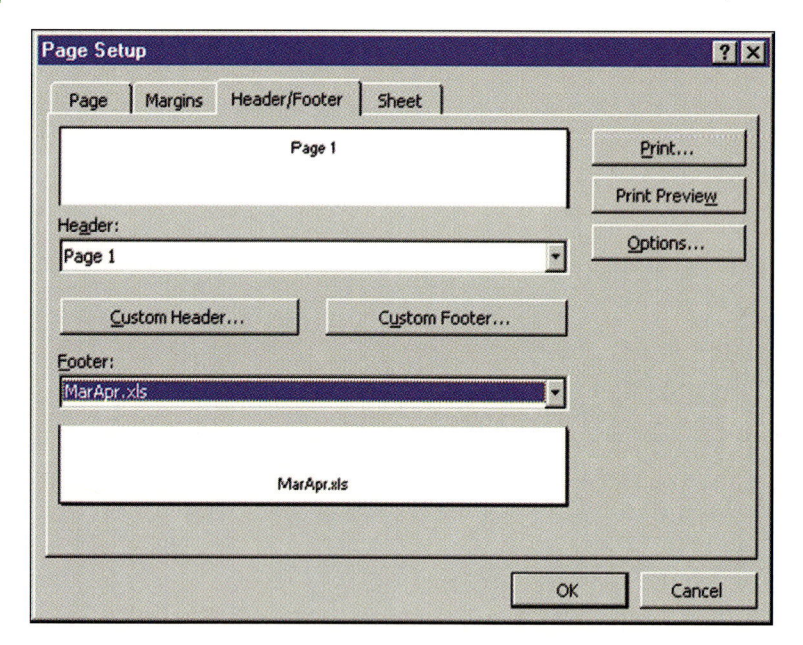

Project 4: Editing the Structure of a Worksheet and a Workbook   EX-117

5 Click Print Preview.

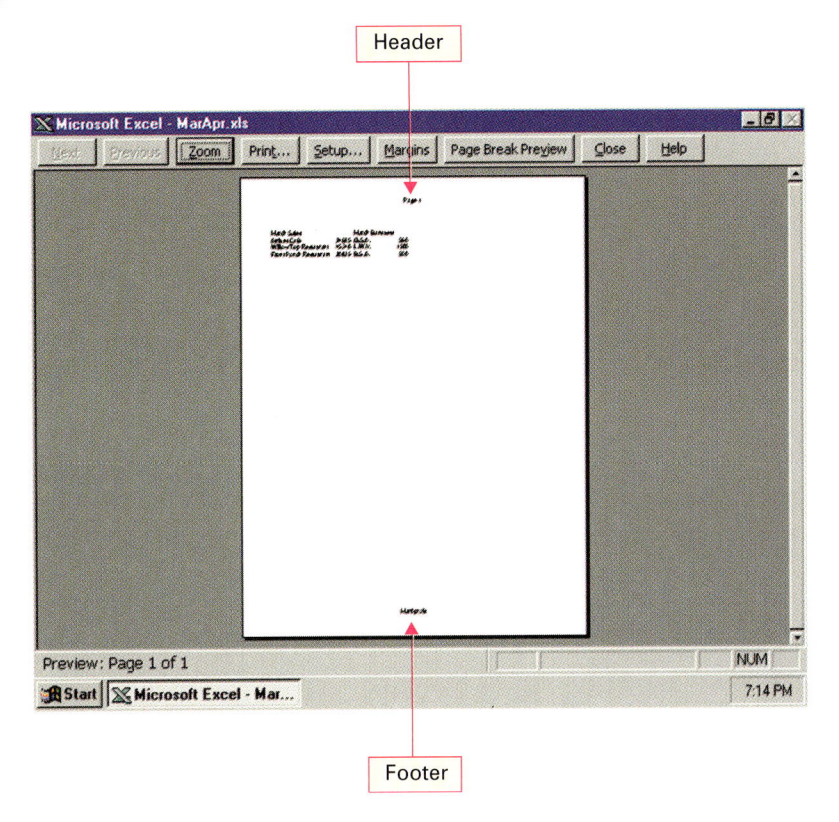

Header

Footer

6 Click Close.
The preview closes, and the worksheet displays in Normal view.

Creating a Custom Header and Footer

If you don't want to use the text supplied for a simple header or footer, you can create a custom header or footer and type the text that you want. Custom headers and footers are divided into three typing areas. The area on the left is left-justified, the area in the middle is centered, and the area on the right is right-justified.

TASK 8: TO CREATE A CUSTOM HEADER AND FOOTER:

1 Click the Atrium Café tab.
The Atrium Café worksheet displays.

2 Choose View, Headers and Footers. The Page Setup dialog box displays.

3 Click Custom Header.

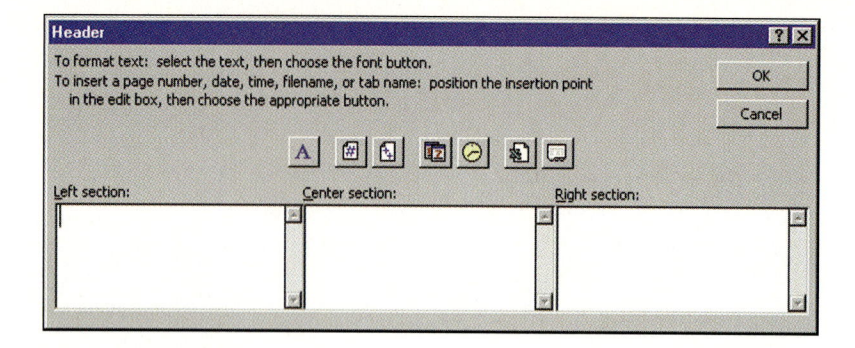

EX-118

4 Type **Sales Report**, press TAB twice, and click the Date button. (When you click the Date button instead of typing the date, Excel adjusts the date to the current date each time the workbook is used.)

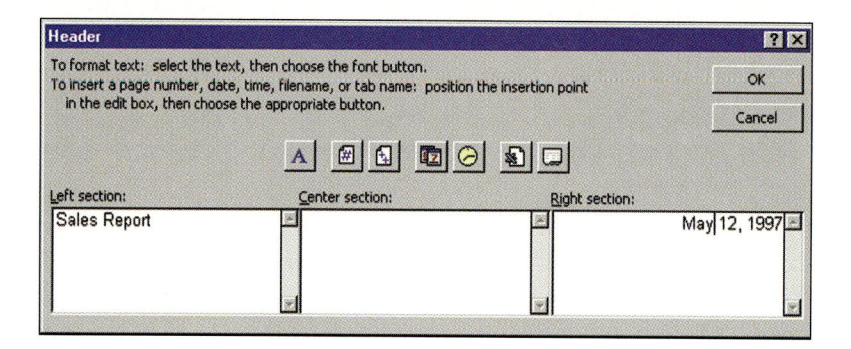

5 Click OK.
The Header dialog box closes and the Page Setup dialog box reappears.

6 Click Custom Footer.

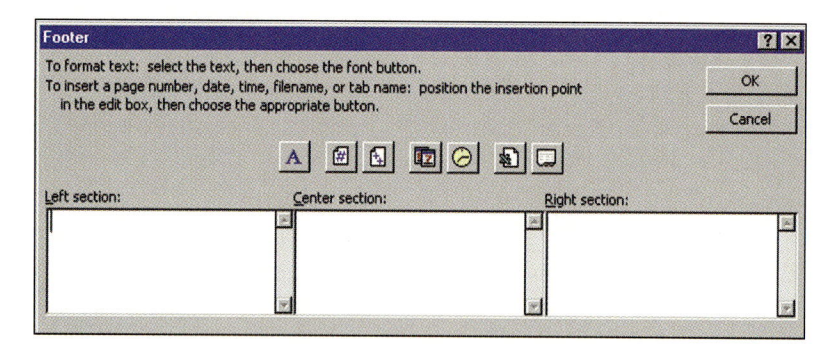

7 Press TAB and type **Prepared by Accounting**.

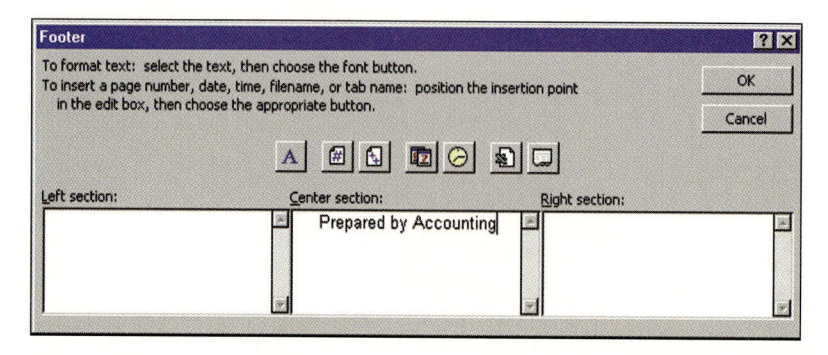

8 Click OK.
The Footer dialog box closes.

9 Click Print Preview.

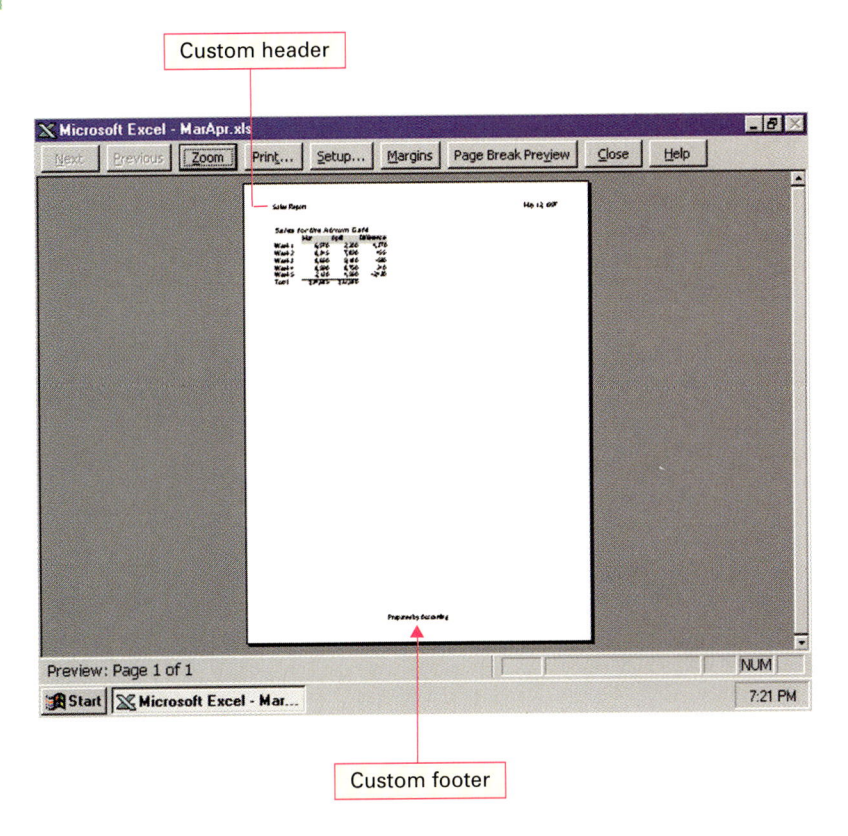

Custom header

Custom footer

10 Click Close.
The Print Preview closes, and the worksheet displays in Normal view.

The Conclusion

Save the worksheet as *MarApr2.xls* and close the file.

Summary and Exercises

Summary

- You can insert and delete worksheets, as well as rearrange them.
- You can change the width of columns and the height of rows.
- You can insert columns, rows, and cells.
- You can delete columns, rows, and cells.
- You can create a header that prints at the top of the page and a footer that prints at the bottom of a page. Headers and footers do not appear on screen in Normal view.

Key Terms and Operations

Key Terms
AutoFit
footer
header

Operations
change the height of a row
change the width of a column
create a footer
create a header
delete a cell
delete a column
delete a row
delete a worksheet
insert a cell
insert a column
insert a row
insert a worksheet
move a worksheet

Study Questions

Multiple Choice

1. A header prints at the
   a. top of every page in a workbook.
   b. bottom of every page in a workbook.
   c. top of every page in a worksheet.
   d. bottom of every page in a worksheet.

2. When you delete a column,
   a. the data in the column is deleted but the cells remain in the worksheet.
   b. the data in the column is deleted and so are the cells.
   c. the column is really just hidden.
   d. the column is moved to the end of the worksheet.

3. When you insert a cell, the other cells move
   a. down.
   b. to the left.
   c. to the right.
   d. down or to the right, as specified by the user.

4. A footer prints at the
   a. top of every page in a workbook.
   b. bottom of every page in a workbook.
   c. top of every page in a worksheet.
   d. bottom of every page in a worksheet.

5. AutoFit can adjust the width of
   a. only one column at a time.
   b. only a row.
   c. columns or rows.
   d. the page.

6. A custom header
   a. is divided into three typing areas.
   b. is created by choosing Format, Header and Footer.
   c. isn't visible in Print Preview mode.
   d. uses default data, such as the page number or the name of the file.

7. If you delete a cell,
   a. the data is deleted.
   b. the cell is deleted and the data displays in the next cell.
   c. the data and the cell are deleted.
   d. None of the above.

8. When you delete a cell, the other cells move
   a. up.
   b. down.
   c. to the left.
   d. up or to the left, as specified by the user.

9. When you drag to change the column width, the pointer displays as
   a. a four-headed arrow.
   b. an arrow.
   c. a two-headed arrow.
   d. a hand.

10. To insert a column, first
    a. select the column where you want the new column to go.
    b. click in the column where you want the new column to go.
    c. A or B
    d. None of the above.

Short Answer
1. How do you insert multiple rows?
2. How do you insert multiple columns?
3. What is a custom header?
4. How do you delete a worksheet?
5. How do you delete a row?
6. How do you delete a cell?
7. How do you create a header with the filename in the center?
8. If the row height adjusts automatically, why would you need to change the height of a row?

9. How do you move a worksheet?

10. How do you see a header or footer without actually printing the worksheet?

For Discussion

1. When would it be an advantage to use AutoFit instead of dragging columns to change the width?

2. Discuss the advantages of using a custom header or footer.

3. Describe a circumstance in which it would be preferable to insert a cell instead of a row.

4. What precautions should you take before deleting a column or a row?

Review Exercises

1. Editing the MarApr2 Workbook

In this exercise you will enhance the worksheet and create a footer.

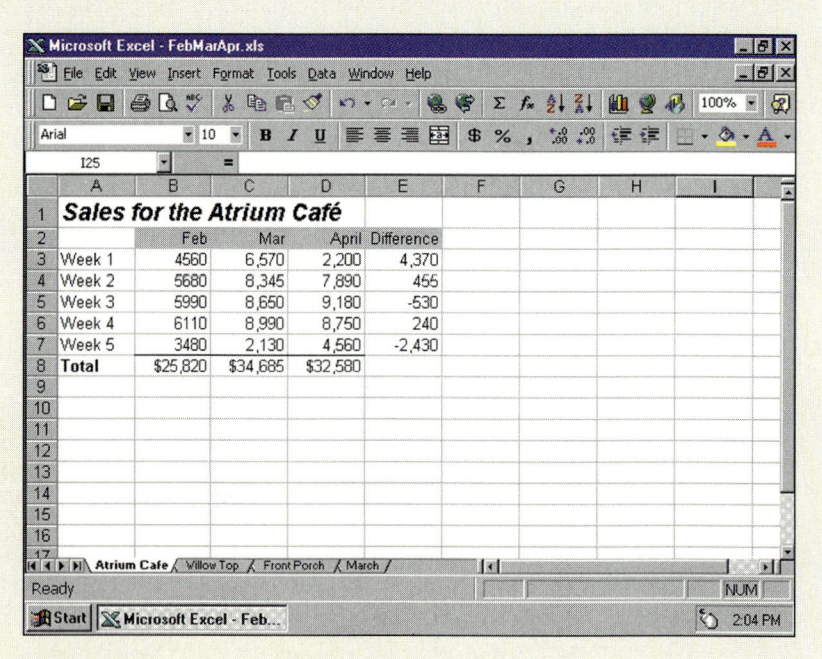

Figure 4.2

1. Open *MarApr2.xls* and click the Atrium Café tab, if necessary.

2. Insert a column before column B and type this information:

    B2: **Feb**

    B3: **4560**

    B4: **5680**

    B5: **5990**

    B6: **6110**

    B7: **3480**

    B8: **=SUM(B3:B7)**

3. Apply a gray fill to cell B2, apply a border to the bottom of cell B7, and format cell B8 with a Currency format (no decimal places) and remove the bold.

4. Create a footer for the Willow Top worksheet that says "Located in The Grande Hotel" and center the footer.

5. Save the file as *FebMarApr.xls* and close it.

2. Creating a Sales Workbook for the Sandwich Shops and Snack Bars

In this exercise, you will create a workbook that can be used to track the sales of all the sandwich shops and snack bars at The Willows Resort.

1. Download the file *Willows.doc* from the Addison Wesley Longman web site (http://www.aw.com./is/select), or ask your instructor for this file. Open the file and find the list of sandwich shops and snack bars.

2. Create a workbook with a worksheet for each of the nine shops and name each worksheet with the name of the shop.

3. Type a title on each worksheet that says "Sales for *xxx*," where *xxx* is the name of the sandwich shop or snack bar. In column A, starting in cell A3, list the weeks in the month (Week 1, Week 2, and so on) and the word "Total" (as in Figure 4.2). In cells B2, C2, and D2, list the first three months of the year (Jan, Feb, and Mar).

4. Create a footer with a centered page number for each worksheet.

5. Save the file as *ShopSales.xls*.

Assignments

1. Creating a Banquet Workbook

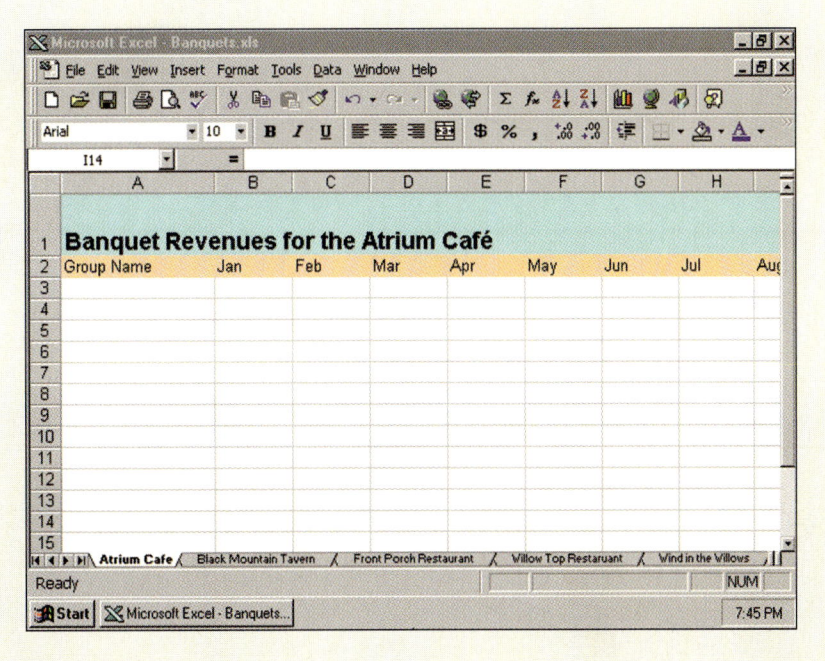

Figure 4.3

Create a workbook with five worksheets and name each worksheet as follows: Atrium Café, Willow Top Restaurant, Wind in the Willows, Front Porch Restaurant, and Black Mountain Tavern. Arrange the worksheets in alphabetical order. Add the text and formatting shown in Figure 4.3 to all the worksheets. (Remember, you can enter the same data on multiple worksheets at the same time.) Save the file as *Banquets.xls* and close it.

2. Creating a Shopping List (Optional Exercise)

Take an international shopping trip via the Planet Shopping Network (http://www.planetshopping.com). Create a workbook that lists the items you would like to buy, their prices (including any shipping, handling, taxes, and duties), and their Web addresses. Use the SUM formula to total the prices and other costs. Create a worksheet for each shopping category (apparel, books, music, jewelry, automobiles, and so on). Save the workbook as *ShopTilYouDrop.xls*.

PROJECT 5

Creating a More Complex Workbook

Well, you're getting pretty good at this, so you're probably ready for something more challenging. This project provides both challenge and fun.

Objectives

After completing this project, you will be able to:

➤ **Copy data from another workbook**
➤ **Sort data**
➤ **Enter formulas with relative references**
➤ **Use headings in formulas**
➤ **Enter formulas with absolute references**
➤ **Create and modify a chart**

The Challenge

Ruth Lindsey, the manager of most of the gift shops at The Willows Resort, would like for you to work on an inventory of the ten top selling items and create some charts for the first quarter sales.

EX-125

The Solution

You will copy data from an existing workbook into the inventory workbook, enter new data, and create formulas to calculate the number of items that you need to order and the wholesale prices of the items. Additionally, you will create a chart for the first quarter sales and a chart for the January sales. Figure 5.1 shows the results.

You can download the files needed for this project form the Addison Wesley Longman web site (http://www.aw.com./is/select) or you can obtain them from your instructor.

The Setup

So that your screen will match the illustrations in this chapter and to ensure that all the tasks in this project will function as described, you should set up Excel as described in Table 5.1. Because these are the default settings for the toolbars and view, you may not need to make any changes to your setup.

Table 5.1: Excel Settings

Location	Make these settings:
View, Toolbars	Deselect all toolbars except Standard and Formatting.
View	Use the Normal view and display the Formula Bar and Status Bar.

Copying Data from Another Workbook

You have copied data from one range to another on the same worksheet, and you have copied data from one worksheet to another in the same workbook. Now you will copy data from one workbook to another. The procedure is very similar to what you have already learned.

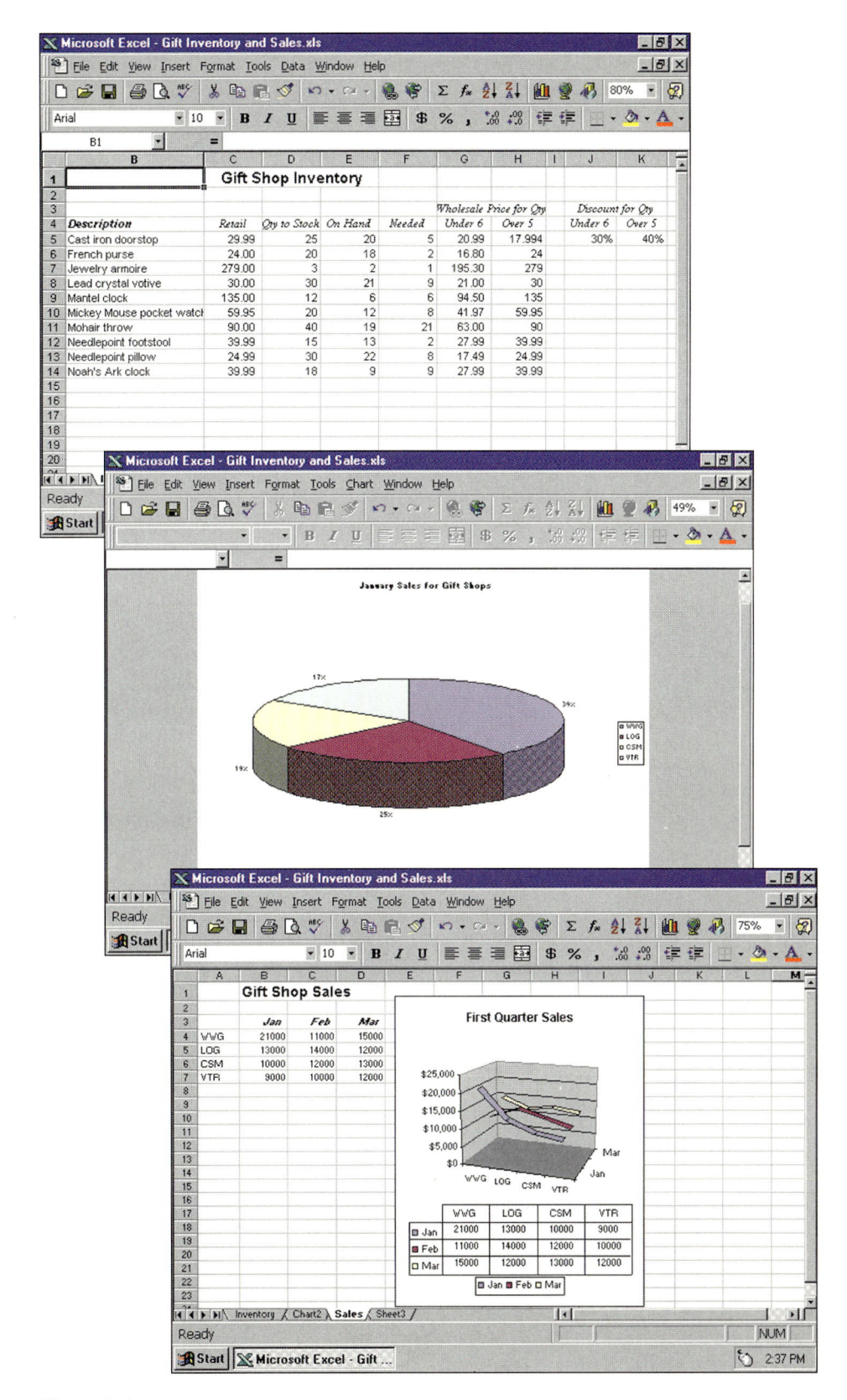

Figure 5.1

EX-128

TASK 1: TO COPY DATA FROM ANOTHER WORKBOOK:

1 Open *Giftinv.xls*.

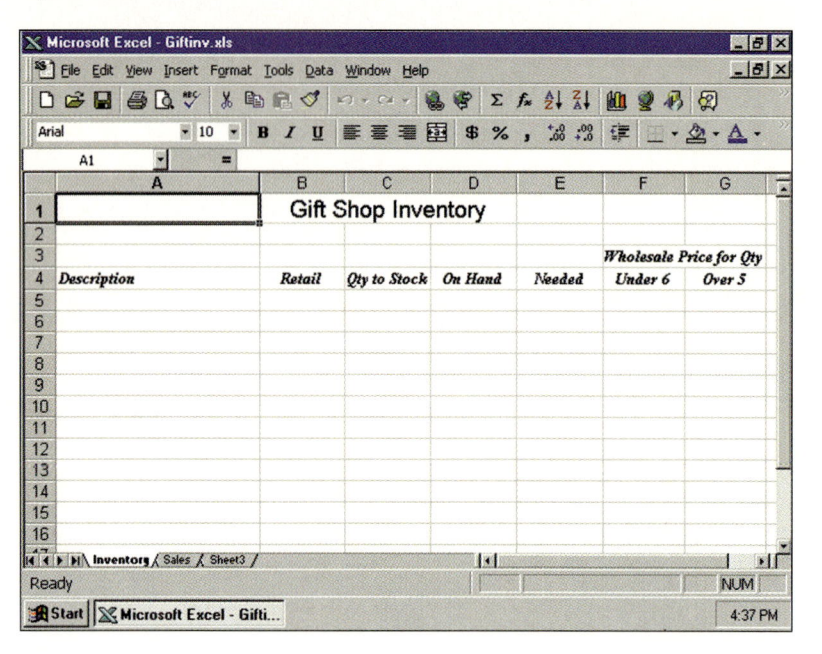

2 Open *TopTen.xls* and select the range A4:B13.

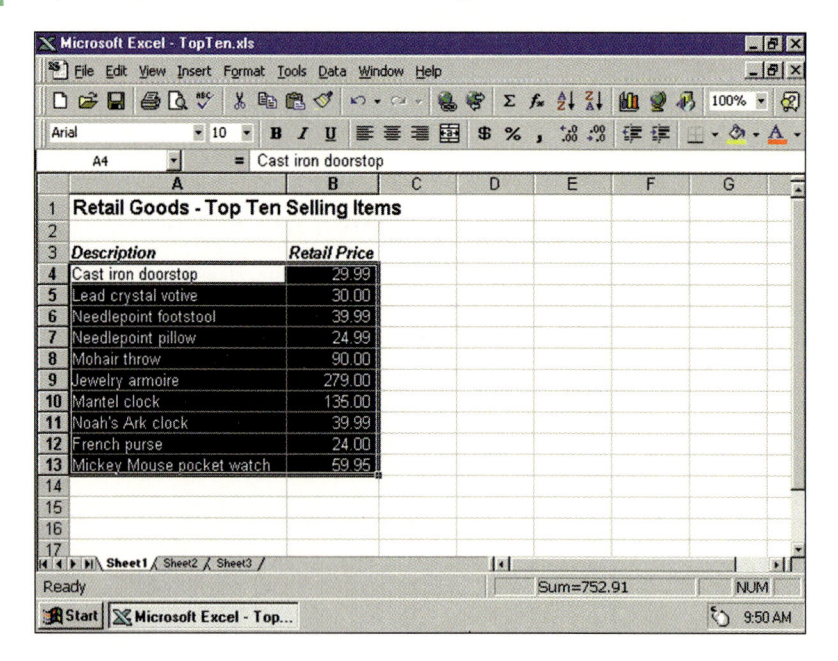

3 Click 📋.
The data is copied to the Clipboard.

4 Choose Window, Giftinv.xls.
The *Giftinv.xls* workbook displays.

5 Click in cell A5 and click 📋.

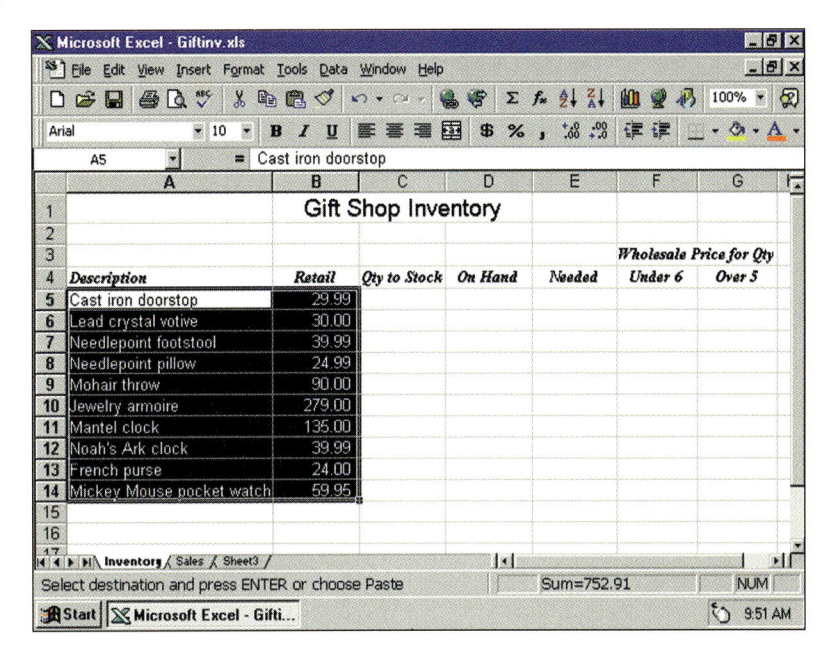

6 Choose Window, TopTen.xls.
The *TopTen.xls* workbook displays.

7 Click ⊠ in the menu bar.
The *TopTen.xls* workbook closes, and the Giftinv.xls workbook displays.

Sorting Data

You can sort columns of data in an Excel worksheet in ascending order or descending order. The Standard toolbar has a button for each function.

TASK 2: TO SORT DATA:

1 Make sure that the range A5:B14 is still selected.
When you sort data, you must be careful to select all the columns that should be included in the sort. When selecting the rows to include, don't include the row with the column headings.

2 Click the Sort Ascending button.

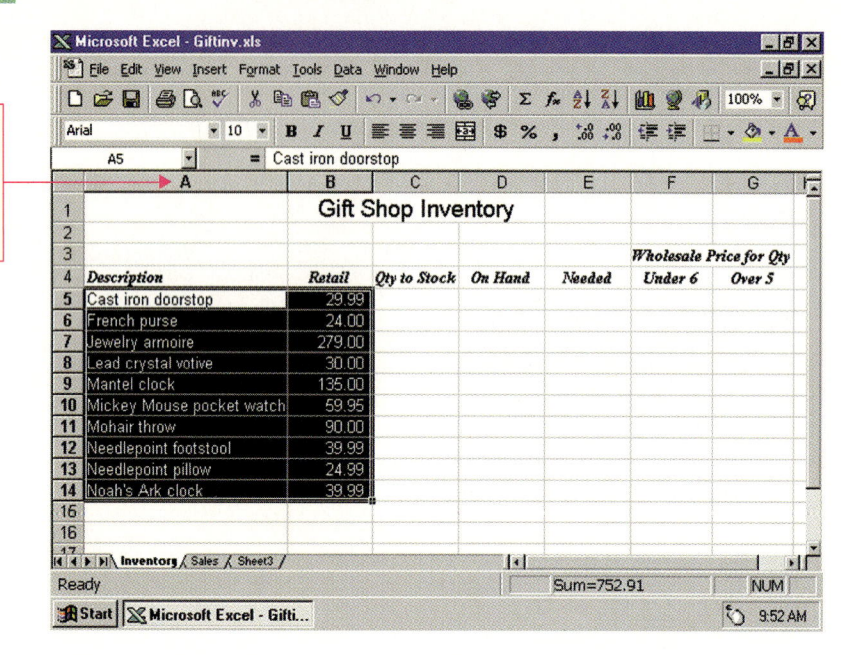

When you use the Sort buttons on the toolbar, Excel automatically sorts by the left-most selected column

Tip If you want to sort a range by any column other than the first column, you must use the Sort command on the Data menu. This command displays a dialog box that allows you to specify the column you want to sort on and the order of the sort. You also can specify two other columns to sort on after the first column is sorted. Check it out. Choose Data, Sort to see the dialog box.

Entering Formulas with Relative References

All the formulas you have used so far have included cell addresses that are relative references. A *relative reference* is an address that Excel automatically changes when the formula is copied to another location. For example, if the formula =A1+A2 is in cell A3 and you copy it to cell B3, Excel changes the formula in column B to refer to the cells in column B, and the formula becomes =B1+B2. Generally, this is precisely what you want, and you are happy that Excel can make such intelligent decisions on its own.

Perhaps you are wondering how this works. Here's the scoop: Excel doesn't interpret a relative cell address in a formula as the actual cell address but rather as a location relative to the location of the formula. For example, Excel interprets the formula =A1+A2 in cell A3 as "Add the cell that is two rows above the formula in the same column to the cell that is one row above the formula in the same column." Therefore, when you copy the formula to any other column, the formula will add the cells that are two rows and one row above the location of the formula.

Project 5: Creating a More Complex Workbook   EX-131

TASK 3: TO ENTER AND COPY A FORMULA WITH RELATIVE ADDRESSES:

1 Enter the following data in the *Qty to Stock* column and the *On Hand* column so that you can write a formula to calculate the value for the *Needed* column.

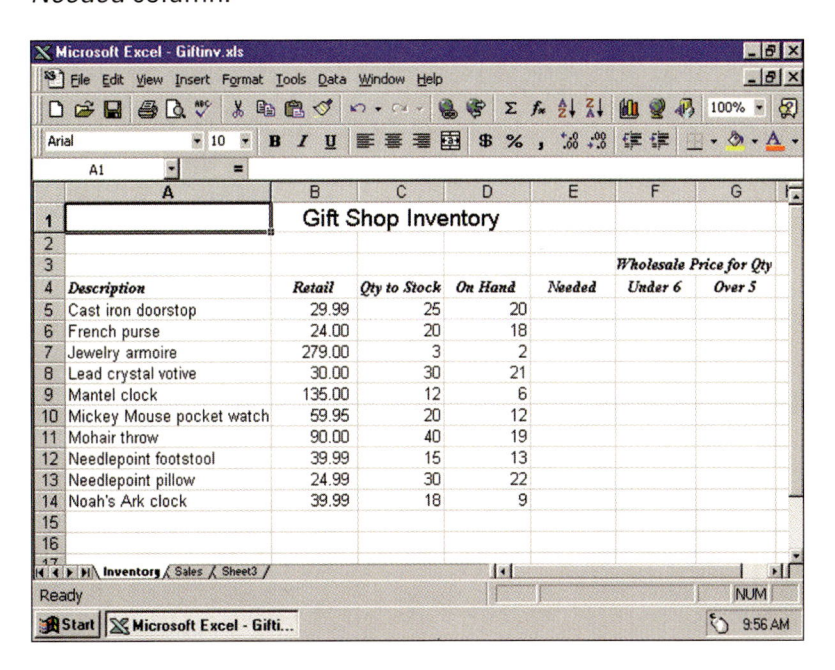

2 Click in cell E5, type **=C5–D5**, and press ENTER.

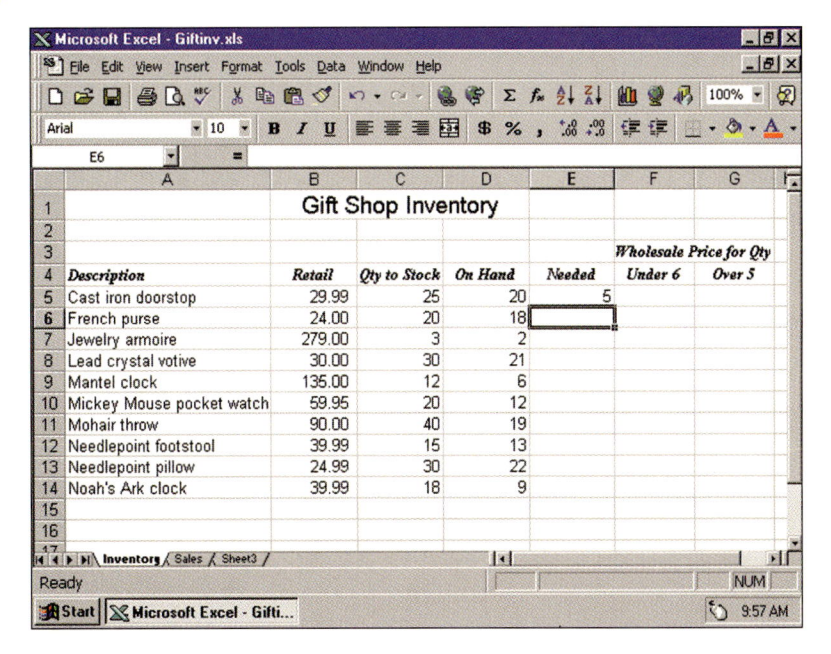

3 Copy cell E5 to the range E6:E8.

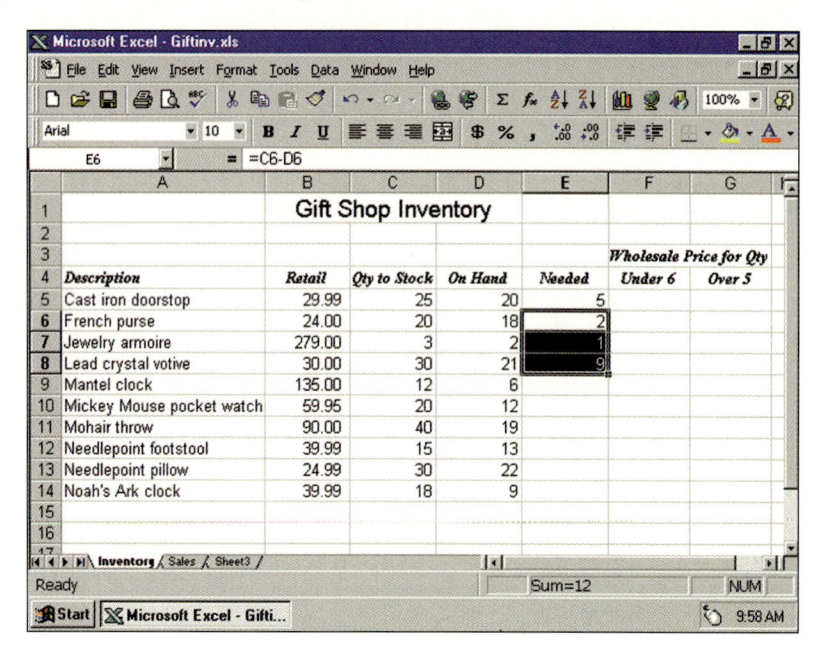

4 Click in cell E6 and notice the formula in the formula bar.

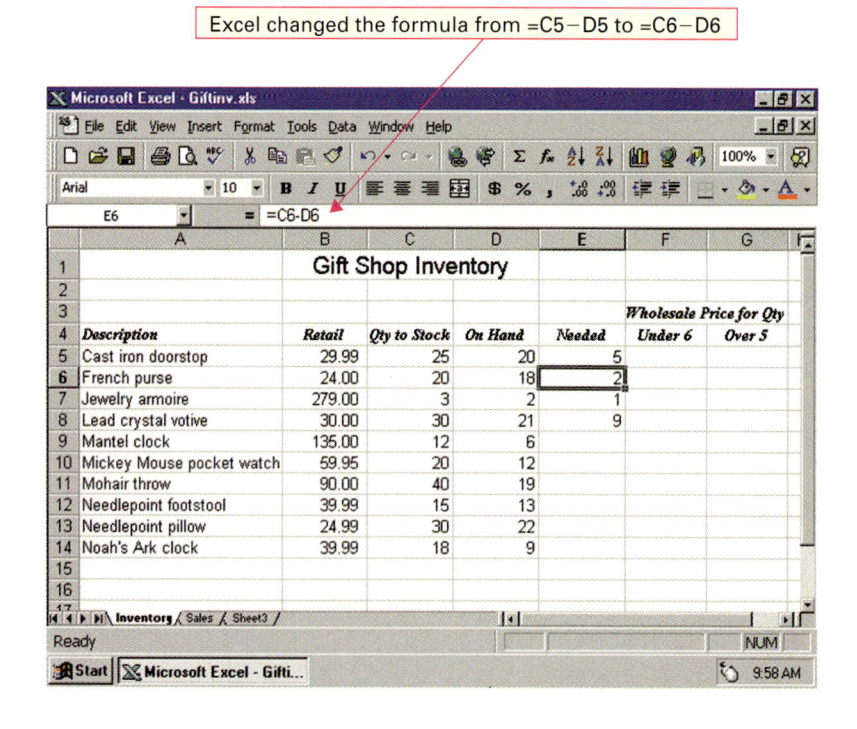

Excel changed the formula from =C5−D5 to =C6−D6

Project 5: Creating a More Complex Workbook   EX-133

Using Headings in Formulas

Using headings in formulas instead of cell addresses is a new feature in Excel 97. The *headings* feature is helpful in two ways: when you create a formula, you can think in logical terms (such as "quantity times cost") and you can easily recognize the purpose of the formula. When you see the formula "Quantity*Cost," you know immediately what it does, but the formula A1*B1 gives you very little information.

TASK 4: TO ENTER A FORMULA THAT USES HEADINGS:

1 Click in cell E9, type **=qty to stock−on hand**, and press (ENTER).
The cell displays the correct calculation.

> **Tip** You do not have to capitalize the headings in formulas.

2 Copy cell E9 to the range E10:E14.
The range also displays the correct calculations relative to the rows.

3 Click in cell E10 and look at the formula in the formula bar.
The formula in cell E10 is the same as in E9.

Entering Formulas with Absolute References

As you have already seen, when formulas with relative references are copied, the cell addresses change appropriately; however, sometimes formulas refer to a cell or range that should never be changed when the formula is copied. To prevent the cell or range address from changing, you must make the address an *absolute reference*. An absolute reference is denoted with the dollar sign symbol, as in A1.

TASK 5: TO ENTER AND COPY A FORMULA WITH AN ABSOLUTE REFERENCE:

1 Scroll the worksheet so that columns B through J are visible.

2 Click in cell F5, type **=B5−(B5*I5)**, and press (ENTER).
This formula calculates the wholesale price of the item using the discount that applies if you are ordering a quantity of less than six. The wholesale price is the retail price minus the discount (which is determined by multiplying the retail price by 30%).

3 Copy cell F5 to F6.
The answer is obviously not correct.

4 Click in cell F6 and look at the formula in the formula bar.

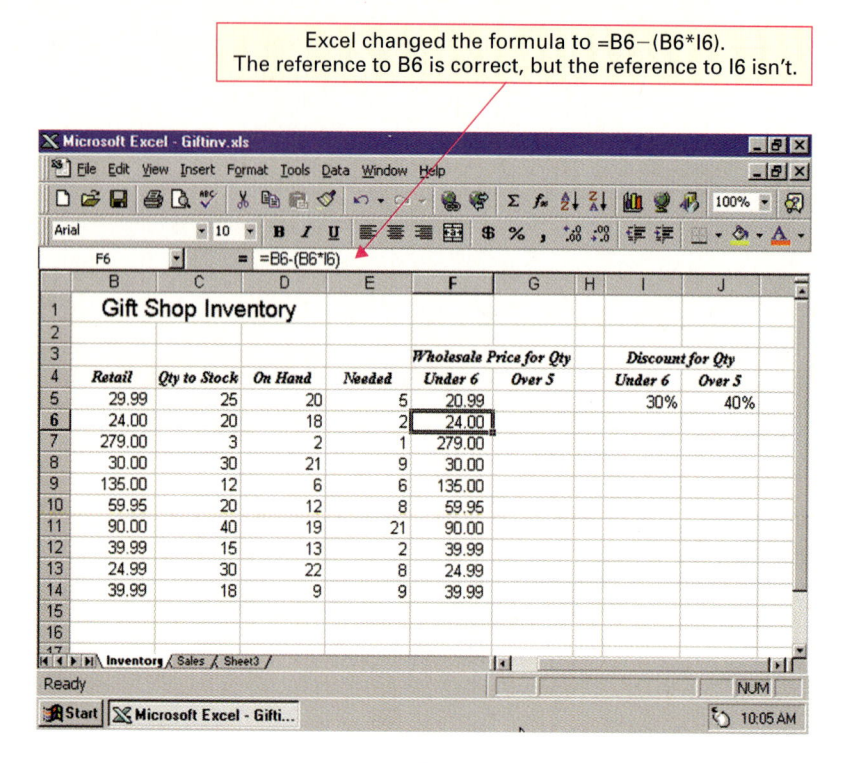

> Excel changed the formula to =B6−(B6*I6).
> The reference to B6 is correct, but the reference to I6 isn't.

5 Edit the contents of cell F5 and insert dollar signs before and after "I" so the formula looks like **=B5−(B5*I5)** and press ENTER.
The result in cell F5 is the same as before, but watch what happens when you copy it.

6 Copy cell F5 to the range F6:F13.

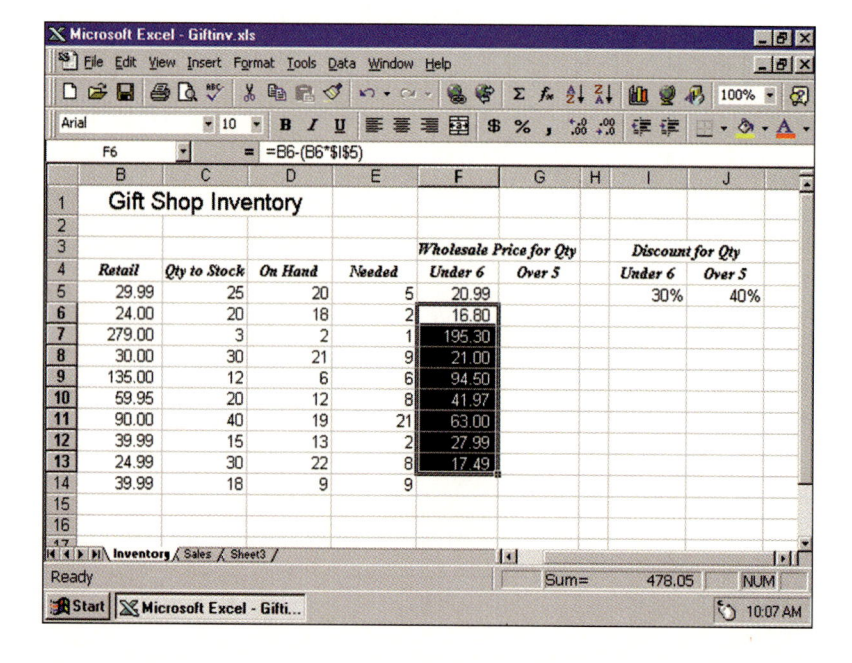

Project 5: Creating a More Complex Workbook   EX-135

Pointing to Enter Absolute References

In the previous task, you typed the complete formula in the cell, but, as you have seen in other projects, you can enter a formula with the pointing method. When you use this method, you can designate an absolute reference with the F4 key.

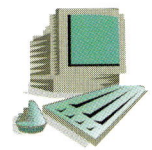

TASK 6: TO ENTER A FORMULA WITH AN ABSOLUTE REFERENCE USING THE POINTING METHOD:

1. Click in cell F14, type an equal sign (=), move to cell B14 using ←, and then type a minus sign followed by an open parenthesis.

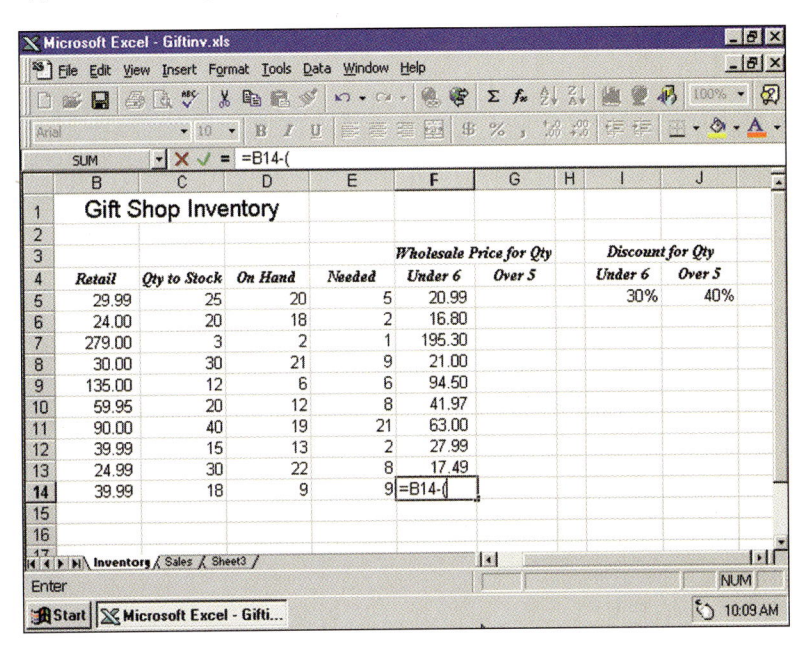

2. Move to cell B14 again, type an asterisk (*), move to cell I5, and then press F4.

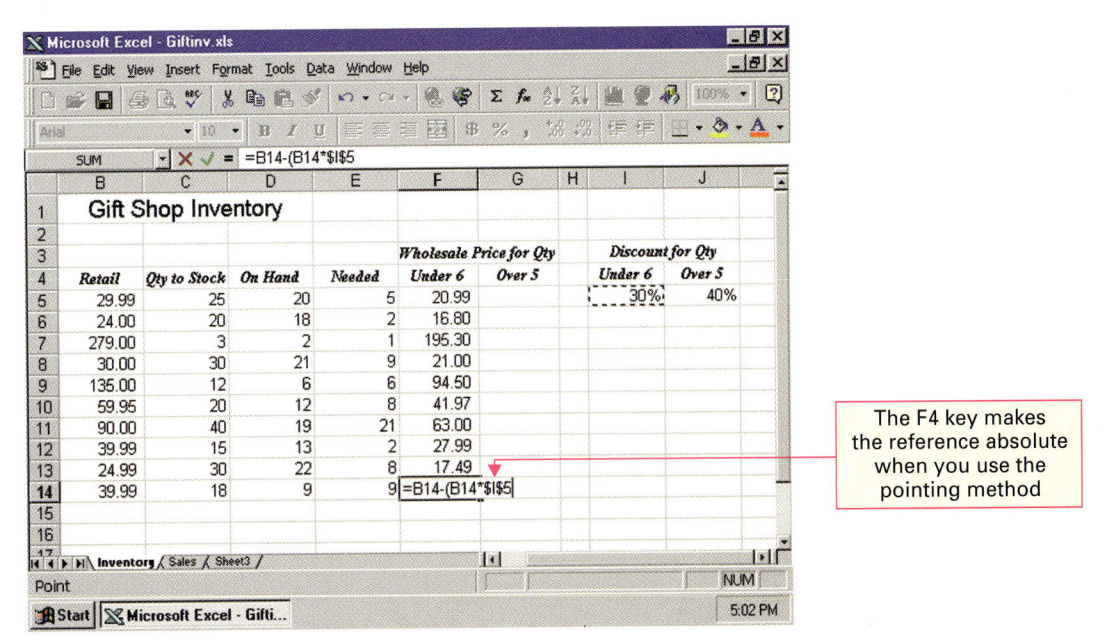

The F4 key makes the reference absolute when you use the pointing method

3 Type a closing parenthesis and press ENTER.
The correct calculation (27.99) displays in the cell.

Using Headings with Absolute References

The heading feature in Excel 97 also works with absolute references. When designating an absolute reference for a heading, only one dollar sign is used, and it precedes the heading.

TASK 7: TO ENTER AND COPY A FORMULA WITH AN ABSOLUTE REFERENCE USING HEADINGS:

1 Click in cell G5, type **=retail−(retail*$over 5)**, and press ENTER.

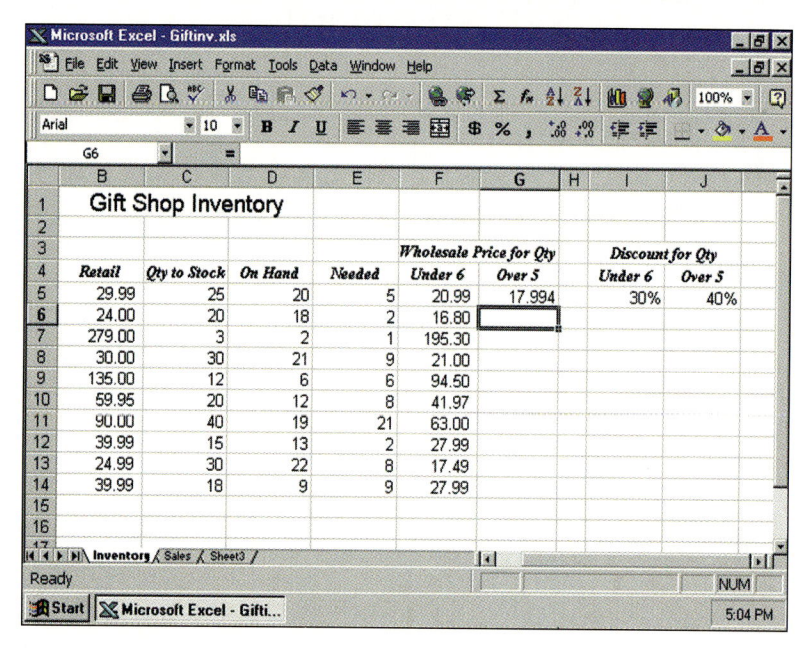

2 Copy cell G5 to the range G6:G14.
The cells display the correct computations.

Creating and Modifying a Chart

Charts present data in a worksheet in a way that numbers never can — visually. Seeing trends and data relationships is so much easier when you look at a chart than when you read numbers. To put a new spin on a tired, old saying, you might say, "A chart is worth 16,777,216 cells." The *Chart Wizard* helps you create charts in Excel.

Project 5: Creating a More Complex Workbook   EX-137

TASK 8: TO CREATE A COLUMN CHART:

1 Click the Sales tab.

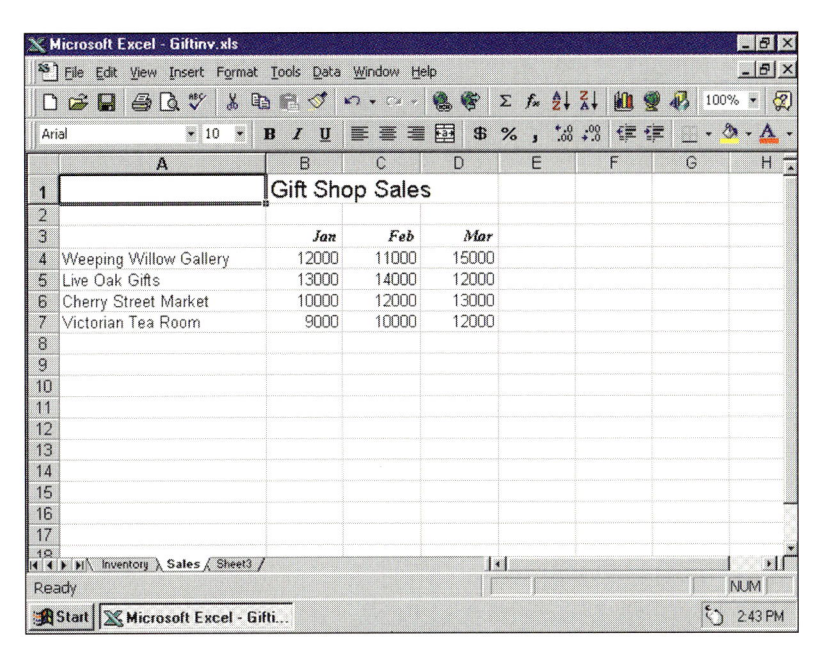

2 Select the range A3:D7 and click the Chart Wizard button.

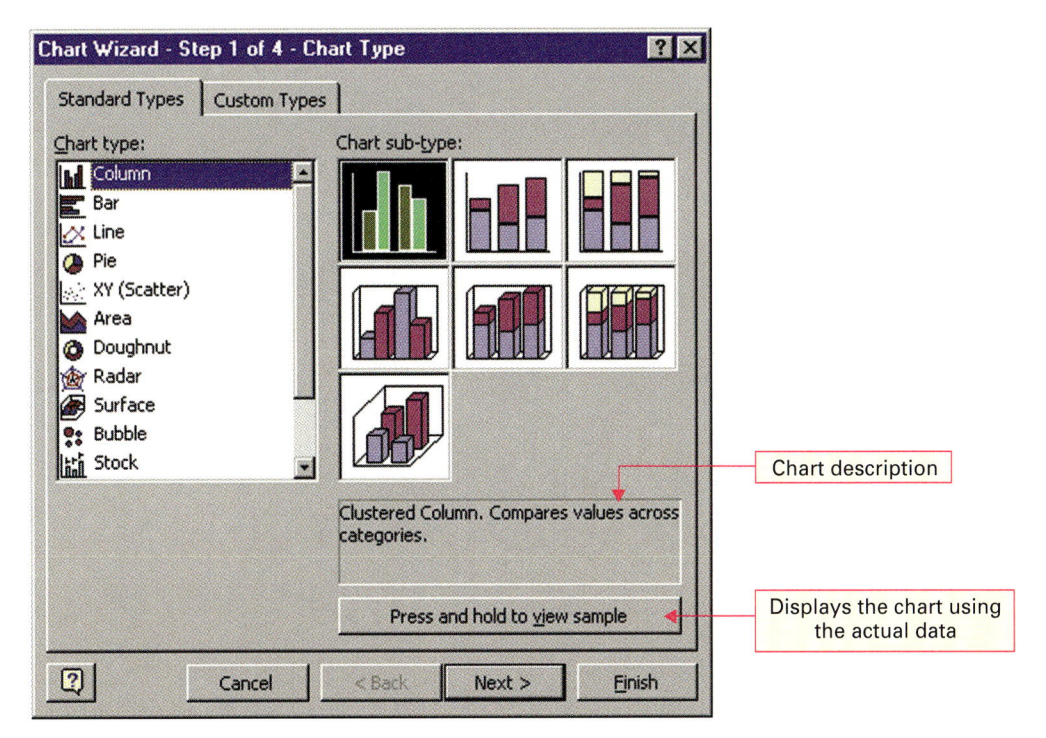

Chart description

Displays the chart using the actual data

EX-138

3 Click Next to accept the chart type.

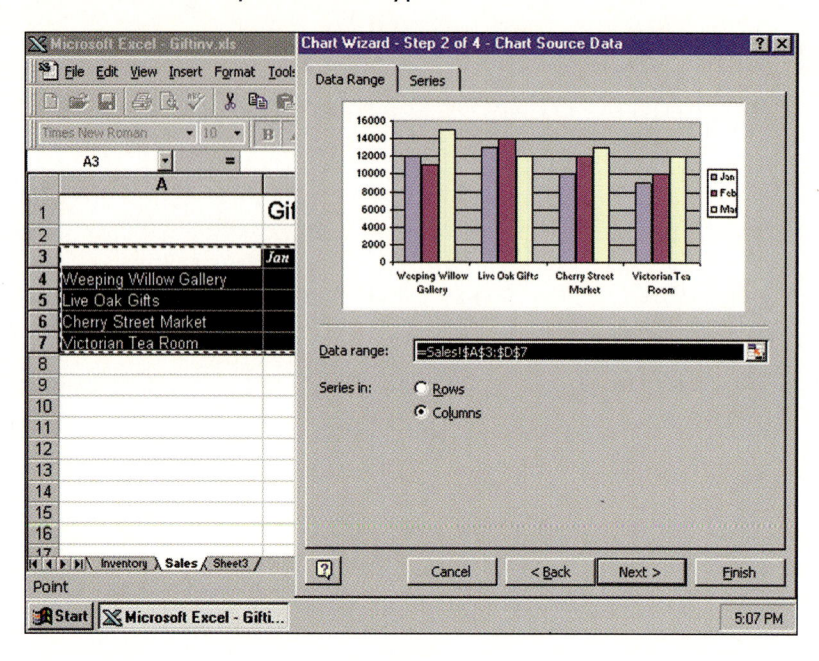

4 Click Next to accept the data range.

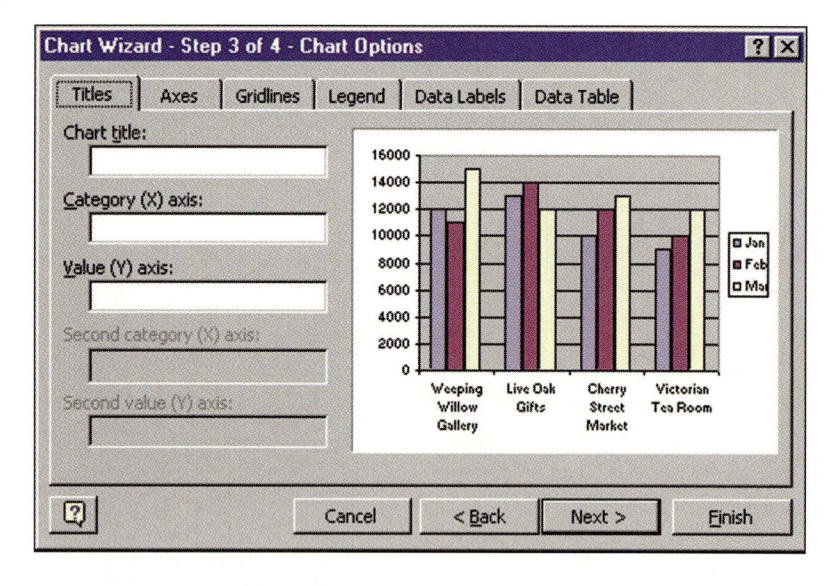

5 Type **First Quarter Sales** for the Chart title and click Next.

The chart will be placed in a new worksheet if you choose this option

The chart will be placed as an object if you choose this option. You also can select another existing sheet for this option

Project 5: Creating a More Complex Workbook   EX-139

6 Click Finish.
The chart displays in the current worksheet with *selection handles*. You may want to close the Chart toolbar to see the complete chart.

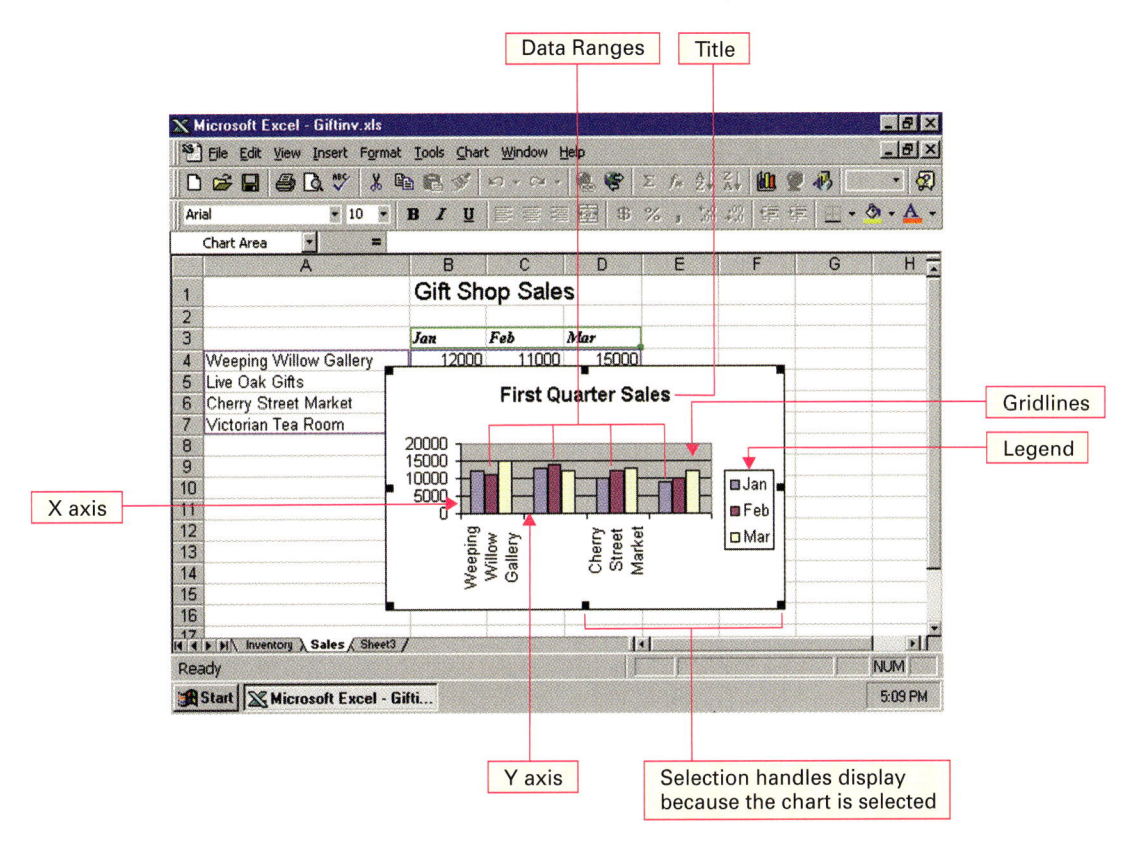

[Screenshot of Excel worksheet with chart labeled: Data Ranges, Title, Gridlines, Legend, X axis, Y axis, and "Selection handles display because the chart is selected"]

Note The Chart Wizard arbitrarily displays every other data label (in this example, Weeping Willow Gallery and Cherry Street Market), because there is too much text to show all the labels.

Moving and Sizing a Chart

When you place a chart on the same page as the worksheet, the Chart Wizard may place the chart in a location that obscures the data in the worksheet, and it may make the chart too small. Because the chart is an object, you can move it and size it however you want.

TASK 9: TO MOVE AND SIZE THE CHART:

1 Point to a blank area of the chart and drag the chart to the right of the data that created the chart.
The chart moves to the new location.

2 Point to a handle at the bottom of the chart and drag the handle down to make the chart about three rows taller.

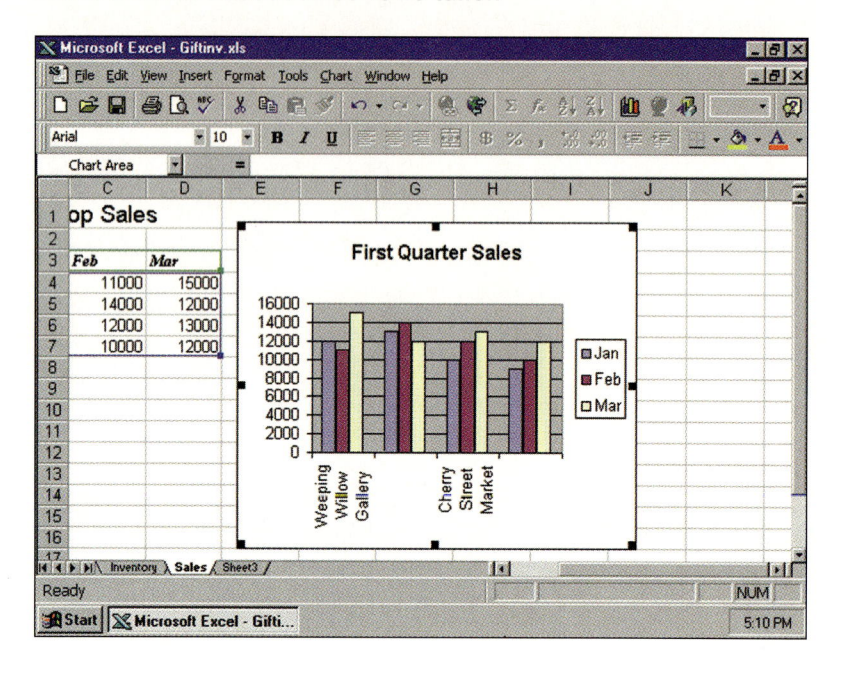

Changing Chart Data

The chart is linked to the data in the worksheet; when you change the data in the worksheet, the chart reflects the change. By the same token, when you change a value in a *data range* in the chart, the data in the worksheet reflects the change.

TASK 10: TO CHANGE CHART DATA:

1 In the worksheet, change the names of the gift shops to abbreviations as follows:
Weeping Willow Gallery: **WWG**;
Live Oak Gifts: **LOG**;
Cherry Street Market: **CSM**;
Victorian Tea Room: **VTR**.
After changing the names, make column A narrower.

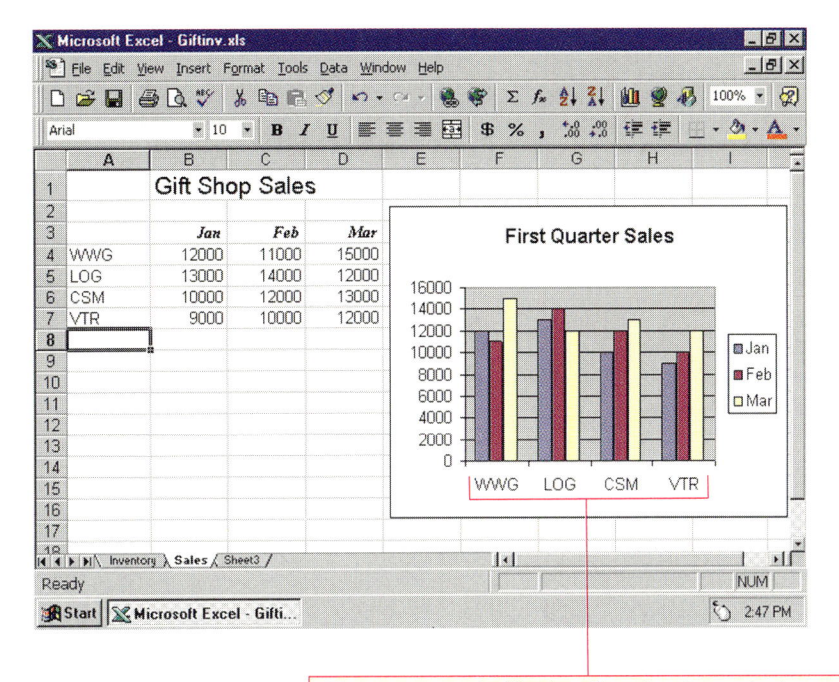

Project 5: Creating a More Complex Workbook   EX-141

The names on the X axis reflect the change in the worksheet

2 Change the value in cell B4 to 18000 and notice the change in the chart. The height of the first column increases when you change the value.

3 Click the first column in the chart to select the data range for January.

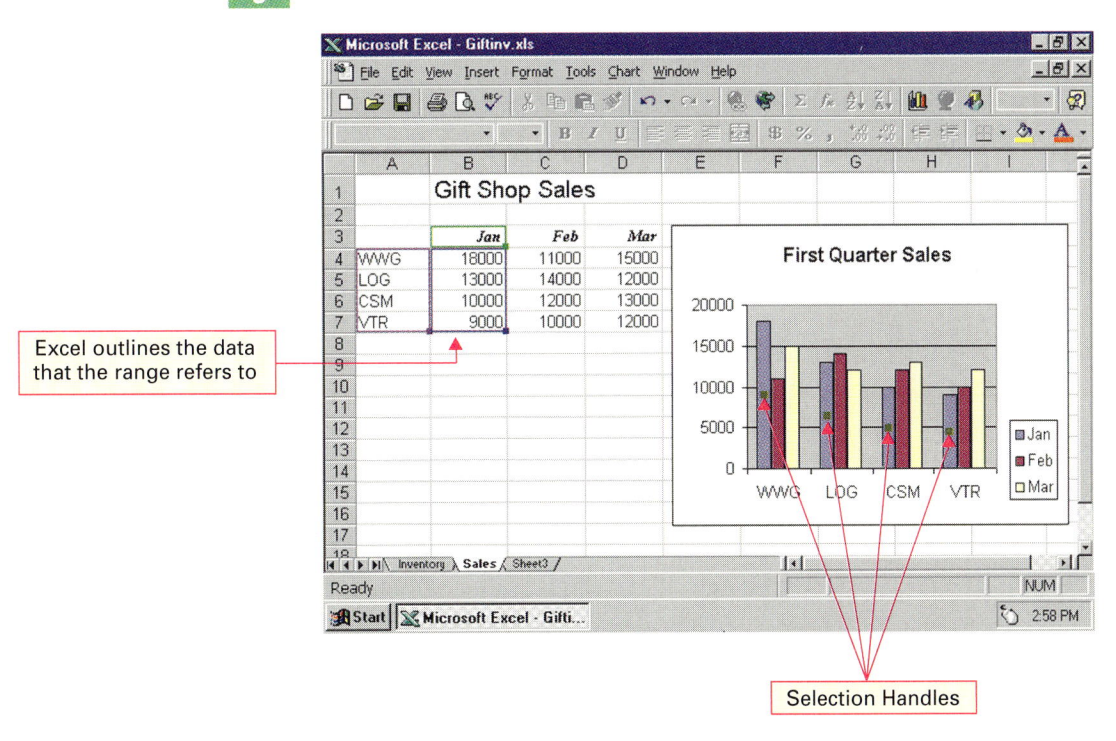

Excel outlines the data that the range refers to

Selection Handles

EX-142

4 Click the first column again.

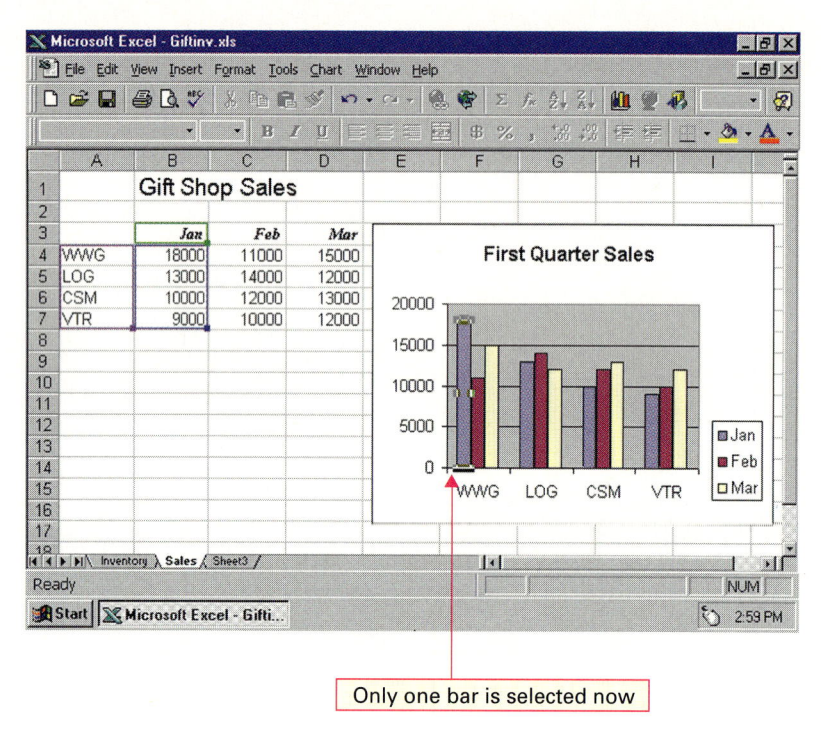

Only one bar is selected now

5 Drag the top of the column up until the value is 21000.

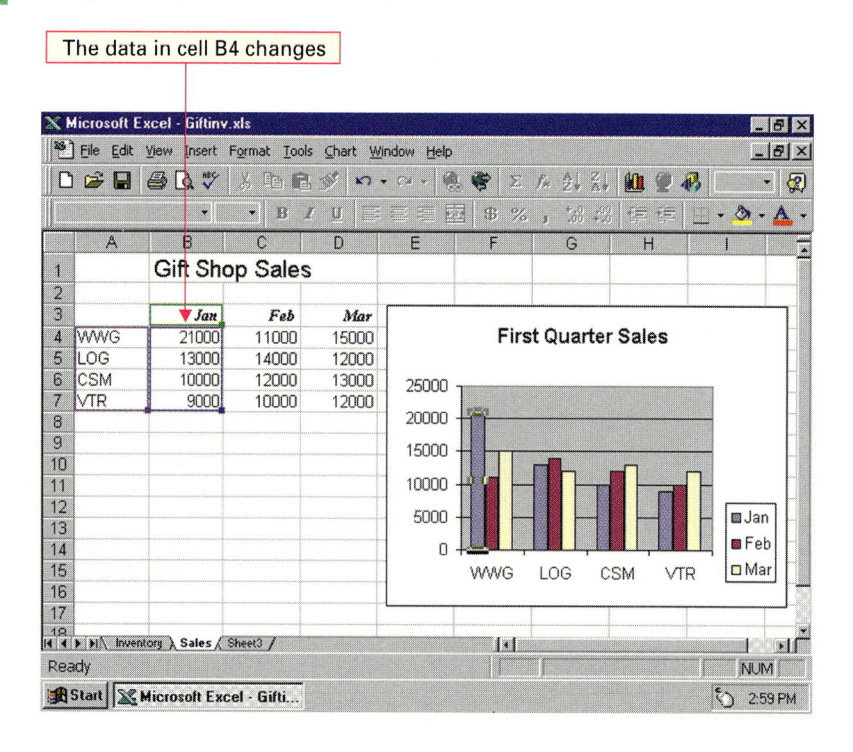

The data in cell B4 changes

Project 5: Creating a More Complex Workbook   EX-143

Formatting Chart Elements

When you create a chart with the Chart Wizard, the Chart Wizard decides how the chart elements will look. For example, the Chart Wizard uses the General number format for the scale on the Y axis. After the chart is created, you can format each element of a chart and use the settings that you want.

TASK 11: TO FORMAT CHART ELEMENTS:

1 Right-click the legend, choose Format Legend, and click the Placement tab.

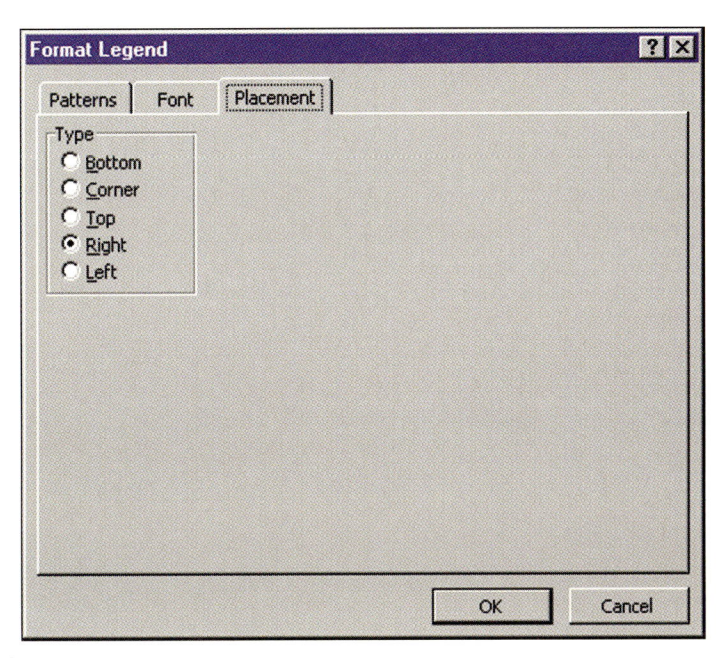

2 Select Bottom and click OK.

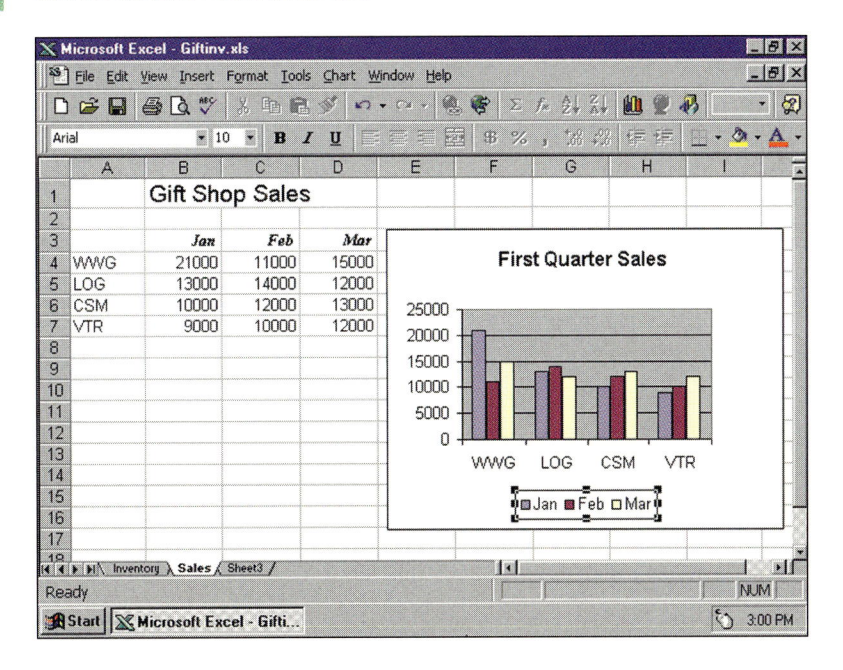

EX-144

3 Right-click the numbers on the Value axis (Y axis), choose Format Axis, and click the Number tab.

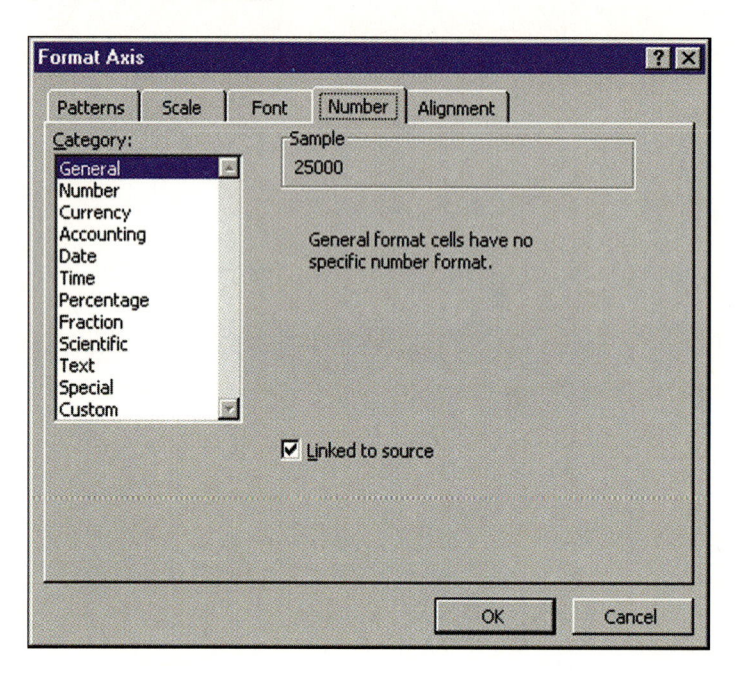

4 Select Currency, 0 decimal places, and click OK.

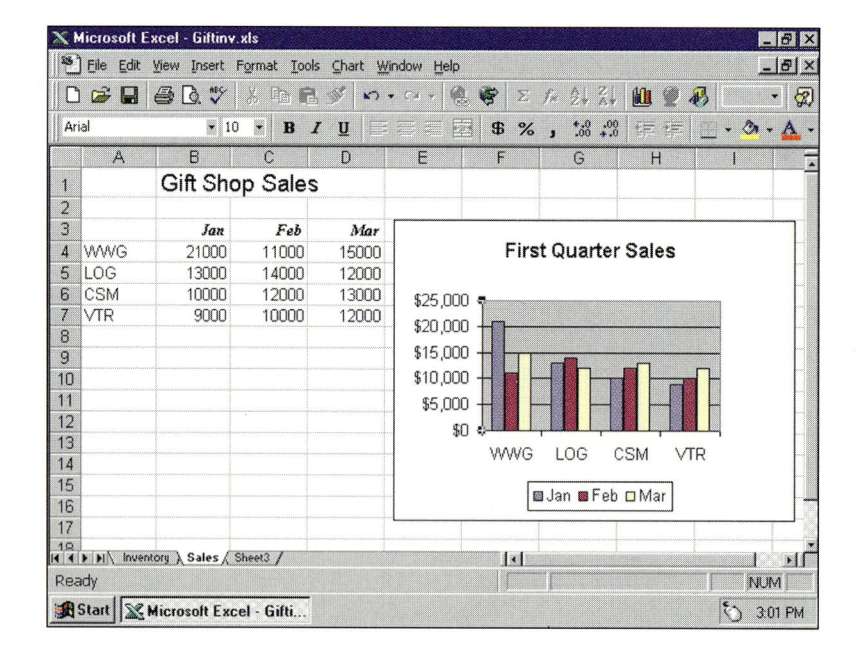

Project 5: Creating a More Complex Workbook   EX-145

5 Right-click the text on the Category axis (X axis), choose Format Axis, and click the Font tab.

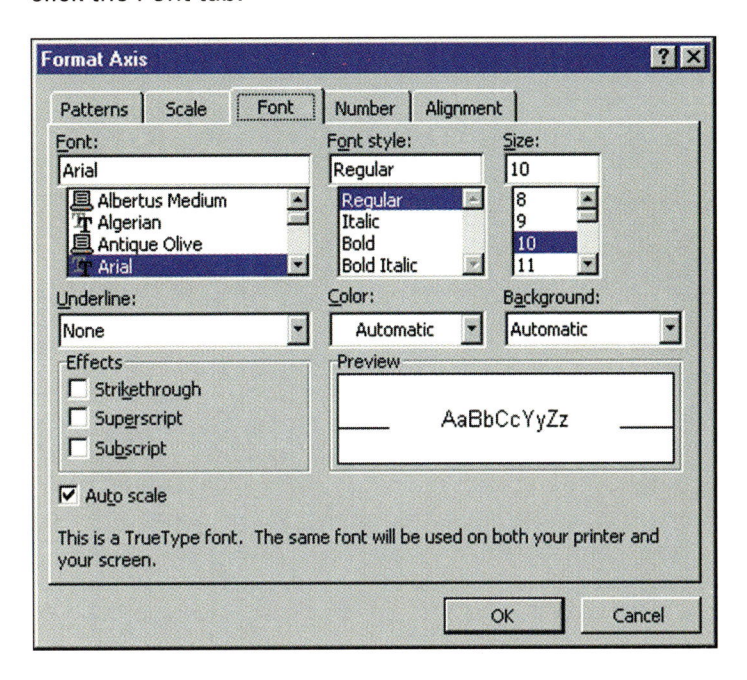

6 Select 8 for the Size and click OK.
The font size of the text is decreased.

Changing the Chart Type

Excel 97 provides many **chart types** and **chart sub-types**. Not all chart types are appropriate for the data in a workbook. Some charts are designed especially for certain types of data. For example, the Stock chart requires three series of data which must be arranged in a specific order: high, low, and close (a stock's high and low values for the day and the closing price of the stock).

TASK 12: TO CHANGE THE CHART TYPE:

1 Right-click a blank area of the chart and choose Chart type.

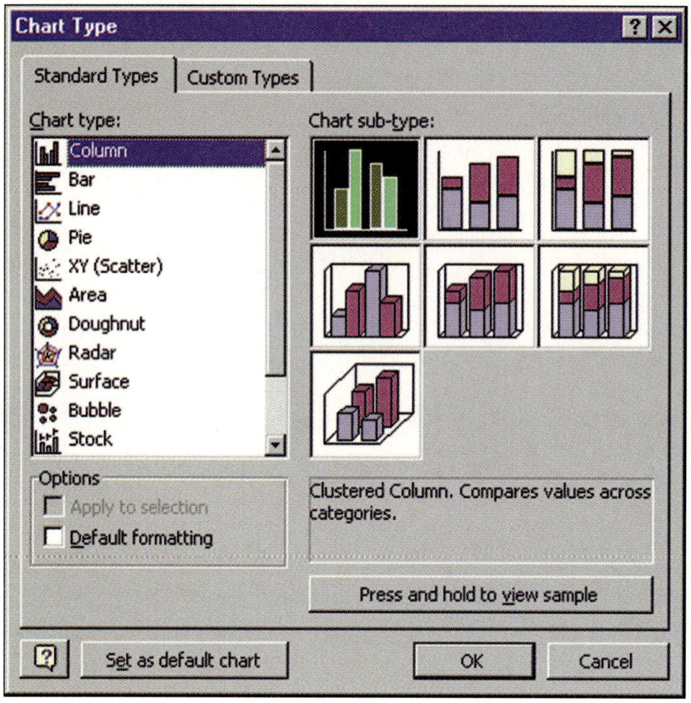

2 Select Line for Chart Type, select the 3-D line sub-type, and click OK.

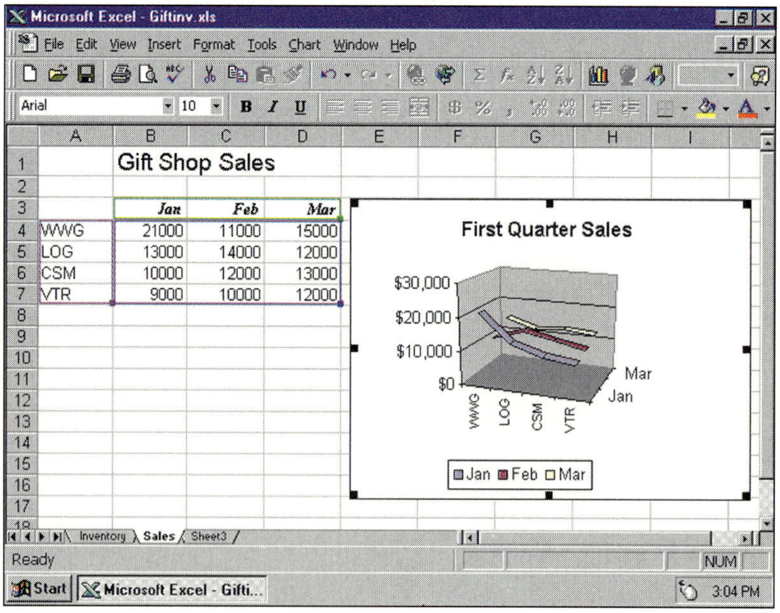

Changing the Chart Options

Settings for the chart ***titles***, ***X axis***, ***Y axis***, ***gridlines***, ***legend***, ***data labels***, and ***data table*** are all contained in the Chart Options dialog box. After you have created a chart, you can select the options that you want.

Project 5: Creating a More Complex Workbook EX-147

TASK 13: TO CHANGE THE CHART OPTIONS:

1 Right-click a blank area of the chart, choose Chart Options, and click the Data Table tab.

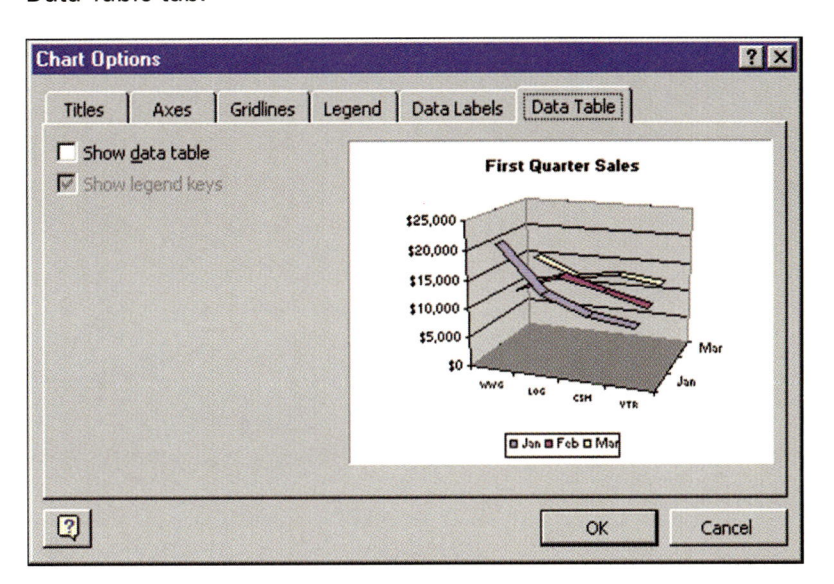

2 Select Show data table and click OK.

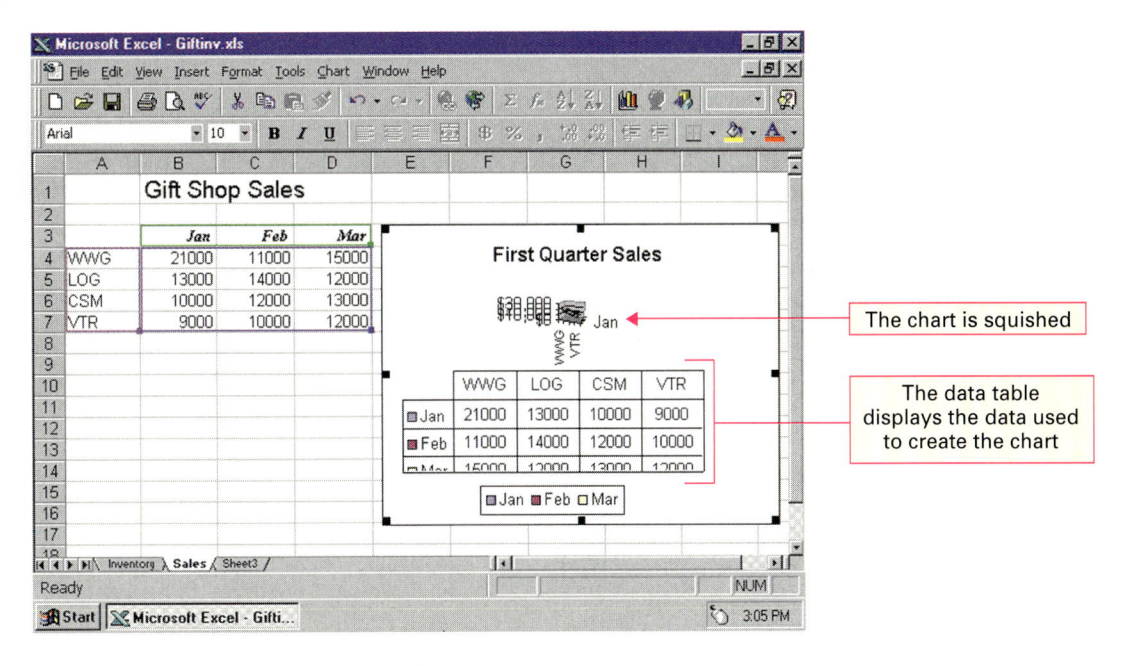

3 Make the chart about 9 rows taller.
The graph returns to its former size.

Creating a Pie Chart

A pie chart is a popular type of chart that shows the relationship of parts to the whole. When selecting data for a pie chart, you will select only one data range.

TASK 14: TO CREATE A PIE CHART:

1 Select the range A4:B7, click [icon], and select Pie as the Chart type and Exploded pie as the sub-type. (A description of the selected chart sub-type shows below the chart sub-type pictures.)

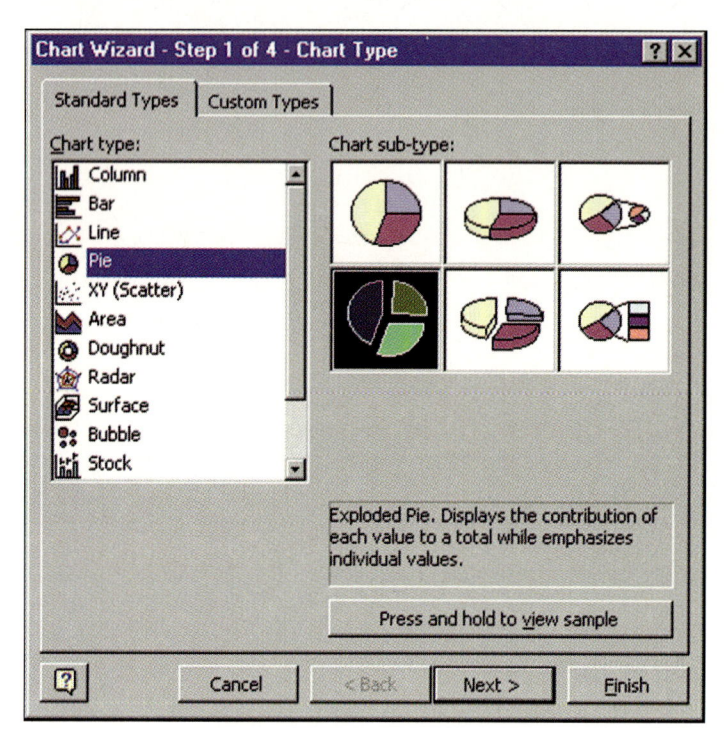

2 Click but don't release the button named Press and hold to view sample. A preview of the chart using your data displays in a Sample box.

Short Answer

1. When you create a chart, what are the two locations where you can place the chart?

2. What is a data table?

3. Where can a legend be placed on a chart?

4. What command do you use if you want to sort on more than one column?

5. How do you move a chart?

6. How do you size a chart?

7. What is the difference between a relative and an absolute reference?

8. Can you use an absolute reference in a formula that uses headings instead of cell addresses?

9. What happens if you change the data in a worksheet after you have created a chart that uses the data?

10. What happens in the worksheet when you select the data ranges in a chart?

For Discussion

1. Discuss the advantages of using headings in formulas.

2. Discuss the advantages of presenting information in charts as opposed to numbers.

3. Name and describe the elements of a chart.

4. Explain how Excel interprets the following formula if it were located in cell H10: =I5+I6*A1.

Review Exercises

1. Revising the Gift Inventory and Sales Workbook
In this exercise, you will make changes to an existing chart.

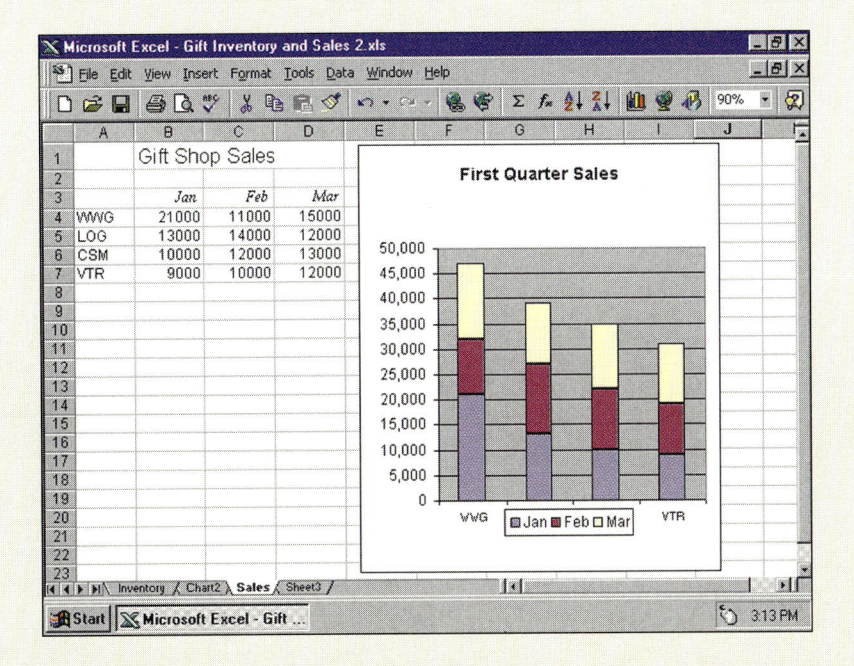

1. Open *Gift Inventory and Sales.xls*.
2. Click the Sales tab if necessary.
3. Change the chart type to a stacked column.
4. Remove the data table.
5. Remove the dollar sign from the numbers on the Y axis.
6. Save the file as Gift Inventory and Sales 2.xls and close the file.

2. Creating a New Items Workbook

In this exercise, you will create a workbook that lists five possible new items and computes the discount on the items.

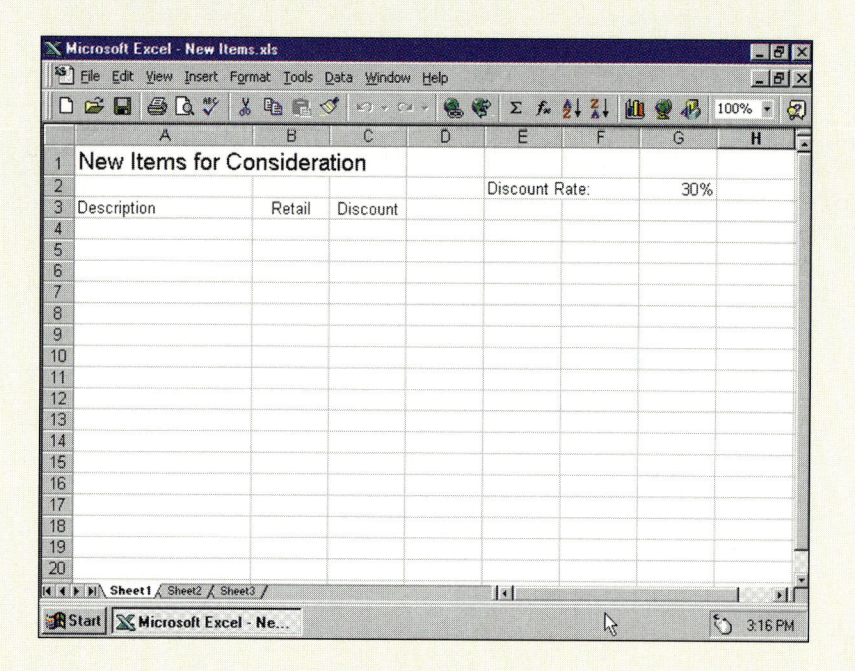

1. Create the workbook shown above.
2. Find five items on the Web that you can suggest as new items for the gift shops to carry. Enter the descriptions of the items and their retail prices in the worksheet in the appropriate columns.
3. In cell C4, enter the formula that multiplies the discount rate in cell G2 times the retail price in cell B4. Copy the formula to the range C5:C8.
4. Save the file as *New Items.xls* and close the file.

Assignments

1. Creating a Chart of Expenditures
Create a workbook that lists your expenditures for the past month. Create a pie chart for the data. Are you spending too much on pizza?

2. Completing a Vacation Package Workbook
Download the workbook *Vacation.xls* from the Addison Wesley Longman web site (http://www.awl.com/is/select/) or ask your instructor for this workbook file. Sort the data in ascending order in the range A4:C8. Enter a formula in cell D4 that multiplies the Price/Person times the appropriate discount rate (cell H4). Copy the formula to the other cells in the column. Enter appropriate formulas for the Travel Agency discounts and the Resort Club discounts. Use headings in the formulas for the Resort Club discounts.

Notes

Notes

Notes

Excel Function Guide

Function	Mouse Action or Button	Menu	Keyboard Shortcut
AutoFormat		Select the cells and choose Format, AutoFormat	
Border, add		Select the cell(s) and choose Format, Cells, Border	
Cell, align	Select the cell(s) and click [icon], [icon], or [icon]	Select the cells(s) and choose Format, Cells, Alignment	
Cell, delete		Select the cells(s) and choose Edit, Delete	
Cell, delete data in		Select the cells(s) and choose Edit, Clear	Select the cells(s) and press DELETE
Cell, copy	Select the cells(s) and click [icon]	Select the cells(s) and choose Edit, Copy	Select the cells(s) and press CTRL+**C**
Cell, cut	Select the cells(s) and click [icon]	Select the cells(s) and choose Edit, Cut	Select the cells(s) and press CTRL+**X**
Cell, format	Select the cells(s) and click appropriate formatting button (**B**, *I*, and so on)	Select the cells(s) and choose Format, Cells, and choose the desired tab	CTRL+1 - (one)
Cell, insert		Select the cells(s) and choose Insert, Cells	
Cell, paste	Select the cells(s) and click [icon]	Select the cells(s) and choose Edit, Paste	Select the cells(s) and press CTRL+**V**
Cell, select	Drag mouse pointer through desired cells		Press SHIFT+any navigation key
Chart, create		Choose Insert, Object, Microsoft Graph 97 Chart	
Chart, move	Select the graph and drag	Select the chart, choose Format, Object, click on the Position tab	
Chart, size	Select a handle and drag	Select the chart, choose Format, Object, click on the Size tab	
Column change the width	Drag the vertical border of the column in the column indicator row	Select the column and choose Format, Column, Width	
Column, delete		Select the column(s) and choose Edit, Delete	
Column, insert		Select the column(s) and choose Insert, Columns	
Comments, add		Select the cell and choose Insert, Comment	
Data, find		Choose Edit, Find	Press CTRL+**F**
Data, sort	Select the cells(s) and click [icon] or [icon]	Select the cells(s) and choose Data, Sort	

Excel Function Guide

Function	Mouse Action or Button	Menu	Keyboard Shortcut
Exit Excel 97	Click ☒	Choose File, Exit	Press ALT+F4
Fill, add	Select the cells(s), click the down arrow on the 🎨, and select a color	Select the cells(s) and choose Format, Cells, Patterns	
Format dates		Select the cells(s) and choose Format, Cells, Number	
Format numbers		Select the cells(s) and choose Format, Cells, Number	
Header, Footer, create		Choose View, Header and Footer	
Page break, change		Choose View, Page Break Preview, and drag the page break line	
Page break, view		Choose View, Page Break Preview	
Preview	Click 🔍	Choose File, Print Preview	
Print	Click 🖨	Choose File, Print	Press [ctrl]+p
Row change the height	Drag the horizontal border of the row indicator	Select the row(s) and choose Format, Row, Height	
Row, delete		Select the row(s) and choose Edit, Delete	
Row, insert		Select the number of rows you want to insert and choose Insert, Rows	
Spell check	Click ABC	Choose Tools, Spelling	Press F7
Workbook close	Click ☒ in the workbook window	Choose File, Close	
Workbook, create	Click 📄	Choose File, New	Press CTRL+END
Workbook, open	Click 📂	Choose File, Open	Press CTRL+O
Workbook, save	Click 💾	Choose File, Save	Press CTRL+S
Worksheet delete		Click the worksheet tab and choose Insert, Worksheet	
Worksheet, insert		Click the worksheet tab that should follow the new worksheet and choose Edit, Delete Sheet	
Worksheet, move	Drag the worksheet tab to new location	Select the worksheet tab and choose Edit, Move or Copy sheet	
Worksheet, name		Right-click the worksheet tab and choose Rename	

INTEGRATED PROJECT

Integrating Word and Excel

One of the advantages of using software programs that are part of a suite is that the programs are designed to work together as a team. You've already discovered a few of the shared components in Microsoft Office — the spelling dictionary, Find, and so on. Now it's time to see how you can use data from an Excel worksheet in a Word document or enhance an Excel worksheet with WordArt.

Objectives

After completing this project, you will be able to:

- ▶ **Create an Excel worksheet**
- ▶ **Create an Excel chart**
- ▶ **Create a Word document**
- ▶ **Add WordArt to a Word document**
- ▶ **Copy Excel data to a Word document**
- ▶ **Link an Excel chart to a Word document**

The Challenge

The golf tournament is now complete, and you need to create a worksheet to display the profits from the tournament. You also need to prepare a report for The Willows Board of Directors that includes the profit figures.

The Solution

To create the documents shown in Figure 1.1, you will enter the final figures for the golf tournament revenues in a new Excel worksheet. Then you will create a chart to visually display profits. After you complete the Excel worksheet and chart, you will create a report in Word that includes the data and chart from Excel.

Integrating data from the worksheet with text in the report is as easy as dragging the data from the worksheet and dropping it on the report. You can also copy the Excel chart to the report and create a link so that the chart in the Word document automatically updates when you change data in the Excel worksheet.

The Setup

To accomplish the tasks outlined in this project, you need to work with both Word and Excel. So that they are available when you need them, launch both applications. Table 1.1 shows the settings you should choose.

Table 1.1   Word and Excel Settings

Element	Setting
Office Assistant	Close Office Assistant in both programs
View, Toolbars	Display the Standard and Formatting toolbars in both programs
View, Ruler	Display the vertical and horizontal rulers in Word
Maximize	Maximize the document windows in both programs
Minimize	The Word program until you are ready for it

When you complete the basic documents in both applications, you can arrange the Excel and Word windows on the screen so that you can drag information from one application to the other and see immediate results.

Integrating Word and Excel   IP1-3

Creating the Excel Worksheet

The first step to accomplishing your goal is to create the Excel worksheet and use the data to create a chart. If necessary, refer to the Excel Function Guide for detailed instructions on tasks required to complete the worksheet.

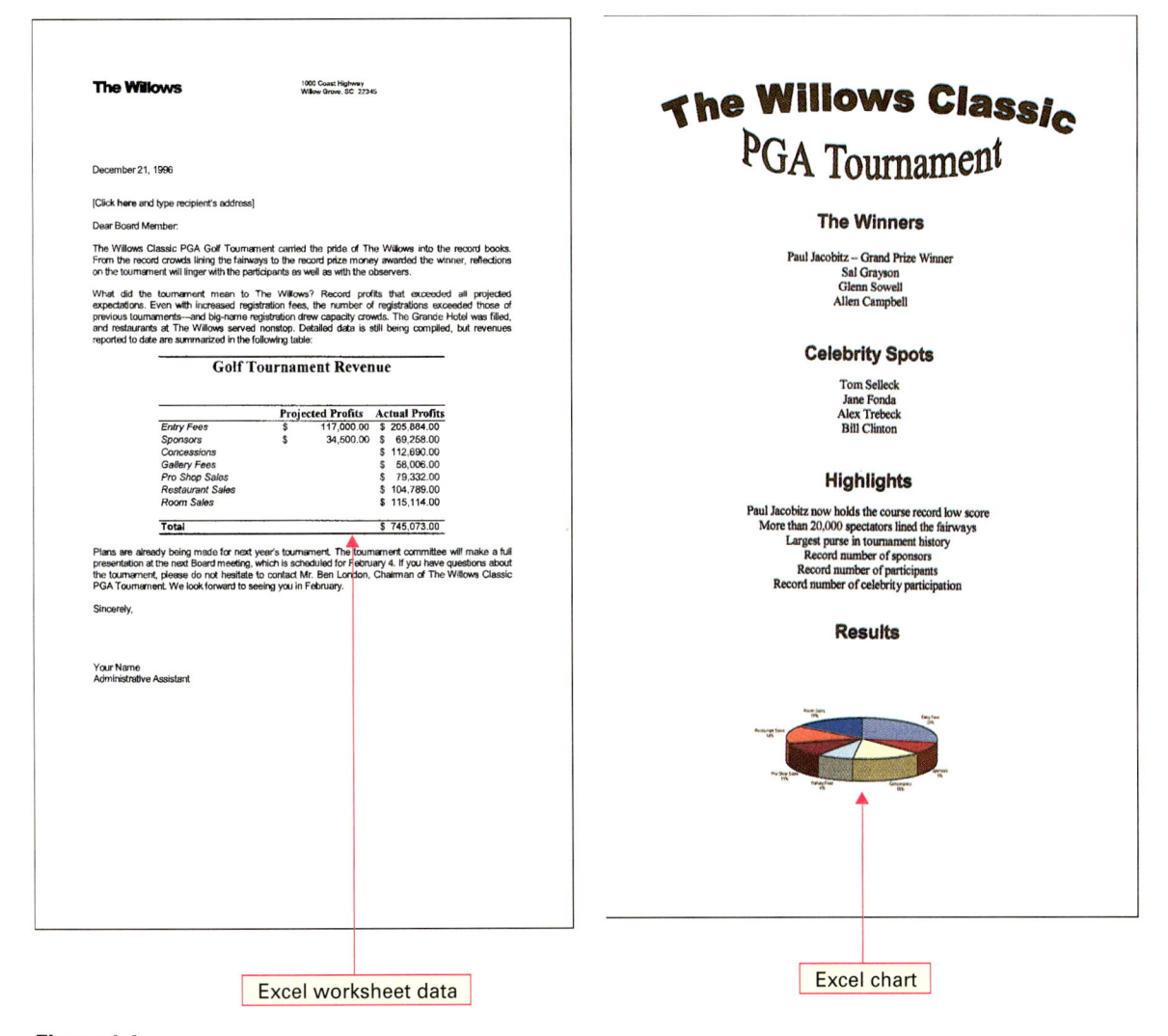

Figure 1.1

IP1-4

TASK 1: TO CREATE THE PROFITS WORKSHEET AND CHART:

1 Select the cells identified on the following illustration and type new data into cells of the worksheet.

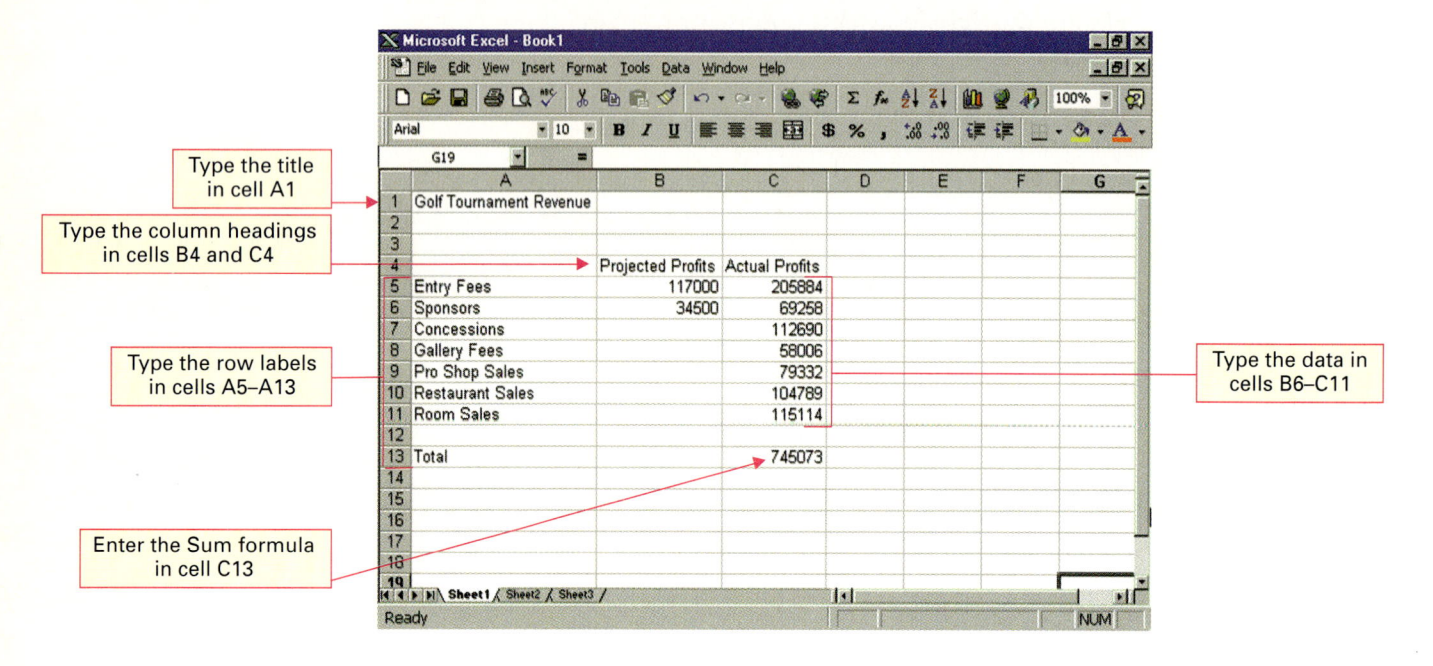

Type the title in cell A1

Type the column headings in cells B4 and C4

Type the row labels in cells A5–A13

Type the data in cells B6–C11

Enter the Sum formula in cell C13

	A	B	C
1	Golf Tournament Revenue		
2			
3			
4		Projected Profits	Actual Profits
5	Entry Fees	117000	205884
6	Sponsors	34500	69258
7	Concessions		112690
8	Gallery Fees		58006
9	Pro Shop Sales		79332
10	Restaurant Sales		104789
11	Room Sales		115114
12			
13	Total		745073

2 Save the worksheet using the filename *Tournament Profits*.

3 Select cells A1 through C13, then choose Format, AutoFormat, and double-click the Simple Table format.

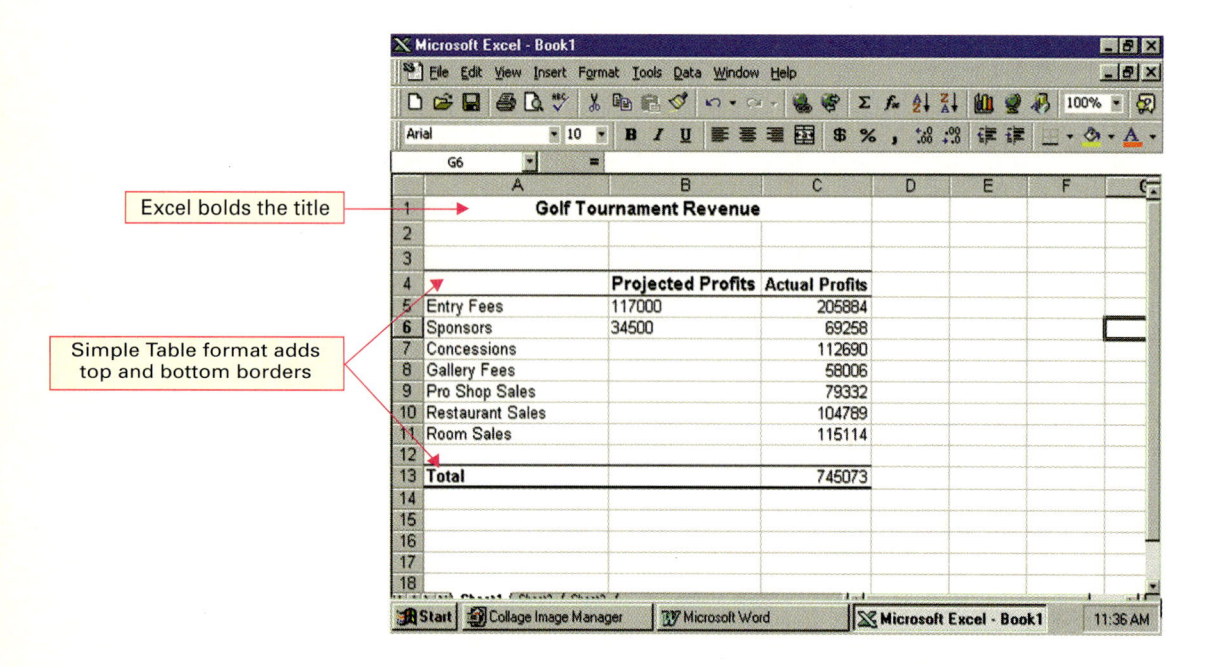

Excel bolds the title

Simple Table format adds top and bottom borders

	A	B	C
1	**Golf Tournament Revenue**		
2			
3			
4		**Projected Profits**	**Actual Profits**
5	Entry Fees	117000	205884
6	Sponsors	34500	69258
7	Concessions		112690
8	Gallery Fees		58006
9	Pro Shop Sales		79332
10	Restaurant Sales		104789
11	Room Sales		115114
12			
13	**Total**		745073

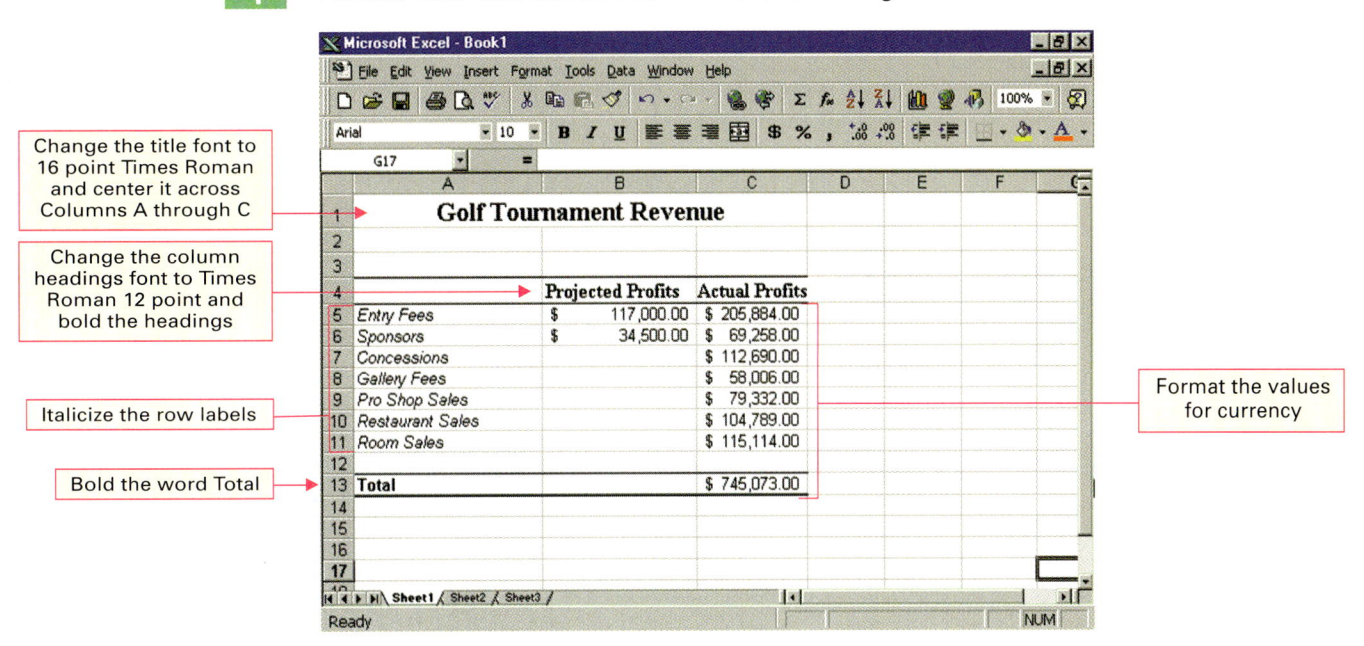

4 Format cells and text as shown in the following illustration:

Change the title font to 16 point Times Roman and center it across Columns A through C

Change the column headings font to Times Roman 12 point and bold the headings

Italicize the row labels

Bold the word Total

Format the values for currency

	A	B	C
1	Golf Tournament Revenue		
2			
3			
4		**Projected Profits**	**Actual Profits**
5	*Entry Fees*	$ 117,000.00	$ 205,884.00
6	*Sponsors*	$ 34,500.00	$ 69,258.00
7	*Concessions*		$ 112,690.00
8	*Gallery Fees*		$ 58,006.00
9	*Pro Shop Sales*		$ 79,332.00
10	*Restaurant Sales*		$ 104,789.00
11	*Room Sales*		$ 115,114.00
12			
13	**Total**		$ 745,073.00

5 Save the changes to the worksheet.

Creating an Excel Chart

Now that you have the data stored in the worksheet, you can select the Actual Profits data and create a pie chart. If necessary, refer to the Excel Function Guide for information about accomplishing specific tasks.

TASK 2: TO CREATE AN EXCEL CHART:

1 Select the data in cells A5 through A11, press (CTRL) and then select cells C5 through C11, and then click the Chart Wizard button on the Standard toolbar.

IP1-6

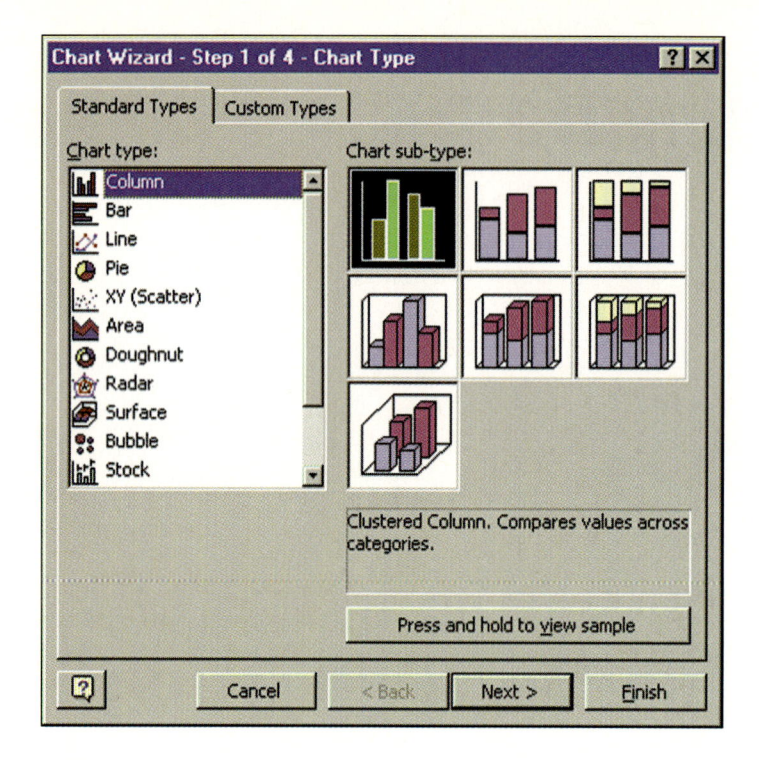

[Screenshot: Chart Wizard - Step 1 of 4 - Chart Type dialog box]

2 Select Pie from the Chart type list, click the 3-D pie on the Chart sub-type palette, and then click Next.

3 Click Next to accept the default values on Steps 2 and 3.

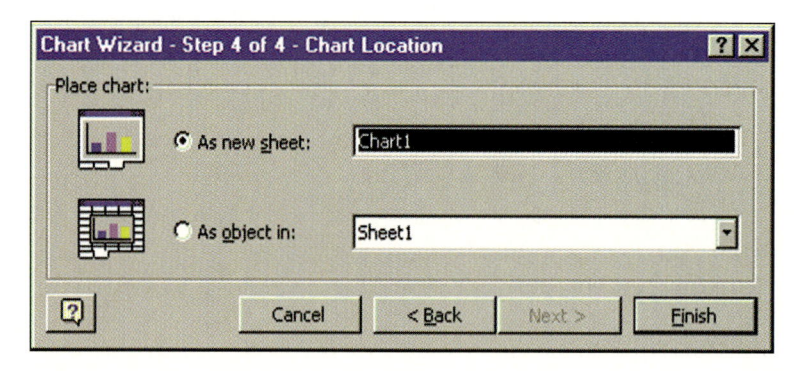

[Screenshot: Chart Wizard - Step 4 of 4 - Chart Location dialog box]

4 Select As new sheet on the Step 4 Wizard page, type **Actual Profits** as the sheet name, and then click Finish.

Integrating Word and Excel IP1-7

Chart toolbar displays automatically

The drop-down list displays chart objects

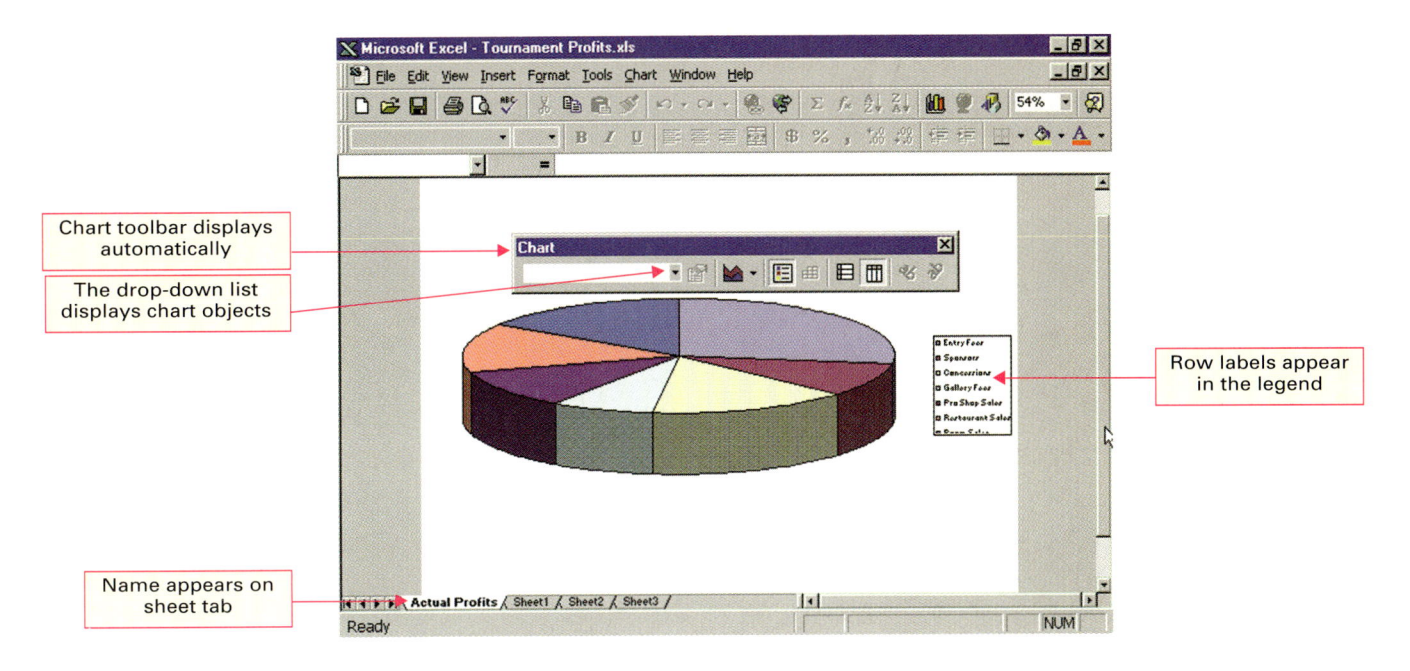

Row labels appear in the legend

Name appears on sheet tab

5 Click the Legend button on the Chart toolbar to turn the legend off, click the drop-down list arrow on the Chart toolbar, select Series 1, and then click the Format Data Series button on the Chart toolbar.

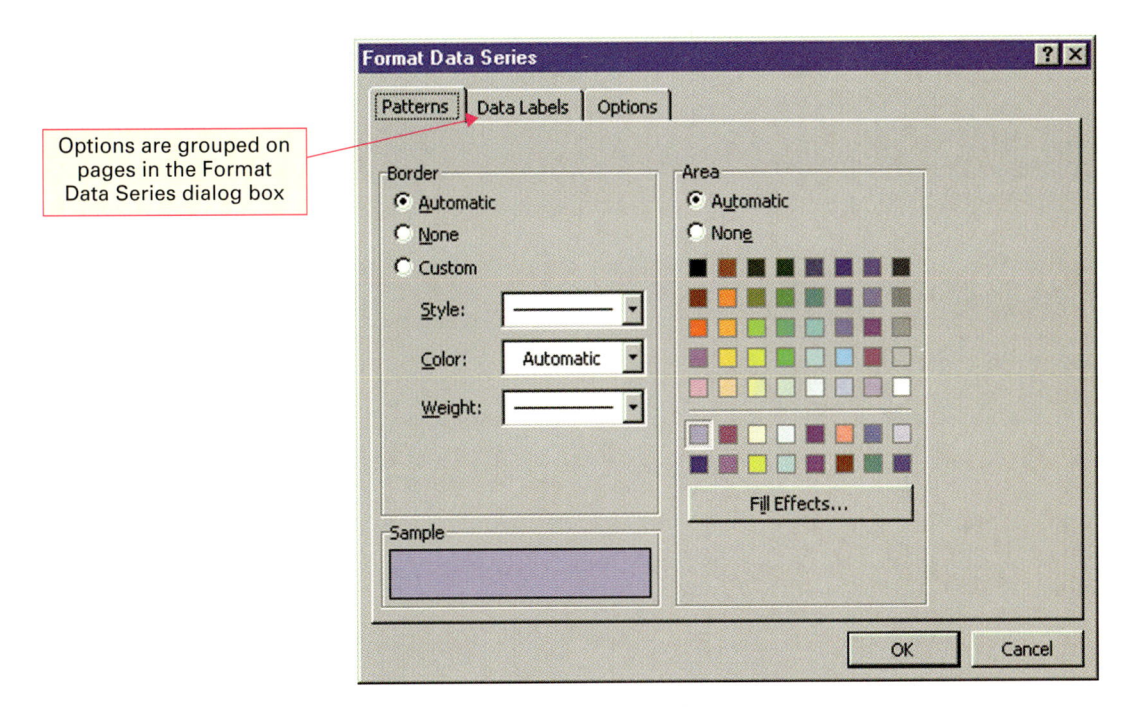

Options are grouped on pages in the Format Data Series dialog box

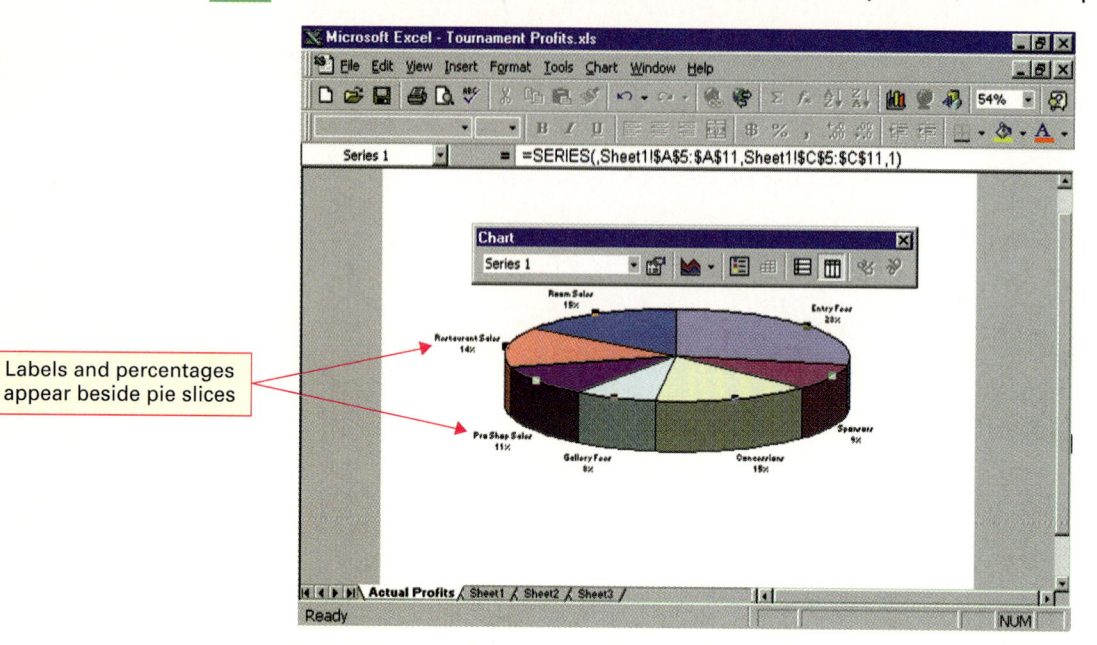

6 Click the Data Labels tab, select Show label and percent, and then press ENTER.

Labels and percentages appear beside pie slices

7 Click the Sheet 1 tab, click cell A1, save changes to the workbook and minimize Excel so that it displays as a button on the Taskbar.

Creating a Word Document

Now that you have completed the Excel worksheet and chart, you need to create the Word document. Refer to the Word and Excel Function Guides for information about how to complete specific tasks.

TASK 3: TO CREATE THE WORD DOCUMENT:

1 Maximize Word and choose File, New to create a new document, if necessary.

> **Tip** If you don't already have Word open, launch the program.

Integrating Word and Excel   IP1-9

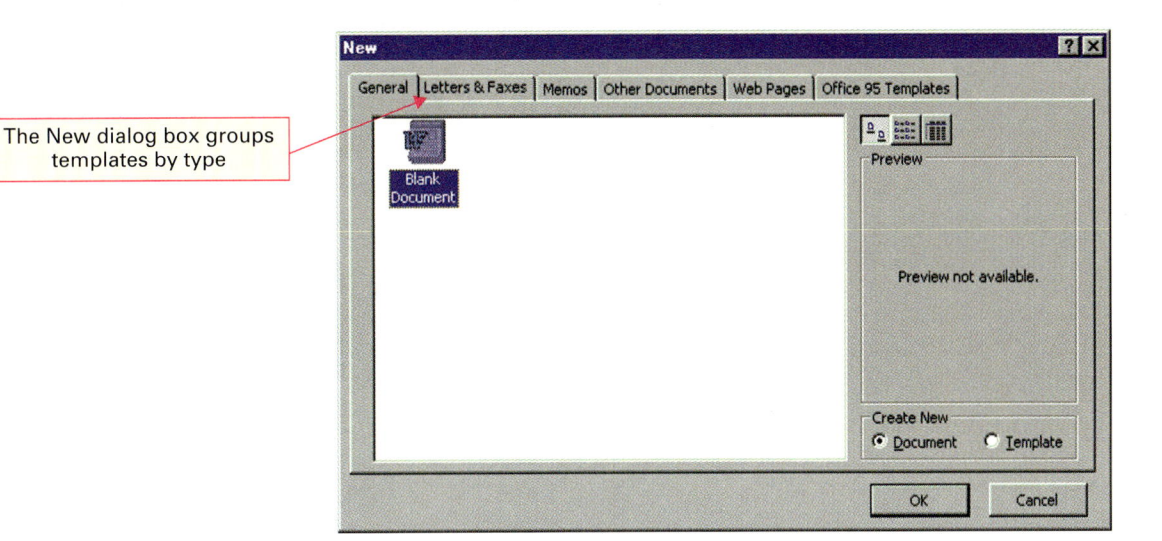

The New dialog box groups templates by type →

[Screenshot of New dialog box with tabs: General, Letters & Faxes, Memos, Other Documents, Web Pages, Office 95 Templates; Blank Document icon; Preview area showing "Preview not available."; Create New: Document/Template radio buttons; OK and Cancel buttons]

2 Click the Letters & Faxes tab and double-click the Professional Letter template.

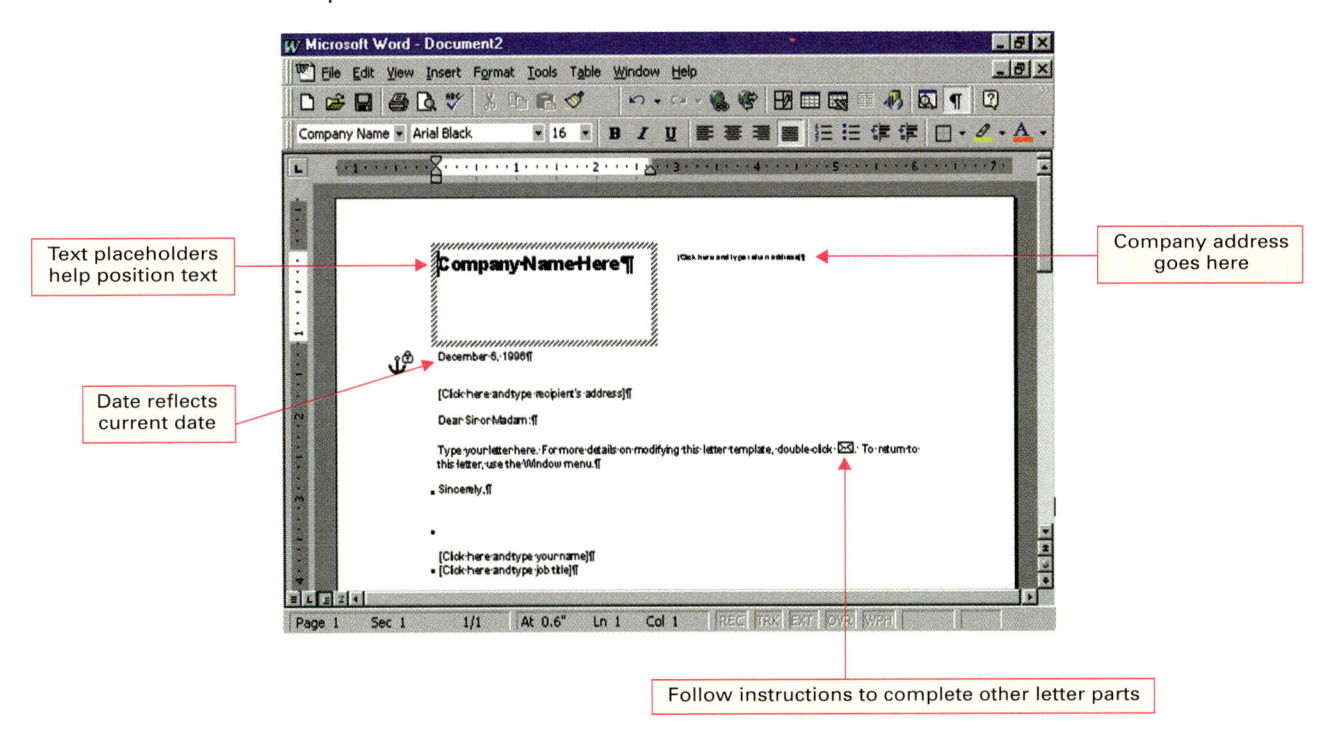

[Screenshot of Microsoft Word - Document2 showing a letter template with "Company Name Here" placeholder, date "December 6, 1996", and placeholder text for recipient's address, "Dear Sir or Madam:", body instructions, "Sincerely,", and placeholders for name and job title]

Text placeholders help position text →

Date reflects current date →

← *Company address goes here*

← *Follow instructions to complete other letter parts*

3 Press (SHIFT)+(END) to select "Company Name Here" and type **The Willows**.

IP1-10

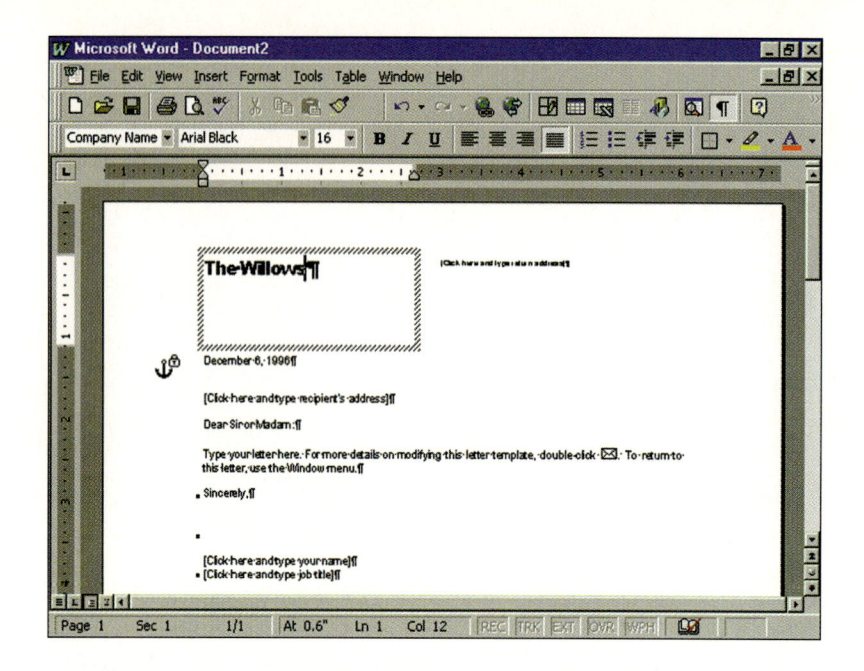

| 4 | Choose a view of 100%, then click [Click here and type return address], type **1000 Coast Highway**, press ENTER, and type **Willow Grove, SC 22345**. |

| 5 | Select "Dear Sir or Madam:" and type **Dear Board Member:** to replace existing text. |

| 6 | Select the "Type your letter here . . ." text and type: |

The Willows Classic PGA Golf Tournament carried the pride of The Willows into the record books. From the record crowds lining the fairways to the record prize money awarded the winner, reflections on the tournament will linger with the participants as well as with the observers.

What did the tournament mean to The Willows? Record profits that exceeded all projected expectations. Even with increased registration fees, the number of registrations exceeded those of previous tournaments - and big-name registration drew capacity crowds. The Grande Hotel was filled, and restaurants at The Willows served nonstop. Detailed data is still being compiled, but revenues reported to date are summarized in the following table:

| 7 | Press ENTER seven times after the second paragraph to leave room for the Excel worksheet and then type the following paragraph: |

Plans are already being made for next year's tournament. The tournament committee will make a full presentation at the next Board meeting, which is scheduled for February 4. If you have questions about the tournament, please do not hesitate to contact Mr. Ben London, Chairman of The Willows Classic PGA Tournament. We look forward to seeing you in February.

| 8 | Type your name as the sender, type **Administrative Assistant** as your job title, and then press CTRL+ENTER to create a new page. |

9 Double-click the header text at the top of page 2 and select the text in the header.

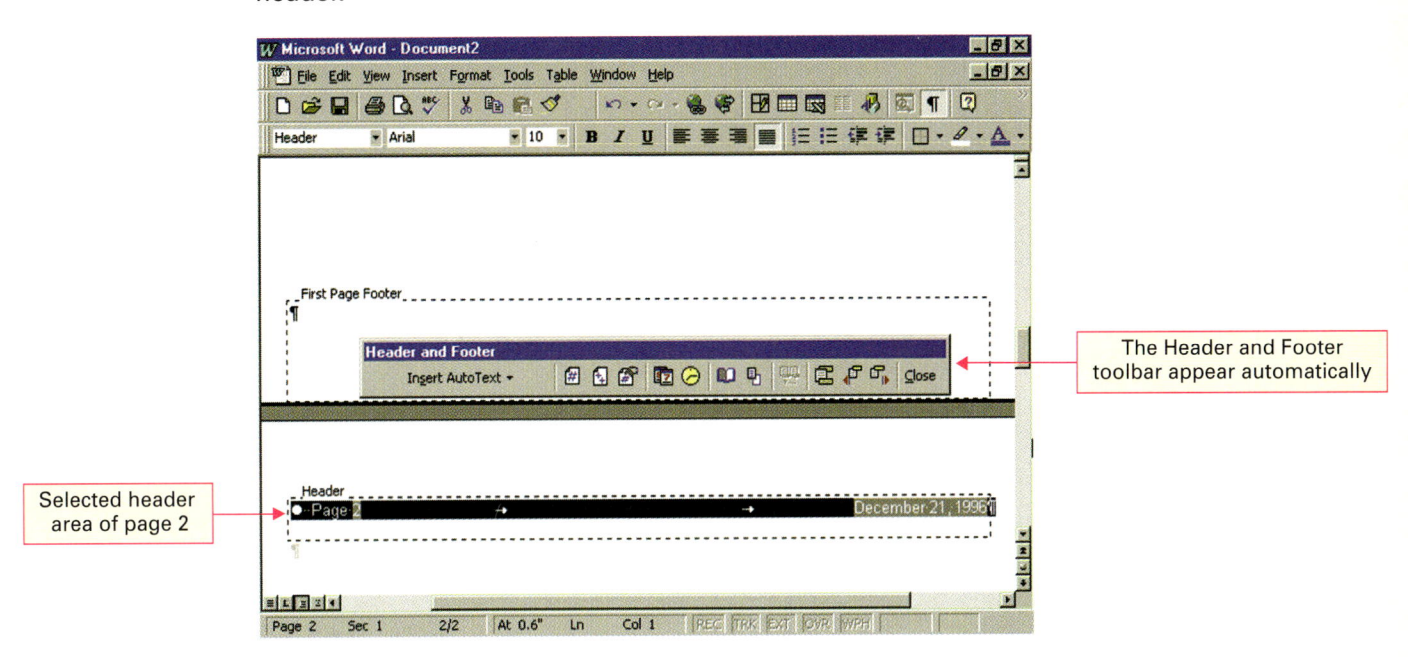

Selected header area of page 2

The Header and Footer toolbar appear automatically

10 Press DEL to delete header text, click the Close button on the Header and Footer toolbar, and change the text style to *Normal*.

11 Press ENTER eight times and then type:

The Winners
Paul Jacobitz - Grand Prize Winner
Sal Grayson
Glenn Sowell
Allen Campbell
Celebrity Spots
Tom Selleck
Jane Fonda
Alex Trebeck
Bill Clinton
Highlights
Paul Jacobitz now holds the course record low score
More than 20,000 spectators lined the fairways
Largest purse in tournament history
Record number of sponsors
Record number of participants
Record number of celebrity participation
Results

12 Format the text as shown in the following illustration:

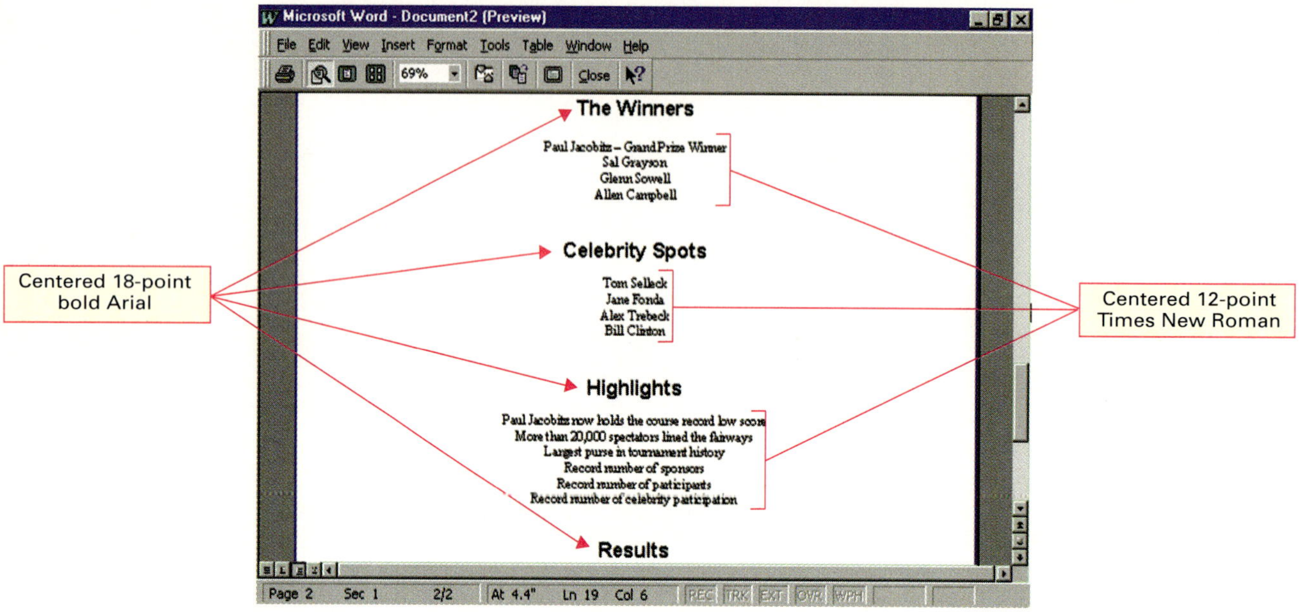
Microsoft Word - Document2 (Preview)
File Edit View Insert Format Tools Table Window Help
69%
Close
The Winners
Paul Jacobitz – Grand Prize Winner
Sal Grayson
Glenn Sowell
Allen Campbell
Celebrity Spots
Tom Selleck
Jane Fonda
Alex Trebeck
Bill Clinton
Highlights
Paul Jacobitz now holds the course record low score
More than 20,000 spectators lined the fairways
Largest purse in tournament history
Record number of sponsors
Record number of participants
Record number of celebrity participation
Results
Page 2 Sec 1 2/2 At 4.4" Ln 19 Col 6
REC TRK EXT OVR WPH
Centered 18-point bold Arial
Centered 12-point Times New Roman

13 Save the document using the filename *Tournament Results to the Board.*

Adding WordArt to a Word Document

WordArt, a feature shared by Word, Excel, and other applications enables you to dress up your Excel worksheets and charts and your Word documents. You can use WordArt to create the graphic text shown in Figure 1.1 at the top of page two on the Word document.

TASK 4: TO ADD WORDART TO A WORD DOCUMENT:

1 Click the Show/Hide ¶ button on the Standard toolbar to turn paragraph symbols on, position the insertion point at the top of Page 2 of the Word document (not in the header area), and click the Drawing button on the Standard toolbar.

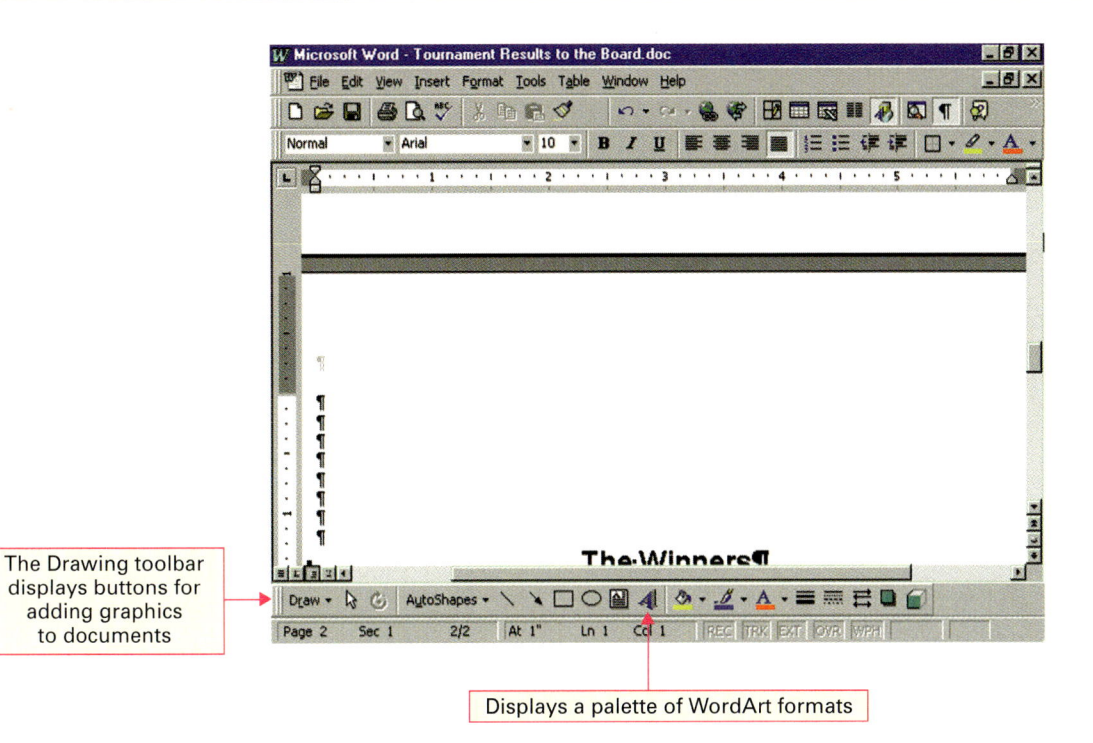

Integrating Word and Excel   IP1-13

The Drawing toolbar displays buttons for adding graphics to documents

Displays a palette of WordArt formats

2   Click the Insert WordArt button.

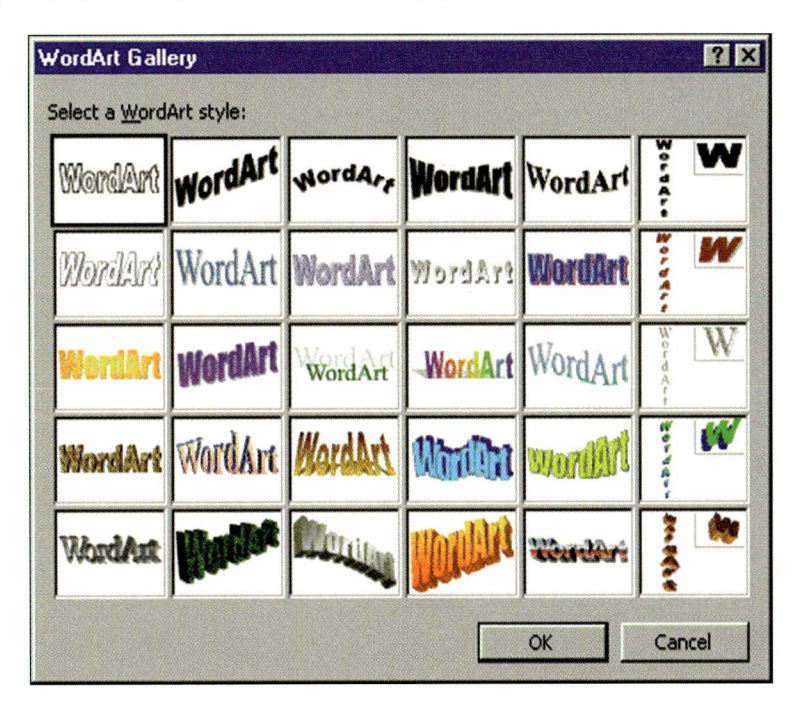

IP1-14

3 Click the third format on the top row and click OK.

4 Type **The Willows Classic** and click OK.

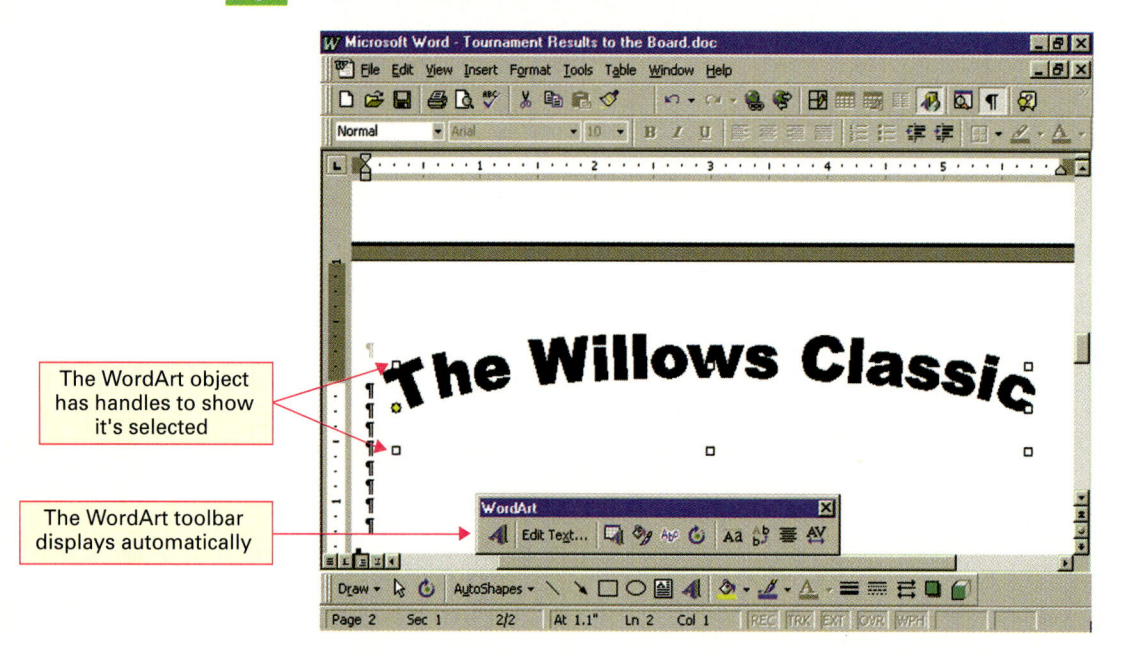

The WordArt object has handles to show it's selected

The WordArt toolbar displays automatically

5 Position the insertion point beside the fourth paragraph symbol just below the WordArt on the left side of your document, click [icon], select the fifth format on the top row, and click OK.

Integrating Word and Excel IP1-15

6 Type **PGA Tournament** and click OK.

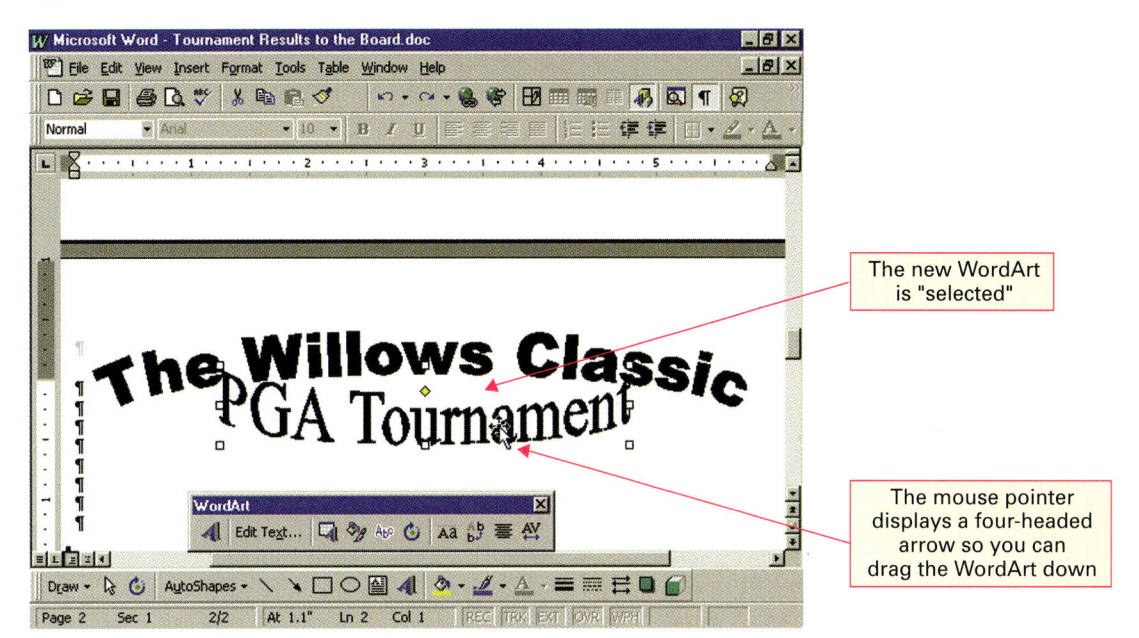

The new WordArt is "selected"

The mouse pointer displays a four-headed arrow so you can drag the WordArt down

7 Point to the new WordArt object, click and drag the WordArt down so that the top left handle appears at about the 0" mark on the vertical ruler, and then press ESC.

8 Preview your document. Click 💾 to save the changes.

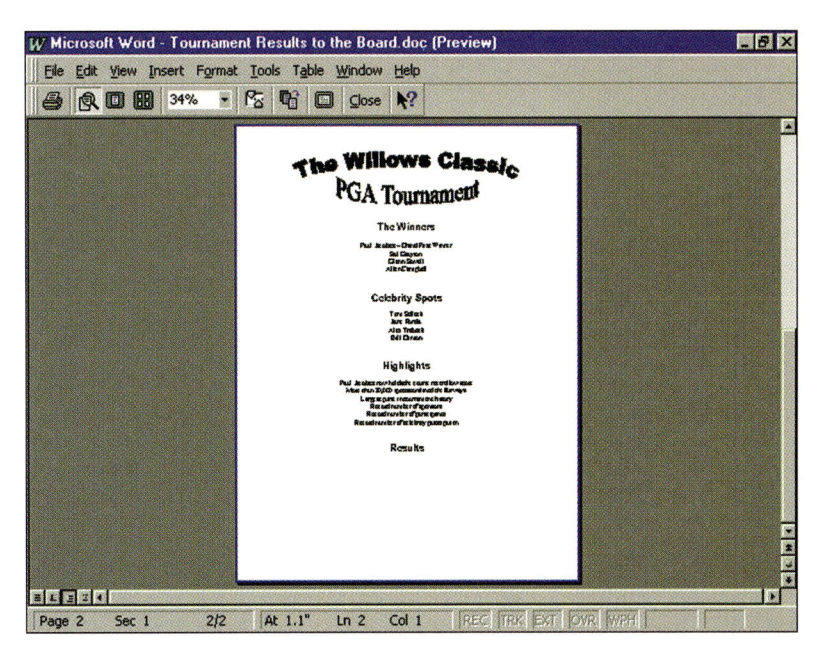

Copying Excel Data to a Word document

After completing and saving the Excel worksheet and the Word documents, you're ready to *integrate*, or combine, the data from the worksheet with the Word document. You can copy the Excel worksheet into the

Word document and actually embed the data in the document. The file you copy is called the *source document* and the file receiving the data is called the *target document*. *Embedded data* (called an *object*) stays with the target document and doesn't change when data in the source document changes.

TASK 5: TO COPY EXCEL DATA TO A WORD DOCUMENT:

1. Close all applications you have opened except Word and Excel, maximize both applications, and ensure that the Tournament Profits worksheet is open and active in Excel and that Tournament Results to the Board document is open and active in Word.

2. Point to an area of the Taskbar away from program buttons and right-click.

> **Troubleshooting** If your mouse pointer is positioned on a program button on the Taskbar, you get a different pop-up menu. Press ESC, reposition the mouse pointer, and try again.

3. Choose Tile Vertically.

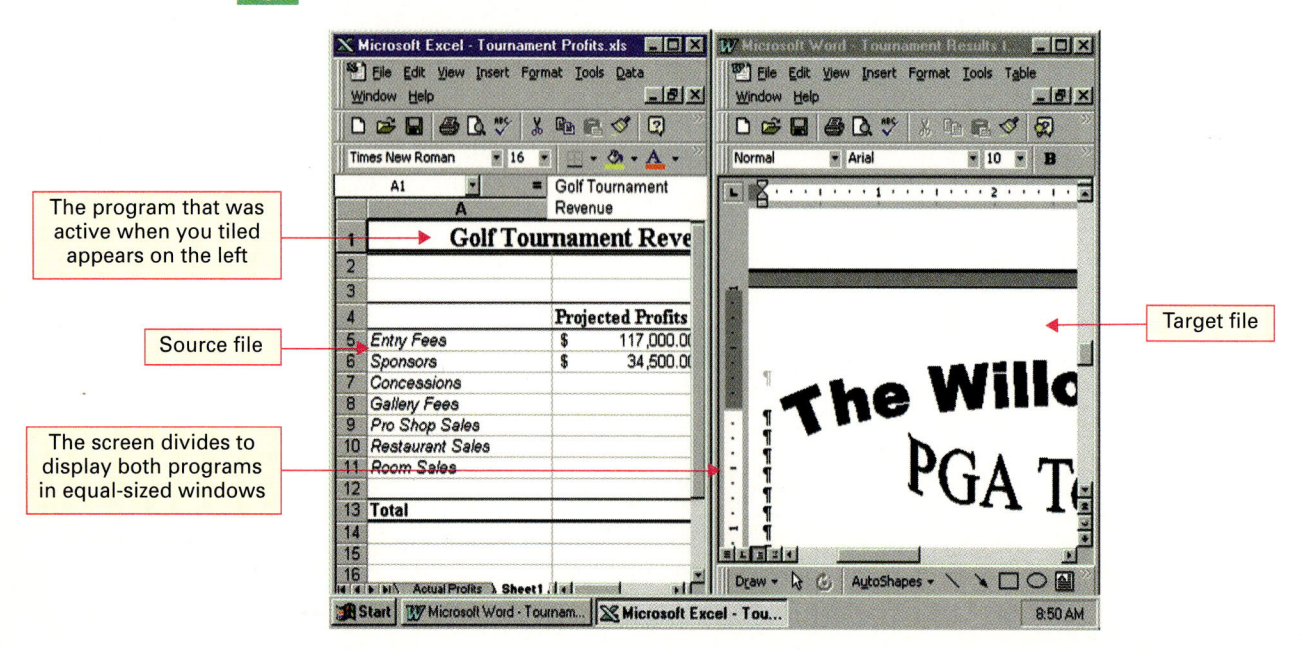

- The program that was active when you tiled appears on the left
- Source file
- The screen divides to display both programs in equal-sized windows
- Target file

Integrating Word and Excel   IP1-17

4 Click the Word title bar to make it active and scroll so that page 1 of the document displays.

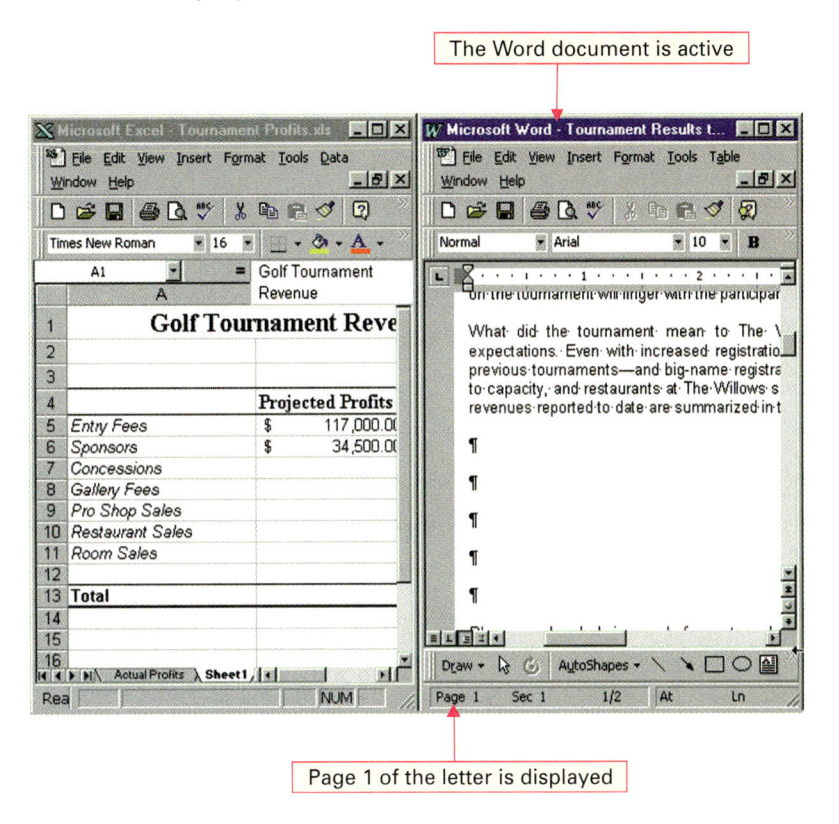

The Word document is active

Page 1 of the letter is displayed

5 Click cell A1 in Excel and drag to select cells A1 through C13.

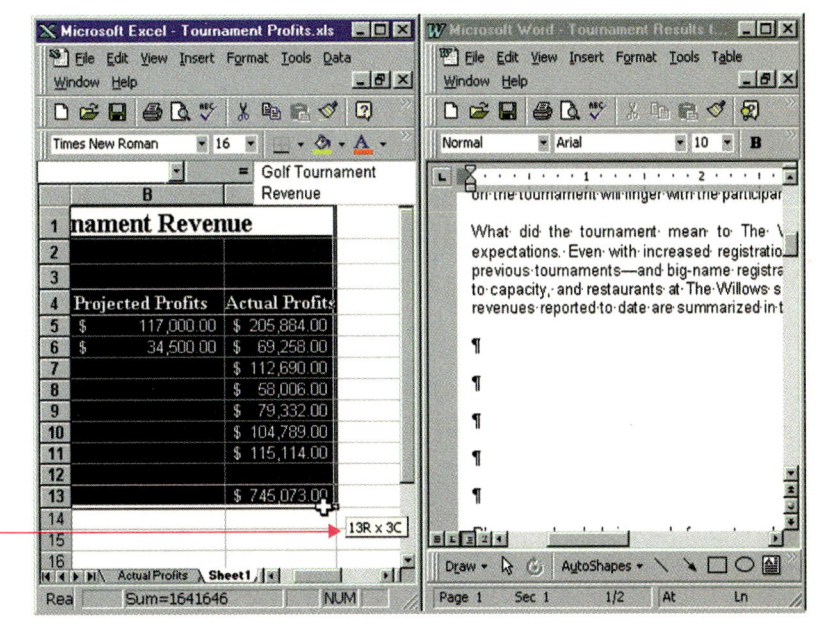

Excel tells you the size of the selected range

6 Position the mouse pointer close to the edge of the selected range so that you see a hollow arrow pointer, press (CTRL) and drag the selection to Word, placing the cursor at the end of the first blank line:

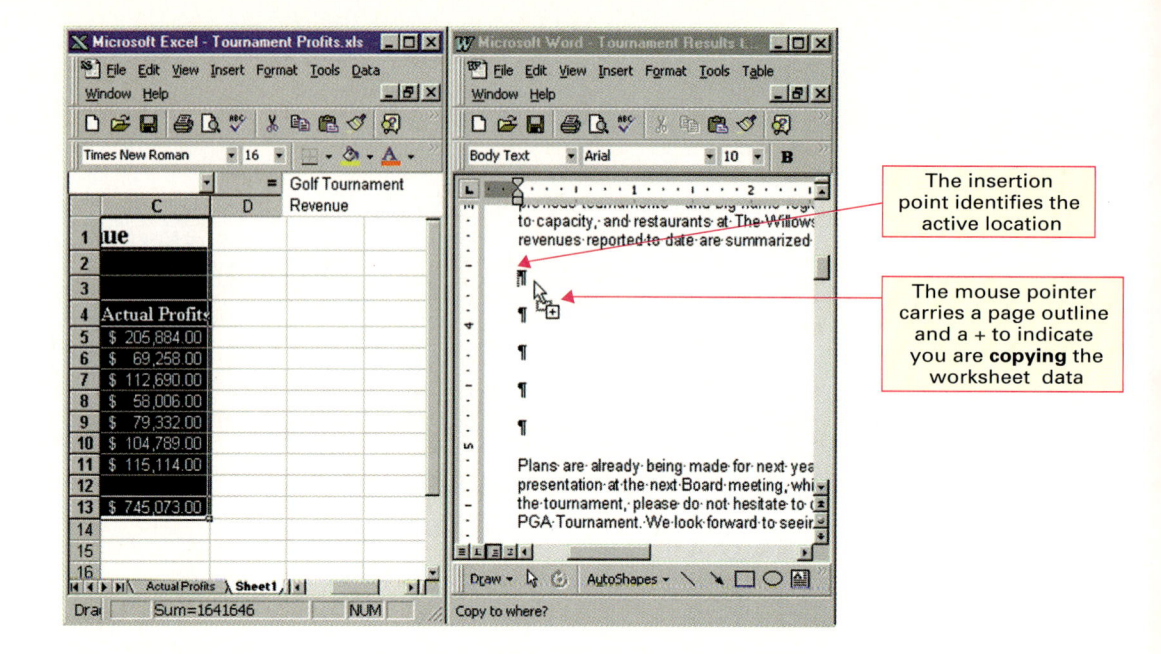

IP1-18

The insertion point identifies the active location

*The mouse pointer carries a page outline and a + to indicate you are **copying** the worksheet data*

Caution If you don't see a + beside the mouse pointer, you are *moving, not copying,* the data from Excel to Word. Move the mouse pointer back to the worksheet and drop the data. Click Undo, if necessary, and then start over.

7 Release the mouse button to drop the data into Word.

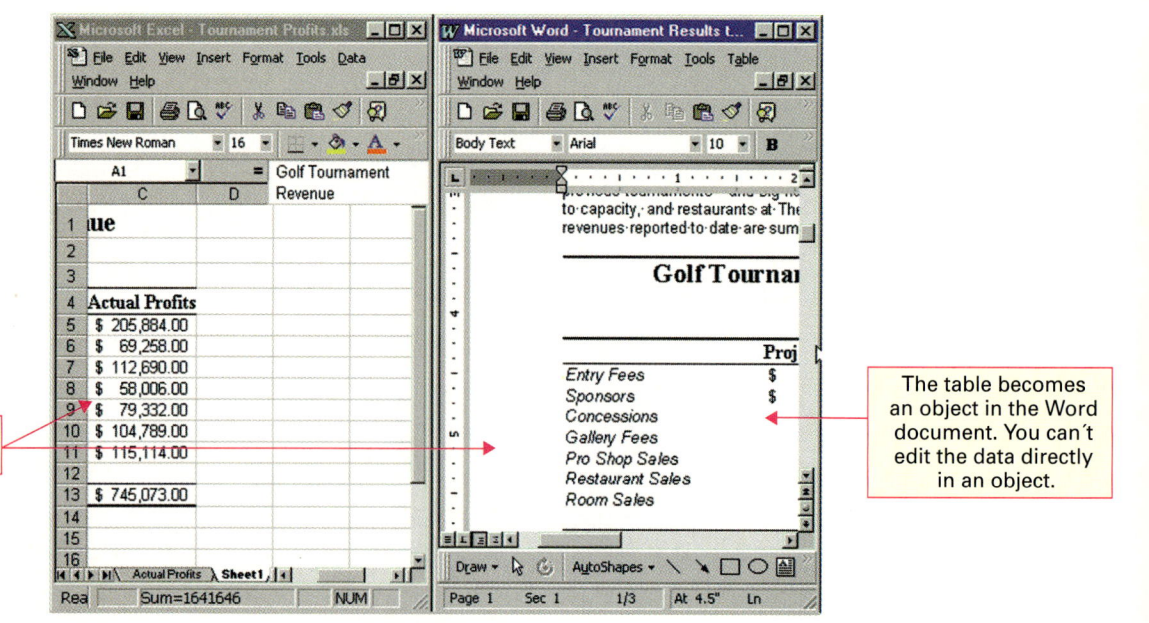

Worksheet data appears in both windows

The table becomes an object in the Word document. You can't edit the data directly in an object.

Integrating Word and Excel **IP1-19**

8 Maximize Word, click the Excel object to select it, click the Center button on the Formatting toolbar, delete extra paragraph symbols between the object and the last paragraph; then preview the letter and print the first page.

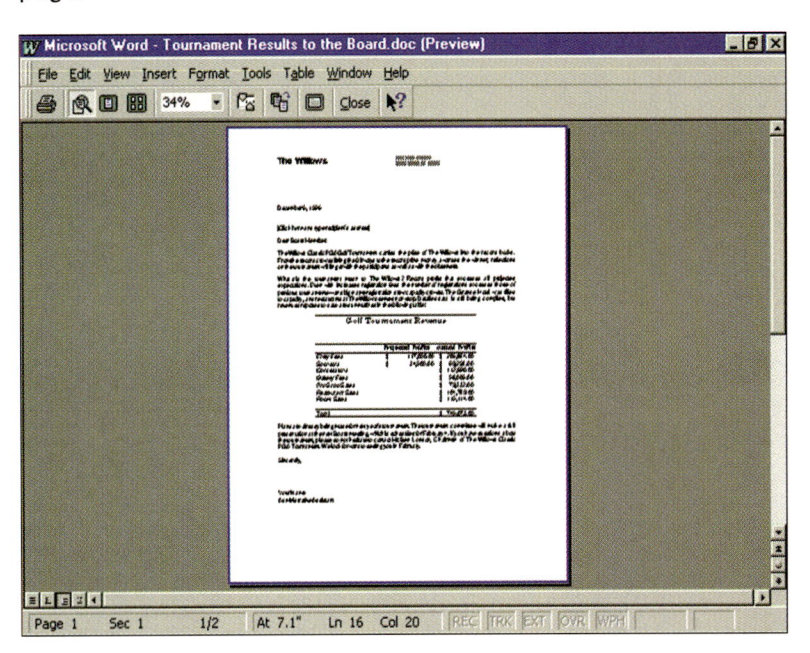

Linking an Excel Chart to a Word Document

The data you copied from the worksheet to the letter is now an embedded object in the letter, and the data in the Word document remains the same regardless of what happens to the worksheet. When you want data in a document to change as data in the original worksheet changes, you have to create a *link* between the worksheet and the document. When you create a link, the document where you place the data checks the original file each time you open the document to see whether changes were made since the data was last updated. You can create a link between the Excel chart and the Word document when you copy the chart to the document.

TASK 6: TO LINK AN EXCEL CHART TO A WORD DOCUMENT:

1 Tile the program windows again, display the Actual Profits chart sheet in Excel, close the Chart toolbar, and scroll the Word document until you see "Results" at the bottom of page 2.

IP1-20

The mouse pointer identifies the active chart area

Handles appear when the chart is selected

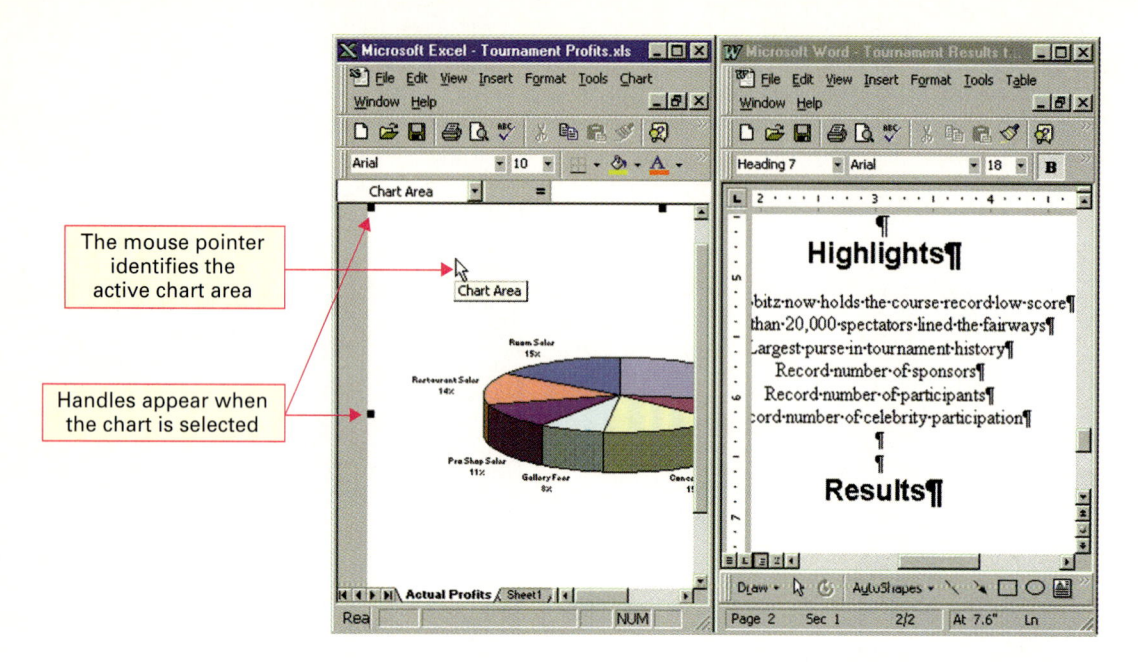

2 Click to select the Chart Area of the Excel chart and click 📋.
A marquee that looks like marching ants displays around the chart area.

3 Click the Word title bar, position the insertion point after the word "Result," and press (ENTER).
The insertion point moves to the left margin of the document and displays a new paragraph symbol.

4 Choose Edit, Paste Special.

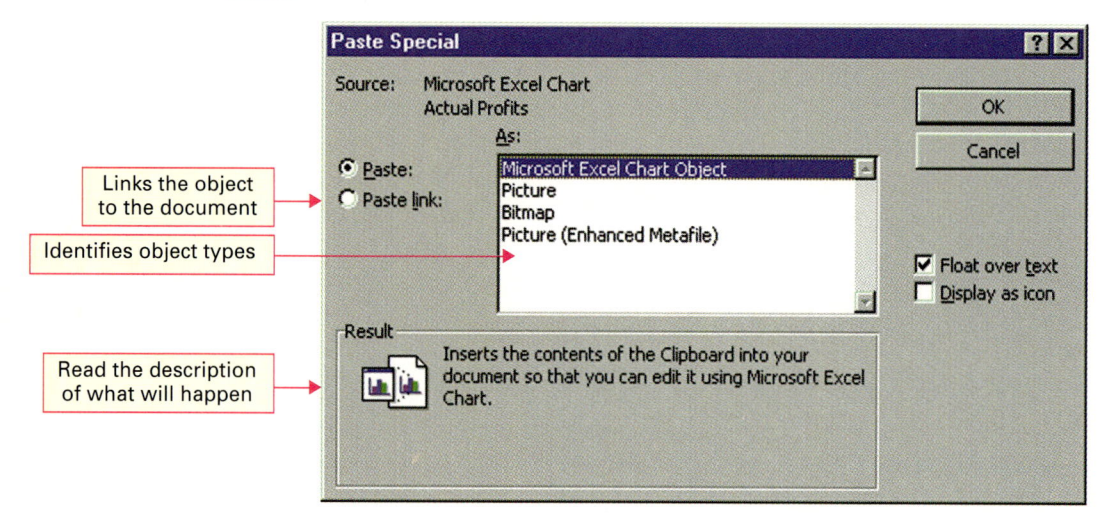

Links the object to the document

Identifies object types

Read the description of what will happen

5 Click the Paste link option, ensure that Microsoft Excel Chart Object is selected in the As list, and click OK.
Wow! Did your screen seem to go nuts? You need to make some adjustments to the size of the chart to bring it back onto the previous page.

6 Maximize Word, click 🔍, scroll to preview the chart, and then close the Preview window.

7 Click the chart to ensure that it is selected, and change the Zoom to Page width.

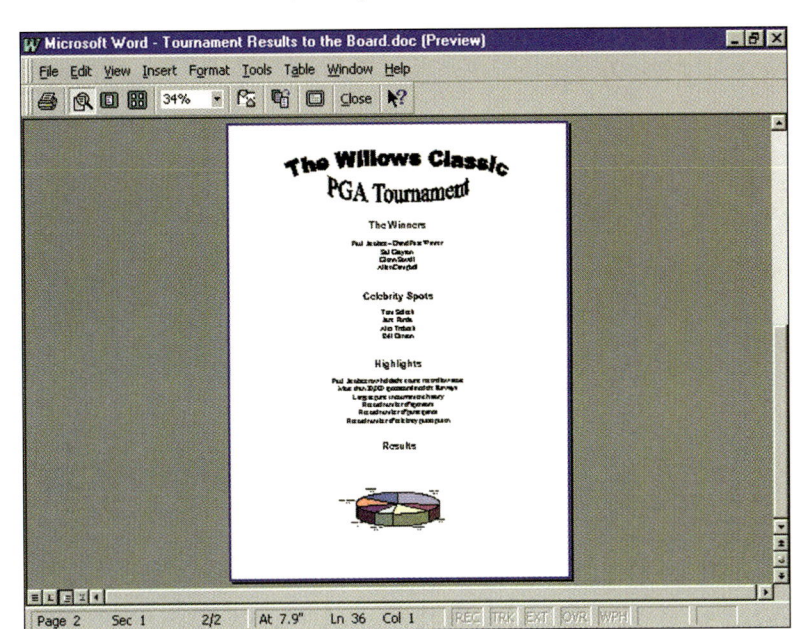

8 Make the chart smaller, and position it at the bottom of page 2.

9 Save changes to the document and print a copy of the second page.

The Conclusion

To see the effects of linking the chart to the document, display the Excel worksheet and change a value in the Actual Profits column. View the changes on the chart and then display the Word document. Choose Edit, Links, Update Now to view the changes to the chart in the Word document. Close the Excel worksheet and the Word document without saving the change you made to the data. If you have completed your work, exit Excel and Word and shut down your computer as instructed.

By the way, when you create a WordArt object or an Excel chart, you are actually embedding new objects in the documents. WordArt is created using the Microsoft WordArt program and the chart is created using the Microsoft Chart.

Double-clicking embedded objects opens the source file in the source program so that you can edit data.

Summary and Exercises

Summary

- One advantage of using programs that are part of an office suite is that the shared features make integrating information quick and easy.
- You can share data between applications using a variety of different techniques: dragging and dropping, copying and pasting, and linking.
- Linking data between applications ensures that data updated in one application is reflected in the other application.
- Embedding creates a copy of the data and places it in the target document without creating a link. Embedded data isn't updated automatically when data changes in the other application.

Key Terms and Operations

Key Terms
embed
integrate
link
source document
target document
tile windows
WordArt

Operations
Create WordArt objects
Drag data from Excel and drop it into a Word document
Link data from Excel to a Word document

Study Questions

Multiple Choice

1. To artistically design text in a document, use
   a. graphics.
   b. the mouse and draw the text.
   c. WordArt.
   d. regular text and change the size.

2. Using data from an Excel worksheet in a Word document is called
   a. integrating data.
   b. AutoFormatting.
   c. tiling.
   d. WordArt.

3. Objects created in one application that are copied to a document in another application are said to be
   a. embedded.
   b. linked.
   c. copied.
   d. placed.

4. The application that created the original file is called the
    a. document.
    b. source.
    c. original.
    d. target.

5. The application into which you copy data from another application is called the
    a. document.
    b. source.
    c. original.
    d. target.

6. To ensure that changes to the source document are automatically reflected in the receiving file, create a(n)
    a. embedded file.
    b. link.
    c. copy.
    d. new object.

7. When you want to link source data to a target file, use the
    a. Clipboard.
    b. Edit, Paste command.
    c. Edit, Paste Special command.
    d. drag and drop technique.

8. The easiest way to arrange the windows so that you can easily drag data from one application to another is to
    a. size the windows separately.
    b. switch back and forth between windows.
    c. close one application and open the other.
    d. open both applications and use the Tile command on the Taskbar shortcut menu.

9. An example of a component shared by all applications contained in an office suite of products is
    a. Office.
    b. Excel.
    c. Word.
    d. WordArt.

10. When you want to use one application to create data that will eventually go into another application,
    a. you should always create the target document first.
    b. you should always create the source document first.
    c. complete and save both documents before linking or embedding the data.
    d. create the data in the target application and then drag it to the source application to save it.

Short Answer

1. What feature in both Word and Excel enables you to create special text effects by graphically arranging and designing text?
2. How do you display the Taskbar shortcut menu?

3. What option from the Taskbar shortcut menu do you choose to arrange applications side by side on the screen?

4. What shape does the mouse pointer take as you drag selected data from Excel to Word?

5. What keyboard key do you press as you drag data between applications to copy the data rather than move the data?

6. What text features can you use to format WordArt objects?

7. What type of object is created when data is dragged from one application to another?

8. How do you ensure that data in a document changes when the source data changes?

9. When you change data in the source application and want to see the changes reflected in the target document, what do you need to do to the target document the next time you open it?

10. On what menu does WordArt appear?

For Discussion

1. What is the difference between linking and embedding?

2. What different methods can you use to take data from one application and place it into a document or file in another application?

3. Discuss the difference between source and target files.

4. How do you open an embedded object to edit it?

Review Exercise

Linking Excel data to a Word document.

Each month, the restaurants at The Willows are required to report earnings to the Board of Directors and compare those earnings with the previous month's earnings. Each restaurant keeps its sales data in an Excel worksheet and data for the month of April for four of the restaurants is stored in the MarApr worksheet you created in an Excel project.

Create a new Word document that you can use to report the sales data and then link the data from the Excel worksheet to create four separate letters to the Board of Directors. The four letters, which will eventually be printed on letterhead, are shown in Figure 1.2.

Integrating Word and Excel IP1-25

Current Date

The Willows Board of Directors
P. O. Box 5456
Willow Grove, SC 22345

Ladies and Gentlemen:

The monthly sales figures for our restaurant are reflected in the following table:

Sales for the Atrium Café

	Mar	April	Difference
Week 1	6,570	2,200	4,370
Week 2	8,345	7,890	455
Week 3	8,650	9,180	-530
Week 4	8,990	8,750	240
Week 5	2,130	4,560	-2,430
Total	$34,685	$32,580	

If you have questions about these figures or would like to receive additional information, please do not hesitate to contact me at the number shown above.

Sincerely,

Your Name

Current Date

The Willows Board of Directors
P. O. Box 5456
Willow Grove, SC 22345

Ladies and Gentlemen:

The monthly sales figures for our restaurant are reflected in the following table:

Sales for the The Front Porch Restaurant

	Mar	April	Difference
Week 1	5,460	4,400	1,060
Week 2	7,250	8,870	-1,620
Week 3	7,670	7,750	-80
Week 4	7,990	8,100	-110
Week 5	2,465	3,100	-635

If you have questions about these figures or would like to receive additional information, please do not hesitate to contact me at the number shown above.

Sincerely,

Your Name

Current Date

The Willows Board of Directors
P. O. Box 5456
Willow Grove, SC 22345

Ladies and Gentlemen:

The monthly sales figures for our restaurant are reflected in the following table:

Sales for the Willow Top Restaurant

	Mar	April	Difference
Week 1	8,560	4,400	4,160
Week 2	10,350	9,870	480
Week 3	10,670	11,150	-480
Week 4	10,990	10,760	230
Week 5	4,670	6,560	-1,890
Total	$45,240	$42,740	

If you have questions about these figures or would like to receive additional information, please do not hesitate to contact me at the number shown above.

Sincerely,

Your Name

Current Date

The Willows Board of Directors
P. O. Box 5456
Willow Grove, SC 22345

Ladies and Gentlemen:

The monthly sales figures for our restaurant are reflected in the following table:

Sales for the Wind in the Willows

	Mar	April	Difference
Week 1	6,460	4,300	2,160
Week 2	7,200	8,800	-1,600
Week 3	7,680	7,760	-80
Week 4	7,890	8,320	-430
Week 5	2,560	3,210	-650
Total	$31,790	$32,390	

If you have questions about these figures or would like to receive additional information, please do not hesitate to contact me at the number shown above.

Sincerely,

Your Name

Figure 1.2

Follow these steps to complete your task:

1. Launch Word so that you can create the letter pictured here, save the letter using the filename *Restaurant Sales to the Board,* and leave the letter open.

December 6, 1996

The Willows Board of Directors
P. O. Box 5456
Willow Grove, SC 22345

Ladies and Gentlemen:

The monthly sales figures for our restaurant are reflected in the following table:

If you have questions about these figures or would like to receive additional information, please do not hesitate to contact me at the number shown above.

Sincerely,

Your Name

---

2. Launch Excel and open your MarApr.xls worksheet.
3. Tile the two applications on-screen.
4. Select the data in the Atrium Cafe worksheet, and copy it to the Clipboard. Then paste the data as a link into the Word document.
5. Format, center, and align the table with paragraphs in the letter and then save the letter using the filename *Atrium Cafe Sales to the Board.*
6. Follow the same procedure to create letters for the Willow Top restaurant, the Wind in the Willow, and the Front Porch restaurant, saving each letter separately with the restaurant name as part of the filename.
7. Print copies of the letters and exit Word and Excel when you have completed your work.

Assignment

Dragging and dropping Word table data to an Excel worksheet and adding WordArt

Figure 1.3 displays data for entry fees for the upcoming golf tournament formatted as a new worksheet which contains WordArt.

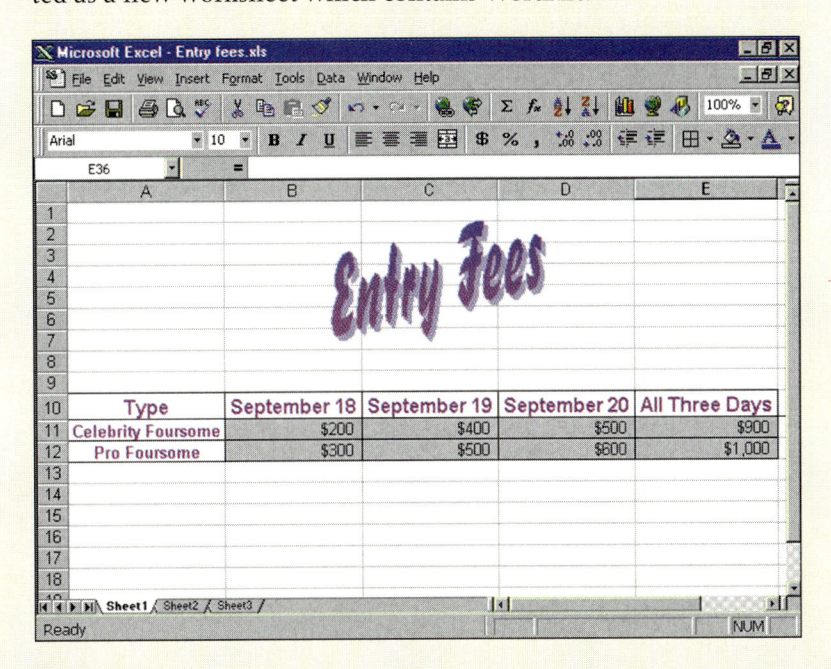

Figure 1.3

The entry fees for the golf tournament were added to a table in your Word Fees-Times-Form.doc document. Use tools presented in this Project to drag the first data table in the document into Sheet 1 of a new Excel workbook. Add a WordArt object, formatting it as shown in Figure 1.3. Save the worksheet using the filename *Tournament Entry Fees* and print a copy of the worksheet. Close the worksheet and exit Excel when you have completed your work.

Notes

Notes

Notes

Notes

Notes

Databases
Using Microsoft Access 97

Overview

Microsoft Access is the database application that comes with Microsoft Office 97. This module identifies many of the basic concepts associated with databases and acquaints you with features of Microsoft Access in particular.

Objectives

After completing this project, you will be able to:

- ➤ **Define database terminology**
- ➤ **Design a database**
- ➤ **Launch Microsoft Access**
- ➤ **Create and save a database**
- ➤ **Identify Microsoft Access screen elements**
- ➤ **Work with menus, dialog boxes, and toolbars**
- ➤ **Get Microsoft Access Help**
- ➤ **Close a database and exit Access**

Defining Database Terminology

Databases are large collections of related data stored together to provide useful information about related topics. You work with a database each time you look up a telephone number or thumb through a catalog.

Microsoft Access is a *relational database management system* (RDBMS) for organizing and storing large volumes of data in a relatively small space so that you can find data more efficiently. Imagine what it would be like if we could use a computer database program to organize our closets!

Defining Database Terms

Database management systems use the basic terms listed in Table O.1.

Table O.1   Database Terms

Term	Description	Examples
Field	One unit or piece of data; the more precise each field is, the more efficient the database management system is when you start searching and manipulating data	First name, middle initial, phone number, catalog number
Record	A collection of all related fields about one person, place, or thing	A driver's license, all the information about each catalog item
File	A collection of records related to the same topic	All drivers licenses for a state, all items in a catalog
Key field	A field containing different (unique) information for each record in a database; if you don't identify a key field, Access can assign one	Social Security number, catalog item number, filename, customer number, numeric count
Objects	Items attached to a database to hold data stored in the database	Tables, forms, reports, queries, macros, modules
Relationship	An association established between tables using fields that the tables have in common	Using Social Security number, item number, or Vendor No. to tie data from one table to data from another table.

Notice how each of these terms applies to information contained in the objects pictured in Figure O.1.

ACC-4

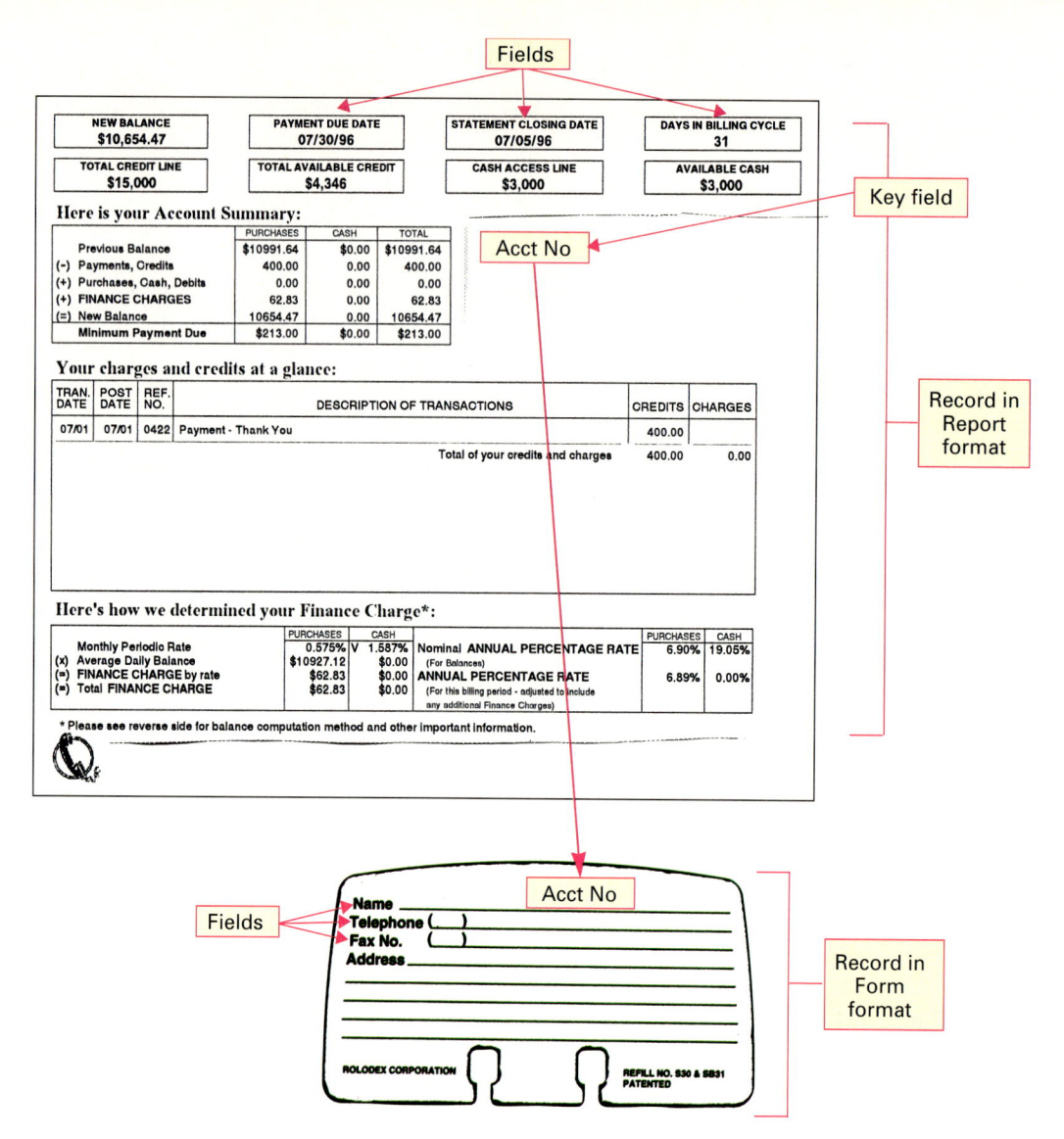

Figure O.1

Access is called an *object-oriented* relational database program because each database you create can contain more than one of each **object** listed in Table O.2.

Table O.2 Database Objects

Object	Description
Table	The primary unit of a database that stores field names, field descriptions, field controls, and field data. Tables display multiple records in a row/column format similar to a spreadsheet layout.
Query	A structured guideline used to search database tables and retrieve records that meet specific conditions.
Form	An aesthetically pleasing layout of table data designed to display one record on-screen at a time.
Report	An organized format of database data designed to generate printouts that provide meaningful information.
Macros *	A mini program that stores a set of instructions designed to perform a particular task.
Module *	A collection of Visual Basic programming procedures stored together to customize the Access environment.

* Macros and modules are advanced topics that extend beyond the scope of this text.

Figure O.2 shows how different objects display the same data.

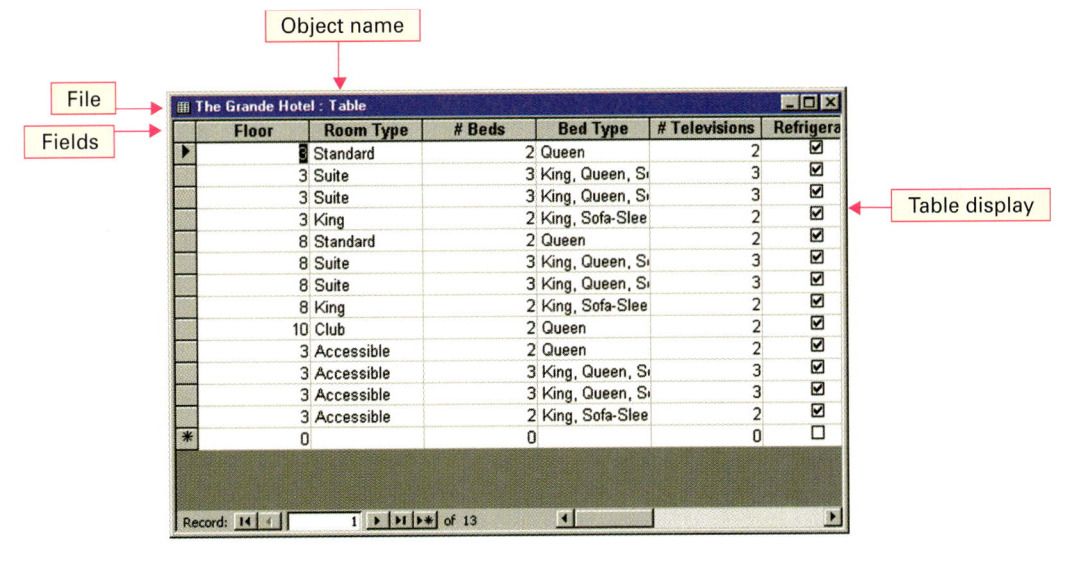

Figure O.2a

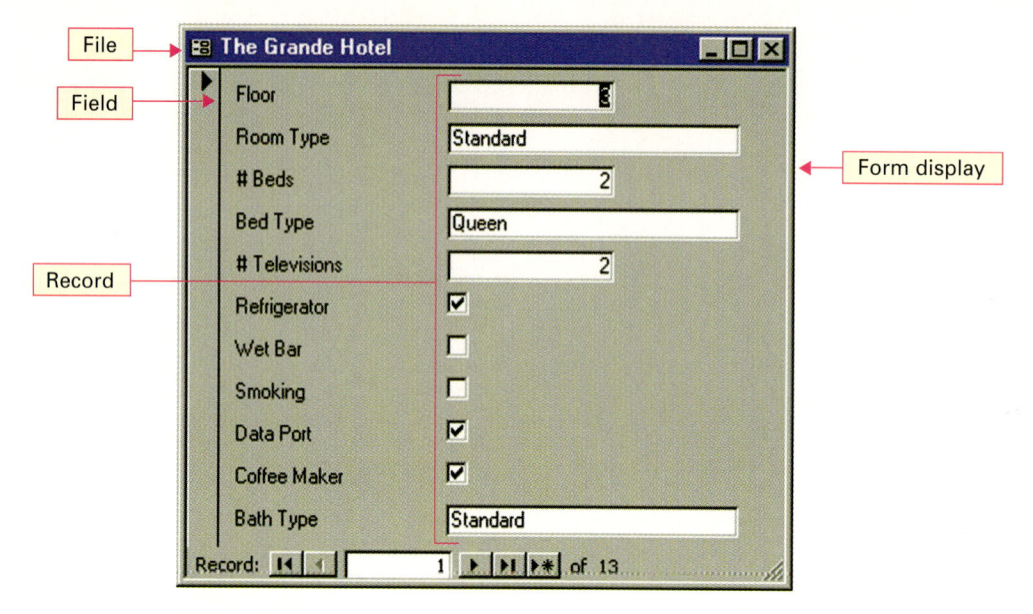

Figure O.2b

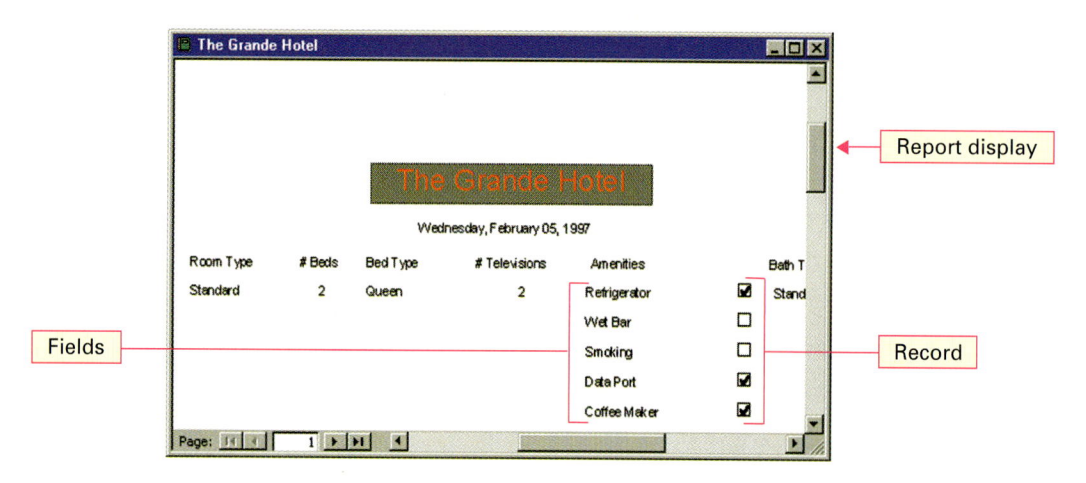

Figure O.2c

Because a database can contain numerous objects, only one database can be open at a time.

Designing a Database

Making the database easier to manage requires careful planning—and the time you spend planning the database reduces the amount of time you spend creating and maintaining the database. Determine the purpose of the database, the data you want to store, and the type of information you want to pull from the database. To print information from a database onto the Rolodex card pictured in Figure O.1, for example, the data must be contained in fields on one of the database tables. You can then create a report format that places the data on the Rolodex-size card.

After you determine the purpose of the database, you're ready to design it. Consider these points as you design the database:

- Determine how many objects (tables, forms, and reports) you need to include in the database file.
- Identify the pieces of information you want to include in each object.
- List the fields you want to include in each object in the database, breaking the information into its smallest pieces; for example, break *Name* into three fields (*First Name, Middle Name, Last Name*).
- Assign names to fields that clearly identify the data the field contains.
- Place key fields first and organize remaining fields in order of importance for each database object.
- Group together similar or related fields, such as those that make up an address, for each database object.
- List all fields for each database object on paper, and next to each field, jot down the maximum number of spaces each field requires and the type of data (text characters, numbers, or dates) each field contains.

Figure O.3 displays field information to be included in an address book.

Field Name	Field Type	Field Length
Last Name	Text	20
First Name	Text	15
Middle Initial	Text	2
Street	Text	25
City	Text	20
State	Text	2
ZIP	Number	5 (or 9)
Home Telephone	Number	12
Business Telephone	Number	12
E-Mail Address	Text	25

Figure O.3

Launching Microsoft Access

After you power up the computer, log onto required networks, and respond to message windows built into the system, Windows 95 starts automatically. Think of the Start button as the launch pad and you'll be able to quickly get Access up and running.

TASK 1: TO LAUNCH ACCESS:

1. Click the Start **Start** button.
2. Point to Programs.

ACC-8

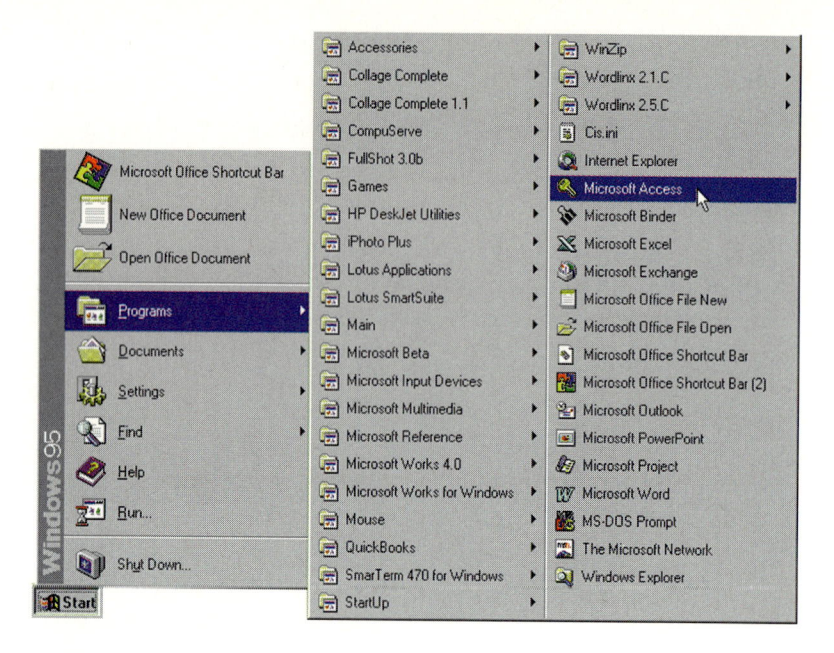

3 Point to Microsoft Access and click.

Clippit offers to help get you started

4 Click Start Using Microsoft Access if the Office Assistant displays.

Creating and Saving a Database

The first time you launch Access, the **Office Assistant** pops up, introduces itself, and offers assistance. After the first launch, the Office Assistant takes a seat up on the toolbar and waits for you to call for help. If you don't see the Office Assistant, that's okay. You learn more about it later in this overview; for now you just want to get started. The dialog box shown in Figure O.4 presents options that enable you to create a new database or open an existing one.

Overview **ACC-9**

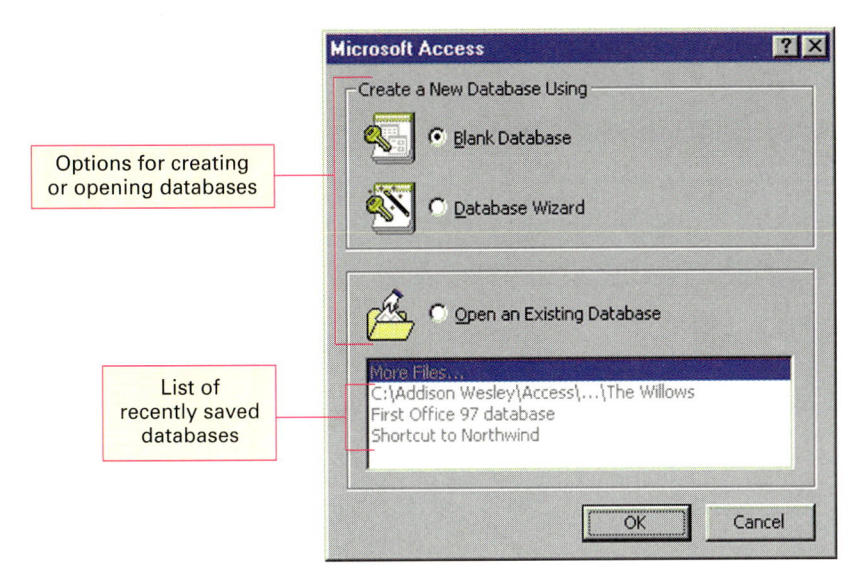

Options for creating or opening databases

List of recently saved databases

Figure O.4

When you create a new database, you have to do your part: you have to name the database and identify the folder you want to use to store the database. Eventually, you will create objects within the database, and Access will store the objects together in the same database file.

> **Note** If you're not ready to create or open a database but just want to learn more about using Access, you can click Cancel in the Access dialog box and then open the Help menu.

TASK 2: TO CREATE AND SAVE A NEW DATABASE FILE:

1 Click Blank Database and then click OK.

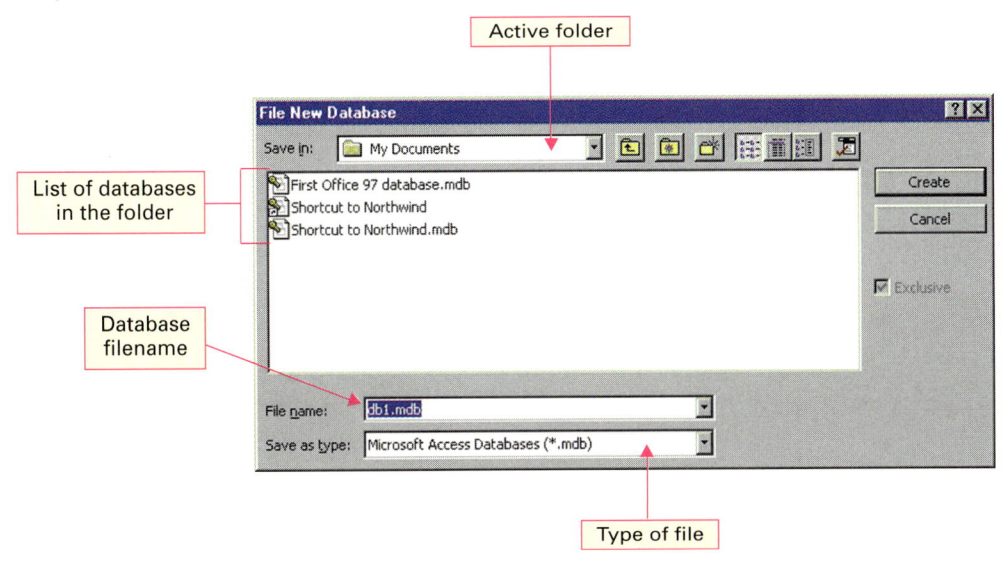

Active folder

List of databases in the folder

Database filename

Type of file

2 Select the folder you want to use to store the database from the Save in drop-down list as directed by your instructor.

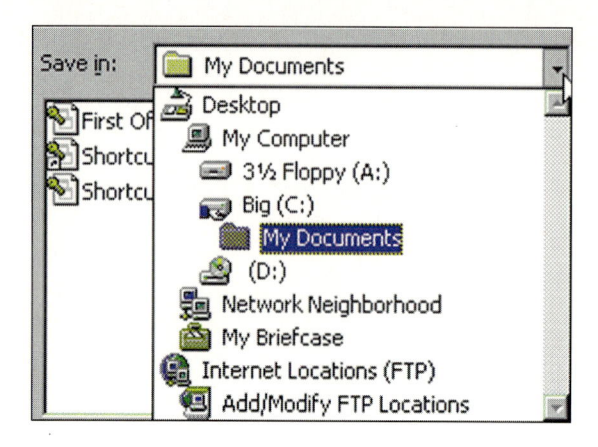

3 Type **The Willows** in the File name text box and press ENTER.
Unless someone has customized your Microsoft Access environment, the screen should resemble the screen shown in Figure O.5.

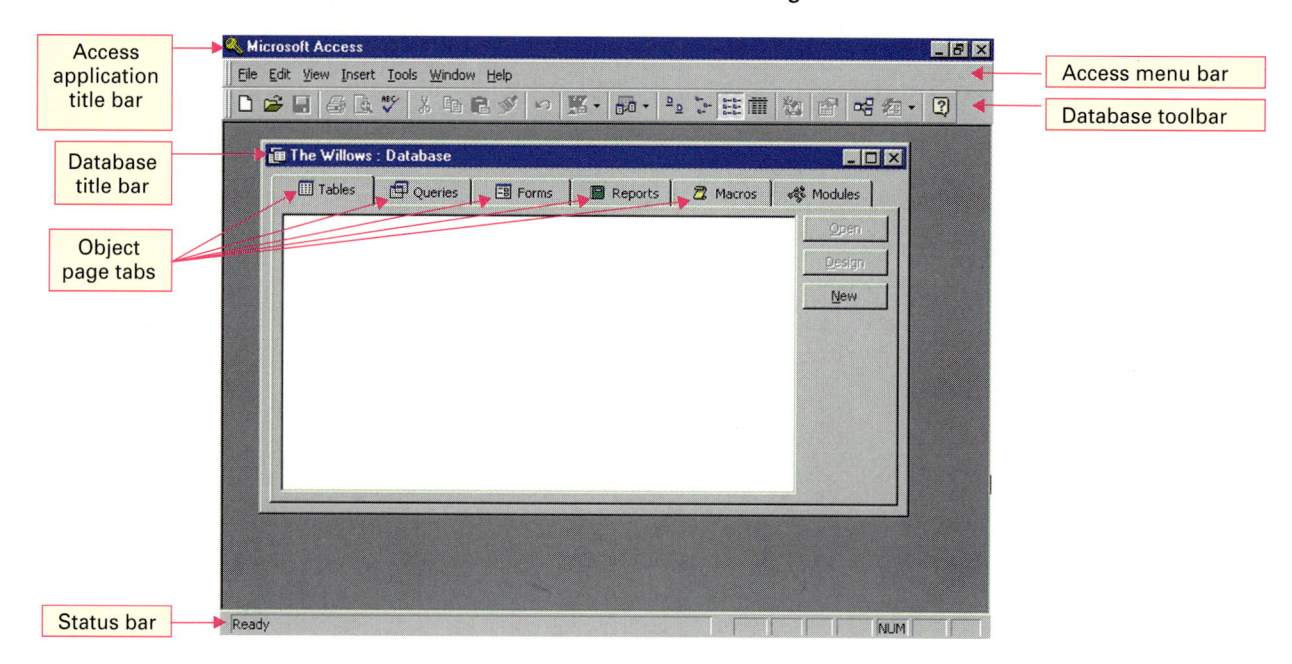

Labels on figure: Access application title bar, Database title bar, Object page tabs, Status bar, Access menu bar, Database toolbar

Figure O.5

Identifying Microsoft Access Screen Elements

The Microsoft Access screen features a number of elements found in other application windows as well as several elements unique to Microsoft Access, as you can see in Table O.3.

Table O.3 Access Screen Features

Screen Feature	Description
Menu bar	Provides access to commands used to perform tasks. The menu bar changes, depending on the task you're performing and the object that is active.
Title bar	Identifies the application name and the name of the active database, and contains the application icon, Maximize/Restore, Minimize, and Close buttons.
Database toolbar	Contains buttons that serve as shortcuts for performing the most common tasks.
Database window	Organizes objects by type to make accessing objects more efficient.
Object Page tabs	Provide access to objects contained in the database.
Status bar	Displays information about the program status, instructions for performing selected tasks, active key information, and trouble messages.

Working with Menus, Dialog Boxes, and Toolbars

Menus and toolbars provide access to features and commands you use as you perform tasks in Access. Dialog boxes present options for you to choose as you create database files and objects, format forms and reports, and build databases.

Identifying Menu Features

The Access *menu bar* appears just below the *title bar* in the Access window. Menu items contained on the menu bar group commands for performing tasks according to type. Don't be surprised when your Access screen seems to change for no reason: in Access, the menu bar changes as you work with different database objects. To display a list of menu commands, point to the menu item and click. Figure O.6 identifies the standard features of Access menus you see.

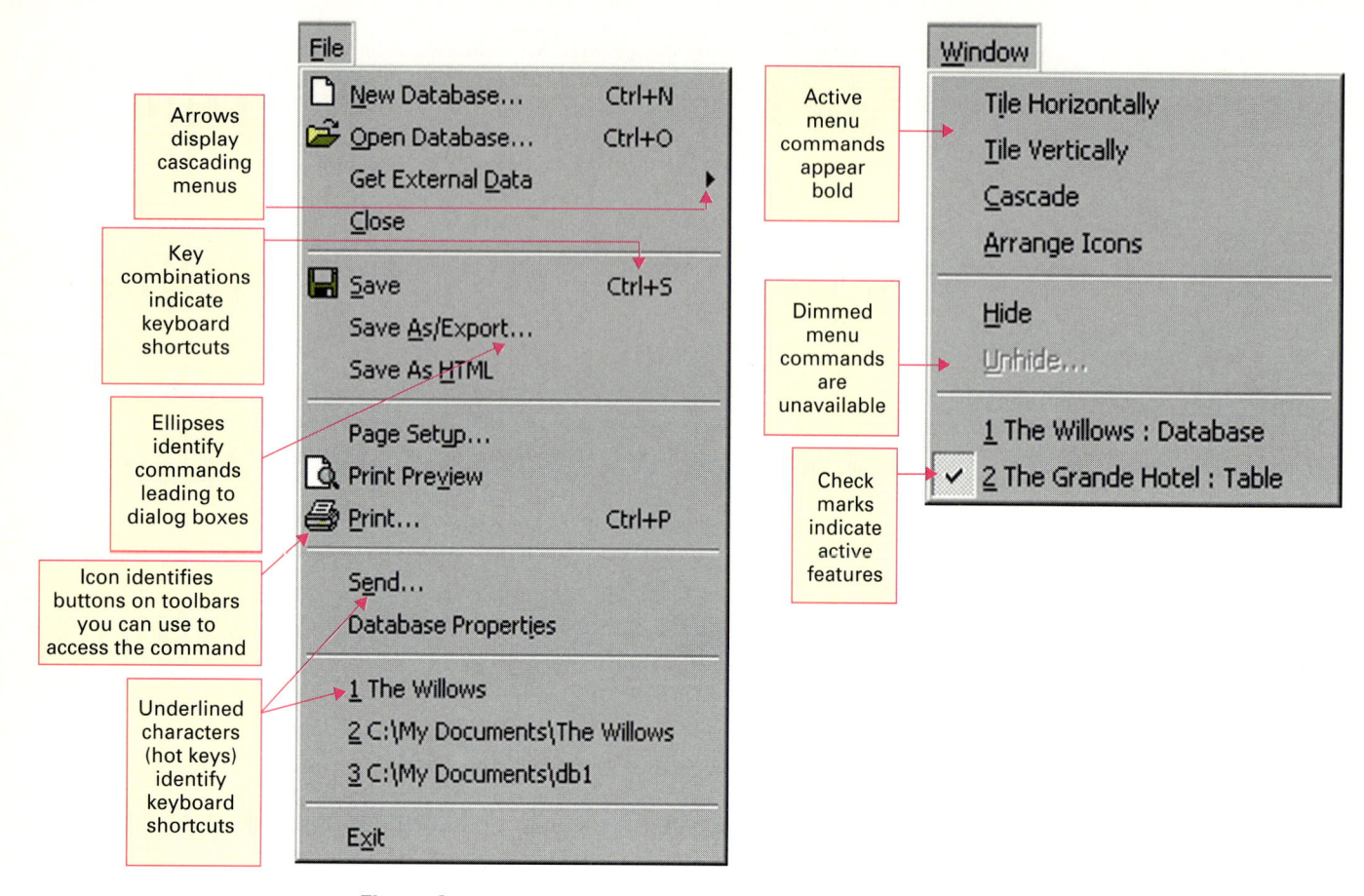

Figure O.6

Working with Toolbars

You can perform many of the most frequently used menu commands or display dialog boxes by clicking buttons on the Access **toolbars**. A *Screen-Tip* pops up when you point to any toolbar button, identifying the task that that button performs. The toolbar displayed in the Access window changes automatically as you work with objects and perform different tasks, just as the menu changes.

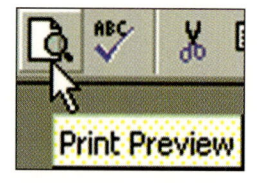

Working with Dialog Boxes

A dialog box appears when you choose a menu command followed by an ellipsis or when you click certain toolbar buttons. Figure O.7 identifies features that you'll see as you work with dialog boxes. Not all features appear in every dialog box.

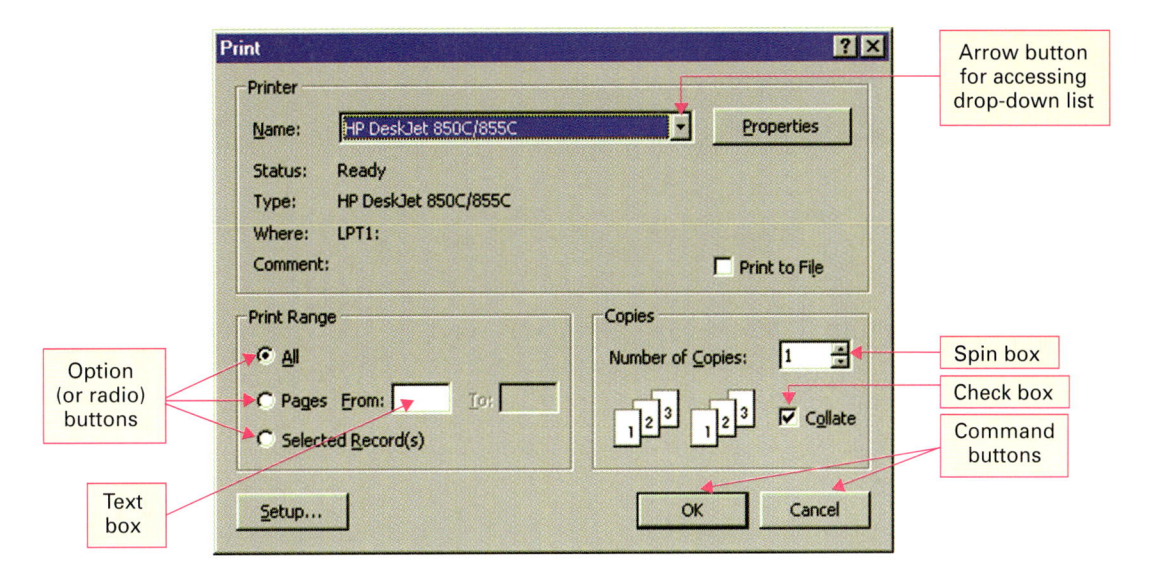

Overview ACC-13

[Figure O.7: Print dialog box with callouts labeling: Arrow button for accessing drop-down list; Spin box; Check box; Command buttons; Option (or radio) buttons; Text box]

Figure O.7

TASK 3: TO DISPLAY MENUS AND DIALOG BOXES AND USE THE TOOLBAR:

1 Point to the File menu and click.
The menu shown in Figure O.6 displays.

2 Click Open Database.

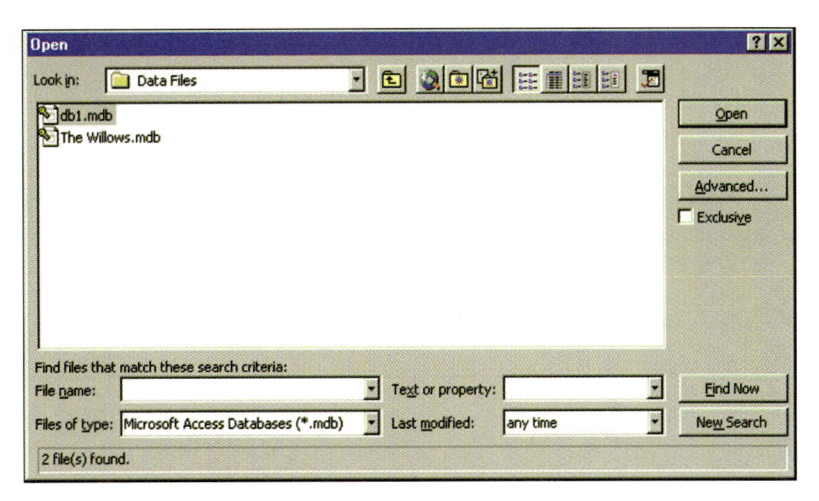

[Open dialog box showing Data Files folder with db1.mdb and The Willows.mdb listed]

3 Press ESC to close the dialog box.

4 Point to the Spelling button on the toolbar and pause to see the ToolTip.

[Spelling button with ToolTip displayed]

5 Click the Open button on the toolbar. The Open dialog box opens again.

6 Close the dialog box again.

Getting Help

Microsoft Access provides numerous ways for you to get *online help* as you work. Simply display the Microsoft Access Help menu and choose the help feature you want to use:

- The Office Assistant, which enables you to ask questions about the task you want to perform.
- The standard three-page Windows 95 Help dialog box, which displays Contents, Index, and Find to search for information on the topic or procedure you need.
- The What's This? feature to obtain a brief description of a button, feature, or command.
- Microsoft on the Web to explore information about new products, obtain answers to frequently asked questions, recommend improvements to the program, and so forth.

In addition, Microsoft Access provides context-sensitive help and tips as you work. Because the Office Assistant automatically pops up as you work with Access, it's the Help feature used to obtain Help in this book.

> **Note** Online help has proven to be a more efficient method for obtaining help than searching through voluminous manuals for tips and information about specific programs and tasks. However, "online help" doesn't refer to connecting to the Internet or communications provider; it simply refers to the help provided by the software and accessible from the computer.

Using the Office Assistant

The Office Assistant is a feature new to Microsoft Office 97 applications. Because you can type questions or topics for which you want help in the Office Assistant's text box, this feature is already growing in popularity. Office Assistant is easy to use, personally animated, and provides a more

Overview   ACC-15

focused list of help topics than the list displayed when you use the Find or Contents features.

TASK 4: TO DISPLAY, USE, AND CLOSE THE OFFICE ASSISTANT:

1 Click the Office Assistant button.

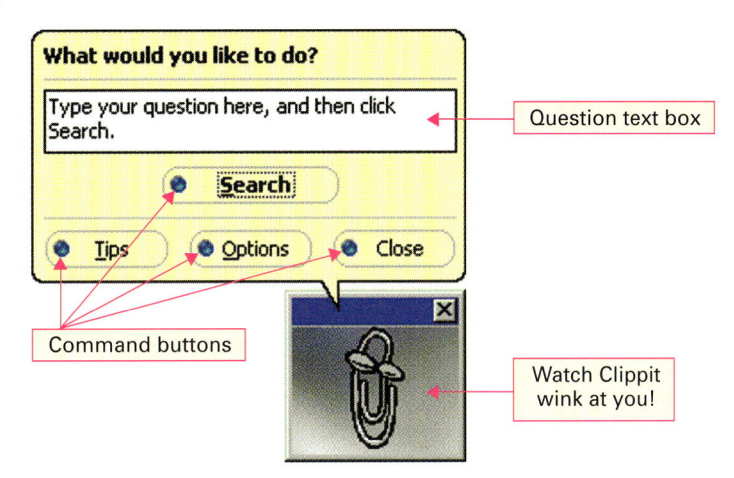

Question text box

Command buttons

Watch Clippit wink at you!

2 Type **Create a Table** in the Question text box; then press (ENTER).

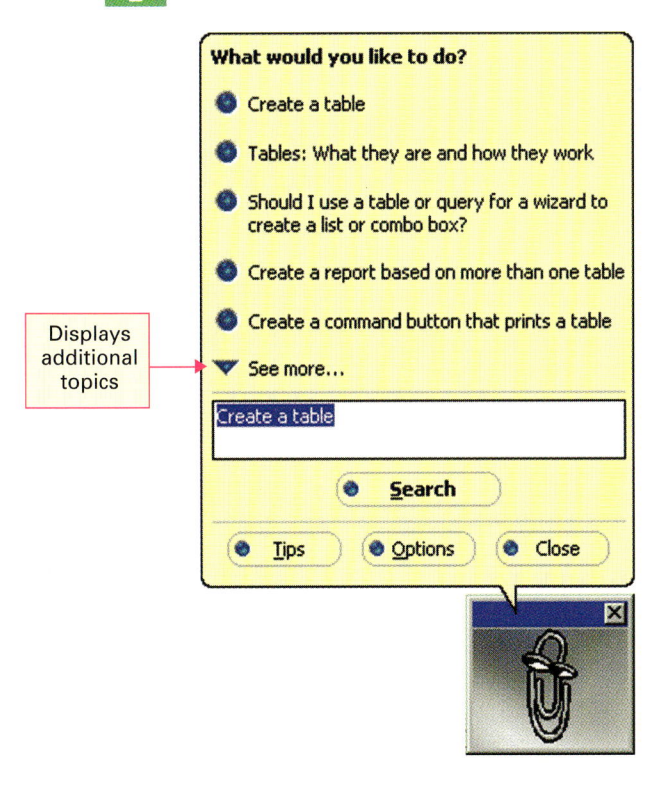

Displays additional topics

3 Click the button beside Create a table, at the top of the related topics list.

ACC-16

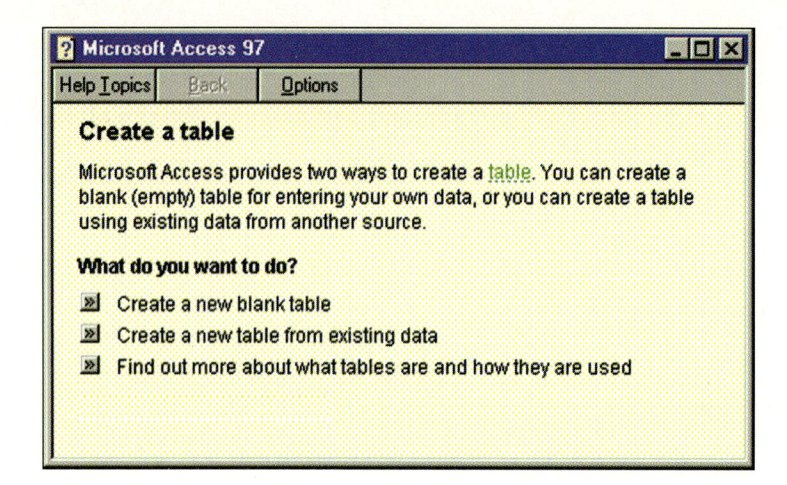

> **Microsoft Access 97**
>
> **Create a table**
>
> Microsoft Access provides two ways to create a table. You can create a blank (empty) table for entering your own data, or you can create a table using existing data from another source.
>
> **What do you want to do?**
> - Create a new blank table
> - Create a new table from existing data
> - Find out more about what tables are and how they are used

4 Review the information in the help dialog box and then click the Close ⊠ button.
The list of related topics disappears; the Office Assistant remains on-screen until you close it.

5 Click ⊠ on the Office Assistant window.

Using What's This? Help

The What's This? Help feature provides a simple, straightforward way for you to point to something on-screen and get a quick definition in a pop-up box. In Access 97, you can select What's This? Help from the Help menu or press Shift+F1.

TASK 5: TO USE WHAT'S THIS? HELP:

1 Press (SHIFT)+(F1).
The pointer changes to an arrow with a question mark attached.

2 Click the Forms tab on the database window.

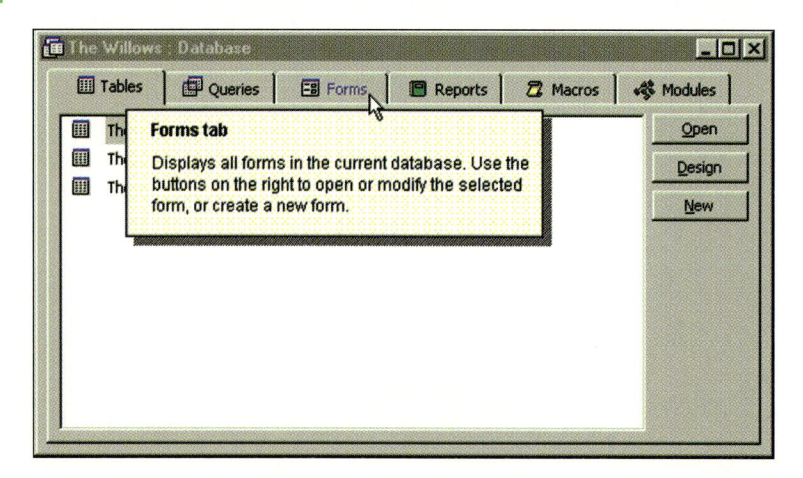

> **The Willows : Database**
>
> Tables | Queries | **Forms** | Reports | Macros | Modules
>
> **Forms tab**
> Displays all forms in the current database. Use the buttons on the right to open or modify the selected form, or create a new form.
>
> Open | Design | New

3 Click again.
The pop-up box closes.

Overview   ACC-17

Using Help Contents

The "Getting Help" section of the Overview of Windows 95 provides a comprehensive overview of how Help features work in most Windows 95 products. This quick review will give you a peek at some of the topics you'll find when you use the Help feature in Access.

TASK 6: TO LOOK UP THE NEW FEATURES OF ACCESS 97:

1 Choose Help.
The Help menu drops down.

2 Choose Contents and Index and click the Contents tab if necessary.

3 Double-click Welcome to Microsoft Access 97 - What's New?

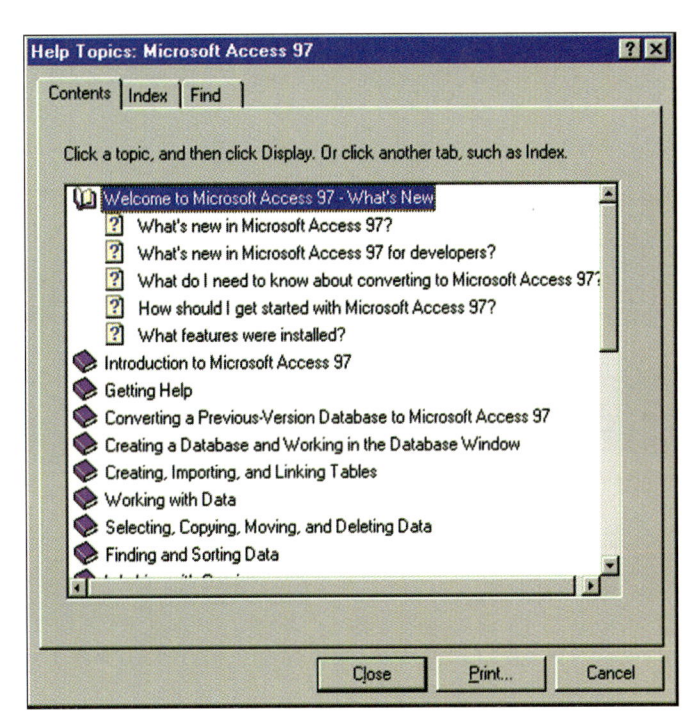

4 Double-click How should I get started with Microsoft Access 97?

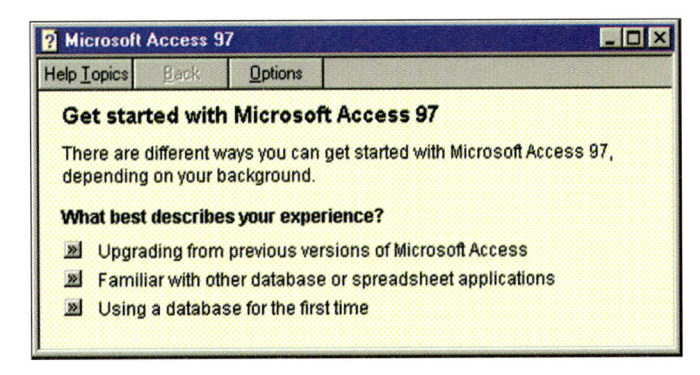

ACC-18

5 Click the button beside Using a database for the first time. Another list of possible topics opens.

6 Review the list of topics and then click ☒ in the Help window.

Using the Help Index

The Help Index feature resembles the Office Assistant in the way it lets you type a topic and see a list of related topics. The basic difference is that you see a comprehensive listing of all Help topics in the Index window—not just the few that Office Assistant identifies when you ask it for help.

TASK 7: TO SEARCH FOR TOPICS IN THE INDEX ABOUT RELATIONSHIPS:

1 Choose Help, Contents and Index, and click on the Index tab if necessary. The Index list opens.

2 Type **relationships** and review the list of topics related to relationships.

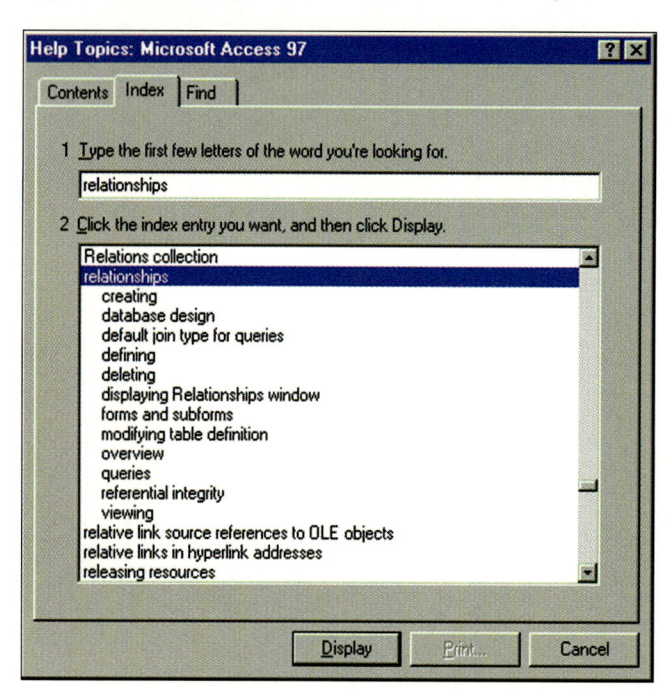

Overview ACC-19

3 Double-click the word *overview* in the list.

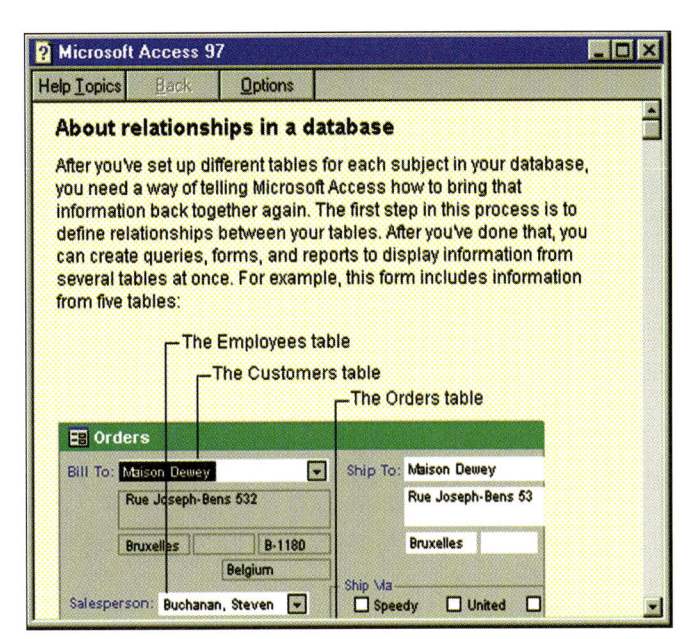

4 Read the Help dialog box and then click ☒.
The dialog box closes.

Getting Help from the Microsoft Web Site

If you're connected to the Internet, you can access the Microsoft World Wide Web site to obtain additional help information. The site provides information directly from Microsoft support team members as well as information from other users.

TASK 8: TO ACCESS ONLINE SUPPORT FROM THE MICROSOFT WEB SITE:

1 Choose Help, Microsoft on the Web.

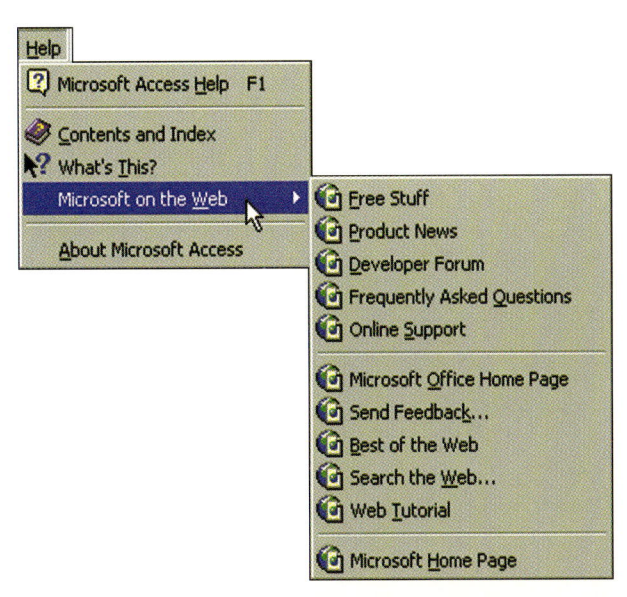

2 Choose Online Support.

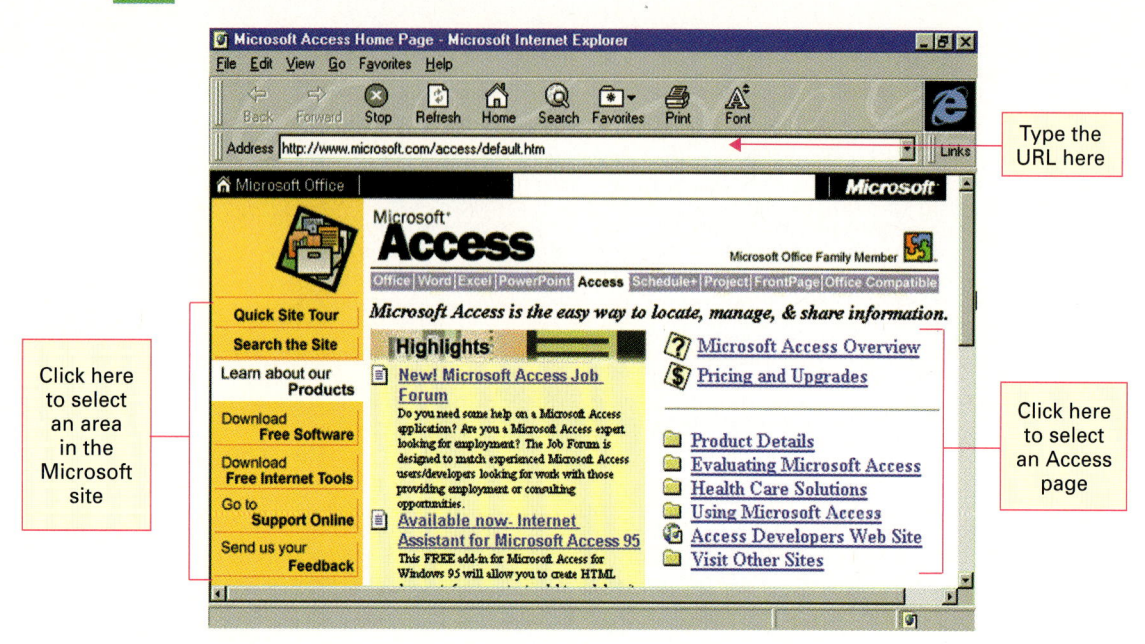

[Screenshot of Microsoft Access Home Page in Internet Explorer, with annotations: "Type the URL here", "Click here to select an area in the Microsoft site", "Click here to select an Access page"]

3 Complete the standard procedure for logging onto the Internet using your service provider.

4 Review the available help topics and then log off the Internet.

Closing a Database and Exiting Microsoft Access

After you've completed your work on a database, you need to close it. When you finish using Access, you need to close the database and exit Access.

TASK 9: TO CLOSE A DATABASE AND EXIT ACCESS:

1 Click ⊠ on the database window.

> **Tip** As you close a database, Access examines each object in the database and reminds you to save changed objects by displaying a message window. Click Yes to save changes to the object, No to discard changes, or Cancel to return to the database.

2 Click ⊠ on the application window.

Summary and Exercises

Summary

- Microsoft Access is an object-oriented relational database program.
- Databases are collections of related data stored together to provide useful information about related topics.
- You must name and save new databases as you create them.
- Each database can contain numerous tables, forms, reports, queries, macros, and modules, each designed to focus on a particular aspect of the broad-based database theme.
- Only one database can be open at a time.
- The toolbar that contains tools needed for specific tasks appears automatically.
- Access offers a variety of resources from which you can get online help.
- Microsoft Access reminds you to save changes to objects you create before you exit the program.

Key Terms and Operations

Key Terms
form
macro
menu bar
module
object
Office Assistant
online help
query
relational database
report
status bar
table
title bar
toolbar
ScreenTips

Operations
exit Microsoft Access
launch Microsoft Access
name and save a Microsoft Access database
retrieve help from the Web
use Office Assistant

Study Questions

Multiple Choice

1. To display the Help dialog box,
   a. choose Help, Contents and Index.
   b. click the Office Assistant button.
   c. press Shift+F1.
   d. choose Help, About Microsoft Access.

2. To start Microsoft Access,
   a. double-click the Outlook icon on the desktop.
   b. click Start and choose Programs, Microsoft Access.
   c. start Windows 95 and then press Alt+W.
   d. open My Computer.

3. What feature identifies toolbar buttons?
    a. the Tipster
    b. Office Assistant
    c. the Objects button
    d. ScreenTips

4. All the following are features of dialog boxes *except*
    a. option buttons.
    b. text boxes.
    c. drop-down lists.
    d. ScreenTips.

5. When you launch Microsoft Access,
    a. a new database appears.
    b. the Open dialog box appears.
    c. the Microsoft Access dialog box appears so that you can tell Access whether you want to create a new database or open an existing database.
    d. a blank table appears so that you can enter field names.

6. How many databases can be open at the same time?
    a. one
    b. ten
    c. as many as the memory installed on the computer can handle
    d. an infinite number

7. All the following procedures can be used to exit Microsoft Access *except*
    a. choosing File, Exit.
    b. clicking the Close button in the menu bar.
    c. pressing Alt+F4.
    d. double-clicking the application control icon.

8. What database term represents a unit of data, such as *First Name?*
    a. field
    b. record
    c. file
    d. key field

9. A unique unit of data can be used as a
    a. field.
    b. record.
    c. file.
    d. key field.

10. To set aside room on a disk to contain the database,
    a. you must save the database as you create it.
    b. type **reserved** in the title field.
    c. open an existing database.
    d. check with your instructor.

Short Answer
1. Why is it necessary to save and name a database as you create it?
2. What's the basic object of a database?
3. How are fields related to files?
4. How many toolbars are available in Microsoft Access?

5. Where does the filename you assign to a database appear?
6. What's the default toolbar displayed in Microsoft Access?
7. How do you find out what task a toolbar button performs?
8. Which Help feature enables you to type a question and displays a narrow range of topics in response to your question?
9. What does an ellipsis following a menu command mean?
10. What's a database management system?

For Discussion
1. How does the procedure for launching Microsoft Access differ from the procedure for launching other Windows 95 applications?
2. Why is planning your database important?
3. What factors should you keep in mind when planning a database?
4. How would you use each of the different objects that can be created in a database?

Review Exercises

1. Designing a New Database
One of the databases that The Willows wants you to create is an employee database. It will be used to keep track of names, addresses, salary information, employment history, and other pertinent information about the people who work for each facility at The Willows. Create a list of data fields you would recommend be included in The Willows' employee database. Include an estimated number of characters required by the data to be entered into each field, and record an example of data that might be typed into the field.

2. Getting Help About Wizards
Because Microsoft Office 97 incorporates the use of wizards to help you create databases and objects within databases, you need to learn more about how wizards can help you with your work. Ask the Office Assistant to locate information about creating a database by using a wizard. Follow these steps:

1. Click the Office Assistant button on the toolbar.
2. Type **Tell me about the Database Wizard** in the question text box of the Office Assistant window and then press (ENTER).
3. Click Create a database in the list of items displayed by the Office Assistant.
4. Click Create a database using a Database Wizard at the bottom of the Create a Database Help window, and then review the information and steps displayed in the Help window.

Assignments

1. Identifying Fields to Include in Database for The Willows
The reception desk of The Grande Hotel at The Willows Resort wants to use the database for The Willows to identify characteristics of the different rooms available at the hotel. Develop a list of field names, field types, and field sizes you think should be included in the database to provide useful information to reception clerks. These data fields will be used in Project 1 to create one of the table objects in the database.

2. Exploring the Microsoft Access Forum on the Web to Look for Jobs
The Microsoft Access Web page contains links to many interesting and helpful sites. (The Microsoft home page is www.Microsoft.com. Click on Product.) One site to which the Microsoft Access page is linked is the Microsoft Access Job Forum. Using Microsoft Access on the Web help, locate the Job Forum and copy job information for five jobs listed on the Forum. If the system permits, you may want to download detailed job descriptions from this forum.

PROJECT 1

Building a Database

Now that you've created a Microsoft Access 97 database, you're ready to build the database by adding objects to the database. In this project, you will create a table to store data and a form to view the data on-screen.

Objectives

After completing this project, you will be able to:

- ➤ Open an Access database
- ➤ Create an Access database table
- ➤ Open an Access database table
- ➤ Add records to an Access database table
- ➤ Check the spelling of data in a database table
- ➤ Create and save a form
- ➤ Navigate datasheets and forms
- ➤ Preview and print database data

The Challenge

As the data-entry specialist for The Willows, you build and maintain databases for The Willows. The first *table* you need to add to the database called *The Willows* will be used by reception clerks at The Grande Hotel to check room descriptions when guests check in. Mr. Gilmore, manager of The Grande Hotel, has developed a list of information he wants you to place in the database table.

The Solution

Your job is to create a new table in the database *The Willows* and define the table fields to hold the information provided by Mr. Gilmore. The table fields are shown in Figure 1.1. After saving the table, you need to enter records in the table, create a form to display table data, and print database data.

The Setup

Just to make sure that you're on the same screen as those pictured in this module, you may want to check some of the settings before you get started. This module assumes that the default settings were in place when the lab guru installed the program on the machine. Because many students work with the lab computers, though, some of the settings may have changed.

If you don't see a toolbar on the screen when you open the Access database, choose View, Toolbars. Then click the toolbar listed at the top of the cascading menu. If you see extra toolbars, close them. After you activate one toolbar, Access should automatically display appropriate toolbars as you work with various features.

If you don't see a status bar, choose Tools, Options. When the Options dialog box displays, click the View page tab and then click the check box beside Status Bar at the top of the page. While you're in the Options dialog box, check the Keyboard page to see which options are selected. If you have Next Field selected in the Move After Enter section in the upper-left corner, you can press Enter as well as Tab to move from one field to the next.

Most of the pictures you see in this project display the screen with objects in their own windows. If you have objects maximized, click the Restore button on each object window.

> **Tip** If your screen still doesn't match the ones shown here, ask your instructor to help you locate those features that appear to be missing.

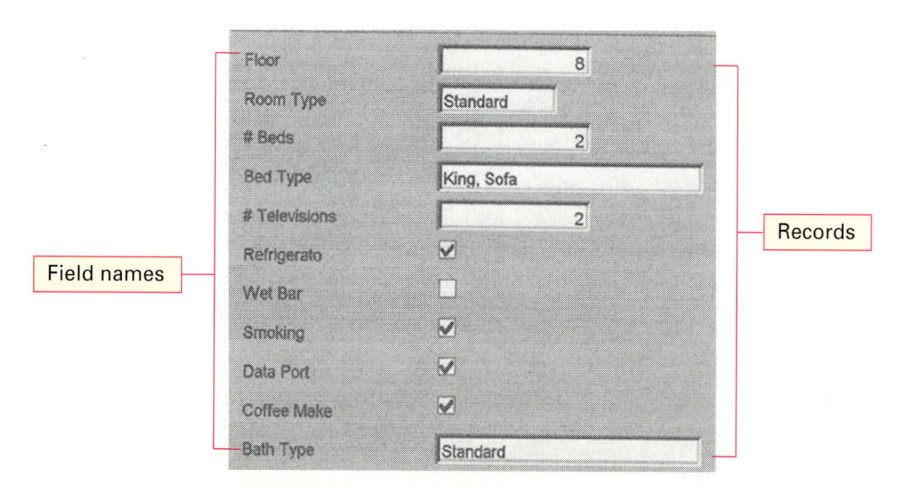

Figure 1.1

Opening an Access Database

When you launch Access, the Microsoft Access dialog box contains an option for opening an existing database. In addition, the last five databases saved on the computer appear in the list box at the bottom of the Microsoft Access dialog box.

TASK 1: TO OPEN A DATABASE:

1 Launch Access.

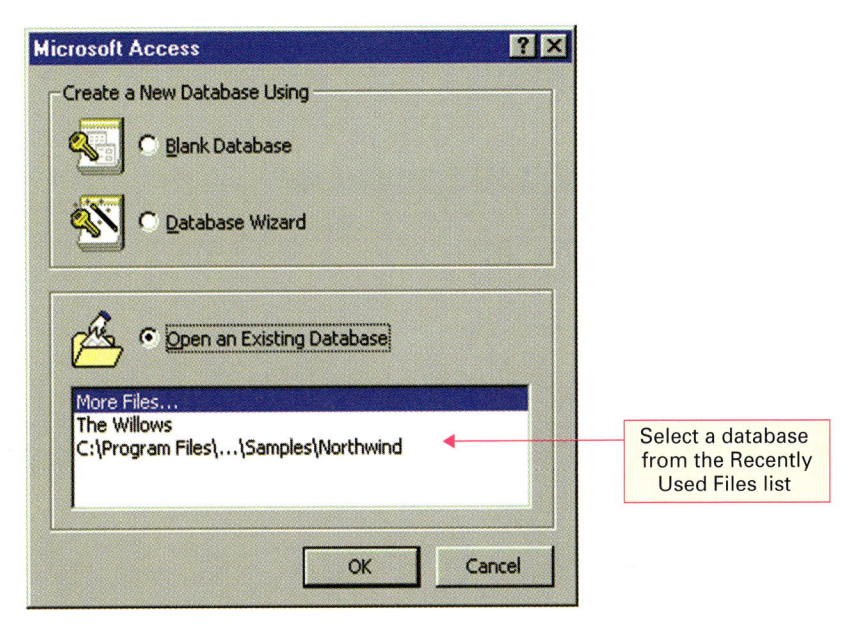

Select a database from the Recently Used Files list

2 Double-click *The Willows* in the list at the bottom of the Microsoft Access dialog box.

The database name appears in the database window title bar

Click to display the Tables page tab

The New button enables you to create a new table

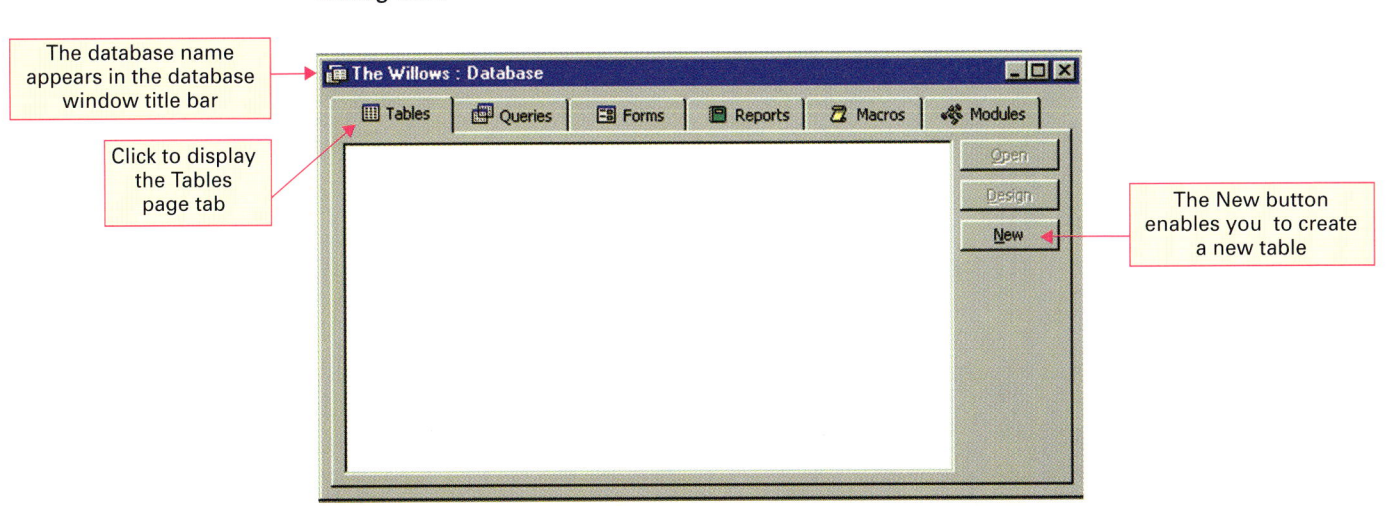

> **Note** If the file you want doesn't appear on the dialog box list, select More Files. From the Open dialog box that appears, select the folder that has the database you want to open and then double-click the database filename.

Creating an Access Database Table

The primary object used to store data in a database is the *database table*. Tables hold the field names, field descriptions, and data for each field of each record. Tables make up the underlying structure for data stored in a database.

The first object you create in the database *The Willows* is a table to hold room descriptions for The Grande Hotel.

TASK 2: TO CREATE A NEW DATABASE TABLE:

1. Click the New button in the database window.

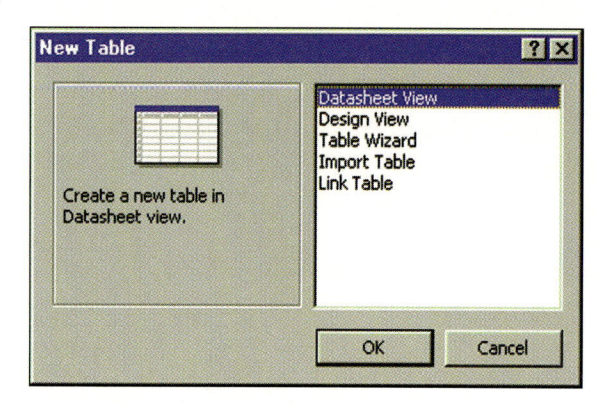

2. Select Design View in the New Table dialog box; then click OK.

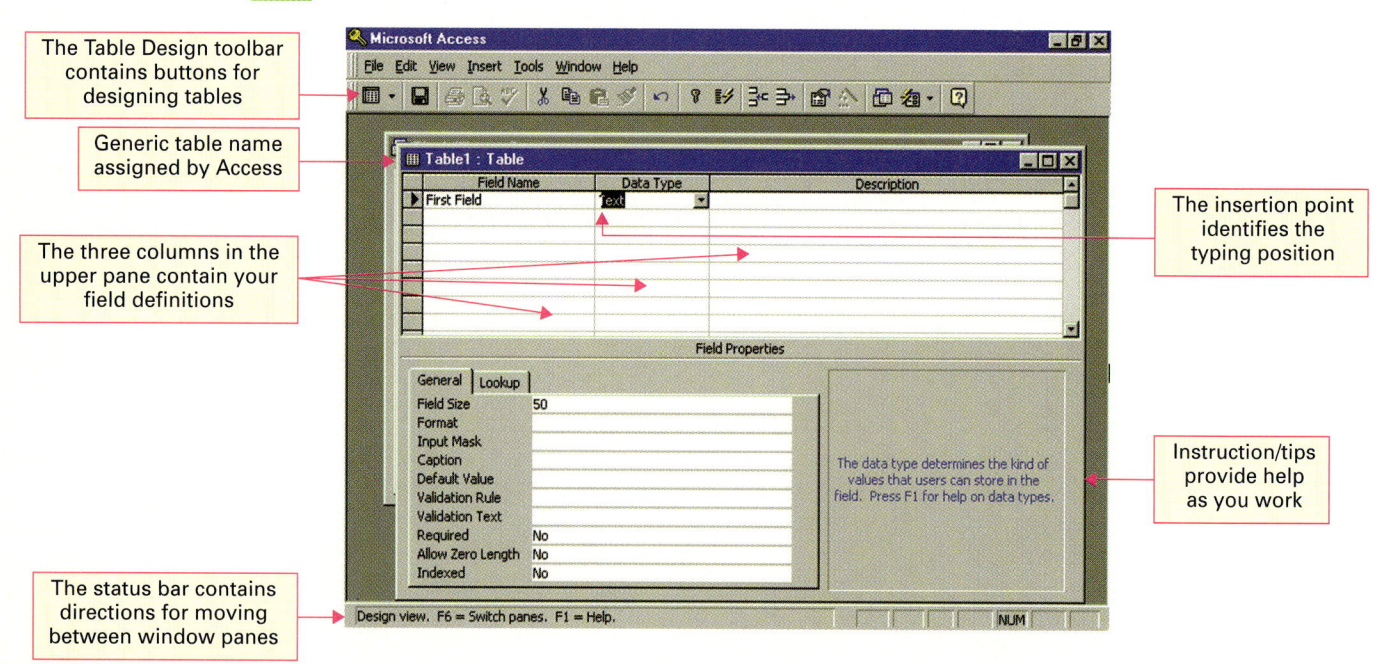

- The Table Design toolbar contains buttons for designing tables
- Generic table name assigned by Access
- The three columns in the upper pane contain your field definitions
- The status bar contains directions for moving between window panes
- The insertion point identifies the typing position
- Instruction/tips provide help as you work

Defining Table Fields

Table 1.1 describes the data types available in Access.

Table 1.1   Access Data Types

Data Type	Description
Text	Any combination of alphabetic and numeric characters, such as names, addresses, and telephone numbers, that aren't used in calculations. Text is the default data type.
Memo	Long entries that require multiple lines of text, such as detailed descriptions and performance notes.
Number	Numeric values, such as the number of items or number of days worked, that might be used in calculations.
Date/Time	Dates, such as date hired, and times, such as 1:00.
Currency	Monetary values, such as a salary, consisting of numbers that might be used in calculations.
AutoNumber	Numbers assigned by Access to uniquely identify each record; these values can't be changed, deleted, or edited.
Yes/No	Single-character entry fields that are marked when the status of the field is true (yes) or left blank when the status is false (no).
OLE Object	Fields that may be linked to an object, such as a picture or a document.
Hyperlink	Fields linked to other objects, Web pages, or documents that appear when the field is clicked.
Lookup Wizard	Fields that enable you to access a value from a table or list of values.

TASK 3: TO DEFINE FIELDS IN THE TABLE DESIGN WINDOW:

1. Type **Floor** in the Field Name column of the first row of the top pane; then press TAB.

> **Tip** Being human, you're bound to make mistakes as you're typing. To correct your errors, press Backspace to remove the incorrect characters and then type the correct characters. If you discover a mistake after you've moved the insertion point to the next column, point to the column containing the error and double-click to select the field contents. Typing the correct data while the field contents are selected automatically replaces the selected data.

ACC-30

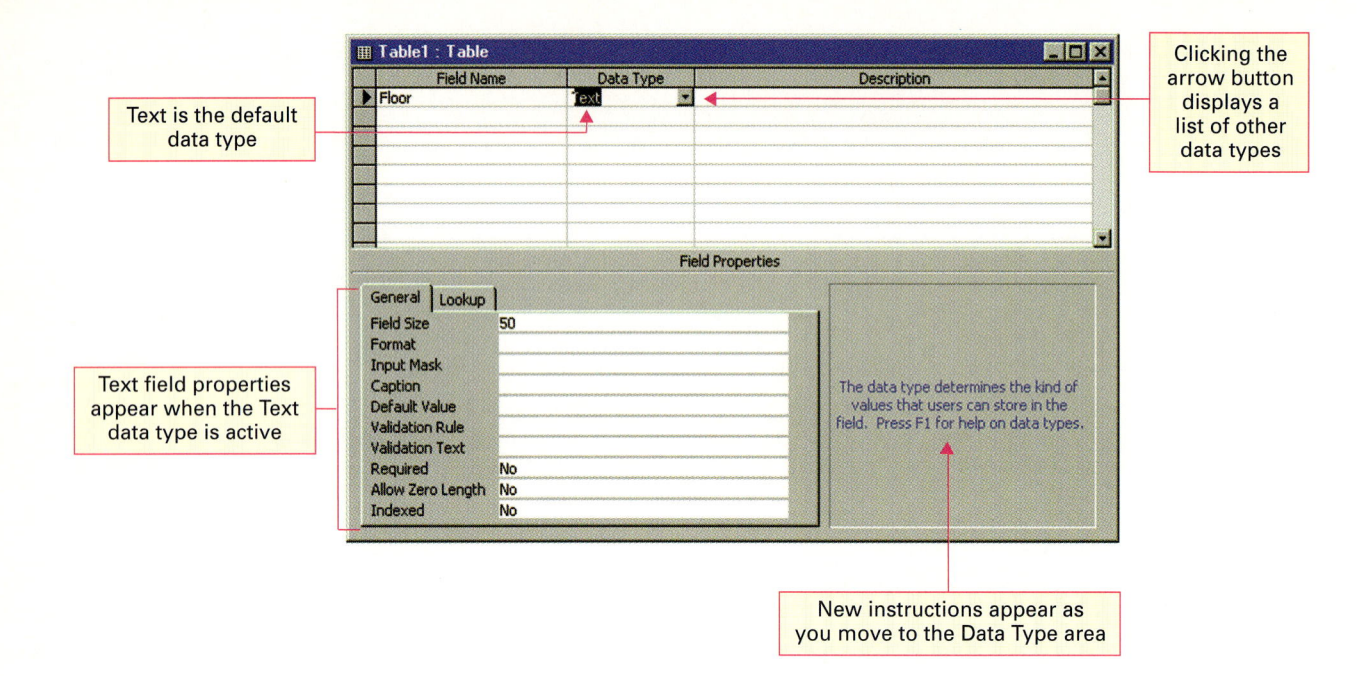

Text is the default data type

Clicking the arrow button displays a list of other data types

Text field properties appear when the Text data type is active

New instructions appear as you move to the Data Type area

2 Click the arrow button at the right side of the Data Type column.

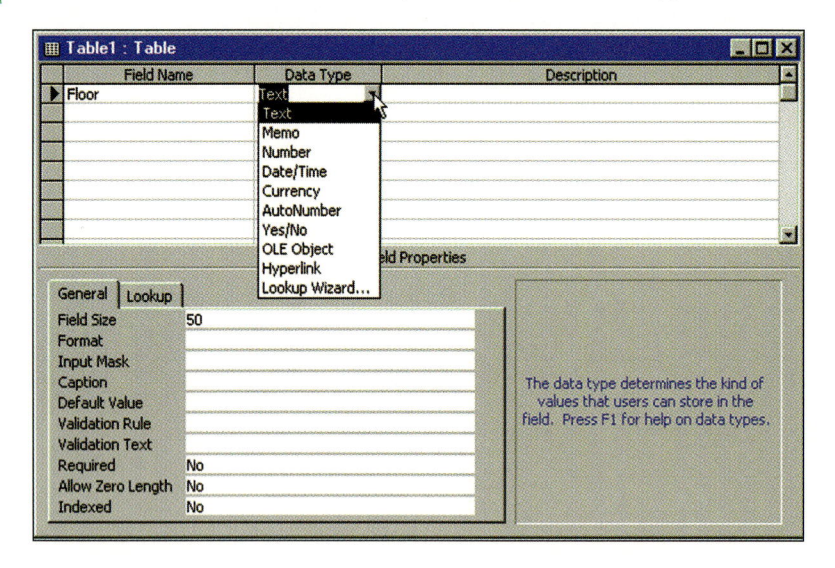

Project 1: Building a Database   ACC-31

3 Click Number to tell Access that the Floor field will contain numeric data.

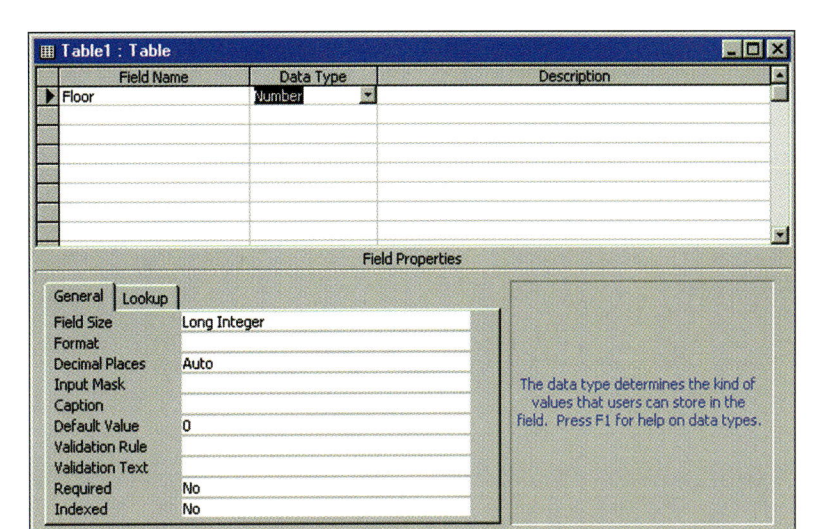

4 Press TAB to move to the Description field. Then type **Valid entries range from 3 through 12** in the text box.

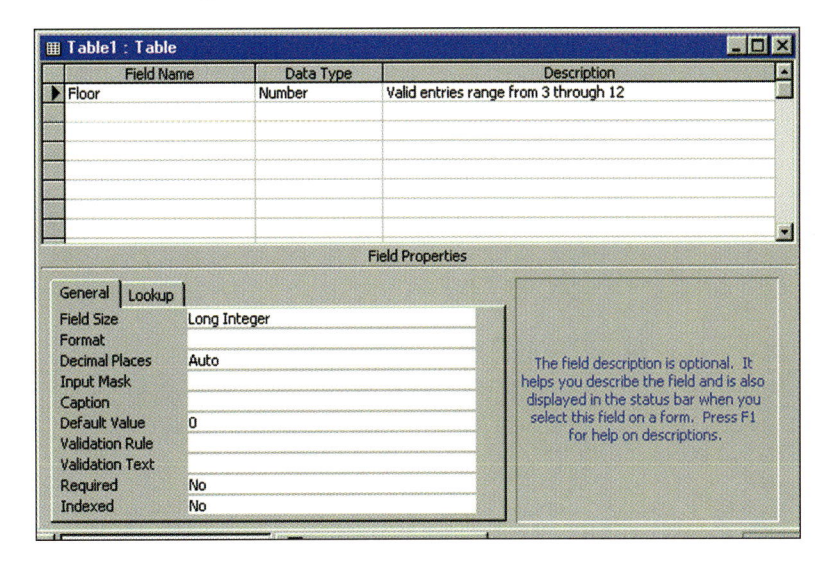

5 Press TAB to move to the Field Name column of the second row.

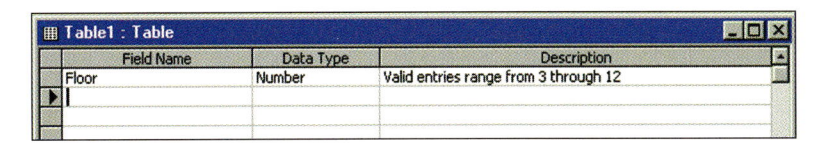

6 Type **Room Type,** press TAB twice, and type **Standard Room or Suite** in the Description text box.

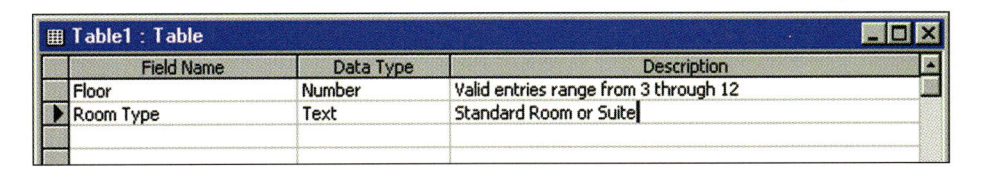

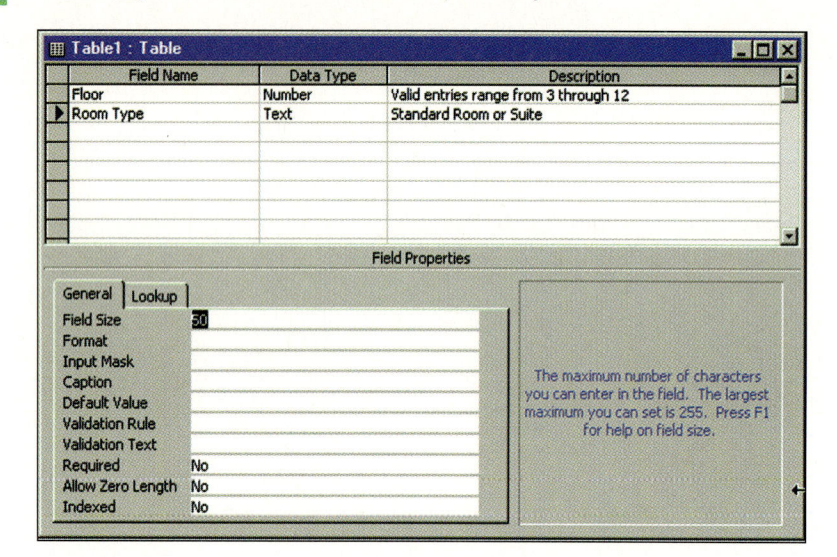

7 Press F6 to move to the Field Properties pane.

8 Type **10** in the Field Size text box; then press F6 to return to the top pane.

9 Press TAB to move to the next row of the Field Name column.

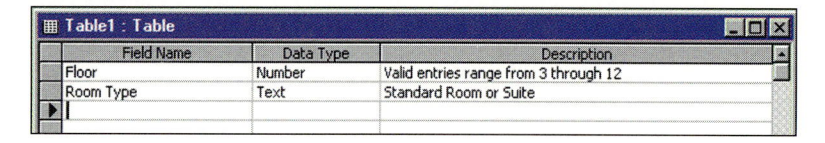

10 Follow the same procedures to add the remaining fields shown in Figure 1.2 to the table design. Accept the default values for field sizes.

Figure 1.2

Saving and Closing a Database Table

After you enter all fields and field descriptions, you need to save the table and close it until you're ready to start entering data into the table.

Project 1: Building a Database   ACC-33

TASK 4: TO SAVE AND CLOSE A DATABASE TABLE:

1 Click the Save button.

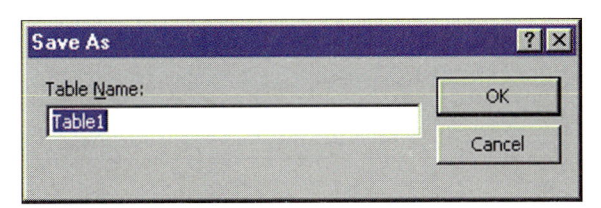

2 Type **The Grande Hotel** in the Table Name text box and press (ENTER).

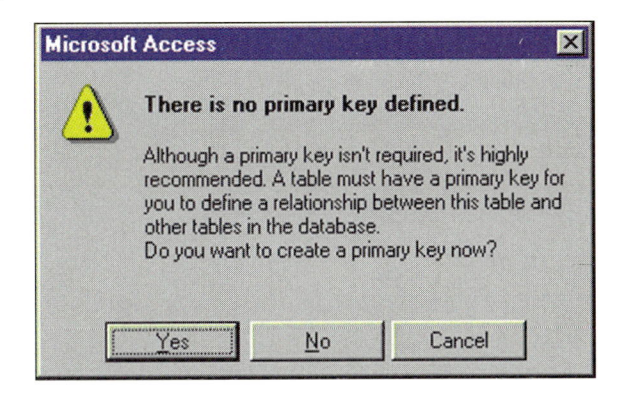

3 Click No to tell Access that you don't want to name a key field.

4 Click the Close button on the table window.

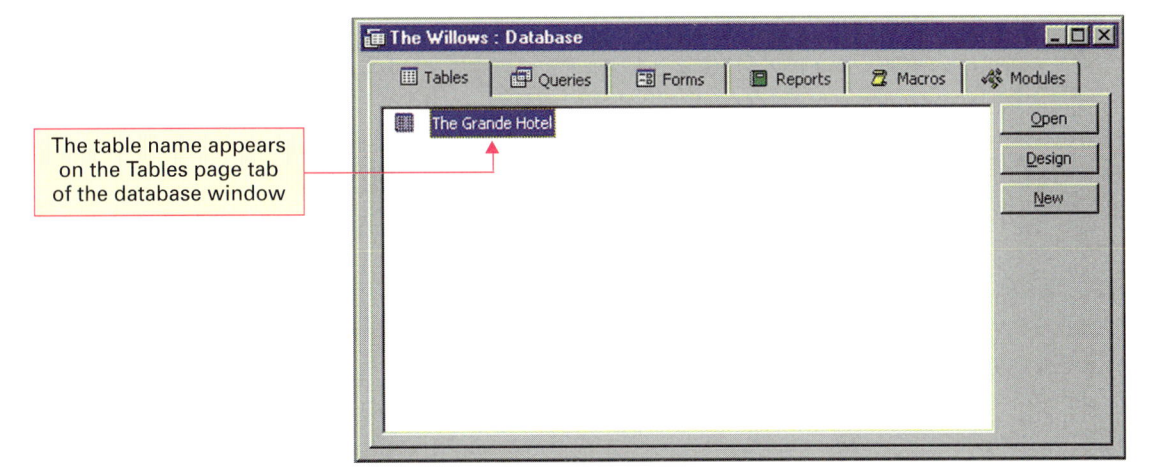

The table name appears on the Tables page tab of the database window

Opening an Access Database Table

Before you can add data to a database table, you need to open the table. Access places an Open button on each page of objects in the database window to make opening objects more efficient.

ACC-34

TASK 5: TO OPEN A DATABASE TABLE:

1 Select The Grande Hotel on the Tables page of the database window, if necessary.

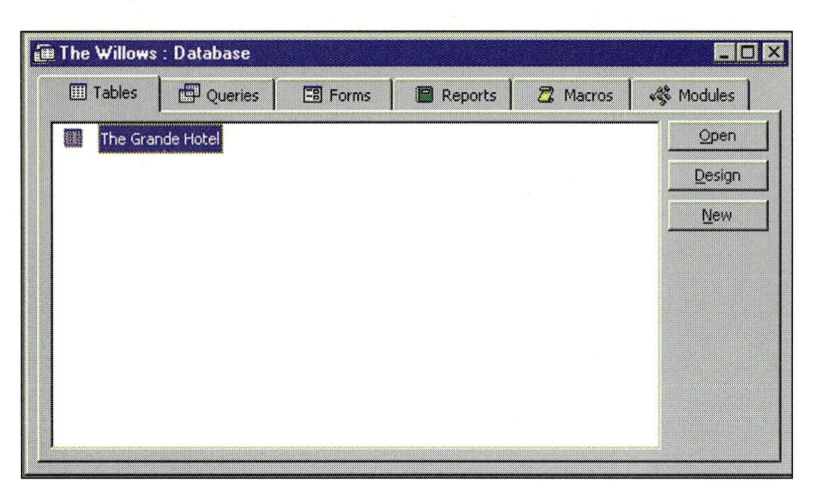

2 Click the Open button.

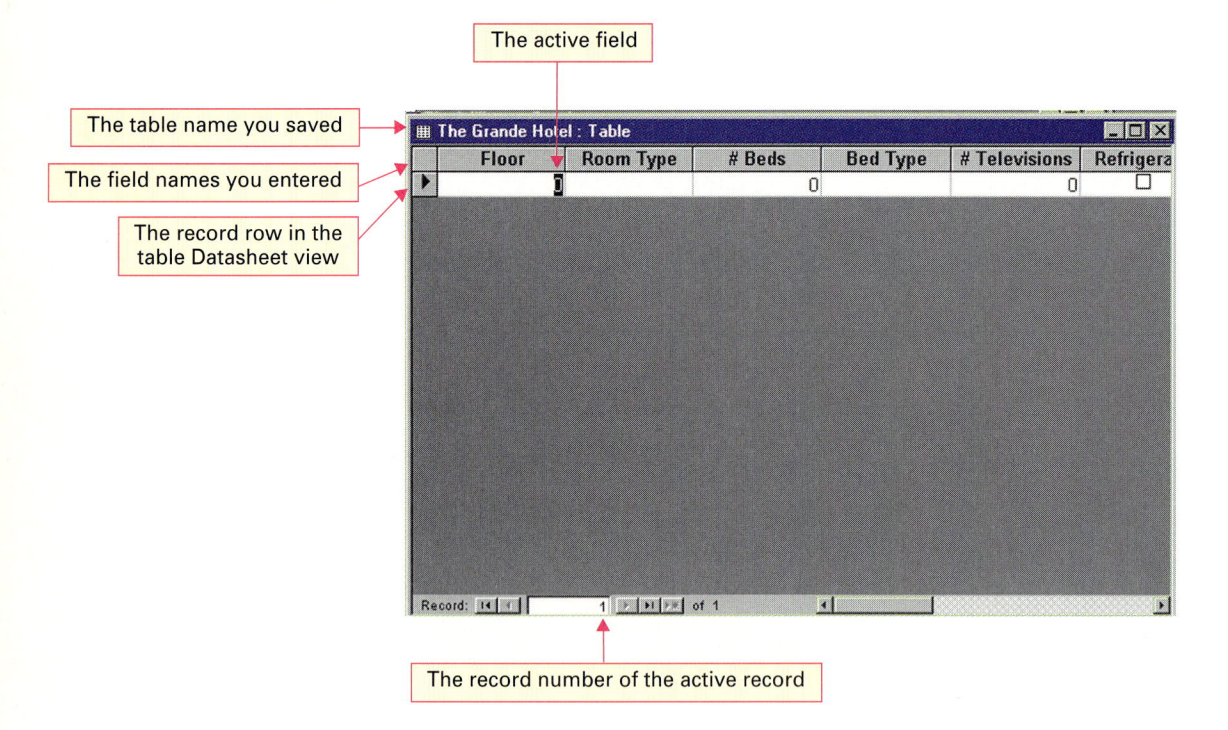

- The active field
- The table name you saved
- The field names you entered
- The record row in the table Datasheet view
- The record number of the active record

Adding Records to an Access Database Table

Mr. Gilmore provided a list of features that describe the rooms in The Grande Hotel. You can use the list to add records to the table. As you enter the data, be consistent in the way you position commas and capitalize words. Any inconsistencies will crop up later when you use the data to create reports and search for data.

Project 1: Building a Database   ACC-35

> **Tip** As you're typing, use the same techniques to correct mistakes that you used to correct errors earlier.

TASK 6: TO ADD RECORDS TO THE DATABASE TABLE:

1 For the first record, type the following entries in the designated fields, pressing TAB to move from one field to the next:

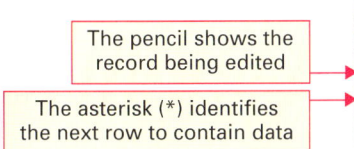

Floor	Room Type	# Beds	Bed Type	# Televisions
3	**Standard**	**2**	**Queen**	**2**

> **Tip** If you set your options to move to the next field when you press Enter, you can press either Enter or Tab to move to the next field.

The pencil shows the record being edited

The asterisk (*) identifies the next row to contain data

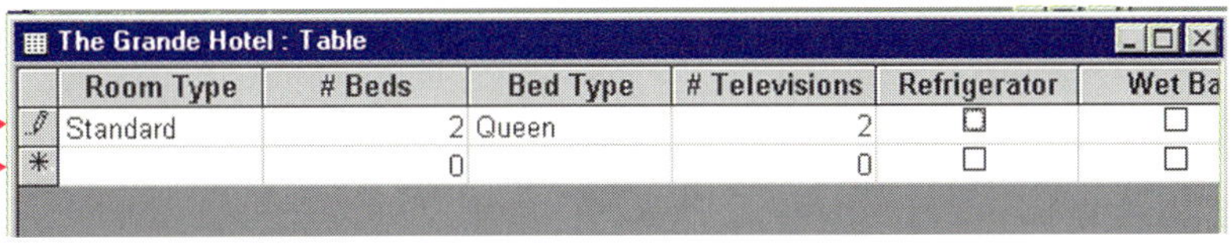

2 Click the check box (or press SPACE) in the Refrigerator column to select the check box; then press TAB three times.
The Data Port field is active.

3 Select the check box in the Data Port column and press TAB.
The Coffee Maker field is active now.

4 Select the check box in the Coffee Maker column.

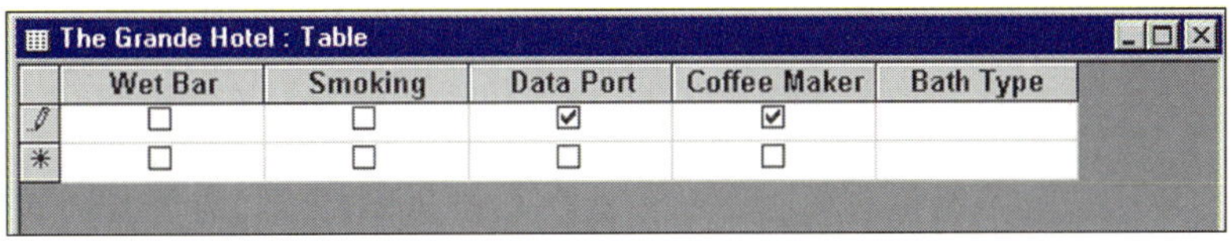

5 Type **Standard** in the Bath Type column, and press TAB to move to the next record.

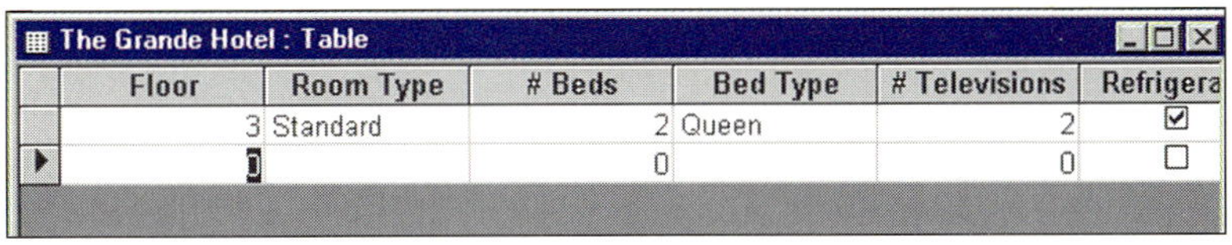

The first record is complete, and you're ready to enter data into the next record. Use the preceding steps to add data to the records as shown in Figure 1.3.

ACC-36

The field names may look a bit bizarre, as Access abbreviates them to cram them all on-screen

Floor	Room	Beds	Bed Type	levisions	Refrige	Wet	Smo	Data	Coffee	Bath Type
3	Standard	2	Queen	2	☑	☐	☐	☑	☑	Standard
3	Suite	3	King, Queen, Sofa	3	☑	☑	☐	☑	☑	Jacuzzi
3	Suite	3	King, Queen, Sofa	3	☑	☑	☐	☑	☑	Standard
3	Standard	2	King, Sofa	2	☑	☐	☐	☑	☑	Standard
8	Standard	2	Queen	2	☑	☐	☑	☑	☑	Standard
8	Suite	3	King, Queen, Sofa	3	☑	☑	☑	☑	☑	Jacuzzi
8	Suite	3	King, Queen, Sofa	3	☑	☑	☑	☑	☑	Standard
8	Standard	2	King, Sofa	2	☑	☐	☑	☑	☑	Standard
10	Club	2	Queen	2	☑	☑	☑	☑	☑	Large Standard

Figure 1.3

> **Note** As you add data to each record, Access saves the data as part of the table. Therefore, after you have completed all records for the table, you don't need to save the table again before closing it.

Checking the Spelling of Data in a Database Table

Access is equipped with a spelling checker that contains a few unique features designed to check the spelling of data in tables.

TASK 7: TO SPELL-CHECK TABLE DATA:

1 Click the Spelling button on the toolbar.

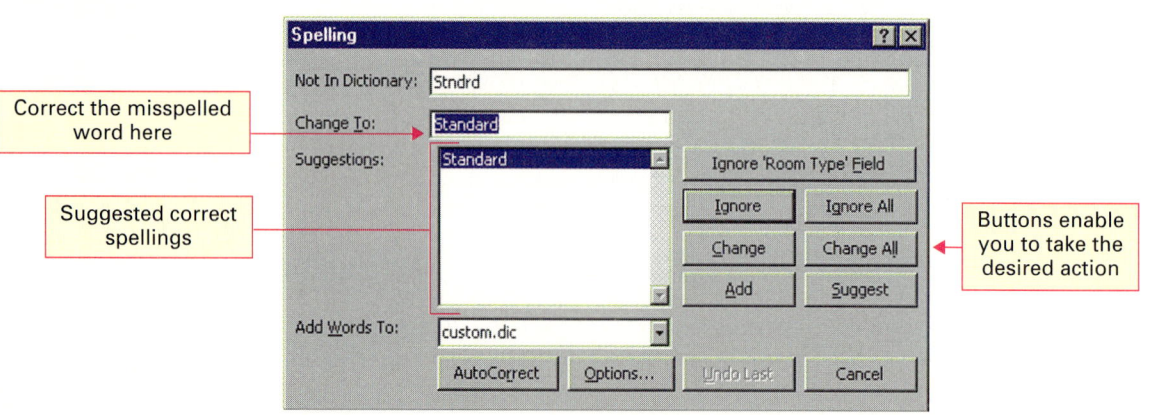

Correct the misspelled word here

Suggested correct spellings

Buttons enable you to take the desired action

2 Click the button for the action you want to take, or select the correct spelling for the word and then click Change.

Project 1: Building a Database   ACC-37

> **Tip** When Access pauses on a word in a field that contains coded data or proper nouns, click the Ignore 'field name' Field button to tell Access not to spell-check the field. You'll get through the table quicker by limiting the fields checked to those that contain meaningful text.

3 Repeat Step 2 each time Access selects a word until all words have been checked.

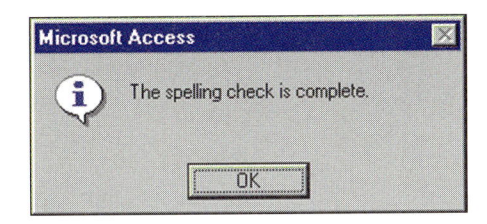

[Microsoft Access dialog box: "The spelling check is complete." with OK button]

4 Click the OK button to close the message box.

Creating and Saving an AutoForm

Access automatically displays new tables using the *Datasheet view* so that you see field names as column headings and records as rows. The Datasheet view enables you to see multiple records on-screen at the same time and makes data entry more efficient. When you want to view records on-screen one at a time, you need to create a *form*. Forms use the fields and data that are stored in database tables. Therefore, you must have a table open to create a form using the AutoForm procedures outlined here. You can save forms as separate objects in the database.

TASK 8: TO CREATE AND SAVE A FORM:

1 Click the New Object: AutoForm button on the Table Datasheet toolbar.

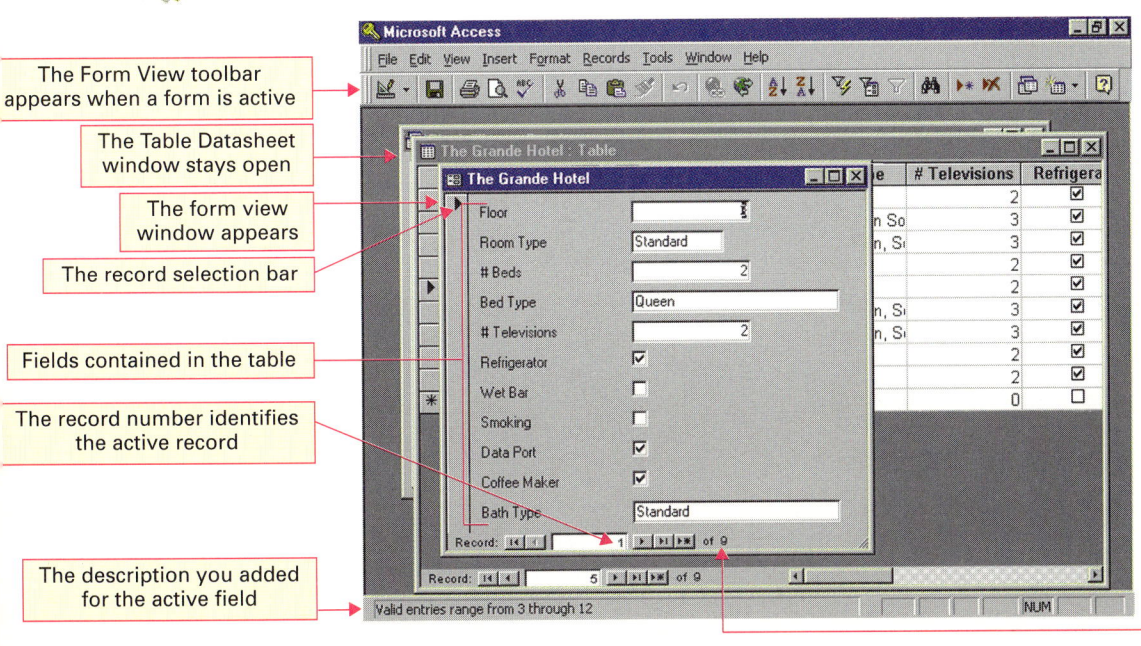

Callouts on screenshot:
- The Form View toolbar appears when a form is active
- The Table Datasheet window stays open
- The form view window appears
- The record selection bar
- Fields contained in the table
- The record number identifies the active record
- The description you added for the active field
- The total number of records in the table

2 Click 💾.

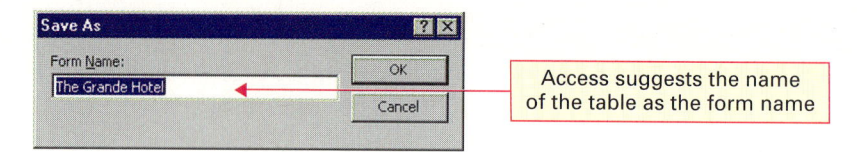

Access suggests the name of the table as the form name

3 Press ENTER to assign the table name to the form; then press CTRL+F6 to display the database window.
Access saves the form and places the form name on the Forms page of the database window.

Navigating Datasheets and Forms

Access displays navigation buttons at the bottom of each form or datasheet; these buttons make moving among the records of a database easy. Figure 1.4 explains the purpose of each navigation button and how to use each one.

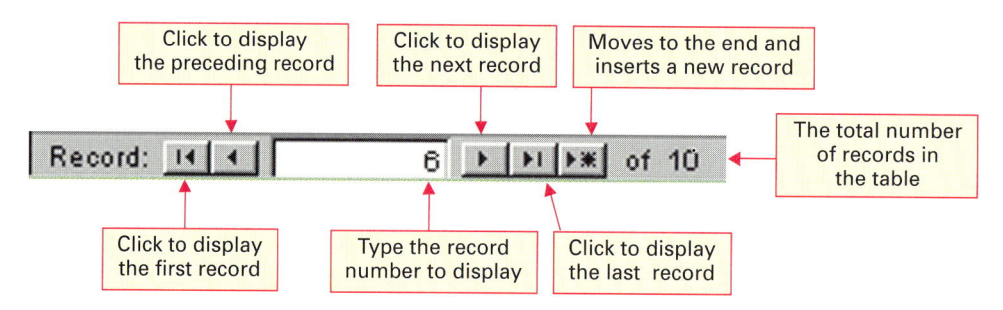

Click to display the preceding record
Click to display the next record
Moves to the end and inserts a new record
The total number of records in the table
Click to display the first record
Type the record number to display
Click to display the last record

Figure 1.4

TASK 9: TO USE NAVIGATION BUTTONS TO NAVIGATE RECORDS:

1 Press CTRL+F6 until the form *The Grande Hotel* appears.

2 Click ▶|.

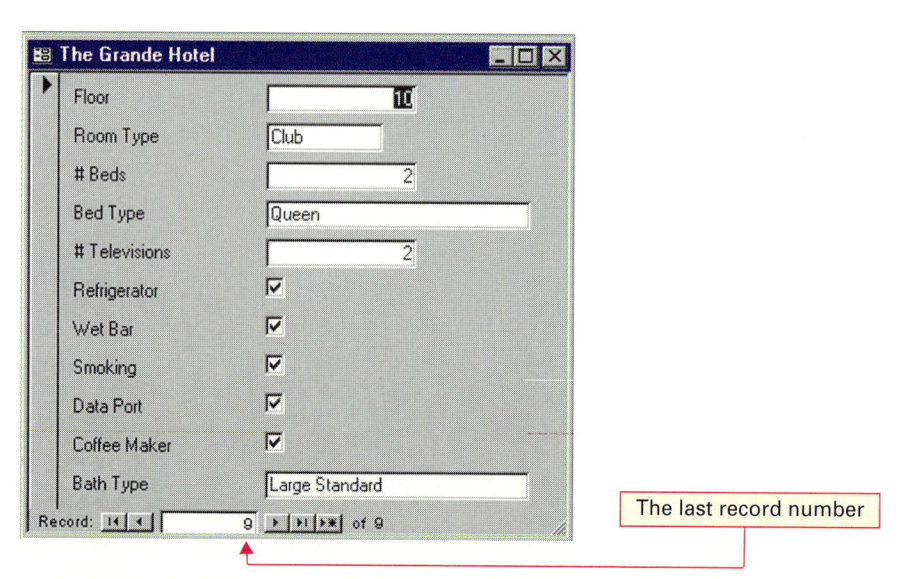

The last record number

3 Click the Previous Record [◀] button.

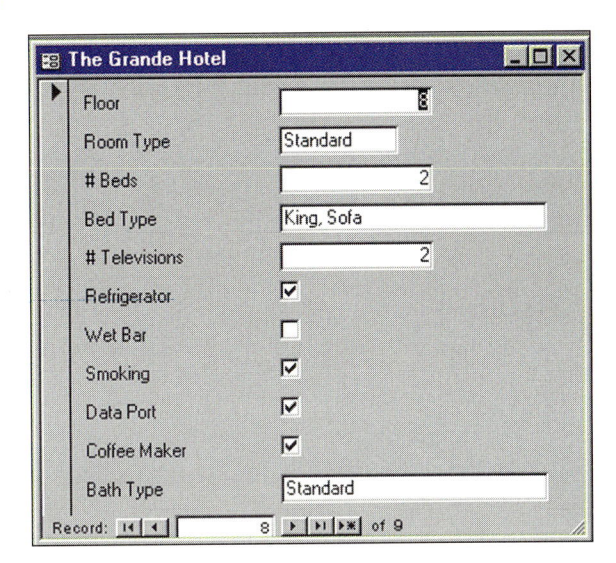

4 Select the Record Number text box, type **5,** and press (ENTER).
Record 5 appears.

5 Choose View, Datasheet View to display the form *The Grande Hotel* as a datasheet.
Notice that record 5 is the active record.

6 Click the Next Record [▶] button.

7 Click [◀◀].
The first table record becomes active.

You can also use keyboard techniques to navigate records in Datasheet view or *Form view*. The records displayed using keyboard techniques depend, to some extent, on whether you're working with the table datasheet or the form and whether you have field data selected, as shown in Table 1.2.

Table 1.2 Keyboard Techniques for Form and Datasheet Views

Keystroke	Form	Datasheet
← →	Left/right one character or to next field if field is highlighted	Left/right one field
↑ ↓	Up/down one record if field is highlighted	Up/down one record (row)
HOME	Beginning of active field or first field in record if data is selected	First field in record (row)
END	End of active field or last field if data is selected	Last field in record (row)
CTRL+HOME	Beginning of active field or first field in active record if data is selected	First field in first record
CTRL+END	End of field or last field in active record if field is selected	Last field in last record
PGUP PGDN	Previous/next record	Previous/next screen of records
CTRL+← CTRL+→	Previous/next field	Previous/next field
CTRL+↑ CTRL+↓	First/last record	Previous/next screen of field columns

Practice each of these keystrokes in both the form and datasheet for The Grande Hotel to see how they work.

Previewing and Printing Database Data

Using the Print Preview feature in Access, you can display data on-screen as it will appear when you print the data on paper. What you see when you preview the printouts in Access depends on which object is active: the table in Datasheet view or the form. After you preview the data, you can print it by clicking the Print button on the Print Preview toolbar, or you can close the Print Preview window and print from the datasheet or form.

TASK 10: TO PREVIEW AND PRINT FORMS AND DATASHEETS:

1 Press CTRL+F6 to display the form *The Grande Hotel.*

Project 1: Building a Database   ACC-41

2 Click the Print Preview button on the toolbar.

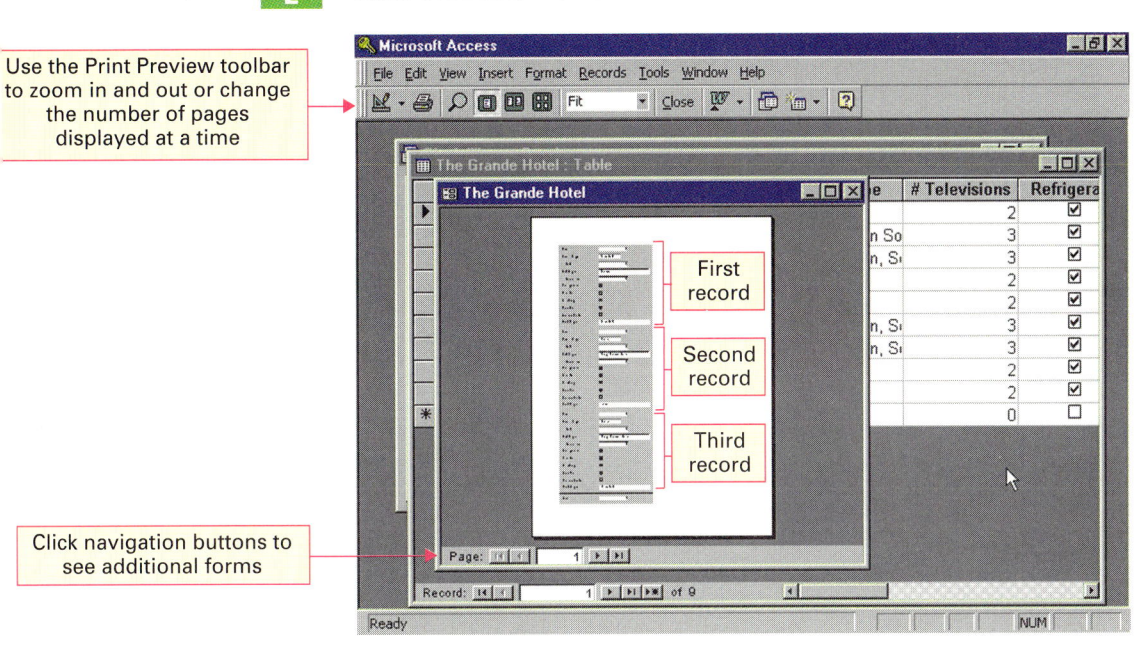

Use the Print Preview toolbar to zoom in and out or change the number of pages displayed at a time

First record
Second record
Third record

Click navigation buttons to see additional forms

3 Click the Close button on the preview window title bar. The form *The Grande Hotel* displays.

4 Press CTRL+F6 until the datasheet for The Grande Hotel displays.

5 Click.

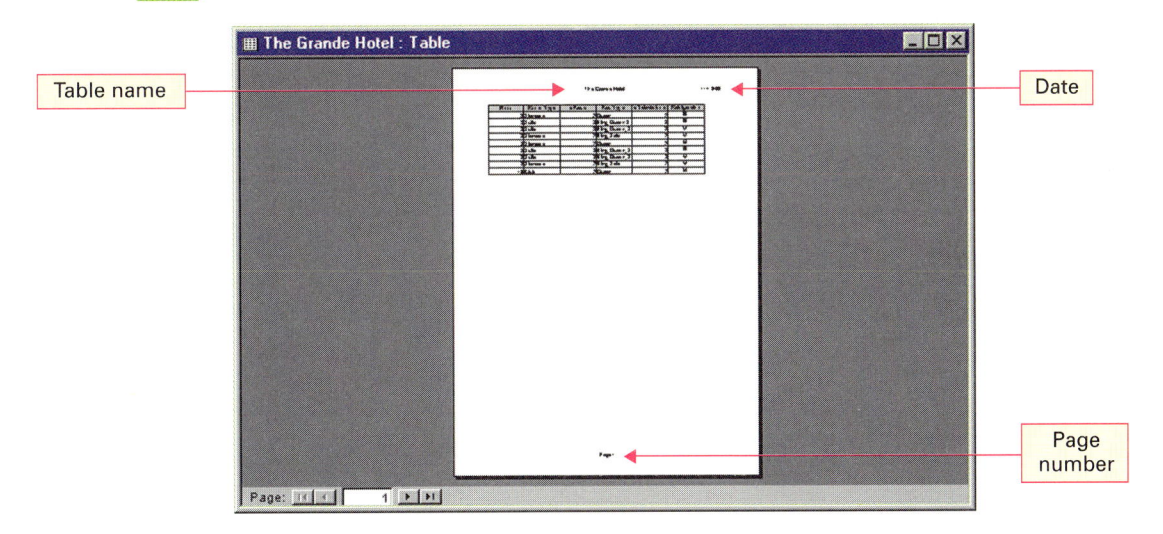

Table name

Date

Page number

6 Click ▶ to display the next page of the printout.

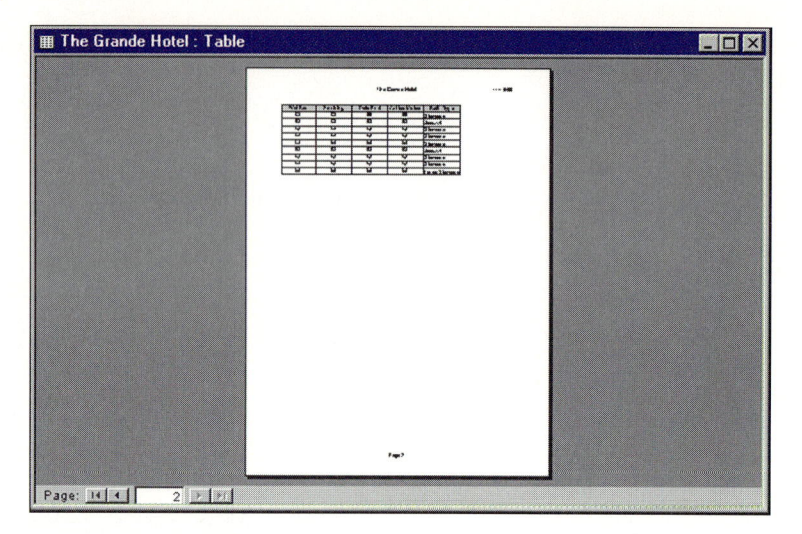

7 Click the Print button on the Print Preview toolbar.

The Conclusion

After completing work in the database, you need to close each object that's open, save changes to objects when reminded to do so, and then close the database. You can click the Close button to close each object as well as to close the database. If you're finished working in Access, exit properly by clicking the Close button for the application. If you plan to continue working on the exercises and assignments, leave Access open.

Summary and Exercises

Summary

- Tables are used to store data in a database.
- You enter field names, field types, field lengths, and field descriptions in the Table Design view.
- To create a new table, you must first open the database that will contain the table.
- After you create a table structure, you must save the table so that you can begin adding data to the table.
- Database tables display information in the Datasheet view by default. The Datasheet view displays multiple records on-screen at a time.
- You create forms by using field definitions and descriptions contained within a table. Forms display information from only one record on-screen at a time.
- Forms are saved as separate objects in a database and appear in the Forms page of the database window.
- Navigation buttons located at the bottom of the form and datasheet windows make navigating records easy. You also can use the keyboard to move among records in a database table.
- You can print table data from both the Datasheet view and Form view.
- The spelling checker in Access enables you to skip fields that contain proper nouns or coded information.

Key Terms and Operations

Key Terms	Operations
AutoForm	add records to a database table
Datasheet view	create and save a database form
Form view	create and save a database table
table	open a database
	open a database table
	preview and print database data
	spell-check database data

Study Questions

Multiple Choice

1. What's the basic object of a database used to store data?
   a. table
   b. form
   c. datasheet
   d. preview

2. To create a table,
   a. you must also create a new database.
   b. you may either create a new database or open an existing one.
   c. you first create a form.
   d. you press Enter.

ACC-43

ACC-44

3. To design your own database table and enter your field names and descriptions, click the New button in the database window and then
   a. press Enter.
   b. click New Form Wizard.
   c. select Design View and press Enter.
   d. select Datasheet View and press Enter.

4. To create a straightforward form that contains all the fields in a table,
   a. display the Forms page of the dialog box and click New.
   b. click the Design View button on the Datasheet toolbar.
   c. choose File, New, and select Form.
   d. click the New Object: AutoForm button on the toolbar.

5. The Table Design window is divided into which of the following panes?
   a. field entry, properties, instructions
   b. field entry, properties
   c. field entry, properties, instructions, help
   d. field description pane only

6. To move from one field in a table or form, press
   a. Tab.
   b. Esc.
   c. F6.
   d. Shift+right arrow.

7. To move to specific records in a database table,
   a. press Ctrl+Page Down.
   b. press F6.
   c. press Ctrl+Home.
   d. click the navigation buttons at the bottom of the window.

8. What special button in the Spelling dialog box lets you skip fields in a database while spell-checking?
   a. Skip button
   b. Ignore button
   c. Ignore *'field name'* Field button
   d. Change button

9. Forms can be saved
   a. as part of a table datasheet.
   b. as separate objects, using the name of the table.
   c. only if they contain different data from data in tables.
   d. outside the database only.

10. What field type places a check box to contain field data?
    a. Text
    b. Number
    c. Date
    d. Yes/No

Short Answer

1. What's the difference between a database and a table?

2. If a table isn't open when you try to create a form, what happens?

3. What page of the database window contains AutoForms?
4. What's the most common data type?
5. What does the Yes/No data type do?
6. What's the quickest way to open a database you've saved recently?
7. To open a database table, what must be open first?
8. What navigation procedure would you use to go directly to a specific record in a database?
9. How do you add a field size to a field in Design view?
10. What's the easiest way to start the Spelling Checker in Access?

For Discussion
1. What are the different field types, and how would you use each?
2. Describe the types of information you might want to include in the Description column of the Table Design view. Where does information entered into the Description column appear when you're entering data?
3. How do the procedures required to create and save a form differ from the procedures for creating and saving a database? A table?
4. What additional information would you include in the table *The Grande Hotel?*
5. What additional tables, if any, could be added to the database *The Willows?*

Review Exercises

1. Creating a Database and a Database Table

Use the Employee database design you created in Exercise 1 in the Overview to create a new database named *The Willows Personnel.* Then create a table named *The Willows Managers* to store employee information contained in Figure 1.5 on the next page. Include fields from the information presented below with your database design.

Field Name	Data Type
First Name	Text
Middle Name	Text
Last Name	Text
Street	Text
City	Text
State	Text
ZIP	Text
Date Employed	Date/Time
Position	Text
Department	Text
Salary	Text
Business Phone	Text
Home Phone	Text

First Name	Middle Name	Last Name	Street	City	State	ZIP	Date	Position	Department	Salary	Business Phone	Home Phone
John	Richard	Gilmore	13951 Field Court	Willow Grove	SC	223	2/4/90	Manager	The Grande Hotel	120000	803-555-1200	803-555-1597
Rebecca	Rae	Jackson	10054 Ruler Court	Smithfield	SC	224	1/19/85	Manager	Willows Beach Cottages	85000	803-555-0850	803-555-3547
Ruth	Smith	Lindsey	15065 Knicker Drive	Willow Grove	SC	223	3/1/81	Manager	All Shops	101000	803-555-1010	803-555-2546
Mark	Edward	Taylor	14419 Brook Street	James Way	SC	243	5/31/88	Manager	The Atrium Grill	65000	803-555-0650	803-555-7854
Brian	Anthony	Atkinson	110 Crozet Street	Smithfield	SC	224	7/5/87	Manager	Willow Top	80000	803-555-0800	803-555-6874
Philip	James	Holmes	15018 Cordell Avenue	James Way	SC	243	8/7/93	Manager	The 18th Hole	70000	803-555-0700	803-555-9658
Marcela	Ann	Bradbury	5622 Forest Glen Road	Willow Grove	SC	223	8/13/96	Manager	Wind in the Willows	50000	803-555-0500	803-555-3574
Henry	Chung	Cho	13411 Reardon Lane	Altamont	SC	222	11/22/86	Manager	All Sandwich Shops	80000	803-555-0801	803-555-1597
Thomas	Nicholas	Williams	9007 Leesburg Pike	Willow Grove	SC	223	9/12/89	Manager	Golf/Tennis Property & Pro Shop	75000	803-555-0750	803-555-8624
Laura	Rene	Carr	9575 Kingsley Road	Smithfield	SC	224	5/16/92	Manager	Exercise/Aerobic Facility	50000	803-555-0501	803-555-9713
Frank	Robert	Davis	14563 Greenridge	James Way	SC	243	6/27/96	Manager	Miniature Golf & Little Tree Playground	30000	803-555-0300	803-555-3179
Chuck	Mercer	Bailey	1275 Garrison Road	Willow Grove	SC	223	4/28/86	Manager	Willow Pond Riding Stables	48000	803-555-0480	803-555-6482
Maria	Suarez	Sanchez	250 Windjammer Drive	Altamont	SC	222	10/15/90	Manager	Willows Water Park	36000	803-555-0360	803-555-3516

Figure 1.5

Follow these steps to create the database and table:

1. Launch Access and select Blank Database from the Microsoft Access dialog box. Then press ENTER.
2. Type the name of the database in the File name text box, select the folder you want to use to store the database, and then press ENTER.
3. Display the Tables page of the database dialog box, and click New.
4. Select Design View from the New Table list, and press ENTER.
5. Type the field names and select field types in the Table Design window.
6. Click the Save button to save the table, type the table name in the Save As dialog box, press ENTER, and respond No to the message about the key field.

2. Adding Records to a Database Table

Record the data from Figure 1.5 in the table *The Willows Managers* in the database *The Willows Personnel.* Follow these steps to add records to the table:

1. Open the database *The Willows Personnel,* and then open the table *The Willows Managers.*
2. Type the information for each field of the first record, pressing TAB to move to the next field.
3. Repeat Step 2 until all records are complete.
4. Spell-check the table, making any necessary changes.
5. Close the table and the database.

Assignments

1. Creating a New Table and Adding Records to the Table

The database called *The Willows* currently contains only one table—called *The Grande Hotel.* Create a new table named *The Grande Hotel Rooms* in the database *The Willows.* Add the following three fields to the table: Floor, Room Number, and Room Type. Use the data in Table 1.3 to add records to the new table. Notice that the Room Number field contains multiple room munbers for some records. Each row in Table 1.3 is a table record.

Table 1.3 Rooms in The Grande Hotel by Type

Floor	Room Number	Room Type
3	3010, 3110, 3210, 3310	Suite
3	3020–3100	Standard
3	3120–3200	King
3	3220–3300	King
3	3320–3400	Standard
4	4010, 4110, 4210, 4310	Suite
4	4020–4100	Standard
4	4120–4200	King
4	4220–4300	King
4	4320–4400	Standard
5	5010, 5110, 5210, 5310	Suite
5	5020–5100	Standard
5	5120–5200	King
5	5220–5300	King
5	5320–5400	Standard
6	6010, 6110, 6210, 6310	Suite
6	6020–6100	Standard
6	6120–6200	King
6	6220–6300	King
6	6320–6400	Standard
7	7010, 7110, 7210, 7310	Suite
7	7020–7100	Standard
7	7120–7200	King
7	7220–7300	King
7	7320–7400	Standard
8	8010, 8110, 8210, 8310	Suite
8	8020–8100	Standard
8	8120–8200	King
8	8220–8300	King
8	8320–8400	Standard

Table 1.3 *(Continued)*

Floor	Room Number	Room Type
9	9010, 9110, 9210, 9310	Suite
9	9020–9100	Standard
9	9120–9200	King
9	9220–9300	King
9	9320–9400	Standard
10	1001–1014	Club King
10	1015–1028	Club Standard
11	1101, 1111, 1121, 1131	Suite
11	1102–1110	Standard
11	1112–1120	King
11	1122–1130	King
11	1132–1140	Standard
12	1201, 1211, 1221, 1231	Suite
12	1202–1210	Standard
12	1212–1220	King
12	1222–1230	King
12	1232–1240	Standard

2. Finding Competitors on the Internet (Optional assignment)

In an effort to ensure that The Willows remains competitive with other resorts along the Atlantic coast, Mr. Gilmore would like for you to search the Internet for information about resorts in the three-state area (North Carolina, South Carolina, and Virginia) that offer golf, water recreation, and beaches. You should download pricing information. Then create a database named Competitors, and add a table that contains fields you can use to record names, locations, facilities, and prices for three of the competitors. Enter data for each of the resorts you locate, and then print a copy of the datasheet data for Mr. Gilmore's approval before adding data for additional records.

PROJECT 2

Maintaining a Database

As addresses and other data stored in the database change and employees come and go, you need to update table data to ensure that the information is accurate and to maintain the usefulness of the database. In this project, you learn how to locate records in large databases, update field data, insert and delete records in database tables, and sort and select records.

Objectives

After completing this project, you will be able to:

- ➤ Find records
- ➤ Update records
- ➤ Insert records
- ➤ Use the Replace feature
- ➤ Delete records
- ➤ Sort records
- ➤ Filter records by selection
- ➤ Filter records by form

The Challenge

As the data-entry specialist for The Willows, you are the jack-of-all-trades: you must edit, update, and maintain the database *The Willows*. Some of the equipment in rooms of The Grande Hotel has changed, and some rooms are now accessible to the handicapped. Mr. Gilmore also wants you to replace the term *Sofa* with *Sofa Sleeper* throughout the table for The Grande Hotel. After you finish making the changes to the table, he wants you to prepare a list of rooms organized by room type, a list of nonsmoking rooms, and a separate list of rooms with king-size beds. He would also like to see a list of nonsmoking rooms with king-size beds. Seems an almost overwhelming task, doesn't it?

The Solution

Access contains features that make updating the table *The Grande Hotel* in the database *The Willows* almost painless. In only a short time you can make the changes in the equipment contained in the guest rooms, change the room type for some of the rooms, and identify those rooms in The Grande Hotel that are accessible to the handicapped. After you make the changes, you can sort and select records to provide the lists that Mr. Gilmore wants. The revised table is shown in Figure 2.1.

Floor	Room Type	# Beds	Bed Type	# Televisions
3	Standard	2	Queen	2
3	Suite	3	King, Queen, Sofa Sleeper	3
3	Suite	3	King, Queen, Sofa Sleeper	3
3	King	2	King, Sofa Sleeper	2
8	Standard	2	Queen	2
8	Suite	3	King, Queen, Sofa Sleeper	3
8	Suite	3	King, Queen, Sofa Sleeper	3
8	King	2	King, Sofa Sleeper	2
10	Club	2	Queen	2
3	Accessible	2	Queen	2
3	Accessible	3	King, Queen, Sofa Sleeper	3
3	Accessible	3	King, Queen, Sofa Sleeper	3
3	Accessible	2	King, Sofa Sleeper	2

Refrigerator	Wet Bar	Smoking	Data Port	Coffee Maker	Bath Type
✔	☐	☐	✔	✔	Standard
✔	✔	☐	✔	✔	Jacuzzi
✔	✔	☐	✔	✔	Standard
✔	☐	☐	✔	✔	Standard
✔	☐	✔	✔	✔	Standard
✔	✔	✔	✔	✔	Jacuzzi
✔	✔	✔	✔	✔	Standard
✔	☐	✔	✔	✔	Standard
✔	✔	✔	✔	✔	Large Standard
✔	☐	☐	✔	✔	Standard
✔	✔	☐	✔	✔	Jacuzzi
✔	✔	☐	✔	✔	Standard
✔	☐	☐	✔	✔	Standard

Figure 2.1

The Setup

So that the screen will match the illustrations and the tasks in this project will function as described, make sure that your Access 97 settings are the same as those listed here:

- If you don't see a toolbar on the screen, choose View, Toolbars, and then select the toolbar listed at the top of the cascading menu.
- If you have objects maximized, click the Restore button on the window for each object.
- If you don't see the status bar, choose Tools, Options and click the View page tab. Click the check box beside Status Bar at the top of the page tab.

Check the data in your database table before you start these activities to ensure that you were consistent in your placement of commas and capitalization. Field data must be consistent to achieve the desired results.

Finding Records

To change the information contained in a database record, you must first display the record in Form view or make it the active row in the Table Datasheet view. The Access Find feature helps you locate specific records.

TASK 1: TO FIND RECORDS IN A DATABASE TABLE:

1. Open the database *The Willows* and then open the table *The Grande Hotel* in Datasheet view.
   A list of records you entered earlier appears in Datasheet view.

2. Click the Find button on the toolbar.

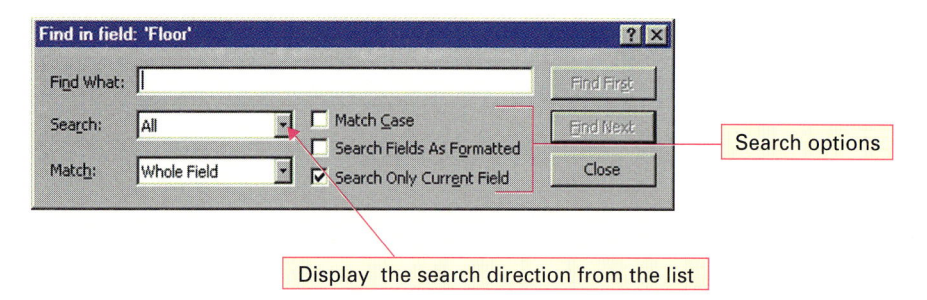

3. Type **King** in the Find What text box, select Any Part of Field from the Match drop-down list, and remove the check mark from the Search Only Current Field check box.

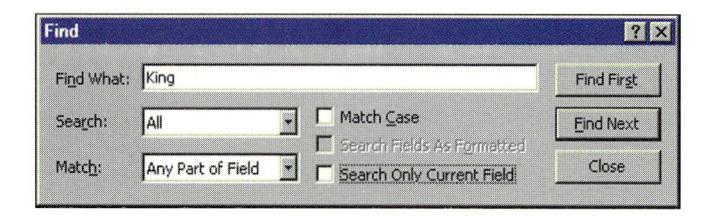

Project 2: Maintaining a Database   ACC-53

4 Click the Find First button.

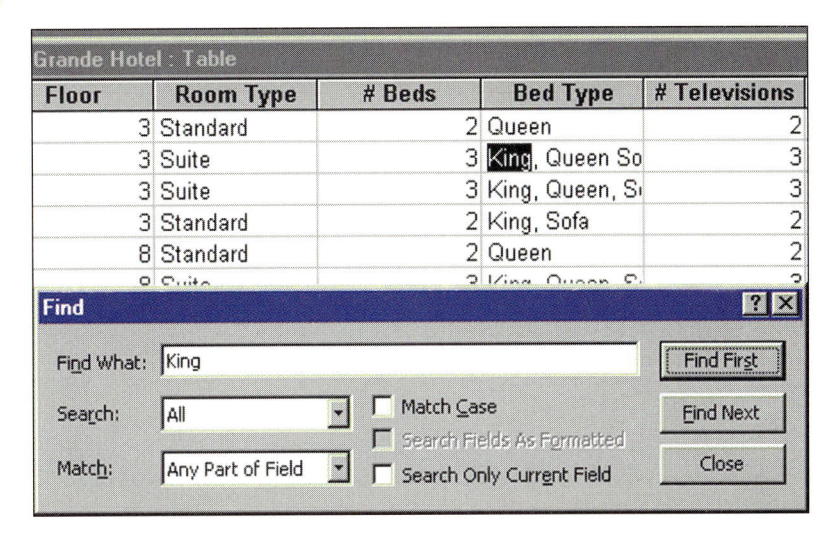

Floor	Room Type	# Beds	Bed Type	# Televisions
3	Standard	2	Queen	2
3	Suite	3	King, Queen So	3
3	Suite	3	King, Queen, S	3
3	Standard	2	King, Sofa	2
8	Standard	2	Queen	2

Find dialog box:
- Find What: King
- Search: All
- Match: Any Part of Field
- Match Case
- Search Fields As Formatted
- Search Only Current Field
- Buttons: Find First, Find Next, Close

Note If your records are arranged differently, Access may find a different first record.

5 Click the Find Next button until you locate a record for a Standard room containing a king-size bed.

Tip Drag the title bar of the Find dialog box to move the dialog box out of the way so that you can see the complete form.

6 Press (ESC) or click the Close ☒ button to close the Find dialog box.

Updating Records

The primary objective of finding data is generally to *update* or change the field data contained in the record. In the table *The Grande Hotel,* you need to change the room type for all Standard rooms with king-size beds to King. You can use either Datasheet view or Form view to edit the data.

TASK 2: TO UPDATE RECORDS:

1 Double-click the word *Standard* in the Room Type field.

Floor	Room Type	# Beds	Bed Type	# Televisions
3	Standard	2	Queen	2
3	Suite	3	King, Queen So	3
3	Suite	3	King, Queen, S	3
3	Standard	2	King, Sofa	2
8	Standard	2	Queen	2

2 Type **King.**

Floor	Room Type	# Beds	Bed Type	# Televisions
3	Standard	2	Queen	2
3	Suite	3	King, Queen So	3
3	Suite	3	King, Queen, Si	3
3	King	2	King, Sofa	2
8	Standard	2	Queen	2

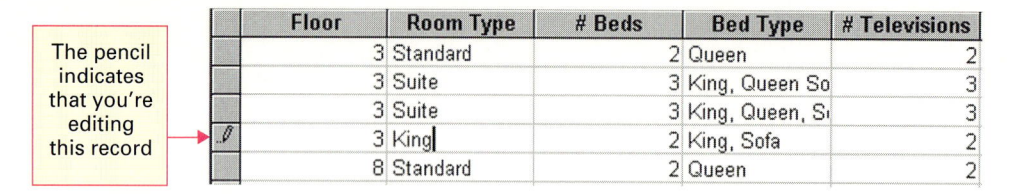

The pencil indicates that you're editing this record

3 Press ⬇ on the keyboard to save changes to the record.

4 Click 🔍 and click Find Next until you find the next occurrence of a record for a Standard room with a king-size bed.

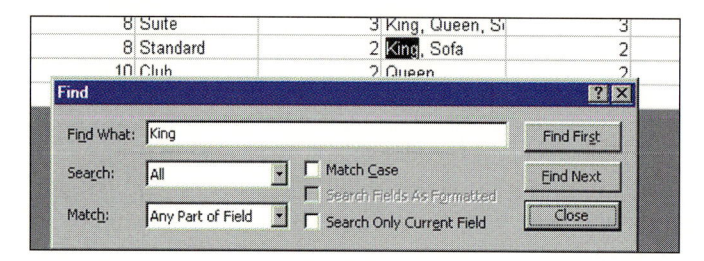

Find dialog box:
- Find What: King
- Search: All
- Match: Any Part of Field
- ☐ Match Case
- ☐ Search Fields As Formatted
- ☐ Search Only Current Field
- Buttons: Find First, Find Next, Close

5 Press ESC to close the Find dialog box, double-click the word *Standard* in the Room Type field, and type **King.**
The Room Type data changes.

6 Click the Database Window button to display the database window, click the Forms tab, and double-click *The Grande Hotel* to open the form.

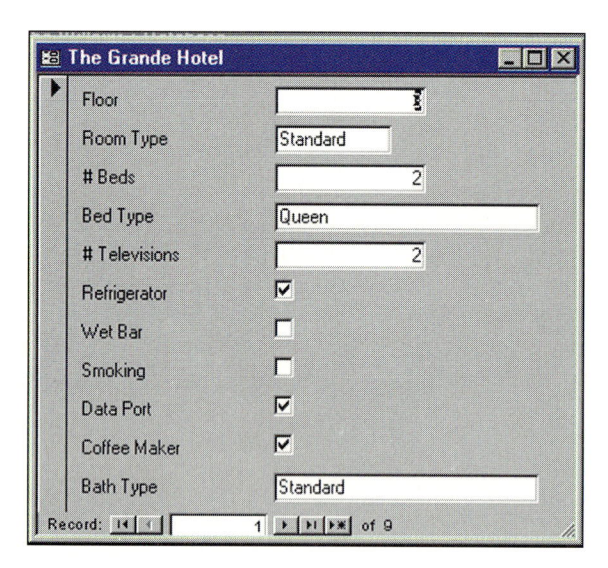

The Grande Hotel form:
- Floor:
- Room Type: Standard
- # Beds: 2
- Bed Type: Queen
- # Televisions: 2
- Refrigerator: ☑
- Wet Bar: ☐
- Smoking: ☐
- Data Port: ☑
- Coffee Maker: ☑
- Bath Type: Standard
- Record: 1 of 9

7 Click 🔍.
The Find window opens again.

8 Click the Find Next button until you identify the next Standard room with a king-size bed.
Access identifies the next record containing the word *King* in any field.

9 Change the room type to King.

Project 2: Maintaining a Database ACC-55

10 Continue finding Standard rooms containing king-size beds and change the room type to *King*.

11 Press ESC to close the Find dialog box when all records are complete.

12 Close the form.

Inserting Records

In Access, you can add records to a database by using the Datasheet view or by entering records on a form. Records you add in either view appear at the bottom of the database table. You can also create new records by copying existing records and updating field data.

TASK 3: TO INSERT RECORDS INTO A DATABASE TABLE:

1 Open the table *The Grande Hotel* in the database *The Willows* in Datasheet view, if necessary.

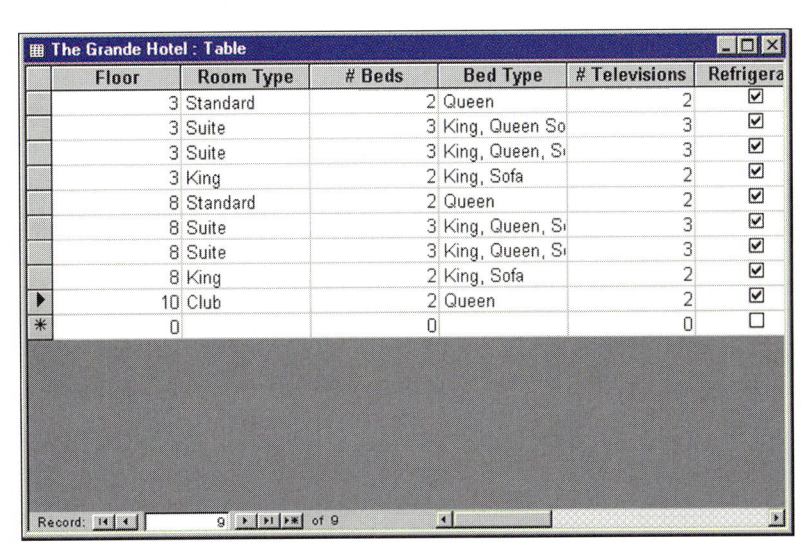

2 Click the New Record navigation button.

3 Type the following data in fields for the new record, pressing TAB to move from field to field:

Floor	Room Type	# Beds	Bed Type	# Telev	Refrig	Wet Bar	Smokin	Data Port	Coffee	Bath Typ
3	Accessible	2	Queen	2	☑	☐	☐	☑	☑	Standard

4 Position the pointer on the frame button beside the first record in the table; then click and drag to select four records.

Click here and drag down to select

Notice the mouse pointer shape when you point to a frame button

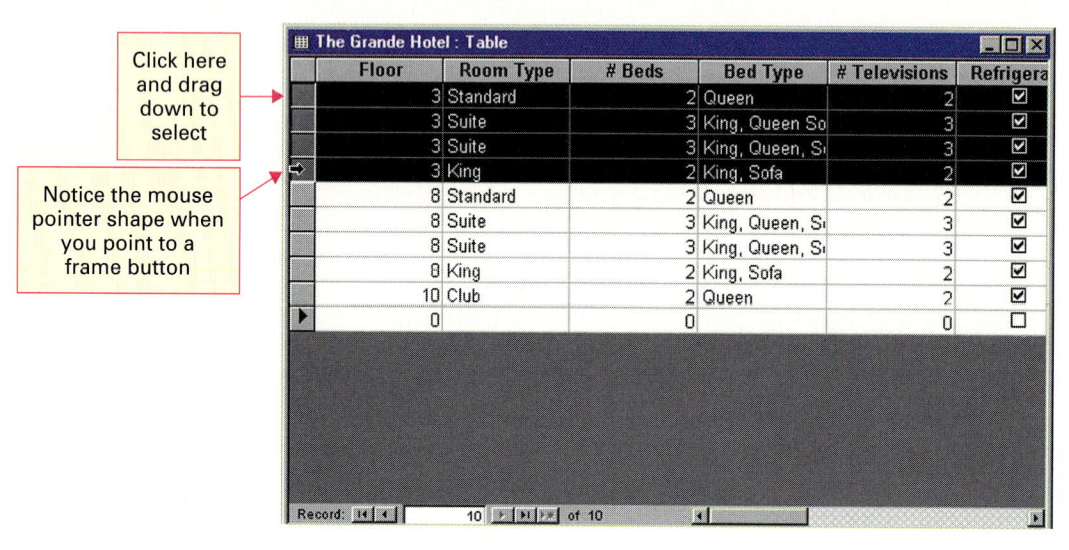

	Floor	Room Type	# Beds	Bed Type	# Televisions	Refrigera
	3	Standard	2	Queen	2	☑
	3	Suite	3	King, Queen So	3	☑
	3	Suite	3	King, Queen, S	3	☑
→	3	King	2	King, Sofa	2	☑
	8	Standard	2	Queen	2	☑
	8	Suite	3	King, Queen, S	3	☑
	8	Suite	3	King, Queen, S	3	☑
	8	King	2	King, Sofa	2	☑
	10	Club	2	Queen	2	☑
▶	0		0		0	☐

5 Click the Copy button on the toolbar.
The selected records are copied to the Windows Clipboard.

6 Click
Access positions the insertion point at the bottom of the table and selects a blank row.

7 Click the Paste button on the toolbar.

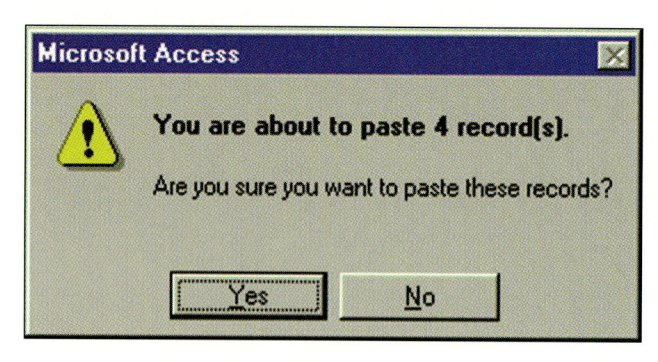

Microsoft Access

⚠ You are about to paste 4 record(s).

Are you sure you want to paste these records?

[Yes] [No]

8 Click Yes to paste the records.

9 Double-click the Room Type field for each copied record and type **Accessible.**

10 Close the table.

Using the Replace Feature

The Replace feature in Access enables you to find occurrences of words, values, or phrases in a database object and replace the information with new data. You can use the Replace feature to change *Sofa* to *Sofa Sleeper* throughout the table *The Grande Hotel,* as Mr. Gilmore requested.

TASK 4: TO REPLACE EXISTING DATA WITH NEW DATA:

1 Open the table *The Grande Hotel* in the database *The Willows* and display the Datasheet view, if necessary.
The table appears as last edited.

ACC-58

2 Choose Edit, Replace.

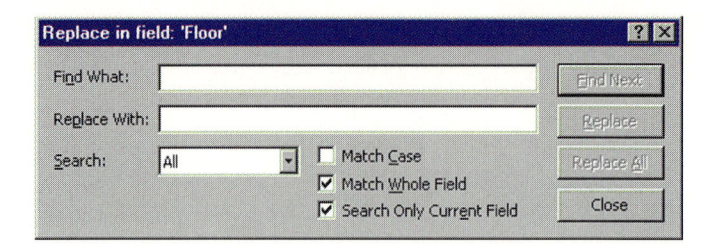

[Replace in field: 'Floor' dialog box shown with Find What, Replace With, Search fields, Match Case, Match Whole Field, Search Only Current Field checkboxes, and Find Next, Replace, Replace All, Close buttons.]

3 Type **Sofa** in the Find What text box, press TAB, type **Sofa Sleeper** in the Replace With text box, and if necessary remove the check marks from the Match Whole Field and Search Only Current Field check boxes.

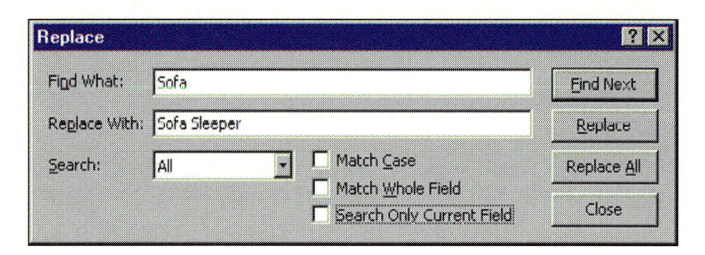

[Replace dialog box with "Sofa" in Find What and "Sofa Sleeper" in Replace With.]

4 Click Find Next.

Floor	Room Type	# Beds	Bed Type	# Televisions
3	Standard	2	Queen	2
3	Suite	3	King, Queen So	3
3	Suite	3	King, Queen, S	3
3	King	2	King, Sofa	2
8	Standard	2	Queen	2
8	Suite	3	King, Queen, S	3

[Replace dialog box with "Sofa" in Find What and "Sofa Sleeper" in Replace With.]

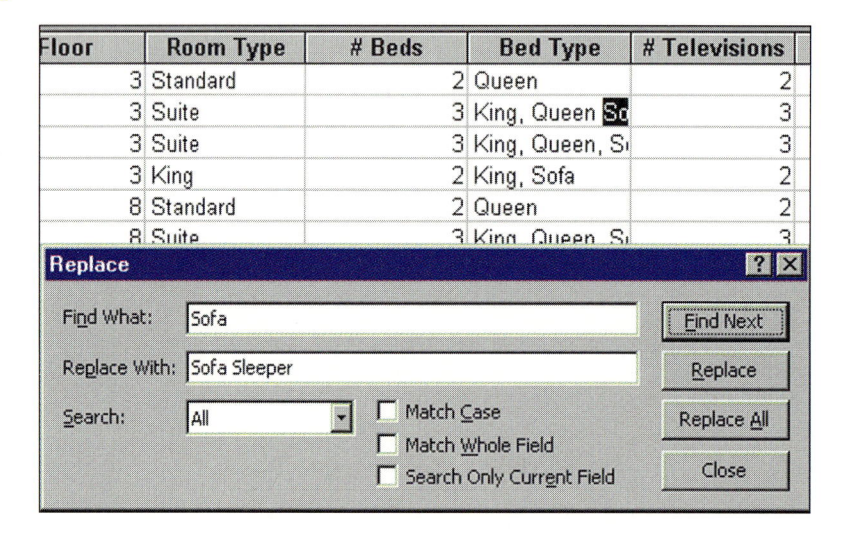

Tip When the Replace dialog box hides the data that Access finds, drag the title bar to move the dialog box to a new location.

Note If your records are in a different order, the record Access finds may differ.

5 Click Replace.
Access makes the substitution and selects the next occurrence of *Sofa.*

Project 2: Maintaining a Database   ACC-59

6 Click Replace All to replace each occurrence of the word *Sofa* with *Sofa Sleeper.*

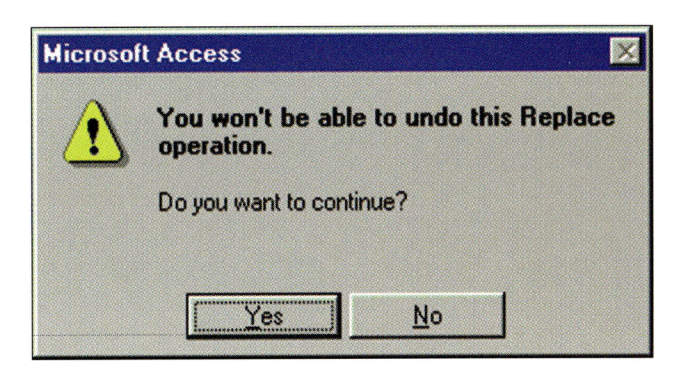

> **Microsoft Access**
>
> ⚠ You won't be able to undo this Replace operation.
>
> Do you want to continue?
>
> [Yes] [No]

7 Click Yes to acknowledge the Access message.

8 Press ESC to close the Replace dialog box.

Deleting Records

When records become obsolete or outdated, you should remove the records to keep the database current. In Access, you can select individual records or multiple records and delete them at the same time, and you can delete records from the Table Datasheet view or from the Form view.

> **Caution** The Undo feature doesn't restore deleted records, nor does deleting records place them on the Clipboard so that you can paste them back into the database table. As a safety measure, you may want to delete a single record by using the Cut button on the toolbar to place the deleted record on the Clipboard, so you can get it back if necessary. Of course, you can always insert a new record and retype the data if you prefer.

TASK 5: TO DELETE RECORDS FROM A DATABASE TABLE:

1 Click the frame button beside the first record showing Accessible as the Room Type.

> **Tip** To delete records in Form view, click the record selection bar on the left side of the form.

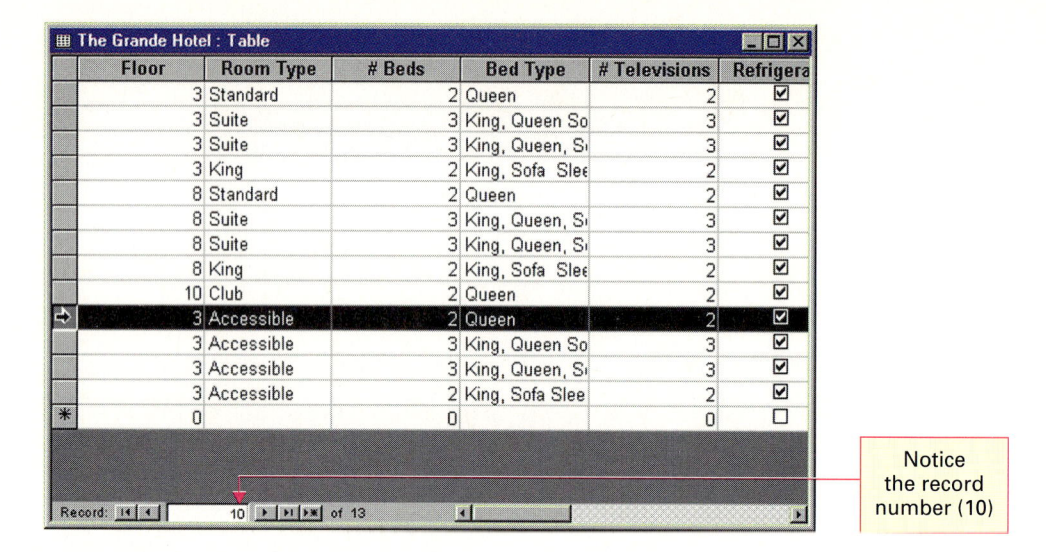

[Screenshot of The Grande Hotel : Table datasheet with record 10 selected]

Notice the record number (10)

2 Press DELETE.

[Screenshot of Microsoft Access confirmation dialog: "You are about to delete 1 record(s). If you click Yes, you won't be able to undo this Delete operation. Are you sure you want to delete these records?" with Yes and No buttons]

3 Click Yes to delete the record.
Records that appear after the deleted record renumber automatically.

Sorting Records

Access enables you to *sort* records in either Datasheet view or Form view on any database field. All you have to do is position the insertion point in the field you want to sort and then click the appropriate Sort button on the toolbar.

TASK 6: TO SORT RECORDS IN A DATABASE TABLE:

1 Click the Room Type field of any record in the table *The Grande Hotel*. Positioning the insertion point in the field that you want to sort makes the field active.

Project 2: Maintaining a Database   ACC-61

2 Click the Sort Ascending button on the toolbar.

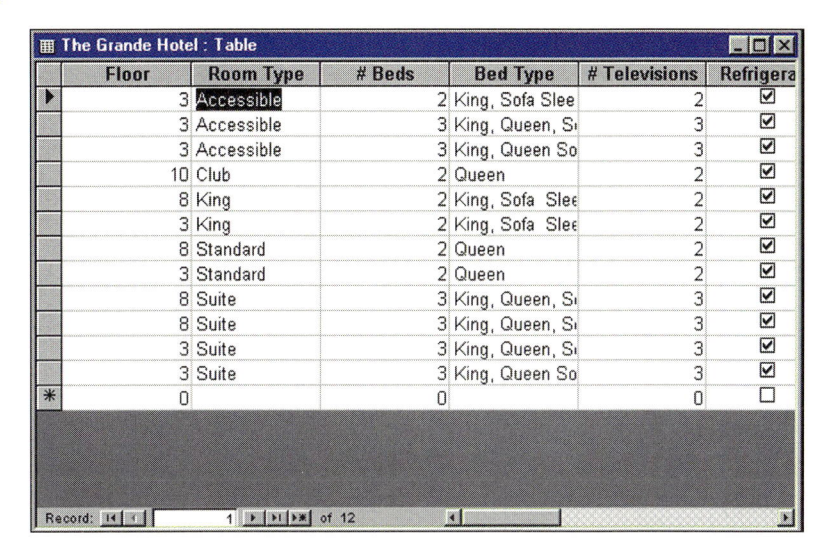

3 Close the table.

4 Click No to leave data stored in its original order. The database window appears.

5 Open the form *The Grande Hotel*.

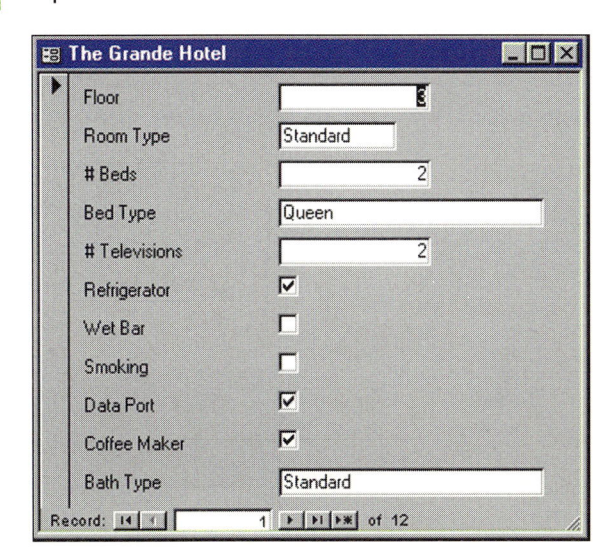

6 Press TAB until the Bed Type field is active.
Pressing TAB to move to a field selects the field contents.

ACC-62

7 Click the Sort Descending button on the toolbar.
Access arranges records with queen-size beds before those with king-size beds.

8 Choose View, Datasheet View to see the results.

Room Type	# Beds	Bed Type	# Tel
Club	2	Queen	
Standard	2	Queen	
Standard	2	Queen	
Accessible	2	King, Sofa Slee	
King	2	King, Sofa Slee	
King	2	King, Sofa Slee	
Accessible	3	King, Queen, S	
Suite	3	King, Queen, S	
Suite	3	King, Queen, S	
Suite	3	King, Queen, S	
Accessible	3	King, Queen So	
Suite	3	King, Queen So	
	0		

Record: 13 of 13

9 Close the datasheet for The Grande Hotel without saving.
The form *The Grande Hotel* (which you were using in Datasheet view) closes.

Filtering Records by Selection

With the Access Filter command, you can identify a value in any field and tell Access to select only those records in the table that contain the same value in the selected field.

TASK 7: TO FILTER DATABASE RECORDS BY SELECTION:

1 Open the table *The Grande Hotel* in the database *The Willows.*

2 Position the mouse pointer close to the left border of a cell in the Smoking field that doesn't contain a check mark.

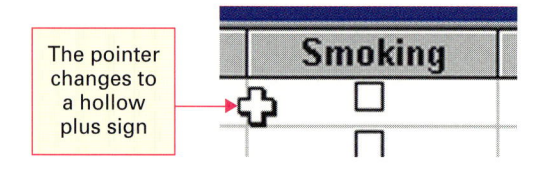

The pointer changes to a hollow plus sign

3 Click to select the field.

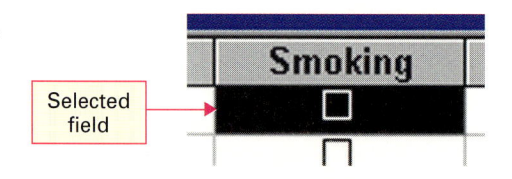

Selected field

> **Note** If you accidentally click the check box as you select the field, a check mark appears in the check box. When this happens, click the check box again to remove the check mark.

4 Click the Filter by Selection button on the toolbar.

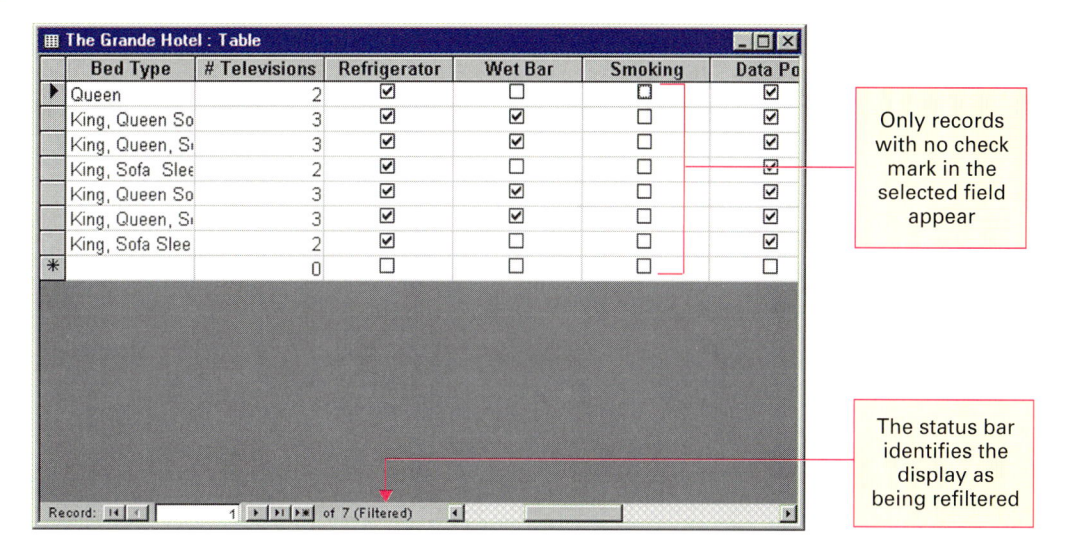

Only records with no check mark in the selected field appear

The status bar identifies the display as being refiltered

5 Preview and print the datasheet for Mr. Gilmore.

6 Click the Remove Filter button on the toolbar. All table records redisplay.

Filtering Records by Form

When you want to filter by more than one field, you have to open the Filter window to select filter values. You can use the Filter command to display nonsmoking rooms, rooms with king-size beds, and nonsmoking rooms with king-size beds in a datasheet, as Mr. Gilmore requested.

ACC-64

TASK 8: TO FILTER RECORDS BY FORM:

1 Click the Filter by Form button on the toolbar.

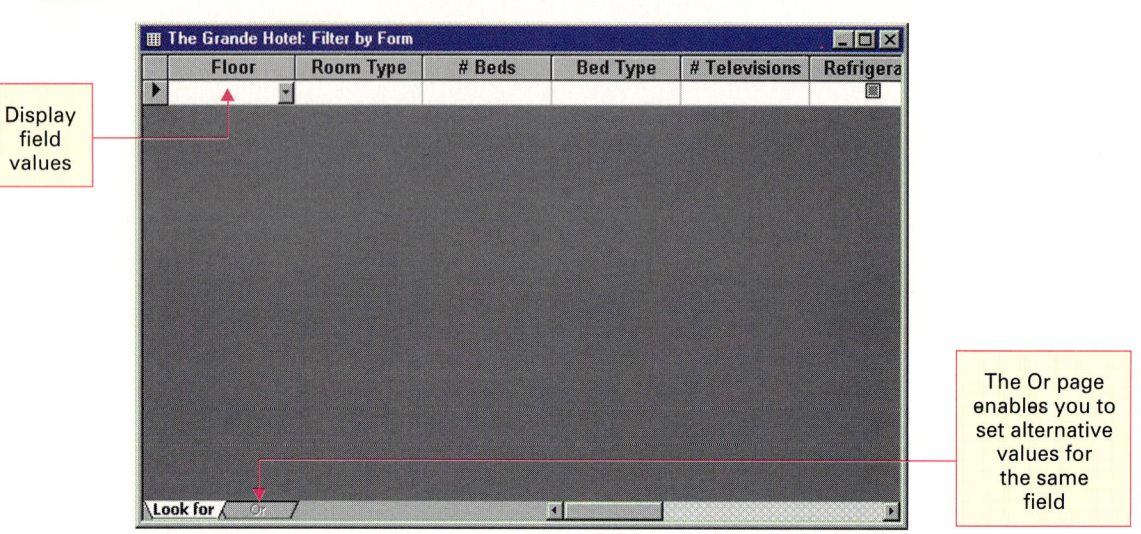

Display field values

The Or page enables you to set alternative values for the same field

2 Click the Bed Type field.

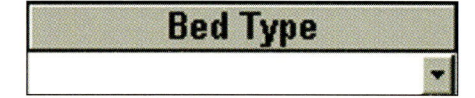

3 Click the arrow button to display valid entries for the Bed Type field.

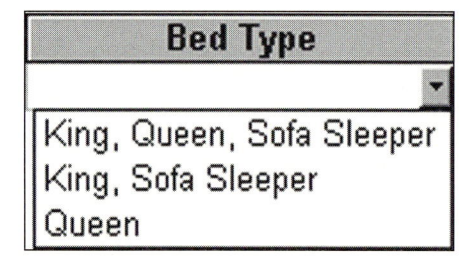

4 Click King, Sofa Sleeper in this list box.

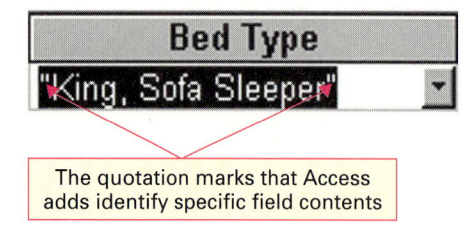

The quotation marks that Access adds identify specific field contents

5 Click the Or tab at the bottom of the window. A blank filter page appears.

Project 2: Maintaining a Database   ACC-65

6 Click the arrow button for Bed Type, and select King, Queen, Sofa Sleeper in the list box.

Bed Type
King, Queen, Sofa Sleep

7 Click the Apply Filter button on the toolbar.

Floor	Room Type	# Beds	Bed Type	# Televisions
3	Suite	3	King, Queen, Sofa Sleeper	3
3	Suite	3	King, Queen, Sofa Sleeper	3
3	King	2	King, Sofa Sleeper	2
8	Suite	3	King, Queen, Sofa Sleeper	3
8	Suite	3	King, Queen, Sofa Sleeper	3
8	King	2	King, Sofa Sleeper	2
3	Accessible	3	King, Queen, Sofa Sleeper	3
3	Accessible	3	King, Queen, Sofa Sleeper	3
3	Accessible	2	King, Sofa Sleeper	2
		0		0

8 Preview and print the list for Mr. Gilmore.

9 Click Remove Filter button to display all records.
All records redisplay in the datasheet.

> **Note** Access remembers the most recent filter values you set. If you want to filter different fields for different values, be sure to remove any filter values previously entered.

10 Click .
The Look For page with previously set filters displays.

11 Click the Smoking field until the check box contains neither shading nor a check mark.

Wet Bar	Smoking	Data Port

The Smoking check box appears clear

12 Click the Or tab at the bottom of the screen, and then click the Smoking check box until it appears clear.

13 Click .

Bed Type	# Televisions	Refrigerator	Wet Bar	Smoking
King, Queen, Sofa-Sleeper	3	☑	☑	☐
King, Queen, Sofa-Sleeper	3	☑	☑	☐
King, Sofa-Sleeper	2	☑	☐	☐
King, Queen, Sofa-Sleeper	3	☑	☑	☐
King, Queen, Sofa-Sleeper	3	☑	☑	☐
King, Sofa-Sleeper	2	☑	☐	☐
	0	☐	☐	☐

Only nonsmoking rooms with king-size beds appear

14 Print a copy of the list for Mr. Gilmore.

15 Click 🔽.
All records in the table redisplay.

16 Close the table *The Grande Hotel,* answer No when prompted to save table changes, and then close the database *The Willows.*
The Access window is blank.

The Conclusion

In the exercises and assignments that follow, you'll continue updating the records in the table *The Grande Hotel* in the database *The Willows.* If you plan to continue working on the exercises and assignments, leave Access running. If you've finished work for the day, close Access, perform the shutdown routine used in your lab, and turn off the computer.

Summary and Exercises

Summary

- You can use the Access Find feature to locate records and the Access Replace feature to update information automatically or to change data.
- Updating data contained in records in a database ensures accuracy of information.
- You can insert and delete records from Form view or Datasheet view and from table objects or form objects. To delete records, be certain that the entire record is selected by clicking the Datasheet view frame button or the Form view record selection bar.
- Records you insert automatically appear at the end of the database table. You can reposition new records by performing a sort routine.
- Sorting enables you to rearrange records by grouping records alphabetically or numerically in *ascending* or *descending* order by selected fields.
- Filtering records enables you to select records that contain specific information in selected fields. You can filter on more than one field in a table or select different values for the same field by using the Or tabbed pages in the Filter by Form window.

Key Terms and Operations

Key Terms	Operations
ascending order	delete records
descending order	filter records
filter	find database records
sort	insert records
update	replace database data
	sort records

Study Questions

Multiple Choice

1. To locate a record in a database table quickly, use the
   a. Find feature.
   b. Replace feature.
   c. Datasheet.
   d. Print Preview feature.

2. Updating records includes all the following activities *except*
   a. changing an address.
   b. creating a new database.
   c. inserting new records.
   d. removing obsolete records.

3. To delete a record from a database,
   a. select a field in the table and press Enter.
   b. select a field in a form and press Delete.
   c. click the frame button or record selection bar and press Delete.
   d. select Datasheet View and press Enter.

4. To identify the field you want to use for sorting records,
   a. click the field frame button and press Ctrl+S.
   b. select the complete table.
   c. choose File, New and then select Sort.
   d. position the insertion point in a row in the field column, and click the sort button that you want on the toolbar.

5. Filtering records in a database
   a. contains field entry, properties, and instructions.
   b. selects records containing specific values in specific fields.
   c. sorts the database automatically.
   d. appears in the field description pane only.

6. The easiest way to filter records in a table is to
   a. filter by the value of the active field.
   b. restore data after accidental loss.
   c. delete all records from the table and copy them to the Clipboard.
   d. select an entire record and click the Sort Ascending button.

7. To restore a deleted record,
   a. press Ctrl+Page Down.
   b. close the database without saving and reopen it.
   c. click the Undo button.
   d. retype the record.

8. Options available in the Find dialog box enable you to do all the following *except*
   a. match any part of the field.
   b. move up or down from the active data field.
   c. replace field contents automatically.
   d. search for text with capitalization that exactly matches the text typed.

9. The filter feature that enables you to select records matching data in multiple fields is the
   a. Apply filter feature.
   b. Filter by Form feature.
   c. Filter by Selection feature.
   d. Sort feature.

10. The filter feature that enables you to select records containing the same value as the selected field is the
    a. Apply filter feature.
    b. Filter by Form feature.
    c. Filter by Selection feature.
    d. Sort feature.

Short Answer
1. What's the difference between finding and replacing?
2. What's the difference between sorting and filtering?
3. What's the selection bar on a form and what does it do?
4. How do you select multiple records in the Datasheet view?
5. What's the most efficient way to add new records that closely resemble existing records?
6. What procedure can you use to remove a record from the database to ensure that you can get it back without retyping it?
7. What's the purpose of the Or pages of the filter window?
8. Which filter feature is the most efficient for finding records that contain a value in only one field?
9. Which filter feature is the most efficient for matching records that contain specific values in more than one field?
10. To sort records from highest to lowest based on numeric values in a Number field, which sort button on the toolbar would you use?

For Discussion
1. What influence do the filter features in Access have on the number of tables you need to include in each database?
2. How do you restore records that have been deleted from a database table?
3. Why is it important to maintain consistency in the way you enter data into your database tables?
4. How does database design affect the way you can sort and filter a database?

Review Exercises

1. Sorting Data, Finding and Replacing Data, and Updating a Database Table

The table *The Grande Hotel* in the database *The Willows* needs to contain room descriptions for rooms on floors 4–7, 9, and 11–12. Because the data required for the new records so closely resembles data found in existing records, you can copy the data from existing records and change the floor numbers for the new records. Mr. Gilmore would also like you to change the Room Type descriptions for the Club rooms on the tenth floor to reflect the types of beds they contain. A portion of the completed datasheet appears in Figure 2.2.

Floor	Room Type	# Beds	Bed Type	# Televisions
3	Suite	3	King, Queen, Sofa Sleeper	3
3	Suite	3	King, Queen, Sofa Sleeper	3
3	King	2	King, Sofa Sleeper	2
3	Accessible	3	King, Queen, Sofa Sleeper	3
3	Accessible	3	King, Queen, Sofa Sleeper	3
3	Accessible	2	King, Sofa Sleeper	2
3	Standard	2	Queen	2
4	King	2	King, Sofa Sleeper	2
4	Standard	2	Queen	2
4	Suite	3	King, Queen, Sofa Sleeper	3
4	Suite	3	King, Queen, Sofa Sleeper	3
5	King	2	King, Sofa Sleeper	2
5	Suite	3	King, Queen, Sofa Sleeper	3
5	Suite	3	King, Queen, Sofa Sleeper	3
5	Standard	2	Queen	2
6	Suite	3	King, Queen, Sofa Sleeper	3
6	Suite	3	King, Queen, Sofa Sleeper	3
6	King	2	King, Sofa Sleeper	2
6	Standard	2	Queen	2
7	King	2	King, Sofa Sleeper	2
7	Suite	3	King, Queen, Sofa Sleeper	3
7	Suite	3	King, Queen, Sofa Sleeper	3
7	Standard	2	Queen	2
8	Suite	3	King, Queen, Sofa Sleeper	3
8	Suite	3	King, Queen, Sofa Sleeper	3
8	King	2	King, Sofa Sleeper	2
8	Standard	2	Queen	2
9	Standard	2	Queen	2
9	Suite	3	King, Queen, Sofa Sleeper	3
9	King	2	King, Sofa Sleeper	2
9	Suite	3	King, Queen, Sofa Sleeper	3
10	Club King	2	King, Sofa Sleeper	2
10	Club Reg	2	Queen	2
11	Standard	2	Queen	2
11	Suite	3	King, Queen, Sofa Sleeper	3
11	King	2	King, Sofa Sleeper	2
11	Suite	3	King, Queen, Sofa Sleeper	3
12	King	2	King, Sofa Sleeper	2
12	Standard	2	Queen	2
12	Suite	3	King, Queen, Sofa Sleeper	3
12	Suite	3	King, Queen, Sofa Sleeper	3

Figure 2.2

Refrigerator	Wet Bar	Smoking	Data Port	Coffee Maker	Bath Type
✓	✓	☐	✓	✓	Jacuzzi
✓	✓	☐	✓	✓	Standard
✓	☐	☐	✓	✓	Standard
✓	✓	☐	✓	✓	Jacuzzi
✓	✓	☐	✓	✓	Standard
✓	☐	☐	✓	✓	Standard
✓	☐	☐	✓	✓	Standard
✓	☐	☐	✓	✓	Standard
✓	☐	☐	✓	✓	Standard
✓	✓	☐	✓	✓	Standard
✓	✓	☐	✓	✓	Jacuzzi
✓	☐	☐	✓	✓	Standard
✓	✓	☐	✓	✓	Standard
✓	✓	☐	✓	✓	Jacuzzi
✓	☐	☐	✓	✓	Standard
✓	✓	☐	✓	✓	Jacuzzi
✓	✓	☐	✓	✓	Standard
✓	☐	☐	✓	✓	Standard
✓	☐	☐	✓	✓	Standard
✓	☐	☐	✓	✓	Standard
✓	✓	☐	✓	✓	Standard
✓	✓	☐	✓	✓	Jacuzzi
✓	☐	☐	✓	✓	Standard
✓	✓	✓	✓	✓	Standard
✓	✓	✓	✓	✓	Jacuzzi
✓	☐	✓	✓	✓	Standard
✓	☐	✓	✓	✓	Standard
✓	☐	✓	✓	✓	Standard
✓	✓	✓	✓	✓	Jacuzzi
✓	☐	✓	✓	✓	Standard
✓	✓	✓	✓	✓	Standard
✓	✓	✓	✓	✓	Large Standard
✓	✓	✓	✓	✓	Large Standard
✓	☐	✓	✓	✓	Standard
✓	✓	✓	✓	✓	Jacuzzi
✓	☐	✓	✓	✓	Standard
✓	✓	✓	✓	✓	Standard
✓	☐	✓	✓	✓	Standard
✓	☐	✓	✓	✓	Standard
✓	✓	✓	✓	✓	Jacuzzi
✓	✓	✓	✓	✓	Standard

Figure 2.2 *(continued)*

Follow these steps to update the table *The Grande Hotel*:

1. Open the table *The Grande Hotel* in the database *The Willows*.

2. Sort the records in the table on the Floor field in ascending order.

3. Copy four records for third floor rooms (two Suite, one King, and one Standard), and paste them to create four new records. Change the floor number for the new records to 4. Don't copy the accessible rooms.

4. Copy and paste the records again to create four new records for floor 5, four new records for floor 6, and four new records for floor 7.

5. Select the field frame buttons Floor and Room Type, and sort the records in ascending order by both fields by clicking the Sort Ascending button on the toolbar.

6. Copy four records for rooms on floor 8 (two Suites, one King, and one Standard), and paste them to create four new records. Change the floor number for the new records to 9.

7. Copy and paste the records again to create records for rooms on floor 11 and four records for rooms on floor 12. (Tenth floor rooms are Club rooms.)
8. Arrange the records by floor number in ascending order.
9. Add a record for Floor 10 that's the same as the current record for Floor 10. Then change the Room Type to Club King, the # Beds to 2, and Bed Type to King, Sofa Sleeper.
10. Sort the records by floor, and then change the Room Type data for Club rooms with queen-size beds to Club Reg.

When you're finished, you should have 41 records in the table *The Grande Hotel*. Print a copy of the Datasheet view of this table. Save and close the database.

2. Filtering Data in a Database Table

Mr. Gilmore has requested an updated list of room types with specific equipment. Filter the table *The Grande Hotel* in the database *The Willows* to provide the following lists:
- Rooms with Jacuzzi baths
- Smoking rooms with wet bars
- Suites with both king- and queen-size beds
- A complete list of room types on all floors arranged by Room Type

To create these lists, follow these instructions:

1. Open the database *The Willows* and display the table *The Grande Hotel* in datasheet view.
2. Make the Bath Type field for a record which contains *Jacuzzi* active and click the Filter by Selection button.
3. Print a copy of the datasheet and then click the Remove Filter button to display all records.
4. Click the Filter by Form button, click the Smoking and Wet Bar check boxes on the Look for page, and click the Apply Filter button.
5. Print a copy of the datasheet and then click the Remove Filter button to display all records.
6. Click the Filter by Form button, click the Clear Grid button to remove previously set values, select Suite from the Room Type list, and King, Queen, Sofa-Sleeper from the Bed Type list; then click the Apply Filter button.
7. Print a copy of the datasheet and then click the Remove Filter button to display all records.
8. Make the Room Type field active and click the Sort Ascending button to arrange the records by Room Type.
9. Print a copy of the datasheet.
10. Close the database without saving changes.

Print a copy of each datasheet for Mr. Gilmore.

Assignments

1. Sorting, Filtering, Finding, and Updating Database Records

You need to make several changes to other tables in the database *The Willows* as well as to the table in the database *The Willows Personnel*. Use techniques learned in this project to make the following corrections to the tables in your databases:

Database	Table	Find	Replace With
The Willows	The Grande Hotel Rooms	3020–3100; Standard 3120–3200; King	3020–3100; Accessible 3120–3200; Accessible
The Willows Personnel	The Willows Managers	Williams 110 Crozet Street Chuck Mercer Bailey	Wilson 759 Azalea Boulevard Delete the record

Chuck Bailey has been replaced by Simpson Arnold Jackson, who lives at 16903 Summertime Lane, Smithfield, SC 22435. He was hired as Manager of the Willow Pond on 9/15/96 at a salary of $36,000. The business phone number for Mr. Jackson is 803-555-0480, and his home phone number is 803-555-3298. Add a new record for Mr. Jackson.

Mr. Gilmore would like for you to prepare an updated list of all managers at The Willows in alphabetical order by last name. Sort the records in the table *The Willows Managers*, and print a copy of the Datasheet view. Then prepare a list of all managers who live in Willow Grove, and print a copy of the Datasheet view. When you're finished, save and close the database.

2. Updating and Sorting a Database (Optional Assignment)

After you receive your *Competitors* database printout back from Mr. Gilmore (from assignment 2 in Project 1), add the approved records to the database. Then perform another search on the Internet to locate similar resorts on the Pacific and Gulf coasts. Sort the records by location, and print a copy of the datasheet. Then print a list of only those resorts that have golf courses on-site. Save and close the database, and then exit Access.

PROJECT 3

Altering the Table Design

As you become more proficient with using Access and more comfortable storing, searching, sorting, and filtering through data in database tables, you may eventually want to add new fields of data to existing tables and customize the way data appears in the table. In this project, you change the table design, set field properties to control the data in the tables, and rearrange the layout of fields in a table.

Objectives

After completing this project, you will be able to:

- ➤ **Insert table fields**
- ➤ **Rearrange table fields**
- ➤ **Delete table fields**
- ➤ **Create a key field**
- ➤ **Create and save an AutoReport**
- ➤ **Copy a table structure**

The Challenge

After reviewing the printout of the table *The Grande Hotel*, Mr. Gilmore realized that he would need to scan numerous fields to identify room types with features most frequently requested. As a result, he would like to change the design of the table to include a code that identifies room features. In addition, he would like to add price fields to the table to make it easier for reception clerks to determine the cost of rooms when guests check in.

ACC-74

Project 3: Altering the Table Design ACC-75

New fields added to the table design

Room Code	Room	#	Bed Type	Low Cost	High Cost	Extension
03ANS	Accessible	2	King, Sofa Sleeper	$85.00	$175.00	30XX
03KNS	King	2	King, Sofa	$95.00	$175.00	30XX
03QNS	Accessible	2	Queen	$85.00	$175.00	30XX
03SNS	Standard	2	Queen	$85.00	$125.00	30XX
03TNJ	Suite	3	King, Queen, Sofa Sleeper	$200.00	$500.00	30XX
03TNS	Suite	3	King, Queen, Sofa Sleeper	$200.00	$500.00	30XX

Format for currency

#	Refrig	Wet Bar	Smokin	Data	Coffe	Bath
2	Yes	No	No	Yes	Yes	Standard
2	Yes	No	No	Yes	Yes	Standard
2	Yes	No	No	Yes	Yes	Standard
2	Yes	No	No	Yes	Yes	Standard
3	Yes	Yes	No	Yes	Yes	Jacuzzi
3	Yes	Yes	No	Yes	Yes	Standard

Figure 3.1

The Solution

As the data-entry specialist at The Willows, you're assigned the task of changing the design of the table *The Grande Hotel* in the database *The Willows* to meet Mr. Gilmore's specifications. You can add a Room Code field and Low Cost and High Cost fields to the table structure, and then add data to the new fields.

The Room Code field presents the greatest challenge because the code must identify rooms by floor and room type, as smoking or non-smoking, and by bath type. You develop a five-digit code to identify the room types so that each code is different, as Mr. Gilmore requested. Before entering the data in all records of the table, you should complete a sample of the codes for Mr. Gilmore's review and approval.

In addition, Mr. Gilmore would like you to add a field to contain the room telephone extension numbers and would like for you to rearrange fields on the table *The Grande Hotel* and change the format for the Costs fields so that data automatically appears in currency format.

The Setup

So that your screen will match the illustrations and the tasks in this project will function as described, make sure that the following Access 97 settings are selected on your computer:

- View menu: If you don't see the toolbars, choose Toolbars and then click the toolbar listed at the top of the cascading menu.
- Screen settings: Click the Restore button on each object window.
- Tools menu: If you don't see the Status bar, choose Options and then click the View page tab. Click the check box beside Status Bar at the top of the page.

Inserting Table Fields

When you need to add fields to a table, you work in Table Design view.

TASK 1: TO INSERT FIELDS INTO A TABLE AND REMOVE FIELDS FROM A TABLE:

1. Open the database *The Willows* and the table *The Grande Hotel*. The table appears as last edited.

2. Click the View button on the toolbar.

> **Tip** For a list of available views, click the arrow button beside the View button.

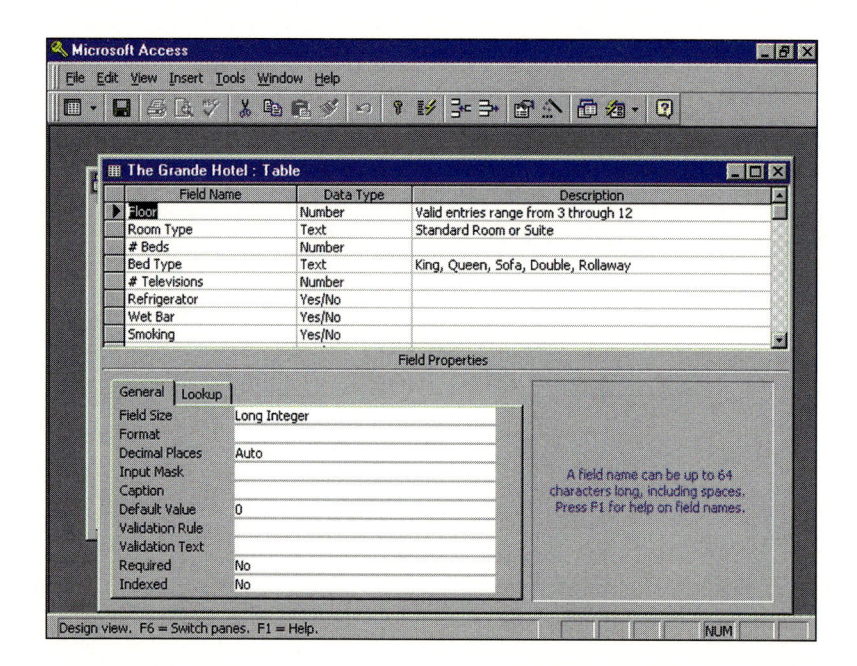

3 Click the frame button for the Floor field.

Field Name	Data Type	Description
Floor	Number	Valid entries range from 3 through 12
Room Type	Text	Standard Room or Suite
# Beds	Number	
Bed Type	Text	King, Queen, Sofa, Double, Rollaway
# Televisions	Number	

4 Click the Insert Rows button on the toolbar.
A blank row appears.

5 Click the Field Name cell, type **Room Code,** and press TAB twice.
The Description cell is active.

6 Type **Floor, Room Type, Smoking Designation, Bath Type.**

Field Name	Data Type	Description
Room Code	Text	Floor, Room Type, Smoking Designation, Bath Type
Floor	Number	Valid entries range from 3 through 12
Room Type	Text	Standard Room or Suite
# Beds	Number	
Bed Type	Text	King, Queen, Sofa, Double, Rollaway

7 Click the frame button for the # Televisions field, and drag to select through the Wet Bar field.

Field Name	Data Type	Description
Room Code	Text	Floor, Room Type, Smoking Designation, Bath Type
Floor	Number	Valid entries range from 3 through 12
Room Type	Text	Standard Room or Suite
# Beds	Number	
Bed Type	Text	King, Queen, Sofa, Double, Rollaway
# Televisions	Number	
Refrigerator	Yes/No	
Wet Bar	Yes/No	

8 Click .
Three blank rows appear.

9 Type three field entries in the blank rows, as in:

Low Cost	Currency	Not less than $85
High Cost	Currency	Not more than $500
Extension	Text	Floor Room Number

10 Click the Save button on the toolbar to save changes to the table design.

11 Click the View button on the toolbar, and maximize the table window.

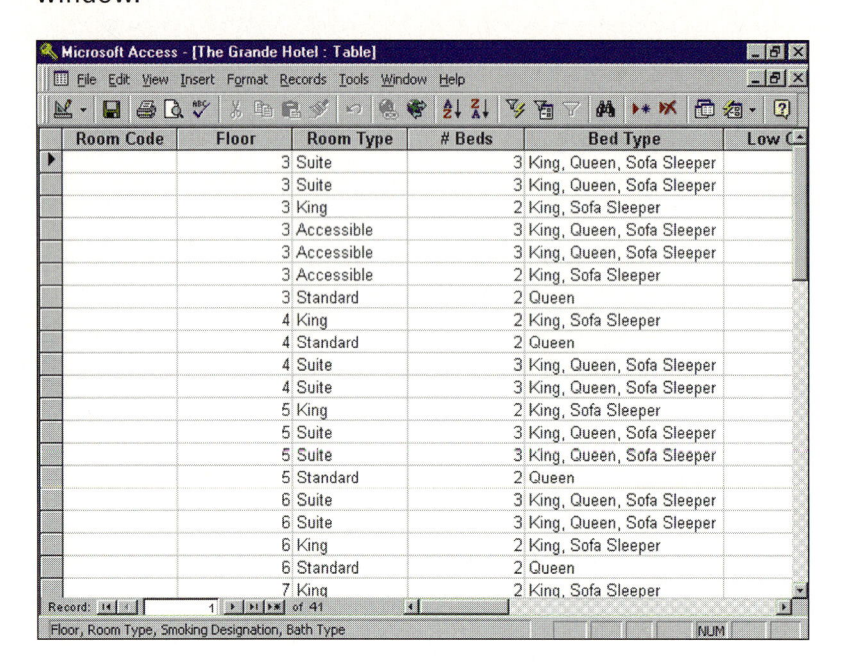

Tip If your records don't appear in the same order as the records shown in the illustration, sort the records by the Floor and Room Type fields.

Rearranging Fields in a Table

Before you delete the Floor field, you need to update each record in the table by entering data for the new fields. You can use the coding scheme identified earlier to update the Room Code field, but because the Smoking and Bath Type fields are off-screen, entering Room Code data could become tedious. By moving the Smoking and Bath Type fields into the table window with the Floor and Room Type fields, you can quickly enter data into the Room Codes field because you can see all fields side-by-side. Rearranging fields in a table doesn't alter the table design.

TASK 2: TO REARRANGE FIELDS IN A TABLE:

1 Click the field frame button for the Smoking field.

Project 3: Altering the Table Design   ACC-79

Field frame buttons →

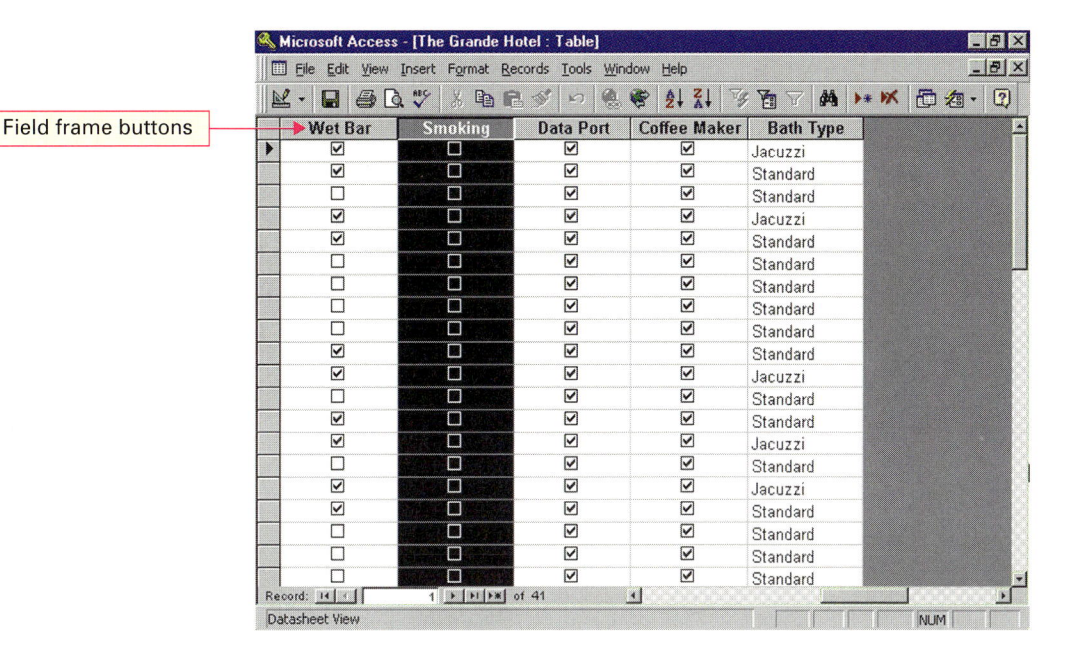

[screenshot of Microsoft Access - The Grande Hotel Table showing columns: Wet Bar, Smoking, Data Port, Coffee Maker, Bath Type]

2 Position the white pointer arrow on the selected frame button; then click and drag the field to the left.

[screenshot of Table showing columns: Room Type, # Beds, Bed Type, Low Cost with rows: Accessible / 2 / King, Sofa Sleeper / $85.00; King / 2 / King, Sofa / $95.00; Accessible / 2 / Queen / $85.00; Standard / 2 / Queen / $85.00; Suite / 3 / King, Queen, Sofa Sleeper / $200.00; Suite / 3 / King, Queen, Sofa Sleeper / $200.00]

The pointer arrow carries the field

The black bar shows the active field position

3 Position the black bar between the Room Type and # Beds fields, and drop the Smoking field by releasing the mouse button.
The Smoking field appears in the new position.

> **Tip** If you accidentally drop the field in the wrong location, simply pick it up by clicking the frame button again and reposition it, or click Undo and start over.

4 Click the frame button for the Bath Type field, and drag it to a position between the Smoking and # Beds fields.

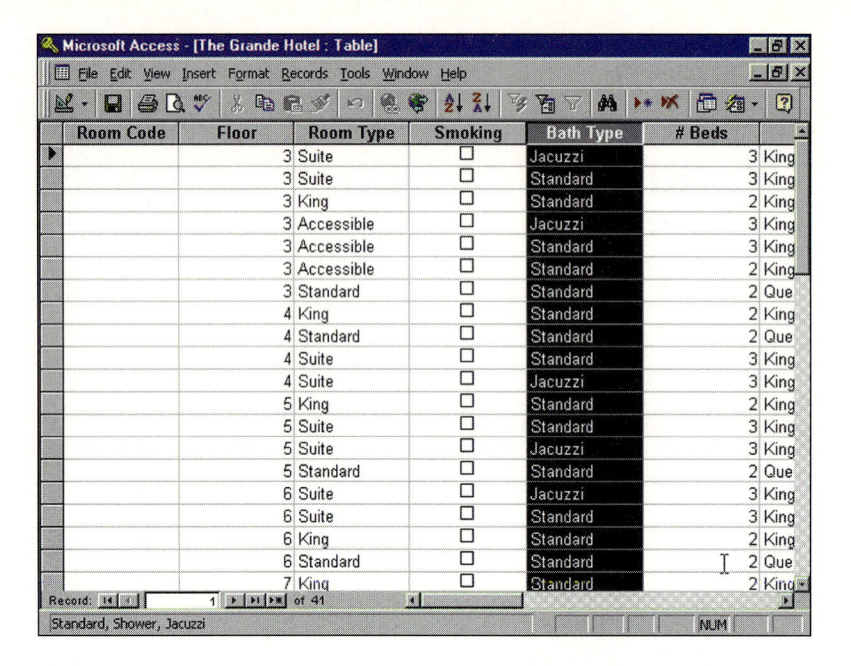

5 Type data into the Room Code field for the third floor rooms, as in:

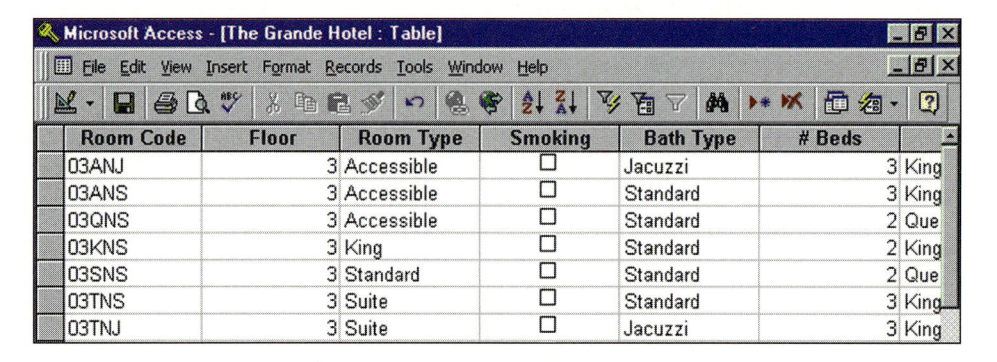

6 Select records for floors 4 through 12 and delete them.
Remember, you want to get Mr. Gilmore's approval before completing the rest of the records.

7 Return the Smoking field to its original position between the Wet Bar and Data Port fields and the Bath Type field to a position after the Coffee Maker field.

8 Use the data in Table 3.1 to enter values into the Low Cost and High Cost fields.

Table 3.1   Low Cost and High Cost Field Data

Room Type	Low Cost	High Cost
Standard	$85	$125
King	$95	$175
Accessible	$85	$175
Suite	$200	$500

9 Type **30xx** into the Extension field for all third-floor records.

Deleting Table Fields

After you add data to the Room Code field in the table *The Grande Hotel,* you can remove the Floor field from the table. After you have completed changes to the table structure, you can save the table design.

TASK 3: TO DELETE FIELDS FROM A TABLE:

1 Click [icon].
The table structure displays in Table Design view.

2 Click the frame button for the Floor field.

Field Name	Data Type	Description
Room Code	Text	Floor, Room Type, Smoking Designation, Bath Type
Floor	Number	Valid entries range from 3 through 12
Room Type	Text	Standard Room or Suite
# Beds	Number	
Bed Type	Text	King, Queen, Sofa, Double, Rollaway
Low Cost	Currency	Note less than $85
High Cost	Currency	Not more than $100
Extension	Text	Floor Room Number

3 Press DELETE.

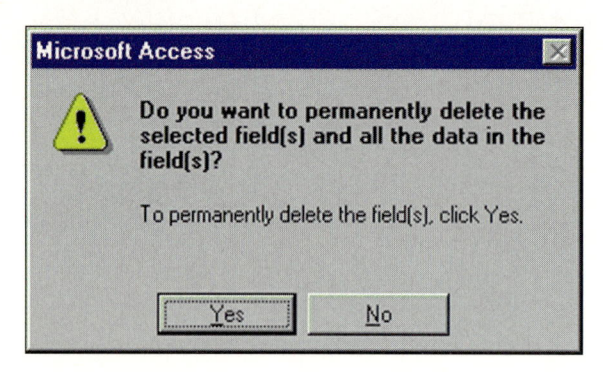

> **Microsoft Access**
> Do you want to permanently delete the selected field(s) and all the data in the field(s)?
> To permanently delete the field(s), click Yes.
> [Yes] [No]

4 Click Yes.
The Floor field is removed from the table design, and other fields move up in the list of fields.

5 Click 💾 and then click 📋 ▾.

Room Code	Room Type	# Beds	Bed Type	Low Cost	High Cost	Extension	# Telev	Refrige	Wet Bar	Smoking	Data Port	Coffee	Bath
03ANS	Accessible	2	King, Sofa Sleeper	$85.00	$175.00	30XX	2	Yes	No	No	Yes	Yes	Standard
03KNS	King	2	King, Sofa	$95.00	$175.00	30XX	2	Yes	No	No	Yes	Yes	Standard
03QNS	Accessible	2	Queen	$85.00	$175.00	30XX	2	Yes	No	No	Yes	Yes	Standard
03SNS	Standard	2	Queen	$85.00	$125.00	30XX	2	Yes	No	No	Yes	Yes	Standard
03TNJ	Suite	3	King, Queen, Sofa	$200.00	$500.00	30XX	3	Yes	Yes	No	Yes	Yes	Jacuzzi
03TNS	Suite	3	King, Queen, Sofa	$200.00	$500.00	30XX	3	Yes	Yes	No	Yes	Yes	Standard

Creating a Key Field

You may have noticed that the records in your table rearrange themselves each time you switch to a different view. Because the table doesn't contain a *key field,* Access isn't quite certain how you want to arrange records, so it automatically chooses the first field in the table and arranges records by that field. When you perform a sort on a different field or filter records based on data in another field, Access appears to arrange your records randomly. Assigning a key field tells Access which field you want to use as the primary field for organizing your records. A key field ensures that your records are arranged or sorted on that field each time you change views. A key field must contain data that's different (unique) for each record, and you can assign only one key field to each table. For the table *The Grande Hotel,* you can use the Room Code field as a key field.

TASK 4: TO CREATE A KEY FIELD:

1 Click 📐 ▾.
The table displays in Table Design view.

2 Click the frame button for the Room Code field.

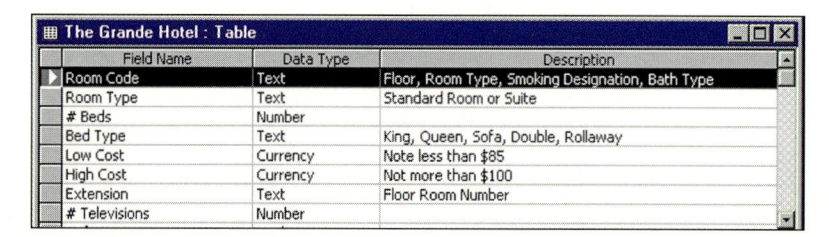

Field Name	Data Type	Description
Room Code	Text	Floor, Room Type, Smoking Designation, Bath Type
Room Type	Text	Standard Room or Suite
# Beds	Number	
Bed Type	Text	King, Queen, Sofa, Double, Rollaway
Low Cost	Currency	Note less than $85
High Cost	Currency	Not more than $100
Extension	Text	Floor Room Number
# Televisions	Number	

Project 3: Altering the Table Design   ACC-83

3 Click the Primary Key button on the toolbar.

A key appears in the frame button for key fields →

Field Name	Data Type	Description
Room Code	Text	Floor, Room Type, Smoking Designation, Bath Type
Room Type	Text	Standard Room or Suite
# Beds	Number	
Bed Type	Text	King, Queen, Sofa, Double, Rollaway
Low Cost	Currency	Note less than $85
High Cost	Currency	Not more than $100
Extension	Text	Floor Room Number
# Televisions	Number	

4 Click 💾 and then click ▦ ▾.
Access displays the table in Datasheet view.

> **Note** If Access determines that data in the key field contains duplicates, a warning message advises you that the key field assignment couldn't be saved. To correct the error, review field values, make the necessary corrections, and then repeat steps 1–4 to assign the key field.

Creating and Saving an AutoReport

Forms you create are designed primarily for on-screen viewing. Reports are database objects designed to print summarized data from database tables on paper. You can design reports using fields in one database table or fields from multiple tables using a query. In this task, you learn how to create, modify, and print **AutoReports.** You can create and save an AutoReport using the same techniques you used to create and save forms. The fields displayed on an AutoReport are the same fields contained in the table on which you base the report.

TASK 5: TO CREATE AND SAVE AN AUTOREPORT:

1 Click the arrow button beside the New Object: AutoForm button on the toolbar.

- AutoForm
- AutoReport
- Table
- Query
- Form
- Report
- Macro
- Module
- Class Module

ACC-84

2 Select AutoReport.

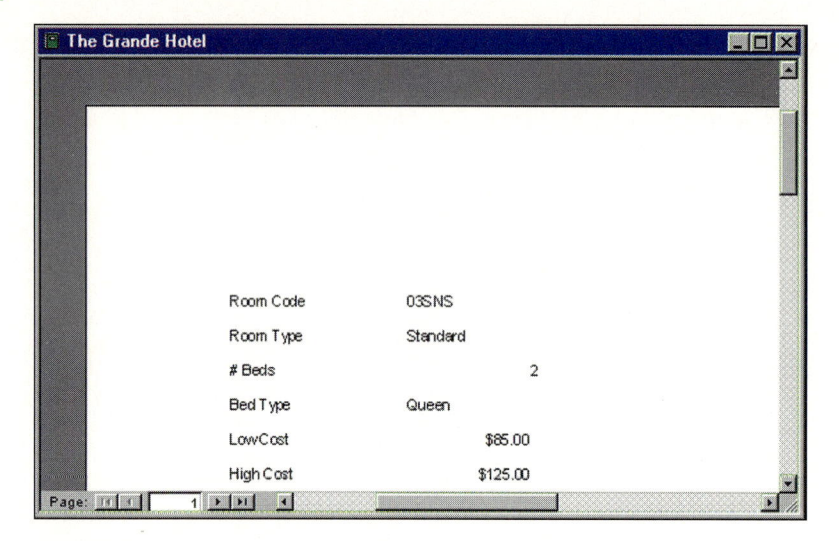

[Screenshot: The Grande Hotel report preview window showing:]

Room Code	03SNS
Room Type	Standard
# Beds	2
Bed Type	Queen
LowCost	$85.00
High Cost	$125.00

3 Choose File, Save to save the report.

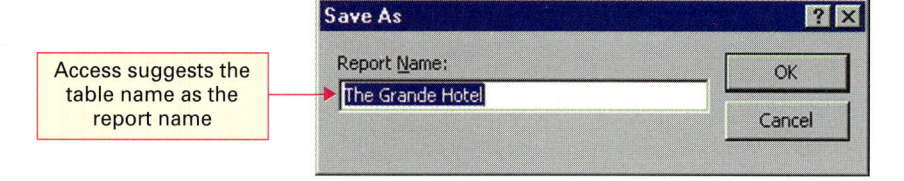

[Screenshot: Save As dialog box with Report Name: "The Grande Hotel", OK and Cancel buttons]

Access suggests the table name as the report name

4 Type **The Grande Hotel** in the Report Name text box and press (ENTER).
The report name appears in the title bar.

5 Click the Close ☒ button on the report window, and then click ☒ on the table window.
The new report name appears alphabetically in the Reports page of the database dialog box.

Copying a Table Structure

When an existing table contains basically the same fields and field structure that you need for a new table, you can copy the structure of the existing table to create the new table.

TASK 6: TO COPY A TABLE STRUCTURE:

1 Click the Tables tab of the database window for *The Willows,* and select the table *The Grande Hotel*—but don't open it.
The table is selected.

2 Click the Copy 🗎 button on the toolbar.
Access stores the table on the Clipboard.

3 Click the Paste button on the toolbar.

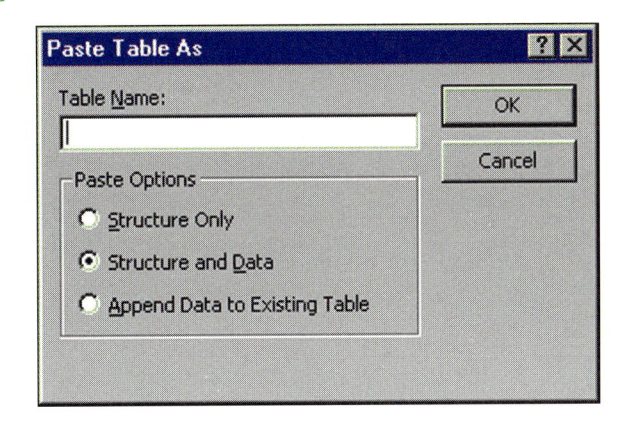

4 Type **The Willows Beach Cottages** in the Table Name text box, and click the Structure Only radio button.

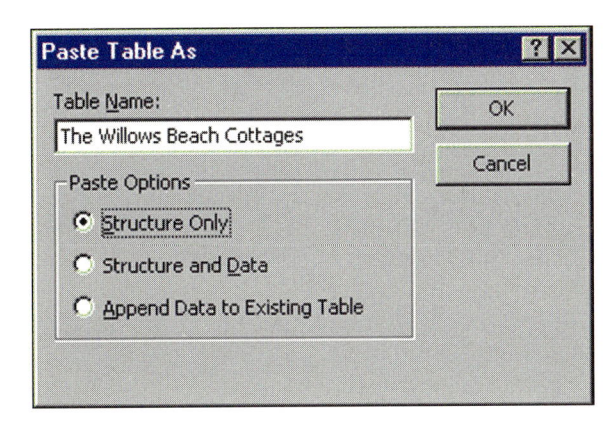

5 Click OK.
The new table name appears in the list of tables on the Tables tab.

After you copy the table, you can open the new table and add records to the table, using the same procedures you used to add records to other tables.

The Conclusion

Because you specified a key field, records rearrange automatically in the correct order each time you open your table. If you plan to continue working on the exercises and assignments, leave Access open and continue after you finish updating the table. If you're finished working in Access, exit Access properly by clicking the Close button on the application window.

Summary and Exercises

Summary

- To change the structure of a table, you must work in Table Design view.
- You can rearrange the display of fields in a table in Datasheet view without affecting the underlying structure of the table.
- When you delete a field, you can't restore it by using the Undo feature; you must insert a new field.
- A key field identifies the primary field you want Access to use to arrange records in a table.
- Reports are database objects designed to print summarized data from database tables on paper. AutoReports create simple report formats using the fields contained in the table you select.
- Key fields prevent important information from being omitted from a record.
- Access enables you to copy the structure of an existing table to create a new table, using the Copy and Paste technique.

Key Terms and Operations

Key Terms
AutoReport
key field
primary key

Operations
add fields to tables
copy a table structure
create an AutoReport
designate a field as a key field
edit fields in tables
remove fields from tables

Study Questions

Multiple Choice

1. The view you use to insert fields in a table is
   a. Table Design view.
   b. Datasheet view.
   c. Form view.
   d. Table view.

2. A warning appears when you
   a. insert a field.
   b. delete a field.
   c. edit field data.
   d. change fields.

3. The Undo feature can't reverse
   a. inserting a field.
   b. editing a field.
   c. deleting a field.
   d. rearranging fields.

4. For a list of available views,
   a. click the field frame button.
   b. select the complete table.
   c. click the View button.
   d. click the arrow button beside the View button on the toolbar.

5. To select a field in Table Design view,
   a. click the Field Entry, Properties, and Instructions text boxes.
   b. click the field frame button.
   c. insert a new field.
   d. enter new properties in the Field Description pane.

6. To insert new fields in a database table,
   a. select the field that follows the new field, and click the Insert Rows button on the toolbar.
   b. select the field that follows the new field, and press Insert.
   c. select a record in the table, and press Enter.
   d. select the field that follows the new field, and choose File, Insert New Record.

7. To move a field in the Datasheet view,
   a. select the field frame button, and press Ctrl+Page Down.
   b. select the field frame button, and press Insert.
   c. select the field frame button, and press the arrow key that represents the direction the field needs to move.
   d. click the field frame button, and drag the field to a new position.

8. AutoReports format and arrange table records for output to the
   a. screen.
   b. database.
   c. printer
   d. form.

9. To sort a table on the same field each time you switch views or open a table,
   a. save the table after you sort on the field.
   b. make the field a primary key field.
   c. filter the field.
   d. make the field a required field.

10. Key fields must contain
    a. filtered data.
    b. default values.
    c. unique data.
    d. presorted information.

Short Answer

1. What effect does rearranging fields in Datasheet view have on the table structure?

2. How does inserting fields in Table Design view affect the Datasheet view?

3. What's a field frame button?

4. How do you format data to appear with dollar signs?

5. What's a key field?
6. What's the quickest type of report format to create?
7. What fields does Access place in an AutoReport?
8. Do you have to identify a key field as you create the field or insert it into an existing table?
9. What button on the toolbar do you use to switch from Datasheet view to Table Design view and back?
10. When you change the table structure, what must you do before returning to Datasheet view?

For Discussion
1. What's the difference between moving fields in Datasheet view and adding fields in Table Design view?
2. How many fields can be identified as primary key fields? Why?
3. What's the difference between key fields and sorted fields?
4. What procedure would you follow if you deleted the wrong field in Table Design view and needed to restore it?
5. Why would you want to copy the structure of a table to create a new table, and when would you want to copy both the structure and data of an existing table to create a new table?

Review Exercises

1. Insert and Delete Fields, Assign a Key Field, and Update a Table

Mr. Gilmore wants you to revise the table *The Willows Managers* in the database *The Willows Personnel*. Because the table title reflects the positions of the people listed in the table, you can delete the Positions field from the table. In addition, Mr. Gilmore would like to add a field for managers' Social Security numbers. Because each person has a different Social Security number, you can make the field a primary key field. Mr. Gilmore would also like to include a field that contains the number of assistant managers assigned to each manager, a field for Termination Date, and a field for Comments/Reason. To make the changes to the database table, follow these instructions:

1. Open the table *The Willows Managers* in the database *The Willows Personnel*.
2. Display the table in Table Design view.
3. Insert the SSN# field as the first field in the table; position the Asst. Mgr. field just after the Salary field.
4. Insert Termination Date as a date field and Comments/Reason as a memo field at the end of the table.
5. Delete the Position field from the table.
   After you finish making changes to the table structure, add the data shown in Table 3.2 to the SSN# field and Asst. Mgr. field.

Table 3.2 Social Security Numbers and Number of Assistant Managers

Manager's Last Name	SSN#	Asst. Mgr.
Gilmore	334–85–1263	10
Jackson, R.	452–47–5920	5
Lindsey	441–34–8840	10
Taylor	441–31–8418	3
Atkinson	452–55–2817	7
Holmes	441–81–8405	2
Bradbury	326–93–1254	2
Cho	541–32–7749	4
Wilson	342–36–0354	3
Carr	331–84–4523	2
Davis	343–44–4675	2
Jackson, S.	548–85–3206	3
Sanchez	338–45–9468	3

6. Make the SSN# field a required key field.
   Print a copy of the table in Datasheet view. Save and close the database.

2. Rearranging Fields in a Table and Creating an AutoReport

Mr. Gilmore would like a report format that lists managers in chronological order with the names of those who have been with The Willows longest at the top and those who have been with The Willows the shortest amount of time at the bottom of the list. He would also like for you to change the Salary data type to Currency so that it displays entries as dollar values. In addition, he would like the list arranged so that the order of fields left to right appears as follows: SSN#, Date Employed, Last Name, First Name, Middle Name, Salary, Asst. Mgr., Department, Business Phone, Home Phone, Street, City, State, ZIP, Termination Date, and Comments/Reasons.

Follow these steps to complete these requests:

1. Open the table *The Willows Managers* in the database *The Willows Personnel*.
2. Sort the table on the Date Employed field, and then display the Table Design view.
3. Change the Data Type for the Salary field to Currency, and save the changes to the table design.
4. Return to Datasheet view, and drag fields to position the fields in the order specified by Mr. Gilmore.
5. Create an AutoReport named *Managers* based on the revised table structure.

Print a copy of the AutoReport.

Assignments

1. Insert Fields, Delete Fields, Set Key Field, and Set Field Properties

For this exercise, ask your instructor for the database *The Willows Updated*, and review the structure of each table in the database. Then add the following fields to the end of the table *The Grande Hotel Rooms:* View, Check-In Date, Scheduled Check-Out, Check-Out Date, Peak Rate, and Off-Season Rate. Make the Room Number field the key field. Suites and Club rooms are Ocean view rooms; Standard and Accessible rooms are Resort view rooms. King rooms with lower numbers on each floor are Ocean view, and King rooms with higher numbers on each floor are Resort view rooms. Enter views for each of the rooms in the table *The Grande Hotel Rooms*.

Print a copy of the Datasheet view for the table *The Grande Hotel Rooms*.

2. Editing and Copying the Structure of a Database Table

You need to add a new table to the database *The Willows Personnel* to hold the information about assistant managers. You can use the structure of the table *The Willows Managers* to create the new table. Name the table *The Willows Assistant Managers*. Then delete the Asst. Mgr., Termination Date, Comments/Reasons, and Salary fields from the new table, and add a Supervisor field to the end of the table. Change the name of the Date Employed field to Date Hired. In Datasheet view, move the Department field to just before the Supervisor field, move the Business Phone field between the Home Phone field and the Department field, and move the Last Name field to the left of the First Name field. Then enter the records shown in Figure 3.3 for the table.

Print a copy of the datasheet for the new table. Save and close the database; then exit Access if you have finished your work.

SSN#	Last Name	First Name	Middle Name	Street	City	State	ZIP	Date Hired	Home Phone	Business	Department	Supervisor
130-50-3005	Lavatto	Marietta	Walana	7302 Centerville Rd.	Ridgelake	SC	22454	4/28/96	803-555-2831	803-555-0855	Willows Beach Cottages	Jackson, R.
138-75-0573	Lancaster	Jodi	Kathleen	2501 N. Century	Willow Grove	SC	22435	5/22/94	803-555-2832	803-555-1011	Victorian Tea Room	Lindsey
141-57-7461	McGrath	Gary	Donald	146 Burges Lane	Smithfield	SC	22435	11/12/87	803-555-4005	803-555-0805	Red Rocker Restaurant	Cho
212-13-1540	Park	William	Prince	1123 North Lake Road	Ridgelake	SC	22454	7/16/72	803-555-2420	803-555-1201	The Grande Hotel	Gilmore
212-19-2016	York	Dennis	Millard	1883 Jones Creek Rd.	Smithfield	SC	22435	5/7/96	803-555-8318	803-555-0850	The Willow Top	Atkinson
212-24-6404	Thibodeaux	Lena	Baugh	3502 West Rockville	Altamont	SC	22234	3/31/86	803-555-2440	803-555-1013	Cherry Street Market	Lindsey
212-26-5436	Warren	Edward	Dwayne	307 Oregon Ridge	Willow Grove	SC	22345	9/11/83	803-555-8095	803-555-1016	Creative Cutlery	Lindsey
212-29-2129	Ritchie	Anna	Jane	16782 Central Ave.	Ridgelake	SC	22454	6/12/70	803-555-1619	803-555-1204	The Grande Hotel	Gilmore
212-40-2875	Lanham	Kevin	Marc	3478 W. Bladen, #15	Smithfield	SC	22435	5/3/91	803-555-5045	803-555-0852	Willows Beach Cottages	Jackson, R.
216-15-6616	Sparks	Robin	Parkton	2095 Oak Street	Willow Grove	SC	22435	5/28/89	803-555-2931	803-555-0520	Wind in the Willows	Bradbury
217-17-7124	Lambrusco	Heather	Marie	112 East Ocean Drive,	Willow Grove	SC	22345	6/10/88	803-555-0626	803-555-0362	Willows Water Park	Sanchez
225-26-9555	Oxley	Gray	Wilbur	2180 N. Century	Altamont	SC	22234	9/26/87	803-555-1521	803-555-0652	The Atrium Grill	Taylor
226-23-2559	Baker	Janet	Burton	3604 Oceanview Dr.	Willow Grove	SC	22345	11/15/94	803-555-1980	803-555-0302	Miniature Golf Courses	Davis
231-98-1535	Fleming	Sherman		726 Hov Drive	Ridgelake	SC	22454	2/5/87	803-555-4621	803-555-0854	Willows Beach Cottages	Jackson, R.
232-35-0252	Pargo	Carlos	Reme	3457 Hereford Dr.	James Way	SC	24354	3/18/90	803-555-2313	803-555-0702	The 18th Hole	Holmes
240-10-6109	Oconnell	Barre	Charles	112 Shoe House Rd.	Willow Grove	SC	22345	2/5/87	803-555-4025	803-555-0482	Bike Rentals	Jackson, S.
252-23-2325	Ashby	Virginia	Lane	2953 Ocean Drive	Willow Grove	SC	22345	6/26/74	803-555-4832	803-555-0751	Game Set Match	Williams
252-72-8419	Knox	Tina	Beth	736 Telegraph Road	Smithfield	SC	22435	6/1/89	803-555-1592	803-555-1210	The Grande Hotel	Gilmore
256-74-2114	Sparks	Mary	Denise	8308 Highway 173	James Way	SC	24354	9/2/93	803-555-2530	803-555-1014	Victorian Tea Room	Lindsey
260-21-1296	Bridges	Andrew	Steel	1507 Allentown Rd.	Willow Grove	SC	22345	4/2/94	803-555-7986	803-555-0820	The Willow Top	Atkinson
261-34-1869	Gadsby	Alexander	Edward	6132 Telegraph Road	Smithfield	SC	22435	10/11/72	803-555-1769	803-555-0810	The Willow Top	Atkinson
263-44-2523	Washington	Mary	Renee	16944 Old Mill Road	Willow Grove	SC	22345	1/2/81	803-555-8599	803-555-1019	Weeping Willows Gallery	Lindsey
274-06-2744	Suitland	Marley	Green	5670 Millage Circle,	James Way	SC	24354	8/13/93	803-555-5478	803-555-0361	Willows Water Park	Sanchez
290-23-2318	Sires	Mayra	Lucille	7414 Millage Circle #5	Willow Grove	SC	22345	6/1/89	803-555-3021	803-555-0483	Riding Stables	Jackson, S.
305-57-0214	Herbert	Benjamin	James	2462 Wrightsville	Ridgelake	SC	22454	7/11/92	803-555-2412	803-555-0870	The Willow Top	Atkinson
311-41-2461	Wilkins	Travis	Edmond	274 Frederick Road	Ridgelake	SC	22454	2/22/92	803-555-3650	803-555-0840	Victorian Tea Room	Lindsey
312-49-3501	Canton	Cally	Riley	831 Plymouth Point	Willow Grove	SC	22345	11/14/86	803-555-5350	803-555-0653	The Atrium Grill	Taylor
313-71-7589	Wright	Douglas	Michael	4981 Walnut Street	Willow Grove	SC	22345	8/23/96	803-555-5180	803-555-1012	Appalachian Crafts	Lindsey
314-35-9401	Towson	Kathleen	Louise	77 East Ocean Drive	Willow Grove	SC	22345	1/3/92	803-555-6170	803-555-0481	Riding Stables	Jackson, S.
322-10-3320	Boudreau	Jonathan	Earl	72 Shoe House Road	Willow Grove	SC	22345	2/28/90	803-555-7867	803-555-0363	Willows Water Park	Sanchez
331-34-4391	Bitts	Lori	Michelle	3638 Bel Air Dr.	Smithfield	SC	22435	1/6/97	803-555-4854	803-555-0802	Willow Green	Cho
334-10-6951	Temple	Henson	Thomas	5509 Outer Loop	Willow Grove	SC	22345	9/7/85	803-555-1251	803-555-0752	Black Mountain Tavern	Williams
337-13-1248	Adams	Valerie	Kay	304 Windy Hill Road	Willow Grove	SC	22345	10/14/90	803-555-0895	803-555-0803	The Cola Shop	Cho
341-21-8195	Canton	Albert	Joseph	831 Plymouth Point	Willow Grove	SC	22345	11/14/86	803-555-5350	803-555-0853	Willows Beach Cottages	Jackson, R.
347-41-1269	Pohick	Gunston	Lee	3691 Hov Drive	Ridgelake	SC	22454	4/3/88	803-555-2411	803-555-0851	Willows Beach Cottages	Jackson, R.
355-89-1019	Pena	Ernest	Toro	1568 Strayer Lane	Altamont	SC	22234	11/27/82	803-555-9309	803-555-0860	The Willow Top	Atkinson
365-86-8365	Springfield	Frank	Dulles	395 W. Rockville	Altamont	SC	22234	4/5/92	803-555-9549	803-555-0651	The Atrium Grill	Taylor
371-92-4247	Smith	Emery	David	5902 Hereford Dr.	James Way	SC	24354	8/19/91	803-555-6524	803-555-0301	Little Tree Playground	Davis
391-16-1716	Concorde	Charles	Edward	1612 Second Street	Willow Grove	SC	22345	10/30/88	803-555-6017	803-555-1207	The Grande Hotel	Gilmore
394-92-4549	Jessup	Glen	Albert	173 New York Ave.	Smithfield	SC	22435	12/14/92	803-555-5402	803-555-0830	The Willow Top	Atkinson
401-20-9324	Forest	Vernon	John	592 Indian Head	James Way	SC	24354	11/12/96	803-555-7791	803-555-1018	Live Oak Gifts	Lindsey
401-22-6849	Marlow	Lesa	Walton	1471 Barnabas Street	Ridgelake	SC	22454	2/12/84	803-555-5095	803-555-1203	The Grande Hotel	Gilmore
403-55-9145	VanDom	Ginger	Mae	1096 Strayer Lane	Altamont	SC	22234	5/30/81	803-555-9968	803-555-1202	The Grande Hotel	Gilmore
414-30-7612	Butler	Parker	William	6371 Mt. Vernon Dr.	Ridgelake	SC	22454	12/23/95	803-555-8442	803-555-1208	The Grande Hotel	Gilmore
414-80-6206	Randal	George	Grayton	4143 North South Blvd	Smithfield	SC	22435	10/9/75	803-555-9252	803-555-0753	The Pro Shop	Williams
419-39-4315	Ho	Chen	Lee	4717 Columbia Pike	Ridgelake	SC	22454	12/7/76	803-555-3018	803-555-0503	Exercise/Aerobic Facility	Carr
423-21-2195	Higgins	Carl	Deaton	136 Silver Circle #10	Altamont	SC	22234	2/4/87	803-555-7295	803-555-1205	The Grande Hotel	Gilmore
441-35-5441	McGrath	Myra	Ellen	146 Burges Lane	Smithfield	SC	22435	2/5/87	803-555-4005	803-555-0804	Grey Fox Deli	Cho
462-81-8180	Anthony	Mark	Edward	538 S. George Street	Ridgelake	SC	22454	7/18/94	803-555-8331	803-555-1209	The Grande Hotel	Gilmore
462-92-3842	Green	Marcia	Rose	980 South Maryland	James Way	SC	24354	11/10/78	803-555-4945	803-555-0502	The Health Bar	Carr
466-93-5350	Timmons	Catherine	Marie	8382 Shawan Road	Altamont	SC	22234	4/15/87	803-555-8131	803-555-1015	Ken's Kids	Lindsey
526-16-7017	Newington	Rocky	James	6495 Baltimore Lane	Willow Grove	SC	22345	12/5/73	803-555-2234	803-555-1020	Newsstand	Lindsey
554-83-2613	Park	Laurel	Kay	4865 First Street	Willow Grove	SC	22345	7/24/95	803-555-5820	803-555-0510	Wind in the Willows	Bradbury
655-55-7821	Rich	Howard	Dean	972 Highway 173	James Way	SC	24354	3/6/95	803-555-5198	803-555-1017	Sindy's Sun Closet	Lindsey
725-77-7355	King	Jose	Filipe	7813 Silver Fox	Altamont	SC	22234	3/10/80	803-555-1769	803-555-0701	The 18th Hole	Holmes
820-53-1289	Skaggs	Elliot	Camp	3525 Tunnel Road	Willow Grove	SC	22345	7/10/96	803-555-2269	803-555-1206	The Grande Hotel	Gilmore

Figure 3.3

PROJECT 4

Creating Queries

The primary objective of a database management system is to enable you to provide meaningful information in a timely manner. You build database tables to include the information you need and then sort, filter, and rearrange the display of *all* fields of table data. Using queries, you can display specific table fields and select records based on conditions. You design and save queries as objects of the database. In this project, you build, save, and run simple queries, and learn how to set query criteria.

Objectives

After completing this project, you will be able to:

➤ Create a new query
➤ Add fields to the query grid
➤ Run a query
➤ Save and close a query
➤ Open and run a query
➤ Set query sort order and criteria
➤ Edit a query

The Challenge

Mr. Gilmore often requests lists that show only specific fields of data contained in tables of the database *The Willows*. He would also like for reception clerks to be able to quickly display a list of rooms available to meet guest requests—to prevent double-booking of rooms and to distribute guests appropriately throughout the hotel.

The Solution

As the data-entry specialist, you are asked to create and save queries to display the fields Mr. Gilmore requests. Figure 4.1 displays two examples of Datasheet views that are the results of queries Mr. Gilmore wants.

Room Code	Room Type	Low Cost	High Cost
03ANJ	Accessible	$85.00	$175.00
03ANS	Accessible	$85.00	$175.00
03KNS	King	$95.00	$175.00
03QNS	Accessible	$85.00	$175.00
03SNS	Standard	$85.00	$125.00
03TNJ	Suite	$200.00	$500.00
03TNS	Suite	$200.00	$500.00
04KNS	King	$95.00	$175.00
04SNS	Standard	$85.00	$125.00
04TNJ	Suite	$200.00	$500.00
04TNS	Suite	$200.00	$500.00
05KNS	King	$95.00	$175.00
05SNS	Standard	$85.00	$125.00
05TNJ	Suite	$200.00	$500.00
05TNS	Suite	$200.00	$500.00
06KNS	King	$95.00	$175.00
06SNS	Standard	$85.00	$125.00
06TNJ	Suite	$200.00	$500.00
06TNS	Suite	$200.00	$500.00
07KNS	King	$95.00	$175.00
07SNS	Standard	$85.00	$125.00
07TNJ	Suite	$200.00	$500.00
07TNS	Suite	$200.00	$500.00
08KSS	King	$95.00	$175.00
08SSS	Standard	$85.00	$125.00
08TSJ	Suite	$200.00	$500.00
08TSS	Suite	$200.00	$500.00
09KSS	King	$95.00	$175.00
09SSS	Standard	$85.00	$125.00
09TSJ	Suite	$200.00	$500.00
09TSS	Suite	$200.00	$500.00
10CSL	Club Reg	$150.00	$300.00
10KSL	Club King	$200.00	$500.00
11KSS	King	$95.00	$175.00
11SSS	Standard	$85.00	$125.00
11TSJ	Suite	$200.00	$500.00
11TSS	Suite	$200.00	$500.00
12KSS	King	$95.00	$175.00
12SSS	Standard	$85.00	$125.00
12TSJ	Suite	$200.00	$500.00
12TSS	Suite	$200.00	$500.00

Room Code	Room Type	Low Cost	High Cost
03KNS	King	$95.00	$175.00
08KSS	King	$95.00	$175.00
04KNS	King	$95.00	$175.00
05KNS	King	$95.00	$175.00
06KNS	King	$95.00	$175.00
07KNS	King	$95.00	$175.00
09KSS	King	$95.00	$175.00
11KSS	King	$95.00	$175.00
12KSS	King	$95.00	$175.00

Four selected fields displayed in a datasheet

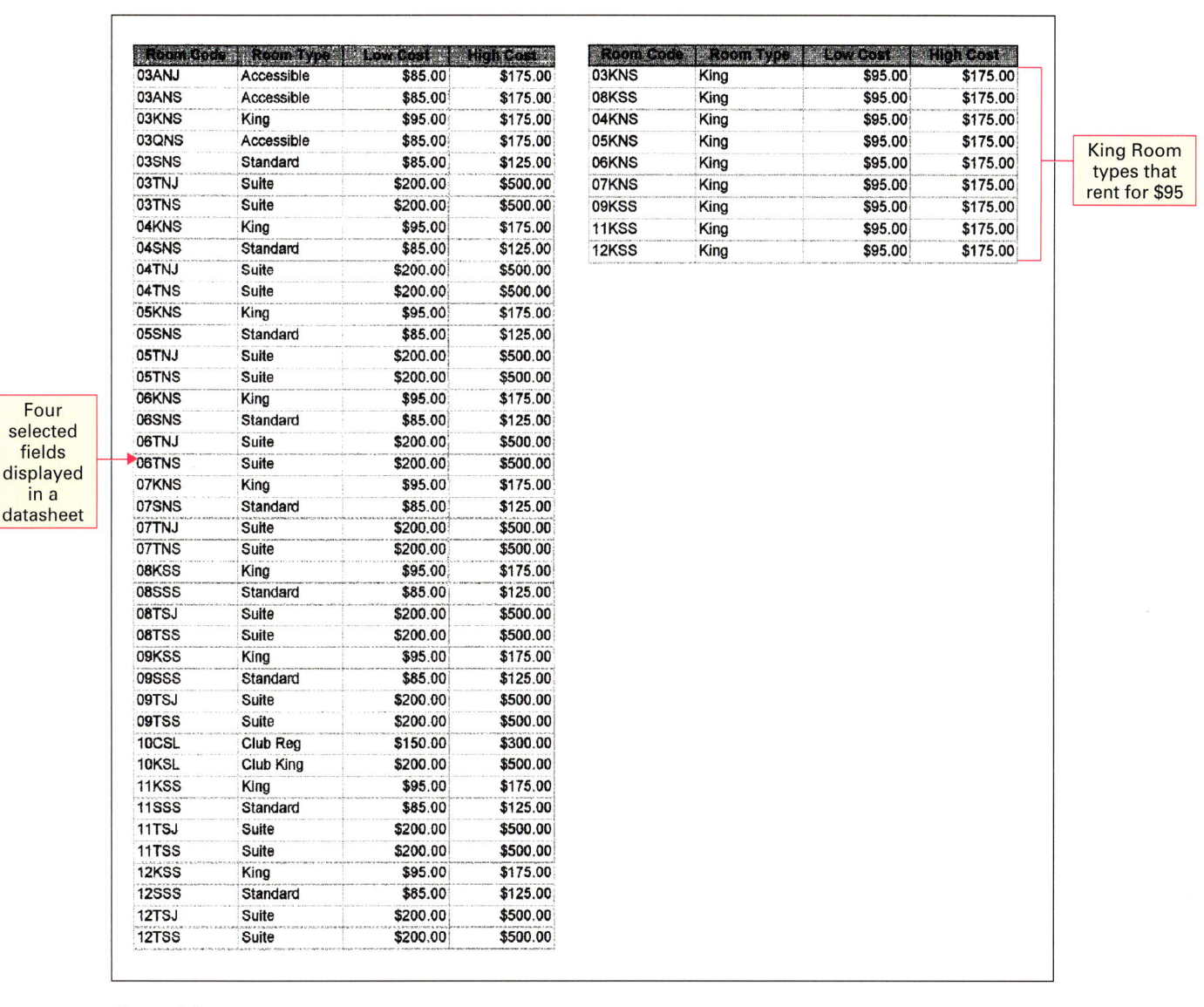

King Room types that rent for $95

Figure 4.1

The Setup

So that your screen will match the illustrations and the tasks in this project will function as described, make sure that the Access 97 settings listed below are selected on your computer:

- View menu: If you don't see the toolbars, choose Toolbars and then click the toolbar listed at the top of the cascading menu.
- Screen settings: Click the Restore button on each object window.
- Tools menu: If you don't see a status bar, choose Options and then click the View page tab. Click the check box beside Status Bar at the top of the page.

You use the database *The Willows Updated* for activities in this Project. If you have not yet downloaded the database, do so before starting these activities or check with your instructor about how to proceed.

Creating a New Query

You create *queries* using the same basic procedures you use to create tables and other database objects. Because queries use data and information stored in database tables, you select the table (or tables) containing fields you want to display in a datasheet and use the table(s) as you create the query. The *select query* is the most common type of query and can be used to display selected fields of data in Datasheet view to make updating easier.

TASK 1: TO CREATE A NEW SELECT QUERY:

1. Open the database *The Willows Updated* and click the Queries tab.

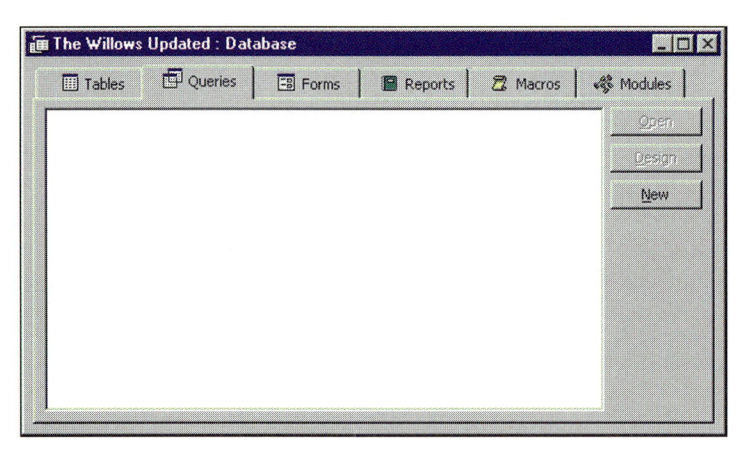

2. Click the New button.

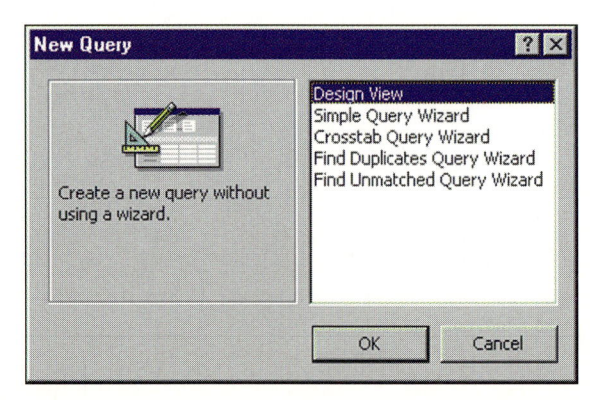

3. Select Design View and click OK.

Project 4: Creating Queries   ACC-95

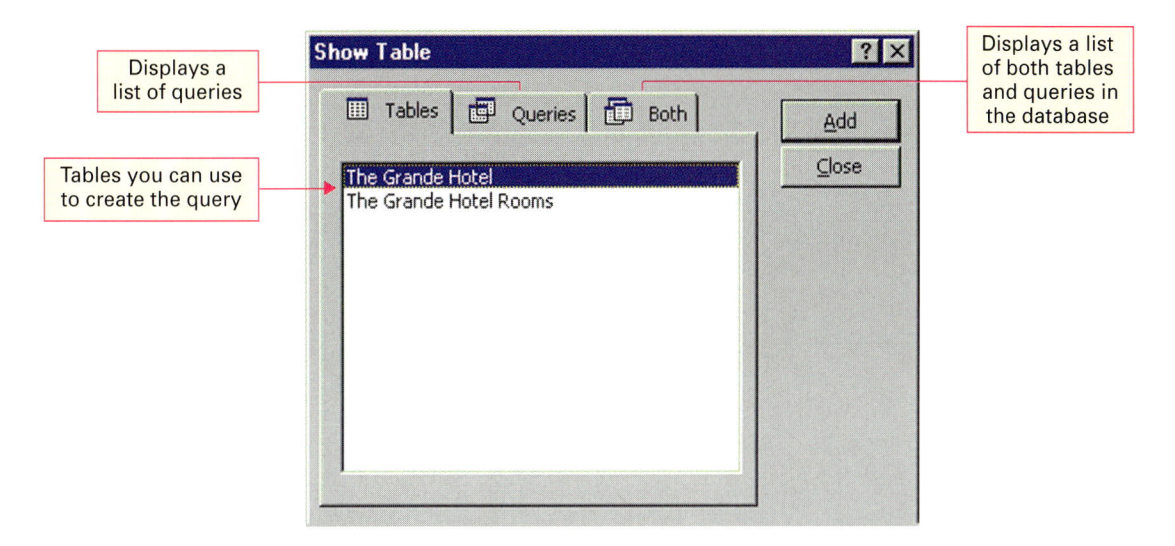

[Show Table dialog box annotations:]
- Displays a list of queries
- Tables you can use to create the query
- Displays a list of both tables and queries in the database

4 Select the table *The Grande Hotel,* click the Add button, and then click the Close button.
The query window shown in Figure 4.2 displays.

> **Tip** If you already have a table open and want to create a query based on fields contained in the open table, click the New Object button and select Query from the drop-down list; then select Design View. Access automatically adds the active table to the query window.

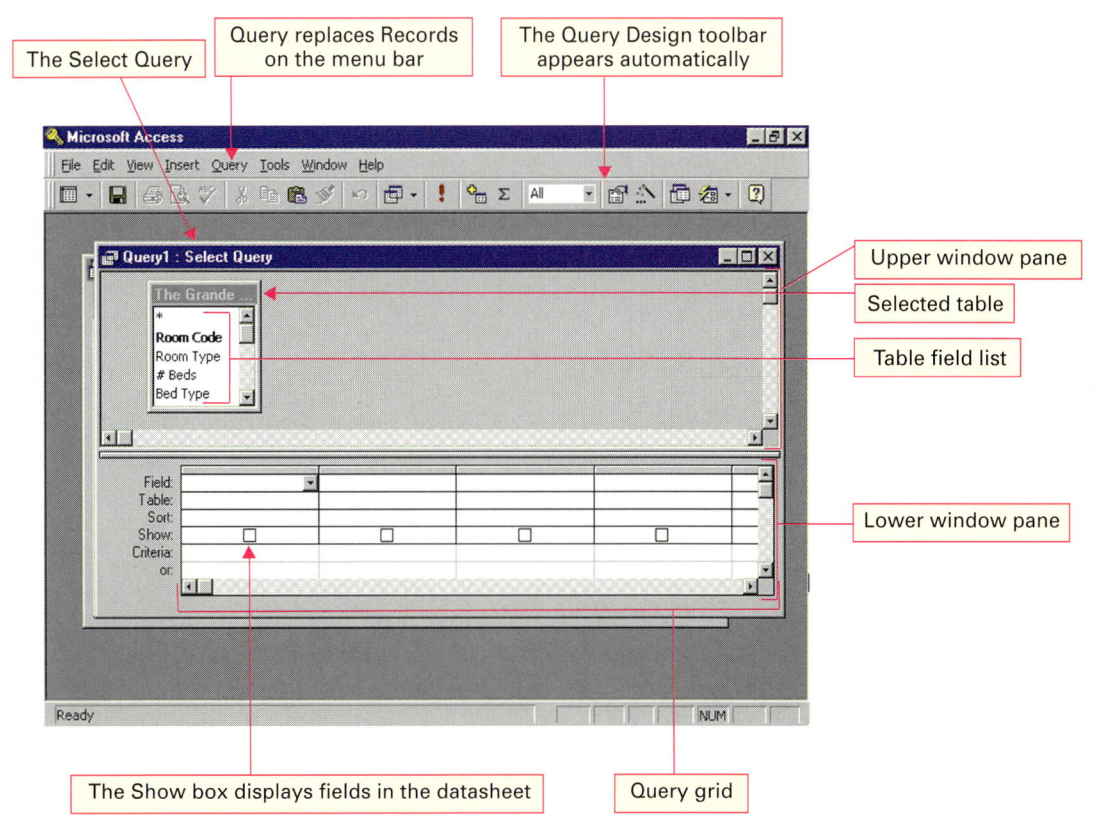

[Query window annotations:]
- The Select Query
- Query replaces Records on the menu bar
- The Query Design toolbar appears automatically
- Upper window pane
- Selected table
- Table field list
- Lower window pane
- The Show box displays fields in the datasheet
- Query grid

Figure 4.2

The query window shown in Figure 4.2 is divided into two panes. The upper pane lists fields contained in tables you add to the query, and the lower pane provides a grid where you tell Access which fields you want to use in the query. You select fields you want to display in the datasheet, identify the table that contains the field, set a sort order (if you want), and tell Access to show the field by clicking the Show box. You also use the grid to set conditions, called *criteria,* to limit the information displayed in the datasheet.

Adding Fields to the Query Grid

You can select the fields to add to a query from the table field list in the upper pane of the query window or from the drop-down list in the Field row of the *query grid.* Only one field appears in each column of the query grid.

TASK 2: TO ADD FIELDS TO THE QUERY GRID:

1 Click the arrow button beside Field in the first column of the query grid.

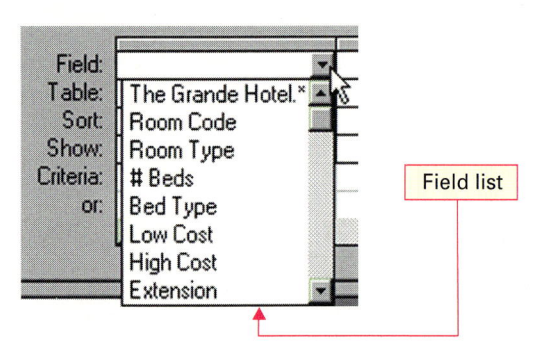

2 Click Room Code.

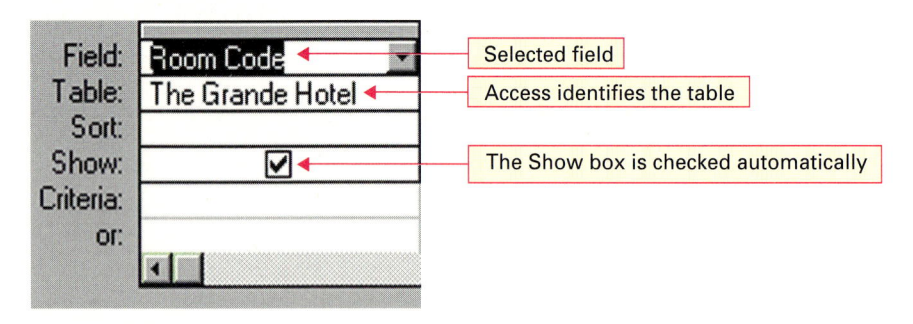

3 Double-click Room Type in the table field list in the upper pane.

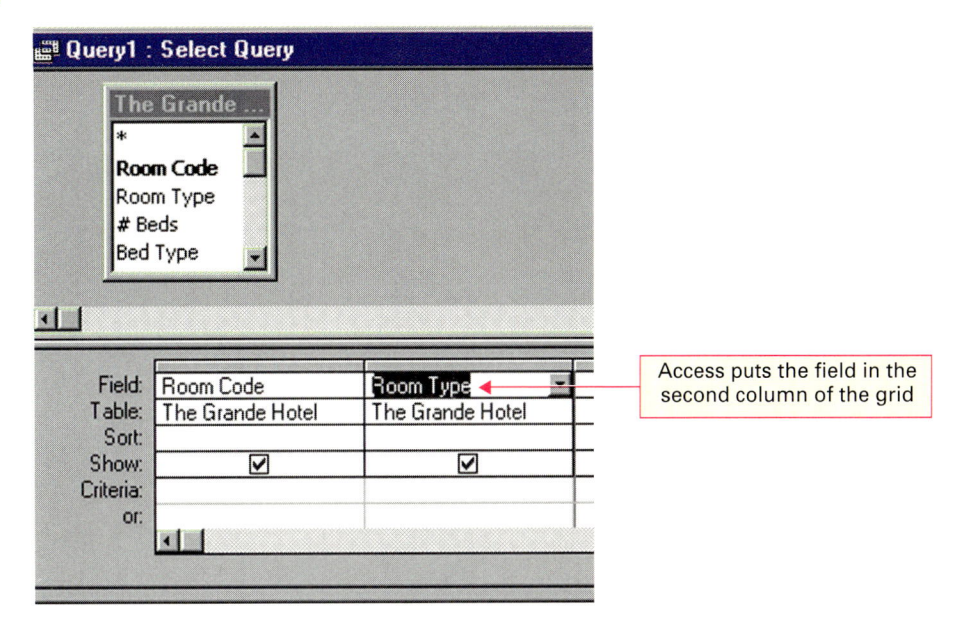

Access puts the field in the second column of the grid

4 Add Low Cost and High Cost to the grid, using the method you prefer.

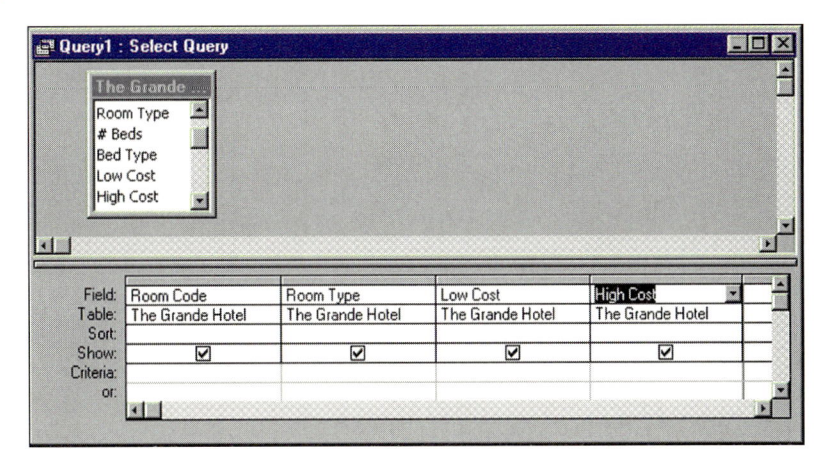

Running a Query

Running the query tells Access to display a datasheet that contains only those fields you've added to the query grid.

TASK 3: TO RUN A QUERY:

1 Click the Run button on the Query design toolbar.

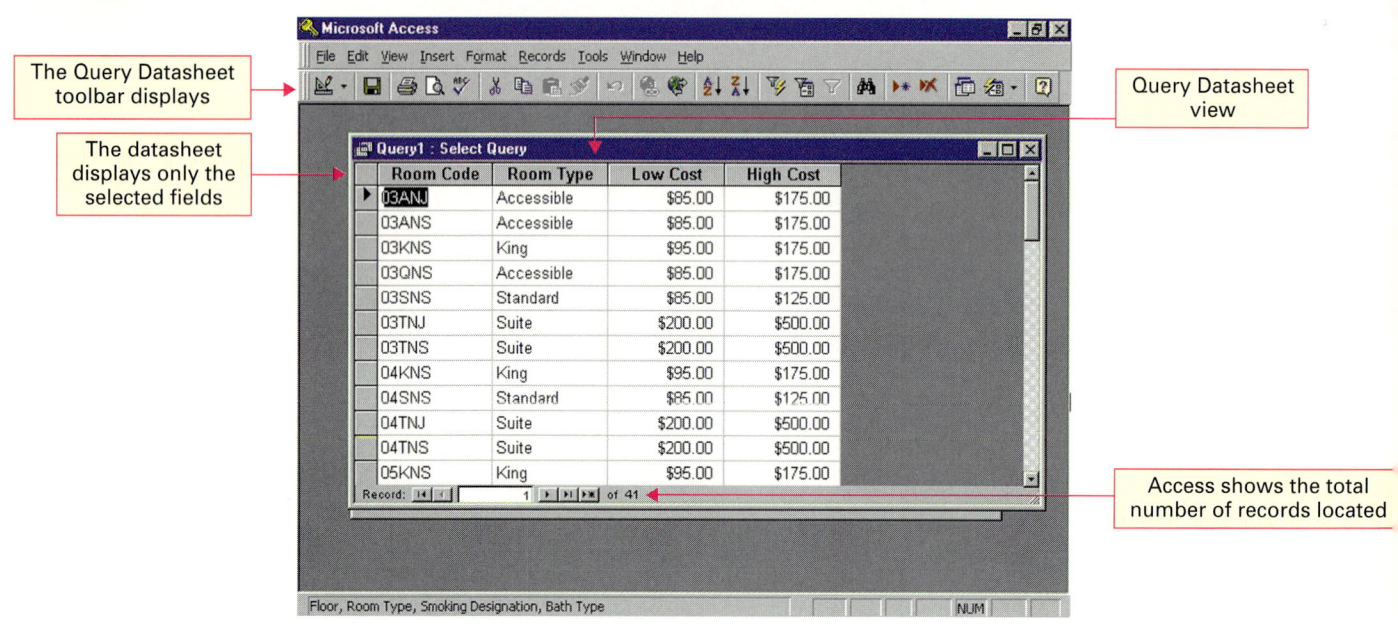

- The Query Datasheet toolbar displays
- Query Datasheet view
- The datasheet displays only the selected fields
- Access shows the total number of records located

2 Click the View button to return to the Query Design window. The Query Design view redisplays.

> **Note** Running a query displays data in a table-like format. You can print the results of a query using the same techniques you use to print a table.

Saving and Closing a Query

Often you'll create a query to use one time; other times you'll find that you use a query frequently. When you create a query that you plan to use again, save the query as an object in the database so that it's available the next time you want to use it. You can save a query from either the Query Datasheet view or the Query Design view. After you save a query, you can close it. Access displays a list of queries on the Queries page tab of the database window.

TASK 4: TO SAVE AND CLOSE A QUERY:

1 Click the Save button to save the query.

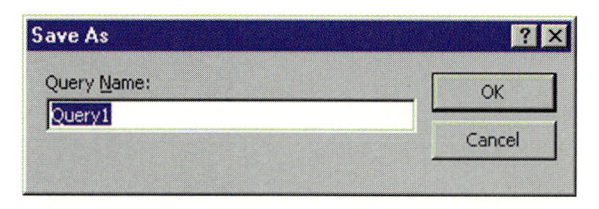

Project 4: Creating Queries   ACC-99

2 Type **Room Type and Price** in the Query Name text box.

> **Tip** Because you frequently create more than one query for each table in a database, choose a query name that describes the information or fields included in the query.

3 Click OK and then click the Close ⊠ button for the query window.

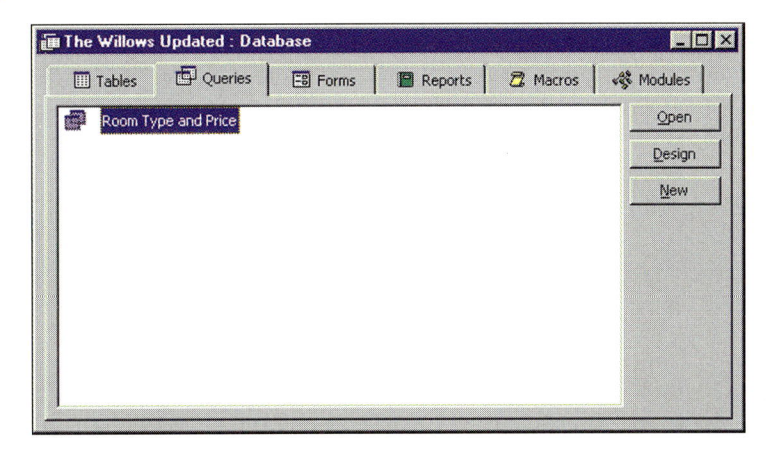

Opening and Running a Query

Saving queries you use frequently reduces the amount of time required to reconstruct the query the next time you need to view the same fields. Access runs the query when you open it.

TASK 5: TO OPEN AND RUN A QUERY:

1 If necessary, display the database window for the database *The Willows Updated* and click the Queries tab.

2 Select the Room Type and Price query and click Open.

3 Close the query.

Setting Query Sort Order and Criteria

When you want Access to run a query and sort records based on data contained in a field at the same time, you can select a sort order for the field in Query Design view. When you want to limit the records displayed to those that contain certain values in specific fields, you can set criteria for the fields in the query grid. Fields you use to set criteria and fields you sort don't have to appear in the Query datasheet. They do, however, need to appear in the query grid. Figure 4.3 displays sample criteria in the query grid.

Use > to find values greater than a specified value

The = sign can be used to find exact data matches, but is not required

Use < to find values less than a specified value

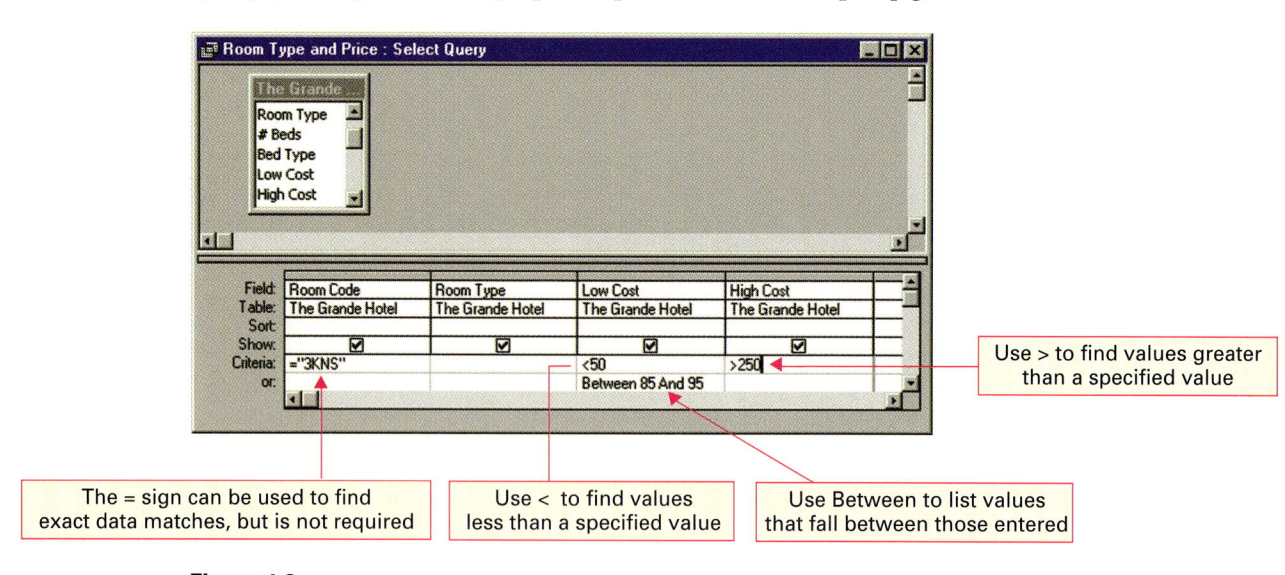

Use Between to list values that fall between those entered

Figure 4.3

Tip In addition to the comparison operators identified in Figure 4.3, you can use <> to find values not equal to the value entered, >= to locate values greater than or equal to the value entered, and <= to find values less than or equal to the value entered. When you use the comparison operators to locate alphanumeric data, > and < locate data that alphabetically follow or come before the value entered.

TASK 6: TO SET CRITERIA AND SORT USING A QUERY:

1 Open the Room Type and Price query.

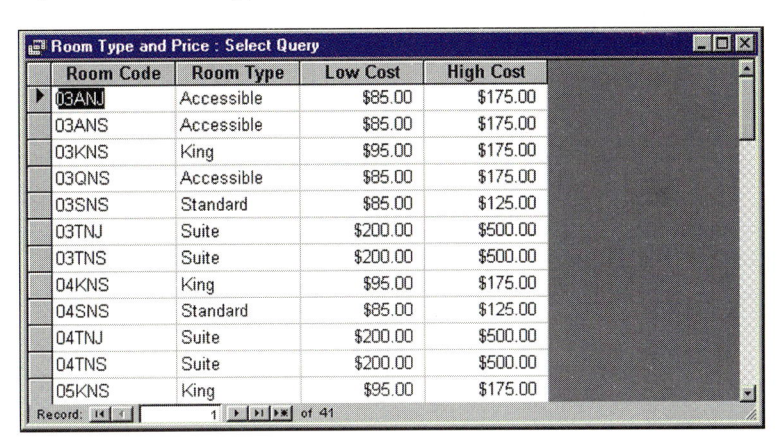

2 Click 🖉 ▾.

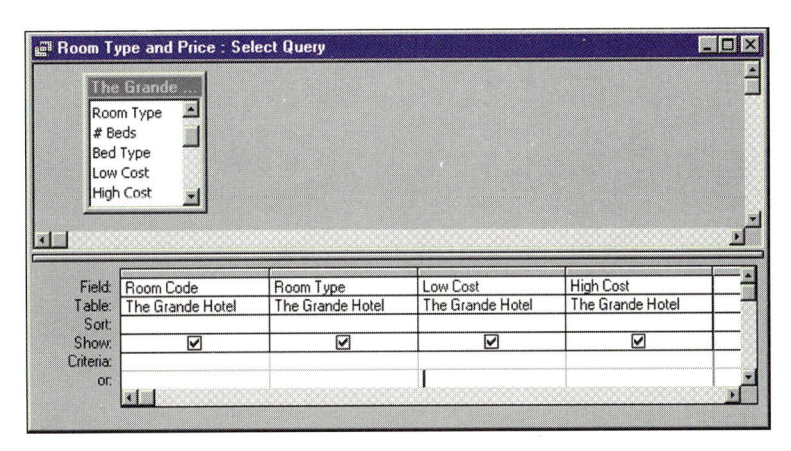

3 Click the Criteria row for the Low Cost field and type **<100**.

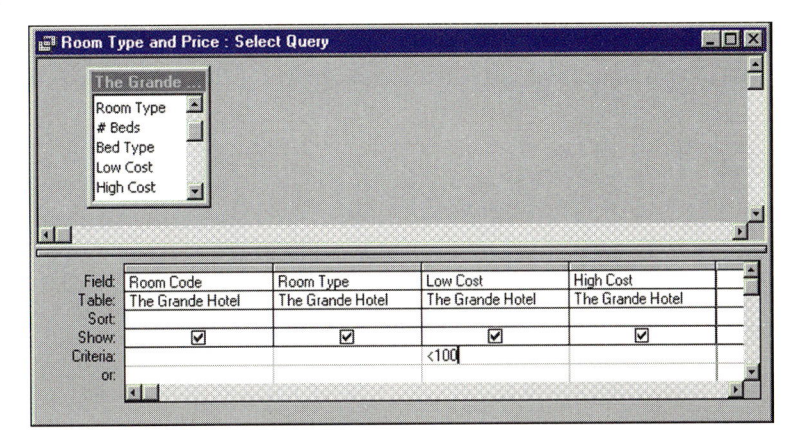

4 Click ⚡.

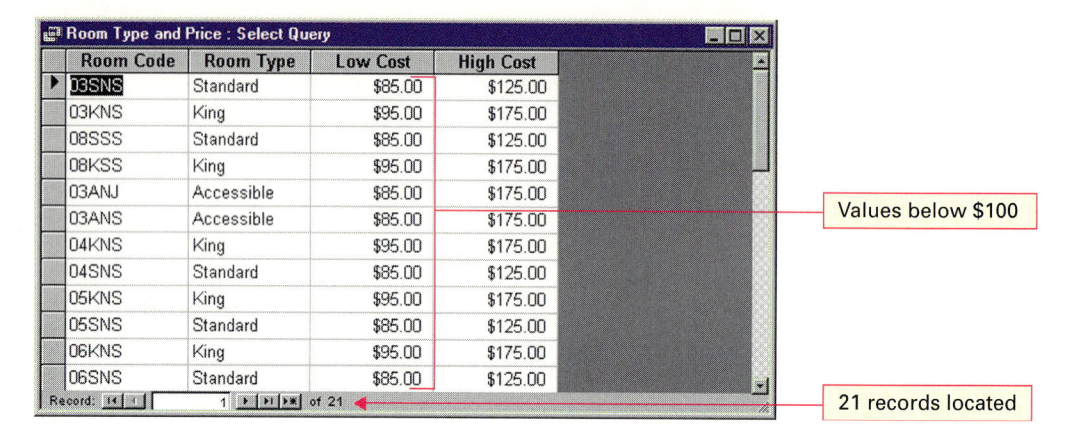

Values below $100
21 records located

5 Click 📝▾.
The Query Design view displays.

6 Type **>100** in the Criteria row for the Low Cost field and click ⚡.

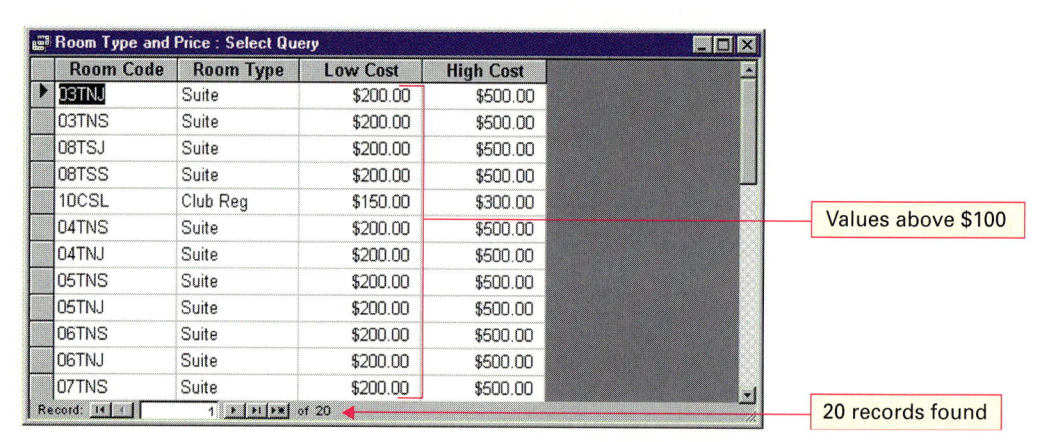

Values above $100
20 records found

7 Click 📝▾, type **95** in the Criteria row for the Low Cost field, and click ⚡.

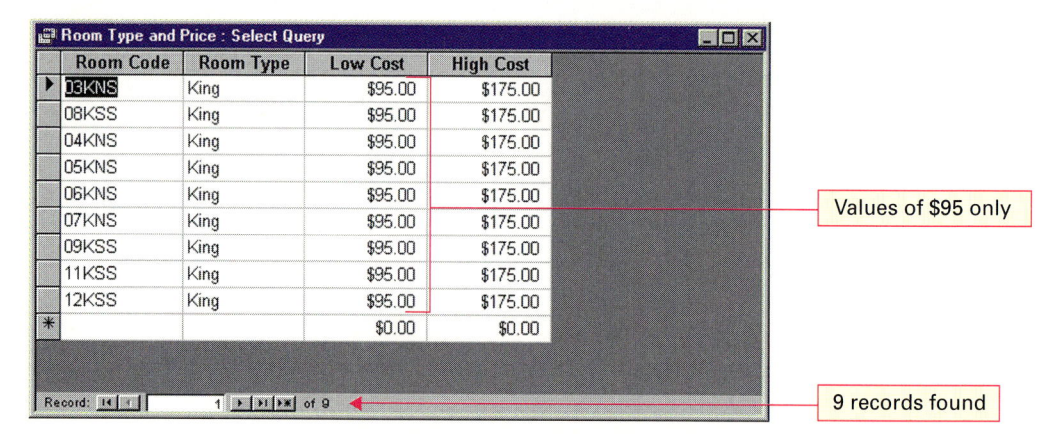

Values of $95 only
9 records found

Project 4: Creating Queries   ACC-103

8 Click [icon], click the Show box for the Low Cost and High Cost fields to remove the check mark, and then click [!].

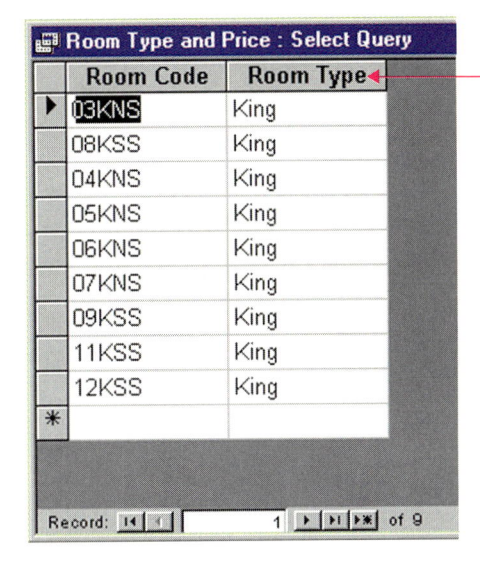

The records are the same, but only two fields appear in the datasheet

Note Access remembers the last query grid settings you ran; be sure to restore or delete those you no longer need before running the next query.

9 Click [icon], delete **95** from the Criteria row, select Ascending from the Sort row for the Room Type field, and click [!].

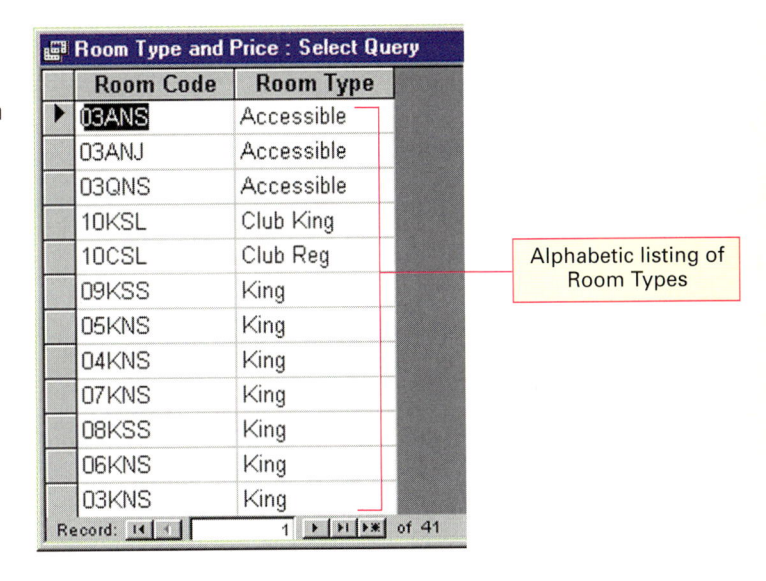

Alphabetic listing of Room Types

10 Click [X] on the query window, and click No when asked to save changes to the query.
Because you want to leave the query in its original format, don't save changes to the query.

Tip To search for data contained in a field when you aren't certain of the exact data contents, use the asterisk (*) wildcard before and after your query criteria. Placing an asterisk in front of and after the value you're trying to match tells Access to find records where the value you enter appears within the field data.

Editing a Query

You can edit the queries you save by adding fields to the query, removing fields from the query, and adding tables to access new fields using the query. You can then discard the changes to the query when you close it, or save the new query using a different query name.

TASK 7: TO EDIT A QUERY:

1 Open the Room Type and Price query.

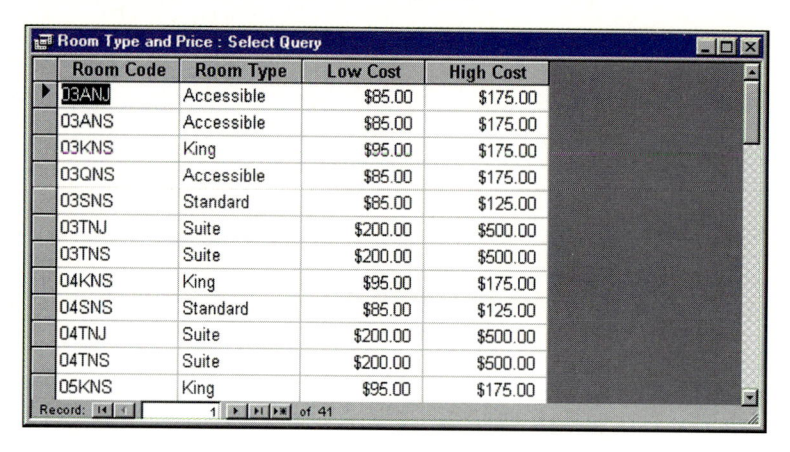

2 Click ▧ ▾.

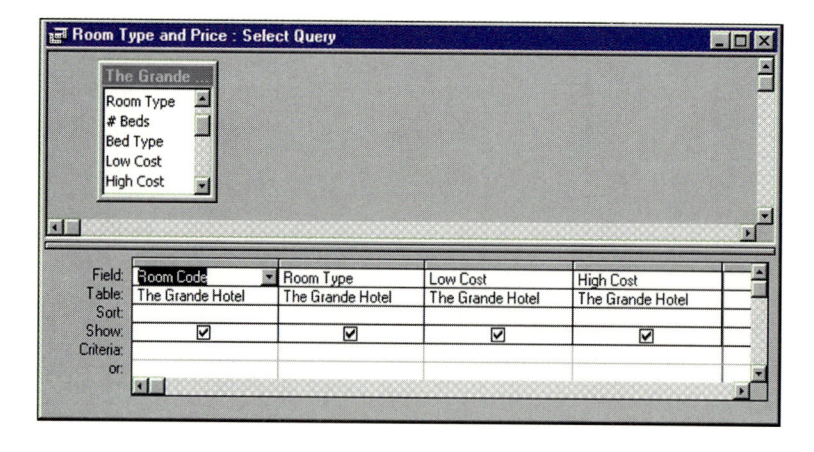

Project 4: Creating Queries   ACC-105

3 Click the frame button for the Low Cost field, and drag across to select the High Cost field.

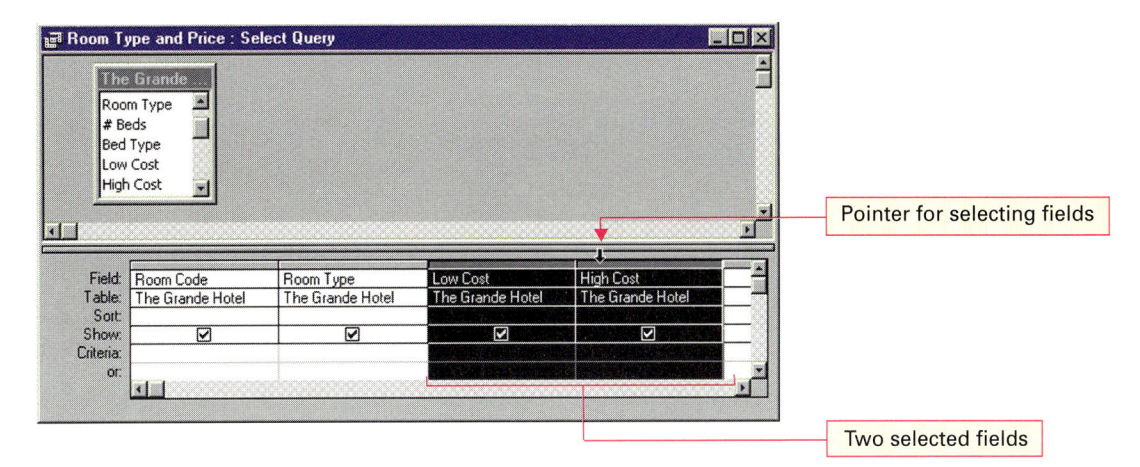

4 Press (DELETE) to clear the fields.

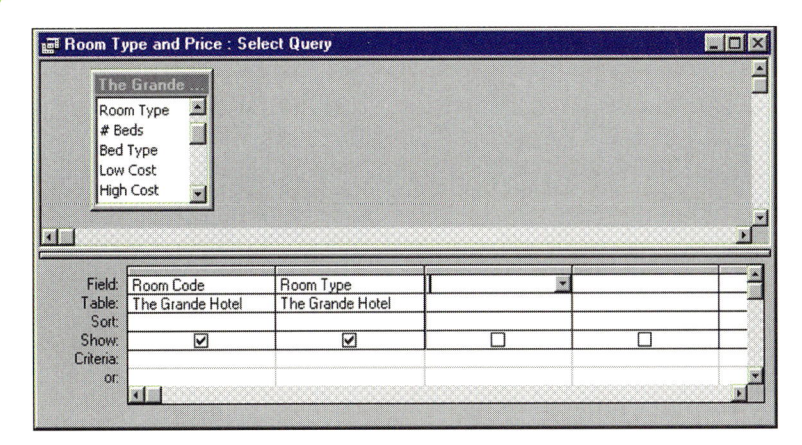

5 Add the Bed Type field to the third column of the query grid, and then run the query.

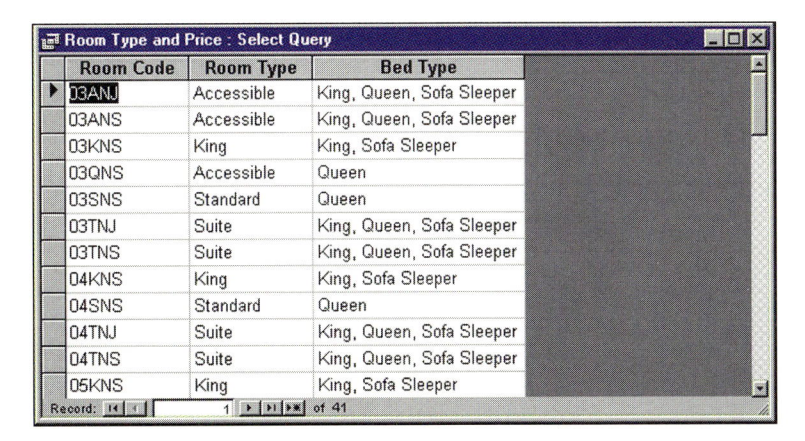

6 Display Query Design view and click the Show Table button on the toolbar.

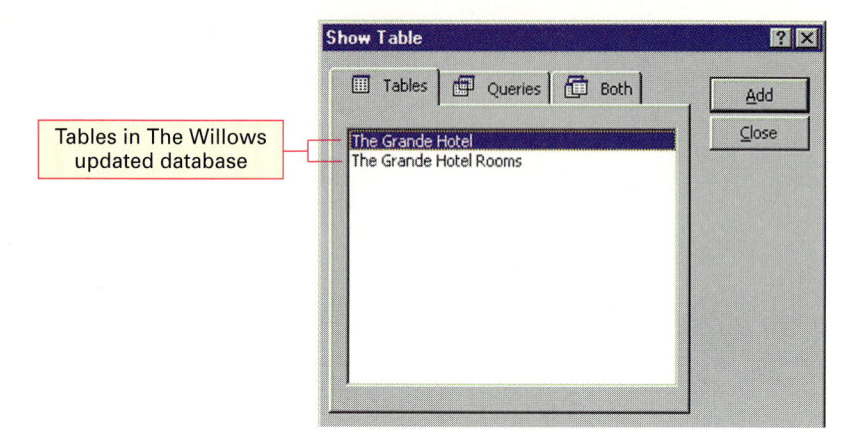

Tables in The Willows updated database

7 Click the table *The Grande Hotel Rooms,* click the Add button, and then click the Close button.

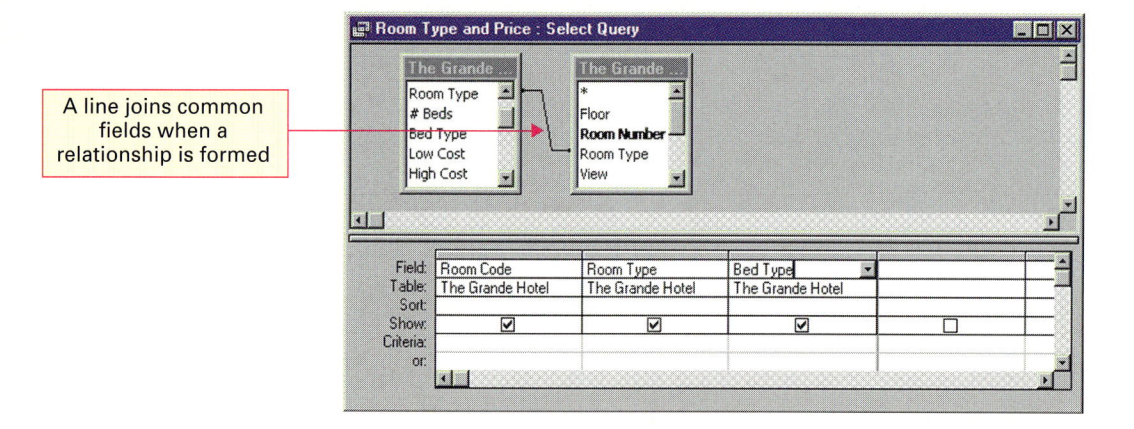

A line joins common fields when a relationship is formed

> **Note** Access tries to establish a connection between fields of tables added to a query window. These connections are sometimes called relationships and are used in advanced database applications.

8 Add the View field from the table *The Grande Hotel Rooms* to the query grid.

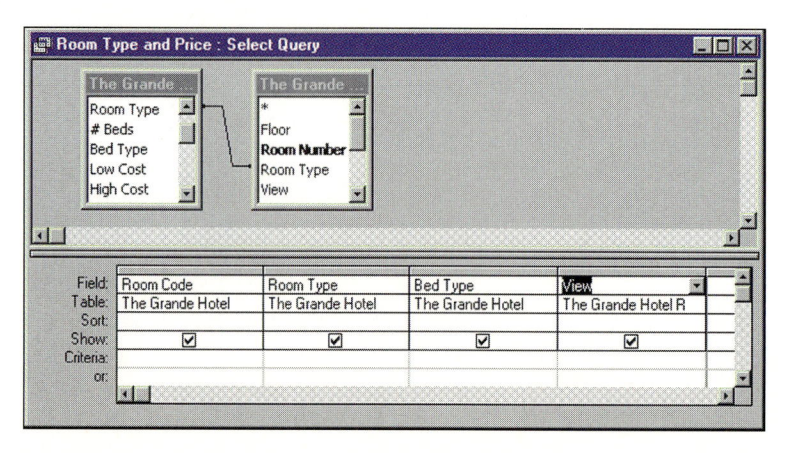

Project 4: Creating Queries   ACC-107

9 Run the query.
Access duplicates records all over the place and displays over 3,500 records because the tables have different key fields.

10 Return to the Query Design view, click a neutral area of the upper pane of the query grid, and then click the Properties button on the toolbar.

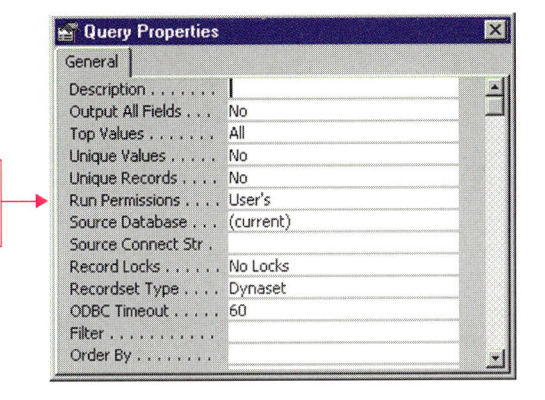

Properties you can set to control records listed when you run a query →

11 Double-click No in the text box beside Unique Values.
Yes displays as the Unique Values property.

12 Close the Query Properties window and run the query again.
49 records with different values in the Room Code field display in the datasheet.

13 Choose File, Save As/Export to save the query using a different query name.

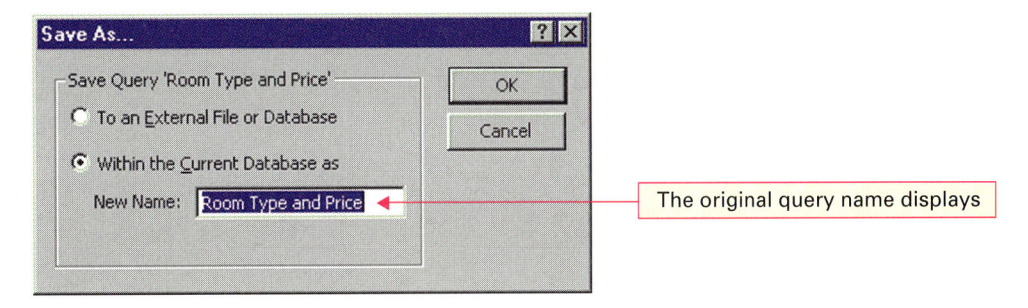

The original query name displays

14 Type **Room, Bed, and View Types** in the New Name text box, press (ENTER), and then close the query.

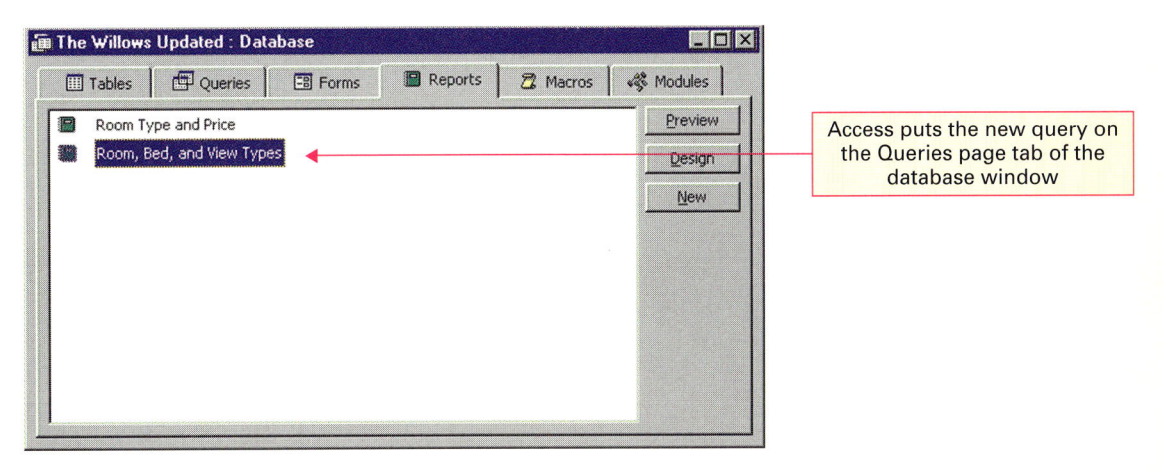

Access puts the new query on the Queries page tab of the database window

The Conclusion

You can create and save additional queries from scratch or edit existing queries to create new queries. After you have completed your work, close the database *The Willows Updated* and exit Access. If you plan to continue working on the exercises and assignments, leave Access open and continue.

Summary and Exercises

Summary

- Queries enable you to select specific fields of a table and display them in a datasheet.
- Queries enable you to sort, filter, and select the fields of a table that you want to display.
- You can select fields from more than one table and display them together on a datasheet by using queries.
- Queries are objects that you can save as part of a database to use again.
- You can set criteria for Access to use to select specific records and display them in a datasheet.

Key Terms and Operations

Key Terms
criteria
query
query grid
relationships
select query

Operations
add fields to a query grid
add tables to queries
create a query
edit queries
run a query
save, close, and open a query

Study Questions

Multiple Choice

1. To display specific fields on a datasheet, create a
   a. table.
   b. form.
   c. query.
   d. module.

2. The query window displays table field lists in
   a. front of other windows.
   b. the upper pane of the query window.
   c. the lower pane of the query window.
   d. another window.

3. The query grid appears in
   a. front of other windows.
   b. the upper pane of the query window.
   c. the lower pane of the query window.
   d. another window.

4. To add fields to a query grid,
   a. double-click the field in the table field list.
   b. select the field from the list in the Field row of the grid.

c. press Enter.
d. double-click the field in the table field list, or select the field from the list in the Field row of the grid.

5. To display records in a datasheet that meet query criteria,
   a. run the query.
   b. choose File, Display.
   c. choose Records, View.
   d. close the query window.

6. To find records with values greater than the value entered in the Criteria row of the query grid, which symbol do you type before the value in the query grid?
   a. <
   b. >
   c. <>
   d. >=

7. To locate records with dates that fall in October and November of the year 1997 into a field, type
   a. **> October** in the Criteria row for the field.
   b. **< November** in the Criteria row for the field.
   c. **between 09/30/97 and 12/01/97** in the Criteria row for the field.
   d. **October** in the first Criteria row and **November** in the second Criteria row.

8. To use a field to set criteria but not display the field in the datasheet,
   a. click the Show box in the grid to remove the check mark.
   b. type **don't show** in the Criteria row for the field.
   c. enter criteria in the Criteria row without adding the field to the grid.
   d. run the query and delete the field from the datasheet.

9. To add a field from a different table to the query grid,
   a. add the field to the table already contained in the query.
   b. create a new query using the table and combine both queries.
   c. copy the field from the table and paste it into the grid.
   d. add the table containing the field to the query and then add the field to the grid.

10. To edit a query,
    a. run the query and edit the data.
    b. open the Query Design view and change fields, criteria, or Show boxes.
    c. delete the existing query and create a new query using the new fields and criteria.
    d. edit the table contained in the query.

Short Answer

1. What's the difference between filtering and creating a query?

2. How do you sort records in a query?

3. When you edit a query, should you save the changes to the query?

4. What fields can you display in a datasheet?

5. What are the comparison operators Access recognizes for comparing field values?

6. What are the two parts of the Query Design view window, and what does each part contain?

7. How do you add a new table to the Query Design view?

8. What's the purpose of the Show box in the query grid?

9. What fields can you use to set criteria in the query grid?

10. Do you have to display fields in the datasheet that you use to set criteria?

For Discussion
1. What's the advantage to creating a query instead of simply filtering records?

2. Why would you want to add additional tables to the same query?

3. How do you save a query?

4. What procedures can be used to run a query? What's the result of running a query?

Review Exercises

1. Creating and Saving a Simple Query
Create two query designs that display the information shown in Figure 4.4. One query should create a phone list of managers, and the second query should create a phone list of assistant managers for The Willows.

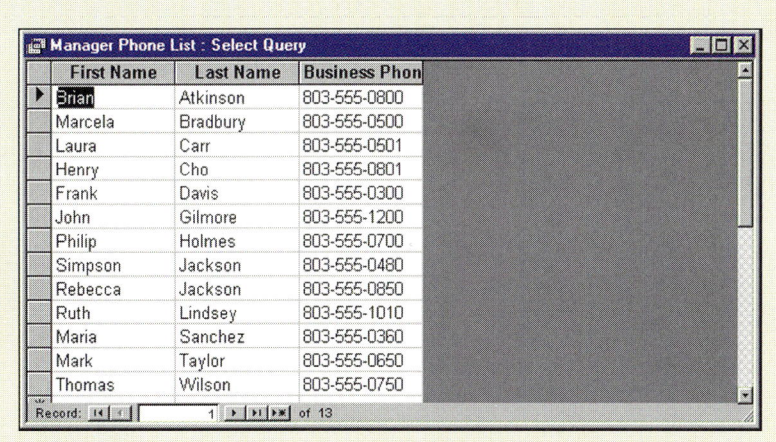

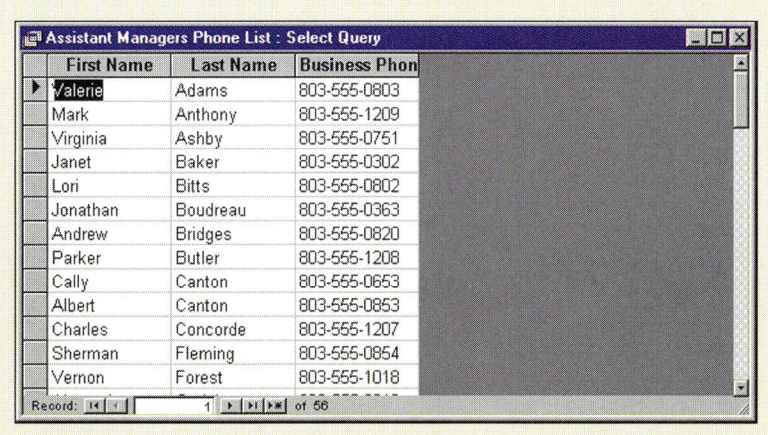

Figure 4.4

Follow these steps to create the queries that generate the lists:

1. Open the database *The Willows Personnel* and create a new query.
2. Add the table *The Willows Managers* to the query design.
3. Add the First Name, Last Name, and Business Phone fields to the query grid.
4. Select Ascending from the Last Name Sort row drop-down list.
5. Run the query and compare the format of your data display with the one shown in Figure 4.4.
6. Print a copy of the Managers phone list.
7. Save the query using the query name *Manager Phone List,* and close the query.
8. Repeat Steps 1–7 using the table *The Willows Assistant Managers* and name the query *Assistant Managers Phone List.*
9. Save and close the database.

2. Creating, Running, Saving, Editing, and Using Criteria in a Multi-Table Query

At the next staff meeting, Mr. Gilmore would like to present awards to the assistant managers who have reached milestones in their employment at The Willows. He needs copies of the lists displayed in Figure 4.5 by the first of next week so that he can prepare the awards.

First Name	Last Name	Date Hired
Kathleen	Towson	1/3/92
Frank	Springfield	4/5/92
Benjamin	Herbert	7/11/92
Travis	Wilkins	2/22/92
Glen	Jessup	12/14/92

◄ Five-year employees in 1997

First Name	Last Name	Date Hired
Barre	Oconnell	2/5/87
Myra	McGrath	2/5/87
Catherine	Timmons	4/15/87
Gary	McGrath	11/12/87
Gray	Oxley	9/26/87
Carl	Higgins	2/4/87
Sherman	Fleming	2/5/87

◄ Ten-year employees in 1997

First Name	Last Name	Date Hired
Ernest	Pena	11/27/82

◄ Fifteen-year employees in 1997

First Name	Last Name	Date Hired
William	Park	7/16/72
Alexander	Gadsby	10/11/72

◄ Twenty-five-year employees in 1997

Figure 4.5

Set up a query that displays the names and hire dates of assistant managers, sorted by department. Save the query using the query name *Employment Anniversaries*. Use the query and set query criteria to print separate lists of the managers and assistant managers who have worked for The Willows for the following lengths of time:

- 5 years
- 10 years
- 15 years
- 25 years

Follow these guidelines to complete this exercise:

1. Open the database *The Willows Personnel*.
2. Create a new query and add the Assistant Managers table to the query.
3. Add the following field names to the query grid: First Name, Last Name, Date Hired, and Department.
4. Click the Show box for Department so that it doesn't appear in the datasheet display when you run the query; select Ascending from the Sort row for the Department field in the grid.
5. Save the query using the name *Employment Anniversaries*.
6. Run the query to verify that the query sorts on the Department field but displays the other three fields.
7. Set criteria in the Date Hired field using the format **Between 12/31/91 and 1/1/93** (for those who have worked for The Willows for five years) and run the query. Print a copy of the datasheet display.
8. Return to Query Design view and use the criteria example in Step 7 to edit the data in the criteria row to generate a list of those who have worked for 10, 15, and 25 years. Print a copy of each datasheet.
9. Save and close the query.

Assignments

1. Creating a Query; Saving, Editing, Opening, and Running a Query

To make locating rooms with specific views easier when guests check into The Grande Hotel, create and save the following queries using the tables in the database *The Willows Updated*:

Query	Description
Ocean View Query	Display Room Number, View, and Check-In Date fields from the table *The Grande Hotel Rooms* for those rooms with an ocean view. Print a copy of the datasheet. Save the query using the name *Ocean View Query*.
Resort View Query	Display Room Number, View, and Check-In Date fields from the table *The Grande Hotel Rooms* for those rooms with a resort view. Print a copy of the query datasheet. Save the query using the name *Resort View Query*.
Vacant Rooms	Display Room Type, Bed Type, and Wet Bar fields from the table *The Grande Hotel,* and Room Number, View, Check-In Date, and Scheduled Check-Out fields from the table *The Grande Hotel Rooms* for rooms with no value in the Check-In Date field of the table *The Grande Hotel Rooms*. Save the query using the name *Vacant Rooms*.

Desk clerks will be able to use the queries you set up when guests check into the hotel and ask for specific types of rooms. Running the *Vacant Rooms* query now would display all records because there are no dates entered in the Check-In Date field. Save and close the database.

2. Creating Queries from Data on the World Wide Web

Ask your instructor how to obtain a database called *Tunes of the Century*. (If you have access to the Internet, you can download the database from the Addison-Wesley site on the World Wide Web.) This database contains a table named *Popular Tunes* that includes a variety of song titles, artists, and song types. Update the list by adding records for your favorite pop, country, jazz, rock, and blues titles.

After you update the database table, create queries to display the title and recording artist for each of the following song categories: Pop, Country, Jazz, Rock, and Blues. Run each query and print a copy of the datasheet. Save each query using the song category as the name of the query. Close all queries and the database, and then exit Access.

PROJECT 5

Creating and Modifying Forms

In Project 1, you learned how to create a simple form using the AutoForm feature in Access. Using forms, you can display individual records on-screen and present the data in a more aesthetically pleasing format. Because you may often want to display data from more than one table in a form, Access enables you to create forms based on fields contained in a table or fields contained in a query. In this project, you learn how to create a new form and modify the layout of fields on a form, using Form Design view.

Objectives

After completing this project, you will be able to:

➤ Create a new form and identify Form Design view features
➤ Select and remove fields from a form
➤ Rearrange fields on a form
➤ Save a form
➤ Align fields on a form
➤ Change form field labels
➤ Adjust field length on a form
➤ Add a title as a form header

The Challenge

Mr. Gilmore would like for you to create a form called *The Grande Hotel* that desk clerks can use to assign rooms as guests check in. He has sketched out the general layout of the form he would like for you to develop and asks you to create the form and design it using the sketch as a guide.

The Solution

After you review the design of the form requested, follow the steps in the tasks shown in this project to create the form. Mr. Gilmore would like for the form to appear as shown in Figure 5.1.

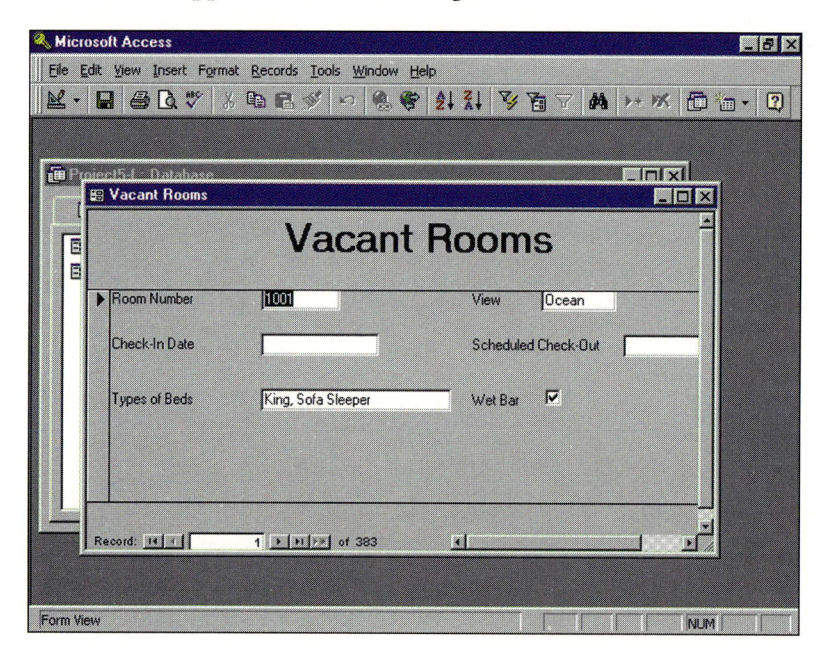

Figure 5.1

The Setup

So that your computer screen will match the illustrations and the tasks in this project will function as described, make sure that the Access 97 settings listed below are selected on the computer:

- View menu: If you don't see toolbars, choose Toolbars and then click the toolbar listed at the top of the cascading menu.
- Screen settings: Click the Restore button on each object window.
- Tools menu: If you don't see the status bar, choose Options and then click the View page tab. Click the check box beside Status Bar at the top of the page.

Project 5: Creating and Modifying Forms   ACC-117

Creating a New Form and Displaying Form Design View

The fields you need to add to the form shown in Figure 5.1 come from two separate tables: *The Grande Hotel* and *The Grande Hotel Rooms*. Both tables appear in the database *The Willows Updated,* and you used both tables to create a query in Project 4. As a result, you need to create a new form using fields contained in the *Vacant Rooms* query. The easiest way to create a form using most of the fields contained in a table or query is to use the AutoForm feature and then reposition fields the way you want them. To arrange fields the way you want them to appear on the form, you must use Form Design view.

TASK 1: TO CREATE A NEW FORM AND DISPLAY FORM DESIGN VIEW:

1 Open the database *The Willows Updated* and then open the *Vacant Rooms* query.

2 Click the New Object: AutoForm button on the toolbar.

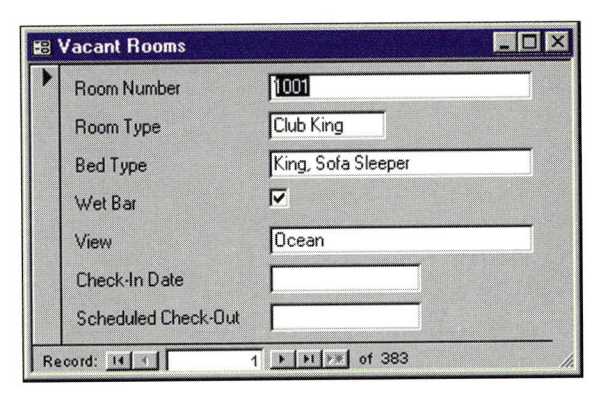

3 Click the View button on the toolbar.
The form displays in Form Design view.

As you study Figure 5.2, notice that each field on the form appears twice. Each field displayed in Form Design view is considered a ***field control*** and consists of two parts:

- *Field labels* identify the data when you display records in the Form view.
- *Field data boxes* hold the actual table data when you display records in Form view.

As you work with Form Design view, you'll also notice different pointer shapes. Each of these shapes has a distinctive purpose, as shown in Table 5.1.

Table 5.1 Pointer Shapes

Mouse Shape	Description
	Selects field controls
	Moves selected label or data box separately
	Moves selected label and data box together
	Sizes selected field label or data box

Identifying Form Design View Features

Form Design view, shown in Figure 5.2, contains a number of new features.

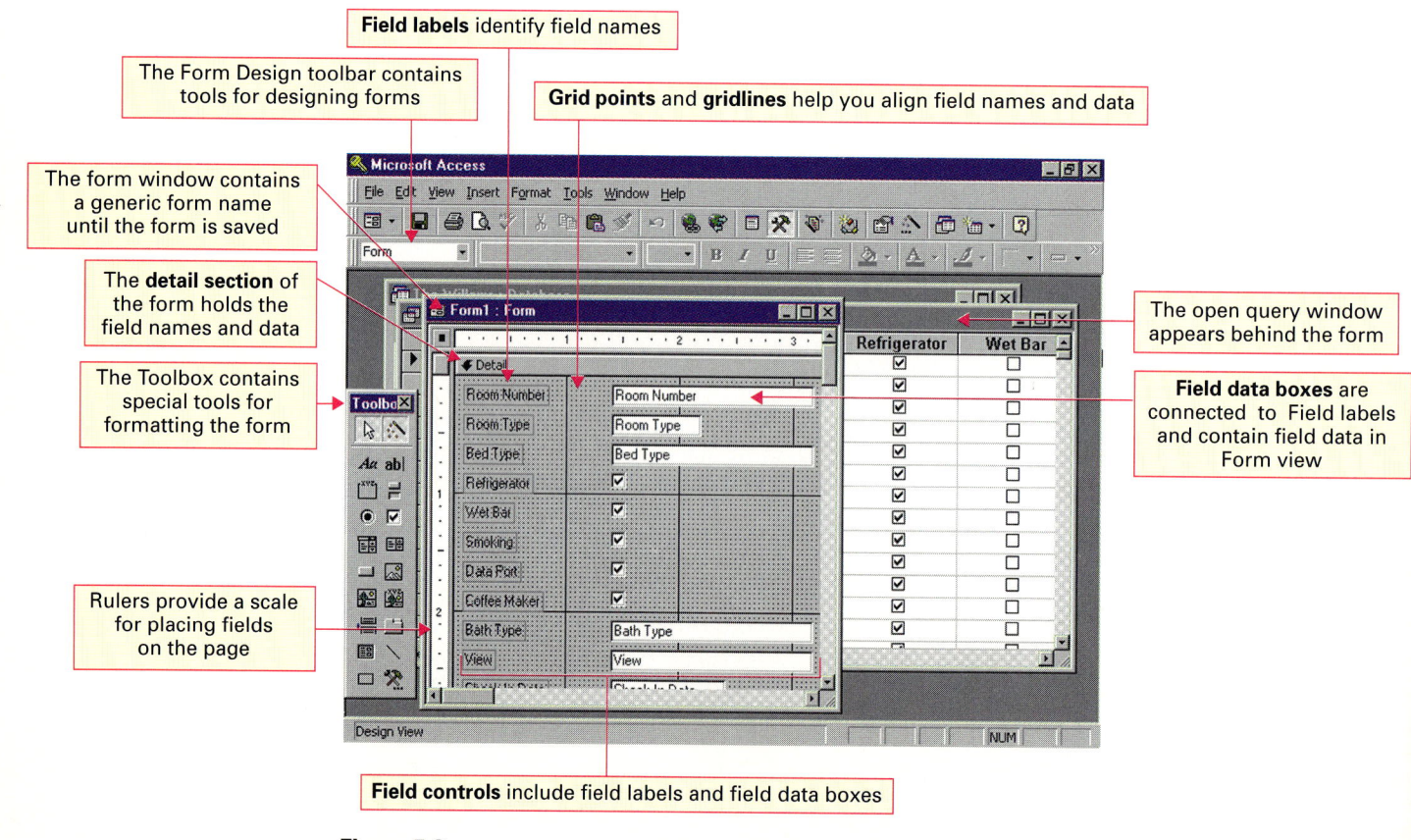

- **Field labels** identify field names
- The Form Design toolbar contains tools for designing forms
- **Grid points** and **gridlines** help you align field names and data
- The form window contains a generic form name until the form is saved
- The **detail section** of the form holds the field names and data
- The Toolbox contains special tools for formatting the form
- Rulers provide a scale for placing fields on the page
- The open query window appears behind the form
- **Field data boxes** are connected to Field labels and contain field data in Form view
- **Field controls** include field labels and field data boxes

Figure 5.2

TASK 2: TO DISPLAY MOUSE POINTER SHAPES:

1 Click the Room Type field data box.

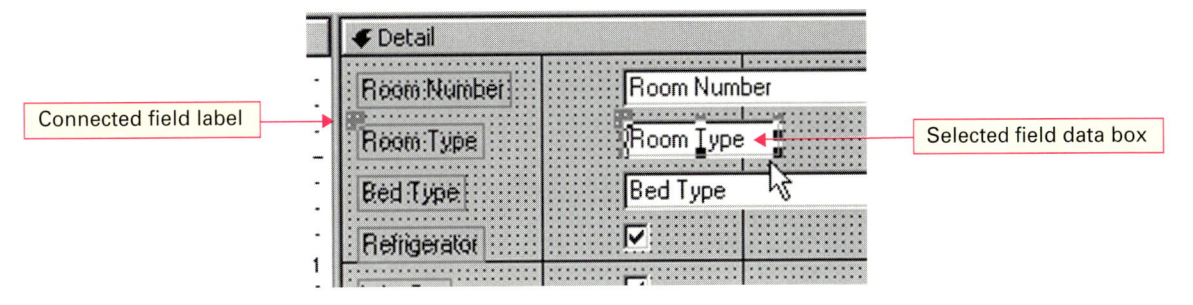

Connected field label — *Selected field data box*

2 Point to a border of the selected data box away from a handle until you see a flat hand, but don't click.

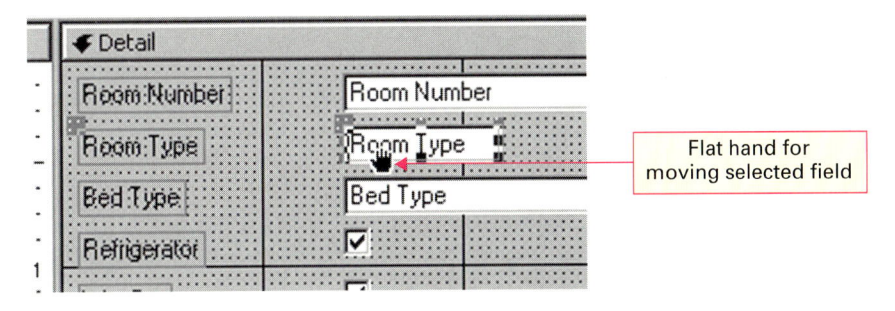

Flat hand for moving selected field

3 Point to the handle in the upper-left corner of the connected field label to see a pointing hand, but don't click.

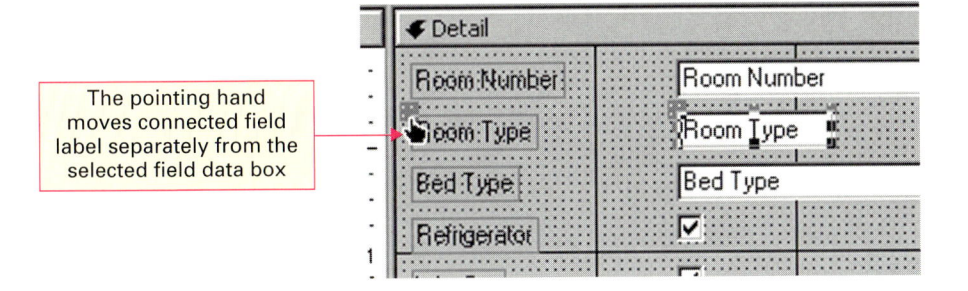

The pointing hand moves connected field label separately from the selected field data box

Selecting and Removing Fields from a Form

In Form Design view, you can quickly and easily select fields you don't need and remove them from the form.

TASK 3: TO SELECT AND DELETE FIELDS FROM A FORM:

1 Click the Room Type field label.

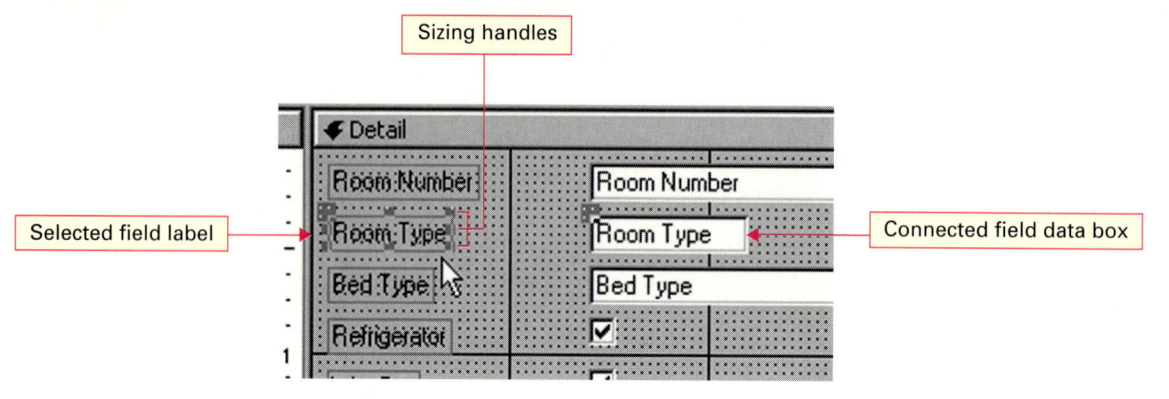

Sizing handles

Selected field label

Connected field data box

2 Press DELETE.
Both parts of the field control are removed from the form.

> **Tip** If you accidentally delete a field in error, reverse the action by using the Undo feature.

Rearranging Fields on a Form

After you delete the unnecessary fields from the new form, you can reposition the remaining fields as you need them. Use Form Design view to rearrange fields on the form. To allow more working room and to see more of the form page, maximize the form window.

TASK 4: TO REARRANGE FIELDS ON A FORM:

1 Select the field data box for the Room Number field.

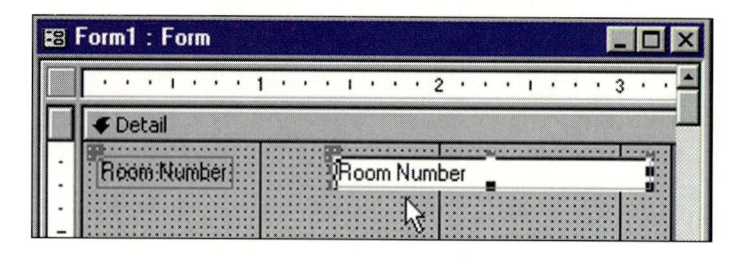

Project 5: Creating and Modifying Forms   ACC-121

2 Point to the top or bottom border of the selected field data box until you see a flat hand; then click and drag the field until the label bumps against the left side of the form and the top of the box is aligned at the top of the screen.

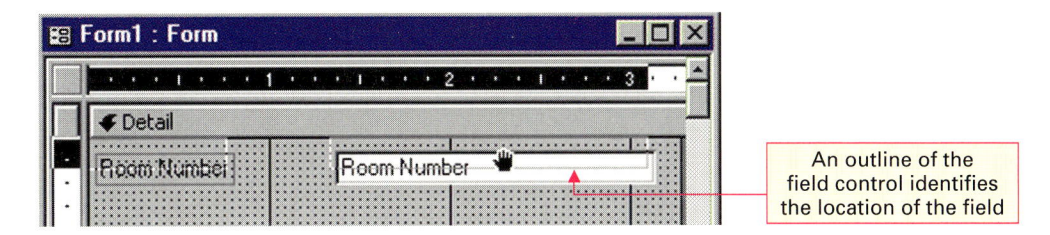

An outline of the field control identifies the location of the field

> **Tip** You can close the Toolbox or drag it out of the way to see the area of the screen you need to access.

3 Point to the View field data box, and drag it to position the field at the top of the form next to the Room Number field. The left edge of the field name should be aligned at about the 3-inch mark on the horizontal ruler at the top of the page.

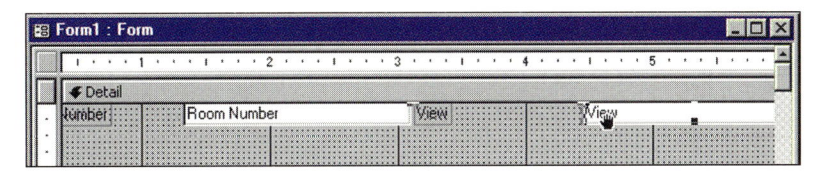

4 Click the large box in the upper-left corner of the View field data box until the pointer changes into a pointing hand; then click and drag the data box closer to the View field label, positioning the left edge of the data box at the 3.75-inch mark on the horizontal ruler.

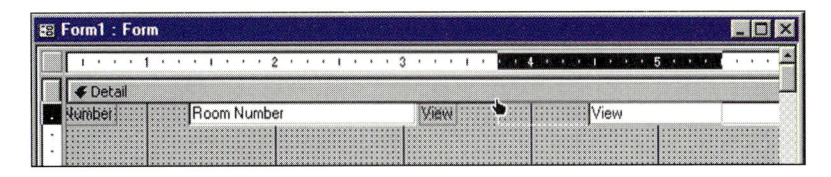

5 Continue to drag field data boxes and labels to position them approximately as in:

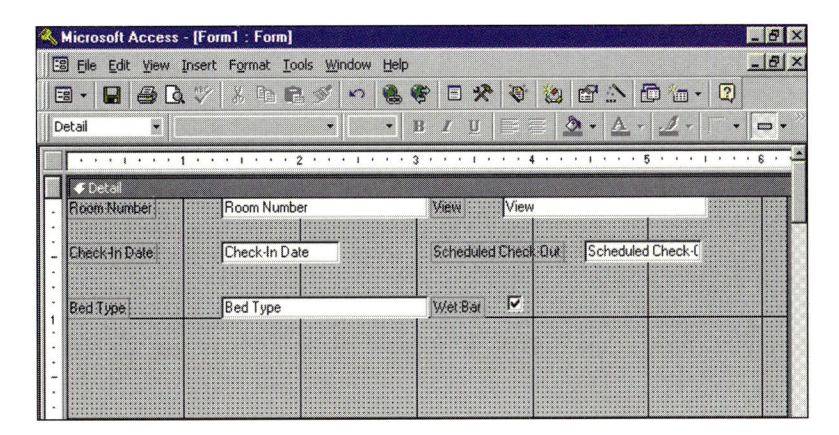

ACC-122

> **Tip** To move more than one field at a time, press Shift to select all field data boxes, and then position the pointer on the border of one selected field data box. Next, click and drag the fields to a general area of the form. Then select each field separately to position it more precisely.
>
> **Note** You learn how to align field labels and data boxes later in this project.

Saving a Form

Because forms are objects in a database, you save them using the same techniques you use to save tables and queries.

TASK 5: TO SAVE A FORM:

1. Click the Save button to save the form design.
   The Save Form dialog box displays.

2. Type **Vacant Rooms** in the Form Name text box and press ENTER.
   The form name appears in the title bar of the window.

3. Close the form by clicking the Close button on the form window, and click the Forms page tab of the database window.

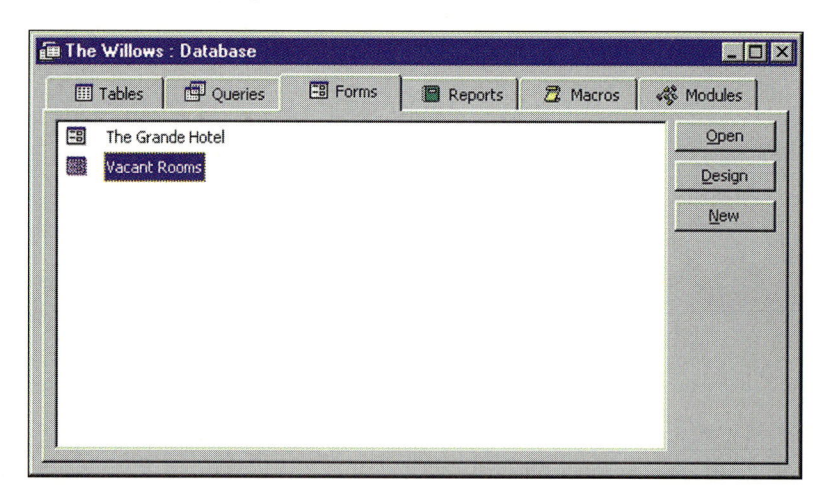

Aligning Fields on a Form

When you need to line up field names or data boxes more precisely than you can place them manually, you can use the Align options to position selected fields.

TASK 6: TO ALIGN SELECTED FIELDS:

1. Open the *Vacant Rooms* form and maximize the form window.
2. Click.

Project 5: Creating and Modifying Forms   ACC-123

3 Press SHIFT and click to select the Check-In Date and Scheduled Check-Out field labels.

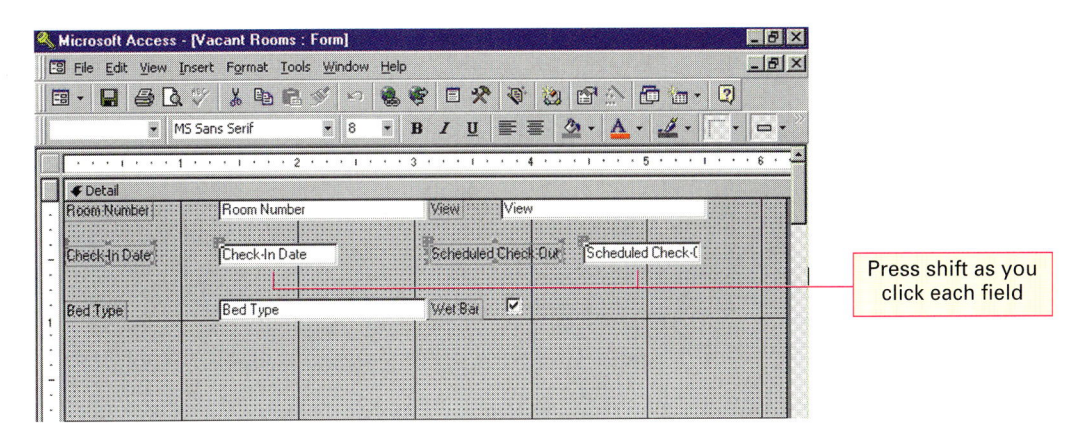

Press shift as you click each field

4 Choose Format, Align.

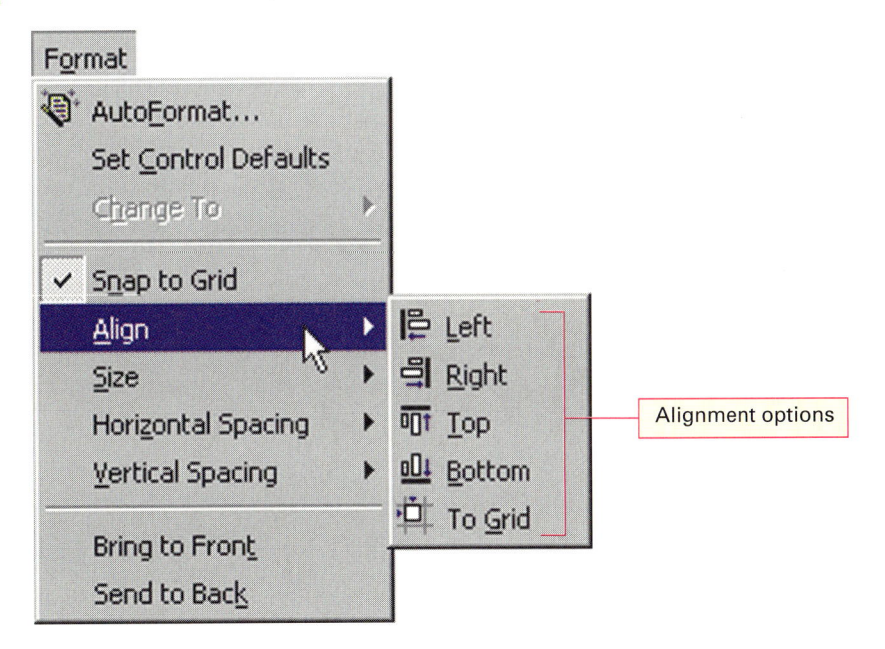

Alignment options

5 Select Top.

Tip If a field label becomes misaligned from its data box, press Shift and click both the field label and the field data box before aligning the objects.

Changing Form Field Labels

When you created the tables to contain the data for the database, you abbreviated some of the field names. When you use the field names on forms, you need to expand or change the labels to make them more descriptive and self-explanatory. Changing the labels on a form doesn't change the field names in database tables; labels on forms simply make identifying the data presented easier.

ACC-124

TASK 7: TO CHANGE A FORM FIELD LABEL:

1 Click to select the Bed Type field label.

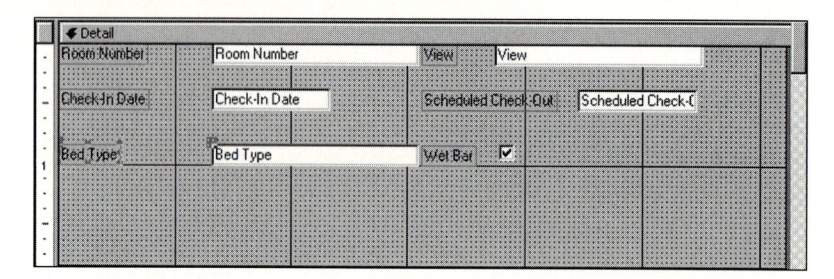

2 Position the pointer on the selected field label until it changes to an I-beam and then click.

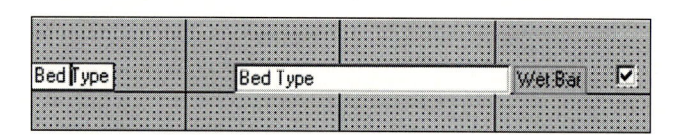

3 Click and drag to select the label text, type **Types of Beds,** and press ENTER.

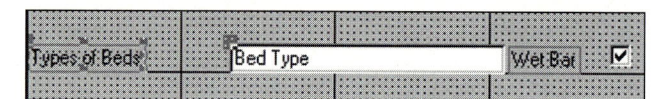

> **Tip** Use the same techniques to select field label text that you use to select text in Access tables: double-click to select a word, Shift+arrow key to select characters, and so forth.

Adjusting Field Length on a Form

When you need to adjust the size of the field data box to accommodate data on a form, you can change the size of the field data box without affecting the structure of the table.

> **Note** Adjusting the field length for Yes/No data types doesn't change the size of the check box.

TASK 8: TO ADJUST FIELD DATA LENGTH ON A FORM:

1 Display the form in Form Design view.

2 Click to select the field data box for Room Number.

3 Position the pointer on the center handle on the right side of the data box so that the pointer appears as a two-headed arrow.

4 Drag the right border of the data box to about the 2-inch mark on the horizontal ruler.

5 Use the techniques presented in steps 2–4 to adjust the size of the View and Bed Type fields, and position them as in:

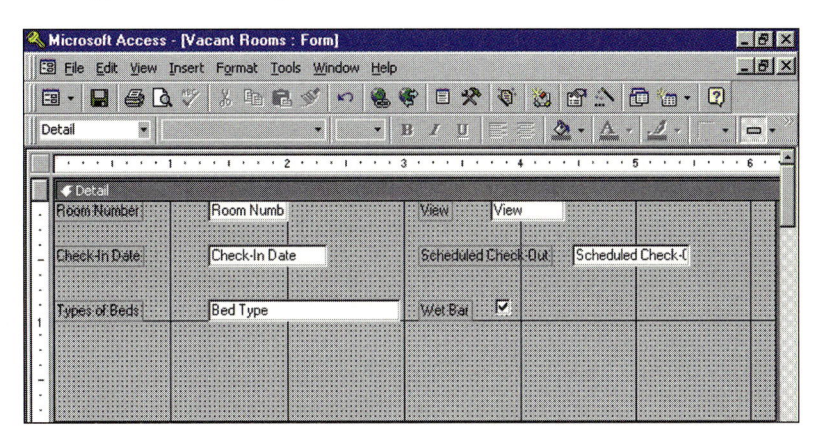

6 Click to save changes to the form.

Adding Titles to Forms

After you complete the Detail section of a form, you can add a title to the form that describes the purpose of or information contained on the form. You could add the form title to the Detail Section of the form so that the title would appear on-screen as each record is displayed. When the form title appears in the Detail section, the title would print multiple times on each printed page — once for each form on the page. If you type the form title into the header area of the form, the title appears on-screen for each record you display and only once at the top of each printed page.

> **Note** Displaying the header section of a form also places the footer section of the form at the bottom of the window. Scroll to see the footer section on the form. Information you add to the footer section prints at the bottom of every printed page in Access just as it does on Word documents.

ACC-126

TASK 9: TO ADD A TITLE TO THE HEADER SECTION OF A FORM:

1 Display the form in Form Design view.

2 Choose View.

3 Click Form Header/Footer.

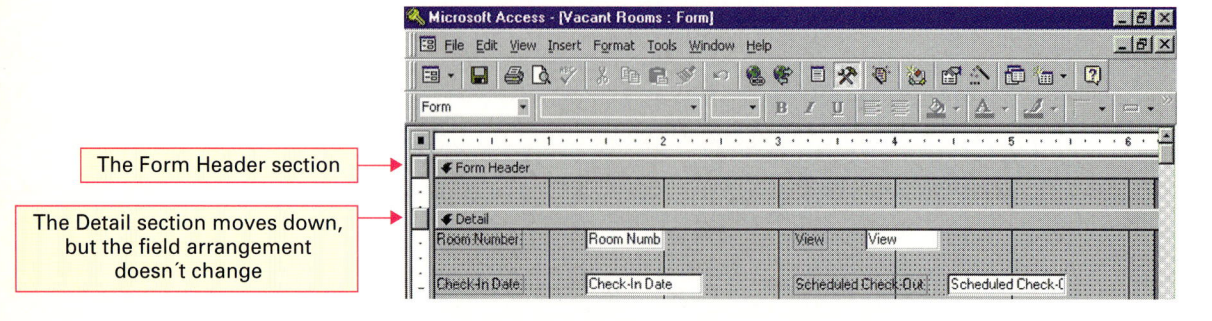

The Form Header section

The Detail section moves down, but the field arrangement doesn't change

4 Click the Label **Aa** tool on the Toolbox palette.
The pointer appears as a crosshair carrying an *A*.

Project 5: Creating and Modifying Forms   ACC-127

> **Note** If the Toolbox palette is nowhere to be seen, click the Toolbox button to display it.

5 Position the crosshair at the top of the Form Header area close to the 2-inch mark; then click and drag diagonally to the 3-inch mark to form a box.

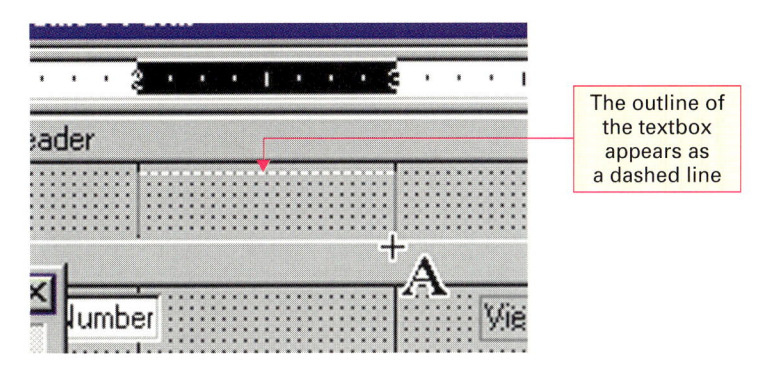

The outline of the textbox appears as a dashed line

6 Type **Vacant Rooms** in the label box.

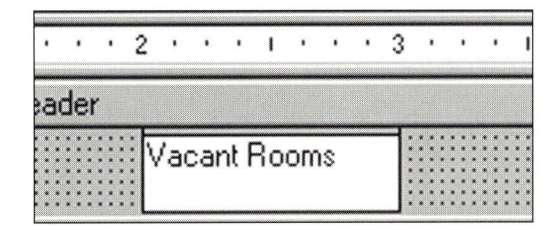

7 Click an area outside the label box, and then click to select the label control.

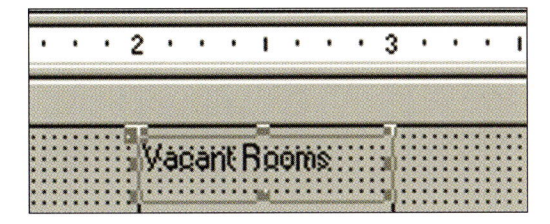

8 Click the Bold [B] button on the Formatting toolbar.
The text appears in bold print.

9 Click the arrow button beside the Font Size box on the Formatting toolbar, and select 24.

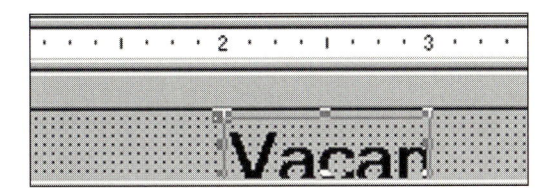

10 Size the box by dragging a corner handle until the complete title is visible, and then position the title in the approximate center of the form.

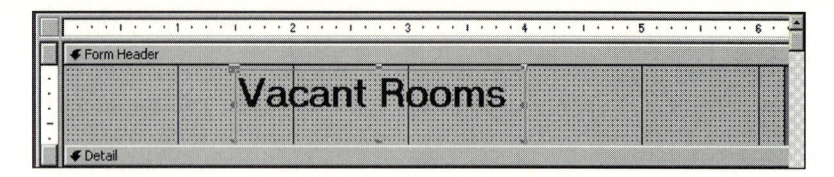

11 Click 💾 to save the changes to the form.

The Conclusion

After you finish designing and saving the form, you're ready to use it to display data, edit records, and add new records to the database. Simply click the View button to return to Form view, and use the techniques described in Project 1 to view individual records. To print a single record form, display the form in Form view and click the Selected Record(s) option in the Print dialog box.

Summary and Exercises

Summary

- You can create a form using fields from tables and queries.
- The easiest type of form to create is the AutoForm.
- To modify a form layout, you must use Form Design view.
- Fields are called *controls* in Form Design view. Controls consist of field labels and field data boxes.
- Form Design view displays rulers, grid points, and gridlines that you can use to position fields.
- Changing field labels and field data box size on a form doesn't change the structure of the field in the table or query.
- Field controls appear in the Detail section of a form.
- To add a title to a form, you can place it at the top of the Detail section or in the Form Header section of the form. To view the header, choose View, Form Header/Footer.

Key Terms and Operations

Key Terms	Operations
control	create an AutoForm
Detail section	edit field labels and field data boxes
field label	move and align field controls
field data box	save a form
grid points	select field controls
gridlines	
header/footer	

Study Questions

Multiple Choice

1. To arrange selected fields on-screen so that records appear individually, create a
    a. table.
    b. form.
    c. query.
    d. module.

2. The easiest way to create a form is to
    a. use Design view and add only the fields you want to include on the form.
    b. create an AutoForm and remove fields you don't want to include on the form.
    c. create a new database to hold the form.
    d. create a report.

3. You can create a form based on
    a. table fields.
    b. query fields.
    c. table or query fields.
    d. other forms.

4. Fields on a form are called
   a. controls.
   b. objects.
   c. fields.
   d. titles.

5. To remove a field from a form,
   a. double-click the field in the table field list.
   b. select the field control and type **REMOVE**.
   c. select the field and press Enter.
   d. select the field control and press Delete.

6. Field controls on forms are made up of
   a. field labels.
   b. field data.
   c. field labels and data.
   d. field names.

7. Field labels
   a. can be changed without affecting the field structure.
   b. pull data from the table or query.
   c. must be aligned with the field data.
   d. can't be changed on forms.

8. Field data boxes
   a. can be changed without affecting the field structure.
   b. pull data from the table or query.
   c. must be aligned with the field label.
   d. can't be moved on forms.

9. To move a field control on a form, the pointer should appear as
   a.
   b.
   c.
   d.

10. To edit a form layout,
    a. display the form and press Page Down or Page Up.
    b. open the form in Design view, select the field control(s) you want to move, and drag the field control(s) to a new position.
    c. delete the existing form and create a new form using new fields.
    d. edit the table or query used in the form.

Short Answer

1. What's the main purpose of a form?

2. What are the three main parts of a form displayed in Form Design view, and what does each part of the form contain?

3. What screen features appear in Form Design view that don't appear in Form view?

4. What are the two parts of a field control, and what does each part control?

5. When do you use a query instead of a table as the basis for a form?

6. How do you add a title to a form?

7. What features are available in Form Design view to help you adjust the placement of fields on the form?

8. How do you save a form?

9. How are form names arranged in the database window?

10. How do you adjust the size of field data length on a form, and what effect does changing the field data length on a form have on the field structure in the table or query?

For Discussion

1. What's the advantage to creating a form based on fields in a query instead of fields in a table?

2. How do the header/footer sections of a form compare to the header/footer sections of a document?

3. How do the procedures for saving and naming a form differ from the procedures used to save tables and queries?

4. How would you limit the records that appear as you browse through records in Form view?

Review Exercises

1. Creating a New Form, Rearranging Fields, and Saving a Form

Create a new form named *Rooms With A View* for the database *The Willows Updated*, based on the *Room, Bed, and View Types* query. Arrange the fields and information on the form so that they appear as shown in Figure 5.3.

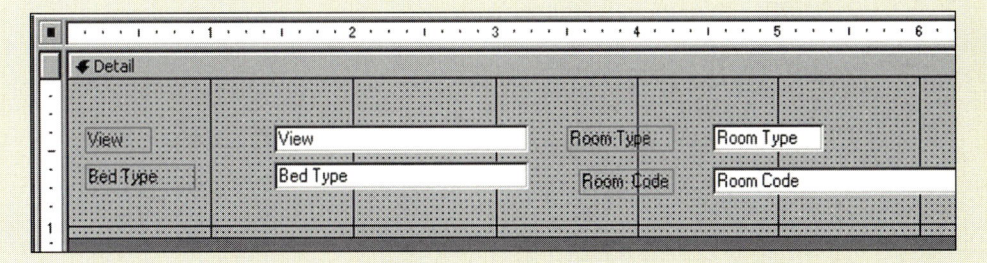

Figure 5.3

Follow these instructions to complete the form:

1. Open the *Room, Bed, and View Types* query and create a new AutoForm.

2. Display the new form in Form Design view.

3. Select and drag the field labels to the locations shown in Figure 5.3.

4. Choose Format, Align and use the ruler to position the fields.

5. Select fields not shown and delete them from the form.

6. Save the form by entering the form name **Rooms With A View.**

7. Print a copy of the form design.

8. Close the database and exit Access after you have completed your work.

2. Editing Field Labels, Adjusting Field Length, and Adding a Form Title

Figure 5.4 displays the edited *Rooms With A View* form. Follow these instructions to edit the form:

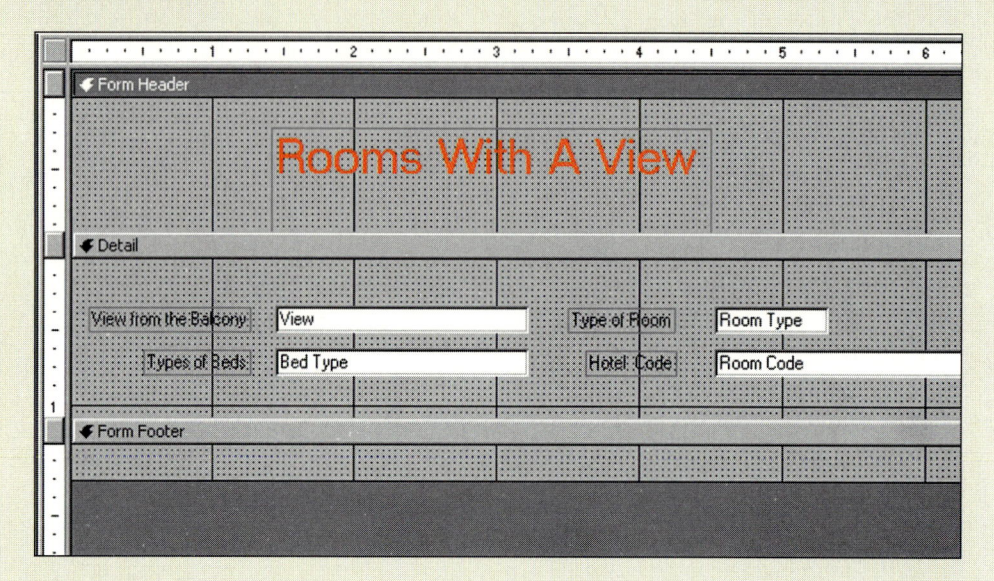

Figure 5.4

1. Display the header/footer sections in Form Design view, and use the Toolbox Label tool to add the title shown in Figure 5.4.
2. Change the field labels to those shown in Figure 5.4.
3. Select and size the field data box, adjusting the length to display the field data more appropriately.
4. Save the changes to the form, and print a copy of the form design.
5. Close the database and exit Access after you've completed your work.

Assignments

1. Creating a Form: Rearranging Fields, Removing Fields, Changing Field Labels, Adjusting Field Length, Adding a Title, and Saving

Open the *Assistant Managers* table in the database *The Willows Personnel*, and create an AutoForm layout to make it easier to enter the names and data for new employees. Group similar fields together on-screen, and format the layout so that all fields are visible on-screen. Adjust the field length of all fields so that data contained in the fields fits the data box more appropriately, and edit the field labels to identify field contents more appropriately. Add a title to the header section of the form, and save the design as a new form by entering the form name *The Willows Assistant Managers*. Print a copy of the form design.

Then open the *Managers* report you created in Project 3, and apply the techniques learned in this project to change the report layout so that it displays the information more attractively. Save changes to the report design, and print a copy of the report. Close the database and exit Access.

2. Locating Forms on the Internet

If you have access to the Web, search the Internet to locate form designs that you might use for each of the following:

- Registering guests at resorts
- Ordering hand-crafted items from specialty shops
- College applications or job applications

Download two examples of each type of form and print a copy of each example.

PROJECT 6

Customizing AutoReports

Forms you create are designed primarily for on-screen viewing. Reports are database objects designed to print summarized data from database tables on paper. You can design reports using fields in one database table or fields from multiple tables using a query. In this project, you learn to open, modify, and print AutoReports.

Objectives

After completing this project, you will be able to:

➤ **Open a report and identify Report Design screen features**
➤ **Select and remove fields from a report**
➤ **Save and view reports**
➤ **Modify a report design**
➤ **Print reports**

The Challenge

Mr. Gilmore wants a report similar to the one pictured in Figure 6.1 for a meeting of The Willows Board of Directors. Because the information he needs to include in the report is currently stored in The Willows Updated database tables, he asks you to design a report in The Willows Updated database to provide the information in the right format.

The Solution

As data-entry specialist at The Willows, you have been asked to design the report Mr. Gilmore wants. Follow the steps in the tasks in this project to make the report look like the one in Figure 6.1.

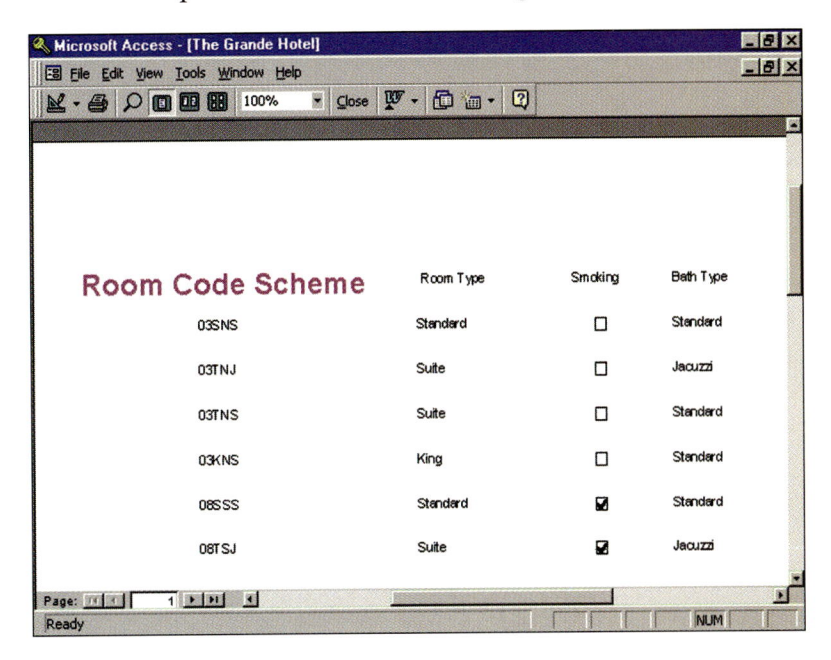

Figure 6.1

The Setup

So that your computer screen will match the illustrations in this project, make sure that the Access 97 settings listed in Table 6.1 are selected on the computer:

Table 6.1 Access Settings

View Menu	Select Toolbars if they are not displayed and then click the toolbar listed at the top of the cascading menu.
Screen Settings	Click the restore icon on each maximized object window.
Tools Menu	If you don't see the Status Bar, select Options and then click the View tab. Click the check box beside "Status Bar" at the top of the page.

Opening a Report and Identifying Report Design Screen Features

In Project 3, you created an AutoReport for The Willows Updated database and saved the report as an object in the database. A list of reports stored as part of the database appears on the Reports page of the Database window. Opening the report places the report in a preview window so that you can view the data. To create reports that display information the way you want them to, you must use Report Design view. Many of the features displayed in the Report Design window shown in Figure 6.2 are the same as those used in Form Design view.

TASK 1: TO OPEN A REPORT:

1. Open *The Willows Updated* database and click the Reports tab of the Database window.

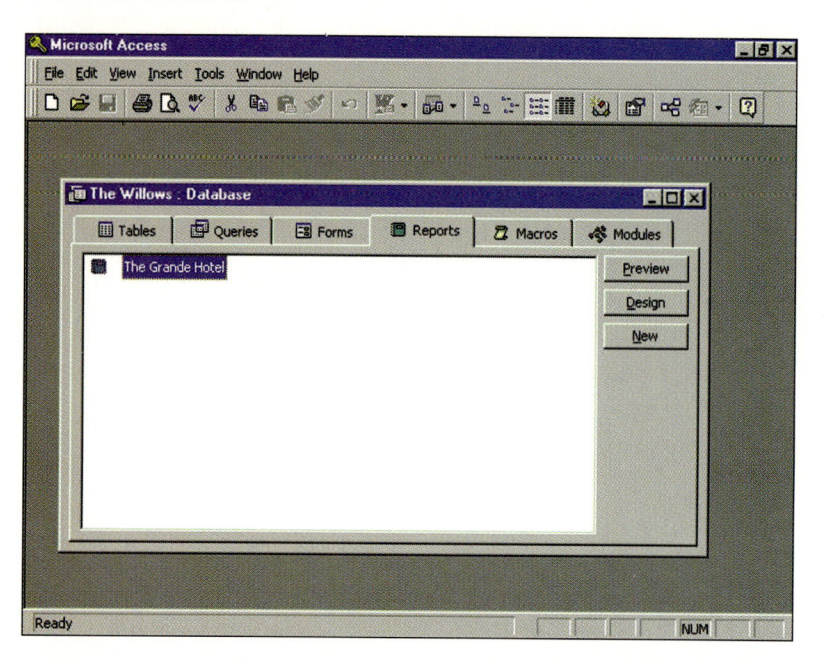

2. Select The Grande Hotel report name and then click Preview.

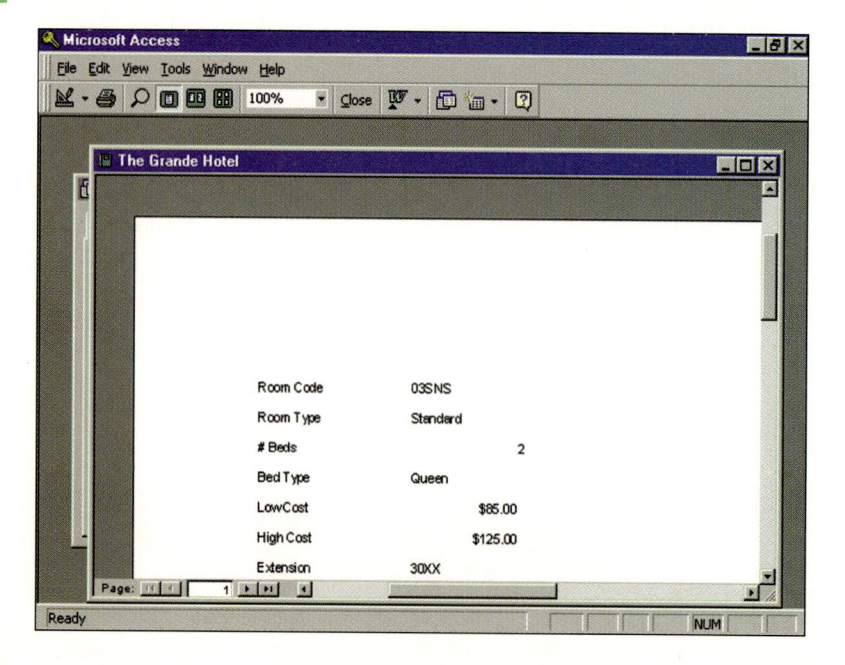

3 Click the toolbar View button.

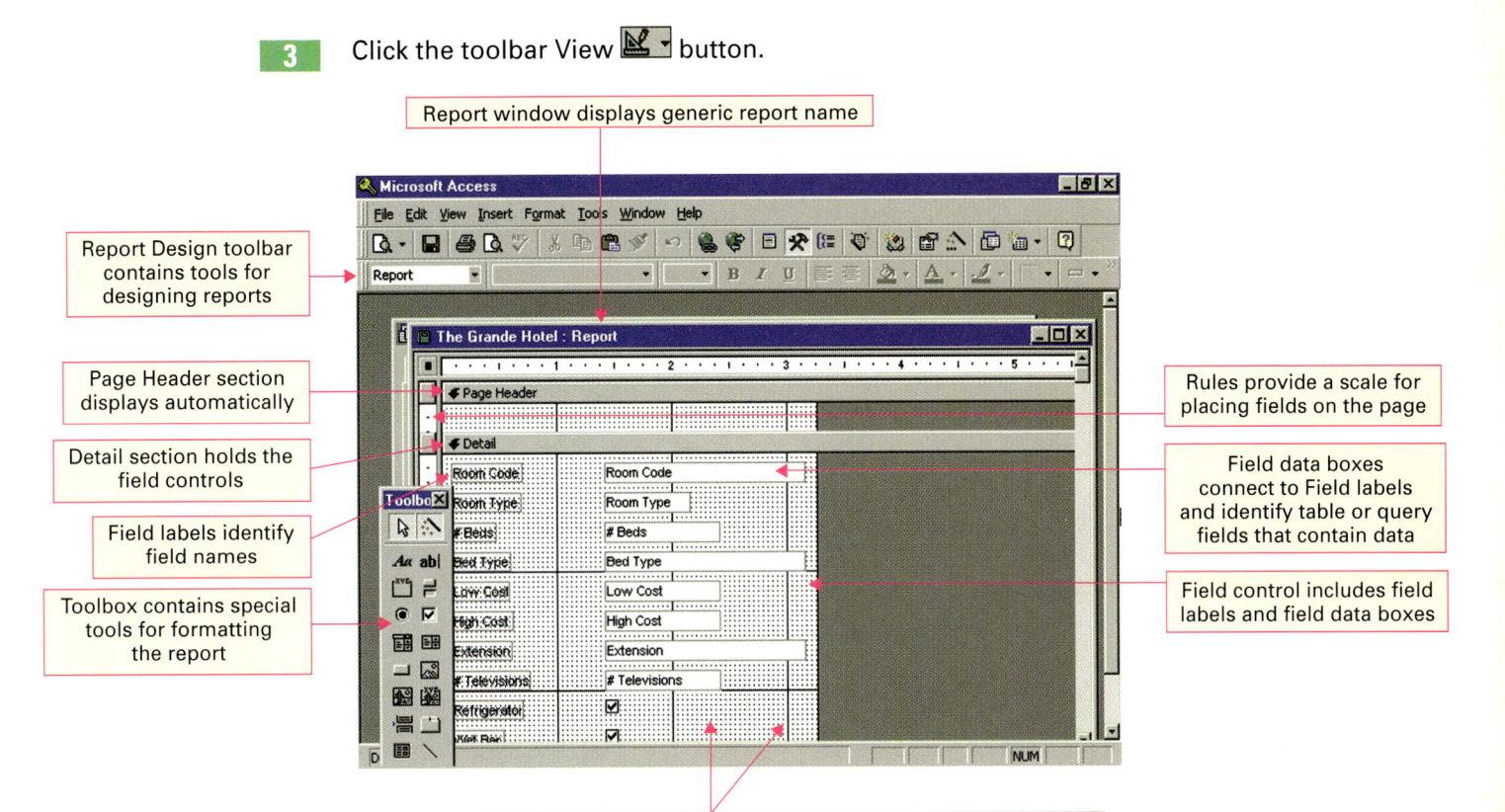

Figure 6.2

- Report window displays generic report name
- Report Design toolbar contains tools for designing reports
- Page Header section displays automatically
- Detail section holds the field controls
- Field labels identify field names
- Toolbox contains special tools for formatting the report
- Rules provide a scale for placing fields on the page
- Field data boxes connect to Field labels and identify table or query fields that contain data
- Field control includes field labels and field data boxes
- Grid points and gridlines help you align field names and data

Note The Page Footer section appears off-screen at the bottom of the report window. Use the scroll bars to view the page footer.

Selecting and Removing Fields from a Report

When you create an AutoReport based on fields contained in a table or query, Access automatically places all fields displayed in the Datasheet view on the report page. You can use the same techniques to remove unnecessary fields from the report page that you used to remove fields from a form. Because reports often display field data without field labels, you need to select the field data box to remove both parts of the field control. Selecting the field label removes the field label and leaves the field data box.

ACC-138

TASK 2: TO SELECT AND DELETE FIELDS FROM A REPORT:

1 Click the # Beds field data box.

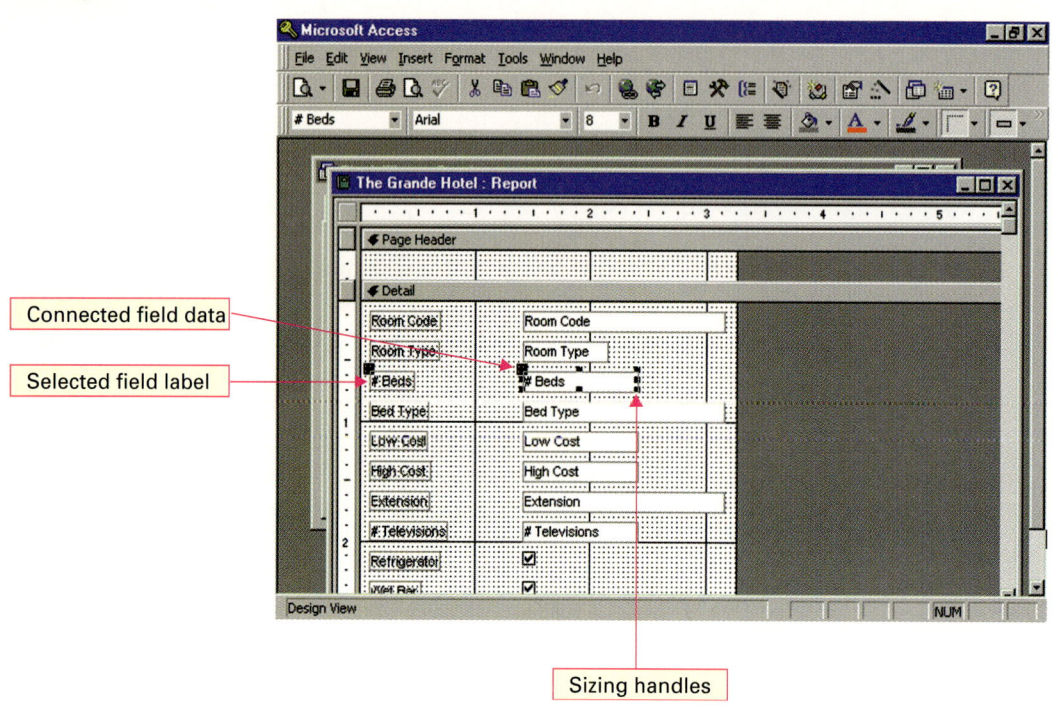

Connected field data

Selected field label

Sizing handles

2 Press (SHIFT) and click to select the field data boxes for all fields *except* Room Code, Room Type, Smoking, and Bath Type fields.
Mr. Gilmore does not want to show the selected fields on the report.

3 Press (DELETE).

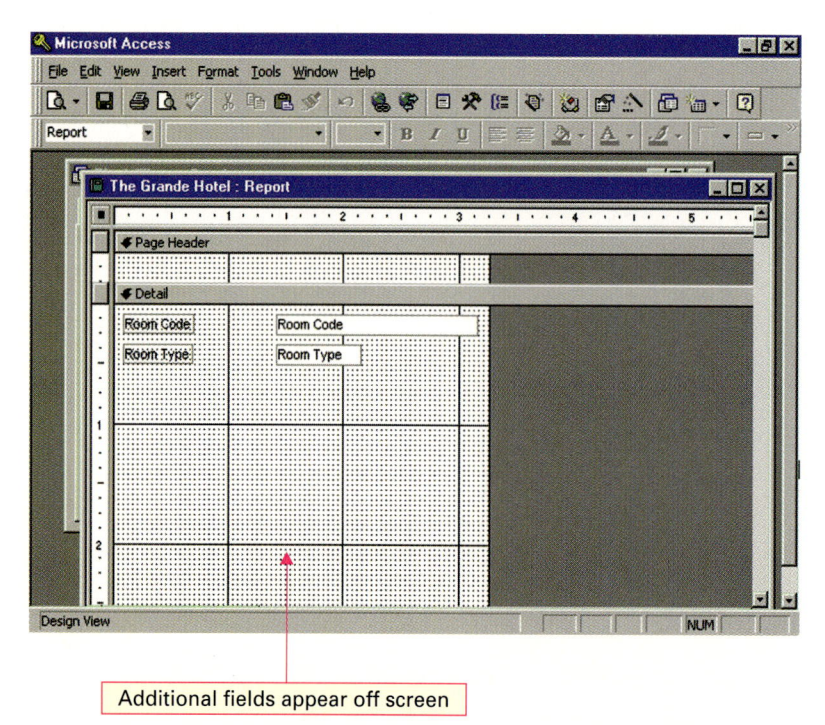

Additional fields appear off screen

Project 6: Creating AutoReports ACC-139

> **Tip** If you accidentally delete a field in error, reverse the action using the Undo feature. In Design view, Access permits you to reverse only the last action.

Saving and Viewing Reports

You need to save reports that you design or modify so that you can use them again. Because reports are objects in a database, you save them using the same techniques you use to save tables, forms, and queries.

Access provides three views for displaying reports: Design view for arranging field controls on the page, Print Preview to display the design with all the data in place as it will print, and *Layout Preview* which displays data from only a few records so that you can check the layout and then make adjustments before printing.

TASK 3: TO SAVE AND VIEW A REPORT:

1. Click 🖫 to save changes to the report design.
2. Click the drop-down list arrow beside the View button on the Report Design toolbar.

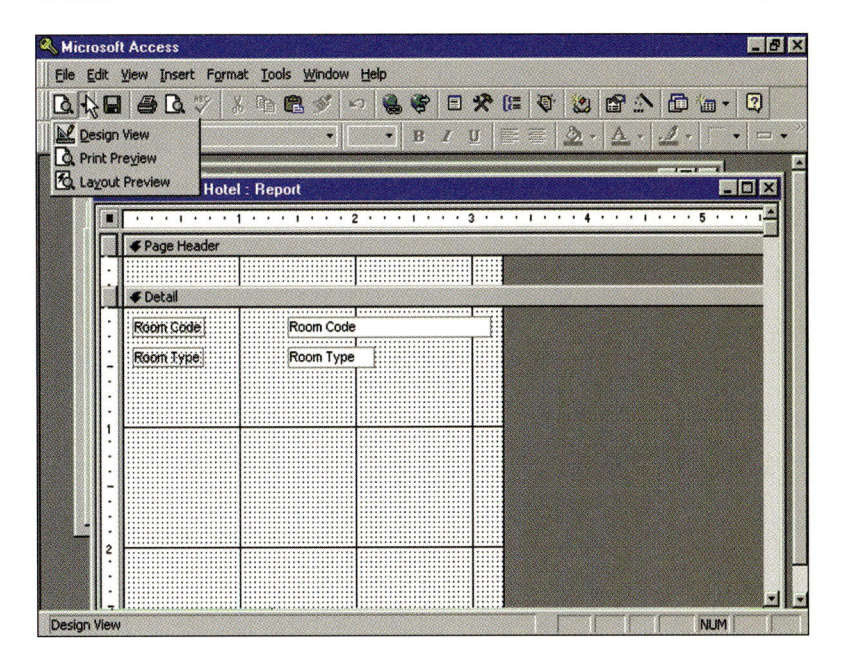

ACC-140

3 Click Layout Preview.

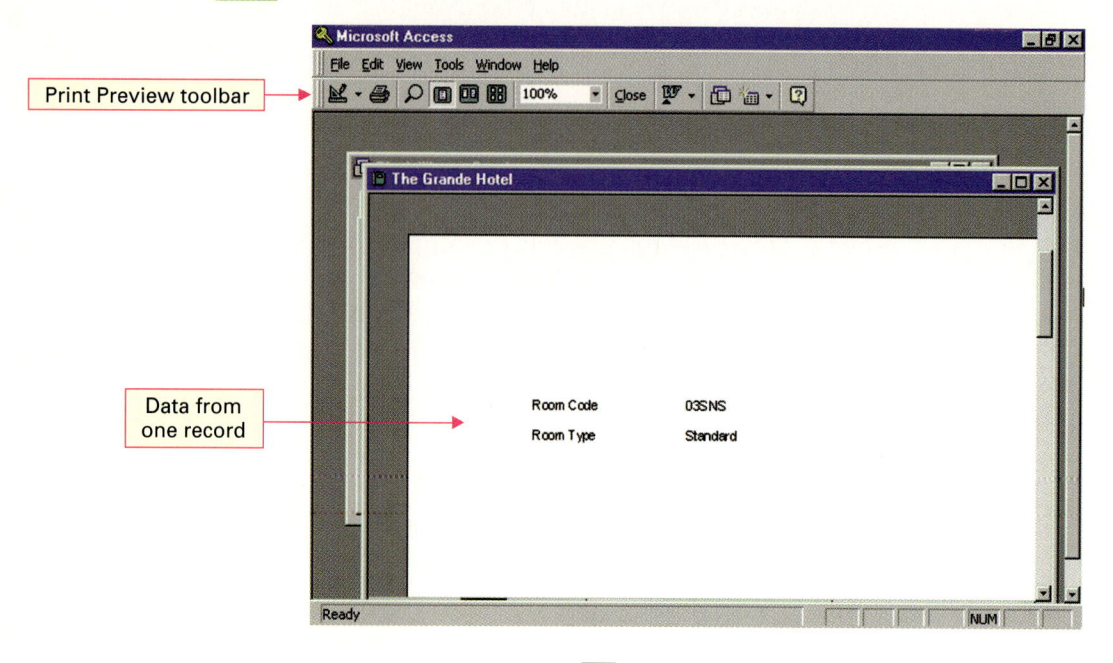

Print Preview toolbar

Data from one record → Room Code   03SNS
Room Type   Standard

4 Click the toolbar Close ⊠ button.
The report appears in Design view again.

Modify a Report Design

After removing unwanted fields from the report design, you need to reposition the remaining fields, move field labels to the *Page Header* section, and reduce the size of the report's Detail section. Maximize the report window so that you have more working area and can see the full width of the report page.

Project 6: Creating AutoReports   ACC-141

TASK 4: TO MODIFY A REPORT DESIGN:

1 Select the label for the Room Code field, and press DELETE.

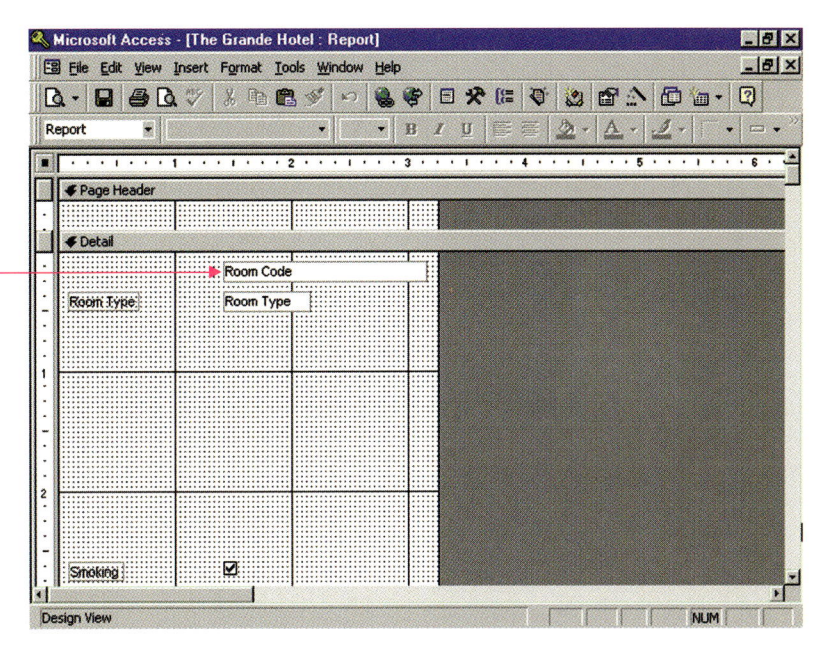

Field data box remains after the label is deleted

2 Select the field data box for the Room Code field, and drag the field data box until the right edge is aligned with the 2-inch mark on the horizontal ruler and the top of the box is aligned at the top of the Detail section.

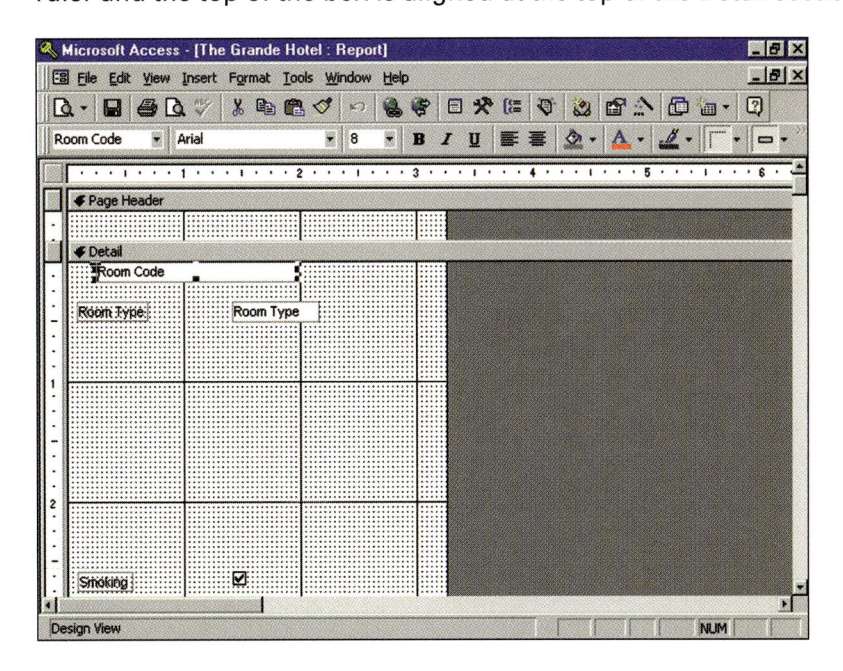

Tip To drag a field data box without deleting the field label, point to the large square in the upper left corner of the field data box until the mouse pointer changes to a pointing hand. Then click and drag the field data box, leaving the field label in its original position.

ACC-142

3 Drag the field data boxes for additional fields until they are positioned as shown here:

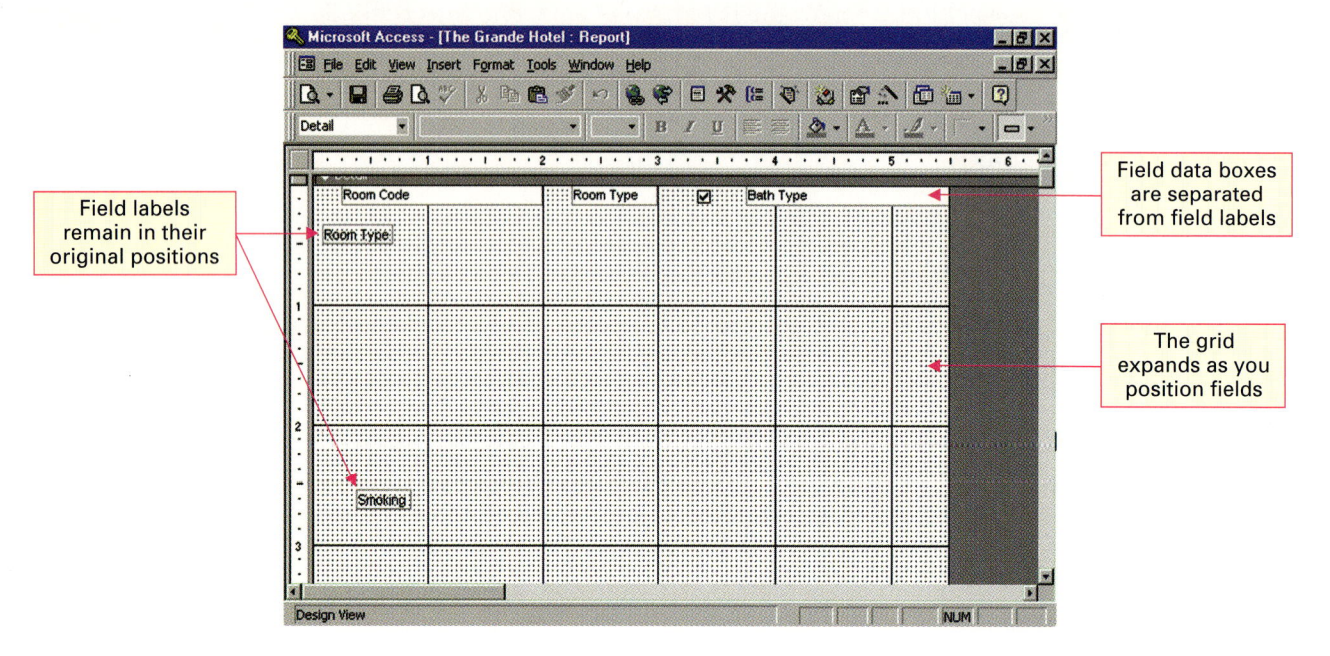

- Field labels remain in their original positions
- Field data boxes are separated from field labels
- The grid expands as you position fields

4 Click the field label for the Room Type control, and click the Cut button. The field label no longer appears on the report Detail section but is available on the Clipboard.

5 Click the Page Header section bar to make the section active.

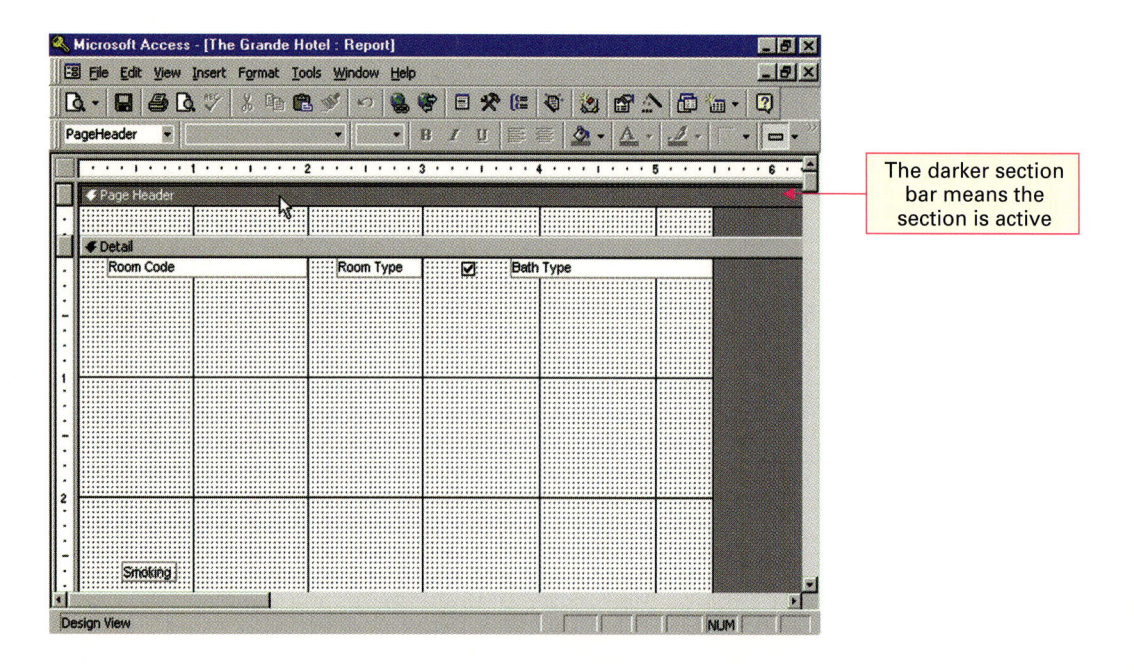

- The darker section bar means the section is active

Project 6: Creating AutoReports   ACC-143

6   Click the Paste button.

The field label appears in the upper left corner of the Page Header section

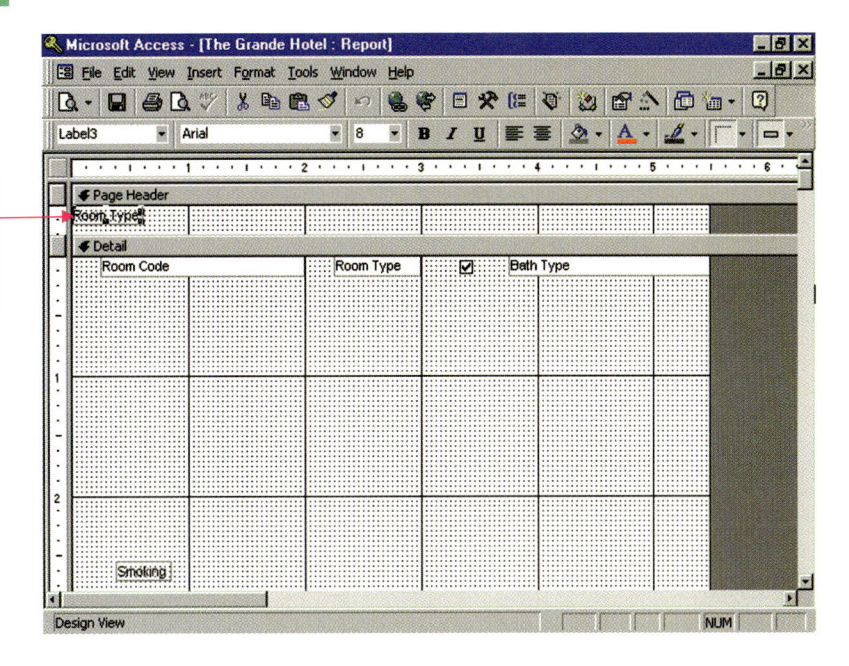

7   Drag the label and position it in the Page Header section centered above the Room Type data box.

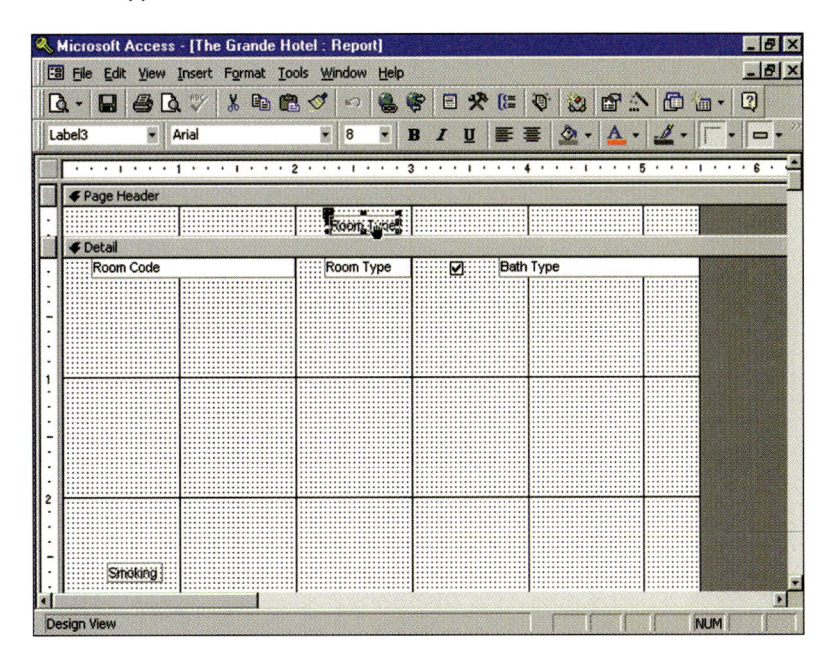

ACC-144

8 Select the field label for the Smoking field, click [icon], click the Page Header section bar, click [icon], and then drag the field label to center it above the Smoking data check box.

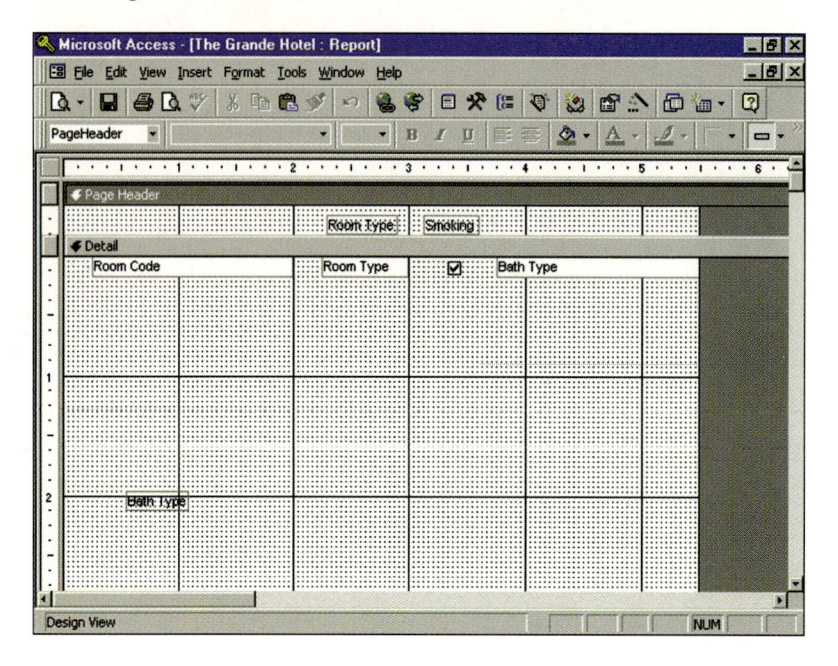

> **Tip** Use the techniques you learned for aligning field controls on Forms to align field controls on reports.

9 Cut and Paste the Bath Type field label in the Page Header above the Bath Type field data box.

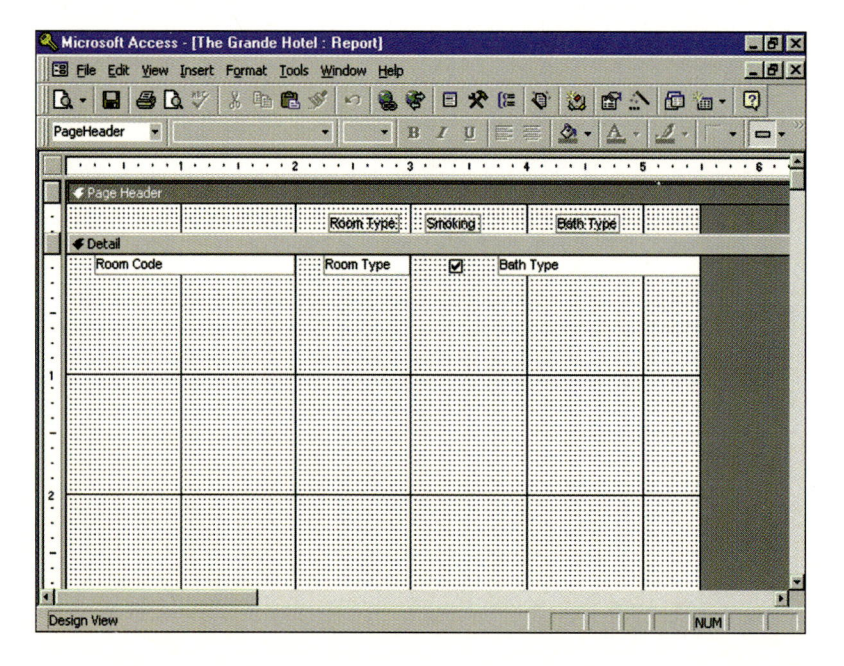

Project 6: Creating AutoReports   ACC-145

10 Preview the printout of the report by clicking the Print Preview button, and then click the Zoom button on the Print Preview toolbar.

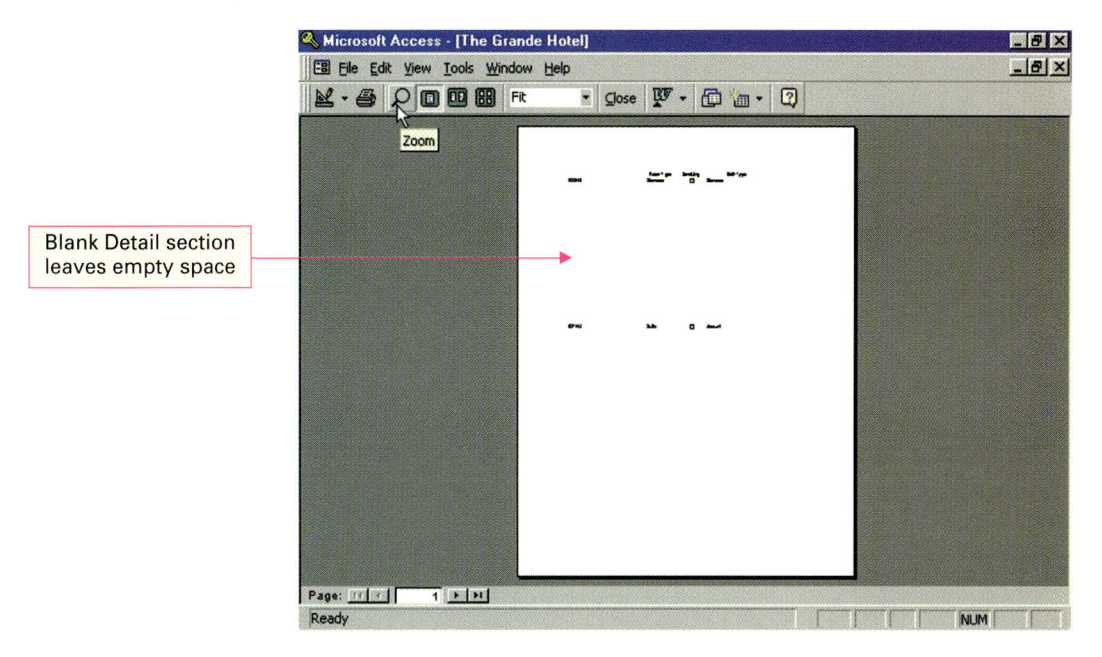

Blank Detail section leaves empty space

11 Click the toolbar Close button to return to Design view, and then scroll to display the bottom of the report design.
The Page Footer area of the report displays at the bottom of the report.

12 Position the pointer on the top edge of the Page Footer section bar until the mouse pointer turns into a ✥.

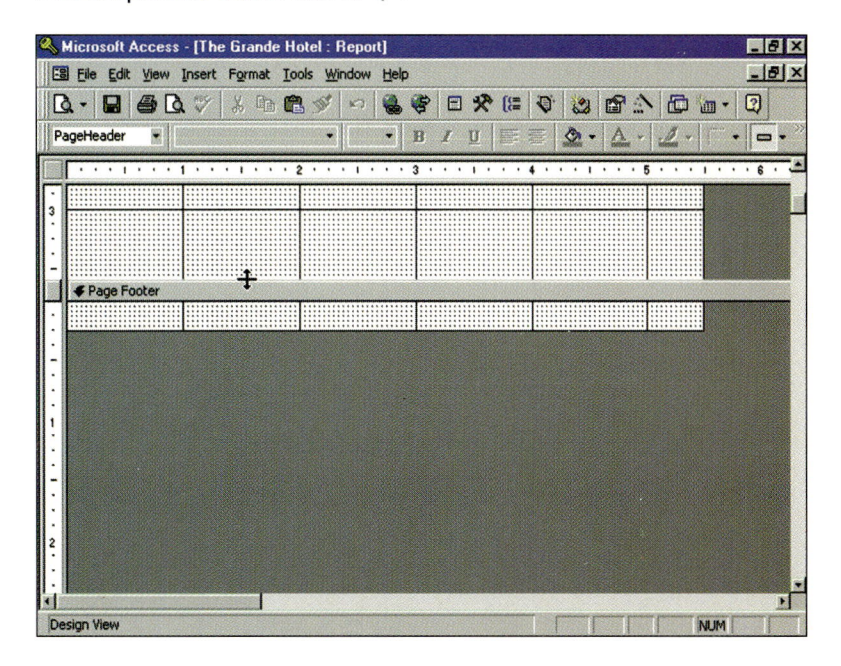

ACC-146

13 Click and drag the Page Footer section bar toward the top of the report to reduce the size of the Detail section.

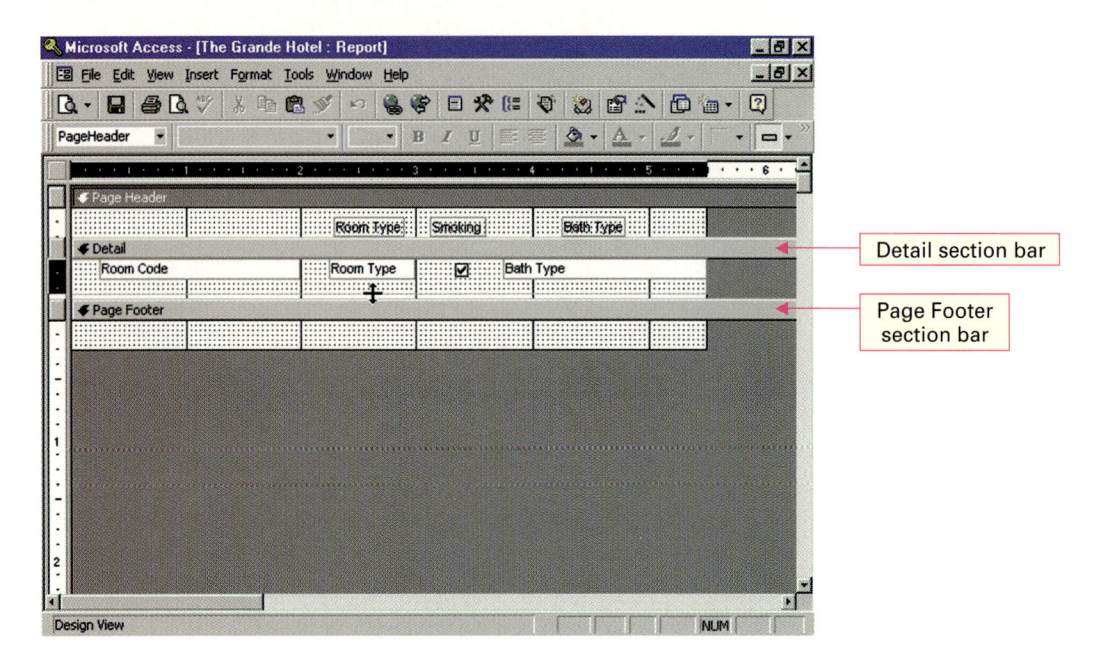

14 Preview the report again.

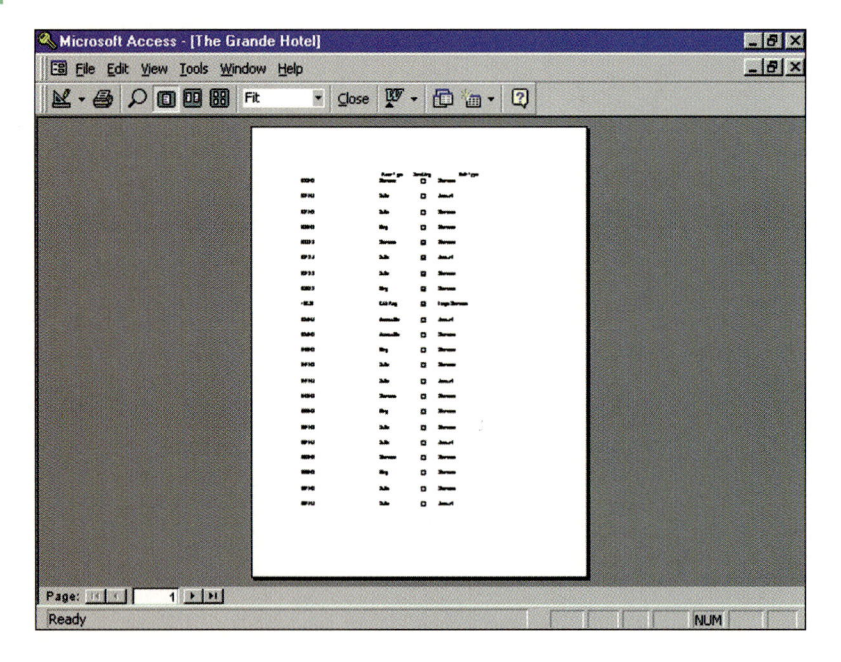

Project 6: Creating AutoReports ACC-147

15 Return to Design view, and adjust the size and position of the field control data boxes so that the data appears centered below the field control labels and at the horizontal positions shown here:

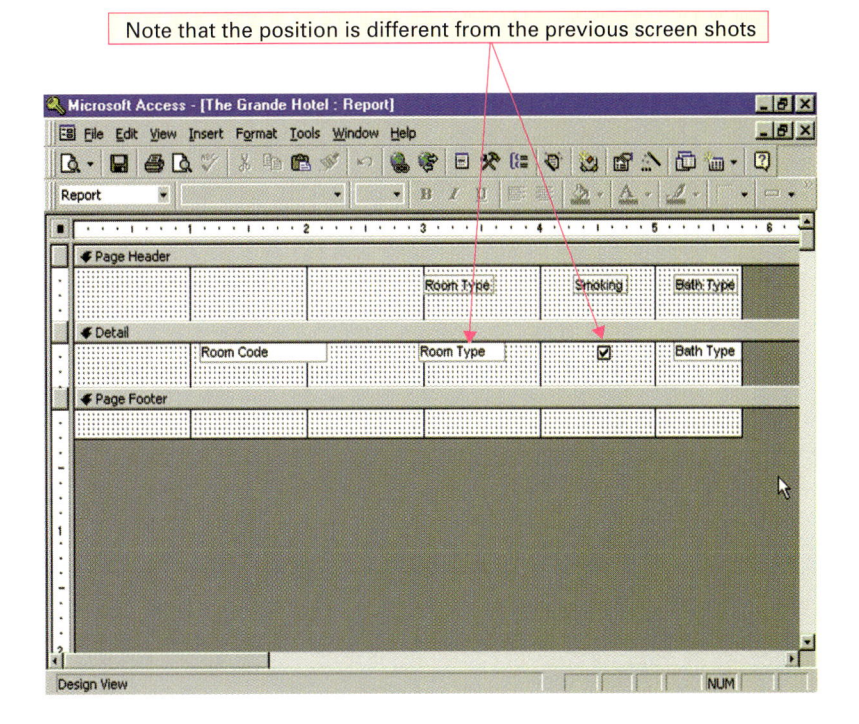

Note that the position is different from the previous screen shots

16 Add the report title displayed here using the Label tool from the Report Toolbox and the same techniques you used to add a title to a form in Project 5.

> **Note** If the Toolbox is not displayed on the screen, click the Toolbox button on the Standard toolbar.

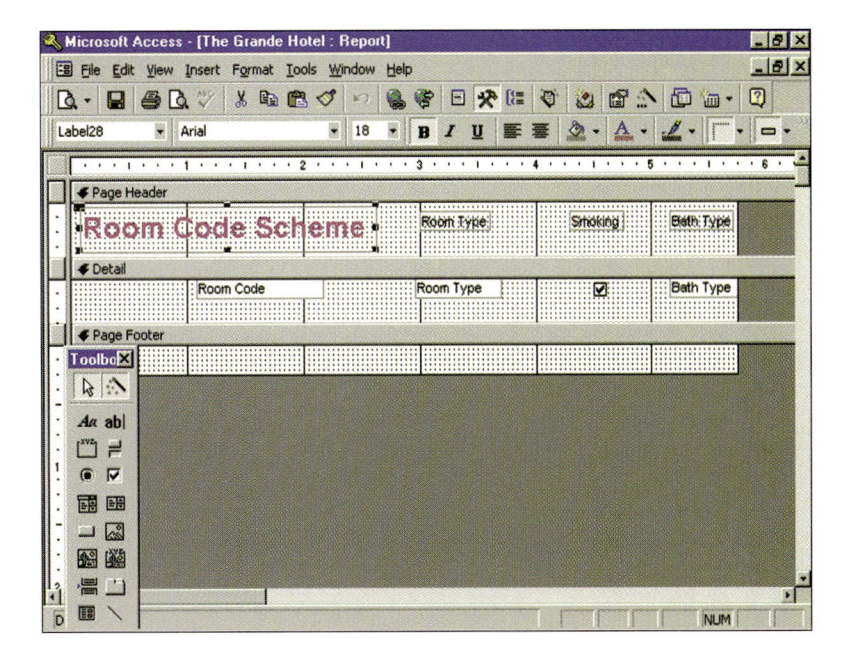

17 Click to save the changes to the report.

Printing Reports

The report design serves as a shell that Access uses to display data contained in the fields of a table or query datasheet. After you have the report designed to display the data in the format you want, you can print the report on paper.

> **Tip** To print a report that was based on a query containing data for records which meet certain criteria, run the query to select those records, and save changes to the query before printing the report.

TASK 5: TO PRINT A REPORT:

1. Click to ensure the report appears as you want it.

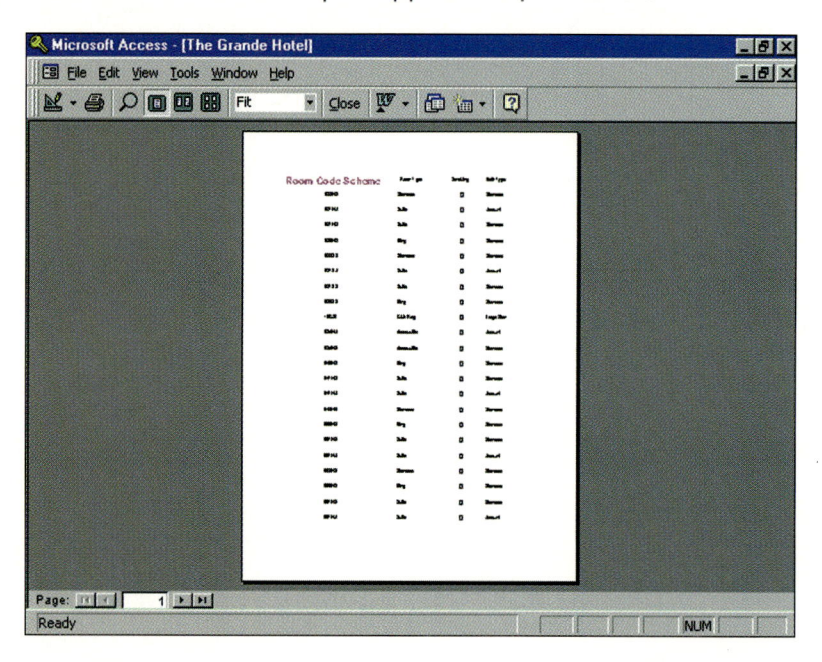

2 Click the Two Pages button.

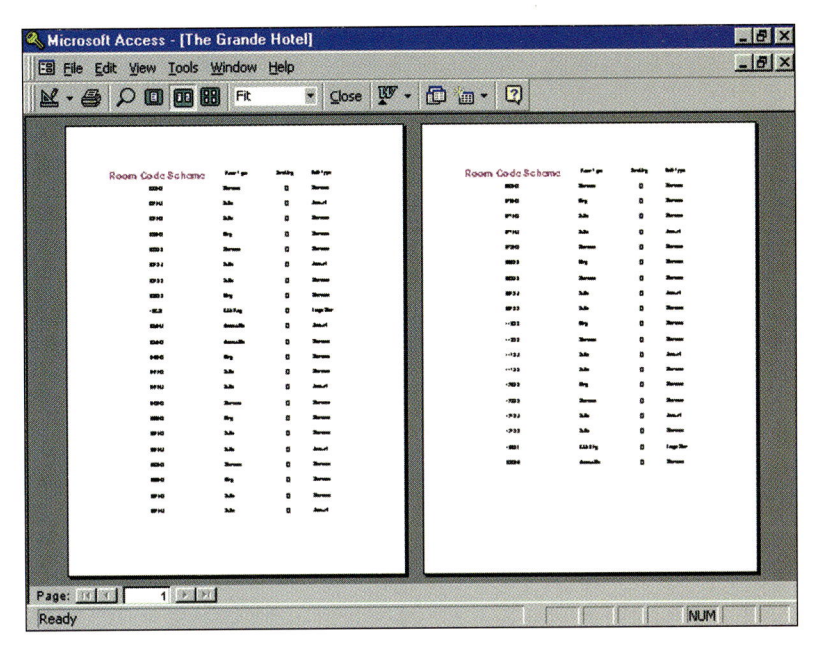

3 Click the Print button to print the report.

The Conclusion

Before closing the report, make final adjustments to the report design to line up the column heading properly, and then print a copy of the report. Save changes to the report design, and then close the report and exit Access if you have finished working.

Summary and Exercises

Summary

- Reports are database objects designed to print summarized data from database tables on paper. You can design reports by using fields in a table or fields in queries.
- You can use a variety of different techniques to create a new report; the easiest type of report to create is the AutoReport.
- To modify a report layout, you must use Report Design view.
- Field controls on reports consist of field labels and field data boxes; you can delete a field label without removing the field data box; deleting the field data box removes the field label attached to it.
- Report Design view displays rulers, grid points, and gridlines you can use to position fields.
- Changing field labels and field data box sizes on a report does not change the structure of the field in the table or query.
- Field controls appear in the Detail section of an AutoReport.
- The Page Header and Page Footer sections appear automatically in Report Design view.
- To change the size of the Detail section of a report, drag the section bar of the Page Footer section up or down.
- To change the size of the Page Header section, drag the Detail section bar up or down.

Key Terms and Operations

Key Terms
Layout Preview
Page Header/Footer

Operations
Create and save an AutoReport
Select, move, cut, paste, and size field controls in Report Design view
Print reports

Study Questions

Multiple Choice

1. To arrange selected fields on-screen so that information from multiple records appears on the same page, create a
   a. table.
   b. form.
   c. query.
   d. report.

2. The easiest way to create a report is to
   a. use Design view and add only the fields you want to include on the report.
   b. create an AutoReport and remove fields you don't want to include on the report.
   c. create a new form and then base the report on form data.
   d. create a new table and base the report on the new table.

3. Creating a report uses many of the same techniques used to create a
   a. form.
   b. query.
   c. table.
   d. database.

4. To arrange fields on a report layout, you must
   a. use controls.
   b. use Form Design view.
   c. display Report Design view.
   d. use Headers and Footers.

5. When you want to place a field label as a column heading,
   a. cut the label from the Detail section, click the Header section bar, and then paste and drag the field label into position.
   b. select the field label and type the column heading.
   c. select the field label and press (DELETE).
   d. drag the field label to the top of the Detail section.

6. To eliminate blank space between records on a report,
   a. drag the column headings closer together.
   b. add multiple field data boxes to the Detail section.
   c. drag the Footer section bar toward the top of the report to reduce the size of the Detail section.
   d. drag the Detail section bar toward the bottom of the report to reduce the size of the Detail section.

7. Reports are designed to
   a. display database data on paper.
   b. pull data from the table or query and print one record per page.
   c. present data on-screen.
   d. summarize data and print totals only.

8. Data entered in the Header section of a report
   a. appears before data from each record.
   b. pulls data from the table or query.
   c. must be aligned across the Header section.
   d. prints at the top of each report page.

9. Reports can be viewed using
   a. two views.
   b. three views.
   c. one view.
   d. four views.

10. Layout view
    a. displays the report with grid points and gridlines.
    b. displays only a sample of data from a few records.
    c. displays all data as it will print on paper.
    d. is unavailable for reports.

Short Answer
1. What is the main purpose of a report?
2. What are the three main parts of a report displayed in Design view, and what does each part of the report contain?
3. What screen features appear in Report Design view that do not appear in other views?
4. How do the two parts of a field control in Report Design differ from the two parts of a field control in Form Design?
5. When do you use a query instead of a table as the basis for a report?
6. How do you move field labels from the Detail section to the Header section of Report Design view?
7. How do the techniques for aligning fields in Report Design view differ from the techniques used to align fields in Form Design view?
8. How do you save a report?
9. What are the views used to display reports, and how do they differ?
10. What view is available for reports that is not available for any other database object?

For Discussion
1. What is the advantage to creating a report based on fields in a query instead of fields in a table?
2. What is the advantage of displaying reports in Layout view rather than Print Preview?
3. What should you consider when determining a report naming scheme?
4. How do you reduce the blank space on each page of a report?

Review Exercises

1. Creating a new AutoReport, rearranging fields, and saving a report
Figure 6.3 shows a confirmation certificate for The Willows Grande Hotel. Create an AutoReport named *Confirmation Certificate* based on The Grande Hotel Rooms table in The Willows Updated database so that reservationists can send it as the confirmation report.

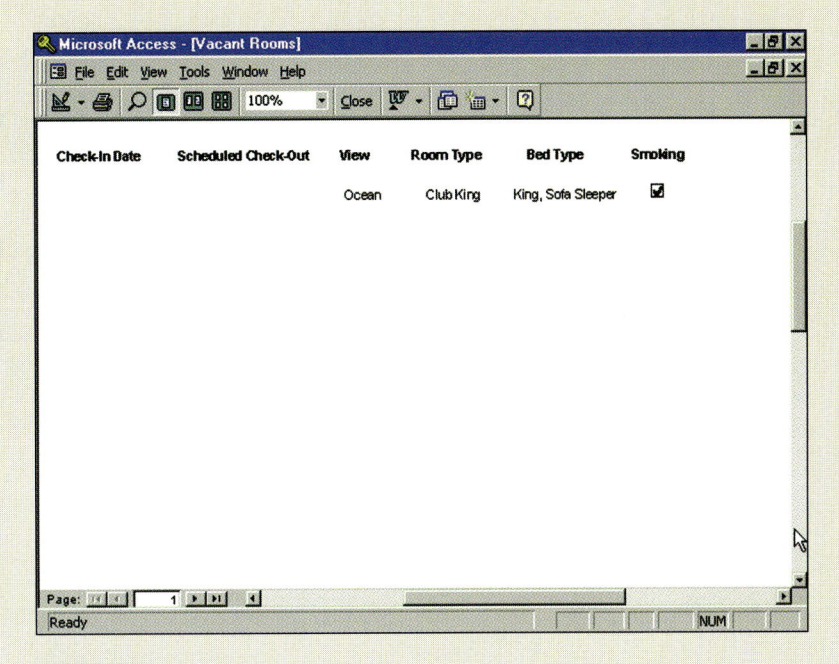

Figure 6.3

Follow these instructions to complete the report:

1. Open The Willows Updated database, display the Vacant Rooms query, and create an AutoReport.
2. Remove all fields except those shown in Figure 6.3.
3. Rearrange remaining fields so that they appear as shown in Figure 6.3.
4. Save the report using the report name *Confirmation Certificate*.
5. Print a copy of the report design.
6. Close the report and the database, and exit Access after you have completed your work.

2. Editing field labels, adjusting field length, and adding a report title

Figure 6.4 displays the edited Confirmation Certificate report. Follow these instructions to edit the report:

ACC-154

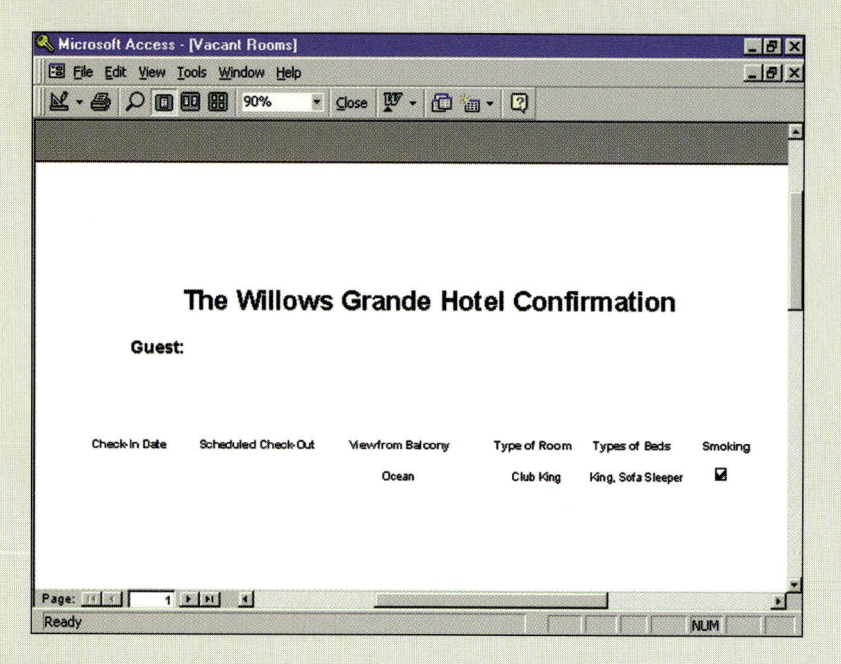

```
┌─────────────────────────────────────────────────────────┐
│ Microsoft Access - [Vacant Rooms]              _ □ ×    │
│ File Edit View Tools Window Help               _ □ ×    │
│ [toolbar icons]   90%   Close                           │
│                                                         │
│                                                         │
│                                                         │
│           The Willows Grande Hotel Confirmation         │
│                                                         │
│     Guest:                                              │
│                                                         │
│                                                         │
│   Check-In Date  Scheduled Check-Out  View from Balcony  Type of Room  Types of Beds  Smoking │
│                                       Ocean              Club King     King, Sofa Sleeper  ☑ │
│                                                         │
│                                                         │
│ Page: |◄ ◄ 1 ► ►|                                       │
│ Ready                                           NUM     │
└─────────────────────────────────────────────────────────┘
```

Figure 6.4

1. Add the title shown in Figure 6.4 to the Page Header section of the report.

2. Adjust the space for the Page Header section to allow room for the recipient's address on blank lines after "Guest:"

3. Set the Footer Section bar so that only two records appear on each page of the report.

4. Change field labels to those shown in Figure 6.4.

5. Adjust the field length of all fields to display data appropriately.

6. Save the changes to the Confirmation Certificate report.

7. Print a copy of pages 1 and 2 of the report.

8. Close the report and the database, and exit Access after you have completed your work.

Assignments

1. Creating a new query to use for creating, designing, modifying, and saving a report

Guests at The Grande Hotel call the front desk to report problems with their rooms. Mr. Gilmore has asked that receptionists report electrical, mechanical, and temperature problems to the Engineering department immediately and record the problems in the Comments field of The Grande Hotel Rooms table of The Willows Updated database. From the table, he wants you to generate a report similar to the one shown in Figure 6.5.

Project 6: Creating AutoReports ACC-155

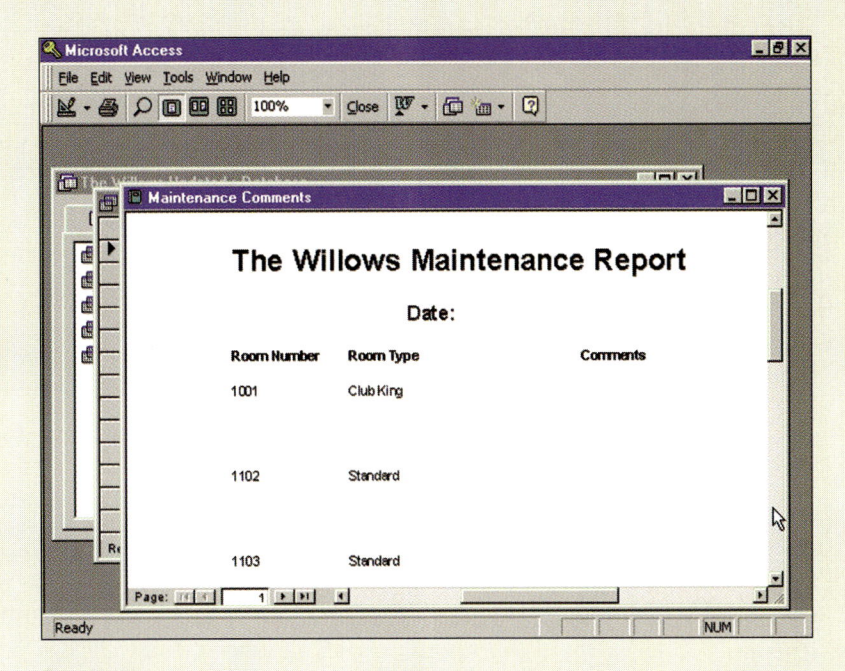

Figure 6.5

Add a Comments field as a text field containing 100 characters to The Grande Hotel Rooms table. Then create a new query for The Willows Updated database that contains the fields shown on the report and selects only those rooms with comments in the Comments field. Use the Help feature in Access to learn how to identify those records with a value in a query field. Save the query using the query name *Maintenance Comments*.

Design and save a report titled *Maintenance Report* using fields contained in the *Maintenance Comments* query. Print a copy of the first page of the report.

Close the report and the database, and exit Access after you have completed your work.

2. Locating report layouts on the Internet
Search the Internet to locate sample report designs for each of the following:

- Company profit/loss statement
- Company annual reports
- Top money winners on the PGA tour

Download examples of each report, and print a copy of each example.

Notes

Notes

Notes

Notes

Notes

Access 97 Function Guide

Function	Mouse Action or Button	Menu	Keyboard Shortcut
Database, close	Click ❌	Choose File, Close	
Database, create new		Choose File, New Database	Press CTRL+**N**
display page of Database window	Click page tab	Choose View, Database Objects, *Object*	Press CTRL+TAB until the database window page appears
Database, open existing	Click 📂	Choose File, Open	Press CTRL+**O**
Exit	Click ❌	Choose File, Exit	
Field, delete	Display table in Design view, click field row, and click 🗑	Display table in Design view, click field row, and choose Edit, Delete Rows	Display table in Design view, click field row, and press DELETE
Field, sort	Activate field and click ↓ or ↑	Activate field and choose Records, Sort, Sort order	
Form, create new	Display table or query and click 📋	Select table or query name in database window and choose Insert, Form	
Form, design	Select form name in database window and click Design button OR Open form and click 📋	Open form an dchoose View, Design View	
Form, open	Select form name in database window and click Open button		Select form name in Forms page of database window and press ENTER
Key Field, assign		Display table in Design view, click field, and choose Edit, Primary Key	
Object, create new	Click New button on object page of database window		Press ALT+**N** on object page of database window
Preview	Click 🔍	Choose File, Print Preview	
Print	Click 🖨	Choose File, Print	Press CTRL+**P**
Query, add fields	Double-click field name		
Query, add table	Click 📋	Choose Query, Show Table	
Query, design	Select query name in database window and click Design button OR Open query and click 📋	Open query and choose View, Design View	
Query, open	Select query name in database window and click Open button		Select query name in Forms page of database window and press ENTER
Query, run	Click ❗	Choose Query, Run	
Query, save	Click 💾	Choose File, Save	Press CTRL+**S**
Query, delete		Select the record and choose Edit, Delete Record	Select record and press DEL

Access 97 Function Guide

Function	Mouse Action or Button	Menu	Keyboard Shortcut
Record, insert	Display table to contain record and click	Open table to contain record and choose Insert, New Record	
Report, create	Display table or query and select AutoReport from drop-down list arrow	Select table or query name in database window and choose Insert, Report	
Report, design	Select report name in database window and click Design button OR Open report and click	Open report and choose View, Design View	
Report, open	Select report name in database window and click Open button		Select report name in Forms page of database window and press (ENTER)
Save	Click	Choose File, Save	Press (CTRL)+S
Send		Choose File, Send	Press (ALT)+F, E
Spelling check	Click	Choose Tools, Spelling and Grammar	Press (F7)
Table align		Click in the table and choose Table, Cell Height and Width	
Table, copy structure	Click table name in database window, click , click and type new table name	Click table name in database window, choose Edit, Paste and type new table name	Click table name in database window, press (CTRL)+C, press (CTRL)+V and type new table name
Table, create		choose Table, Insert Table	
Table, design	Select table name in database window and click Design button OR Open table and click	Open table and choose View, Design View	
Table, open	Select table name in database window and click Open button		Select table name in Forms page of database window and press (ENTER)
Text, copy	Select the text and click	Select the text and choose Edit, Copy	Press (CTRL)+C
Text, cut	Select the text and click	Choose Edit, Cut	Press (CTRL)+X
Text, find	Click	Choose Edit, Find	Press (CTRL)+F
Text, paste	Select the text and click	Choose Edit, Paste	Press (CTRL)+V
Text, replace		Choose Edit, Replace	Press (CTRL)+H
Text, select	Drag through text		Press (SHIFT)+any cursor movement key, such as → or (END)
Undo	Click	Choose Edit, Undo	Press (CTRL)+Z
View, change	Click or	Choose View, Type View	
Web	Click	Choose Help, Microsoft on the Web	

INTEGRATED PROJECT 2

Integrating Word, Excel, and Access

In Integrated Project 1, you learned how to share Word and Excel data using linking and embedding techniques. Many of the techniques you used to copy and paste data between Word and Excel can also be used when you want to share data between Access and Word or Excel. In addition, you'll appreciate the features built into Access that make sharing data automatic.

Objectives

After completing this project, you will be able to:

➤ Copy Excel data to an Access database

➤ Update the Access table design

➤ Merge data from an Access database table with a Word document

The Challenge

Ruth Lindsey, Manager of the retail shops at The Willows, would like to thank distributors of the top ten selling items by sending each distributor a thank-you letter.

The Solution

To fulfill Ms. Lindsey's simple request, you'll need to jump through quite a few hoops. First you will take the data for the top ten items stored in the Topten worksheet you created in Excel Project 5 and use it to create a database. Then you will add fields to the database so you can merge the data to a Word document.

Figure 2.1 displays one of the thank-you notes you'll create.

Current Date

Iron Works Unlimited
1550 North State Street
Ogden, Utah 84404

Ladies and Gentlemen:

It is with pleasure that we announce the success of one of your products in our retail shops at The Willows resort. Your Cast iron doorstop (Product Number CID 11126) was recently listed as one of the top ten selling products at the resort.

The success of your products is a reflection of the dependability of your staff in meeting the demands of your customers. Such service does not go unnoticed.

Best wishes for continued success in all your endeavors.

Sincerely,

Ms. Ruth Lindsey, Manager
Retail Sales

Figure 2.1

The Setup

To accomplish the tasks outlined in this project, you need to work with Word, Excel, and Access. So that they are available when you need them, launch all three applications and create a new blank database named *Retail Sales* in Access. As you work with each application, maximize the application and document windows. Minimize applications you aren't using. Table 2.1 shows the settings you need to use.

Integrating Word, Excel, and Access   **IP2-3**

Table 2.1   Settings in Word, Excel, or Access

Element	Setting
Office Assistant	Close Office Assistant in all programs.
View, Toolbars	Display the Standard and Formatting toolbars in Word and Excel and the default toolbar in Access.

Copying Excel Data to an Access Database

You can drag data from Excel into the Access database using the same basic techniques you used to drag Excel data into Word. When you drag the Excel worksheet into Access, Access creates a new table using the worksheet data. Access *imports* the data, converting it to a format you can use to perform standard database activities.

TASK1: TO IMPORT EXCEL DATA TO A NEW ACCESS DATABASE:

1. Maximize Excel and open your *Topten.xls* worksheet.

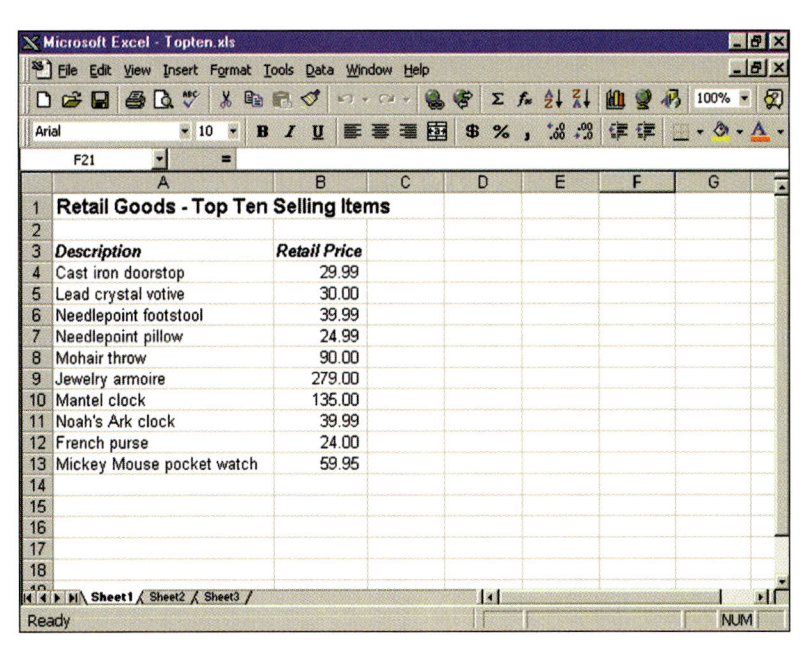

2. Maximize Access.

IP2-4

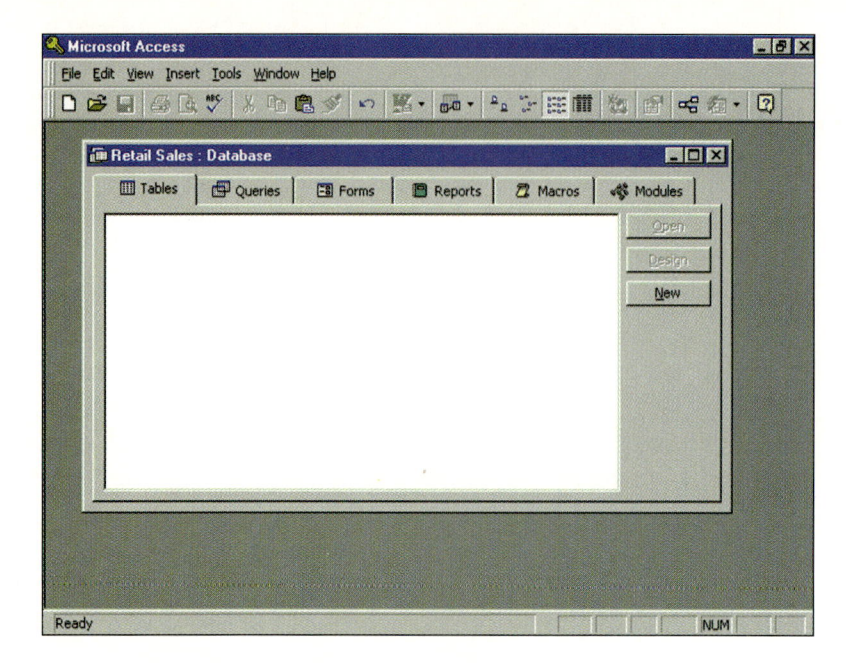

3 Position the mouse pointer on the Taskbar and right-click.

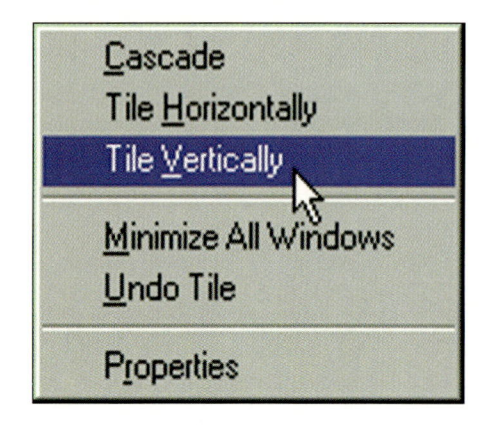

4 Choose Tile Vertically.

Integrating Word, Excel, and Access **IP2-5**

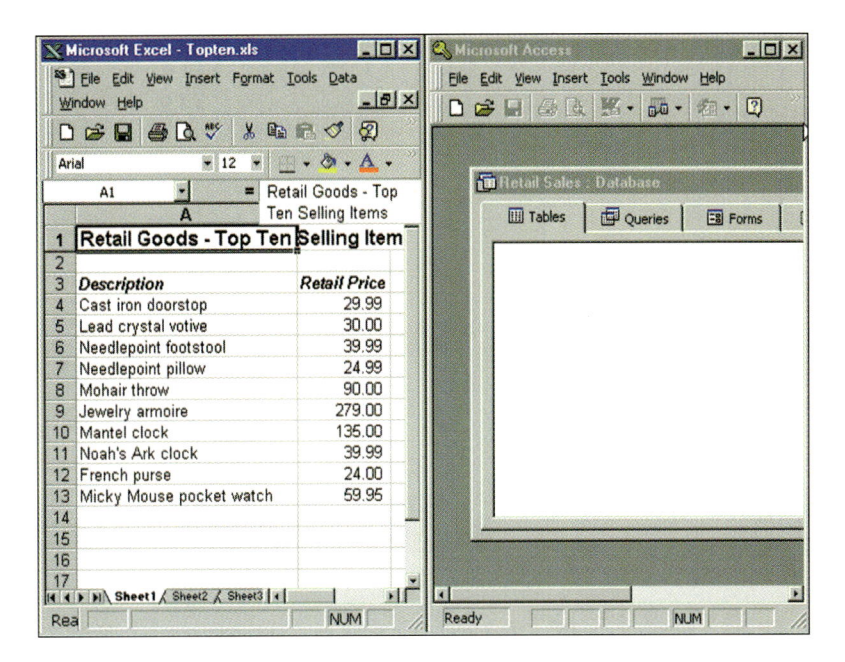

5 Select the Excel data in rows 3 through 13 and columns A and B.

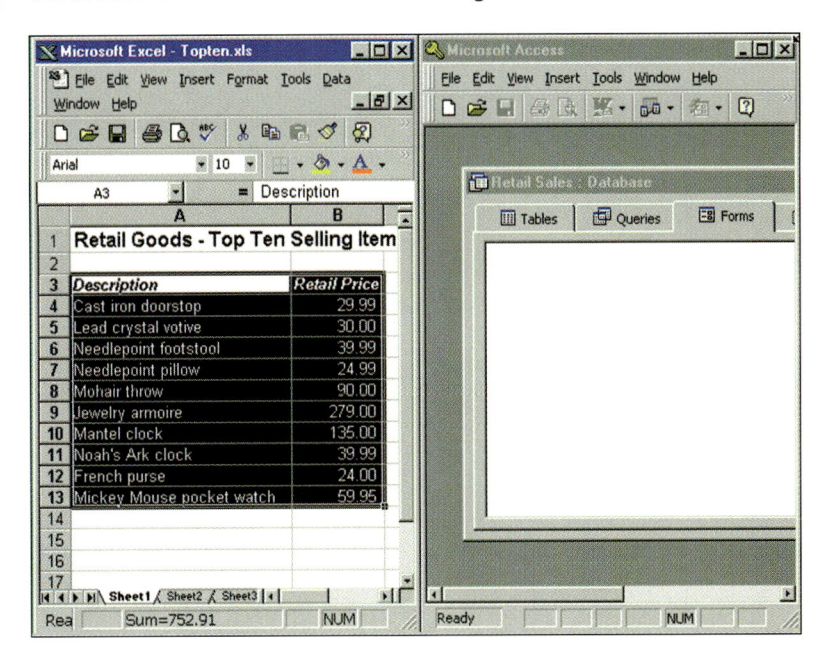

6 Position the mouse pointer on the right border of the selected Excel data, press CTRL, and drag the data to the Access database window.

IP2-6

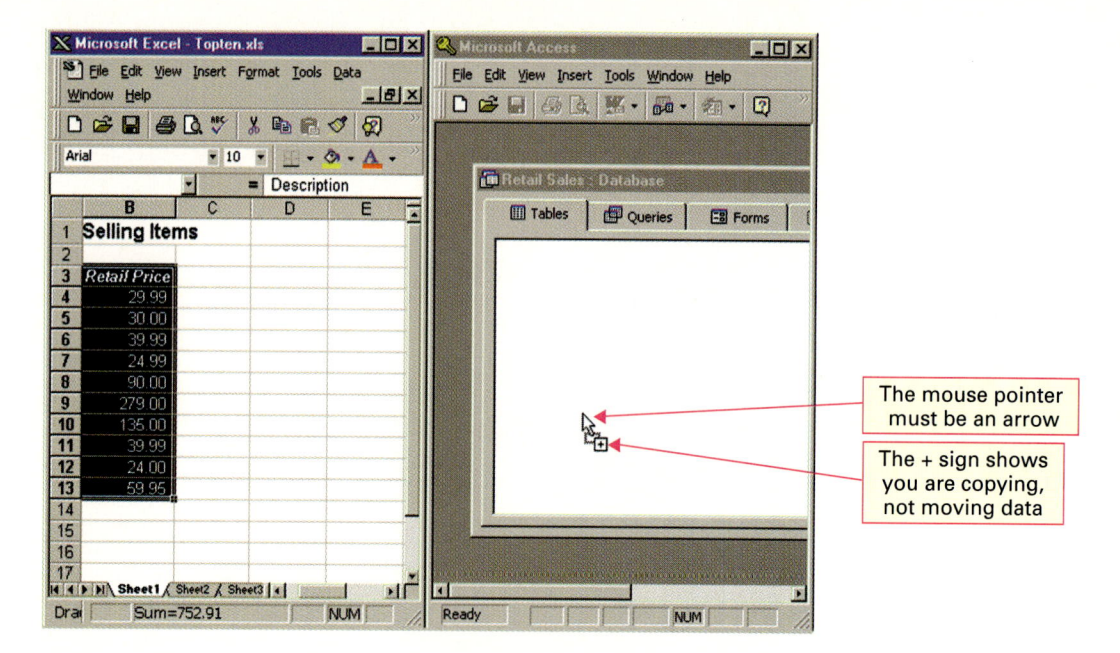

> The mouse pointer must be an arrow
>
> The + sign shows you are copying, not moving data

7 Release the mouse button and then the CTRL key.

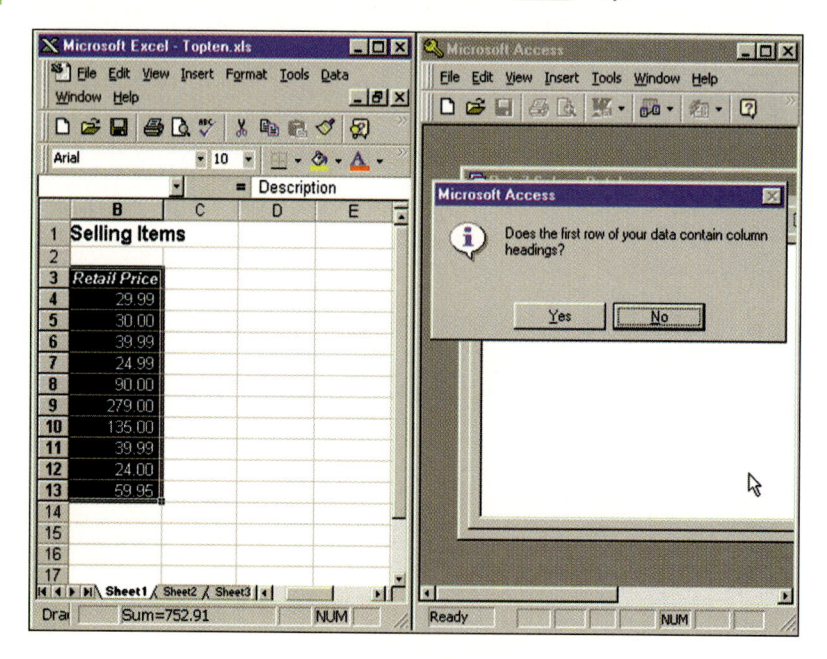

8 Select Yes to indicate that the top row does contain column headings. Access informs you that the import was successful.

9 Click OK to acknowledge the import message.
Sheet1 appears as the table name in the database window.

10 Click Sheet1, type **TopTen Selling Products** as the table name, and press ENTER.
The table name in the database window changes.

11 Close Excel and maximize Access.

Integrating Word, Excel, and Access   IP2-7

Updating the Access Table Design

Dragging worksheet data into Access creates a new table that identifies fields by column headings contained in the Excel worksheet. You can add fields to the table design and update table data without affecting the data or structure of the worksheet.

TASK 2: TO UPDATE THE ACCESS TABLE DESIGN:

1 Click the Design button on the Retail Sales database window.

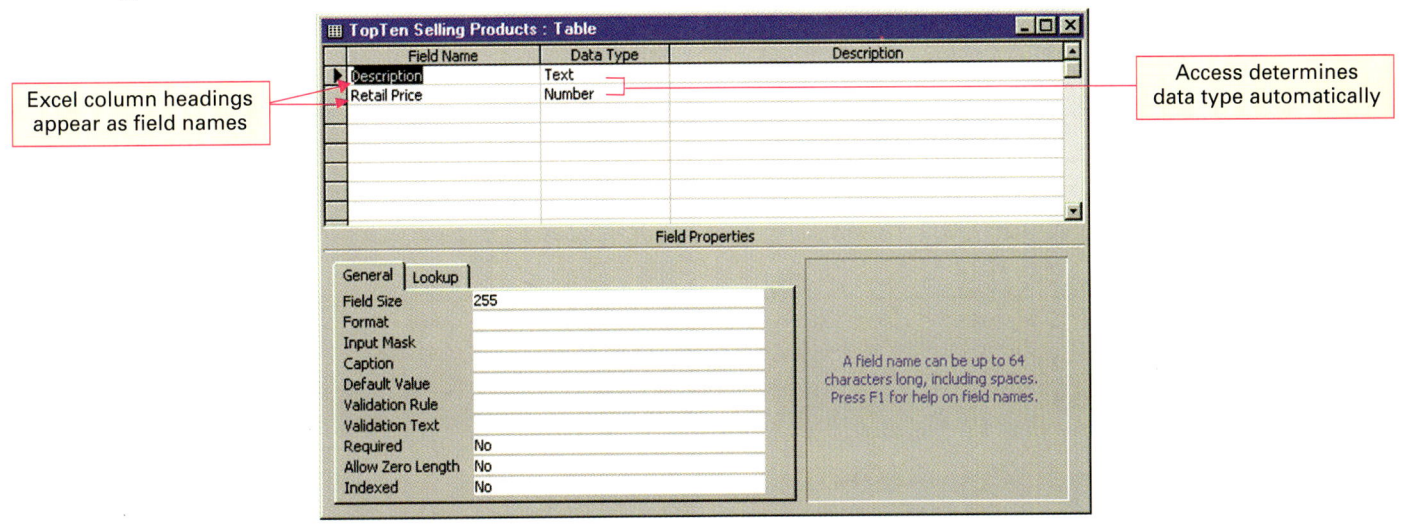

Excel column headings appear as field names

Access determines data type automatically

2 Position the mouse pointer on the first blank row of the table design and add the field names and data types shown in the following illustration:

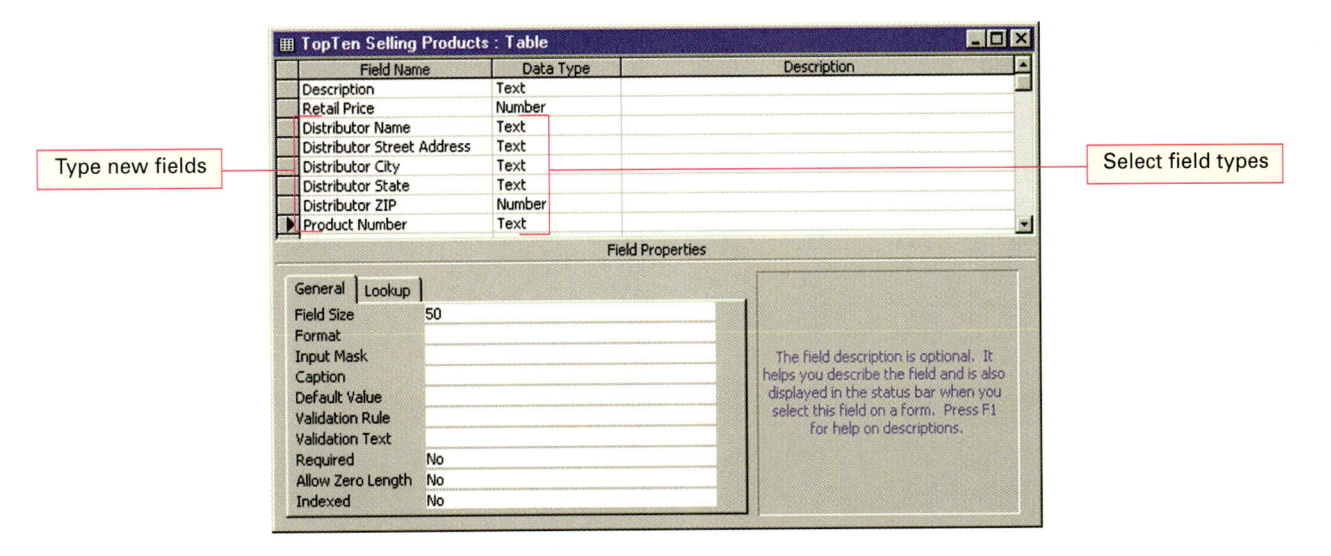

Type new fields

Select field types

3 Click 💾 to save design changes and then click 🔲 to display table data.

Field column width hides some data

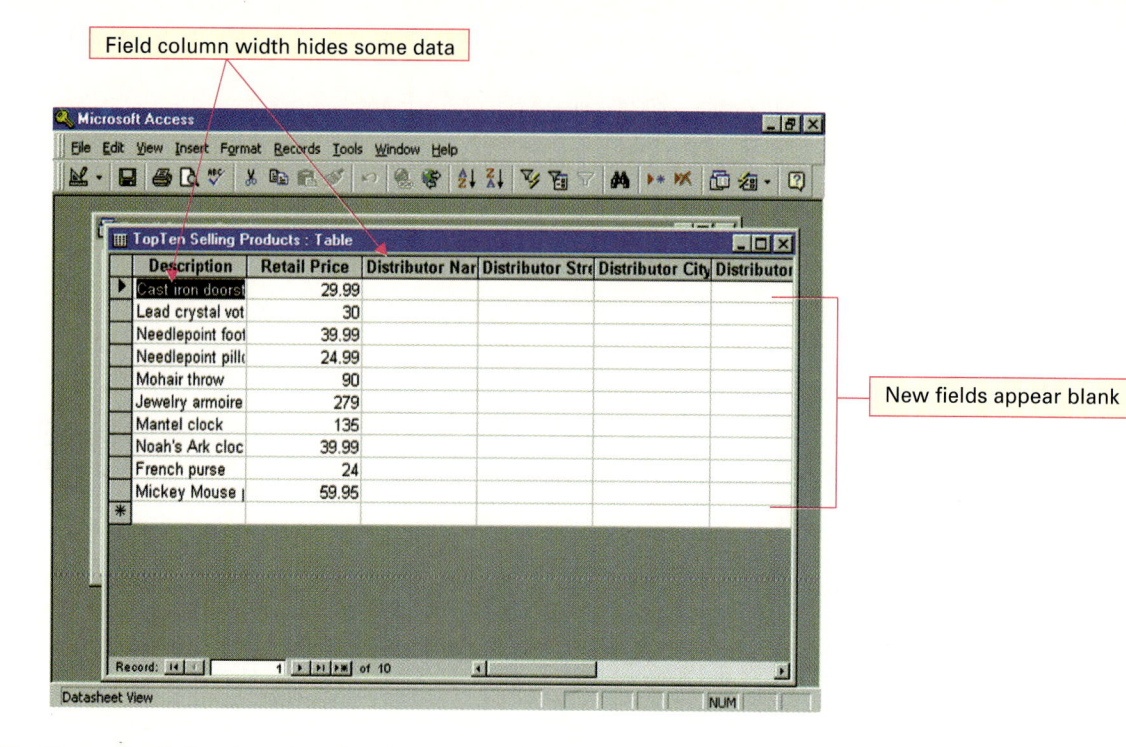

New fields appear blank

4 Type the following data for the ten products:

Description	Distributor	Product Number
Cast iron doorstop	Iron Works Unlimited 1550 North State Street Ogden, Utah 84404	CID 11126
Lead crystal votive	Anna's China & Crystal Distributors 20953 Orleans Boulevard Alexandria, VA 22201	LCV 88496
Needlepoint footstool	Furniture Outfitters 33380 Elm Street Simi Valley, CA 92265	NPF 16000
Needlepoint pillow	Furniture Outfitters 33380 Elm Street Simi Valley, CA 92265	NPP 15600
Mohair throw	Far East Imports 88 Mountain Drive Sioux City, SD 57049	MHT 99981
Jewelry armoire	Furniture Outfitters 33380 Elm Street Simi Valley, CA 92265	JYA 16445
Mantel clock	Southside Specialties One Alpha Plaza Houston, TX 77074	MCK 01234
Noah's Ark clock	Custom Works, Inc. 168 Main Street Portland, ME 01234	NAC 01034

Integrating Word, Excel, and Access   IP2-9

Description	Distributor	Product Number
French purse	TML France, Esq. 1616 Madison Avenue New York, NY 10001	FHP 85848
Mickey Mouse pocket watch	Finer Things, Inc. 8 Southside Bay Miami, FL 11101	MPW 57483

Merging Access Data with a Word Document

After updating the Access database so that it contains the data you need, you can use the data to create the thank-you letters. When you merge data from Access tables to Word documents, field names in the table are inserted into the document to tell Word where to look for the data in the Access database. The document to which you add merge fields is the *merge document* and the database table that contains the data and fields is the *merge data source file*.

TASK 3: TO MERGE DATA FROM THE ACCESS DATABASE TO A NEW WORD DOCUMENT:

1 Close the *TopTen Selling Products* table and click the drop-down list arrow beside the OfficeLinks button on the Standard toolbar.

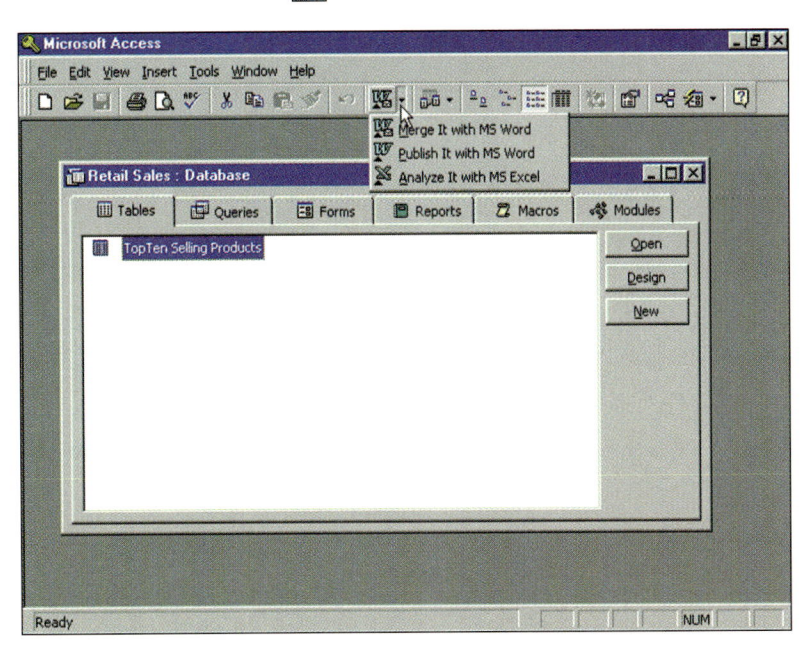

2 Select Merge It with MS Word to launch the Microsoft Word Mail Merge Wizard.

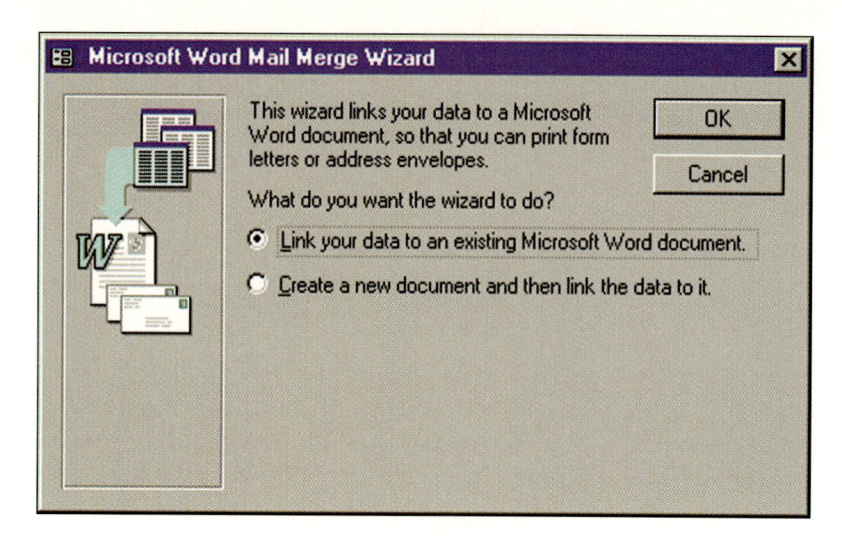

IP2-10

[Dialog box: Microsoft Word Mail Merge Wizard]

This wizard links your data to a Microsoft Word document, so that you can print form letters or address envelopes.

What do you want the wizard to do?

- ○ Link your data to an existing Microsoft Word document.
- ○ Create a new document and then link the data to it.

[OK] [Cancel]

3 Select *Create a new document and then link the data to it* and press (ENTER). Word launches and displays a new document with the Merge toolbar active and database table fields available on the Insert Merge Field list.

4 Type the text shown in the following figure, choose the field names from the Insert Merge Field list, press (ENTER) to move to the next line, and add punctuation and spacing.

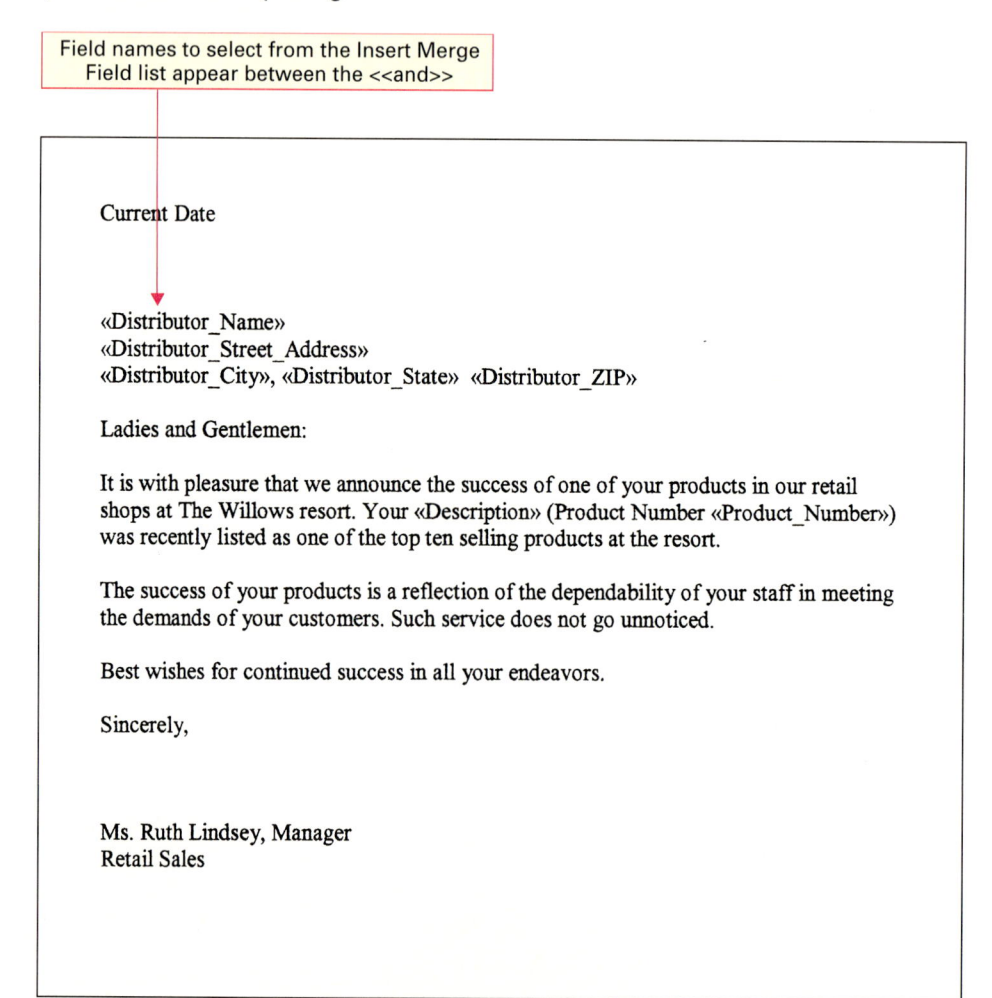

> Field names to select from the Insert Merge Field list appear between the <<and>>

Current Date

«Distributor_Name»
«Distributor_Street_Address»
«Distributor_City», «Distributor_State» «Distributor_ZIP»

Ladies and Gentlemen:

It is with pleasure that we announce the success of one of your products in our retail shops at The Willows resort. Your «Description» (Product Number «Product_Number») was recently listed as one of the top ten selling products at the resort.

The success of your products is a reflection of the dependability of your staff in meeting the demands of your customers. Such service does not go unnoticed.

Best wishes for continued success in all your endeavors.

Sincerely,

Ms. Ruth Lindsey, Manager
Retail Sales

5. Save the document using the filename *TopTen Thank You Letter,* merge the database data to a new document, review the form letters and print them.

6. Close the form letters after printing without saving them and exit Word, saving changes to the merge document.

7. Close the database, saving the changes, and then exit Access.

The Conclusion

While you used an Access table as the merge data source to merge data to a document, remember that the data originated in an Excel worksheet. When you need to pull data from more than one table in an Access database, you can create a query that displays data from multiple tables and then use the query as the merge data source. In addition, you can use data from an Access report in a Word document by selecting Publish It with MS Word from the OfficeLinks button on the Access toolbar. When you choose Publish It with MS Word, Office displays your Access report as a document in Word.

If you have completed your work for the day, shut down the computer according to standard lab procedures or continue working on the summary exercise and assignment.

Summary and Exercises

Summary

- You can use the same techniques to drag and drop Excel worksheet data to an Access database that you used to drag worksheet data to a Word document.
- When you drag and drop data from a worksheet to a database, Access creates a new table in the active database.
- When you use data from an Access database as the merge file for a Word Merge document, you have the choice of selecting an existing Word file or creating a new Word document.
- Using an Access database table as a data source file automatically creates a link between the database table and the merge document.
- To use data from multiple tables in a database as a data source file, you can create a query and select the query as the file to merge to Word.
- You can also publish data from an Access report to a Word document.

Key Terms and Operations

Key Terms
import
merge data source
merge document
Merge to Word
publishing

Operations
Copy data from an Excel worksheet to create a new Access database table
Update an Access database table design
Merge Access database table data with a new Word document

Study Questions

Multiple Choice

1. To change an Access database table design,
   a. delete the table and create a new one.
   b. select the table in the database window and click the Design button.
   c. copy the data from another table and use it to create a new table.
   d. position the insertion point on a table name and press ENTER.

2. All of the following techniques can be used to copy data from Excel to Access *except*
   a. cutting the data from the Excel worksheet and choosing Edit, Paste Special.
   b. dragging and dropping the data from Excel to Access.
   c. copying the Excel data to the Clipboard and pasting the data into Access.
   d. retyping the data from Excel into an Access table.

3. To copy data using drag and drop data from Excel to Access, press
   a. ESC.
   b. ENTER.
   c. ALT.
   d. CTRL.

4. Field names you type in the Table Design view of a table appear as
   a. inserts in the table.
   b. data entered in the fields.
   c. column headings in table datasheet view.
   d. row headings in table datasheet view.

5. As you enter data into new fields of an Access table,
   a. you have to save each field.
   b. Access saves data automatically when you move to a different record.
   c. data in existing fields changes.
   d. data automatically appears in queries.

6. When you merge Access table data to a Word document,
   a. a link is created automatically.
   b. data automatically appears in a Word table.
   c. the Access table appears in the Word document.
   d. nothing happens.

7. The toolbar that appears in Word when you merge Access table data to a Word document is the
   a. Standard toolbar.
   b. Formatting toolbar.
   c. Drawing toolbar.
   d. Merge toolbar.

8. Data from an Excel worksheet dragged into Access creates
   a. new field names.
   b. a chart.
   c. a new table.
   d. a new report.

9. Table data from multiple tables can appear together by creating a
   a. new table.
   b. query.
   c. report.
   d. new database.

10. To include summarized data from an Access database in a Word document, copy
    a. an Access report into a Word document.
    b. a query into a Word document.
    c. a form into a Word document.
    d. data to Excel and then drag it into the Word document.

Short Answer

1. To include data from multiple tables in a data source file, what database object should you merge?

2. What special toolbar appears when you merge Access data with a Word document?

3. What button do you click in Word to select a field name?

4. What special characters appear before and after a merge field in the Word document?

5. Does the table or query you use to merge with a Word document have to be open to complete the merge?
6. What does dragging Excel worksheet data create in an Access database?
7. Can you change the structure of a database table that is created from Excel worksheet data?
8. What database object do you drag to Word to include database summarized data in a Word report?
9. What Access toolbar button enables you to merge data from Access to Word automatically?
10. How do you tile applications on-screen?

For Discussion
1. How do you create a link between Access database table data and a Word document?
2. What techniques do you use to drag and drop data between an Excel worksheet and either Word or Access?
3. What happens when you drop data from an Excel worksheet into an Access database?
4. How do you merge data from multiple tables in an Access database to a Word document?

Exercise

Creating a new Access database and tables from Excel data
The board of directors of The Willows would like to see a summarization of data for sales of the three major restaurants at the resort. Figure 2.2 displays a report that Mark Taylor, manager of The Atrium Café, compiled to send to the board.

Sales Figures

	March Totals	April Totals
Atrium Cafe	$34,685.00	$32,580.00
Front Porch	$30,835.00	$32,220.00
Willow Top	$45,240.00	$42,740.00

Figure 2.2

Use the techniques explored in this project to create the report based on data contained in the *Restaurant Sales.xls* Excel worksheet you created in Excel Project 4.

1. Launch Excel, open the *Restaurant Sales.xls* worksheet, and maximize the application on-screen.
2. Launch Access, create a new blank database named *Restaurant Sales Figures*, and maximize the application on-screen.
3. Right-click the Taskbar and select Tile Vertically to tile the applications on-screen.
4. Click the Atrium Café worksheet, select the range from cells A8 through C8, drag the worksheet data into the Access database, and tell Access that the first row does NOT contain column headings.
5. Follow the same procedures to create two additional tables, one for the Willow Top and one for the Front Porch.
6. Close the worksheet and exit Excel; then maximize Access.
7. Change the field name of F1 in each table to *Restaurant Name,* F2 to *March,* and F3 to *April.*
8. Create a new query named *Sales Summary* in Access, add all three tables to the query, and design the query to contain all the fields in each table as shown here:

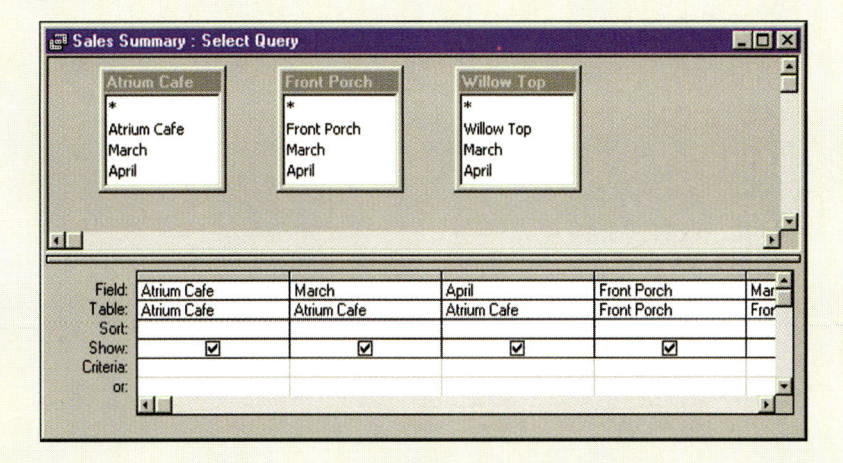

9. Create a report named *Sales Summary* based on the *Sales Summary* query and design it to appear as shown in Figure 2.2.

Assignment

Merging Access database table data with a Word document and publishing Access report data to a Word document

Before sending the report of restaurant sales to the Board of Directors, Mr. Taylor would like to have the managers of different programs and facilities at The Willows review the data. Create the document pictured in Figure 2.3 by merging name and address data from The Willows Managers table in The Willows Personnel database. Then use the OfficeLinks button in Access while previewing the report to publish the Sales Summary report in the Word document, positioning it as shown in Figure 2.3.

> Current Date
>
> «First_Name» «Middle_Name» «Last_Name»
> «Street»
> «City», «State» «ZIP»
>
> Dear Friends:
>
> Before sending the data summarized below to the members of The Willows Board of Directors, I thought you might want to review it. Please send any comments you have to the manager of the restaurant and voice any concerns you have to me before Friday.
>
> ## Sales Figures
>
> | | March Totals | April Totals |
> |---|---|---|
> | Atrium Cafe | $34,685.00 | $32,580.00 |
> | Front Porch | $30,835.00 | $32,220.00 |
> | Willow Top | $45,240.00 | $42,740.00 |
>
> Sincerely,
>
>
> Mark Taylor, Manager
> The Atrium Cafe

Figure 2.3

Save the document using the filename *Preliminary Sales Report to Board* and print the merged data form letters. Attach a copy of the main merge document to an e-mail message to your instructor, using the Outlook Mail feature.

Presentation Software
Using Microsoft PowerPoint 97

Overview

Microsoft PowerPoint 97 is a presentation graphics program that enables you to prepare slide shows and present them with style and impact. You can use PowerPoint to print handouts for the audience, speaker notes to aid presentation delivery, and overhead transparencies to use when you have no computer available. In this overview, you identify features unique to PowerPoint and see some old friends from other programs. After you get better acquainted with these basics, you'll be able to put them to use in the other projects in this module and unveil some of the power of PowerPoint.

Objectives

After completing this project, you will be able to:

- ➤ Design a presentation
- ➤ Launch Microsoft PowerPoint
- ➤ Identify PowerPoint screen elements
- ➤ Create a presentation
- ➤ Display presentations in different views
- ➤ Work with menus, dialog boxes, and toolbars
- ➤ Get Microsoft PowerPoint Help
- ➤ Exit PowerPoint

Defining PowerPoint Terminology

Presentations are collections of related slides that summarize key points of a report or act as a visual aid during an oral presentation. Whether you display slides on a computer screen, project slides onto a flat surface, or use transparencies to present slide images, PowerPoint can help you develop your presentation.

To use PowerPoint effectively, you need to become familiar with the PowerPoint terminology (see Figure O.1):

Term	Description
Slide	Basic unit of a presentation, which may contain numerous slides. Each slide in a presentation is equivalent to a page of a document, workbook, or database record.
Placeholder	Predefined area outlined on a slide, containing slide text, bulleted lists, and objects such as graphs, tables, and charts.
AutoLayout	Preformatted layouts that contain object placeholders.
Masters	Layouts that contain formats for text, bullets, placeholder alignment, headers/footers, and backgrounds.
Templates	Professionally developed slide designs that you can apply to presentations to give a consistent look to all slides in a presentation.

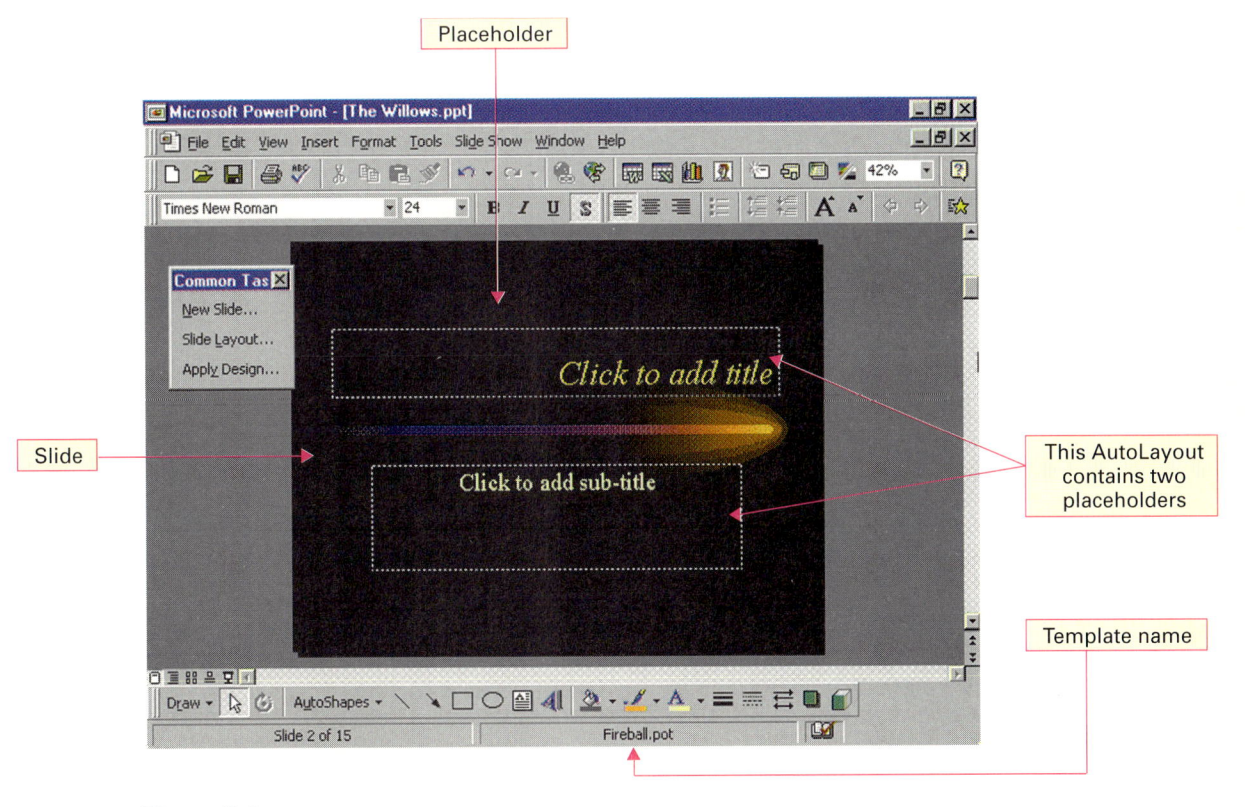

Figure O.1

Designing a Presentation

Because Microsoft PowerPoint comes with a variety of designs you can use to dress up your presentation, you can focus on the content of your presentation as you design it. Some things to consider as you plan your presentation:

- *Who* will be in your audience and how many people will attend: managers, corporate executives, salespeople, peers, and so forth.
- *What* materials do you want to use with the presentation: slides, handouts, notes, and overhead transparencies.
- *Where* is the presentation to be given: consider the size of the room, acoustics of the room, location of the speaker platform, and other factors. Remember that small printed characters are difficult to see from the back of the room, so limit lists to short statements rather than complete sentences and make the characters larger.
- *When* will the presentation occur: identify the time of day, placement of the presentation in relation to other presentations, and so on.
- *Why* are you giving the presentation: determine the message you want to communicate and the action you want the audience to take.
- *How* does the method you will use to deliver the presentation affect the presentation design: color can be used more effectively in on-screen shows than in transparencies; if no color printer is available, handouts and color transparencies might be too dark.

After you consider each of these points, you can develop a presentation targeted to your audience, design a look for the presentation that best conveys the purpose of the presentation, and jot down a brief outline of the topics you want to include in the presentation. Then you're ready to launch PowerPoint.

Launching Microsoft PowerPoint

After you have powered up your computer, logged onto required networks, and responded to messages built into your system, Windows 95 starts automatically.

Overview **PP-5**

TASK 1: TO LAUNCH POWERPOINT:

1. Click the Start button.
2. Point to Programs.

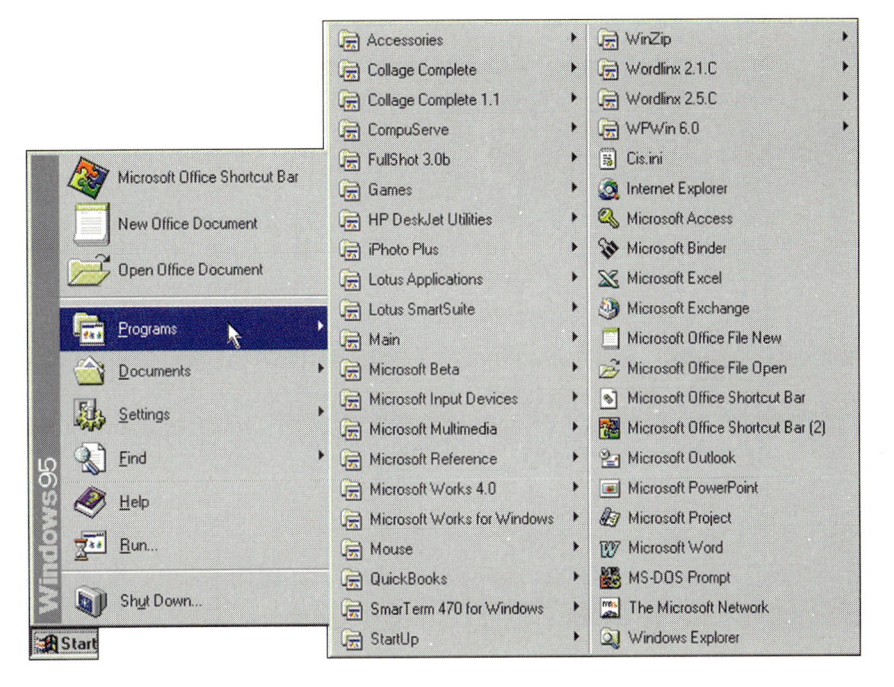

3. Point to Microsoft PowerPoint and click.

Identifying PowerPoint Screen Elements

The PowerPoint screen features a number of elements found in other application windows as well as several elements unique to PowerPoint (see Figure O.2). The first time you launch PowerPoint after it's installed on a computer, the Office Assistant pops up, introduces itself, and offers assistance. After the first time, the Office Assistant sits quietly by or hops up on the toolbar until you need it.

Figure O.2

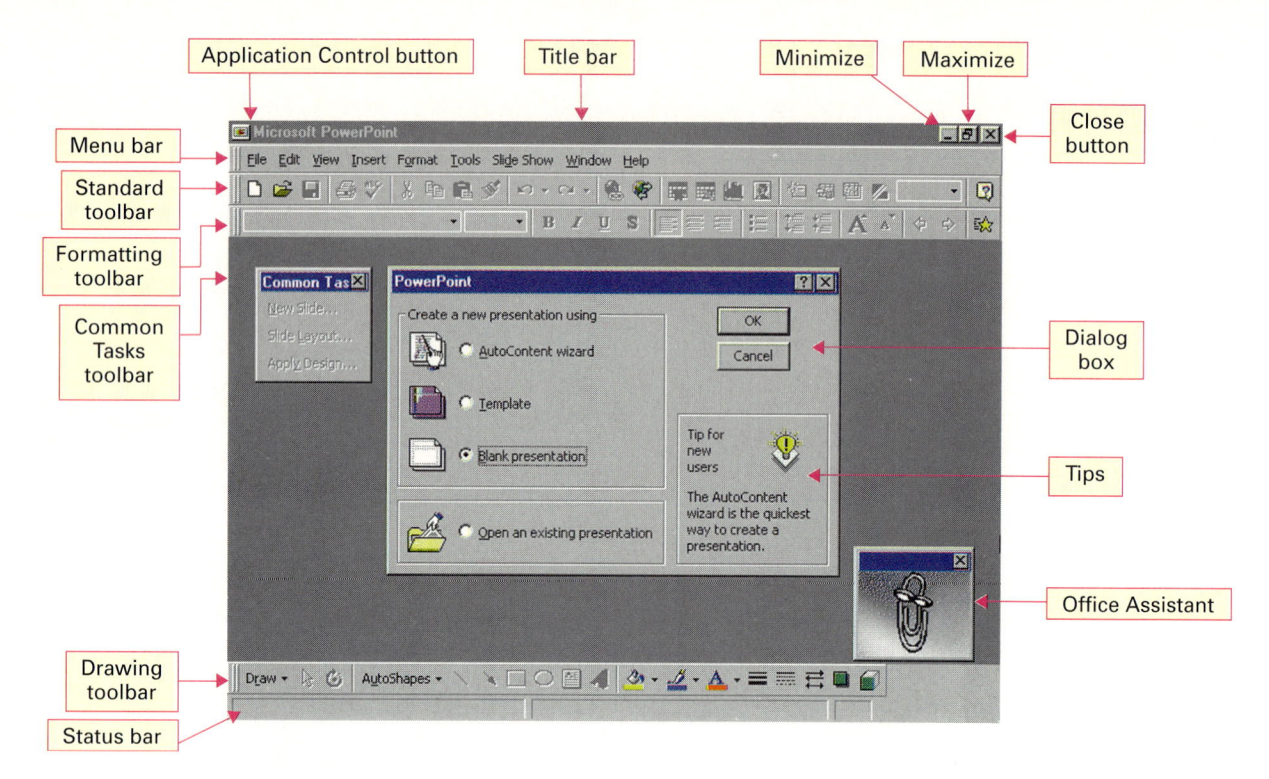

Table 0.1 contains a brief description of each PowerPoint screen feature.

Table 0.1 PowerPoint Screen Features

Screen Feature	Description
Menu bar	Provides access to commands used to perform tasks.
Title bar	Identifies the application name and contains the application icon, Maximize/Restore, Minimize, and Close buttons. Until you save a presentation, PowerPoint names the presentations consecutively, using the generic names Presentation1, Presentation2, and so forth. After you save a presentation, the filename you assign appears in the title bar.
Standard toolbar	Contains buttons that serve as shortcuts for performing common menu commands, displaying special toolbars, or changing screen features.
Formatting toolbar	Displays buttons and list boxes to access the most frequently used formatting commands.
Common Tasks toolbar	Displays commands to accomplish the three most frequently performed tasks.
Drawing toolbar	Displays tools for creating and formatting drawn objects.
View buttons	Provides an easy way to display your presentation in a different format. You'll see these after you create your first slide or open a presentation.
Office Assistant	Provides tips as you work and can answer some of your questions about the program.
Status bar	Displays information about the program status, instructions for performing selected tasks, active key information, functions of the toolbar buttons when you point to them, and trouble messages.

Creating a Presentation

Each time you launch PowerPoint, the PowerPoint dialog box shown in Figure O.3 presents options that enable you to create a new presentation or open an existing one.

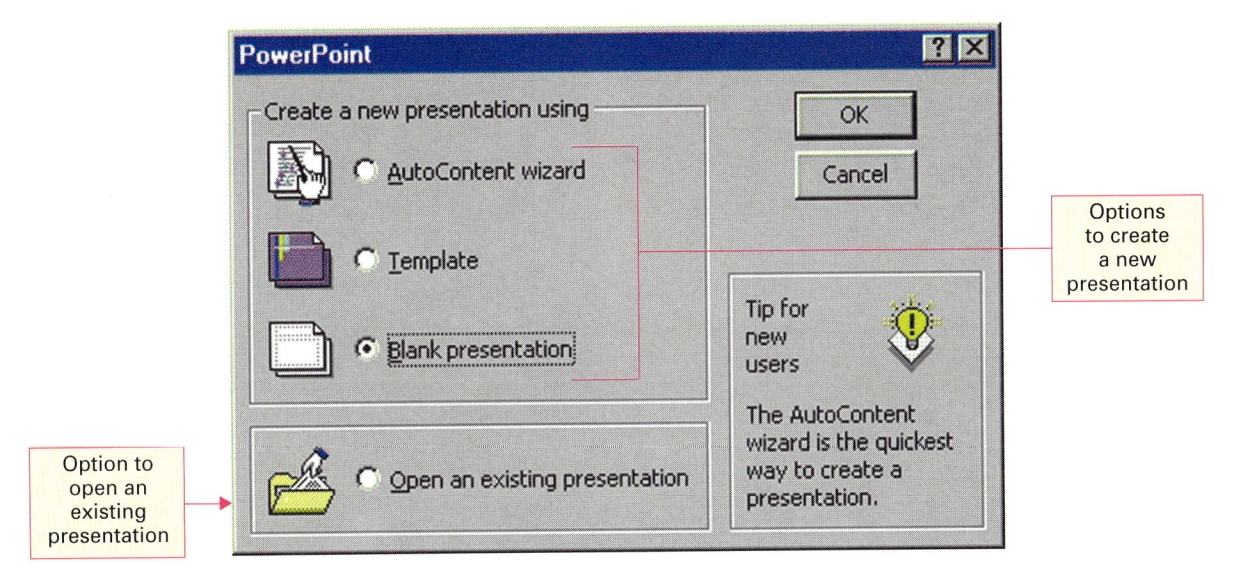

Figure O.3

[Screenshot of PowerPoint dialog box with options: AutoContent wizard, Template, Blank presentation (selected), and Open an existing presentation. Annotations indicate "Options to create a new presentation" and "Option to open an existing presentation."]

Options for creating a new presentation include:

- AutoContent wizard: The wizard creates a presentation, based on the purpose of the presentation and choices you select from options the wizard presents. The wizard formats slides in the presentation to contain instructions and information about the presentation content. You then replace that instructional and informative text with the text you want to include on each slide.

- Template: Lets you choose a design for your presentation and then build the presentation from scratch by adding your own text and objects to slides you create.

- Blank presentation: Creates a plain presentation that formats slides with placeholders to contain text and objects.

When you choose to create a new presentation, PowerPoint presents a series of formats for the first slide with the title slide selected. Each placeholder on the title slide contains instructions to help you add text to the slide.

PP-**8**

TASK 2: TO CREATE A NEW, BLANK PRESENTATION:

1 Click Blank presentation and then click OK.

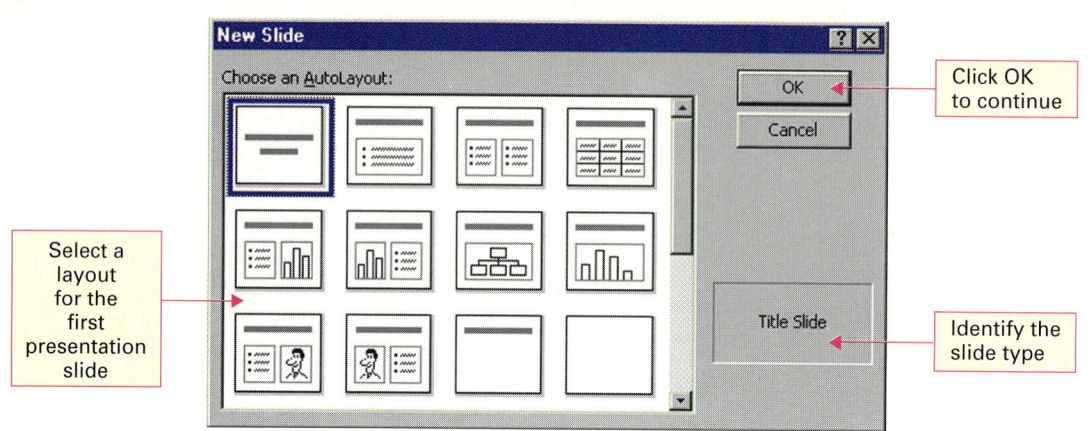

Click OK to continue

Select a layout for the first presentation slide

Identify the slide type

2 Click OK to accept the Title Slide AutoLayout format for the first slide in the presentation.

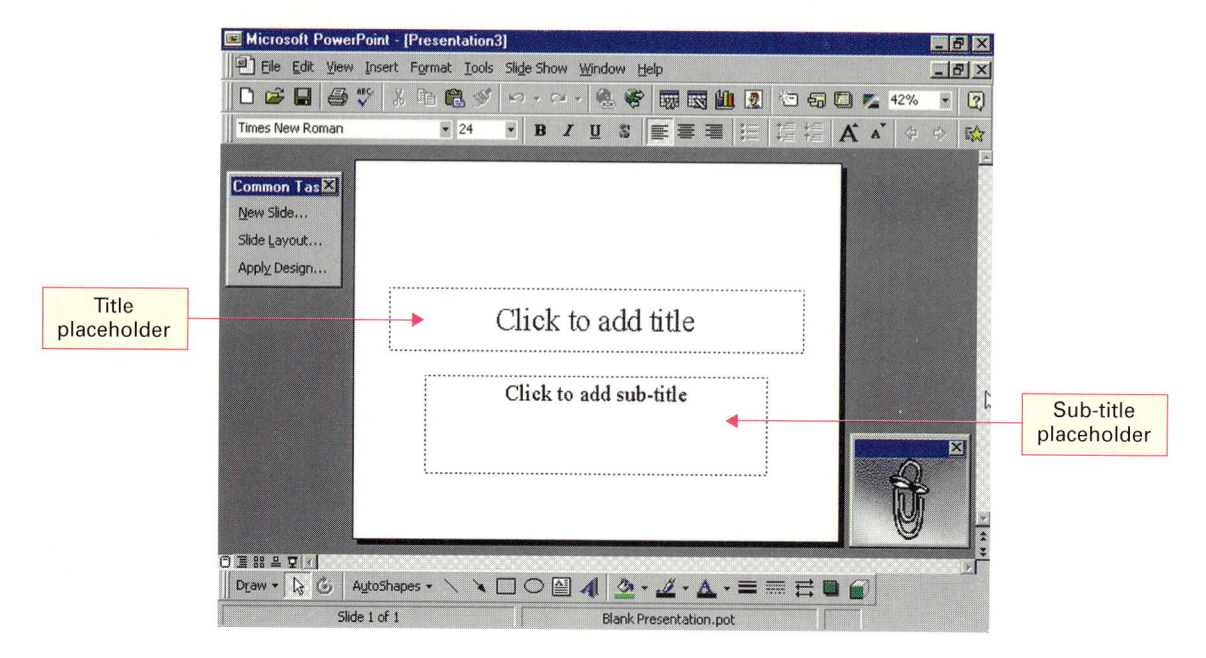

Title placeholder

Sub-title placeholder

Displaying Presentations in Different Views

PowerPoint provides several views that allow you to display your presentation in different ways. Each view is designed to make working with specific features of a presentation easier:

- Slide view: Displays all slide text, formatting, graphics, charts, and other objects individually on-screen. Slide view lets you add and edit text, create new slides, create drawings, access slide objects, and change the slide format.

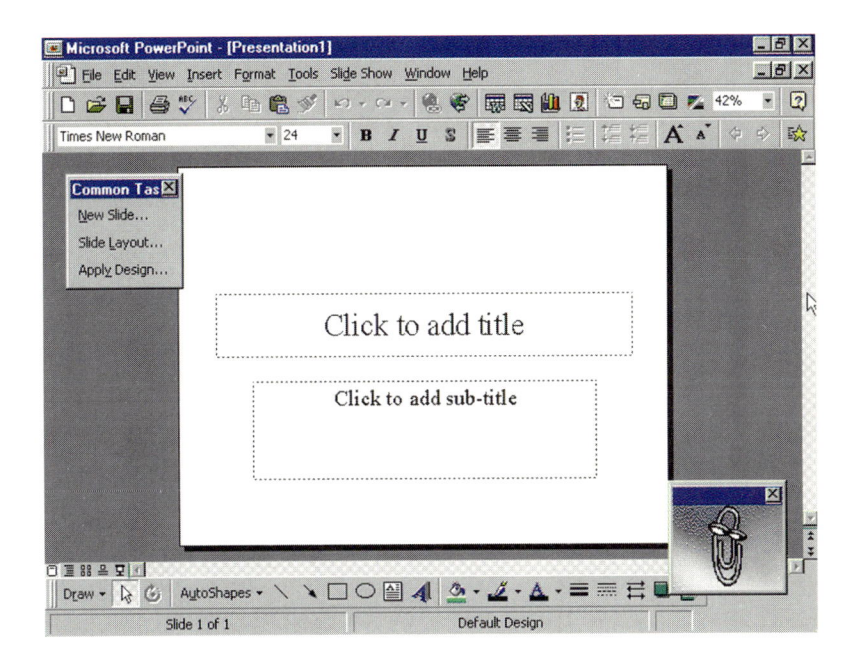

- Outline view: Displays the slide text you type into placeholders in an outline structure. Typing text in Outline view makes creating text for multiple slides more efficient. You can add and edit text, create new slides, and rearrange slides in Outline view, but you can't add other objects to slides.

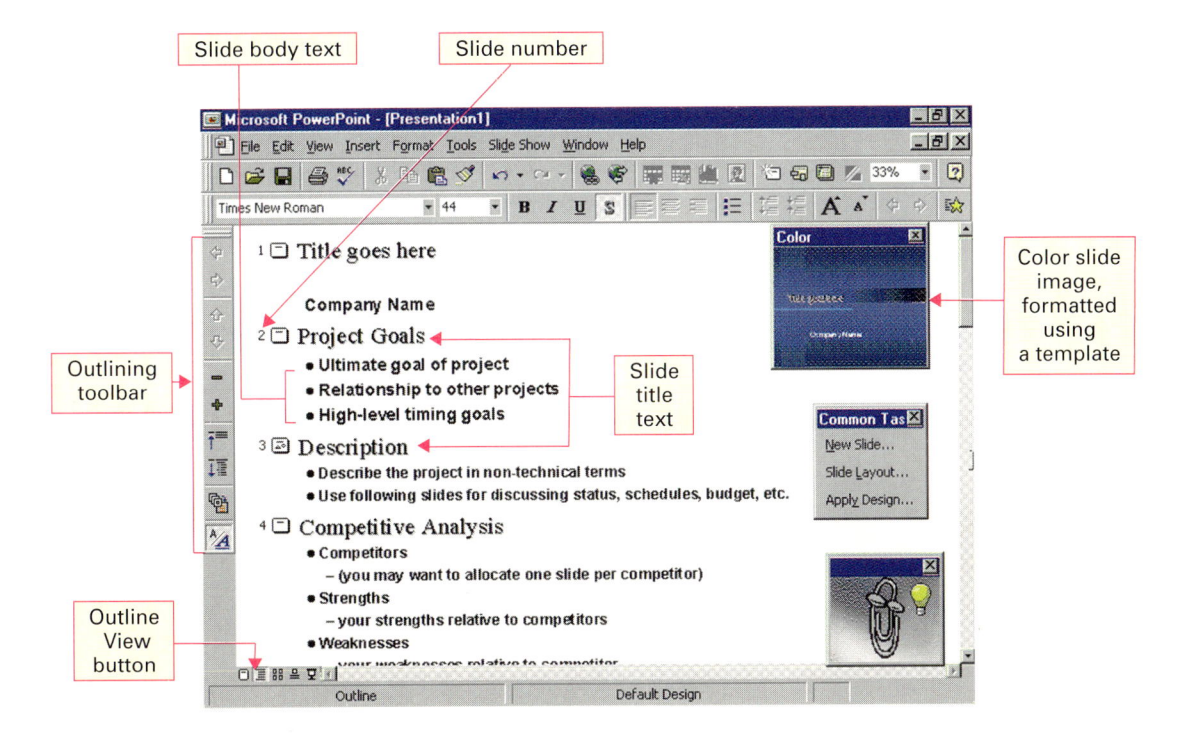

- Slide Sorter view: Displays thumbnail images of multiple slides on-screen at the same time. Slide Sorter view makes rearranging slides more efficient, but slides can't be edited in Slide Sorter view.

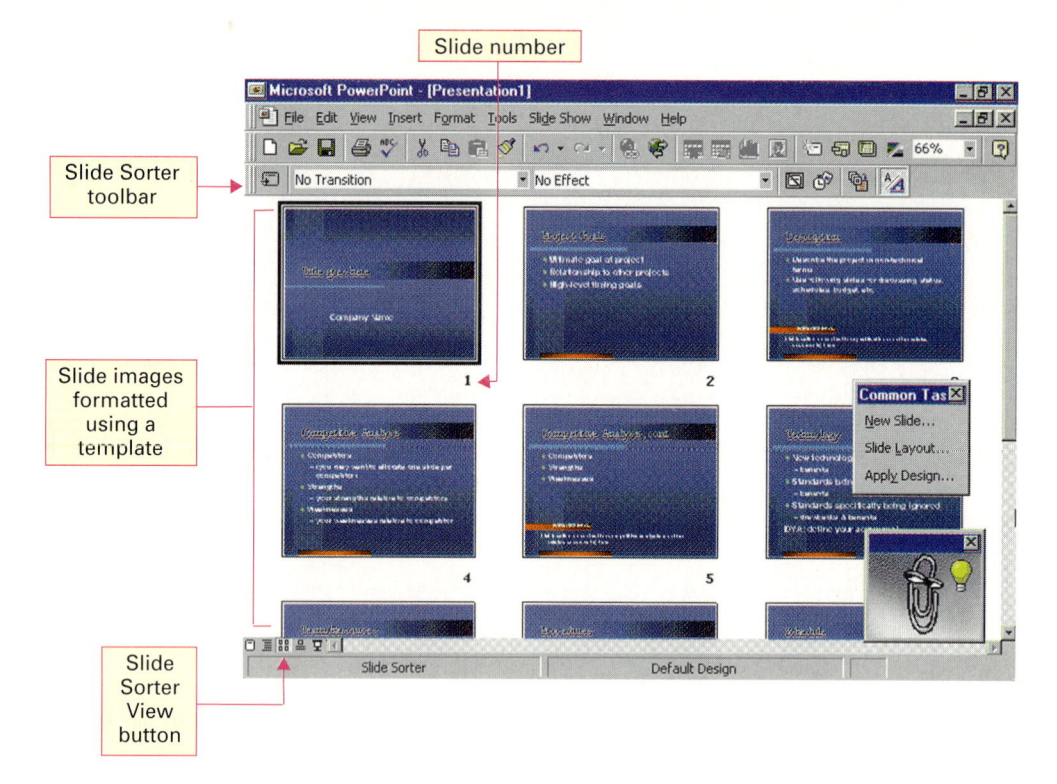

- Notes Pages view: Displays a small slide image at the top of the page and provides space below the image to type notes and supportive information about the slide contents.

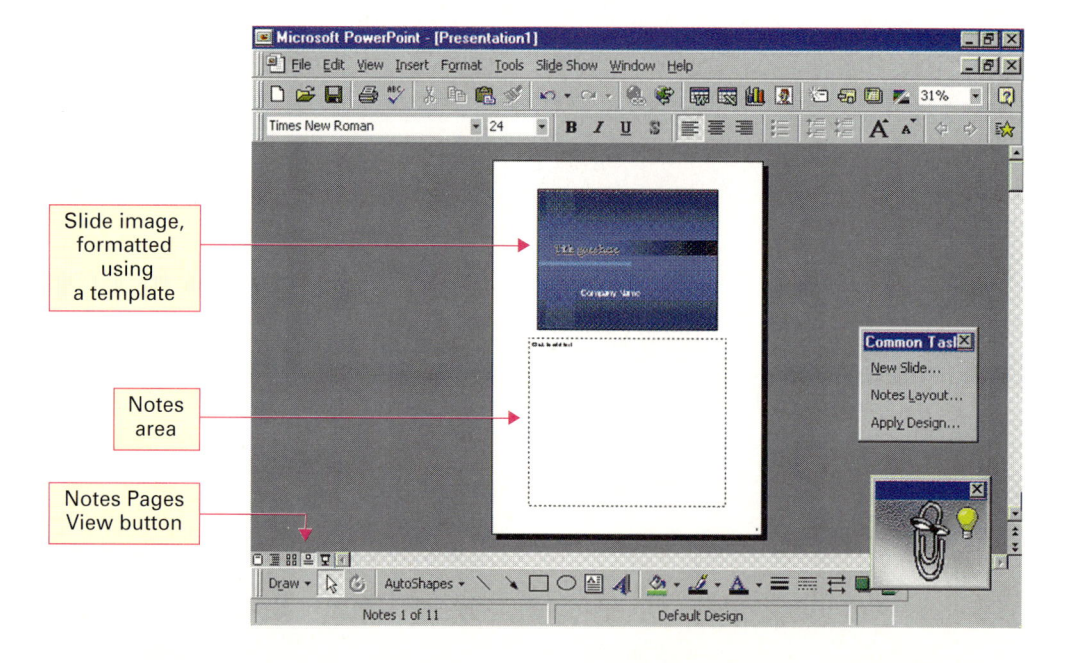

Overview   PP-11

Working with Menus, Dialog Boxes, and Toolbars

Just as menus in restaurants display food items by type, menus and toolbars in PowerPoint group features and commands you use as you perform tasks in PowerPoint. Dialog boxes present options for you to choose as you create presentation files and objects, create format slides and handouts, and build your presentations.

Identifying Menu Features

Menus group commands for performing tasks according to type. In PowerPoint, the menu bar remains constant as you work with different presentation objects, but available menu commands change as you switch views and work with objects. To display a list of menu commands, point to the menu item and click. Figure O.4 identifies the standard features of PowerPoint menus you will see:

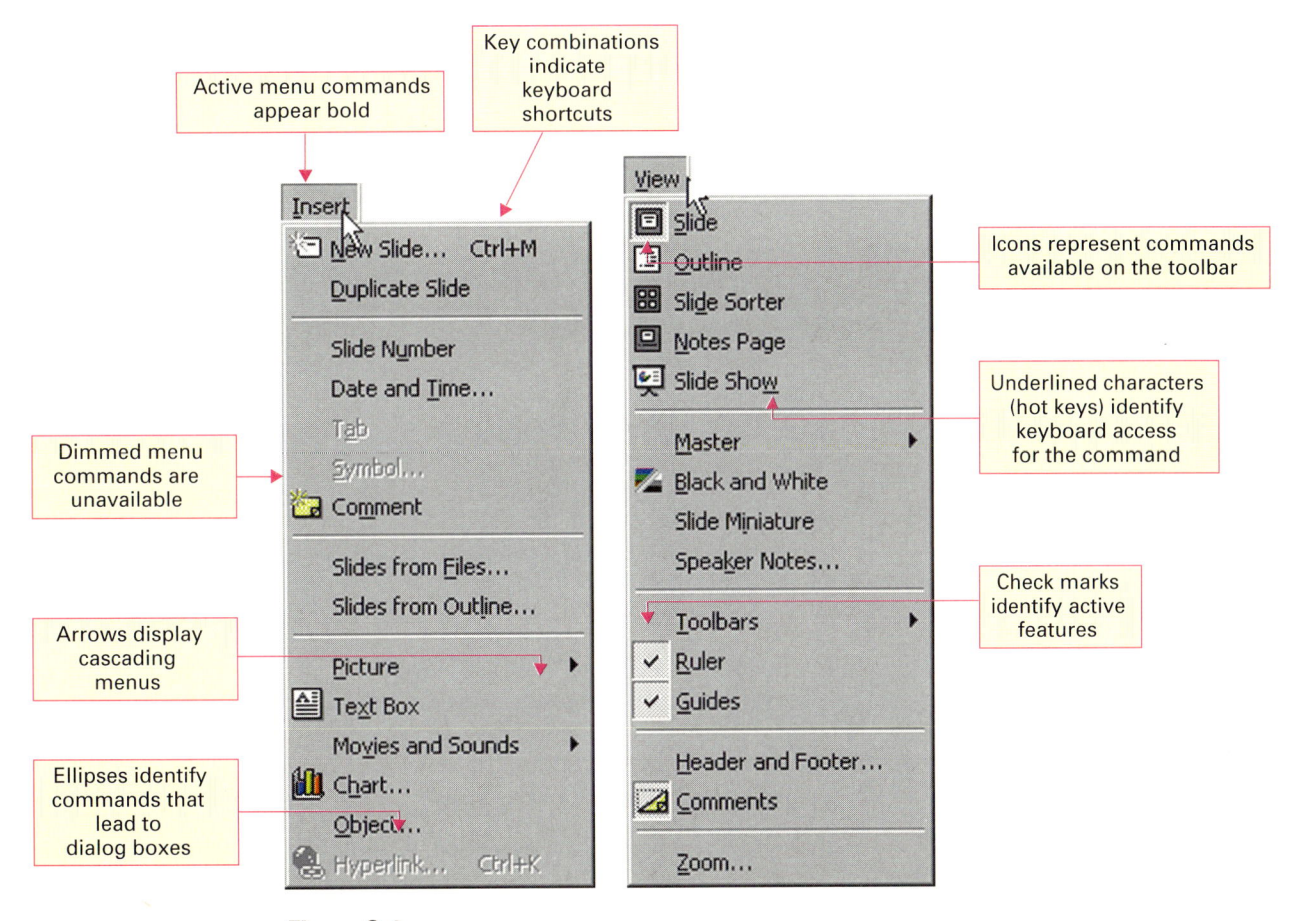

Figure O.4

Working with Toolbars

Tools on the toolbars provide easy access to many of the most frequently used menu commands and dialog boxes. To use the toolbar buttons, point to the button that represents the command you want to perform or feature you want to display, and click. **ScreenTips** identify the name of each button on the toolbar, and pop up when you point to the toolbar button.

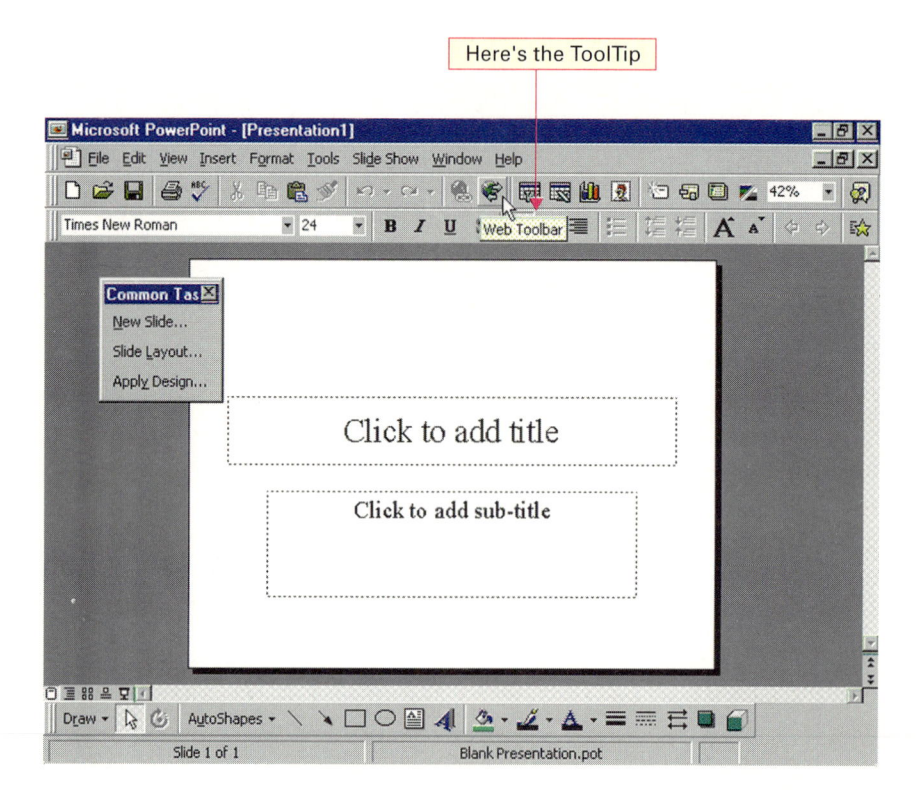

The view buttons at the bottom of the presentation window operate in much the same way as toolbar buttons. When you point to a view button, a ScreenTip identifies the view; when you click a view button, PowerPoint automatically switches to the selected view.

> **Note** The toolbars displayed in the PowerPoint window change automatically as you work with objects and perform different tasks.

Toolbars (such as the Common Tasks toolbar) that display on-screen with title bars are called *floating toolbars*; toolbars that appear on-screen with no title bar are called *docked toolbars*. You can dock a floating toolbar by dragging its title bar until the toolbar forms a narrow horizontal or vertical rectangle on any side of the PowerPoint window. You can also float toolbars by grabbing the toolbar's grip and dragging the toolbar to a new position.

Overview **PP-13**

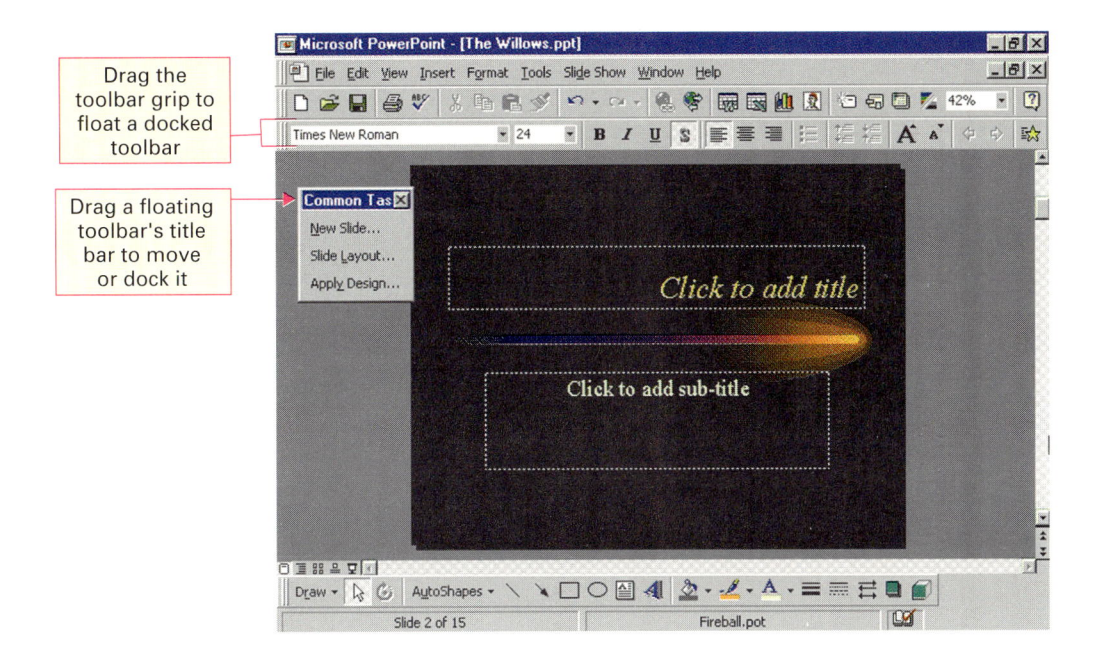

[Screenshot of Microsoft PowerPoint window with annotations:
- Drag the toolbar grip to float a docked toolbar
- Drag a floating toolbar's title bar to move or dock it]

Working with Dialog Boxes

Dialog boxes appear when you select a menu command that's followed by an ellipsis and when you click certain toolbar buttons. Figure O.5 identifies features you'll see as you work with dialog boxes. Not all features will appear in every dialog box.

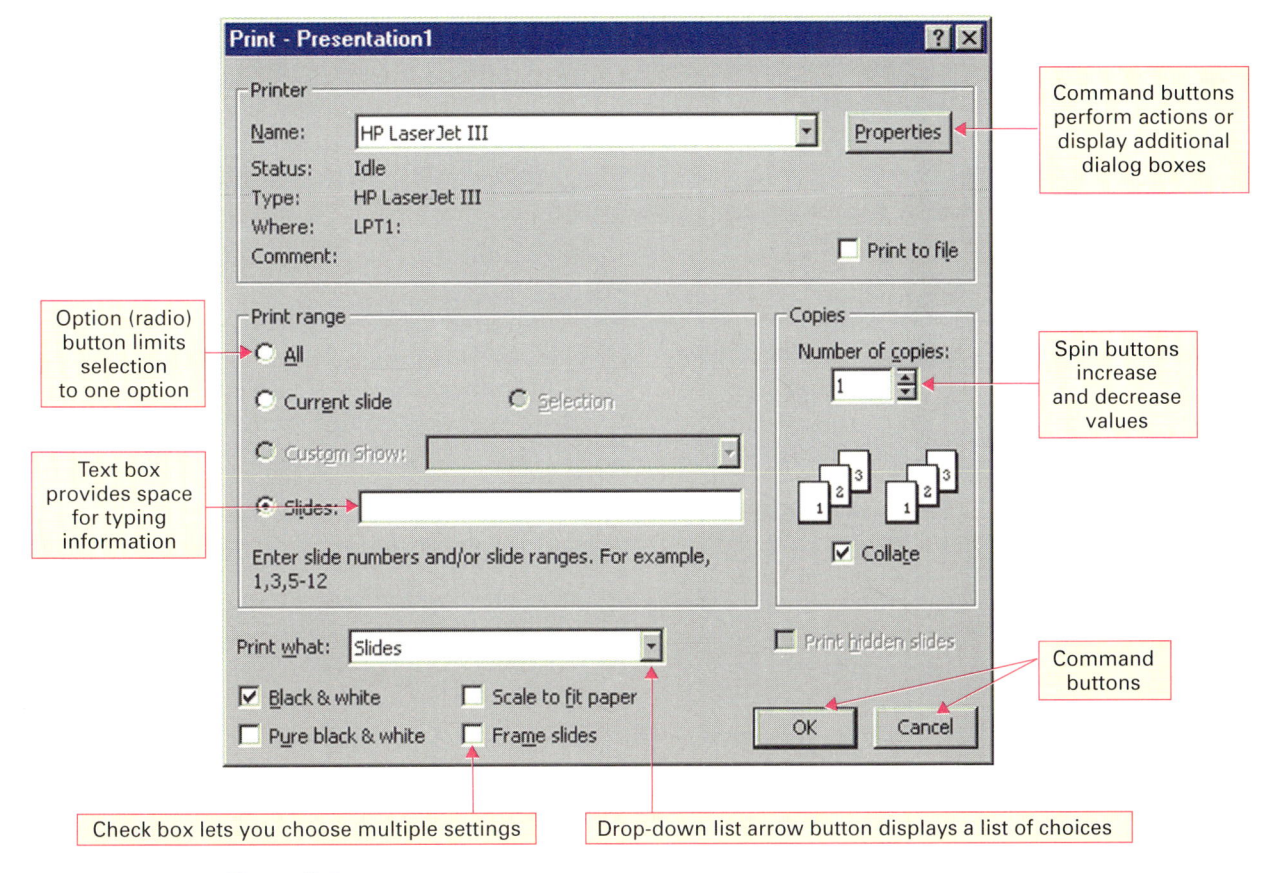

[Screenshot of Print dialog box with annotations:
- Command buttons perform actions or display additional dialog boxes
- Spin buttons increase and decrease values
- Option (radio) button limits selection to one option
- Text box provides space for typing information
- Command buttons
- Check box lets you choose multiple settings
- Drop-down list arrow button displays a list of choices]

Figure O.5

PP-14

TASK 3: TO DISPLAY MENUS OR DIALOG BOXES AND USE THE TOOLBAR:

1 Point to the File menu and click.

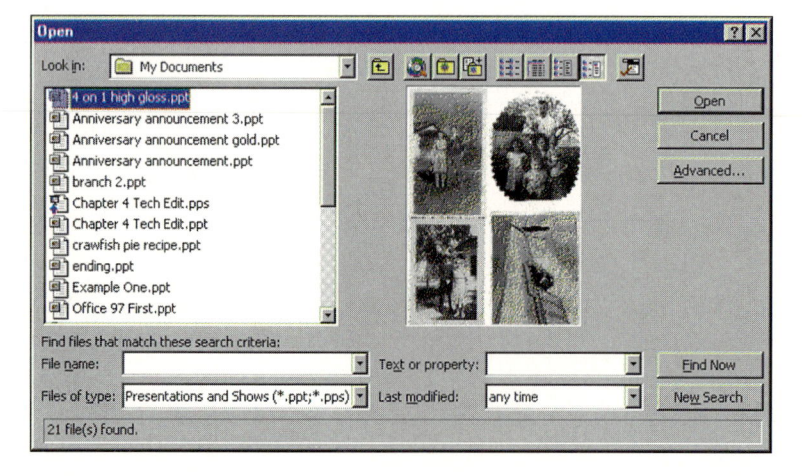

2 Choose Open.

3 Click the Cancel button.
The dialog box closes and the PowerPoint presentation reappears.

4 Point to the Spelling button on the Standard toolbar and pause.

Overview **PP-15**

5 Click the title bar of the Common Tasks toolbar and drag it to the lower-right corner of the window.
The toolbar appears where you drop it.

6 Drag the Common Tasks title bar toward the top of the window until it becomes a flat, horizontal toolbar.

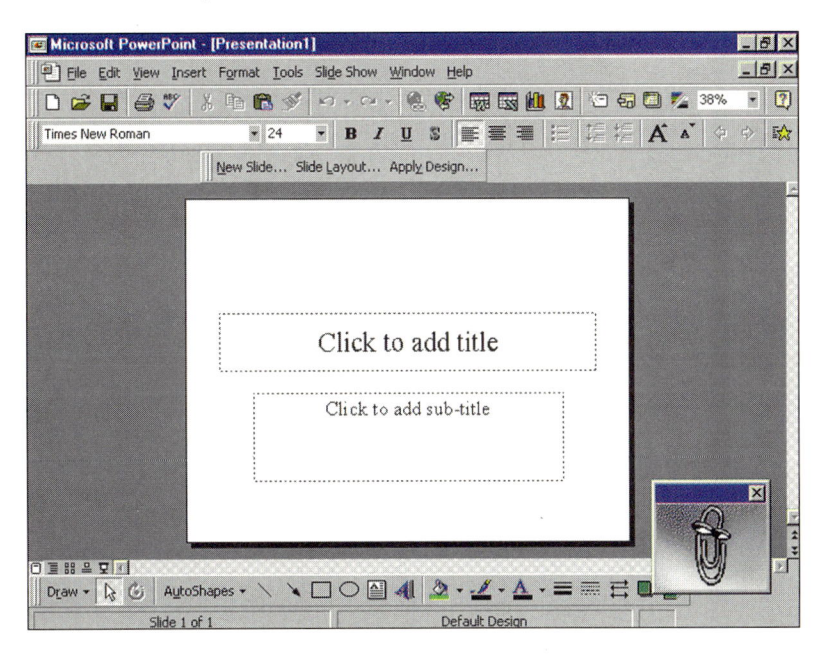

7 Grab the grip on the Common Tasks toolbar and drag it down until the toolbar is shaped as a square.

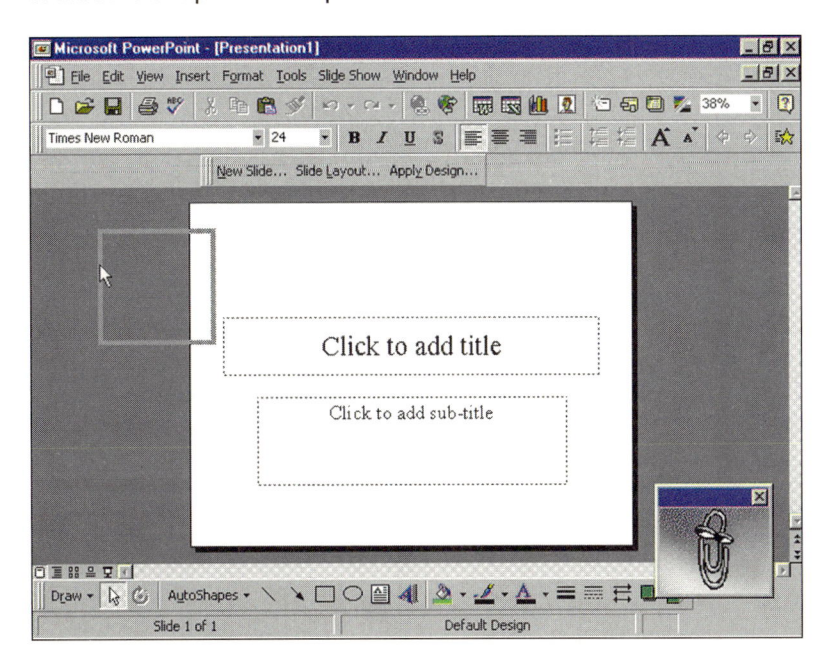

8 Release the mouse button.

9 Choose the Tools menu.

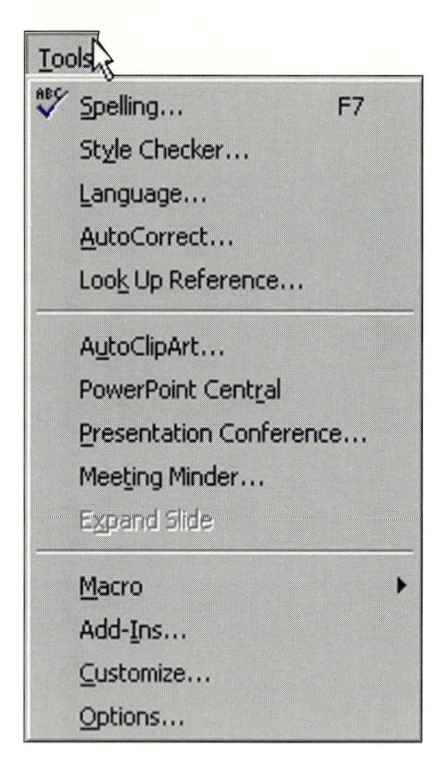

```
Tools
 ABC  Spelling...           F7
      Style Checker...
      Language...
      AutoCorrect...
      Look Up Reference...

      AutoClipArt...
      PowerPoint Central
      Presentation Conference...
      Meeting Minder...
      Expand Slide

      Macro              ▶
      Add-Ins...
      Customize...
      Options...
```

10 Press `ESC` twice to close the Tools menu.

Getting Help

PowerPoint provides numerous ways for you to get online help as you work. From the PowerPoint Help menu, you can access standard features available on the Help menus of other Microsoft Office 97 applications:

- The Office Assistant, which enables you to ask questions about the task you want to perform.
- The standard three-page Windows 95 Help dialog box, which displays Contents, Index, and Find to search for information on the topic or procedure you need.
- What's This?, to obtain a brief description of a button, feature, or command.
- Microsoft on the Web to explore information about new products, obtain answers to frequently asked questions, recommend improvements to the program, and so forth.

In addition, PowerPoint provides context-sensitive help and tips as you work. You will primarily use the Office Assistant to access Help in PowerPoint.

Note Online help has proven to be a more efficient method for obtaining help than searching through voluminous manuals for tips and information about specific programs and tasks. However, "online help" doesn't refer to connecting to the Internet or a communications provider; it simply refers to the help provided by the software that's accessible from your computer.

Using the Office Assistant

The Office Assistant is a feature new to Microsoft Office 97 applications, and already the Office Assistant is growing in popularity. The Office Assistant is easy to use, is personably animated, and provides a focused list of help topics. It opens the first time you launch PowerPoint. After that, it makes eyes at you or waits on the Standard toolbar and appears as a Johnny-on-the-spot each time you call for help.

TASK 4: TO DISPLAY, USE, AND CLOSE THE OFFICE ASSISTANT:

1 Click the Office Assistant button on the toolbar.

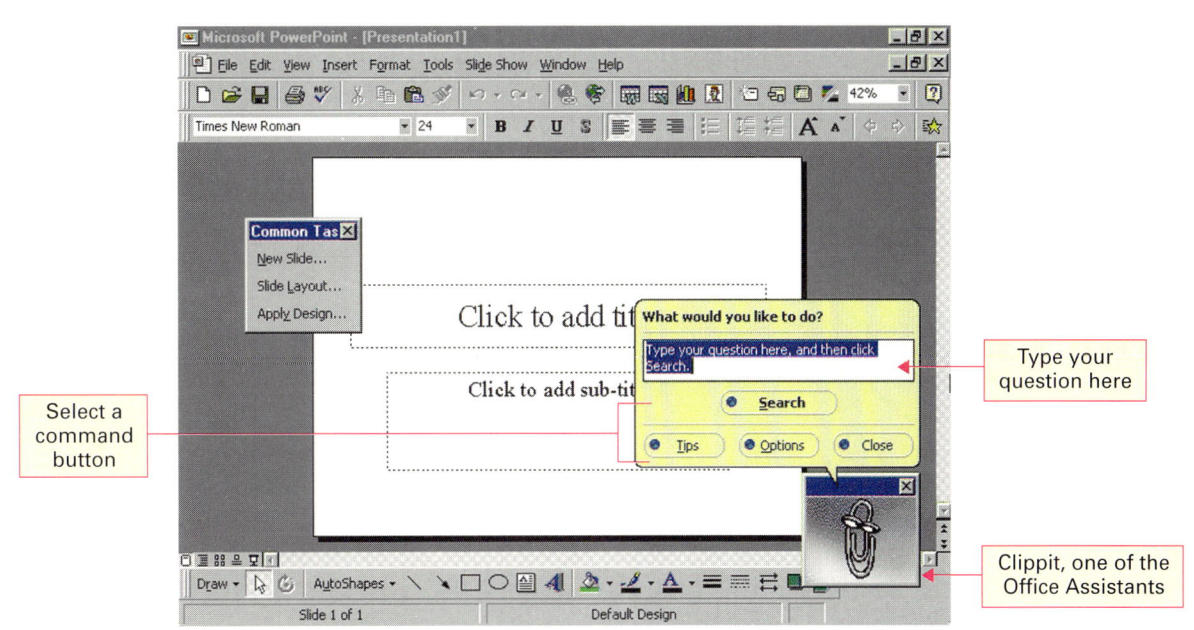

2 Type **Add a slide** in the question textbox; then press ENTER.

PP-18

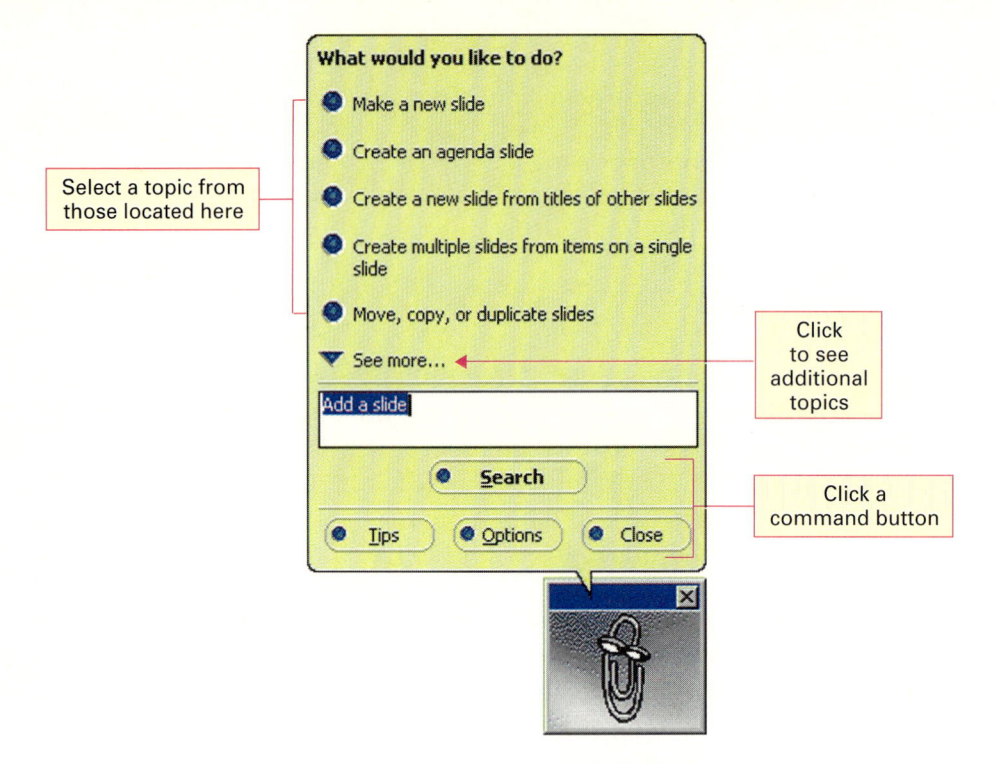

Select a topic from those located here

Click to see additional topics

Click a command button

3 Click the button beside Make a new slide, at the top of the related topics list.

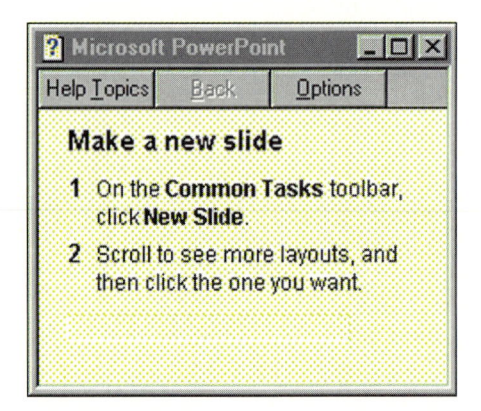

4 Review the information in the help dialog box and then click the Close ⊠ button.
The list of related topics no longer appears on-screen; the Office Assistant remains on-screen until you close it.

5 Click ⊠ on the Office Assistant window.

Getting Help from the Microsoft Web Site

If you're connected to the Internet, you can access the Microsoft Web site to obtain additional help information. The Web provides information directly from Microsoft support team members as well as information from other users.

Overview PP-19

TASK 5: TO ACCESS ONLINE SUPPORT FROM THE WEB:

1 Choose Help, Microsoft on the Web.

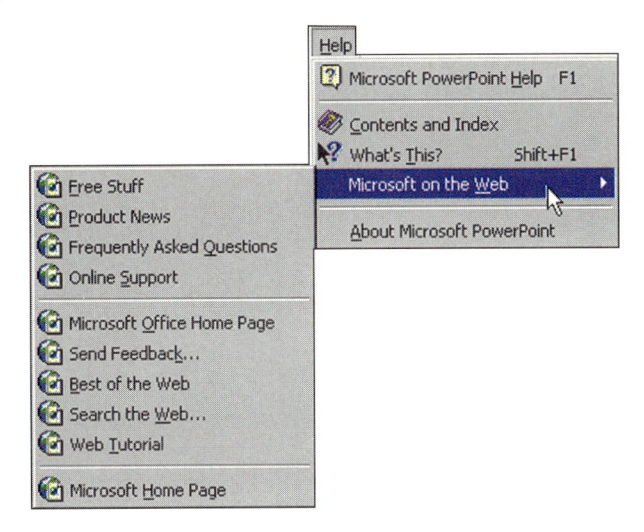

2 Choose Online Support.
Your Internet access window appears.

3 Complete the standard procedure for logging onto the Internet using your service provider.

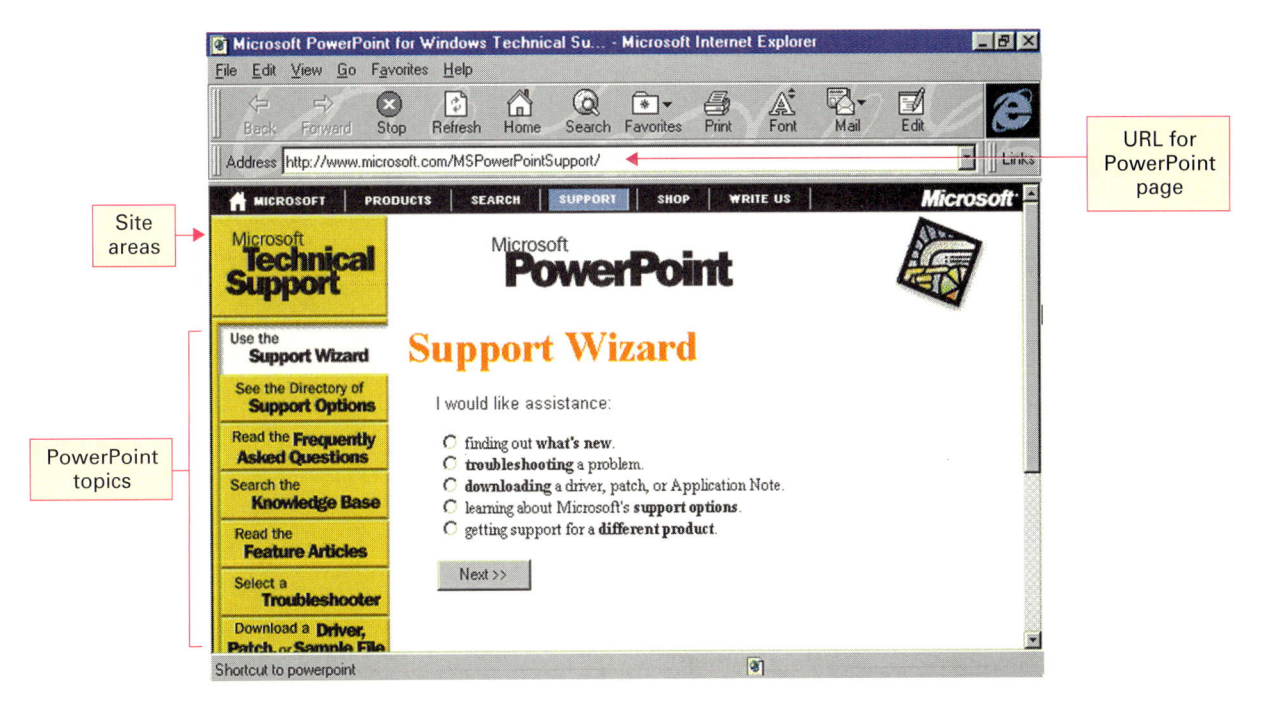

4 Select an option for which you would like assistance and click Next. Explore several help topics when you log on and get a feel for how to navigate online support and find the information you need. Then log off the Internet.

Closing a Presentation and Exiting Microsoft PowerPoint

When you have completed your work on a presentation, you should close it. When you're finished using PowerPoint, you need to exit PowerPoint.

TASK 6: TO CLOSE A PRESENTATION AND EXIT POWERPOINT:

1. Click ⊠ on the presentation window.
   As you close a presentation, PowerPoint examines the presentation and reminds you to save changes by displaying a message window. Click Yes to save changes to the presentation, No to discard changes, or Cancel to return to the presentation.

2. Click ⊠ on the application window.
   If you don't save and close your presentation before exiting, PowerPoint reminds you to save changes you have made since you last saved the presentation.

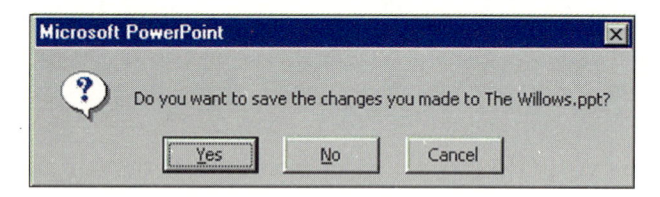

Summary and Exercises

Summary

- Microsoft PowerPoint is a presentation graphics program designed to prepare slide shows.
- Presentations may include handouts, speaker notes, slides, and outlines.
- PowerPoint displays presentations in four different views: Slide View, Outline View, Slide Sorter View, and Notes Pages View. Each view is designed to help you accomplish specific tasks.
- Each presentation may contain numerous slides, each designed to focus on a particular aspect of the broad-based presentation theme.
- Toolbars containing tools needed to accomplish specific tasks appear automatically.
- PowerPoint offers a variety of resources from which you can get online help.
- PowerPoint reminds you to save your changes before you exit the program.

Key Terms and Operations

Key Terms
AutoLayout
master
menu bar
Office Assistant
online help
placeholder
ScreenTip
status bar
template
title bar
toolbar
view

Operations
create a blank PowerPoint presentation
exit Microsoft PowerPoint
get help with Office Assistant
launch Microsoft PowerPoint
retrieve help from the Web

Study Questions

Multiple Choice

1. To display the Help dialog box,
   a. choose Help, Contents, and Index.
   b. click the Office Assistant button.
   c. press Shift+F1.
   d. choose Help, About Microsoft PowerPoint.

2. To start PowerPoint,
   a. double-click the Outlook icon on the desktop.
   b. click Start and choose Microsoft PowerPoint.
   c. start Windows 95 and then press Alt+W.
   d. open My Computer.

3. PowerPoint presentations can be used to generate all of the following except
   a. slides.
   b. handouts.
   c. outlines.
   d. Masters.

4. The PowerPoint view that displays a small slide image at the top of a page and provides space for speaker notes is
   a. Slide view.
   b. Outline view.
   c. Slide Sorter view.
   d. Notes Pages view.

5. When you launch Microsoft PowerPoint,
   a. a new presentation appears.
   b. the Open dialog box appears.
   c. the PowerPoint dialog box appears so that you can tell PowerPoint whether you want to create a presentation or open an existing presentation.
   d. a blank slide appears so that you can enter your title slide.

6. The PowerPoint view that displays only title and body placeholder text is
   a. Slide view.
   b. Outline view.
   c. Slide Sorter view.
   d. Notes Pages view.

7. The PowerPoint view that makes rearranging slides easier is
   a. Slide view.
   b. Outline view.
   c. Slide Sorter view.
   d. Notes Pages view.

8. The term that refers to the layout of objects on slides is
   a. AutoLayout.
   b. Master.
   c. template.
   d. slide.

9. Professional designs that contain graphics and background color schemes you can use to dress up a presentation are called
   a. AutoLayouts.
   b. Masters.
   c. templates.
   d. slides.

10. The basic unit of a presentation is a
    a. slide.
    b. placeholder.
    c. picture.
    d. template.

Short Answer
1. What are the three default toolbars displayed in the Slide view of a presentation?
2. What's the basic object of a presentation?
3. What supporting materials can you generate from a presentation?
4. How many views are available in PowerPoint?
5. Which view allows you to type text into placeholders, create drawings on a slide, and insert other objects on the slide?
6. What toolbar is displayed in Outline view that doesn't appear in Slide View?
7. What are AutoLayouts?
8. What six things should you consider as you plan your presentation?
9. What does a grayed menu command indicate?
10. What features are available on the World Wide Web to help you as you work with PowerPoint?

For Discussion
1. How does the procedure for launching Microsoft PowerPoint differ from the procedure for launching other Windows 95 applications?
2. Why is planning your presentation important?
3. What's the difference between AutoLayout formats, templates, and Masters?
4. How does the phrase "Less is more" relate to presentations?

Review Exercises

1. Designing a New Presentation
The Willows Marketing department needs a presentation about the sports facilities at the resort. Marketing representatives will use the presentation during sales conferences and trade shows to provide an overview of the resort to prospective guests and convention planners. The Willows sporting facilities are listed in Table 0.2 on the next page. Use this list to develop a plan for the Marketing department presentation.

Table 0.2 The Willows Sporting Facilities

Facility	Features
Golf	Three 18-hole PGA courses Two driving ranges Five practice putting greens
Tennis	Ten asphalt courts Two clay courts Two grass courts
Exercise/Aerobic Center	Three saunas Four whirlpools Three massage beds scheduled by appointment Personal trainers Step aerobic classes twice daily Low impact aerobic classes daily
Miniature golf	Two 18-hole courses (Bye Bye Birdie and The Eagle's Nest)
Little Tree Playground	Heavy duty playground equipment for young children
Willow Pond Riding Stables	Fifteen horses One-, two-, and three-hour bridle paths Bicycle rentals
Willows Water Park	Wave pool Water slides Olympic-size swimming pool
The Willows Beach Front	Five miles of Atlantic Coast beach with lifeguards, a boardwalk, jet-ski rentals, surfing, etc.

2. Getting Help

Because PowerPoint comes with professionally designed templates you can use to dress up your presentation, you need to know how to apply the templates to presentations you develop. Ask the Office Assistant to locate information about applying a template to an existing presentation.

1. Click the Office Assistant button on the toolbar.

2. Type **How do I apply a template to a presentation?** in the question box of the Office Assistant window and press (ENTER).

3. Click Apply a different design to a presentation in the list of items the Office Assistant displays.

4. Review the information in the Help window.

5. Click the Show me button at the top of the Help window and watch as PowerPoint identifies the Apply Design button on the toolbar.

6. Click the Apply Design button twice to display the Apply Design dialog box.

7. Click a template name in the list of templates to display a sample of the template in the view area of the dialog box.

> **Tip** If the view area isn't displayed in the Apply Design dialog box, click the Preview button on the Apply Design toolbar to display the view area.

Assignments

1. Designing a Personal Presentation
The Willows posted a notice in the newspaper, advertising the position of design specialist in the Marketing department. As a response to the advertisement, develop a presentation outline on paper, based on your résumé, to accompany your official résumé and letter of application. Design the presentation so that it adequately relates your skills and talents.

2. Searching the Internet for Images
The Willows would like to vary the graphics included in its presentations and publications to better reflect the topics presented. Search the World Wide Web for pictures that relate to sports that you might want to include in the Sports Facilities presentation you designed earlier. Download these images to a floppy disk and make a list of filenames for the images you find.

Do not download copyrighted images.

PROJECT 1

Building a Presentation

To be effective, each presentation you create should be designed to achieve an objective. Whether the objective of the presentation is to sell a product or provide information, you can sketch out the presentation plan on paper and then create the presentation on the computer using PowerPoint. In this project, you create a blank presentation and begin building the presentation using both the Slide view and the Outline view.

Objectives

After completing this project, you will be able to:

➤ Create a blank presentation and a title slide
➤ Save and close a presentation
➤ Open a presentation and add slides
➤ Navigate a presentation
➤ Apply a template
➤ Switch views
➤ Add text in Outline view
➤ Print slides as handouts and presentation outlines

The Challenge

The managers at The Willows decided at a recent meeting that they would like to have someone develop a graphic presentation describing some of the features available at The Willows. The presentation should identify each of the facilities and give a brief description of them.

PP-26

The Solution

As the graphic artist employed by The Willows, you have been asked to put your creative talents to work designing an effective presentation. Use PowerPoint to create a new presentation, add text to the slides, and format and save your presentation by following the steps presented in the tasks that follow. Figure 1.1 shows the first five slides one of the managers sketched for the presentation.

Slide 1 — The Willows
Where Neighbors Become Friends

Slide 2 — Featuring...
- Lodging
- Fine Dining
- A Taste of the Land
- The Joys of the Sea

Slide 3 — The Grande Hotel
- Guest Rooms
- Shops
- Restaurants
- Meeting Rooms
- Exercise Facility
- Pool and Sun Deck

Slide 4 — Willows Beach Cottages
- Luxury living in a cottage setting
  - Two Bedrooms in each Cottage
  - Additional Sofa Bed in the Living Area
  - King and Queen Size Beds
- Fully Stocked Kitchen Facilities
- Nestled Among the Links

Slide 5 — The Facilities
- Golf and Tennis
- Exercise and Aerobics
- Miniature Golf
- Playground
- Riding Stables
- Water Park

Figure 1.1

The Setup

Just to make sure that you're on the same screen as your book, you may want to check some of the settings before you get started. This book assumes that the default settings were in place when the lab guru installed PowerPoint on the machine. However, because some students nose around where they shouldn't, some of the settings may have changed.

If you don't see the default toolbars on the screen when you open a blank presentation, choose View, Toolbars. Then click Standard, Formatting, and Common Tasks and/or Drawing to display the missing toolbar(s). If you see extra toolbars, close them. PowerPoint automatically displays appropriate toolbars as you work with different views and features in the presentation, so don't be surprised when something new pops up.

If you don't see a status bar, choose Tools, Options. When the Options dialog box displays, click the View page tab and then click the check box beside Status Bar at the top of the page. While you're in the Options dialog box, check to make sure that all options on the View page tab of the dialog box are checked except the last one—end with black slide.

If rulers appear below the toolbars and down the left side of your presentation window, you can hide them, if desired, by choosing View, Ruler. You can close the Office Assistant, or leave it active. Most of the illustrations and figures don't show the Office Assistant, but you know it's there when you need it.

Creating a Blank Presentation and a Title Slide

The Blank presentation option in the opening PowerPoint dialog box lets you create a "plain vanilla" presentation with standard text format, no color, and no graphics.

Each time you create a new presentation or add a slide to an existing presentation, PowerPoint displays the New Slide dialog box, which contains 24 *AutoLayout* formats. Each AutoLayout format contains placeholders that outline the areas of the slide set aside to contain text and graphic *objects* you can include on the slide. The first slide in a presentation is generally formatted with the Title AutoLayout format.

Project 1: Building a Presentation PP-29

TASK 1: TO CREATE A NEW BLANK PRESENTATION WITH A TITLE SLIDE:

1. Launch PowerPoint.

2. Click the Blank presentation option in the PowerPoint dialog box and then click OK.

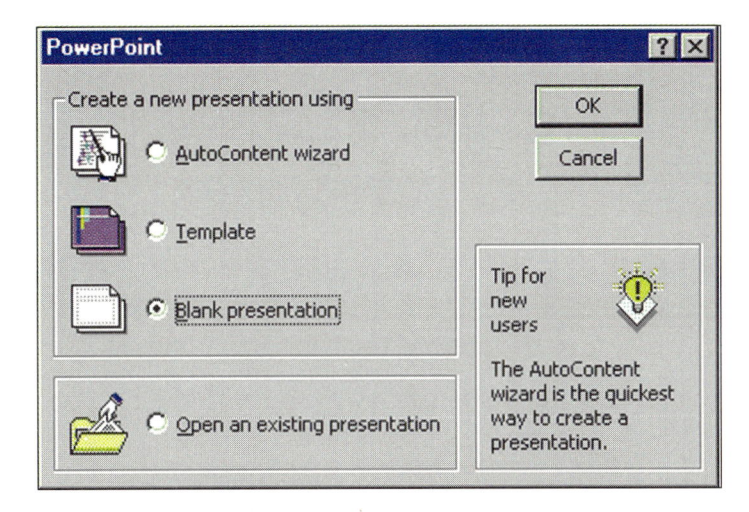

3. Click OK to accept the Title Slide AutoLayout format for the first slide.

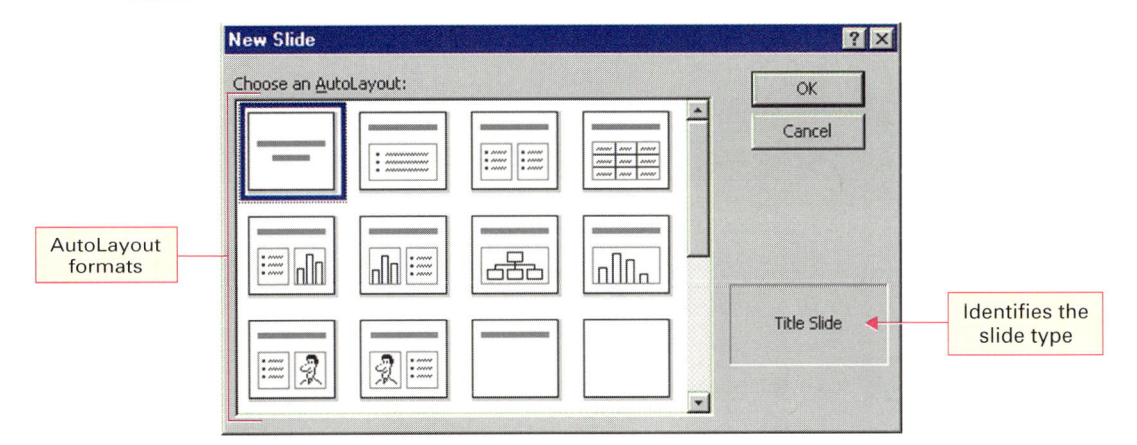

AutoLayout formats

Identifies the slide type

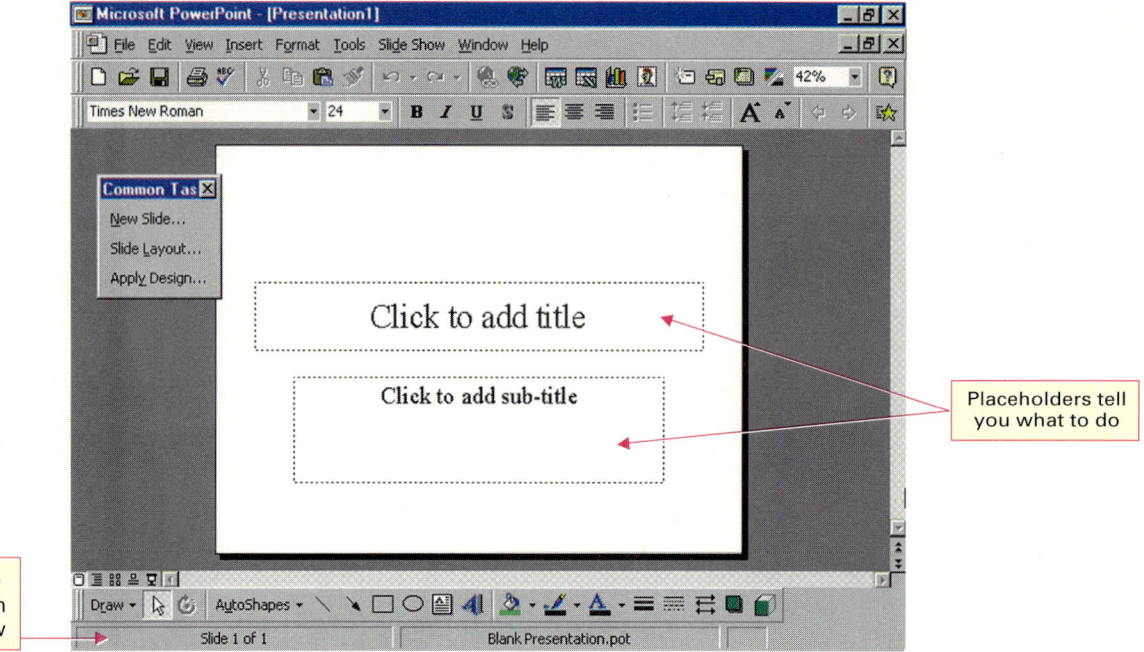

PP-30

Slide one appears in Slide view

Placeholders tell you what to do

4 Click the title placeholder.
The placeholder border is selected and the insertion point appears at the center, replacing the instruction text.

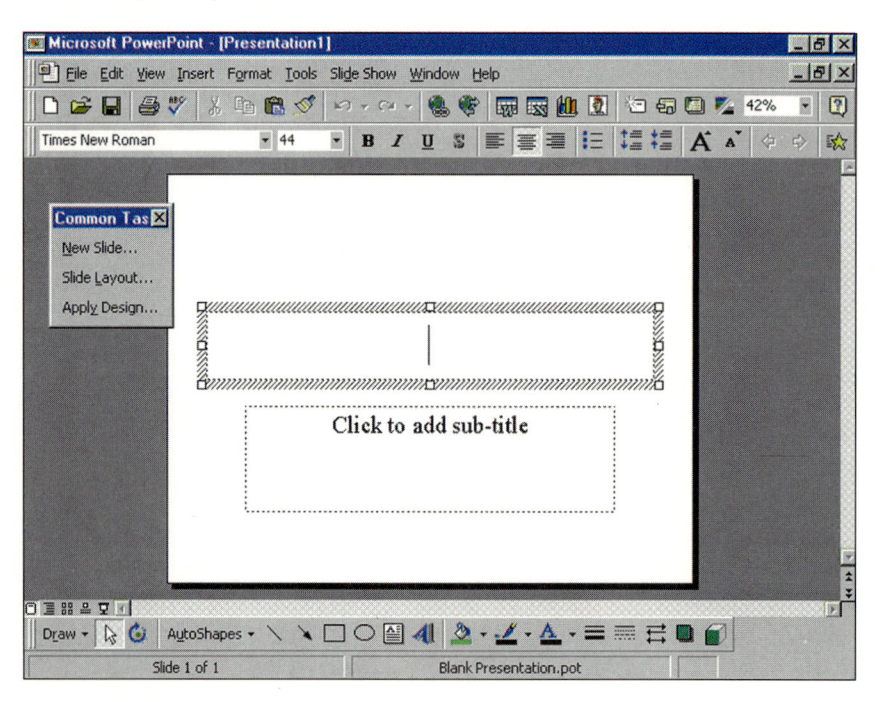

Project 1: Building a Presentation   PP-31

5 Type **The Willows** in the title placeholder.

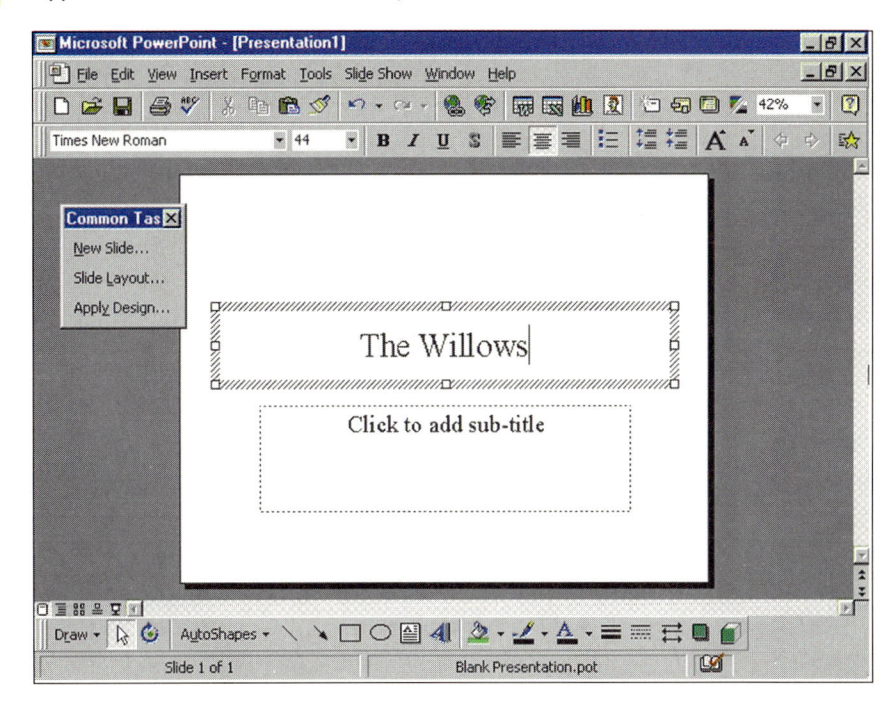

6 Press (CTRL)+(ENTER) to move to the subtitle placeholder. This area is selected and the instruction text is replaced by the insertion point.

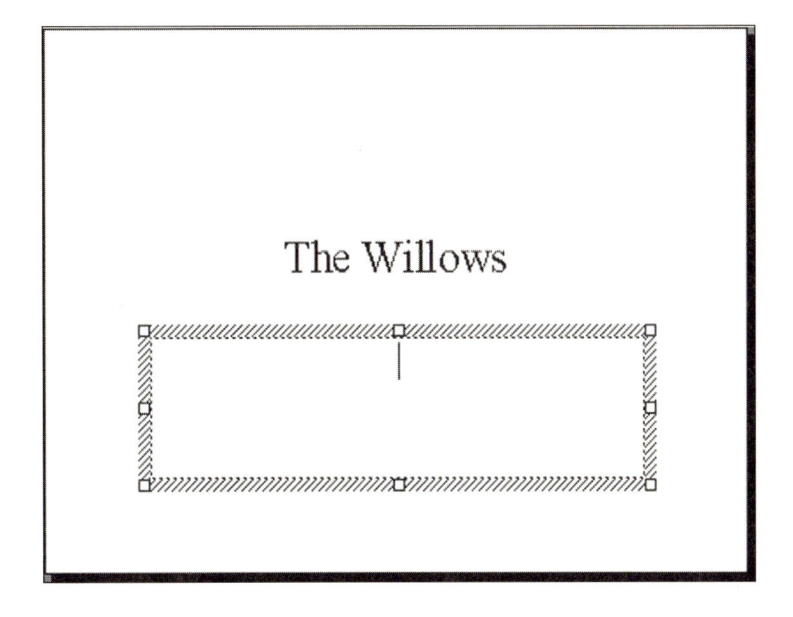

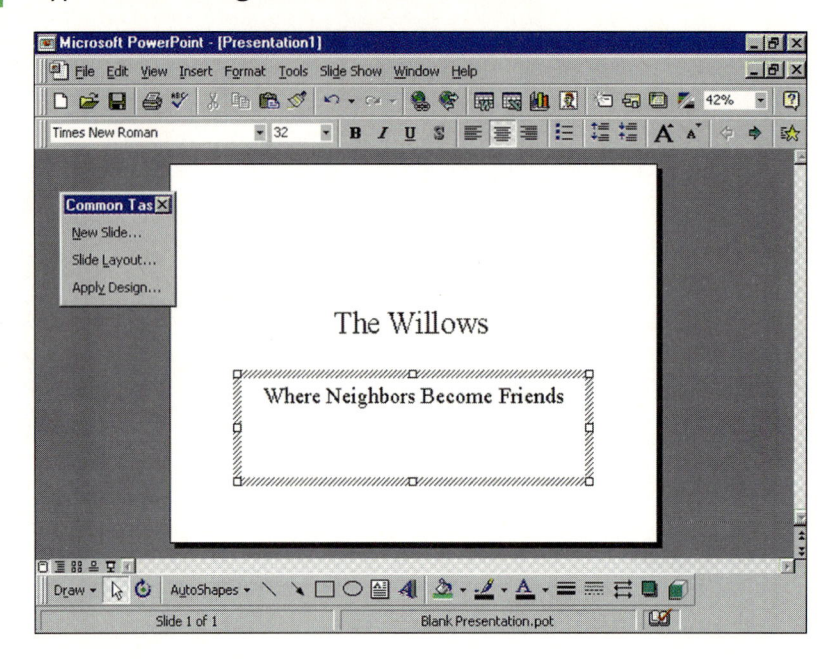

7 Type **Where Neighbors Become Friends**.

Saving and Closing a Presentation

You can use the same procedures to save a presentation in PowerPoint that you use to save files in other Windows 95 applications. All slides in the presentation are stored in one file. When you save a presentation for the first time, the Save dialog box opens the *My Documents* folder unless someone told PowerPoint to store files somewhere else. If you want to store your presentation in a different folder or on a different disk, you need to open the disk and folder before saving.

TASK 2: TO SAVE AND CLOSE A PRESENTATION:

1 Click the Save button on the Standard toolbar.

2 Select a folder to store the presentation.
The folder you choose to store your document should appear in the Save in text box at the top of the Save window.

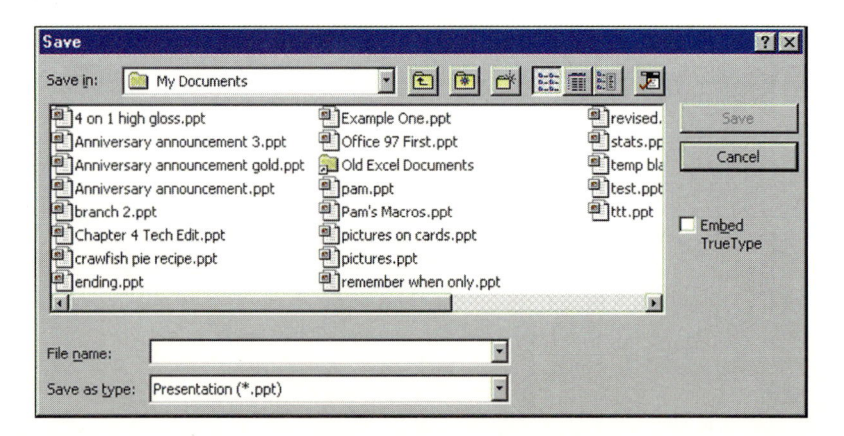

3 Type **The Willows** in the file name box and press (ENTER) or click the Save button.

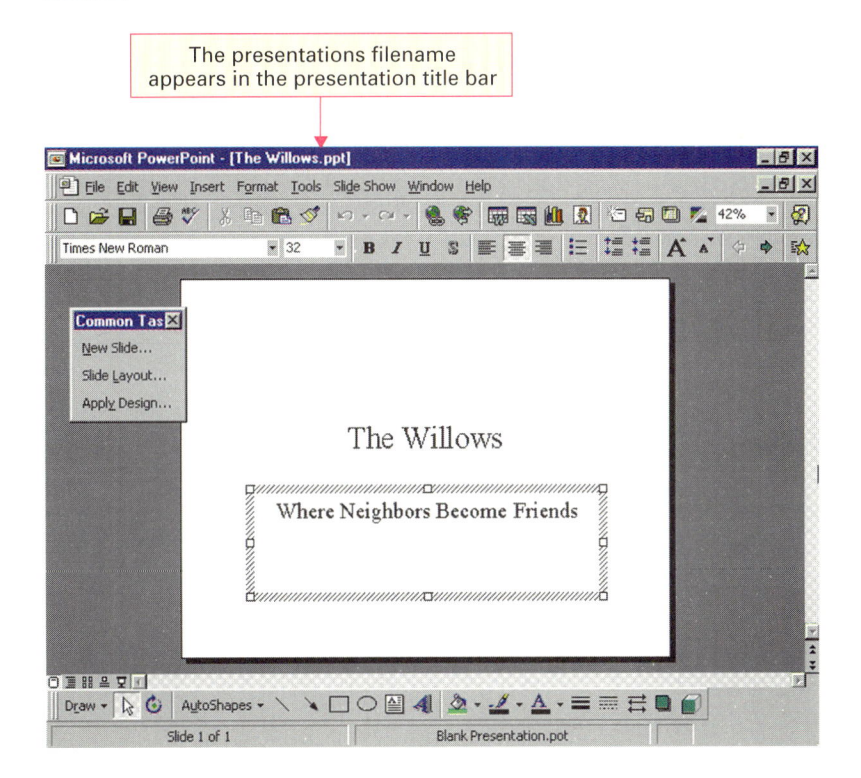

The presentations filename appears in the presentation title bar

4 Click the Close ⊠ button for the presentation window to close the presentation.

> **Note** To create a new blank presentation after closing a presentation, click the New button on the Standard toolbar.

Opening a Presentation and Adding Slides

Most presentations consist of a series of slides, each devoted to a particular topic you want to cover in the presentation. Behind each topic slide you often need to add slides to provide explanatory information about the topic, or supporting documentation. When you want to add slides to an existing presentation, you need to open the presentation and display the slide that the new slide(s) will follow.

The procedures you use to open a presentation when PowerPoint is running are the same procedures you use to open files in most Windows 95 applications. You can also select the Open an existing presentation option from the PowerPoint dialog box when you launch PowerPoint.

PP-34

TASK 3: TO OPEN A PRESENTATION AND ADD SLIDES:

1 Click the Open button.

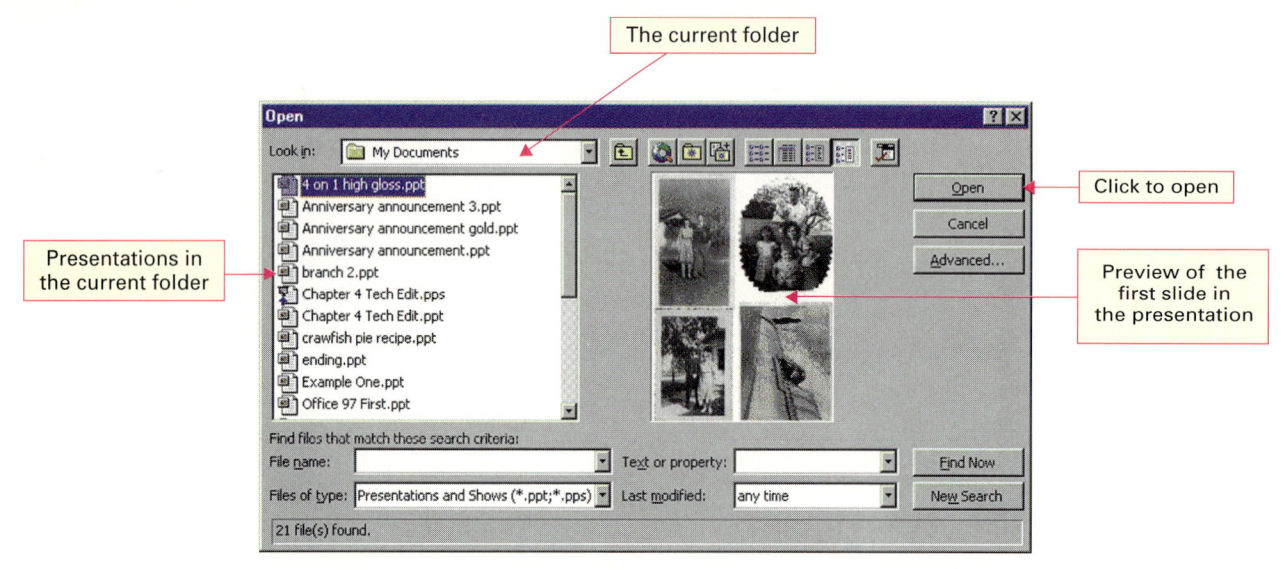

- The current folder
- Presentations in the current folder
- Click to open
- Preview of the first slide in the presentation

2 Select the folder containing your presentation from the Look in drop-down list and double-click the presentation called *The Willows*.

3 Click New Slide in the Common Tasks toolbar.

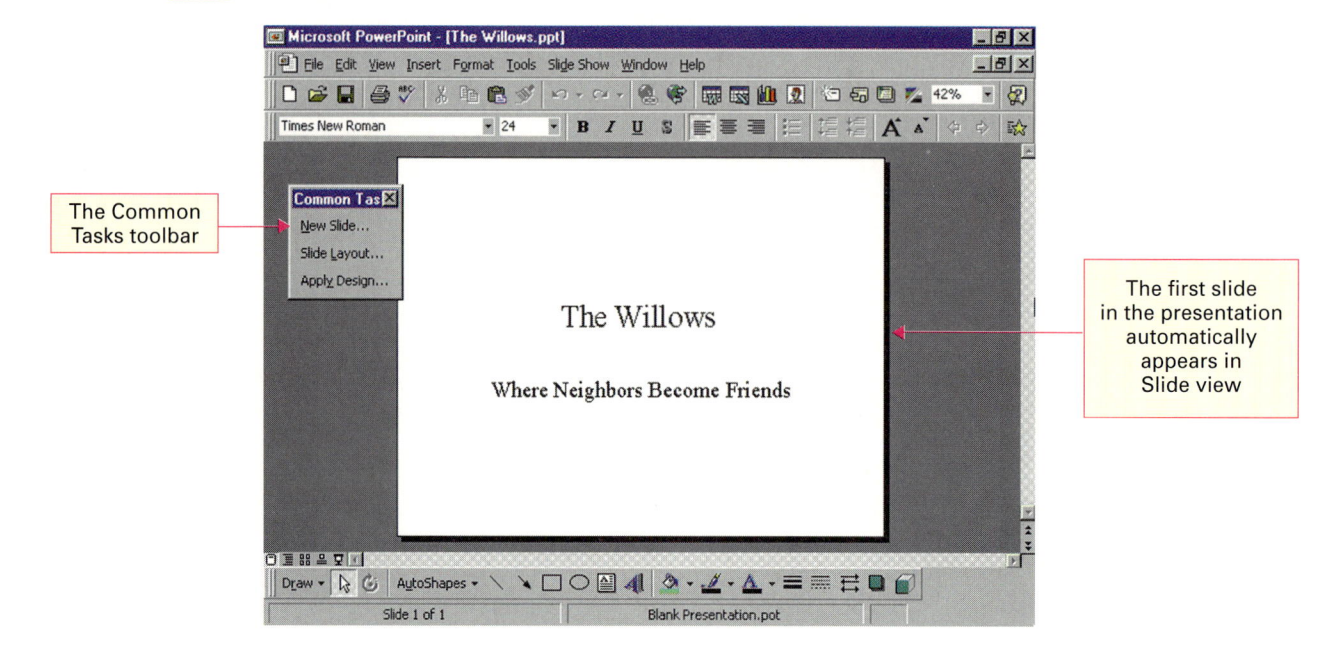

- The Common Tasks toolbar
- The first slide in the presentation automatically appears in Slide view

Project 1: Building a Presentation   **PP-35**

4 Click the Bulleted List AutoLayout format, if necessary, and click OK.

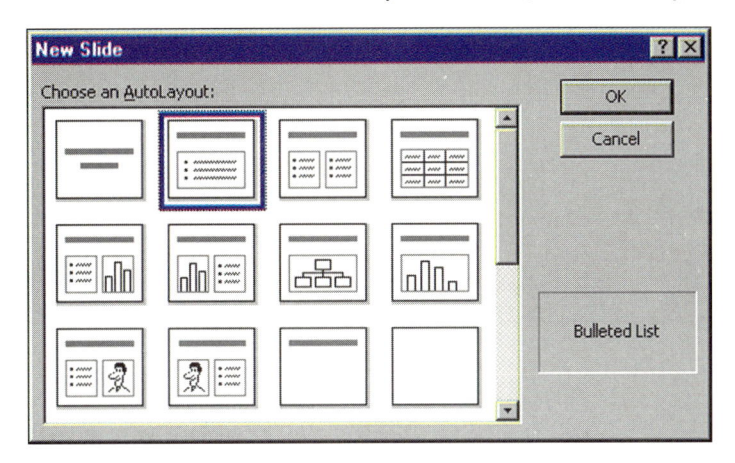

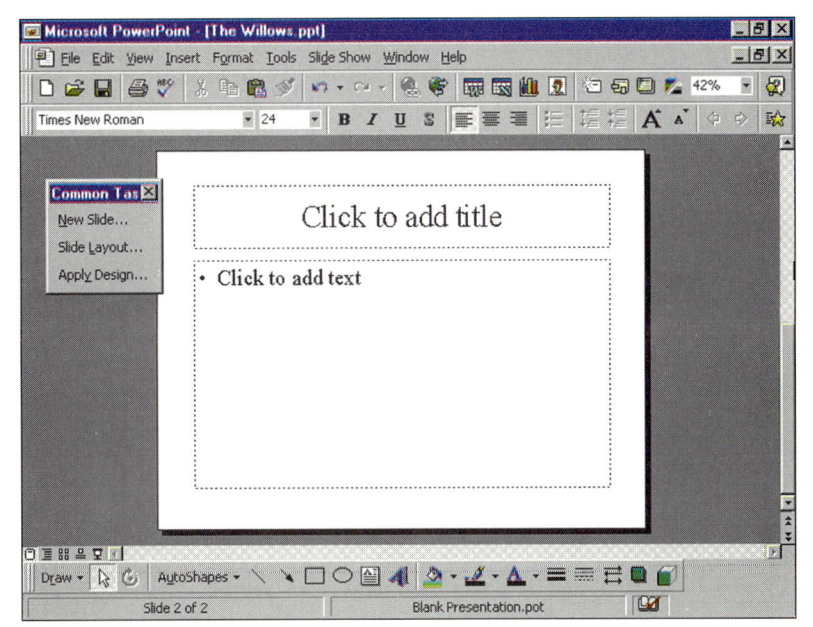

5 Click the title placeholder and type **Featuring . . .**

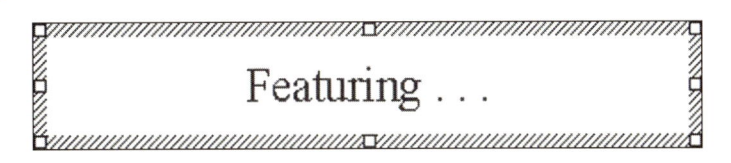

6 Click the bulleted list placeholder; then type **Lodging** and press ENTER.

- Lodging

7 Type **Fine Dining** and press ENTER.

- Lodging
- Fine Dining

8 Repeat step 7, substituting the text shown below for the last two bulleted items:

- Lodging
- Fine Dining
- A Taste of the Land
- The Joys of the Sea

9 Press CTRL+ENTER to create another new bulleted list slide.

> **Note** Pressing Ctrl+Enter from any other placeholder activates the next placeholder on the slide instead of creating a new slide.

Project 1: Building a Presentation   PP-37

Navigating a Presentation

As you build your presentation and your presentation begins to grow, you need to be able to navigate among the slides to display the slides you need to edit or review. You can use both the mouse and keyboard to display different slides in Slide view. Figure 1.2 identifies techniques for navigating slides using the mouse.

Check the status bar to identify the active slide number and the total number of slides in the presentation

Drag to display the slide number and a portion of the slide title

Click to display the previous slide

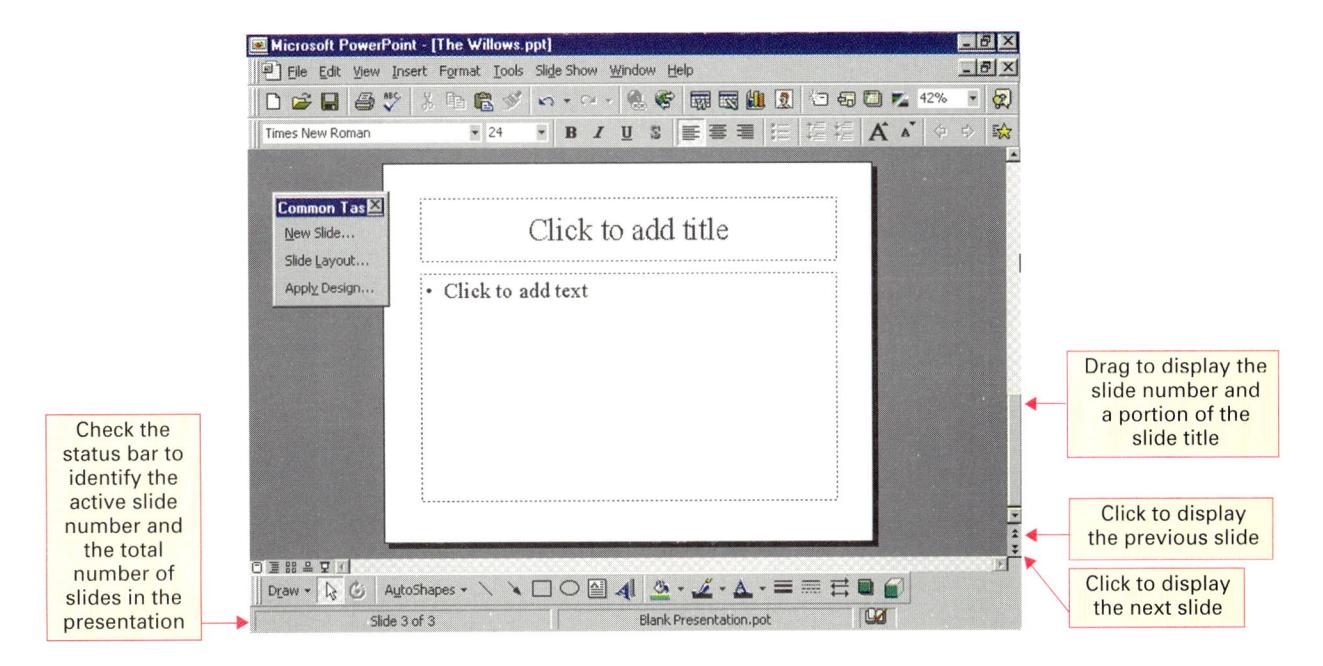

Click to display the next slide

Figure 1.2

TASK 4: TO NAVIGATE SLIDES IN A PRESENTATION:

1. Press (PGUP) to display Slide 2 of the presentation *The Willows*.
2. Press (CTRL)+(HOME) to display the first slide in the presentation.
3. Press (PGDN) to display Slide 2 of the presentation.
4. Press (CTRL)+(END) to display the last slide in the presentation.
5. Click the Show Previous Slide button to display Slide 2.
6. Click the scroll box and drag it to the top of the scroll bar to display Slide 1.

Applying a Template

PowerPoint provides a number of ***templates*** that you can use to enhance the look of your presentation. Templates provide the style, color, and pizzazz your presentation needs to attract the attention of your audience. Templates hold special font formats and text alignments, background color, and bullet formats for text contained in placeholders of the presentation. Applying a template to a presentation helps maintain consistency among the slides in your presentation.

Templates are stored in a special *Templates* folder that automatically opens when you choose a template command from the menu or toolbars. When you apply a template, all slides in the presentation are automatically formatted with the template design.

TASK 5: TO APPLY A TEMPLATE TO A PRESENTATION:

1 Click Apply Design in the Common Tasks toolbar.

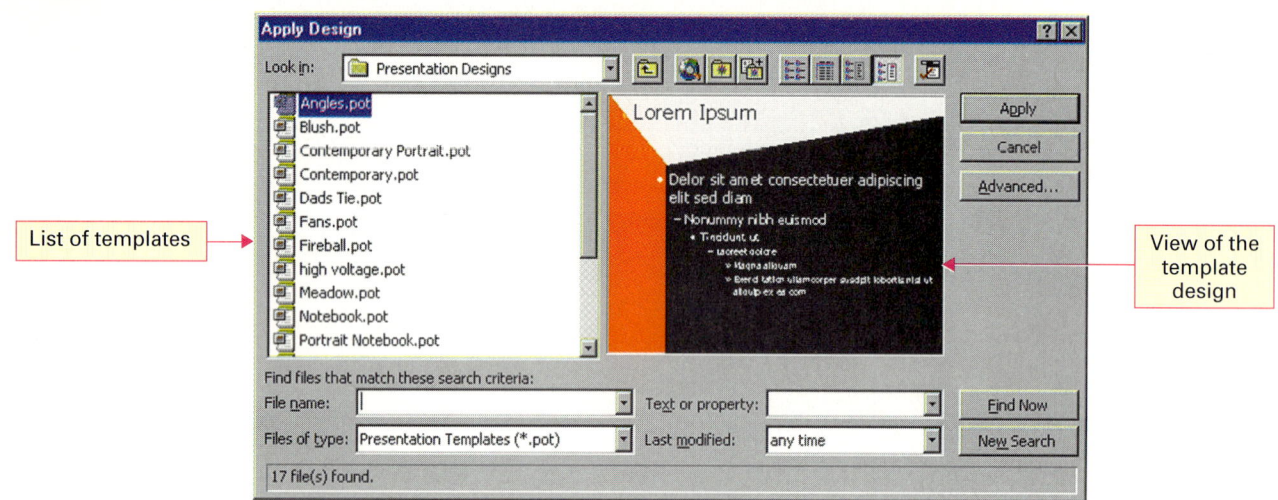

List of templates

View of the template design

2 Click Fireball.pot and view the template design.

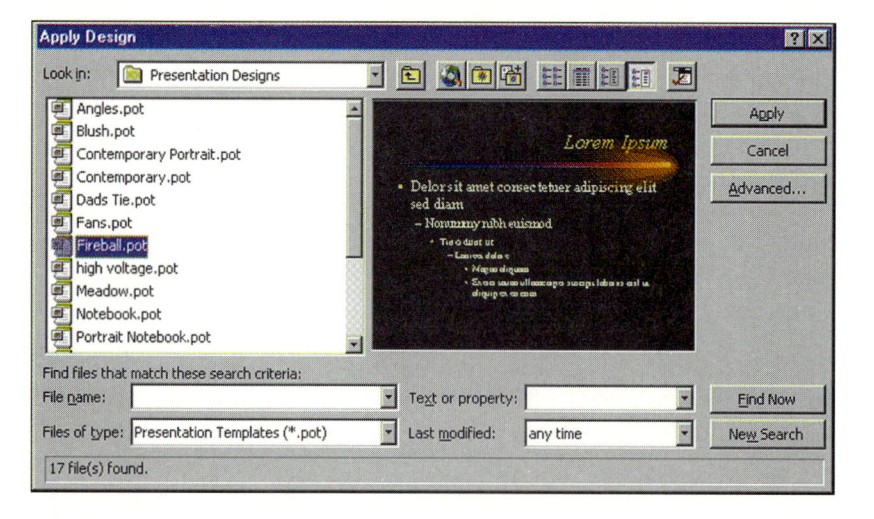

Project 1: Building a Presentation   PP-39

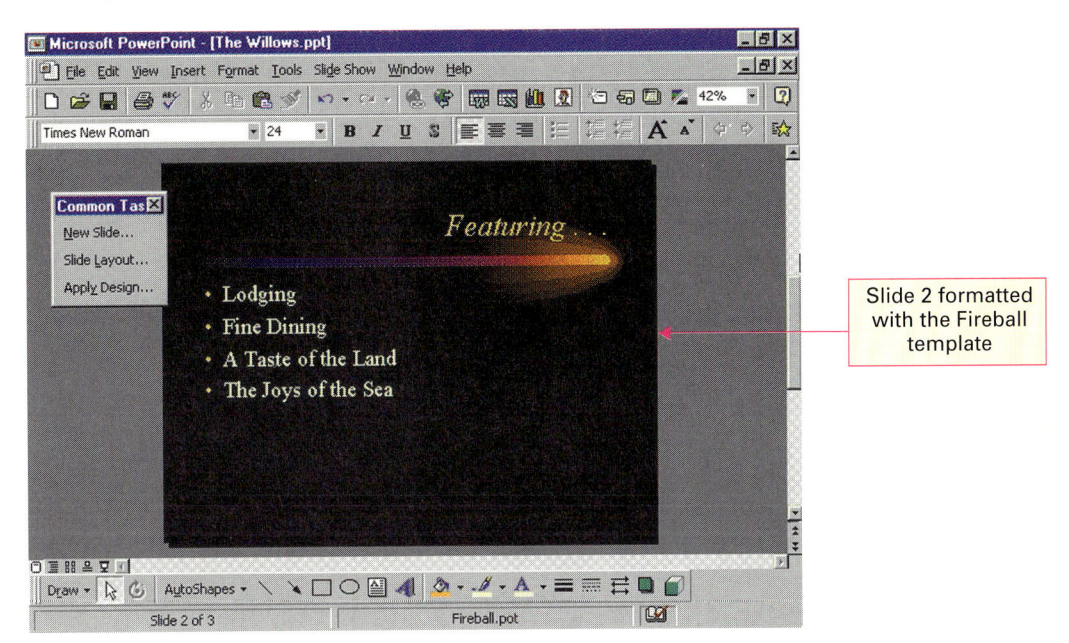

3 Click Apply to apply the template to the presentation.

Slide 2 formatted with the Fireball template

Switching Views

When you want to review the flow of a presentation or view all slides after applying a new slide format or design, you can display your presentation using a different view. The default view, the view you have been working in, is called slide view. Slide Sorter view displays small images (often called *thumbnail images*) of each slide in the presentation so that you can review the effects of applying a template design to all the slides in the presentation. Outline view displays the title and body text you add to placeholders in a notebook-like format so you can review the content of the presentation.

TASK 6: TO SWITCH VIEWS:

1 Position the mouse pointer on the third view button at the bottom of the presentation window.

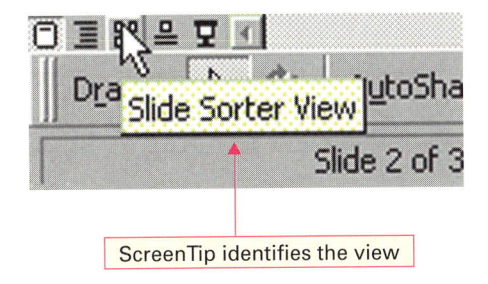

ScreenTip identifies the view

2 Click the Slide Sorter View button.

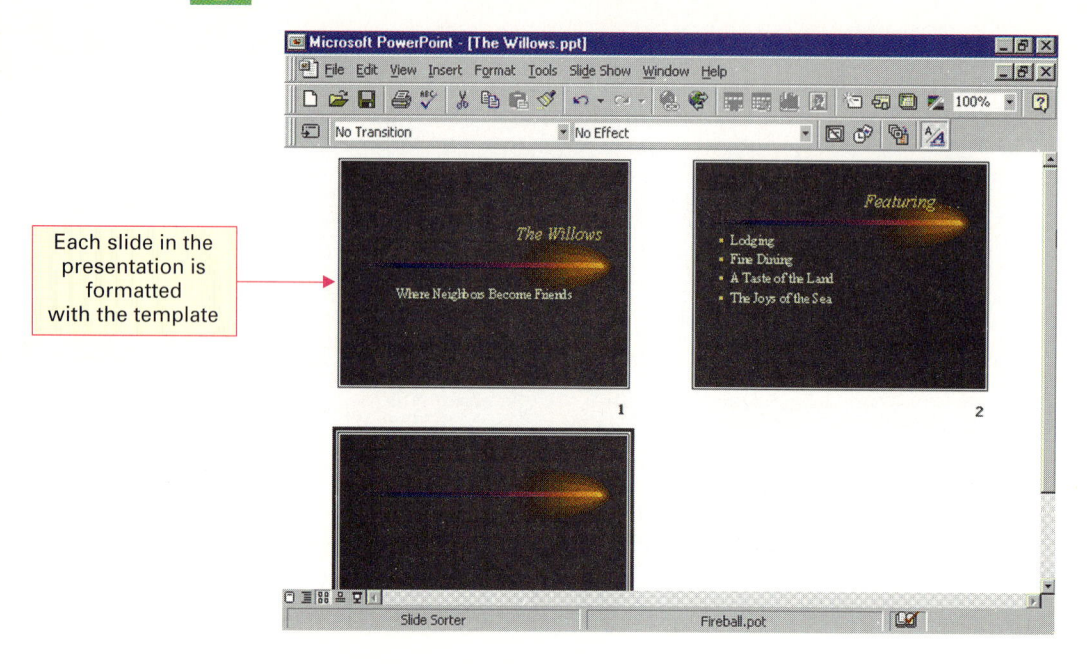

Each slide in the presentation is formatted with the template

Tip If the Common Tasks toolbar gets in your way, point to the toolbar's title bar and drag it out of the way.

3 Click Slide 3 and then click the Outline View button. Title and body placeholder text shows the slide content.

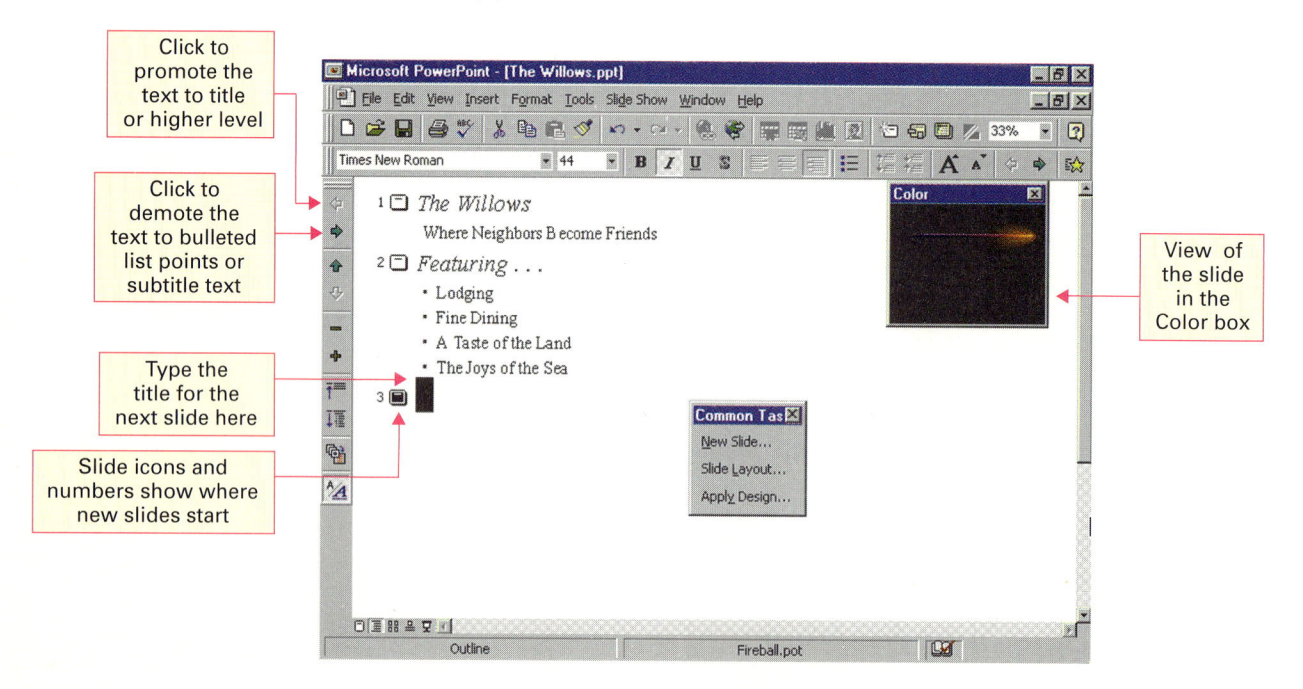

Click to promote the text to title or higher level

Click to demote the text to bulleted list points or subtitle text

Type the title for the next slide here

Slide icons and numbers show where new slides start

View of the slide in the Color box

PP-40

Adding Text in Outline View

When you have developed an outline of text and information you want to include in a presentation, you'll find that Outline view enables you to type the title and body text for your slides more quickly. PowerPoint provides formatting for five levels of text plus the title text on a slide. You can move to the next text level by pressing Tab and return to a higher text level by pressing Shift+Tab. When you finish typing the outline text, you can view the slides in Slide view and add graphics and other enhancements to individual slides or apply a presentation design to all slides.

TASK 7: TO ADD TEXT IN OUTLINE VIEW:

1. Type **The Grande Hotel** as the title for Slide 3 and press ENTER.

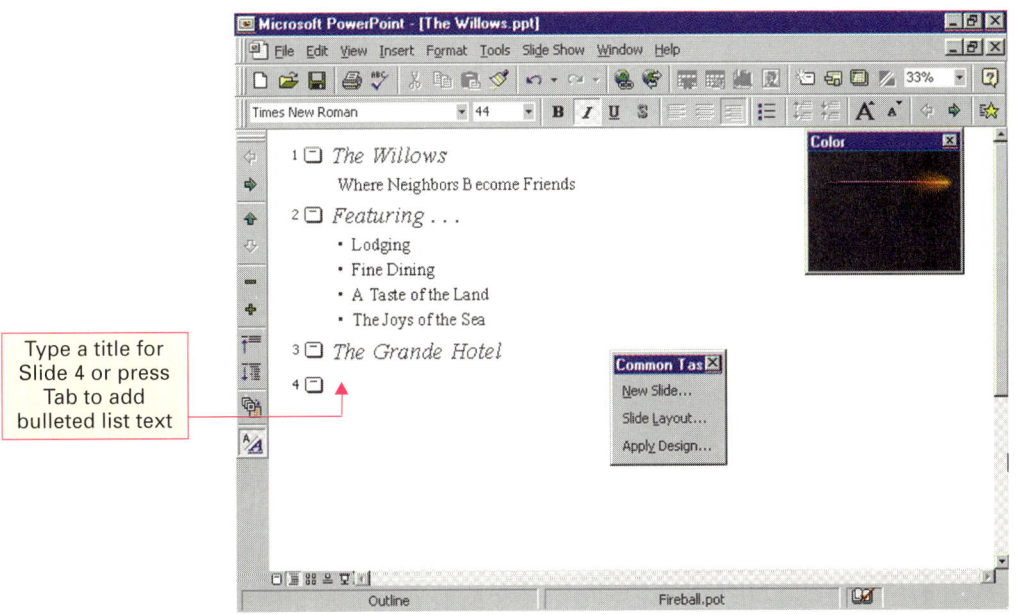

    Type a title for Slide 4 or press Tab to add bulleted list text

2. Press TAB to add the bulleted list text and then type:

    Guest Rooms
    Shops
    Restaurants
    Meeting Rooms
    Exercise Facility
    Pool and Sun Deck

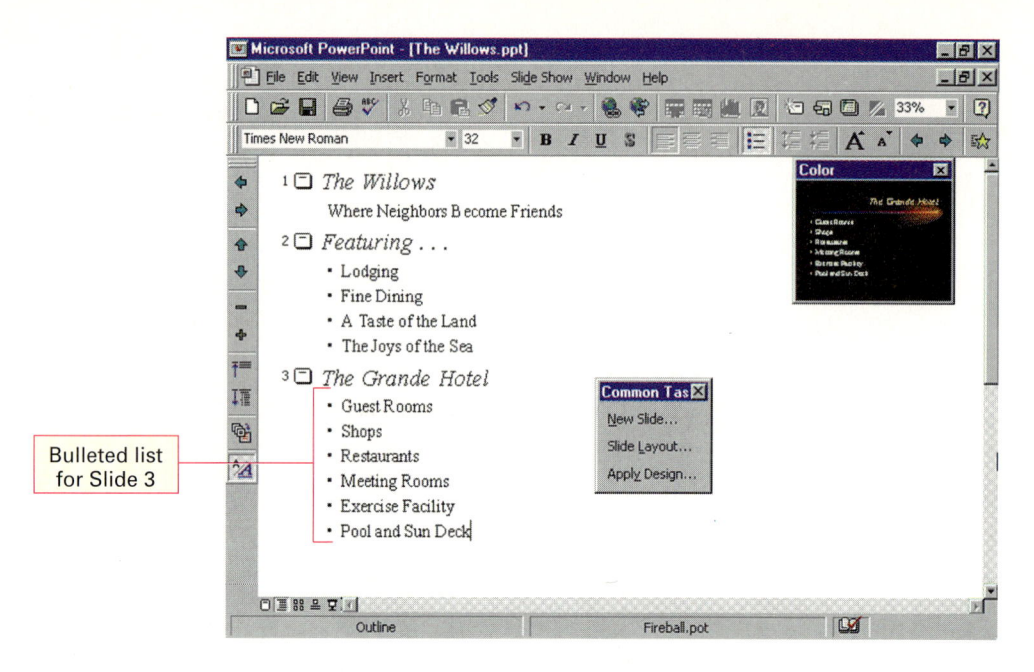

PP-42

Bulleted list for Slide 3 (annotation pointing to Slide 3 bullets)

Screenshot — Microsoft PowerPoint - [The Willows.ppt]:

1. *The Willows*
   - Where Neighbors Become Friends
2. *Featuring . . .*
   - Lodging
   - Fine Dining
   - A Taste of the Land
   - The Joys of the Sea
3. *The Grande Hotel*
   - Guest Rooms
   - Shops
   - Restaurants
   - Meeting Rooms
   - Exercise Facility
   - Pool and Sun Deck

3 Press ENTER after typing the last bullet point and then press CTRL+ENTER to start a new slide. Continue typing to create the following slides:

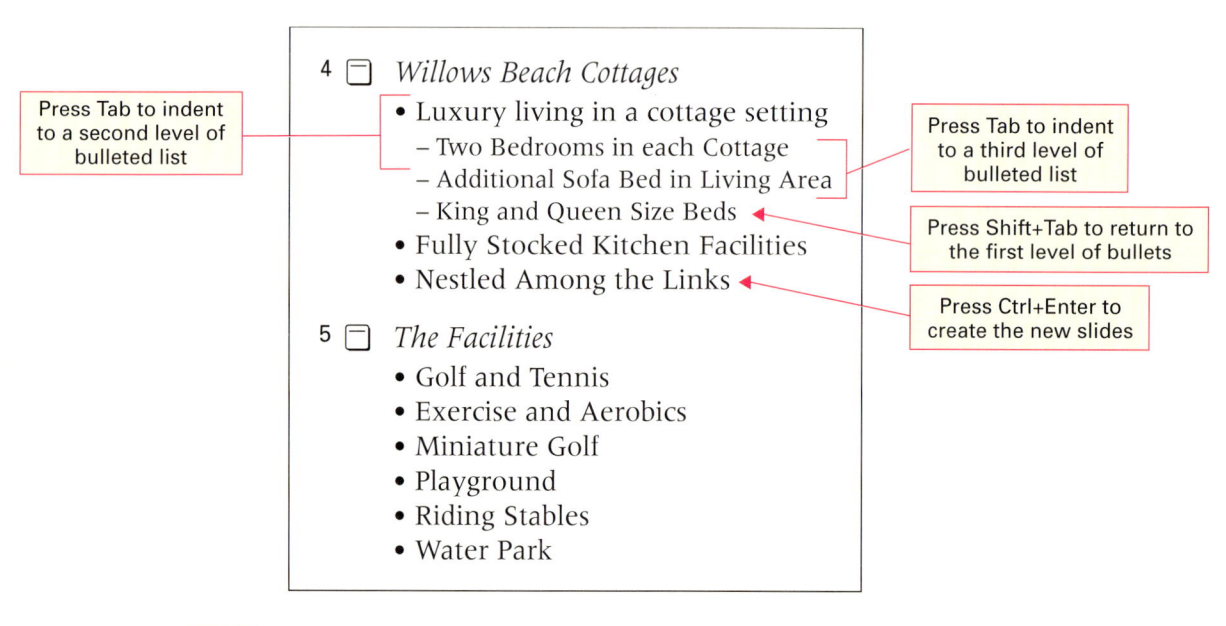

4. *Willows Beach Cottages*
   - Luxury living in a cottage setting
     – Two Bedrooms in each Cottage
     – Additional Sofa Bed in Living Area
     – King and Queen Size Beds
   - Fully Stocked Kitchen Facilities
   - Nestled Among the Links

5. *The Facilities*
   - Golf and Tennis
   - Exercise and Aerobics
   - Miniature Golf
   - Playground
   - Riding Stables
   - Water Park

Press Tab to indent to a second level of bulleted list

Press Tab to indent to a third level of bulleted list

Press Shift+Tab to return to the first level of bullets

Press Ctrl+Enter to create the new slides

4 Save the changes to the presentation.

Project 1: Building a Presentation   PP-43

Printing Slides, Handouts, and Presentation Outlines

Because PowerPoint is primarily a graphically oriented program and can print your presentation in a variety of formats, the Print dialog box contains features and options unique to PowerPoint. For example, you can print each slide individually on a sheet of paper, print multiple slides on the same page in a format called *handouts*, or print the Outline view of your presentation. Figure 1.3 identifies additional print options that you can set to control the quality of the print for different types of printers.

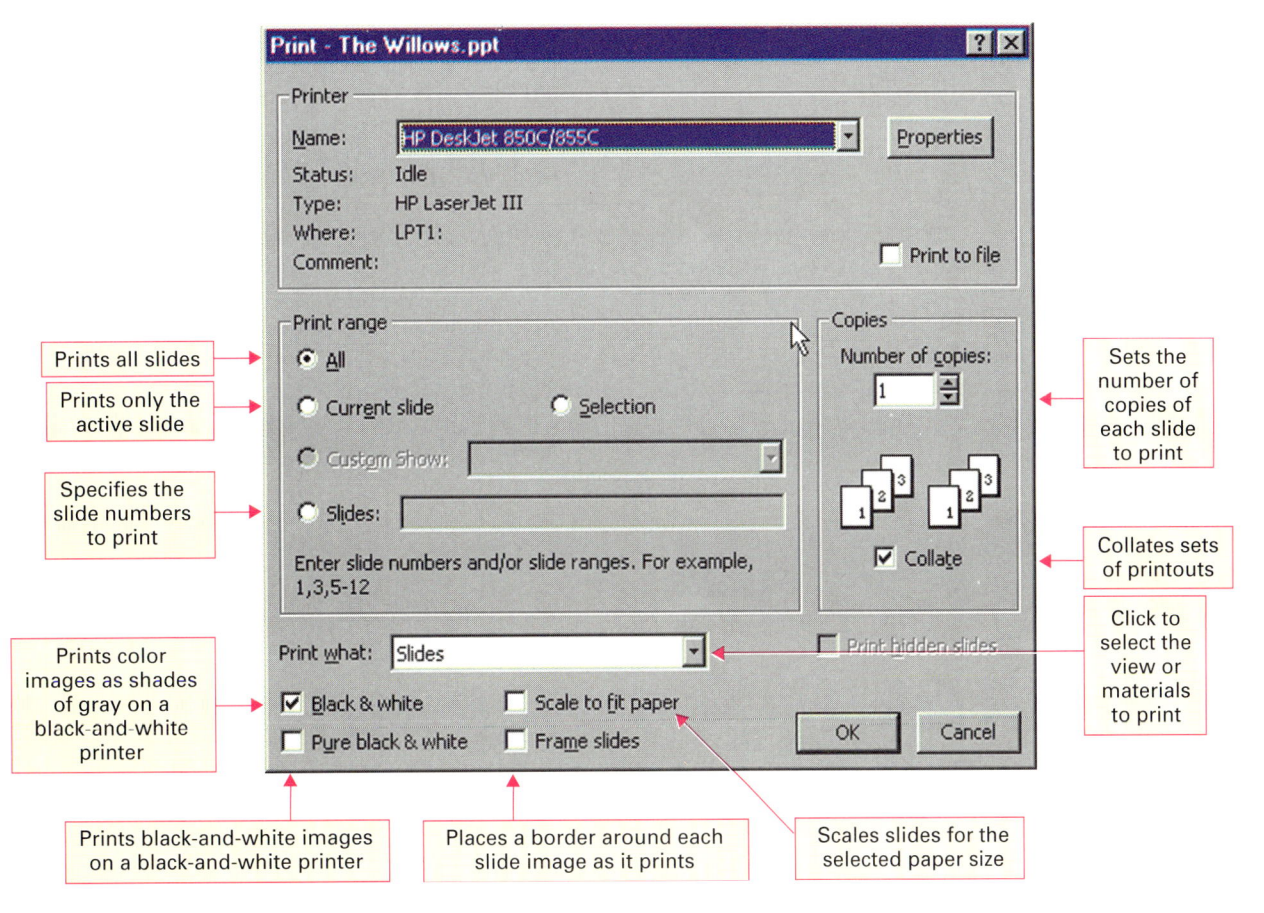

Callouts around the Print dialog box:
- Prints all slides → All
- Prints only the active slide → Current slide
- Specifies the slide numbers to print → Slides:
- Prints color images as shades of gray on a black-and-white printer
- Prints black-and-white images on a black-and-white printer
- Places a border around each slide image as it prints
- Scales slides for the selected paper size
- Sets the number of copies of each slide to print
- Collates sets of printouts
- Click to select the view or materials to print

Figure 1.3

TASK 8: TO PRINT SLIDES AND OUTLINES:

1. Choose File, Print to display the Print dialog box shown in Figure 1.3.

   Tip To bypass the Print dialog box and print the complete presentation using the print settings last set, click the Print button on the Standard toolbar. Each time you launch PowerPoint, the print settings return to the default settings.

2. Click the drop-down arrow at the end of the Print What text box.

PP-44

3 Click Handouts (Six Slides per Page).

4 Click the Black & White check box, if necessary, and click OK. PowerPoint compiles the slides, sizes them for printing together on one page, and then prints the slides (see Figure 1.4).

Featuring...

The Willows

Where Neighbors Become Friends

- Lodging
- Fine Dining
- A Taste of the Land
- The Joys of the Sea

The Grande Hotel

- Guest Rooms
- Shops
- Restaurants
- Meeting Rooms
- Exercise Facility
- Pool and Sun Deck

Willows Beach Cottages

- Luxury Living in a Cottage Setting
  – Two Bedrooms in each Cottage
  – Additional Sofa Bed in the Living Area
  – King and Queen Size Beds
- Fully Stocked Kitchen Facilities
- Nestled Among the Links

The Facilities

- Golf and Tennis
- Exercise and Aerobics
- Miniature Golf
- Playground
- Riding Stables
- Water Park

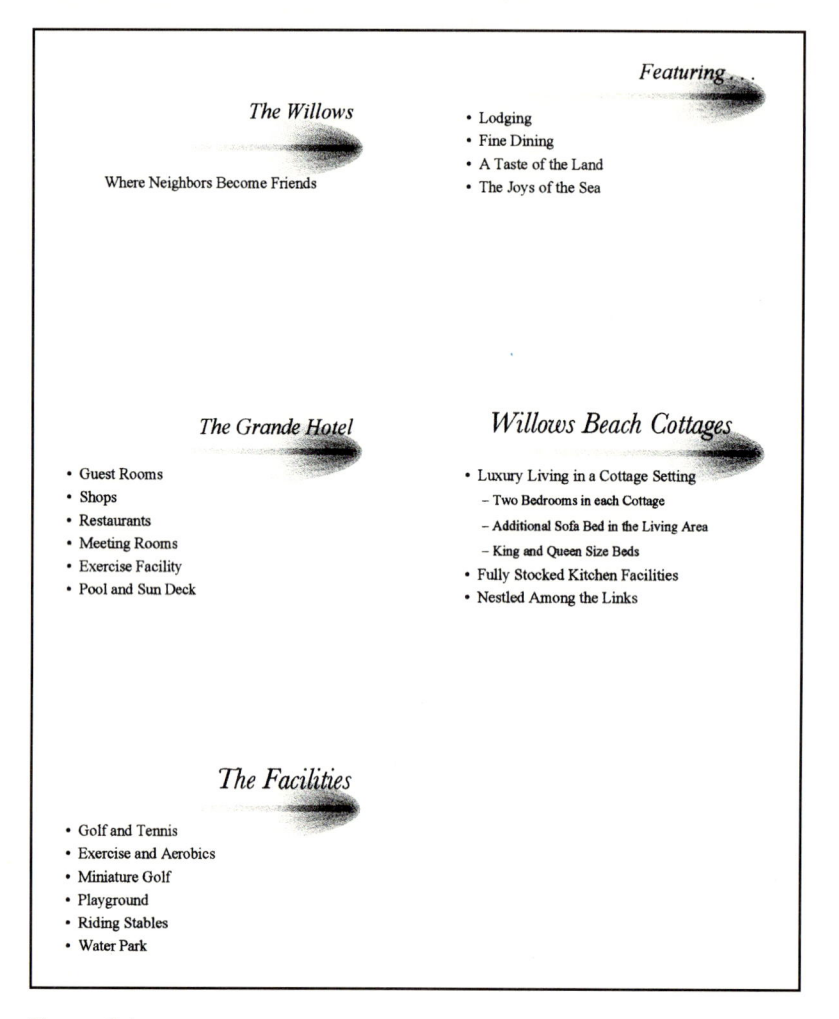

Figure 1.4

5 Choose File, Print again, select Outline View from the Print What drop-down list, and click OK (see Figure 1.5).

1. *The Willows*
   Where Neighbors Become Friends
2. *Featuring . . .*
   - Lodging
   - Fine Dining
   - A Taste of the Land
   - The Joys of the Sea
3. *The Grande Hotel*
   - Guest Rooms
   - Shops
   - Restaurants
   - Meeting Rooms
   - Exercise Facility
   - Pool and Sun Deck
4. *Willows Beach Cottages*
   - Luxury Living in a Cottage Setting
     - Two Bedrooms in each Cottage
     - Additional Sofa Bed in the Living Area
     - King and Queen Size Beds
   - Fully Stocked Kitchen Facilities
   - Nestled Among the Links
5. *The Facilities*
   - Golf and Tennis
   - Exercise and Aerobics
   - Miniature Golf
   - Playground
   - Riding Stables
   - Water Park

Figure 1.5

The Conclusion

If time permits, practice printing different materials and setting different options in the Print dialog box to see the effects they have on the way your slides print. When you're done, save changes to the presentation and close the presentation. If you've completed your work in PowerPoint, exit the program and shut down your computer as instructed.

Summary and Exercises

Summary

- PowerPoint enables you to create blank presentations formatted with no special design as well as presentations formatted using special designs called templates. You can change the look of slides in a presentation by selecting a different template design.
- AutoLayout formats make creating slides with preformatted text easier.
- You can add, delete, format, and select presentation text using many of the same techniques used in other Windows-based programs.
- PowerPoint displays presentation slides using four different views: Slide view, Slide Sorter view, Notes Pages view, and Outline view. Each view is designed to help you accomplish specific tasks.
- Presentations normally contain numerous slides; you can add slides and move from slide to slide in a presentation using a variety of different mouse and keyboard techniques.
- You save, open, close, and print presentations using many of the same procedures used in other Windows applications; you can print a variety of different presentation materials by selecting the desired format from the Print dialog box.

Key Terms and Operations

Key Terms	Operations
AutoLayout	add slides to a presentation
handouts	create, save, open, and close a presentation
Outline view	move around a presentation
Notes Pages view	print slides and handouts
Slide Sorter view	switch presentation views
template	use templates to change the look of a presentation

Study Questions

Multiple Choice

1. To create a new, blank presentation,
   a. simply launch PowerPoint—a new presentation automatically appears.
   b. choose New Presentation from the PowerPoint dialog box.
   c. select Blank presentation from the PowerPoint dialog box and press Enter.
   d. select Template from the PowerPoint dialog box and press Enter.

2. Slides added to a presentation are formatted using
   a. an AutoLayout format.
   b. text and title boxes.
   c. blank slides that resemble blank pieces of paper.
   d. outlines.

3. New slide layouts contain
   a. fields.
   b. placeholders.
   c. tables.
   d. templates.

4. Placeholders identify
   a. slide names.
   b. slide fields.
   c. slide titles.
   d. slide objects.

5. To add a new slide to a presentation, use any of the following techniques *except*
   a. double-clicking the active slide.
   b. clicking the New Slide button on the toolbar.
   c. clicking the New Slide command on the Common Tasks toolbar.
   d. choosing Insert, New Slide from the menu.

6. Most slides contain
   a. slide tables.
   b. pictures.
   c. slide titles.
   d. slide names.

7. Outline view displays
   a. all slide objects.
   b. slide title and body text only.
   c. small slide images.
   d. slide images and notes about the slide.

8. Slide Sorter view displays
   a. all slide objects.
   b. slide title and body text only.
   c. small slide images.
   d. slide images and notes about the slide.

9. Notes Pages view displays
   a. all slide objects.
   b. slide title and body text only.
   c. small slide images.
   d. slide images and notes about the slide.

10. Slide view displays
    a. all slide objects.
    b. slide title and body text only.
    c. small slide images.
    d. slide images and notes about the slide.

Short Answer

1. How do you create a new presentation if PowerPoint is already running?
2. What's a template?
3. What are AutoLayout formats and what do they contain?
4. What are the four presentation views and when should you use each view?
5. How do you switch views?
6. How do you print handouts?
7. How can you use the vertical scroll bar to display a specific slide?

8. How do you apply a template?
9. How do you open a presentation when you launch PowerPoint?
10. How do you move from one placeholder on a slide to another without using the mouse?

For Discussion
1. What are the four options in the PowerPoint dialog box when you launch PowerPoint and what does each option enable you to do?
2. How do you identify the material you want to print, and what options should you check if you're using a black-and-white printer?
3. What are the advantages of formatting a presentation by using a template?
4. What kind of presentations could you create with PowerPoint for your other classes?

Review Exercises

1. Creating, Saving, and Adding Slides and Text to Presentations

Ruth Lindsey, Manager of The Willows Shops, has been asked to display the diversity of gift items available in different shops at The Willows. She has developed the preliminary outline shown in Figure 1.6 and asks you to create a presentation using the outline.

1. **The Willows Shops**
   Where Exploring Becomes an Adventure
2. **The Newsstand**
   - Newspapers
   - Magazines
   - Recent Publications
   - The Willows Post Office
3. **Sindy's Sun Closet**
   - Swimsuits
   - Bathing Accessories
   - Lotions
   - Towels
   - Flippers
4. **Weeping Willow Gallery**
   - Paintings
   - Sculpture
   - Iron Works
   - Local Artists

5. **Live Oak Gifts**
6. **Creative Cutlery**
   - A Wide Assortment of Kitchen Wares
7. **Cherry Street Market**
   - Home Grown Produce
   - Natural Flora from the Carolinas
8. **Victorian Tea Room**
   - Victorian gifts and clothing
   - Victorian High Tea Served Daily
9. **Ken's Kids**
   - Children's games and toys
   - Children's clothing
10. **Appalachian Crafts**
    - Treasures from the Hills
    - Displays of local artists

Figure 1.6

Using PowerPoint, create a new blank presentation named *The Willows Shops*. Follow these instructions to complete the presentation:

1. Launch PowerPoint and create a new blank presentation that contains a title slide.

Project 1: Building a Presentation   PP-49

2. Switch to Outline view and add the text shown in Figure 1.6.

3. Save the presentation using the filename *The Willows Shops*.

4. Close the presentation and exit PowerPoint when you have completed your work.

2. Switching Views, Navigating Presentation Slides, Applying a Template, and Printing Handouts

Ms. Lindsey would like a copy of the slides in the presentation *The Willows Shops* for her assistant managers to review before she makes the presentation. She would like to have the presentation slides formatted using the template shown in Figure 1.7.

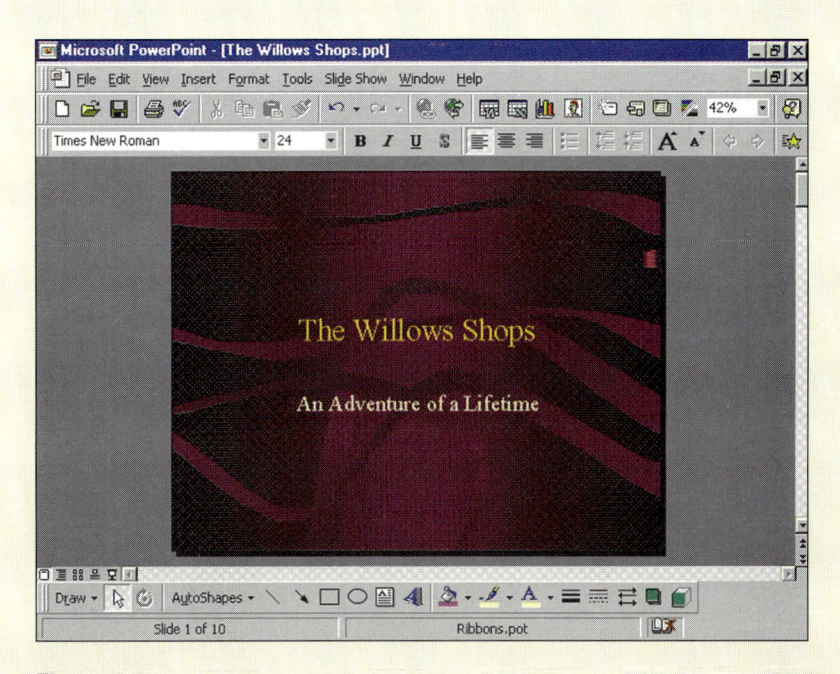

Figure 1.7

She asks you to reformat the presentation with the template and print copies for her assistant managers. Follow these instructions to meet Ms. Lindsey's request:

1. Open the presentation *The Willows Shops* and review the presentation in Outline view.

2. Display Slide 1 in Slide view and apply the Ribbons template to the presentation.

3. Review each slide on-screen using different navigation tools.

4. Save changes to the presentation and print a copy of the presentation as black-and-white handouts with six slides per page.

5. Close the presentation and exit PowerPoint when you have completed your work.

Assignments

1. Creating, Formatting, and Saving a Multi-Slide Presentation

The Willows area of South Carolina features a number of festivals and attractions. Create a presentation named *Festivals and Attractions* that contains the slides pictured in Figure 1.8.

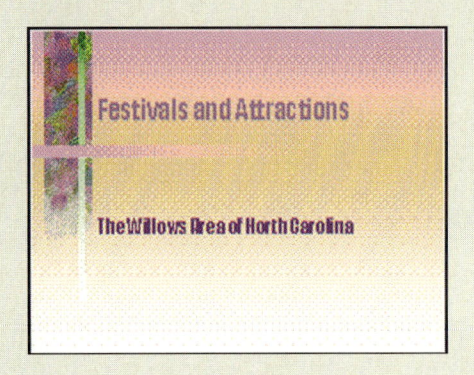

Figure 1.8

Apply the Blush template and view the presentation in all four views. Save the presentation and print a copy of the presentation as black-and-white handouts with three slides per page. Close the presentation and exit PowerPoint when you have completed your work.

2. Finding Templates on the Internet

Search the PowerPoint Internet site and locate additional templates that you can use to format presentations. (Go to Microsoft's home page at WWW.Microsoft.com and then click on Products.) Download a template and apply it to the Festivals and Attractions presentation created in the preceding assignment. Save the presentation and print a copy of the title slide.

PROJECT 2

Editing Slide Text

PowerPoint contains a variety of tools that you can use to edit text you add to slides. The techniques you use to edit text are similar to the techniques you use to edit text in other Windows 95 applications. In this project, you apply different techniques to edit and enhance text, format text placeholders, and change the setup of your slide page.

Objectives

After completing this project, you will be able to:

- ➤ Select and edit placeholder text
- ➤ Change the appearance of text
- ➤ Find and replace text
- ➤ Check the style and spelling of text
- ➤ Format text placeholders
- ➤ Change the page setup
- ➤ Create a presentation using a wizard

The Challenge

Francesca Savoy has been hired to coordinate a marketing campaign designed to promote The Willows resort. She has reviewed the presentation slides you created in Project 1 and has made changes to the slide text. In addition, she has recommended changes to the text format and text placeholder positions to improve the display of information on slides in the presentation. Slides in the presentation should appear as shown in Figure 2.1 after you complete your edits.

PP-51

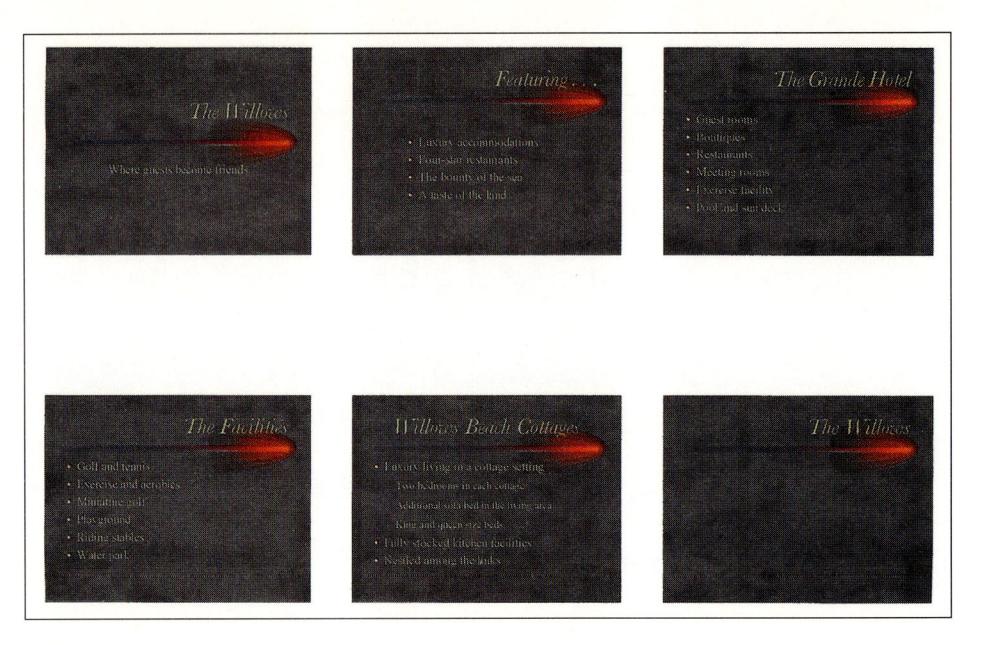

Figure 2.1

In addition, Ms. Savoy would like you to create the structure of a new presentation designed to be used as a marketing tool for the resort. She plans to use the presentation as a guide and will provide the text she wants to include in the new presentation from the presentation outline that you prepare. Your completed presentation outline appears in Figure 2.2.

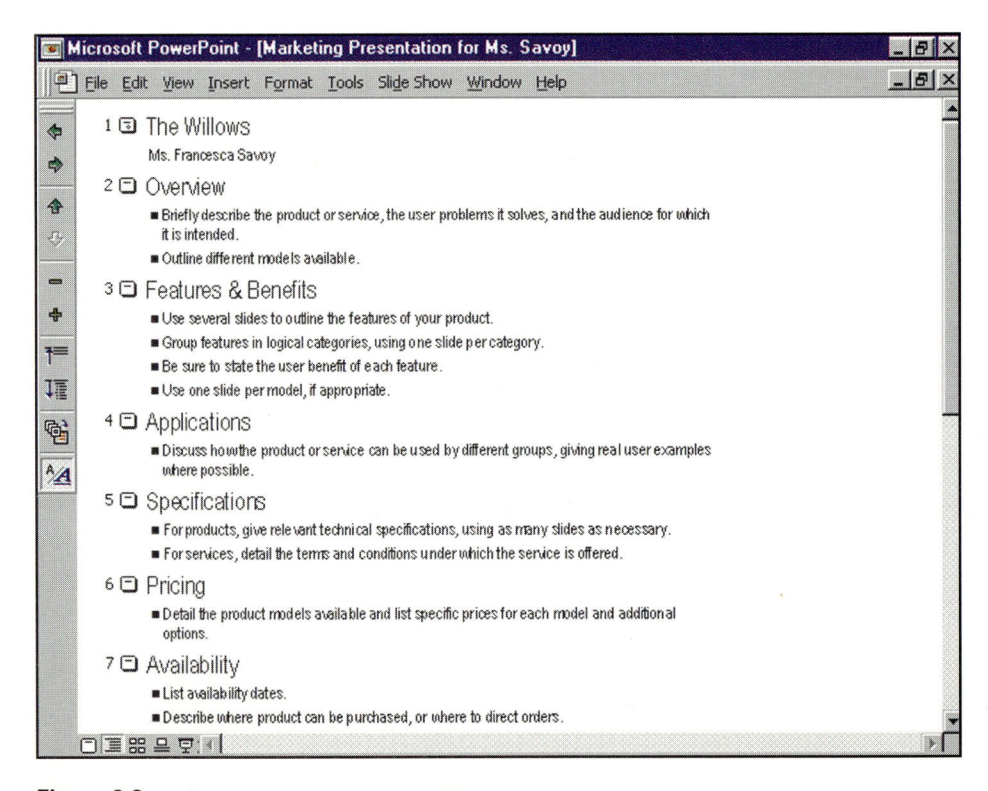

Figure 2.2

The Solution

As the graphic artist at The Willows, it's your responsibility to edit text on each slide in the presentation for The Willows, format text and text placeholders on the slides, and ensure that there are no spelling or formatting errors on the slides. Follow the steps in the tasks in this project to make the edits required by Ms. Savoy. When you complete the edits, you can create the outline for Ms. Savoy's marketing presentation using the PowerPoint AutoContent Wizard.

The Setup

Before starting this project, you may want to make sure that the following settings are active so that your presentations display in a format that matches the pictures in this book. Figures and illustrations use the default settings installed automatically with the PowerPoint program. If someone has fiddled with these settings, you may find that your screen looks different from those pictured here. Here are a few things to check:

- Do you see the four default toolbars—Standard, Formatting, Common Tasks, and Drawing? If not, choose View, Toolbars and then select the ones that are missing. Close any extra toolbars displayed.
- Display the status bar, if you don't see it, by choosing Tools, Options, and then checking the options on the View page tab. Make sure that all options on the View page tab of the dialog box are checked except the last one.
- If rulers appear, hide them by choosing View, Ruler.
- Make sure that your presentation window is maximized by clicking the Maximize button on the presentation window.

Selecting and Editing Placeholder Text

To edit text or to change the appearance of text, you must first **select** the text. PowerPoint offers a variety of techniques to select text. You can edit the text in slide placeholders using either Slide view or Outline view.

TASK 1: TO SELECT AND EDIT PLACEHOLDER TEXT:

1 Open the presentation *The Willows* and display the first slide in Slide view.

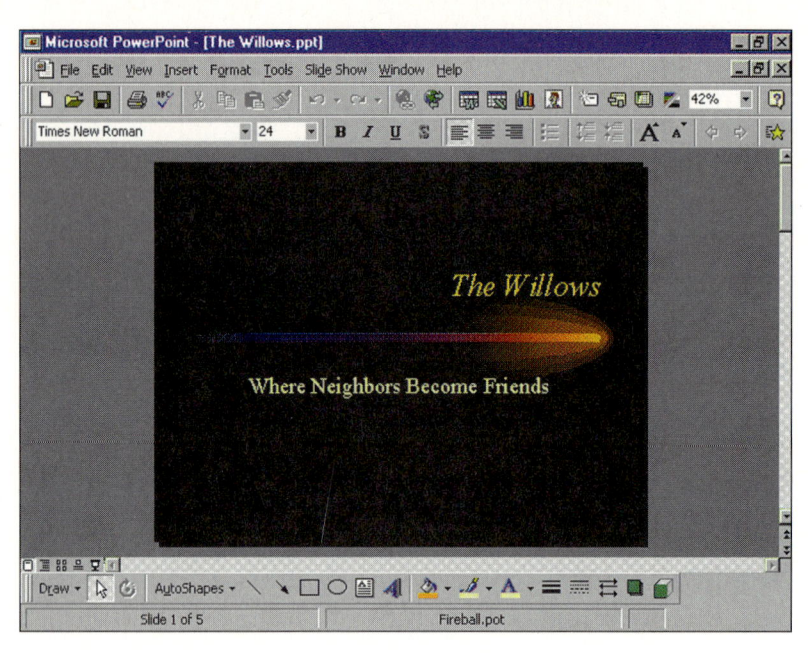

2 Double-click the word "Neighbors" and press (DELETE) to remove the word. The text appears as "Where Become Friends."

3 Position the insertion point between "Where" and "Become" and type **Guests.**

4 Display Slide 2, double-click the word "Lodging," and type **Luxury Accommodations**.

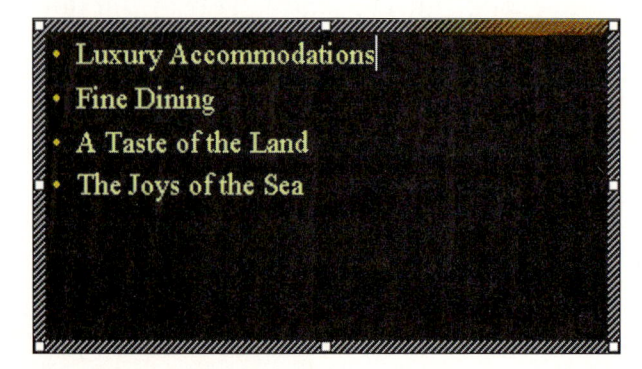

5 Select the text for the second bullet point and type **Four-Star Restaurants.**

Featuring...
- Luxury Accommodations
- Four-Star Restaurants
- A Taste of the Land
- The Joys of the Sea

6 Switch to Outline view and click the bullet beside the third bulleted item in Slide 2.

2 *Featuring...*
- Luxury Accommodations
- Four-Star Restaurants
- A Taste of the Land
- The Joys of the Sea

3 *The Grande Hotel*
- Guest Rooms
- Shops
- Restaurants

7 Drag the bullet to the bottom of the Slide 2 bulleted list and drop it.

> 2 *Featuring...*
> - Luxury Accommodations
> - Four-Star Restaurants
> - A Taste of the Land
> - The Joys of the Sea
>
> 3 *The Grande Hotel*
> - Guest Rooms
> - Shops
> - Restaurants

The mouse pointer changes shape

A line identifies the active position

8 Click the slide icon beside Slide 4.

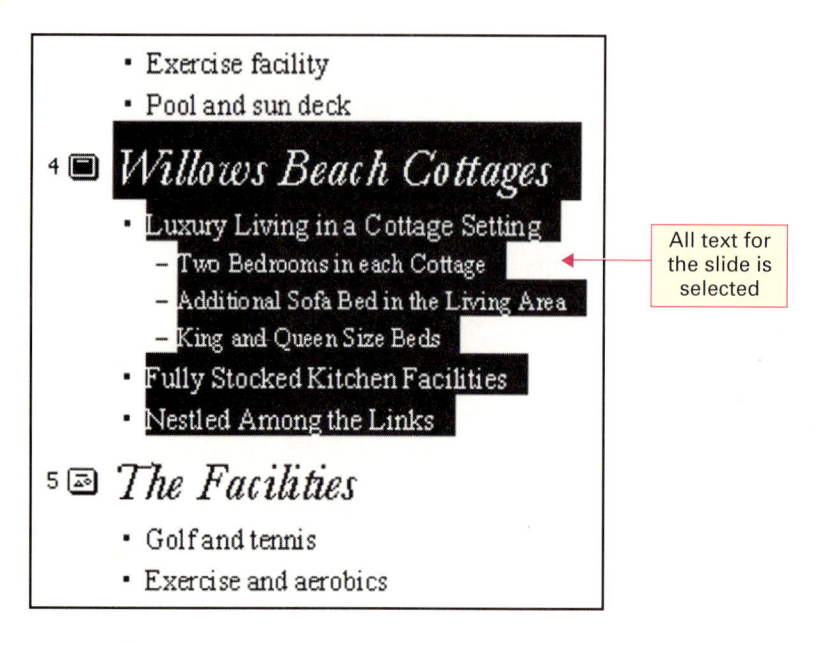

> - Exercise facility
> - Pool and sun deck
>
> 4 *Willows Beach Cottages*
> - Luxury Living in a Cottage Setting
>   - Two Bedrooms in each Cottage
>   - Additional Sofa Bed in the Living Area
>   - King and Queen Size Beds
> - Fully Stocked Kitchen Facilities
> - Nestled Among the Links
>
> 5 *The Facilities*
> - Golf and tennis
> - Exercise and aerobics

All text for the slide is selected

9 Position the mouse pointer on the selected slide icon, click, and drag the text to the bottom of the outline.

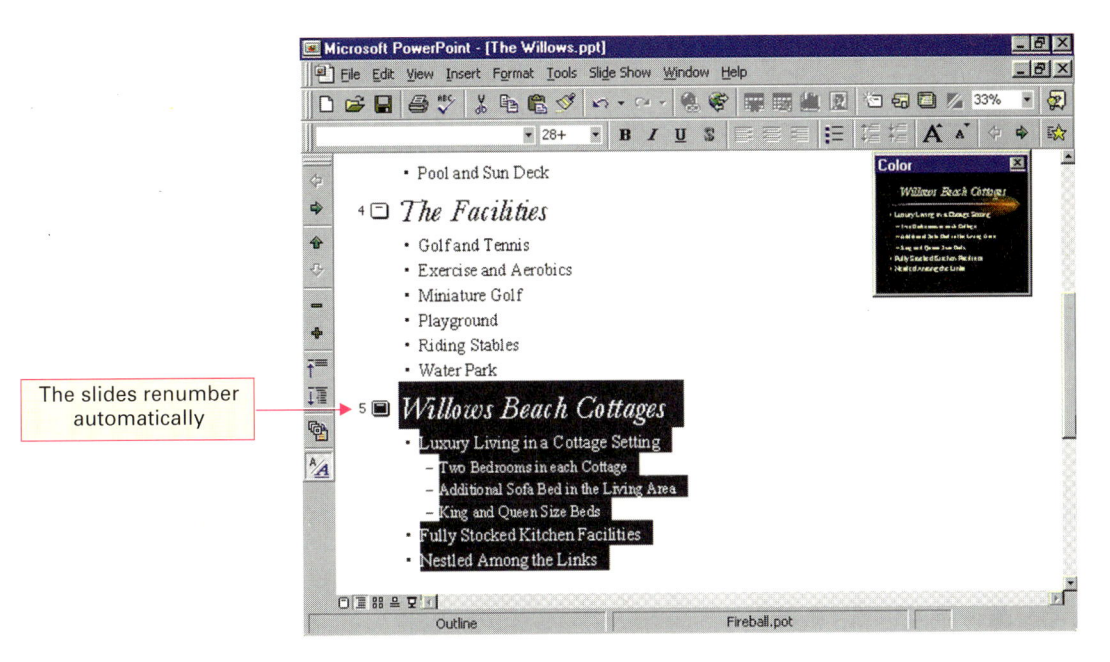

The slides renumber automatically

10 Return to Slide view, display Slide 1, and triple-click the title placeholder.

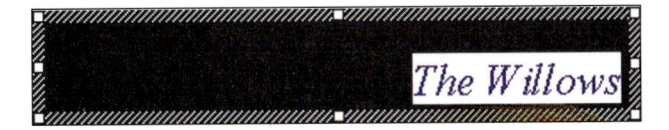

11 Click the Copy button on the Standard toolbar.

12 Display Slide 5 and add a new bulleted list slide at the end of the presentation.
A new slide appears, formatted with a title placeholder and bulleted list placeholder.

13 Click the title placeholder and then click the Paste button on the Standard toolbar.

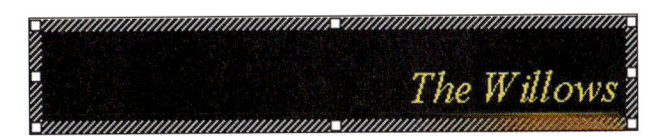

Changing the Appearance of Text

To make the changes to the appearance of the text that Ms. Savoy requested, you need to change the font, change the font size, apply enhancements, and change the color of the text. You can apply many of these features using tools on the Formatting toolbar, as shown in Figure 2.3.

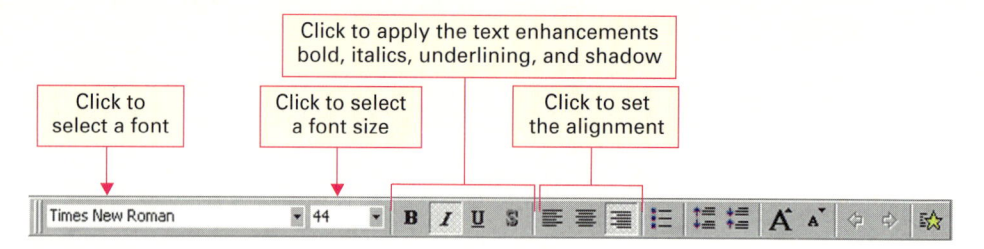

Figure 2.3

Enhancements and changes you make to slide text affect only text you select before making the change. If an enhancement you want to apply doesn't have a button on the toolbar, you can open the Font dialog box and select additional options. You can then copy the text format and apply it to text on other slides by using the Format Painter to ensure consistency.

TASK 2: TO CHANGE THE APPEARANCE OF TEXT IN A PRESENTATION:

1. Display Slide 1 of the presentation *The Willows* in Slide view and select the slide title text.

2. Click the arrow button beside the Font box on the Formatting toolbar to open the drop-down list.

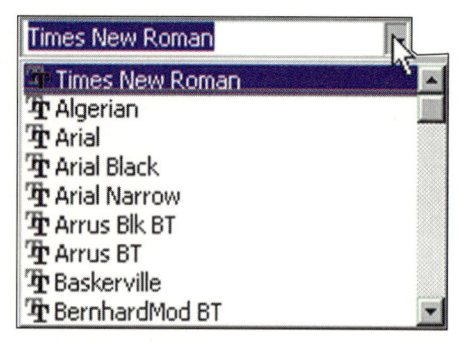

3. Select Baskerville from the Font list.

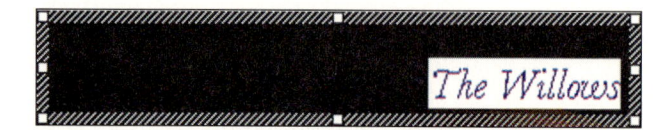

Project 2: Editing Slide Text   PP-**59**

4 Click the arrow button beside the Font Size box on the Formatting toolbar to open the drop-down list.

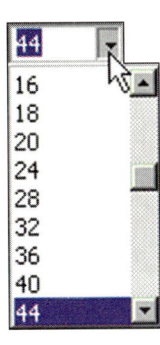

5 Scroll as necessary and select 60 from the font size list and then click the Bold **B** button on the Formatting toolbar.

The Willows

6 Choose Format, Font to display the Font dialog box.

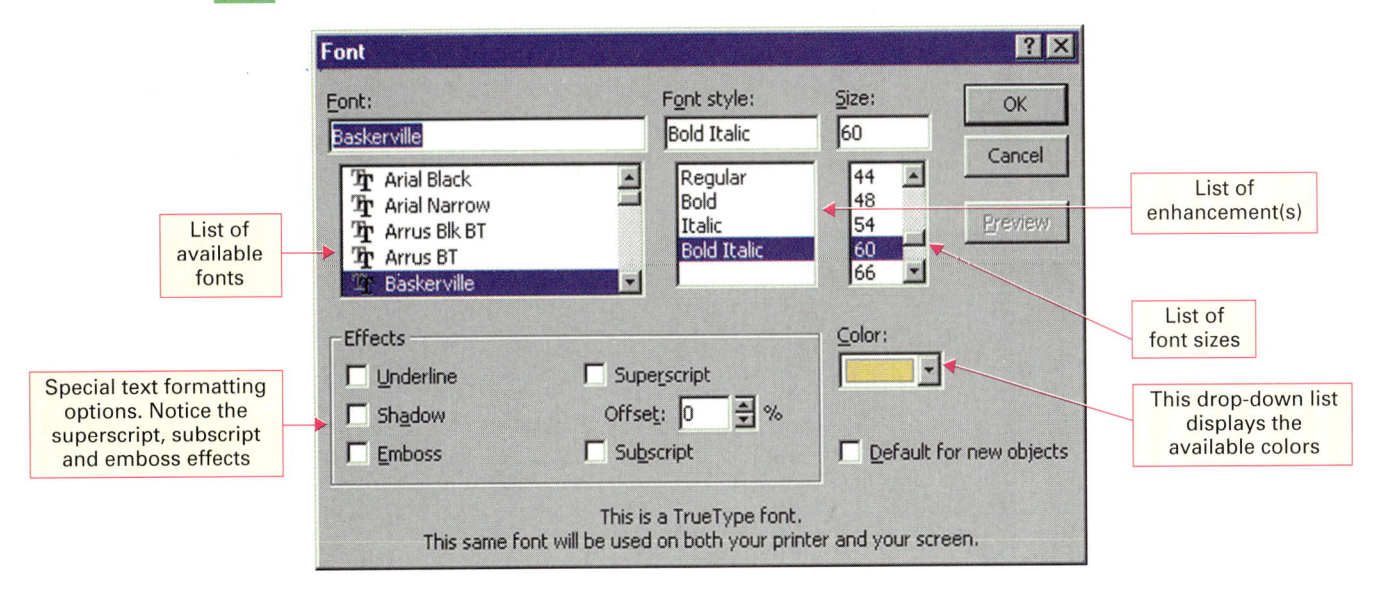

- List of available fonts
- List of enhancement(s)
- List of font sizes
- Special text formatting options. Notice the superscript, subscript and emboss effects
- This drop-down list displays the available colors

7 Click the arrow button beside the Color box, click the lighter yellow color, and press ENTER.

8 Click B to remove the bold and then double-click the Format Painter button.

The mouse pointer carries a paintbrush to paint other text with the text format of the selected text

9 Display Slide 2 and select the slide title.
The title text appears reformatted.

10 Repeat step 9 to change the format of title text for all slides in the presentation.

11 Press ESC to drop the paintbrush.

12 Save the changes to the presentation.

Finding and Replacing Text

The Find feature in PowerPoint enables you to search for text contained in text placeholders on slides, in outlines, or in the notes area of notes pages. The Replace feature enables you to substitute different text for the text PowerPoint finds. Take, for example, a presentation that contains the company name that you've misspelled throughout the presentation. Using the Replace feature, you can quickly change all occurrences of the misspelled name to the correct spelling.

Project 2: Editing Slide Text PP-61

TASK 3: TO FIND AND REPLACE TEXT:

1 Press CTRL+HOME to display the first slide in the presentation.
You can start the Find and Replace feature from any location in the presentation; starting at the first slide in this task ensures that your screen will resemble the figures shown here.

> **Note** If a placeholder is active when you press Ctrl+Home, PowerPoint places the insertion point at the top of the active placeholder. Click outside all placeholders and then press Ctrl+Home to display the first slide.

2 Choose Edit, Find.

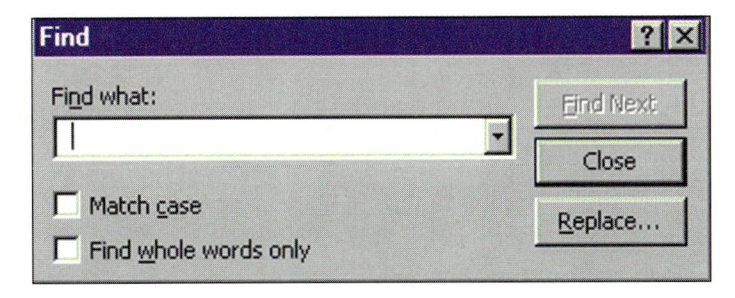

3 Type **Joys** in the Find what textbox, click the Match case check box, and press ENTER.

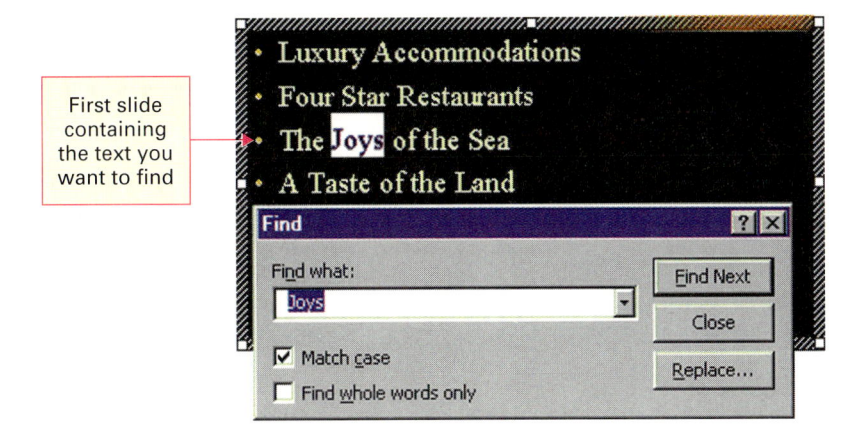

First slide containing the text you want to find

- Luxury Accommodations
- Four Star Restaurants
- The Joys of the Sea
- A Taste of the Land

Tip Drag the Find dialog box out of the way to view the text behind it.

4 Press ESC to close the Find dialog box and type **Bounty** to replace the word *Joys*.

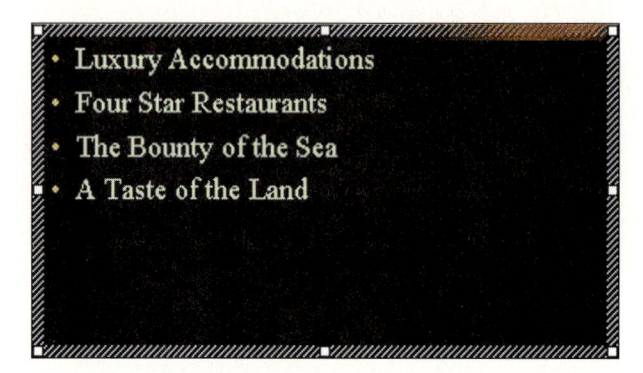

- Luxury Accommodations
- Four Star Restaurants
- The Bounty of the Sea
- A Taste of the Land

5 Choose Edit, Replace.

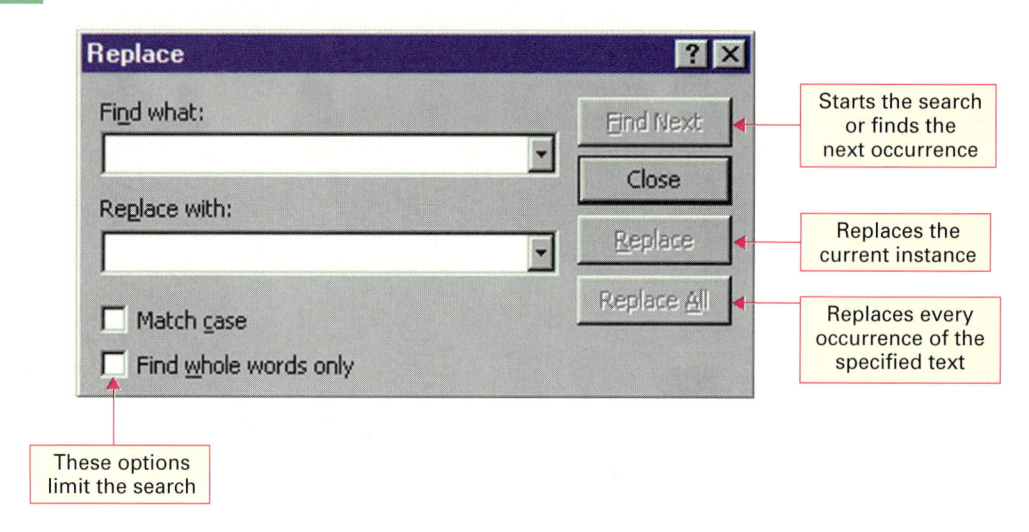

Starts the search or finds the next occurrence

Replaces the current instance

Replaces every occurrence of the specified text

These options limit the search

6 Type **Shops** in the Find what text box, press (TAB), type **Boutiques** in the Replace with text box, and press (ENTER).

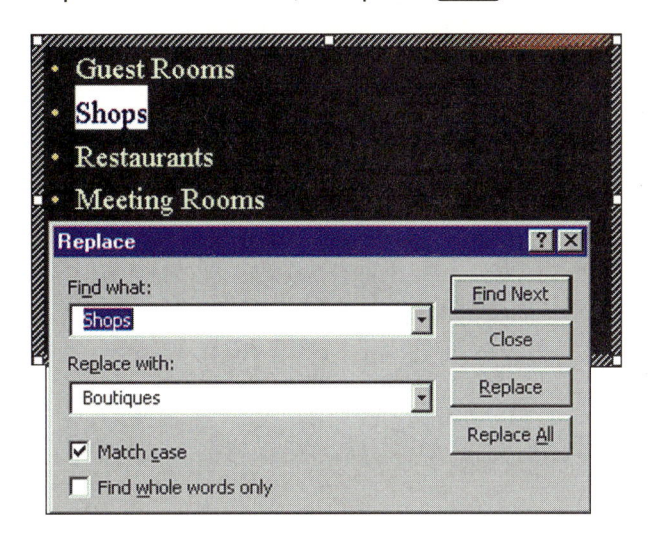

7 Click Replace.
"Shops" changes to "Boutiques."

8 Click Find Next, if necessary.

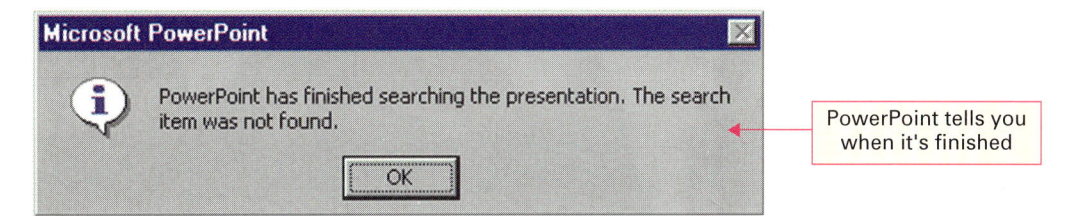

PowerPoint tells you when it's finished

9 Click OK to acknowledge the message, press (ESC) to close the Replace dialog box, and click the Save button to save the changes to the presentation.

Checking the Style and Spelling of Text

The PowerPoint Spelling feature proofs all the materials in your presentation and locates words in text placeholders that it doesn't recognize.

The PowerPoint Style Checker checks placeholder text on presentation slides for consistency in end punctuation, capitalization, and spelling. When you use the Style Checker to check capitalization, PowerPoint automatically formats all words except the first word in each bulleted item in lowercase. Checking the Spelling option in the Style Checker dialog box eliminates the need to run the Spelling feature separately.

TASK 4: TO CHECK A PRESENTATION FOR STYLE AND SPELLING:

1 Press CTRL+HOME to display the first slide in the presentation. You can start the Style Checker from any location in the presentation; starting at the first slide in this activity ensures that your screen will resemble the figures shown here.

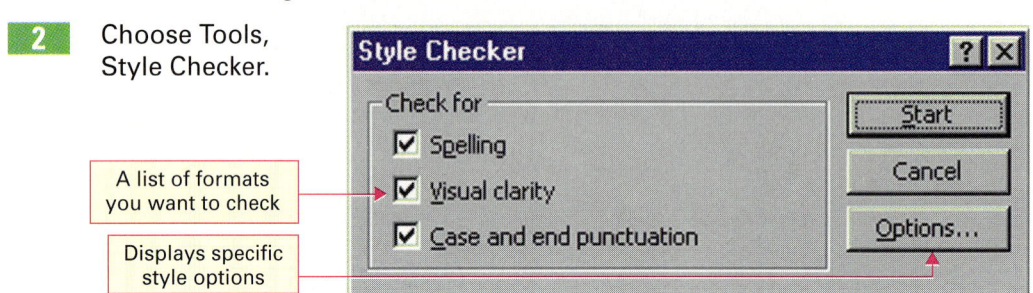

2 Choose Tools, Style Checker.

- A list of formats you want to check
- Displays specific style options

3 Select the check boxes for Spelling, Visual Clarity, and Case and End Punctuation, and click Options.

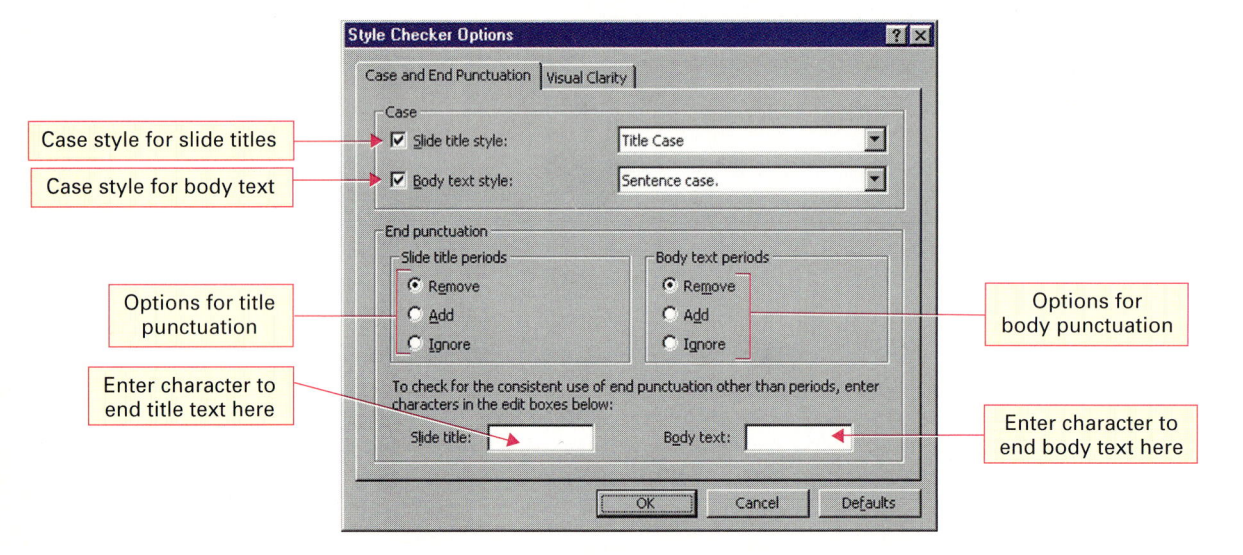

- Case style for slide titles
- Case style for body text
- Options for title punctuation
- Options for body punctuation
- Enter character to end title text here
- Enter character to end body text here

4 Set the options shown above on the Case and End punctuation page of the style checker options dialog box and then click the Visual Clarity page tab.

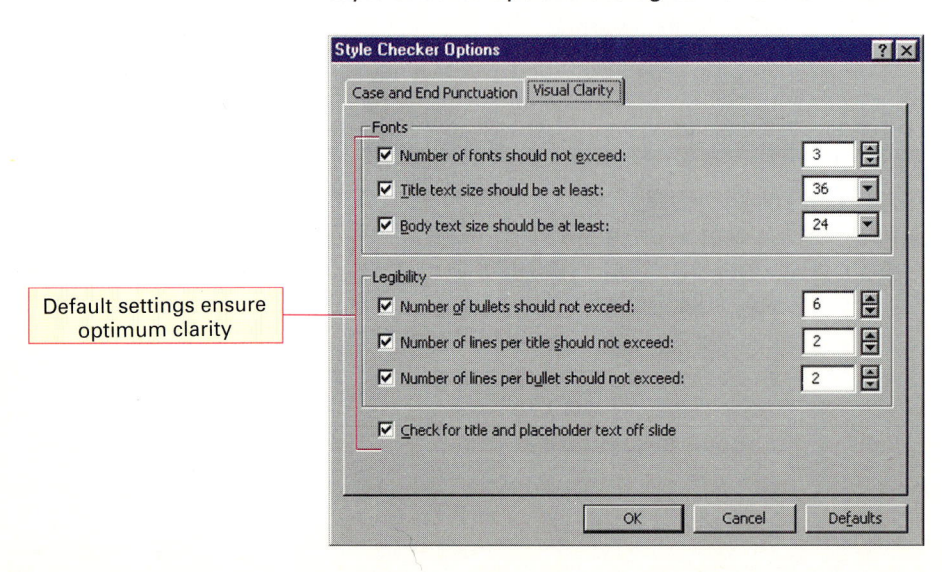

- Default settings ensure optimum clarity

5 Select each option on the Visual Clarity page and change option values to those shown earlier, if necessary. Then press (ENTER) and click the Start button.

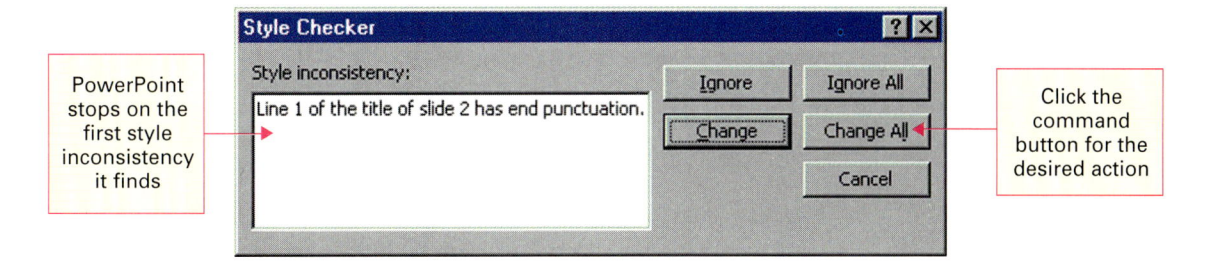

PowerPoint stops on the first style inconsistency it finds

Click the command button for the desired action

Tip To see the slide text identified, drag the dialog box out of the way.

6 Click the command button for the action you want to take.
PowerPoint locates the next style error and displays a message identifying the error.

7 Repeat step 6 until you've reviewed all style errors.

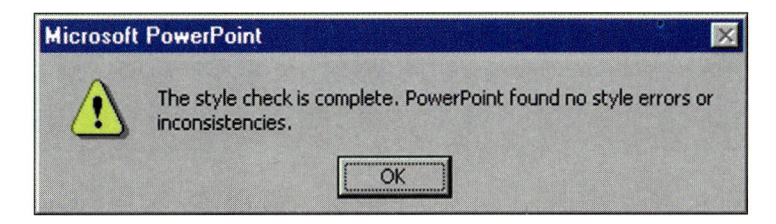

8 Click OK to close the message box and then click 💾 to save changes to the presentation.

Formatting Text Placeholders

Placeholder objects contained on slides in your presentation can be selected, sized, and moved using the same techniques you use to size other objects. Changing the size of the text placeholder makes it possible to adjust the position of slide text and can be compared to setting margins on word processing documents. In addition, you can change the alignment and *line spacing* of all text in a placeholder by first selecting the placeholder and then adjusting the setting. Selected placeholders display *handles* on their corners and sides, as shown in Figure 2.4.

Tip Displaying the ruler helps to position and size placeholders more precisely. To display the ruler, choose View, Ruler.

PP-66

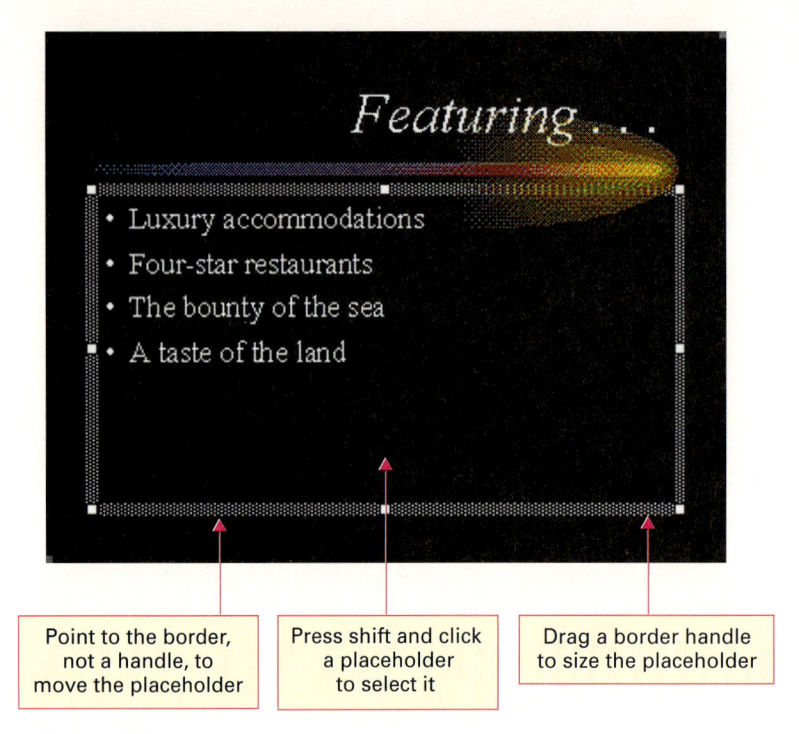

[Figure: slide showing "Featuring..." with bulleted list: Luxury accommodations, Four-star restaurants, The bounty of the sea, A taste of the land. Callouts: "Point to the border, not a handle, to move the placeholder"; "Press shift and click a placeholder to select it"; "Drag a border handle to size the placeholder"]

Figure 2.4

TASK 5: TO FORMAT TEXT PLACEHOLDERS:

1. Display Slide 5 of the presentation *The Willows*, press SHIFT, and click the title placeholder.

   [Image: "Willows Beach Cottages" title placeholder selected — labeled "Selected title placeholder"]

2. Click the Center button on the Formatting toolbar.

   [Image: "Willows Beach Cottages" title, centered]

3. Display Slide 2 and select the bulleted list placeholder.

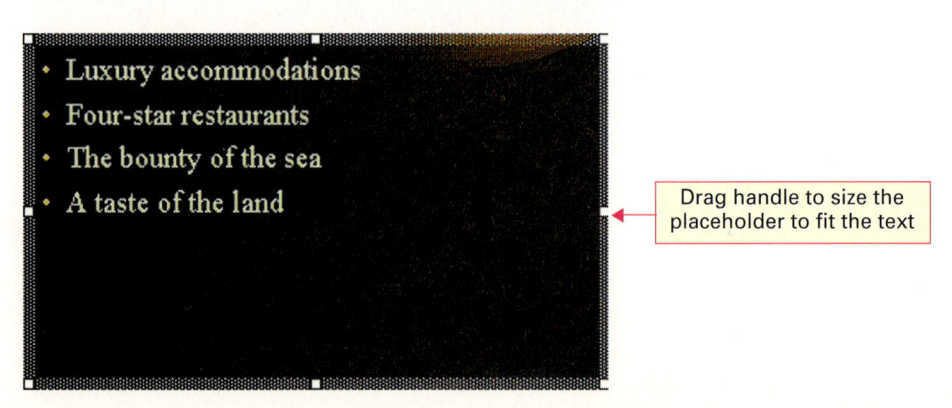

   [Image: bulleted list placeholder with Luxury accommodations, Four-star restaurants, The bounty of the sea, A taste of the land — labeled "Drag handle to size the placeholder to fit the text"]

4 Drag the lower-right corner handle diagonally toward the placeholder text.

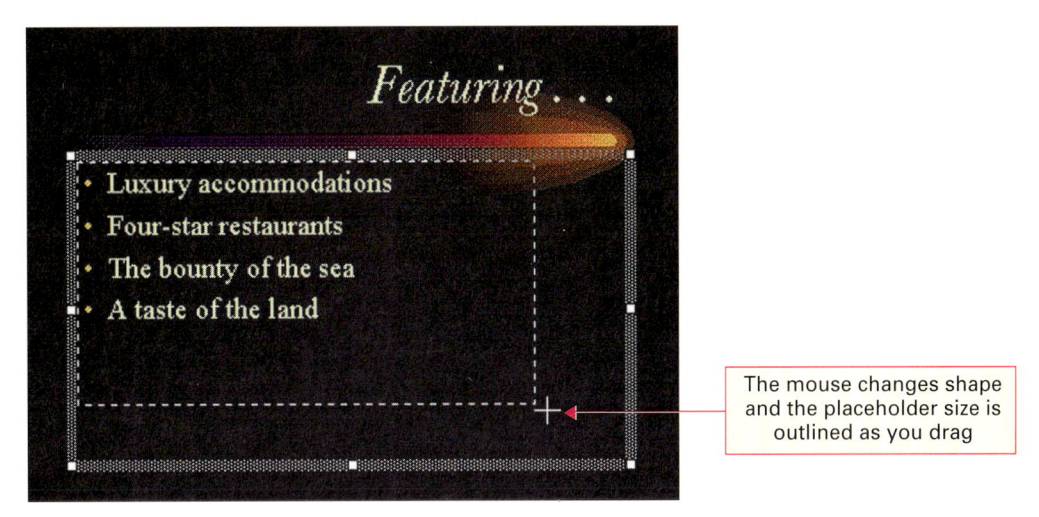

The mouse changes shape and the placeholder size is outlined as you drag

5 Position the mouse pointer on a border of the placeholder away from a handle and drag the placeholder diagonally down and right.

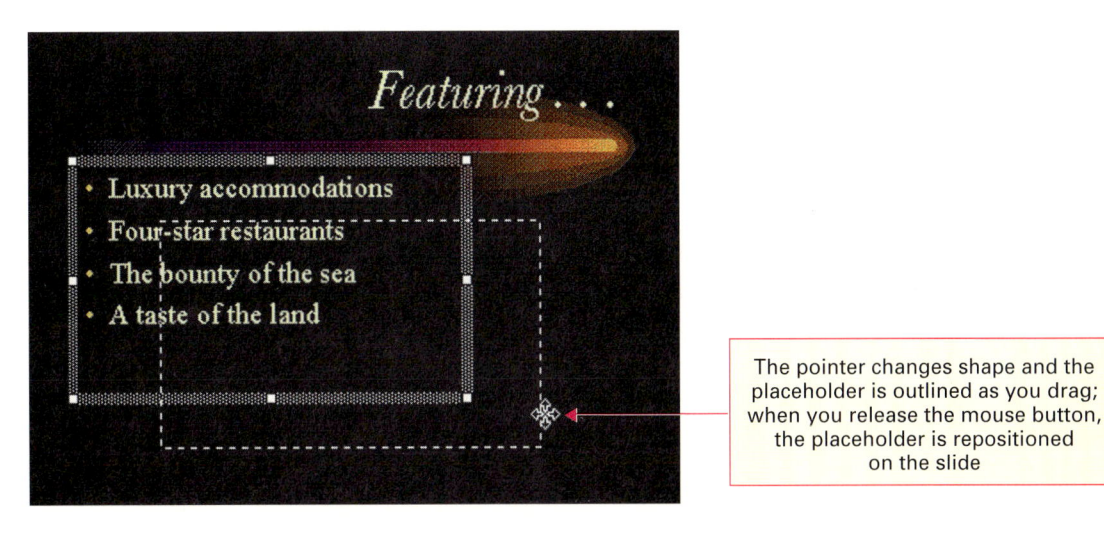

The pointer changes shape and the placeholder is outlined as you drag; when you release the mouse button, the placeholder is repositioned on the slide

6 Display Slide 5 and select the three second-level bulleted items following "Luxury living in a cottage setting."

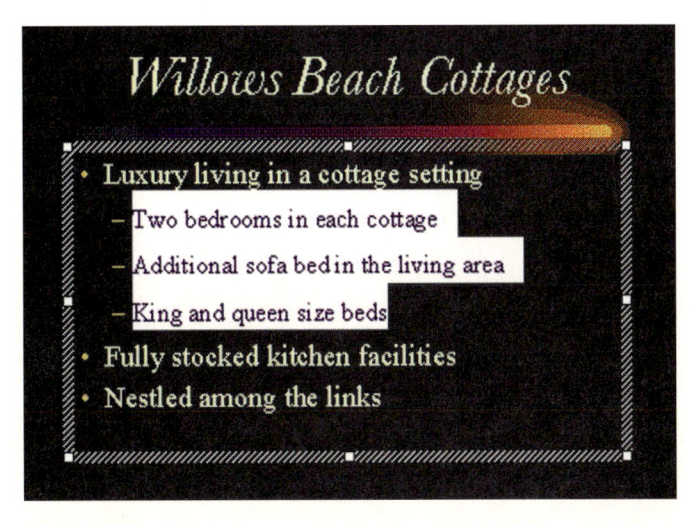

7 Choose Format, Line Spacing.

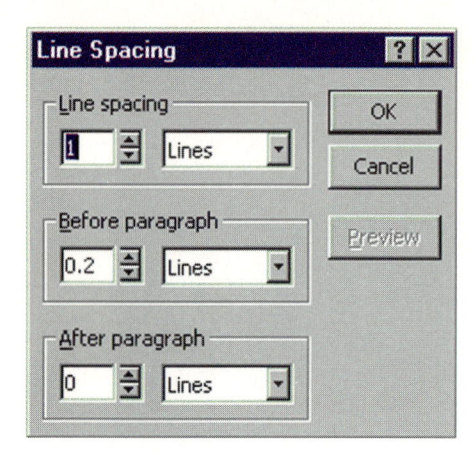

8 Click the spin buttons to increase the Line spacing to 1.5 and to decrease the Before paragraph spacing to 0; then click OK.

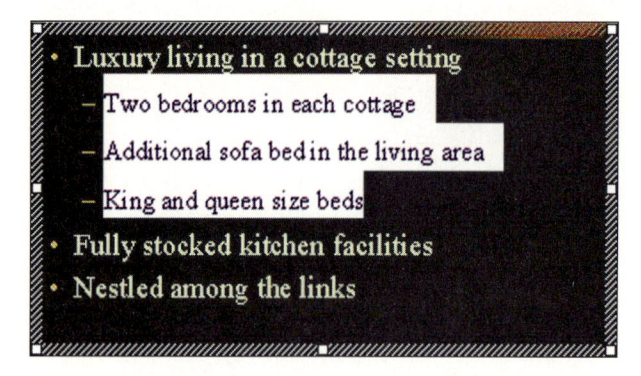

9 Save changes to the presentation.

Changing the Page Setup

To change the size and *orientation* (direction) of paper you want to use to print slides and other materials, you need to change the *page setup*. The Page Setup dialog box presents a set of options for setting the orientation of text on slides and a separate set of options for setting the page orientation for outlines, handouts, and notes pages, as shown in Figure 2.5. You can also format slides to print on different size paper by selecting the paper size from the Slides Sized For drop-down list, enter values in the Width and Height value boxes, and set the page number for the first slide in the presentation.

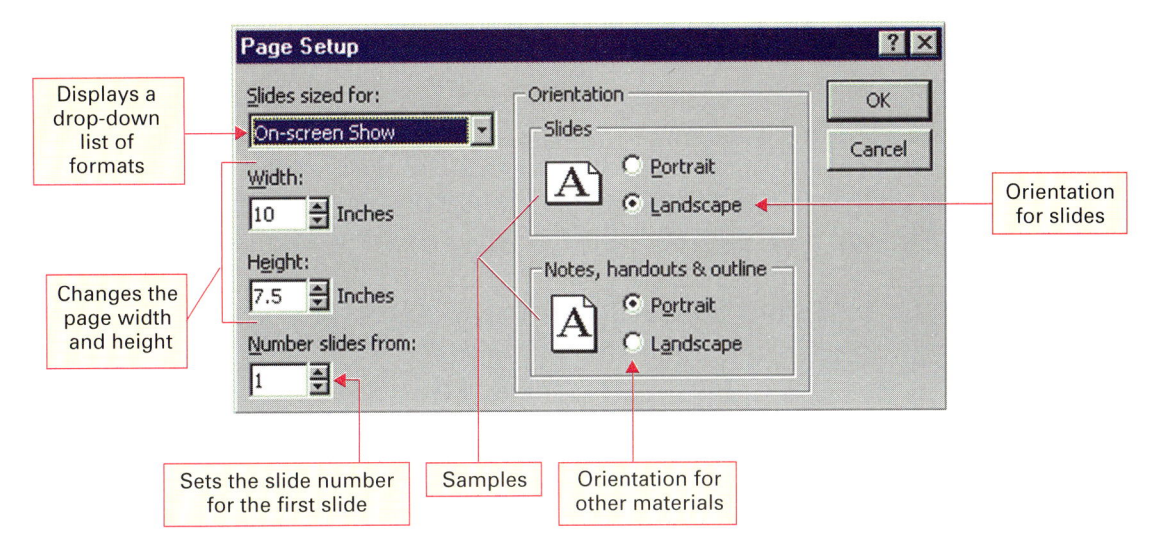

Project 2: Editing Slide Text   PP-69

Figure 2.5 — Page Setup dialog box with callouts:
- Displays a drop-down list of formats
- Changes the page width and height
- Sets the slide number for the first slide
- Samples
- Orientation for other materials
- Orientation for slides

TASK 6: TO CHANGE THE PAGE SETUP FOR MATERIALS IN A PRESENTATION:

1 Choose File, Page Setup.
The dialog box in Figure 2.8 displays.

2 Change the settings in the Page Setup dialog box as in:

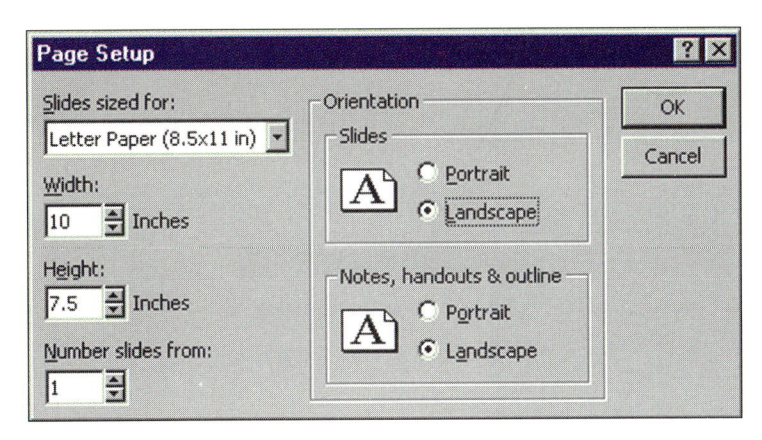

(Page Setup dialog box showing: Slides sized for: Letter Paper (8.5x11 in); Width: 10 Inches; Height: 7.5 Inches; Number slides from: 1; Orientation Slides: Landscape; Notes, handouts & outline: Landscape)

3 Click OK, save the changes to the presentation, and close the presentation.

Creating a Presentation Using a Wizard

The PowerPoint AutoContent Wizard helps you build an outline for specific types of presentations by presenting options for you to choose and enabling you to fill in specific pieces of information about the presentation. You can choose the AutoContent Wizard from the PowerPoint dialog box when you launch PowerPoint, or select the AutoContent Wizard from the New Presentation dialog box.

Using the Wizard, you can quickly and easily create the presentation outline for the marketing presentation Ms. Savoy requested.

PP-70

TASK 7: TO CREATE A PRESENTATION USING THE AUTOCONTENT WIZARD:

1 Close all open presentations.
You don't have to close all presentations to use the wizard; doing so now ensures that your screen resembles those shown in this section.

2 Choose File, New, and click the Presentations tab.

Click the Presentations tab to display sample presentations

Select the Wizard

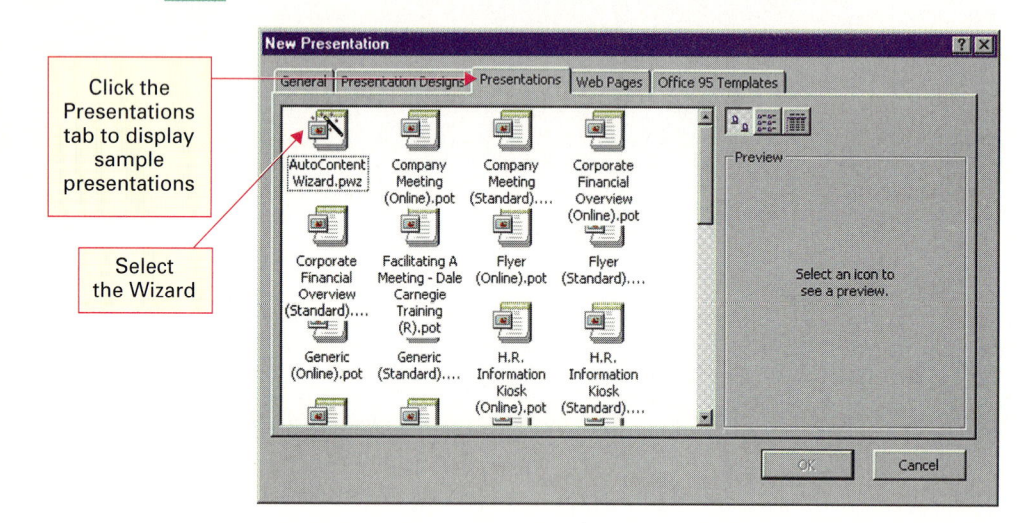

Note: Files listed on the Presentations page that have a .pot extension are sample presentation templates.

3 Doubleclick the *AutoContent Wizard.pwz*.

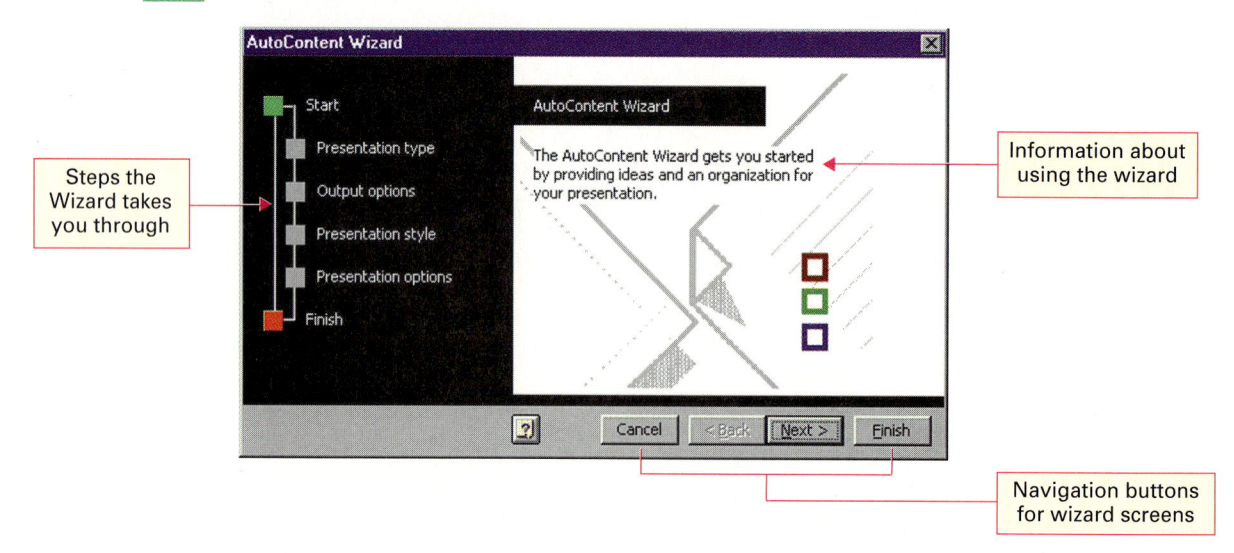

Steps the Wizard takes you through

Information about using the wizard

Navigation buttons for wizard screens

Project 2: Editing Slide Text   PP-71

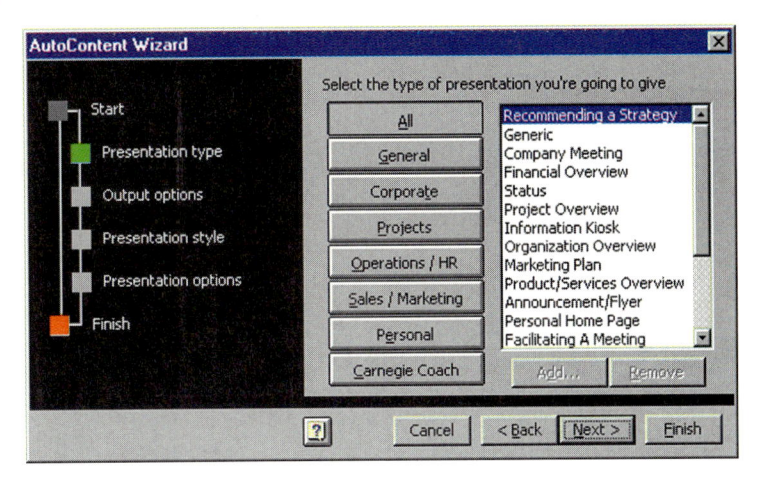

4 Click Next.

5 Click the Sales/Marketing button, select Product/Services Overview, and then click Next.

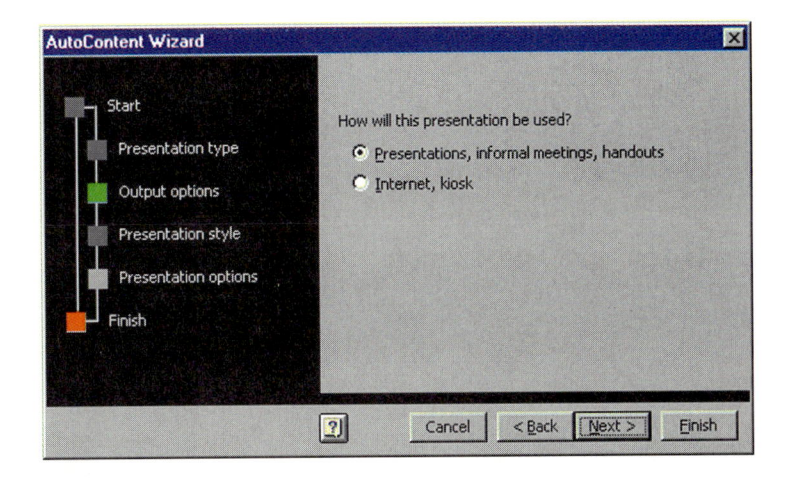

6 Select Presentations, informal meetings, handouts and then click Next.

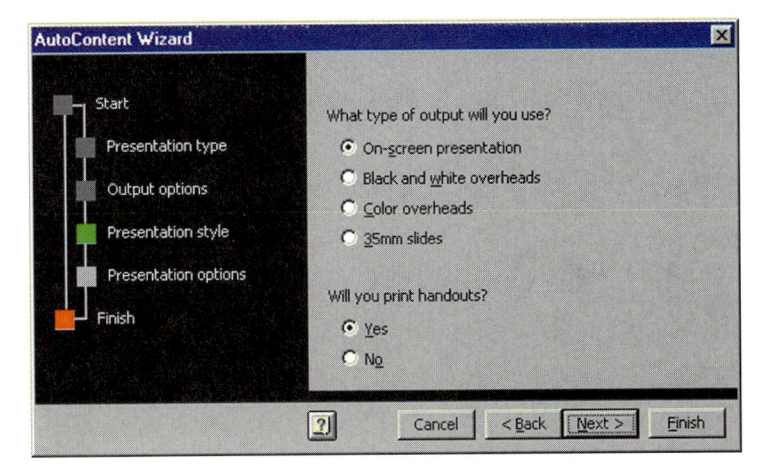

PP-72

7 Click Next to accept the default presentation style options.

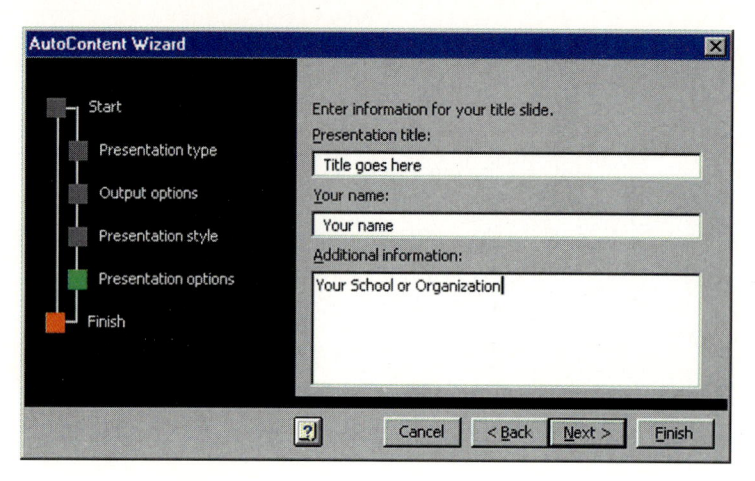

8 Type **The Willows** in the Presentation title text box, **Ms. Francesca Savoy** in the Your name text box, delete the text in the Additional information box, and then click Next.
The last screen the wizard presents instructs you to click Finish to continue. If you need to make changes to previous wizard screens, click the Back button until the screen appears, make the changes, and then click Finish from any screen.

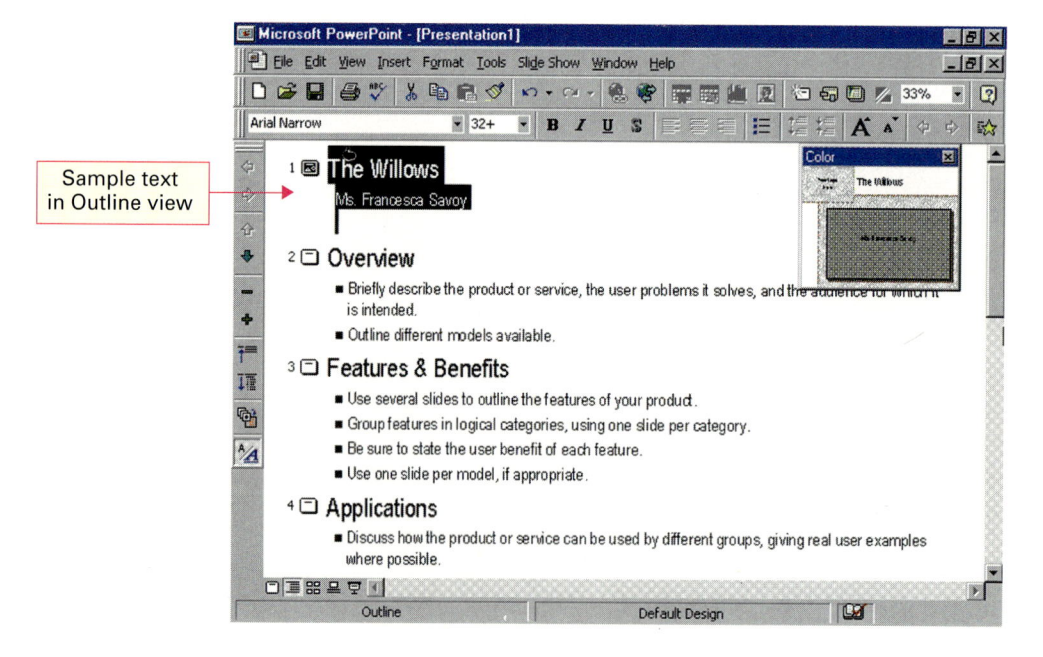

9 Click Finish.

Sample text in Outline view

10 Save the presentation using the filename *Marketing Presentation for Ms. Savoy* and close the presentation.

The Conclusion

Print copies of Slides 1, 2, 4, and 5 in the presentation *The Willows* as black-and-white slides. Print a copy of the marketing presentation in Outline view for Ms. Savoy. When you're done, save changes to both presentations and close the presentations.

Summary and Exercises

Summary

- Many of the techniques used to select, insert, delete, enhance, move, and copy text used in other Windows applications can be used to work with text in PowerPoint as well.
- You can use the Find and Replace commands to automatically substitute new text for existing text in a presentation.
- PowerPoint comes complete with features that enable you to check the spelling and style of slide text.
- You can change the size of object placeholders on slides by selecting the placeholder and dragging a handle; you can move the object placeholder on a slide by selecting the placeholder and dragging it to a new location.
- The Page Setup dialog box enables you to change the orientation of slides and other presentation materials and to set different dimensions for slides and presentation materials.
- Wizards enable you to create a new presentation based on the purpose of a presentation, and to format the presentation using a template appropriate to the presentation type. Presentations created using wizards include sample and instructive text that you can replace with specific text to complete your presentation.

Key Terms and Operations

Key Terms
AutoContent Wizard
font
handles
line spacing
orientation
page setup

Operations
change the size and orientation of slides and presentation materials
create a presentation using the AutoContent Wizard
edit placeholder format
select and edit text
use PowerPoint tools to check a presentation

Study Questions

Multiple Choice

1. To select text,
   a. you must use the keyboard.
   b. you must use the mouse.
   c. you can use either the mouse or keyboard.
   d. position the insertion point on a word and press Enter.

2. To insert a word between existing words in a bulleted list,
   a. position the insertion point where you want the new word and type the word.
   b. delete existing text and retype all text, adding the new word where you want it.
   c. create a new blank line to contain the new word.
   d. you must use Outline view.

3. Text enhancements in PowerPoint include all the following *except*
   a. bold.
   b. strikethrough.
   c. italics.
   d. superscripts.

4. The easiest way to copy text formatting is to use
   a. copy/paste.
   b. drag and drop.
   c. menu commands.
   d. the Format Painter.

5. To copy the font for selected text in a presentation to different text, use
   a. the Format Painter.
   b. the Replace Fonts command.
   c. copy/paste commands.
   d. drag and drop techniques.

6. To ensure consistency for end punctuation among bulleted lists, use the
   a. Spell Checker.
   b. Find command.
   c. Style Checker.
   d. Format Painter.

7. To ensure that capitalization of specific terms remains consistent throughout a presentation, use the
   a. Spell Checker only.
   b. Spell Checker or Style Checker.
   c. Style Checker only.
   d. Format Painter.

8. To place extra space between bulleted list items in a placeholder,
   a. change the font.
   b. make the placeholder larger.
   c. change the line spacing for text within the placeholder.
   d. press Enter two times between list items.

9. Instead of setting margins for text on slides,
   a. click the placeholder border.
   b. use the ruler.
   c. use a dialog box.
   d. size the text placeholder.

10. The Page Setup dialog box enables you to set
    a. the orientation for slides separately from that of other presentation materials.
    b. one orientation for all materials.
    c. the size of body text placeholders.
    d. one paper size for all materials.

Short Answer

1. How do you select all text for a bulleted list item?

2. What features are copied when you use the Format Painter?

3. What's the easiest way to apply the most frequently used text enhancements?

4. What text formatting features are found on the Formatting toolbar in PowerPoint that aren't usually found on the Formatting toolbar in other Windows applications?

5. What options can you set to limit the instances of text found using the Find feature in PowerPoint?

6. How do you change the size of paper you plan to use to print a presentation?

7. What are the two basic alignment settings you can apply to a placeholder?

8. How do you move a placeholder?

9. What settings can you change using the Page Setup dialog box?

10. What's the advantage of using the AutoContent Wizard to create a new presentation?

For Discussion

1. How do you choose a wizard to use for creating a presentation?

2. What's the difference between sizing a placeholder and sizing objects in other Windows applications?

3. What features does PowerPoint check when you use the Style Checker?

4. Which of PowerPoint's wizards will be most helpful to you in your area of study?

Review Exercises

1. Editing Text in an Existing Presentation

Based on the response received from her assistant managers, Ruth Lindsey, Manager of The Willows Shops, would like you to edit text contained on some of the slides in the presentation *The Willows Shops*. Revisions to slide text appear in the outline shown in Figure 2.6.

1. The Willows Shops
    Where Exploring Becomes an Adventure
2. Sindy's Sun Closet
    - Swimsuits and Accessories
    - Sun Cosmetics
    - Beach and Pool Toys
3. Weeping Willow Gallery
    - Paintings
    - Sculpture
    - Iron Works
    - Local Artisans
4. Live Oak Gifts
5. Creative Cutlery
    - A Large Assortment of Kitchen Wares
6. Cherry Street Market
    - Home Grown Produce
    - Natural Flora from the Carolinas
7. Victorian Tea Room
    - Victorian gifts and clothing
    - Victorian High Tea Served Daily
8. Ken's Kids
    - Children's games and toys
    - Children's clothing
9. Appalachian Crafts
    - Treasures from the Hills
    - Displays of local Artisans
10. The Newsstand
    - Newspapers
    - Magazines
    - Recent Publications
    - The Willows Post Office

Figure 2.6

Use the techniques explored in this project to edit the slides. Follow these instructions to complete the presentation:

1. Launch PowerPoint, if necessary, and open the presentation *The Willows Shops*.

2. Display the presentation in Outline view; select, edit, and enhance text on each slide as indicated in Figure 2.10.

3. Use the Find and Replace feature to change each occurrence of "Artists" in the presentation to "Artisans."

4. Move Slide 2 to the end of the outline.

5. Use the Spelling feature to check the spelling of your presentation.

6. Save changes to the presentation and print a copy of the presentation in Outline view.

7. Close the presentation and exit PowerPoint when you've completed your work.

2. Formatting Placeholders, Changing the Page Setup, and Checking the Style of Slides in a Presentation

Ms. Lindsey requests the format changes shown in Figure 2.7 for slides in the presentation *The Willows Shops*.

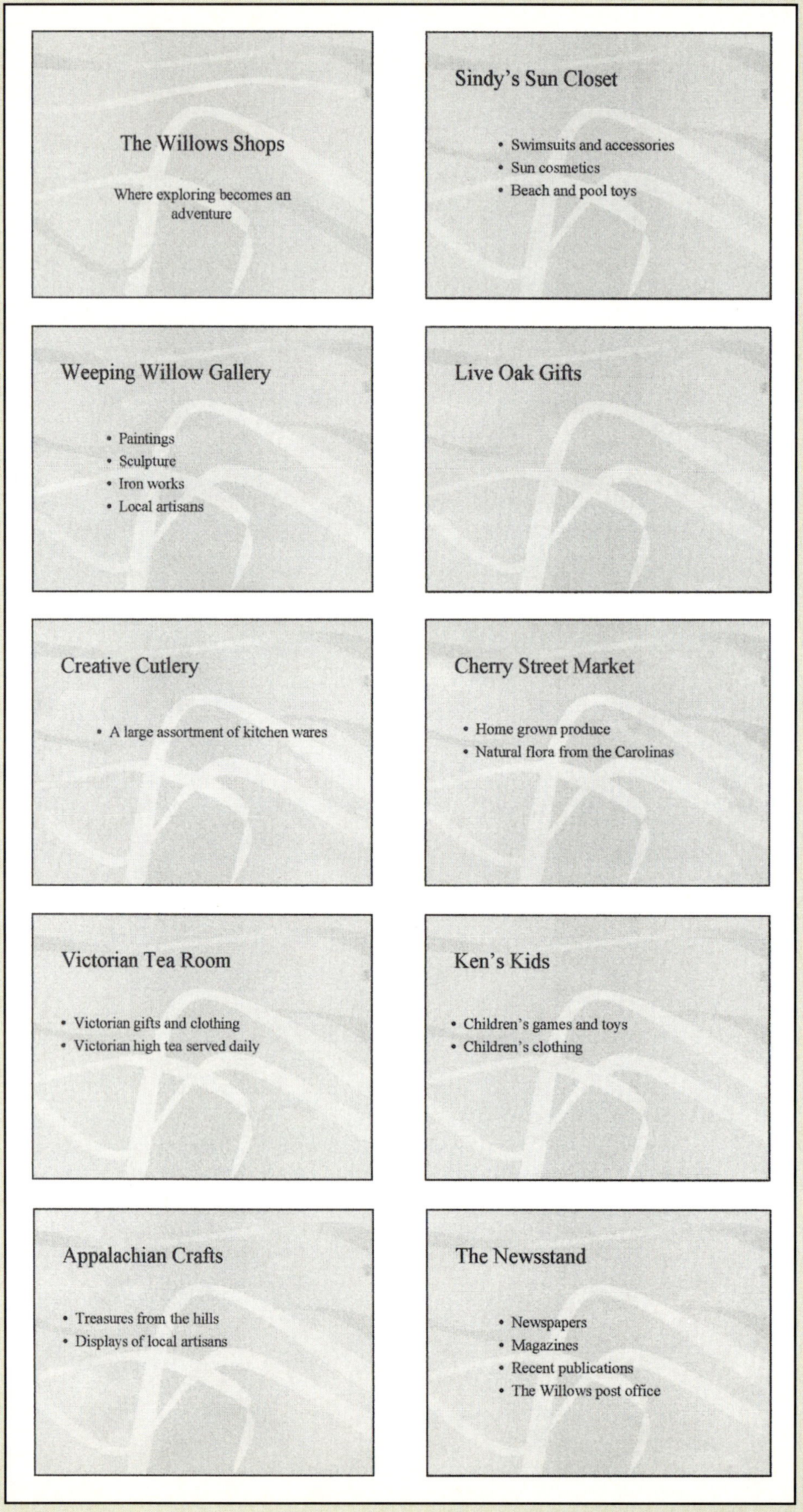

The Willows Shops

Where exploring becomes an adventure

Sindy's Sun Closet

- Swimsuits and accessories
- Sun cosmetics
- Beach and pool toys

Weeping Willow Gallery

- Paintings
- Sculpture
- Iron works
- Local artisans

Live Oak Gifts

Creative Cutlery

- A large assortment of kitchen wares

Cherry Street Market

- Home grown produce
- Natural flora from the Carolinas

Victorian Tea Room

- Victorian gifts and clothing
- Victorian high tea served daily

Ken's Kids

- Children's games and toys
- Children's clothing

Appalachian Crafts

- Treasures from the hills
- Displays of local artisans

The Newsstand

- Newspapers
- Magazines
- Recent publications
- The Willows post office

Figure 2.7

Follow these steps to complete the formatting:

1. Launch PowerPoint, if necessary, and open the presentation *The Willows Shops*.
2. Display Slide 5 in Slide view, select the bulleted list placeholder, and set the alignment of text to center horizontally in the placeholder.
3. Size placeholders to better fit the text each bulleted list placeholder contains. Position the placeholder on Slides 2, 3, and 10 so that the left edge of the placeholder aligns at the 3" mark on the horizontal ruler and the top of the placeholder aligns at the 1" mark above center on the vertical ruler.
4. Position the bulleted list placeholders for Slides 5–9 so that the top edge of the placeholder aligns with the 1" mark above center on the vertical ruler.
5. Left-align text in the title placeholder of Slide 2. Select the placeholder (not the text) and use the Format Painter to copy the alignment to title placeholders of all slides except Slide 1.
6. Use the Style Checker to check the style of text on slides in the presentation.
7. Save changes to the presentation and print slides as black-and-white handouts with six framed slides per page.
8. Close the presentation when you've completed your work.

Assignments

1. Editing and Formatting Slide Text and Placeholders
The revised *Festivals and Attractions* presentation slides appear in Figure 2.8.

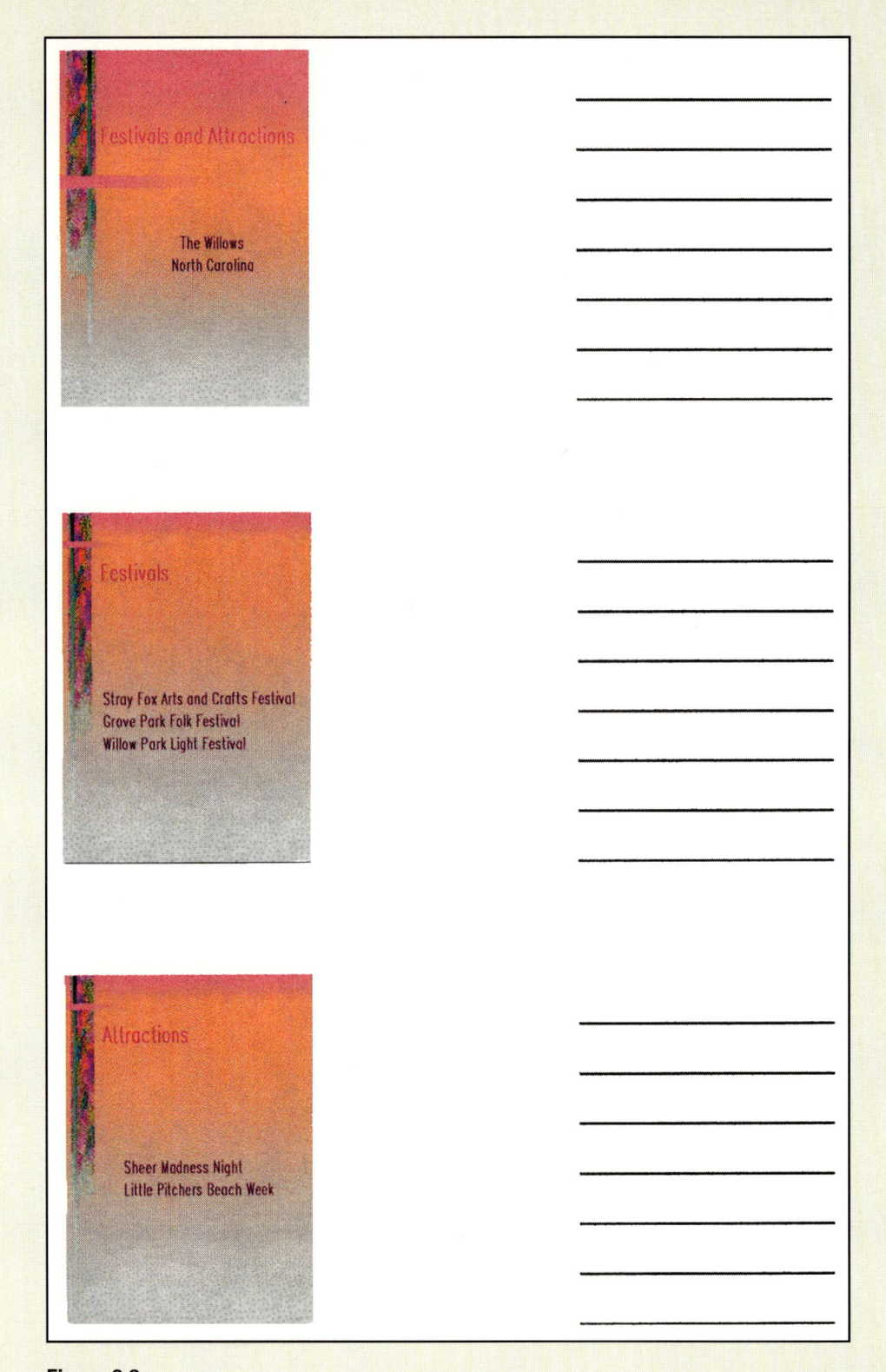

Figure 2.8

Use tools presented in this project to edit your presentation. Size, position, and format the text placeholders using the double-spaced, bold Modern font. Change the page setup of the presentation to format slides in portrait orientation. Check the spelling and style of the presentation. Because most of the features and attractions are proper names, however, don't check the presentation style for case. Save changes to the presentation and print black-and-white handouts with three framed slides per page. Close the presentation and exit PowerPoint when you've completed your work.

2. Creating a Presentation Using the Wizard

Ask your instructor how to obtain a presentation named *Resume.ppt*. The presentation contains an outline structure of information you should include in a résumé. Compare the sample résumé presentation to the one you designed in the Overview of PowerPoint to ensure that you've included all the necessary information. Then use the sample presentation and your own personal résumé to create a new presentation about yourself. Check the spelling and style of your presentation and format text and placeholders as desired. Apply a template to dress up the presentation. Save your presentation using your first and last names as the filename. Print a copy of your presentation as black-and-white handouts with three framed slides per page.

Close the presentation when you have completed your work.

3

PROJECT

Adding Art to a Presentation

PowerPoint makes dressing up your presentation with pictures quick and easy. Not only can you apply your own artistic talents to design powerful creations, but you can pull designs from the Clip Gallery or download them from the Internet. You can also use the PowerPoint WordArt module to change text into "words of art." In this project, you learn how to add graphics to your presentation slides and how to change the appearance of graphics to better fit your presentation needs.

Objectives

After completing this project, you will be able to:

➤ **Insert clip art into a slide**

➤ **Move and size clip art**

➤ **Download and insert clip art from the PowerPoint Web site**

➤ **Create WordArt**

➤ **Format WordArt**

➤ **Create drawings**

➤ **Manipulate art on a slide**

The Challenge

The template you applied to your presentations in Project 2 dressed up the design of your presentation but did nothing to fill in the blank space on presentation slides. Ms. Savoy would like for you to add appropriate graphics to slides in the presentation *The Willows*.

Project 3: Adding Art to a Presentation   PP-83

The Solution

As the graphics artist at The Willows, you get to add art to the slides in the presentation *The Willows*. Your dressed-up slides will appear as shown in Figure 3.1.

Figure 3.1

The Setup

So that your screen will match the illustrations shown in this project, make sure that the PowerPoint settings in the following table are selected on your computer:

Setting	Description
View menu	Choose Toolbars and then click the toolbar name for the one(s) you want to display. The four default toolbars and other toolbars that pop up automatically are displayed in this project.
Screen settings	Click the Maximize button to maximize the presentation window.
Tools menu	If you don't see the status bar, choose Options and then click the View tab. Select the check box beside Status Bar at the top of the page.

Inserting Clip Art

PowerPoint comes with a gallery of *clip art* images that you can use to enhance your presentation. You can use an AutoLayout that contains a clip art placeholder to add an image to a slide, or add an image to a slide that contains other types of placeholders. When you add a clip art image to a slide that contains a clip art placeholder, PowerPoint places the image in the placeholder and sizes it to fill the placeholder. When you add an image to a slide that doesn't contain a clip art placeholder, PowerPoint places the image in the middle of the slide and sizes it according to the default size of the clip art image.

The first time you access the Clip Gallery, PowerPoint takes a few moments to build the gallery and then presents thumbnail images of pictures.

TASK 1: TO INSERT CLIP ART IMAGES FROM THE CLIP GALLERY:

1. Open the presentation *The Willows* and display Slide 3 in Slide view.

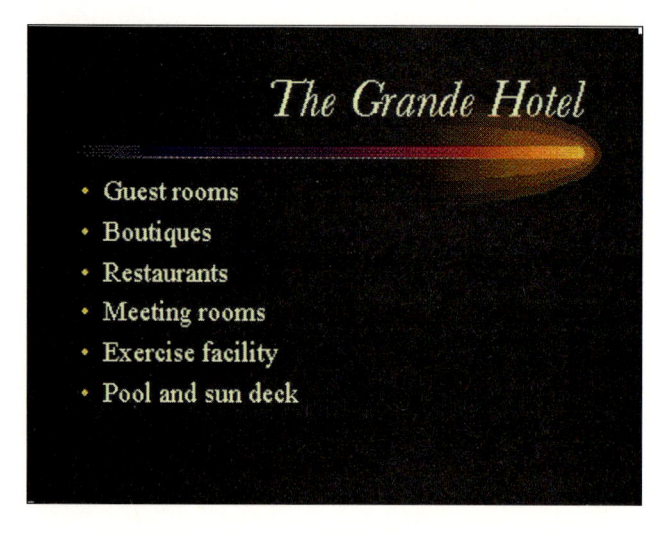

The Grande Hotel
- Guest rooms
- Boutiques
- Restaurants
- Meeting rooms
- Exercise facility
- Pool and sun deck

Project 3: Adding Art to a Presentation   **PP-85**

2 Choose Insert, Picture.

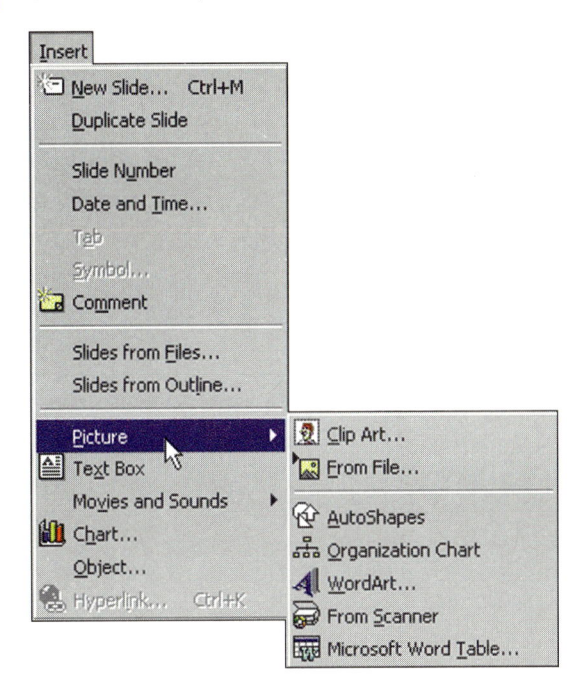

3 Choose Clip Art.

> **Note** You may see a message box telling you where you can find additional clips on the CD-ROM. Click OK to acknowledge the message.

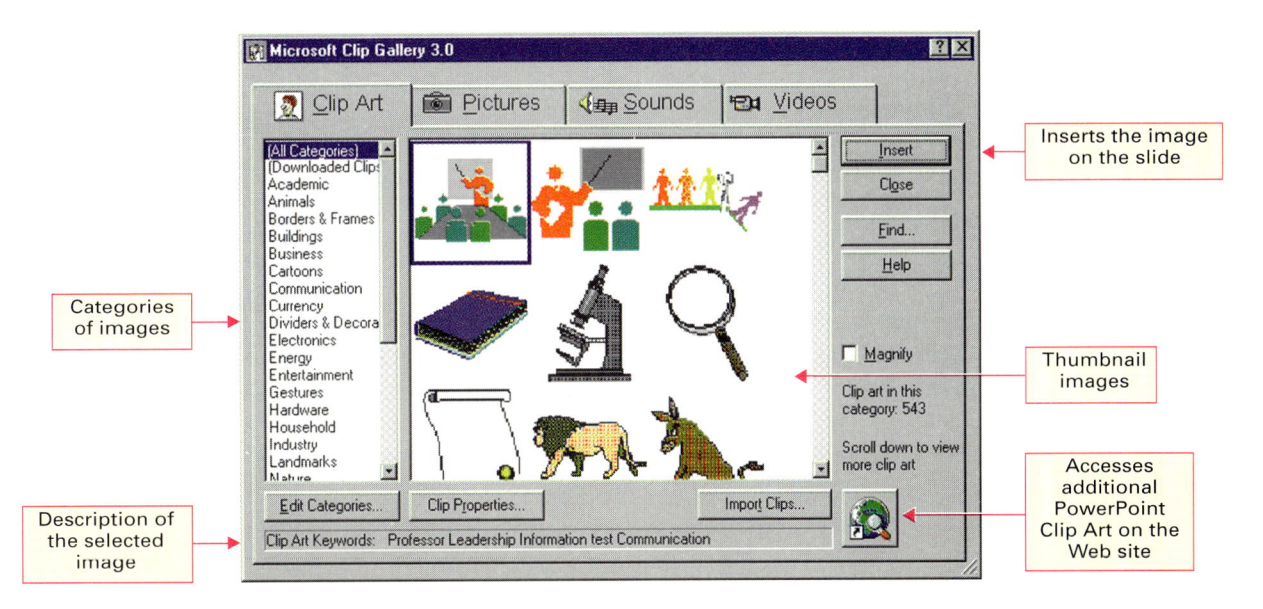

4 Click the Screen Beans category and then scroll until you see the Strong Powerful Invincible Superior Human image.

> **Note** If you don't see the image in your Clip Gallery, select a different image as directed by your instructor.

PP-86

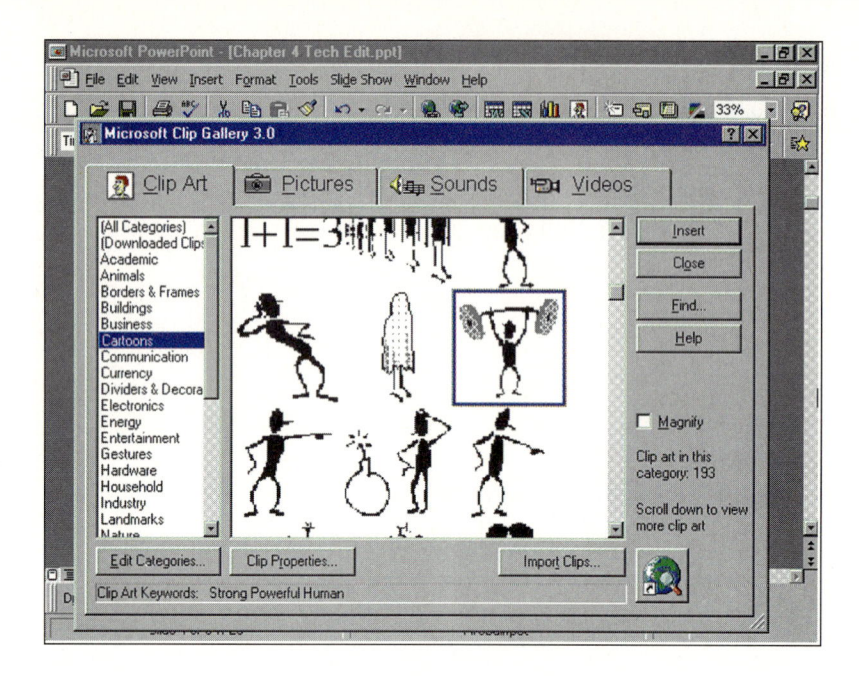

5 Click Insert.

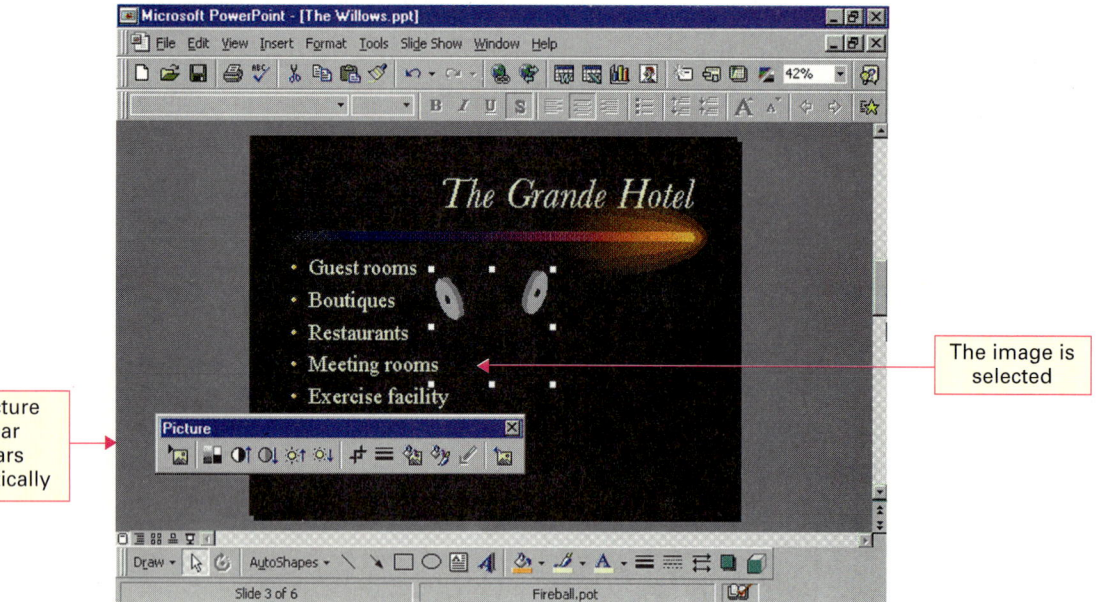

The Picture toolbar appears automatically

The image is selected

Project 3: Adding Art to a Presentation   PP-87

6 Click the Black and White View button on the Standard toolbar.

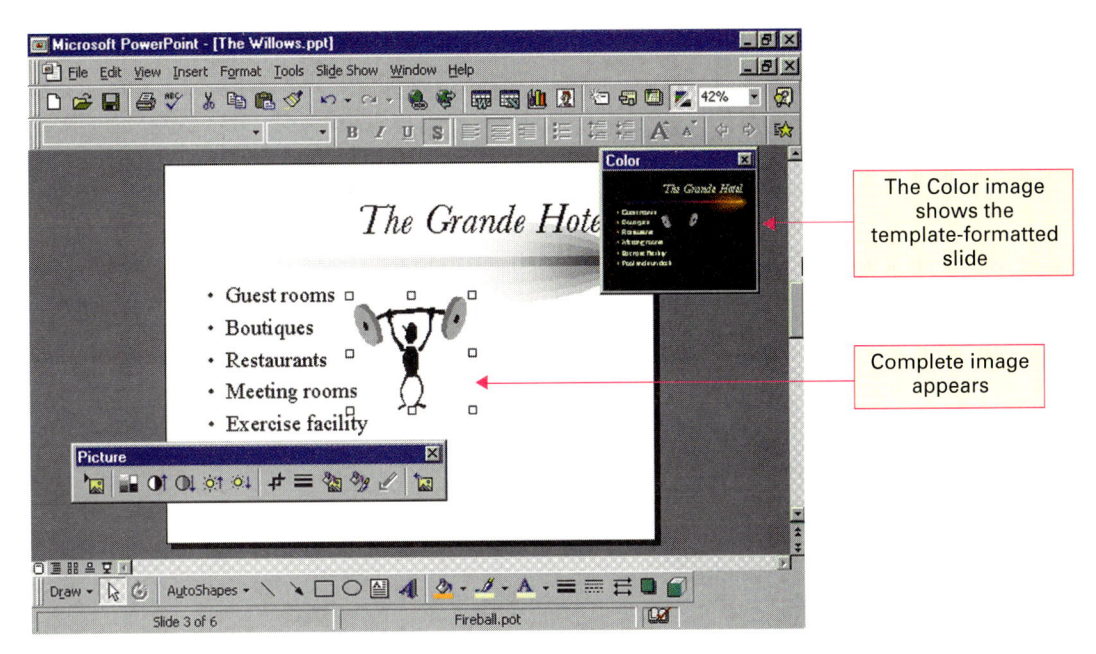

The Color image shows the template-formatted slide

Complete image appears

7 Save the changes to the presentation.

Moving and Sizing Clip Art

Clip art images that you add to slides often need to be positioned and sized so that they don't interfere with the text on the slide. When you add a clip art image to a slide, the image remains selected until you select another object or display a different slide. Selected images display handles on the corners and sides that you can use to size the image. To get a full-screen view of your slides as you work with the graphics, close the Color view box and the Picture toolbar.

TASK 2: TO MOVE AND SIZE A CLIP ART IMAGE:

1 Position the pointer on the selected image added to Slide 3.

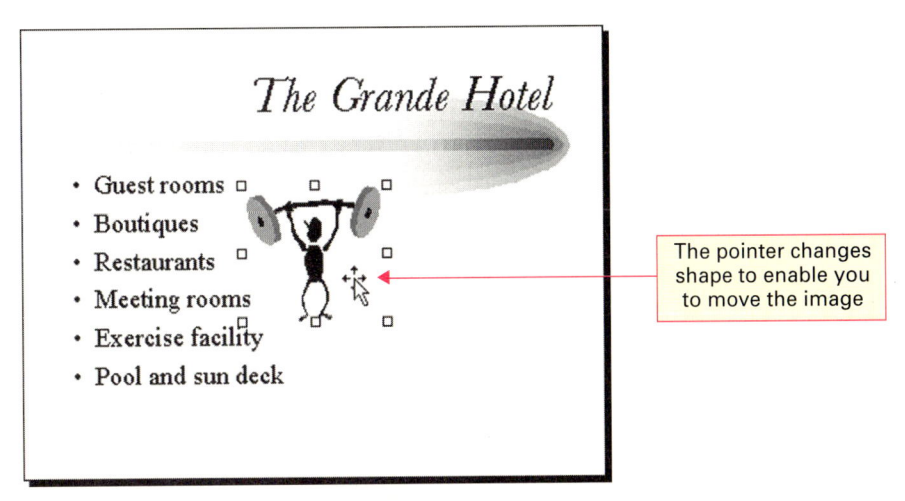

The pointer changes shape to enable you to move the image

2 Click and drag the image to the lower-right corner of the slide.

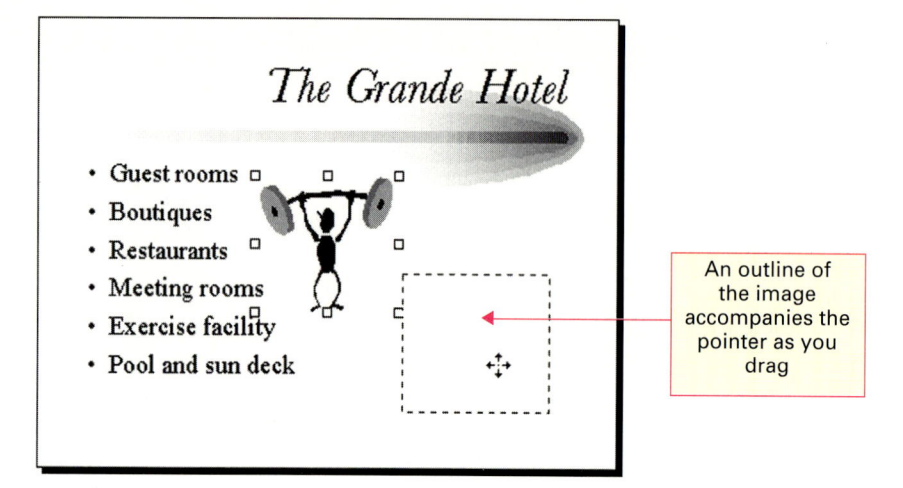

An outline of the image accompanies the pointer as you drag

3 Release the mouse button to drop the image.

4 Position the pointer on the handle in the upper-left corner.

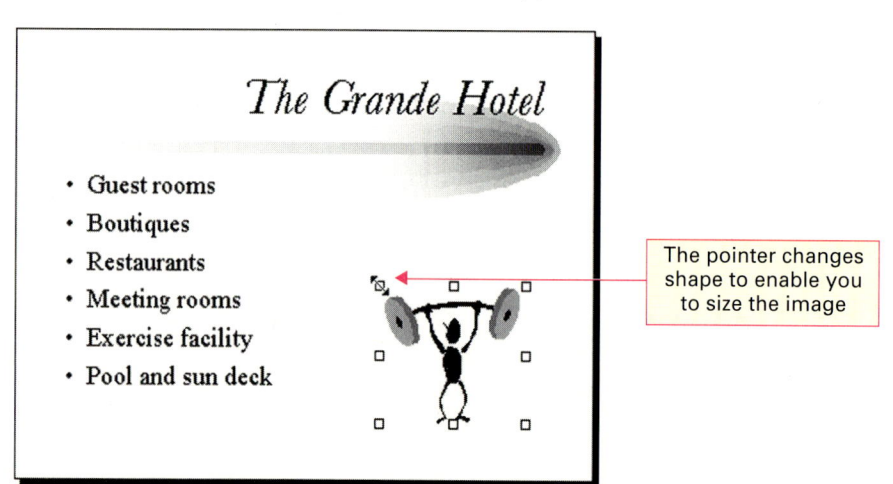

The pointer changes shape to enable you to size the image

Project 3: Adding Art to a Presentation   PP-89

5 Click and drag the corner handle to size the image.

6 Save the changes to the presentation.

Downloading and Inserting Clip Art from the PowerPoint Web Site

When the Clip Gallery that comes with PowerPoint doesn't contain the pictures you need, you can search the PowerPoint Web site for additional graphics.

TASK 3: TO DOWNLOAD CLIP ART FROM THE POWERPOINT WEB SITE:

1 Display Slide 4 of the presentation *The Willows* in Slide view.

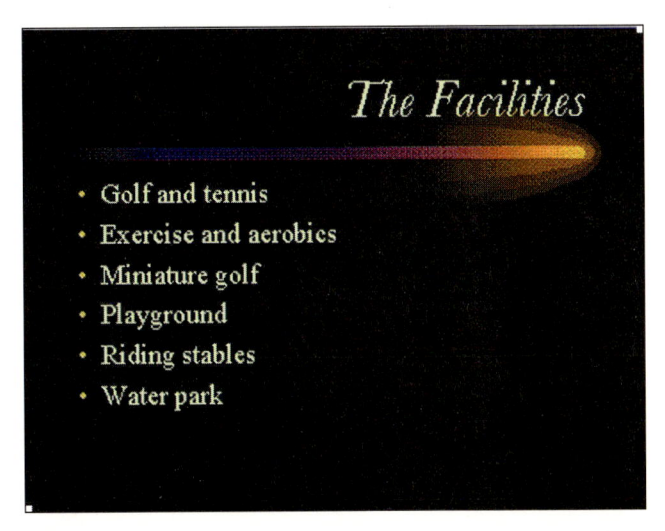

2 Choose Insert, Picture, Clip Art to open the Clip Gallery. The Clip Gallery window opens.

3 Click the globe icon representing a shortcut to the Web.

> **Note** Depending on how your computer is set up, you may see the following message box. Simply click OK to acknowledge the message.

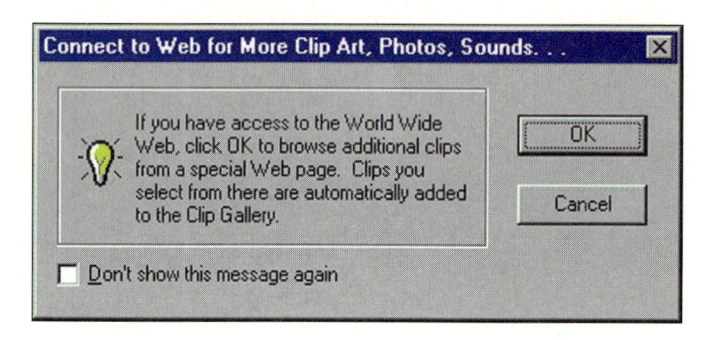

4 Log on to the Internet, using standard logon procedures.

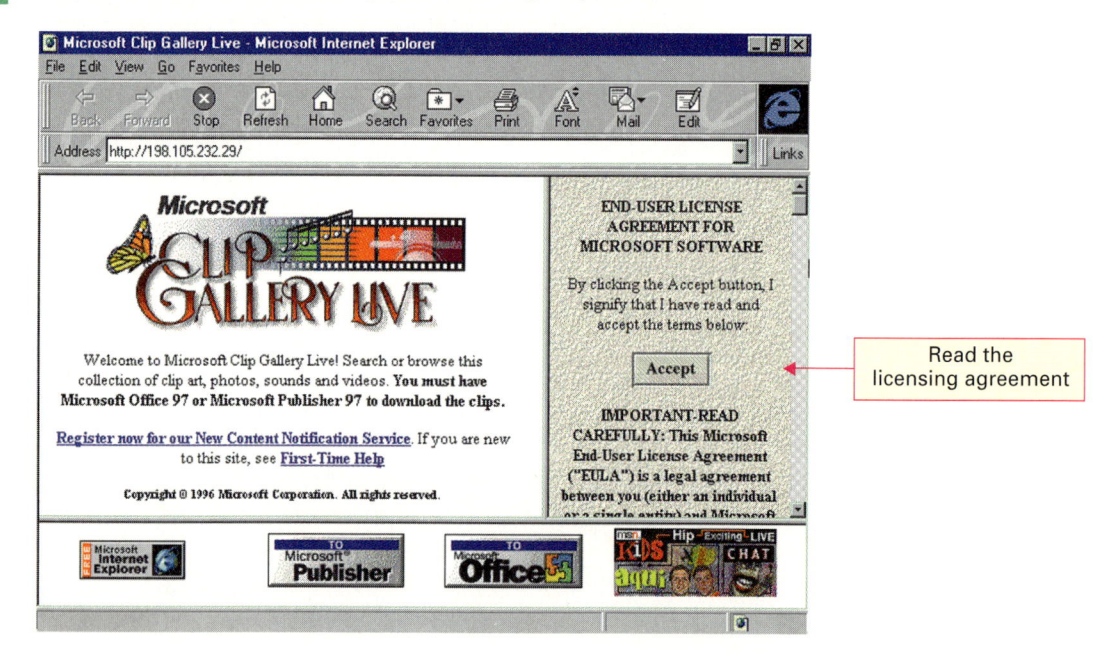

Read the licensing agreement

Project 3: Adding Art to a Presentation   PP-91

5 Read the license agreement and then click the Accept button.

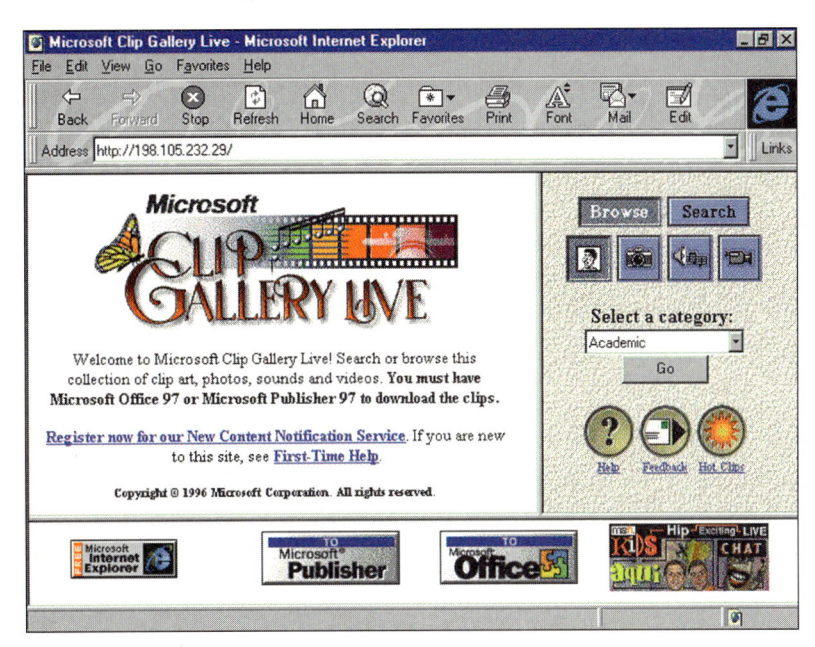

Note The Web page you see may differ from the one pictured here. Microsoft changes Web pages regularly to reflect updates to software and to add new clips.

6 Click the arrow button beside the Select a category list box, select Animals, and click Go.

Total number of pictures found

Number displayed

Click the Search button to start the search

7 Click the Search button.

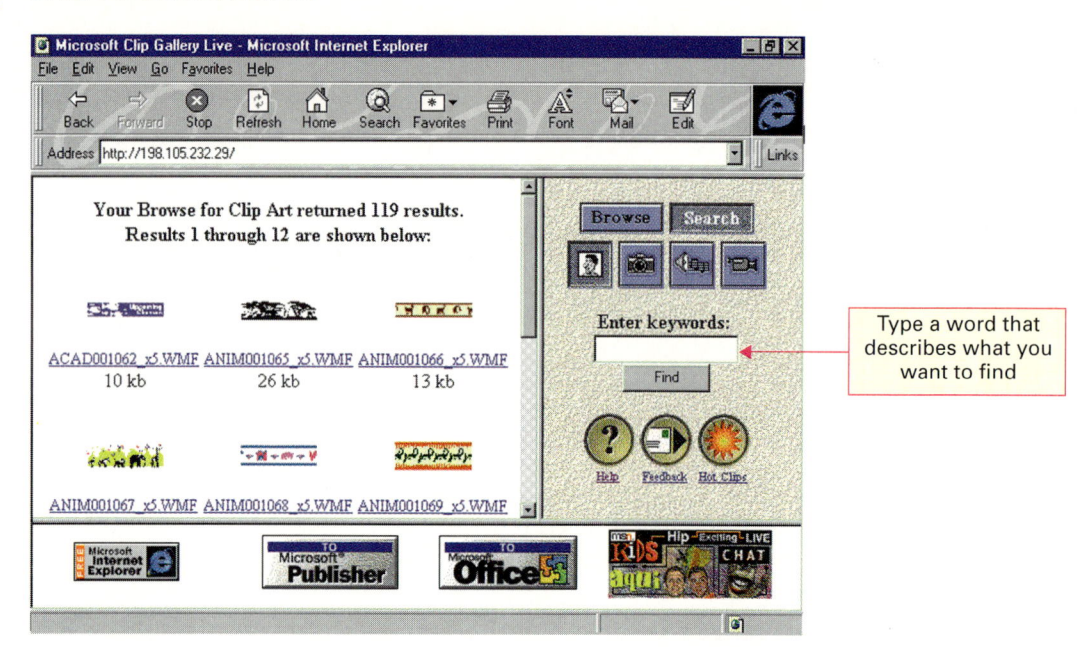

Type a word that describes what you want to find

8 Type **Golf** in the Enter keywords text box and then click the Find button.

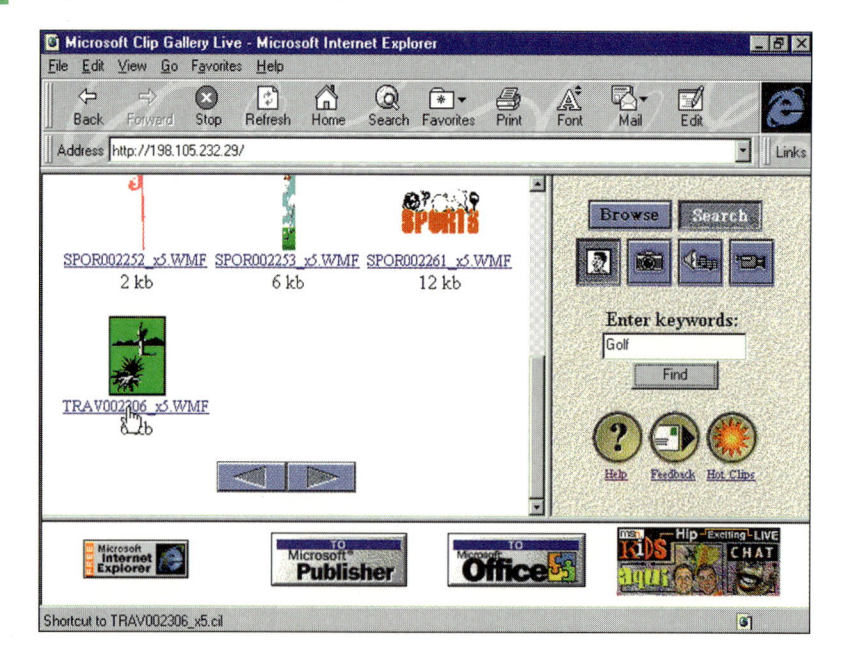

Project 3: Adding Art to a Presentation   PP-93

9 Scroll until you see the filename *TRAV002306_x5.wmf* and then click the filename to select the image.

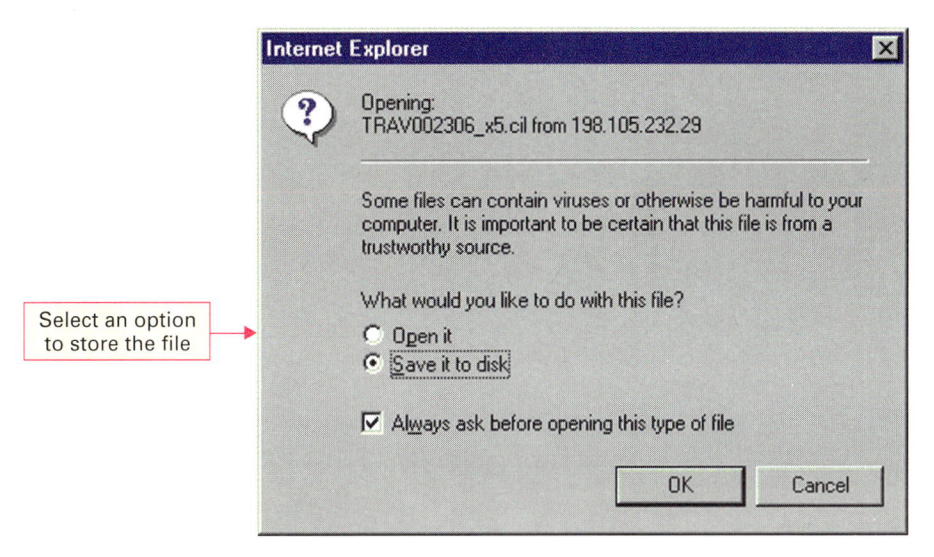

Select an option to store the file

10 Click the Open it option and then click OK.
PowerPoint adds the image to the Downloaded Clips category of the Clip Gallery 3.0 window.

11 Select the downloaded image and click Insert.
PowerPoint places the image on the slide that was active when you launched the Web site.

12 Log off the Internet and display Slide 4 in PowerPoint Slide view.

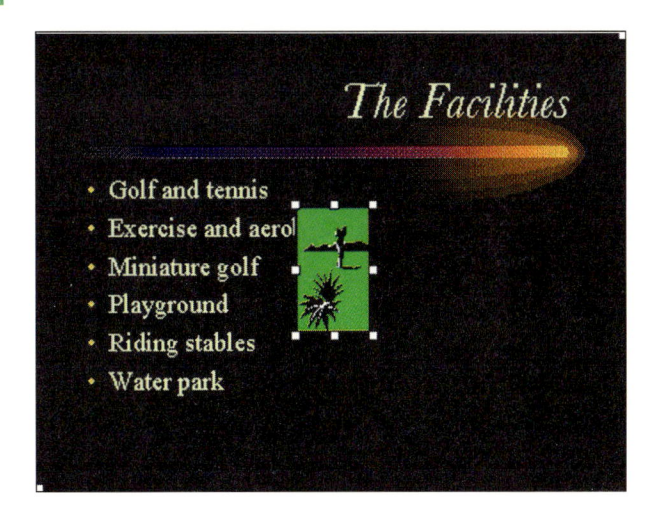

The Facilities
- Golf and tennis
- Exercise and aerobics
- Miniature golf
- Playground
- Riding stables
- Water park

13 Size and position the graphic as shown and then save the changes to the presentation.

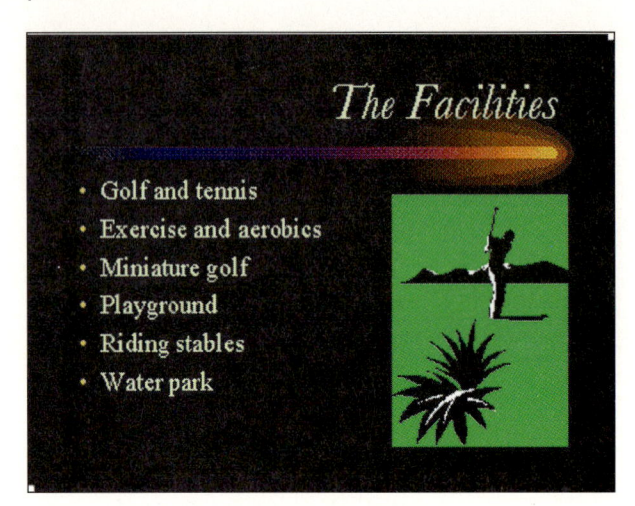

Creating WordArt

The *WordArt* module available in PowerPoint is the same module you may have used in other Microsoft applications. WordArt enables you to type text, curve, skew, or mold the text into a shape that better fits the area of the slide you want it to occupy. It's a great way to grab someone's attention.

TASK 4: TO CREATE WORDART:

1 Display Slide 6 in Slide view.

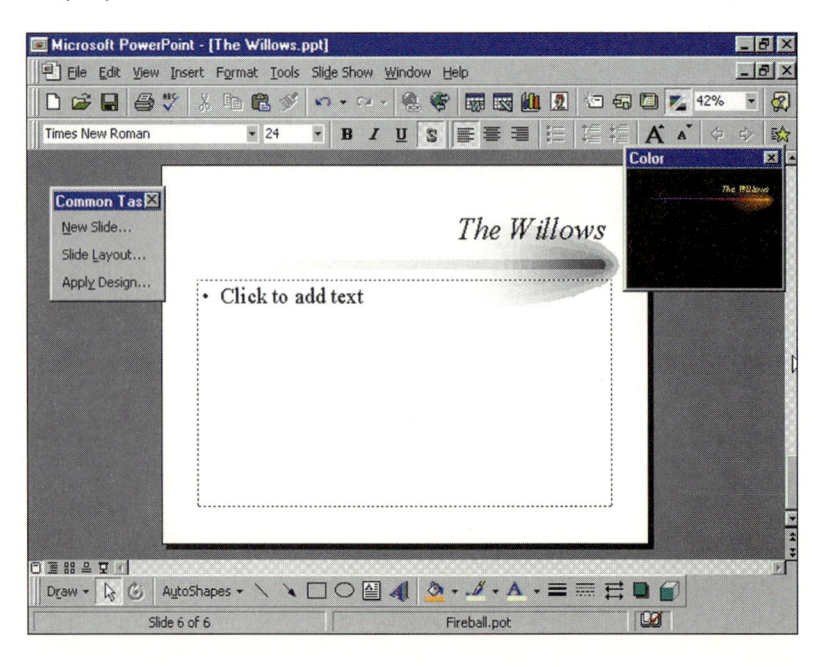

Project 3: Adding Art to a Presentation   PP-95

2 Press SHIFT and click the bulleted list placeholder; then press DEL. The title placeholder is now the only object on the slide.

3 Choose Insert, Picture, WordArt.

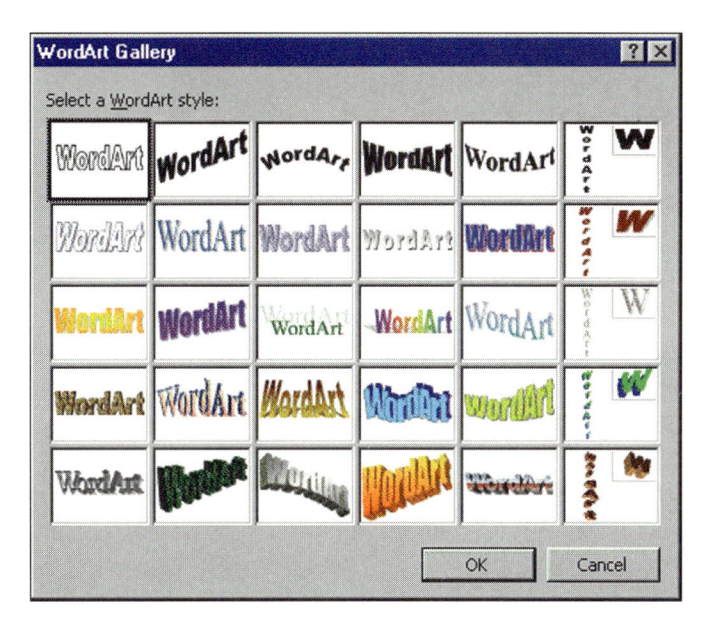

4 Select the fifth style in the top row and press ENTER.

5 Type **A Symbol of Genteel Quality** and click OK.

PP-96

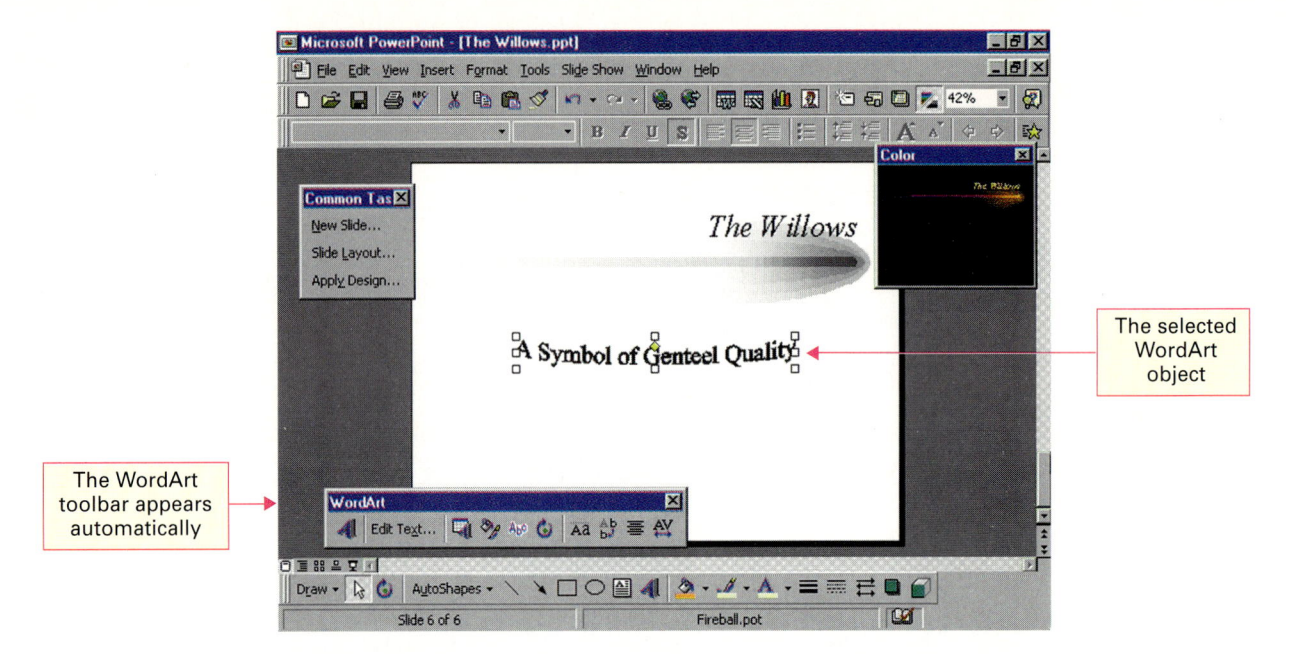

The WordArt toolbar appears automatically

The selected WordArt object

6 Drag the WordArt object to a position at the bottom of the slide.

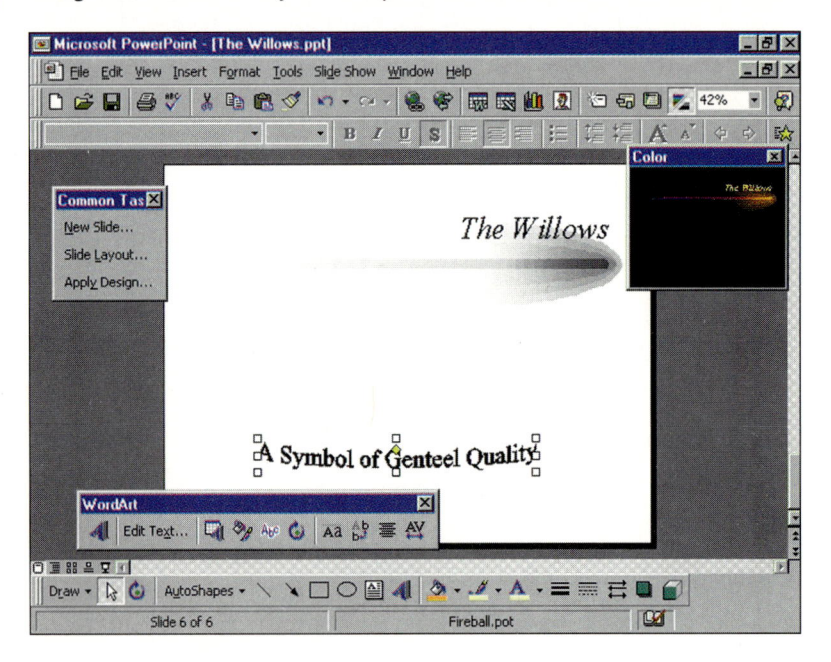

7 Save the changes to the presentation.

Formatting WordArt

After you get the WordArt object on the slide, you need to format the WordArt so that it appears the way you want it. You can use the WordArt toolbar to edit WordArt text as well as to change the shape, format, and angle of the WordArt object.

Project 3: Adding Art to a Presentation   PP-97

TASK 5: TO FORMAT WORDART OBJECTS:

1 Click the WordArt object on Slide 6, if necessary, to select it. The WordArt object displays handles on the corners and sides.

2 Click the Format WordArt button on the WordArt toolbar.

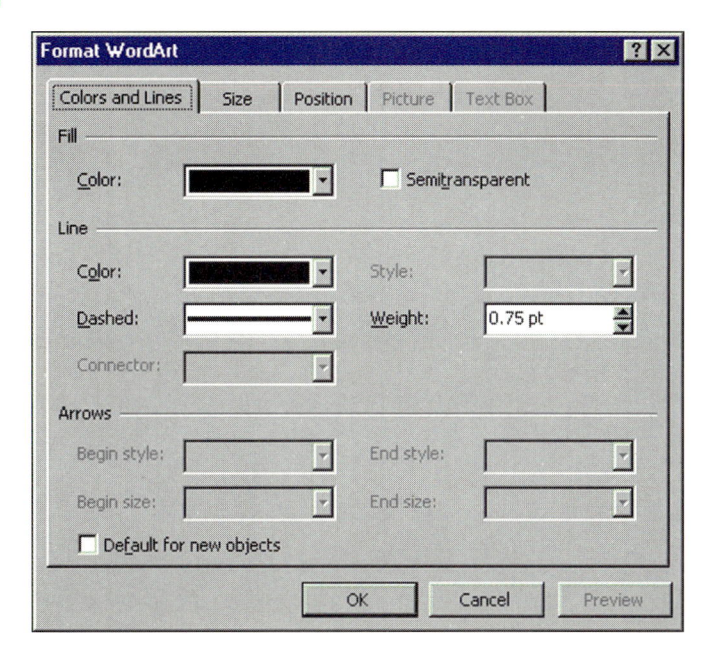

3 Click the arrow button for the Fill Color option.

> **Note** The color you select from the Fill palette controls the color of the WordArt text.

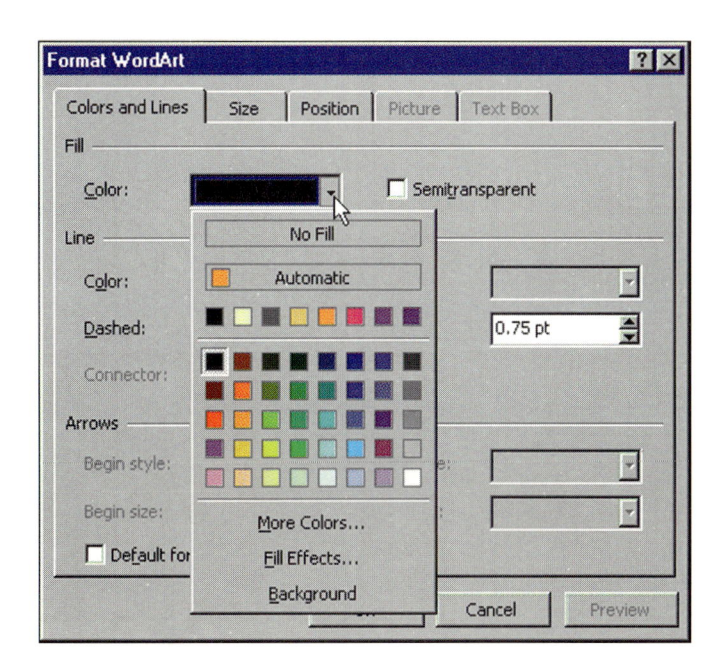

4 Click the second color box on the bottom row of the color palette and then click the arrow button to open the Line Color option.

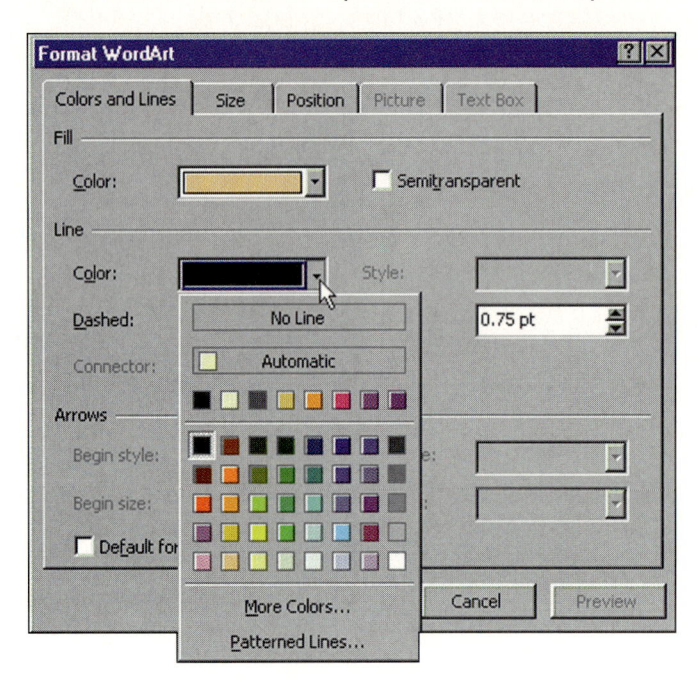

5 Click the second color box on the bottom row of the color palette and then click OK.

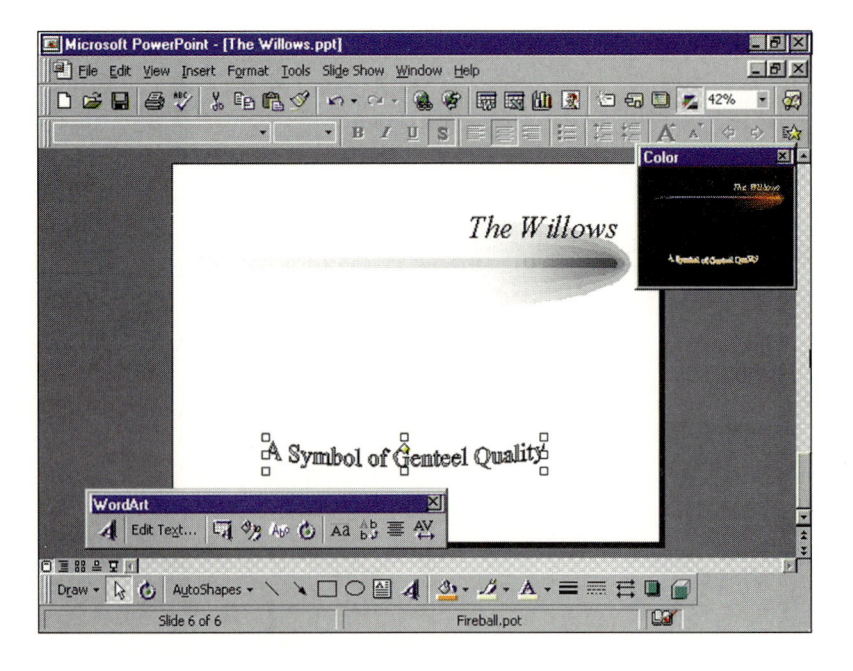

6 Click ▨ to display the slide in color.

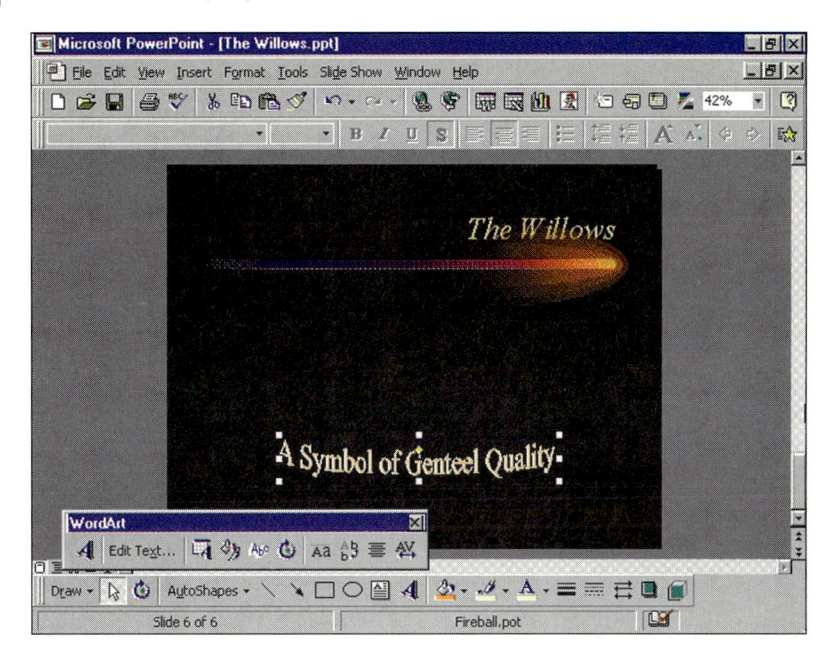

7 Drag the top center handle of the WordArt object to expand the size of the object.

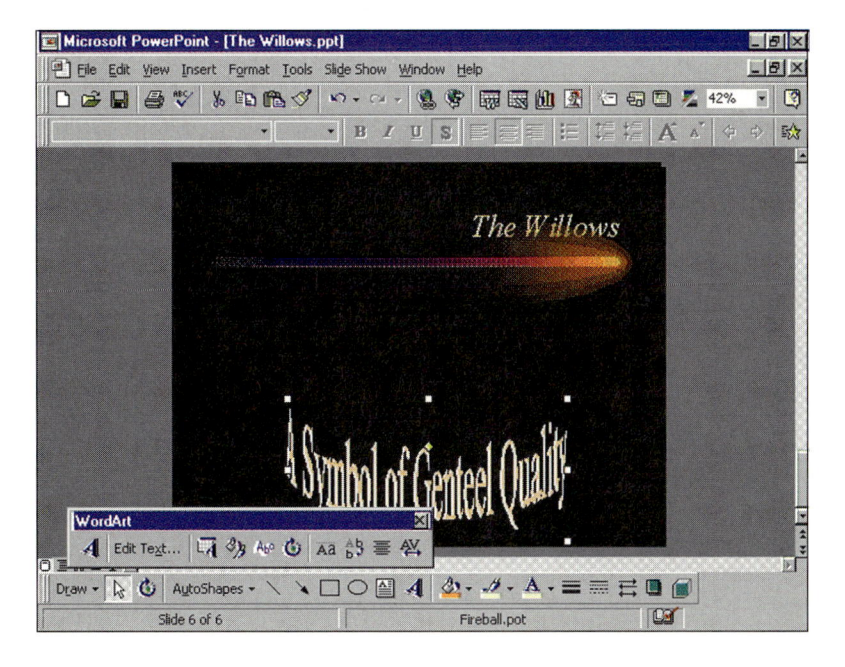

8 Save the changes to the presentation.

Creating Drawings

In addition to the special features such as WordArt, you'll also find quite a sophisticated drawing module that enables you to enhance your slides with original *freehand* creations. Even if you're no artist, you'll find the tools on the Drawing toolbar easy to use. Simply select the tool that represents the shape you want to draw, position the pointer where you want to start the drawing, click, and drag the pointer to the point where you want the shape to end.

TASK 6: TO CREATE DRAWINGS USING THE DRAWING TOOLBAR:

1   Display Slide 2 in Slide view.

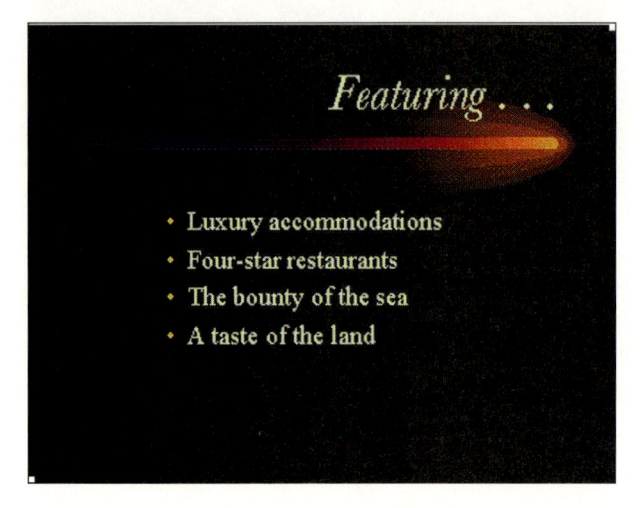

Note If you don't see the Drawing toolbar on your screen, position the pointer on any active toolbar, right-click, and then select the Drawing toolbar.

2   Click the AutoShapes button on the Drawing toolbar and select Stars and Banners.

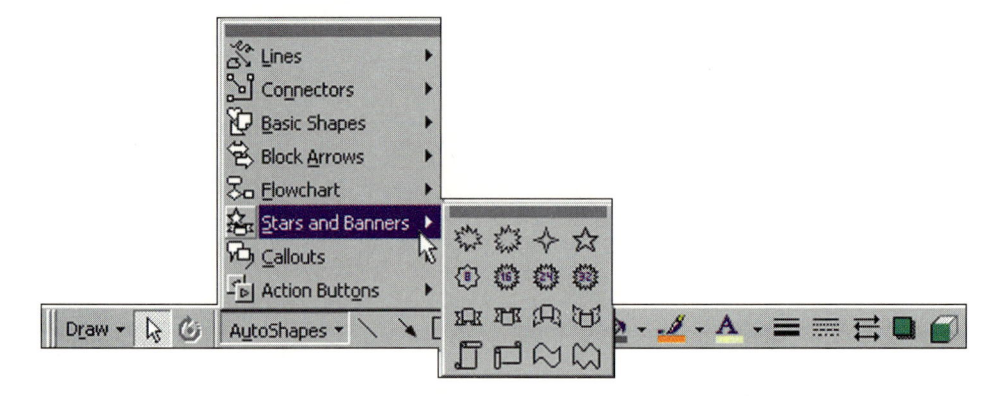

3   Click the 5-Point Star shape on the first row of the palette.
    The mouse pointer changes shape and looks like a plus (+) sign.

4   Position the pointer below and to the left of the last bulleted item, click, and drag diagonally to draw the shape.

Project 3: Adding Art to a Presentation   PP-101

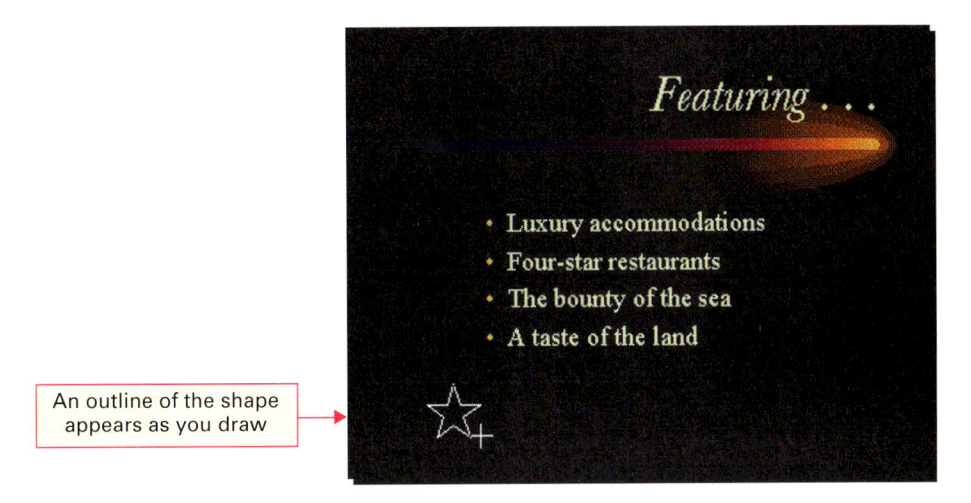

An outline of the shape appears as you draw

5   Click the Arrow button on the Drawing toolbar, press (SHIFT), and draw an arrow below the second bulleted item.

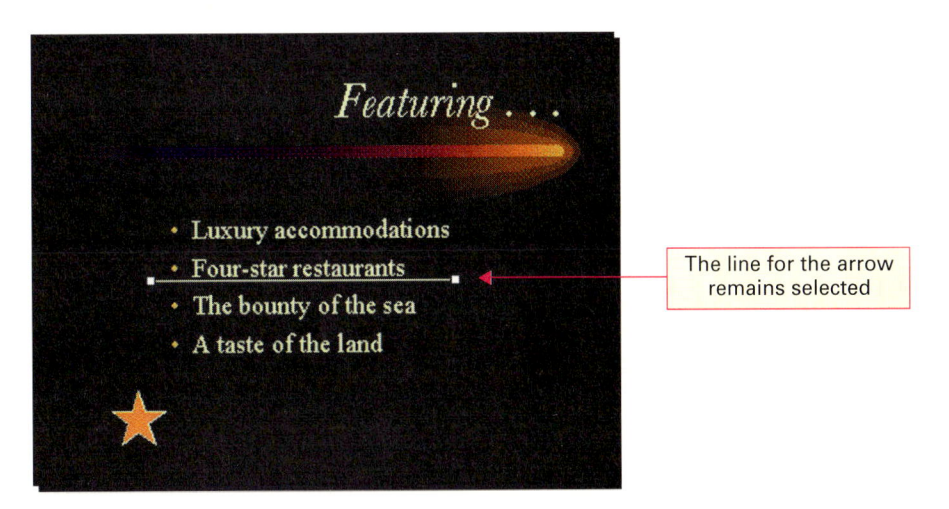

The line for the arrow remains selected

6   Click the Arrow Style button on the Drawing toolbar.

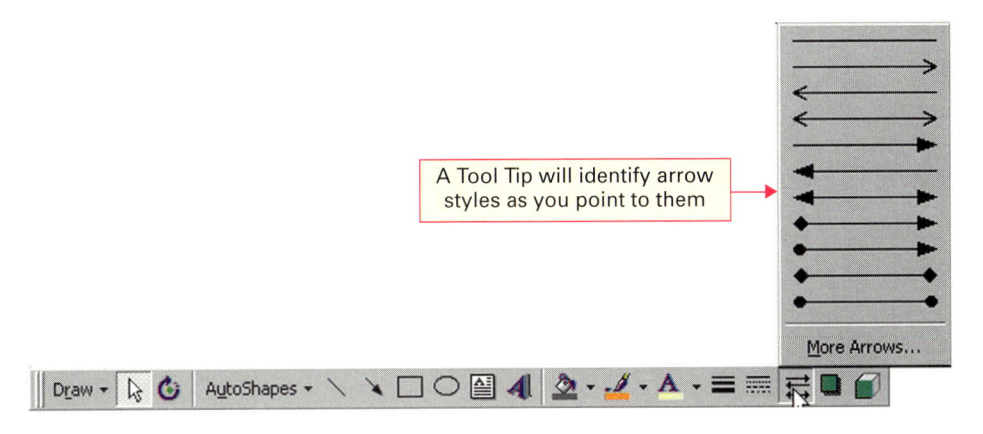

A Tool Tip will identify arrow styles as you point to them

7   Select Arrow Style 10 and then double-click the line for the arrow you just drew.

8 Click the spin buttons beside the Line Weight text box to increase the weight to 2 pt, if necessary; then click OK.
The arrow on the slide appears thicker.

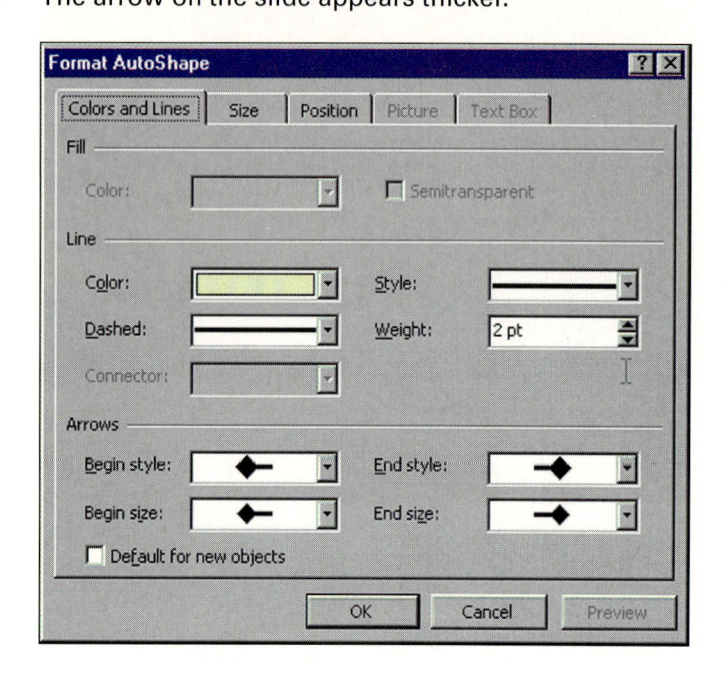

9 Click the star shape you drew earlier to select it and then click the Line Color arrow button.

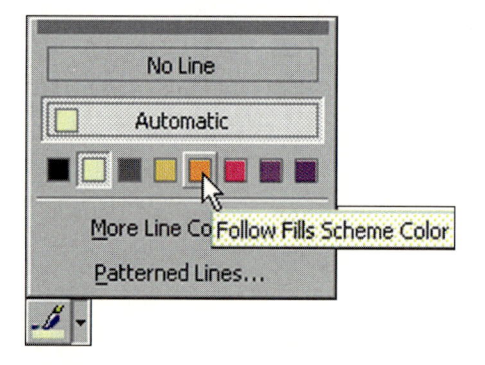

10 Click the Follow Fills Scheme Color box on the Line Color palette.
Changing the line color for the star to the same color as the star fill color makes the shape a more cohesive unit by hiding the shape's outline.

Project 3: Adding Art to a Presentation **PP-103**

11 Click the 3-D button on the Drawing toolbar and select 3-D Style 6.

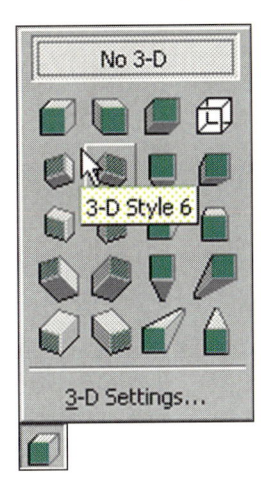

12 Press CTRL+**D** to duplicate the star.

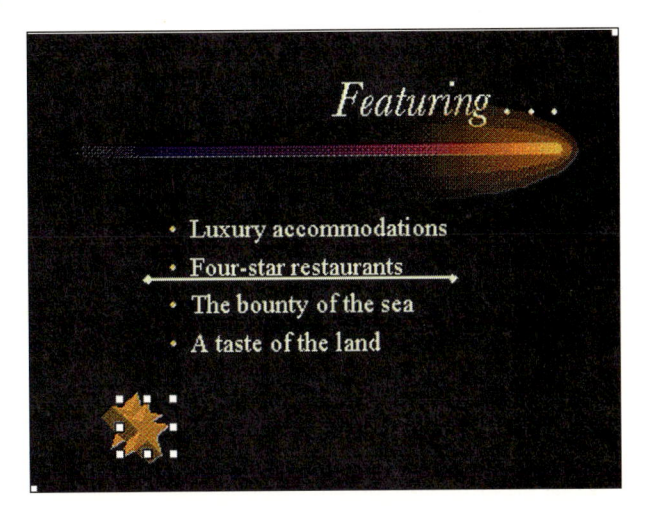

13 Drag the new star slightly up and to the right of the first star.

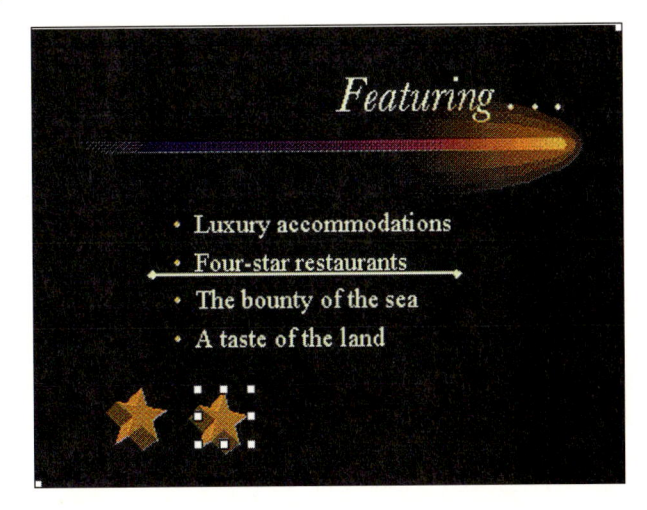

14 Repeat step 12 two more times and arrange the stars as in:

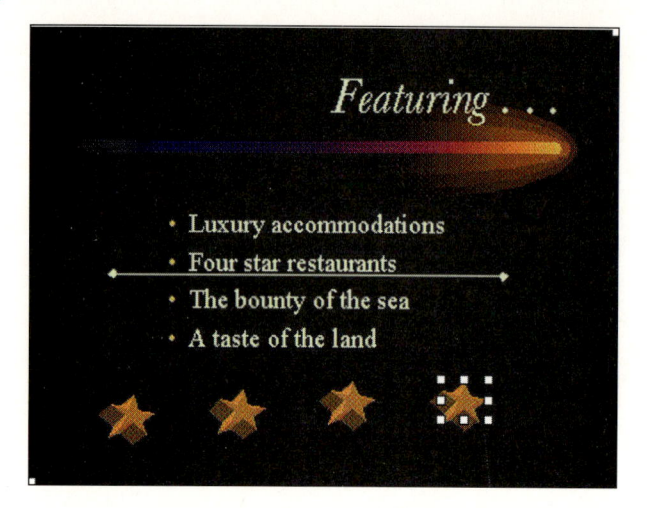

15 Save the changes to the presentation.

Manipulating Art

Clip art images that you add to slides and drawings that you create freehand often need to be adjusted so that they display appropriately on the slides. Using PowerPoint's special features, you can *flip* images to make them face the opposite direction, turn them upside down, *rotate* them to create special effects, *group* separate objects to make them stick together, and *ungroup* grouped objects to change pieces of the objects. You can also rearrange the objects so that different objects appear in front of or behind other objects.

TASK 7: TO MANIPULATE ART OBJECTS:

1 Display Slide 3 in Slide view.

The clip art image you added is lost in the background color

Project 3: Adding Art to a Presentation   PP-105

2 Click the clip art image to select it and then click the Draw button on the Drawing toolbar.

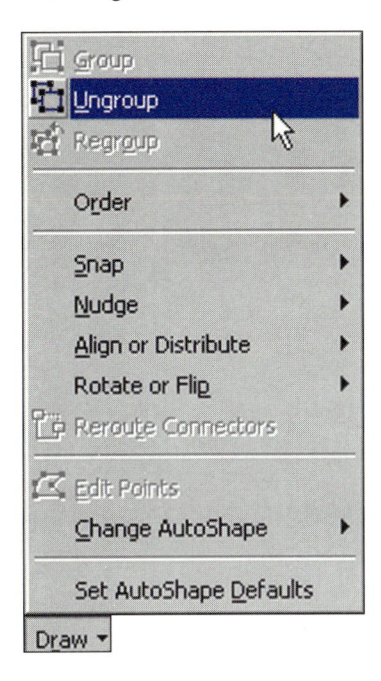

```
  Group
  Ungroup
  Regroup
  Order          ▶
  Snap           ▶
  Nudge          ▶
  Align or Distribute ▶
  Rotate or Flip ▶
  Reroute Connectors
  Edit Points
  Change AutoShape ▶
  Set AutoShape Defaults
Draw ▼
```

3 Click Ungroup.
A message box tells you that you are about to convert the image to a PowerPoint image. By converting the object, you can edit pieces of the object.

4 Choose Yes to convert the object to a PowerPoint image.

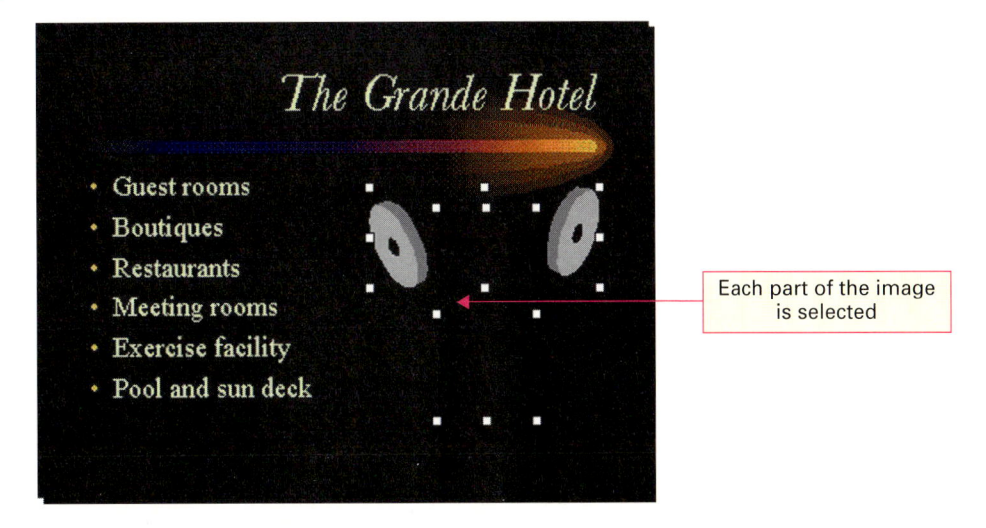

The Grande Hotel
- Guest rooms
- Boutiques
- Restaurants
- Meeting rooms
- Exercise facility
- Pool and sun deck

Each part of the image is selected

5 Press (SHIFT) and click the barbells to deselect them.
Only the body of the clip art image remains selected.

6 Click the Fill Color button arrow on the Drawing toolbar.

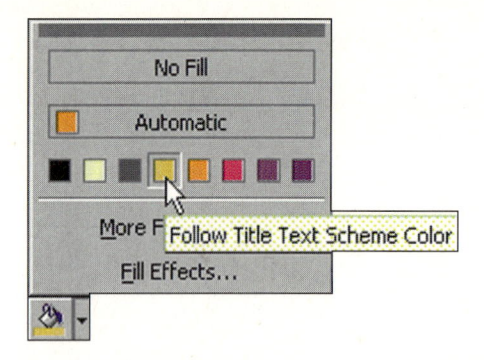

7 Click the Follow Title Text Scheme Color button on the Fill Color palette.

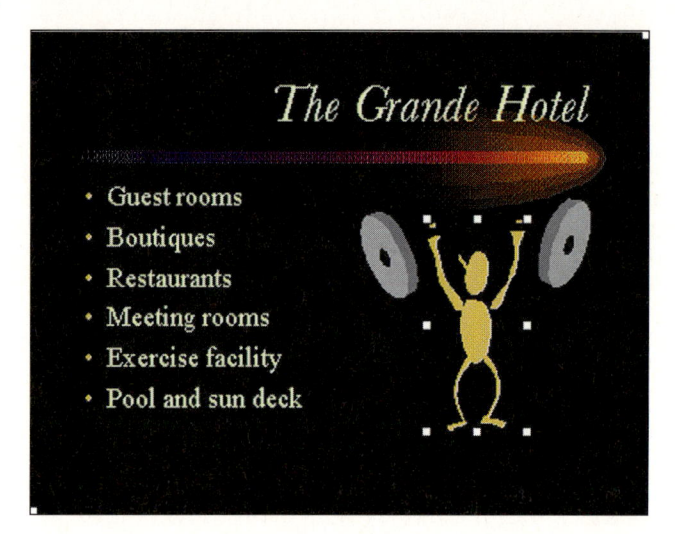

8 Click the barbells and ungroup the object.

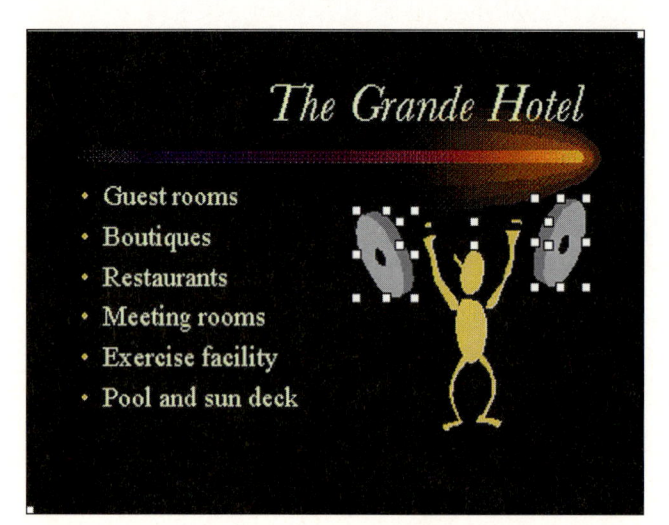

Tip If the selected object isn't made up of smaller objects, the Ungroup command on the Draw menu isn't available.

9 Press (SHIFT) and click each of the gray barbells, leaving only the bar selected.

10 Click the fill color button arrow and click the dark gray color.

Project 3: Adding Art to a Presentation PP-107

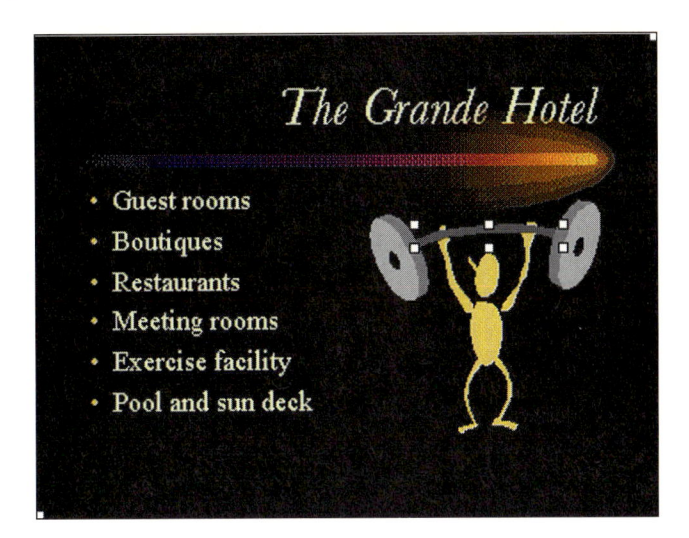

11 Click the body of the clip art image and then click the Draw button on the Drawing toolbar and select Rotate or Flip.

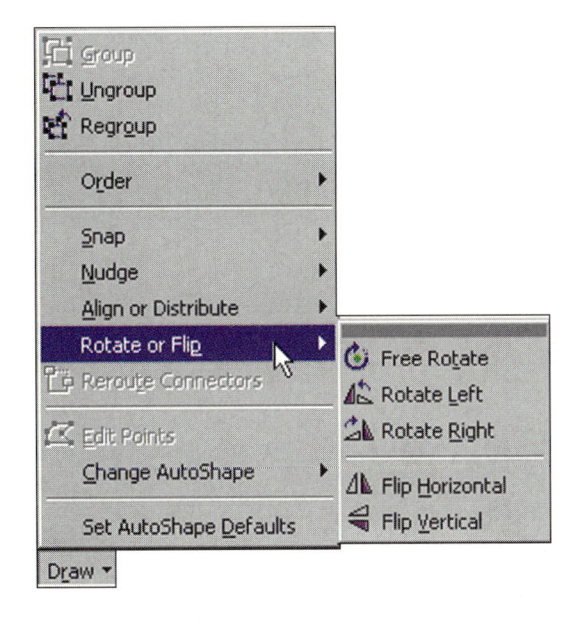

12 Click Flip Horizontal.

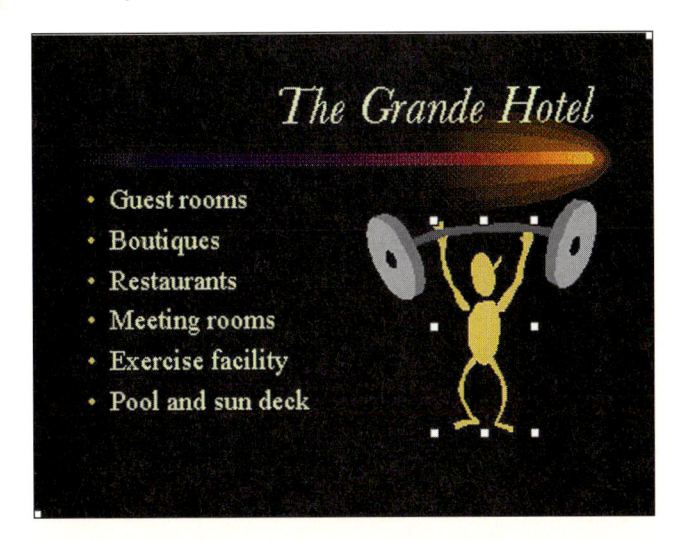

PP-108

13 Position the pointer slightly above and to the left of the leftmost barbell; then click and drag across the clip art image.

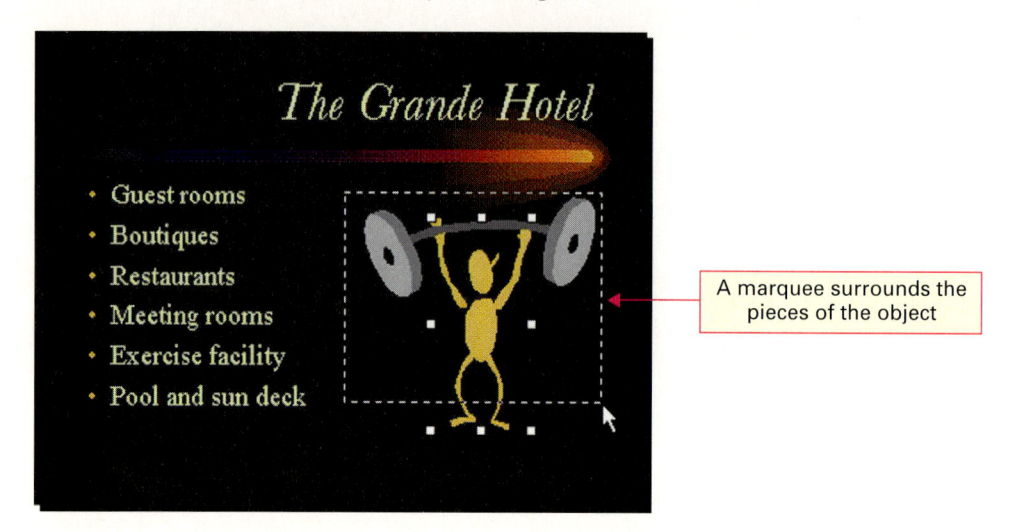

A marquee surrounds the pieces of the object

14 Release the mouse button when all pieces of the image are within the marquee.
All pieces of the original clip art image are selected.

15 Click the Draw button on the Drawing toolbar and select Group.
The image is one object again.

16 Display Slide 2, press (SHIFT), and click each of the star shapes.
All four stars are selected.

17 Click the Draw button on the Drawing toolbar and select Align or Distribute.

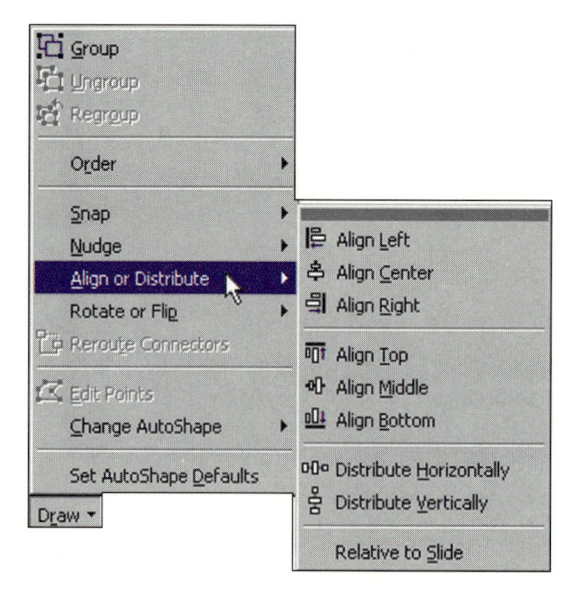

18 Select Align Top.

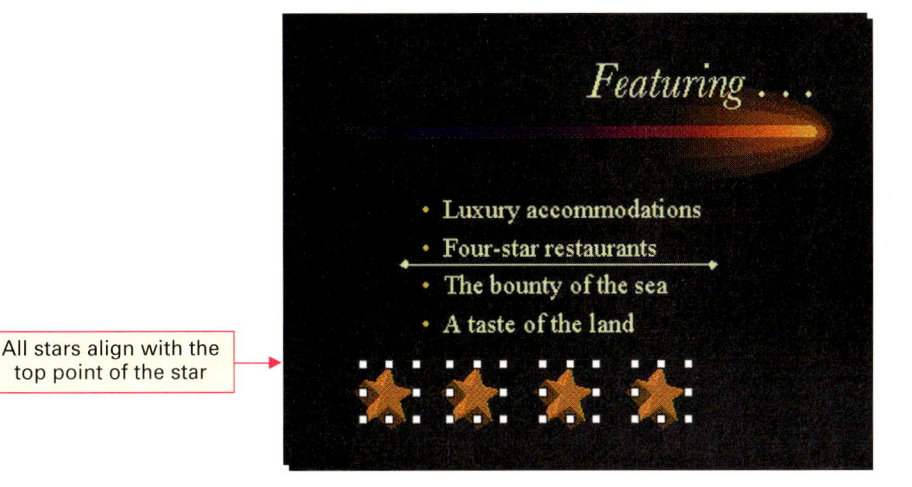

All stars align with the top point of the star

> **Tip** If you want to position an image behind text on a slide, select the image and choose Draw, Order, and then select the Send to Back option from the cascading menu.

19 Click the Draw button on the Drawing toolbar, select Align or Distribute, and then select Distribute Vertically.
The stars are evenly spaced from each other.

20 Save the changes to the presentation.

The Conclusion

Before closing the presentation *The Willows*, print a copy of the presentation as black-and-white handouts with six framed slides per page. Then, if you've completed your work, close the presentation and exit PowerPoint. If you plan to continue with the Exercises and Assignments, close the presentation and leave PowerPoint running.

Summary and Exercises

Summary

- You can add clip art to any slide in Slide view; AutoLayout formats make accessing the Clip Gallery easy.
- WordArt lets you shape text to fit creatively on your slides. You can apply many of the techniques you use to format slide text to WordArt text.
- PowerPoint's Drawing toolbar provides tools for drawing and formatting shapes and adding special effects.
- Manipulating graphic images includes grouping, ungrouping, flipping, rotating, and aligning.

Key Terms and Operations

Key Terms	Operations
clip art	add, select, move, size, and delete presentation art
flip	create and manipulate WordArt
group	create drawings
rotate	group, ungroup, flip, and rotate art
ungroup	
WordArt	

Study Questions

Multiple Choice

1. PowerPoint comes with a number of images known as
   a. clip art.
   b. pictures.
   c. drawings.
   d. multimedia clips.

2. You can use any of the following techniques to add clip art images to your slide *except*
   a. choose an AutoLayout format that contains a clip art placeholder.
   b. choose File, Import.
   c. click the Insert Clip Art toolbar button.
   d. choose Insert, Picture, Clip Art.

3. To move a clip art image,
   a. delete the existing image, reposition the insertion point, and reinsert the image.
   b. select the image and drag a handle.
   c. select the image, position the pointer on the image away from a handle, and drag the image to a new location.
   d. outline the position you want the image to occupy and then double-click the image to make it move to the new position.

4. When you add clip art images to a document, what toolbar appears?
   a. The Formatting toolbar.

    b. The Drawing toolbar.
    c. The Insert Clip Art toolbar.
    d. The Picture toolbar.

5. To swirl title text on a slide, use PowerPoint's
    a. WordArt feature.
    b. Text Rotate command.
    c. Drawing toolbar.
    d. Clip Gallery.

6. You can edit clip art images to change the color of part of the image by first
    a. redrawing a shape on top of the part you want to change.
    b. ungrouping the image.
    c. changing the size of the image.
    d. editing the image, using Paint.

7. When you want to move two objects together and retain their current position relative to each other,
    a. delete one object, move the other, and then redraw the second object.
    b. ungroup the objects.
    c. group the objects.
    d. relayer the objects.

8. To select multiple drawn objects, WordArt, or clip art images,
    a. simply click each object.
    b. save the slide as a picture and then select the picture object.
    c. position all objects on top of each other and then outline the group of objects.
    d. press Shift and click each object.

9. When you want to draw an object from the center point,
    a. press Ctrl, position the pointer at the object's center point, and draw the shape.
    b. draw the object and then move it so that the center is where you want it.
    c. draw the object and then double-click it.
    d. ungroup all objects on the slide.

10. To size a drawn object, WordArt object, or clip art image,
    a. delete and then redraw the object.
    b. ungroup the object.
    c. select the object and then drag a handle.
    d. select the object, position the pointer in the middle of the object, and drag.

Short Answer

1. What Drawing toolbar button accesses a palette of shapes?

2. How do you copy a drawn object?

3. How do you make a clip art image face the other way?

4. How do you add WordArt to a slide?

5. How do you change the shape of a WordArt object?

6. Name the three basic ways to insert a clip art image.

7. In what shape does the pointer appear when you draw a freehand shape?

8. How does layering affect objects on a slide?
9. How do you change the border color and fill color of a drawn object?
10. What procedure do you use to group objects?

For Discussion
1. What additional formatting techniques can you use to enhance WordArt that are not available for formatting placeholder text?
2. How do the techniques for adding WordArt to slides differ from the techniques used to add text to placeholders?
3. How do you access additional clip art on the Internet?
4. Which of the art features presented in this project do you believe will benefit you the most?

Review Exercises

1. Adding, Moving, and Sizing Clip Art Images
Ruth Lindsey, Manager of The Willows Shops, would like you to add clip art images to slides to enhance the presentation *The Willows Shops*. Suggested graphics are shown in Figure 3.2.

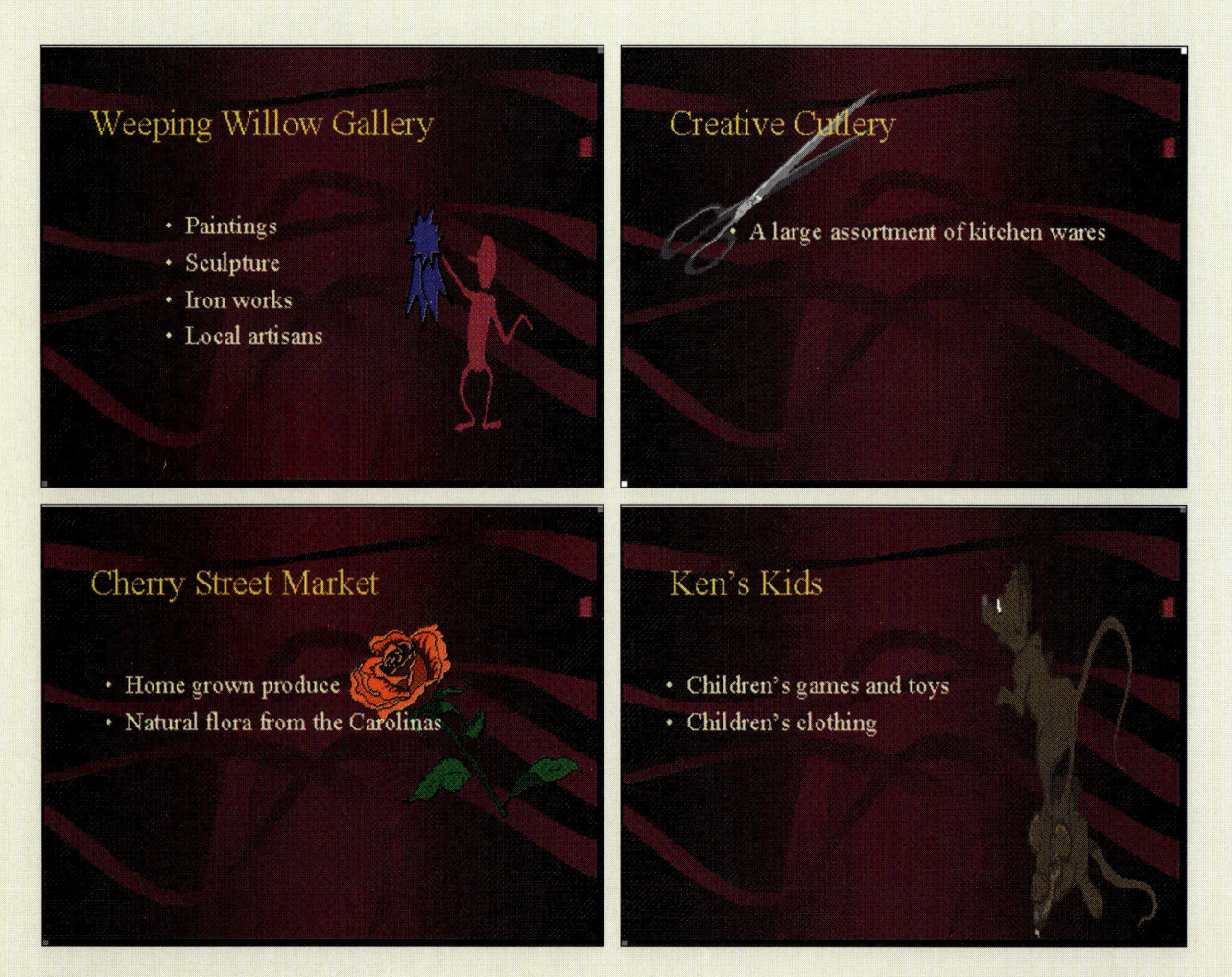

Figure 3.2

Project 3: Adding Art to a Presentation   PP-113

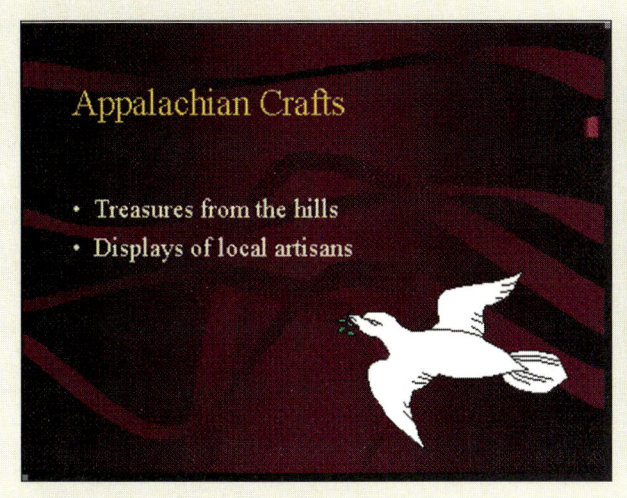

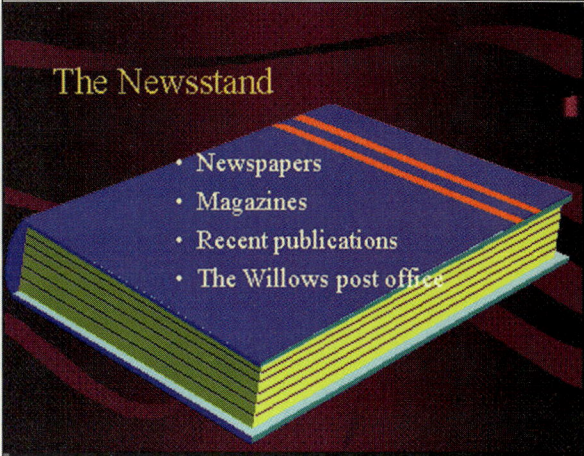

Figure 3.2 *(continued)*

If you do not have the images displayed, insert graphics of your choice or those chosen by your instructor. Use the techniques explored in this project to locate appropriate clip art to add to slides. Follow these instructions to complete the presentation:

1. Launch PowerPoint, if necessary, and open the presentation *The Willows Shops*.
2. Display the presentation in Slide view, display the slides pictured in Figure 3.2, and choose Insert, Picture, Clip Art to locate the image in the Clip Gallery.
3. Position and size the clip art images to appear as shown in Figure 3.2. Rotate and flip items as necessary to create the images displayed in the figure. Ungroup the object on Slide 3 and change the color of the character so it can be seen.
4. Save changes to the presentation and print a copy of the six slides containing clip art.
5. Close the presentation and exit PowerPoint when you've completed your work.

2. Adding WordArt and Drawings to Slides

Ms. Lindsey would also like to change the titles of the three slides pictured in Figure 3.3 from the presentation *The Willows Shops* to WordArt.

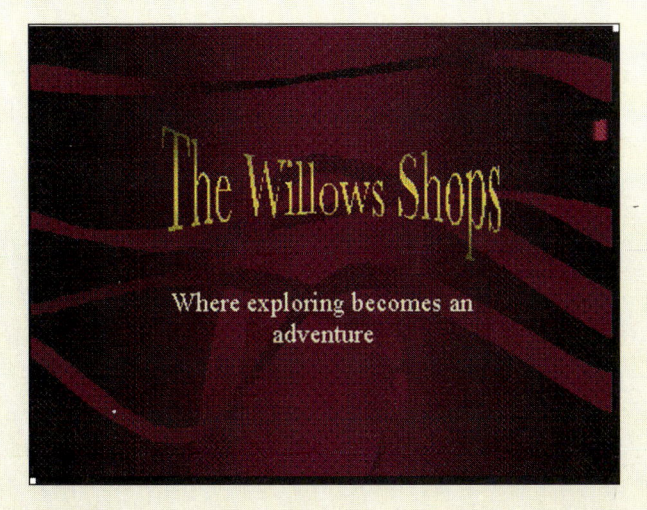

Figure 3.3

PP-114

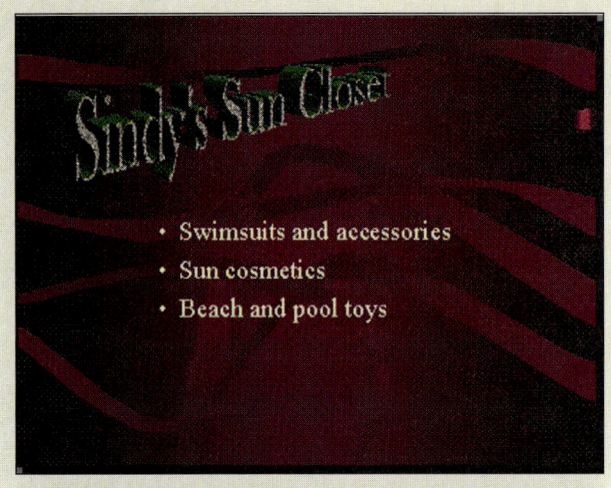

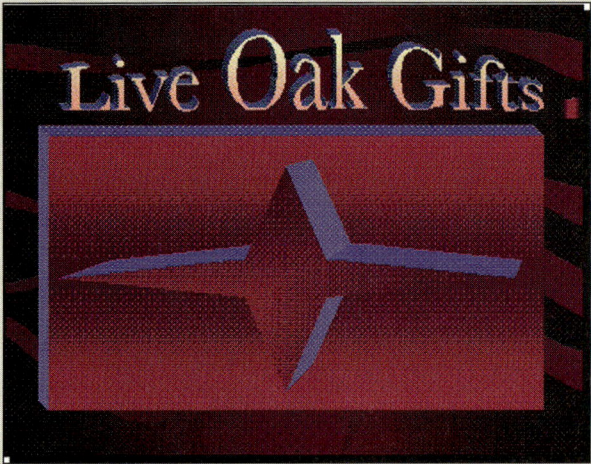

Figure 3.3 *(continued)*

Follow these steps to complete the task.

1. Launch PowerPoint, if necessary, and open the presentation *The Willows Shops*.
2. Display Slide 1 in Slide view, delete the title placeholder, add the title text as a WordArt object, and format the WordArt so that it appears as shown in Figure 3.3.
3. Repeat step 2 for Slides 2 and 4.
4. Display Slide 4 and create and format the drawn object shown in Figure 3.3, using a shadowed rectangle and a shaded four-pointed AutoShape star. Edit the colors to show gradient fill effects.
5. Save the changes to the presentation and print copies of the three slides containing WordArt titles as black-and-white handouts with three slides per page.
6. Close the presentation and exit PowerPoint when you've completed your work.

Assignments

1. Adding, Formatting, and Manipulating Clip Art, WordArt, and Drawings

The slides from the *Festivals and Attractions* presentation enhanced with suggested graphics appear in Figure 3.4.

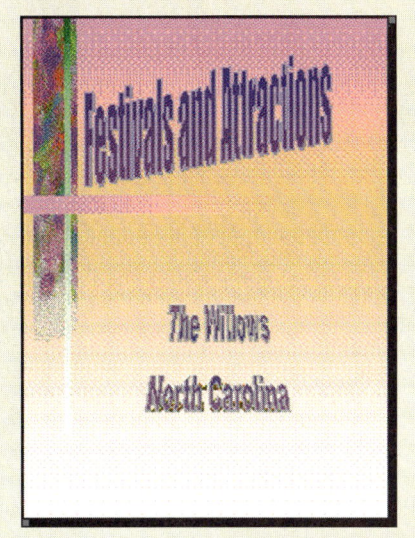

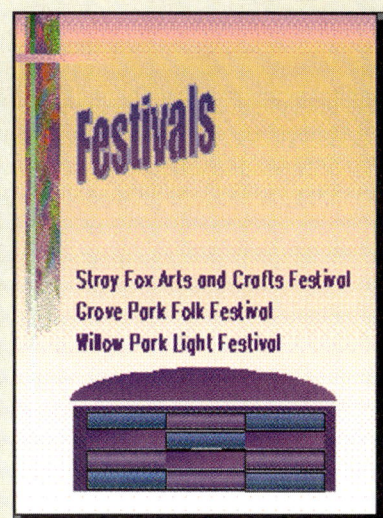

Figure 3.4

Use tools presented in this project to add clip art images, WordArt objects, and drawings to your presentation slides. Edit the clip art images by ungrouping them and changing the colors. Size and position the graphics as shown in Figure 3.4. Save changes to the presentation and print black-and-white handouts with three slides per page. Close the presentation and exit PowerPoint when you've completed your work.

2. Searching the Internet for Pictures to Enhance Presentations

Check with your instructor on how and where to download the Willow graphic. If you have access to the Internet, click the Globe button on the Clip Gallery window to search the Internet Clip Gallery for images you can use in your résumé presentation. Otherwise, search the Clip Art Gallery that is provided in the program.

Add drawings to presentation slides and change the titles of all slides in your presentation to WordArt, formatted to create special effects. Save changes to the presentation and print a copy of your presentation as black-and-white handouts with three slides per page.

Close the presentation and exit PowerPoint when you've completed your work.

PROJECT 4

Viewing and Editing a Presentation

Most of the presentations you create are designed to provide powerful visuals to enhance oral presentations. Slides in a presentation can be formatted and shown on-screen by individuals or projected on an audiovisual screen or flat surface as you present a report to an audience.

Showing your presentations with style has a positive impact on your audience. The PowerPoint slide show feature enables you to show your presentation on a computer screen. Seeing your presentation "live" the first time can be quite satisfying—and exciting. In this project, you learn how to dress up your presentation for on-screen viewing and how to use Slide Sorter view to rearrange slides in the presentation.

Objectives

After completing this project, you will be able to:

- ➤ **Present a slide show**
- ➤ **Use the slide show shortcut menu**
- ➤ **Rearrange slides in a presentation**
- ➤ **Add slide transitions**
- ➤ **Animate text**
- ➤ **Expand slides**
- ➤ **Hide slides and display hidden slides**

Project 4: Viewing and Editing a Presentation PP-117

The Challenge

Francesca Savoy has reviewed the presentation *The Willows* and has approved the design, graphics, and format of slides in the presentation. She now asks that the presentation be tweaked into its final form so that she can present it to the managers at their next meeting.

The Solution

To get the presentation *The Willows* into shape, you need to view the presentation as a slide show and then use Slide Sorter view to make final edits to the presentation. Figure 4.1 shows the final presentation in Slide Sorter view.

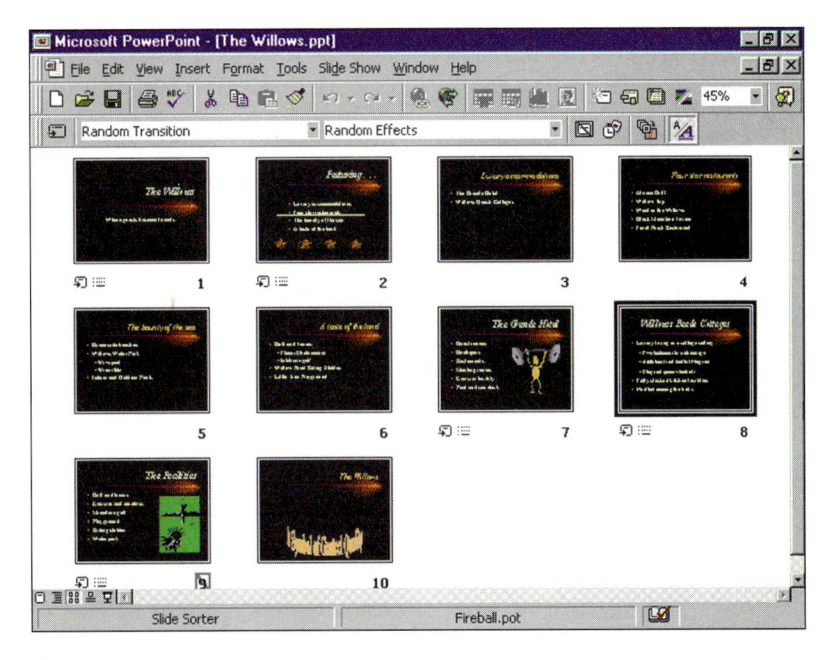

Figure 4.1

The Setup

You're switching to a different view for many of the activities in this section, and you're also going to be using the slide show feature in PowerPoint. As a result, you need to select some different settings to ensure that your screen will match the illustrations shown in this project.

When you switch to Slide Sorter view, make sure that the Standard and Slide Sorter toolbars display. If you don't see them, choose View, Toolbars, and then select them. Close the Common Tasks toolbar if it's open.

You'll also need to work with your presentation window maximized in Slide Sorter view. Click the Maximize button on the presentation window, if necessary. Then set the Zoom control to 66%.

Presenting a Slide Show

Viewing your presentation as a slide show makes it come to life. Slide shows display slides in the presentation window without the PowerPoint toolbars, title bar, and status bar. During a slide show, each slide literally fills the screen and you can focus on slide contents to determine impact. PowerPoint offers a number of ways to launch a slide show:

- Choose View, Slide Show
- Choose Slide Show, View Show
- Click the Slide Show button at the bottom of the presentation window

TASK 1: TO VIEW A PRESENTATION AS A SLIDE SHOW:

1. Open the presentation *The Willows* and display the first slide in Slide view. Slide 1 of the presentation appears as last shown in Project 3.
2. Click the Slide Show button at the bottom of the presentation window.

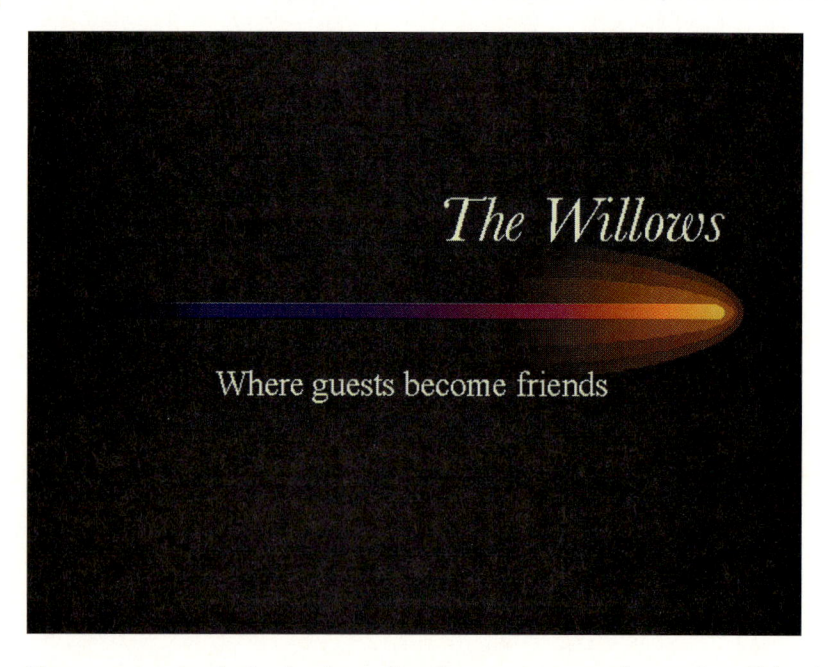

The Willows

Where guests become friends

You can use both the keyboard and mouse to navigate the slides in a presentation during a slide show. Table 4.1 compares the actions for using both techniques. Practice each technique to identify the ones you like best.

> **Note** The slide show starts with the slide displayed in Slide or Notes Pages view or the slide selected in Slide Sorter or Outline view.

Project 4: Viewing and Editing a Presentation   PP-119

Table 4.1   Mouse and Keyboard Techniques for Navigating Slides in a Slide Show

Movement	Mouse Action	Keyboard Action(s)
Advance to the next slide	Click the left mouse button	Press **N**, ENTER, SPACE, PGDN, ↓, or →
Return to the previous slide	Right-click and choose Previous	Press **P**, BACKSPACE, PGUP, ←, or ↑
Specific slide number		Type the slide number; then press ENTER. For example, type **5** to go to slide 5 and then press ENTER.
Stop the slide show	Right-click and choose End Show	Press ESC

Using the Slide Show Shortcut Menu

The *slide show shortcut menu* displays commands for accessing navigation features as well as for controlling on-screen features such as the mouse pointer and slide meter. To display the slide show shortcut menu, click the right mouse button during the slide show or press SHIFT+F10.

TASK 2: TO USE THE SLIDE SHOW SHORTCUT MENU:

1. Click 🖥 to start the slide show, if necessary.
   The slide that was active in Slide view appears in full-screen view.

2. Right-click anywhere on the screen.

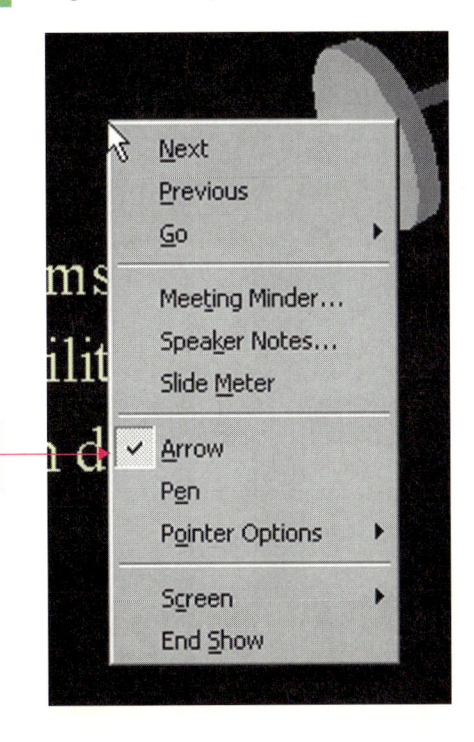

The arrow pointer shape is active

- Next
- Previous
- Go ▶
- Meeting Minder...
- Speaker Notes...
- Slide Meter
- ✓ Arrow
- Pen
- Pointer Options ▶
- Screen ▶
- End Show

Tip You can also access the slide show shortcut menu by moving the mouse pointer on-screen until a shortcut menu button displays in the lower-left corner of the slide; then click the shortcut menu button.

PP-120

3 Choose Screen, Black Screen.
The entire screen becomes black so that the audience focuses on you, the speaker, rather than on the same slide for an extended period of time.

> **Tip** You could also display a black screen while you draw or annotate.

4 Click the left mouse button to redisplay the slide.
The slide redisplays.

5 Right-click again, and then choose End Show.
The slide displayed when you chose End Show appears in Slide view.

Rearranging Slides in a Presentation

After viewing the presentation as a slide show, you may find that you need to rearrange slides so that the flow is smoother or to match changes in the oral presentation. Slide Sorter view displays miniature images (these are called *thumbnail* images, remember?) of presentation slides that you can drag to new positions. Slide Sorter view prevents slide editing; as a result, you must return to Slide view to edit slide text and graphics.

TASK 3: TO REARRANGE SLIDES USING SLIDE SORTER VIEW:

1 Click the Slide Sorter View button at the bottom of the presentation window.

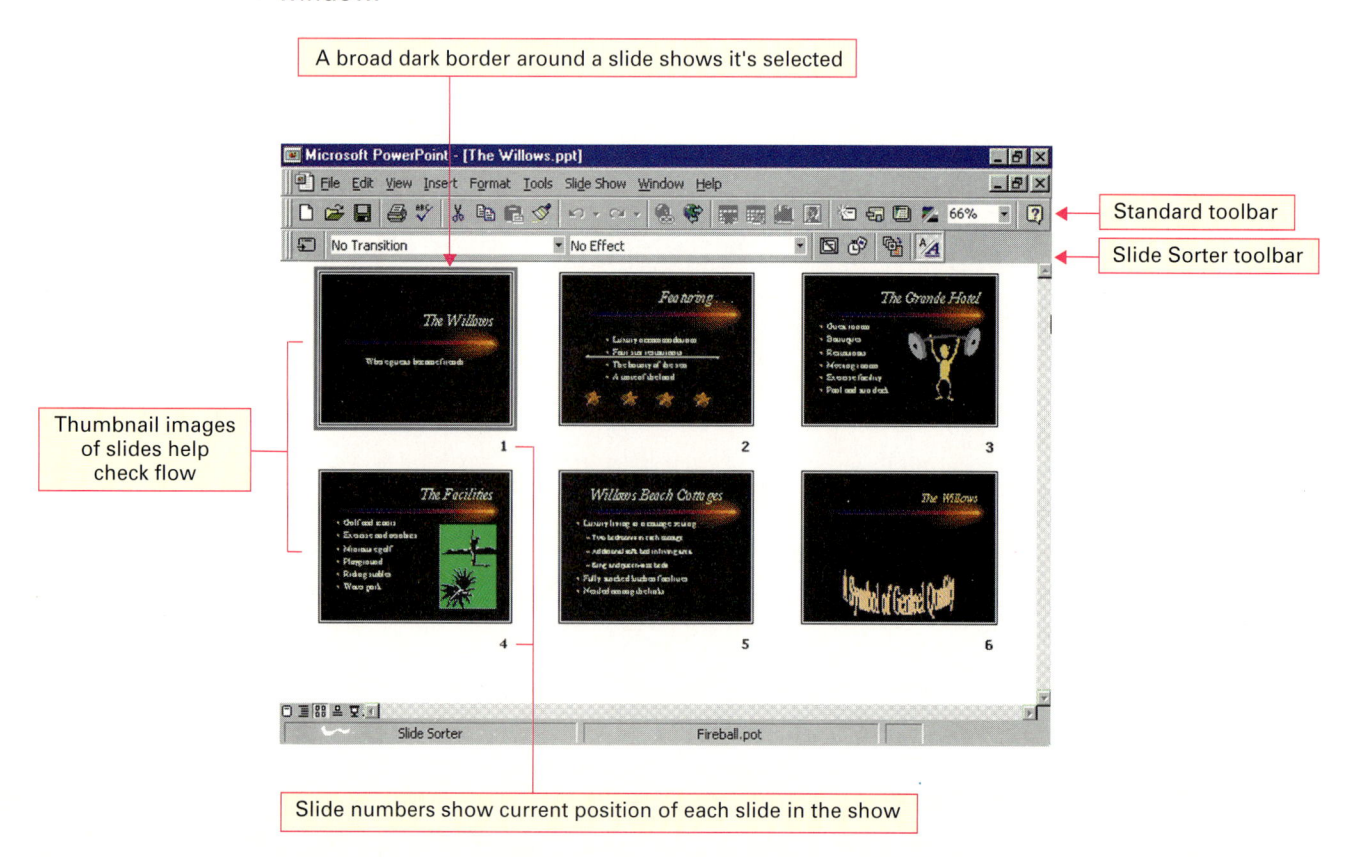

A broad dark border around a slide shows it's selected

Thumbnail images of slides help check flow

Standard toolbar
Slide Sorter toolbar

Slide numbers show current position of each slide in the show

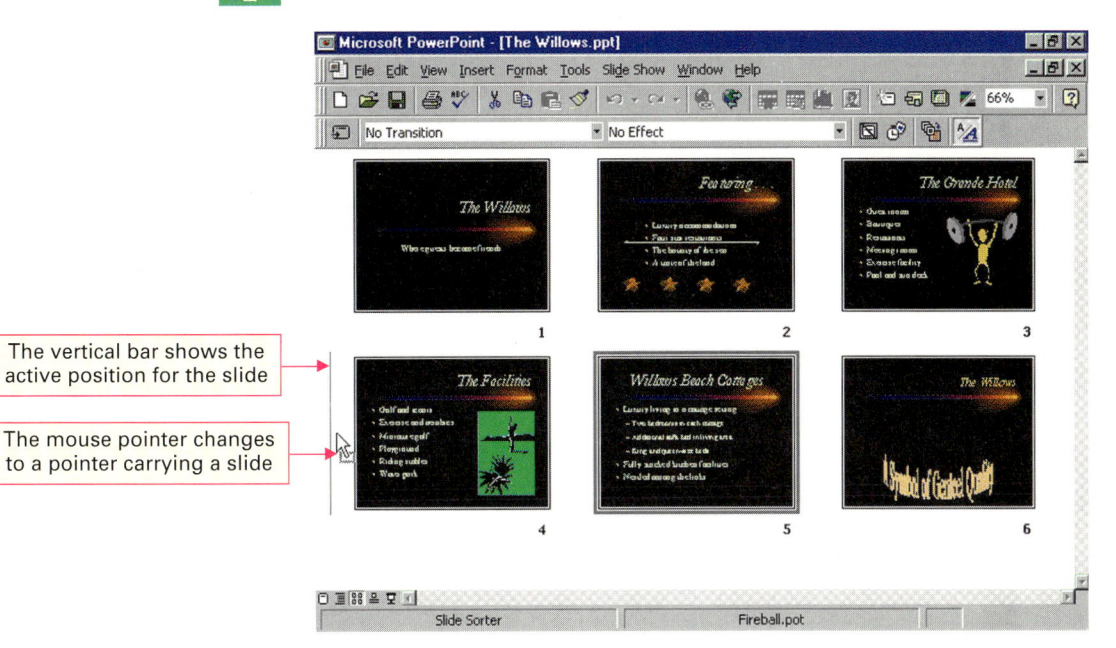

Project 4: Viewing and Editing a Presentation   PP-121

2 Click Slide 5 to select it, and then drag it to the left of Slide 4.

The vertical bar shows the active position for the slide

The mouse pointer changes to a pointer carrying a slide

3 Drop Slide 5 when the vertical bar appears as shown in step 4.

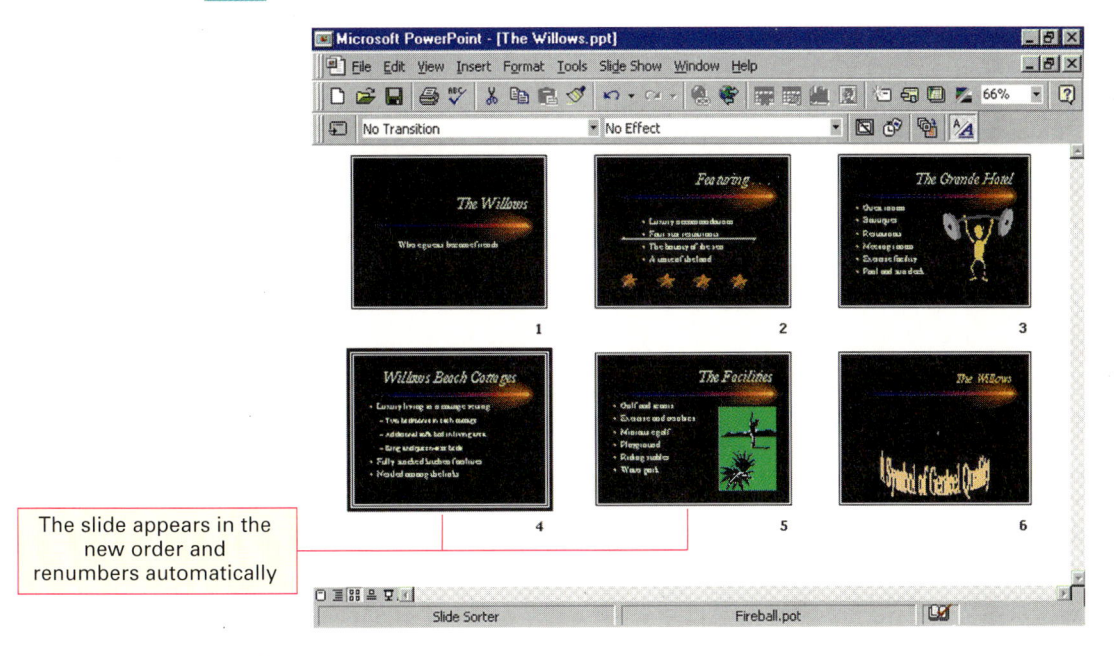

The slide appears in the new order and renumbers automatically

4 Click 🖫 to save changes to the presentation, and leave it open.

Adding Slide Transitions

Slide *transitions* create special effects as your slides go on and off the screen during a slide show. You can use the Slide Sorter toolbar to add transitions to your slides.

PP-122

TASK 4: TO ADD SLIDE TRANSITIONS:

1 Display the presentation *The Willows* in Slide Sorter view, if necessary.

2 Click Slide 1 to select it and then click the arrow button beside the Slide Transition Effects list box on the Slide Sorter toolbar.

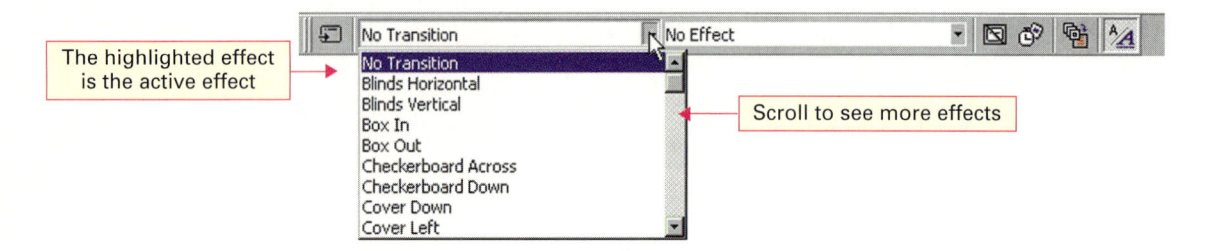

The highlighted effect is the active effect

Scroll to see more effects

3 Scroll down the effects list, if necessary, click *Dissolve,* and watch Slide 1 closely to view the effect.

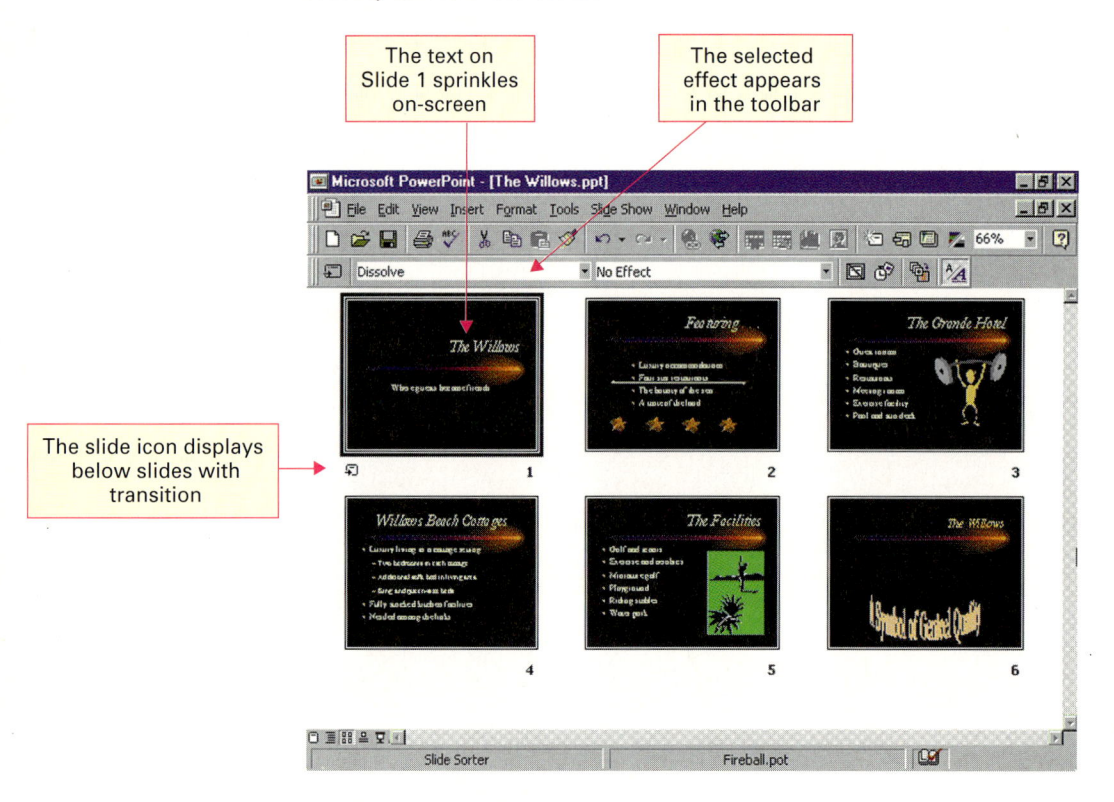

The text on Slide 1 sprinkles on-screen

The selected effect appears in the toolbar

The slide icon displays below slides with transition

4 Click the slide icon below Slide 1.
The transition effect repeats to show the effect.

5 Click to select Slide 2, and then press (SHIFT) and click Slides 3, 4, and 5.
The four selected slides appear with broad dark borders.

6 Click the Slide Transition Effect arrow button, scroll down the list, and select Random Transition from the bottom of the transition effects list.
An icon appears below each selected slide.

7 Click the transition slide icon below each slide and view the transition effect.
The effect changes each time you click the icon below a slide when you use Random transition.

8 Click 🖫.

Project 4: Viewing and Editing a Presentation   PP-123

Animating Text

When you apply *text preset animations* (formerly known as *builds*) to slides, each slide title displays on-screen by itself and each bulleted list item is presented separately during a slide show. Text preset animations help focus the attention of your audience on each individual bulleted item as you discuss it and removes the distractions of presenting all bulleted points at once. Text that appears in text placeholders is affected when you apply the text preset animation effects.

TASK 5: TO ANIMATE SLIDE TEXT:

1 Click Slide 1 in Slide Sorter view.
Slide 1 is selected.

2 Click the arrow button for the Text Preset Animation list box in the Slide Sorter toolbar.

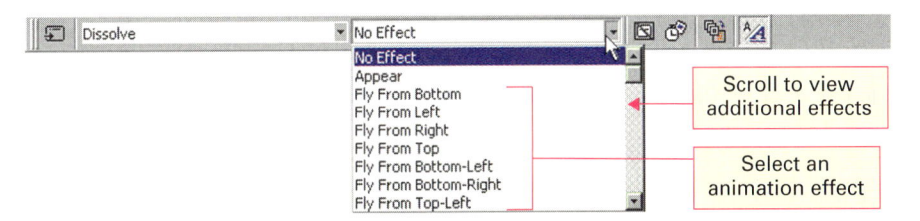

Scroll to view additional effects

Select an animation effect

3 Scroll down the list, if necessary, and select Crawl From Right.

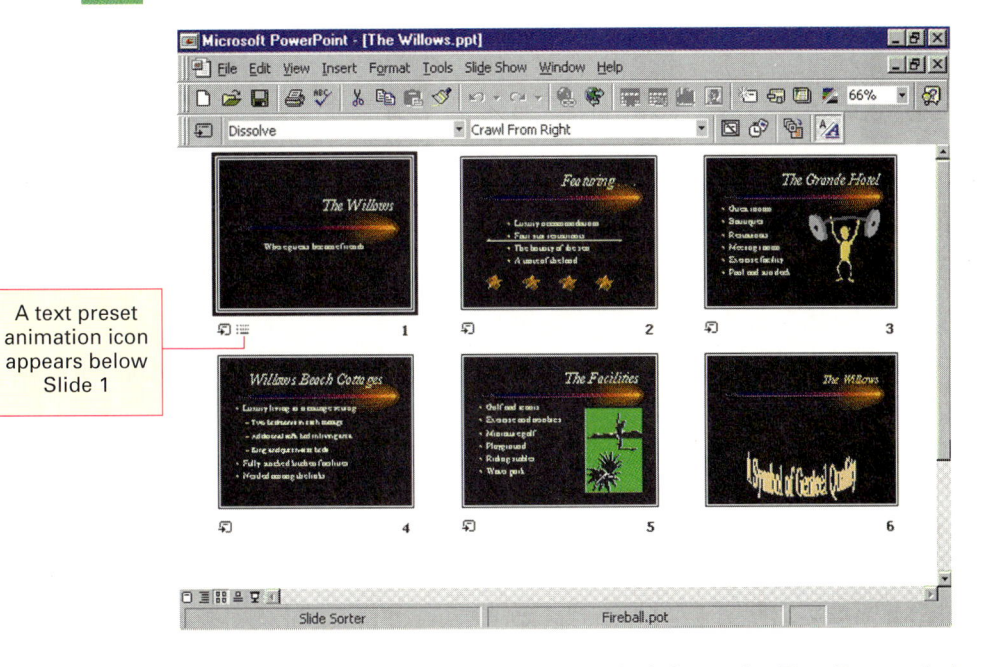

A text preset animation icon appears below Slide 1

4 Select Slide 2 and select Peek From Left from the Text Preset Animations list.

5 Add text preset animations of your choice to Slides 3, 4, and 5.
Text preset animation icons appear below each slide.

6 Select Slide 1 and then click 🖳 to view the special effects applied to each slide.
Use navigation techniques to review all slides and end the slide show.

7 Click 💾 when the slide show finishes.

Expanding Slides

When a bulleted list slide contains points that you need to expand (or expound upon), you can use the PowerPoint *expand* feature to create new slides. When you expand a slide, each bulleted list item appears as the title of a new slide. Slides you expand are often referred to as *parent slides* and new slides created from the parent slide are called *children*. When you expand a slide, the children appear in bulleted list order immediately following the parent slide.

TASK 6: TO EXPAND BULLETED LISTS:

1 Select Slide 2 in Slide Sorter view.
Slide 2 appears with a broad dark border.

2 Choose Tools, Expand Slide.

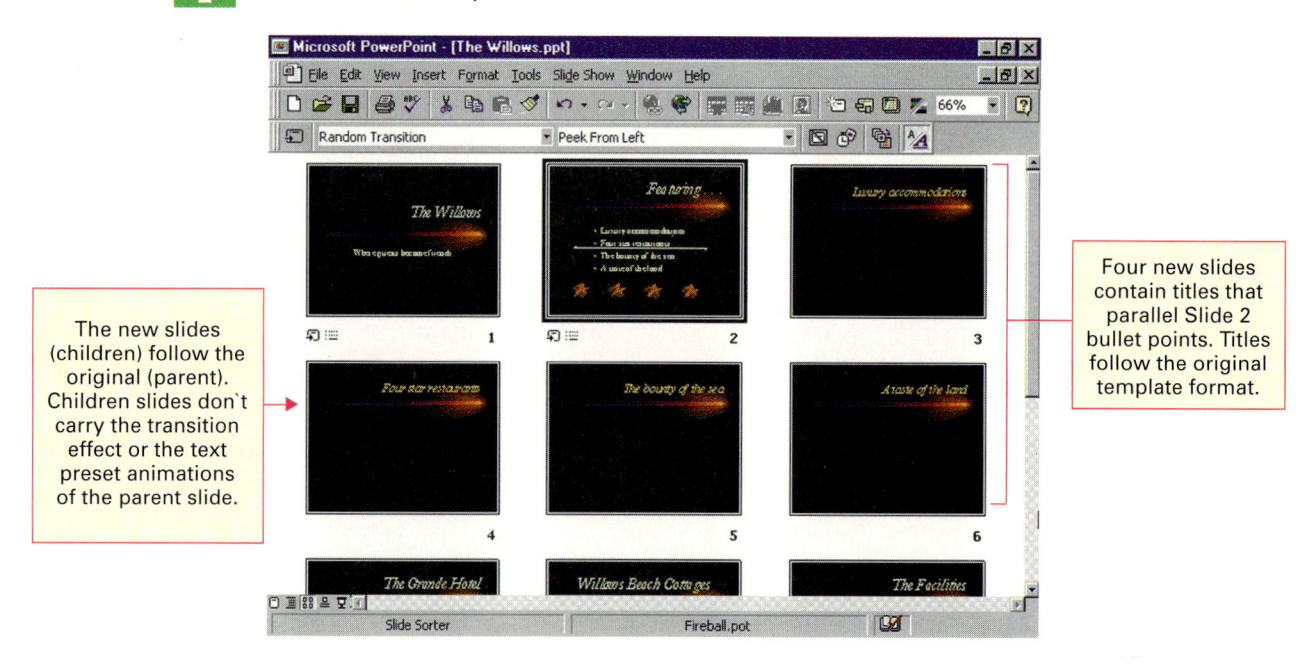

The new slides (children) follow the original (parent). Children slides don't carry the transition effect or the text preset animations of the parent slide.

Four new slides contain titles that parallel Slide 2 bullet points. Titles follow the original template format.

Project 4: Viewing and Editing a Presentation   PP-125

3 Click ▤ to switch to Outline view.

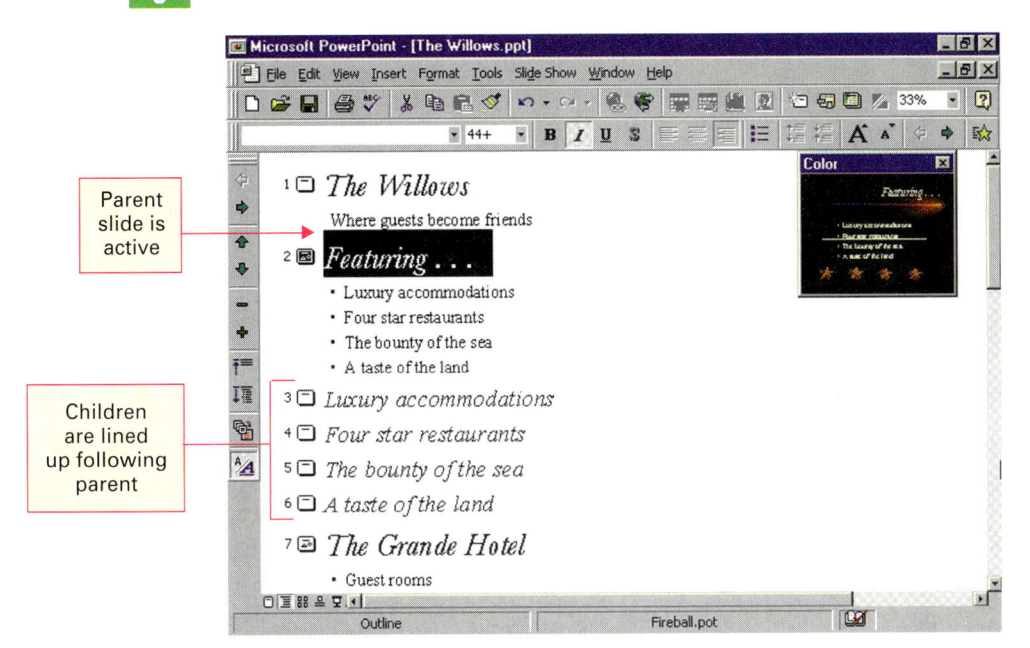

Parent slide is active

Children are lined up following parent

The Willows
Where guests become friends

Featuring . . .
- Luxury accommodations
- Four star restaurants
- The bounty of the sea
- A taste of the land

Luxury accommodations
Four star restaurants
The bounty of the sea
A taste of the land

The Grande Hotel
- Guest rooms

4 Position the I-beam after the word "accommodations" in Slide 3, press (ENTER) and then (TAB), and type additional text, as in:

3 ▢ *Luxury accommodations*
- The Grande Hotel
- Willows Beach Cottages

5 Position the I-beam after the last word in the slide titles for Slides 4, 5, and 6, press ENTER, and then press TAB and type the additional text shown here as bulleted lists:

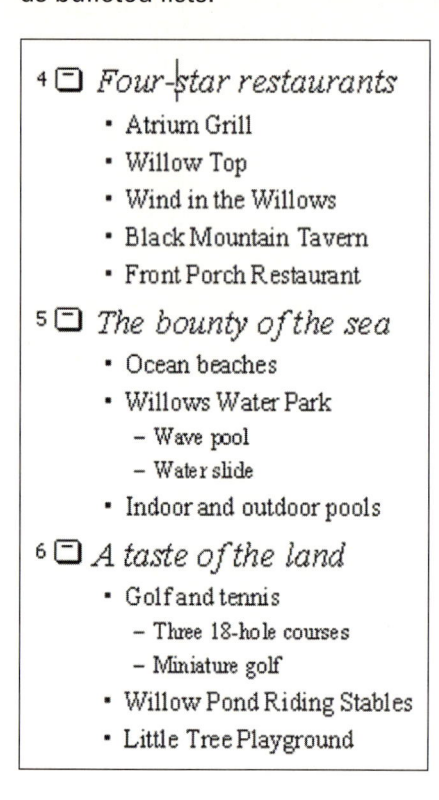

4. *Four-star restaurants*
   - Atrium Grill
   - Willow Top
   - Wind in the Willows
   - Black Mountain Tavern
   - Front Porch Restaurant

5. *The bounty of the sea*
   - Ocean beaches
   - Willows Water Park
     – Wave pool
     – Water slide
   - Indoor and outdoor pools

6. *A taste of the land*
   - Golf and tennis
     – Three 18-hole courses
     – Miniature golf
   - Willow Pond Riding Stables
   - Little Tree Playground

6 Click [icon] to return to Slide Sorter view, click the Zoom box on the Standard toolbar, type **45**, and press ENTER.

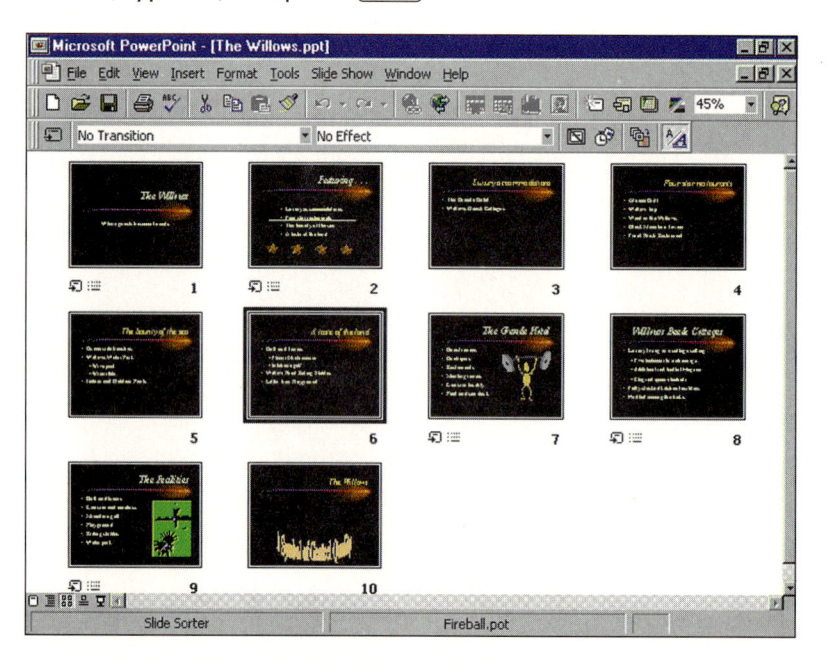

Hiding Slides and Displaying Hidden Slides

Hiding slides enables you to include slides containing detailed information or data in your presentation but display the slides during a slide show only when the audience asks questions or when you need more details about a topic. Hidden slides remain in the background during a slide show and show only when you access them.

TASK 7: TO HIDE SLIDES AND DISPLAY THEM DURING A SLIDE SHOW:

1. Select Slide 9 in Slide Sorter view.
   Slide 9 appears with a broad dark border.

2. Click the Hide Slide ![icon] button on the Slide Sorter toolbar.

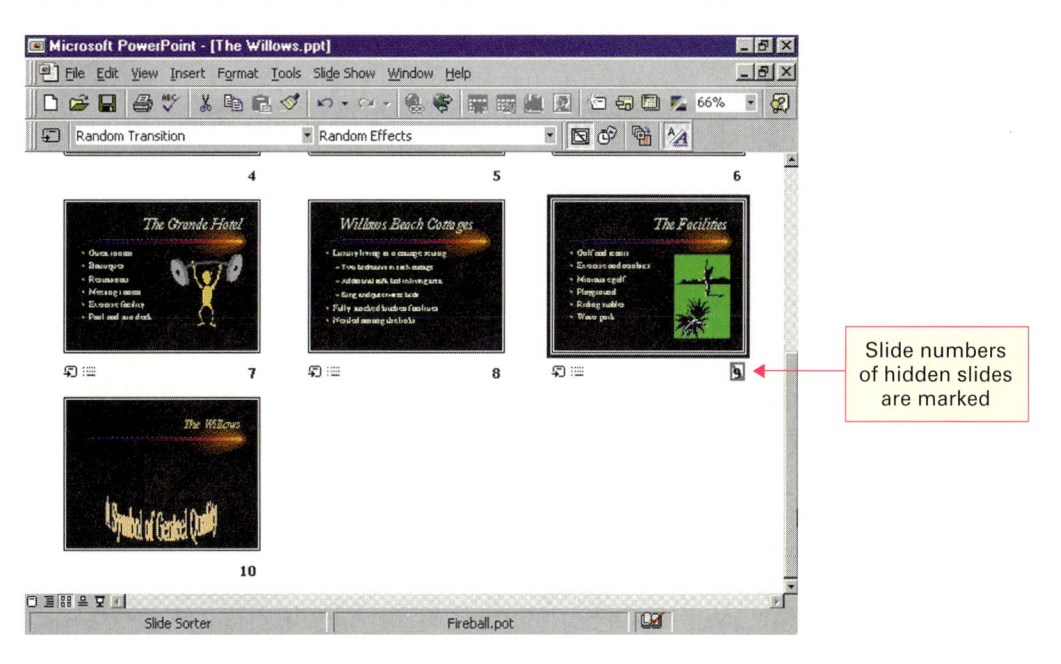

   Slide numbers of hidden slides are marked

3. Select Slide 8 and then click ![icon].
   Slide 8 displays in the slide show window.

4. Click the left mouse button until the next slide displays.
   Slide 10 now displays after Slide 8 during the slide show unless you call up Slide 9.

5. Press (ESC) to stop the slide show, select Slide 8, if necessary, and then click ![icon] to start the show again.
   Slide 8 displays in the slide show window.

6. Press **H** to display the hidden Slide 9.
   Slide 9 title and graphic display immediately.

7. Press (ESC) to stop the slide show, select Slide 8, if necessary, and then click ![icon] again.
   Slide 8 displays in the slide show window.

8. Right-click on the screen and choose Go.

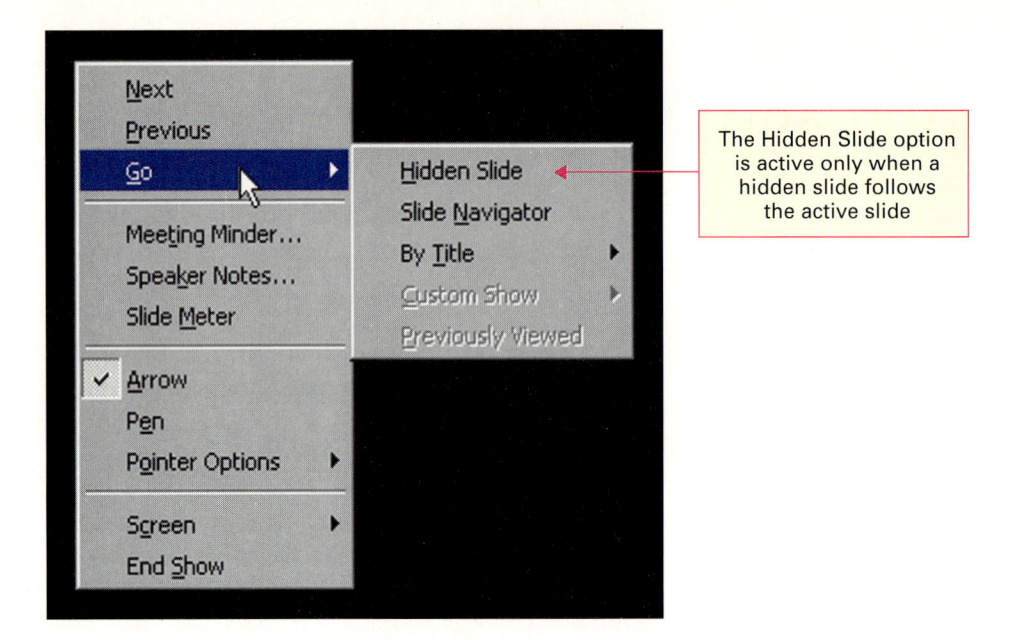

[Screenshot of slide show context menu with Go submenu expanded showing Hidden Slide, Slide Navigator, By Title, Custom Show, Previously Viewed]

The Hidden Slide option is active only when a hidden slide follows the active slide

9 Choose Hidden Slide.
The Slide 9 title and graphic display immediately.

10 Press ESC to stop the slide show and then click 💾.
PowerPoint saves changes to the presentation.

The Conclusion

Before closing the presentation *The Willows*, print a copy of the presentation in Outline view. Then, if you've completed your work, close the presentation and exit PowerPoint. If you plan to continue with the Exercises and Assignments, close the presentation and leave PowerPoint running.

Summary and Exercises

Summary

- The PowerPoint slide show feature enables you to show your presentation on-screen.
- Slide shows display slides in the presentation window without the PowerPoint toolbars, title bar, and status bar.
- The easiest way to start a slide show is to click the Slide Show button at the bottom of the presentation window.
- You can use both mouse and keyboard techniques to navigate slides during a slide show.
- You can display the slide show shortcut menu during a slide show by clicking the right mouse button. The slide show shortcut menu displays commands for controlling on-screen features.
- You can also access the slide show shortcut menu by moving the mouse pointer on-screen until a shortcut menu button displays and then clicking the shortcut menu button.
- Slide Sorter view is the most efficient view to use when you need to rearrange slides or apply transitions and special effects.
- Slide transitions affect the way slides move on and off the screen during a slide show.
- Text preset animations present text on slides one bullet point at a time during a slide show. You can also set an animation to dim previously presented bullet points to enable the audience to focus on the point being discussed.
- You can use the expand slide feature to create new slides that use the bulleted list text from a parent slide. Each bulleted list item appears as the title of a new slide.
- Hiding slides enables you to include slides with supplemental information in the presentation and display the slides only when you need them.

Key Terms and Operations

Key Terms
expand
hidden slides
slide show
slide show shortcut menu
Slide Sorter view
text preset animation
transition

Operations
add transitions to slides
animate slide text using text preset animations
display different slides in a presentation
end a slide show
expand and hide slides
rearrange slides in a presentation using Slide Sorter view
start a slide show

Study Questions

Multiple Choice

1. To start a slide show,
   a. click a button on the Standard toolbar.
   b. press Enter after the last slide is completed.
   c. use the slide show shortcut menu.
   d. click the Slide Show button at the bottom of the presentation window.

2. Showing slides as a slide show displays slides
    a. all on-screen together.
    b. in Print Preview mode.
    c. one at a time, using the full screen.
    d. one at a time, as in Slide view.

3. The view that makes it easy to rearrange slides is
    a. Print Preview.
    b. Slide Sorter view.
    c. Outline view.
    d. Slide view.

4. To move a slide in Slide Sorter view,
    a. select the slide and drag it to a new location.
    b. press Delete and then press Insert.
    c. press Ctrl+Insert.
    d. press Ctrl+D.

5. As you move a slide in Slide Sorter view, what identifies the active location of the slide?
    a. The mouse pointer
    b. The slide outline
    c. The ruler scale
    d. A vertical bar

6. To create special effects as slides move onto the screen,
    a. use the slide show shortcut menu.
    b. press the left mouse button.
    c. add a transition.
    d. press Page Down.

7. To advance to the next slide during a slide show, use any of the following techniques *except*
    a. click the left mouse button.
    b. press E.
    c. press Page Down.
    d. press N.

8. To leave a slide in a presentation but display it only when it's needed,
    a. hide the slide.
    b. build the slide text.
    c. skip the slide.
    d. branch out to the slide.

9. One way to move to a specific slide during a slide show is to
    a. press Home and the slide number.
    b. press Ctrl and the slide number.
    c. press Esc.
    d. type the slide number and press Enter.

10. To stop a presentation,
    a. press Enter.
    b. press Ctrl+S.
    c. press Esc.
    d. press Home.

Short Answer
1. Which view enables you to select a transition from a special toolbar?
2. In what shape does the pointer appear when you move a slide in Slide Sorter view?
3. What feature do you apply to slide text so that bullet items appear one at a time?
4. When you drag and drop a slide in Slide Sorter view, how do you know where the slide will appear?
5. On what menu does the Expand Slide feature appear?
6. Name the three basic ways to launch a slide show.
7. To what view in other applications might you compare viewing slides as a slide show?
8. What's the difference between a transition and text preset animation?
9. How do you display the slide show shortcut menu?
10. What view displays the presentation when the show ends?

For Discussion
1. What design concerns should you consider when applying transitions?
2. Why do you add hidden slides to a presentation?
3. What's the advantage of applying text preset animations to slides?
4. How can you control which slide appears first during a slide show?

Review Exercises

1. Rearranging, Hiding, and Expanding Slides and Showing a Presentation
The presentation *The Willows* is almost ready for Ms. Savoy to show to the managers, but it needs a bit more editing. The final presentation outline appears in Figure 4.2.

1 *The Willows*
- Where guests become friends

2 *Featuring...*
- Luxury accommodations
- Four-star restaurants
- The bounty of the sea
- A taste of the land

3 *Luxury accommodations*
- The Grande Hotel
- Willows Beach Cottages

4 *The Grande Hotel*
- Guest rooms
- Boutiques
- Restaurants
- Meeting rooms
- Exercise facility
- Pool and sun deck

5 *Willows Beach Cottages*
- Luxury living in a cottage setting
  - Two bedrooms in each cottage
  - Additional sofa bed in the living area
  - King and queen size beds
- Fully stocked kitchen facilities
- Nestled among the links

6 *Four-star restaurants*
- Atrium Grill
- Willow Top
- Wind in the Willows
- Black Mountain Tavern
- Front Porch Restaurant

7 *Sandwich Shops*
- Willow Green on the golf course
- The Cola Shop on the Mezzanine
- Grey Fox Deli at The Grande Hotel
- The 18th Hole on the golf course

- Red Rocker at the pool
- The Boardwalk on the beach

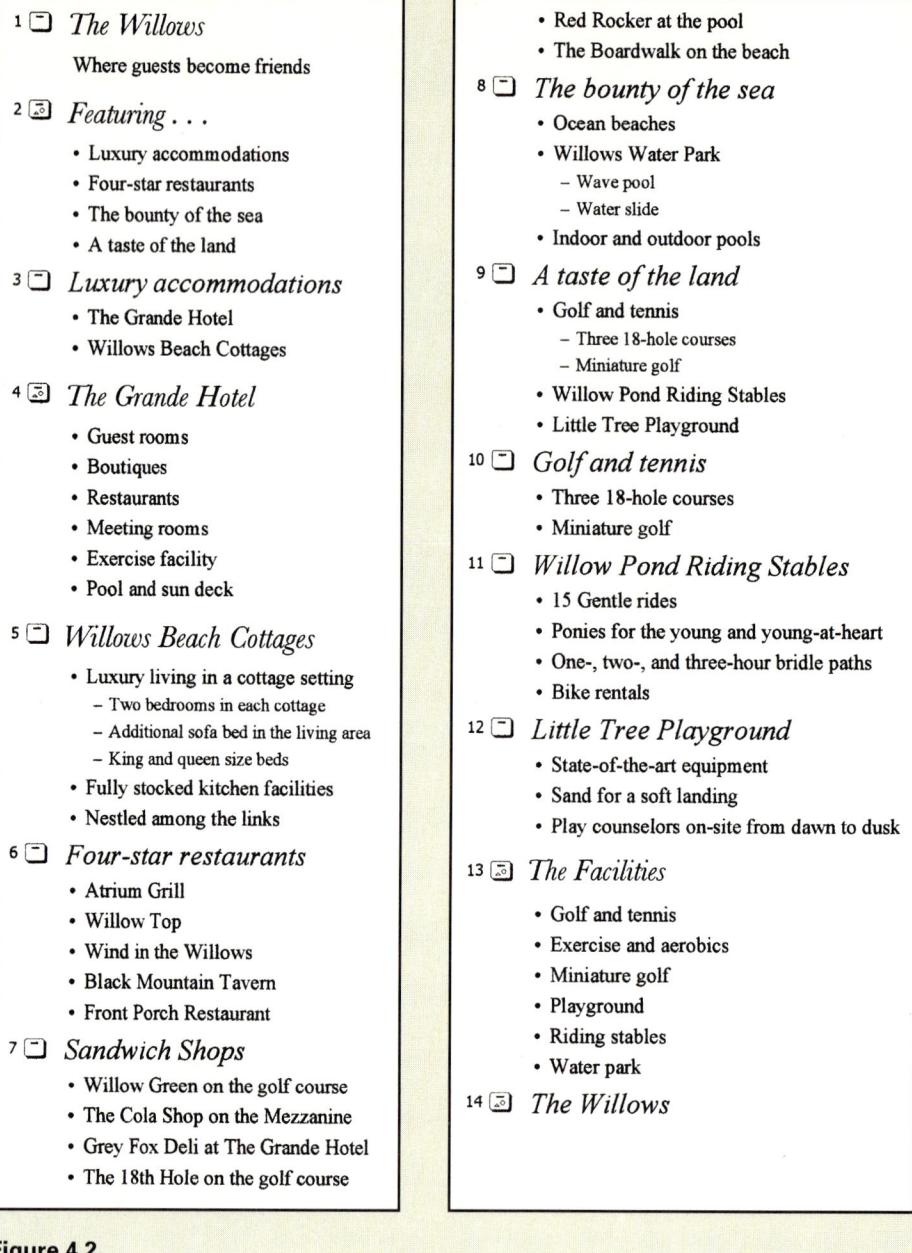

8 *The bounty of the sea*
- Ocean beaches
- Willows Water Park
  - Wave pool
  - Water slide
- Indoor and outdoor pools

9 *A taste of the land*
- Golf and tennis
  - Three 18-hole courses
  - Miniature golf
- Willow Pond Riding Stables
- Little Tree Playground

10 *Golf and tennis*
- Three 18-hole courses
- Miniature golf

11 *Willow Pond Riding Stables*
- 15 Gentle rides
- Ponies for the young and young-at-heart
- One-, two-, and three-hour bridle paths
- Bike rentals

12 *Little Tree Playground*
- State-of-the-art equipment
- Sand for a soft landing
- Play counselors on-site from dawn to dusk

13 *The Facilities*
- Golf and tennis
- Exercise and aerobics
- Miniature golf
- Playground
- Riding stables
- Water park

14 *The Willows*

Figure 4.2

Follow these steps to complete the presentation:

1. Launch PowerPoint, if necessary, and open the presentation *The Willows*.

2. Display the presentation in Slide Sorter view and move Slide 7 so that it becomes Slide 4. Then move Slide 8 so that it becomes Slide 5.

3. Select Slide 6; then click the New Slide button on the Standard toolbar and choose the Bulleted List AutoLayout. Double-click the plain new slide to display it in Slide view so that you can add slide text.

4. Type **Sandwich Shops** in the title placeholder and then add the following bulleted list to the bulleted list placeholder:
   - Willow Green on the golf course
   - The Cola Shop on the Mezzanine

- Grey Fox Deli at The Grande Hotel
- The 18th Hole on the golf course
- Red Rocker at the pool
- The Boardwalk on the beach

5. Display Slide Sorter view again, hide Slide 7, and expand Slide 9.

6. Switch to Outline view and add the text for new Slides 11 and 12 as shown in Figure 4.2.

7. View the slide show and then display the presentation in Slide Sorter view to add transitions and text preset animations you find most effective to each slide.

8. Save the changes to the presentation and print a copy of the presentation outline. Demonstrate the slide show for your instructor.

2. Editing, Enhancing, and Viewing a Presentation as a Slide Show

Ms. Lindsey would also like to fine-tune the presentation *The Willows Shops* so that she can include it in her presentation to the managers. Figure 4.3 displays the finished presentation in Slide Sorter view.

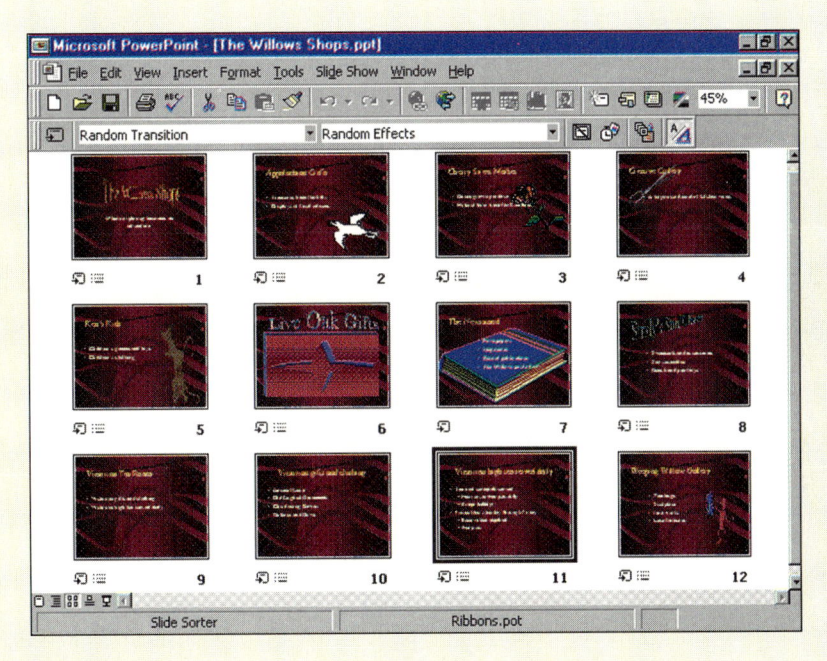

Figure 4.3

Follow these steps to complete the task:

1. Launch PowerPoint, if necessary, and open the presentation *The Willows Shops*.

2. Display Slide Sorter view and rearrange the bulleted list slides into alphabetical order by titles as follows:
   - Slide 9 becomes Slide 2
   - Slide 7 becomes Slide 3
   - Slide 7 (new) becomes Slide 4
   - Slide 9 becomes Slide 5
   - Slide 8 becomes Slide 6
   - Slide 10 becomes Slide 7
   - Slide 10 (new) becomes Slide 9

3. Expand Slide 9. Display the new Slide 10 in Slide view and add the following text to the bulleted list placeholder:
   - Ancient Lace
   - Old English Ornaments
   - Christening Gowns
   - Buttons and Bows

4. Display Slide 11 and add the following bulleted list items:
   - Tea and crumpets
     - 9:00 a.m. to 4:00 p.m. daily
     - Except holidays
   - Formal tea Monday through Friday
     - Reservations required
     - 4:00 p.m.

5. Show the presentation as a slide show and then display Slide Sorter view. Add transitions and text preset animations to the bulleted list slides and show the presentation again.

6. Make any necessary adjustments to the presentation and then save the changes to the presentation.

7. Show the presentation to your instructor and print copies of presentation slides as handouts with six framed pure black-and-white slides per page.

8. Close the presentation and exit PowerPoint when you've completed your work.

Assignments

1. Editing and Enhancing a Presentation and Viewing a Slide Show

The slides from the *Festivals and Attractions* presentation appear in Figure 4.4. Use the tools presented in this project to expand slides, rearrange slides, and add text to slides. Add slide transitions and text preset animations to slides in the presentation. Then view the presentation as a slide show and save changes to the presentation. Present the slide show to your instructor and print pure black-and-white handouts with six framed slides per page. Close the presentation and exit PowerPoint when you've completed your work.

2. Editing and Enhancing a Presentation and Posting It to the WWW (Optional Assignment. Ask your instructor how to proceed.)

Edit and enhance your résumé presentation and then follow one or both of the following options, as directed by your instructor:
- Post the presentation to the Web site identified by your instructor.
- Choose File, Send To, Exchange Folder to file the presentation in Outlook. Select Microsoft Outlook from the Profile Name list and save the presentation in the Journal folder of the Personal Folders drawer or create a new personal folder with your name as the folder name (according to your instructor's directions) and store the presentation in your personal folder. Then launch Outlook, if available, and verify that the presentation name appears on the list of files in the Journal folder or in your personal folder.

Project 4: Viewing and Editing a Presentation PP-135

Slide 1: Festivals and Attractions
The Willows
North Carolina

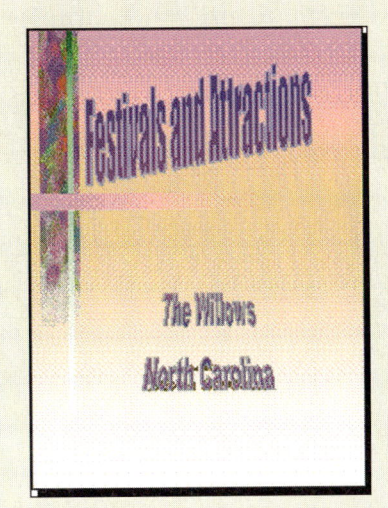

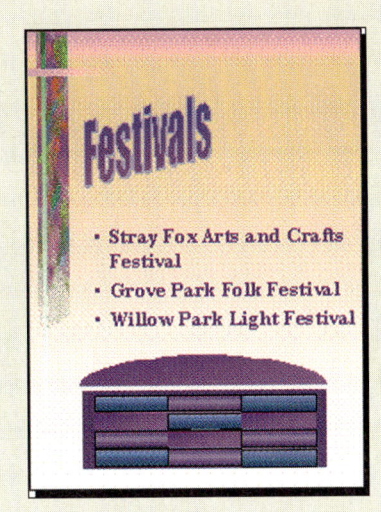

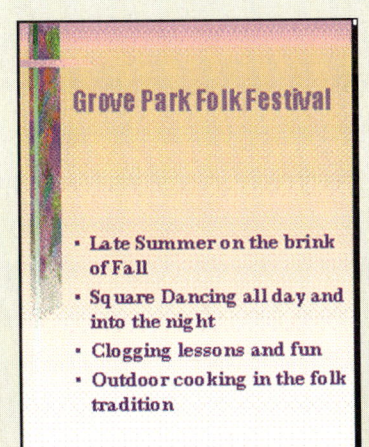

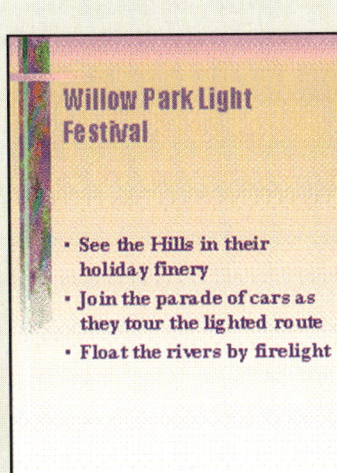

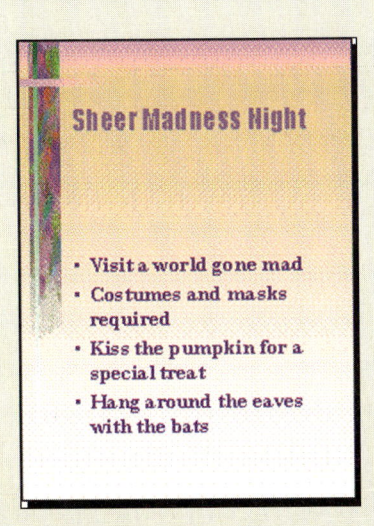

Slide 2: Festivals
- Stray Fox Arts and Crafts Festival
- Grove Park Folk Festival
- Willow Park Light Festival

Slide 3: Stray Fox Arts and Crafts Festival
- In the Spring when the blush is on the roses
- Costumes for an "Old World" fox hunt encouraged
- Treasures crafted for those who appreciate "Old World" charm
- Antiques and Hunt objects featured

Slide 4: Grove Park Folk Festival
- Late Summer on the brink of Fall
- Square Dancing all day and into the night
- Clogging lessons and fun
- Outdoor cooking in the folk tradition

Slide 5: Willow Park Light Festival
- See the Hills in their holiday finery
- Join the parade of cars as they tour the lighted route
- Float the rivers by firelight

Slide 6: Attractions
- Sheer Madness Night
- Little Pitchers Beach Week

Slide 7: Sheer Madness Night
- Visit a world gone mad
- Costumes and masks required
- Kiss the pumpkin for a special treat
- Hang around the eaves with the bats

Slide 8: Little Pitchers Beach Week
- Midsummer fun for the young and the young-at-heart
- Activities focus on children 12 years old and under
- Teen dance Friday night

Figure 4.4

5

PROJECT

Enhancing a Presentation

Okay! You've created a fantastic presentation, edited it, and dressed it up so that you can deliver it with style, and you're ready to take the presentation on the road. A few more features are buried within PowerPoint that will help you set up your presentation to run in different environments. In this project, you learn how to fine-tune your presentations and create materials to use as you show the presentation.

Objectives

After completing this project, you will be able to:

- ➤ **Animate slides with sound**
- ➤ **Set action buttons**
- ➤ **Add slide timings**
- ➤ **Set a presentation to run continuously**
- ➤ **Create notes pages**
- ➤ **Pack a presentation to go**

The Challenge

Francesca Savoy impressed the managers when she made her presentation last week. Now the Board of Directors of The Willows wants the presentation to be set up at strategic locations throughout the resort so that guests and visitors can stop and view it. In addition, the Board has authorized Ms. Savoy, as Marketing Director, to market the resort to large organizations interested in locating resort settings for conventions. She comes to you for help.

The Solution

To get the presentation for The Willows ready for viewing throughout the resort, you need to set the presentation to run automatically. To draw the attention of guests and visitors to the presentation, you need to add some sound to your text animation. Because Ms. Savoy will be traveling with the presentation, you need to package the presentation to take on the road and develop a set of notes pages for her to use as she shows the presentation. A sample notes page appears in Figure 5.1.

Figure 5.1

The Setup

Most of the default settings you've been using throughout this part of the book should be active as you complete the activities in this project. You'll be using Notes Pages view for part of the project, and the toolbars for Notes Pages view are the same toolbars you see in Slide view. Display the Standard, Formatting, and Drawing toolbars and close the Common Tasks toolbar so that what you see on your computer screen will match the illustrations shown here.

You'll also need to work with your presentation window maximized in Slide and Notes Pages views. Click the Maximize button on the presentation window, if necessary.

Animating Slides with Sound

In Project 4, you animated the slide text using text preset animations. The Animation Effects toolbar contains buttons that you can use to add sound to the animated text automatically or to customize the animation effect and select a sound. When you choose to add *custom animation,* you'll use the Custom Animation dialog box. The Custom Animation dialog box displays options that also enable you to dim bullet points for animated text as new bullet points display.

TASK 1: TO ANIMATE SLIDES WITH SOUND:

1. Open the presentation *The Willows* and display Slide 1 in Slide view. Slide 1 displays as last edited.

2. Click the Animation Effects button on the Formatting toolbar.

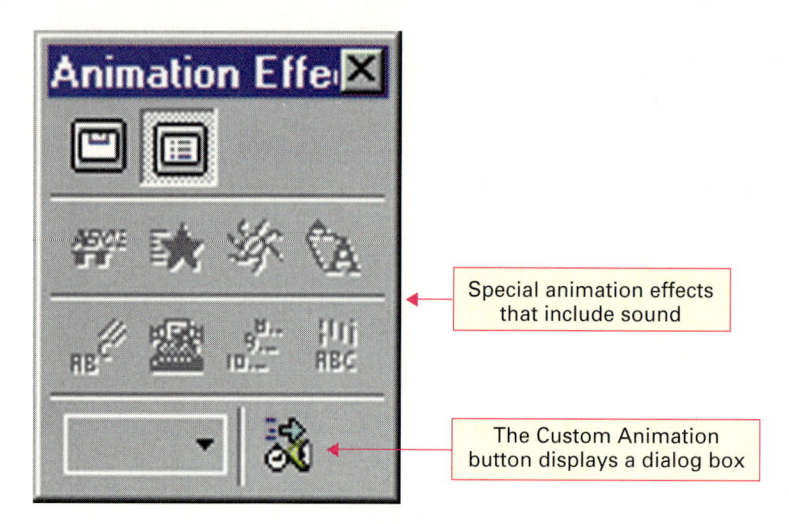

   Special animation effects that include sound

   The Custom Animation button displays a dialog box

3. Click the Custom Animation button.

   Text already animated

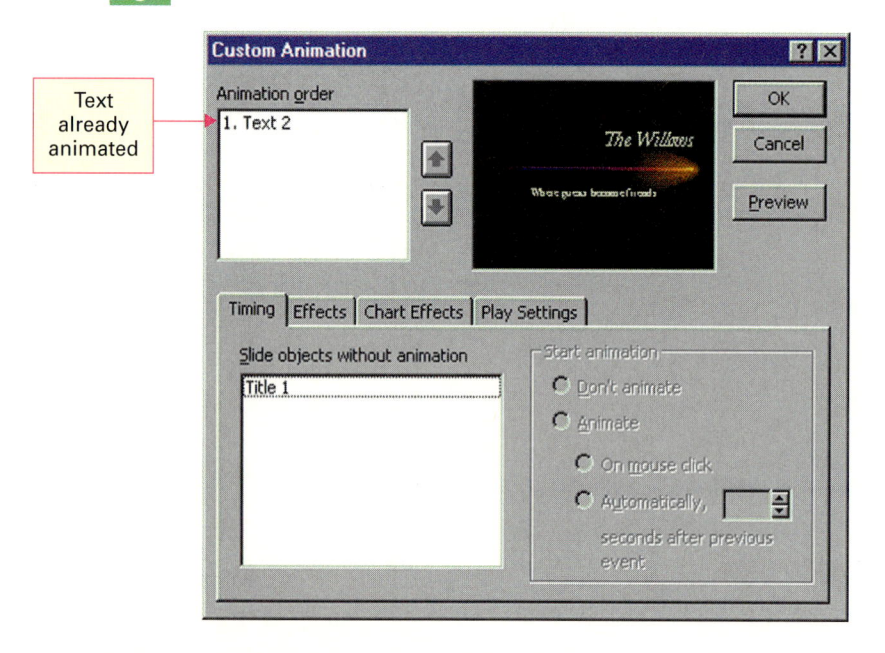

4. Click the Effects tab and then click "1. Text 2" in the Animation order list box.

Project 5: Enhancing a Presentation   PP-139

The Text 2 placeholder appears selected

Click to select a new animation effect

Animation buttons become available

Click to select a sound

Click to dim bullet points when new bullet points appear

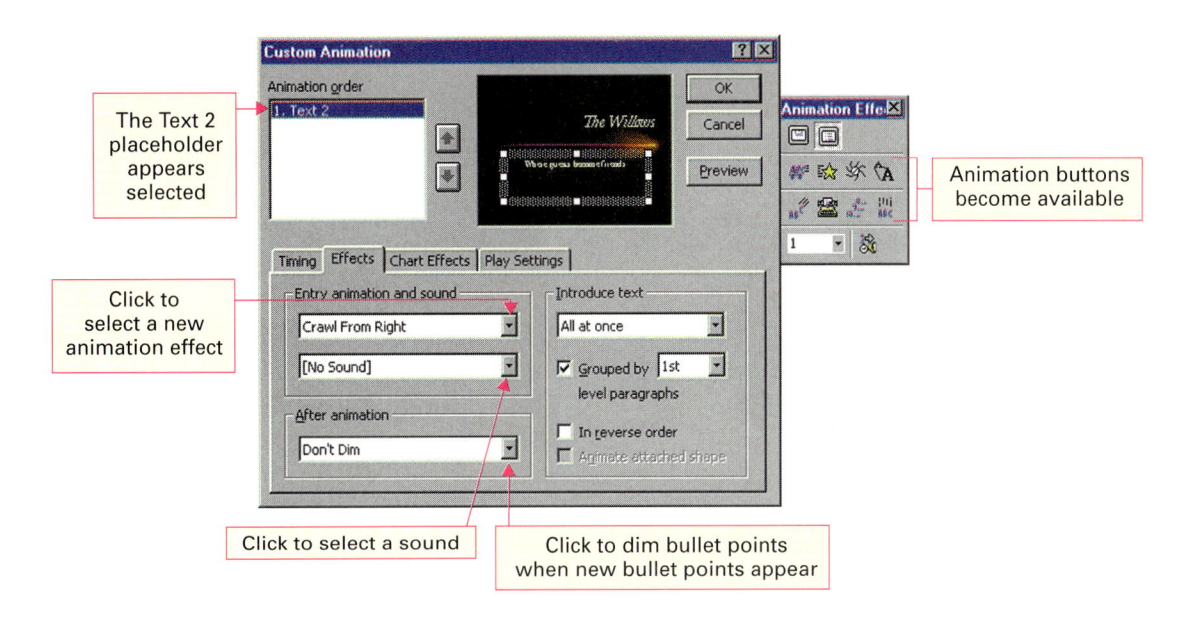

5 Click the arrow button for the sound option and point to Whoosh.

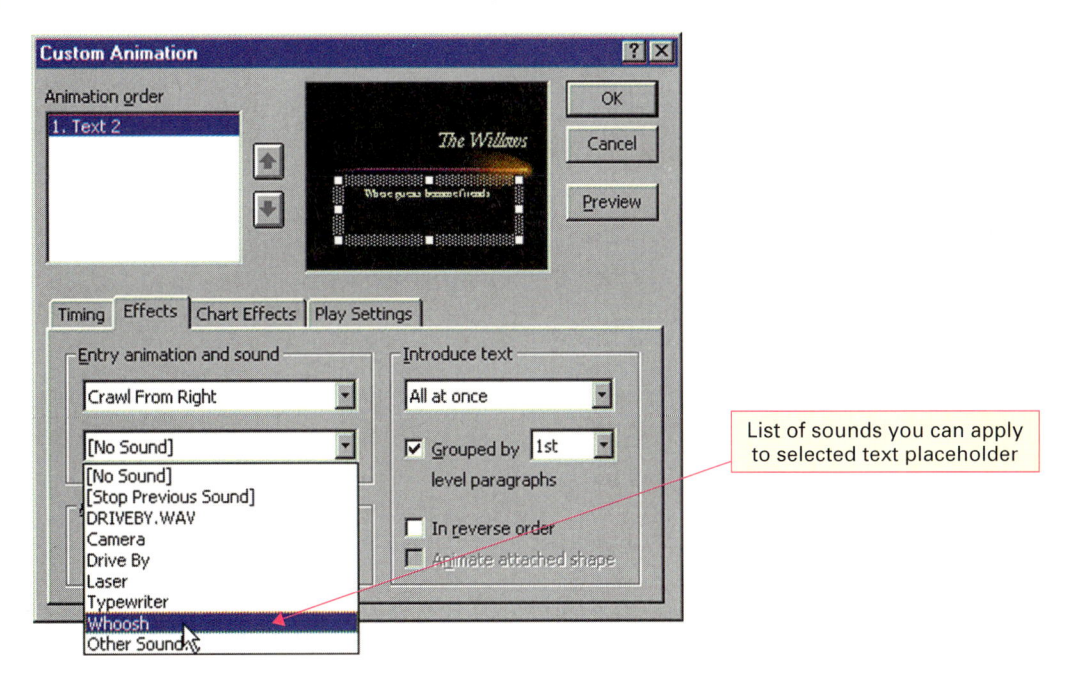

List of sounds you can apply to selected text placeholder

6 Click Whoosh to apply the sound to the animated text.
Whoosh appears in the text box.

7 Click OK to return to Slide 1 and then click the Slide Show View button to show the slide.
Slide 1 displays in full-screen view.

8 Press (ENTER) to display the animated text and hear the sound; then press (ESC) to return to Slide view.
Slide 1 displays in Slide view.

PP-140

9 Display Slide 2, select the bulleted list placeholder, and click the Typewriter Text Effect button on the Animation Effects toolbar.

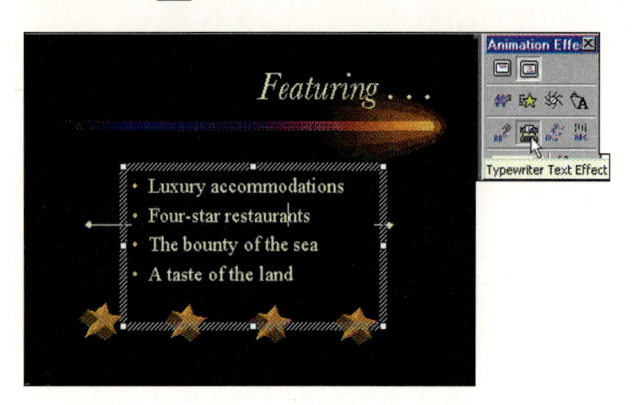

10 Click to open the Custom Animation dialog box.

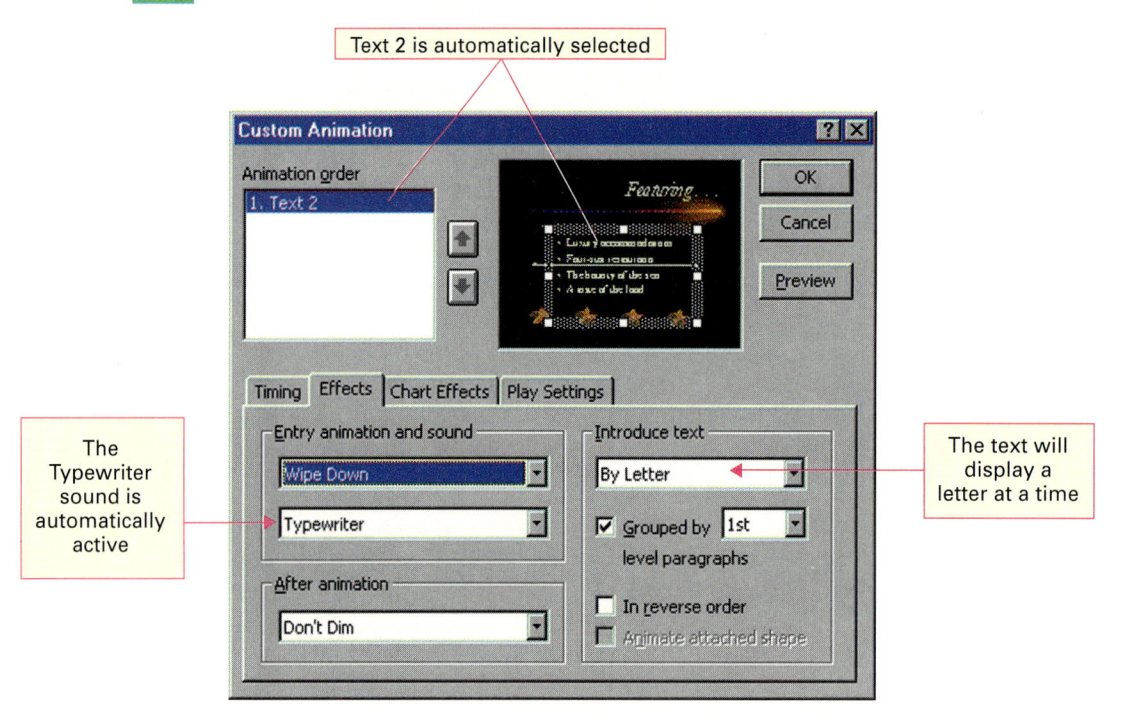

Text 2 is automatically selected

The Typewriter sound is automatically active

The text will display a letter at a time

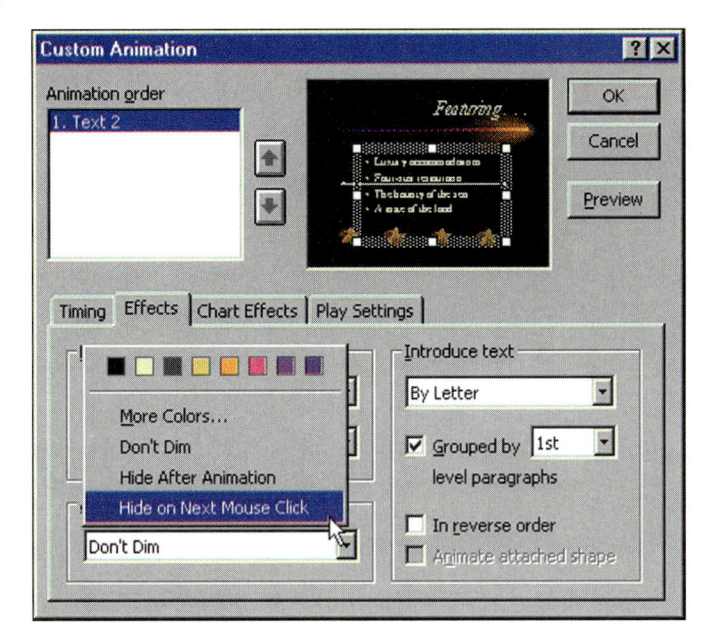

11 Click the arrow button beside the After animation option.

12 Click Hide on Next Mouse Click and then click OK to return to the slide. Slide 2 appears in Slide view.

13 Show the slide to view the effects, press (ESC), and then save the changes to the presentation.
The text displays one character at a time and you can hear the sound of a typewriter as each character appears. Each bullet point disappears when the next bullet point displays.

Setting Action Buttons

Action buttons enable you to control the slide PowerPoint displays when you click the button during a slide show. For the presentation *The Willows,* you can add an action button to display a hidden slide that follows Slide 8. PowerPoint creates a *hyperlink* to the slide so that clicking the action button automatically displays the desired slide.

> **Tip** You can also add action buttons to enable users to choose the section of a presentation they want to view or to display documents from other applications. Explore these advanced features as you become more comfortable with PowerPoint.

PP-142

TASK 2: TO CREATE AND SET AN ACTION BUTTON:

1 Display Slide 6 of the presentation *The Willows* in Slide view.

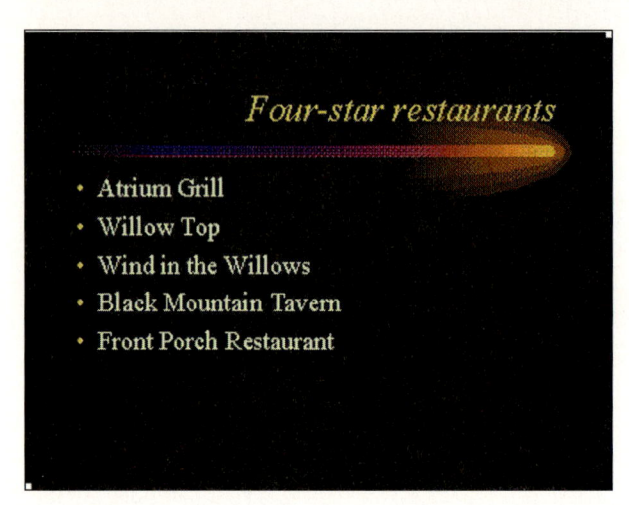

2 Choose Slide Show, Action Buttons.

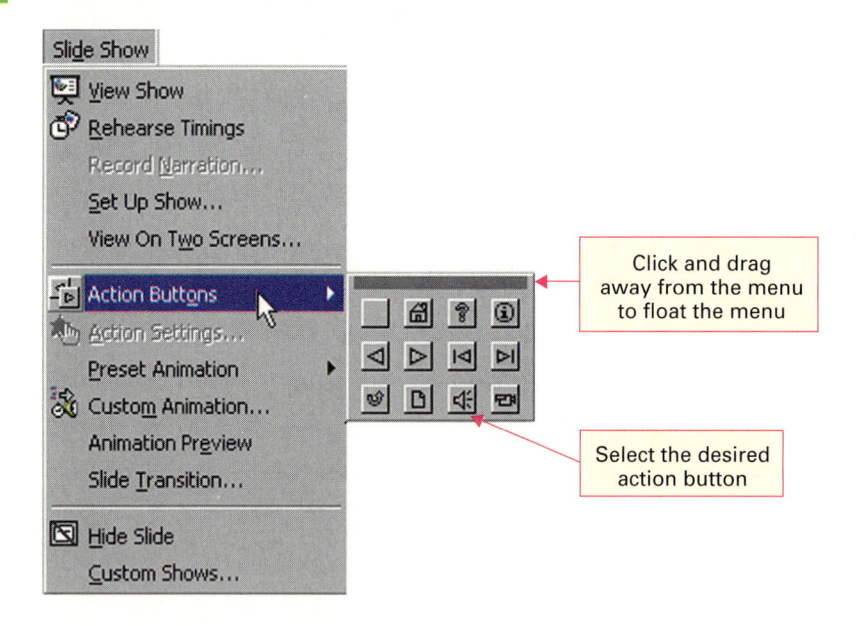

Click and drag away from the menu to float the menu

Select the desired action button

3 Click the Action Button: Forward or Next button.
The pointer changes to a plus (+).

Project 5: Enhancing a Presentation   PP-143

4 Position the pointer in the lower-right corner of the slide, click, and draw a small square shape.

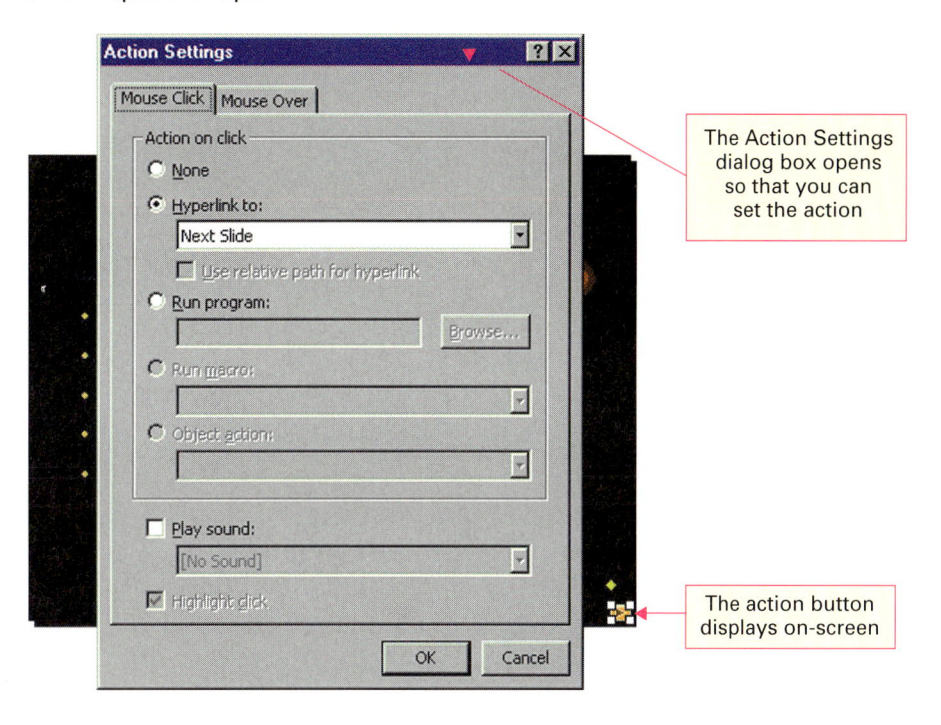

The Action Settings dialog box opens so that you can set the action

The action button displays on-screen

5 Click the arrow button beside the Hyperlink to option and select Slide.

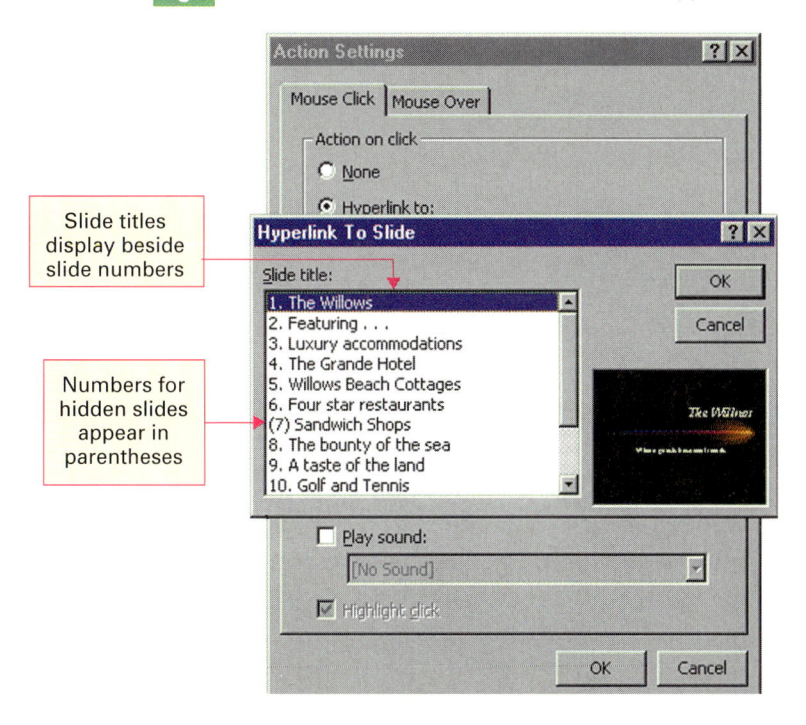

Slide titles display beside slide numbers

Numbers for hidden slides appear in parentheses

6 Select (7) Sandwich Shops and then click OK.
The slide title appears in the Hyperlink to text box.

7 Press ENTER to close the Action Settings dialog box and then click 🖫 to show the slide.

8 Point to the action button and click to display the hidden slide. Slide 7 displays immediately.

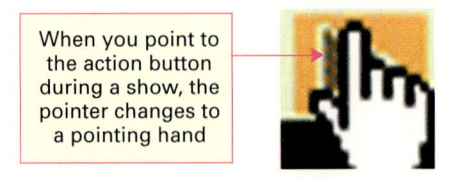

When you point to the action button during a show, the pointer changes to a pointing hand

9 Press ESC to stop the show, save the changes to the presentation, and close the Animation Effects toolbar.

Adding Slide Timings

Before you set the presentation to run automatically, you need to add slide timings so that each slide displays for a set amount of time before advancing to the next slide. After you add timings, slides move on and off the screen automatically. Of course, viewers can advance slides manually, even when timings are present.

TASK 3: TO ADD SLIDE TIMINGS:

1 Display the presentation *The Willows* in Slide Sorter view. Thumbnail images appear in Slide Sorter view.

2 Select Slide 1 and then click the Slide Transition 🖫 button on the Slide Sorter toolbar.

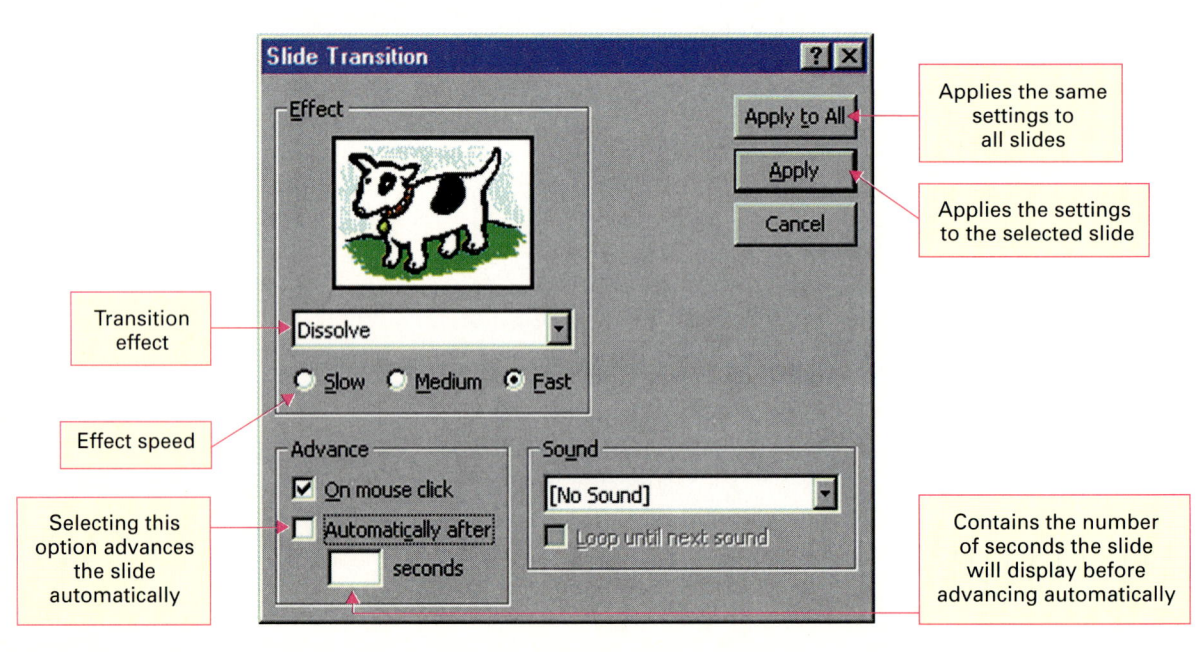

Applies the same settings to all slides

Applies the settings to the selected slide

Transition effect

Effect speed

Selecting this option advances the slide automatically

Contains the number of seconds the slide will display before advancing automatically

Project 5: Enhancing a Presentation PP-145

3 Click the check box beside Automatically after, type **25** in the seconds value box, and click Apply.

The slide timing appears below the slide

4 Apply the slide timings shown here to all the slides in the presentation.

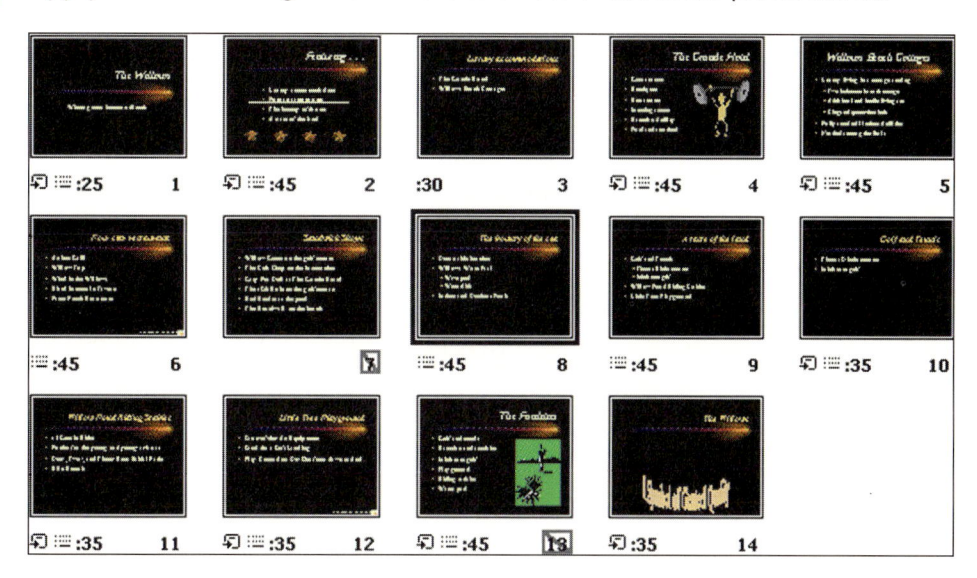

> **Note** If slide text is formatted with a text preset animation, PowerPoint distributes the timing you set among the bulleted list items on the slide. As a result, a four-point bulleted list set to display for 60 seconds would display each bulleted item for 15 seconds before displaying the next bullet point.

5 Save the first few changes to the presentation and then show the presentation, letting the slides advance automatically.

Setting a Presentation to Run Continuously

You may have seen computer monitors set up in stores or at conferences or trade shows that displayed information automatically and gave you an opportunity to review the information. Now that you have the presentation set up to run automatically with timings, you can set it to start over after the last slide displays, so that it runs continuously—or *loops* back to the first slide in a never-ending circle.

TASK 4: TO SET UP A PRESENTATION TO RUN CONTINUOUSLY:

1 Choose Slide Show, Set Up Show.

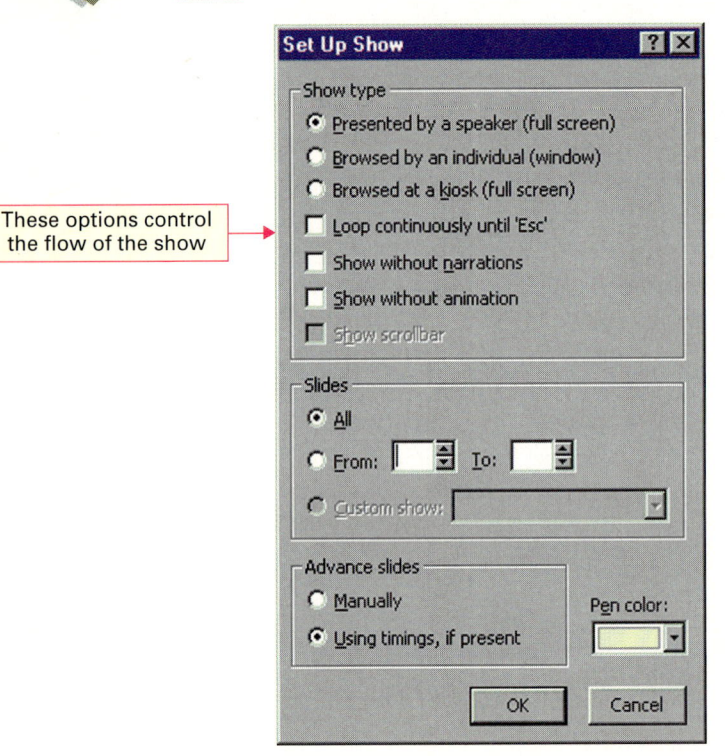

These options control the flow of the show

2 Click the Loop continuously until 'Esc' option and click OK.

> **Tip** Selecting the Browsed at a kiosk (full screen) option in the Set Up Show dialog box restricts slide advancement to timings only; manual clicking won't advance slides. Selecting Loop continuously until 'Esc' lets you advance slides manually as well as automatically.

3 Save the changes to the presentation and show the presentation, letting some slides advance automatically and advancing some slides manually.

4 Press (ESC) to stop the presentation, display Slide 6 in Slide view, and then click the Text Box button on the Drawing toolbar.

Project 5: Enhancing a Presentation   PP-147

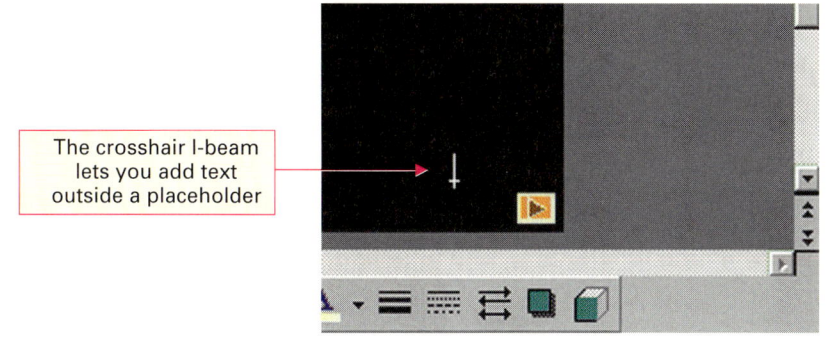

The crosshair I-beam lets you add text outside a placeholder

5 Position the I-beam to the left of the action button, click, and type **Click to see facilities summary.**
The text appears shadowed and too large for the slide area.

6 Select the text in the text box, click the Shadow button on the Formatting toolbar to turn off shadowing, and select 14 from the Font Size list box.

7 Click to view the slide and click the action button to display Slide 7.

8 Press ESC to stop the presentation and then save the changes to the presentation.

Creating Notes Pages

Your presentation is ready to be set up at strategic locations throughout the resort and is almost ready to take on the road. All Ms. Savoy needs now is a set of notes to take with her so she doesn't forget important points she wants to make during the presentation. The PowerPoint Notes Pages view enables you to add notes to the bottom of a page that contains an image of the slide at the top.

TASK 5: TO CREATE NOTES PAGES:

1 Display Slide 1 in Slide view and then click the Notes Pages View button at the bottom of the presentation window.
A small image of Slide 1 appears on-screen with a Notes placeholder at the bottom. The zoom percentage makes reading difficult.

2 Change the Zoom control setting to 75%.

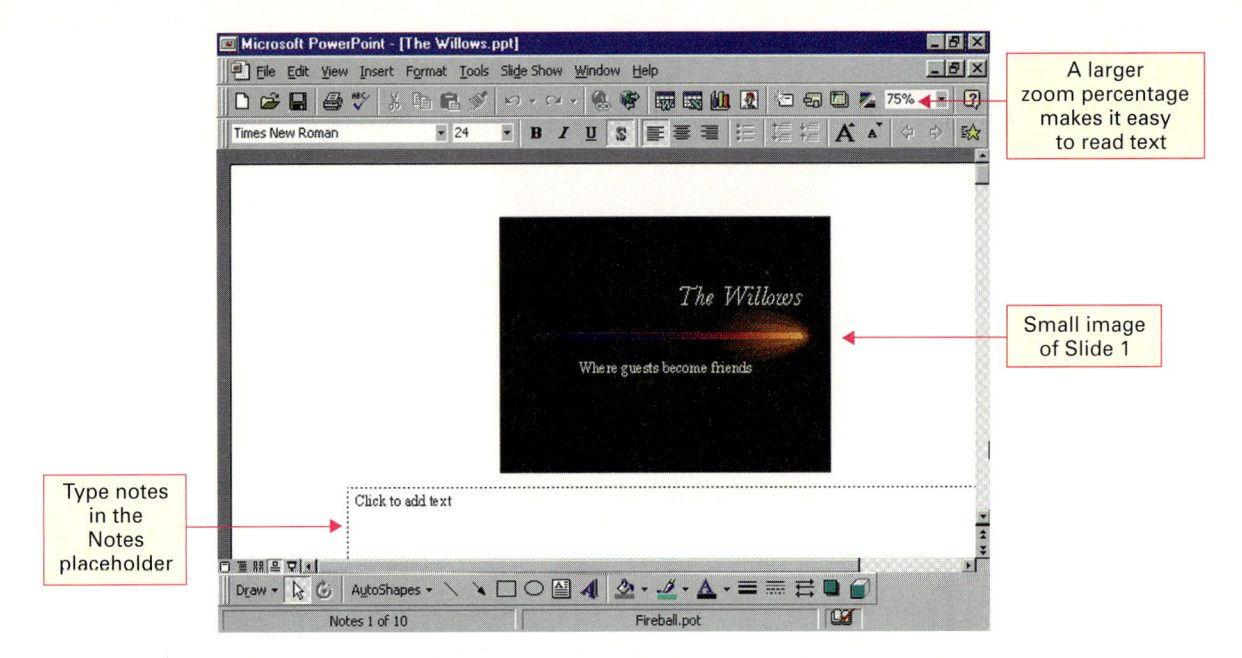

Screenshot callouts:
- A larger zoom percentage makes it easy to read text
- Small image of Slide 1
- Type notes in the Notes placeholder

3 Point to the Notes placeholder, click, and type **Introduce myself and explain the purpose of the presentation. Ask audience what facilities they require for their conference.**
The text appears in the notes placeholder below the slide image.

4 Press (PGDN) to display Slide 2, click the Notes placeholder, and type **Review basic features of The Willows.**
The notes appear in the Notes placeholder of Slide 2.

5 Add the following text as notes to the following slides:

Slide 3: **Emphasize that The Grande Hotel has more than 400 rooms to accommodate large gatherings and that the cottages offer more private settings. Review specific features of The Grande Hotel and the cottages as next two slides appear.**

Slide 6: **Cite accolades of recent publications about the quality of our restaurants. Emphasize that there are less formal eateries available as well. Mention catering for special dinners. A hidden slide follows this slide and lists sandwich shops in case someone asks about them.**

Slide 8: **Ask audience what types of activities they like to explore.**

Slide 9: **Compare on-shore activities to the water sports. Stress the "something for everyone" aspect of the resort to show that families will have plenty to do while businesspeople attend meetings.**

Slide 14: **Summarize The Willows features and ask for questions.**

6 Choose File, Print.
The Print dialog box displays.

7 Select Notes Pages from the Print what drop-down list, select the Pure black & white option, click the Slides option, type **1–3,6,8,9,14** in the Slides text box, and press (ENTER).
The notes pages for the selected slides print.

Project 5: Enhancing a Presentation   PP-149

Packing a Presentation to Go

Everything is set—and, as usual, just in the nick of time! Ms. Savoy is about to take off on her first marketing trip and needs the presentation on a disk to take with her. You're in luck—PowerPoint has a Pack and Go Wizard that can have her on the road in just a few minutes with disk in hand. Graphics, templates, and animation effects increase the size of presentations and make them difficult to copy to a disk. When you pack a presentation using the Pack and Go Wizard, however, PowerPoint *compresses* the presentation, making it more compact and easier to fit on one disk.

TASK 6: TO PACK A PRESENTATION TO GO:

1. Choose File, Pack and Go.

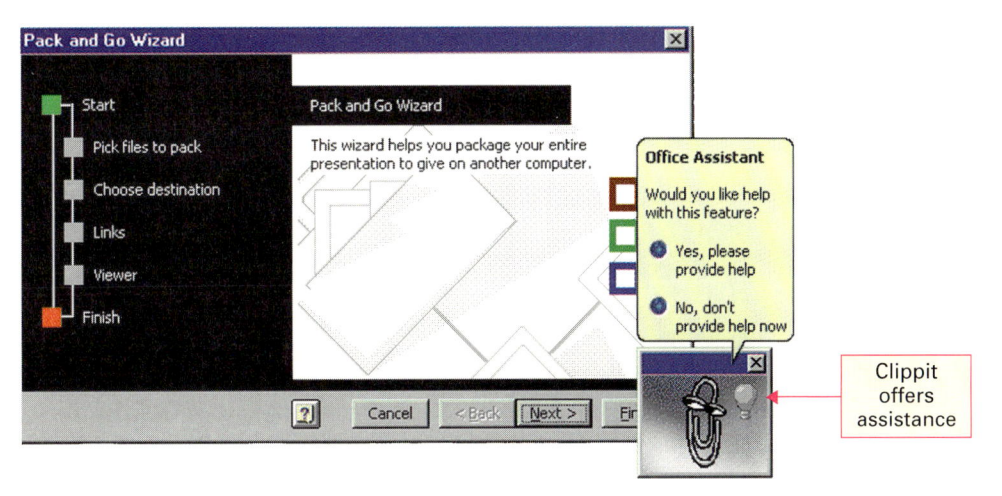

   Clippit offers assistance

2. Click No, don't provide help now to close the Office Assistant; then click Next.

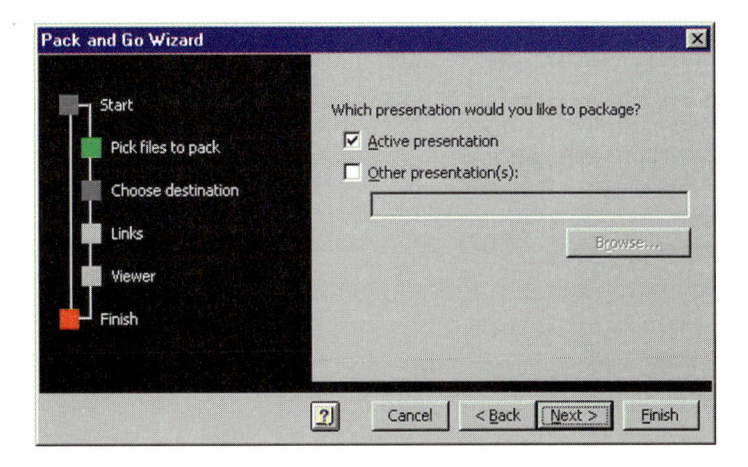

3 Ensure that Active presentation is selected and click Next.

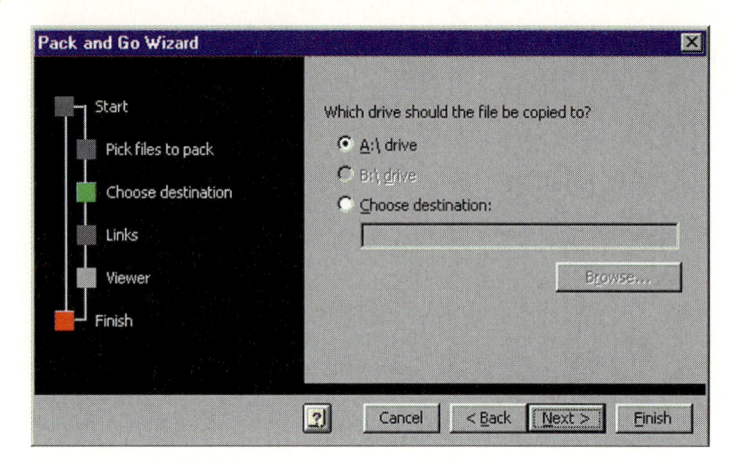

4 Ensure that the floppy drive for your computer is active, place a disk in the floppy drive, and click Next.

> **Note** The disk you use should contain no other files, otherwise your presentation might not fit.

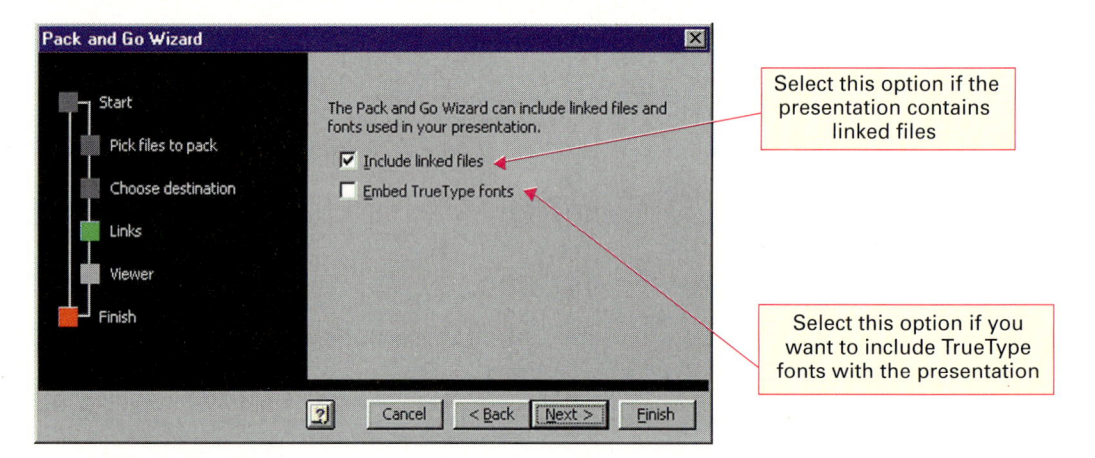

Select this option if the presentation contains linked files

Select this option if you want to include TrueType fonts with the presentation

5 For this exercise, deselect the Include linked files option because your presentation doesn't contain links, and select Embed TrueType fonts to ensure that your presentation displays properly; then click Next.

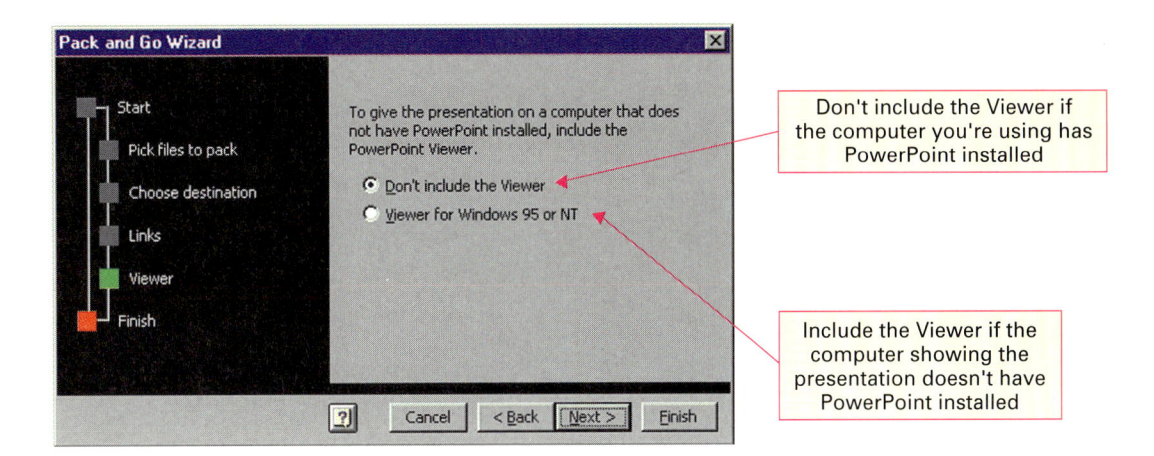

Project 5: Enhancing a Presentation PP-151

Don't include the Viewer if the computer you're using has PowerPoint installed

Include the Viewer if the computer showing the presentation doesn't have PowerPoint installed

Note If the PowerPoint Viewer isn't installed on your computer, you'll need the original PowerPoint CD to access the Viewer so that the Pack and Go Wizard can find it and pack it with the presentation(s).

6 For this example, click Don't include the Viewer and then click Next.

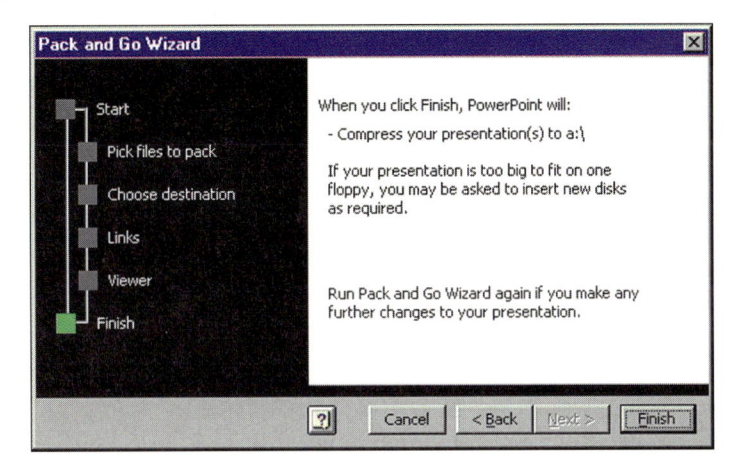

7 Click Finish.
PowerPoint whirs and burps a bit as it packages the presentation on the disk. When the presentation is packaged, a message window tells you that Pack and Go has successfully packed your presentation. If your presentation is too large to fit on one disk, you'll be told when to insert another disk.

8 Click OK to acknowledge the message.
Your presentation is ready to turn in to your instructor.

The Conclusion

Now that you have the presentation on disk, you can show it from any computer that has PowerPoint installed. Simply launch PowerPoint and open the presentation. If you've completed your work, close the presentation for The Willows and exit PowerPoint. If you plan to continue with the Review Exercises and Assignments, close the presentation and leave PowerPoint running.

Summary and Exercises

Summary

- PowerPoint comes equipped with animation effects that can contain sounds. You can apply these effects to slide text by using the Animation Effects toolbar.
- You can use action buttons to control the slides presented and to jump to different parts of a presentation.
- To prepare a presentation to run automatically, add slide timings to each slide to tell PowerPoint how long to leave the slide on the screen. When slide text is animated, each bullet point or animated object gets an equal share of the time allotted to the slide.
- To show a presentation at a trade show or in a location where no one is available to monitor the presentation, you can set the presentation to run continuously until someone stops the show.
- Create notes pages to type reminder notes to use during a show. Notes Pages view presents pages with slide images at the top and a notes placeholder at the bottom of the page for you to use.
- The Pack and Go Wizard prepares presentations for showing at another location. You can include a PowerPoint Viewer with the presentation if necessary.

Key Terms and Operations

Key Terms
action button
compress
custom animation
dim effect
hyperlink
loop
Pack and Go Wizard
timings
Viewer

Operations
add sound to slide text animations
add timings to slides so that they automatically advance
create notes pages to accompany a presentation
pack up a presentation using the Pack and Go Wizard
set action buttons to control the flow of the presentation
set a presentation to run continuously

Study Questions

Multiple Choice

1. To jump to a different slide than the one that normally follows the active slide,
   a. create a mini-program that runs the link.
   b. add a text box to a slide.
   c. add a graphic to the slide.
   d. add an action button to the slide.

2. To select a sound for a text preset animation,
   a. record the sound using a microphone.
   b. create an action button.
   c. customize the animation.
   d. add a graphic to the slide.

3. To create a set of notes to use during a slide show, display
   a. Slide Sorter view.
   b. Notes Pages view.
   c. Outline view.
   d. Slide view.

4. You can set up a presentation to advance slides automatically by setting
   a. slide timings.
   b. a hyperlink.
   c. a loop.
   d. an action button.

5. A hyperlink attached to an action button is called
   a. an animation effect.
   b. the slide outline.
   c. slide timings.
   d. a loop.

6. When you want to set up a presentation to run without constant monitoring, set up the presentation
   a. as a slide show.
   b. with timings only.
   c. to run continuously, using a loop.
   d. to advance manually.

7. Notes Pages view displays
   a. a notes placeholder only.
   b. a notes placeholder and a slide image.
   c. a slide image only.
   d. three slides on each page.

8. To prepare a presentation to show on another computer,
   a. use the Pack and Go Wizard.
   b. copy the slide to a disk.
   c. use the Send to command.
   d. branch out to the slide.

9. Slide timings
   a. must all be set exactly the same.
   b. don't work during a regular presentation.
   c. don't let you advance slides manually.
   d. can be different for each slide.

10. When you want to disable the manual advance for a presentation,
    a. simply set slide timings.
    b. set the presentation to loop continuously.
    c. set the presentation to run at a kiosk.
    d. You can't disable the manual advance for a presentation.

Short Answer
1. How can you quickly access the Animation Effects toolbar?
2. How does the slide number for hidden slides appear in a list of slide titles?

3. What page of the Custom Animation dialog box displays sounds and animation effects?

4. What tool do you use to add text to a slide outside a text placeholder?

5. How does the Pack and Go Wizard fit a large presentation onto one floppy disk?

6. To help focus the attention of your audience on the bullet point you're discussing during a slide show, what should you do to other bullet points already presented?

7. What view makes it easy to add slide timings?

8. Where do slide timings appear on-screen?

9. How do you stop a show set to run continuously?

10. What can you change to make the text in Notes Pages view easier to read?

For Discussion

1. What does the dim feature do?

2. What advantage does applying timings to slides in a presentation provide when the time you have for a presentation is limited?

3. Where have you seen presentations set up to run unmonitored?

4. How does attaching an action button help keep track of hidden slides?

Review Exercises

1. Adding Sound Effects to Animated Text, Setting Action Buttons to Display Hidden Slides, Adding Text to a Slide

The presentation *The Willows* includes numerous slides that contain animated text and a hidden slide that you need to format an action button to access. Follow these steps to complete the presentation:

1. Launch PowerPoint, if necessary, open the presentation *The Willows* in Slide view, and display the Animation Effects toolbar.

2. Display Slides 3 through 14 individually and apply an animated sound to the text preset animations already applied to the slides. Select different options to dim bullet points.

3. Display Slide 12 and add an action button to hyperlink to hidden Slide 13.

4. Display Slide 6, press (SHIFT), select the text box next to the action button, and copy the text box to the Windows Clipboard. Then display Slide 12 again and paste the text box onto the slide. Adjust the size and placement of the text box as needed.

5. Show the slide show to view your changes, and make final adjustments to the presentation.

6. Save changes to the presentation and print a copy of Slide 12 in pure black-and-white. Close the presentation.

2. Adding Action Buttons, Animating with Sound, Adding Slide Timings, Setting a Presentation to Run Continuously, Creating Notes Pages

Ms. Lindsey was so impressed with your work on the presentation for The Willows that she would like you to develop the presentation for The Willows Shops using the same techniques, and add a list of notes to notes pages in the presentation. A sample notes page appears in Figure 5.2.

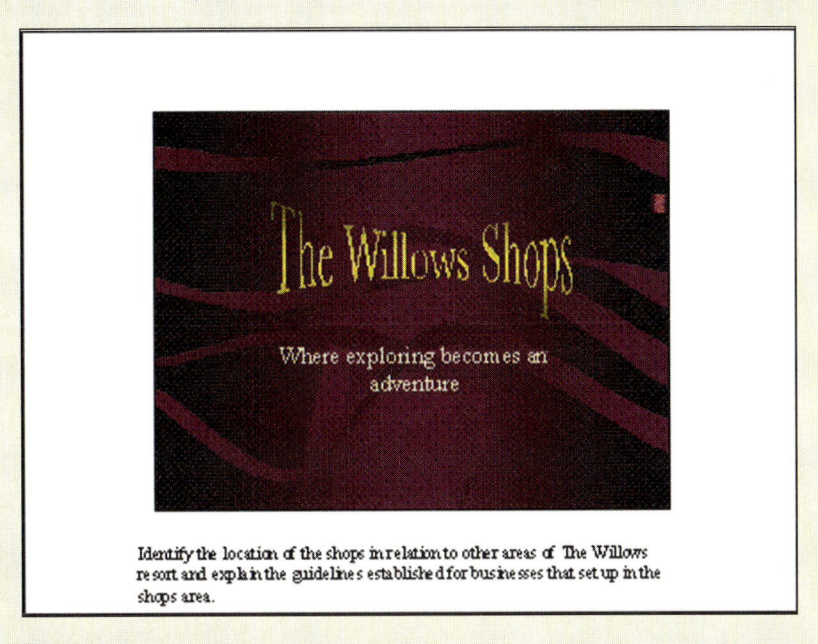

Figure 5.2

Follow these steps to format each slide in the presentation with a sound animation effect, dim bulleted list points, add timings to the all slides in the presentation, and create notes pages for the presentation.

1. Launch PowerPoint, if necessary, and open the presentation *The Willows Shops*.

2. Display Slide Sorter view and review the presentation settings. Then switch to Slide view and display the Animation Effects toolbar.

3. Display each slide in the presentation individually and apply a custom animation effect to the text already formatted with a preset animation. Apply a dim option to bulleted list text.

4. View the slide show and assess the effects. Then return to slide view and make any adjustments to slides in the presentation.

5. Display the presentation in Slide Sorter view and apply slide timings to each slide. Hide Slide 6.

6. Switch back to Slide view and add an action button to Slide 5 to access the hidden slide. Double-click the action button and change the fill and line color to make the action button blend in with the slide background.

7. View the presentation again and make certain that the action button displays the correct slide.

8. Display Notes Pages view and add the following notes to the slides:

   Slide 1: **Identify the location of the shops in relation to other areas of The Willows resort and explain the guidelines established for businesses that set up in the shops area.**

   Slide 2: **A series of slides about different shops starts with this slide and extends through Slide 12.**
   Emphasize that the wares displayed in this craft shop are original creations of people living in the Appalachian Mountains.

   Slide 3: **Stress that produce is brought to market daily.**

   Slide 5: **Mention that sizes for children range from newborn to about age 12.**

   Slide 7: **Mention daily delivery of all major newspapers from across the country, delivered on time, and available for room delivery.**

   Slide 11: **Review operating hours and explain that special arrangements can be made for organizations holding meetings at the resort.**

9. Set the presentation to loop continuously, using the Set Up Show dialog box, and then save changes to the presentation.

10. Print a copy of all notes pages containing notes, close the presentation, and exit PowerPoint when you've completed your work.

Assignments

1. Finalizing a Presentation to Run Continuously

The slides from the *Festivals and Attractions* presentation appear in Slide Sorter view in Figure 5.3.

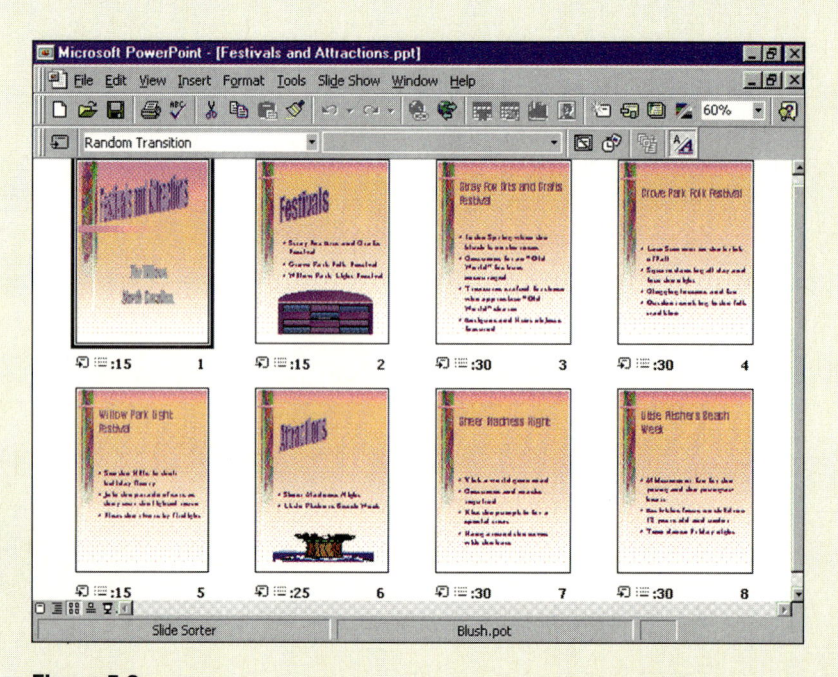

Figure 5.3

Use tools presented in this project to animate slide text with sound, add slide timings, and set the presentation to run continuously. Then view the presentation as a slide show and save changes to the presentation. Use your imagination to develop notes pages for the presentation and print copies of the notes pages that display slides in black-and-white. Set up the presentation on your computer during the next class session so that your instructor can review the special effects you've applied. Close the presentation and exit PowerPoint when you've completed your work.

2. Packing Presentations to Go and Sending Them Via a Mail Message

Package the *Festivals and Attractions* and *The Willows Shops* presentations to go, using the same disk. Exit PowerPoint and launch Outlook or your school mail program.

Create a mail message to your instructor. From the floppy that contains your presentations, attach the *Pngsetup.exe* file to the mail message. Send the message to your instructor.

Notes

Notes

Notes

PowerPoint 97 Function Guide

Function	Mouse Action or Button	Menu	Keyboard Shortcut
AutoLayout, select	Click [icon] and select format	Choose Format, Slide Layout and select format	
Bold	Select text and click [B]	Select text, choose Format, Font, and slect Bold	Select text and press CTRL+**B**
Bulleted list, format	Select item, right-click on screen, select Bullet, select bullet font category, and select bullet shape	Select item, choose Format, Bullet, select bullet font category, and select bullet shape	
indent			Press TAB
Font, change size	Select text, click Font Size drop-down list, select size OR select text and click [A] or [A]	Select text, choose Format, Font, select font size	Select text and press CTRL+**[** to decrease font size or CTRL+**]** to increase font size
Italicize	Select text and click [I]	Select text, choose Format, Font, and select Italic	Select text and press CTRL+**I**
Notes Pages, create	Click [icon] and type notes in area at bottom of page	Choose View, Notes Pages, and type notes in area at bottom of page	
Objects, group		Select all objects and choose Draw, Group	
Objects, move	Select object, position mouse pointer on object away from handle, click and drag		Press TAB until object is selected and press cursor arrows until object is positioned
Objects, ungroup		Select object and choose Draw, Ungroup	
Outline, indent	Click [icon] or [icon]		Press TAB or SHIFT+**[T**
Placeholder, add text	Click placeholder and type text		Press TAB to select placeholder and type text.
Placeholder, select text	Double-click to select word; triple-click to select bulleted item or title		Press SHIFT+arrow keys to highlight text
Presentation, add slide	Click [icon]	Choose Insert, New Slide	Press CTRL+**M**
Presentation, create new	Click [icon]	Choose File, New	Press CTRL+**N**
Presentation, pack to go		Choose File Pack and Go and follow screen prompts	
Presentation, save as template		Choose File, Save As, Select Presentation Template from Files of type list	
Presentation, show	Click [¶]	Choose View, Slide Show OR choose Slide Show, View Show	
Preview	Click [icon]	Choose File, Print Preview	
Print	Click [icon]	Choose File, Print	Press CTRL+**P**

PowerPoint 97 Function Guide

Function	Mouse Action or Button	Menu	Keyboard Shortcut
Save	Click	Choose File, Save	Press CTRL+**S**
Send		Choose File, Send	Press ALT+**F, E**
Slide, create	Click	Choose Insert, New Slide	Press CTRL+**M**
Slide, delete		Select slide and choose Edit, Delete Slide	
Slide, delete object on slide			Select object (placeholder, graphic, etc.) and press DELETE
Slide, display next	Click		Press PGDN
Slide, display previous	Click		Press PGUP
Slide, display Master	Press SHIFT and click view button	Choose View, Master, and select Master	
Slide, hide	In Slide Sorter view, select slide(s) to hide and click	In all views, select or display slide to hide and choose Slide Show, Hide Slide	
Slide, move in Slide Sorter view	Click slide to select it and drag it to a new position		
Slide, select in Outline or Slide Sorter view	Click slide icon or slide image		Press arrow keys until slide is selected
Select multiple slides in Outline or Slide Sorter view	Click first slide icon or slide image; press SHIFT and click addition slide icons or images		
Spelling check	Click	Choose Tools, Spelling and Grammar	Press F7
Style Check		Choose Tools, Style Checker	
Text, copy	Select text and click	Select text and choose Edit, Copy	Press CTRL+**C**
Text, cut	Select text and click	Choose Edit, Cut	Press CTRL+**X**
Text, paste	Select text and click	Choose Edit, Paste	Press CTRL+**V**
Template, apply	Click and select template	Choose Format, Apply Design	
Transitions, add	Display presentation in Slide Sorter view, select slide, click drop-down arrow, and select effect	Choose Slide Show, Slide Transition and select a transition from Effect drop-down list	
Underline	Select text and click	Select text, choose Format, Font, and select Underline	Select text and press CTRL+**U**
Undo	Click	Choose Edit, Undo	Press CTRL+**Z**
Web	Click	Choose Help, Microsoft on Web	
Zoom	Click in Preview	Choose View, Zoom	

INTEGRATED PROJECT

Integrating Word, Excel, Access, and PowerPoint

3

As you've already discovered, you can save valuable time by sharing data that already exists in other applications with documents and files in different applications. In this integrated project, you learn to integrate data among all Office products, learn how to share outlines between Word and PowerPoint, and how to save a file in HTML format so that you can use it on the Internet.

Objectives

After completing this project, you will be able to:

➤ **Embed a Word table on a PowerPoint slide**

➤ **Link data from Excel to a PowerPoint slide**

➤ **Create a Word document from a PowerPoint presentation outline**

➤ **Save a PowerPoint slide as a graphic and add the image to a Word document**

➤ **Create a hyperlink between a Word document and a PowerPoint presentation**

➤ **Save a presentation as an HTML file**

The Challenge

Ruth Lindsey, manager of the retail shops at The Willows resort, wants to add two slides to the The Willows presentation and create an outline using the text from slides contained in the presentation *The Willows*. In addition, Ms. Lindsey wants to include the first slide from the presentation as a graphic for the outline so that she can launch the presentation from the Word document.

IP3-1

The Solution

Figure 3.1 shows the two slides you will add to the presentation. Because you are comfortable with the features from all Office applications, you will use Word to add the table to a new slide in the presentation *The Willows*. The Excel worksheet contains the data shown in the second slide, so you will copy the data from Excel and link it to the slide.

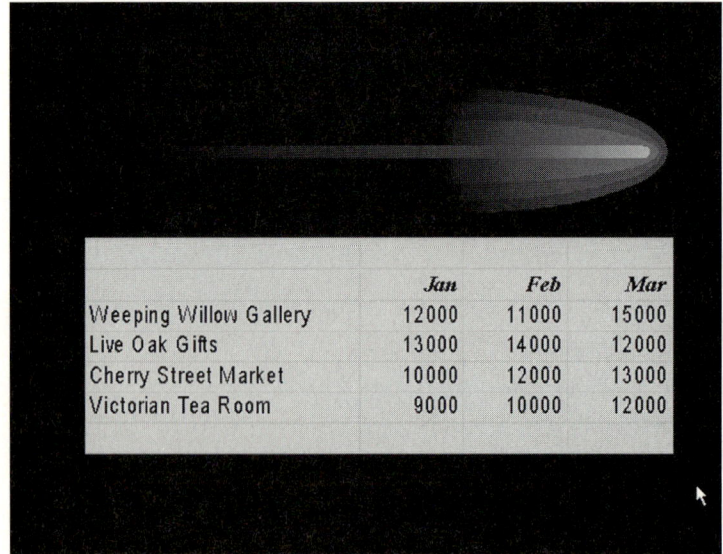

Figure 3.1

After you complete the presentation, you will use the presentation text to create the Word outline shown in Figure 3.2, capture the first slide from the presentation as a graphic, and then place the graphic in the Word outline. Finally, you create a hyperlink in Word that launches the presentation.

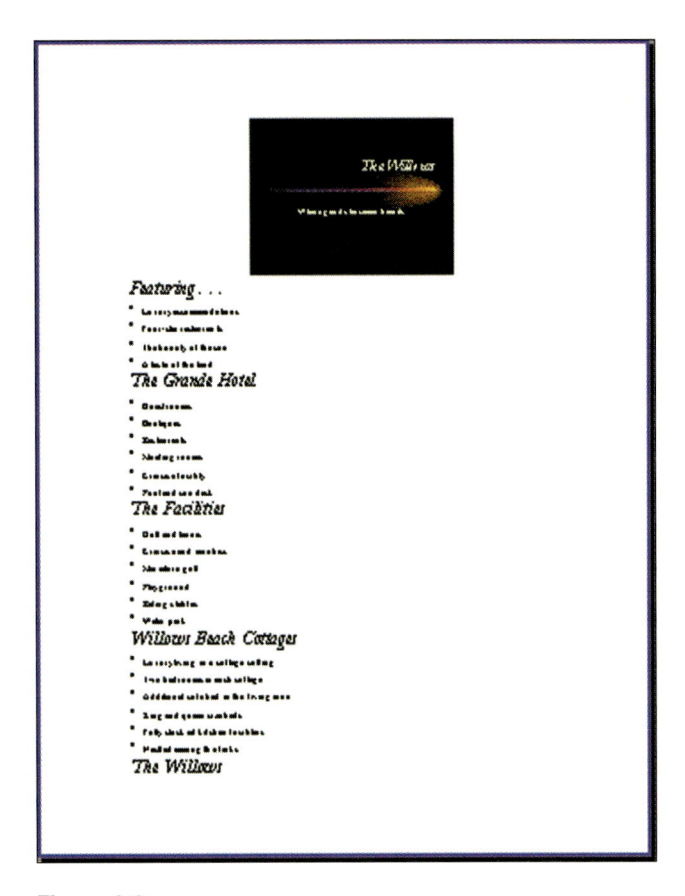

Figure 3.2

The Setup

To accomplish the tasks outlined in this project, you'll work with Word, Excel, and PowerPoint. You can launch applications as you need them and tile them on-screen. When you are working with only one application, maximize that application and its document window. Table 3.1 shows the settings you use.

Table 3.1 Settings

Element	Setting
Office Assistant	Close Office Assistant in all programs.
View, Toolbars	Display the Standard and Formatting toolbars in Word, Excel, and PowerPoint.
View, Toolbars	Display the Drawing toolbar in PowerPoint.
View, Ruler	Display the ruler in Word.

Embedding a Word Table on a PowerPoint Slide

When you want to include data from a Word document or an Excel worksheet on a PowerPoint slide, you can create the data in PowerPoint using tools from Word or Excel. Objects you create in PowerPoint using tools from other applications are embedded on the slide and become a part of the presentation. They aren't saved as individual files.

> **Note** When you add an object to a presentation slide using tools from Word or Excel, you can copy the data to a Word document or to an Excel worksheet and then save them as separate files using standard procedures for saving files in the application, if desired.

TASK 1: TO EMBED A WORD TABLE ON A POWERPOINT SLIDE:

1. Open the presentation *The Willows* in Slide view.

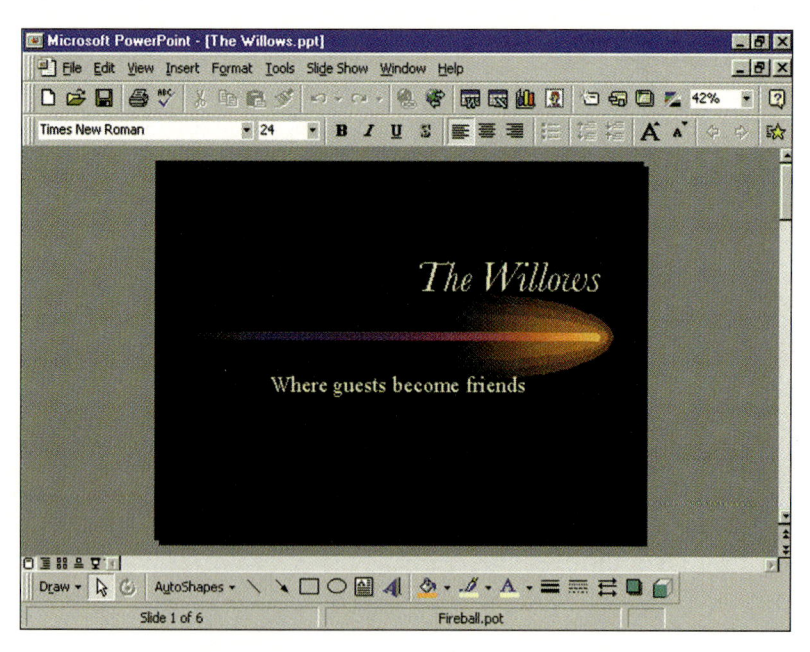

2. Click the New Slide button on the Standard toolbar and then select the Table AutoLayout format.

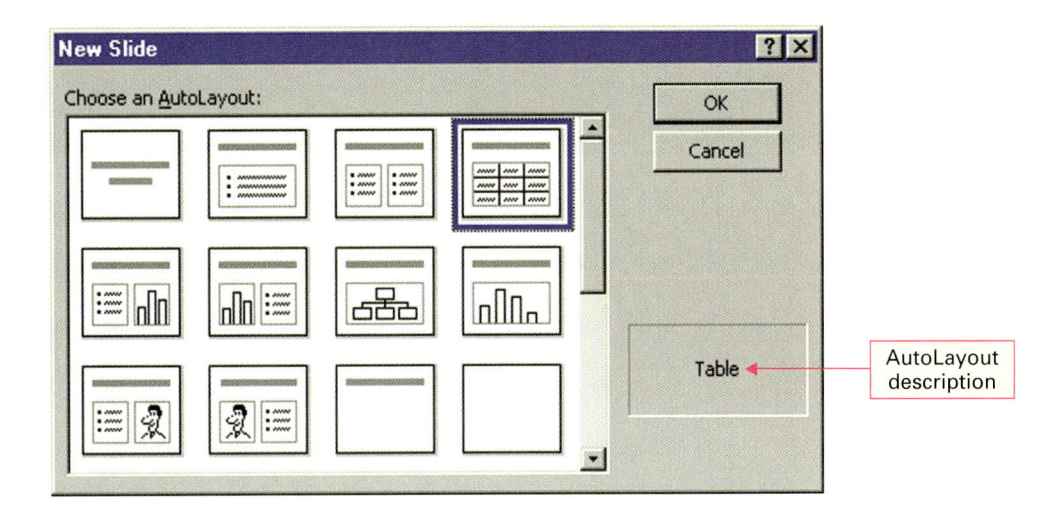

Integrating Word, Excel, Access and PowerPoint **IP3-5**

AutoLayout description

3 Click OK.

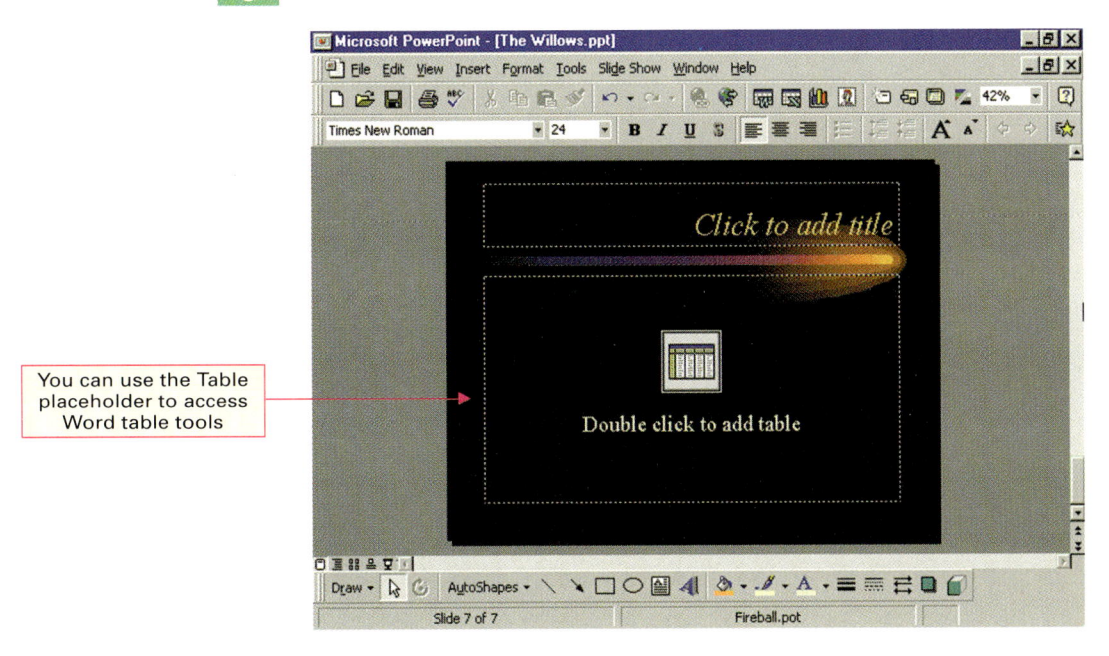

You can use the Table placeholder to access Word table tools

4 Double-click the Table placeholder.

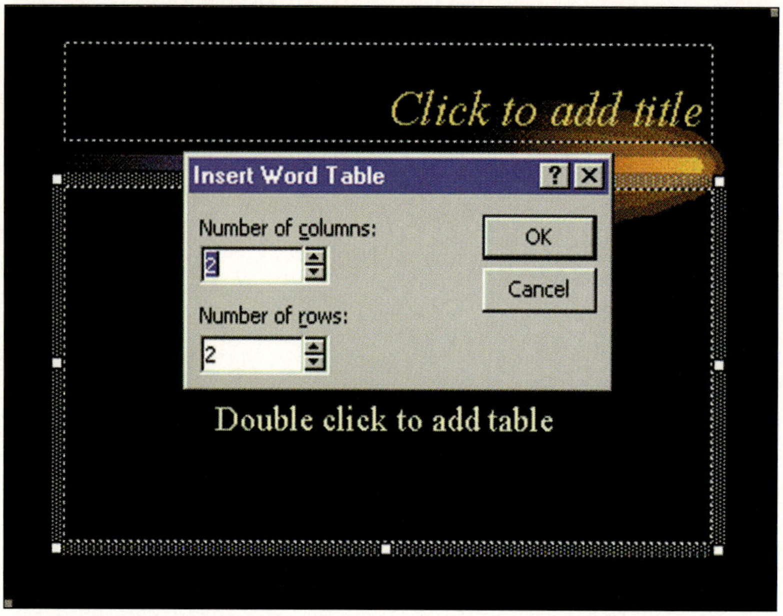
Click to add title
Insert Word Table
Number of columns:
2
Number of rows:
2
OK
Cancel
Double click to add table

5 Type **3** in the Number of rows value box and press ENTER.

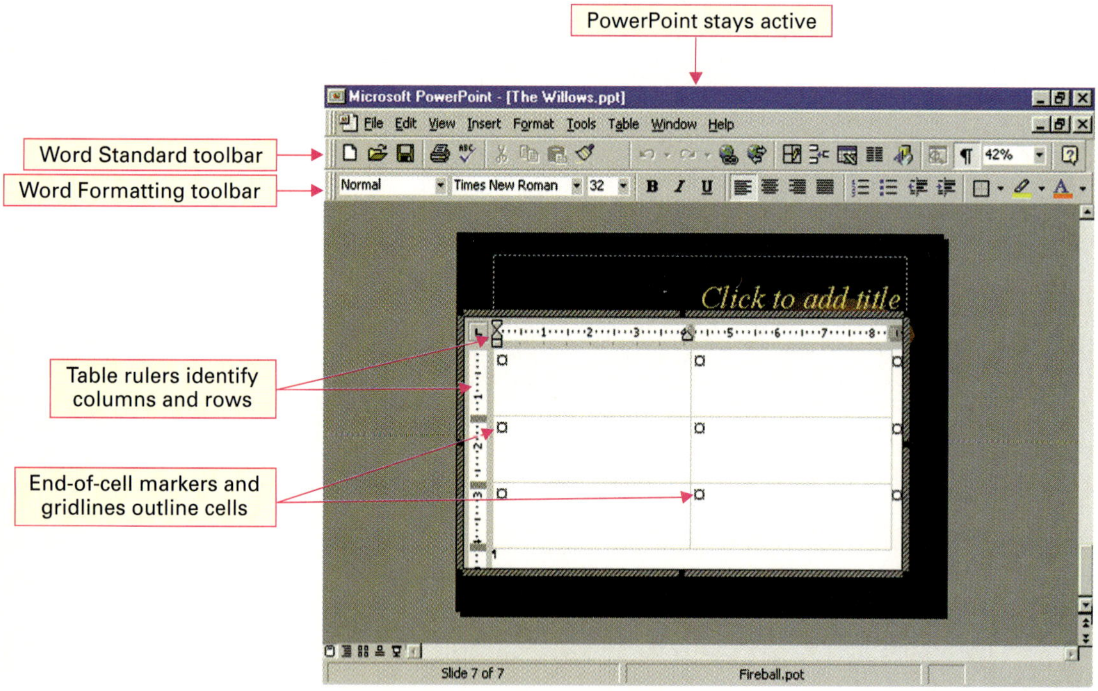
PowerPoint stays active
Word Standard toolbar
Word Formatting toolbar
Table rulers identify columns and rows
End-of-cell markers and gridlines outline cells
Microsoft PowerPoint - [The Willows.ppt]
File Edit View Insert Format Tools Table Window Help
Normal
Times New Roman
32
42%
Click to add title
Slide 7 of 7
Fireball.pot

Note If you don't see gridlines, choose Table, Gridlines.

6 Type the text shown in the following illustration into cells, and change the text color to red.

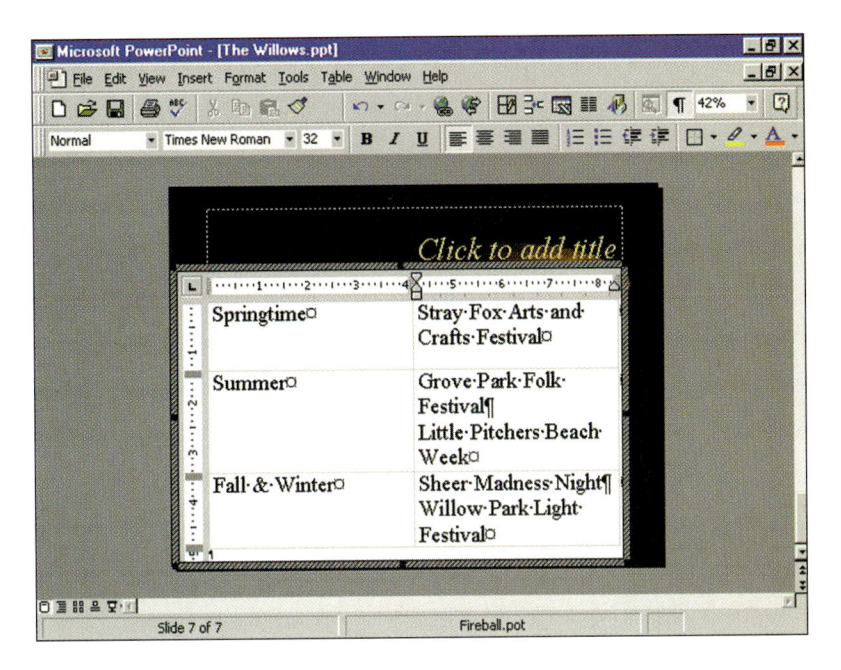

Integrating Word, Excel, Access and PowerPoint   IP3-7

[screenshot of PowerPoint slide showing a table with Springtime / Stray Fox Arts and Crafts Festival; Summer / Grove Park Folk Festival, Little Pitchers Beach Week; Fall & Winter / Sheer Madness Night, Willow Park Light Festival]

7 Press ESC to return to the PowerPoint slide.
PowerPoint toolbars reappear and the table text displays on the slide.

8 Double-click the table to display the Word tools again and double-click the border between the columns to adjust the width of the first column.

> **Note** If you see a dialog box when you double-click the column border, check the box beside AutoFit and then click OK.

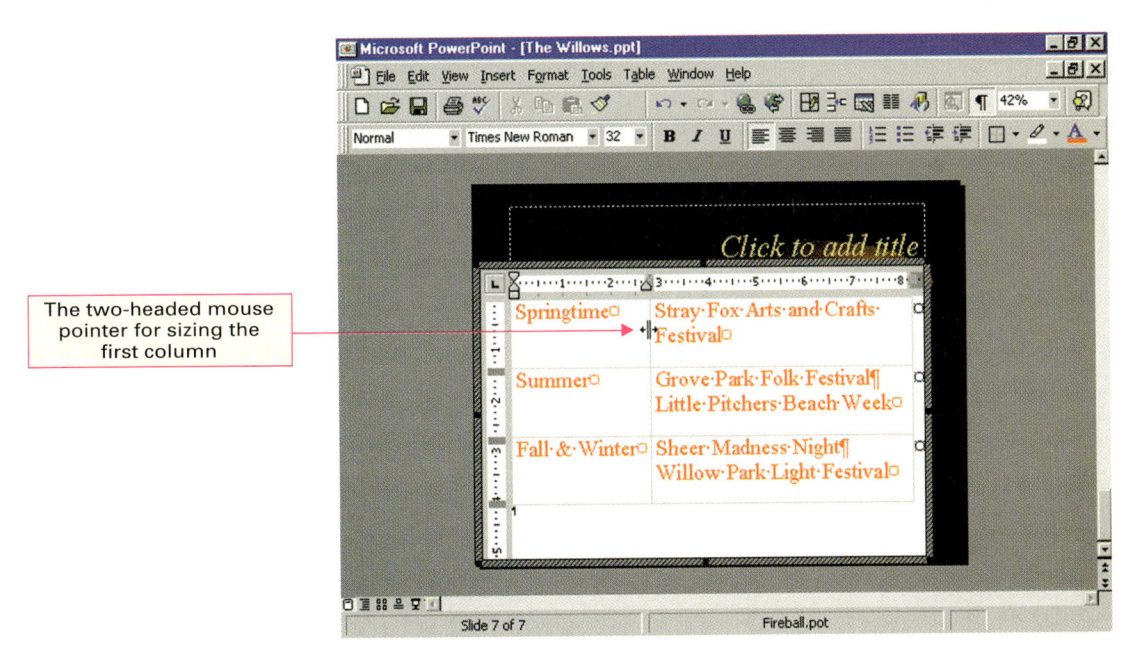

[screenshot of PowerPoint slide with table after column adjustment; annotation: "The two-headed mouse pointer for sizing the first column"]

9 Press ESC to return to the slide and type **Willows Area Festivals** in the title placeholder for the slide.

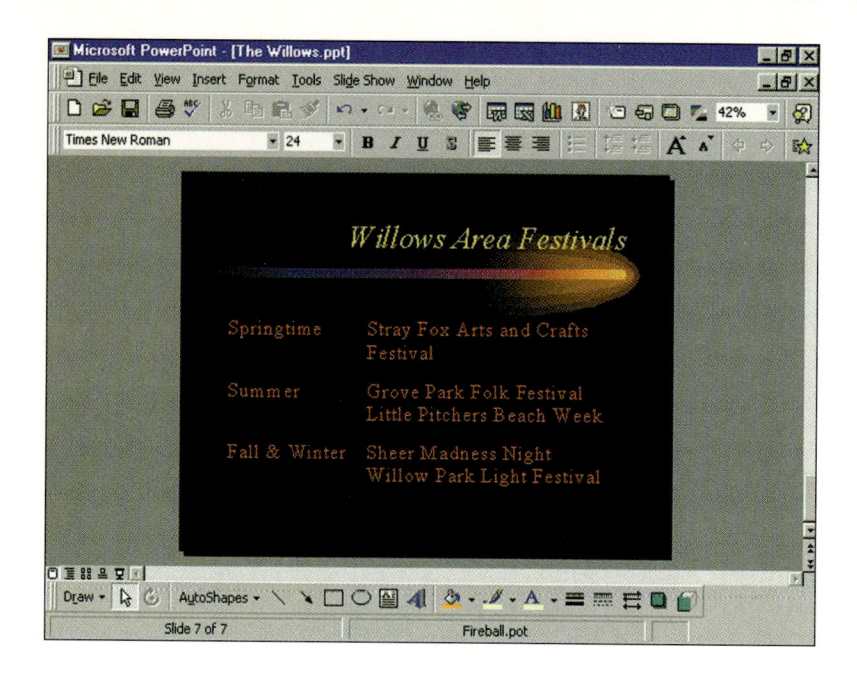

Linking Data from Excel to a PowerPoint Slide

When data you want to add to a slide exists in an Excel worksheet, you can copy the data from Excel onto the PowerPoint slide. Linking the data ensures that it can be updated in PowerPoint when the source file changes.

TASK 2: TO LINK DATA FROM EXCEL TO A POWERPOINT SLIDE:

1. Create another new slide in the presentation *The Willows,* formatting the slide with the Title Only AutoLayout.
   A new slide with only a title placeholder appears on-screen.

2. Maximize Excel, open the *GiftInv.xls* workbook, and display the Sales worksheet.

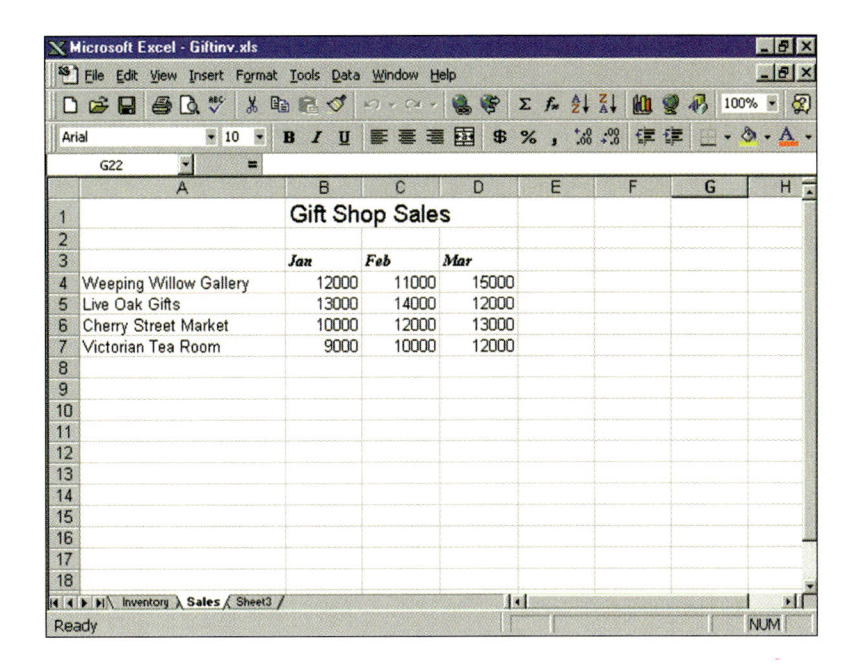

Integrating Word, Excel, Access and PowerPoint   IP3-9

3 Tile the applications on-screen and select the cells containing text and data in the Sales worksheet.

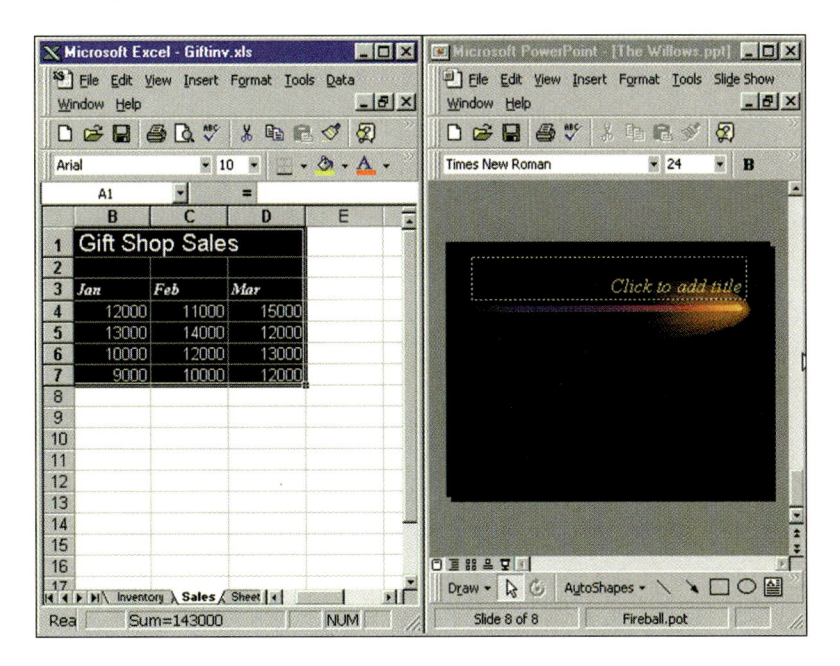

4 Click 📋.
The worksheet data is copied to the Clipboard.

5 Close Excel, maximize PowerPoint, and choose Edit, Paste Special.

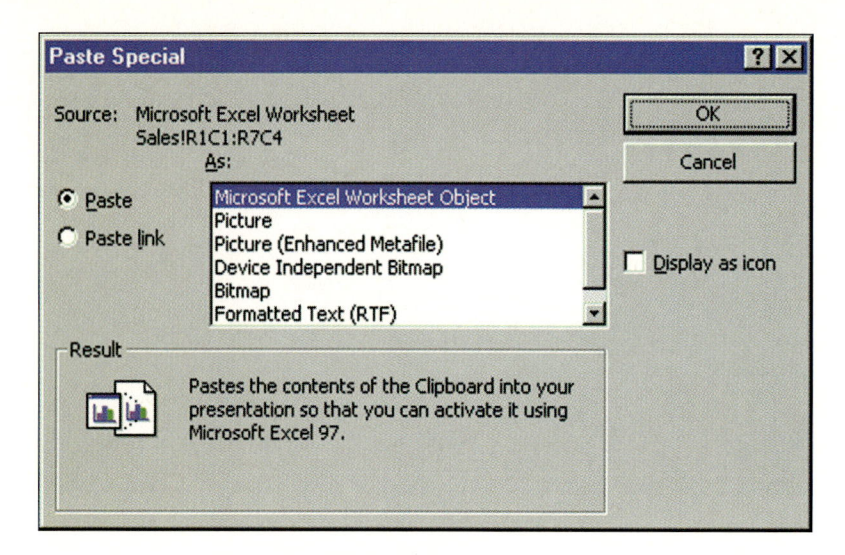

6 Choose Paste link, ensure that Microsoft Excel Worksheet Object is selected in the As list box, and click OK.

7 Right-click on the Excel worksheet object.

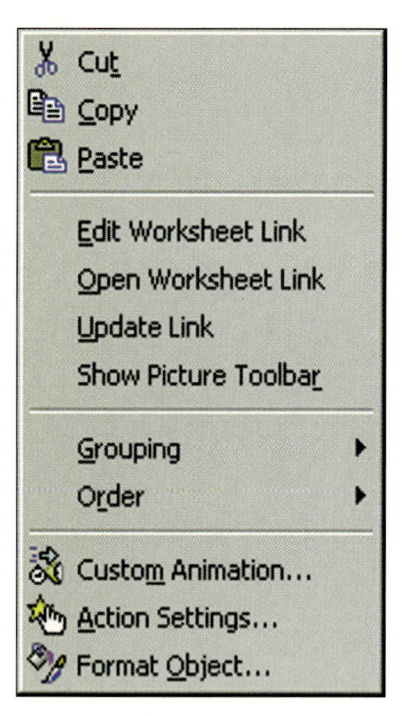

Integrating Word, Excel, Access and PowerPoint **IP3-11**

8 Select Format Object.

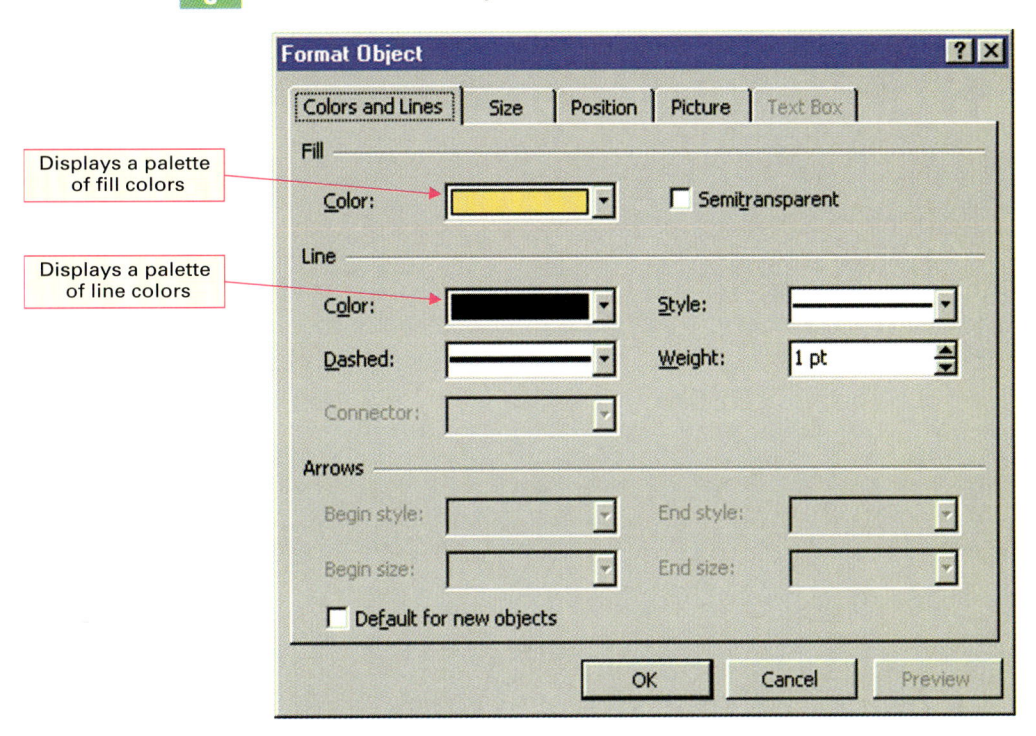

Displays a palette of fill colors

Displays a palette of line colors

9 Click the drop-down list arrow for Fill Color and select the Follow Title Text Scheme Color; then click the drop-down list arrow for Line Color, select black, and click OK.
Text is now visible in the worksheet object.

10 Point to a corner handle on the worksheet object, click and drag the handle to size the worksheet and position it as shown in the following illustration:

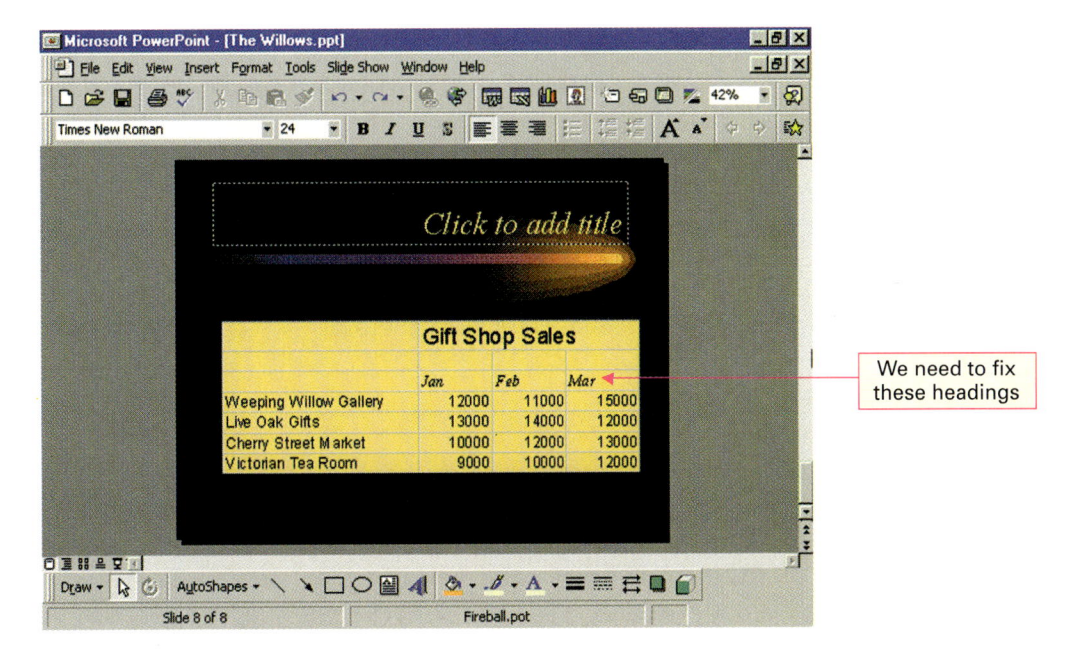

We need to fix these headings

11 Double-click the Excel object.
The worksheet opens in Excel.

12 Select cells B3 through D7 and click the Right Align button.

Creating a Word Document from a PowerPoint Presentation Outline

Outlines from PowerPoint presentations often make effective guides for reports. Because the Outline view in PowerPoint prints extraneous information and slide icons, you can send the outline from PowerPoint to Word with the touch of a button and eliminate the need to retype the entire outline in Word. When you send the outline to Word, a Write-Up window opens and displays a list of formats for the Word document.

TASK 3: TO CREATE A WORD DOCUMENT FROM A POWERPOINT PRESENTATION OUTLINE:

1 Display the presentation *The Willows* in Outline view.

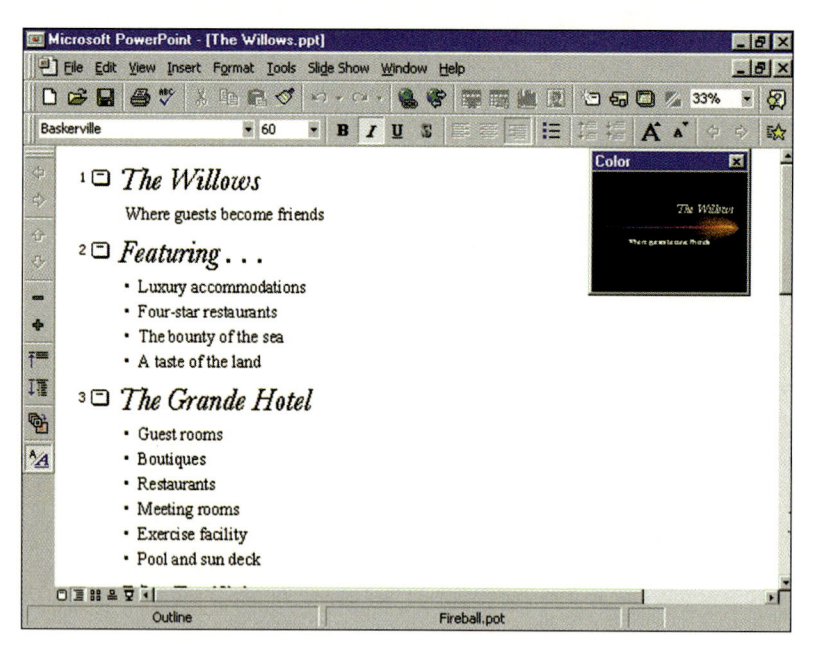

2 Choose File, Send To, Microsoft Word.

Integrating Word, Excel, Access and PowerPoint IP3-13

Formats for the Word layout → [Page layout in Microsoft Word options: Notes next to slides (selected), Blank lines next to slides, Notes below slides, Blank lines below slides, Outline only]

Linking options → [Add slides to Microsoft Word document: Paste (selected), Paste link]

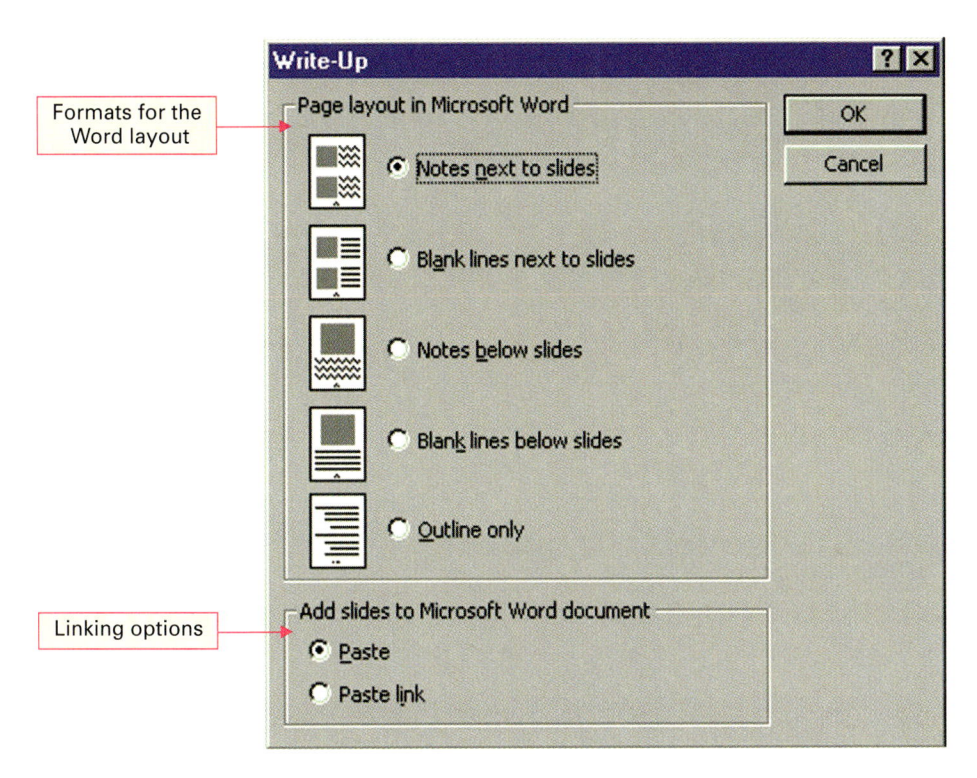

3 Click the Outline only option button and then click OK.
The outline appears in a new Word document.

4 Delete the text from the last slide title, press CTRL+**A** to select all text, and left-align the text in the outline; then press CTRL+HOME to position the insertion point at the top of the outline.

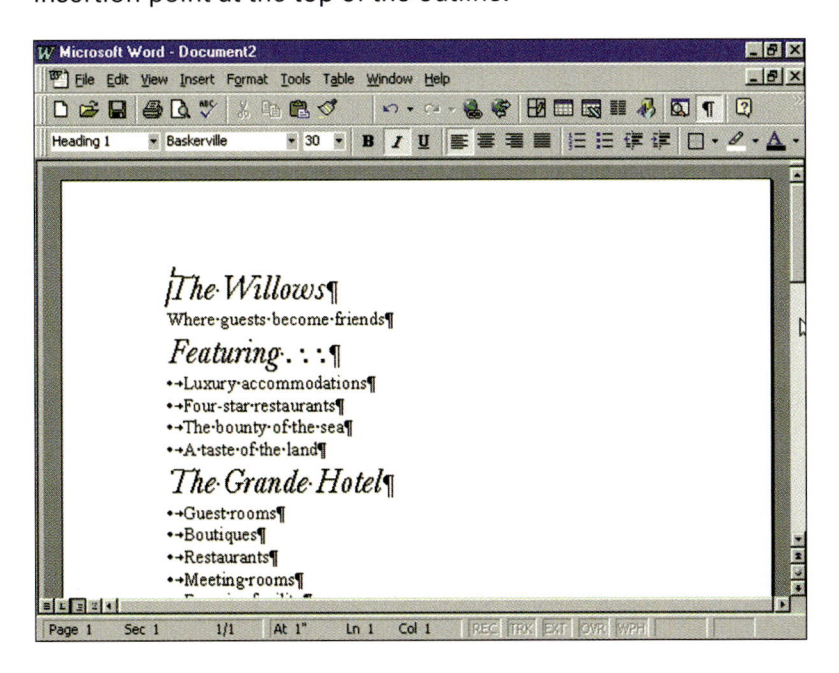

[Screenshot of Microsoft Word - Document2 showing outline with:
The Willows
Where guests become friends
Featuring...
• Luxury accommodations
• Four-star restaurants
• The bounty of the sea
• A taste of the land
The Grande Hotel
• Guest rooms
• Boutiques
• Restaurants
• Meeting rooms]

5 Delete the Slide 1 title and subtitle text.
Featuring appears at the top of the outline.

6 Save the Word document using the filename *The Willows Outline*.

Saving a PowerPoint Slide as a Graphic and Adding the Image to a Word Document

Another way to share data between Office applications is to capture information from one application as a graphic and place it into another application file. PowerPoint slides make effective graphics that not only enhance a document but also relay a message. PowerPoint includes a file option that enables you to save your slides as Windows *Metafiles,* a graphic type recognized as pictures by most Windows applications.

TASK 4: TO SAVE A POWERPOINT SLIDE AS A GRAPHIC AND ADD IT TO A WORD DOCUMENT:

1. Press ALT+TAB to access PowerPoint and display Slide 1 in Slide view. Slide 1 appears in Slide view.

2. Choose File, Save As, and click the drop-down list arrow for the Save as type text box.

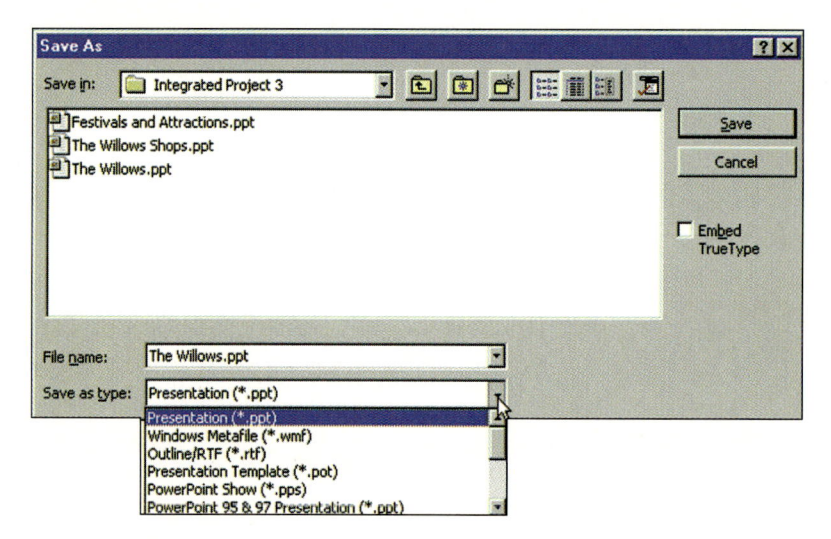

3. Select Windows Metafile (*.wmf) from the file type list, select a folder to contain the file, ensure that *The Willows* appears in the File name text box, and click Save.

Integrating Word, Excel, Access and PowerPoint   IP3-15

Saves each slide as a graphic

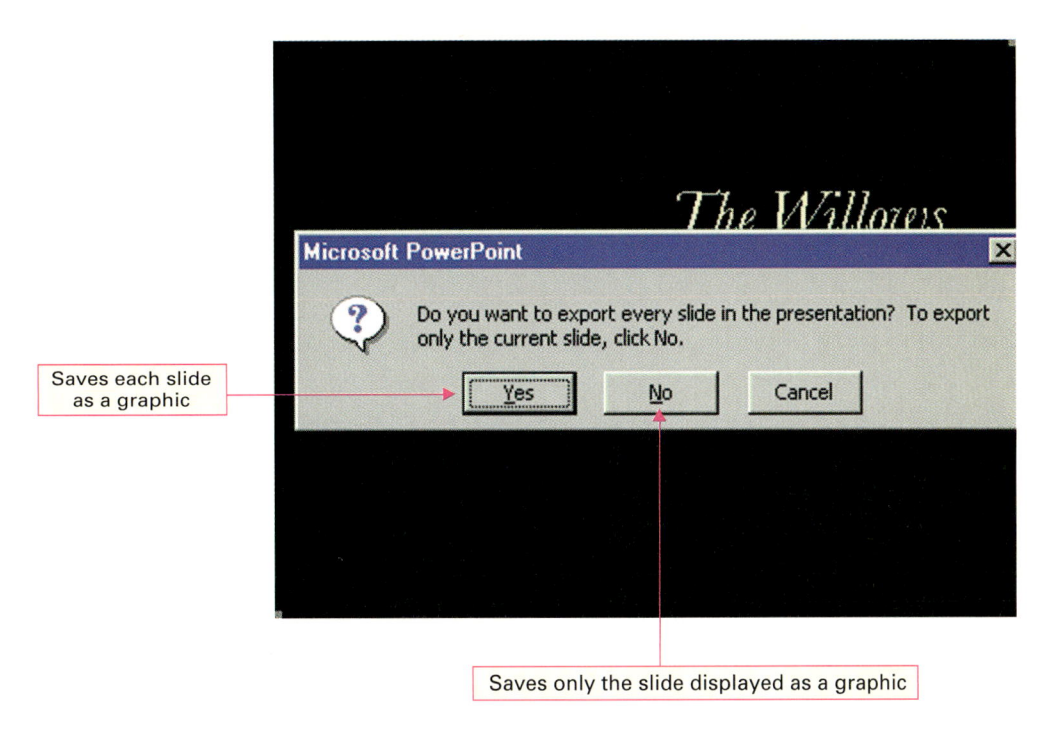

Saves only the slide displayed as a graphic

4 Click No to export only Slide 1, close the presentation, and exit PowerPoint. Word displays *The Willows Outline* document.

5 Press CTRL+HOME, choose Insert, Picture, From File and then select the folder that contains *The Willows* graphic file.
The insertion point appears at the top of the Word outline, and a list of files in the folder displays in the Insert Picture dialog box.

6 Select *The Willows.wmf* file and then click the Insert button.
The slide image appears at the top of the document.

7 Click the image to select it.

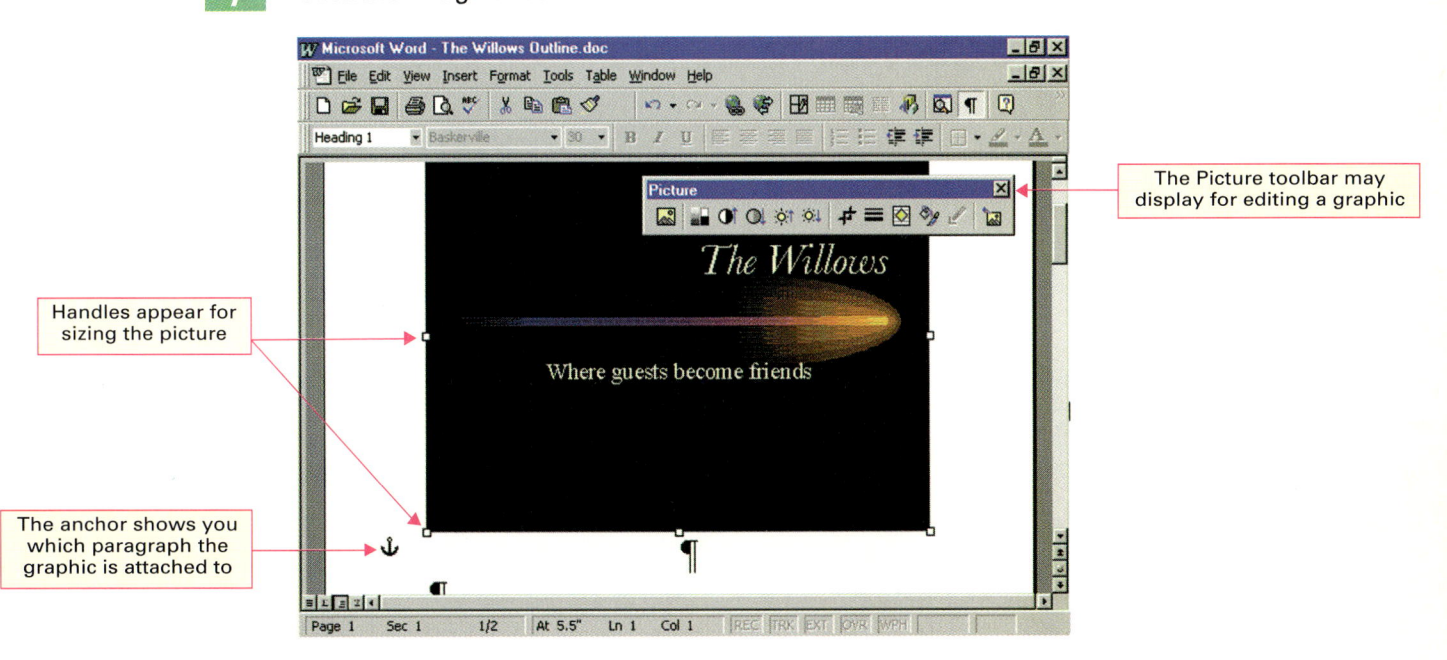

The Picture toolbar may display for editing a graphic

Handles appear for sizing the picture

The anchor shows you which paragraph the graphic is attached to

8 Close the Picture toolbar, click and drag a handle on the graphic to size the image so that it is approximately 3" wide; then drag the image so that the left edge appears at approximately the 1.5" mark on the horizontal ruler at the top of the document.
More of the outline appears on Page 1 of the document.

9 Select the word *Featuring* in the first line of the outline and change the font size to 20; then copy the format to other slide titles using the Format Painter.
All outline text appears on one page.

10 Follow the same procedure to change all bulleted list text to 10 points; then click to preview the document.

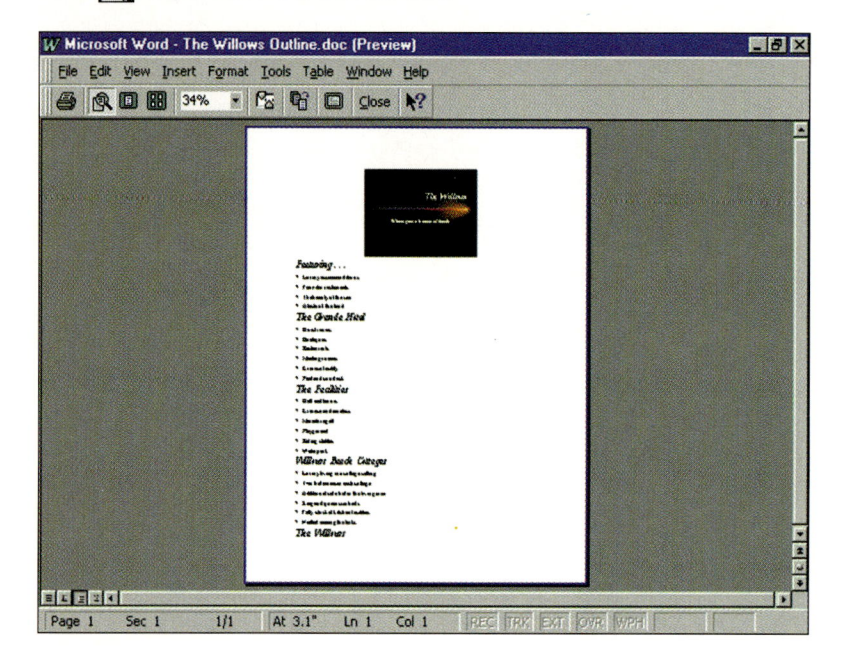

11 Save and close the document.

Creating a Hyperlink Between a Word Document and a PowerPoint Presentation

To launch the PowerPoint presentation *The Willows* from the Word document *The Willows Outline,* you can create a hyperlink between the two files. Hyperlinks in Office work the same way hyperlinks on the Internet or World Wide Web pages work—they enable you to jump from one location to another by clicking on text or graphics.

TASK 5: TO CREATE A HYPERLINK BETWEEN WORD AND POWERPOINT

1 Display the Word document *The Willows Outline* in Page Layout view, if necessary, and select the graphic slide image at the top of the document. The graphic appears with handles to show it's selected.

2 Choose Insert, Hyperlink.

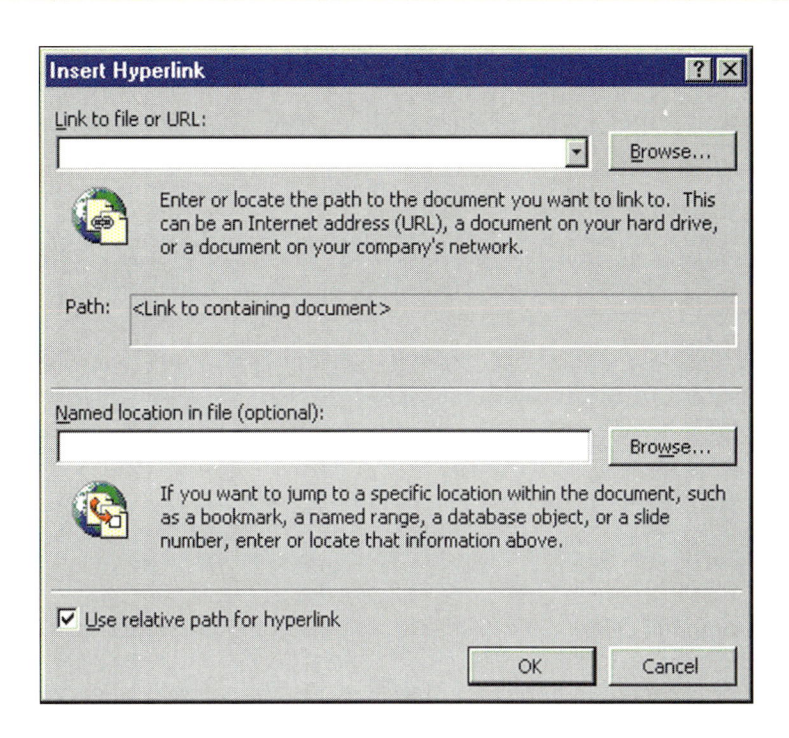

Integrating Word, Excel, Access and PowerPoint   IP3-**17**

3 Click the Browse button beside the Link to file or URL text box, locate and select the presentation *The Willows*, and click OK.
The filename and location appear in the textbox.

4 Click OK.
The presentation is hyperlinked to the graphic and when you point to the graphic on the Word document, the mouse pointer changes to a pointing hand.

5 Click the graphic on the Word document.

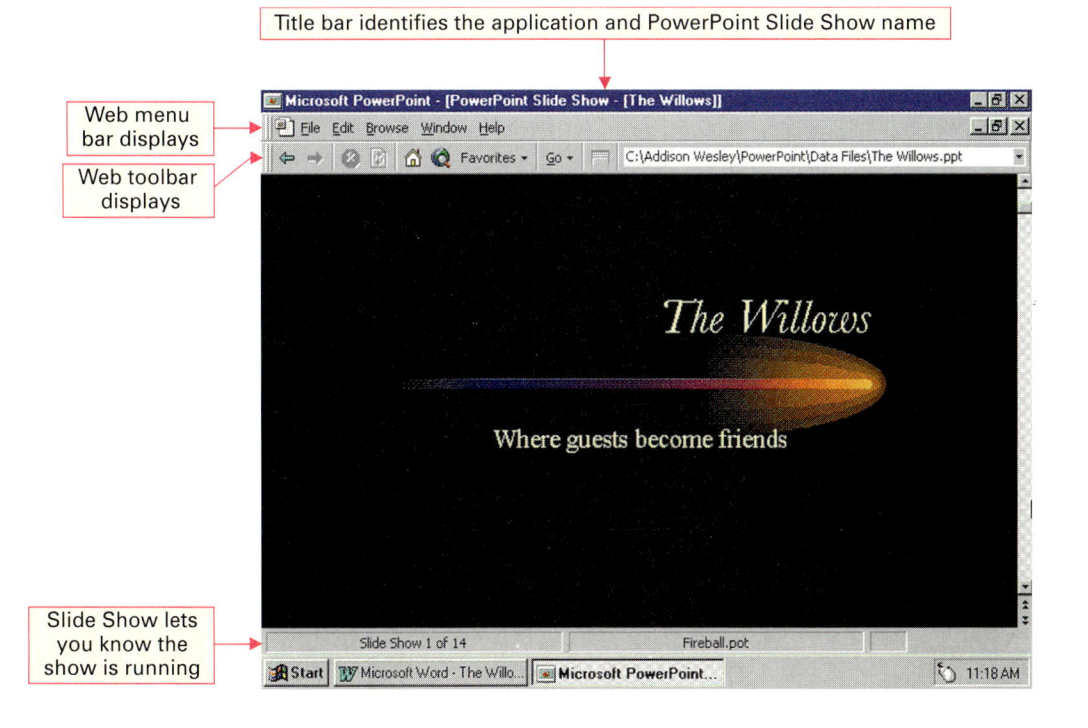

6 Press ESC to stop the slide show, click OK to close the show, close PowerPoint, and maximize Word.
The Word document displays with the Web toolbar active and the name of the hyperlink document displayed in the Address text box.

7 Save and close the document.

Saving a Presentation as an HTML File

You can save a file you create in any application as an HTML file so that, if you have a home page and the necessary browsers, you can send your work to a Web site. Office 97 offers Wizards to help you save your PowerPoint presentations, Access database objects, and Excel workbooks in an HTML format; Word converts documents to HTML format directly.

TASK 6: TO SAVE A FILE IN AN HTML FORMAT:

1 Launch PowerPoint, if necessary, and open the presentation *The Willows,* if necessary.
Your presentation appears in the view that was active when you last saved it.

2 Choose File, Save as HTML.

> **Note** Saving files in HTML format is a special feature not automatically installed with Office 97. If saving files in HTML format does not appear or is not available on your File menu, the module of Office required to save documents in HTML format was not installed. Check with your instructor or lab assistant for installation procedures.

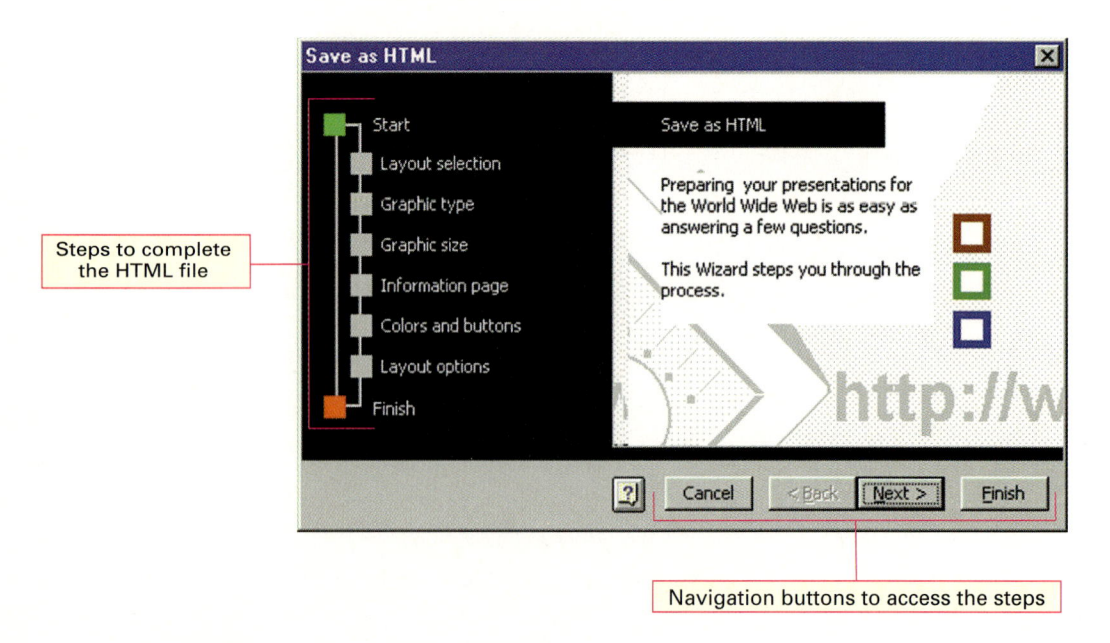

3 Click the Next button.

4 Check New layout and click Next.

5 Select Standard and click Next.

Integrating Word, Excel, Access and PowerPoint **IP3-19**

6 Choose PowerPoint animation and click Next.

7 Choose 640 by 480 to ensure that the graphics can be viewed by most computers, select 1/2 width of screen for the graphic width, and click Next.

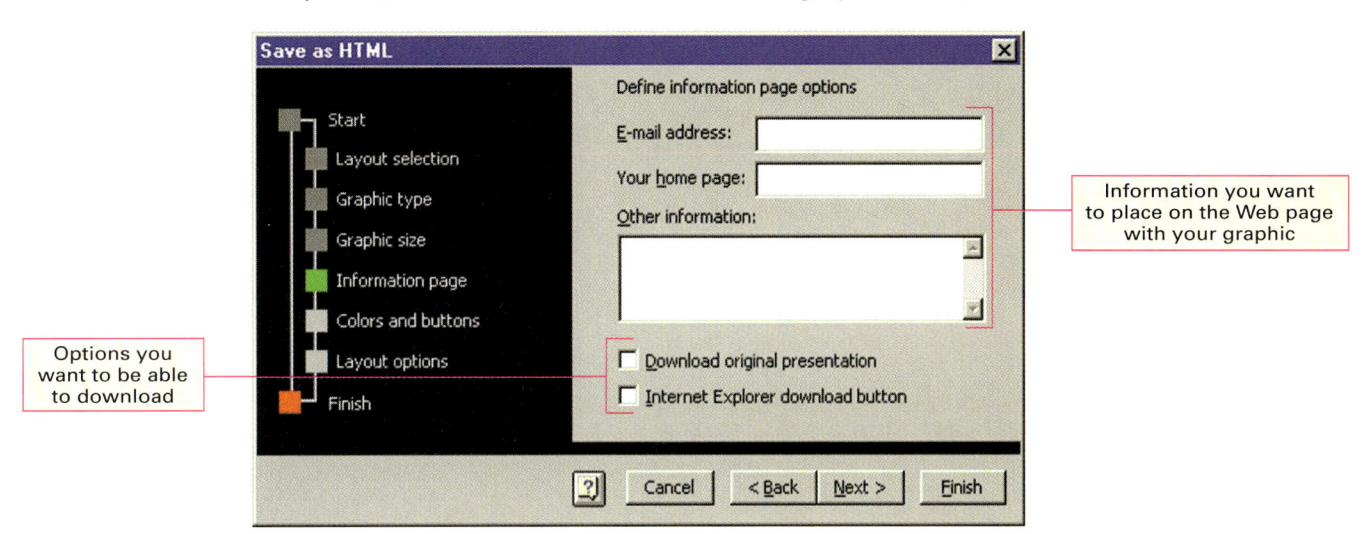

Options you want to be able to download

Information you want to place on the Web page with your graphic

8 Type your e-mail address, home page address, and other information you want displayed with the graphic on the Web and select options that enable users to download the presentation and/or the Internet Explorer; then click Next.

9 Choose Use browser colors and click Next.

10 Select the circle button style and click Next.

11 Select the button position you like best and then click Next.

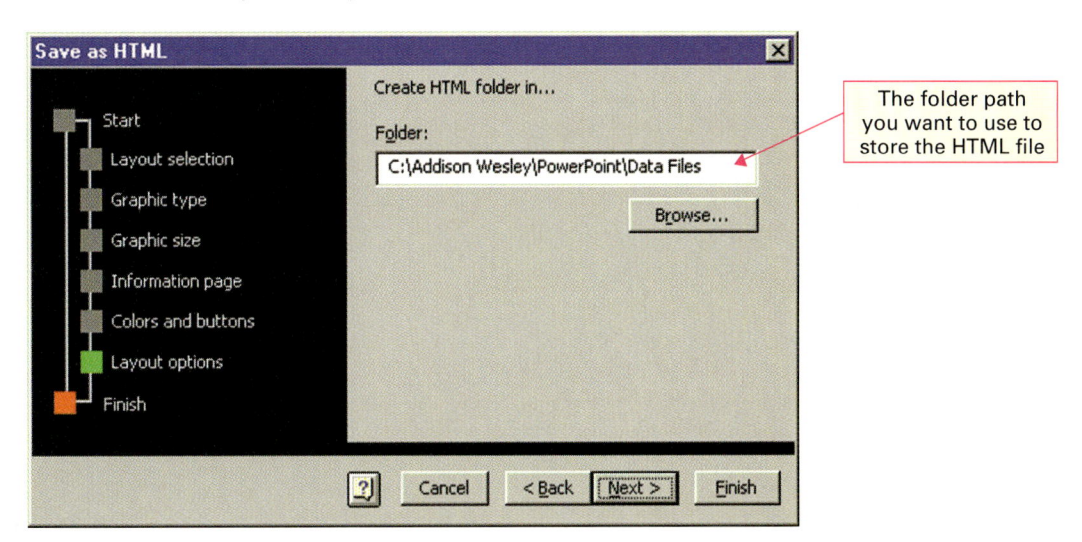

The folder path you want to use to store the HTML file

12 Click Browse, select the folder to store the HTML file, click Select, and then click Next.
The last page of the Save as HTML Wizard provides additional information and instruction for completing your HTML file.

13 Click Finish.

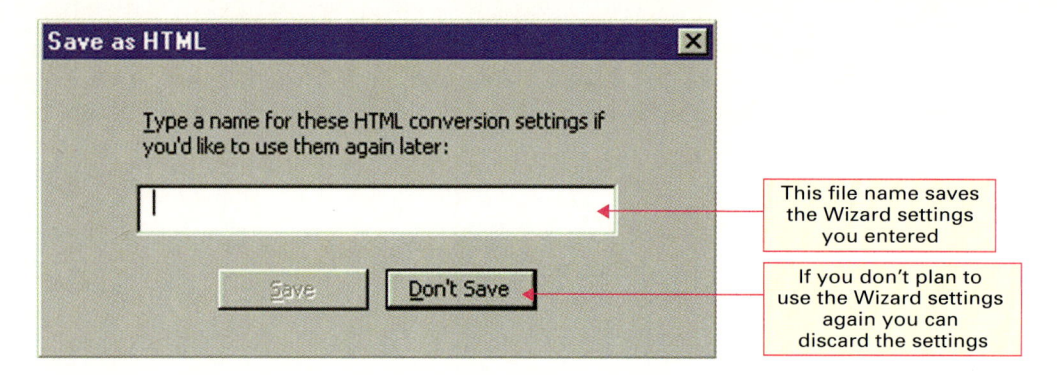

14 Type **PowerPoint Presentation** in the text box and click Save. PowerPoint displays a message indicating that it is creating the files required for your Web page and asks you to wait. A message window appears when the page is complete.

15 Click OK to close the message window.
The files PowerPoint creates when you save a presentation as an HTML file are stored in a folder named The Willows — the presentation file name. You can send these files to a World Wide Web page using procedures defined and available at your school.

The Conclusion

In this project, you created a new Word document using an outline of a PowerPoint presentation. You can also create a PowerPoint presentation by sending text from a Word document to PowerPoint using the Word File, Send To command. When you want to include only a small portion of data or information from a Word document in a PowerPoint presentation, you can select, drag, and drop text from Word to a slide. You can use the File, Save as HTML command from any Office 97 application to save a finished file in a format you can use on the World Wide Web.

If you have completed your work for the day, exit all programs and shut down the computer according to standard lab procedures.

Summary and Exercises

Summary

- You can drag and drop Excel worksheet data to a PowerPoint slide.
- You can use the File, Send To command to share information among Office applications.
- When you want to add data using tools from other applications to create objects on slides in a PowerPoint presentation, you can select an AutoLayout format for the slide and then double-click the object placeholder to access the tools.
- You can save a PowerPoint presentation slide as a graphic file and then use it to enhance Word documents and files in other applications.
- The File, Save as HTML command saves documents, worksheets, databases, and presentations in a format you can use to upload the files to a Web site.
- Hyperlinks enable you to display files by launching them from another document.

Key Terms and Operations

Key Terms
hyperlink
metafile
Write Up feature

Operations
Create an embedded object in PowerPoint using tools from Word
Link Excel worksheet data to a PowerPoint slide
Send a presentation outline to Word to create a new document
Save a presentation slide as a graphic.
Insert a presentation slide graphic as a picture in a Word document
Create a hyperlink

Study Questions

Multiple Choice

1. To send a PowerPoint outline to Word, use the
    a. File menu.
    b. Edit menu.
    c. Tools menu.
    d. Insert menu.

2. All the following techniques can be used to copy data from Excel to PowerPoint *except*
    a. dragging and dropping the data from Excel to PowerPoint.
    b. cutting the data from the Excel worksheet and choosing Edit, Paste Special.
    c. copying the Excel data to the Clipboard and pasting it into PowerPoint.
    d. retyping the data from Excel into PowerPoint.

3. To create a link between data from Excel and PowerPoint,
    a. press (CTRL) as you drag and drop.
    b. press (ENTER).
    c. choose Edit, Paste Special.
    d. choose File, Export.

IP3-21

4. When you want to create a new object and imbed it in a presentation, you can
   a. choose Insert, Table.
   b. use the drag-and-drop technique to copy it from Word.
   c. use the Clipboard.
   d. choose an AutoLayout format that contains the object placeholder you want to add.

5. When you create a new object in a PowerPoint presentation using tools from another application,
   a. the object is embedded in the presentation.
   b. the object becomes a separate file.
   c. the source application opens as a button on the toolbar.
   d. you can't create new data in a PowerPoint slide.

6. After you format a slide using an AutoLayout format that contains an object placeholder, what action do you take to access the other application tools?
   a. Press (ENTER).
   b. Double-click the object placeholder.
   c. Choose Insert, Object.
   d. Click the object placeholder and type the data.

7. When you add a Word table to a PowerPoint slide, the toolbars that appear are
   a. PowerPoint default toolbars.
   b. the Word Formatting toolbar.
   c. the Word Standard and Formatting toolbars.
   d. no toolbars.

8. To access a linked or embedded object copied from another application and added to a PowerPoint slide,
   a. close the presentation and exit PowerPoint.
   b. launch the source application and open the file.
   c. press (ENTER).
   d. double-click the object.

9. To save a slide as a graphic, choose
   a. File, Save As and select Windows Metafile from the Save as type list.
   b. Insert, Picture, From File.
   c. File, Send To.
   d. Edit, Paste Special.

10. To place a slide graphic in a Word document, choose
    a. File, Save As and select Windows Metafile from the Save as type list.
    b. Insert, Picture, From File.
    c. File, Send To.
    d. Edit, Paste Special.

Short Answer

1. What option do you choose from the Paste Special dialog box to create a link between the source and target files?

2. What application toolbars appear when you insert a Word table in a PowerPoint slide?

3. What appears on graphic objects to enable you to change the size of the graphic?

4. What dialog box appears when you send a PowerPoint presentation outline to Word?

5. How do you tell PowerPoint the type of object you plan to add to a new slide?

6. How do you access the shortcut pop-up menu for an object in a presentation slide?

7. Where does data have to be held to enable you to use the Paste Special feature?

8. How many slides in a presentation can you save as graphics at the same time?

9. How do you redisplay tools from the source application after you return an object to the slide?

10. On what menu does the hyperlink command appear?

For Discussion

1. How do you create a new document using a presentation outline?

2. What is the difference between linked files and hyperlinked files?

3. What techniques do you use to ensure that a link is created when you add data from Word or Excel to a PowerPoint slide?

4. Discuss the benefits of hyperlinking files to other files.

Exercises

Creating a PowerPoint presentation from a Word outline and saving a slide as a graphic

The Board of Directors at The Willows requests that you create a broader scope presentation to advertise The Willows on the World Wide Web. The presentation, entitled *The Most Inviting Resort,* should contain the slides pictured in Figure 3.3.

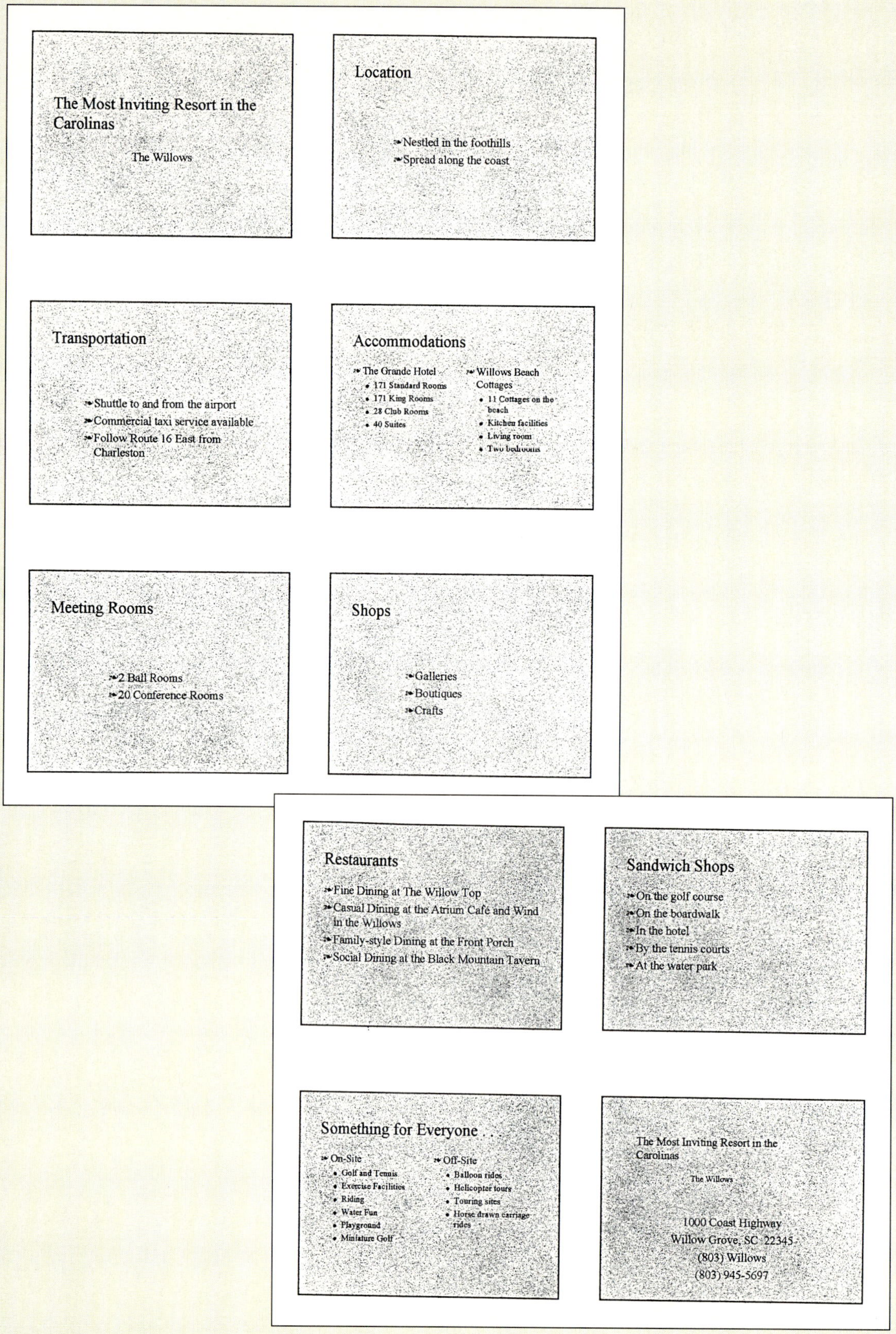

The Most Inviting Resort in the Carolinas
The Willows
Location
Nestled in the foothills
Spread along the coast
Transportation
Shuttle to and from the airport
Commercial taxi service available
Follow Route 16 East from Charleston
Accommodations
The Grande Hotel
171 Standard Rooms
171 King Rooms
28 Club Rooms
40 Suites
Willows Beach Cottages
11 Cottages on the beach
Kitchen facilities
Living room
Two bedrooms
Meeting Rooms
2 Ball Rooms
20 Conference Rooms
Shops
Galleries
Boutiques
Crafts
Restaurants
Fine Dining at The Willow Top
Casual Dining at the Atrium Café and Wind in the Willows
Family-style Dining at the Front Porch
Social Dining at the Black Mountain Tavern
Sandwich Shops
On the golf course
On the boardwalk
In the hotel
By the tennis courts
At the water park
Something for Everyone . . .
On-Site
Golf and Tennis
Exercise Facilities
Riding
Water Fun
Playground
Miniature Golf
Off-Site
Balloon rides
Helicopter tours
Touring sites
Horse drawn carriage rides
The Most Inviting Resort in the Carolinas
The Willows
1000 Coast Highway
Willow Grove, SC 22345
(803) Willows
(803) 945-5697

Figure 3.3

The *Most Inviting Resort* outline is stored as a Word document on the Addison Wesley Web site (www.awl.com/is/select). You can download the outline and use it to develop the presentation. If you are unable to download this file, ask your instructor for it. Follow these steps to create the presentation:

1. Launch the Internet Explorer, access the Addison Wesley Web site, locate and download the Word document *Most Inviting Resort*.

2. Launch Word and open the Most Inviting Resort document.

3. Choose File, Send To, Microsoft PowerPoint to automatically create a presentation using information from the Word outline.

4. Position the insertion point beside Slide 2 in the PowerPoint Outline view and press TAB to make *The Willows* a subtitle for Slide 1; then display Slide 1 in Slide view.

5. Click the Slide Layout button on the Standard Toolbar and double-click the Title AutoLayout format in the Slide Layout dialog box.

6. Display each slide in the presentation to ensure that the text fits appropriately on each slide, making the following adjustments:
   - Slide 4: Format the slide using the 2 Column Text AutoLayout and then cut the information for the Willows Beach Cottages bullet point and paste it into the placeholder on the right.
   - Slide 9: Format the slide using the 2 Column Text AutoLayout and place the Off-Site information in the placeholder on the right.

7. Apply a template to the presentation. The presentation pictured in Figure 3.3 is formatted using the Serene template.

8. Add a new title slide to the end of the presentation and type the following information on the slide:

   1000 Coast Highway
   Willow Grove, SC 22345
   (803) Willows
   (803) 945-5697

9. Adjust text placeholders on each slide to display the information shown in Figure 3.3.

10. Display Slide 1 and save it as a Windows Metafile graphic; then insert it as a graphic on Slide 10, as shown in Figure 3.3.

11. Save the presentation using the filename *Most Inviting Resort* and print a copy of the presentation as handouts with six framed slides per page.

Assignments

Embedding a new object in a PowerPoint presentation, linking an Excel worksheet to a PowerPoint slide, and creating a hyperlink to display the Excel worksheet.

Mr. Gilmore wants you to add the two slides shown in Figure 3.4 to *The Willows Shops* presentation.

Weekend Specials at The Grande

Package	Club Rooms	Suites
Bonnie & Clyde	$ 745	$ 840
The Grande Romance	$ 525	$ 615

- Bonnie & Clyde
  - Two nights with all meals included
  - Champagne, candles, flowers, chocolates
- The Grande Romance
  - Two nights with dinner and breakfast
  - Champagne cocktails

Retail Goods - Top Ten Selling Items

Description	Retail Price
Cast iron doorstop	29.99
Lead crystal votive	30.00
Needlepoint footstool	39.99
Needlepoint pillow	24.99
Mohair throw	90.00
Jewelry armoire	279.00
Mantel clock	135.00
Noah's Ark clock	39.99
French purse	24.00
Mickey Mouse pocket watch	59.95

Figure 3.4

Create a new slide at the end of the presentation *The Willows Shops* and format it using the Object over Text AutoLayout. Select the Object placeholder and delete it. Then click the Insert Microsoft Word Table button on the toolbar and create a table with three columns and two rows. Type and format the text in the table; then add the text to the text placeholder.

Create another new slide and format it using the Blank AutoLayout. Link the Excel worksheet *TopTen* to the slide. Format, size, and change the colors of the worksheet object to match those shown in Figure 3.4.

Save the presentation and print a copy of the two new slides as handouts with two slides per page.

Create a hyperlink that opens the Excel *TopTen* worksheet when you click the Excel object on the slide. Save changes to the presentation and then save the presentation again in HTML format.

Close the presentation and exit PowerPoint.

Glossary

Absolute reference In Excel, an address you use to reference a specific cell or range of cells in a worksheet; this reference, which doesn't change, is denoted with the dollar sign symbol, as in A1.

Action button The button that enables you to control the slide PowerPoint displays during a slide show.

Active cell In Excel, the cell in which you can enter data or formulas. You make the cell active by clicking in the cell or by moving to the cell with keystrokes. This cell is outlined with a black border.

Application title bar The bar at the top of the window that displays the name of the application and the Minimize, Maximize/Restore, and Close buttons.

Arithmetic operators The operators you use to perform calculations in formulas and functions: + (addition), − (subtraction), * (multiplication), / (division), % (percent), and ^ (exponentiation).

Ascending order A sort order in which you arrange data alphabetically from A to Z or numerically from smallest to largest.

AutoComplete A feature that automatically completes many common words and phrases as you type.

AutoContent Wizard A PowerPoint feature that helps you build an outline for specific types of presentations by presenting options for you to choose and enabling you to fill in specific pieces of information about the presentation.

AutoCorrect A feature that automatically corrects many common typographical errors.

AutoCalculate A feature in Excel that displays a calculation in the status bar when you select a range with values.

AutoFit An Excel feature that automatically adjusts the column or row to be just wide enough to accommodate the widest or tallest entry.

AutoForm An Excel feature that you use to create forms using the fields and information stored as part of the table or query.

AutoFormat A Word feature that provides many different formats for a table and enables you to preview the format before you select it.

AutoLayout A PowerPoint feature that contains object placeholders.

AutoReport An Access feature you use to create simple report formats using the fields contained in a table or query.

Bold The style you attach to text to make the font appear heavier so that it stands out.

Border In Excel, a line that displays on any side of a cell or group of cells. You can use borders to draw rectangles around cells, to create dividers between columns, to create a total line under a column of numbers, and so on. In Word, the top, bottom, left, and right lines you add to draw attention to important text; any of these lines can be displayed or hidden.

Bulleted list A list set off with symbols (usually black circles) that precede the text.

Cell The intersection of a column and a row in a worksheet or table.

Center To align text with equal amounts of white space on each side of the text.

Center tab A tab that distributes text equally to the left and right of the tab location.

Chart A visual representation of data in a worksheet.

Chart sub-type A variation on a Chart type. For example, the column type chart has these sub-types in both 2-D and 3-D: Clustered Column, Stacked Column, and 100% Stacked Column.

Chart Title The name of the chart. You define this setting in the Chart Options dialog box.

Chart type A chart that represents data in a specific format, such as columns, a pie, scatter points, etc.

Chart Wizard A feature you use to create charts. When you create a chart with the Chart Wizard, the Chart Wizard decides how the chart elements will look.

Clip art A graphic provided in a file format such as tif, wpg, bmp, and so on. Office 97 provides many clip art files and stores them in the Clip Art Gallery which is available to all Office 97 programs.

Clipboard A memory area in which data, text, graphics, and other objects that have been cut or copied is stored.

Column A vertical block of cells in a worksheet or a table.

Column indicators The letters associated with the columns on a worksheet or field names in database tables.

Comment Text that you can attach to cells in a worksheet or text in a Word document or PowerPoint slide to provide additional information.

Compress To arrange data more tightly so that it will fit on a disk; for example, the Pack and Go Wizard compresses presentations.

GL-1

Context-sensitive help Help on the task you're performing provided by the Office Assistant. If the Office Assistant doesn't display the help you want, you can type a question to obtain the desired help.

Controls Field labels and field data boxes that appear in sections of a form or report Design view in Access.

Criteria In Access, conditions you set in a grid to limit the information displayed in the datasheet.

Custom animation In PowerPoint, the special effects you add to animation settings using the Custom Animation dialog box. The Custom Animation dialog box displays options that also enable you to dim bullet points for animated text as new bullet points display.

Data labels The names you attach to different types of data in a chart. You define this setting in the Chart Options dialog box.

Data range A block of cells used to create an element in a chart.

Data Source document In Word, a document that contains the variable information that will be used to "fill in the blanks" in a mail merge document.

Data table A table containing the data that is used to create a chart.

Datasheet view In Access, the view in which you can see multiple records on-screen at the same time; this view makes data entry more efficient.

Decimal tab A type of tab that aligns text on a decimal.

Descending order A sort order in which you arrange data alphabetically from Z to A or numerically from largest to smallest.

Detail section In Access, the part of a form or report that holds the field data controls and pulls information from database tables.

Dim effect The setting that causes animated text to lighten or dim as new bullet points display on a slide during a slide show.

Document Map A new Word 97 tool that lists all the document headings, similar to an outline, in a pane on the left. The headings are linked to the document so that you can click a heading and go directly to the text in the document.

Document title bar The bar at the top of the document window that displays the document title and the Minimize, Maximize/Restore, and Close buttons. If the window is maximized, no document title bar displays and the document buttons display in the menu bar.

Edit mode In Excel, the mode in which you edit the contents of a cell.

Endnotes In Word, notes (comments or references) grouped together at the end of the document. The reference in the text to which the endnote applies is generally numbered, and the endnote displays the same number.

Enter mode In Excel, the mode in which you enter data in a worksheet.

Error mode The mode Excel switches to if you make an error when entering data in a cell.

Expand To create new slides in PowerPoint, using bullet list text from another slide. When you expand a slide, each bulleted list item appears as the title of a new slide.

Field A piece of data in an Access table, such as the last name or zip code or the variable information for each record in a Data Source document in Word.

Field data box The part of the field control that connects data from a table to a form or report in Access.

Field label The part of the field control that identifies data in a form or report in Access.

Fill A color or a shade of gray that you apply to the background of a cell or data. Also called *shading* or *patterns*.

Filter In Access, to select only those records in a table that contain the same value in the selected field.

Flip To turn images so they face the opposite direction vertically or horizontally.

Floating palette A palette of toolbar buttons that "floats" in the window instead of being displayed as a bar that spans the width of the window.

Font The type and style of text.

Footer Text that prints at the bottom of every page.

Footnotes Comments or references that appear at the bottom of the page. The reference in the text to which the footnote applies is generally numbered, and the footnote displays the same number.

Form In Access, an aesthetically pleasing layout of table data designed to display one record on-screen at a time.

Form Header/Footer In Access, the area of a form in which you supply information such as the form title that you want to display on each screen or printed page.

Form view In Access, the view which displays records on-screen one at a time in an aesthetically pleasing format.

Formatting toolbar Contains buttons and controls for formatting. To use the toolbar, click a button to perform a command or view a dialog box.

Formula A mathematical statement that performs calculations. You create and enter formulas to perform the specific calculations needed.

Formula bar The area at the top of the window in Excel that displays the cell address and the contents of the active cell. You can use it to enter and edit data and formulas.

Function A type of formula included in Office 97 that is designed to perform a special calculation.

Graphic A piece of art that adds interest to a document, slide, report, etc.

Gridlines In Access, cell borders in Datasheet view used to separate fields of data and records. Also, lines displayed in Form Design View and Report Design View to mark sections of the form or report to help align fields. In Excel, the vertical and horizontal lines in a chart that mark the values.

Grid points Dots displayed on-screen in Form Design or Report Design view that help you align field controls.

Group To combine separate graphic or drawn objects into one.

Handles The squares on the corners and sides of selected placeholders, graphics, drawn objects, or charts that enable you to size the object.

Handouts Printed versions of your PowerPoint presentation. You can display two, three, or six slides on each printed handout page.

Hard page break A user-defined page break.

Header Text that prints at the top of every page.

Hidden slides Slides that remain part of a presentation but don't display unless you specifically access them.

Hyperlink The connection that enables you to jump to a desired location when you click an action button, text, or object.

Indent To move lines of text in from the left or right.

Insertion point The blinking, vertical line that marks the current typing position.

Italic The style you apply to text to make the font appear slanted so that it stands out.

Justify To change the alignment of text so that it is spread evenly between the margins.

Key field In Access, a field that contains different (unique) data for each record and that you can use to organize records. You can assign only one key field to each table.

Kiosk A booth at a convention or shopping mall where you can set up a presentation to run continuously.

Layout Preview The view in which Access displays data from only a few records so that you can check the layout and then make adjustments before printing.

Leader Characters, such as periods, that appear before the tab. Any type of tab can have a leader.

Left-align To change the alignment of text so it is on the left margin of the document, cell, placeholder, etc.

Left tab A tab type that causes text to align on the left.

Legend The description of elements in a chart. You define this setting in the Chart Options dialog box.

Line spacing The amount of space between lines of text.

Loop To play back continuously in a slide show or to go back to the first slide after the last slide has played in a never-ending circle.

Macro A mini program that stores a set of instructions designed to perform a particular task.

Mail merging A process in which you insert text from a file containing a list of information into a form file such as a form letter. The process involves three steps: creating the file that contains the list of information, creating the form, and merging the two files.

Main document The document, usually a letter, with which you merge the list of names in the Data Source document when you use the mail merge feature.

Margin The white space around text. The default margins in Word are 1 inch for the top and bottom and 1.25 inches for the left and right.

Master In PowerPoint, a layout that contains formats for text, bullets, placeholder alignment, headers and footers, and backgrounds.

Menu bar The bar at the top of the window that provides access to commands used to perform tasks. The menu bar may change, depending on the task you're performing and the program you're using.

Mode indicator In Excel, a feature displayed on the far left side of the status bar. It shows a word that describes the current working condition of the program.

Module A collection of Visual Basic programming procedures stored together to customize the Access environment.

New document A new blank Word document. Document 1 is automatically opened for you when you open Word.

Newspaper columns The style of columns in which text flows from one column to the next as columns fill up. Word can create multiple newspaper columns of equal or unequal widths.

Normal view In Word, the view you use to examine text. Normal view doesn't show the white space for margins or the area on a page that hasn't been used.

Notes Pages view The PowerPoint view that displays a small slide image at the top of the page and provides space below the image so that you can type notes about the slide contents.

Numbered list A list set off with numbers, often to indicate a sequence of steps.

Object A table, query, form, report, macro, or module in a database.

Office Assistant The new Help feature that offers help on the task you're performing, often referred to as context-sensitive help. Office Assistant enables you to ask questions about the task you want to perform.

Online help The help provided by the software and accessible from the computer.

Order of precedence The sequence in which each operation should be performed when a formula has more than one operation. The order of precedence is as follows: exponentiation, then multiplication or division (from left to right), and finally addition or subtraction (from left to right). If the formula has parentheses, the operation(s) in the parentheses are performed first.

Orientation The direction in which text prints on a page. Orientation can be Portrait or Landscape.

Outline view The PowerPoint view that displays the title and body text you add to placeholders in a notebook-like format so that you can review the content of the presentation.

Pack and Go Wizard A PowerPoint feature that prepares presentations for showing at another location. The Pack and Go Wizard compresses the presentation, making it easier to fit on one disk.

Page break A break that separates pages of text.

Page Break Preview In Excel, the view in which you can see where the pages will break when the worksheet prints.

Page Header/Footer In Access, the part of a page displayed in Report Design view in which you place information you want to appear on each printed report page.

Page Layout view In Word, the view you use to see margins and unused space as well as a visual page break between pages.

Page setup Options for margins, orientation, and size of paper used.

Paper size The size of the paper on which you will print.

Pattern A color or a shade of gray that you apply to the background of a cell or data. Also called *fill* or *shading*.

Placeholder A predefined area outlined on a slide for placing text, bulleted lists, and objects such as graphs, tables, and charts.

Point mode In Excel, the mode in which you're pointing to cells to build a formula or function in a worksheet.

Print Preview mode The mode that shows the full page view of the current page of the current worksheet. In this mode you can view additional pages of the worksheet, or you can zoom in on the page so that you can actually read the data, if necessary.

Query A structured guideline used to search database tables and retrieve records that meet specific conditions.

Query grid The lower pane of the Query window where you tell Access which fields you want to use in a query or display in a datasheet.

Range In Excel, a block of cells selected as a group.

Ready mode In Excel, the mode in which the worksheet is ready to receive data or execute a command.

Record Fields of related data stored in each row of a table, Data Source document, or worksheet.

Relational database A database that enables you to store data using a variety of different objects all related to the central theme of the database.

Relationships Connections between fields of tables contained in a database to identify common field data.

Relative reference A worksheet address that Excel automatically changes when a formula is copied to another location.

Report In Access, an organized format for summarizing and grouping database data to provide meaningful information.

Right-align To change the alignment of text so it aligns on the right of the margin, cell, placeholder, etc.

Right tab A tab type that causes text to align on the right.

Rotate To turn or spin objects to create special effects.

Row A horizontal block of cells in a worksheet or table.

Row indicators The numbers associated with the rows on a worksheet.

Ruler The scale that displays the settings for the margins, tabs, and indents. The ruler also can be used to make these settings.

Scientific notation A number format used for very large numbers and very small decimal numbers. For example, the scientific notation for 1,000,000,000 is 1E+09 which means 1 times 10 to the ninth power.

ScreenTips Short explanations that pop up when you point to any toolbar button, identifying the tasks the buttons perform.

Scroll bars The bars on the side or the bottom of the window that enable you to scroll the screen vertically and horizontally.

Section break In Word, a break that defines a new section in a document. You need to create a new section in a document if you want to use different formats, such as paper size and orientation, or if you want to create different headers and footers for each section.

Select Browse Object button In Word, a button you use to change the navigation buttons.

Select query The most common type of query in Access; it can be used to display selected fields of data in Datasheet view to make it easier to update.

Selection bar In Word, the white space in the left margin of the document window where you can click to select text.

Shading A color or a shade of gray that you apply to the background of a cell or data. Also called *fill* or *pattern*.

Slide show The display of slides in the presentation window without the PowerPoint toolbars, title bar, and status bar. During a slide show, each slide fills the screen, and you can focus on slide contents.

Slide show shortcut menu A list that displays commands for accessing navigation features as well as for controlling on-screen features such as the mouse pointer and slide meter. To display the slide show shortcut menu, click the right mouse button during the slide show.

Slide Sorter view The PowerPoint view that displays small images (often called *thumbnail images*) of each slide in the presentation so that you can apply and review special and template designs.

Soft page break A break automatically inserted by Word 97 when a page fills up with text.

Sort To arrange data in ascending or descending order.

SpellIt The automatic spell-checking feature. When you type a word that isn't in the dictionary, a wavy red line appears. Instead of erasing the word with the Backspace key, you can correct it by selecting the correct spelling from a shortcut menu.

Standard toolbar Contains buttons and controls used to the most common perform commands. To use the toolbar, click a button to perform a command or view a dialog box.

Status bar The bar at the bottom of the program window that displays information about the program and the current file. Instructions for performing selected tasks, active key information, and trouble messages.

Style A collection of format settings that are grouped together and given a name. When you apply a style, the text takes on all the formatting stored in the style.

Tab Preset stop points set on the ruler or with a dialog box used to align text.

Tab key The key on the keyboard you use to indent paragraphs.

Table In Access, the primary object of a database that stores field names, field descriptions, and field data. Tables display multiple records in a row/column format similar to a spreadsheet layout. In Word, a grouping of columns and rows (like a spreadsheet).

Tables and Borders toolbar In Word, the tools for drawing a table. When you draw a table, the Tables and Borders toolbar displays automatically. It may appear as a palette.

Template A professionally developed slide design that you can apply to presentations to give a consistent look to all slides in a presentation. In Word, a predesigned document you can use to create a new document.

Text preset animation A slide presentation (formerly known as a *build*) in which each slide title displays on-screen by itself and each bulleted list item is presented separately during a slide show. Text preset animations help focus the attention of your audience on each individual bulleted item as you discuss it and removes the distractions of presenting all bulleted points at once.

Timing The set amount of time a slide appears before automatically advancing to the next slide.

Title bar The bar at the top of the program window document or object window that identifies the application name and contains the application icon, Maximize/Restore, Minimize, and Close buttons.

Toolbar A bar that contains buttons for performing commands. To use the toolbar, click a button to perform a command or view a dialog box.

Toolbar grip The vertical lines on the left side of a toolbar that can be used to drag the toolbar to a new location.

Transitions Special effects that appear as your slides go on and off the screen during a slide show.

Underline The rule added under text so that it stands out.

Ungroup To separate a grouped object into its individual pieces so that individual pieces of the object can be changed.

Update In Access, to change the field data contained in a record.

View The way in which Office 97 programs display presentations, documents, worksheets, and database objects on screen.

Viewer A software program with which you view slide shows.

Wait mode In Excel, the mode in effect when the worksheet is busy and cannot accept data or commands.

Web toolbar The toolbar containing buttons for Internet use. To display the Web toolbar, click the Web Toolbar button in the Standard toolbar. To hide the Web toolbar, click the Web Toolbar button again.

Word processing program A program used to create documents such as memos, letters, envelopes, reports, manuals, and so on.

WordArt A feature you use to change text into words of art. WordArt enables you to curve, skew, or mold the text into a shape.

Workbook A file that contains Excel worksheets. By default, a new workbook file has three worksheets.

Worksheet A page in a workbook file.

Worksheet scroll buttons The buttons you use on the scroll bar to scroll the tabs for the worksheets.

Worksheet tab A part of the window that displays the names of worksheets in the current workbook. Clicking a tab displays the worksheet.

X axis The horizontal axis in a chart. You define this setting in the Chart Options dialog box.

Y axis The vertical axis in a chart. You define this setting in the Chart Options dialog box.

Windows 95, Outlook, and Internet Explorer 3.0

Addresses, Internet, IE-4, IE-6, IE-7–IE-8
ALT, WIN-8
Applications. *See* Programs
Appointments, scheduling, OL-6–OL-7

Calendar feature, OL-6–OL-7
CD-ROM drives, WIN-11
Chat, Internet Relay, IE-4
Clicking, WIN-4
Clip, in e-mail message list, OL-17
Close buttons, OL-7, OL-18, WIN-5
Commands, WIN-5, WIN-8–WIN-9. *See also specific command or operation*
Computer activities, tracking, OL-10–OL-12
Contacts List, OL-12–OL-15
Contents, Help, WIN-23
Context-sensitive help, WIN-22
Copying files, WIN-12–WIN-14

Dates
   in Calendar entries, OL-7
   in Journal entries, OL-11
   in Task List, OL-9
Deleted Items feature, OL-3
Deleting files, WIN-16
Desktop, WIN-3
Dialog boxes, WIN-9–WIN-11
Directories, WIN-12. *See also* Files
Disk drives
   copying files between, WIN-14
   overview, WIN-11
Downloading Internet files, IE-13–IE-15

E-mail
   Outlook feature for handling, OL-12, OL-15–OL-18
   sending and receiving over Internet, IE-22–IE-25
ENTER, OL-8, WIN-14
Envelopes, in e-mail message list, OL-17
Exiting
   Internet Explorer, IE-25
   Microsoft Windows, 29
   Outlook, OL-20
   Outlook tools, OL-7, OL-18

Favorites menu, IE-10–IE-11
Files
   copying, WIN-12–WIN-14
   deleting, WIN-16
   discarded, Recycle Bin and, WIN-3
   downloading from Internet, IE-13–IE-15
   folders for, WIN-12
   moving, WIN-14–WIN-15
   opening, WIN-19–WIN-20
   overview, WIN-11
   renaming, WIN-14
   restoring deleted, WIN-16–WIN-17
   saving, WIN-22
   separating data files from program files, WIN-12
Finding
   help info, WIN-26–WIN-27
   Internet info, IE-11–IE-12, IE-16–IE-18
   text, IE-12

Floppy disk drives, WIN-11
Folders, WIN-12. *See also specific folder*
Formatting disks, WIN-11
FTP, IE-13–IE-15

Go menu, IE-8–IE-9
Gopher sites, IE-15–IE-18
Graphics, in Web pages, IE-8
GUI (Graphical User Interface), WIN-2

Hard disk drives, WIN-11
Help, for Windows, WIN-22–28
History folder, IE-9–IE-10
Home pages, IE-5, IE-7
Hypertext links, IE-6, IE-7

Icons, WIN-2, WIN-8–WIN-9
Inbox (e-mail), OL-15–OL-18
Index, Help, WIN-24–WIN-26
Internet
   connecting to, IE-3
   downloading files from, IE-13–IE-15
   e-mail via, IE-22–IE-25
   etiquette in using, IE-22
   newsgroups, IE-18–IE-21
   overview and available resources, IE-3–IE-4
   printing info from, IE-12–IE-13
   searching, IE-11–IE-12, IE-16–IE-18
   tool for using. *See* Internet Explorer
   World Wide Web. *See* World Wide Web
Internet Explorer. *See also specific component or operation*
   exiting, IE-25
   main screen for, IE-5–IE-6
   overview, IE-4–IE-5
   starting, IE-5
Internet Mail, IE-23–IE-25
Internet News, IE-18
Internet Relay Chat, IE-4

Journal, OL-10–OL-12

Launching. *See* Starting
Links, IE-6, IE-7

Maximize button, WIN-6–WIN-7
Menus, WIN-5, WIN-8–WIN-9. *See also specific menu*
Messages
   e-mail. *See* E-mail
   newsgroup, IE-18–IE-22
Microsoft Windows. *See also specific component or operation*
   desktop elements, WIN-3
   exiting, 29
   starting, WIN-3
Minimize button, WIN-6–WIN-7
Mouse, basic use of, WIN-3–WIN-4
Moving files, WIN-14–WIN-15
Multitasking, WIN-17
My Computer, WIN-3, WIN-4

Netiquette, IE-22
Networks, IE-3
Newsgroups, IE-18–IE-22

Notes
   for Calendar entries, OL-7
   Notes feature, OL-3
   for Task List entries, OL-9

Opening files, WIN-19–WIN-20
Operating systems, WIN-2
Outlook. *See also specific component or operation*
   exiting, OL-20
   features
      accessing, OL-4–OL-6
      overview, OL-3
   main window for, OL-4
   printing info from, OL-18–OL-19
   starting, OL-3–OL-4
Outlook Bar, OL-3, OL-4–OL-6

Paper clip, in e-mail message list, OL-17
Passwords, OL-4, IE-13
Paste, WIN-14
Printing
   Internet info, IE-12–IE-13
   Outlook info, OL-18–OL-19
Programs
   starting, WIN-6
   switching between, WIN-17–WIN-22

Recycle Bin, WIN-3, WIN-16–WIN-17
Renaming files, WIN-14
Restoring deleted files, WIN-16–WIN-17

Saving work, OL-7, OL-14, WIN-22
Scrolling windows, WIN-6–WIN-7
Searching. *See* Finding
Sites
   FTP sites, IE-13–IE-15
   Gopher sites, IE-15–IE-18
   Web sites. *See* World Wide Web, sites
Starting
   Internet Explorer, IE-5
   Microsoft Windows, WIN-3
   Outlook, OL-3–OL-4
   Outlook components, OL-4–OL-6
Start menu, WIN-5–WIN-6
Start pages, IE-5, IE-7

TAB, OL-7
Taskbar, WIN-3
Task List, OL-8–OL-10
Telnet, IE-4
Time
   in Calendar entries, OL-7
   in Journal entries, OL-11
   in Task List, OL-9
Toolbars, WIN-8–WIN-9
ToolTips, WIN-8
Transferring Internet files, IE-13–IE-15

URLs, IE-4
Usenet newsgroups, IE-19

Web. *See also* Internet
   as component of Internet, IE-4
   pages
      graphics and, IE-8

INDEX-1

links and, IE-7
navigating open pages, IE-11
printing, IE-13
sites
　Favorites folder for, IE-10–IE-11
　selecting from Go Menu, IE-8–IE-9
　selecting from History folder, IE-9–IE-10
What's This? feature, WIN-22, WIN-27
Windows
　operating system based on. *See* Microsoft Windows
　overview and components, WIN-6
　sizing and scrolling, WIN-6–WIN-7
　switching between, WIN-17–WIN-22
World Wide Web. *See* Web

Word 97

Aligning
   tables and table components. *See* Tables
   text, 53–54. *See also* Tabs
Applications
   starting, 4
Application title bar, 5
Arrow keys, 45, 110–111
Asterisk (*), prohibited from document names, 30
AutoComplete, 27–28
AutoCorrect, 25
AutoFormat, 115–116
AutoText, 6–7, 56–57

BACKSPACE, 25
Bars, in tabs, 83
Boldface, 47
Borders, 95–97, 98
Break, 76
Breaks, in pages. *See* Pages, breaks in
Browsing pages, 135, 140
Bulleted lists, 92–93

Cells, in tables, 107, 112. *See also* Tables
Centering. *See* Aligning
Characters. *See also* Text
   prohibited, in document names, 30
   special, 27
Clicking, 112
Clip art. *See* Graphics
Clipboard, 53, 55, 56
Clipit, 13
Closing. *See also* Exiting
   documents, 4, 14–15, 34–35
   headers and footers, 147
Columns
   in documents, 75–76
   in tables. *See* Tables, columns
Commands. *See also specific command or operation*
   in menus. *See* Menus
   in toolbars. *See* Toolbars
Context-sensitive Help, 11
Convert Text to Table, 110
Copying text, 55–56
Cut, 52

Database toolbar, 7
Data source documents. *See* Merging documents
Dates, 23–25, 144
Decimal tabs, 83
Deleting
   page breaks, 140–142
   section breaks, 143
   table columns and rows, 114–115
   text, 25, 28, 50–51
Document Map, 136–138
Documents. *See also* Pages; Paragraphs; Text
   closing, 4, 14–15, 34–35
   columns in, 75–76
   correcting, via AutoCorrect, 25
   creating, 22–23
   data source documents. *See* Merging documents
   envelopes, 59–60
   finding, 44

   graphics in. *See* Graphics
   insertion point in, moving, 44–45
   main, in merging, 159. *See also* Merging documents
   merging. *See* Merging documents
   naming, 30–31
   opening, 43–44
   previewing, 32–33
   printing. *See* Printing
   saving. *See* Saving
   section breaks in, 142–143
   selecting entire, 46
   tables in. *See* Tables
   views of, changing, 60–62
Document title bar, 5
Drawing toolbar, 7
Draw Table, 119–124

END, 45
Endnotes, 148–151
ENTER, 23, 28, 162
Envelopes, 59–60
Exiting. *See also* Closing
   Word, 4, 14–15

F1, Help via, 11
F3, in using AutoText, 57
Field names, in data source documents, 160. *See also* Merging documents
Files
   Word. *See* Documents
Finding
   documents, 44
   pages, 135, 136–138
   text, 135–136
Fonts, 48–50
Footers, 142, 143–147
Footnotes, 148–151
Formatting. *See also* Styles
   paragraphs, 81–83
   tables, 115–117
   text. *See* Text
Form letters. *See* Merging documents

Go To, 135, 136
Grammar checker, 57–59
Graphics
   gallery of, 76
   inserting, 77–78
   sizing and moving, 79–80
Grip, toolbar, 7

Handles, sizing, 78
Hard page breaks, 138
Headers, 142, 143–147
Headings, in finding pages, 135, 136–138
Help
   for Word, 9–14
Hiding
   Ruler, 8–9
   toolbars, 8
HOME, 23, 45
Hyphenation, 11

Indenting, 81–83, 93, 110
Insert Columns, 113
Insertion point, 5, 23, 44–45

Insert Row, 112
Insert Table, 108
Italics, 48

Landscape orientation, 75
Leaders, in tabs, 83, 85–86
Lists
   bulleted, 92–93
   numbered, 94–95
   overview, 92

Magnifying glass pointer, 33
Mail merge. *See* Merging documents
Main documents, in merging, 159. *See also* Merging documents
Margins, 73–74
Menus
   menu bars, 5
Merging documents
   data source documents for
     creating, 160–164, 169–171
     selecting, 172
   main documents for, creating, 164–167, 168–169
   merge procedure, 167–168
   overview and components, 159–160
   printing merged documents, 167
   toolbar for, 164
   utility for, accessing, 161
Microsoft
   Windows. *See also specific component or operation*
   Word. *See* Word
Mouse, *See specific operation*
Moving
   graphics, 80
   text, 51–53

New, 23
Newspaper columns, 75–76
Next Heading button, 135
Normal Body style, 89
Normal view, 60, 134, 139, 140
Numbered lists, 94–95
Numbers, page, 144, 146

Office Assistant, 11–13
Opening documents, 43–44
Orientation, page, 73, 75

Page Layout view, 60, 61, 134
Pages. *See also* Documents; Paragraphs; Text
   breaks in
     deleting, 140–142
     inserting, 138–140
     soft vs. hard, 138
     viewing, 60, 61
   browsing, 135, 140
   footnotes, 148–151
   headers and footers, 142, 143–147
   locating, 135, 136–138
   margins, 73–74
   moving between, 134–135
   numbers, 144, 146
   orientation, 73, 75
Paper size, 75

INDEX-3

Paragraphs
    borders and shading, 95–98
    formatting, 81–83. *See also* Styles
    indenting, 81–82
    text in, working with. *See* Text
Paste, 53, 56
PGDN and PGUP, 45
Pictures. *See* Graphics
Portrait orientation, 73, 75
Previewing
    printouts, 32–33
    spacing and indent changes, 82
    table formatting changes, 116
Printing
    basic procedure, 33–34
    document merge and, 167
    envelopes, 60
    page setup for. *See* Pages
    paper size, 75
    previewing document before, 32–33
Programs, starting, 4

Question mark (?), prohibited from filenames, 30

Records, in data source documents, 160. *See also* Merging documents
Red lines, denoting spelling errors, 29–30
Redo, 28
References, footnote, 148–150
Replace, Find and, 135–136
Ruler, 5, 8–9, 84–87

Save As, 32
Saving
    existing documents, 31–32
    new documents, 30–31
    recommended frequency of, 31
    upon closing documents, 14
Scrolling, 5, 44, 45
Searching. *See* Finding
Sections, 142–143
Select Browse Object button, 136, 140
Sentences. *See* Text
Shading, 95, 97–98
Show/Hide button, 95
Sizing
    graphics, 79–80

Soft page breaks, 138
Spaces, prohibited in field names, 162
Spacing, text, 81–83
Special characters, 27
Spell-checking
    automatic, with Spellit, 29–30
    with Spelling and Grammar checker, 57–59
Standard toolbar, 7
Starting
    Word, 4
Status bar, 5
Styles. *See also* Formatting
    applying, 87–89
    modifying, 90–92
    overview, 87
    in tables, 117
Symbols, 27

TAB
    indenting text with, 23, 26
    navigating tables with, 110, 111
Tables
    aligning, 119
    columns
        centering text in, 117
        deleting, 115
        inserting, 113
        overview, 107
        width, 117–118
    creating from existing text, 109–110
    drawing freehand, 119–124
    entering data in, 111–115
    formatting, 115–117
    inserting and basic setup, 107–109
    navigating, 110–111
    overview and components, 107
    rows
        deleting, 114
        inserting, 112–113
        moving between, 110
        overview, 107
    selecting contents of, 112, 122
Tabs, 83–87, 109, 110
Text. *See also* Documents; Pages
    aligning, 53–54
    AutoText, 56–57
    boldface, 47

columns of, 75–76
completing, via AutoComplete, 27–28
copying, 55–56
deleting, 25, 28, 50–51
entering, 23, 25–26, 56–57
finding, 135–136
fonts, 48–50
headings, in finding pages, 135, 136–138
hyphenating, 11
indenting, 81–82, 93
italic, 48
in lists. *See* Lists
moving, 51–53
replacing, 54–55
selecting, 45–46
spacing around, 82–83
special characters, 27
spell-checking. *See* Spell-checking
styles and. *See* Styles
in tables. *See* Tables
underlined, 47
undoing changes in, 28
Time, 24, 144
Title bars, 5
Toolbars. *See also specific operation*
    overview, 5
    using, 6–8
Triple-clicking, 112

Underlining text, 47
Undo, 28

Variables, in data source documents, 160. *See also* Merging documents
Views, changing, 60–62

What's This? feature, 11
Windows interface. *See* Microsoft, Windows
Word
    exiting, 4, 14–15
    overview of capabilities, 2–3
    screen elements, 4–9
    starting, 4
World Wide Web, Help via, 13–14

Excel 97

Absolute references, 133–136
Accounting format, 82
Active cell, 3, 4, 5, 19–23
Addition, operator for, 33
Addresses, cell. *See* Cells, addresses
Aligning cell contents, 78–81
Applications title bar, 4, 5
Arguments, 33
Arithmetic operators, 32–33
Arrow keys, 20, 21
Asterisk (*), as operator, 33
AutoComplete, 26
AutoFit, 106–107, 108
AutoFormat, 92–93
AutoSum, 36
AVERAGE, 33
Axes, in charts, 139, 142–143, 146. *See also* Charts

Boldface, 77
Borders, 88–89

Caret (^), as operator, 33
Cells. *See also* Worksheets
   addresses
      absolute references and, 133
      overview, 33
      relative addresses and, 130
   borders and fill for, 88–90
   comments for. *See* Comments
   contents
      aligning, 78–81
      copying, 58–61
      deleting, 61–63
      editing, 52–55
      moving, 63–65
   deleting, 112, 114
   inserting, 109, 111–112
   merging, 78, 80–81
   overview, 2, 3, 5
   ranges of, 33, 55–57. *See also* Cells, contents; Columns; Rows
   selecting, 55–57
Centering cell contents, 78, 80–81
Charts
   column charts, 137–139
   creating, 137–139, 147–152
   data changes in, 140–142
   elements of
      formatting, 143–145
      options for, 146–147
      overview, 139
   examples, 127
   moving and sizing, 139–140
   overview, 136
   pie charts, 127, 147–152
   type, changing, 145–146
Chart Wizard, 136, 137
Clear, 61
Clipboard, 58, 63
Clippit, 10
Closing
   Excel, 5
   workbooks, 5, 11
Colon (:), in cell ranges, 33
Color, 78, 89–90

Column charts, 137–139
Columns. *See also* Worksheets
   deleting, 112, 113
   inserting, 109–110
   overview, 2, 3, 5
   selecting, 55
   sorting, 129–130
   width, 104–107
Comments
   adding to cells, 65–68
   overview, 65
   viewing and hiding, 68–69
Contents (Help), 8
Context-sensitive help, 8, WIN-10, WIN-14
Copying
   cell contents, 58–61
   data, between workbooks, 126–129
   formulas, 130–132, 133–134
COUNT, 33
CTRL, extending selections with, 55, 57
Currency format, 82
Custom format, 82
Cut, 64

Data ranges, in charts, 139, 140. *See also* Charts
Dates, 25, 82, 84–85
Deleting
   cell contents, 23, 26, 61–63
   cells, 112, 114
   columns, 112, 113
   rows, 112
   worksheet pages, 102
Dialog boxes, *See specific operation*
Division, operator for, 33
Document title bar, 4, 5

Edit mode, 5
END, 20, 22
ENTER, 22
Enter mode, 5
Equal sign (=), in formulas and functions, 32, 33
Error mode, 5
ESC, 26
Excel. *See also specific component or operation*
   exiting, 5, 11
   launching, 3–4
   screen elements, 4–6
Exiting
   Excel, 5, 11
Exploded pie charts, 148–150
Exponentiation, operator for, 33

Files
   Excel. *See* Workbooks
Fill, 88, 89–90
Finding
   Help info, 8–9,
   worksheet data, 50–52
Fonts, 77–78, 145
Footers. *See* Headers and footers
Formatting
   chart elements, 143–145
   dates, 82, 84–85
   numbers, 81–83, 86–87

   with pre-set formats, 92–93
   text, 77–78
   toolbar for, 4, 5
Formulas. *See also* Functions
   entering in worksheets
      using absolute references, 133–136
      basic procedure, 34–37
      using relative references, 130–132
   formula bar, 4, 5
   headings in, 133, 136
   order of operations in, 37
   overview and components, 32–33
Fractions, 25, 82
Functions. *See also* Formulas
   common, list of, 33
   entering in worksheets, 35–37
   overview and components, 32–33

General format, 82
Gridlines, in charts, 139, 146. *See also* Charts
Grips, toolbar, 7
Group indicator, 27

Headers and footers
   custom, 117–119
   overview, 114
   simple, 115–117
Headings, in formulas, 133, 136
Help
   Excel, 8–10
HOME, 20, 22

Index (Help), 8
Italics, 77

Launching. *See* Starting
Legends, in charts, 139, 143, 146. *See also* Charts
Lines, around cells, 88–89

MAX, 33
Menus
   menu bars, 4, 5,
Merging cells, 78, 80–81
Microsoft
   Excel. *See* Excel
   Web site, for Excel help, 10
MIN, 33
Minus sign (-), as operator, 33, 34
Mode indicators, 4, 5
Mouse, *See specific operation*
Moving
   cell contents, 63–65
   charts, 139–140
Multiplication, operator for, 33

Naming worksheets, 23–24
New button, 19
Normal view, 92
Number format, 82
Numbers
   entering in worksheets. *See* Worksheets, entering data in
   formatting, 81–83, 86–87
   fractions, 25
   serial numbers, 87

INDEX-5

Office Assistant, 8–10
Opening workbooks, 49–50
Operators, arithmetic, 32–33

Pages. See also Worksheets
   breaks in, 91–92
   deleting, 102
   headers and footers for. See Headers and footers
   inserting, 102–103
   rearranging, 103–104
Paste, 59, 61, 64
Patterns, 88, 89–90
Percentages
   format for, 82
   operator for, 33
PGDN, 20, 21
PGUP, 20
Pie charts, 147–152. See also Charts
Plus sign (+), as operator, 33
Point mode, 5
Pound sign (#), in cells, 31
Previewing
   headers and footers, 117
   page breaks, 91
   worksheet printouts, 39–40
Printing
   Excel worksheets, 39–41

Ready mode, 5
Relative references, 130–132
Rename, 24
Rows. See also Worksheets
   deleting, 112
   height, 107–108
   inserting, 109, 110
   overview, 2, 3, 5. See also Worksheets
   selecting, 55

Saving work
   basic procedure, 37–39
   recommended frequency of, 39
   under another name or in another location, 39
   upon exiting, 11
Scientific format, 82

Scientific notation, 31
Scrolling, 4, 5,
Searching. See Finding
Serial numbers, 87
Shading, 88, 89–90
Sizing
   charts, 139, 140
   columns, 104–107
   rows, 107–108
Slash (/), as operator, 33
Sorting worksheet data, 129–130
Special format, 82
Spell-checking, 69–70
Spreadsheets. See Worksheets
Standard toolbar, 4, 5
Starting
   Excel, 3–4
Status bar, 4, 5
Subtraction, operator for, 33
SUM, 33, 35

TAB, 118
Tabs, worksheet, 4, 5
Text. See also Cells, contents
   in charts. See Charts
   entering in worksheets. See Worksheets, entering data in
   formatting, 77–78
   formatting numbers as, 82, 86–87
3-D charts, 151
Time format, 82
Title bars, 4, 5
Titles, chart, 139, 146
Toolbars. See also specific toolbar or operation
   Excel, 4, 5, 6–7

Underlined text, 77
Undo, 61, 62

Values. See Numbers

Wait mode, 5
Web
   Help via, 10
   Web toolbar, 6

What's This feature, 8
Workbooks. See also Worksheets
   closing, 11, 41
   copying data between, 126–129
   creating, 19
   naming, 37–38
   navigating, 19–23
   open, list of, 49
   opening, 49–50
   overview, 3
   saving. See Saving work
Worksheets
   cells in. See Cells
   changes in, linked to charts, 140–142
   charts from. See Charts
   columns in. See Columns
   comments for. See Comments
   entering data in
      on multiple worksheets, 26–31
      numbers, 31–32
      overview, 25
      text, 25–31
   finding data in, 50–52
   formulas and functions in. See Formulas; Functions
   headers and footers for. See Headers and footers
   multiple, entering data in, 26–31
   naming, 23–24
   navigating, 19–23
   overview and components, 2–3
   pages in. See Pages
   printing, 39–41
   rows in. See Rows
   saving. See Saving work
   scrolling, 4, 5
   sorting data in, 129–130
   spell-checking, 69–70
   tabs for, 4, 5
World Wide Web. See Web

X axis, 139, 145, 146. See also Charts

Y axis, 139, 144, 146. See also Charts

Access 97

Access 97; *See* Access
Access
   dialog box, 9
   exiting, 20
   launching Microsoft, 7–8
   learning about, 9
   looking up new features of, 17–18
   object-oriented relational database program, 4
   starting, 7–8
Accessing online support, 19–20
Adding
   fields to query grids, 96–97
   records to database tables, 34–36
   titles to forms, 125–128
Adjusting field lengths on forms, 124–125
Aligning
   field controls on reports, 144
   fields on forms, 122–123
Altering table design, 74–91
AutoForm
   creating, 37–38
   saving, 37–38
AutoReports
   creating, 83–84, 134–155
   saving, 83–84

Bars; *See also* Toolbars
   menu, 11–12
   title, 11–12
Building databases, 25–49

Changing
   field data, 53–55
   form field labels, 123–124
Check box, clicking, 63
Checking spelling, 36–37
Check mark, removing, 63
Choosing query names, 99
Clicking,
   check box, 63
Closing
   databases, 20
   database tables, 32–33
   Office Assistant, 15–16
   queries, 98–99
   Toolbox, 121
Comparison operators, 100
Copying table structures, 84–85
Correcting mistakes, 35
Creating
   AutoForm, 37–38
   AutoReports, 83–84, 134–155
   databases, 8–10
   database tables, 28–33
   forms, 37–38, 115–133
   key fields, 82–83
   new forms, 117–118
   new queries, 94–96
   queries, 92–114
   queries based on fields, 95
Criteria
   defined, 96
   setting, 100–103

Data
   hidden, 58

previewing, 40–42
printing, 40–42
replacing, 57–59
saving, 36
searching for, 103
Databases
   building, 25–49
   closing, 20
   creating, 8–10
   designing, 6–7
   maintaining, 50–73
   opening, 27
   programs, 4
   saving, 8–10
   terminology defined, 2–6
Database tables; *See also* Tables
   adding records to, 34–36
   checking spelling in, 36–37
   closing, 32–33
   creating, 28–33
   opening, 33–34
   saving, 32–33
Datasheets
   navigating, 38–40
   views, 37, 39
Defining table fields, 29–32
Deleting
   fields, 120, 139
   records, 59–60
   table fields, 81–82
Designing databases, 6–7
Dialog boxes
   Access, 9
   displaying, 13–14
   Find, 53
   Replace, 58
   working with, 12–14
Displaying
   dialog boxes, 13–14
   Form Design view, 117–118
   header sections of forms, 125
   menus, 13–14
   Office Assistant, 15–16

Editing queries, 104–107
Exiting
   Access, 20

Features, looking up new, 17–18
Fields
   adding to query grids, 96–97
   aligning, 122–123
   creating key, 82–83
   creating queries based on, 95
   data, changing, 53–55
   deleting, 120, 139
   deleting table, 81–82
   dropping in wrong locations, 79
   filtering different, 65
   labels, 123–124
   lengths, adjusting, 124–125
   moving, 122
   moving to, 35
   not spell checking, 37
   rearranging, 78–81
   rearranging on forms, 120–122
   removing from forms, 119–120

searching for data contained in, 103
selecting, 63
   from forms, 119–120
   from reports, 137–139
   of tables, 106
Filtering
   different fields, 65
   records by
      Form, 63–66
      selection, 62–63
Find dialog box, 53
Finding
   records, 52–53
Form Design view
   displaying, 117–118
   features, identifying, 118–119
Forms
   adding titles to, 125–128
   adjusting field lengths on, 124–125
   aligning fields on, 122–123
   creating, 37–38, 115–133
   displaying header sections of, 125
   field labels, changing, 123–124
   filtering records by, 63–66
   modifying, 115–133
   navigating, 38–40
   rearranging fields on, 120–122
   removing fields from, 119–120
   saving, 37–38, 122
   viewing complete, 53
Form view, 39

Getting Help, 14–20
Grid settings, query, 103

Header sections, displaying, 125
Help
   contents, using, 17–18
   getting, 14–20
   Index, using, 18–19
   menu, 9
   online, 14
   Using What's This?, 16
Hidden data, 58

Identifying
   Form Design view features, 118–119
   menu features, 11–12
   Report Design screen features, 135–137
   screen elements, 10–11
Index, searching for topics in, 18–19
Inserting
   records, 55–57
   table fields, 76–78

Key fields, creating, 82–83

Labels
   changing form field, 123–124
   field, 123
Launching Microsoft Access, 7–8
Learning about Access, 9
Looking up new features, 17–18

Maintaining databases, 50–73
Menu bar, 11–12

INDEX-7

Menus
	displaying, 13–14
	features, identifying, 11–12
	Help, 9
	working with, 11–12
Microsoft Access: See also Access
	exiting, 20
	launching, 7–8
Microsoft Web site, getting Help from, 19–20
Mistakes, correcting, 35
Modifying forms, 115–133
Modifying report designs, 140–147
More Files, selecting, 27
Moving
	fields, 122
	to next field, 35

Names, choosing query, 99
Navigating
	datasheets, 38–40
	forms, 38–40
	records, 38–40

Objects, saving changes to, 20
Office Assistant, 8, 18
	closing, 15–16
	displaying, 15–16
	using, 14–16
Online
	help, 14
	support, accessing, 19–20
Opening
	databases, 27
	database tables, 33–34
	queries, 99–100
	reports, 135–137
Operators, comparison, 100

Page Footer section, 137
Page Header section, 140
Previewing database data, 40–42
Printing
	database data, 40–42
	reports, 148–149

Queries
	based on fields, 95
	closing, 98–99
	creating, 92–114
	editing, 104–107
	opening, 99–100
	printing reports based on, 148
	running, 97–100
	saving, 98–99
	selecting, 94
	windows, 106
Query grids
	adding fields to, 96–97
	settings, 103
Query sort order, setting, 100–103

RDBMS (relational database management system), 2
Rearranging fields
	on forms, 120–122
	in tables, 78–81
Records
	arrangements of, 53
	deleting, 59–60
	filtering, 62–66
	finding, 52–53
	inserting, 55–57
	navigating, 38–40
	order of, 58
	sorting, 60–62, 78
	updating, 53–55
Relationships
	defined, 106
	searching for topics about, 18–19
Removing
	check marks, 63
	fields
		from forms, 119–120
		from reports, 137–139
Replace dialog box, 58
Replace feature, using, 57–59
Replacing, data, 57–59
Report Design screen features, identifying, 135–137
Reports
	aligning field controls on, 144
	designs, modifying, 140–147
	opening, 135–137
	printing, 148–149
	removing fields from, 137–139
	saving, 139–140
	viewing, 139–140
Running queries, 97–100

Saving
	AutoForm, 37–38
	AutoReports, 83–84
	changes to objects, 20
	data, 36
	databases, 8–10
	database tables, 32–33
	forms, 37–38, 122
	queries, 98–99
	reports, 139–140
Screen
	accessing area of, 121
	elements, identifying, 10–11
	Tip, 12
Searching
	for data contained in fields, 103
	for relationship topics, 18–19
Selecting
	fields, 63
		from forms, 119–120
		from reports, 137–139
	More Files, 27
Select query, 94

Setting
	criteria, 100–103
	query sort order, 100–103
Sorting records, 60–62, 78
Sort order, setting query, 100–103
Spell checking, 36–37
Starting
	Access, 7–8

Table design, altering, 74–91
Table fields, 106
	defining, 29–32
	deleting, 81–82
	inserting, 76–78
Tables; See also Database tables
	rearranging fields in, 78–81
	structures, copying, 84–85
	The Willows, 25–26
Title bars, 11–12
Titles, adding to forms, 125–128
Toolbars
	working with, 12
Toolbox
	closing, 121
	displaying a, 147
	palette, 127

Undo feature, 59, 120, 139
Updating records, 53–55
Using
	comparison operators, 100
	help contents, 17–18
	Help Index, 18–19
	Office Assistant, 14–16
	Replace feature, 57–59
	the toolbar, 13–14
	What's This? Help, 16

Viewing
	forms, 53
	reports, 139–140
Views
	datasheet, 37, 39
	displaying Form Design, 117–118
	Form, 39
	list of available, 76

Web site, getting Help from Microsoft, 19–20
Willows table, The, 25–26
Windows
	query, 106
Working with
	dialogue boxes, 12–14
	menus, 11–12
	toolbars, 12
World Wide Web; See Web site

PowerPoint 97

Action buttons, setting, 141–144
Action Settings dialog box, 141
Adding
  art, 82–115
  slides, 18, 33–36
  slide timings, 144–145
  slide transitions, 121–122
  text in Outline view, 41–42
Animating
  slides with sound, 137–141
  text, 123–124
Animation Effects toolbar, 142
Animations
  custom, 137–138
  text preset, 123
Art
  adding, 82–115
  manipulating, 104–109
AutoContent Wizard, 69–72
AutoLayout format, 28, 35–36

Black screens, displaying, 120
Blank presentation option, 29
Builds (animation), 123

Changing
  line spacing of text, 65
  page setup, 68–69
  paper size and orientation, 68–69
  text appearance, 57–60
Checking
  spelling of text, 63–64
  style of text, 63–64
Children, 124
Choosing View, Ruler, 65
Clip art
  downloading from Web site, 89–94
  inserting, 84–87
  inserting from Web site, 89–94
  moving, 87–89
  sizing, 87–89
Clippit, using, 17–18
Closing
  presentations, 20, 32–33
Common Tasks toolbar, 15, 34, 40
Compressing presentations, 151
Creating
  drawings, 99–104
  notes pages, 147–148
  presentations using Wizard, 69–72
  title slides, 28–32
  WordArt, 94–96
Creations, freehand, 99
Custom animation, 137–138
Custom Animation dialog box, 142

Dialog boxes
  Action Settings, 141
  custom animation, 142
  displaying, 14–16
  New Slide, 28
  PowerPoint, 7, 29
  Print, 43
  Style Checker Options, 64
  working with, 13–16
Displaying
  Dialog Boxes, 14–16

hidden slides, 127–128
  menus, 14–16
  ruler, 65
Docked toolbars, 12
Downloading clip art from Web site, 89–94
Drawings, creating, 99–104
Drawing toolbar, 100–104

Editing
  placeholder text, 53–57
  presentations, 116–135
  slide text, 51–81
Enhancing presentations, 136–157
Exiting PowerPoint, 20
Expanding slides, 124–126

Finding
  text, 60–63
Flip images, 104
Floating toolbars, 12
Folders
  My Documents, 32
  templates, 38
Formats
  AutoLayout, 28, 35–36
  Title AutoLayout, 28
Formatting
  text placeholders, 64–68
  WordArt, 96–99
Freehand creations, 99

Group separate objects, 104

Handouts, printing, 43–45
Help
  getting, 16–20
    Microsoft on the Web, 19
    Microsoft Web Site, 18–20
    using Clippit, 17–18
    using the Office Assistant, 17–18
  menu, 16
Hidden slides, displaying, 127–128
Hiding slides, 127–128
Hyperlink, 141, 143

Images
  flip, 104
  miniature, 120
  rotate, 104
  thumbnail, 39, 120
Inserting
  clip art, 84–87
  clip art from Web site, 89–94

Manipulating art, 104–109
Menus
  displaying, 14–16
  Help, 16
  identifying features, 11
Microsoft
  PowerPoint; See PowerPoint
  Web site, 18–20
Miniature images, 120
Moving clip art, 87–89
My Documents folder, 32

Navigating presentations, 37
New Slide dialog box, 28
Notes Pages
  creating, 147–148
  view, 10

Objects
  group separate, 104
  ungroup grouped, 104
Office Assistant, using the, 17–18
Online support, accessing, 19
Opening presentations, 33–36
Outline views, 9, 41–42

Packing presentations to go, 149–151
Pages
  creating notes, 147–148
  setups, changing, 68–69
Parent slides, 124
Placeholders
  formatting text, 64–68
  selecting and editing text, 53–57
PowerPoint
  AutoContent Wizard, 69–72
  dialog box, 7, 29
  exiting, 20
  launching, 4–5
  starting, 4–5
  Style Checker, 63
  terminology, defining, 2–3
  Web site; See Web site
Presentations
  adding art to, 82–115
  applying templates, 37–39
  building, 26–50
  changing text appearance, 57–60
  closing, 20, 32–33
  compressing, 151
  creating, 7–8
  creating blank, 28–32
  defined, 2
  designing, 3
  displaying in different views, 8–10
  editing, 116–135
  enhancing, 136–157
  navigating, 37
  opening, 33–36
  outlines, printing, 43–45
  packing to go, 149–151
  rearranging slides in, 120–121
  saving, 32–33
  setting to run continuously, 146–147
  setup, 28–45
  slide shows, 118–119
  viewing, 116–135
Print dialog box, 43
Printing
  handouts, 43–45
  presentation outlines, 43–45
  slides, 43

Question textbox, 18

Rearranging slides in presentations, 120–121
Replacing text, 60–63
Rotating images, 104

INDEX-9

Ruler, displaying, 65
Running presentations continuously, 146–147

Saving
   changes to presentations, 69
   presentations, 32–33
Screen elements, identifying, 5–6
Screen Tips, 12
Selecting placeholder text, 53–57
Setting
   action buttons, 141–144
   presentations to run continuously, 146–147
Sizing
   clip art, 87–89
Slides
   adding, 18, 33–36
   animating with sound, 137–141
   creating title, 28–32
   displaying hidden, 127–128
   expanding, 124–126
   hiding, 127–128
   parent, 124
   printing, 43
   rearranging in presentations, 120–121
   shows
      presenting, 118–119
      using shortcut menu, 119–120
   Sorter views, 10, 39, 120
   text
      editing, 51–81
      seeing, 64
   timings, adding, 144–145

transitions, adding, 121–122
views, 9
Sound, animating slides with, 137–141
Spelling of text, 63–64
Standard toolbar, 33
Starting
   PowerPoint, 4–5
Style Checker
   Options dialog box, 64
   PowerPoint, 63
Style of text, 63–64
Switching views, 39–40
Templates
   applying, 37–39
   folders, 38
Text
   animating, 123–124
   changing
      appearance of, 57–60
      line spacing of, 65
   checking
      spelling of, 63–64
      style of, 63–64
   editing slide, 51–81
   finding, 60–63
   in Outline view, adding, 41–42
   placeholders, formatting, 64–68
   replacing, 60–63
   seeing slide, 64
   selecting and editing placeholder, 53–57
Textbox, question, 18
Thumbnail images, 39, 120
Timings, adding slide, 144–145
Title
   AutoLayout format, 28

Toolbars
   Animation Effects, 142
   Common Tasks, 15, 34, 40
   docked, 12
   drawing, 100–104
   floating, 12
   standard, 33
   using, 14–16
   working with, 12–13

Ungroup grouped objects, 104
Using toolbars, 14–16

Viewing presentations, 116–135
Views
   displaying presentations in different, 8–10
   Notes Pages, 10
   outline, 9, 41–42
   slide, 9
   Slide Sorter, 10, 39, 120
   switching, 39–40
Visual Clarity, 64

Web site
   accessing online support from the, 19
   site, 18–20, 89–94
Wizard, creating, presentation using, 69–72
WordArt
   creating, 94–96
   formatting, 96–99
Working with
   Dialog Boxes, 13–16
   toolbars, 12–13

Integrated Projects

Access databases. *See* Databases
Art. *See* Graphics

Charts
   creating, IP1-5–IP1-8
   linking to documents, IP1-19–IP1-21
Copying
   worksheet data to databases, IP2-3–IP2-6
   worksheet data to documents, IP1-15–IP1-19

Databases
   copying worksheet data to, IP2-3–IP2-6
   merging with documents, IP2-9–IP2-11
   updating worksheet data in, IP2-7–IP2-9
Documents
   adding art to, IP1-12–IP1-15, IP3-15–IP3-16
   copying worksheet data to, IP1-15–IP1-19
   creating
      basic procedure, IP1-8–IP1-12
      from presentation outlines, IP3-12–IP3-13
   linking charts to, IP1-19–IP1-21
   linking to presentations, IP3-16–IP3-18
   merging with database, IP2-9–IP2-11

Excel
   charts. See Charts
   worksheets. See Worksheets

Files, saving in HTML, IP3-18–IP3-20

Graphics
   adding to documents, IP1-12–IP1-15, IP3-15–IP3-16
   metafiles and, IP3-14
   saving slides as, IP3-14–IP3-15

HTML files, saving files as, IP3-18–IP3-20
Hyperlinks, IP3-16–IP3-18

Importing data, IP2-3–IP2-6

Linking
   charts to documents, IP1-19–IP1-21
   documents to presentations, IP3-16–IP3-18
   worksheet data to slides, IP3-8–IP3-11

Merging documents with database data, IP2-9–IP2-11
Metafiles, IP3-14
Microsoft
   Access. See Databases
   Excel. See Excel
   PowerPoint. See PowerPoint
   Word. See Word

Paste Special, IP1-20
PowerPoint. See Presentations; Slides
Presentations. See *also* Slides
   linking documents to, IP3-16–IP3-18
   outlines of, creating documents from, IP3-12–IP3-13
   saving as HTML files, IP3-18–IP3-20

Saving
   files, in HTML, IP3-18–IP3-20
   slides, as graphics, IP3-14–IP3-15
Send To, IP3-12
Slides. *See also* Presentations
   embedding tables in, IP3-4–IP3-8
   linking worksheet data to, IP3-8–IP3-11
   saving as graphics, IP3-14–IP3-15

Tables
   database. See Access
   Word, embedding in slides, IP3-4–IP3-8
Tiling windows, IP2-4

Web
   saving files for use on, IP3-18–IP3-20
   toolbar, IP3-17
Windows, tiling, IP2-4
Word
   documents. See Documents
   tables, embedding in slides, IP3-4–IP3-8
   WordArt, IP1-12–IP1-15
World Wide Web. *See* Web
Worksheets
   adding data to slides, IP3-4
   charts from. See Charts
   copying data to databases, IP2-3–IP2-6
   copying data to documents, IP1-15–IP1-19
   creating, IP1-4–IP1-5
   linking data to slides, IP3-8–IP3-11
   updating, in database, IP2-7–IP2-9